The Penguin Pocket Thesaurus

Rosalind Fergusson is a freelance editor and lexicographer. She has written for both *The Penguin English Dictionary* (2000; 2003) and *The Encarta World English Dictionary* (1999). She is also the author of *The Penguin Rhyming Dictionary* (1985), *The Penguin Dictionary of Synonyms and Antonyms* (1992), *The Chambers Dictionary of Foreign Words and Phrases* (1995), *The Cassell Dictionary of English Idioms* (1999) and other reference works. She lives in Kent.

Martin Manser is the author and editor of over eighty reference books. These include *The Chambers Dictionary of Synonyms and Antonyms* (1991), *The Oxford Pocket Learner's Dictionary* (1992), *The NIV Thematic Study Bible* (Hodder & Stoughton, 1996), *The Chambers English Thesaurus* (1997) and *The Penguin Writer's Manual* (with Stephen Curtis, 2001). He lives in Aylesbury.

David Pickering has written and contributed to over 150 reference books. These include *The Cassell Dictionary of Abbreviations* (1996), *The Cassell Dictionary of Proverbs* (1997), *The Cassell Thesaurus* (1998) and *The Penguin Dictionary of First Names* (1999; 2004). He lives in Buckingham.

THE PENGUIN
POCKET THESAURUS

Edited by
Rosalind Fergusson
Martin Manser
David Pickering

PENGUIN BOOKS

PENGUIN BOOKS

Published by the Penguin Group
Penguin Books Ltd, 80 Strand, London WC2R 0RL, England
Penguin Group (USA) Inc., 375 Hudson Street, New York, New York 10014, USA
Penguin Books Australia Ltd, 250 Camberwell Road, Camberwell, Victoria 3124, Australia
Penguin Books Canada Ltd, 10 Alcorn Avenue, Toronto, Ontario, Canada M4V 3B2
Penguin Books India (P) Ltd, 11 Community Centre, Panchsheel Park, New Delhi – 110 017, India
Penguin Group (NZ), cnr Airborne and Rosedale Roads, Albany, Auckland 1310, New Zealand
Penguin Books (South Africa) (Pty) Ltd, 24 Sturdee Avenue, Rosebank 2196, South Africa

Penguin Books Ltd, Registered Offices: 80 Strand, London WC2R 0RL, England

www.penguin.com

The New Penguin Thesaurus first published 2000
Published without antonyms or appendices as *The Penguin Concise Thesaurus* 2002
This edition published as *The Penguin Pocket Thesaurus* 2004
4

Set in Linotype ITC Stone
Typeset by Rowland Phototypesetting Ltd, Bury St Edmunds, Suffolk
Printed in England by Clays Ltd, St Ives plc

aback *adv* **taken aback** surprised, startled, astonished, dumbfounded, speechless, flabbergasted (*inf*).

abandon *verb* **1** desert, leave, strand, maroon, leave high and dry (*inf*), leave in the lurch (*inf*), forsake, discard, ditch (*inf*), drop, jilt, quit, vacate, evacuate. **2** give up, stop, abort, scrap (*inf*), kick (*inf*), forgo, renounce, abdicate, resign, yield, surrender, cede, waive, relinquish.
➤*noun* recklessness, carelessness, unrestraint, immoderation, wildness, verve, impulsiveness, wantonness.

abandoned *adj* **1** left, discarded, cast away, cast aside, rejected, unused, deserted, vacant, empty, derelict, stranded, marooned, forsaken, forlorn. **2** unrestrained, uninhibited, immoderate, reckless, wild, wanton, shameless, dissolute, debauched.

abase *verb* lower, disgrace, dishonour, humiliate, mortify, humble, demean, degrade, debase, disparage, belittle, demote.

abash *verb* embarrass, disconcert, discomfit, humiliate, humble, overawe, intimidate, confuse, bewilder, dumbfound.

abate *verb* **1** subside, let up, die down, remit, moderate, lessen, reduce, decrease, diminish, decline, wane, weaken, ease, relieve, alleviate, soothe, calm, pacify, quell. **2** abolish, terminate, suppress, control, restrain, limit.

abbey *noun* monastery, friary, priory, nunnery, convent, cloister, church, minster, cathedral.

abbreviate *verb* shorten, curtail, truncate, clip, cut, abridge, reduce, contract, compress, paraphrase, summarize.

abbreviation *noun* short form, contraction, acronym, initialism, shortening, paraphrase.

abdicate *verb* **1** resign, retire, stand down, quit. **2** give up, relinquish, renounce, forgo, abandon, repudiate, reject, refuse, surrender, cede, waive.

abdomen *noun* belly, paunch (*inf*), stomach, midriff, gut, intestines, viscera.

abduct *verb* kidnap, carry off, run away with, snatch, seize, seduce, spirit away.

aberrant *adj* irregular, abnormal, atypical, anomalous, freakish, rogue, unusual, eccentric, deviant, perverted, deviating, divergent.

aberration *noun* **1** deviation, divergence, irregularity, abnormality, anomaly, freak, variation, mistake. **2** delusion, vagary, hallucination, instability, derangement.

abet *verb* aid, assist, help, back, support, advocate, promote, encourage, incite, urge.

abeyance *noun* suspension, deferment, postponement, dormancy, latency, remission.

abhor *verb* loathe, detest, execrate, abominate, spurn, hate, dislike, despise.

abhorrent *adj* loathsome, detestable, execrable, abominable, odious, repugnant, repulsive, revolting, disgusting, hateful, horrid.

abide *verb* **1** stand, bear, tolerate, suffer, brook, endure, accept. **2** last, endure, persist, remain, continue, survive. **3** live, dwell, reside, lodge, sojourn, settle, tarry, stay.
abide by 1 comply with, conform to, observe, obey, keep, accept. **2** hold to, stick to, stand by, fulfil, carry out.

abiding *adj* lasting, enduring, persisting, continuing, long-term, long-lasting, durable, changeless, steadfast, constant.

ability *noun* **1** capacity, capability, power, potential, propensity, facility, faculty. **2** competence, proficiency, skill, adeptness, dexterity, cleverness. **3** talent, gift, knack, flair, aptitude, skill.

abject *adj* **1** contemptible, despicable, ignoble, ignominious, mean, low, base, degraded, miserable, wretched, pitiable, pathetic, forlorn, destitute. **2** grovelling, servile, sycophantic, obsequious, ingratiating, cringing, slavish, submissive.

abjure *verb* retract, recant, withdraw, deny, disclaim, disavow, forswear, renounce, give up, eschew, forgo, relinquish, abandon, repudiate, disown.

ablaze *adj* **1** blazing, burning, on fire, alight, aflame. **2** illuminated, lit up, alight, incandescent, brilliant, radiant. **3** aroused, impassioned, inflamed, ardent, fiery, furious, raging.

able *adj* **1** capable, competent, efficient, fit, qualified, adept, proficient, skilled. **2** skilful, clever, talented, gifted, expert, masterly.

able-bodied *adj* fit, healthy, robust, hardy, strong, sound, tough, powerful.

ablution *noun* **1** washing, bathing, showering. **2** cleansing, purification.

abnegate *verb* renounce, deny, reject, relinquish, surrender, eschew, forgo.

abnormal *adj* irregular, unusual, extraordinary, aberrant, deviant, atypical, anomalous, exceptional, unnatural, freakish, strange, eccentric, idiosyncratic.

abode *noun* dwelling, home, residence, domicile, habitation, quarters, house.

abolish *verb* destroy, do away with, annihilate, eradicate, eliminate, stamp out, terminate, discontinue, stop, scrap (*inf*), axe (*inf*), cancel, suppress, revoke, repeal, annul, quash, nullify.

abominable *adj* **1** detestable, loathsome, abhorrent, hateful, execrable, odious, repulsive, revolting, disgusting. **2** terrible, atrocious, foul, vile, horrible, unpleasant, disagreeable, nasty.

abominate *verb* abhor, detest, loathe, execrate, hate, condemn, despise.

abomination *noun* **1** abhorrence, detestation, loathing, execration, aversion, repugnance, repulsion, disgust. **2** evil, villainy, atrocity, obscenity, disgrace, offence, torment, bugbear, anathema.

aboriginal *adj* native, indigenous, autochthonous, original, first, primitive, primeval, primordial.

abort *verb* **1** terminate. **2** miscarry. **3** abandon, call off, stop, halt, suspend, fail.

abortion *noun* **1** termination, foeticide. **2** miscarriage, stillbirth. **3** failure, termination, end, abandonment.

abortive *adj* failed, unsuccessful, futile, vain, fruitless, unavailing, ineffectual.

abound *verb* **1** be plentiful, proliferate, flourish, thrive. **2** teem, swarm, be crawling (*inf*), overflow.

about *prep* **1** concerning, relating to, pertaining to, connected with, to do with, on, re, touching, regarding, with respect to, with reference to. **2** over, throughout, round, around. **3** around, round, encircling, surrounding. **4** with, near, by, beside.
➤ *adv* **1** approximately, roughly, in the region of, circa. **2** almost, nearly, wellnigh, more or less. **3** around, round, here and there, to and fro, hither and thither. **4** near, nearby, close, in the vicinity, around.

about to 1 on the point of, on the verge of, on the brink of, ready to. **2** prepared to, going to, intending to.

above *prep* **1** over, on top of, higher than, atop. **2** exceeding, over, greater than, more than, in excess of. **3** surpassing, transcending, beyond. **4** superior to, over, higher than. **5** beyond, not open to, not liable to, not subject to.
➤ *adv* **1** higher, high up, on top. **2** earlier, before, previously, formerly. **3** overhead, aloft, on high.

aboveboard *adj* honest, legitimate, straight, on the level (*inf*), honourable, reputable, trustworthy.

abrasion *noun* **1** erosion, friction, rubbing, scraping, attrition, grinding. **2** graze, scratch, scrape, cut.

abrasive *adj* **1** rough, scratching, scraping, grating, frictional, erosive. **2** biting, caustic, cutting, nasty, unpleasant, irritating, annoying.

abreast *adv* **1** alongside, beside, side by side, shoulder to shoulder, level. **2** acquainted, familiar, informed, conversant, up to date, in touch.

abridge *verb* **1** shorten, condense, compress, cut, prune, summarize, précis, digest. **2** reduce, lessen, diminish, decrease.

abroad *adv* **1** overseas, in foreign parts, out of the country. **2** widely, extensively, everywhere, far and wide. **3** about, around, at large, in circulation. **4** away, elsewhere, out, forth.

abrogate *verb* repeal, revoke, rescind, countermand, annul, nullify, quash, abolish.

abrupt *adj* **1** sudden, unexpected, unforeseen, quick, swift, hasty, precipitate. **2** steep, sheer, precipitous. **3** curt, brusque, terse, gruff, blunt, rude.

abscess *noun* sore, pustule, boil, ulcer.

abscond *verb* run away, run off, do a runner (*inf*), do a bunk (*inf*), decamp, bolt, escape, flee, leave, disappear.

absence *noun* **1** nonattendance, nonappearance, absenteeism, truancy. **2** lack, want, need, default, unavailability, nonexistence.

absent *adj* **1** away, off, missing, truant, out. **2** missing, lacking, wanting. **3** inattentive, abstracted, in a world of one's own (*inf*), absorbed, preoccupied, distracted, oblivious, unaware, daydreaming, woolgathering, miles away (*inf*).

absentminded *adj* **1** forgetful, scatterbrained, scatty (*inf*), with a mind like a sieve (*inf*). **2** inattentive, distracted, abstracted, absent, dreaming, faraway, oblivious, unaware, unconscious, unthinking.

absolute *adj* **1** complete, utter, total, full, sheer, rank, consummate, perfect, pure, unadulterated. **2** unlimited, unrestricted, unconditional, unqualified. **3** despotic, autocratic, tyrannical, dictatorial, arbitrary, authoritative, supreme, sovereign.

absolutely *adv* completely, utterly, totally, fully, thoroughly, perfectly, positively, definitely, undoubtedly, really, certainly, indeed.

absolution *noun* forgiveness, pardon, exoneration, exculpation, acquittal, amnesty, remission, reprieve.

absolve *verb* **1** forgive, pardon, exonerate, exculpate, acquit, reprieve. **2** remit, forgive, pardon, excuse. **3** release, discharge, liberate, free.

absorb *verb* **1** soak up, suck up, blot up, imbibe, ingest. **2** assimilate, incorporate, swallow, engulf. **3** take in, assimilate, incorporate, digest, retain. **4** engross, preoccupy, engage, rivet, fascinate.

absorbent *adj* porous, permeable, pervious, absorptive, sorbefacient.

absorbing *adj* engrossing, engaging, interesting, riveting, fascinating, enthralling, gripping.

abstain *verb* refrain, forbear, desist, decline, refuse, forgo, renounce, shun, eschew, avoid, resist.

abstemious *adj* abstinent, temperate, moderate, self-restrained, self-denying, self-disciplined, sparing, frugal.

abstention *noun* abstaining, refraining, forbearing, refusal, avoidance, resistance.

abstinence *noun* teetotalism, temperance, moderation, abstemiousness, continence, self-restraint, self-discipline, self-denial.

abstract *adj* theoretical, hypothetical, unreal, conceptual, imaginary, notional, indefinite, metaphysical.
➤*noun* summary, synopsis, précis, résumé, digest.
➤*verb* **1** remove, extract, take out, draw off, separate, detach, isolate. **2** summarize, synopsize, précis, digest, condense, abridge.

abstracted *adj* preoccupied, inattentive, distracted, absentminded, daydreaming, thoughtful, pensive, unaware.

abstraction *noun* **1** preoccupation, inattention, distraction, absentmindedness, absence. **2** idea, concept, notion, theory, hypothesis. **3** removal, extraction, separation, detachment, isolation.

abstruse *adj* obscure, recondite, esoteric, arcane, cryptic, puzzling, incomprehensible, unfathomable.

absurd *adj* ridiculous, ludicrous, preposterous, nonsensical, irrational, incongruous, foolish, silly, laughable, risible, comical.

abundance *noun* **1** plenty, profusion, plethora, lots (*inf*), masses (*inf*), loads (*inf*).

2 plentifulness, copiousness, exuberance, luxuriance. **3** wealth, affluence, richness.

abundant *adj* **1** plentiful, copious, lavish, profuse, ample, galore. **2** rich, replete, overflowing, teeming.

abuse *verb* **1** misuse, misapply, exploit. **2** ill-treat, maltreat, mistreat, harm, molest. **3** insult, swear at, curse, revile, defame, libel, slander.
➤ *noun* **1** misuse, misapplication, exploitation. **2** ill-treatment, maltreatment, mistreatment, ill-use, harm, molestation. **3** insults, curses, expletives, invective, slander, libel, defamation, tirade, diatribe.

abusive *adj* insulting, offensive, rude, vulgar, blasphemous, defamatory, libellous, slanderous, vituperative, opprobrious.

abut *verb* adjoin, touch, meet, join, border, verge.

abysmal *adj* **1** shocking, appalling, awful, dreadful, disgraceful. **2** deep, unfathomable, immeasurable, bottomless.

abyss *noun* gulf, gorge, chasm, ravine, bottomless pit, abysm, void.

academic *adj* **1** scholarly, erudite, intellectual, highbrow, collegiate, educational, pedagogical. **2** intellectual, learned, well-read, bookish, studious, donnish. **3** abstract, theoretical, hypothetical, conjectural, artificial, unreal, irrelevant.
➤ *noun* scholar, professor, lecturer, don, master, fellow, tutor.

academy *noun* **1** school, college, university, seminary. **2** institution, institute.

accede *verb* **1** agree, concur, assent, acquiesce, grant. **2** attain, inherit, assume, succeed, ascend.

accelerate *verb* **1** speed up, go faster, step on it (*inf*), give it some welly (*sl*). **2** quicken, hurry, hasten, step up. **3** stimulate, precipitate, advance, forward, promote.

accent *noun* **1** pronunciation, inflection, modulation, intonation, brogue, twang (*inf*). **2** stress, emphasis, accentuation, rhythm, cadence. **3** priority, importance, highlighting, underlining.
➤ *verb* **1** stress, emphasize. **2** accentuate, highlight, underline.

accentuate *verb* accent, stress, emphasize, highlight, underline, underscore, point up, heighten.

accept *verb* **1** take, say yes to, jump at (*inf*), receive. **2** take on, assume, bear, undertake. **3** agree to, accede to, assent to, comply with. **4** acknowledge, recognize, admit, allow. **5** believe, credit, buy (*inf*), swallow (*inf*). **6** tolerate, put up with, stand, suffer. **7** welcome, receive, embrace.

acceptable *adj* **1** satisfactory, adequate, passable, all right, OK (*inf*). **2** tolerable, bearable, permissible, admissible. **3** welcome, desirable, agreeable, pleasing.

accepted *adj* approved, authorized, sanctioned, recognized, received, standard, established, conventional, orthodox, normal, correct, appropriate.

access *noun* **1** approach, way in, entrance, passage, door, path. **2** admission, admittance, entrance, entry. **3** attack, fit, paroxysm, spasm, outburst.

accessible *adj* **1** approachable, reachable, nearby, available, getatable (*inf*). **2** understandable, intelligible, comprehensible, fathomable.

accession *noun* **1** succession, inheritance, inauguration, investiture, installation. **2** acquisition, addition, gain.

accessory *noun* **1** supplement, addition, appendage, attachment, fitting, extra, ornament, trimming. **2** accomplice, abettor, confederate, associate.
➤ *adj* supplementary, additional, extra, auxiliary, ancillary, secondary.

accident *noun* **1** mishap, misadventure, disaster, crash, collision, pile-up (*inf*). **2** chance, fluke (*inf*), coincidence. **3** luck, chance, hazard, fortune, serendipity.

accidental *adj* **1** chance, fortuitous, random, haphazard, serendipitous. **2** unintentional, inadvertent, unwitting, unplanned, unexpected.

acclaim *verb* applaud, cheer, praise, commend, extol, hail, welcome.

acclamation *noun* acclaim, praise, commendation, applause, ovation, plaudits, congratulations, tribute, homage.

acclimatize *verb* habituate, familiarize, accustom, adjust, adapt, inure.

acclivity *noun* ascent, upward slope, incline, hill.

accommodate *verb* **1** house, lodge, put up, quarter, billet. **2** take, receive, hold, contain. **3** oblige, help, assist, serve, supply, indulge. **4** adapt, adjust, modify, fit, harmonize.

accommodating *adj* obliging, helpful, cooperative, compliant, willing, friendly, hospitable.

accommodation *noun* **1** housing, lodgings, digs (*inf*), quarters, billet. **2** agreement, settlement, compromise, reconciliation. **3** adaptation, adjustment, modification, harmonization.

accompaniment *noun* **1** backing, support, obbligato. **2** complement, supplement, addition, adjunct, accessory.

accompany *verb* **1** escort, attend, usher, chaperon, partner, convoy. **2** supplement, complement. **3** coincide with, coexist with. **4** back, support, play with.

accomplice *noun* accessory, abettor, collaborator, associate, confederate, partner, mate.

accomplish *verb* **1** complete, finish, achieve, attain, consummate. **2** execute, perform, discharge, fulfil, realize.

accomplished *adj* **1** talented, gifted, skilled, expert, masterly, practised, proficient, able, qualified. **2** refined, polished. **3** finished, done, completed.

accomplishment *noun* **1** achievement, attainment, exploit, feat, coup. **2** talent, gift, skill, ability. **3** completion, execution, performance, achievement, fulfilment, realization.

accord *verb* **1** grant, yield, concede, allow. **2** give, confer, bestow, present, offer. **3** agree, correspond, tally, match, fit.
➤*noun* **1** agreement, conformity, unanimity, consensus. **2** harmony, concord, sympathy, rapport.
of one's own accord voluntarily, freely, willingly.
with one accord unanimously, concertedly, of one mind.

accordance *noun* accord, agreement, conformity, compliance.

according *adj* **according to 1** as stated by, on the authority of, on the report of. **2** in accordance with, in compliance with, in line with, in keeping with. **3** depending on, on the basis of. **4** commensurate with, in proportion to, in relation to.

accordingly *adv* **1** correspondingly, consistently, appropriately. **2** consequently, therefore, so, thus.

accost *verb* **1** approach, address, stop, waylay, buttonhole (*inf*). **2** solicit, importune.

account *noun* **1** narration, story, description, report, statement, record. **2** statement, ledger, book, balance sheet, tally. **3** profit, advantage. **4** importance, note, consequence, worth, value.
➤*verb* judge, deem, regard, consider, reckon.
account for 1 explain, clear up. **2** justify, vindicate.
on account of because of, owing to.
on no account under no circumstances, certainly not.

accountable *adj* responsible, answerable, liable.

accredit *verb* **1** license, certify, authorize, recognize. **2** appoint, commission, delegate. **3** approve, sanction, endorse. **4** attribute, ascribe, assign.

accretion *noun* growth, increase, accumulation, agglomeration.

accrue *verb* **1** accumulate, amass, increase, grow. **2** result, ensue, come, proceed.

accumulate *verb* **1** gather, collect, assemble, amass, hoard. **2** increase, grow, build up, aggregate, accrue.

accumulation *noun* **1** aggregation, accretion, increase, build-up. **2** heap, pile, hoard, stockpile, collection.

accurate *adj* **1** exact, precise, correct, true, faithful.

accursed *adj* damned, wretched, detestable, execrable.

accusation *noun* **1** charge, allegation, imputation, indictment, complaint. **2** incrimination, arraignment, blame, denunciation, recrimination.

accuse *verb* charge, blame, indict, impeach, point the finger at (*inf*).

accustom *verb* familiarize, acquaint, habituate, inure, adapt.

accustomed *adj* **1** customary, habitual, usual, set, traditional. **2** used, habituated, given, wont.

ace noun expert, master, virtuoso, dab hand (inf), professional, champion.
> adj excellent, first-rate, great, brilliant.

acerbic adj 1 bitter, sour, tart, acid, sharp. 2 harsh, caustic, biting, trenchant, bitter, vitriolic.

ache verb 1 hurt, pain, be sore, throb. 2 suffer, agonize, sorrow. 3 long, yearn, pine, hanker, itch.
> noun pain, soreness, hurt, discomfort.

achieve verb 1 accomplish, complete, execute, fulfil, realize. 2 attain, gain, win, obtain.

achievement noun 1 accomplishment, attainment, exploit, feat. 2 fulfilment, realization, accomplishment, performance, completion.

acid adj 1 sour, tart, sharp, acerbic, acidulous. 2 biting, cutting, trenchant, mordant, caustic.

acknowledge verb 1 recognize, admit, grant, confess, concede, declare. 2 answer, reply to, respond to. 3 greet, hail, notice.

acknowledgment noun 1 recognition, admission, acceptance. 2 answer, reply, response, thanks. 3 declaration, avowal, confession.

acme noun top, summit, pinnacle, zenith, height.

acolyte noun follower, admirer, attendant, assistant.

acquaint verb familiarize, inform, notify, apprise, enlighten.

acquaintance noun 1 associate, contact, friend. 2 familiarity, awareness, knowledge, experience.

acquiesce verb assent, accept, accede, comply, submit.

acquire verb 1 obtain, come by, buy, gain, secure. 2 gain, get, pick up.

acquisition noun 1 purchase, buy, prize, gain, addition. 2 acquirement, attainment, procurement, appropriation.

acquisitive adj greedy, grasping, rapacious, covetous, mercenary.

acquit verb 1 exonerate, exculpate, pardon, discharge, free, release. 2 behave, conduct, comport, act, perform.

acrid adj 1 pungent, sharp, harsh, bitter, sour. 2 bitter, vitriolic, astringent, acerbic, acrimonious.

acrimonious adj bitter, sour, caustic, malignant, virulent, vitriolic.

acrimony noun bitterness, sourness, asperity, vitriol, spleen, gall.

acrobatics noun agility, gymnastics, tumbling.

across adv crosswise, transversely.
prep athwart, astride, over.

act verb 1 do, move, take action. 2 behave, perform. 3 operate, work, function, serve. 4 play, portray, perform, enact. 5 impersonate, imitate, mimic. 6 assume, affect, feign, simulate, pretend.
> noun 1 action, deed, feat, exploit, achievement. 2 performance, execution. 3 judgment, ruling, resolution. 4 bill, statute, law, ordinance. 5 show, performance, turn, routine. 6 pretence, show, front, pose.

act for represent, deputize for, stand in for.

act on obey, carry out, comply with, heed.

act up misbehave, play up (inf), malfunction.

acting adj substitute, temporary, interim, provisional, supply.

action noun 1 act, deed, exploit, undertaking. 2 operation, performance, activity, work. 3 effort, move, step, measure. 4 activity, energy, exertion, movement. 5 combat, fighting, conflict, warfare. 6 battle, fight, engagement, skirmish, encounter. 7 lawsuit, case, litigation, proceedings.

activate verb 1 trigger, set off, turn on, trip, fire. 2 stimulate, energize, drive, actuate, initiate.

active adj 1 busy, bustling, occupied, on the go (inf). 2 energetic, lively, vigorous, spirited. 3 operative, working, running. 4 effective, effectual. 5 involved, committed, engaged.

activity noun 1 movement, motion, action, industry. 2 bustle, stir, life, animation, commotion. 3 pursuit, hobby, pastime, undertaking, enterprise, project, task.

actor noun player, trouper, performer, thespian, star.

actress *noun* player, comedienne, tragedi-enne, leading lady.

actual *adj* 1 real, true, authentic, factual, physical, concrete. 2 current, present, existent.

actually *adv* really, truly, indeed, in fact, in reality.

actuate *verb* 1 activate, trigger, set off. 2 motivate, stimulate, move, prompt, incite, spur.

acumen *noun* sharpness, shrewdness, astuteness, insight, perspicacity, judgment, discrimination.

acute *adj* 1 quick, shrewd, astute, discern-ing, incisive, smart. 2 keen, sharp, dis-criminating. 3 intense, sharp, cutting, stabbing, piercing. 4 severe, grave, serious, critical, dangerous. 5 critical, crucial, urgent, pressing.

adage *noun* saying, proverb, truism, maxim, precept.

adamant *adj* determined, resolute, unyielding, inflexible, firm, intransigent.

adapt *verb* adjust, accommodate, conform, modify, convert, fit.

adaptation *noun* 1 adjustment, accom-modation, habituation, conformity. 2 alteration, modification, change. 3 conversion, remodelling, reworking.

add *verb* 1 append, annex, attach, affix, join, combine. 2 increase, augment, sup-plement, amplify. 3 sum, total, add up, tot up (*inf*). 4 reckon, tally, compute, calculate.

add up 1 constitute, comprise, amount to, come to. 2 make sense, stand to rea-son, hold water (*inf*).

addendum *noun* addition, appendix, sup-plement, codicil, postscript, rider.

addict *noun* 1 user, junkie (*inf*). 2 enthusiast, devotee, buff (*inf*), freak (*inf*).
➤*verb* 1 habituate, hook (*inf*). 2 devote, dedicate.

addition *noun* 1 adding, attachment, aug-mentation, summing, totalling. 2 adjunct, extra, supplement, increment, annex, addendum.
in addition also, as well, too, besides.

additional *adj* supplementary, extra, added, further, more.

address *noun* 1 home, residence, domicile, location, place, whereabouts. 2 speech, discourse, lecture, presentation, oration, sermon.
➤*verb* 1 speak to, talk to, lecture, harangue. 2 greet, hail, call, name. 3 communicate, direct, convey. 4 direct, send. 5 attend to, get down to, deal with, undertake.
address oneself attend, apply oneself, concentrate, focus.

adduce *verb* cite, quote, mention, offer, put forward.

adept *adj* proficient, competent, skilled, expert, good, able.
➤*noun* expert, master, dab hand (*inf*), ace (*inf*), professional, specialist.

adequate *adj* 1 enough, sufficient, ample, requisite, suitable. 2 satisfactory, passable, fair, mediocre, so-so (*inf*), unexceptional, no great shakes (*inf*).

adhere *verb* 1 stick, cohere, hold fast, cling, cleave. 2 be faithful, follow, stand by. 3 follow, observe, comply with, fulfil, abide by.

adherent *noun* disciple, follower, hanger-on (*inf*), supporter, advocate, partisan.
➤*adj* adhering, sticking, adhesive.

adhesion *noun* adherence, sticking, cohe-sion, bond.

adhesive *noun* glue, gum, paste, fixative.
➤*adj* sticky, gummed, stick-on, tacky, clinging, adherent.

adieu *interj and noun* goodbye, farewell, cheerio (*inf*), parting, leave-taking.

adjacent *adj* 1 adjoining, contiguous, abutting, juxtaposed, bordering, next-door. 2 neighbouring, near, close, proximate.

adjoin *verb* abut, touch, border, connect, link, join.

adjourn *verb* 1 suspend, interrupt, discon-tinue, stop, break. 2 postpone, put off, defer, shelve. 3 withdraw, retire, repair.

adjudge *verb* 1 pronounce, declare, judge, decide. 2 grant, award, allot, assign.

adjudicate *verb* 1 decide, settle, adjudge, determine. 2 judge, arbitrate, umpire, referee.

adjunct *noun* addition, extra, appendage, attachment, accessory, supplement.

adjure *verb* charge, command, enjoin, entreat, implore.

adjust *verb* 1 alter, change, regulate, set, tweak (*inf*), arrange, tailor. 2 adapt, conform, accommodate, become accustomed, reconcile oneself.

ad-lib *verb* improvise, extemporize, make up.
>*adj* improvised, impromptu, extemporaneous, spontaneous.
>*adv* impromptu, extempore, off the cuff (*inf*), off the top of one's head (*inf*).

administer *verb* 1 manage, run, direct, supervise, oversee. 2 give, supply, dispense, mete out, impose, execute.

administration *noun* 1 management, running, organization, direction, government. 2 executive, board, management, directors. 3 government, executive. 4 regime, term of office. 5 supply, dispensing, imposition, execution.

administrator *noun* manager, director, leader, organizer, controller, governor.

admirable *adj* praiseworthy, commendable, worthy, estimable, excellent, masterly.

admiration *noun* esteem, regard, reverence, awe, appreciation, liking.

admire *verb* esteem, regard, value, appreciate, revere, worship, like, commend.

admissible *adj* 1 acceptable, allowable, permissible, allowed, permitted. 2 lawful, legitimate.

admission *noun* 1 acknowledgment, recognition, acceptance, confession, avowal. 2 admittance, access, entrance, introduction, initiation.

admit *verb* 1 acknowledge, recognize, concede, grant, own, confess. 2 let in, accept, receive, welcome.

admittance *noun* 1 admission, reception, welcome. 2 entry, entrance, access, passage.

admonish *verb* 1 reprimand, rebuke, reprove, scold, chide, upbraid. 2 warn, caution, advise, counsel, urge, exhort.

ado *noun* fuss, bother, trouble, commotion, tumult, excitement.

adolescent *adj* 1 teenage, teenaged, young, youthful, pubescent, juvenile. 2 immature, puerile, childish.
>*noun* teenager, youth, young person, minor, juvenile.

adopt *verb* 1 take in, foster, parent. 2 take up, embrace, espouse, support. 3 appropriate, take over, assume, affect. 4 accept, endorse, ratify, sanction. 5 choose, select, elect, nominate.

adorable *adj* lovable, charming, appealing, sweet, dear, darling, delightful, enchanting.

adore *verb* 1 love, cherish, hold dear, revere, esteem, dote on, think the world of (*inf*). 2 worship, idolize, venerate, revere. 3 like, love, relish, enjoy, delight in.

adorn *verb* 1 decorate, ornament, embellish, trim, deck, festoon. 2 enhance, grace, enrich.

adrift *adj* 1 drifting, floating, unmoored, loose. 2 rootless, unsettled, aimless, purposeless, directionless.

adroit *adj* 1 dexterous, skilful, adept, able, masterly, deft. 2 clever, shrewd, ingenious, resourceful.

adulate *verb* flatter, blandish, fawn, worship, idolize, adore.

adult *noun* grown-up, man, woman.
>*adj* 1 grown-up, of age, mature, fully grown, fully developed. 2 pornographic, obscene, salacious, dirty.

adulterate *verb* debase, vitiate, alloy, tamper with, contaminate, pollute, corrupt, taint.

adultery *noun* infidelity, unfaithfulness, extramarital sex, affair, bit on the side (*inf*).

adumbrate *verb* 1 outline, sketch, delineate, silhouette. 2 foreshadow, presage, indicate, suggest.

advance *verb* 1 go on, move forward, progress, make headway, proceed. 2 develop, improve, thrive, flourish, prosper. 3 hasten, expedite, speed up, accelerate, further, boost. 4 promote, raise, elevate, upgrade. 5 suggest, put forward, propose. 6 lend, loan, pay, give.
>*noun* 1 advancement, progress, headway. 2 development, progress, improvement, breakthrough, innovation, discovery. 3 loan, retainer, deposit, credit. 4 proposition, approach, overture, move.

in advance ahead, beforehand, earlier, previously.

advanced *adj* **1** forward, ahead. **2** complex, high-level, sophisticated, state-of-the-art, leading-edge.

advancement *noun* **1** advance, progress, headway. **2** development, improvement, furtherance. **3** promotion, preferment, betterment.

advantage *noun* **1** asset, plus, trump card, benefit, superiority, ascendancy. **2** gain, profit, good, use, benefit, convenience.

advantageous *adj* beneficial, profitable, useful, worthwhile, valuable, favourable, superior, dominant.

advent *noun* arrival, coming, approach, onset, beginning, dawn.

adventitious *adj* accidental, fortuitous, incidental, extraneous.

adventure *noun* **1** exploit, feat, venture, undertaking. **2** risk, hazard, danger, chance. **3** venture, enterprise, risk, gamble, speculation.

adventurous *adj* daring, bold, brave, intrepid, enterprising, venturesome.

adversary *noun* opponent, antagonist, enemy, foe, rival, competitor.

adverse *adj* **1** antagonistic, opposing, contrary, negative. **2** unfavourable, disadvantageous, hostile, injurious, untoward, inauspicious.

adversity *noun* misfortune, affliction, trouble, hardship, suffering, distress.

advertise *verb* **1** promote, publicize, push (*inf*), plug (*inf*), hype (*inf*). **2** announce, declare, proclaim, broadcast, publicize.

advertisement *noun* commercial, advert (*inf*), ad (*inf*), publicity, promotion, plug (*inf*).

advice *noun* **1** guidance, counsel, caution, warning, recommendation, suggestion, hint, tip. **2** notification, news, communication, information.

advisable *adj* prudent, sensible, judicious, wise, politic, recommended.

advise *verb* **1** counsel, guide, direct, instruct. **2** recommend, suggest, urge, warn. **3** inform, tell, notify, apprise.

advisory *adj* **1** consultative, counselling. **2** guiding, helpful.

advocate *verb* recommend, advise, support, endorse, champion, promote, uphold, defend, campaign for, lobby for. ➤ *noun* **1** supporter, backer, champion, defender, campaigner, proponent. **2** lawyer, counsel, solicitor, attorney.

aegis *noun* support, patronage, sponsorship, auspices, protection, guardianship.

aerial *adj* **1** high, lofty. **2** airy, ethereal.

aeronautics *noun* aviation, flying, flight.

aeroplane *noun* plane, aircraft, airliner, jet.

aesthetic *adj* **1** tasteful, classic, artistic, beautiful. **2** cultured, refined.

afar *adv* far away, yonder, abroad.

affable *adj* **1** friendly, amiable, pleasant, approachable, easygoing, sociable, kindly, good-natured, benevolent. **2** amicable, friendly, congenial, cordial, agreeable.

affair *noun* **1** concern, business, duty, responsibility. **2** matter, issue, question. **3** incident, event, episode, circumstance. **4** liaison, intrigue, relationship, fling (*inf*). **5** party, reception, function, do (*inf*).

affairs *pl noun* business, commerce, finances, operations, proceedings, activities.

affect[1] *verb* **1** influence, alter, act on, attack, apply to, concern, involve. **2** move, touch, impress, stir, disturb, trouble.

affect[2] *verb* **1** put on, pretend, feign, simulate, counterfeit. **2** adopt, assume, sham, fake.

affectation *noun* **1** pretence, sham, show, display, insincerity, hypocrisy. **2** mannerism, air, posturing, posing, artificiality, pretension.

affected *adj* **1** insincere, mannered, pretentious, pompous, ostentatious. **2** unnatural, artificial, sham, put-on, feigned, studied.

affecting *adj* moving, touching, stirring, poignant, distressing.

affection *noun* **1** love, devotion, attachment, fondness, liking, favour, warmth, tenderness. **2** emotion, feeling, passion.

affectionate *adj* **1** loving, devoted, caring, doting, friendly. **2** tender, passionate, loving, fond, warm.

affiance *verb* betroth, engage, pledge, promise.

affidavit *noun* declaration, statement, deposition, testimony.

affiliate *verb* 1 join, merge, amalgamate, incorporate, annex. 2 associate, ally, unite, combine.

affinity *noun* 1 liking, rapport, sympathy, empathy. 2 attraction, taste, fondness, liking, partiality, predilection. 3 relationship, connection, correspondence, analogy, resemblance, similarity.

affirm *verb* 1 confirm, corroborate, certify, vouch for. 2 assert, declare, state, profess, aver. 3 ratify, confirm, uphold.

affirmation *noun* 1 assertion, declaration, statement, asseveration. 2 testimony, deposition, attestation.

affirmative *adj* positive, confirming, corroborative, approving, favourable.

affix *verb* 1 attach, fasten, pin, stick, join. 2 add, append, annex.
➤*noun* addition, prefix, suffix.

afflict *verb* 1 trouble, distress, hurt, grieve, torment. 2 try, harass, vex, plague.

affliction *noun* 1 distress, suffering, torment, anguish, adversity, hardship. 2 trouble, trial, ordeal, scourge, disease, disorder.

affluent *adj* wealthy, moneyed, rich, prosperous, moneyed, well-off, flush (*inf*), rolling in it (*inf*), loaded (*sl*).

afford *verb* 1 pay for, support. 2 spare, allow. 3 give, supply, provide, produce, generate.

affray *noun* fight, brawl, mêlée, scrap, scuffle, clash, row, disturbance, breach of the peace.

affront *verb* insult, outrage, slight, hurt, offend, annoy, anger.

afoot *adv and adj* going on, about, around, abroad, in circulation, up, astir.

aforementioned *adj* aforesaid, above-mentioned, preceding, foregoing.

afraid *adj* 1 frightened, scared, fearful, alarmed, apprehensive, daunted, intimidated. 2 sorry, regretful, concerned.

afresh *adv* again, anew, once more, over again.

after *prep* 1 following, behind. 2 succeeding, later than. 3 about, regarding, concerning. 4 imitating, in the style of, on the model of.
➤*adv* afterwards, later, subsequently.

aftermath *noun* 1 wake, after-effects, repercussions. 2 result, consequence, outcome, upshot.

afterthought *noun* 1 reflection, second thought, hindsight, retrospect. 2 postscript, addition, appendix.

afterwards *adv* after, subsequently, later, thereafter.

again *adv* 1 anew, afresh, once more. 2 besides, moreover, furthermore. 3 on the other hand, conversely, on the contrary.
again and again repeatedly, over and over again, time and time again, often, continually.

against *prep* 1 opposing, versus, at odds with, anti (*inf*). 2 touching, on, in contact with, abutting. 3 counter to, opposite to.

agape *adj* 1 gaping, yawning, wide open. 2 open-mouthed, dumbfounded, thunderstruck.

age *noun* 1 span, duration, years. 2 phase, stage, period. 3 period, time, era, date, generation. 4 a long time, hours on end, donkey's years (*inf*), an eternity.
➤*verb* 1 grow old, decline, fade. 2 mature, mellow, ripen, season.

aged *adj* 1 old, elderly, getting on (*inf*), over the hill (*inf*). 2 senile, geriatric.

agency *noun* 1 bureau, office, business, company. 2 means, medium, instrumentality, intervention, mediation, intercession. 3 action, operation, effect, influence, power, force.

agenda *noun* plan, schedule, programme, timetable.

agent *noun* 1 representative, delegate, proxy, factor, broker, middleman, go-between. 2 envoy, emissary. 3 instrument, cause, vehicle, medium, agency, author, perpetrator.

agglomerate *verb* gather, collect, cluster, accumulate, aggregate, conglomerate.

agglutinate *verb* adhere, stick, glue, bond, fuse, unite, attach, cling.

aggrandize verb 1 magnify, amplify, exalt, elevate, ennoble, dignify. 2 inflate, exaggerate, glorify, glamorize.

aggravate verb 1 worsen, exacerbate, compound, increase, intensify, inflame. 2 irritate, annoy, provoke, rub up the wrong way (inf), vex, exasperate.

aggregate noun 1 total, sum, whole, entirety. 2 collection, assemblage, agglomeration, conglomeration.
➤adj 1 total, whole, combined, gross. 2 composite, compound, massed, collective.
➤verb collect, gather, accumulate, amass, agglomerate, cluster.

aggression noun 1 invasion, encroachment, infringement, provocation. 2 attack, assault, offensive, raid, foray, onslaught. 3 aggressiveness, hostility, belligerence, pugnacity.

aggressive adj 1 hostile, offensive, argumentative, provocative. 2 pugnacious, belligerent, bellicose, militant. 3 assertive, bold, forceful, dynamic, go-ahead, pushy (inf), in-your-face (sl).

aggrieved adj 1 annoyed, angry, indignant, resentful, bitter, hurt. 2 wronged, ill-used, maltreated.

aghast adj horrified, appalled, shocked, thunderstruck, dumbfounded, flabbergasted (inf).

agile adj 1 nimble, spry, sprightly, lithe, supple, fit. 2 alert, smart, clever, sharp, acute, quick-witted.

agitate verb 1 stir, beat, shake, churn, toss. 2 excite, work up, provoke, trouble, upset, fluster, alarm, worry. 3 campaign, fight, argue, stir.

agitator noun troublemaker, agent provocateur, subversive, firebrand, demagogue, rabble-rouser.

agnostic noun 1 sceptic, doubter, doubting Thomas. 2 unbeliever, freethinker, pagan, heathen.

ago adv past, gone by, earlier, before now, previously.

agog adj eager, impatient, excited, expectant, curious, on tenterhooks.

agonize verb 1 suffer, be in agony. 2 labour, struggle, strive, worry.

agony noun torment, pain, throes, suffering, anguish, distress.

agree verb 1 concur, accord, see eye to eye, be of the same mind. 2 arrange, decide on. 3 assent, give the go-ahead (inf), allow, permit. 4 consent, acquiesce, promise, engage. 5 correspond, tally, match, concur, coincide. 6 settle, fix.

agreeable adj 1 pleasant, pleasing, charming, delightful, nice. 2 in agreement, consenting, compliant, willing, amenable.

agreement noun 1 accord, concord, harmony, unison, unanimity, consensus. 2 correspondence, consistency, conformity, congruity. 3 assent, consent, permission, approval. 4 treaty, pact, deal, bargain. 5 contract, undertaking, covenant, bond.

agriculture noun farming, husbandry, cultivation, agronomy.

aground adj grounded, beached, stranded, high and dry, on the rocks.

ahead adv and adj 1 in front, leading, before. 2 forward, onward. 3 in advance, beforehand. 4 winning, in the lead, superior, in the forefront.
ahead of in front of, in advance of, before, earlier than.

aid verb 1 help, assist, lend a hand, support, relieve, rally round. 2 facilitate, ease, promote, expedite.
➤noun 1 help, assistance, succour, support, service. 2 relief, benefit, subsidy, charity, sponsorship, patronage.

aide noun helper, assistant, abettor, adviser, right-hand man, associate.

ail verb 1 afflict, trouble, pain, distress, bother. 2 suffer, sicken, be ill, be unwell.

ailing adj suffering, sick, ill, unwell, indisposed, poorly, sickly, infirm.

ailment noun illness, sickness, complaint, malady, disease, disorder.

aim verb 1 point, direct, level, focus, train. 2 mean, intend, propose, plan, aspire, try, seek.
➤noun 1 intention, purpose, plan, target, objective, goal, aspiration, ambition, desire. 2 pointing, sighting.

air noun 1 atmosphere, aerospace, sky, ether. 2 breeze, draught, puff of wind, zephyr. 3 aspect, appearance, demeanour,

bearing, aura, impression, quality. **4** tune, melody, strain, song.
➤*verb* **1** ventilate, freshen, fan, aerate. **2** display, expose, reveal, make known, communicate, express, vent.

aircraft *noun* aeroplane, glider, helicopter, balloon, airship.

airing *noun* **1** ventilation, aeration, drying. **2** stroll, walk, outing, jaunt, drive, ride. **3** expression, communication, publication, dissemination, declaration, disclosure.

airs *pl noun* affectation, posing, pretentiousness, haughtiness, hauteur, pomposity.

airtight *adj* **1** sealed, closed, impermeable. **2** unassailable, indisputable, incontrovertible.

airy *adj* **1** open, well-ventilated. **2** spacious, roomy. **3** nonchalant, offhand, flippant, breezy. **4** light, weightless, graceful, lithe. **5** flimsy, delicate, insubstantial, ethereal.

aisle *noun* passageway, gangway, passage, lane, alley.

ajar *adj* unclosed, half open, open, unfastened.

akin *adj* **1** related, kindred, cognate, consanguineous. **2** similar, like, corresponding, analogous.

alacrity *noun* speed, haste, promptness, readiness, willingness, eagerness, enthusiasm.

alarm *verb* frighten, scare, startle, terrify, shock, dismay, unnerve, perturb.
➤*noun* **1** fear, fright, shock, terror, panic, trepidation, dismay, disquiet. **2** siren, bell, alert, danger signal.

alarmist *noun* scaremonger, doomster, pessimist.

albeit *conj* although, even though, notwithstanding that.

album *noun* **1** book, folder, scrapbook, file. **2** record, disc, CD, LP.

alcohol *noun* drink, liquor, intoxicant, booze (*inf*), the bottle (*inf*).

alcoholic *adj* intoxicating, inebriating, hard, strong, distilled, brewed.
➤*noun* drunkard, inebriate, dipsomaniac, boozer (*inf*), wino (*inf*), alkie (*inf*).

alcove *noun* recess, niche, nook, cubbyhole, bay, arbour.

alert *adj* **1** watchful, vigilant, observant, on the lookout, wide-awake, wary, on one's guard, ready. **2** smart, quick, brisk, on the ball (*inf*), sharp, agile, active, on one's toes (*inf*).
➤*noun* alarm, warning, signal, siren.
➤*verb* **1** signal, warn. **2** notify, inform, tell.

alias *adv* also called, also known as, otherwise.
➤*noun* pseudonym, false name, nom de guerre, sobriquet, nickname.

alibi *noun* defence, excuse, explanation, justification, story.

alien *adj* **1** foreign, exotic. **2** extraterrestrial, remote. **3** strange, unfamiliar, unknown. **4** contrary, conflicting, opposed, incompatible, antagonistic.
➤*noun* **1** foreigner, immigrant. **2** stranger, outsider.

alienate *verb* **1** estrange, disaffect, turn away, cut off. **2** divert, sever, separate, cut off.

alienation *noun* estrangement, disaffection, withdrawal, remoteness, separation, rupture.

alight[1] *verb* **1** get off, disembark, dismount, descend. **2** land, settle, come to rest, light.

alight[2] *adj* lit, ignited, burning, on fire.

align *verb* **1** straighten, range, line up, even up, adjust, arrange. **2** associate, ally, unite, side, sympathize, cooperate.

alike *adj* similar, resembling, like, comparable, allied, equivalent, identical, equal.
➤*adv* the same, similarly, identically, equally.

alimony *noun* maintenance, support, keep.

alive *adj* **1** living, live, breathing, animate, in the land of the living (*inf*). **2** extant, active. **3** quick, sharp, lively, animated, active, energetic, spirited, vital. **4** crawling, teeming, swarming, bristling.
alive to aware of, cognizant of, alert to, awake to.

all *adj* **1** each, every. **2** the whole of, every bit of. **3** complete, total, utter, perfect.
➤*adv* wholly, entirely, completely, totally, altogether, utterly, quite, fully.

pron **1** whole, total, entirety, the lot (*inf*). **2** everybody, everyone, everything.

allay *verb* **1** soothe, alleviate, ease, relieve, abate, assuage. **2** lessen, reduce, moderate, suppress, calm, quell.

allegation *noun* assertion, statement, declaration, accusation, charge, claim.

allege *verb* assert, state, maintain, avow, aver, claim.

allegiance *noun* **1** support, adherence, loyalty, faithfulness, devotion. **2** duty, fealty, homage.

allegorical *adj* metaphorical, figurative, parabolic, symbolic.

allegory *noun* **1** fable, parable. **2** symbolism, metaphor, analogy.

allergic *adj* **1** sensitive, hypersensitive, susceptible, affected. **2** disinclined, loath, averse, opposed.

allergy *noun* **1** sensitivity, hypersensitivity, susceptibility. **2** dislike, aversion, opposition, antipathy.

alleviate *verb* allay, soothe, relieve, ease, assuage, quell, abate, dull.

alley *noun* **1** alleyway, passage, passageway, back street. **2** path, pathway, footpath, walk.

alliance *noun* **1** union, coalition, league, federation, partnership, association, bloc, consortium. **2** affinity, association, relationship, connection, bond.

allied *adj* **1** confederate, associated, amalgamated, in league. **2** united, combined, joint. **3** alike, similar, analogous, related, linked. **4** akin, kindred, related.

allocate *verb* **1** apportion, divide, distribute, give out, share out. **2** assign, allot, allow. **3** designate, earmark, set aside.

allot *verb* **1** assign, allocate, give out, deal out, dispense. **2** designate, earmark, set aside.

allotment *noun* **1** allocation, apportionment, distribution, assignment, portion, quota, share, ration, allowance. **2** plot, patch.

all-out *adj* complete, exhaustive, intensive, wholesale, full-scale, vigorous, utmost.

allow *verb* **1** permit, let, authorize, sanction, approve, agree to, OK (*inf*). **2** allot,

allocate, assign, set aside, grant, spare. **3** acknowledge, concede, grant, admit, own.
allow for consider, take into account, keep in mind, make provision for, plan for, foresee.

allowance *noun* **1** ration, quota, share, portion, allocation. **2** payment, grant, pocket money, maintenance, benefit, weighting. **3** reduction, rebate, concession.
make allowances for take into consideration, take into account, consider, allow for, excuse.

alloy *noun* compound, mixture, blend, amalgam, composite.
verb **1** mix, blend, combine, amalgamate, compound. **2** adulterate, debase, impair.

all right *adj* **1** acceptable, satisfactory, OK (*inf*), adequate, passable, fair, average. **2** well, healthy, safe and sound, OK (*inf*), unharmed, unhurt.
adv satisfactorily, well enough, OK (*inf*), adequately, reasonably.
interj yes, very well, OK (*inf*).

allude *verb* refer, mention, touch on, suggest, intimate.

allure *verb* tempt, entice, lure, seduce, attract, fascinate, captivate, enchant.
noun attraction, appeal, charm, fascination, lure, temptation.

allusion *noun* reference, mention, suggestion, hint, insinuation, implication.

ally *verb* **1** unite, join forces, band together, team up, league, federate, associate. **2** combine, join, unite, merge.
noun **1** confederate, associate. **2** colleague, partner, friend, accomplice, assistant.

almanac *noun* yearbook, annual, calendar, annals, ephemeris.

almighty *adj* **1** all-powerful, omnipotent, supreme, absolute. **2** great, terrible, severe, intense.

almost *adv* nearly, well-nigh, virtually, practically, as good as, pretty well (*inf*), all but, not quite.

alms *pl noun* charity, bounty, donation, handout.

aloft *adv* above, overhead, on high, skyward, up.

alone *adj and adv* **1** solitary, lonely, isolated, apart, separate, single, sole, lone.

2 only, solely, exclusively. **3** solo, unaided, single-handed, unaccompanied, by oneself, on one's own.

along *prep* **1** alongside, beside, by. **2** through, during.
➤*adv* **1** forward, onward, on. **2** together, in company.
along with 1 together with, accompanied by. **2** in addition to, plus, as well as.

aloof *adj* distant, detached, apart, remote, unapproachable, standoffish, unsociable, uninvolved.

aloud *adj* audibly, distinctly, clearly, out loud.

already *adv* **1** by now, by this time, before now. **2** before, hitherto, previously.

also *adv* as well, too, in addition, additionally, besides, furthermore.

alter *verb* change, modify, adjust, adapt, revise, vary, transform, turn.

altercation *noun* quarrel, argument, dispute, row, wrangle, disagreement.

alternate *verb* rotate, take turns. **2** interchange, substitute, replace. **3** reciprocate, oscillate, fluctuate, chop and change (*inf*).
➤*adj* **1** alternating, every other, every second. **2** in rotation, interchanging, reciprocal, sequential.

alternative *noun* **1** choice, option, recourse. **2** substitute, backup.
➤*adj* **1** different, other, substitute, backup. **2** unorthodox, unconventional, fringe.

although *conj* **1** though, notwithstanding, while. **2** even though, even if.

altitude *noun* height, elevation, loftiness.

altogether *adv* **1** completely, entirely, fully, perfectly, thoroughly, absolutely. **2** in all, all told, in toto.

altruism *noun* unselfishness, selflessness, philanthropy, public-spiritedness.

always *adv* **1** every time, unfailingly, repeatedly, again and again. **2** without exception, invariably, consistently. **3** continuously, incessantly, constantly. **4** perpetually, forever, eternally.

amalgam *noun* compound, alloy, composite, mixture, combination, blend, synthesis.

amalgamate *verb* unite, join, combine, mix, alloy, incorporate, merge, coalesce.

amanuensis *noun* copyist, transcriber, scribe, clerk, secretary.

amass *verb* **1** collect, garner, hoard, stash away (*inf*). **2** gather, accumulate, accrue, aggregate, agglomerate.

amateur *noun* nonprofessional, layperson, dabbler.
➤*adj* nonprofessional, lay, unqualified, unpaid.

amateurish *adj* unprofessional, inexpert, unskilled, incompetent, crude, inferior.

amatory *adj* amorous, loving, romantic, passionate.

amaze *verb* astonish, astound, stagger, stun, flabbergast (*inf*), bowl over (*inf*), knock for six (*inf*).

amazing *adj* astonishing, astounding, remarkable, striking, extraordinary, wonderful.

ambassador *noun* diplomat, envoy, emissary, plenipotentiary, consul, attaché.

ambience *noun* atmosphere, air, aura, mood, tone, vibes (*inf*).

ambient *adj* surrounding, environmental.

ambiguity *noun* double meaning, double entendre, enigma, puzzle. **2** equivocacy, uncertainty, imprecision, doubt.

ambiguous *adj* **1** equivocal, two-edged, double-edged. **2** unclear, indefinite, indeterminate, imprecise, vague.

ambition *noun* **1** goal, objective, desire, hope, dream, aspiration. **2** enterprise, initiative, drive, get-up-and-go (*inf*), zeal, commitment.

ambitious *adj* **1** aspiring, zealous, committed, enterprising, go-ahead, assertive, pushy (*inf*). **2** challenging, demanding, formidable, bold, grandiose.

ambivalence *noun* **1** uncertainty, doubt, irresolution, indecision, vacillation. **2** conflict, clash, contradiction, mixed feelings.

amble *verb* saunter, stroll, toddle (*inf*), meander, ramble, mosey (*inf*).

ambush *noun* **1** ambuscade, surprise

attack, trap, pitfall. **2** hiding, concealment, cover.
➤*verb* lie in wait for, surprise, pounce on, waylay.

ameliorate *verb* improve, better, enhance, mend, alleviate.

amenable *adj* **1** agreeable, acquiescent, willing, accommodating, flexible, tractable, docile. **2** liable, accountable, answerable, responsible.

amend *verb* **1** correct, put right, rectify, improve. **2** alter, change, modify, revise.

amendment *noun* alteration, modification, revision, correction, addition.

amends *pl noun* **make amends** compensate, recompense, atone, make good, indemnify, repay, redress.

amenity *noun* facility, utility, convenience, service, resource.

amiable *adj* friendly, affable, pleasant, likeable, genial, good-natured, benevolent, sociable.

amicable *adj* friendly, good-natured, cordial, peaceable, civilized, polite.

amid *prep* amidst, among, between, with, surrounded by, in the middle of.

amiss *adv and adj* wrong, badly, unsatisfactory, inappropriate, out of order, faulty, awry, astray.

amity *noun* friendship, amicableness, cordiality, comity, concord, goodwill, peace, fellowship.

ammunition *noun* munitions, shells, cartridges, bullets, rounds, shot.

amnesty *noun* **1** pardon, remission, acquittal, reprieve. **2** immunity, dispensation, indulgence.

amok *adv* berserk, in a frenzy, wildly, uncontrollably, madly, violently.

among *prep* amongst, between, amid, with, surrounded by, in the middle of.

amorous *adj* **1** romantic, amatory, erotic. **2** fond, affectionate, loving, tender, passionate, randy (*inf*).

amorphous *adj* shapeless, formless, unstructured, vague, nebulous, chaotic.

amount *noun* **1** quantity, number, measure, magnitude, extent. **2** total, sum, aggregate.

verb **1** add up, come, total, equal. **2** correspond, be equivalent, be tantamount, boil down.

ample *adj* **1** enough, sufficient, plenty of, substantial, considerable, abundant, generous, unlimited. **2** large, big, spacious, capacious.

amplify *verb* **1** increase, raise, heighten. **2** boost, intensify, strengthen. **3** expand, enlarge on, develop, flesh out, expatiate on, elaborate on, add to, supplement.

amplitude *noun* ampleness, abundance, magnitude, dimensions, size, largeness, extent, range, scope.

amputate *verb* cut off, sever, lop, dock, remove.

amulet *noun* charm, talisman, fetish, protector.

amuse *verb* **1** please, entertain, divert, tickle (*inf*). **2** occupy, absorb, interest, distract.

amusement *noun* **1** mirth, laughter, merriment, fun, enjoyment, recreation. **2** entertainment, diversion, pastime, game.

amusing *adj* funny, droll, comical, humorous, witty, entertaining.

anaemic *adj* colourless, pale, pallid, wan, pasty.

anaesthetic *noun* painkiller, sedative, narcotic, stupefacient.
➤*adj* numbing, deadening, painkilling, sedative, narcotic, soporific.

anaesthetize *verb* deaden, numb, desensitize, dope, stupefy.

analogous *adj* **1** similar, like, resembling, related. **2** corresponding, matching, equivalent, comparable.

analogy *noun* **1** comparison, simile, parallel. **2** similarity, likeness, resemblance, correspondence, correlation.

analyse *verb* break down, dissect, examine, investigate, evaluate, sift.

analysis *noun* **1** breakdown, decomposition, dissection, separation. **2** examination, scrutiny, investigation, evaluation.

analytical *adj* **1** searching, in-depth, detailed, diagnostic, evaluative. **2** logical, systematic, methodical, organized, investigative, problem-solving.

anarchic *adj* **1** lawless, nihilistic, libertarian, revolutionary. **2** disorganized, confused, chaotic, disorderly, riotous, rebellious.

anarchist *noun* **1** rebel, insurgent, revolutionary, agitator. **2** nihilist, libertarian.

anarchy *noun* **1** lawlessness, misrule, anarchism, nihilism, riot, disorder. **2** confusion, chaos, mayhem, pandemonium.

anathema *noun* **1** abomination, bane, bugbear, bête noire. **2** curse, excommunication, ban, proscription.

anatomize *verb* **1** dissect, dismember, cut up, vivisect. **2** analyse, examine, scrutinize.

anatomy *noun* **1** structure, framework, composition, make-up. **2** dissection, vivisection, zootomy. **3** analysis, examination, scrutiny.

ancestor *noun* **1** forebear, progenitor, predecessor, forerunner. **2** precursor, antecedent, prototype.

ancestral *adj* inherited, hereditary, patrimonial, familial, lineal, genealogical.

ancestry *noun* **1** ancestors, forebears, progenitors, family. **2** line, lineage, pedigree, stock, blood, descent, extraction.

anchor *noun* kedge, grapnel, hook (*inf*).
➤*verb* fasten, secure, make fast, fix.

anchorage *noun* mooring, harbour, refuge, shelter.

ancient *adj* **1** old, aged, age-old, antique, archaic. **2** primeval, primordial, antediluvian, olden, bygone. **3** antiquated, superannuated, obsolete, old-fashioned, out-of-date.

ancillary *adj* **1** auxiliary, accessory, supplementary, contributory. **2** subordinate, subservient, subsidiary, secondary.

and *conj* **1** plus, in addition, along with. **2** besides, furthermore.

androgynous *adj* hermaphrodite, epicene, bisexual, gynandrous.

anecdote *noun* story, tale, yarn, account, reminiscence, incident.

anew *adv* **1** again, once again, over again. **2** afresh, newly.

angel *noun* **1** seraph, cherub, archangel, divine messenger. **2** saint, darling, dear, treasure.

angelic *adj* **1** seraphic, cherubic, divine, heavenly. **2** adorable, delightful, lovely, pure, innocent, saintly.

anger *noun* rage, wrath, ire, fury, annoyance, vexation, indignation, spleen.
➤*verb* enrage, infuriate, incense, madden, exasperate, annoy, antagonize, vex.

angle[1] *noun* **1** intersection, fork, bend, crook, elbow. **2** corner, nook. **3** inclination, slope, obliquity. **4** viewpoint, aspect, slant, perspective. **5** approach, method, technique.
➤*verb* **1** slope, slant, incline, tilt. **2** slant, distort, skew, bias.

angle[2] *verb* **1** fish, cast. **2** seek, fish for, solicit, be after (*inf*).

angry *adj* furious, irate, incensed, mad (*inf*), livid, fuming, annoyed, hot under the collar (*inf*), up in arms (*inf*), cross, bad-tempered.

angst *noun* anxiety, foreboding, disquiet, unease.

anguish *noun* agony, torment, pain, suffering, distress, grief, heartache, desolation.

anguished *adj* afflicted, stricken, suffering, wretched, tormented, agonized.

angular *adj* bony, gaunt, lean, spare, rangy, gawky.

animadvert *verb* censure, rebuke, reprove, criticize.

animal *noun* **1** creature, beast. **2** beast, brute, pig (*inf*), monster, savage.

animate *verb* enliven, liven up, vitalize, invigorate, pep up (*inf*), energize, fire, rouse, stir.
➤*adj* alive, living, live, breathing, moving.

animated *adj* lively, spirited, energetic, active, vivacious, excited, enthusiastic, ardent, impassioned.

animation *noun* liveliness, life, spirit, vitality, vivacity, verve, zest, excitement, enthusiasm, ardour, passion.

animosity *noun* ill feeling, bad blood, antagonism, animus, antipathy, hostility, enmity, malice, acrimony, rancour, resentment.

annals *pl noun* **1** records, accounts, reports, rolls. **2** archives, chronicles, memoirs, history.

annex *verb* **1** add, append, adjoin, attach, affix. **2** occupy, conquer, seize, take over. ➤*noun* **1** extension, wing. **2** addition, supplement, postscript, codicil.

annihilate *verb* **1** abolish, exterminate, wipe out, eradicate, extirpate, erase, extinguish, destroy. **2** conquer, defeat, rout, beat, thrash (*inf*), trounce (*inf*).

annotate *verb* comment on, gloss, explain, interpret, illustrate.

announce *verb* **1** declare, proclaim, make known, publish, broadcast, advertise, report, disclose, divulge. **2** herald, presage, augur, foretell, betoken, signify.

announcer *noun* presenter, broadcaster, commentator, reporter, newsreader, anchorman, anchorwoman, host, compere.

annoy *verb* **1** irritate, vex, irk, nettle, exasperate, anger, rile, tease, provoke, get someone's back up (*inf*). **2** harass, pester, badger, harry, plague, torment, bug (*inf*). **3** bother, trouble, disturb, get on someone's nerves (*inf*), drive up the wall (*inf*), get to (*inf*).

annual *adj* yearly, every year, once a year. ➤*noun* yearbook, almanac.

annul *verb* **1** nullify, invalidate, void, declare null and void, countermand, overrule. **2** abolish, repeal, revoke, cancel, quash, rescind.

annular *adj* circular, ring-shaped, round.

anodyne *adj* mild, bland, inoffensive, innocuous, neutral. ➤*noun* painkiller, analgesic, opiate, palliative.

anoint *verb* ordain, consecrate, sanctify, hallow, bless.

anomalous *adj* abnormal, irregular, atypical, unusual, exceptional, inconsistent, aberrant, deviating.

anomaly *noun* abnormality, irregularity, exception, freak, aberration, deviation, peculiarity, quirk.

anon *adv* soon, shortly, presently, before long, by and by, in a little while.

anonymous *adj* **1** nameless, unnamed, unidentified, unspecified, unknown, unsigned. **2** featureless, nondescript, undistinguished, unexceptional.

another *adj* **1** a second, a further, an additional, an extra. **2** a different, not the same. **3** some other, an alternative.

answer *verb* **1** reply, respond, acknowledge, retort, retaliate. **2** respond, react. **3** satisfy, meet, serve, suit. **4** correspond to, conform to, match. **5** be responsible, be accountable, be liable, take the blame. **6** pay, suffer, make amends. ➤*noun* **1** reply, response, acknowledgment, retort, riposte, rejoinder. **2** solution, resolution, key, explanation.

answerable *adj* liable, responsible, accountable, amenable.

antagonism *noun* hostility, animosity, antipathy, enmity, opposition, rivalry, friction, discord.

antagonist *noun* opponent, adversary, enemy, rival, competitor.

antagonize *verb* anger, annoy, provoke, offend, alienate, disaffect.

antecedent *adj* preceding, prior, previous, earlier, foregoing. ➤*noun* precedent, precursor, forerunner.

antecedents *pl noun* ancestors, forebears, ancestry, extraction, genealogy, background.

antedate *verb* predate, precede, forego, come before.

antediluvian *adj* **1** archaic, antiquated, old-fashioned, out of the ark (*inf*). **2** ancient, age-old, prehistoric, primeval, primordial.

anterior *adj* **1** front, fore, forward. **2** prior, preceding, earlier, previous, foregoing.

anteroom *noun* antechamber, vestibule, foyer, lobby.

anthem *noun* hymn, song, chant, paean.

anthology *noun* collection, compilation, treasury, miscellany, selection.

anticipate *verb* **1** foresee, predict, forestall, intercept, prevent. **2** pre-empt, beat to it (*inf*). **3** contemplate, prepare for, reckon on. **4** await, look forward to, expect.

anticipation *noun* **1** expectation, prospect, prediction, foresight, presentiment. **2** expectancy, hope, excitement.

anticlimax *noun* comedown, letdown, disappointment, bathos.

antics *pl noun* pranks, tricks, capers, horseplay, tomfoolery, buffoonery.

antidote *noun* **1** remedy, cure, corrective, countermeasure. **2** antivenin, antitoxin, antibody.

antipathy *noun* dislike, aversion, loathing, hatred, repugnance, distaste.

antiquated *adj* old-fashioned, out-of-date, passé, old hat (*inf*), obsolete, archaic, fossilized.

antique *adj* **1** vintage, veteran, antiquarian. **2** old, ancient, early, primitive. ►*noun* curio, objet d'art, relic, antiquity.

antiseptic *adj* **1** germicidal, bactericidal, disinfectant, medicated. **2** aseptic, sterile, germ-free, hygienic, sanitary, uncontaminated. ►*noun* disinfectant, germicide, bactericide.

antisocial *adj* **1** unsociable, uncommunicative, withdrawn, unfriendly, misanthropic. **2** asocial, lawless, rebellious, disruptive, disorderly.

antithesis *noun* **1** opposite, reverse, converse, contrary. **2** contrast, opposition.

anxiety *noun* **1** worry, disquiet, uneasiness, apprehension, nervousness, stress. **2** trouble, care, misgiving.

anxious *adj* **1** worried, concerned, troubled, uneasy, on edge, nervous, tense, apprehensive. **2** eager, keen, yearning, impatient.

any *pron* some, one. ►*adv* at all, in the least, somewhat, to some extent.

anyhow *adv* **1** anyway, in any case, at any rate, in any event. **2** haphazardly, at random, carelessly, negligently.

anyway *adv* **1** in any case, at any rate, in any event, anyhow. **2** however, nevertheless, nonetheless.

apace *adv* quickly, rapidly, swiftly, fast.

apart *adv* **1** aside, to one side, away, afar, alone, separately. **2** asunder, to pieces, to bits.

apart from 1 besides, other than. **2** except, but, save, excluding.

apartment *noun* **1** flat, room. **2** suite, rooms, lodging.

apathetic *adj* **1** unfeeling, unresponsive, impassive, listless, lethargic, passive. **2** indifferent, unconcerned, uninterested.

apathy *noun* **1** impassivity, unresponsiveness, insensibility, listlessness, lethargy, inertia. **2** indifference, unconcern.

ape *noun* anthropoid, gorilla, gibbon, chimpanzee. ►*verb* imitate, mimic, copy, parrot.

aperture *noun* opening, hole, orifice, gap, space, slot, vent.

apex *noun* **1** vertex, top. **2** tip, point. **3** top, pinnacle, peak, acme, apogee, zenith, culmination.

aphorism *noun* proverb, saying, dictum, adage, saw.

apiece *adv* each, individually, respectively.

aplomb *noun* poise, self-possession, self-assurance, composure, calmness, sangfroid.

apocalyptic *adj* **1** revelatory, prophetic, oracular. **2** dire, catastrophic, cataclysmic.

apocryphal *adj* unsubstantiated, dubious, spurious, untrue, fictitious, imaginary.

apologetic *adj* sorry, regretful, remorseful, contrite, penitent.

apologist *noun* advocate, champion, defender.

apologize *verb* beg pardon, say sorry, be sorry, regret.

apology *noun* **1** excuse, explanation, confession, acknowledgment. **2** defence, vindication, plea, argument, apologia. **3** travesty, mockery, substitute, excuse.

apophthegm *noun* maxim, dictum, saying, axiom, precept.

apostasy *noun* desertion, defection, backsliding, recidivism, disloyalty, treachery.

apostate *noun* renegade, turncoat, backslider, recidivist, defector, traitor.

apostle *noun* **1** missionary, preacher, evangelist. **2** crusader, pioneer, champion, advocate.

apotheosis *noun* **1** deification, exaltation, glorification. **2** idealization, quintessence.

appal *verb* horrify, outrage, shock, stun, dismay, alarm.

apparatus *noun* **1** equipment, gear, tackle, machinery, device, appliance, contraption, mechanism. **2** system, organization, set-up.

apparel *noun* clothes, garments, attire, dress, outfit, costume.

apparent *adj* **1** obvious, evident, plain, manifest, visible, discernible. **2** seeming, ostensible.

apparition *noun* **1** ghost, spectre, phantom, spirit, visitant. **2** appearance, manifestation, materialization, illusion, hallucination.

appeal *noun* **1** attraction, allure, charm, fascination. **2** entreaty, plea, prayer, supplication. **3** request, call. **4** application, petition. **5** suit, claim.
➤*verb* **1** request, solicit, entreat, beg, beseech, plead. **2** address, call on, invoke, petition. **3** attract, interest, fascinate, charm, invite.

appear *verb* **1** come into view, come into sight, loom, emerge, surface, materialize. **2** arrive, turn up, show up. **3** seem, look. **4** be present, attend.

appearance *noun* **1** arrival, emergence, materialization, manifestation, presence, attendance. **2** look, aspect, demeanour, air, image. **3** impression, semblance, illusion, show, front, facade.

appease *verb* **1** pacify, lull, still, calm. **2** placate, propitiate, conciliate, mollify. **3** satisfy, quench, quell, assuage, allay, relieve.

appellation *noun* name, title, designation, denomination.

append *verb* add, attach, affix, adjoin, annex, tack on.

appendage *noun* **1** attachment, addition, accessory, appurtenance. **2** part, projection, limb, member.

appendix *noun* addition, supplement, addendum, postscript, codicil, rider.

appertain *verb* belong, pertain, refer, relate, concern, apply.

appetite *noun* **1** hunger, taste, palate, stomach. **2** desire, lust, craving, hankering, hunger, thirst, inclination, proclivity.

appetizer *noun* apéritif, hors d'oeuvre, antipasto.

appetizing *adj* savoury, mouth-watering, delicious, succulent, tempting, appealing.

applaud *verb* clap, cheer, praise, commend, congratulate.

applause *noun* clapping, ovation, standing ovation, a big hand (*inf*).

appliance *noun* **1** device, machine, gadget, instrument, apparatus, piece of equipment. **2** application, use, exercise, practice.

applicable *adj* appropriate, apt, apposite, germane, relevant, pertinent.

applicant *noun* candidate, interviewee, aspirant, petitioner, claimant.

application *noun* **1** request, claim, petition, appeal, enquiry. **2** appliance, use, exercise, practice. **3** relevance, pertinence, bearing, significance, appropriateness. **4** purpose, function, use. **5** dedication, commitment, diligence, industry, effort.

apply *verb* **1** use, utilize, employ, exercise, administer, exert, bring to bear. **2** ask, request, claim, appeal, enquire. **3** dedicate, devote, commit, direct, address. **4** refer, be relevant, relate, appertain. **5** spread, smear, daub.

appoint *verb* **1** select, assign, elect, install, employ, engage, commission. **2** name, designate, fix, set, arrange, decide, establish, decree.

appointment *noun* **1** meeting, consultation, date, rendezvous, engagement. **2** office, position, job, situation. **3** engagement, recruitment, selection, election, installation.

apportion *verb* divide, share, allot, allocate, administer, dispense, distribute, dole out (*inf*).

apposite *adj* apt, appropriate, fitting, suitable, applicable, relevant, apropos, to the point.

appraisal *noun* evaluation, assessment, inspection, review, valuation, judgment.

appraise *verb* **1** evaluate, assess, size up (*inf*), inspect, review, judge. **2** value, price, rate.

appreciable *adj* noticeable, perceptible, discernible, marked, significant, substantial, considerable.

appreciate *verb* 1 value, prize, cherish, treasure. 2 esteem, respect, recognize, acknowledge, be grateful for. 3 see, understand, grasp, realize, be aware of, be sensitive to, sympathize with. 4 go up, increase, gain.

appreciation *noun* 1 esteem, regard, admiration, acknowledgment, gratitude, thanks, approval, approbation. 2 recognition, perception, grasp, realization, awareness, sensitivity, sympathy. 3 rise, increase, growth, gain. 4 review, critique, evaluation, assessment, judgment.

apprehend *verb* 1 seize, catch, capture, arrest, detain, take into custody. 2 understand, comprehend, grasp, perceive, recognize, realize.

apprehension *noun* 1 fear, alarm, dread, trepidation, anxiety, nervousness, misgiving, disquiet. 2 seizure, capture, arrest, detention. 3 understanding, comprehension, grasp, perception, recognition, realization.

apprehensive *adj* anxious, nervous, fearful, frightened, troubled, uneasy.

apprentice *noun* trainee, student, pupil, probationer, learner, novice.

apprise *verb* inform, tell, notify, acquaint, enlighten, brief.

approach *verb* 1 near, come near, move towards, catch up, gain on, reach. 2 tackle, undertake, set about, start, broach. 3 come close to, border on, verge on, approximate, resemble. 4 appeal to, apply to, contact, make advances to, make overtures to, proposition, accost, address. ►*noun* 1 advent, coming, advance, arrival. 2 access, entrance, way, road, path, drive. 3 method, procedure, technique, way, manner, strategy. 4 appeal, application, proposition, proposal, advances, overtures.

approachable *adj* friendly, sociable, affable, easygoing, communicative, talkative.

approbation *noun* 1 approval, sanction, assent, consent. 2 praise, commendation, recognition, acclaim.

appropriate *adj* 1 suitable, timely, opportune. 2 apt, fitting, right, proper, seemly, apposite, pertinent, germane.

►*verb* 1 seize, take, requisition, commandeer, arrogate, expropriate, confiscate, impound. 2 assign, allot, allocate, earmark, set aside, ring-fence.

approval *noun* 1 approbation, admiration, esteem, appreciation, favour, liking, praise, acclamation. 2 sanction, authorization, consent, agreement, acceptance, endorsement, blessing, green light (*inf*), OK (*inf*), thumbs-up (*inf*).

approve *verb* 1 admire, esteem, favour, like, be pleased with, think well of, praise, acclaim. 2 sanction, authorize, ratify, rubber-stamp (*inf*), consent to, agree to. 3 accept, endorse, support.

approximate *adj* 1 rough, estimated, near, close. 2 inexact, imprecise, loose. ►*verb* 1 approach, border on, verge on. 2 resemble, be similar to, compare with.

appurtenance *noun* accessory, attachment, fitting.

apropos *prep* regarding, with regard to, with reference to, with respect to, in connection with, on the subject of, re.

apt *adj* 1 appropriate, suitable, fitting, proper, felicitous, apropos, apposite, relevant. 2 disposed, inclined, prone, liable, subject, given, likely. 3 able, clever, smart, bright, intelligent, astute, adroit, adept.

aptitude *noun* 1 ability, faculty, capacity, skill, gift, talent, flair, disposition. 2 aptness, suitability, fitness, appositeness, pertinence, relevance.

aquatic *adj* 1 marine, water, sea, river. 2 maritime, nautical, water.

aquiline *adj* hooked, bent, curved, Roman.

arable *adj* cultivable, farmable, tillable, fertile.

arbiter *noun* judge, adjudicator, arbitrator, referee, umpire, authority, expert.

arbitrary *adj* 1 random, capricious, whimsical, subjective, personal, unreasoned, irrational, inconsistent. 2 despotic, dictatorial, autocratic, tyrannical, absolute, imperious.

arbitrate *verb* 1 judge, adjudicate, referee, umpire, decide, settle, mediate, intervene. 2 negotiate, conciliate.

arbitration *noun* judgment, adjudication, settlement, mediation, intervention, negotiation, conciliation.

arbitrator *noun* judge, adjudicator, arbiter, referee, mediator, negotiator, intermediary, go-between.

arbour *noun* bower, pergola, shelter, alcove.

arc *noun* bend, curve, arch, bow.

arcade *noun* 1 colonnade, peristyle. 2 portico, cloister, gallery. 3 precinct, mall.

arcane *adj* 1 mysterious, cryptic. 2 occult, esoteric, recondite, secret, hidden.

arch[1] *noun* archway, vault, span.
➤ *verb* curve, bend, bow, arc, vault.

arch[2] *adj* roguish, artful, waggish, mischievous, playful, saucy.

archaic *adj* 1 ancient, old, antiquated, superannuated, outmoded, old hat (*inf*). 2 obsolete, obsolescent.

archetype *noun* 1 original, prototype, standard, model, pattern. 2 paradigm, exemplar, paragon, ideal, epitome.

architect *noun* 1 designer, planner, draughtsman, draughtswoman. 2 creator, originator, founder, engineer, mastermind.

architecture *noun* 1 design, planning, building, construction, architectonics. 2 structure, composition, make-up, design, arrangement.

archive *noun* collection, records, documents, papers.

arctic *adj* 1 polar, hyperborean. 2 cold, freezing, frozen, glacial, icy.

ardent *adj* 1 fervent, passionate, avid, zealous, earnest, intense. 2 burning, hot, fiery, glowing.

ardour *noun* 1 fervour, passion, feeling, emotion, warmth, fire, intensity. 2 eagerness, avidity, enthusiasm, zeal, devotion, dedication.

arduous *adj* difficult, hard, tough, taxing, laborious, tiring, strenuous, gruelling.

area *noun* 1 district, region, zone, sector, territory, arena. 2 sphere, field, domain, province, department, scope, range. 3 extent, surface, space, dimensions. 4 expanse, stretch, tract, plot.

arena *noun* 1 stadium, ground, field, ring, amphitheatre, hippodrome. 2 sphere, world, realm, domain.

argue *verb* 1 dispute, disagree, quarrel, wrangle, squabble, bicker, row. 2 debate, discuss, reason, maintain, assert, claim, plead.

argument *noun* 1 dispute, disagreement, quarrel, row, altercation, tiff (*inf*). 2 discussion, debate, polemic, controversy. 3 case, reasoning, rationale, reasons. 4 defence, contention, plea, claim.

argumentative *adj* contentious, quarrelsome, disputatious, belligerent, stroppy (*inf*).

arid *adj* 1 dry, parched, baked, scorched, desert, barren. 2 dull, boring, flat, dry, insipid, barren.

aright *adv* rightly, correctly, properly, exactly.

arise *verb* 1 originate, derive, spring, stem, begin, proceed, result. 2 appear, emerge, occur. 3 rise, stand up, go up.

aristocracy *noun* nobility, gentry, peerage, ruling class, upper class.

aristocrat *noun* noble, nobleman, noblewoman, gentleman, lady, patrician.

aristocratic *adj* noble, titled, upper class, patrician, blue-blooded, highborn, genteel, well-bred.

arm[1] *noun* 1 limb, forelimb, member, appendage. 2 branch, wing, division, department, section. 3 inlet, sound, estuary, firth.

arm[2] *verb* 1 equip, provide, supply, issue. 2 fortify, strengthen, reinforce, protect, brace.

armada *noun* fleet, flotilla, navy.

armament *noun* weaponry, ordnance, matériel.

armistice *noun* truce, cease-fire, peace.

armour *noun* 1 mail, chain mail. 2 covering, protection, armour plate.

armoured *adj* reinforced, ironclad, armour-plated, bulletproof.

armoury *noun* 1 arsenal, magazine, ammunition dump, ordnance depot, depository, cache. 2 store, stockpile, supply.

arms *pl noun* 1 weapons, weaponry, firearms, guns, artillery. 2 shield, escutcheon, insignia, blazonry, armorial bearings, heraldic device.

army *noun* **1** soldiers, troops, military. **2** multitude, host, crowd, throng, mob.

aroma *noun* odour, smell, scent, bouquet, redolence, savour.

aromatic *adj* **1** fragrant, scented, perfumed, sweet-smelling. **2** spicy, pungent.

around *prep* **1** round, surrounding, encircling, encompassing. **2** all over, throughout, about.
➤*adv* **1** about, here and there, to and fro. **2** near, nearby, at hand, close. **3** roughly, approximately, about, circa.

arouse *verb* **1** wake, awaken, rouse. **2** cause, prompt, provoke, stimulate, kindle, trigger. **3** stir, animate, rouse, spur, goad, incite. **4** stimulate, excite, turn on (*inf*).

arraign *verb* summon, prosecute, accuse, charge, indict, impeach.

arrange *verb* **1** order, dispose, group, sort, classify, systematize, place, lay out. **2** fix, prepare, plan, organize, coordinate, set up. **3** adapt, set, orchestrate, score.

arrangement *noun* **1** order, array, disposition, layout, design, pattern, system, structure. **2** plan, preparation, provision, measure. **3** agreement, settlement, understanding, compact. **4** adaptation, setting, interpretation, version.

arrant *adj* utter, total, absolute, downright, out-and-out, thoroughgoing, brazen, gross.

array *verb* **1** arrange, dispose, display, marshal, assemble, line up, rank, position. **2** dress, clothe, attire, garb, apparel, adorn, deck.
➤*noun* **1** display, collection, assemblage. **2** arrangement, disposition, line-up, formation, parade. **3** dress, clothing, garments, attire, apparel, garb, finery, regalia.

arrears *pl noun* debt, amount overdue, outstanding payment, deficit.
in arrears behind, late, in debt, in the red, overdue, outstanding, owed.

arrest *verb* **1** seize, catch, capture, apprehend, take into custody, detain, nick (*inf*), run in (*inf*). **2** stop, stem, halt, impede, obstruct, block. **3** restrain, inhibit, delay, hold back. **4** attract, catch, capture, engage, grip, hold.
➤*noun* **1** seizure, capture, apprehension, detention. **2** stoppage, cessation, halt, inhibition, suppression, obstruction, blockage.

arresting *adj* striking, stunning, impressive, remarkable, extraordinary, conspicuous.

arrival *noun* **1** appearance, entrance, advent, coming, occurrence, approach. **2** newcomer, visitor, caller, incomer.

arrive *verb* **1** get there, enter, check in, clock in, land, dock, appear, roll up (*inf*). **2** come, appear, turn up, occur. **3** succeed, make it (*inf*), reach the top, prosper.
arrive at reach, get to, come to, attain, realize.

arrogant *adj* proud, haughty, self-important, full of oneself (*inf*), supercilious, stuck-up (*inf*), overbearing, high and mighty (*inf*), lordly, pompous.

arrogate *verb* appropriate, seize, claim, assume, usurp, commandeer.

arrow *noun* **1** shaft, dart, bolt. **2** pointer, marker, indicator.

arsenal *noun* armoury, magazine, ammunition dump, arms depot, depository.

arson *noun* fire-raising, incendiarism, pyromania.

art *noun* **1** painting, drawing, sculpture, design, fine arts, graphic arts. **2** skill, technique, craft, knack, expertise, mastery, finesse.

artful *adj* cunning, sly, wily, subtle, shrewd, crafty, clever, ingenious.

article *noun* **1** item, thing, object, commodity, unit. **2** story, report, piece, feature, column, paper, review. **3** section, division, clause, point, paragraph.

articulate *verb* **1** pronounce, enunciate, utter, speak, say, voice. **2** express, verbalize, state. **3** join, unite, connect, link, couple. **4** interlock, hinge.
➤*adj* **1** distinct, intelligible, eloquent, well-spoken, fluent. **2** clear, coherent, comprehensible, lucid.

artifice *noun* **1** trick, stratagem, wile, device, tactic, ruse. **2** trickery, guile, craftiness, strategy, skill, ingenuity.

artificial *adj* **1** synthetic, man-made, manufactured, simulated, imitation, mock, ersatz, fake. **2** affected, insincere, unnatural, contrived, studied, mannered.

artillery *noun* gunnery, cannonry, ordnance, battery.

artisan *noun* craftsman, craftswoman, artificer, skilled worker, technician.

artist *noun* 1 painter, sculptor, designer. **2** master, expert. **3** artiste, performer, entertainer, singer, musician, player, trouper.

artistic *adj* 1 creative, sensitive, imaginative. **2** tasteful, aesthetic, attractive, decorative, stylish, elegant.

artistry *noun* art, craftsmanship, talent, flair, genius, virtuosity, finesse, creativity.

artless *adj* 1 simple, natural, unaffected, unpretentious. **2** honest, truthful, sincere, frank, naive, ingenuous. **3** awkward, clumsy, inexpert, untaught, crude, primitive.

as *conj* 1 while, when. **2** because, since, seeing that. **3** like, in the same way that. ➤*prep* like, being, in the role of.
as for as to, with regard to, with respect to, in relation to.
as yet up to now, until now.

ascend *verb* 1 rise, slope upwards. **2** go up, climb, scale. **3** soar, mount, rise.

ascendancy *noun* superiority, dominance, advantage, upper hand, control, sway, supremacy, command.

ascendant *noun* ascendancy, superiority, dominance, authority, control, power. ➤*adj* 1 dominant, prevailing, superior, powerful, commanding, ruling. **2** rising, ascending, climbing, mounting, soaring.

ascent *noun* 1 ascension, rise, climb, scaling. **2** gradient, incline, slope, acclivity, rising ground, ramp.

ascertain *verb* discover, find out, learn, determine, identify, establish, verify, confirm.

ascetic *adj* 1 abstemious, abstinent, self-denying, continent, celibate, temperate. **2** austere, spartan, severe, rigorous, harsh, strict.

ascribe *verb* 1 put down, attribute, blame, refer. **2** assign, attribute. **3** credit, accredit, attribute.

ashamed *adj* abashed, embarrassed, sheepish, guilty, remorseful, sorry, bashful, self-conscious.

ashen *adj* ashy, pale, pallid, livid, ghastly, white, blanched, colourless.

ashore *adv* to the shore, shoreward, landward, on shore, aground, beached.

aside *adv* 1 to the side, alongside. **2** away, out of the way, apart. **3** in reserve, on one side.
➤*noun* 1 stage whisper, soliloquy, monologue. **2** digression, departure.

asinine *adj* stupid, foolish, idiotic, silly, daft (*inf*), senseless, inane, brainless, dumb (*inf*).

ask *verb* 1 question, quiz, interrogate, cross-examine, interview, poll. **2** inquire, query. **3** put, pose. **4** request, desire, crave, solicit. **5** approach, apply to, appeal to, beg. **6** demand, seek, require, expect. **7** invite, bid, summon.

askew *adv and adj* awry, crooked, aslant, lopsided, off-centre, out of line, skew-whiff (*inf*).

asleep *adj* 1 sleeping, slumbering, dozing, napping, having forty winks (*inf*), dead to the world (*inf*), dormant, inactive. **2** numb, insensible.

aspect *noun* 1 side, angle, point, feature, facet, factor. **2** appearance, look, air, slant, viewpoint, outlook. **3** direction, orientation, position, view, prospect.

asperity *noun* 1 harshness, sharpness, sourness, irascibility. **2** roughness, coarseness, ruggedness.

aspersion *noun* cast aspersions on slander, defame, vilify, denigrate, disparage, deprecate, smear.

asphyxiate *verb* suffocate, smother, stifle, choke, strangle, throttle.

aspiration *noun* desire, longing, hope, dream, ambition, goal, aim, objective.

aspire *verb* desire, long, yearn, hope, dream, seek, strive, aim.

ass *noun* donkey, jackass, dolt, fool, idiot, dunce, blockhead, twit (*inf*), wally (*sl*), dickhead (*sl*).

assail verb 1 attack, assault, set about, lay into, berate, lambaste, bombard, strike. 2 beset, plague, bedevil, prey on, worry, trouble, torment.

assailant noun attacker, assaulter, accoster, mugger, aggressor, opponent.

assassin noun killer, murderer, liquidator, executioner, hitman (inf).

assassinate verb kill, murder, slay, liquidate, eliminate (inf), execute, hit (inf).

assault verb 1 attack, assail, set about, strike, hit, mug, charge, storm. 2 molest, interfere with, abuse, rape.
➤noun 1 attack, onslaught, onset, charge, strike, offensive. 2 violence, battery, mugging, actual bodily harm, grievous bodily harm, GBH (inf). 3 molestation, interference, abuse, rape.

assay verb 1 analyse, examine, scrutinize, probe. 2 test, prove, inspect, check, assess, evaluate. 3 try, attempt, essay.
➤noun test, analysis, examination, inspection, assessment, evaluation.

assemblage noun assembly, gathering, crowd, collection, combination, medley, accumulation, cluster.

assemble verb 1 come together, collect, gather, congregate, meet, convene, rally. 2 bring together, collect, gather, accumulate, marshal, muster, convoke. 3 construct, make, manufacture, put together, join, connect, build.

assembly noun 1 gathering, meeting, rally, convention, congress, congregation, body, crowd. 2 construction, fabrication, manufacture, building.

assent verb agree, acquiesce, concur, accept, consent, allow.
➤noun 1 agreement, acceptance, approval, sanction, consent, permission. 2 acquiescence, compliance.

assert verb 1 declare, affirm, aver, swear, maintain, state, announce, claim. 2 insist on, push for, emphasize, stress, support, defend.
assert oneself make one's presence felt, exert one's influence.

assertion noun declaration, statement, avowal, proclamation, allegation, claim.

assertive adj 1 positive, dogmatic, opinionated, emphatic, insistent, forceful.

2 self-confident, self-assured, not backward in coming forward (inf), strong-willed, firm, aggressive, self-assertive, pushy (inf).

assess verb 1 estimate, weigh up, size up, judge, appraise, evaluate. 2 value, rate. 3 calculate, compute, determine, fix.

asset noun 1 possession, chattel. 2 advantage, benefit, plus (inf), blessing, virtue, strength, resource, help.

assets pl noun property, estate, belongings, effects, capital, securities, holdings, reserves.

asseverate verb declare, affirm, attest, avow, aver, assert.

assiduity noun industry, diligence, application, devotion, effort, care, attention, conscientiousness.

assiduous adj industrious, diligent, sedulous, zealous, persistent, painstaking, attentive, conscientious.

assign verb 1 appoint, nominate, select, detail, charge, commission. 2 allot, allocate, give, designate, earmark. 3 fix, set, decide, specify. 4 attribute, ascribe, put down, accredit, impute. 5 transfer, convey, consign, make over.

assignation noun 1 meeting, rendezvous, tryst, appointment, date. 2 allotment, allocation, designation, assignment, appointment, selection.

assignment noun 1 task, job, project. 2 mission, errand, post, appointment. 3 transfer, conveyance, consignment.

assimilate verb 1 absorb, take in, digest, incorporate, learn. 2 adapt, adjust, accommodate, conform, fit. 3 naturalize, merge, integrate. 4 blend, mingle.

assist verb help, aid, lend a hand, support, cooperate, serve, advance, facilitate.

assistance noun help, aid, service, support, cooperation, collaboration, relief.

assistant noun 1 helper, aide, accomplice, collaborator, partner, auxiliary, right-hand man, deputy. 2 salesperson, checkout operator.

associate verb 1 relate, link, connect. 2 affiliate, incorporate, amalgamate, merge, ally, league. 3 consort, fraternize, socialize, mix, mingle, rub shoulders (inf), keep company, hang out (inf). 4 unite,

join, attach, combine.
➤ *noun* colleague, co-worker, partner, ally, fellow, friend, companion.

association *noun* **1** society, organization, guild, league, federation, alliance, syndicate, company, partnership, corporation, club, fellowship. **2** relationship, correlation, connection, link.

assorted *adj* mixed, various, miscellaneous, multifarious, heterogeneous, diverse, motley, sundry.

assortment *noun* mixture, variety, miscellany, medley, hotchpotch, selection, range, collection.

assuage *verb* **1** ease, relieve, alleviate, allay, soothe, moderate, abate, dull. **2** quell, quench, slake, satisfy.

assume *verb* **1** presume, suppose, surmise, deduce, postulate, hypothesize. **2** affect, feign, put on, pretend, counterfeit, simulate. **3** accept, take on, undertake, shoulder. **4** adopt, embrace. **5** acquire, develop. **6** seize, take over, usurp, arrogate.

assumption *noun* **1** presumption, supposition, conjecture, surmise, deduction, acceptance, belief. **2** hypothesis, theory, postulate, premise. **3** assuming, taking, adoption, undertaking. **4** appropriation, seizure, usurpation, arrogation.

assurance *noun* **1** promise, word, guarantee, pledge, vow, oath, declaration, undertaking. **2** assuredness, self-assurance, self-confidence, self-possession, poise, boldness, presumption, arrogance. **3** certainty, sureness, conviction, confidence, belief.

assure *verb* **1** promise, guarantee, vow, swear, attest, certify, aver, affirm. **2** convince, persuade, reassure, comfort, encourage, hearten. **3** ensure, make certain, guarantee, secure.

assured *adj* **1** self-assured, self-confident, confident, complacent, assertive, bold, presumptuous, arrogant. **2** certain, sure, guaranteed, secure.

astir *adj* active, on the move, awake, alert, up and about.

astonish *verb* amaze, astound, stagger, flabbergast (*inf*), dumbfound, gobsmack (*inf*), daze, stun, knock for six (*inf*).

astound *verb* amaze, astonish, stagger, dumbfound, take someone's breath away (*inf*), bowl over (*inf*), bewilder, confound, nonplus.

astral *adj* stellar, sidereal, starry, starlike.

astray *adv* **1** off course, off the right track, wandering, lost, missing, absent. **2** wrong, amiss, off course, off the rails (*inf*).

astringent *adj* sharp, acerbic, caustic, mordant, trenchant, harsh, stern, severe.

astronaut *noun* spaceman, spacewoman, cosmonaut.

astute *adj* shrewd, sharp, acute, quick-witted, intelligent, discerning, perceptive, subtle, artful, clever.

asunder *adv* apart, to pieces, to bits.

asylum *noun* **1** refuge, sanctuary, haven, retreat, shelter, protection, safety. **2** institution, home, hospital, mental hospital, psychiatric hospital, loony bin (*inf*).

asymmetric *adj* unsymmetrical, unbalanced, lopsided, uneven, irregular, disproportionate.

atheism *noun* irreligion, godlessness, unbelief, freethinking, rationalism, heathenism, paganism.

athlete *noun* sportsman, sportswoman, runner, gymnast, player, contestant.

athletic *adj* **1** muscular, sinewy, brawny, strapping, strong, powerful. **2** sporty, energetic, vigorous, active, fit, able-bodied.

athwart *adv* across, crosswise, transversely, obliquely.
➤ *prep* across, over.

atmosphere *noun* **1** air, aerospace, sky, heavens. **2** environment, surroundings, background, setting, ambience, aura, climate, mood, tone, tenor, vibrations, vibes (*inf*).

atom *noun* particle, scrap, bit, jot, iota, shred, grain, trace, hint.

atone *verb* expiate, pay, make amends, make reparation, redress, do penance.

atonement *noun* expiation, redemption, amends, reparation, restitution, propitiation, redress, penance.

atrocious *adj* **1** monstrous, villainous, wicked, evil, brutal, inhuman, savage, barbaric. **2** abominable, detestable, horrifying, shocking, outrageous, heinous, appalling, disgraceful. **3** appalling, terrible, dreadful, awful, abysmal.

atrocity noun **1** outrage, monstrosity, enormity, horror. **2** brutality, crime, violation. **3** infamy, villainy, wickedness, evil, cruelty, inhumanity, savagery, barbarity.

atrophy noun **1** wasting, emaciation, shrivelling, withering. **2** decline, degeneration, decay, diminution, dwindling.
➤*verb* decline, degenerate, waste away, shrivel, wither, diminish, dwindle.

attach verb **1** fasten, join, connect, secure, fix, stick, append, add. **2** affiliate, associate, ally, unite. **3** assign, second, detail, appoint. **4** attribute, ascribe, associate, impute, put, lay.

attached adj fond, loving, affectionate, devoted, enamoured, infatuated.

attachment noun **1** accessory, fitting, extension, part, appendage, appurtenance. **2** fondness, tenderness, love, affection, liking, affinity, bond, fidelity. **3** assignment, secondment, posting, appointment. **4** fastening, connection, coupling, link.

attack verb **1** assault, assail, ambush, mug, strike, invade, raid, charge. **2** criticize, run down (*inf*), censure, slate (*inf*), slander, malign, abuse, berate. **3** affect, infect, infest, destroy. **4** embark on, undertake, tackle, set about.
➤*noun* **1** invasion, offensive, assault, raid, onslaught, strike, criticism, censure, slander, abuse. **2** assault, ambush, mugging, beating up (*inf*). **3** bout, spasm, access, fit, paroxysm.

attain verb **1** achieve, realize, accomplish, fulfil, secure, gain, win. **2** reach, arrive at, get to.

attainment noun accomplishment, achievement, exploit, feat, success, qualification, skill, proficiency

attempt verb try, endeavour, essay, have a go, strive, seek.
➤*noun* try, effort, endeavour, bid, go, stab (*inf*), crack (*inf*), shot (*inf*).

attend verb **1** be present, appear, show up (*inf*). **2** go, visit, frequent. **3** accompany, escort, chaperon, guard, serve, wait on. **4** minister to, tend, nurse, look after, care for. **5** listen, watch, pay attention, concen-

trate, mark, mind. **6** result from, arise from, go with, accompany, be associated with.

attend to deal with, see to, handle, take care of, look after.

attendant noun escort, companion, servant, steward, guard, aide.
➤*adj* accompanying, concomitant, associated, related, incidental, resultant.

attention noun **1** attentiveness, heed, mind, vigilance, notice, thought, concentration, application. **2** regard, consideration, care, ministration, treatment, service. **3** thought, consideration, handling, processing. **4** respect, courtesy, gallantry, compliment, address.

attentive adj **1** heedful, alert, mindful, observant, vigilant, concentrating, intent. **2** considerate, thoughtful, kind, solicitous, gallant, chivalrous.

attenuate verb **1** diminish, reduce, weaken, dilute, rarefy. **2** taper, thin, draw out.

attest verb **1** affirm, aver, confirm, corroborate. **2** authenticate, certify, ratify, endorse. **3** bear witness to, show, demonstrate, prove, bear out, substantiate.

attic noun loft, garret.

attire noun dress, clothing, wear, garb, outfit, costume.
➤*verb* dress, clothe, garb, array, apparel, rig out.

attitude noun **1** opinion, viewpoint, stance, position, approach, mood, mentality. **2** pose, posture, position, stance.

attorney noun agent, deputy, substitute, proxy.

attract verb **1** draw, pull, bring in. **2** allure, entice, seduce, charm, captivate, win. **3** tempt, engage, interest, fascinate.

attraction noun **1** draw, pull, magnetism. **2** charm, appeal, allure, lure, glamour. **3** activity, diversion, entertainment.

attractive adj **1** pleasing, lovely, good-looking, beautiful, handsome, pretty, charming, enchanting, picturesque, seductive, alluring, sexy. **2** tempting, inviting, appealing, desirable, interesting, pleasant.

attribute verb **1** ascribe, assign, credit, accredit. **2** blame, charge, put down.

➤*noun* **1** quality, virtue, characteristic, trait, feature. **2** property, peculiarity, mark, sign, indicator.

attrition *noun* **1** abrasion, friction, wear, rubbing, grinding, erosion. **2** weakening, enfeebling, debilitation, enervation, sapping, wearing down.

attune *verb* **1** accustom, assimilate, acclimatize, familiarize, adjust, adapt. **2** harmonize, coordinate.

atypical *adj* unusual, exceptional, uncharacteristic, abnormal, anomalous.

auburn *adj* reddish-brown, copper-coloured, chestnut, russet, Titian.

audacious *adj* **1** bold, daring, fearless, dauntless, intrepid, venturesome, adventurous. **2** rash, reckless, foolhardy. **3** forward, brazen, impertinent, insolent, arrogant, presumptuous.

audible *adj* perceptible, discernible, detectable, distinct.

audience *noun* **1** crowd, turnout, house, gate, spectators, viewers, listeners, patrons. **2** interview, hearing, reception, meeting, consultation.

audit *verb* inspect, examine, scrutinize, check, verify, go over.
➤*noun* inspection, examination, scrutiny, verification.

audition *noun* hearing, test, trial, tryout.

augment *verb* add to, raise, boost, intensify, increase, multiply, expand, grow, rise

augur *verb* **1** predict, forecast, foretell, prophesy. **2** portend, presage, bode, herald, signify, betoken.
➤*noun* prophet, soothsayer, seer, oracle.

augury *noun* **1** divination, soothsaying, prophecy, prediction, prognostication. **2** omen, portent, presage, herald, sign, token.

august *adj* dignified, grand, magnificent, stately, majestic, venerable, exalted, solemn.

aura *noun* air, atmosphere, ambience, feeling, mood, quality.

auspicious *adj* favourable, bright, rosy, promising, encouraging, hopeful, optimistic, propitious.

austere *adj* **1** stern, severe, harsh, forbidding, serious, solemn, aloof. **2** abstemious, self-denying, Spartan, frugal, ascetic, abstinent, puritanical. **3** plain, simple, unadorned, basic, stark.

authentic *adj* **1** genuine, true, veritable, real, legitimate, valid, bona fide. **2** truthful, honest, trustworthy, accurate, factual, true, faithful, authoritative.

authenticate *verb* **1** verify, prove, substantiate, validate, ratify, endorse. **2** confirm, corroborate, attest, vouch for.

author *noun* **1** writer, novelist, essayist, poet, playwright, journalist, contributor, composer. **2** creator, originator, initiator, founder, mastermind, inventor, architect.

authoritarian *adj* **1** oppressive, strict, harsh, tough, draconian. **2** despotic, autocratic, tyrannical, dictatorial, absolute, imperious, domineering, overbearing.
➤*noun* despot, autocrat, tyrant, dictator.

authoritative *adj* **1** official, legitimate, valid, authentic, genuine, true, scholarly, definitive. **2** reliable, dependable, trustworthy, decisive, conclusive, certain. **3** assertive, confident, masterful, dogmatic, dictatorial, imperious, overbearing.

authorities *pl noun* establishment, administration, management, government, state, powers that be (*inf*).

authority *noun* **1** power, control, command, jurisdiction, management, direction, government, rule, influence, sway. **2** expert, consultant, specialist, professional, scholar, pundit, connoisseur. **3** source, reference, documentation.

authorize *verb* **1** empower, enable, accredit, entitle, license. **2** sanction, approve, rubber-stamp (*inf*), ratify, permit, allow.

autobiography *noun* life story, memoirs, diary, journal.

autocracy *noun* dictatorship, despotism, tyranny, absolutism, totalitarianism.

autocrat *noun* **1** dictator, despot, tyrant, totalitarian. **2** authoritarian, dictator, tyrant, little Hitler (*inf*).

autograph *noun* signature, name, initials.
➤*verb* sign, initial, make one's mark.

automatic *adj* **1** automated, mechanized, self-activating, self-regulating, push-button. **2** mechanical, robotic. **3** involuntary, unconscious, spontaneous,

instinctive, reflex, knee-jerk (*inf*).
4 inevitable, unavoidable, certain, assured.

autonomous *adj* self-governing, self-ruling, autarchic, independent, free.

autonomy *noun* **1** self-government, self-rule, home rule, autarchy. **2** self-reliance, self-sufficiency, independence, freedom.

autopsy *noun* postmortem, necropsy, dissection.

auxiliary *adj* **1** ancillary, subsidiary, secondary, subordinate. **2** supplementary, additional, extra, spare, reserve, back-up.
➤ *noun* ancillary, accessory, subordinate, assistant, helper.

avail *noun* use, benefit, good, profit, advantage, help, service.
➤ *verb* benefit, profit, help, serve.
avail oneself of use, exploit, make use of, take advantage of.

available *adj* **1** ready, to hand, at one's disposal, free, vacant, usable. **2** obtainable, accessible, within reach, handy, convenient.

avalanche *noun* cascade, deluge, flood.

avant-garde *adj* experimental, innovative, progressive, modernistic, futuristic, advanced.

avarice *noun* greed, rapacity, cupidity, materialism, acquisitiveness, covetousness, miserliness.

avenge *verb* revenge, retaliate, requite, repay, punish, get even (*inf*).

avenue *noun* **1** approach, way, path, course. **2** drive, boulevard.

aver *verb* assert, affirm, avow, state, declare, maintain, claim.

average *noun* **1** mean, median, midpoint. **2** norm, standard, par, rule, yardstick.
➤ *adj* **1** mean, medial. **2** medium, middle, intermediate, middling, mediocre, satisfactory, fair, moderate. **3** normal, standard, typical, ordinary, usual, common, unexceptional.

averse *adj* reluctant, indisposed, disinclined, loath, opposed, hostile.

aversion *noun* loathing, repugnance, hate, antipathy, dislike, distaste, hostility.

avert *verb* **1** turn away, turn aside, divert. **2** deflect, ward off, avoid, forestall, thwart, prevent.

aviation *noun* flight, flying, aeronautics.

aviator *noun* airman, airwoman, flier, pilot, aeronaut.

avid *adj* keen, eager, enthusiastic, ardent, passionate, fanatical, greedy, insatiable.

avoid *verb* **1** evade, dodge, shirk, shun, steer clear of. **2** escape, avert, circumvent. **3** refrain from, abstain from.

avow *verb* **1** affirm, assert, aver, declare, swear. **2** admit, acknowledge, recognize, confess.

await *verb* wait for, expect, anticipate.

awake *adj* **1** wakeful, waking, aroused, attentive, active. **2** conscious, aware, alert.
➤ *verb* wake, wake up, awaken, stir.

awaken *verb* **1** wake, wake up, rouse. **2** arouse, stimulate, provoke, stir up.

award *verb* **1** give, present, grant, bestow, confer. **2** assign, allot, apportion.
➤ *noun* **1** prize, trophy, medal, decoration, grant, endowment. **2** decision, judgment, verdict.

aware *adj* **1** mindful, conscious, cognizant, sensitive, alert. **2** enlightened, informed, knowledgeable, acquainted, conversant.

away *adv* **1** out, elsewhere, abroad. **2** far, distantly, remotely, apart. **3** off, aside. **4** continuously, incessantly, relentlessly, persistently.

awe *noun* admiration, wonder, reverence, veneration, dread.
➤ *verb* impress, overwhelm, daunt, intimidate, subdue.

awesome *adj* **1** awe-inspiring, impressive, formidable, daunting, overwhelming. **2** splendid, wonderful, marvellous, excellent.

awful *adj* **1** abominable, abysmal, ghastly, horrendous, foul, disgusting. **2** dreadful, terrible, frightful, appalling, atrocious, bad.

awhile *adv* briefly, for a moment, for a while.

awkward *adj* **1** clumsy, maladroit, bungling, ham-fisted. **2** ungainly, graceless, lumbering, uncoordinated, oafish. **3** gauche, uncouth, coarse, unrefined. **4** inconvenient, embarrassing, delicate. **5** unwieldy, unmanageable, cumbersome. **6** difficult, tricky, problematic. **7** perverse, contrary, obstinate, bloody-minded (*inf*), uncooperative, obstructive.

awry *adv and adj* **1** askew, crooked, distorted, to one side, skew-whiff (*inf*). **2** wrong, amiss.

axe *noun* chopper, hatchet, cleaver, tomahawk.
➤*verb* cancel, terminate, discontinue, get rid of, dismiss, discharge.

axiom *noun* **1** truism, truth. **2** principle, precept, maxim, adage.

axiomatic *adj* self-evident, true, incontestable, certain, given, presupposed.

axis *noun* **1** pivot, hinge. **2** vertical, horizontal.

axle *noun* shaft, rod, spindle, pin.

azure *adj* blue, sky-blue, cerulean.

babble *verb* **1** burble, gabble, gibber. **2** chatter, jabber, prattle. **3** ripple, murmur, gurgle.
➤*noun* gabble, prattle, gibberish.

babe *noun* baby, infant, suckling.

babel *noun* hubbub, uproar, tumult, commotion, pandemonium.

baby *noun* **1** infant, babe, newborn, child, tot. **2** tiny, miniature, mini, dwarf, small, little.
➤*verb* mollycoddle, pamper, spoil, cosset.

bacchanalia *noun* revelry, orgy, carousal, debauch.

back *noun* rear, stern, reverse, end.
➤*adj* rear, hind, hindmost, last.
➤*adv* backwards, to the rear, behind.
➤*verb* **1** reverse. **2** support, stand by, help, assist, approve, finance, sponsor. **3** bet on, wager on.
back down withdraw, yield, give in, concede.
back out give up, withdraw, renege, chicken out (*inf*).
back up support, stand by, side with, help, assist.

backbite *verb* malign, defame, run down, bitch (*inf*), slag off (*inf*).

backbone *noun* **1** spine, spinal column, vertebrae. **2** foundation, basis, mainstay. **3** determination, resolution, firmness, courage, moral fibre, bottle (*inf*).

backfire *verb* rebound, recoil, boomerang, blow up in one's face (*inf*).

background *noun* **1** setting, context, circumstances. **2** upbringing, family, education, experience.

backhanded *adj* equivocal, ambiguous, two-edged, ironic.

backing *noun* **1** support, aid, help, sponsorship, finance, funding. **2** approval, endorsement.

backlash *noun* reaction, retaliation, kickback.

backlog *noun* accumulation, arrears.

backpedal *verb* back down, have second thoughts, do a U-turn (*inf*).

backslide *verb* relapse, regress, lapse, go astray.

backup *noun* support, reinforcements, help, assistance.

backward *adj* **1** reverse, regressive, retrograde. **2** slow, retarded, dull, stupid. **3** reluctant, hesitant, loath.

backwash *noun* wash, wake, swell.

backwoods *pl noun* **1** bush, outback. **2** back of beyond (*inf*), middle of nowhere (*inf*).

bacterium *noun* germ, virus, microorganism, microbe, bug (*inf*).

bad *adj* **1** wicked, evil, immoral, dishonest, criminal, crooked. **2** harmful, pernicious, detrimental, destructive. **3** inferior, poor, inadequate, substandard, unsatisfactory, ropy (*inf*), lousy (*inf*). **4** naughty, mischievous, disobedient. **5** unpleasant, disagreeable, distressing, unwelcome. **6** serious, critical, severe, terrible. **7** inconvenient, unfortunate, difficult, inappropriate, inauspicious. **8** decayed, rotten, mouldy, rancid, off. **9** sick, ill, unwell, poorly, under the weather (*inf*).
not bad fair, all right, so-so (*inf*), OK (*inf*).

badge *noun* emblem, device, insignia, shield.

badger *verb* harass, plague, pester, nag, hassle (*inf*).

badinage *noun* banter, raillery, teasing.

badly *adv* **1** poorly, inadequately, unsatisfactorily. **2** seriously, severely, acutely. **3** very much, extremely, greatly.

bad-tempered *adj* cross, irritable, grumpy, touchy, prickly, stroppy (*inf*).

baffle *verb* perplex, bewilder, confuse, puzzle.

bag *noun* handbag, sack, pouch, container, satchel, case.

baggage *noun* luggage, suitcases, bags, things.

baggy *adj* loose, ill-fitting, roomy, shapeless.

bail[1] *noun* surety, security, guarantee, pledge.

bail[2] *verb* escape, get out, quit.

bail out release, rescue, help, relieve.

bait *noun* lure, decoy.
➤*verb* tease, torment, needle (*inf*).

bake *verb* 1 cook, roast. 2 dry, parch, harden.

balance *verb* 1 steady, poise, stabilize, level. 2 counterbalance, offset, counteract, compensate, make up for. 3 weigh, compare, consider, ponder.
➤*noun* 1 equilibrium, equipoise, steadiness, stability. 2 evenness, symmetry, equivalence, correspondence. 3 remainder, rest, residue, difference. 4 equanimity, composure, self-possession, poise.

balcony *noun* terrace, veranda, loggia.

bald *adj* 1 hairless. 2 bare, barren, bleak. 3 plain, unadorned, unvarnished, straightforward, blunt.

balderdash *noun* rubbish, nonsense, humbug, poppycock (*inf*), piffle (*inf*).

bale *noun* bundle, package, parcel, truss.

baleful *adj* 1 harmful, injurious, pernicious, deadly. 2 menacing, threatening, ominous, sinister.

balk *verb* 1 hesitate, shrink, recoil, jib. 2 thwart, frustrate, baffle, foil.

ball[1] *noun* sphere, orb, globe.

ball[3] *noun* dance, hop (*inf*), party.

ballad *noun* song, folk song, poem.

ballast *noun* weight, packing, filling, counterweight.

balloon *noun* airship, dirigible, blimp, zeppelin.
➤*verb* swell, inflate, distend, bag, belly.

ballot *noun* poll, vote, election.

ballyhoo *noun* 1 fuss, excitement, commotion, to-do (*inf*), song and dance (*inf*). 2 hype.

balm *noun* 1 ointment, lotion, salve. 2 comfort, consolation, solace.

balmy *adj* calm, mild, pleasant, temperate.

bamboozle *verb* 1 cheat, trick, dupe, con (*inf*). 2 confuse, baffle, perplex, stump.

ban *verb* prohibit, forbid, veto, outlaw, bar.
➤*noun* prohibition, embargo, veto, restriction, taboo.

banal *adj* trite, commonplace, clichéd, hackneyed, corny (*inf*).

band[1] *noun* 1 strip, fillet, ribbon. 2 strip, bar, stripe. 3 tie, cord, strap.

band[2] *verb* join, unite, combine, associate, gather.

band[3] *noun* 1 group, company, gang. 2 group, ensemble, combo.

bandage *noun* dressing, compress, plaster.
➤*verb* dress, bind up, cover.

bandit *noun* brigand, outlaw, robber, marauder, highwayman.

bandy *verb* exchange, swap, trade.
➤*adj* bent, curved, bow-legged.

bane *noun* affliction, curse, plague, scourge, torment, blight.

bang *noun* 1 explosion, boom, shot, report, thump, crash. 2 blow, knock, bump, thump, slap, wallop (*inf*).
➤*verb* 1 knock, hit, bump, strike, thump. 2 rap, hammer, pound. 3 boom, crash, thump, clatter.
➤*adv* 1 right, directly, straight, smack (*inf*). 2 exactly, precisely.

bangle *noun* band, bracelet, armlet.

banish *verb* 1 expel, exile, deport, outlaw. 2 dispel, drive away, get rid of.

banister *noun* rail, railing, handrail.

bank[1] *noun* 1 side, shore, edge, embankment. 2 heap, mound, ridge. 3 slope, incline, rise.
➤*verb* 1 form, accumulate, gather. 2 turn, tilt.

bank[2] *noun* 1 financial institution, finance house. 2 store, stock, fund, reserve.
➤*verb* deposit, save, put by, lay by, stash away (*inf*).

bank on depend on, count on, rely on, trust.

bank³ *noun* row, series, array, panel.

bankrupt *adj* 1 insolvent, broke (*inf*), failed, bust (*inf*), on the rocks (*inf*), ruined. 2 empty, lacking, deficient, devoid. ➤*verb* cripple, ruin, impoverish.

bankruptcy *noun* insolvency, liquidation, ruin, failure.

banner *noun* standard, flag, streamer, pennant.

banquet *noun* feast, dinner, repast, spread (*inf*).

banter *verb* chaff, tease, rib (*inf*), kid (*inf*), pull someone's leg (*inf*). ➤*noun* badinage, raillery, chaff, teasing, ribbing (*inf*), kidding (*inf*).

baptism *noun* christening, immersion, naming, initiation.

baptize *verb* christen, immerse, name, initiate.

bar *noun* 1 rod, rail, pole, shaft. 2 barrier, obstacle, hindrance, obstruction, ban, prohibition, embargo, boycott. 3 saloon, lounge. 4 counter, buffet, table. 5 band, strip, line, stripe, streak. 6 barristers, advocates. ➤*verb* 1 lock, bolt, secure, barricade. 2 confine, exclude. 3 prohibit, forbid, ban, stop, prevent. ➤*prep* except, but for, apart from, excluding, barring.

barb *noun* 1 point, bristle, thorn, prickle. 2 gibe, insult, dig (*inf*).

barbarian *noun* 1 savage, brute. 2 ignoramus, philistine.

barbaric *adj* 1 savage, brutal, cruel, ruthless, inhuman. 2 uncivilized, wild, primitive.

barbarism *noun* 1 primitiveness, lack of civilization, uncouthness, barbarity. 2 cruelty, harshness, savagery, brutality, barbarity.

barbarous *adj* 1 uncivilized, primitive, uncouth, ignorant, uncultured, unsophisticated, crude. 2 brutal, savage, cruel, inhuman.

barbed *adj* 1 prickly, spiky, pointed. 2 snide, hostile, cutting, caustic.

bare *adj* 1 naked, nude, undressed, stripped, uncovered, exposed, unprotected. 2 open, exposed, unprotected. 3 unfurnished, empty, austere. 4 plain, simple, stark, bald, unadorned. 5 basic, least, mere, scant.

barefaced *adj* impudent, brazen, shameless, blatant, flagrant.

barely *adv* scarcely, only just, hardly, by the skin of one's teeth (*inf*).

bargain *noun* 1 agreement, arrangement, pact, contract, deal, promise. 2 discount, snip (*inf*), steal (*inf*), good buy. ➤*verb* negotiate, haggle, barter, trade.
bargain for anticipate, expect, foresee, allow for.
bargain on expect, anticipate, count on.
into the bargain in addition, as well, besides.

barge *noun* 1 lighter. 2 canal boat, narrow boat. ➤*verb* 1 push, shove, jostle, elbow. 2 intrude, interrupt, butt in, burst in.

bark¹ *verb* 1 yelp, yap, woof. 2 shout, yell, bawl, snap. ➤*noun* yelp, yap, woof.

bark² *noun* covering, casing, rind.

barmy *adj* crazy, idiotic, mad, daft, nuts (*inf*), batty (*inf*), dotty, off one's head (*inf*), round the bend (*inf*).

barn *noun* shed, stable, outhouse.

baron *noun* 1 noble, nobleman, lord, peer. 2 tycoon, magnate, mogul.

baroque *adj* elaborate, ornate, florid, fussy, extravagant.

barrack *noun* camp, quarters, encampment.

barrage *noun* 1 bombardment, cannonade, shelling. 2 deluge, stream, avalanche, torrent.

barrel *noun* cask, keg, vat, butt, tun.

barren *adj* 1 infertile, sterile, childless. 2 unproductive, infertile, arid, waste. 3 futile, useless, fruitless, dull, boring.

barricade *noun* barrier, obstruction, roadblock. ➤*verb* obstruct, block, bar, shut in.

barrier *noun* **1** barricade, obstacle, obstruction, fence, railing, wall, rampart. **2** hindrance, impediment, obstacle, hurdle.

barrister *noun* lawyer, counsel, advocate, attorney.

barrow *noun* handcart, truck, wheelbarrow, handbarrow.

barter *verb* exchange, trade, haggle, bargain.
➤*noun* trade, traffic, exchange, swapping.

base¹ *noun* **1** bottom, foot, foundation, support, pedestal. **2** basis, foundation, source, root. **3** home, headquarters, centre, starting point.
➤*verb* **1** establish, found, build, ground. **2** station, locate, situate, post.

base² *adj* **1** low, mean, abject, worthless, menial. **2** despicable, bad, contemptible, ignoble, dishonourable. **3** alloyed, adulterated, impure, debased.

baseless *adj* groundless, unfounded, uncorroborated, unsubstantiated.

basement *noun* cellar, crypt, vault.

bashful *adj* **1** shy, timid, coy, diffident. **2** reticent, shrinking, self-effacing.

basic *adj* **1** fundamental, essential, underlying. **2** rudimentary, primary, elementary. **3** standard, starting, lowest, minimum. **4** simple, plain, spartan, austere.
➤*noun* fundamental, essential, rudiment, nitty-gritty (*inf*), nuts and bolts (*inf*).

basically *adv* fundamentally, essentially, intrinsically.

basin *noun* **1** container, vessel, bowl, dish. **2** depression, dip.

basis *noun* starting point, premise, base, foundation, ground, reason, principle, essence, root.

bask *verb* **1** wallow, lounge, relax. **2** revel, luxuriate, delight, relish.

basket *noun* container, hamper, punnet, creel.

bass *adj* deep, low, low-pitched.

bastard *adj* **1** illegitimate, natural, baseborn. **2** inferior, impure, debased, adulterated. **3** counterfeit, fake.
➤*noun* **1** illegitimate child, love child, natural child. **2** scoundrel, wretch, rotter (*inf*).

bastardize *verb* adulterate, debase, degrade.

bastion *noun* **1** citadel, bulwark. **2** protector, defender, bulwark.

bat *noun* stick, club, racket.

batch *noun* **1** set, lot, quantity, amount. **2** group, bunch, set, collection.

bath *noun* **1** tub, bathtub, sauna, Jacuzzi®, whirlpool. **2** wash, soak, dip, scrub.
➤*verb* wash, bathe, scrub, soak.

bathe *verb* **1** bath, wash. **2** swim, go for a swim, go for a dip. **3** clean, wash, rinse, immerse. **4** suffuse, envelop, flood.
➤*noun* swim, dip.

bathing suit *noun* swimming costume, bathing costume, trunks, bikini, swimsuit.

bathos *noun* anticlimax, letdown, triteness.

baton *noun* **1** stick, wand, rod. **2** club, truncheon.

battalion *noun* **1** force, unit, section. **2** throng, crowd, horde.

batten¹ *noun* bar, strip.
➤*verb* fix, fasten, secure.

batten² *verb* exploit, thrive on, gain from.

batter *verb* beat, pound, pummel, buffet, hit, strike, abuse, assault, attack.

battered *adj* **1** damaged, worn. **2** abused, beaten, assaulted, injured.

battery *noun* **1** series, group, set, sequence. **2** assault, grievous bodily harm, violence. **3** cannons, guns, artillery.

battle *noun* **1** fight, conflict, combat, engagement, skirmish, action. **2** conflict, struggle, controversy, strife, clash, dispute.
➤*verb* **1** fight, struggle, combat, contend. **2** fight, struggle, strive.

battle-axe *noun* dragon, virago, harridan, tartar.

battlefield *noun* battleground, front, war zone, combat zone, theatre.

battlement *noun* parapet, castellation, wall.

battleship *noun* warship, man-of-war, dreadnought.

batty *adj* eccentric, odd, peculiar, crazy, foolish, daft (*inf*), nutty (*inf*), barmy (*inf*), bonkers (*inf*).

bauble *noun* trinket, trifle, toy, gewgaw, knick-knack, ornament.

bawdy *adj* obscene, blue, lewd, indecent, risqué, salacious, racy, suggestive, smutty.

bawl *verb* **1** yell, shout, cry, roar, bellow, holler (*inf*). **2** cry, weep, wail.

bay[1] *noun* cove, inlet, gulf, bight.

bay[2] *noun* recess, alcove, niche.

bay[3] *verb* bark, yelp, howl, cry.

bazaar *noun* **1** market, mart, souk. **2** fete, fair, sale, bring and buy.

be *verb* **1** exist, live, breathe, prevail, be situated. **2** occur, happen, take place.

beach *noun* shore, seashore, seaside, strand.
➤*verb* run aground, ground, strand.

beachcomber *noun* forager, scavenger, gatherer.

beacon *noun* **1** signal, bonfire, warning. **2** sign, mark, landmark, guide.

bead *noun* **1** spherule, pellet, ball. **2** drop, droplet, globule, blob.

beak *noun* **1** bill, mandible, nib. **2** ram, prow.

beaker *noun* cup, glass, mug, tankard.

beam *noun* **1** timber, rafter, joist. **2** ray, streak, shaft.
➤*verb* **1** shine, gleam, radiate. **2** emit, transmit, send. **3** smile, grin.

bear *verb* **1** carry, convey, transport, take, bring. **2** support, sustain, hold up. **3** endure, stand, tolerate, put up with. **4** give birth to, bring forth, breed. **5** produce, yield, provide. **6** display, show, exhibit, have. **7** harbour, cherish, entertain. **8** accept, take on, shoulder. **9** turn, veer, go, curve. **10** affect, concern, regard, relate to. **11** make allowances for, be patient with, indulge.
bear out confirm, substantiate, corroborate.
bear up cope, persevere, grin and bear it (*inf*).

beard *noun* facial hair, whiskers, stubble, goatee, five o'clock shadow.
➤*verb* confront, face, defy, brave.

bearer *noun* **1** carrier, porter. **2** holder, beneficiary, payee.

bearing *noun* **1** behaviour, conduct, deportment, carriage, manner. **2** relevance, connection, relation. **3** direction, course, aim. **4** whereabouts, position, location.

bearish *adj* surly, gruff, bad-tempered. clumsy, rough, uncouth.

beast *noun* **1** brute, animal, creature. **2** monster, brute, swine.

beastly *adj* **1** nasty, mean, rotten, terrible, awful. **2** brutal, cruel, inhuman.

beat *verb* **1** strike, hit, thrash, whip, flog, lash, spank, smack, cane, belt (*inf*). **2** strike, hit, bang, pound. **3** defeat, overcome, vanquish, trounce, rout, hammer (*inf*), slaughter (*inf*). **4** throb, pulsate, pound, thump. **5** whisk, whip, blend. **6** flap, flutter, vibrate. **7** hammer, work, fashion, shape, flatten. **8** surpass, exceed, top, outdo.
➤*noun* **1** throb, pulsation, pulse. **2** accent, rhythm, stress, metre, time, tempo. **3** round, circuit, route.
➤*adj* tired out, worn out, exhausted.
beat up attack, assault, batter, mug (*inf*), do over (*inf*), rough up (*inf*).

beatific *adj* **1** ecstatic, blissful, rapturous. **2** blessed, heavenly.

beatitude *noun* ecstasy, delight, rapture, bliss, felicity, blessedness.

beau *noun* **1** admirer, escort, sweetheart, boyfriend, lover. **2** dandy, fop.

beautiful *adj* attractive, lovely, gorgeous, elegant, handsome, pretty, good-looking, ravishing, stunning.

beautify *verb* adorn, embellish, prettify, enhance, decorate.

beauty *noun* **1** attractiveness, loveliness, prettiness, glamour. **2** belle, Venus, stunner (*inf*), knockout (*inf*), peach (*inf*), smasher (*inf*). **3** advantage, benefit, attraction.

beaver *verb* **beaver away** work hard, persevere, slog (*inf*), graft (*inf*).

becalm *verb* bring to a standstill, leave stuck, maroon.

because *conj* as, since, seeing that.
because of owing to, on account of, thanks to, as a result of.

beckon *verb* **1** summon, invite, signal, wave, gesture, gesticulate. **2** attract, call, draw.

become verb 1 grow, turn, get, develop into, change into, come to be. 2 suit, flatter, look good on, set off.
become of happen to, befall.

becoming adj attractive, pretty, flattering, stylish, tasteful, suitable, appropriate.

bed noun 1 bunk, couch, berth, cot, cradle, kip (inf). 2 bottom, base, floor, layer. 3 area, plot, patch, border, row.
➤verb 1 settle down, turn in (inf), hit the hay (inf), hit the sack (inf), kip down (inf). 2 sleep with, have sex with, seduce, make love to, have it off with (sl), hump (sl), screw (sl), shag (sl). 3 embed, fix, set.

bedclothes pl noun sheets, covers, bed linen, bedding.

bedding noun 1 bedclothes, covers, bed linen. 2 litter, straw, hay.

bedeck verb decorate, adorn, embellish.

bedevil verb afflict, beset, plague, vex.

bedlam noun uproar, pandemonium, hubbub, turmoil, commotion.

bedraggled adj untidy, unkempt, dishevelled, wet, soaked, dripping.

bedridden adj incapacitated, housebound, laid up (inf).

bedrock noun 1 foundation, substratum. 2 foundation, basis, essentials, nitty-gritty (inf).

beef noun 1 brawn, strength, muscle, effort. 2 complaint, grumble, grievance, gripe.
➤verb 1 strengthen, consolidate, reinforce. 2 complain, grumble, moan, gripe, grouse.

beefy adj brawny, muscular, strong, sturdy, strapping.

beetling adj overhanging, jutting, projecting, prominent.

befall verb happen to, overtake, betide.

befit adj be suitable for, fit, become.

befog verb 1 confuse, muddle. 2 obscure, blur.

before prep 1 prior to, previous to. 2 in front of, ahead of. 3 in preference to, rather than.
➤adv 1 earlier, previously, formerly, already. 2 ahead, in advance.

beforehand adv before, in advance, previously, earlier.

befriend verb make friends with, look after, keep an eye on, stand by.

befuddle verb 1 confuse, muddle, bewilder. 2 intoxicate, inebriate, stupefy.

beg verb 1 ask, request, solicit. 2 ask, entreat, beseech, plead, implore. 3 cadge, scrounge (inf), sponge off (inf).

beget verb 1 father, sire, procreate. 2 engender, create, cause.

beggar noun 1 down-and-out, mendicant, tramp, vagrant, bum (inf). 2 fellow, chap, person, guy (inf).
➤verb 1 impoverish, ruin, bankrupt. 2 surpass, exceed.

beggarly adj miserable, pitiful, contemptible, paltry, petty, mean.

beggary noun poverty, ruin, penury, destitution.

begin verb 1 start, commence, embark on, set about, set the ball rolling (inf), take the plunge (inf). 2 start, arise, appear, emerge, come into being, inaugurate, initiate.

beginning noun 1 start, starting point, commencement, opening, outset, dawn, birth, onset, inception, the word go (inf), square one (inf). 2 origin, source, spring, root. 3 start, opening, chapter one.

begrudge verb envy, grudge, resent.

beguile verb 1 deceive, cheat, mislead, dupe. 2 charm, delight, entertain, solace. 3 pass, spend, while away.

behalf noun on behalf of for, representing, in the interests of, for the sake of.

behave verb 1 act, perform, conduct oneself, acquit oneself, comport oneself. 2 be good, be well-behaved, mind one's manners, toe the line (inf), keep one's nose clean (inf).

behaviour noun conduct, deportment, manners, actions, operation, functioning.

behead verb decapitate, guillotine, execute.

behest noun injunction, command, order, demand, bidding.

behind prep 1 at the back of, on the other side of, after, following, in the wake of. 2 later than, after, slower than. 3 responsible for, at the back of, at the bottom of. 4 supporting, for, on the side of.

➤*adv* 1 following, after, afterwards, next. 2 behindhand, late, slow. 3 in arrears, overdue.

behindhand *adv* late, slow, behind, overdue, in arrears.

behold *verb* see, observe, view, witness, perceive.
➤*interj* lo, look.

beholden *adj* obliged, indebted, bound.

behove *verb* befit, become, be necessary, be incumbent upon.

beige *adj* buff, fawn, sandy, biscuit, oatmeal, mushroom, neutral.

being *noun* 1 existence, actuality, reality. 2 life, animation. 3 essence, soul, spirit, nature. 4 creature, animal, individual.

belabour *verb* 1 labour, dwell on, harp on. 2 attack, criticize, lay into. 3 pummel, beat, strike, thrash.

belated *adj* late, overdue, behindhand, delayed.

belch *verb* 1 burp (*inf*), eruct, bring up wind. 2 emit, discharge, spew, give off. 3 gush, issue, spew.

beleaguer *verb* 1 besiege, hem in, beset. 2 harass, badger, plague.

belie *verb* 1 disprove, contradict. 2 disguise, conceal, hide, gloss over.

belief *noun* 1 faith, conviction, credence. 2 confidence, assurance, trust. 3 creed, doctrine, dogma, tenet, faith, opinion, view, conviction.

believe *verb* 1 be convinced of, trust, credit, accept, swallow (*inf*), buy (*inf*). 2 think, reckon, maintain, hold, gather, understand. 3 be sure of the existence of, have faith in. 4 support, favour, set great store by, swear by.

belittle *verb* disparage, depreciate, scorn, sneer at, underestimate, undervalue, underrate.

bellicose *adj* aggressive, belligerent, pugnacious, combative.

belligerent *adj* 1 aggressive, pugnacious, argumentative, quarrelsome. 2 at war, warring, combatant.

bellow *verb* roar, bawl, yell, shout.

belly *noun* abdomen, paunch, stomach, tummy (*inf*), corporation (*inf*), beer gut (*inf*).

belong *verb* 1 be owned by, be someone's. 2 be a member of, be affiliated to, be an adherent of. 3 go with, fit, be part of.

belongings *pl noun* possessions, property, effects, things (*inf*), stuff (*inf*), gear (*inf*).

beloved *adj* dear, dearest, darling, precious.
➤*noun* sweetheart, dear, pet, boyfriend, girlfriend.

below *prep* 1 under, underneath, beneath. 2 inferior to, subordinate to. 3 unworthy of, unbecoming.
➤*adv* 1 underneath, beneath, lower down. 2 later, further on.

belt *noun* 1 band, girdle, sash, cummerbund. 2 zone, region, area. 3 band, conveyor belt, fan belt.
➤*verb* 1 hit, thump, punch, wallop (*inf*), whack (*inf*), bash (*inf*). 2 dash, rush, hurry, tear.

bemoan *verb* lament, mourn, grieve over, bewail, deplore.

bemuse *verb* bewilder, baffle, confuse, muddle, perplex, astonish.

bench *noun* 1 form, pew, seat, settle. 2 workbench, worktable. 3 court, tribunal. 4 judiciary, judicature.

benchmark *noun* criterion, standard, norm, guideline, yardstick.

bend *verb* 1 curve, bow, crook, twist, flex, deviate, veer, turn. 2 stoop, crouch, bow, hunch. 3 subdue, overwhelm, sway, influence. 4 yield, submit, give way, concede.
➤*noun* curve, bow, arc, turn, twist, corner, deviation, zigzag.

beneath *prep* 1 below, under, underneath. 2 inferior to, subordinate to. 3 unworthy of, unbecoming.
➤*adv* below, under, underneath, lower.

benediction *noun* blessing, thanksgiving.

benefaction *noun* donation, gift, bequest, legacy, endowment, alms.

benefactor *noun* patron, sponsor, donor, backer, philanthropist, angel (*inf*).

benefice *noun* living, cure.

beneficent *adj* generous, liberal, munificent, charitable.

beneficial *adj* helpful, useful, profitable, good, salutary.

benefit *noun* 1 advantage, good, profit, boon, blessing. 2 good, sake, interest, service, welfare, well-being. 3 allowance, payment, credit.
➤*verb* help, avail, serve, profit, improve, advantage.

benevolent *adj* kind, kindly, benign, kind-hearted, good, unselfish, charitable, philanthropic.

benighted *adj* unenlightened, uncivilized, uneducated, ignorant, backward.

benign *adj* 1 kind, kindly, benevolent, friendly, gracious. 2 favourable, propitious, beneficial. 3 treatable, curable, harmless.

bent *adj* 1 crooked, twisted, curved, bowed, arched, hunched, stooped. 2 corrupt, crooked, dishonest. 3 determined to, set on, fixed on.
➤*noun* 1 inclination, tendency, disposition, penchant, predilection. 2 aptitude, forte, talent.

benumb *verb* deaden, numb, anaesthetize.

bequeath *verb* 1 leave, will, make over. 2 pass on, hand on, hand down.

bequest *noun* 1 bestowal, gift. 2 legacy, inheritance, settlement.

berate *verb* reprove, chide, scold, rebuke, upbraid, censure, tell off (*inf*).

bereave *verb* deprive, rob, dispossess, strip.

bereft *adj* deprived, devoid, stripped, destitute.

berserk *adj* **go beserk** go mad, run amok, go on the rampage, lose it (*inf*).

berth *noun* 1 bed, bunk. 2 mooring, anchorage, harbour.
➤*verb* dock, anchor, moor, tie up.

beseech *verb* 1 implore, beg, entreat, plead, appeal to. 2 beg, entreat, crave, solicit.

beset *verb* 1 harass, trouble, bother, pester. 2 beleaguer, surround, besiege.

besetting *adj* habitual, persistent, inveterate.

beside *prep* 1 next to, alongside, adjacent to. 2 compared with, next to, in contrast to.
beside oneself frenzied, frantic, distraught, demented, hysterical.

besides *prep* 1 apart from, other than, except. 2 in addition to, over and above.
➤*adv* 1 in addition, as well, too, also. 2 moreover, furthermore, what's more.

besiege *verb* 1 surround, hem in, lay siege to. 2 surround, enclose, mob. 3 harass, plague, hound.

besmirch *verb* sully, defame, stain, tarnish.

besotted *adj* 1 infatuated, doting, smitten, obsessed. 2 intoxicated, befuddled, drunk.

bespatter *verb* splash, spatter, splatter, spray.

bespeak *verb* 1 denote, signify, indicate, betoken. 2 order, engage, request.

best *adj* finest, outstanding, top, first-rate, first-class, supreme, unsurpassed, second to none (*inf*), number one (*inf*).
➤*adv* 1 superlatively, supremely, outstandingly. 2 most, by preference.
➤*noun* choice, flower, elite, cream, prime, peak, height, top form.
➤*verb* defeat, beat, thrash, trounce, hammer (*inf*).

bestial *adj* 1 brutal, savage, inhuman, depraved, degenerate, vile, sordid, low. 2 brutish, animal.

bestir *verb* stir, rouse, get going (*inf*).

bestow *verb* confer, give, grant, present, bequeath, endow.

bestrew *verb* strew, scatter, sprinkle.

bestride *verb* 1 straddle, span. 2 dominate, tower over.

bet *verb* 1 wager, stake, gamble, risk, speculate, hazard. 2 be sure, be certain, be convinced, expect.
➤*noun* 1 wager, gamble, flutter (*inf*), speculation. 2 ante, stake. 3 opinion, belief, expectation, prediction. 4 choice, option, alternative.

bête noire *noun* bane, bugbear, anathema, aversion.

betide *verb* befall, chance, come to pass, ensue.

betoken *verb* 1 denote, indicate, signify. 2 presage, augur, portend.

betray *verb* 1 inform on, double-cross, shop (*inf*), rat on (*inf*), blow the whistle on (*inf*), sell out (*inf*), stab in the back (*inf*).

2 disclose, reveal, divulge. **3** show, exhibit, display. **4** tell, blab, give away, let slip. **5** abandon, desert, walk out on, jilt.

betroth *verb* **be betrothed** be engaged, be affianced, be promised.

better *adj* **1** superior, finer, greater, higher, preferable. **2** improving, recovering, healthier, cured, on the mend (*inf*).
➤*verb* **1** improve, ameliorate, correct, rectify, reform. **2** surpass, exceed, excel, beat, improve on.

betterment *noun* improvement, amelioration, reform.

between *prep* **1** amidst, in the middle of, betwixt, among. **2** connecting, joining, linking.

bevel *noun* chamfer, angle, slant.

beverage *noun* drink, liquid, potation.

bevy *noun* group, throng, bunch, collection, party.

bewail *verb* lament, mourn, grieve for, regret, weep over.

beware *verb* take care, watch out, look out, be careful, mind, avoid, steer clear of, guard against.

bewilder *verb* confuse, puzzle, perplex, bemuse, baffle, nonplus, mystify, faze (*inf*), stump (*inf*).

bewitch *verb* enchant, fascinate, captivate, entrance, mesmerize, charm, enrapture.

beyond *prep* **1** on the far side of, past. **2** over, above, greater than. **3** out of reach of, outside, surpassing. **4** besides, over and above.
➤*adv* farther, further.

bias *noun* **1** tendency, predisposition, propensity, prejudice, bigotry, narrow-mindedness, favouritism, one-sidedness. **2** diagonal, slant, angle.
➤*verb* predispose, incline, prejudice.

bible *noun* **1** testament, Scriptures, Scripture, Holy Writ, the Good Book, Old Testament, New Testament. **2** handbook, manual, textbook, guide.

bibliography *noun* catalogue, book list, references.

bibulous *adj* alcoholic, boozy (*inf*), intemperate.

bicker *verb* quarrel, squabble, row, spat, argue.

bicycle *noun* cycle, bike, two-wheeler, tandem, push-bike (*inf*).

bid *verb* **1** offer, tender, put forward. **2** attempt, try, endeavour. **3** command, order, enjoin. **4** summon, invite, ask. **5** say, wish.
➤*noun* **1** offer, tender, proposal, proposition, price, amount. **2** attempt, try, endeavour.

biddable *adj* willing, amenable, cooperative, pliant, tractable.

bidding *noun* order, command, behest, injunction.

big *adj* **1** large, great, huge, massive, vast, spacious, extensive, substantial, sizeable, tall, burly, well-built, fat. **2** older, elder. **3** grown-up, adult. **4** important, significant, major, weighty, prominent, influential, powerful, eminent, famous, well-known, principal, main. **5** generous, kind, magnanimous, unselfish. **6** arrogant, boastful, pompous, inflated, pretentious.

bigot *noun* fanatic, zealot, dogmatist, racist, jingoist, chauvinist.

bigwig *noun* VIP, celebrity, nob (*inf*), big noise (*inf*), big shot (*inf*), big cheese (*inf*).

bile *noun* spleen, ill humour, irritability, irascibility, peevishness.

bilge *noun* nonsense, rubbish, drivel, twaddle, piffle (*inf*), rot (*inf*).

bilious *adj* **1** queasy, sick, nauseated. **2** bad-tempered, ill-tempered, crotchety, irritable, peevish, grumpy. **3** garish, nauseating, sickly.

bilk *verb* deceive, cheat, defraud.

bill[1] *noun* **1** account, statement, invoice, reckoning. **2** poster, notice, placard, advertisement, flier, handbill, leaflet, brochure. **3** programme, card. **4** measure, proposal, proposed law.
➤*verb* **1** charge, invoice, debit, send a statement. **2** advertise, announce, publicize.

bill[2] *noun* beak, nib.

billet *noun* **1** quarters, accommodation, lodgings. **2** job, position, post, office.
➤*verb* quarter, put up, house.

billow *verb* roll, surge, swell, swirl, balloon.
➤*noun* **1** wave, breaker, surge. **2** mass, swirl, cloud.

|

bin *noun* receptacle, container, box.

bind *verb* **1** tie, secure, fasten, attach, strap, rope, tether, lash. **2** tie up, truss up. **3** bandage, dress. **4** unite, join. **5** oblige, force, compel, obligate, require. **6** stick, glue, paste, cement. **7** edge, hem, trim, border, finish.
➤*noun* nuisance, bore, inconvenience, drag (*inf*).
in a bind in a predicament, in a spot (*inf*), in a pickle (*inf*).

binding *adj* obligatory, compulsory, mandatory.
➤*noun* **1** fastening. **2** cover

binge *noun* spree, orgy, jag (*inf*), bender (*inf*).

biography *noun* life, life history, profile, bio (*inf*).

birth *noun* **1** childbirth, parturition, delivery, confinement. **2** genesis, origin, beginning, emergence, appearance. **3** ancestry, descent, extraction, line, lineage, family, parentage, background.

birthmark *noun* blemish, mole, discoloration, naevus.

birthright *noun* prerogative, privilege, inheritance.

bisect *verb* cut in two, divide, split.

bisexual *adj* androgynous, hermaphroditic, epicene. **2** AC/DC (*inf*), bi (*inf*).

bishop *noun* prelate, patriarch, suffragan.

bishopric *noun* **1** diocese, see. **2** episcopacy, episcopate.

bit[1] *noun* **1** scrap, sliver, fragment, piece, morsel, jot, speck, trace, hint. **2** moment, minute, little while, second, jiffy (*inf*).

bit[2] *noun* restraint, check, curb, snaffle.

bitch *noun* **1** shrew, vixen, virago, cow (*sl*). **2** nightmare, nuisance, sod (*sl*).
➤*verb* complain, gripe, grouse, beef (*inf*).

bitchy *adj* nasty, snide, malicious, vindictive, catty.

bite *verb* **1** chew, gnaw, champ, munch, crunch, nibble. **2** nip, sting. **3** grip, hold, grasp. **4** have an effect, take effect, work.
➤*noun* **1** nip, snap, nibble. **2** sting, wound. **3** morsel, mouthful, piece. **4** snack, refreshment. **5** piquancy, sharpness, spiciness, kick (*inf*).

biting *adj* **1** piercing, keen, nipping, penetrating, freezing. **2** caustic, cutting, mordant, sarcastic, withering, scathing.

bitter *adj* **1** acrid, pungent, sharp, sour, vinegary. **2** acrimonious, resentful, vindictive, rancorous, embittered, morose, sullen. **3** intense, severe, harsh, fierce, virulent. **4** distressing, sad, painful, grievous, tragic. **5** icy, freezing, intense, severe, biting.

bizarre *adj* strange, odd, weird, grotesque, fantastic, outlandish, ridiculous, eccentric.

blab *verb* **1** divulge, let slip, blurt out. **2** squeal (*inf*), tell, tattle.

black *adj* **1** dark, inky, sooty, ebony, jet, pitch-black. **2** dark, dark-skinned, Negroid, swarthy, coloured. **3** dark, moonless, starless, unlit, gloomy, sombre, tenebrous, Cimmerian, stygian. **4** depressing, mournful, tragic, ominous. **5** dirty, filthy, soiled, grubby, grimy, sooty. **6** angry, hostile, belligerent, aggressive, menacing, threatening. **7** bad, vile, evil, villainous, heinous, wicked. **8** macabre, grim, sick, cynical.
➤*verb* bar, ban, embargo, boycott, blacklist.
in the black solvent, in credit, out of debt.

black-and-white *adj* **1** monochrome. **2** clear-cut, absolute, categorical, uncompromising.

blackball *verb* **1** ban, bar, exclude, blacklist. **2** ostracize, snub, give the cold shoulder (*inf*).

blacken *verb* **1** soil, dirty, darken. **2** defame, sully, malign, traduce, run down, drag through the mud.

blackguard *noun* scoundrel, rogue, villain, swine (*inf*).

blacklist *verb* exclude, ban, bar, black, boycott, ostracize, snub.

blackmail *noun* extortion, intimidation, hush money (*inf*), protection money (*inf*).
➤*verb* squeeze, bleed (*inf*), lean on (*inf*), compel, force.

blackout *noun* **1** faint, loss of consciousness. **2** power failure, power cut. **3** embargo, suppression, censorship.

blame *verb* **1** censure, criticize, find fault with, reproach, reprove. **2** hold

responsible, accuse, charge, pin on (*inf*).
➤*noun* **1** responsibility, culpability, fault, guilt, rap (*inf*). **2** censure, condemnation, disapproval, criticism, reproach.

blameless *adj* innocent, guiltless, in the clear, irreproachable, unsullied, unblemished, above suspicion.

blanch *verb* **1** whiten, bleach, pale, blench. **2** scald, boil.

bland *adj* **1** tasteless, insipid, flavourless. **2** dull, boring, uninteresting, insipid, mediocre, unexciting. **3** mild, gentle, soft, soothing. **4** benign, suave, glib.

blandishment *noun* flattery, compliment, soft soap (*inf*), sweet talk (*inf*).

blank *adj* **1** empty, void, vacant, unfilled, unmarked. **2** expressionless, deadpan, vacant, poker-faced, impassive. **3** at a loss, perplexed, dazed, disconcerted, uncomprehending, nonplussed. **4** outright, absolute, utter, unqualified.
➤*noun* void, emptiness, space, vacancy, nothingness, gap.

blanket *noun* **1** cover, covering, coverlet, bedcover. **2** cover, carpet, cloak, mantle, sheet, coating, layer.
➤*verb* cover, overlay, envelop, cloak, carpet, shroud.
➤*adj* all-inclusive, all-embracing, comprehensive, general, across-the-board.

blare *verb* **1** blast, roar, clamour, blow. **2** proclaim, broadcast, trumpet.

blarney *noun* blandishments, cajolery, soft soap (*inf*), sweet talk (*inf*).

blasé *adj* offhand, nonchalant, unmoved, indifferent, jaded, bored, weary.

blaspheme *verb* swear, curse, damn, cuss (*inf*), profane.

blasphemy *noun* impiety, profanity, swearing, sacrilege, irreverence.

blast *noun* **1** explosion, burst, boom, bang. **2** gust, squall, draught, rush, gale. **3** blare, boom, roar, bellow, clamour.
➤*verb* **1** blow up, explode. **2** shatter, demolish, destroy, ruin. **3** criticize, denounce, attack, castigate, slam (*inf*). **4** blight, wither, shrivel, kill.
blast off lift off, take off, be launched.

blatant *adj* **1** conspicuous, obvious, glaring. **2** brazen, flagrant, shameless.

blaze *verb* **1** flame, burn, flare up, burst into flames. **2** shine, glitter, gleam, flash.
➤*noun* **1** fire, inferno, conflagration. **2** glitter, radiance, brilliance, flash. **3** outburst, outbreak, explosion, flare-up.

blazon *verb* proclaim, make known, broadcast, publicize, trumpet.

bleach *verb* blanch, whiten, fade, lighten.

bleak *adj* **1** bare, exposed, open, desolate, windswept. **2** cold, raw, chilly. **3** gloomy, dismal, dreary, cheerless, depressing, hopeless.

bleary *adj* blurred, hazy, cloudy, indistinct.

bleed *verb* **1** lose blood, haemorrhage, ooze, trickle, flow. **2** draw blood, let blood. **3** extort, extract, milk, fleece, squeeze. **4** drain, exhaust, suck dry.

blemish *noun* **1** spot, mark, stain, scratch, discoloration. **2** defect, fault, imperfection, taint.
➤*verb* tarnish, taint, sully, spoil, mar, disfigure, mark, spot, stain.

blench *verb* shrink, recoil, flinch, wince, hesitate, falter.

blend *verb* **1** mix, mingle, combine, amalgamate, fuse, merge, unite. **2** harmonize, go with, suit, complement.
➤*noun* mixture, mix, combination, fusion, synthesis.

bless *verb* **1** praise, extol, glorify. **2** sanctify, consecrate. **3** bestow, grant, give.

blessed *adj* **1** sacred, holy, hallowed, consecrated. **2** beatified. **3** happy, glad, joyful, fortunate, lucky.

blessing *noun* **1** benediction, grace, invocation. **2** approval, backing, support, sanction. **3** boon, advantage, benefit, godsend.

blight *noun* **1** disease, infestation, canker, fungus. **2** scourge, plague, bane, calamity, curse, affliction.
➤*verb* **1** destroy, ruin, wreck, frustrate. **2** blast, wither, shrivel, kill.

blind *adj* **1** sightless, unseeing, unsighted, visually impaired. **2** indifferent, ignorant, unaware, unconscious, oblivious, heedless. **3** unreasoning, unthinking, rash, reckless, impetuous, careless, mindless. **4** closed, blocked, impassable.
➤*verb* **1** render sightless, dazzle, obscure one's vision, block one's line of vision.

2 confuse, bewilder, deceive, mislead.
➤*noun* **1** shade, screen, curtain. **2** mask, disguise, feint, stratagem, ruse.

blink *verb* **1** wink, nictitate, flutter, bat. **2** flicker, twinkle, glitter, glimmer, sparkle. **3** ignore, disregard, overlook, turn a blind eye.
➤*noun* glimpse, wink.

bliss *noun* **1** ecstasy, happiness, joy, euphoria, rapture, elation, felicity. **2** paradise, heaven, Eden.

blister *noun* pustule, vesicle, bleb, boil, carbuncle, ulcer, cyst, bubble, swelling.

blistering *adj* extreme, intense, searing, scathing, savage, severe.

blithe *adj* **1** merry, cheerful, carefree, jolly, buoyant, jaunty. **2** heedless, indifferent, casual.

blitz *noun* **1** attack, bombardment, onslaught, offensive, blitzkrieg. **2** all-out effort, set-to, campaign.

blizzard *noun* snowstorm, storm.

bloat *verb* swell, puff up, inflate, balloon, distend, enlarge.

blob *noun* drop, globule, glob, bead, ball, lump, spot, splash, blotch.

bloc *noun* alliance, federation, coalition.

block *noun* **1** lump, mass, chunk, piece, cake, bar, brick. **2** building, complex, development. **3** set, cluster, batch. **4** blockage, obstruction, bottleneck, stoppage, barrier.
➤*verb* **1** obstruct, stop, clog, plug. **2** obstruct, impede, hinder, thwart.

blockade *noun* closure, siege.
➤*verb* block, close, besiege.

blockage *noun* block, obstruction, jam, stoppage.

blockhead *noun* dunce, dolt, idiot, numskull.

bloke *noun* fellow, man, boy, chap (*inf*), guy (*inf*).

blonde *adj* fair, flaxen, fair-haired.

blood *noun* **1** gore, lifeblood, plasma. **2** ancestry, descent, family, parentage, extraction, pedigree.

bloodcurdling *adj* terrifying, horrifying, horrific, hair-raising, spine-chilling.

bloodless *adj* **1** pale, wan, pallid, anaemic. **2** lifeless, listless, apathetic. **3** unfeeling, cold, indifferent. **4** peaceful, non-violent.

bloodshed *noun* killing, carnage, slaughter, butchery.

bloodthirsty *adj* murderous, ferocious, vicious, sadistic, ruthless.

bloody *adj* **1** gory, sanguinary, bleeding, bloodstained. **2** bloodthirsty, murderous, savage.

bloom *noun* **1** blossom, flower. **2** prime, heyday, peak. **3** glow, sheen, blush, radiance.
➤*verb* **1** blossom, flower, blow, open. **2** flourish, prosper, succeed, get on, thrive.

blossom *noun* bloom, flower, efflorescence.
➤*verb* **1** bloom, flower. **2** bloom, thrive, flourish, prosper, get on.

blot *noun* **1** spot, stain, smudge, mark, blotch. **2** blemish, taint, stain, disgrace.
➤*verb* **1** absorb, dry, soak up. **2** spot, stain. **3** sully, tarnish, stain, blacken, dishonour.

blot out 1 obscure, hide, conceal, eclipse. **2** erase, expunge, obliterate.

blotch *noun* patch, splodge, smudge, smear.

blow[1] *verb* **1** gust, puff, blast. **2** waft, fan, drive, whisk, whirl. **3** breathe, exhale, pant, puff, gasp. **4** sound, blare, toot, play. **5** squander, misspend, fritter away. **6** spoil, bungle, ruin, wreck.
➤*noun* blast, gust, gale.

blow out extinguish, snuff, put out.

blow over 1 subside, die down. **2** pass, vanish, cease.

blow up 1 explode, go off, detonate, burst. **2** pump up, inflate, swell, enlarge. **3** exaggerate, amplify, embroider. **4** enlarge, make bigger. **5** lose one's temper, flip (*inf*), blow one's top (*inf*), hit the roof (*inf*), fly off the handle (*inf*), go off the deep end (*inf*).

blow[2] *noun* **1** hit, knock, thump, slap, punch, smack, wallop (*inf*). **2** shock, disaster, bombshell, catastrophe, disappointment, setback.

blowout *noun* **1** puncture, flat tyre. **2** feast, binge, bash (*inf*).

blubber *verb* sob, cry, weep.

bludgeon *noun* cudgel, club.
➤*verb* **1** hit, club, beat, cudgel. **2** coerce, force, intimidate, bully, browbeat.

blue *adj* **1** azure, sapphire, turquoise, aquamarine, ultramarine, navy. **2** dejected, depressed, unhappy, sad, glum, downcast, despondent, in the dumps (*inf*). **3** obscene, dirty, pornographic. **4** risqué, bawdy, near the knuckle (*inf*).

blueprint *noun* design, pattern, template, plan.

blues *pl noun* sadness, unhappiness, depression, dejection, melancholy, despondency.

bluff[1] *verb* mislead, deceive, sham, feign.
➤*noun* deception, pretence, sham, show, bravado.

bluff[2] *adj* open, frank, candid, outspoken, straightforward.
➤*noun* cliff, slope, scarp, escarpment.

blunder *noun* mistake, oversight, gaffe, clanger (*inf*), boob (*inf*).
➤*verb* **1** slip up (*inf*), mess up (*inf*), foul up (*inf*). **2** botch, bungle, mismanage. **3** stumble, lurch, stagger.

blunt *adj* **1** dull, unsharpened, worn. **2** unceremonious, plainspoken, direct, frank, brusque. **3** straightforward, to the point.
➤*verb* **1** dull, take the edge off. **2** soften, dampen.

blur *verb* **1** dim, obscure, fog, cloud, make indistinct. **2** smear, smudge.
➤*noun* **1** haze, fog, indistinct shape. **2** smear, smudge.

blurt out *verb* blab, come out with, let slip.

blush *verb* redden, flush, colour.
➤*noun* **1** flush, reddening, colour. **2** rosiness, pinkness.

bluster *verb* **1** gust, blast, storm. **2** storm, bully, threaten, domineer, throw one's weight about.
➤*noun* bravado, bluff, bombast.

board *noun* **1** plank, panel. **2** food, meals, provisions. **3** committee, council, panel, directors.
➤*verb* **1** get on, embark, go aboard. **2** lodge, put up, accommodate. **3** stay, live, lodge. **4** cover, close up, shut up.

boast *verb* **1** brag, vaunt, show off, blow one's own trumpet, swank (*inf*). **2** possess, have, pride oneself on.
➤*noun* **1** brag, vaunt. **2** pride, treasure, pride and joy.

boat *noun* vessel, craft, dinghy, canoe, ferry.

bob *verb* float, bounce, jump, jerk, duck.

bode *verb* presage, portend, augur, foreshadow.

bodily *adj* physical, corporeal, material, carnal, tangible.
➤*adv* wholly, entirely, completely, altogether, en masse.

body *noun* **1** physique, build, frame, figure. **2** corpse, cadaver, stiff (*inf*). **3** trunk, torso. **4** organization, group, party, association, corporation. **5** main part, principal part. **6** density, solidity, firmness.

bog *noun* swamp, marsh, quagmire, morass, slough.
bog down obstruct, halt, stop, impede, delay, stall.

bogey *noun* **1** ghost, evil spirit, hobgoblin. **2** bugbear, bête noire, pet hate.

boggle *verb* hesitate, falter, waver, hang back.

bogus *adj* false, counterfeit, sham, fake, phoney.

Bohemian *noun* hippy, dropout, nonconformist.

boil[1] *verb* **1** seethe, bubble, foam, froth, simmer, cook, stew. **2** fume, rage, seethe, lose one's temper.

boil[2] *noun* carbuncle, ulcer, blister, sore.

boiling *adj* scorching, roasting, baking, sweltering, blistering.

boisterous *adj* **1** lively, unruly, rowdy, high-spirited, exuberant, uproarious. **2** stormy, blustery, turbulent.

bold *adj* **1** brave, daring, audacious, adventurous. **2** impudent, pert, cheeky, forward. **3** prominent, striking, conspicuous, eye-catching.

bolshie *adj* awkward, perverse, uncooperative, unhelpful, bloody-minded (*inf*).

bolster *verb* support, brace, shore up, buttress, reinforce, strengthen, boost.
➤*noun* pillow, cushion.

bolt *noun* **1** bar, latch, catch. **2** fastening, rivet, pin. **3** flash, blaze, burst. **4** arrow, dart, shaft. **5** roll.
➤*verb* **1** fasten, secure, lock, bar. **2** devour, wolf, gobble. **3** escape, run away, abscond. **4** dash, dart, rush.

bomb *noun* explosive device, mine, incendiary.
➤*verb* bombard, blow up, blitz.

bombard *verb* **1** bomb, shell, blitz, pound. **2** inundate, pester, harass.

bombast *noun* pomposity, verbosity, grandiloquence, fustian.

bona fide *adj* genuine, real, authentic, valid, legitimate.

bonanza *noun* windfall, stroke of luck, godsend.

bond *noun* **1** cord, band, tie, fastening, chain, fetter. **2** link, tie, connection, affinity, attachment. **3** contract, agreement, obligation, pledge, guarantee.
➤*verb* connect, join, stick, fuse, weld, cement.

bondage *noun* slavery, servitude, captivity, imprisonment, serfdom.

bonny *adj* fair, pretty, comely, beautiful, handsome.

bonus *noun* **1** premium, extra, plus. **2** tip, gratuity, reward, perk (*inf*).

bony *adj* lean, thin, skinny, scraggy, scrawny, skeletal.

booby *noun* dunce, fool, simpleton.

book *noun* **1** volume, tome, text, work, publication, title. **2** notebook, jotter, pad. **3** accounts, ledgers, finances.
➤*verb* **1** reserve. **2** engage, charter.
book in register, enter.

bookish *adj* studious, intellectual, academic, highbrow, pedantic.

boom *verb* **1** resound, reverberate, roar, thunder. **2** prosper, flourish, succeed, grow, rocket.
➤*noun* **1** roar, thunder, bang, reverberation. **2** rise, increase, upsurge, upturn, spurt, boost.

boomerang *verb* rebound, recoil, backfire.

boon *noun* blessing, benefit, advantage, godsend.

boor *noun* lout, oaf, barbarian, yob (*inf*).

boost *verb* **1** increase, expand, amplify, jack up (*inf*), hike up (*inf*). **2** raise, encourage, inspire, uplift.
➤*noun* **1** encouragement, inspiration, stimulus, shot in the arm. **2** increase, expansion, development.

boot *verb* kick out, expel, dismiss, sack (*inf*).

booth *noun* **1** stall, stand. **2** cubicle, compartment, carrel.

bootless *adj* unavailing, useless, pointless.

booty *noun* spoils, plunder, pillage, loot.

booze *noun* drink, alcohol, liquor.

border *noun* **1** boundary, frontier, marches. **2** edge, margin, fringe, hem.
➤*verb* **1** adjoin, abut, touch. **2** verge on, approach, resemble.

bore[1] *verb* drill, mine, burrow, dig.
➤*noun* **1** hole, tunnel, shaft. **2** calibre, diameter.

bore[2] *verb* tire, weary, turn off (*inf*).
➤*noun* pest, nuisance, drag (*inf*), pain (*inf*).

boredom *noun* dullness, tedium, monotony, dreariness, ennui.

borough *noun* town, municipality.

borrow *verb* **1** take, cadge, scrounge, sponge (*inf*). **2** copy, plagiarize, pirate. **3** appropriate, adopt, acquire, take over.

bosh *noun* nonsense, balderdash, rubbish.

bosom *noun* **1** chest, breasts, breast, bust. **2** heart, soul, emotions, feelings. **3** centre, core, depths.

boss[1] *noun* employer, supervisor, overseer, manager, director, chief, head, governor (*inf*), gaffer (*inf*).
➤*verb* **1** supervise, manage, head. **2** order about, push around, bully.

boss[2] *noun* stud, knob, protuberance.

bossy *adj* domineering, overbearing, authoritarian, dictatorial.

botch *verb* bungle, mismanage, mess up, make a hash of, louse up (*inf*), cock up (*sl*).
➤*noun* mess, hash, blunder.

bother *verb* **1** disturb, inconvenience, trouble, hassle (*inf*), annoy, irritate, pester, harass. **2** perplex, disconcert. **3** make the effort, take the time, go to the trouble.

➤*noun* **1** trouble, nuisance, hassle (*inf*), inconvenience. **2** fuss, flurry. **3** trouble, aggravation (*inf*).

bottleneck *noun* constriction, narrowing, blockage.

bottle up *verb* suppress, keep back, hide.

bottom *noun* **1** base, foot, foundation, support. **2** bed, floor, depths, end, far end. **3** underside, underpart, underneath. **4** seat, rump, rear, posterior, backside (*inf*), behind (*inf*). **5** lowest level, lowest position.
➤*adj* lowest, last.

bottomless *adj* **1** unfathomable, abysmal, fathomless. **2** immeasurable, infinite, boundless.

bough *noun* branch, limb, stem.

boulder *noun* rock, stone.

boulevard *noun* avenue, road, drive, thoroughfare.

bounce *verb* **1** rebound, recoil, spring back. **2** jump, leap, bob, spring.
➤*noun* **1** springiness, elasticity. **2** spring, leap, jump, bound. **3** vitality, energy, liveliness, zip (*inf*).

bouncing *adj* healthy, strong, fit.

bound[1] *adj* **1** confined, limited. **2** obliged, compelled, constrained, obligated. **3** certain, sure, likely.
bound up with tied up with, connected with, related to.

bound[2] *verb* spring, leap, jump, skip.
➤*noun* spring, leap, jump, skip.

bound[3] *verb* **1** limit, restrict, circumscribe. **2** border, enclose, surround.
noun **1** boundary, confines. **2** restrictions, limitations.
out of bounds off limits, forbidden.

bound[4] *adj* heading, headed, off to.

boundary *noun* **1** border, frontier. **2** limit, confine, bound, edge, perimeter.

boundless *adj* unlimited, infinite, endless, vast, immeasurable.

bountiful *adj* **1** plentiful, abundant, lavish. **2** generous, kind, liberal, open-handed, unstinting.

bounty *noun* **1** generosity, liberality, beneficence. **2** gift, donation, largess. **3** reward, recompense, inducement.

bouquet *noun* **1** bunch, posy, nosegay. **2** aroma, fragrance, scent.

bourgeois *adj* **1** middle-class. **2** conservative, conventional, traditional. **3** materialistic, capitalistic.

bout *noun* **1** fight, contest, match. **2** spell, period, session. **3** attack, spell, fit.

bovine *adj* cowlike, stupid, dull, slow-witted.

bow[1] *verb* **1** submit, yield, surrender, give in. **2** bend the knee, salaam, kowtow, make obeisance.
➤*noun* salaam, obeisance.
bow out withdraw, leave, retire, step down.

bow[2] *verb* **1** bend, curve, warp, droop. **2** subdue, depress, humble, weigh down.

bow[3] *noun* prow, front.

bowdlerize *verb* censor, expurgate, blue-pencil.

bowel *noun* **1** intestines, entrails, guts, innards (*inf*). **2** depths, interior.

bower *noun* arbour, alcove, pergola.

bowl[1] *noun* **1** basin, container, vessel, dish. **2** hollow, dip, depression. **3** stadium, arena.

bowl[2] *verb* **1** throw, pitch, deliver. **2** roll.
bowl over 1 knock down, floor, topple. **2** overwhelm, dumbfound, astound.

box[1] *noun* **1** carton, case, trunk, crate. **2** cubicle, compartment.
➤*verb* **1** encase, pack. **2** shut in, confine, enclose.

box[2] *verb* **1** spar, fight. **2** cuff, hit, slap, clout (*inf*).
➤*noun* cuff, blow, slap, clout (*inf*).

boxer *noun* fighter, prizefighter, pugilist.

boy *noun* lad, youth, youngster, kid.

boycott *verb* black, blacklist, blackball, embargo, bar, exclude.

boyfriend *noun* date, young man, sweetheart, beau.

brace *verb* **1** support, prop, reinforce, hold up, shore up. **2** prepare, make ready, steel.
➤*noun* **1** support, prop, reinforcement, buttress. **2** pair, couple.

bracelet *noun* bangle, circlet, band.

bracing *adj* invigorating, reviving, restorative, refreshing, exhilarating.

bracket *noun* 1 support, strut, corbel, console. 2 group, grouping, category, division.

brackish *adj* salty, briny.

brag *verb* boast, crow, blow one's own trumpet, talk big (*inf*).
➤*noun* boast, vaunt.

braggart *noun* boaster, show-off, big mouth (*inf*), loudmouth (*inf*).

braid *verb* weave, plait, twine.
➤*noun* 1 cord, ribbon, tape. 2 plait.

brain *noun* 1 encephalon, grey matter. 2 mind, head, intellect, reason, intelligence, common sense, nous (*inf*), savvy (*inf*). 3 thinker, intellectual, egghead (*inf*). 4 mastermind.

brainless *adj* stupid, foolish, thoughtless, senseless.

brainwash *noun* indoctrinate, re-educate.

brainy *adj* clever, intelligent, smart, bright.

brake *noun* curb, restraint, check.
➤*verb* slow down, slow, decelerate, moderate, check.

branch *noun* 1 limb, bough, offshoot, ramification. 2 tributary, feeder, affluent. 3 division, subdivision, section.
➤*verb* diverge, divide, ramify, fork.
branch out expand, extend, diversify.

brand *noun* 1 kind, sort, type, make, variety. 2 mark, stamp, emblem, label, trademark, symbol, identification.
➤*verb* 1 mark, label, stamp, burn in. 2 stigmatize, denounce, discredit.

brandish *verb* flourish, wield, swing, wave.

brash *adj* insolent, bold, self-confident, self-assertive, forward, brazen, cocky, pushy (*inf*).

brassy *adj* 1 harsh, loud, blaring, strident. 2 brazen, shameless, presumptuous, cheeky, bold, pushy (*inf*).

brat *noun* urchin, rascal, imp, whippersnapper.

bravado *noun* bragging, boasting, showing-off, swagger, bluster.

brave *adj* courageous, valiant, heroic, gallant, daring, fearless, intrepid, bold, resolute, plucky, spunky (*inf*).
➤*verb* confront, face, defy, stand up to.

bravery *noun* courage, valour, heroism, gallantry, daring, fearlessness, pluck, guts (*inf*), spunk (*inf*).

brawl *verb* fight, tussle, scuffle, scrap (*inf*), quarrel, row (*inf*).
➤*noun* fight, scrap (*inf*), punch-up (*inf*), fracas, scuffle, row, rumpus, tussle.

brawn *noun* muscle, strength, heftiness, beef (*inf*).

brawny *adj* strong, powerful, muscular, strapping, hefty, sturdy.

bray *verb* hee-haw, neigh, whinny, blare.

brazen *adj* bold, forward, brassy, barefaced, shameless, impudent, insolent, saucy.
brazen it out be defiant, be unrepentant, stand one's ground.

breach *noun* 1 rupture, break, crack, cleft, hole, gap, opening. 2 violation, infringement, infraction, contravention, transgression. 3 rift, break-up, estrangement, falling-out, difference, disagreement, quarrel.
➤*verb* 1 violate, break, disobey, infringe, contravene. 2 rupture, burst, break, split.

bread *noun* money, dough (*inf*), dosh (*inf*).

breadth *noun* 1 width, span, spread. 2 extent, range, scope, scale, spread. 3 latitude, openness, broad-mindedness.

break *verb* 1 smash, shatter, fracture, snap, crack, shiver, splinter, disintegrate, demolish, destroy, wreck, pierce. 2 violate, infringe, disobey, breach. 3 fail, malfunction, stop working, pack up (*inf*), go on the blink (*inf*), conk out (*inf*). 4 interrupt, pause, stop, rest, halt. 5 surpass, excel, beat, cap (*inf*). 6 reveal, disclose, make known, release. 7 crush, overcome, defeat, rout. 8 crush, tame, cow, subdue. 9 decipher, crack, solve, work out. 10 change, alter. 11 soften, cushion. 12 begin, dawn.
➤*noun* 1 fracture, crack, split, gap, breach, rupture, rift, opening. 2 pause, interruption, recess, respite, rest, halt, breather (*inf*), letup (*inf*), time-out (*inf*). 3 holiday, vacation, time off. 4 opportunity, chance, opening, stroke of luck.
break away 1 escape, run away, make a run for it (*inf*). 2 leave, part company, secede, split off.
break down 1 fail, malfunction, stop working, pack up (*inf*), conk out (*inf*).

2 collapse, fail, fall through, come to nothing. **3** analyse, dissect, itemize. **4** lose control, crack up (inf), go to pieces (inf).

break in 1 interrupt, intervene, interfere, butt in, cut in, barge in. **2** burgle, rob, break and enter. **3** initiate, prepare, train, accustom, tame. **4** wear in.

break off 1 detach, sever, separate, snap off, remove. **2** stop, desist. **3** end, finish, stop, terminate, discontinue, suspend.

break out 1 start, begin, erupt, burst out. **2** escape, run away, abscond.

break up 1 dismantle, take apart, disband, split up. **2** disperse, split up, separate, go their separate ways. **3** adjourn, finish, stop, terminate.

breakable adj fragile, brittle, flimsy, frail.

breakdown noun **1** stoppage, failure, malfunction. **2** collapse, failure, ruin. **3** collapse, crack-up (inf). **4** analysis, itemization, dissection, review, summary.

breaker noun wave, comber, billow, roller.

break-in noun burglary, robbery.

breakneck adj rapid, reckless, dangerous.

breakthrough noun advance, success, step forward, quantum leap, discovery, invention.

breakwater noun mole, groyne, jetty.

breast noun **1** teat, tit (inf), boob (inf), knocker (sl). **2** bust, chest, bosom.

breath noun **1** inhalation, exhalation, respiration, gasp, pant, wheeze. **2** breeze, gust, puff, waft, draught. **3** hint, suggestion, whisper.

breathe verb **1** respire, inhale, exhale, gasp, wheeze, pant, puff. **2** say, whisper, murmur.

breather noun rest, break, pause, respite, breathing space.

breathless adj **1** gasping, panting, winded, out of breath, puffed out. **2** excited, in suspense, with bated breath, on tenterhooks.

breathtaking adj awesome, awe-inspiring, impressive, magnificent, astounding, stunning, exciting, thrilling.

breed verb **1** reproduce, multiply, procreate. **2** rear, raise, propagate, bring up. **3** create, produce, generate, give rise to, arouse. **4** inculcate, instil.

➤noun **1** race, stock, strain, variety, species, pedigree, line. **2** kind, sort, type, class.

breeding noun **1** manners, refinement, culture, cultivation, polish, civility, courtesy, politeness. **2** background, ancestry, lineage.

breeze noun light wind, flurry, breath of wind, draught.
➤verb drift, glide, sweep, sail.

breezy adj **1** windy, fresh, blustery, blowy. **2** carefree, casual, light-hearted, cheerful, confident, easygoing, relaxed, jaunty.

brevity noun **1** conciseness, terseness, succinctness, pithiness. **2** shortness, transience, transitoriness, impermanence.

brew verb **1** steep, ferment, prepare, make. **2** infuse, boil. **3** gather, develop, build up, threaten. **4** foment, plot, contrive, devise, concoct.
➤noun drink, beverage, infusion, concoction.

bribe verb buy, buy off, suborn, corrupt, fix (inf), grease someone's palm (inf).
➤noun inducement, enticement, back-hander (inf), graft, sweetener, carrot (inf), payoff (inf), payola (inf).

bric-a-brac noun knick-knacks, trinkets, curios, antiques.

bridal adj nuptial, conjugal, matrimonial, marital.

bride noun newlywed, wife, spouse.

bridegroom noun groom, newlywed, husband, spouse.

bridge noun flyover, viaduct, overpass.
➤verb **1** span, traverse, cross, go over. **2** connect, join, link.

bridle noun curb, restraint, halter.
➤verb **1** curb, restrain, check, hold back, govern. **2** bristle, be indignant, raise one's hackles.

brief adj **1** short, fleeting, transitory, transient, momentary, temporary. **2** concise, short, terse, succinct, pithy, laconic, curt, abrupt.
➤noun **1** remit, instructions, directions, mandate, terms of reference. **2** case, argument, evidence, defence.
➤verb instruct, inform, fill in (inf), enlighten, prepare, put in the picture.

briefing *noun* meeting, conference, discussion, seminar.

brigade *noun* **1** force, section, unit. **2** group, squad, team, bunch.

brigand *noun* bandit, robber, outlaw, marauder, plunderer, highwayman.

bright *adj* **1** luminous, shining, brilliant, radiant, gleaming, glittering, glowing, glossy, resplendent, dazzling, vivid, intense. **2** strong, vivid, intense, bold, brilliant, rich, glowing. **3** intelligent, clever, smart, sharp, brainy, astute, quick. **4** radiant, beaming, happy. **5** lively, vivacious, genial. **6** favourable, promising, good, encouraging, rosy, auspicious.

brighten *verb* **1** illuminate, lighten, light up, clear, shine, enhance, enliven, cheer, cheer up, encourage, perk up, buck up (*inf*).

brilliant *adj* **1** bright, radiant, shining, sparkling, glittering, lustrous, intense, vivid, dazzling, splendid, magnificent, resplendent, refulgent. **2** intelligent, clever, bright, brainy, smart, learned, accomplished, expert, talented, gifted. **3** successful, exceptional, outstanding, distinguished, illustrious, eminent. **4** great, superb, wonderful, fantastic, excellent, marvellous.

brim *noun* rim, lip, edge, brink. ➤*verb* be filled with, overflow with.

brindled *adj* mottled, dappled, tabby.

brine *noun* **1** saline solution, pickle. **2** salt water, seawater.

bring *verb* **1** fetch, carry, convey, conduct, lead, escort, accompany. **2** cause, engender, produce, result in, provoke. **3** initiate, propose, lay.
bring about cause, effect, occasion, result in, produce, accomplish, realize.
bring down 1 reduce, decrease, lower, cut. **2** overthrow, unseat, oust, depose.
bring forward 1 introduce, raise, propose, suggest. **2** advance.
bring in 1 earn, yield, fetch, gross, net, realize. **2** introduce, establish, inaugurate, institute.
bring off achieve, pull off, accomplish, carry out.
bring on 1 help, encourage, foster. **2** produce, cause, lead to.
bring out 1 publish, issue, launch, release. **2** reveal, show up. **3** emphasize, highlight, accentuate.
bring round 1 revive, resuscitate. **2** win over, persuade, convince, convert.
bring up raise, rear, nurture, educate, foster.

brink *noun* **1** border, edge, rim, margin, verge, bank, shore. **2** verge, edge, threshold.

brisk *adj* **1** energetic, lively, animated, vigorous, nimble, spry, quick, fast. **2** businesslike, efficient, no-nonsense. **3** keen, crisp, fresh, invigorating, bracing.

bristle *noun* hair, whisker, spine. ➤*verb* **1** stand up, stand on end. **2** be indignant, bridle, flare up. **3** swarm, abound, be thick (*inf*).

bristly *adj* hairy, whiskery, stubbly, rough, prickly, spiky.

brittle *adj* **1** fragile, frail, delicate, crisp, breakable. **2** sharp, hard, harsh, grating, strident. **3** tense, irritable, edgy, on edge, uptight (*inf*).

broach *verb* **1** introduce, mention, bring up, raise. **2** open, tap, pierce, uncork.

broad *adj* **1** wide, ample, vast, large, extensive, spacious, roomy. **2** comprehensive, inclusive, sweeping, all-embracing, universal, general. **3** general, rough, loose, vague, inexact, imprecise. **4** clear, explicit, obvious, direct, plain. **5** extensive, wide, wide-ranging, widespread, vast. **6** strong, regional, dialectal. **7** vulgar, coarse, indecent, indelicate.

broadcast *verb* **1** transmit, relay, show, air, beam, televise. **2** publish, make known, disseminate, proclaim, announce, advertise. **3** sow, scatter. ➤*noun* show, programme, transmission.

broaden *verb* widen, enlarge, amplify, expand, open up, increase.

broad-minded *adj* liberal, tolerant, indulgent, forbearing, permissive, unprejudiced, unbiased, open-minded.

broadside *noun* **1** bombardment, salvo, volley. **2** attack, criticism, diatribe, philippic, harangue, flak (*inf*), stick (*inf*).

brochure *noun* leaflet, pamphlet, booklet, flyer, handbill, notice, circular, advertisement.

broil *verb* **1** grill, cook, fry, roast, barbecue. **2** roast, bake, swelter.

broke *adj* penniless, bankrupt, cash-strapped, skint (*inf*), bust (*inf*), stony-broke (*inf*), cleaned out (*inf*), on one's beam ends (*inf*), on one's uppers (*inf*).

broken *adj* halting, hesitant, disjointed, faltering, stammering.

brokenhearted *adj* inconsolable, desolate, grief-stricken, miserable, wretched, heartbroken, despairing, devastated.

broker *noun* middleman, intermediary, agent, negotiator, go-between.

brooch *noun* pin, clasp, clip.

brood *verb* **1** think, ponder, ruminate, dwell on, worry. **2** sit on, incubate, hatch. ➤*noun* **1** litter, clutch, offspring, family, young. **2** children, family, kids (*inf*).

brook¹ *noun* stream, beck, rivulet, rill, burn, gill.

brook² *verb* bear, endure, stand, stomach, put up with (*inf*).

brothel *noun* house of ill repute, bordello, whorehouse, knocking shop (*inf*).

brother *noun* **1** sibling, kinsman, bro (*inf*). **2** comrade, partner, companion, colleague, associate. **3** monk, friar.

brotherhood *noun* **1** fraternity, society, fellowship, association, league. **2** brotherliness, friendship, comradeship, fellowship, camaraderie.

brow *noun* **1** forehead, temple. **2** crown, summit, peak, top, brink, edge.

browbeat *verb* bully, coerce, intimidate, cow, overbear, domineer, bulldoze (*inf*).

brown *adj* **1** chestnut, bronze, copper, tan, tawny, chocolate, coffee, walnut, bay, brunette, sorrel, roan. **2** tanned, bronzed, sunburnt. ➤*verb* grill, fry, toast.

browned off *adj* fed up, bored, cheesed off (*inf*), hacked off (*inf*).

browse *verb* **1** scan, skim, dip into, thumb, leaf, look around. **2** nibble, crop, graze.

bruise *verb* injure, damage, hurt, mark, blemish, discolour, blacken, contuse. ➤*noun* injury, contusion, discoloration, mark, blemish, black eye, shiner (*inf*).

brunt *noun* full force, impact, stress, strain, pressure.

brush¹ *noun* **1** broom, besom, sweeper. **2** touch, stroke, contact. ➤*verb* **1** sweep, clean, groom. **2** touch, graze, stroke, kiss. **brush off** reject, spurn, snub, rebuff, dismiss, cold-shoulder, disregard, ignore. **brush up** revise, read up, go over, relearn, bone up on (*inf*).

brush² *noun* scrub, thicket, undergrowth, bushes.

brush³ *noun* skirmish, clash, encounter, tussle, scrap (*inf*).

brusque *adj* curt, abrupt, short, gruff, rude, unceremonious.

brutal *adj* **1** cruel, savage, vicious, ruthless, callous, heartless, unfeeling. **2** harsh, severe, merciless.

brute *noun* **1** animal, beast, creature. **2** beast, savage, monster, devil, swine. ➤*adj* **1** physical, bodily, carnal. **2** bestial, savage, cruel. **3** instinctive, unthinking.

bubble *noun* drop, bead, globule, glob, blister. ➤*verb* **1** sparkle, foam, froth, seethe, boil, fizz, effervesce. **2** gurgle, burble. **3** be excited, sparkle.

bubbly *adj* **1** effervescent, sparkling, fizzy, carbonated, foaming, frothy. **2** lively, sparkling, vivacious, ebullient.

buccaneer *noun* pirate, corsair, freebooter, privateer.

buck *verb* spring, jump, leap, jerk. **buck up 1** cheer up, perk up. **2** hurry, speed up, get a move on. **3** encourage, hearten.

bucket *noun* pail, can, scuttle.

buckle *noun* clasp, clip, fastener. ➤*verb* **1** bow, bend, warp, distort, bulge. **2** crumple, collapse, cave in. **3** fasten, secure.

bucolic *adj* rural, rustic, pastoral.

bud *noun* shoot, germ, sprout. ➤*verb* sprout, shoot, burgeon, grow, develop.

budding *adj* promising, up-and-coming, fledgling.

budge *verb* **1** move, stir, shift, dislodge, give way. **2** change one's mind, be swayed, give in, yield.

budget *noun* **1** estimate, statement, plan. **2** funds, resources, allocation.
➤*verb* plan, cost, estimate, allocate, apportion, set aside.

buff *adj* yellowish-brown, beige, sandy.
➤*verb* polish, shine, burnish.
➤*noun* enthusiast, fan, expert, devotee, addict, aficionado, freak (*inf*).

buffer *noun* bumper, shock absorber, cushion, fender, bulwark.

buffet[1] *noun* **1** snack bar, counter, bar. **2** meal, smorgasbord. **3** sideboard, cabinet, cupboard.

buffet[2] *verb* strike, hit, thump, pound.

buffoon *noun* jester, clown, fool, comedian, joker, wag.

bug *noun* **1** insect, flea, creepy-crawly. **2** germ, virus, infection. **3** craze, obsession, fad, mania. **4** flaw, defect, fault, imperfection, gremlin. **5** listening device, tap, phone-tap, wire-tap.
➤*verb* **1** irritate, annoy, bother, pester, irk, plague, needle (*inf*). **2** eavesdrop, tap, listen in.

bugbear *noun* bogey, nightmare, bête noire, anathema.

build *verb* erect, put up, construct, make, assemble, put together.
➤*noun* physique, body, figure, frame.
build up 1 boost, strengthen, reinforce, expand. **2** accumulate, accrue, develop, increase, mount.

building *noun* edifice, structure, house, pile.

buildup *noun* **1** increase, growth, expansion, enlargement, development, intensification, accumulation. **2** publicity, promotion, hype (*inf*).

built-in *adj* **1** integral, fitted. **2** inherent, essential.

bulbous *adj* rounded, swollen, bulging.

bulge *verb* swell, balloon, expand, dilate, distend.
➤*noun* **1** swelling, lump, bump, protuberance. **2** increase, rise, surge.

bulk *noun* **1** size, volume, mass, weight, magnitude, dimensions. **2** majority, preponderance, greater part, most.
➤*verb* expand, fill out, pad.

bulky *adj* large, big, massive, cumbersome, unwieldy.

bulldoze *verb* **1** knock down, level, flatten, raze. **2** force, pressurize, bully, browbeat.

bulletin *noun* **1** announcement, statement, communiqué, dispatch. **2** newsflash, update. **3** newsletter, leaflet, pamphlet.

bullish *adj* confident, optimistic, positive, upbeat (*inf*).

bully *noun* tormentor, persecutor, oppressor.
➤*verb* browbeat, intimidate, domineer, terrorize, persecute, harass, push around (*inf*).

bulwark *noun* rampart, fortification, bastion, defence, safeguard.

bum[1] *noun* bottom, backside, behind (*inf*), arse (*sl*).

bum[2] *noun* **1** tramp, vagrant, hobo. **2** idler, loafer, layabout.
➤*verb* laze, lounge, loaf.

bumble *verb* blunder, lurch, shamble.

bump *verb* **1** knock, bang, strike, hit. **2** collide with, crash into, slam into (*inf*). **3** bounce, jolt, rattle.
➤*noun* **1** blow, knock, bang, crash, collision, shock, jar, jolt. **2** swelling, lump, protuberance, bulge.
bump into come across, meet, run into, chance upon.

bumper *adj* abundant, rich, exceptional.

bumpkin *noun* rustic, peasant, yokel, clodhopper.

bumptious *adj* conceited, vain, arrogant, self-assertive, pushy (*inf*), cocky.

bumpy *adj* **1** rough, uneven, rutted, potholed. **2** rough, jerky, bouncy.

bunch *noun* **1** bouquet, posy, spray, collection, assortment, group, bundle, sheaf. **2** group, set, crowd (*inf*), gang (*inf*).
➤*verb* cluster, gather, bundle, huddle.

bundle *noun* bunch, collection, pack, bale, pile, accumulation.

➤*verb* **1** pack, wrap, tie, package, parcel, fasten, gather. **2** hurry, push, thrust, shove.

bungle *verb* botch, mismanage, mess up, make a mess of, mishandle, louse up (*inf*), cock up (*sl*).

bunker *noun* **1** container, bin, chest. **2** obstacle, hazard.

buoy *noun* float, marker, guide.
➤*verb* **1** sustain, support. **2** cheer up, encourage, boost, rally, hearten.

buoyant *adj* **1** light, floating. **2** cheerful, breezy, lighthearted, carefree.

burden *noun* **1** duty, responsibility, charge, encumbrance, weight, millstone, affliction, trial. **2** weight, load.
➤*verb* load, weigh down, oppress, afflict, trouble, encumber.

burdensome *adj* onerous, heavy, taxing, troublesome, trying, weighty.

bureau *noun* **1** desk, writing desk. **2** department, office, agency, branch.

bureaucracy *noun* **1** red tape, rules and regulations, officialdom. **2** civil service, administration.

bureaucrat *noun* **1** official, civil servant, functionary. **2** mandarin, apparatchik.

burgeon *verb* **1** bud. **2** grow, develop, expand, proliferate.

burglar *noun* housebreaker, robber, thief, pilferer.

burglary *noun* housebreaking, breaking and entering, theft, robbery.

burial *noun* interment, inhumation, entombment, funeral.

burlesque *noun* caricature, parody, takeoff (*inf*), send-up (*inf*).

burly *adj* sturdy, stocky, thickset, brawny, beefy, hefty, strapping.

burn *verb* **1** be ablaze, be on fire, flame, blaze, smoulder, light, set on fire, set alight. **2** scorch, char, singe, sear, reduce to ashes, incinerate. **3** smart, sting, prick, tingle. **4** yearn, long, itch, be eager, simmer, smoulder.

burning *adj* **1** on fire, flaming, blazing, fiery, hot, glowing, smouldering. **2** ardent, fervent, intense, passionate, eager. **3** urgent, important, critical, pressing.

burnish *verb* polish, shine, rub, buff, furbish.

burp *verb* belch, eruct.

burrow *noun* tunnel, hole, den, lair, retreat.
➤*verb* **1** dig, excavate, tunnel. **2** search, hunt, rummage, ferret.

bursar *noun* treasurer.

burst *verb* **1** puncture, rupture, crack, break, shatter, blow up, explode. **2** erupt, rush, push one's way, gush, pour, surge. **3** exclaim, cry out, call out, blurt out. **4** break out, begin suddenly.
➤*noun* eruption, outburst, gush, outbreak, fit.

bury *verb* **1** inter, lay to rest. **2** cover, conceal, hide, secrete. **3** sink, embed, implant. **4** occupy, absorb, immerse, engross.

bush *noun* **1** shrub. **2** thicket, undergrowth. **3** brush, scrub, scrubland, wilds.

bushy *adj* rough, thick, shaggy, luxuriant.

business *noun* **1** occupation, trade, profession, line, work, job, vocation. **2** company, firm, organization, concern, partnership, industry, enterprise, multinational. **3** commerce, trade, buying and selling. **4** affair, concern, responsibility, function. **5** subject, issue, matter, question, task.

businesslike *adj* efficient, organized, methodical, systematic, professional.

bust[1] *noun* **1** chest, bosom, breast. **2** sculpture, statue.

bust[2] *verb* **1** break, damage, burst, crack. **2** arrest, capture, nab (*inf*), collar (*inf*).
➤*adj* bankrupt, insolvent, ruined, broke (*inf*).

bustle *verb* hurry, dash, rush, fuss.
➤*noun* fuss, flurry, stir, ado, hurry, haste.

busy *adj* **1** occupied, engaged, employed. **2** active, on the go (*inf*), bustling, full, eventful, hectic.

busybody *noun* meddler, snooper, nosy parker (*inf*).

but *conj* **1** however, on the other hand. **2** yet, still, nevertheless.
➤*prep* except, bar, barring.
➤*adv* only, merely.

butch *adj* mannish, masculine.

butcher *noun* killer, murderer.
➤*verb* slaughter, massacre, kill, murder.

butt[1] *noun* 1 shaft, handle, end. 2 stub, end, dog-end (*inf*). 3 behind (*inf*), ass (*inf*), arse (*sl*).

butt[2] *noun* object, victim, laughing stock.

butt[3] *verb* push, shove, ram.
butt in 1 interfere, meddle, intrude. 2 interrupt, chip in (*inf*).

butt[4] *noun* cask, barrel.

buttock *noun* rump, rear, posterior, seat.

button *noun* 1 fastener, clasp. 2 knob, switch.

buttonhole *verb* accost, waylay, detain.

buttress *noun* support, stay, reinforcement, abutment.
➤*verb* 1 support, strengthen, reinforce. 2 support, back, bolster, uphold.

buxom *adj* plump, healthy, full-bosomed, voluptuous.

buy *verb* purchase, pay for, obtain, acquire.
➤*noun* purchase, acquisition, bargain.

buzz *verb* 1 hum, murmur, drone, whirr. 2 rush, hurry, bustle.
➤*noun* 1 hum, drone, whirr, murmur. 2 ring, call. 3 thrill, excitement, kick (*inf*). 4 rumour, gossip, latest.

by *prep* 1 near, next to, alongside. 2 through, by way of, via. 3 by means of, through. 4 before, no later than. 5 past, beyond.

bygone *adj* past, previous, former, erstwhile.

bylaw *noun* local law, local regulation, rule.

bypass *noun* ring road, detour, diversion.
➤*verb* 1 go round, avoid. 2 get round, evade, circumvent, overlook, pass over, ignore.

bystander *noun* onlooker, spectator, observer, passer-by.

byword *noun* 1 embodiment, personification. 2 saying, maxim, slogan, motto.

cab *noun* **1** taxi, minicab, hackney carriage. **2** compartment, cabin, cubicle.

cabal *noun* clique, coterie, set, ring, band, camp, faction.

cabaret *noun* **1** show, floor show, entertainment. **2** club, nightclub, nightspot.

cabin *noun* **1** hut, chalet, shack, shanty, shelter, refuge. **2** compartment, berth, sleeping quarters, stateroom.

cabinet *noun* **1** case, dresser, cupboard, chest. **2** council, committee, administration, executive, government, ministry.

cable *noun* **1** line, rope, chain. **2** wire, flex, lead. **3** cablegram, wire, telegram, telegraph, message.
➤*verb* wire, telegraph.

cache *noun* hiding place, repository, storehouse, stockpile.

cachet *noun* prestige, distinction, reputation, renown, esteem, seal of approval.

cackle *verb* **1** cluck, squawk. **2** chatter, jabber, prattle, babble.

cacophony *noun* discord, dissonance, disharmony, stridency, caterwauling.

cad *noun* scoundrel, rogue, rascal, blackguard, rotter (*inf*), bounder (*inf*).

cadaver *noun* corpse, dead body, stiff (*inf*).

cadaverous *adj* **1** deathly, corpselike, ghastly, pallid, ashen, emaciated, skeletal. **2** haggard, gaunt, drawn, hollow-cheeked.

cadence *noun* **1** intonation, tone, inflection, accent. **2** rhythm, metre. **3** beat, tempo.

cadge *verb* scrounge, beg, sponge (*inf*), freeload (*inf*).

café *noun* cafeteria, snack bar, buffet, tearoom, coffee bar.

cafeteria *noun* canteen, buffet, self-service restaurant, café.

cage *noun* enclosure, pen, hutch, aviary.
➤*verb* confine, imprison, coop up, hem in, restrict.

cagey *adj* secretive, guarded, circumspect, discreet, noncommittal, evasive.

cajole *verb* coax, wheedle, persuade, dupe, inveigle, flatter, sweet-talk (*inf*).

cake *noun* **1** pastry, bun, gateau. **2** lump, chunk, block, bar, slab.
➤*verb* **1** solidify, harden, congeal, coagulate. **2** encrust, plaster, cover, coat.

calamity *noun* disaster, catastrophe, cataclysm, tragedy, misfortune, blow, trouble, affliction.

calculate *verb* **1** compute, work out, reckon, figure, determine. **2** estimate, gauge, judge, weigh up. **3** rely, depend, count, bank.

calculated *adj* **1** aimed, intended, designed, contrived. **2** intentional, deliberate, planned, premeditated.

calculating *adj* scheming, devious, crafty, cunning, shrewd, manipulative.

calculation *noun* **1** computation, working out, reckoning, estimation, judgment, deliberation. **2** planning, design, forethought, shrewdness, craft, cunning.

calendar *noun* chronology, agenda, schedule, diary.

calibre *noun* **1** diameter, bore, gauge. **2** capacity, ability, talent, endowments. **3** quality, worth, excellence.

call *noun* **1** shout, yell, cry, exclamation. **2** cry, signal. **3** summons, invitation. **4** request, appeal, demand, requirement. **5** need, cause, reason, excuse, justification. **6** attraction, lure, calling. **7** phone call, ring, buzz (*inf*), bell (*inf*).
➤*verb* **1** shout, cry, yell, roar, proclaim, announce. **2** hail, summon, rouse. **3** convene, convoke, summon, invite,

send for. **4** name, dub, entitle, designate, term, style, brand. **5** ring, ring up, telephone, phone, contact. **6** visit, stop by, drop in.
call for 1 necessitate, need, require, involve, warrant, demand, campaign for. **2** fetch, pick up, collect.
call off cancel, abandon, postpone, defer, shelve (*inf*).
call on/upon appeal to, invoke, ask, request, urge, require.
call up 1 evoke, recall, bring to mind, summon up. **2** enlist, recruit, draft, sign up.
on call on duty, standing by, ready.

calling *noun* **1** vocation, mission, call. **2** career, profession, occupation, trade, business, work, line.

callous *adj* unfeeling, insensitive, cold, unsympathetic, uncaring, harsh, hard-hearted, heartless.

callow *adj* inexperienced, naive, ingenuous, innocent, immature, green, unsophisticated.

calm *adj* **1** still, windless, tranquil, peaceful, smooth, like a millpond. **2** placid, composed, self-possessed, self-controlled, cool, collected, poised, unruffled, relaxed, laid back (*inf*), imperturbable, unflappable (*inf*).
➤*noun* **1** calmness, composure, self-possession, cool (*inf*), equanimity, poise. **2** stillness, smoothness, tranquillity, peace, quiet, hush, lull.
➤*verb* pacify, appease, still, lull, relax, sedate, tranquillize, compose oneself, simmer down (*inf*).

calumniate *verb* slander, libel, defame, vilify, malign, abuse, insult.

calumny *noun* **1** slander, libel, misrepresentation, slur, smear. **2** calumniation, defamation, vilification, denigration, mudslinging.

camaraderie *noun* comradeship, companionship, fellowship, friendliness, esprit de corps.

camber *noun* curve, arch, curvature, convexity.

camouflage *noun* **1** disguise, concealment, mask, cloak, facade. **2** screening, covering.
➤*verb* disguise, mask, cloak, screen, cover, conceal, hide.

camp[1] *noun* **1** encampment, cantonment, bivouac. **2** campsite, camping ground. **3** faction, clique, coterie, set, party, group.
➤*verb* **1** encamp, pitch camp. **2** sleep out, rough it (*inf*).

camp[2] *adj* **1** effeminate, limp-wristed (*inf*), homosexual, gay. **2** mannered, affected, exaggerated, theatrical, extravagant, flamboyant, posturing.
camp it up overact, ham it up, overdo it, posture.

campaign *noun* **1** battle, war, operation, exercise, manoeuvre, attack, offensive. **2** drive, push, movement, crusade.
➤*verb* fight, battle, crusade, push, press, strive, agitate.

can *noun* tin, jar, container, receptacle.
➤*verb* tin, preserve.

canal *noun* **1** channel, waterway, watercourse. **2** tube, duct, pipe, passage.

cancel *verb* **1** call off, abandon, abort, drop, scrap (*inf*), axe (*inf*). **2** annul, nullify, revoke, repeal, rescind, countermand, negate. **3** obliterate, expunge, delete, cross out. **4** neutralize, counteract, counterbalance, offset.

cancer *noun* **1** tumour, carcinoma, malignancy, growth. **2** canker, blight, bane, evil, scourge, corruption, sickness.

candid *adj* frank, open, direct, honest, truthful, sincere, blunt, forthright.

candidate *noun* applicant, aspirant, nominee, contender, entrant, runner.

candour *noun* frankness, openness, directness, honesty, truthfulness, sincerity, bluntness, forthrightness.

cane *noun* **1** stick, staff. **2** rod, stick. **3** stem, stalk.
➤*verb* beat, thrash, flog.

canker *noun* **1** abscess, ulcer, infection, lesion, sore, chancre. **2** blight, bane, evil, scourge, curse, sickness, cancer.

cannabis *noun* marijuana, hemp, hashish, ganja, grass (*inf*), pot (*inf*), hash (*inf*).

cannonade *noun* bombardment, battery, barrage, broadside, volley, salvo.

canny *adj* astute, shrewd, knowing, discerning, sharp, clever, artful, wise, prudent, cautious.

canon *noun* **1** law, statute, rule, convention, precept, standard, principle, criterion. **2** catalogue, list, enumeration, litany.

canonical *adj* official, recognized, orthodox, conventional, standard, regular.

canopy *noun* tester, baldachin, awning, cover, tarpaulin.

cant[1] *noun* **1** hypocrisy, insincerity, sanctimoniousness. **2** jargon, lingo, argot, slang, vernacular.

cant[2] *noun* inclination, slope, slant, tilt, angle.
➤*verb* incline, slope, slant, tilt, tip.

cantankerous *adj* irritable, irascible, testy, bad-tempered, grumpy, crotchety (*inf*), ill-humoured, peevish, quarrelsome, argumentative.

canteen *noun* cafeteria, restaurant, dining room.

canticle *noun* hymn, song, psalm.

canvas *noun* sailcloth, tarpaulin, ticking, drill.

canvass *verb* **1** electioneer, campaign, poll, survey. **2** debate, discuss, air.
➤*noun* poll, survey.

canyon *noun* ravine, gully, gorge, valley, chasm, gulf.

cap *noun* **1** hat, skullcap, baseball cap. **2** lid, top, cover, stopper.
➤*verb* **1** top, crown, surmount, cover. **2** surpass, exceed, transcend, eclipse, outdo, better. **3** restrict, limit, curb. **4** complete, perfect, consummate, round off.
to cap it all as a finishing touch, as the last straw, on top of everything else.

capability *noun* **1** ability, competence, proficiency, adeptness, skill, experience. **2** capacity, faculty, potential, aptitude, talent, gift.

capable *adj* **1** able, competent, proficient, skilful, experienced, qualified, talented. **2** apt, fitted, suited, inclined, disposed. **3** likely, liable, susceptible.

capacious *adj* spacious, roomy, commodious, ample, large, vast, voluminous.

capacitate *verb* enable, empower, qualify, entitle, authorize.

capacity *noun* **1** volume, dimensions, size, space, room. **2** ability, aptitude, talent, gift, skill. **3** power, potential, capability. **4** position, office, function, role.

cape[1] *noun* cloak, mantle, wrap, poncho.

cape[2] *noun* headland, ness, mull, promontory, point.

caper *verb* frolic, frisk, gambol, hop, skip, cavort, prance.
➤*noun* **1** frolic, gambol, skip, leap, spring. **2** prank, practical joke, trick, stunt, lark.

capital *adj* excellent, first rate, super (*inf*), splendid, fine.
➤*noun* **1** money, finance, funds, resources, stock. **2** capital letter, block letter, uppercase letter. **3** seat of government, administrative centre.

capitalist *noun* financier, investor, banker, tycoon, mogul.

capitalize *verb* finance, fund, back, sponsor.
capitalize on take advantage of, profit from, turn to account, exploit.

capitulate *verb* **1** surrender, yield, give in, throw in the towel (*inf*). **2** back down, submit, accede, acquiesce.

caprice *noun* whim, vagary, impulse, fancy, notion, fad.

capricious *adj* fickle, inconstant, changeable, unpredictable, mercurial, volatile, impulsive, whimsical, fanciful.

capsize *verb* **1** overturn, invert, upset. **2** turn over, keel over, turn turtle.

capsule *noun* **1** lozenge, tablet, pill, bolus. **2** case, sheath, shell, pod, receptacle. **3** craft, probe, compartment, section.

captain *noun* **1** skipper, master. **2** commander, leader, head, chief, number one (*inf*).

caption *noun* **1** legend, heading, inscription, gloss. **2** subtitle, explanation, comment.

captious *adj* carping, cavilling, quibbling, fault-finding, nit-picking (*inf*).

captivate *verb* fascinate, charm, enchant, enthral, allure, win, delight, ravish.

captive *noun* prisoner, hostage, convict, slave.
➤*adj* **1** captured, in captivity, imprisoned, interned. **2** confined, restricted, restrained, caged.

capture verb catch, take, seize, arrest, collar (inf), take prisoner, trap, net, bag (inf).
➤ noun catching, taking, seizure, arrest, imprisonment.

car noun automobile, motor, banger (inf), wheels (inf).

carafe noun flask, decanter, bottle, flagon.

caravan noun 1 mobile home, camper, trailer, wagon. 2 troop, band, group, company. 3 convoy, motorcade.

carcass noun 1 corpse, body, cadaver. 2 skeleton, hulk, shell. 3 framework, structure.

card noun cardboard, pasteboard.
on the cards possible, likely, probable.

cardinal adj principal, chief, key, crucial, essential, fundamental, central, pivotal, primary, paramount.

care noun 1 concern, anxiety, worry, distress, strain. 2 trouble, problem, burden, responsibility. 3 attention, heed, diligence, pains, effort, carefulness, caution. 4 safekeeping, charge, management, control, supervision. 5 custody, guardianship, wardship, protection. 6 regard, consideration, thoughtfulness, concern, solicitude, sympathy.
➤ verb 1 worry, be concerned, bother, trouble, mind, give a damn (sl). 2 like, enjoy, love, cherish. 3 tend, nurse, attend to, mind, look after, take care of, protect. 4 want, desire, wish.

career noun calling, vocation, profession, work, occupation, métier.
➤ verb rush, dash, hurtle, race, tear.

carefree adj cheerful, light-hearted, unworried, untroubled, happy-go-lucky, nonchalant, airy, blithe.

careful adj 1 wary, watchful, heedful, alert. 2 attentive, thoughtful, considerate, concerned, painstaking, meticulous, thorough, precise. 3 cautious, prudent, circumspect, judicious.

careless adj 1 negligent, neglectful, slipshod, slapdash, heedless, unthinking, inattentive, reckless. 2 carefree, happy-go-lucky, nonchalant, insouciant. 3 indifferent, uncaring, unconcerned, unworried. 4 artless, unstudied, natural, simple, spontaneous, casual.

caress noun stroke, fondle, pat, touch.
➤ verb stroke, fondle, pet, pat, touch, grope (inf).

caretaker noun 1 keeper, warden, steward. 2 janitor, concierge, porter, curator.

careworn adj tired, weary, gaunt, haggard, troubled, anxious.

cargo noun load, lading, freight, consignment, shipment, goods, merchandise.

caricature noun 1 distortion, exaggeration, burlesque, parody. 2 cartoon, lampoon, travesty, send-up (inf).
➤ verb distort, exaggerate, lampoon, burlesque, parody, mock, send up (inf).

carnage noun slaughter, massacre, butchery, bloodshed.

carnal adj sexual, sensual, lascivious, fleshly, physical, bodily.

carnival noun 1 festival, fête, gala, jamboree, fiesta. 2 celebration, festivity, revel, Mardi Gras.

carol noun song, hymn, lay.
➤ verb sing, chorus, warble, trill.

carouse verb revel, roister, party, celebrate, make merry, live it up (inf), paint the town red (inf), drink, booze (inf).
noun carousal, revel, celebration, party, rave-up (inf), spree, booze-up (inf).

carp verb complain, cavil, criticize, find fault, pick holes, quibble, nit-pick (inf).

carpenter noun joiner, woodworker.

carpet noun 1 rug, mat, carpeting, matting. 2 covering, layer, blanket, mantle.
➤ verb cover, blanket, mantle, overlay, overspread.

carriage noun 1 vehicle, coach, cab, trap, chariot. 2 posture, bearing, demeanour, deportment. 3 carrying, conveyance, transport, transportation, freight, delivery.

carrier noun 1 bearer, porter, messenger, runner. 2 transporter, haulier, courier. 3 conveyor, vehicle. 4 vector, transmitter, bearer.

carry verb 1 bear, take, transport, convey, cart (inf), tote (inf), transmit, conduct. 2 support, hold up, bear. 3 accept, shoulder, take. 4 maintain, uphold, accomplish, effect. 5 extend, reach, spread. 6 affect, influence, persuade, convince, win over.

7 secure, pass, accept. **8** print, publish, broadcast, cover. **9** hold, bear, deport, comport.

carry on 1 continue, go on, keep on, persist, restart, resume. **2** conduct, run, manage, operate. **3** have an affair, commit adultery, be involved. **4** make a fuss, create (*inf*), misbehave, play up (*inf*).

carry out effect, implement, discharge, accomplish, achieve, realize, perform, execute.

cart *noun* barrow, handcart, wagon, dray.
➤*verb* **1** carry, transport, convey, bear. **2** haul, drag. **3** lug (*inf*), hump (*inf*), tote (*inf*).

carton *noun* box, packet, pack, case.

cartoon *noun* **1** animation, animated film. **2** caricature, lampoon, satire. **3** sketch, drawing, draft.

cartridge *noun* **1** case, container, cassette. **2** shell, cylinder, tube.

carve *verb* **1** cut, chisel, whittle, hew. **2** sculpt, fashion, shape, incise, engrave. **3** slice, cut up, divide, chop.

carve up divide, share out, split up, separate.

cascade *noun* **1** waterfall, cataract, chute, fountain. **2** torrent, deluge, flood, avalanche.
➤*verb* fall, tumble, plunge, pour, shower, spill, rush, surge.

case¹ *noun* **1** instance, occasion, example, illustration, specimen. **2** situation, state of affairs, circumstances, conditions. **3** event, occurrence, situation, circumstance. **4** action, suit, lawsuit, dispute, cause. **5** testimony, evidence, claim, plea. **6** argument, presentation, exposition, thesis. **7** patient, sufferer, victim.

case² *noun* **1** box, crate, carton, casket, cabinet, container, receptacle, holder. **2** suitcase, valise, holdall, grip, bag, trunk. **3** casing, housing, covering, sheath, shell, capsule, jacket, cover.

cash *noun* money, currency, coins, banknotes, ready money, dosh (*sl*).
➤*verb* encash, change, exchange, liquidate, realize.

cashier¹ *noun* clerk, teller, bursar, treasurer.

cashier² *verb* dismiss, discharge, expel, drum out.

cask *noun* barrel, keg, vat, butt.

casket *noun* **1** box, chest, coffer, case. **2** coffin, sarcophagus.

cast *verb* **1** throw, fling, toss, pitch, sling, hurl. **2** direct, project. **3** emit, send out, radiate, distribute. **4** put, place, confer, impart. **5** shed, drop, throw off, slough off, discard, get rid of. **6** mould, found, shape. **7** form, fashion, model.
➤*noun* **1** actors, players, performers, characters, dramatis personae, company. **2** casting, mould, form. **3** throw, fling, toss, pitch.

cast about hunt, look, search, grope.

cast away shipwreck, maroon, strand.

cast down depress, deject, sadden, dispirit, crush.

caste *noun* class, group, rank, grade, status, station.

castigate *verb* chastise, punish, reprimand, chide, berate, dress down (*inf*).

castle *noun* citadel, fortress, keep, palace, château, stately home.

castrate *verb* geld, emasculate, neuter.

casual *adj* **1** accidental, chance, fortuitous, incidental, contingent, random. **2** informal, relaxed, comfortable, leisure. **3** nonchalant, insouciant, blasé, offhand, unconcerned, couldn't-care-less (*inf*). **4** part-time, short-term, temporary, occasional, irregular.

casualty *noun* **1** fatality, death, loss, injury, wounded person, missing person. **2** victim, sufferer, loser, injured person.

casuistry *noun* sophistry, sophism, speciousness, equivocation, subtlety, chicanery.

cat *noun* feline, mouser, tabby, tom, puss (*inf*), moggy (*inf*).

cataclysm *noun* **1** earthquake, upheaval, convulsion. **2** catastrophe, disaster, calamity, debacle.

catacomb *noun* **1** crypt, vault, underground cemetery. **2** tunnel, passage, underground labyrinth.

catalogue *noun* list, inventory, schedule, register, file, index, directory, brochure, prospectus.
➤*verb* **1** list, record, register, file. **2** index, classify, categorize.

catapult *verb* shoot, launch, propel, hurl, pitch, fling.

cataract *noun* cascade, waterfall, rapids.

catastrophe *noun* disaster, calamity, cataclysm, blow, tragedy, ruin, fiasco.

catcall *noun* boo, hiss, whistle, jeer.

catch *verb* **1** take, seize, corner, arrest. **2** capture, snare, trap, hook, net. **3** discover, find out, expose, unmask, surprise. **4** entangle, snag. **5** intercept, clutch, hold, grip. **6** snatch, grab, grasp. **7** receive, collect. **8** contract, develop, get, pick up, go down with (*inf*). **9** attract, draw, hold. **10** hear, perceive, make out, take in, grasp, understand.
➤*noun* **1** clasp, fastener, clip, hook, hasp, latch. **2** snag, drawback, obstacle, problem, trap, trick. **3** bag, net, trophy, prize, haul (*inf*).

catch on 1 become popular, become fashionable. **2** understand, comprehend, get the picture (*inf*), twig (*inf*).

catch up gain on, reach, draw level with.

catching *adj* infectious, contagious, communicable, transmissible.

catchword *noun* slogan, motto, byword, watchword.

catchy *adj* memorable, unforgettable, tuneful, melodious.

catechism *noun* questioning, examination, drill, instruction.

catechize *verb* question, quiz, examine, test, drill.

categorical *adj* positive, definite, emphatic, unqualified, unconditional, absolute, utter, downright.

categorize *verb* class, classify, group, pigeonhole, stereotype, sort, rank.

category *noun* class, classification, group, division, section, heading, type.

cater *verb* **1** provision, victual, feed. **2** serve, supply, satisfy, indulge, humour, gratify.

caterwaul *verb* yell, howl, yowl, scream, wail, cry.

catharsis *noun* **1** purification, purgation. **2** release, abreaction.

catholic *adj* **1** general, universal, comprehensive, all-inclusive, all-embracing, eclectic. **2** liberal, tolerant, broad-minded, open-minded.

cattle *pl noun* cows, bulls, oxen, livestock.

catty *adj* spiteful, malicious, nasty, mean, snide, bitchy (*inf*).

caucus *noun* **1** group, faction, cabal, clique. **2** meeting, conference, conclave.

cauldron *noun* pot, kettle, copper.

cause *noun* **1** source, origin, root, prime mover, agent, factor. **2** reason, basis, justification, grounds, occasion, motive. **3** principle, ideal, conviction, movement, purpose, objective. **4** case, lawsuit, action.
➤*verb* occasion, bring about, generate, originate, produce, effect, precipitate, trigger off, give rise to, result in.

caustic *adj* **1** corrosive, burning, mordant, acid. **2** biting, cutting, trenchant, mordant, scathing, bitter.

caution *noun* **1** care, wariness, vigilance, attention, heed, prudence, circumspection. **2** admonition, warning, advice, injunction.
➤*verb* warn, advise, counsel, urge.

cautious *adj* careful, wary, chary, vigilant, watchful, prudent, circumspect, discreet, guarded.

cavalcade *noun* procession, parade, cortege, column, file, caravan.

cavalier *noun* courtier, gentleman, gallant, escort, beau.
➤*adj* haughty, supercilious, condescending, disdainful, offhand, casual.

cavalry *noun* horsemen, dragoons, hussars.

cave *noun* cavern, grotto, hollow, pothole, tunnel.

caveat *noun* warning, caution, admonition.

cavern *noun* cave, grotto, underground chamber.

cavil *verb* carp, object, complain, quibble, nit-pick (*inf*).
➤*noun* objection, complaint, quibble.

cavity *noun* hole, hollow, pit, crater, gap.

cease *verb* stop, end, finish, terminate, conclude, halt, let up, leave off.

ceaseless *adj* unceasing, incessant, constant, continuous, uninterrupted, nonstop, endless, interminable, everlasting.

cede *verb* yield, surrender, give up, relinquish, hand over, convey.

ceiling *noun* **1** roof, vault, dome, rafters. **2** upper limit, maximum, cut-off point.

celebrate *verb* **1** observe, keep, mark, remember, commemorate, honour. **2** rejoice, make merry, party, revel, have a ball (*inf*), paint the town red (*inf*). **3** perform, solemnize, bless. **4** praise, extol, exalt, glorify, proclaim, advertise.

celebrated *adj* famous, well-known, distinguished, eminent, renowned, great, legendary.

celebrity *noun* **1** star, personality, famous person, somebody, personage, household name, living legend. **2** fame, renown, eminence, glory, acclaim, popularity, stardom.

celerity *noun* speed, swiftness, rapidity, quickness, haste.

celestial *adj* **1** heavenly, divine, godly, angelic, immortal, spiritual, supernatural. **2** ethereal, empyrean, astral, stellar, extraterrestrial.

celibate *adj* **1** abstinent, continent, chaste, pure. **2** single, unmarried.

cell *noun* **1** room, chamber, cubicle, dungeon. **2** recess, cavity, hole, compartment. **3** nucleus, unit, section, faction.

cellar *noun* basement, vault, crypt, storeroom.

cement *verb* join, connect, attach, affix, bind, stick, glue, bond.
➤*noun* **1** mortar, plaster, grout, concrete. **2** adhesive, glue, gum.

cemetery *noun* graveyard, burial ground, necropolis.

cenotaph *noun* monument, memorial, shrine.

censor *verb* cut, delete, edit, expurgate, bowdlerize.
➤*noun* editor, expurgator, bowdlerizer.

censorious *adj* critical, fault-finding, disapproving, condemnatory.

censure *verb* criticize, blame, condemn, denounce, reprove, admonish, castigate, berate.
➤*noun* **1** criticism, stricture, rebuke, repri-

mand. **2** blame, condemnation, obloquy, reproof, admonition, castigation.

central *adj* **1** middle, mid, inner, interior. **2** focal, pivotal, core, crucial, key, cardinal, principal, essential, fundamental.

centralize *verb* concentrate, focus, centre, converge, consolidate.

centre *adj* **1** middle, midpoint, midst, core, heart, kernel, nucleus. **2** focus, focal point, hub, pivot, linchpin.
➤*verb* focus, hinge, pivot, revolve.

cereal *noun* **1** crop, grain, corn. **2** grain, seed, meal.

ceremonial *adj* formal, official, ritual, solemn, stately, liturgical, sacramental.
➤*noun* **1** ceremony, ritual, rite, sacrament. **2** protocol, etiquette, custom, tradition.

ceremonious *adj* punctilious, scrupulous, formal, stiff, courteous, deferential.

ceremony *noun* **1** ritual, rite, ceremonial, observance, commemoration, service, liturgy, sacrament. **2** formality, protocol, etiquette, form, decorum, propriety.

certain *adj* **1** sure, positive, convinced, confident, assured, persuaded. **2** unquestionable, indubitable, indisputable, irrefutable, conclusive, definite, decided, established. **3** bound, destined, fated. **4** inevitable, unavoidable, inexorable, ineluctable. **5** infallible, unfailing, reliable, dependable, foolproof, sure-fire (*inf*). **6** particular, specific. **7** special, individual. **8** moderate, reasonable, partial.

certainly *adv* **1** undoubtedly, without doubt, unquestionably, positively, assuredly, definitely. **2** yes, of course, by all means, naturally, surely.

certainty *noun* **1** conviction, sureness, confidence, assurance, certitude, positiveness. **2** fact, truth, reality. **3** sure thing (*inf*), safe bet (*inf*), dead cert (*inf*).

certificate *noun* document, credential, testimonial, diploma, licence, warrant, authorization.

certify *verb* **1** attest, avow, aver, confirm. **2** corroborate, substantiate, verify, authenticate, document, guarantee, warrant. **3** license, charter, accredit.

certitude *noun* certainty, sureness, assurance, conviction.

cessation *noun* end, stoppage, termination, conclusion, halt, pause.

cession *noun* surrender, capitulation, submission, relinquishment, transfer, conveyance.

chafe *verb* 1 rub, inflame, excoriate. 2 abrade, wear, erode. 3 warm, rub. 4 fume, rage, fret, brood.

chaff[1] *noun* 1 husks, hulls, shells, cases. 2 waste, rubbish, detritus, dregs.

chaff[2] *noun* banter, badinage, joking, jesting, teasing, raillery.
➤*verb* tease, josh, kid (*inf*), rib (*inf*), rag (*inf*).

chagrin *noun* vexation, exasperation, disappointment, discomfiture, mortification, embarrassment, humiliation, shame.
➤*verb* annoy, vex, irk, exasperate, aggrieve, disappoint, mortify, humiliate.

chain *noun* 1 fetter, shackle, manacle. 2 series, succession, sequence, string, train, cycle.
➤*verb* tether, hitch, fasten, secure, fetter, shackle, restrain, confine.

chair *noun* 1 seat, bench, pew, throne. 2 professorship, professorate. 3 chairperson, chairman, chairwoman, president, master of ceremonies.
➤*verb* preside over, lead, direct, control.

chalk *verb* **chalk up** 1 attribute, ascribe, credit, put down, impute. 2 achieve, attain, score.

challenge *verb* 1 dare, defy, throw down the gauntlet (*inf*). 2 confront, accost, question. 3 stretch, tax, test, stimulate, inspire. 4 question, query, dispute, disagree with. 5 object to, take exception to, protest against.
➤*noun* 1 dare, defiance, ultimatum, confrontation. 2 test, trial, problem, obstacle, hurdle. 3 question, dispute, opposition, stand. 4 objection, protest.

chamber *noun* 1 room, bedroom, boudoir. 2 hall, room. 3 cavity, hollow, cell, compartment. 4 assembly, council, legislature, house.

champ *verb* 1 chew, gnaw, bite. 2 munch, crunch.

champion *noun* 1 winner, victor, titleholder, champ (*inf*). 2 defender, supporter, advocate, sponsor.
➤*verb* defend, protect, fight for, support, advocate, promote.

chance *noun* 1 luck, fortune, providence, fate, serendipity, hazard, uncertainty. 2 accident, coincidence, fluke (*inf*). 3 opportunity, opening, occasion, break (*inf*). 4 possibility, likelihood, probability, prospect, odds.
➤*verb* 1 happen, occur, befall, come about. 2 risk, hazard, venture, stake.
➤*adj* accidental, unintentional, coincidental, fortuitous, unexpected, unpremeditated, casual, arbitrary.
chance on find, discover, stumble on, come across.

chancy *adj* risky, hazardous, speculative, uncertain, dicey (*inf*), iffy (*inf*).

change *verb* 1 alter, vary, modify, revise, amend, adjust, evolve, mutate, fluctuate. 2 replace, substitute, exchange, transpose, switch, swap. 3 transform, convert, transmute, transfigure, remodel, adapt. 4 exchange, swap.
➤*noun* 1 alteration, modification, difference, variation, transformation, metamorphosis, reform, revision, transition, flux. 2 exchange, switch, swap, replacement, substitution. 3 variety, innovation, novelty. 4 coins, silver, coppers, cash.

changeable *adj* 1 variable, changeful, inconstant, unsettled, fluctuating, unstable, protean. 2 modifiable, convertible, mutable, adjustable, adaptable. 3 fickle, capricious, mercurial, unpredictable, inconstant.

channel *noun* 1 duct, conduit, main. 2 gutter, groove, furrow, trough. 3 ditch, culvert, watercourse. 4 waterway, fairway. 5 strait, sound. 6 avenue, path, way, medium, vehicle.
➤*verb* 1 direct, guide. 2 conduct, convey, transmit. 3 groove, furrow, flute.

chant *noun* 1 song, psalm, canticle. 2 plainsong, incantation. 3 shout, chorus, slogan, mantra.
➤*verb* sing, intone, chorus, recite.

chaos *noun* disorder, confusion, shambles (*inf*), upheaval, havoc, pandemonium, anarchy.

chap *noun* man, fellow, bloke (*inf*), guy (*inf*).

chaperon noun escort, companion, duenna, governess.
➤**verb** escort, accompany, shepherd, attend, mind, supervise, keep an eye on.

chaplet noun wreath, garland, coronal, circlet.

chapter noun 1 part, division, section, episode. 2 phase, period, stage, series, sequence, chain. 3 branch, lodge, wing, section, division.

char verb burn, scorch, singe, sear.

character noun 1 personality, temperament, disposition, nature, calibre, constitution. 2 nature, attributes, ethos, qualities. 3 reputation, repute, name, standing. 4 honour, integrity, uprightness, rectitude, moral fibre. 5 person, individual, sort, type, customer (*inf*), eccentric, original, card (*inf*). 6 role, part, persona. 7 letter, figure, symbol, device.

characteristic adj distinctive, distinguishing, peculiar, individual, idiosyncratic, typical, symptomatic.
➤**noun** peculiarity, idiosyncrasy, quirk, trait, feature, quality, property, sign, symptom.

characterize verb 1 typify, distinguish, mark, stamp, identify, indicate. 2 represent, describe, portray, depict.

charade noun travesty, pretence, sham, farce, parody.

charge verb 1 accuse, arraign, impeach, indict. 2 ask, demand, levy, impose. 3 bill, invoice. 4 debit, put down. 5 rush, storm, attack, assault. 6 fill, load. 7 suffuse, imbue, permeate, pervade.
➤**noun** 1 accusation, indictment, allegation. 2 fee, levy, toll, price, tariff. 3 attack, assault, onslaught, sortie. 4 custody, care, safekeeping, guardianship, control, supervision. 5 obligation, responsibility, duty. 6 command, order, direction, instruction, mandate.
charge with entrust with, burden with, saddle with.
in charge responsible, in control, in command, directing, supervising.

charger noun horse, mount, steed.

charitable adj 1 generous, liberal, bountiful, munificent, open-handed. 2 philanthropic, humanitarian, almsgiving, eleemosynary. 3 kind, benevolent, considerate, sympathetic, gracious, magnanimous, tolerant, lenient.

charity noun 1 almsgiving, benefaction, philanthropy, generosity, altruism. 2 trust, foundation. 3 alms, relief, aid, assistance. 4 kindness, benevolence, goodwill, compassion, humanity. 5 magnanimity, leniency, indulgence, tolerance.

charlatan noun fake, fraud, impostor, quack, mountebank.

charm verb 1 delight, please, enchant, captivate, entrance, allure. 2 win over, cajole.
➤**noun** 1 attractiveness, desirability, pleasantness, suavity, charisma. 2 attraction, appeal, allure. 3 spell, incantation. 4 amulet, talisman.

charming adj delightful, pleasing, lovely, attractive, enchanting, suave, urbane, courteous.

chart noun 1 map, plan. 2 diagram, graph, table. 3 hit parade, top twenty.
➤**verb** 1 map, plot, draw, outline. 2 record, register, note, monitor.

charter noun 1 licence, warrant, permit, franchise, concession. 2 privilege, right, prerogative, sanction, authorization. 3 constitution, code, canon.
➤**verb** 1 hire, lease, commission. 2 certify, accredit, license.

chary adj 1 cautious, circumspect, guarded, wary, leery. 2 slow, reluctant, unwilling.

chase verb 1 pursue, follow, run after, hunt, track. 2 drive, expel, send packing, put to flight. 3 rush, hurry.
➤**noun** pursuit, hunt.

chasm noun 1 abyss, gorge, crevasse, ravine, gulf, rift, fissure, crater. 2 gulf, rift, breach, gap.

chassis noun 1 framework, skeleton, substructure. 2 frame, mounting, support.

chaste adj 1 pure, undefiled, virginal, celibate, continent, abstinent. 2 virtuous, decent, decorous, modest, innocent. 3 simple, plain, austere, severe.

chasten verb 1 humble, humiliate, subdue, repress, restrain. 2 punish, correct, discipline, chastise, castigate.

chastise verb 1 punish, correct, beat, flog, cane, thrash. 2 berate, upbraid, chide, reprove, haul over the coals (*inf*).

chastity *noun* **1** purity, virtue, modesty, innocence. **2** celibacy, continence, abstinence. **3** virginity, maidenhood.

chat *verb* talk, gossip, natter (*inf*), chew the fat (*inf*), chatter, gab (*inf*).
➤ *noun* **1** talk, conversation, gossip, natter (*inf*), chinwag (*inf*). **2** chatter, chitchat, small talk.

chatter *verb* prattle, jabber, gab (*inf*), witter (*inf*), rabbit (*inf*), talk, chat, natter (*inf*).
➤ *noun* prattle, babble, jabber, talk.

chatterbox *noun* chatterer, babbler, gossip, prattler, windbag (*inf*), motormouth (*inf*).

chatty *adj* **1** talkative, loquacious, voluble, garrulous, gabby (*inf*). **2** gossipy, conversational, informal, friendly, newsy (*inf*).

chauvinism *noun* **1** jingoism, flag-waving, nationalism. **2** partisanship, bias, prejudice.

cheap *adj* **1** inexpensive, low-cost, reasonable, affordable, reduced, cut-price, going for a song (*inf*), budget, economy. **2** shoddy, inferior, second-rate, trashy, tawdry, tacky (*inf*). **3** mean, shabby, contemptible, despicable.

cheapen *verb* **1** degrade, debase, demean, lower. **2** reduce, cut, discount, mark down, devalue, depreciate.

cheat *verb* **1** deceive, trick, hoax, dupe, defraud, swindle, double-cross, two-time (*inf*). **2** deprive, deny. **3** escape, dodge, avoid, thwart, frustrate, foil.
➤ *noun* **1** swindler, trickster, rogue, fraud, charlatan, liar. **2** trick, artifice, con (*inf*), fraud, swindle.

check *verb* **1** inspect, examine, test, screen, vet, scan, monitor. **2** verify, confirm, make sure, ascertain. **3** compare, cross-check. **4** halt, arrest, stop, stem. **5** hinder, impede, obstruct, block. **6** inhibit, repress, curb, restrain, limit, control.
➤ *noun* **1** inspection, examination, once-over (*inf*), test, screening, verification, audit. **2** stoppage, arrest, halt, delay. **3** curb, restraint, limitation, hindrance, impediment, barrier.

checkmate *noun* defeat, rout, conquest, victory.

checkup *noun* examination, inspection, assessment, appraisal.

cheek *noun* impertinence, impudence, insolence, disrespect, effrontery, audacity, temerity, nerve.

cheeky *adj* impertinent, impudent, insolent, disrespectful.

cheep *verb* chirp, chirrup, tweet, peep.

cheer *verb* **1** shout, yell, whoop. **2** applaud, acclaim, hail. **3** encourage, urge, root for (*inf*). **4** hearten, buck up (*inf*), comfort, console, elate, exhilarate, uplift.
➤ *noun* **1** shout, yell, cry, hurrah, acclamation. **2** cheerfulness, happiness, joy, gaiety, merriment, good spirits.

cheerful *noun* happy, glad, joyful, buoyant, sunny, breezy, hopeful, optimistic.

cheerio *interj* goodbye, bye (*inf*), so long (*inf*), see you later (*inf*), ciao.

cheerless *adj* dreary, dull, gloomy, dismal, bleak, depressing, glum, miserable.

cheers *interj* your good health, all the best, skol, bottoms up (*inf*), down the hatch (*inf*).

cheery *adj* hearty, jovial, genial, cheerful, happy, merry, jolly, sunny.

chemist *noun* pharmacist, apothecary.

chequered *adj* varied, diverse, mixed, eventful, full of ups and downs.

cherish *verb* **1** treasure, prize, hold dear, love. **2** cosset, pamper, look after, tend, nurture. **3** harbour, entertain, cling to, foster, nurse.

cherub *noun* **1** angel, seraph. **2** child, baby, innocent, darling, dear.

chest *noun* **1** breast, thorax, sternum, bosom, bust. **2** box, case, coffer, casket.

chew *verb* masticate, munch, champ, grind, gnaw.

chew over ponder, consider, ruminate on, reflect on, weigh up, mull over.

chic *adj* fashionable, modish, stylish, smart, elegant.

chicanery *noun* trickery, dishonesty, fraud, sharp practice, deception, guile, artifice, subterfuge, sophistry.

chide *verb* scold, reprimand, tell off (*inf*), tick off (*inf*), rebuke, reprove, upbraid.

chief *noun* leader, head, chieftain, ruler, overlord, captain, commander, president.

➤*adj* **1** head, supreme, grand, arch. **2** main, principal, foremost, primary, cardinal, key.

chiefly *adv* **1** especially, above all, principally. **2** mainly, mostly, predominantly, on the whole.

child *noun* **1** boy, girl, kid (*inf*), nipper (*inf*), youngster, juvenile, minor. **2** baby, infant. **3** son, daughter, offspring, descendant.

childbirth *noun* labour, delivery, parturition, confinement.

childhood *noun* boyhood, girlhood, infancy, youth, minority.

childish *adj* **1** young, youthful, boyish, girlish. **2** babyish, infantile, puerile, juvenile, immature, silly.

childlike *adj* innocent, artless, ingenuous, credulous, trustful.

chill *noun* **1** cold, coldness, chilliness, coolness, crispness, nip. **2** cold, flu, fever. **3** aloofness, frostiness, coldness, coolness. **4** chilliness, shiver, shudder.
➤*verb* **1** cool, ice, refrigerate. **2** depress, dishearten, dispirit, dampen. **3** frighten, scare, terrify, horrify.

chill out calm down, relax, take it easy (*inf*).

chilly *adj* **1** cold, cool, chill, nippy (*inf*), parky (*inf*), raw, wintry, bleak. **2** frosty, cool, aloof, distant, unfriendly, unwelcoming.

chime *verb* **1** toll, sound, strike, peal, ring, clang, jingle. **2** strike, indicate, mark. **3** harmonize, accord, agree, coordinate.
chime in interrupt, interpose, chip in (*inf*), butt in (*inf*).

chimera *noun* hallucination, fantasy, dream, delusion, fancy, illusion.

china *noun* **1** porcelain, pottery, ceramics. **2** crockery, tableware, dishes.

chink[1] *noun* gap, slit, crack, fissure, crevice.

chink[2] *noun* clink, jingle, tinkle, ring.
➤*verb* clink, jingle, tinkle, ring.

chip *noun* **1** piece, fragment, flake, sliver, splinter, shard. **2** nick, notch, flaw, defect. **3** token, counter, disc.
➤*verb* chisel, whittle, cut, hew, break off.
chip in 1 contribute, donate, pay. **2** interrupt, chime in, cut in, butt in (*inf*).

chirp *verb* chirrup, cheep, tweet, pipe, peep.

chirpy *adj* bright, cheerful, happy, jaunty, perky (*inf*).

chisel *verb* carve, sculpt, hew, whittle, engrave, shape.

chit *noun* note, slip, voucher, receipt.

chitchat *noun* chat, small talk, gossip, tittle-tattle.

chivalrous *adj* **1** knightly, heroic, valiant, gallant, courtly. **2** gracious, gallant, gentlemanly, courteous. **3** generous, magnanimous, noble, high-minded, honourable.

chivalry *noun* **1** knighthood, heroism, nobility. **2** valour, courage, honour, integrity, loyalty. **3** gallantry, courtesy, graciousness, generosity.

chivvy *verb* urge, goad, hurry, badger, nag, pester, harass, hassle (*inf*).

choice *noun* **1** selection, pick, preference, decision. **2** option, alternative. **3** range, selection, variety, supply.
➤*adj* **1** select, hand-picked, elite. **2** excellent, first-rate, prime, superior, fine, special.

choke *verb* **1** strangle, throttle, stifle, asphyxiate. **2** retch, gasp, cough. **3** block, obstruct, congest, clog. **4** suppress, repress, hold back, fight back.

choleric *adj* irritable, bad-tempered, crotchety, angry, hot-tempered, irate.

choose *verb* **1** select, pick, opt for, single out, decide on, take. **2** desire, wish, want, fancy, prefer, favour.

choosy *adj* discriminating, selective, picky (*inf*), particular, fussy.

chop *verb* **1** cut, hack, fell, lop, sever. **2** cut up, slice, dice, cube, mince.

choppy *adj* rough, turbulent, stormy, tempestuous.

chore *noun* **1** job, task, duty. **2** burden, bother, fag (*inf*).

chortle *verb* laugh, chuckle, snigger, crow.

chorus *noun* **1** choir, choristers, singers, vocalists. **2** refrain, burden, response.
in chorus in unison, all together, as one.

christen *verb* baptize, name, call, dub, style.

Christian name *noun* first name, forename, given name.

Christmas *noun* Xmas, Noel, Yuletide, festive season.

chronic *adj* **1** recurring, perennial, long-lasting, lingering, incurable. **2** persistent, constant, incessant, deep-seated, permanent. **3** inveterate, habitual, hardened. **4** appalling, dreadful, terrible, awful, atrocious.

chronicle *noun* **1** journal, diary, log, record, archive, history. **2** account, narrative, story, saga.
➤*verb* record, set down, document, report, recount, narrate.

chronological *adj* consecutive, sequential, serial, progressive, historical.

chubby *adj* plump, tubby, podgy, fat, flabby, fleshy.

chuck *verb* **1** throw, toss, hurl, sling. **2** discard, throw away, get rid of. **3** give up, quit, abandon, pack in (*inf*), drop (*inf*), dump (*inf*).

chuckle *verb* giggle, titter, chortle, snigger, laugh, smile.

chum *noun* friend, pal (*inf*), mate (*inf*), buddy (*inf*).

chummy *adj* friendly, close, pally (*inf*), matey (*inf*).

chunk *noun* lump, block, slab, wedge.

church *noun* **1** chapel, kirk, cathedral, abbey, house of God. **2** denomination, faith, sect, cult.

churchyard *noun* graveyard, cemetery, burial ground, God's acre.

churl *noun* **1** boor, lout, oaf. **2** rustic, peasant, bumpkin, yokel.

churlish *adj* **1** rude, impolite, uncivil, surly, ill-tempered, sullen, unfriendly, mean. **2** uncouth, boorish, vulgar, ill-bred.

churn *verb* **1** stir, agitate, shake, beat. **2** convulse, writhe, toss, turn, swirl, seethe.

chute *noun* slide, slope, incline, channel, gutter.

cigarette *noun* fag (*inf*), ciggy (*inf*), smoke (*inf*), coffin nail (*inf*), joint (*inf*).

cinch *noun* child's play, doddle (*inf*), piece of cake (*inf*).

cinder *noun* ash, ember, coal.

cinema *noun* **1** film theatre, multiplex, fleapit (*inf*). **2** films, pictures, movies, big screen (*inf*), silver screen (*inf*).

cipher *noun* **1** code, cryptogram. **2** symbol, device. **3** nonentity, nobody, nothing. **4** nil, zero, nought.

circle *noun* **1** ring, round, cycle, revolution. **2** hoop, wreath, coil, disc. **3** set, clique, coterie, crowd, club, society, realm, sphere.
➤*verb* **1** revolve, rotate, gyrate, wheel, orbit, circumnavigate. **2** ring, encircle, surround, gird, circumscribe.

circuit *noun* **1** revolution, lap, orbit, loop, circle. **2** tour, round, beat. **3** boundary, compass, ambit, circumference, perimeter. **4** track, course.

circuitous *adj* roundabout, indirect, tortuous, winding, serpentine, meandering, rambling.

circular *adj* round, annular, ring-shaped, hoop-shaped.
➤*noun* notice, advertisement, flier, handbill, leaflet.

circulate *verb* **1** circle, rotate, revolve, move round. **2** flow, move round, go round. **3** spread, go round, be disseminated.

circulation *noun* **1** spread, dissemination, diffusion, transmission, publication, distribution. **2** flow, movement, motion, circling, rotation.

circumference *noun* **1** perimeter, circuit, girth. **2** outline, border, fringe, skirt, periphery, boundary.

circumlocution *noun* **1** verbosity, wordiness, long-windedness, prolixity, tautology, pleonasm. **2** periphrasis, equivocation.

circumscribe *verb* **1** restrict, restrain, confine, limit, curb, curtail. **2** encircle, enclose, outline, delineate.

circumspect *adj* cautious, wary, careful, chary, prudent, judicious, politic, wise.

circumstance *noun* **1** incident, case, element, factor, detail, particular. **2** fate, destiny, lot, fortune.

circumstances *pl noun* situation, condition, state, background, means, status, station, lifestyle.

circumstantial *adj* **1** inferential, conjectural, implied, indirect. **2** incidental, contingent. **3** detailed, specific, precise.

circumvent *verb* **1** bypass, get round, sidestep. **2** dodge, avoid, evade, elude, outwit.

citadel *noun* fortress, stronghold, castle, keep, tower, bastion.

citation *noun* **1** quotation, passage, excerpt, extract, reference. **2** commendation, award, mention, honour.

cite *verb* **1** quote, mention, allude to, refer to, adduce. **2** name, mention, refer to. **3** summon, call, subpoena, arraign.

citizen *noun* **1** subject, national. **2** townsman, townswoman, inhabitant, denizen, local, resident.

city *noun* metropolis, municipality, megalopolis, concrete jungle, big smoke (*inf*).

civic *adj* municipal, borough, town, city, metropolitan, urban.

civil *adj* **1** national, state, civilian, nonmilitary, secular, lay, public, local. **2** polite, well-mannered, respectful, gracious, obliging, pleasant.

civility *noun* politeness, courtesy, manners, breeding, respect.

civilization *noun* **1** development, progress, sophistication, cultivation. **2** society, people, way of life, culture. **3** edification, enlightenment, humanization, socialization.

civilize *verb* refine, sophisticate, cultivate, improve, educate, enlighten, humanize, socialize.

clack *verb* **1** clatter, click, rap, rattle. **2** chatter, prattle, prate, jabber.

clad *adj* dressed, clothed, wearing, covered.

claim *verb* **1** ask for, request, put in for, apply for. **2** demand, require, requisition, commandeer, appropriate. **3** lay claim to, take. **4** assert, insist, maintain, contend, allege, profess.
➤*noun* **1** demand, requisition, request, application. **2** right, title, entitlement, privilege, prerogative. **3** assertion, contention, allegation, declaration.

claimant *noun* applicant, candidate, pretender, litigant.

clairvoyance *noun* extrasensory perception, sixth sense, second sight, fortune-telling.

clamber *verb* climb, scramble, crawl, shin.

clammy *adj* **1** damp, moist, sticky, sweaty. **2** dank, close, humid, muggy.

clamour *noun* **1** uproar, shouting, yelling, hubbub. **2** noise, din, racket, hullabaloo. **3** demand, call, protest, outcry, fuss.
➤*verb* **1** demand, call, insist, press. **2** shout, cry, yell.

clamp *noun* vice, brace, clasp, grip.
➤*verb* **1** secure, fasten, fix, press, squeeze. **2** hold, clasp, grip, clench.
clamp down restrict, limit, control, suppress, crack down.

clan *noun* **1** family, tribe, line, house. **2** band, gang, set, coterie, sect, faction.

clandestine *adj* furtive, surreptitious, stealthy, cloak-and-dagger, secret, undercover, underground, covert.

clang *verb* ring, resound, toll, clank, clash.

clanger *noun* mistake, error, slip, blunder, gaffe, faux pas.

clangour *noun* clang, clash, ringing, reverberation, clamour, din.

clank *verb* clash, ring, clink, chink, rattle.

clannish *adj* cliquish, exclusive, insular, provincial, parochial, sectarian.

clap *verb* **1** applaud, put one's hands together. **2** slap, strike, hit, pat.
➤*noun* **1** applause, ovation. **2** slap, blow, pat, whack. **3** burst, peal, explosion, bang.

claptrap *noun* nonsense, rubbish, drivel, bunk (*inf*), bombast, humbug, blarney, flannel (*inf*).

clarify *verb* **1** explain, make clear, elucidate, simplify, demystify, clear up. **2** purify, refine, filter, strain, clear.

clarity *noun* clearness, transparency, lucidity, comprehensibility, plainness, sharpness, definition.

clash *noun* **1** brush, confrontation, fight, struggle, showdown. **2** conflict, disagreement, discord, opposition. **3** clang, clank, crash, bang, clatter.
➤*verb* **1** disagree, quarrel, fight, cross swords, lock horns. **2** differ, conflict, collide. **3** jar, scream (*inf*), not match, not go. **4** clang, clank, crash, bang, clatter.

clasp verb **1** hold, grip, clutch, grasp, seize. **2** hug, embrace, enfold. **3** fasten, clip, pin, hook.
➤noun **1** fastener, hook, catch, hasp, clip. **2** hold, hug, embrace.

class noun **1** set, group, category, kind, sort, type. **2** division, grade, rank, league. **3** status, standing, caste, stratum. **4** form, grade, set, study group. **5** lesson, seminar, workshop. **6** excellence, distinction, quality, style, elegance, refinement.
➤verb classify, rank, grade, group, categorize, designate, pigeonhole.

classic adj **1** excellent, first-class, outstanding, exemplary, ideal, finest. **2** typical, archetypal, stock, model, definitive, quintessential. **3** traditional, enduring, timeless, ageless.
➤noun exemplar, paradigm, archetype, model, standard.

classical adj Greek, Grecian, Attic, Roman, Latin.

classification noun **1** categorization, grouping, ranking, arrangement, codification, systematization, taxonomy. **2** category, group, class, division, set.

classify verb **1** sort, group, rank, grade, codify, systematize, catalogue. **2** categorize, class, pigeonhole, designate.

classy adj stylish, elegant, chic, refined, high-class, upmarket, posh (*inf*).

clatter verb rattle, crash, bang.

clause noun subsection, passage, paragraph, item, provision, specification, condition, term.

claw noun **1** nail, talon. **2** pincer, nipper.
➤verb scratch, tear, gouge, scrape, scrabble.

clean adj **1** spotless, immaculate, unsoiled, washed, laundered, scrubbed. **2** sterilized, decontaminated, sterile, uncontaminated, unpolluted, aseptic, hygienic, sanitary. **3** total, complete, utter, decisive, final. **4** innocent, moral, virtuous, reputable, honest, unblemished, unspotted, squeaky-clean (*inf*). **5** decent, respectable. **6** fair, proper, legal. **7** blank, empty, unused, unmarked.
➤verb cleanse, wash, launder, scrub, dust, sweep, valet.
➤adv completely, absolutely, totally, utterly, altogether.

cleanse verb **1** clean, wash, scrub, disinfect, decontaminate. **2** clear, purify, purge.

clear adj **1** fine, fair, cloudless, bright, fresh. **2** transparent, see-through, crystalline, glassy, colourless. **3** audible, plain, distinct, perceptible. **4** lucid, explicit, coherent, intelligible, understandable, obvious, indisputable, unambiguous. **5** visible, sharp, plain, conspicuous, apparent, evident, plain, manifest. **6** free, empty, unobstructed, open. **7** innocent, guiltless. **8** untroubled, tranquil, serene. **9** clean, pure, unpolluted, immaculate, unsullied, unblemished, faultless, perfect. **10** sharp, keen, quick, logical, rational. **11** certain, sure, convinced, confident, positive. **12** whole, complete, full.
➤adv clearly, plainly, distinctly.
➤verb **1** brighten, lighten, clear up, improve. **2** acquit, exonerate, exculpate, absolve, pardon, discharge. **3** sweep, wipe, free, rid, disencumber, unblock, decongest. **4** empty, vacate, evacuate. **5** remove, take, throw away, get rid of. **6** filter, refine, purify, clarify. **7** settle, square, pay off, discharge. **8** earn, make, net, take home. **9** jump, vault, miss. **10** authorize, sanction, permit, pass, approve.

clear out 1 leave, depart, go, decamp, withdraw, get out. **2** empty, evacuate, clean, tidy.

clear up 1 clarify, elucidate, explain, solve, iron out. **2** remove, take away, clean up, tidy up.

clearance noun **1** authorization, sanction, permission, green light (*inf*), go-ahead (*inf*). **2** headroom, gap, space. **3** evacuation, eviction, clearing, removal, demolition.

clear-cut adj **1** plain, distinct, sharp, well-defined. **2** specific, precise, explicit, unambiguous.

cleave[1] verb **1** split, divide, separate, part. **2** cut, hack, chop, slash.

cleave[2] verb cling, stick, adhere, hold fast, remain faithful.

cleaver noun chopper, hatchet, axe, knife.

cleft noun rift, crack, split, fissure, gap, opening.

clement adj **1** merciful, lenient, forgiving, indulgent, compassionate, benevolent, magnanimous, generous. **2** mild, temperate, balmy, warm, fair.

clench verb 1 close, shut, grit. 2 grip, grasp, clutch. 3 contract, tighten.

clergy pl noun clerics, ecclesiastics, ministry, priesthood, the cloth.

cleric noun clergyman, clergywoman, churchman, churchwoman, ecclesiastic, preacher, minister, priest.

clerical adj 1 administrative, office, white-collar, secretarial. 2 ecclesiastical, priestly, sacerdotal, canonical.

clerk noun 1 office worker, pen pusher (inf), secretary, typist, bookkeeper, receptionist. 2 official, recorder, registrar.

clever adj 1 bright, smart, intelligent, brainy (inf), quick-witted, shrewd, resourceful, knowledgeable. 2 ingenious, inventive, cunning. 3 talented, able, adroit, dexterous, adept, skilful, expert, masterly.

cliché noun platitude, commonplace, truism, bromide.

click verb 1 clack, snap, crack, tick. 2 get on, hit it off, be on the same wavelength. 3 be popular, be successful, go down well. 4 make sense, fall into place. ➤noun clack, snap, crack, tick.

client noun 1 customer, patron, regular, user. 2 patient, case.

clientele noun clients, customers, patrons, market.

cliff noun crag, bluff, precipice, scar.

climate noun 1 weather, temperature. 2 clime, place, region, zone. 3 feeling, mood, ethos, atmosphere, trend, tendency.

climax noun culmination, acme, zenith, apogee, peak, height, crisis, turning point.

climb verb 1 ascend, mount, scale, clamber. 2 rise, soar, bank. 3 increase, rise, go up, soar.
climb down back down, eat one's words, withdraw.

clinch verb 1 conclude, complete, close, sew up (inf), settle, decide. 2 fix, secure, fasten. 3 hold, grip, clutch. 4 hug, embrace.
➤noun 1 hold, grip, clasp, clutch. 2 hug, embrace, cuddle.

cling verb 1 hold, grip, clasp, clutch. 2 stick, adhere, cleave. 3 hold fast, abide by, stand by, defend.

clinical adj 1 unemotional, dispassionate, detached, objective, scientific, analytic. 2 simple, basic, stark, impersonal.

clink verb ring, jingle, tinkle, chink, clank.

clip[1] verb fasten, pin, staple, attach. ➤noun pin, staple, grip, clasp.

clip[2] verb 1 cut, trim, pare, shear, crop. 2 prune, dock, shorten, truncate. 3 shorten, abbreviate, abridge. 4 hit, cuff, box, smack, clout (inf). ➤noun 1 blow, cuff, box, smack, clout (inf). 2 extract, excerpt, trailer, snippet, passage, piece. 3 cut, trim, pruning, shearing. 4 speed, pace, rate, lick (inf).

clipping noun cutting, snippet, passage, piece, clip.

clique noun set, circle, crowd, coterie, gang, ring, party, faction.

cloak verb hide, conceal, shroud, veil, screen, mask. ➤noun 1 cape, mantle, robe, coat. 2 cover, veil, screen, blind, front, disguise.

clock noun 1 timepiece, chronometer, timer. 2 dial, meter, speedometer, milometer.
verb 1 record, register. 2 reach, attain, achieve, do (inf).

clod noun 1 lump, mass, sod, turf. 2 fool, idiot, dolt, fathead (inf).

clog verb 1 block, obstruct, choke, congest. 2 hinder, hamper, impede, encumber, restrain. ➤noun hindrance, impediment, encumbrance, burden, handicap.

cloister noun colonnade, arcade, gallery, ambulatory.

cloistered adj 1 secluded, sequestered, sheltered, protected, reclusive, solitary. 2 monastic, cloistral.

close[1] verb 1 shut, fasten, latch. 2 cover, plug, cork, seal. 3 block, obstruct. 4 finish, conclude, end, stop, terminate, round off, wind up (inf). 5 shut down, cease trading, cease operating, fail, fold (inf). 6 come together, grapple. ➤noun end, finish, conclusion, termination, completion, finale.

close in approach, draw near, encircle, surround.

close[2] *adj* **1** near, neighbouring, hard by, imminent, impending, at hand. **2** similar, alike, comparable. **3** dear, intimate, bosom, devoted, inseparable, matey (*inf*), pally (*inf*). **4** dense, solid, compact, tight, packed, congested, cramped. **5** oppressive, muggy, sultry, sticky, airless, stuffy. **6** well-matched, hard-fought, neck-and-neck. **7** fixed, concentrated, keen, intent, careful, thorough, painstaking, minute. **8** mean, miserly, tight-fisted, niggardly, stingy. **9** secretive, uncommunicative, unforthcoming, reticent, reserved.

close[3] *noun* **1** cul-de-sac, dead end. **2** precinct, courtyard, quadrangle.

closet *noun* cupboard, wardrobe, cabinet, locker.
➤*adj* secret, private, hidden, undisclosed, covert.
➤*verb* shut away, sequester, cloister.

closure *noun* close, closing, shutdown, end, finish, termination, stoppage.

clot *noun* **1** lump, mass. **2** coagulation, thrombus. **3** fool, ass, blockhead, dolt, wally (*sl*).
➤*verb* coagulate, congeal, curdle, solidify.

cloth *noun* fabric, textile, material, stuff.

clothe *verb* dress, attire, garb, deck, array, apparel.

clothes *pl noun* clothing, garments, dress, attire, wear, wardrobe, outfit, costume.

cloud *noun* **1** haze, mist, fog, vapour. **2** pall, shroud, shadow, gloom. **3** swarm, flock, crowd, horde.
➤*verb* **1** dim, darken, obscure, shadow, eclipse, veil, shroud. **2** blur, mist, fog. **3** confuse, muddle.

cloudy *adj* **1** overcast, dull, grey, lowering, leaden. **2** murky, misty, foggy, opaque, milky, muddy.

clout *verb* hit, strike, thump, smack, wallop (*inf*), clobber (*inf*).
➤*noun* **1** blow, thump, smack, wallop (*inf*), whack (*inf*). **2** influence, power, muscle (*inf*), authority, prestige.

clown *noun* **1** buffoon, jester, fool, harlequin, pierrot. **2** joker, comic, comedian, wag.
verb fool around, joke, jest, act the goat (*inf*).

cloy *verb* **1** surfeit, satiate, sate, glut. **2** sicken, nauseate.

club *noun* **1** society, association, organization, group, circle, guild. **2** cudgel, truncheon, bludgeon, cosh. **3** stick, bat, iron.
➤*verb* beat, batter, bash, cudgel, bludgeon, cosh.

club together unite, combine, join forces, pool resources, have a whip-round (*inf*).

clue *noun* hint, tip, lead, pointer, tip-off, suggestion.

clump *noun* **1** bunch, cluster, group, bundle, tuft. **2** mass, lump, accumulation, agglomeration.
➤*verb* **1** clomp, stump, stomp, tramp, plod, trudge. **2** cluster, mass, collect, accumulate.

clumsy *adj* **1** awkward, maladroit, ham-fisted (*inf*), cack-handed (*inf*), uncoordinated, ungainly, gauche, accident-prone. **2** bulky, cumbersome, unwieldy, awkward. **3** gauche, tactless, insensitive, crass.

cluster *noun* clump, bunch, knot, huddle, group, accumulation.
➤*verb* **1** clump, bunch, bundle, gather, collect. **2** assemble, throng, collect, accumulate, agglomerate.

clutch *verb* **1** hold, grip, hang on to, clasp, grasp. **2** snatch, grab, catch at, reach for.
➤*noun* hold, grip, clasp, grasp.

clutches *pl noun* power, control, custody, possession, hands.

clutter *verb* litter, strew, scatter, make untidy, encumber.
➤*noun* **1** litter, mess, rubbish. **2** muddle, disorder, disarray, confusion, chaos.

coach *noun* **1** bus, charabanc. **2** carriage, wagon, car. **3** carriage, chariot. **4** instructor, trainer. **5** tutor, teacher.
➤*verb* train, drill, instruct, teach, cram (*inf*).

coagulate *verb* clot, thicken, curdle, congeal, solidify.

coalesce *verb* unite, combine, join, amalgamate, merge, fuse.

coalition *noun* alliance, confederation, association, league, bloc, compact.

coarse *adj* **1** rough, scaly, bristly, lumpy, crude. **2** rude, vulgar, obscene, dirty, crude, gross, ribald, bawdy. **3** boorish, loutish, rude, uncouth, unsophisticated, unrefined, common, vulgar.

coarsen *verb* roughen, thicken, toughen, harden.

coast *noun* **1** seaside, seashore, beach, strand. **2** shoreline, seaboard.
➤*verb* sail, glide, taxi, freewheel.

coat *noun* **1** overcoat, jacket, anorak, mackintosh. **2** fur, hair, pelt, hide, skin, fleece. **3** covering, coating, layer, film.
➤*verb* cover, spread, paint, finish.

coating *noun* coat, layer, dusting, film, covering, finish.

coax *verb* cajole, wheedle, persuade, prevail upon, induce, tempt.

cobble *verb* mend, repair.
cobble together make, improvise, knock up.

cock *noun* rooster, cockerel.
➤*verb* raise, prick up, tilt, tip.

cock-eyed *adj* **1** crooked, askew, awry, lopsided, skew-whiff (*inf*). **2** crazy, absurd, preposterous, mad.

cocky *adj* cocksure, overconfident, arrogant, vain, presumptuous, self-important.

cocoon *verb* envelop, wrap, cover, protect, isolate, insulate.

coddle *verb* pamper, cosset, mollycoddle, overprotect, baby, spoil.

code *noun* **1** system, canon, laws, rules, ethics, morals, customs, manners. **2** cipher, cryptograph. **3** numbers, letters, characters, symbols.

codicil *noun* supplement, appendix, addendum, rider.

codify *verb* systematize, organize, classify, collect.

coerce *verb* force, constrain, compel, pressure, lean on (*inf*), browbeat, bully, dragoon.

coffer *noun* chest, trunk, case, casket, safe, strongbox.

coffin *noun* casket, sarcophagus, box, wooden overcoat (*inf*).

cogent *adj* forceful, strong, convincing, persuasive, powerful, weighty, compelling.

cogitate *verb* ponder, ruminate, meditate, reflect, deliberate, mull over.

cognate *adj* **1** related, akin, kindred, consanguine. **2** connected, related, allied, corresponding. **3** alike, similar, akin.

cognition *noun* perception, awareness, judgment, intuition, reasoning, comprehension, knowledge.

cognizance *noun* **1** awareness, consciousness, knowledge, perception, comprehension. **2** notice, heed, acceptance, recognition, acknowledgment.

cognizant *adj* informed, knowledgeable, versed, familiar, conversant.

cohabit *verb* live together, live in sin (*inf*), shack up (*sl*).

cohere *verb* **1** stick, adhere, cling, unite, fuse, coalesce. **2** be consistent, follow, make sense, hang together.

coherent *adj* **1** articulate, intelligible, lucid. **2** consistent, systematic, logical, rational, reasoned.

cohesion *noun* union, fusion, coalescence, consolidation.

cohort *noun* **1** troop, division, squadron, regiment, company, band. **2** friend, companion, associate, accomplice.

coil *noun* spiral, roll, curl, loop.
➤*verb* **1** wind, twine, loop, wreathe. **2** twist, snake, wind, curl, spiral.

coin *verb* **1** formulate, make up, think up, invent, originate. **2** mint, stamp, forge.
➤*noun* **1** piece, bit. **2** money, specie, cash, change.

coincide *verb* **1** be concurrent, clash, synchronize, coexist. **2** correspond, tally, harmonize, match. **3** agree, concur, accord.

coincidence *noun* **1** chance, fluke, accident. **2** synchronism, simultaneity, concurrence, coexistence. **3** correspondence, harmony, agreement.

coincident *adj* **1** synchronous, simultaneous, concurrent, coexistent. **2** corresponding, harmonious, in accordance, matching.

coitus *noun* coition, copulation, mating, sexual intercourse.

cold *adj* **1** cool, chill, chilly, nippy (*inf*), parky (*inf*), freezing, frozen. **2** distant, aloof, frigid, glacial, unfriendly, inhospitable, hostile. **3** unresponsive, indifferent, unmoved, uninterested, unemotional,

impassive, unfeeling, callous.
➤*noun* **1** coldness, chill. **2** wintriness, chilliness, frost.

cold-blooded *adj* cruel, barbaric, brutal, savage, ruthless, pitiless, heartless, callous.

collaborate *verb* **1** cooperate, work together, join forces, team up. **2** conspire, collude, connive, fraternize.

collapse *verb* **1** subside, cave in, give way, disintegrate. **2** founder, fail, fold (*inf*), flop (*inf*). **3** faint, pass out, keel over, drop, slump.
➤*noun* **1** subsidence, cave-in, disintegration. **2** failure, flop (*inf*), fall, breakdown, faint, blackout, exhaustion, prostration.

collar *verb* grab, seize, nab (*inf*), catch, apprehend.

collate *verb* collect, gather, sort, arrange, compare, check.

collateral *noun* security, surety, deposit, pledge.
➤*adj* accompanying, subordinate, secondary, indirect.

collation *noun* **1** collection, gathering, sorting, organization, comparison, verification. **2** snack, light meal.

colleague *noun* partner, associate, co-worker, workmate, teammate.

collect *verb* **1** assemble, amass, accumulate, hoard, save. **2** gather, glean, raise, acquire. **3** congregate, gather, muster, rally, assemble, convene. **4** fetch, pick up, call for.

collected *adj* calm, composed, self-possessed, serene, cool, unruffled.

collection *noun* set, series, assortment, accumulation, hoard, cluster, gathering, assembly.

collective *adj* joint, combined, united, concerted, cooperative, shared, common, communal.

college *noun* **1** school, university. **2** academy, institution, institute. **3** association, society, guild, league.

collide *verb* **1** crash, smash, bump, bang. **2** clash, conflict, differ, be at variance.

collision *noun* crash, impact, accident, prang (*inf*), clash, conflict, confrontation.

collocate *verb* arrange, dispose, group, juxtapose.

collocation *noun* grouping, arrangement, juxtaposition, phrase, expression.

colloquial *adj* informal, conversational, familiar, idiomatic, vernacular, demotic.

colloquy *noun* conversation, discourse, dialogue, discussion.

collude *verb* connive, conspire, intrigue, plot, collaborate, cooperate.

collusion *noun* connivance, complicity, collaboration, cooperation, conspiracy, intrigue.

colonist *noun* settler, pioneer, colonial, expatriate, migrant.

colonize *verb* settle, occupy, populate, people.

colony *noun* **1** settlement, community. **2** dominion, territory, dependency, protectorate, outpost. **3** group, community, commune. **4** district, quarter, ghetto.

colossal *adj* enormous, huge, immense, vast, massive, gigantic, tremendous, monumental.

colour *noun* **1** tint, hue, shade, coloration. **2** paint, pigment, colorant, dye, tincture. **3** rosiness, ruddiness, flush, blush, glow. **4** complexion, pigmentation, colouring. **5** flag, ensign, standard, insignia, badge. **6** animation, vitality, vividness, richness.
➤*verb* **1** dye, tint, paint, stain. **2** blush, flush, redden. **3** distort, garble, misrepresent, embroider, exaggerate, slant. **4** influence, affect, bias, prejudice.

colourful *adj* **1** bright, gaudy, multicoloured, psychedelic, vivid, vibrant. **2** rich, lively, interesting, exciting.

colourless *adj* **1** achromatic, hueless, neutral, monochrome, transparent, pale, washed-out, anaemic. **2** dull, dreary, lacklustre, monotonous, uninteresting, characterless.

coltish *adj* frisky, frolicsome, playful, lively, spirited.

column *noun* **1** pillar, post, shaft, obelisk, monolith. **2** line, file, queue, procession, train. **3** article, feature, item, review.

columnist *noun* journalist, correspondent, reviewer.

coma *noun* unconsciousness, insensibility, oblivion, stupor.

comatose adj 1 unconscious, insensible, out. 2 torpid, lethargic, sluggish, somnolent.

comb verb 1 untangle, tidy, groom, arrange, curry. 2 search, sift, rake, scour.

combat verb 1 fight, oppose, resist, battle, struggle, strive.
➤ noun 1 war, battle, action, hostilities. 2 fight, encounter, clash, skirmish, engagement, bout.

combatant noun fighter, soldier, warrior, enemy, adversary, opponent, contestant.
➤ adj fighting, warring, belligerent.

combative adj aggressive, militant, warlike, belligerent, argumentative, quarrelsome.

combination noun 1 mixture, blend, compound, synthesis, amalgam, composite. 2 mixing, blending, amalgamation, integration, fusion.

combine verb 1 blend, synthesize, integrate, homogenize, fuse, merge. 2 compound, alloy. 3 mix, mingle, unite, amalgamate, pool. 4 ally, join forces, team up, cooperate.
➤ noun union, alliance, coalition, league, consortium, syndicate.

combustible adj inflammable, flammable, incendiary.

combustion noun burning, incineration, cremation, ignition.

come verb 1 approach, advance, near, draw near. 2 arrive, enter, attend, appear, turn up. 3 happen, occur, befall. 4 reach, extend, stretch. 5 be available, be made, be produced.
come about occur, happen, take place, come to pass, transpire, arise.
come across find, discover, stumble upon, chance upon, meet, run into.
come by get, obtain, acquire, get hold of (inf).
come clean own up, confess, admit, make a clean breast of it (inf).
come down 1 fall, drop, decrease. 2 descend, alight, touch down, land, crash.
come down on criticize, censure, reproach, reprimand, upbraid, jump on (inf).
come down to mean, amount to, boil down to, end up as.

come into inherit, be left, succeed to, receive.
come of result from, arise from, proceed from, develop from.
come off 1 succeed, work, happen. 2 finish, end up.
come out 1 appear, become available, be published, be issued, be released, be launched, become known, be disclosed. 2 end, finish, terminate.
come out with say, utter, declare, exclaim, blurt out.
come over visit, call, drop in (inf).
come round 1 regain consciousness, revive, recover, come to. 2 submit, yield, give way, relent, acquiesce.
come through survive, endure, succeed, triumph.
come to 1 regain consciousness, revive, recover, come round. 2 total, add up to, amount to, equal.
come up arise, crop up, occur, present itself.
come up with produce, provide, supply, offer, advance, present, propose.

comeback noun 1 return, reappearance, resurgence, revival, recovery, rally. 2 reply, rejoinder, retort, riposte.

comedian noun comic, wit, humorist, entertainer, clown.

comedown noun 1 degradation, demotion, humiliation, descent. 2 reverse, setback, blow, disappointment, anticlimax.

comedy noun 1 farce, slapstick, satire, burlesque, light entertainment. 2 humour, funniness, drollery, hilarity.

comely adj pretty, attractive, fair, lovely, pleasing.

come-on noun attraction, enticement, lure, inducement, encouragement.

comeuppance noun just deserts, retribution, nemesis, punishment.

comfort verb 1 cheer, gladden, hearten, encourage, invigorate, refresh. 2 console, solace, reassure, relieve, ease, soothe.
➤ noun 1 consolation, solace, sympathy, commiseration, cheer, encouragement, support, help, reassurance, relief. 2 ease, repose, well-being, contentment, cosiness, luxury.

comfortable adj 1 snug, cosy, comfy (inf), pleasant, easy, relaxing, roomy, luxurious.

2 satisfied, contented, happy, prosperous.
3 relaxed, at ease, serene, tranquil.

comic *adj* **1** funny, humorous, amusing, entertaining, light, witty, facetious, comical. **2** zany, farcical, slapstick.
➤*noun* comedian, wit, humorist, entertainer, clown.

comical *adj* funny, amusing, comic, droll, hilarious, absurd, laughable.

command *verb* **1** order, bid, direct, charge, instruct. **2** compel, require, demand. **3** overlook, dominate. **4** lead, head, control, direct, supervise.
➤*noun* **1** order, injunction, directive, instruction, decree, edict. **2** leadership, government, rule, control, mastery, ascendancy, dominion. **3** charge, authority, power.

commandeer *verb* **1** seize, take, hijack, confiscate, impound. **2** appropriate, requisition.

commander *noun* captain, chief, leader, head.

commanding *adj* **1** leading, directing. **2** dominant, superior, advantageous, strong, powerful. **3** forceful, assertive, compelling, impressive, authoritative, masterful.

commemorate *verb* **1** celebrate, observe, keep, mark, honour, pay tribute to. **2** solemnize, immortalize, perpetuate, memorialize, remember.

commence *verb* begin, start, go ahead, embark on, set about, open, launch, instigate.

commencement *noun* beginning, start, opening, outset, launch, origin, dawn, birth.

commend *verb* **1** praise, extol, applaud, acclaim, speak highly of, compliment. **2** recommend, advocate, endorse, promote. **3** entrust, commit, hand over, deliver.

commensurate *adj* **1** equal, equivalent, comparable, consistent. **2** corresponding, proportionate, to scale, in accordance.

comment *noun* remark, observation, opinion, criticism, annotation, note, gloss, explanation.
➤*verb* **1** remark, observe, say, point out, note, mention, interject. **2** annotate, gloss, explain, interpret, clarify, illustrate.

commentary *noun* **1** narration, voiceover, description, account, report, analysis. **2** notes, exposition, interpretation, analysis, exegesis, critique, review.

commentator *noun* reporter, broadcaster, sportscaster, narrator, expositor, critic.

commerce *noun* **1** business, trade, traffic, exchange, dealings, transactions, industry, enterprise. **2** communication, intercourse, relations.

commercial *adj* **1** business, trade, trading, merchant, mercantile, entrepreneurial. **2** profitable, profit-making, saleable, marketable.
➤*noun* advertisement, advert (*inf*), ad (*inf*), promotion, publicity.

commiserate *verb* sympathize, condole, pity, feel for, console, comfort.

commission *noun* **1** assignment, task, appointment, board, charge, mission. **2** committee, board, council. **3** fee, share, dividend, percentage, cut (*inf*). **4** mandate, authority, warrant, permit, licence. **5** perpetration, execution, performance.
➤*verb* authorize, empower, appoint, assign, detail, engage, contract, order.

commissioner *noun* agent, representative, envoy, ambassador, official, officer.

commit *verb* **1** do, perpetrate, effect, execute, carry out. **2** entrust, consign, hand over, deliver, commend. **3** pledge, promise, bind, obligate, engage, align, devote, dedicate. **4** confine, put away, lock up, imprison, incarcerate, hospitalize, institutionalize.

commitment *noun* **1** pledge, promise, covenant, vow, undertaking, guarantee. **2** obligation, duty, responsibility, engagement, tie. **3** dedication, devotion, involvement, loyalty, allegiance.

committal *noun* consignment, charge, custody, confinement, imprisonment, incarceration, hospitalization, institutionalization.

committee *noun* board, commission, panel, working party, task force, think tank (*inf*).

commodious *noun* spacious, roomy, capacious, ample, large.

commodity *noun* thing, item, article, product.

common *adj* 1 joint, shared, mutual, collective, universal, general. 2 public, communal, community, popular. 3 widespread, prevalent, general, universal. 4 familiar, accepted, conventional, stock, normal, run-of-the-mill. 5 frequent, routine, everyday, typical, unexceptional, ten a penny (*inf*). 6 ordinary, regular, standard. 7 vulgar, ill-bred, coarse, uncouth.

commonplace *adj* ordinary, everyday, common, normal, widespread, undistinguished, unexceptional, unremarkable, trite, banal.
➤*noun* cliché, platitude, truism, banality.

common sense *noun* sense, good sense, intelligence, wisdom, nous (*inf*), pragmatism, realism, prudence, shrewdness.

commotion *noun* 1 turmoil, tumult, upheaval, disorder. 2 fuss, ado, rumpus, bustle, uproar, clamour, brouhaha.

communal *adj* 1 public, community, common, shared 2 joint, collective.

commune[1] *verb* communicate, talk, confide, feel at one, relate, empathize.

commune[2] *noun* community, collective, cooperative, kibbutz, colony.

communicable *adj* infectious, contagious, catching, transmittable.

communicate *verb* 1 impart, make known, announce, divulge, talk, correspond, contact, interface, liaise. 2 spread, transmit, pass on, convey, bestow. 3 connect, adjoin, abut.

communication *noun* 1 language, conversation, intercourse, correspondence, contact, liaison, dissemination, transmission. 2 message, note, memorandum, letter, call, fax, e-mail, announcement, report, bulletin.

communicative *adj* open, forthcoming, frank, talkative, chatty, outgoing, extrovert.

communion *noun* 1 rapport, affinity, empathy, intimacy, fellowship, harmony, accord. 2 Eucharist, Lord's Supper, Mass.

communiqué *noun* bulletin, dispatch, announcement, communication, report, statement.

communism *noun* 1 socialism, collectivism. 2 Marxism, Leninism.

community *noun* 1 population, people, residents, inhabitants, neighbourhood, parish, settlement. 2 group, body, society, fellowship, colony. 3 society, state, public.

commute *verb* 1 travel, journey, shuttle. 2 change, modify, convert. 3 exchange, substitute, replace, reduce, remit.

compact[1] *adj* 1 close, dense, compressed, condensed, packed, tight. 2 small, portable, pocket.
➤*verb* 1 compress, condense, pack, cram, tamp. 2 consolidate, fuse, bind.

compact[2] *noun* contract, treaty, pact, entente, agreement, bargain, deal.

companion *noun* 1 associate, comrade, friend, intimate, buddy (*inf*), partner. 2 escort, attendant, aide, chaperon. 3 fellow, counterpart, match, mate.

companionable *adj* friendly, amiable, gregarious, sociable, convivial, congenial, informal, familiar.

company *noun* 1 business, firm, corporation, establishment, house. 2 group, body, crew, circle, unit, detachment, troop, troupe. 3 companionship, fellowship, society, togetherness, conviviality. 4 visitors, guests, callers.

comparable *adj* 1 like, similar, alike, analogous, corresponding, equivalent, tantamount. 2 akin, related, in the same league.

comparative *adj* relative, by comparison, approximate.

compare *verb* 1 correlate, collate, juxtapose, contrast, balance. 2 liken, equate, link, relate.
compare with 1 resemble, equal, correspond to, parallel. 2 approach, be in the same league as, hold a candle to (*inf*).

comparison *noun* 1 likeness, resemblance, similarity, relation, parallel. 2 likening, analogy, simile. 3 correlation, collation, juxtaposition, contrast.

compartment *noun* 1 cubbyhole, pigeonhole, booth, stall, cell, chamber. 2 part, section, division, partition.

compass *noun* range, scope, reach, span, boundary, limits, sphere, field.

compassion *noun* sympathy, pity, fellow feeling, concern, understanding, kindness, humanity, mercy.

compassionate *adj* kind, tender, gentle, sympathetic, soft-hearted, humane, charitable, merciful.

compatible *adj* 1 congruous, consistent, in keeping, consonant, accordant. 2 well-suited, well-matched, like-minded, in tune.

compel *verb* 1 force, coerce, dragoon, drive, pressure, make, oblige, constrain. 2 exact, insist on, force, necessitate.

compelling *adj* absorbing, fascinating, enthralling, gripping, riveting, forceful, convincing, powerful.

compendious *adj* summary, compact, concise, succinct, pithy.

compendium *noun* synopsis, summary, digest, abstract, résumé, précis.

compensate *verb* 1 recompense, reimburse, repay, indemnify, make amends, make up, make good. 2 offset, balance, counterbalance, cancel out.

compensation *noun* recompense, reimbursement, repayment, indemnity, reparation, damages, amends.

compere *noun* host, presenter, master of ceremonies.

compete *verb* contest, contend, vie, rival, strive, fight, enter, participate, be in the running (*inf*).

competence *noun* ability, capacity, proficiency, skill, aptitude, adequacy, suitability.

competent *adj* 1 able, capable, trained, qualified, proficient, skilled, accomplished, knowledgeable, fit, equal. 2 satisfactory, acceptable, skilful, masterly.

competition *noun* 1 contest, championship, event, race, match. 2 rivalry, opposition, contention, strife, competitiveness, survival of the fittest. 3 rivals, opposition, opponents, challengers, competitors, contestants, field.

competitive *adj* 1 rival, competing, vying, aggressive, cutthroat, dog-eat-dog (*inf*). 2 combative, aggressive, ambitious, assertive, pushy (*inf*).

competitor *noun* rival, opponent, adversary, contestant, contender, challenger, entrant, candidate.

compilation *noun* 1 collection, anthology, album, assortment, omnibus. 2 compiling, composition, preparation, collection, assembly, collation.

compile *verb* 1 collect, gather, assemble, put together, collate. 2 compose, prepare, write, edit.

complacency *noun* smugness, self-satisfaction, contentment, satisfaction, serenity, ease.

complacent *adj* smug, self-satisfied, triumphant, contented, satisfied, serene, at ease, unconcerned.

complain *verb* grumble, moan, whine, bleat (*inf*), bellyache (*inf*), lament, deplore, carp, criticize, protest, object.

complaint *noun* 1 grievance, lament, grouse, gripe (*inf*), beef (*inf*), criticism, protest, objection. 2 disorder, disease, illness, ailment, affliction, trouble.

complaisant *adj* 1 agreeable, accommodating, obliging, compliant. 2 acquiescent, amenable, biddable, deferential.

complement *noun* 1 quota, total, sum, entirety, whole, capacity. 2 companion, counterpart, match, coordinate. 3 supplement, addition, accessory, finishing touch.
➤*verb* complete, round off, match, coordinate with, supplement, add to.

complementary *adj* 1 completing, finishing, perfecting, consummating. 2 matching, coordinating, corresponding, reciprocal.

complete *adj* 1 entire, whole, total, full, integral, intact, unabridged, undivided. 2 finished, completed, ended, concluded, finalized, accomplished, done, over. 3 absolute, utter, total, downright, perfect, consummate, unqualified, unconditional.
➤*verb* 1 finish, end, conclude, terminate, finalize, wind up (*inf*). 2 consummate, crown, cap, round off. 3 execute, discharge, fulfil, realize, achieve, accomplish.

complex *adj* 1 complicated, intricate, involved, elaborate, convoluted. 2 composite, compound, multiple, manifold.
➤*noun* 1 structure, network, system, synthesis, composite. 2 obsession, fixation, preoccupation, thing (*inf*). 3 phobia, hang-up (*inf*).

complexion *noun* **1** skin, colouring, pigmentation. **2** appearance, aspect, cast, stamp, character, nature.

compliance *noun* **1** obedience, conformity, accordance, fulfilment, discharge, performance, execution, agreement, consent. **2** acquiescence, submission, docility, passivity, deference, complaisance.

complicate *verb* confuse, involve, entangle, muddle, compound.

complicated *adj* **1** confused, involved, convoluted, tortuous, difficult, problematic, tangled, knotty. **2** complex, intricate, elaborate, fiddly (*inf*).

complication *noun* **1** complexity, intricacy, confusion, muddle, involvement, entanglement. **2** difficulty, problem, obstacle, drawback, snag.

complicity *noun* collusion, conspiracy, connivance, collaboration, involvement.

compliment *noun* praise, commendation, tribute, accolade, bouquet, congratulation, flattery.
>*verb* flatter, admire, congratulate, praise, commend, acclaim, salute.

complimentary *adj* **1** flattering, admiring, congratulatory, appreciative, favourable, laudatory. **2** free, gratis, courtesy, on the house (*inf*).

compliments *pl noun* greetings, respects, regards, good wishes, best wishes.

comply *verb* **1** submit, agree, consent, accede, obey, conform, observe, respect, follow, abide by. **2** meet, satisfy, fulfil.

component *noun* part, section, piece, constituent, element, ingredient, factor.
>*adj* constituent, integral, intrinsic.

comport *verb* **comport oneself** act, behave, conduct oneself, bear oneself, acquit oneself.

compose *verb* **1** form, make, produce, put together, assemble, construct. **2** constitute, make up. **3** write, compile, formulate, invent, think up, create, devise. **4** calm, pacify, steady, settle, soothe, control, collect. **5** arrange, align, put in order.

composed *adj* calm, tranquil, cool, collected, poised, self-possessed, unruffled, unperturbed.

composite *adj* **1** compound, complex, manifold, multiple, heterogeneous, mixed. **2** combined, blended, synthesized, hybrid.

composition *noun* **1** formation, make-up, structure, form, character, constitution. **2** writing, formulation, production, configuration, organization, arrangement, balance, symmetry. **3** work, opus, piece. **4** essay, story. **5** combination, mixture, blend, synthesis, compound, amalgam.

compost *noun* fertilizer, manure, mulch, dressing.

composure *noun* calmness, serenity, poise, aplomb, sang-froid, self-possession, ease, equanimity.

compound *noun* mixture, blend, alloy, amalgam, synthesis, composite.
>*adj* composite, complex, multiple, mixed, combined, hybrid.
>*verb* **1** mix, blend, alloy, combine, amalgamate, synthesize. **2** intensify, magnify, add to, aggravate, exacerbate, complicate.

comprehend *verb* **1** understand, fathom, grasp, see, assimilate. **2** include, encompass, embrace, cover, involve.

comprehensible *adj* understandable, intelligible, accessible, clear, simple, explicit, coherent.

comprehension *noun* **1** understanding, grasp, apprehension, conception, awareness, realization. **2** sense, intelligence, intellect, ken (*inf*).

comprehensive *adj* broad, extensive, general, universal, inclusive, all-embracing, thorough, full.

compress *verb* **1** compact, press, squeeze, squash, flatten, constrict. **2** condense, reduce, shorten, abridge, summarize.

compression *noun* pressurization, squeezing, squashing, constriction, condensation, reduction, abridgment.

comprise *verb* **1** consist of, be composed of, contain, include. **2** form, compose, constitute, make up.

compromise *verb* **1** meet halfway, strike a balance, come to terms, make a deal, adjust, accommodate. **2** discredit, bring into disrepute, endanger, jeopardize, risk, expose, prejudice, damage.
>*noun* **1** middle ground, happy medium, terms, agreement, deal, trade-off.

2 mutual concession, give-and-take, adjustment, accommodation, settlement, negotiation.

compulsion *noun* **1** obligation, duress, pressure, force, constraint, coercion. **2** urge, drive, impulse, necessity, desire, obsession.

compulsive *adj* compelling, overpowering, uncontrollable, irresistible, addictive, obsessive, inveterate, pathological (*inf*).

compulsory *adj* obligatory, mandatory, de rigueur, essential, required, enforced, unavoidable.

compunction *noun* **1** remorse, regret, contrition, penitence, sorrow, guilt, shame. **2** qualm, scruple, misgiving.

computation *noun* **1** calculation, reckoning, adding up, counting. **2** computing, data processing, information technology.

compute *verb* calculate, work out, reckon, add up, count, estimate, measure.

computer *noun* processor, terminal, workstation, PC, laptop.

comrade *noun* companion, associate, fellow, peer, confederate, ally, friend, mate (*inf*), buddy (*inf*).

con *verb* swindle, do (*inf*), cheat, deceive, dupe, hoodwink, mislead.
➤*noun* swindle, fraud, racket, scam (*inf*), confidence trick, hoax, cheat.

concave *adj* hollowed, sunken, depressed, cupped, scooped.

conceal *verb* **1** hide, cover, obscure, screen, mask, camouflage, secrete. **2** suppress, dissemble, keep secret, cover up, hush up (*inf*).

concede *verb* **1** accept, recognize. **2** admit, acknowledge, confess, own, grant, allow. **3** yield, surrender, cede, give up, hand over.

conceit *noun* **1** vanity, conceitedness, immodesty, pride, egotism, self-adulation, narcissism, big-headedness (*inf*). **2** simile, metaphor, ornament, decoration. **3** idea, notion, fancy, whim, caprice.

conceited *adj* vain, immodest, proud, egotistical, self-important, narcissistic, big-headed (*inf*), full of oneself (*inf*), boastful, cocky, smug.

conceivable *adj* possible, likely, imaginable, credible.

conceive *verb* **1** devise, contrive, invent, originate, think up, formulate, design, plan. **2** understand, comprehend, grasp, see, appreciate, imagine, visualize, envisage, think, fancy.

concentrate *verb* **1** focus, converge, centre, direct, bring to bear. **2** centralize, consolidate, cluster, amass, gather, assemble, muster. **3** condense, reduce, boil down, thicken. **4** pay attention, apply oneself, think, meditate.

concentration *noun* **1** attention, application, absorption, thought, mind, focus, convergence. **2** cluster, mass, conglomeration, accumulation, collection, gathering.

concept *noun* idea, notion, thought, conception, impression, image, hypothesis, theory, plan, design.

conception *noun* **1** idea, notion, concept, image, visualization, understanding, appreciation, inkling, clue. **2** invention, origination, birth, genesis. **3** fertilization, impregnation, insemination, reproduction.

concern *verb* **1** regard, relate to, pertain to, apply to, touch, be about, deal with, have to do with. **2** interest, involve, affect, influence. **3** worry, perturb, alarm, bother, disturb, trouble. **4** occupy, busy, engage, devote.
➤*noun* **1** business, duty, responsibility, job, field, domain, interest, regard. **2** anxiety, worry, care, trouble. **3** affair, matter, problem. **4** company, firm, business, enterprise, organization, establishment.

concerned *adj* **1** anxious, worried, perturbed, uneasy, bothered, troubled. **2** involved, implicated, affected, interested.

concerning *prep* about, re, relating to, with reference to, regarding, apropos of, to do with.

concert *noun* performance, recital, show, engagement, gig (*inf*).
in concert together, jointly, collectively, concertedly, cooperatively, in collaboration, side by side.

concerted *adj* combined, united, joint, collective, cooperative, collaborative, coordinated, synchronized.

concession *noun* **1** grant, right, privilege, favour, exemption, dispensation.

2 discount, reduction. **3** admission, acknowledgment, recognition, acceptance, allowance, compromise, surrender, relinquishment.

conciliate verb **1** mediate, negotiate, reconcile, reunite. **2** placate, appease, propitiate, pacify, mollify.

concise adj brief, short, terse, compact, pithy, succinct, condensed, abridged, summary.

conclave noun council, assembly, meeting, session.

conclude verb **1** close, end, terminate, finish, round off, wind up (inf). **2** settle, resolve, negotiate, close, complete, clinch. **3** decide, determine, work out. **4** infer, deduce, assume, guess, surmise, gather, reckon, judge.

conclusion noun **1** close, end, ending, finish. **2** settlement, resolution, completion. **3** inference, deduction, assumption, supposition, opinion, judgment, decision, verdict. **4** outcome, issue, result, consequence, upshot.

conclusive adj final, decisive, convincing, indisputable, irrefutable, incontestable, definite, positive.

concoct verb **1** contrive, devise, invent, think up, brew, hatch, formulate, make up. **2** prepare, mix, make, put together, rustle up (inf).

concomitant adj attendant, accompanying, accessory, incidental, associated, related.

concord noun agreement, harmony, accord, unity, unanimity, consensus, peace, amity.

concordant adj **1** harmonious, accordant, consonant. **2** in agreement, unanimous.

concordat noun covenant, treaty, compact, pact, convention, agreement.

concourse noun assembly, gathering, meeting, convergence, confluence.

concrete adj **1** real, actual, substantial, tangible, material, physical, solid. **2** specific, particular, precise, explicit, definite, positive.

concubine noun mistress, lover, paramour, kept woman, courtesan.

concupiscence noun desire, passion, libido, lust, lechery, lasciviousness.

concur verb **1** agree, assent, acquiesce, accede, accord, be in harmony. **2** coincide, clash, synchronize, coexist.

concurrent adj **1** simultaneous, synchronous, contemporaneous, parallel, coincident, coexistent. **2** convergent, confluent, meeting, joining, intersecting.

concussion noun collision, impact, shock, blow, jolt, jar.

condemn verb **1** criticize, censure, reproach, reprove, deplore, deprecate, slam (inf), slate (inf), denounce, proscribe. **2** sentence, punish, convict, find guilty. **3** doom, damn, force, compel.

condensation noun **1** liquefaction, deliquescence, distillation. **2** mist, fog, droplets, liquid. **3** abridgment, summary, synopsis, précis, résumé, abstract, digest.

condense verb **1** concentrate, reduce, boil down, evaporate, thicken, compress, compact, abridge, shorten, summarize, encapsulate. **2** liquefy, deliquesce, be distilled.

condescend verb deign, vouchsafe, stoop, descend, lower oneself, demean oneself, patronize, talk down.

condign adj fitting, appropriate, just, deserved, merited.

condiment noun sauce, relish, dressing, seasoning.

condition noun **1** stipulation, proviso, term, restriction, requirement, prerequisite, demand. **2** state, shape, form, order, nick (inf). **3** fitness, health, fettle, shape, form, trim. **4** disorder, complaint, problem, disease, disability, defect.
➤verb **1** accustom, habituate, adapt, adjust, prepare, groom. **2** train, teach, indoctrinate, brainwash. **3** improve, tone up, treat, restore.

conditional adj provisional, qualified, restricted, relative, dependent, subject, contingent.

conditions pl noun circumstances, situation, surroundings, environment, setting, context, atmosphere, climate.

condolence noun commiseration, sympathy, pity, compassion, comfort, solace.

condom noun sheath, contraceptive, prophylactic, French letter (inf), rubber (inf).

condone verb pardon, excuse, make allowances for, overlook, ignore.

conduce verb lead, tend, contribute, aid, advance.

conducive adj leading, tending, contributory, instrumental, helpful, useful, favourable.

conduct noun 1 behaviour, manners, ways, habits, actions, practices. 2 management, administration, control, handling, leadership, direction. ➤verb 1 guide, lead, steer, usher, escort, accompany. 2 convey, transmit, carry, bear. 3 carry out, perform, execute, do. 4 lead, direct, supervise, manage, run, control.
conduct oneself act, behave, comport oneself, acquit oneself.

conduit noun duct, passage, pipe, main, channel.

confab noun conversation, talk, chat, gossip, discussion, debate.

confabulate verb talk, chat, gossip, natter (inf).

confectionery noun sweets, sweetmeats, candy, confections.

confederacy noun alliance, league, confederation, coalition, bloc.

confederate adj allied, associated, united, federated, confederated. ➤noun ally, associate, partner, accomplice. ➤verb ally, combine, unite, merge, amalgamate, federate.

confederation noun 1 alliance, league, coalition. 2 federation, confederacy, union.

confer verb 1 bestow, award, present, grant, accord. 2 discuss, debate, consult, talk, parley.

conference noun 1 meeting, convention, forum, symposium, colloquium, seminar. 2 consultation, discussion, debate, talk, parley, dialogue.

confess verb 1 acknowledge, admit, own, grant, recognize, declare, reveal, make known. 2 own up, admit guilt, come clean (inf), unburden oneself, make a clean breast of it (inf).

confession noun acknowledgment, admission, recognition, declaration, revelation, disclosure.

confidant noun intimate, friend, crony, mate (inf), buddy (inf).

confide verb 1 disclose, reveal, tell, impart, whisper, confess. 2 entrust, commit, commend, consign, hand over.
confide in open one's heart to, unburden oneself to.

confidence noun 1 trust, dependence, reliance, faith. 2 conviction, assurance, certainty, belief. 3 self-confidence, self-assurance, self-possession, self-reliance, courage, boldness.

confident adj 1 sure, certain, positive, assured, convinced, satisfied, optimistic. 2 self-confident, self-assured, sure of oneself, self-reliant, assertive, bold.

confidential adj 1 private, secret, personal, sensitive, off-the-record, classified, restricted, hush-hush (inf). 2 trustworthy, trusty, dependable, reliable, faithful.

configuration noun 1 figure, form, shape, pattern, formation, outline, contour. 2 structure, arrangement, disposition.

confine verb 1 imprison, incarcerate, intern, lock up, cage, pen, keep in. 2 restrict, limit, circumscribe, hem in, constrain, control, shackle, inhibit.

confines pl noun limits, bounds, circumference, perimeter, limitations, restrictions.

confirm verb 1 verify, corroborate, validate, authenticate, ratify, endorse, underwrite. 2 prove, evidence, bear out, substantiate, back up. 3 vindicate, strengthen, reinforce, support. 4 establish, settle, pledge, promise, guarantee.

confirmation noun 1 verification, corroboration, validation, ratification, substantiation, proof, evidence, endorsement, support. 2 affirmation, assurance, pledge.

confirmed adj habitual, chronic, incurable, inveterate, hardened, dyed-in-the-wool, entrenched.

confiscate verb seize, take, sequester, distrain, impound, appropriate, commandeer.

conflagration noun fire, blaze, inferno, holocaust.

conflict noun 1 battle, war, hostilities, action, fight, combat, strife, encounter, engagement, skirmish. 2 disagreement, discord, clash, friction, antagonism, opposition, difference, variance. ➤verb clash, collide, disagree, differ, be at variance, oppose.

conflicting adj opposed, antagonistic, at odds, at variance, different, incompatible, inconsistent, contradictory, paradoxical, contrary.

confluence noun convergence, meeting, union, concurrence.

conform verb 1 obey, comply, toe the line (inf), be conventional, follow the crowd (inf), go with the flow (inf), adapt, adjust. 2 agree, correspond, match, fit, accord, comply.

conformist noun conventionalist, traditionalist.

conformity noun 1 conventionality, traditionalism, orthodoxy, adaptation, adjustment. 2 compliance, accordance, correspondence, observance. 3 likeness, resemblance, similarity.

confound verb 1 astonish, amaze, surprise, perplex, confuse, disconcert. 2 defeat, beat, overthrow, upset, thwart, frustrate. 3 contradict, refute, demolish, explode.

confounded adj wretched, accursed, damned, execrable, odious.

confront verb 1 face up to, challenge, defy, brave, beard, accost, address, tackle, resist, stand up to, meet head on (inf). 2 threaten, trouble, harass, face.

confuse verb 1 bewilder, perplex, puzzle, confound, mystify, baffle, bemuse, nonplus. 2 muddle, disorientate, throw (inf), disconcert, fluster. 3 complicate, jumble, disorder, tangle, garble. 4 mistake, muddle, mix up.

confused adj 1 bewildered, perplexed, puzzled, mystified, baffled, all at sea (inf). 2 muddled, mixed up, disorientated, dazed, flustered. 3 disorganized, muddled, jumbled, disorderly, untidy, garbled.

confusing adj puzzling, baffling, muddling, complicated, involved, unclear, ambiguous, misleading.

confute verb refute, disprove, rebut, contradict, controvert. 2 defeat, overwhelm.

congeal verb coagulate, clot, cake, set, gel, thicken, stiffen, solidify.

congenial adj 1 pleasant, agreeable, amiable, companionable, sympathetic, compatible, well-suited, comfortable, homely. 2 suitable, fit, favourable.

congenital adj 1 inborn, inbred, innate, inherited, hereditary, natural. 2 habitual, chronic, incurable, inveterate, ingrained, hardened, confirmed, thoroughgoing.

congested adj 1 full, packed, overcrowded, overflowing, teeming, blocked, obstructed, jammed, gridlocked. 2 blocked, clogged, choked.

conglomerate verb cluster, gather, collect, amass, accumulate, aggregate, agglomerate.
➤ noun multinational, corporation, cartel, consortium.

congratulate verb compliment, felicitate, pat on the back (inf), acclaim, praise, take one's hat off to (inf).

congratulations pl noun and interj compliments, felicitations, best wishes, well done, bravo, congrats (inf).

congregate verb collect, gather, assemble, convene, rendezvous, muster, rally, throng, flock, converge.

congregation noun 1 gathering, assembly, meeting, convention, convocation, rally. 2 parish, parishioners, flock.

congress noun 1 assembly, conference, convention, convocation, conclave, synod, council. 2 legislature, parliament, senate, diet. 3 meeting, gathering, assembly.

congruous adj agreeing, accordant, congruent, consonant, consistent, harmonious, compatible, suitable.

conical adj conic, cone-shaped, funnel-shaped, tapering, pointed.

conjecture verb 1 guess, surmise, suppose, assume, suspect, imagine. 2 infer, theorize, hypothesize, postulate.
➤ noun 1 speculation, guesswork, surmise, supposition, inference. 2 guess, assumption, suspicion, hypothesis, fancy, belief, conclusion.

conjoin verb join, connect, link, unite, tie, bind, combine, associate.

conjugal adj connubial, matrimonial, married, wedded, marital, nuptial.

conjunction *noun* **1** connection, union, combination, association, alliance, collaboration, cooperation. **2** coincidence, concurrence, coexistence, simultaneity, juxtaposition.
in conjunction with with, together with, alongside, in association with, combined with.

conjuncture *noun* juncture, stage, turning point, crossroads, crisis, emergency.

conjure *verb* **1** perform magic, do tricks. **2** invoke, call up, summon, rouse. **3** beseech, implore, entreat, beg.
conjure up 1 evoke, call to mind, bring to mind, recall. **2** imagine, create, produce.

conjurer *noun* magician, illusionist, sorcerer, wizard.

conk *verb* **conk out** break down, fail, pack up (*inf*), go on the blink (*inf*).

conman *noun* confidence trickster, swindler, cheat, fraud, impostor.

connect *verb* **1** join, attach, fasten, unite, link, couple, affix, combine. **2** link, relate, associate, ally, identify, bracket. **3** communicate, adjoin, abut, border, neighbour.

connection *noun* **1** joint, junction, union, link, coupling, tie, bond, fastening. **2** relationship, link, liaison, association, correspondence, analogy, context, relation. **3** contact, acquaintance, friend, ally, patron, relative.

connive *verb* **1** conspire, intrigue, plot, scheme, collude, collaborate. **2** overlook, disregard, ignore, turn a blind eye to, condone, allow.

conniving *adj* scheming, plotting, unscrupulous, unprincipled.

connoisseur *noun* expert, authority, specialist, cognoscente, devotee, aficionado, arbiter, gourmet, aesthete.

connotation *noun* implication, significance, nuance, undertone, overtone, association, suggestion, allusion.

connote *verb* **1** signify, betoken, involve. **2** imply, indicate, suggest, intimate.

connubial *adj* conjugal, matrimonial, married, wedded, marital, nuptial.

conquer *verb* **1** defeat, vanquish, best, worst, overcome, rout. **2** seize, take, possess, annex, occupy, subjugate.

3 overcome, surmount, master, suppress, triumph over, vanquish.

conquest *noun* **1** victory, win, triumph, defeat, rout, mastery, subjugation, invasion, occupation, annexation. **2** catch, prize, acquisition, trophy, booty, spoils.

conscience *noun* scruples, principles, morals, ethics, integrity, honour.

conscientious *adj* **1** diligent, assiduous, industrious, painstaking, scrupulous, meticulous, thorough, precise. **2** honest, upright, scrupulous, principled, moral, high-minded, responsible, honourable.

conscious *adj* **1** aware, alert, cognizant, mindful, heedful. **2** deliberate, intentional, premeditated, calculated, wilful, voluntary. **3** awake, aware, responsive, sentient, alive.

consciousness *noun* **1** awareness, alertness, realization, recognition, cognizance, knowledge, perception. **2** wakefulness, awareness, responsiveness, sentience.

conscript *verb* recruit, enlist, draft, call up, mobilize.
➤*noun* recruit, enlistee, draftee.

consecrate *verb* **1** sanctify, bless. **2** hallow, make holy, dedicate. **3** ordain, anoint, exalt.

consecutive *adj* successive, sequential, serial, continuous, uninterrupted, progressive.

consensus *noun* agreement, concurrence, unanimity, accord, common consent.

consent *verb* **1** agree, assent, accede, acquiesce, submit, give in. **2** permit, allow, approve, grant, authorize.
➤*noun* agreement, assent, acquiescence, compliance, permission, clearance, go-ahead (*inf*), thumbs-up (*inf*), approval, authorization.

consequence *noun* **1** result, outcome, issue, effect, upshot, repercussion. **2** importance, significance, concern, moment, import, value. **3** distinction, standing, esteem, eminence, influence, prestige.

consequent *adj* resultant, resulting, consequential, ensuing, following.

consequently *adv* therefore, ergo, thus, hence, as a result.

conservation noun 1 preservation, protection, care, saving, husbandry, economy. 2 maintenance, upkeep, preservation, safekeeping.

conservative adj 1 moderate, cautious, prudent. 2 conventional, traditional, orthodox, unprogressive, hidebound, reactionary, diehard. 3 Tory, right-wing, reactionary.
➤ noun Tory, right-winger, reactionary, traditionalist, establishmentarian.

conservatory noun 1 greenhouse, glasshouse, hothouse. 2 conservatoire, academy.

conserve verb 1 preserve, protect, safeguard. 2 save, spare, go easy on (inf), store, reserve.

consider verb 1 reflect, ponder, deliberate, contemplate, think about, examine, weigh up, mull over. 2 regard, deem, think, believe, judge, rate, count, hold. 3 respect, heed, mark. 4 remember, bear in mind, take into account, take into consideration.

considerable adj 1 great, large, big, substantial, ample, decent, respectable, goodly. 2 important, significant, noteworthy, remarkable.

considerate adj thoughtful, kind, compassionate, caring, attentive, solicitous, obliging, sensitive, tactful, patient, charitable, unselfish.

consideration noun 1 reflection, deliberation, contemplation, thought, examination, analysis, attention, heed. 2 thoughtfulness, kindness, compassion, care, solicitude, concern, sensitivity, discretion. 3 account, reckoning, estimation, respect, regard. 4 issue, factor, circumstance, concern. 5 payment, fee, reward, perquisite, emolument, gratuity.

considering prep in view of, in the light of, bearing in mind, taking into account.
➤ adv all things considered, all in all.

consign verb 1 commit, entrust, hand over, deliver, transfer. 2 assign, banish, relegate, deposit. 3 send, dispatch, ship, convey, mail.

consignment noun load, shipment, delivery, batch.

consist verb **consist in** lie in, reside in. **consist of** comprise, be composed of, contain, include, involve, amount to.

consistency noun 1 thickness, density, viscosity, firmness. 2 accordance, agreement, correspondence, conformity, correlation, congruity. 3 regularity, constancy, uniformity, steadiness.

consistent adj 1 accordant, agreeing, corresponding, consonant, congruous, compatible. 2 regular, constant, unchanging, uniform, steady, reliable, unfailing.

consolation noun comfort, solace, commiseration, encouragement, reassurance, relief, help.

console[1] verb comfort, solace, commiserate with, cheer, hearten, soothe, reassure, relieve, support.

console[2] noun control panel, instrument panel, dashboard, switchboard, controls, switches, buttons, dials.

consolidate verb 1 unite, join, combine, amalgamate, merge. 2 strengthen, fortify, reinforce. 3 compact, fuse, coalesce, harden, solidify.

consonance noun consistency, compatibility, congruity, accord, harmony, agreement, correspondence.

consonant adj consistent, compatible, congruous, in harmony, in agreement, in accordance, correspondent, appropriate.

consort noun 1 partner, spouse, husband, wife. 2 companion, associate, fellow, comrade.
➤ verb associate, fraternize, mix, keep company, go around.

consortium noun syndicate, cartel, league, alliance, partnership, association.

conspicuous adj 1 obvious, evident, plain, clear, manifest, visible, noticeable, perceptible. 2 showy, flashy, garish, loud, bold, striking, prominent, glaring, flagrant, blatant.

conspiracy noun 1 plot, intrigue, scheme, stratagem, machination. 2 plotting, intrigue, machination, collaboration, collusion, connivance.

conspirator noun plotter, intriguer, schemer, collaborator, traitor.

conspire verb 1 plot, intrigue, scheme, collaborate, collude, connive. 2 combine, unite, act together, work together, gang up.

constant adj 1 faithful, loyal, steadfast, staunch, dependable, trusty, dogged, resolute, persevering, tenacious, unwavering, unshaken. 2 uniform, even, unchanging, invariable, fixed, stable, steady. 3 regular, continual, perpetual, continuous, incessant, ceaseless, interminable, uninterrupted, unrelenting, sustained, persistent.

constellation noun galaxy, cluster, group, assemblage.

consternation noun dismay, distress, shock, alarm, horror, anxiety, confusion, bewilderment.

constituent adj component, integral, intrinsic, elemental.
➤noun 1 component, ingredient, element, part, unit, factor. 2 voter, elector.

constitute verb 1 compose, make up, form. 2 be, represent, amount to, be tantamount to, be regarded as. 3 empower, authorize, commission, charter. 4 found, establish, set up, institute.

constitution noun 1 composition, make-up, structure. 2 formation, foundation, establishment, institution. 3 code, charter, bill of rights, laws, statutes, rules.
4 health, physique, make-up, disposition, temperament, character.

constitutional adj 1 lawful, legitimate, legal, statutory, authorized, ratified.
2 inherent, intrinsic, natural, organic.

constrain verb 1 compel, force, oblige, make, drive, impel, urge. 2 restrain, hold back, curb, check, hinder, impede, restrict, confine.

constrained adj unnatural, forced, stiff, inhibited, reserved, embarrassed.

constraint noun 1 compulsion, force, obligation, coercion, duress, pressure.
2 restraint, curb, check, hindrance, restriction. 3 unnaturalness, inhibition, repression, embarrassment.

constrict verb 1 tighten, narrow, contract, shrink. 2 squeeze, compress, pinch, strangulate.3 impede, hinder, restrict, limit, restrain, inhibit.

construct verb 1 build, erect, raise, put up, assemble, make, fabricate. 2 formulate, compose, put together, frame, create, devise.

construction noun 1 erection, building, assembly, fabrication. 2 building, edifice, erection, structure.

constructive adj positive, useful, helpful, practical, productive, valuable.

construe verb interpret, explain, translate, analyse, read, take, infer, deduce.

consult verb 1 ask, refer to, turn to, seek advice from. 2 refer to, turn to, look up.
3 confer, talk, discuss, debate, deliberate.

consultant noun specialist, expert, authority, adviser, guru.

consume verb 1 devour, eat, drink, swallow, ingest, scoff (inf), down (inf). 2 use, utilize, use up, exhaust, drain, devour, eat up, swallow up, deplete, spend. 3 destroy, demolish, devastate, lay waste, ravage, gut.
4 absorb, engross, preoccupy, obsess, monopolize, grip.

consumer noun buyer, purchaser, shopper, user, customer, client, patron.

consummate verb accomplish, achieve, realize, execute, complete, finish, conclude.
➤adj 1 accomplished, skilled, expert, masterly, proficient, practised, polished, perfect. 2 supreme, ultimate, utter, complete, absolute, total, unqualified.

consumption noun ingestion, swallowing, eating, drinking, use, utilization, exhaustion, depletion, expenditure, dissipation, destruction, demolition.

contact noun 1 touch, union, junction, connection, juxtaposition, touching, exposure. 2 communication, correspondence, association. 3 connection, acquaintance, associate.
➤verb get in touch with, get hold of, reach, speak to, communicate with, notify, call, write to, e-mail.

contagion noun infection, communication, transmission, spread, contamination, corruption, pollution.

contagious adj infectious, catching, communicable, transmissible, transferable, spreading.

contain verb 1 hold, carry, accommodate, enclose. 2 include, incorporate, embrace, comprise, consist of, embody. 3 restrain, hold back, keep back, check, curb, control.
4 repress, suppress, stifle.

container *noun* receptacle, holder, vessel, repository.

contaminate *verb* **1** pollute, adulterate, debase, infect, poison, foul, defile, taint. **2** corrupt, deprave.

contemplate *verb* **1** consider, ponder, think about, reflect on, meditate on, mull over, deliberate, ruminate, muse. **2** stare at, gaze at, view, survey, regard, observe, scrutinize, study, examine. **3** intend, plan, mean, propose, envisage, have in mind.

contemplation *noun* thought, consideration, deliberation, reflection, meditation, rumination, observation, scrutiny, examination, prospect, expectation, intention.

contemplative *adj* thoughtful, pensive, reflective, meditative, ruminative, introspective, lost in thought, in a brown study (*inf*).

contemporary *adj* **1** contemporaneous, coexistent, concurrent, synchronous, simultaneous. **2** modern, up-to-the-minute, fashionable, trendy (*inf*), current, present, avant-garde, futuristic.

contempt *noun* **1** scorn, derision, disrespect, disdain, contemptuousness, dislike, disgust. **2** disrespect, disregard, disobedience.

contemptible *adj* despicable, base, mean, low, abject, shameful, paltry, derisory, pathetic, wretched, ignominious.

contemptuous *adj* scornful, derisive, sneering, disrespectful, insolent, disdainful, withering, patronizing, supercilious.

contend *verb* **1** compete, vie, contest, challenge, oppose, fight, combat, wrestle, strive. **2** deal, cope, grapple, struggle, face, confront, tackle, address. **3** argue, maintain, hold, aver, assert, claim, allege, declare.

content[1] *noun* contentment, contentedness, satisfaction, gratification, ease, comfort, peace of mind, pleasure, happiness. ➤*adj* contented, satisfied, gratified, tranquil, pleased, happy, glad, willing. ➤*verb* satisfy, gratify, appease, pacify, placate, humour, indulge, please.

content[2] *noun* **1** matter, substance, essence, gist, burden, text, material, subject matter. **2** amount, quantity, proportion.

contented *adj* content, satisfied, gratified, fulfilled, at ease, comfortable, relaxed, complacent.

contention *noun* **1** competition, rivalry, opposition, conflict, combat, struggle, strife, antagonism. **2** conflict, discord, dissension, disagreement, controversy, quarrel, argument. **3** assertion, claim, allegation, declaration, belief, conviction, opinion, view, thesis, argument, point.

contentious *adj* **1** quarrelsome, argumentative, disputatious, belligerent, combative, litigious, querulous, contrary. **2** controversial, polemical, debatable, disputable.

contents *pl noun* **1** load, filling, items, elements, ingredients. **2** chapters, sections, parts, topics, subjects.

contest *noun* **1** competition, tournament, championship, match, event. **2** struggle, battle, fight, tussle, conflict, dispute. ➤*verb* **1** dispute, argue, litigate, oppose, challenge, question. **2** compete, contend, vie, fight, struggle, strive.

contestant *noun* competitor, contender, aspirant, candidate, entrant, opponent, adversary, rival.

context *noun* **1** frame of reference, connection, relation, subject, topic. **2** background, setting, situation, conditions, circumstances, state of affairs.

contiguous *adj* **1** touching, in contact. **2** meeting, abutting, adjoining, adjacent, juxtaposed, bordering, neighbouring. **3** next, near, close.

continent *adj* self-restrained, self-controlled, moderate, temperate, abstinent, self-denying, chaste, celibate.

contingency *noun* **1** possibility, eventuality, occurrence, event, accident, emergency, circumstance, case. **2** chance, fortuity, uncertainty.

contingent *adj* **1** dependent, subject, based, conditional. **2** accidental, casual, chance, fortuitous, random, unforeseen, unpredictable, uncertain. ➤*noun* group, party, deputation, detachment, batch, quota, share.

continual *adj* **1** recurrent, repeated, regular, constant, persistent. **2** perpetual, constant, incessant, unremitting, sustained.

continuance *noun* continuation, constancy, permanence, persistence, endurance, survival.

continuation *noun* **1** sequel, supplement, postscript, appendix, extension. **2** continuance, maintenance, protraction, prolongation. **3** resumption, recommencement, renewal.

continue *verb* **1** carry on, go on, persist, persevere, sustain, keep up, maintain, perpetuate. **2** resume, recommence, start again, carry on, proceed. **3** last, endure, survive, hold out. **4** abide, stay, remain, persist.

continuity *noun* connection, interrelationship, coherence, flow, progression, sequence.

continuous *adj* unbroken, uninterrupted, solid, consecutive, nonstop, endless, sustained, prolonged, perpetual, constant.

contort *verb* deform, twist, warp, distort.

contour *noun* outline, silhouette, profile, shape, figure, line, curve.

contraception *noun* birth control, family planning, safe sex.

contract *verb* **1** reduce, decrease, compress, compact, squeeze. **2** shrink, shorten, narrow, constrict, tighten, tense. **3** shorten, condense, compress, abbreviate. **4** agree, arrange, engage, undertake, pledge, promise, covenant. **5** catch, get, pick up, develop, go down with (*inf*). **6** incur, acquire.
➤*noun* agreement, compact, covenant, bond, undertaking, engagement, arrangement, bargain, transaction, deal.

contraction *noun* **1** tightening, tensing, shortening, narrowing, constriction. **2** shortening, short form, elision, abbreviation.

contradict *verb* **1** deny, gainsay, dispute, oppose, challenge, contest, rebut. **2** go against, disagree with, conflict with, negate, belie, disprove, refute, fly in the face of (*inf*).

contradiction *noun* **1** denial, opposition, refutation, rebuttal, conflict, variance, discrepancy, disagreement. **2** inconsistency, paradox.

contradictory *adj* contrary, opposing, at variance, conflicting, clashing, incompatible, inconsistent, paradoxical.

contraption *noun* contrivance, device, gadget, gizmo (*inf*), apparatus, machine, appliance.

contrariety *noun* opposition, conflict, disagreement, discord, contradiction, incompatibility, inconsistency.

contrary *adj* **1** opposed, opposite, conflicting, contrasting, incompatible, inconsistent, at variance, at odds. **2** perverse, awkward, difficult, stroppy (*inf*), obstinate, refractory, wayward, wilful. **3** adverse, unfavourable, hostile, inimical.
contrary to against, in opposition to, counter to, at variance with.
on the contrary in contrast, quite the opposite, quite the reverse.

contrast *verb* **1** compare, differentiate, distinguish, discriminate. **2** juxtapose, set off. **3** stand out, differ, oppose, clash, conflict, be at variance.
➤*noun* **1** comparison, juxtaposition, distinction, differentiation. **2** difference, disparity.

contravene *verb* break, infringe, violate, flout, contradict, oppose, run counter to.

contravention *noun* infringement, violation, breach, transgression, contradiction, opposition.

contretemps *noun* disagreement, altercation, squabble, row, tiff (*inf*), clash, brush, confrontation.

contribute *verb* **1** give, donate, pay, subscribe, offer, chip in (*inf*). **2** lead, be conducive, add, help, advance, play a part, be instrumental, cause. **3** write, compose, compile, prepare, supply, provide.

contributory *adj* instrumental, accessory, conducive, helpful, participatory, responsible.

contrite *adj* penitent, repentant, sorry, regretful, remorseful, conscience-stricken, guilt-ridden, chastened, shamefaced.

contrition *noun* penitence, repentance, sorrow, regret, remorse, compunction, shame.

contrivance *noun* device, invention, contraption, gadget, machine, apparatus, instrument, scheme, ruse, ploy, stratagem, expedient.

contrive *verb* **1** invent, design, create, fabricate, construct, improvise. **2** devise, formulate, think up, plan, plot, scheme.

3 engineer, manoeuvre, wangle (*inf*), arrange, orchestrate, stage-manage, effect, bring about.

contrived *adj* artificial, forced, unnatural, strained, laboured, overdone, mannered, affected.

control *verb* **1** direct, lead, head, preside over, govern, rule, manage, supervise, oversee, pull the strings (*inf*), call the shots (*inf*). **2** restrain, curb, check, bridle, suppress, contain, restrict, handle, discipline, dominate, master. **3** regulate, monitor, verify, adjust. **4** operate, work, drive, steer, pilot.
➤*noun* **1** direction, leadership, command, rule, authority, jurisdiction, charge, power, influence. **2** management, supervision, monitoring, regulation. **3** restraint, restriction, constraint, mastery, dominance, discipline. **4** curb, check, brake. **5** lever, switch, knob, button, instrument, dial. **6** base, headquarters, centre of operations.
in control in charge, in the driving seat (*inf*), in the saddle (*inf*).

controversial *adj* contentious, disputed, at issue, debatable, questionable, controvertible, polemic.

controversy *noun* dispute, debate, polemic, war of words, disagreement, contention, dissension, strife.

controvert *verb* deny, rebut, oppose, challenge, contest, dispute, contradict.

contumacious *adj* stubborn, obstinate, contrary, refractory, recalcitrant, rebellious, insubordinate, intractable.

contumely *noun* abuse, invective, obloquy, opprobrium, contempt, disdain, arrogance, insolence.

contusion *noun* bruise, discoloration, ecchymosis, knock, bump.

conundrum *noun* **1** riddle, puzzle, poser, brainteaser (*inf*). **2** enigma, mystery, problem.

convalesce *verb* recover, recuperate, improve, get better, mend, get well.

convene *verb* call, summon, convoke, rally, muster, assemble, meet, gather, congregate.

convenience *noun* **1** expedience, utility, usefulness, handiness, suitability, fitness, availability, accessibility, proximity. **2** advantage, benefit, aid, help, assistance, service, use, comfort, ease. **3** facility, amenity, appliance, device, gadget.

convenient *adj* **1** suitable, fitting, appropriate, timely, opportune, favourable, advantageous. **2** handy, expedient, useful, helpful, suited, adapted. **3** accessible, available, handy, to hand, near by, within reach.

convent *noun* nunnery, cloister, abbey, priory.

convention *noun* **1** meeting, assembly, conference, convocation, congress, council. **2** agreement, treaty, pact, entente, concordat, arrangement. **3** custom, tradition, practice, usage, protocol, etiquette, code, formality, propriety. **4** method, technique, practice, style.

conventional *adj* **1** accepted, received, approved, proper, correct, official, orthodox, traditional, customary, conservative, mainstream, standard, regular. **2** commonplace, run-of-the-mill, stereotypical, trite, banal, prosaic, pedestrian, unoriginal.

converge *verb* **1** meet, join, unite, merge, become one. **2** focus, concentrate, coincide, come together, gather, flock, approach, close in.

conversant *adj* familiar, acquainted, informed, au fait, versed, knowledgeable, experienced, practised.

conversation *noun* **1** talk, dialogue, exchange, chat, natter (*inf*), chinwag (*inf*), confab (*inf*), heart-to-heart, tête-à-tête. **2** communication, discussion, discourse, colloquy, chitchat, small talk.

converse[1] *verb* talk, communicate, discuss, confer, confabulate, chat, gossip, natter (*inf*).

converse[2] *noun* opposite, reverse, contrary, antithesis, other side of the coin (*inf*).
➤*adj* opposite, reverse, contrary, counter, antithetical.

conversion *noun* **1** change, transformation, metamorphosis, alteration, modification, adaptation, reorganization, reconstruction, exchange. **2** persuasion, reformation, rebirth, proselytization, baptism.

convert *verb* **1** change, transform, alter, modify, adapt, remodel, rebuild.

2 transmute, metamorphose, make, turn. **3** exchange, swap, change. **4** convince, persuade, win over. **5** reform, proselytize, baptize.

convex *adj* bulging, rounded, humped, swollen.

convey *verb* **1** carry, bear, transfer, transport, move, take, conduct, transmit, pipe, send, deliver. **2** transmit, pass on, communicate, impart, express, disclose. **3** transfer, grant, cede, devolve, bequeath, will.

conveyance *noun* **1** vehicle, means of transport, car, carriage, truck, bus. **2** carriage, transportation, shipping, haulage, transmission, communication, expression, disclosure. **3** transfer, transmission, cession, devolution, demise.

convict *verb* condemn, find guilty, sentence, imprison.
➤*noun* criminal, felon, offender, lawbreaker, crook (*inf*), prisoner, jailbird, con (*inf*), old lag (*inf*).

conviction *noun* **1** condemnation, judgment, sentence, punishment, imprisonment. **2** assurance, confidence, certainty, persuasion, belief, faith. **3** opinion, idea, belief, creed, principle, tenet.

convince *verb* **1** persuade, satisfy, assure. **2** prevail upon, bring round, persuade, sway, win over.

convincing *adj* **1** plausible, credible, likely, persuasive, powerful, forceful, impressive, telling. **2** conclusive, decisive.

convivial *adj* sociable, congenial, jolly, merry, festive, hearty, cordial, friendly.

convocation *noun* assembly, meeting, convention, congress, council.

convoke *verb* call, summon, convene, muster, assemble, gather, rally.

convoluted *adj* **1** intricate, complex, complicated, involved, tortuous. **2** twisting, turning, winding, twisted, coiled.

convolution *noun* **1** coil, curl, twist, turn, loop, whorl, spiral, roll. **2** intricacy, complexity, complication, involvement, entanglement, tortuousness.

convoy *noun* fleet, company, line, train, procession, escort, guard, entourage.
➤*verb* escort, accompany, guard, protect, defend, usher, pilot, guide.

convulse *verb* **1** shake, heave. **2** agitate, discompose, unsettle, shake.

convulsion *noun* **1** seizure, fit, paroxysm, spasm, tic, tremor. **2** agitation, disturbance, upheaval, upset, commotion, turbulence, turmoil.

cook *verb* **1** bake, stew, boil, fry, roast, grill. **2** falsify, forge.

cook up concoct, devise, invent, contrive, make up, prepare, create, improvise.

cool *adj* **1** chilly, cold, nippy, unheated, chilled, refrigerated. **2** fresh, refreshing, bracing. **3** composed, calm, collected, unperturbed, relaxed, laid back (*inf*), serene, self-possessed, poised, level-headed, unemotional, dispassionate. **4** unfriendly, cold, frosty, chilly, unresponsive, undemonstrative, aloof, standoffish, lukewarm, unenthusiastic. **5** smart, elegant, stylish, fashionable, trendy (*inf*). **6** excellent, marvellous, wonderful, great.
➤*verb* chill, refrigerate, ice, get cold, lose heat.
➤*noun* **1** coolness, chill, cold, freshness. **2** composure, calmness, self-possession, self-control, poise, serenity.

coop *noun* cage, pen, enclosure, pound, box.
➤*verb* cage, pen, confine, shut up, enclose, imprison.

cooperate *verb* **1** help, lend a hand, abet, collaborate, work together, combine, join forces, contribute, participate. **2** go along, play ball (*inf*).

cooperative *adj* **1** helpful, supportive, obliging, accommodating, willing, responsive. **2** collective, communal, combined, joint, shared.

coordinate *verb* **1** organize, arrange, integrate, mesh, synchronize, harmonize, match, correspond. **2** work together, act together, collaborate, cooperate.

cope *verb* manage, succeed, get by, make out (*inf*), deal, handle, hack (*inf*).

copious *adj* abundant, plentiful, ample, profuse, lavish, full, bountiful, liberal.

coppice *noun* copse, thicket, grove, wood.

copulate *verb* mate, couple, have sex, make love, have it off (*sl*).

copy *verb* **1** duplicate, replicate, reproduce, photocopy, scan, transcribe. **2** plagiarize,

pirate, counterfeit, imitate, mimic, ape, echo, mirror. **3** follow, emulate.
➤*noun* **1** duplicate, replica, facsimile, reproduction, photocopy, print, transcription, counterfeit, likeness, imitation. **2** issue, example, sample, specimen.

cord *noun* **1** line, string, twine, rope. **2** cable, flex, wire.

cordial *adj* **1** friendly, warm, pleasant, gracious, sociable, genial, amiable, affable. **2** sincere, earnest, ardent, hearty, heartfelt, wholehearted.

cordon *noun* line, chain, ring, barrier.
cordon off close off, isolate, separate, enclose, surround.

core *noun* centre, heart, kernel, nucleus, nub, crux, essence.

cork *noun* stopper, bung.

corn *noun* **1** cereal, grain, arable crop. **2** maize, sweet corn, corn on the cob.

corner *noun* **1** angle, bend, crook, niche, nook, crevice. **2** junction, intersection, turn, turning. **3** predicament, plight, hole (*inf*), spot (*inf*). **4** part, region, hideout, retreat.
➤*verb* **1** trap, bring to bay, run to earth, block off. **2** monopolize, control, dominate, hog (*inf*).

corny *adj* **1** trite, banal, mawkish, sentimental, feeble. **2** hackneyed, stale, unoriginal, commonplace, platitudinous.

corollary *noun* **1** inference, deduction, conclusion. **2** consequence, result, upshot.

coronation *noun* crowning, enthronement, accession, investiture.

coronet *noun* **1** crown, diadem, circlet, tiara. **2** wreath, garland.

corporal *adj* bodily, fleshly, physical, carnal, somatic, corporeal.

corporate *adj* combined, joint, shared, collective, united, pooled.

corporation *noun* **1** company, firm, concern, establishment, trust, partnership. **2** council, local authority, governing body.

corporeal *adj* **1** physical, material, corporal. **2** real, tangible, substantial.

corps *noun* **1** company, troupe, body, group. **2** unit, detachment, troop, squadron, platoon.

corpse *noun* cadaver, body, stiff (*inf*), carcass, remains.

corpulent *adj* fat, stout, plump, tubby, rotund, portly, obese, overweight.

correct *adj* **1** accurate, true, right, unerring, exact, precise, spot on (*inf*). **2** proper, fitting, appropriate, seemly, decorous, accepted, conventional, standard.
➤*verb* **1** put right, rectify, right, redress, amend. **2** alter, adjust, improve, remedy, counteract, compensate for. **3** discipline, punish, chastise, castigate, admonish, reprove.

corrective *adj* remedial, therapeutic, curative, rectifying, reparatory, disciplinary, punitive, penal.

correlate *verb* **1** relate, correspond, agree, coordinate, interact. **2** connect, associate. **3** compare, equate.

correlation *noun* **1** correspondence, equivalence, interrelationship, reciprocity, mutuality. **2** interdependence, connection, association.

correlative *noun* corresponding, equivalent, interrelated, reciprocal, mutual, complementary.

correspond *verb* **1** agree, accord, harmonize, conform, tally, match, square, correlate. **2** be similar, be comparable, be equivalent, be analogous. **3** communicate, write, exchange letters, keep in touch.

correspondence *noun* **1** agreement, accord, harmony, conformity, correlation. **2** similarity, resemblance, comparison, equivalence, analogy. **3** letters, mail, communication, writing.

correspondent *noun* **1** journalist, reporter, columnist, contributor. **2** letter writer, pen-friend, pen pal (*inf*).

corridor *noun* passage, hall, aisle.

corroborate *verb* confirm, substantiate, verify, validate, bear out, support, back up, document, authenticate, prove.

corrode *verb* **1** erode, wear away, eat away, consume. **2** weaken, impair, destroy, ruin. **3** rust, disintegrate, crumble.

corrosive *adj* corroding, erosive, wearing, consuming, destructive, acid, caustic.

corrugate *verb* wrinkle, crinkle, furrow, groove, ridge, flute.

corrupt *adj* **1** dishonest, unscrupulous, unprincipled, dishonourable, bribable, venal, crooked, bent (*inf*). **2** immoral, depraved, perverted, warped, degenerate, debauched, decadent, dissolute. **3** impure, adulterated, contaminated, polluted, tainted, rotten.
➤*verb* **1** bribe, suborn, buy, square (*inf*), deprave, pervert, warp, debauch, lead astray. **2** alter, doctor, tamper with. **3** contaminate, pollute, taint, spoil, blight, adulterate.

corsair *noun* pirate, buccaneer, freebooter, privateer, raider.

corset *noun* girdle, foundation, belt, stays.

cortège *noun* procession, line, column, train.

coruscate *verb* sparkle, flash, glint, gleam, scintillate, glitter, twinkle, glimmer.

cosmetic *adj* **1** beautifying, improving. **2** surface, superficial, external, peripheral.

cosmonaut *noun* astronaut, spaceman, spacewoman.

cosmopolitan *adj* **1** universal, global, worldwide, international. **2** international, multiracial, multicultural. **3** urbane, sophisticated, worldly, worldly-wise, well-travelled, globe-trotting, jet-setting.

cosmos *noun* universe, solar system, macrocosm.

cosset *verb* pamper, mollycoddle, baby, indulge, spoil.

cost *noun* **1** price, charge, rate, fee, expense, expenditure, outlay, payment, damage (*inf*), valuation, quotation, estimate. **2** loss, sacrifice, penalty, price, damage, harm, pain, suffering.
➤*verb* **1** sell for, be priced at, be worth, fetch, go for, come to, set one back (*inf*). **2** price, value, evaluate, estimate, quote for.

costly *adj* **1** dear, expensive, valuable, fine, luxurious, opulent, lavish, extravagant. **2** damaging, harmful, injurious, deleterious, destructive, ruinous, disastrous, catastrophic.

costume *noun* dress, garb, attire, clothing, outfit, uniform, livery, robes.

cosy *adj* **1** snug, comfortable, warm, sheltered, secure, homely. **2** intimate, congenial, relaxed.

coterie *noun* set, circle, crowd, clique, gang, cabal, faction, camp.

cottage *noun* lodge, chalet, cabin, shack, shanty.

couch *noun* sofa, settee, chaise longue.
➤*verb* state, express, phrase, word, frame, style.

cough *verb* hack, bark, clear one's throat.
cough up pay, stump up (*inf*), fork out (*inf*).

council *noun* **1** board, panel, committee, commission, advisory body, working party, parliament, congress. **2** local authority, governing body, corporation.

counsel *noun* **1** advice, guidance, warning, caution, admonition, recommendation, opinion. **2** consultation, deliberation, discussion, conference. **3** advocate, attorney, lawyer, barrister.
➤*verb* advise, urge, warn, suggest, recommend, advocate.

counsellor *noun* adviser, mentor, guide.

count *verb* **1** add up, total, tot up (*inf*), number, enumerate, reckon, tally. **2** include, take into account, allow for, number among, embrace. **3** consider, regard, deem, judge, think, reckon, hold. **4** matter, signify, be important, tell, cut ice (*inf*).
➤*noun* **1** enumeration, calculation, reckoning, tally, score, poll. **2** sum, total, aggregate.
count on 1 depend on, rely on, trust. **2** bank on, take for granted.

countenance *noun* **1** face, features, physiognomy, expression, look, air. **2** approval, sanction, favour, support, encouragement, aid.
➤*verb* approve, favour, support, accept, tolerate, allow.

counter¹ *adv* against, versus, in opposition, at variance, contrarily, conversely.
➤*adj* contrary, adverse, opposite, contradictory, conflicting, contrasting.
➤*verb* **1** oppose, resist, offset. **2** retaliate, hit back, respond, combat, contradict. **3** parry, ward off.

counter² *noun* **1** table, worktop, bar, checkout. **2** disc, token, piece.

counteract *verb* neutralize, counterbalance, offset, negate, oppose, resist, check.

counterbalance *verb* balance, equalize, offset, counteract, compensate for, counterpoise.

counterfeit *verb* forge, fake, feign, simulate, copy, pirate, imitate.
➤*adj* forged, fake, false, feigned, simulated, imitation, pirate, bogus.
➤*noun* forgery, fake, copy, imitation, sham, fraud.

countermand *verb* revoke, rescind, quash, retract, reverse, override.

counterpart *noun* equivalent, equal, opposite number, partner, fellow, match, double, analogue.

counterpoise *verb* counterbalance, balance, equilibrate, offset, countervail.
➤*noun* counterweight, counterbalance.

countless *adj* innumerable, numberless, myriad, legion, incalculable, untold, infinite, umpteen (*inf*).

country *noun* **1** nation, state, republic, kingdom, realm, people, homeland. **2** land, terrain, territory, area, region, locality. **3** countryside, green belt, provinces, rural areas, outback, bush, sticks (*inf*).

countryman *noun* **1** rustic, provincial, yokel, bumpkin, peasant, farmer. **2** compatriot, citizen, national, native.

countryside *noun* country, farmland, moorland, green belt, great outdoors (*inf*), landscape, scenery.

county *noun* province, shire, region, area, administrative unit.

coup *noun* **1** feat, exploit, masterstroke, tour de force, accomplishment, stunt. **2** coup d'état, putsch, revolution, uprising, insurgence, takeover, overthrow.

couple *noun* **1** pair, brace, duo. **2** twosome, partners, lovers, husband and wife. **3** two or three, a few.
➤*verb* **1** unite, link, yoke, bracket, pair, marry, wed, match. **2** attach, hitch, fasten, connect. **3** mate, copulate.

coupon *noun* **1** voucher, token, ticket. **2** slip, form.

courage *noun* bravery, valour, fearlessness, boldness, pluck, mettle, guts (*inf*), bottle (*inf*), heroism, gallantry.

courageous *adj* brave, valiant, fearless, bold, plucky, intrepid, dauntless, daring, heroic, gallant.

courier *noun* **1** messenger, bearer, carrier, dispatch rider. **2** guide, escort.

course *noun* **1** route, path, track, way, channel, orbit, round. **2** direction, line, tack, trajectory. **3** progression, sequence, advance, march, flow, development, passage, duration. **4** procedure, system, method, way, conduct. **5** policy, plan, programme, approach, line, tack. **6** classes, lectures, lessons, studies, curriculum, syllabus. **7** dish, part, stage. **8** series, succession, period, spell. **9** circuit, track, area, field.
➤*verb* **1** run, flow, pour, rush. **2** chase, pursue, follow, hunt.

court *noun* **1** tribunal, trial, assize. **2** lawcourt, bar, bench. **3** retinue, train, suite, entourage, attendants, royal household. **4** palace, castle. **5** enclosure, arena, ground.
➤*verb* **1** woo, pay court to, date, go out with, go steady with (*inf*). **2** invite, solicit, ask for, provoke, prompt, attract. **3** cultivate, curry favour with, butter up (*inf*), flatter, sweet-talk (*inf*).

courteous *adj* polite, civil, well-mannered, gallant, chivalrous, respectful, gracious, cordial, obliging, considerate.

courtesan *noun* prostitute, whore, mistress, kept woman, demimondaine, paramour.

courtesy *noun* politeness, civility, manners, gallantry, chivalry, respect, graciousness, cordiality, generosity, benevolence.

courtier *noun* noble, attendant, steward, squire, lady-in-waiting.

courtly *adj* refined, well-bred, dignified, ceremonious, stately, gallant, chivalrous, gentlemanly, ladylike, noble, aristocratic, elegant, polite.

courtship *noun* wooing, suit, romance, affair, dating.

courtyard *noun* court, quadrangle, yard, enclosure, area, square.

cove *noun* bay, bight, inlet.

covenant *noun* agreement, contract, treaty, convention, promise, pledge, bond, commitment.

➤*verb* agree, contract, promise, pledge, undertake, guarantee.

cover *verb* 1 mask, screen, shield, shelter, protect, house, sheathe, overlay. 2 hide, conceal, obscure, veil, shroud, disguise, camouflage, cover up, whitewash (*inf*). 3 spread, plaster, coat, overlie, envelop, wrap. 4 include, embrace, incorporate, comprise, take in, encompass, involve, deal with, treat, consider, examine, study. 5 blanket, mantle, carpet. 6 cross, traverse, pass through, travel over. 7 insure, indemnify, protect. 8 defend, guard, protect. 9 mark, obstruct.
➤*noun* 1 lid, top, cap. 2 covering, coat, layer, film, veneer, blanket, carpet, case, sheath, shell, shield, guard. 3 jacket, case, wrapper. 4 cloak, veil, mask, screen, shroud. 5 disguise, camouflage, facade, front, pretext, smokescreen. 6 shelter, refuge, sanctuary, hiding place. 7 covert, undergrowth, thicket, woodland. 8 defence, protection, shield, guard. 9 insurance, assurance, indemnity, protection.

cover for replace, deputize for, stand in for, fill in for.

coverage *noun* reporting, articles, stories, accounts.

covert *adj* clandestine, secret, private, concealed, hidden, disguised, underground, surreptitious, furtive.

cover-up *noun* concealment, smokescreen, whitewash (*inf*), pretence, front, suppression, secrecy, conspiracy.

covet *verb* envy, desire, wish for, hanker after, crave, set one's heart on, aspire to, dream of.

covetous *adj* envious, jealous, desirous, acquisitive, grasping, rapacious, avid, craving.

covey *noun* brood, flight, flock, bevy.

cow *verb* frighten, unnerve, overawe, daunt, intimidate, browbeat, bully, terrorize, oppress, discourage, dishearten.

coward *noun* craven, poltroon, renegade, chicken (*inf*), yellow-belly (*inf*), baby, weakling, wimp (*inf*).

cowboy *noun* 1 cowhand, cowherd, drover, stockman. 2 scoundrel, rogue, bungler, amateur.

cower *verb* cringe, shrink, recoil, flinch, quail, crouch, stoop, skulk.

coy *adj* 1 shy, bashful, modest, self-effacing, demure, prudish. 2 arch, coquettish, flirtatious, skittish. 3 reserved, reticent.

crabbed *adj* 1 crabby, irritable, irascible, bad-tempered, ill-humoured, testy, touchy, waspish, crusty, cantankerous, crotchety (*inf*), grouchy (*inf*). 2 cramped, illegible, unreadable, indecipherable.

crack *verb* 1 break, fracture, split, shatter, craze, chap. 2 snap, pop, clap, crash, bang, burst, explode. 3 yield, give way, break down, collapse. 4 solve, puzzle out, work out, decipher, decode, unravel.
➤*noun* 1 break, split, cleft, rift, breach, fissure, chink, slit. 2 snap, pop, clap, crash, bang, detonation, report. 3 bang, blow, knock, bump, clout (*inf*). 4 try, attempt, go, bash (*inf*), shot (*inf*). 5 joke, gag (*inf*), quip, witticism, jibe, dig (*inf*).
➤*adj* expert, ace (*inf*), first-rate, brilliant, elite, top-notch (*inf*).

crack down on restrict, limit, control, curb, suppress, clamp down on, put a stop to.

crack up break down, collapse, go to pieces, go mad.

cracked *adj* 1 broken, fractured, split, crazed, chapped, damaged, imperfect. 2 mad, crazy, insane, out of one's mind, nuts (*inf*), round the bend (*inf*).

crackers *adj* mad, crazy, insane, out of one's mind, nuts (*inf*), round the bend (*inf*).

crackle *verb* snap, crack, pop, crepitate.

cradle *noun* 1 cot, crib, bassinet, Moses' basket. 2 birthplace, origin, source, fount, spring.
➤*verb* 1 hold, support. 2 shelter, rock, nurse, foster.

craft *noun* 1 art, handicraft, skill, ability. 2 trade, vocation, calling, occupation, business, work. 3 skill, technique, talent, flair, expertise, artistry, workmanship, handiwork. 4 craftiness, cunning, artfulness, guile, wiliness, trickery, artifice, subterfuge. 5 vessel, boat, ship, aircraft, spacecraft.

craftsman *noun* 1 artisan, artist, technician. 2 expert, master.

crafty adj cunning, artful, sly, wily, foxy, shrewd, calculating, tricky, devious.

crag noun rock, tor, cliff, escarpment, ridge, peak.

craggy noun rugged, rough, uneven, jagged, rocky.

cram verb **1** push, shove, thrust, force, ram, stuff, press, squeeze. **2** fill, stuff, pack, crowd, jam, choke. **3** study, revise, swot (inf), mug up (inf), bone up (inf).

cramp[1] verb handicap, check, restrain, restrict, limit, confine.
cramp somebody's style hinder, hamper, constrain, inhibit.

cramp[2] noun spasm, contraction, twinge, pang, stitch, crick, pain, stiffness.

cramped adj small, narrow, poky (inf), tight, restricted, confined, overcrowded.

crane noun derrick, davit, winch, hoist.

crank noun **1** lever, arm, shaft, handle. **2** eccentric, character, weirdo (inf), oddball (inf), fanatic, enthusiast, devotee, nut (inf).
➤verb start, turn over, rev (inf).
crank up increase, intensify, accelerate, speed up.

cranky adj **1** eccentric, odd, strange, bizarre, weird, unconventional, wacky (inf). **2** bad-tempered, cross, irritable, awkward, difficult.

cranny noun chink, crevice, crack, slit, gap, interstice.

crash verb **1** break, smash, shatter, splinter, dash, batter. **2** clatter, clash, bang, boom, roar, thunder. **3** wreck, write off (inf). **4** collide, hit. **5** hurtle, rush, smash, plough. **6** fall, topple, tumble, plunge. **7** go down, fail, malfunction, pack up.
➤noun **1** clatter, clash, bang, thud, boom, roar. **2** collision, accident, shunt (inf), prang (inf), pile-up (inf). **3** collapse, failure, fall, ruin.
➤adj intensive, rapid, accelerated, concentrated.

crass adj insensitive, tactless, coarse, unrefined, uncouth, boorish.

crate noun case, box, chest, basket.

crater noun hole, cavity, pit, hollow, depression.

crave verb **1** want, desire, long for, hanker after, fancy (inf), be dying for (inf), need, require. **2** ask, beg, beseech, implore, pray, solicit.

craven adj cowardly, dastardly, pusillanimous, timorous, fearful, chicken (inf), yellow (inf), faint-hearted, lily-livered, spineless.

craving noun desire, longing, yearning, hankering, hunger, thirst, urge, need.

crawl verb **1** worm, slither, go on all fours. **2** creep, inch, steal, sneak. **3** swarm, teem, seethe, bristle. **4** grovel, fawn, toady, curry favour, suck up (inf).

craze noun fashion, vogue, fad, rage, thing (inf), mania, enthusiasm, obsession.

crazy adj **1** mad, insane, deranged, unhinged, lunatic, nuts (inf), crackers (inf), bonkers (inf), off one's rocker (inf). **2** silly, foolish, absurd, ridiculous, preposterous, idiotic, senseless, impractical, foolhardy, harebrained (inf), daft (inf), barmy (inf). **3** strange, odd, peculiar, bizarre, weird. **4** infatuated, enamoured, smitten, wild, mad, passionate, enthusiastic, fanatical.

creak verb squeak, grate, scrape, groan.

cream noun **1** emulsion, lotion, ointment, salve, liniment. **2** best, pick, prime, flower, elite.

crease noun wrinkle, pucker, fold, line, ridge, furrow, corrugation.
➤verb **1** wrinkle, crinkle, pucker, crumple, line, ridge, furrow, corrugate. **2** amuse, entertain, laugh, fall about (inf), be in stitches (inf).

create verb **1** constitute, establish, found, institute, originate, initiate, engender, beget. **2** produce, generate, cause, bring about, start. **3** appoint, install, invest, ordain. **4** invent, devise, concoct, design, make, build, construct.

creation noun **1** invention, conception, concoction, design, construction, development. **2** work, opus, concept, brainchild, masterpiece, chef-d'oeuvre. **3** the universe, the cosmos, the world, nature, life.

creative adj **1** artistic, inventive, resourceful, talented, productive, fertile. **2** original, innovative, ingenious, imaginative.

creator noun **1** maker, producer, inventor, originator, author, architect, designer, founder. **2** prime mover, first cause, God.

creature *noun* **1** being, living thing, animal, organism, individual. **2** person, human being, mortal, soul, body, character. **3** minion, lackey, parasite, hanger-on, puppet, tool, sycophant, toady.

credence *noun* belief, credit, acceptance, faith, trust.

credential *noun* certificate, diploma, permit, pass, identity card, testimonial, letter of introduction.

credibility *noun* **1** plausibility, probability, likelihood. **2** trust, reliability, honesty, integrity, sincerity.

credible *adj* believable, plausible, imaginable, tenable, probable, likely, convincing.

credit *noun* **1** praise, commendation, recognition, acknowledgement, honour, glory, tribute, homage. **2** reputation, standing, influence, prestige, respect, esteem, name, character. **3** asset, pride and joy (*inf*), feather in the cap (*inf*). **4** credence, belief, acceptance, faith, trust, credibility, plausibility.
➤*verb* **1** ascribe, attribute, accredit, assign, impute, put down. **2** believe, accept, buy (*inf*), swallow (*inf*).
in credit solvent, in the black (*inf*).
on credit on account, on the slate (*inf*), by instalments, on the never-never (*inf*).

creditable *adj* praiseworthy, commendable, admirable, estimable, meritorious, deserving, worthy, respectable.

credulity *noun* credulousness, gullibility, naivety, trustfulness.

credulous *adj* gullible, naive, trustful, unsuspecting, simple.

creed *noun* **1** belief, faith, credo, dogma, doctrine, articles of faith. **2** tenet, principle, rule.

creek *noun* **1** inlet, estuary, bay. **2** stream, brook, watercourse.

creep *verb* **1** slither, wriggle, worm, crawl. **2** inch, edge. **3** steal, sneak, tiptoe. **4** grovel, fawn, crawl, toady, kowtow, curry favour.
➤*noun* sycophant, toady, bootlicker (*inf*).

creeper *noun* climber, rambler, trailing plant, runner, liana.

creepy *adj* **1** eerie, ghostly, macabre, scary (*inf*), hair-raising, spine-chilling. **2** sinister, ominous, menacing, disturbing.

crest *noun* **1** top, apex, summit, peak, ridge, crown. **2** tuft, comb, topknot. **3** plume, tassel. **4** badge, emblem, symbol, device, insignia.

crestfallen *adj* disappointed, dispirited, disheartened, dejected, depressed, downcast, despondent, disconsolate.

crevasse *noun* chasm, abyss, ravine, gorge, fissure, cleft.

crevice *noun* chink, cranny, crack, cleft, split, gap, opening.

crew *noun* **1** company, team, squad, unit. **2** gang, band, crowd, pack, bunch, lot.

crib *noun* **1** cot, cradle, bed. **2** stall, pen, enclosure. **3** rack, manger.
➤*verb* **1** copy, duplicate, plagiarize, lift (*inf*). **2** steal, pilfer, purloin, pinch (*inf*).

crick *noun* cramp, spasm, twinge, pang, pain, stiffness.

crime *noun* **1** felony, offence, misdemeanour, violation, transgression. **2** lawbreaking, wrongdoing, misconduct, delinquency, vice. **3** offence, atrocity, outrage, wrong, sin.

criminal *noun* felon, offender, lawbreaker, wrongdoer, malefactor, miscreant, delinquent, villain, crook (*inf*).
➤*adj* **1** unlawful, illegal, illicit, wrong, dishonest, crooked (*inf*). **2** guilty, culpable. **3** deplorable, scandalous, shameful, reprehensible, wicked, iniquitous, sinful.

crimp *verb* curl, wave, frizz.

cringe *verb* **1** flinch, wince, shrink, recoil, cower, duck, quail, blench. **2** fawn, grovel, toady, crawl (*inf*), creep (*inf*), kowtow, bow and scrape.

crinkle *verb* wrinkle, crease, pucker, furrow, flute, corrugate.

cripple *verb* **1** lame, disable, handicap, paralyse, injure, maim, hamstring, debilitate. **2** hamper, impede, paralyse, hamstring, damage, ruin.

crisis *noun* **1** emergency, exigency, quandary, predicament, strait, extremity, disaster, catastrophe. **2** turning point, climax, height.

crisp *adj* **1** brittle, friable, crumbly. **2** crunchy, crispy, firm, fresh. **3** cold, fresh, brisk, bracing, invigorating. **4** sharp, brusque, curt, abrupt, clear, incisive.

criterion *noun* standard, norm, measure, scale, touchstone, benchmark, yardstick, rule, principle.

critic *noun* 1 reviewer, commentator, analyst, authority, pundit, arbiter. 2 censurer, attacker, detractor, knocker (*inf*), faultfinder, nit-picker (*inf*).

critical *adj* 1 censorious, derogatory, disapproving, judgmental, carping, nit-picking (*inf*). 2 analytical, evaluative, interpretative, expository, discerning, penetrating. 3 crucial, decisive, pivotal, vital, essential, all-important. 4 urgent, pressing, serious, grave, dangerous, precarious, touch-and-go.

criticism *noun* 1 censure, animadversion, condemnation, disapproval, fault-finding, nit-picking (*inf*), knocking (*inf*). 2 objection, stricture, slating (*inf*), panning (*inf*), brickbat (*inf*). 3 appraisal, analysis, review, critique, notice, write-up (*inf*). 4 judgment, evaluation, assessment, appreciation, analysis, interpretation, exposition.

criticize *verb* 1 censure, condemn, denounce, find fault with, pick holes in (*inf*), knock (*inf*), slate (*inf*), pan (*inf*). 2 judge, evaluate, appraise, analyse, comment on, examine, review.

critique *noun* evaluation, assessment, appraisal, analysis, commentary, interpretation, exposition, review.

croak *verb* 1 squawk, caw. 2 rasp, wheeze, gasp, murmur.

crockery *noun* pottery, earthenware, china, tableware, dishes.

crone *noun* hag, witch, old woman, old bat (*inf*).

crony *noun* friend, pal (*inf*), mate (*inf*), associate, ally, sidekick (*inf*).

crook *noun* 1 criminal, rogue, villain, thief, swindler, cheat. 2 bend, angle, hook, bow, curve, turn.
➤*verb* 1 bend, flex, angle, hook, bow. 2 curve, turn, twist, wind.

crooked *adj* 1 bent, hooked, curved, twisting, winding, zigzag, warped, distorted, lopsided, askew. 2 dishonest, fraudulent, corrupt, bent (*inf*), criminal, illegal, dubious, shady (*inf*).

croon *verb* sing, warble, hum.

crop *noun* 1 yield, produce, fruits, harvest, vintage. 2 batch, lot, group. 3 gullet, throat, craw, maw.
➤*verb* 1 cut, trim, clip, shear. 2 harvest, gather, cut, mow.

crop up happen, occur, take place, arise, turn up, emerge.

cross *noun* 1 crucifix, rood. 2 hybrid, mongrel, crossbreed. 3 blend, amalgam, combination, mixture.
➤*verb* 1 go across, pass over, traverse, ford. 2 span, bridge, crisscross, interweave, lace. 3 intersect, meet. 4 delete, strike out, cancel, eliminate. 5 hybridize, interbreed, crossbreed, mongrelize, cross-pollinate, mix, blend. 6 hinder, impede, obstruct, frustrate, thwart, oppose.
➤*adj* 1 angry, annoyed, vexed, upset, put out. 2 bad-tempered, ill-humoured, irritable, irascible, crusty, crotchety (*inf*), cantankerous, grumpy.

cross-examine *verb* interrogate, question, cross-question, quiz, grill (*inf*).

crossing *noun* 1 junction, intersection, crossroads. 2 zebra crossing, pelican crossing, subway, underpass. 3 journey, trip, sail, passage.

crosswise *adv* crossways, diagonally, obliquely, athwart, transversely, across, over.

crotch *noun* 1 crutch, groin. 2 angle, fork.

crotchety *adj* cross, irritable, peevish, fractious, bad-tempered, ill-humoured, irascible, cantankerous.

crouch *verb* squat, kneel, stoop, hunker down, bend, cower.

crow *verb* 1 gloat, exult, triumph, rejoice. 2 boast, brag, show off, swagger, strut.

crowd *noun* 1 throng, mob, multitude, herd, flock, assembly, gathering. 2 majority, masses, populace, general public, common people, hoi polloi, rabble. 3 group, bunch, gang, lot, set. 4 spectators, audience, turnout, gate.
➤*verb* 1 cluster, huddle, press, pack. 2 gather, assemble, congregate, mass, throng, flock. 3 cram, pack, stuff, jam, squeeze. 4 fill, pack, congest, throng. 5 push, shove, jostle, elbow.

crowded *adj* 1 packed, full, overflowing, jam-packed (*inf*), congested, swarming. 2 busy, full.

crown noun **1** diadem, coronet, tiara. **2** circlet, wreath, garland. **3** award, reward, prize, trophy, laurels, honour. **4** sovereign, monarch, ruler, king, queen, royalty. **5** top, apex, brow, crest, summit, peak. **6** acme, zenith, pinnacle, peak, culmination, height, climax.
➤verb **1** invest, install, enthrone, anoint. **2** complete, finish, conclude, round off, consummate, perfect. **3** top, cap, surmount.

crucial adj **1** critical, decisive, central, key, pivotal, essential, urgent, pressing. **2** all-important, imperative, momentous, high-priority.

crucify verb **1** execute, put to death, nail to a cross. **2** persecute, torture, torment. **3** defeat, thrash, trounce. **4** mock, ridicule, attack, tear to pieces (inf), criticize, slam (inf).

crude adj **1** rude, vulgar, bawdy, smutty, gross, offensive, coarse, uncouth. **2** raw, natural, unrefined, unprocessed. **3** primitive, simple, makeshift, rough-and-ready, inexpert, amateurish.

cruel adj **1** savage, brutal, inhuman, cold-blooded, sadistic, merciless, heartless, unfeeling, callous. **2** unpleasant, painful, distressing, harrowing, harsh, severe, bitter.

cruelty noun savagery, barbarity, brutality, inhumanity, sadism, harshness, callousness, malice.

cruise noun sail, voyage, trip, holiday.
➤verb sail, travel, journey, voyage.

crumb noun scrap, morsel, bit, shred, particle, grain, atom, iota.

crumble verb **1** grind, pulverize, comminute, granulate, break up, fragment. **2** collapse, break down, disintegrate, fall to pieces, fade away.

crummy adj inferior, third-rate, poor, pathetic (inf), shoddy, grotty (inf).

crumple verb **1** rumple, ruffle, wrinkle, crease, crush, crinkle. **2** collapse, fall, break down, go to pieces, cave in.

crunch verb munch, gnaw, chew, champ, grind, crush.
➤noun crisis, crux, test, moment of truth.

crusade noun campaign, mission, movement, cause, struggle, drive.
➤verb campaign, fight, battle, struggle, push, advocate.

crush verb **1** squeeze, press, squash, compress, crumple. **2** grind, pulverize, powder, crumble, pulp, mash, pound. **3** overwhelm, overcome, subdue, suppress, quash, defeat, conquer.
➤noun **1** crowd, throng, pack, press, congestion. **2** infatuation, passion, love, fancy.

crust noun **1** top, lid, topping. **2** incrustation, exterior, shell, casing.

crusty adj bad-tempered, crabby, cantankerous, surly, curt, gruff, brusque.

crux noun heart, core, nucleus, nub, essence.

cry verb **1** sob, weep, wail, bawl, howl, whimper, lament, keen. **2** call, shout, yell, scream, shriek, exclaim.
➤noun **1** sob, weep, tears, lamentation. **2** exclamation, ejaculation. **3** call, shout, yell, scream, shriek, roar. **4** plea, petition, appeal, request, demand, call.

cry off 1 call off, cancel. **2** withdraw, back out, change one's mind.

cry out for need, require, want, demand, call for.

crypt noun vault, tomb, burial chamber, sepulchre.

cryptic adj **1** secret, hidden, occult, esoteric, arcane, recondite. **2** obscure, vague, enigmatic, mysterious, ambiguous, equivocal.

cub noun offspring, young, pup, whelp.

cubbyhole noun compartment, pigeon-hole, slot, recess, niche.

cube noun dice, hexahedron.

cuddle verb **1** hug, embrace, clasp, hold, caress, pet. **2** snuggle, nestle.

cuddly adj cuddlesome, lovable, soft, plump, warm, cosy.

cudgel noun club, bludgeon, cosh, truncheon, stick, shillelagh.
➤verb beat, batter, drub, club, bludgeon, cosh.

cue noun signal, sign, nod, hint, reminder, prompt.

cuff[1] *noun* **off the cuff** impromptu, extempore, ad lib, off the top of one's head (*inf*).

cuff[2] *verb* hit, strike, box, slap, smack, knock.
➤*noun* hit, blow, slap, smack.

cuisine *noun* cookery, cooking, food, fare.

cul-de-sac *noun* dead end, blind alley, no through road, close.

cull *verb* **1** pick, choose, select, gather, collect. **2** kill, slaughter, thin out.

culminate *verb* end, close, conclude, climax, peak.

culpable *adj* blameworthy, to blame, reprehensible, wrong, at fault, guilty, responsible.

culprit *noun* offender, guilty party, wrongdoer, miscreant, criminal, felon.

cult *noun* **1** sect, belief, faith, persuasion, religion, denomination. **2** worship, veneration, adoration, devotion, craze, trend, mania, obsession.

cultivate *verb* **1** farm, till, work, plough, prepare, fertilize, sow. **2** plant, sow, grow, raise, produce. **3** improve, better, develop, refine, enrich, enlighten, educate, train. **4** court, woo, curry favour with, butter up (*inf*), suck up to (*inf*), pursue, get in with (*inf*).

cultivated *adj* cultured, refined, civilized, enlightened, educated, erudite, sophisticated, urbane, discerning.

cultural *adj* **1** artistic, intellectual, educational, edifying, enlightening, civilizing. **2** national, traditional, ethnic, folk.

culture *noun* **1** refinement, cultivation, sophistication, urbanity, taste, discernment, education, enlightenment, edification. **2** civilization, society, way of life, lifestyle, customs, traditions, habits, mores. **3** arts, humanities, intellectual pursuits. **4** growing, production, cultivation, farming, agriculture.

cultured *adj* cultivated, refined, genteel, civilized, enlightened, educated, intellectual, highbrow, artistic, sophisticated.

culvert *noun* channel, conduit, passage, drain, sewer, watercourse.

cumbersome *adj* awkward, clumsy, unwieldy, bulky, heavy, large, unmanageable.

cumulative *adj* collective, aggregate, increasing, accruing, growing, mounting.

cunning *adj* **1** artful, crafty, sly, wily, shrewd, canny, devious, calculating. **2** ingenious, resourceful, inventive, imaginative, clever, deft, dexterous.
➤*noun* **1** artfulness, craftiness, slyness, wiliness, guile, trickery, shrewdness, subtlety. **2** ingenuity, resourcefulness, inventiveness, skill, art, dexterity.

cup *noun* mug, beaker, tankard, chalice, goblet, trophy.

cupboard *noun* cabinet, locker, closet.

cupidity *noun* greed, avarice, acquisitiveness, rapacity, covetousness, desire, yearning, avidity.

cur *noun* **1** dog, hound, mongrel, mutt (*inf*). **2** scoundrel, rogue, blackguard, villain, cad, rotter (*inf*).

curative *adj* healing, restorative, remedial, therapeutic, medicinal.

curator *noun* custodian, keeper, caretaker, conservator.

curb *verb* restrain, check, control, suppress, contain, restrict, moderate.
➤*noun* restraint, check, control, limit, restriction, constraint.

curdle *verb* separate, coagulate, clot, go sour, turn.

cure *verb* **1** heal, restore, make better, make well. **2** heal, treat, alleviate, relieve. **3** remedy, correct, rectify. **4** preserve, dry, salt, smoke.
➤*noun* **1** treatment, therapy, antidote, remedy, medicine, drug. **2** healing, restoration, recovery. **3** panacea, cure-all, remedy, antidote.

curio *noun* curiosity, novelty, objet d'art, bibelot, knick-knack.

curiosity *noun* **1** inquisitiveness, prying, nosiness (*inf*), meddling, interference. **2** curio, novelty, oddity, rarity, phenomenon, freak, spectacle, wonder.

curious *adj* **1** inquiring, questioning, interested, searching. **2** inquisitive, prying, nosy (*inf*), meddlesome, interfering. **3** odd, strange, funny, weird, extraordinary, unusual, exotic, novel.

curl verb **1** wave, kink, crimp, frizz. **2** twist, wind, coil, spiral, twine, wreathe, loop, curve.
➤*noun* **1** wave, kink, ringlet, lock, tress. **2** coil, spiral, whorl, curlicue, loop.

curly adj curled, wavy, kinky, permed, crimped, frizzy.

currency noun **1** money, legal tender, cash, specie. **2** acceptance, popularity, vogue, prevalence, circulation.

current adj **1** present, ongoing, in progress, existing, up-to-date, contemporary. **2** accepted, widespread, general, common, popular, prevailing, in circulation.
➤*noun* **1** flow, stream. **2** drift, trend, tendency, course.

curriculum noun syllabus, course of study, programme.

curse noun **1** oath, expletive, swearword, four-letter word (*inf*), profanity, obscenity. **2** charm, spell, jinx, voodoo, imprecation, anathema, incantation, malediction. **3** scourge, bane, blight, evil, affliction, trouble, plague, misfortune, calamity.
➤*verb* **1** swear, blaspheme, use bad language. **2** jinx, voodoo, denounce, excommunicate, damn, blast (*inf*). **3** scourge, blight, afflict, trouble, plague, beset.

cursed adj accursed, confounded, wretched, damnable, blasted (*inf*), abominable, execrable, devilish, infernal.

cursory adj superficial, perfunctory, summary, hasty, quick, brief, desultory, fleeting.

curt adj brusque, abrupt, terse, short, brief, blunt, rude, gruff.

curtail verb shorten, cut short, truncate, abridge, cut, dock, pare, prune, reduce, decrease, restrict, limit.

curtain noun **1** hanging, screen, drape, blind. **2** veil, cloak, mantle, screen, cover, shield.
➤*verb* conceal, screen, veil, cloak, shroud, shield.

curtsy noun bob, genuflection.

curvaceous adj shapely, well-rounded, buxom, voluptuous.

curvature noun curve, concavity, convexity, flexure.

curve verb bend, arc, arch, vault, bow, turn, wind, curl.
➤*noun* bend, arc, arch, camber, bow, curl, crescent, curvature.

cushion noun **1** pad, squab, bolster, hassock, headrest. **2** buffer, shock absorber.
➤*verb* **1** lessen, soften, deaden, muffle, dampen, absorb, suppress. **2** protect, shield, bolster, brace.

cushy adj easy, undemanding, soft, comfortable.

custodian noun guardian, protector, keeper, curator, conservator, caretaker.

custody noun **1** care, protection, keeping, safekeeping, charge, guardianship, trusteeship, surveillance. **2** confinement, imprisonment, incarceration, captivity, detention.

custom noun **1** convention, tradition, institution, practice, ritual, rite, ceremony. **2** usage, procedure, formality, policy, rule. **3** habit, routine, wont, practice, way, style. **4** duty, tariff, toll, levy, tax. **5** trade, business, patronage, goodwill.

customary adj usual, habitual, wonted, accustomed, routine, conventional, traditional, established, normal, usual.

customer noun client, patron, regular (*inf*), shopper, consumer.

customize verb adapt, modify, convert, alter, tailor.

cut verb **1** slash, slit, nick, pierce, penetrate, incise. **2** lacerate, gash, wound. **3** slice, carve, hack, chop, divide, cleave, sever, trim, clip, shear, mow, prune. **4** whittle, hew, sculpt, carve, chisel, engrave. **5** reduce, lower, decrease, prune, slash. **6** shorten, abridge, curtail, truncate, edit, condense. **7** break, stop, discontinue, interrupt. **8** cross, intersect, meet. **9** snub, ignore, cold-shoulder, rebuff, cut dead (*inf*), look right through (*inf*).
➤*noun* **1** wound, gash, laceration. **2** slash, nick, incision. **3** reduction, decrease, retrenchment, economy, saving. **4** share, percentage, slice, piece, ration, quota. **5** style, fashion.
cut back retrench, economize, cut down, rationalize, downsize.
cut down 1 fell, hew, chop down, raze. **2** reduce, lower, decrease, curb, curtail.
cut in interpose, interrupt, butt in, intervene.

cut off 1 block, interrupt, discontinue, stop, suspend, disconnect. **2** isolate, seclude, separate. **3** amputate, sever, chop off, detach, remove.

cut out 1 remove, excise, eliminate, delete, edit out, exclude, drop. **2** stop, desist, abstain from, refrain from, quit (*inf*), pack in (*inf*).

cut up chop, dice, mince, slice, carve, dissect, dismember.

cute *adj* sweet, appealing, winsome, pretty, delightful, charming.

cut out *adj* suited, fitted, qualified, equipped.

cut-price *adj* reduced, discount, bargain, cheap.

cutthroat *adj* ruthless, fierce, keen, competitive, dog-eat-dog (*inf*).

cutting *adj* **1** sharp, keen. **2** trenchant, mordant, incisive, caustic, barbed, scathing, sarcastic, cruel, hurtful, wounding. **3** keen, piercing, biting, bitter, stinging, raw, chill, icy.
➤*noun* clipping, piece, snippet, excerpt, extract, clip.

cycle *noun* circle, revolution, rotation, round, series, sequence, order, rota.

cynic *noun* **1** sceptic, doubter, misanthrope, scoffer, mocker. **2** pessimist, doomster, wet blanket (*inf*).

cyst *noun* sac, vesicle, blister, bleb, wen.

dab verb **1** pat, tap, press, touch. **2** daub, spot.
➤noun **1** spot, drop, daub, bit. **2** pat, tap, touch.

dabble verb **1** dip, paddle, splash, wet. **2** potter, tinker, toy, play at, dip into.

dab hand noun expert, master, ace (inf).

daft adj silly, foolish, stupid, idiotic, crazy, absurd, senseless, potty (inf), crackpot (inf), crackers (inf), nuts (inf), nutty (inf).

dagger noun dirk, stiletto, poniard, knife.

daily adj diurnal, quotidian, circadian, regular, routine.
➤adv every day, day by day, day after day.

dainty adj **1** delicate, fine, exquisite, petite. **2** elegant, refined, exquisite, beautiful. **3** fastidious, particular, fussy, finicky, choosy.
➤noun delicacy, titbit.

dais noun platform, rostrum, stage, podium.

dale noun valley, dell, dingle, glen.

dally verb **1** dawdle, loiter, linger, dilly-dally, delay, waste time, hang around. **2** flirt, fool around. **3** trifle, toy, play.

dam noun barrage, barrier, barricade.
➤verb block, confine, obstruct, staunch, stem.

damage noun **1** harm, injury, hurt, impairment, loss, destruction, devastation, ruin. **2** compensation, reparation, indemnity, costs.

➤verb **1** harm, hurt, injure, impair, mar, spoil, vandalize, devastate, ruin, wreck, deface. **2** harm, injure.

dame noun **1** lady, peeress, baroness. **2** matron, dowager.

damn verb **1** condemn, denounce, censure, criticize, abuse, inveigh against, slate (inf), slam (inf), knock (inf), pan (inf). **2** curse, swear, blaspheme, cuss (inf). **3** doom, sentence, condemn, excommunicate, anathematize.
➤noun jot, whit, hoot (inf), brass farthing (inf).

damnable adj **1** abominable, vile, detestable, despicable, atrocious. **2** cursed, accursed.

damnation noun condemnation, perdition, doom, excommunication, anathema.

damned adj confounded, accursed, infernal, abominable, detestable, blasted (inf), darned (inf).

damning adj incriminating, condemning, conclusive.

damp adj moist, wet, dank, humid, clammy, soggy.
➤noun dampness, moisture, humidity, wetness, clamminess, dankness.
➤verb **1** moisten, dampen, wet. **2** discourage, restrain, moderate, dull, deaden, muffle. **3** extinguish, stifle, smother, bank.

dampen verb **1** damp, wet, moisten. **2** moderate, restrain, dull, deaden, stifle, discourage, put a damper on.

damper noun put a damper on dampen, discourage, restrain.

damsel noun girl, maiden, maid, young lady.

dance verb **1** sway, jig, whirl, pirouette, shake a leg (inf). **2** caper, skip, hop, jig, prance, frisk, frolic, gambol, play, flicker, twinkle, sparkle.
➤noun ball, disco, hop (inf), knees-up (inf).

dandle verb dance, bounce, rock, cradle.

dandy noun beau, fop, man about town.
➤adj fine, excellent, splendid, great.

danger noun **1** peril, risk, jeopardy. **2** threat, menace, hazard.

dangerous adj **1** perilous, risky, hazardous, unsafe, precarious. **2** threatening, menacing, harmful, ominous.

dangle *verb* **1** hang, swing, droop, trail. **2** hang, suspend, brandish, wave. **3** flaunt, hold out.

dank *adj* damp, clammy, moist, wet.

dapper *adj* smart, spruce, elegant, well-groomed, natty (*inf*).

dapple *verb* mottle, mark, dot, fleck, spot, speckle.

dare *verb* **1** challenge, provoke, goad, taunt. **2** risk, venture, attempt, presume.
➤*noun* challenge, provocation, ultimatum.

daredevil *noun* desperado, madcap, adventurer, stunt man.

daring *adj* bold, brave, adventurous, audacious, intrepid, fearless, rash, reckless, daredevil, death-defying.
➤*noun* boldness, audacity, bravery, intrepidity, nerve, guts (*inf*), temerity, rashness, recklessness.

dark *adj* **1** dim, unlit, shadowy, murky, overcast, dusky. **2** black, swarthy. **3** rich, full, sombre. **4** dismal, sad, gloomy, cheerless, bleak, grim. **5** secret, hidden, abstruse, profound, unfathomable, obscure, mysterious, enigmatic, occult, arcane. **6** evil, wicked, vile, atrocious, hellish, sinister, threatening, forbidding, ominous, menacing.
➤*noun* **1** darkness, dimness, blackness, gloom, obscurity. **2** twilight, dusk, evening, night.

darken *verb* **1** dim, obscure, eclipse, overshadow, blacken. **2** deject, depress, dishearten, discourage, oppress.

darling *noun* **1** dear, dearest, sweetheart, beloved, pet, love, honey, sweetie (*inf*). **2** favourite, pet, apple of one's eye, blue-eyed boy (*inf*).
➤*adj* **1** dear, dearest, beloved, precious, adored, pet, favourite. **2** charming, lovely, sweet, adorable, cute.

darn *verb* mend, repair, sew up.
➤*noun* mend, patch, repair.

dart *verb* dash, rush, sprint, shoot, fly, run, tear.
➤*noun* **1** arrow, bolt. **2** rush, dash, run, sprint.

dash *verb* **1** rush, run, dart, hurry, tear, fly, bolt, sprint. **2** hurl, throw, fling, smash, shatter, splinter. **3** frustrate, thwart, ruin, destroy, shatter.

➤*noun* **1** run, dart, rush, sprint. **2** tinge, touch, trace, soupçon, hint, drop, bit. **3** élan, flair, verve, panache, vigour, gusto.

dashing *adj* **1** lively, spirited, energetic, impetuous, gallant, daring. **2** smart, stylish, elegant, sporty, chic, dapper.

dastard *noun* coward, craven, cur, worm.

dastardly *adj* cowardly, craven, base, despicable, low, underhand.

data *pl noun* **1** facts, figures, information, material, statistics. **2** input.

date *noun* **1** age, period, era, epoch, time. **2** appointment, engagement, meeting, assignation, rendezvous. **3** partner, escort, boyfriend, girlfriend.
➤*verb* **1** become old-fashioned, become obsolete. **2** go out with, take out, go steady with. **3** come from, go back to.
to date until now, up to now, so far.

dated *adj* old-fashioned, outdated, outmoded, passé, old hat (*inf*).

daub *verb* smear, paint, plaster, cover, spatter.
➤*noun* smear, smudge, spot, blotch.

daunt *verb* intimidate, unnerve, dismay, scare, frighten, cow, overawe, discourage, deter.

dauntless *adj* undaunted, bold, daring, brave, fearless.

dawdle *verb* **1** lag, loiter, dillydally (*inf*). **2** waste time, idle, potter.

dawn *noun* **1** daybreak, sunrise, sunup, first light, cockcrow. **2** beginning, start, rise, appearance, birth, genesis, emergence.
➤*verb* **1** break, grow light. **2** begin, start, appear, emerge, come into being. **3** occur to, come to, strike.

day *noun* **1** daylight, daytime. **2** generation, age, period, era, time.
day in day out continually, endlessly, relentlessly, persistently.

daybreak *noun* dawn, sunrise, sunup, first light.

daydream *noun* **1** reverie, musing, woolgathering, fancy, vision. **2** pipe dream, figment, fantasy.
➤*verb* dream, muse, fantasize, imagine.

daylight *noun* **1** sunshine, sunlight, day, daytime. **2** dawn, daybreak, sunrise.

daze *verb* stun, stupefy, shock, bewilder, dumbfound, astound, flabbergast (*inf*).
➤*noun* stupor, trance.

dazzle *verb* 1 blind, bedazzle. 2 stun, amaze, impress, overwhelm, bowl over (*inf*), knock out (*inf*).
➤*noun* brilliance, splendour, glare, glitter.

dead *adj* 1 lifeless, defunct, deceased, late, departed, passed away, passed on. 2 insensitive, unresponsive, unsympathetic, cold, indifferent. 3 numb, paralysed, gone to sleep. 4 obsolete, lapsed, disused, irrelevant, ineffective, inactive, inert, not working. 5 dull, boring, uninteresting, quiet. 6 complete, utter, downright, total, absolute.
➤*noun* midst, depths.
➤*adv* completely, utterly, totally, exactly, absolutely, thoroughly.
dead on one's feet tired out, exhausted, worn out, dead beat (*inf*).

deaden *verb* 1 damp, dampen, muffle. 2 reduce, diminish, alleviate, mitigate, dull. 3 numb, anaesthetize, paralyse.

deadlock *noun* stalemate, impasse, standstill, stop.

deadly *adj* 1 mortal, fatal, lethal, death-dealing, malignant, poisonous, venomous. 2 implacable, mortal, murderous, remorseless, unrelenting. 3 intense, serious, extreme, great. 4 accurate, true, unerring, unfailing. 5 boring, dull, tedious, monotonous.
➤*adv* extremely, utterly, totally, absolutely.

deaf *adj* 1 hard of hearing. 2 heedless, unmoved, indifferent.

deafening *adj* earsplitting, piercing, thunderous.

deal *verb* 1 distribute, hand out. 2 distribute, dispense, mete, dole out, give out, divide, share out. 3 give, deliver, administer. 4 trade, traffic, do business.
➤*noun* agreement, bargain, transaction, contract, understanding.
deal with 1 handle, sort out, tackle, see to, take care of. 2 manage, cope with. 3 be about, discuss, concern.

dealer *noun* 1 merchant, salesperson, trader, wholesaler, retailer. 2 trafficker, pusher.

dealings *pl noun* business, trade, relations, contact.

dear *adj* 1 beloved, adored, cherished, treasured, intimate, close. 2 expensive, costly, exorbitant, pricey (*inf*), steep (*inf*).
➤*noun* darling, beloved, love, sweetheart, precious, pet.
➤*adv* at great cost, at a high price.

dearly *adv* 1 greatly, deeply, fondly, devotedly. 2 at great cost, at a high price.

dearth *noun* lack, scarcity, shortage, famine.

death *noun* 1 decease, demise, passing. 2 end, cessation, close, disappearance, extinction, destruction.

deathless *adj* immortal, undying, everlasting, eternal.

deathly *adj* ghastly, pale, wan, haggard.

debacle *noun* ruin, failure, fiasco, disaster, catastrophe, rout, defeat.

debar *verb* bar, exclude, blackball, forbid, prevent, disallow, stop.

debase *verb* 1 degrade, shame, drag down, disgrace, dishonour, demean, discredit. 2 reduce, devalue, depreciate, adulterate.

debatable *adj* disputable, questionable, undecided, moot, controversial, doubtful.

debate *verb* 1 discuss, deliberate, consider, kick around (*inf*). 2 dispute, argue, wrangle.
➤*noun* 1 discussion, deliberation, exchange of views. 2 argument, dispute, controversy, wrangle.

debauch *verb* deprave, corrupt, deflower, seduce, lead astray.
➤*noun* spree, orgy, binge (*inf*).

debauchery *noun* depravity, immorality, dissipation, licentiousness, promiscuity, intemperance, profligacy, excess.

debilitate *verb* enfeeble, weaken, enervate, undermine.

debility *noun* feebleness, weakness, enervation, exhaustion, frailty.

debonair *adj* 1 suave, urbane, elegant, smart. 2 nonchalant, jaunty, carefree, breezy, light-hearted.

debris *noun* 1 remains, rubble, wreckage. 2 rubbish, litter.

debt *noun* 1 liability, obligation, debit, arrears, score. 2 indebtedness, obligation.

debunk verb expose, mock, puncture, deflate.

debut noun beginning, launch, premiere.

decadence noun 1 wane, fall, decline, decay. 2 dissipation, debauchery, immorality, depravity, licentiousness.

decadent adj 1 dissolute, dissipated, immoral, corrupt, debauched, licentious. 2 decaying, declining, waning.

decamp verb abscond, bolt, make off, scarper (inf), do a runner (inf), do a moonlight flit (inf).

decant verb pour, pour out, draw off.

decapitate verb behead, guillotine, execute.

decay verb 1 rot, decompose, spoil, perish, go bad. 2 decline, fail, deteriorate, wither, dwindle.
➤noun 1 rot, decomposition, caries. 2 decomposition, spoilage, deterioration, degeneration, decline, wane.

decease noun death, demise, passing, end.

deceased adj dead, departed, late.

deceit noun 1 fraud, deception, duplicity, cheating, trickery, double-dealing. 2 trick, ruse, stratagem, wile, imposture, fraud, swindle. 3 deceitfulness, craftiness, dishonesty.

deceitful adj dishonest, false, insincere, two-faced, double-dealing, cheating, sly, crafty, scheming.

deceive verb mislead, cheat, trick, fool, dupe, hoodwink, con (inf), double-cross (inf), take in (inf), lead up the garden path (inf).

decelerate verb slow, slow down, brake, reduce speed.

decency noun propriety, modesty, decorum, respectability.

decent adj 1 respectable, proper, seemly, decorous, modest. 2 nice, kind, helpful, generous, thoughtful. 3 adequate, fair, reasonable, not bad, acceptable.

deception noun 1 deceit, fraud, cheating, duplicity, double-dealing, hypocrisy, trickery, deceitfulness, dishonesty. 2 trick, ruse, wile, fraud, dodge, swindle, hoax, bluff.

deceptive adj misleading, deceiving, unreliable, ambiguous.

decide verb 1 make up one's mind, come to a decision, resolve, conclude. 2 determine, adjudicate, judge, rule. 3 determine, settle.

decided adj 1 definite, certain, unquestionable, unambiguous, distinct, clear, categorical. 2 determined, resolute, firm, decisive.

decipher verb 1 decode, translate. 2 solve, unravel, explain, understand, read, crack (inf).

decision noun 1 resolution, conclusion, verdict, judgment, ruling. 2 determination, resolution. 3 determination, resolution, resolve, decisiveness.

decisive adj 1 conclusive, definitive, categorical, final. 2 critical, crucial, significant. 3 resolute, decided, determined, firm.

deck verb adorn, decorate, clothe, dress, dress up.

declaim verb 1 orate, make a speech, hold forth. 2 rant, spout, sound off (inf).

declamation noun 1 oratory, grandiloquence. 2 oration, speech, harangue, tirade.

declamatory adj rhetorical, oratorical, high-flown, grandiloquent, bombastic, pompous.

declaration noun 1 proclamation, announcement, statement, decree, pronouncement. 2 statement, affirmation, avowal, assertion, acknowledgment.

declare verb 1 proclaim, announce, broadcast, make known. 2 state, affirm, avow, assert, profess, allege, testify, certify.

decline verb 1 refuse, turn down, reject. 2 decrease, diminish, lessen, dwindle, fall off. 3 weaken, degenerate, decay, deteriorate. 4 descend, sink, dip, slope. 5 fade, wane, ebb.
➤noun decrease, diminution, waning, deterioration, fall, degeneration, decay.

declivity noun descent, downward slope.

decompose verb 1 rot, go bad, putrefy, decay. 2 break down, break up, separate, resolve.

decor noun decoration, furnishings, furniture, colour scheme.

decorate *verb* **1** ornament, embellish, adorn, deck, trim. **2** paint, wallpaper, paper, renovate, do up (*inf*). **3** cite, honour.

decoration *noun* **1** embellishment, ornamentation, beautification. **2** adornment, trimming, ornament, flourish, frill. **3** medal, order, award, honour, ribbon.

decorous *adj* proper, seemly, decent, becoming, tasteful, appropriate, well-behaved, genteel, respectable.

decorum *noun* propriety, seemliness, decency, etiquette, good taste, good manners, respectability.

decoy *verb* lure, entice, tempt, inveigle, entrap.
➤*noun* lure, enticement, temptation, bait.

decrease *verb* lessen, diminish, reduce, dwindle, decline, lower, fall, drop, let up, slacken, ease, cut down, cut back, taper off, shrink.
➤*noun* lessening, diminution, reduction, decline, lowering, slackening, fall, cutback, shrinkage.

decree *noun* **1** edict, order, command, law, act, rule, regulation, injunction. **2** judgment, decision, ruling, verdict.
➤*verb* order, command, ordain, rule, enact, lay down, decide.

decrement *noun* decrease, diminution, reduction.

decrepit *adj* **1** infirm, feeble, weak, frail, old, doddering. **2** dilapidated, ramshackle, broken-down, run-down, rickety. **3** worn-out, in bad condition, superannuated.

decry *verb* disparage, deprecate, run down, abuse, criticize, condemn, denounce, knock (*inf*).

dedicate *verb* **1** devote, pledge, commit, consecrate. **2** consecrate, sanctify, hallow. **3** inscribe, address.

dedicated *adj* **1** committed, devoted, enthusiastic, zealous. **2** customized, custom-built, exclusive.

dedication *noun* **1** devotion, commitment, enthusiasm, loyalty. **2** devotion, consecration, sanctification. **3** inscription, message.

deduce *verb* conclude, infer, gather, conclude.

deduct *verb* subtract, take away, take off.

deduction *noun* **1** conclusion, inference, finding. **2** inference, reasoning. **3** subtraction, taking-off. **4** reduction, allowance, discount.

deed *noun* **1** action, act, undertaking. **2** feat, exploit, achievement. **3** title, document, instrument.

deem *verb* consider, judge, regard, think, believe.

deep *adj* **1** profound, bottomless, yawning, extensive. **2** low, low-pitched, bass, resonant, rich. **3** dark, rich, intense, vivid, full. **4** grave, great, intense, extreme, profound, heartfelt, ardent, fervent. **5** abstruse, obscure, difficult, mysterious, unfathomable, arcane. **6** learned, intellectual, perceptive, penetrating, shrewd, wise.
➤*adv* a long way, far.
➤*noun* **1** sea, ocean, main. **2** middle, midst, dead.

deepen *verb* hollow out, excavate, dredge, intensify, grow, add to, heighten.

deface *verb* disfigure, mar, spoil, damage, vandalize.

de facto *adj* real, actual, existing.
➤*adv* in fact, in effect, actually.

defame *verb* cast aspersions on, insult, slander, libel, denigrate, run down, vilify, discredit, dishonour, malign, abuse, smear.

default *noun* failure, omission, neglect, non-payment.
➤*verb* fail, evade, cheat, welsh (*inf*).

defaulter *noun* offender, non-payer, cheat, welsher (*inf*).

defeat *verb* **1** beat, conquer, vanquish, overcome, rout, overwhelm, crush, thrash, trounce, clobber (*inf*), wipe the floor with (*inf*). **2** thwart, foil, frustrate, prevent, ruin, dash.
➤*noun* **1** conquest, overthrow, rout. **2** reverse, setback, failure.

defecate *verb* excrete, move one's bowels, pass a motion, do a poo (*inf*), shit (*sl*), crap (*sl*).

defect *noun* **1** imperfection, flaw, fault, blemish, failing, weakness, shortcoming. **2** deficiency, lack, insufficiency.
➤*verb* desert, change sides, turn traitor, apostatize.

defective *adj* faulty, imperfect, flawed, broken, out of order, not working.

defence *noun* **1** resistance, protection, safeguarding. **2** guard, safeguard, shelter, cover, shield, bulwark, rampart. **3** vindication, justification, excuse, explanation, extenuation, rebuttal, apology.

defend *verb* **1** protect, guard, watch over, safeguard, shield, screen, shelter, secure, fortify. **2** support, endorse, uphold, maintain, justify, make a case for, champion, stand by, stick up for.

defendant *noun* accused, offender, prisoner, respondent.

defensible *adj* tenable, justifiable, pardonable, excusable, secure, unassailable, impregnable.

defensive *adj* **1** protective, protecting, shielding. **2** oversensitive, self-justifying, self-defensive, prickly (*inf*).

defer¹ *verb* delay, postpone, put off, adjourn, suspend, hold over, put on ice (*inf*).

defer² *verb* yield, submit, bow, surrender, give in, give way.

deference *noun* **1** respect, regard, honour, reverence, homage. **2** compliance, submission, acquiescence, obedience.

deferential *adj* **1** respectful, reverential, submissive, compliant, obedient. **2** obsequious, subservient, fawning.

defiance *noun* resistance, opposition, insubordination, disobedience, insolence, rebelliousness, recalcitrance.

deficiency *noun* **1** lack, shortage, insufficiency, scarcity, inadequacy. **2** weakness, failing, shortcoming, fault, defect.

deficient *adj* **1** lacking, short of, wanting, inadequate. **2** defective, imperfect, flawed.

deficit *noun* **1** shortage, shortfall, deficiency. **2** arrears, debt.

defile *verb* pollute, soil, dirty, sully, taint, corrupt, desecrate.

define *verb* **1** describe, explain, identify, specify, determine, fix. **2** delineate, outline. **3** demarcate, limit, establish, fix.

definite *adj* **1** certain, fixed, settled, positive, guaranteed. **2** clear, clear-cut, marked, obvious, unmistakable.

definition *noun* **1** description, explanation, meaning. **2** distinctness, clarity, sharpness, focus. **3** demarcation, determination, specification.

definitive *adj* **1** final, conclusive, decisive. **2** authoritative, exhaustive, ultimate, best.

deflate *verb* **1** collapse, let down, empty, puncture. **2** chasten, humble, humiliate, squash. **3** reduce, devalue, depreciate.

deflect *verb* divert, sidetrack, turn aside, glance off, ricochet.

deflection *noun* deviation, refraction, ricochet.

deflower *verb* rape, ravish, violate, debauch, seduce.

deform *verb* **1** disfigure, deface, mar. **2** distort, buckle, warp, misshape, twist.

deformed *adj* misshapen, disfigured, ugly, twisted, warped.

deformity *noun* **1** malformation, abnormality, misshapenness, distortion. **2** disfigurement, blemish, defect.

defraud *verb* cheat, swindle, fleece, rob, rook (*inf*), rip off (*inf*), con (*inf*).

defray *verb* meet, pay, cover.

deft *adj* adept, dextrous, skilful, handy, nimble.

defunct *adj* **1** dead, gone, deceased, departed. **2** gone, finished, obsolete.

defy *verb* **1** flout, disregard, ignore, disobey, resist, oppose. **2** challenge, dare. **3** elude, frustrate, baffle.

degenerate *verb* deteriorate, lapse, slip, go downhill (*inf*), go the dogs (*inf*).
➤*adj* dissolute, debauched, depraved, corrupt, decadent, immoral, wicked.
➤*noun* deviant, pervert, reprobate.

degradation *noun* **1** misery, shame, disgrace, ignominy, squalor, degeneracy. **2** degeneration, abasement, debasement. **3** decline, deterioration, decadence.

degrade *verb* **1** dishonour, demean, disgrace, discredit, lower, cheapen. **2** demote, downgrade.

degrading *adj* demeaning, dishonourable, shameful, humiliating.

degree noun **1** extent, measure, amount, intensity, level. **2** stage, step, rung, level, point. **3** grade, rank, class, standing, status.
by degrees gradually, step by step, little by little.

dehydrate verb **1** dry, desiccate. **2** dry up, parch.

deify verb **1** elevate, exalt, apotheosize. **2** worship, revere, venerate, idolize.

deign verb condescend, stoop, see fit.

deity noun **1** god, goddess, immortal, divinity. **2** God, supreme being.

dejected adj downcast, despondent, downhearted, disheartened, depressed, sad, unhappy, miserable, glum.

dejection noun despondency, misery, wretchedness, depression, unhappiness, sadness, gloom, sorrow.

delay verb **1** defer, postpone, put off, adjourn, hold over. **2** hold up, slow down, set back, detain. **3** procrastinate, stall, dawdle, dillydally (inf).
➤noun **1** deferment, postponement, suspension, procrastination, dawdling. **2** holdup, interruption, stoppage, pause, break, hiatus.

delectable adj **1** delicious, luscious, tasty, appetizing, scrumptious (inf). **2** delightful, attractive, charming.

delectation noun delight, enjoyment, pleasure, gratification.

delegate noun representative, envoy, ambassador, spokesperson.
➤verb **1** give, transfer, entrust, assign. **2** depute, appoint, commission.

delegation noun **1** deputation, embassy, mission. **2** assignment, transference, commissioning, appointment, nomination.

delete verb cross out, strike out, cancel, rub out, erase, cut.

deleterious adj harmful, noxious, injurious, disadvantageous, damaging, detrimental.

deliberate verb consider, ponder, reflect, discuss, debate.
➤adj **1** intentional, premeditated, calculated, planned, conscious, studied. **2** careful, considered, painstaking, methodical. **3** unhurried, slow, measured.

deliberation noun **1** consideration, reflection, thought, study. **2** discussion, debate, consultation. **3** care, thoughtfulness, steadiness.

delicacy noun **1** fineness, daintiness, lightness, exquisiteness, grace. **2** fragility, flimsiness, frailty. **3** tact, sensitivity, consideration. **4** fastidiousness, prudishness, squeamishness. **5** discrimination, refinement, finesse, subtlety. **6** morsel, titbit, treat.

delicate adj **1** fine, dainty, exquisite, graceful. **2** flimsy, fragile. **2** weak, frail, infirm, sickly. **3** faint, muted, pale, subdued, subtle, pastel. **4** tricky, difficult, ticklish. **5** sensitive, tactful, diplomatic, considerate, discreet. **6** fastidious, finicky, choosy. **7** sensitive, accurate, precise.

delicious adj **1** tasty, appetizing, luscious, mouth-watering, scrumptious (inf), yummy (inf). **2** delightful, exquisite, enchanting.

delight verb **1** enjoy, love, like, relish, savour. **2** gladden, charm, enchant, thrill, please, gratify.
➤noun joy, happiness, gladness, pleasure, bliss, ecstasy, elation.

delighted adj happy, glad, pleased, elated, overjoyed, ecstatic, thrilled, over the moon (inf), tickled pink (inf).

delightful adj pleasing, pleasant, charming, enchanting, captivating, attractive, lovely, agreeable, enjoyable.

delineate verb **1** portray, draw, sketch, outline. **2** describe, set out.

delinquency noun **1** crime, offence, misdeed. **2** misconduct, wrongdoing. **3** dereliction, omission, negligence.

delinquent noun offender, wrongdoer, criminal, lawbreaker, culprit.
➤adj offending, criminal, lawbreaking.

delirious adj **1** raving, incoherent, hallucinating. **2** ecstatic, carried away, euphoric.

delirium noun **1** raving, incoherence, hallucination, fever. **2** frenzy, hysteria, euphoria.

deliver verb **1** take, send, convey, transport, carry. **2** utter, speak, read, declare, announce. **3** transfer, entrust, commit, hand over, surrender, yield, cede. **4** release, liberate, set free, rescue, save, redeem. **5** deal, inflict, strike.

deliverance *noun* release, liberation, rescue, salvation, redemption.

delivery *noun* **1** transport, transportation, conveyance, carriage, distribution, surrender, handing over. **2** consignment, shipment. **3** articulation, enunciation, diction. **4** childbirth, confinement, labour.

delude *verb* deceive, mislead, dupe, cheat, fool, trick, take in, hoodwink, bamboozle (*inf*), take for a ride (*inf*).

deluge *noun* **1** flood, inundation. **2** downpour, cloudburst. **3** flood, torrent, avalanche.
➤ *verb* **1** flood, inundate, overwhelm, engulf. **2** flood, inundate, overwhelm, swamp.

delusion *noun* **1** illusion, hallucination, mirage, misapprehension, misconception. **2** deception, trickery, fraud.

delusive *adj* misleading, deceptive, illusory.

de luxe *adj* luxurious, luxury, select, superior.

delve *verb* **1** dig, burrow, search, rummage. **2** examine, investigate, probe.

demagogue *noun* orator, agitator, rabble-rouser, populist.

demand *verb* **1** ask, claim, insist on, order, command, enjoin. **2** call for, press for, insist on. **3** require, need, call for.
➤ *noun* **1** request, claim, order, command, charge, behest, insistence. **2** need, call, desire.
in demand sought-after, requested, popular, fashionable.

demanding *adj* **1** challenging, difficult, hard, exacting. **2** insistent, nagging, trying.

demarcation *noun* delimitation, marking off, definition, separation.

demean *verb* lower, humble, abase.

demeanour *noun* behaviour, bearing, manner.

demented *adj* insane, deranged, unhinged, unbalanced, mad, crazy, out of one's mind, touched.

demerit *noun* fault, defect, blemish, misdeed.

demesne *noun* **1** estate, land, property. **2** realm, domain.

demise *noun* **1** death, decease, passing. **2** end, collapse, downfall. **3** transfer, conveyance.

democracy *noun* **1** representative government, popular government. **2** republic, commonwealth.

democratic *adj* egalitarian, republican, popular, representative.

demolish *verb* **1** knock down, destroy, level, flatten, bulldoze. **2** refute, discredit, explode.

demolition *noun* destruction, flattening, bulldozing, refutation, discrediting.

demon *noun* **1** fiend, devil, evil spirit. **2** fiend, devil. **3** fiend, wizard, ace (*inf*).

demonic *adj* **1** demoniacal, evil, fiendish, diabolical, devilish. **2** frenzied, frenetic, frantic, maniacal, demented.

demonstrable *adj* verifiable, provable.

demonstrate *verb* **1** show, prove, establish. **2** show, display, exhibit, indicate, manifest. **3** explain, illustrate, show, teach. **4** protest, march, rally.

demonstration *noun* **1** display, exhibition, evidence, proof, indication, explanation, presentation, illustration. **2** march, rally, protest, demo (*inf*).

demonstrative *adj* **1** emotional, loving, warm, affectionate. **2** illustrative, indicative, symptomatic.

demoralize *verb* dishearten, dispirit, discourage, depress, daunt.

demote *verb* downgrade, degrade, depose, relegate.

demur *verb* object, protest, be reluctant, balk.
➤ *noun* objection, protest, hesitation, misgivings, reservations.

demure *adj* **1** modest, diffident, shy, bashful, decorous. **2** coy, priggish, prim.

den *noun* **1** lair, hole, hideaway. **2** haunt, meeting place, dive (*inf*), joint (*inf*). **3** study, retreat, sanctum.

denial *noun* **1** contradiction, negation, disclaimer. **2** refusal, rejection, withholding. **3** disowning, repudiation, rejection.

denigrate *verb* disparage, defame, run down, blacken, vilify, speak ill of.

deprave

denizen *noun* citizen, resident, inhabitant, dweller.

denominate *verb* designate, name, call.

denomination *noun* 1 church, faith, religion, sect. 2 grade, unit, value. 3 designation, name, title.

denote *verb* 1 indicate, show, be evidence of. 2 symbolize, stand for, represent, signify.

denouement *noun* climax, culmination, conclusion, resolution.

denounce *verb* 1 condemn, criticize, decry, censure. 2 accuse, charge, inform against, incriminate.

dense *adj* 1 compacted, solid, thick, packed, crowded. 2 stupid, dull, slow, thick (*inf*).

density *noun* thickness, solidity, bulk, compactness.

dent *verb* depress, press in, hollow. ➤*noun* hollow, depression, pit, impression.

denude *verb* strip, divest, bare, expose.

denunciation *noun* condemnation, criticism, censure, accusation.

deny *verb* 1 contradict, dispute, disprove, disclaim, negate. 2 refuse, withhold, forbid, veto. 3 reject, turn down. 4 disown, renounce, disavow, repudiate.

deodorant *noun* antiperspirant, deodorizer.

depart *verb* 1 go, leave, go away, take one's leave, exit, withdraw, retreat, retire, make tracks (*inf*), hit the road (*inf*). 2 leave, start, set out, set off. 3 deviate, diverge, differ, digress.

departed *adj* dead, deceased, late.

department *noun* 1 branch, division, section, agency, unit. 2 sphere, realm, responsibility, speciality.

departure *noun* exit, leaving, setting out, setting off, withdrawal, deviation, divergence, difference, innovation.

depend *verb* 1 rely on, count on, bank on. 2 be dependent, hinge on, turn on, be subject to. 3 rely on, trust in, have confidence in, put one's faith in.

dependable *adj* reliable, trusty, trustworthy, unfailing.

dependant *noun* child, minor, relative.

dependence *noun* 1 reliance, trust, faith, confidence. 2 reliance, need, helplessness, vulnerability, defencelessness. 3 reliance, connection, relationship. 4 addiction, habit, abuse.

dependency *noun* 1 reliance, dependence, addiction. 2 colony, province, protectorate.

dependent *adj* 1 reliant, clinging, helpless, weak, vulnerable. 2 contingent, conditional, subject to.

depict *verb* 1 portray, sketch, draw, paint, represent. 2 portray, describe, relate, recount, tell, record.

deplete *verb* 1 empty, drain. 2 decrease, lessen, reduce, expend, spend, consume.

deplorable *adj* 1 lamentable, miserable, unfortunate, sad, pitiable, wretched. 2 scandalous, disgraceful, shameful, reprehensible.

deplore *verb* lament, regret, grieve for, condemn, criticize, censure.

deploy *verb* 1 arrange, position, dispose, spread out. 2 use, utilize.

deport *verb* 1 expel, exile, expatriate. 2 conduct, behave, comport.

deportment *noun* carriage, bearing, posture, stance.

depose *verb* 1 dethrone, oust, unseat. 2 declare, testify, swear.

deposit *verb* 1 lay, lay down, drop, place, put down, set down. 2 save, store, put away, put by. 3 bank, pay in. 4 settle, precipitate. ➤*noun* 1 sediment, layer, silt, alluvium, dregs. 2 down payment, part payment, retainer, instalment.

depositary *noun* trustee, guardian, fiduciary.

deposition *noun* 1 affidavit, statement, testimony. 2 dethronement, ousting, removal.

depository *noun* depot, store, storehouse, repository.

depot *noun* 1 storehouse, warehouse, depository, repository. 2 station, terminus, garage.

deprave *verb* corrupt, debauch, pervert, lead astray, debase.

deprecate *verb* 1 deplore, condemn, criticize, frown on, disapprove of. 2 disparage, denigrate, depreciate.

deprecatory *adj* 1 apologetic, regretful, rueful. 2 disapproving, condemnatory, critical.

depreciate *verb* 1 devalue, devaluate, deflate. 2 lose value, fall. 3 disparage, deprecate, denigrate, decry, belittle.

depredation *noun* plunder, pillage, despoliation, robbery.

depress *verb* 1 deject, sadden, dishearten, discourage, cast down, upset, get down (*inf*). 2 weaken, debilitate, exhaust, drain. 3 depreciate, devalue, reduce, bring down. 4 press down, push down.

depressant *noun* sedative, tranquillizer, calmative, downer (*inf*).

depressed *adj* 1 dejected, dispirited, discouraged, disheartened, unhappy, low, despondent, down, downcast, gloomy, pessimistic, miserable, sad. 2 poor, disadvantaged, deprived, run-down.

depression *noun* 1 dejection, gloom, despondency, melancholy, sadness, unhappiness, hopelessness, discouragement, pessimism, the blues (*inf*). 2 indentation, hollow, pit, dent, dimple, basin, valley. 3 recession, slump, crash, downturn.

deprivation *noun* 1 denial, withdrawal, withholding, expropriation, confiscation, dispossession, robbing. 2 hardship, destitution, privation, penury, need.

deprive *verb* 1 deny, refuse, withhold. 2 take away, strip, dispossess, rob.

deprived *adj* poor, destitute, impoverished, needy, underprivileged, disadvantaged.

depth *noun* 1 deepness, profundity. 2 wisdom, insight, sagacity, understanding, profundity, penetration, discernment. 3 intensity, strength, passion, fervour, gravity, seriousness, severity. 4 intensity, vividness, richness, warmth. 5 deep, bowels, bottom, middle, midst.

deputation *noun* delegation, embassy, legation, commission, committee.

depute *verb* 1 appoint, nominate, designate, second, authorize. 2 delegate, transfer, assign.

deputize *verb* stand in for, replace, substitute for, represent, understudy, cover for.

deputy *noun* substitute, stand-in, agent, representative, surrogate, locum, assistant, second-in-command.

deranged *adj* mad, crazy, demented, distracted, disturbed, berserk, unhinged, unbalanced, insane, touched, loony (*inf*), barking (*inf*), cracked (*inf*), nuts (*inf*).

derelict *adj* 1 abandoned, neglected, dilapidated, crumbling, ruined, ramshackle, run-down. 2 remiss, negligent, irresponsible, lax, careless.
➤*noun* tramp, vagrant, beggar, down-and-out.

dereliction *noun* 1 dilapidation, ruin, disrepair. 2 neglect, negligence, carelessness, slackness, laxity, remissness, omission. 3 fault, failure.

deride *verb* mock, ridicule, scoff at, laugh at, scorn, disdain, sneer at, poke fun at, make fun of, insult, abuse, lampoon, pooh-pooh (*inf*).

derision *noun* mockery, ridicule, scorn, sneering, contempt, disdain, disrespect, abuse.

derisive *adj* scornful, contemptuous, disdainful, mocking, scoffing, jeering, sarcastic, irreverent.

derisory *adj* 1 laughable, absurd, ridiculous, contemptible, insulting, tiny, inadequate, paltry. 2 derisive, mocking, scornful.

derivation *noun* 1 source, origin, root, spring, beginnings, ancestry, descent, extraction. 2 acquisition, extraction, collection, obtaining, gathering, deduction. 3 etymology.

derivative *adj* 1 derived, acquired, borrowed, deduced, inferred. 2 unoriginal, hackneyed, secondhand, trite, imitative, copied, plagiaristic, rehashed (*inf*).
➤*noun* offshoot, by-product, spin-off, development.

derive *verb* 1 draw, extract, get, obtain, acquire, elicit, borrow. 2 deduce, infer, follow. 3 originate, arise, proceed, emanate, come, stem, develop.

derogatory *adj* disparaging, critical, insulting, offensive, abusive, disapproving, uncomplimentary, unfavourable, pejorative.

descend *verb* **1** go down, sink, fall, drop, plunge, tumble, swoop, sink, subside, dismount, alight, get down. **2** dip, incline, slope, slant. **3** attack, swoop, pounce, invade. **4** originate, issue, spring, stem. **5** lower oneself, sink, stoop, deteriorate, decline, go downhill (*inf*).

descendant *noun* scion, child, successor.

descent *noun* **1** fall, drop, plunge, dip, decline, deterioration, degeneration. **2** slope, slant, decline, declivity, drop. **3** ancestry, parentage, extraction, stock, heredity, lineage, line, pedigree. **4** source, origin, derivation. **5** attack, assault, incursion, raid, invasion.

describe *verb* **1** portray, depict, draw, outline, detail, explain, tell, narrate, relate, recount, report, define, set out, present, characterize, call, label. **2** mark out, trace, outline, draw.

description *noun* **1** portrayal, depiction, characterization, illustration, account, narrative, relation, report, statement, outline, profile, sketch, portrait. **2** sort, kind, type, variety, category, genre, ilk.

descriptive *adj* **1** expressive, graphic, striking, vivid. **2** illustrative, depictive, explanatory.

descry *verb* discern, make out, distinguish, espy, glimpse, see, spot.

desecrate *verb* **1** profane, violate, blaspheme. **2** profane, defile, despoil, pollute, violate, vandalize.

desert[1] *noun* **1** wilderness, waste, wasteland. **2** wilderness, solitude, void.

desert[2] *verb* **1** abandon, leave, forsake, relinquish, jilt, walk out on, run out on (*inf*). **2** run away, abscond, go AWOL. **3** abandon, renounce, relinquish, give up, forsake, betray, rat on (*inf*).

desert[3] *noun* due, right, reward, retribution, comeuppance.

deserve *verb* earn, merit, be worthy of, be entitled to, justify, qualify for.

deserving *adj* worthy, meritorious, estimable, admirable, creditable, commendable, good.

desiccate *verb* **1** dry, dry up, parch. **2** dehydrate, evaporate, powder.

design *verb* **1** plan, draw, sketch, outline, draft. **2** invent, devise, conceive, think up, formulate, develop. **3** intend, plan, purpose, mean, aim.
➤*noun* **1** plan, sketch, drawing, diagram, outline, pattern, guide, blueprint. **2** style, form, shape, format, arrangement, organization, composition, make-up. **3** motif, pattern, device. **4** plan, plot, scheme, project, intrigue, stratagem. **5** proposal, aim, goal, intention, object, objective, purpose.

designate *verb* **1** call, name, title, entitle, style. **2** appoint, nominate, choose, depute, select, elect.

designation *noun* **1** name, title, denomination, description, label, tag (*inf*). **2** indication, specification, description, appointment, nomination, selection.

designer *noun* inventor, deviser, planner, creator, originator, producer, couturier, stylist.

designing *adj* artful, crafty, sly, scheming, cunning, Machiavellian, underhand, unscrupulous, calculating, insidious, devious.

desirable *adj* **1** profitable, advantageous, beneficial, sought-after, popular, advisable, preferable, expedient, sensible. **2** attractive, fetching, glamorous, seductive, sexy.

desire *verb* **1** wish for, want, long for, covet, crave, hanker after, yearn for, fancy, like, aspire to. **2** ask for, request, demand. **3** want, lust after, fancy (*inf*), have a crush on (*inf*), have the hots for (*inf*).
➤*noun* **1** longing, craving, yearning, wish, want, need, hankering, fancy, inclination, aspiration, appetite, thirst, yen (*inf*), lust, libido, passion, ardour. **2** appeal, request, petition. **3** wish, hope, need, aspiration.

desirous *adj* eager, enthusiastic, keen, longing, itching, wishing, hopeful, ambitious.

desist *verb* stop, cease, break off, halt, pause, refrain, give up, leave off, give over.

desolate *adj* **1** deserted, abandoned, uninhabited, empty, lonely, godforsaken. **2** desert, wild, waste, barren, bare, lifeless. **3** forlorn, forsaken, abandoned, bereft, lonely, friendless, depressed, dejected, brokenhearted, unhappy, grieving, wretched, disconsolate, inconsolable.
➤*verb* **1** destroy, devastate, lay waste, ravage, ruin. **2** depopulate, empty.

3 devastate, overwhelm, upset, depress, dismay, grieve, sadden.

despair *noun* hopelessness, desperation, despondency, gloom, dejection, depression, misery, defeatism, pessimism, resignation.
➤*verb* lose hope, lose heart, resign oneself, give up, give in, throw in the towel.

desperado *noun* bandit, outlaw, brigand, thug, gangster, criminal, cutthroat.

desperate *adj* **1** rash, reckless, headstrong, impetuous, mad, foolhardy, frantic, frenzied, wild, violent. **2** drastic, extreme, frantic, last-ditch, eleventh-hour, do-or-die. **3** grave, serious, critical, urgent, pressing, dire, acute, severe, hopeless, irredeemable. **4** despairing, hopeless, anguished, distraught, desolate, wretched, heartbroken, inconsolable, depressed, suicidal.

desperately *adv* **1** critically, gravely, seriously, severely, badly, dangerously, extremely, dreadfully, frightfully. **2** despairingly, in despair, in desperation, forlornly.

desperation *noun* **1** recklessness, rashness, foolhardiness, panic, frenzy, fury. **2** despair, hopelessness, misery, distress, wretchedness, depression.

despicable *adj* contemptible, low, mean, base, cheap, shabby, ignoble, vile, sordid, reprehensible, disgraceful, infamous, shameful.

despise *verb* scorn, disdain, look down on, spurn, deride, dislike, detest, hate, loathe, shun.

despite *prep* in spite of, notwithstanding, regardless of, in defiance of.

despoil *verb* pillage, plunder, loot, ravage, ransack, sack, devastate, desolate, lay waste.

despondent *adj* depressed, dejected, gloomy, miserable, low, down, downcast, downhearted, wretched, dispirited, discouraged, disheartened, defeatist, down in the dumps (*inf*).

despot *noun* tyrant, autocrat, dictator, absolutist.

dessert *noun* sweet, pudding, pud (*inf*), afters (*inf*).

destination *noun* goal, objective, journey's end, terminus.

destine *verb* **1** direct, schedule, consign, send. **2** fate, doom, ordain, preordain, predestine, mean, intend, set apart, dedicate, designate.

destiny *noun* **1** fate, fortune, future, doom, lot. **2** fate, fortune, chance, luck, the stars, karma, kismet.

destitute *adj* **1** poor, impoverished, poverty-stricken, penniless, insolvent, bankrupt, indigent, penurious, needy, down-and-out, skint (*inf*), broke (*inf*). **2** devoid, bereft, without, deficient, lacking, wanting.

destroy *verb* **1** demolish, raze, dismantle, knock down, pull down, tear down, flatten, level, obliterate, blow up, ruin, wreck, smash, shatter, total (*inf*), trash (*inf*). **2** kill, slay, slaughter, wipe out, annihilate, decimate. **3** put down, put to sleep. **4** ruin, wreck, devastate, shatter, sabotage, neutralize, put an end to, torpedo.

destruction *noun* demolition, ruin, razing, levelling, devastation, havoc, wreckage, vandalism, overthrow, undoing, annihilation, elimination, extermination, liquidation, killing, slaughter.

destructive *adj* **1** damaging, devastating, disastrous, ruinous, catastrophic, detrimental, deleterious, disruptive, harmful, injurious, dangerous, pernicious, noxious. **2** deadly, fatal, lethal. **3** negative, adverse, unfavourable, hostile, unfriendly.

desultory *adj* **1** random, haphazard, spasmodic, fitful. **2** haphazard, aimless, rambling, erratic, vague, undirected, unmethodical, unsystematic, disconnected.

detach *verb* **1** separate, disconnect, uncouple, unfasten, unhitch, remove, tear off, cut off, free, disentangle. **2** sever, separate, disaffiliate, divide. **3** dissociate, separate, cut off, divorce.

detached *adj* **1** separate, unconnected, disconnected, discrete, free-standing, loose, isolated. **2** uninvolved, objective, impartial, unbiased, unprejudiced, disinterested, neutral, unconcerned, dispassionate, indifferent, aloof, clinical.

detachment noun **1** separation, disconnection, uncoupling, unfastening, disentangling, disengagement, severance, removal. **2** objectivity, impartiality, disinterestedness, neutrality, coolness, aloofness, indifference, unconcern. **3** squad, patrol, unit, group, detail, task force.

detail noun **1** particular, item, specific, particularity. **2** fact, component, ingredient, element, point, feature, aspect, circumstance. **3** technicality, minutia, nicety. **4** precision, thoroughness, exactitude. **5** detachment, group, task force.
➤verb **1** list, catalogue, enumerate, particularize, itemize, specify, spell out, point out, set out, recount. **2** appoint, assign, delegate, commission, nominate.
in detail point by point, in depth, at length, comprehensively, fully, thoroughly.

detailed adj complex, elaborate, intricate, involved, circumstantial, comprehensive, exhaustive, thorough, full, in-depth, precise, specific, particular, itemized.

detain verb **1** delay, hold up, retard, slow down, keep, stop. **2** hold, confine, imprison, lock up, arrest.

detect verb **1** discover, perceive, discern, make out, see, spot, notice, sense, scent, smell, hear, identify. **2** discover, expose, reveal, identify, unmask, uncover, unearth, bring to light.

detective noun plain-clothes officer, police officer, private investigator, private eye (inf), sleuth (inf), gumshoe (inf), dick (inf), tec (inf).

detention noun custody, imprisonment, captivity, restraint, arrest.

deter verb **1** discourage, prevent, stop, put off, restrain, dissuade, intimidate, scare off, turn off (inf). **2** discourage, prevent, stop, forestall, restrain, foil, thwart.

detergent noun cleaner, cleanser, soap powder, washing powder, washing-up liquid.
➤adj cleaning, cleansing, purifying.

deteriorate verb decline, degenerate, worsen, get worse, degrade, decay, disintegrate, decompose, spoil, go bad, fall off, lapse, slide, slump, slip, go downhill (inf).

determination noun **1** resolution, resolve, resoluteness, firmness, conviction, single-mindedness, persistence, perseverance, conviction, dedication, drive, doggedness, backbone, tenacity, willpower, grit (inf). **2** resolution, resolve, intention, purpose. **3** decision, judgment, verdict, ruling. **4** settlement, solution, resolution.

determine verb **1** settle, decide, resolve, conclude, clinch (inf). **2** ascertain, detect, find out, identify, discover, establish, calculate, work out. **3** establish, fix, dictate, condition, control, influence, affect, shape.

determined adj resolute, resolved, single-minded, set, fixed, intent, bent, dogged, persevering, persistent, steadfast, stubborn, indomitable, tenacious, strong-willed, strong-minded.

deterrent noun disincentive, repellent, impediment, obstacle, restraint, curb.

detest verb abhor, loathe, abominate, execrate, hate.

detestable adj abhorrent, loathsome, abominable, execrable, hateful, odious, repugnant, repulsive, repellent, obnoxious, vile.

detestation noun abhorrence, loathing, abomination, execration, hate, hatred, aversion, antipathy, disgust.

dethrone verb **1** depose, overthrow. **2** unseat, oust, topple.

detonate verb **1** explode, go off, blow up, burst. **2** explode, trigger, set off, let off.

detour noun diversion, deviation, roundabout way, scenic route.

detract verb diminish, lessen, reduce, take away from, devalue, spoil.

detractor noun enemy, opponent, critic, backbiter, slanderer, muckraker.

detriment noun damage, harm, injury, hurt, loss, disadvantage, prejudice.

detrimental adj damaging, harmful, injurious, deleterious, inimical, prejudicial, disadvantageous, adverse, unfavourable.

detritus noun waste, debris, rubble, remains, ruins, wreckage, refuse, rubbish.

devastate verb **1** desolate, despoil, ravage, lay waste, waste, destroy, demolish, wreck, ruin, trash (inf). **2** overwhelm, shatter, shock, crush, traumatize, knock sideways (inf), knock for six (inf).

devastating *adj* **1** destructive, damaging, ruinous, disastrous, catastrophic, savage, fierce. **2** shattering, overwhelming, shocking, traumatic, horrifying, savage, withering. **3** stunning, dazzling, glamorous, ravishing, gorgeous.

develop *verb* **1** grow, expand, branch out, spread, evolve, improve, progress. **2** mature, blossom, ripen, evolve. **3** foster, nurture, cultivate. **4** elaborate, amplify, expand, supplement, reinforce, work out. **5** begin, start, set in motion, found, institute, establish, invent, design, generate, produce. **6** appear, emerge, ensue, arise, unfold. **7** catch, go down with, pick up, contract.

development *noun* **1** growth, evolution, progress, maturation, expansion, extension, spread, enlargement, elaboration, unfolding, creation, design, invention, establishment. **2** incident, occurrence, event, happening, change. **3** outcome, result, upshot, innovation. **4** block, complex, estate.

deviant *adj* **1** divergent, aberrant, anomalous, abnormal. **2** warped, twisted, perverse, perverted, kinky (*inf*), sick (*inf*). ➤*noun* freak, misfit, pervert, oddball (*inf*), weirdo (*inf*).

deviate *verb* diverge, wander, stray, err, go astray, depart, digress, differ, vary.

deviation *noun* **1** divergence, aberration, departure, variance, abnormality, irregularity, digression, detour, change, shift. **2** deviancy, perversion, eccentricity. **3** difference, disparity, discrepancy.

device *noun* **1** contrivance, contraption, gadget, tool, machine, instrument, implement, apparatus, gizmo (*inf*). **2** ruse, stratagem, plan, plot, scheme, subterfuge, manoeuvre, gambit, machination, trick, ploy, dodge (*inf*). **3** emblem, symbol, motif.

devil *noun* **1** Satan, Lucifer, Beelzebub, Mephistopheles, Prince of Darkness, Evil One, Old Nick (*inf*). **2** demon, fiend, imp, evil spirit. **3** villain, brute, fiend, monster. **4** demon, imp, rascal, scamp, terror, monkey (*inf*). **5** wretch, creature, beggar.

devilish *adj* diabolical, demonic, evil, fiendish, infernal, satanic, wicked, hellish, accursed.

devil-may-care *adj* careless, rash, reckless, impetuous, impulsive, heedless, casual, cavalier, happy-go-lucky, unconcerned.

devious *adj* **1** underhand, deceitful, dishonest, artful, crafty, sly, scheming, calculating, conniving, double-dealing, treacherous, evasive, shifty, insincere, slippery (*inf*), tricky (*inf*). **2** underhand, surreptitious, tortuous, confusing. **3** rambling, circuitous, roundabout, indirect, crooked.

devise *verb* **1** invent, contrive, formulate, work out, prepare, put together, design, concoct, come up with, think up, cook up (*inf*). **2** plan, plot, contrive.

devoid *adj* lacking, without, destitute, bereft, void, empty.

devolve *verb* **1** delegate, transfer, deliver, entrust. **2** pass, fall to.

devote *verb* **1** dedicate, consecrate, allocate, reserve, set aside. **2** dedicate, consecrate, commit, pledge.

devoted *adj* **1** faithful, loyal, true, staunch, steadfast, unswerving. **2** loving, affectionate, caring, attentive, ardent. **3** dedicated, committed, tireless, zealous.

devotee *noun* **1** enthusiast, fan, admirer, aficionado, follower, supporter, addict. **2** disciple, votary, zealot.

devotion *noun* **1** dedication, commitment. **2** attachment, affection, love, fondness, adoration, loyalty, allegiance, fidelity, support, zeal, ardour, passion, enthusiasm. **3** devoutness, piety, faith. **4** prayer, worship, religious observance.

devour *verb* **1** consume, eat, eat up, gobble, guzzle, bolt, wolf (*inf*), scoff (*inf*), polish off (*inf*). **2** destroy, consume, engulf, swallow up. **3** take in, drink in, enjoy, appreciate.

devout *adj* **1** pious, godly, religious, committed, practising, church-going. **2** sincere, genuine, heartfelt, earnest, serious, wholehearted.

dexterity *noun* **1** skill, skilfulness, adroitness, handiness, expertise, proficiency, mastery, ingenuity, facility, finesse, deftness. **2** ingenuity, inventiveness, resourcefulness, shrewdness, astuteness.

dexterous *adj* **1** deft, adroit, adept, skilled, skilful, clever, expert, accomplished, proficient, nimble-fingered, handy, nifty (*inf*). **2** clever, shrewd, astute, smart, ingenious, inventive, resourceful.

diabolical *adj* **1** devilish, demonic, satanic, fiendish, infernal, hellish, evil, wicked. **2** outrageous, appalling, atrocious, monstrous, dreadful, abominable, shocking, nasty, awful.

diadem *noun* crown, coronet, circlet, tiara.

diagnose *verb* identify, determine, recognize, isolate, detect.

diagnosis *noun* **1** identification, recognition, detection, explanation, interpretation, opinion, judgment, conclusion. **2** investigation, analysis, scrutiny.

diagonal *adj* slanting, sloping, oblique, angled.

diagram *noun* **1** plan, chart, drawing, representation, outline, cutaway. **2** figure, table, graph.

dial *verb* telephone, phone, ring, call.

dialect *noun* language, idiom, vernacular, patois, accent.

dialectic *noun* argument, argumentation, analysis, logic, reasoning, ratiocination.

dialogue *noun* **1** conversation, colloquy, talk, duologue, conference, exchange, debate, discussion, tête-à-tête. **2** lines, script, conversation.

diaphanous *adj* translucent, gauzy, gossamer, filmy, sheer, see-through, transparent.

diarrhoea *noun* loose motions, dysentery, gippy tummy (*inf*), Montezuma's revenge (*inf*), Delhi belly (*inf*), the runs (*inf*).

diary *noun* **1** journal, log, chronicle, daybook, yearbook. **2** personal organizer, appointment book.

diatribe *noun* tirade, harangue, tongue-lashing, philippic, attack, onslaught, denunciation.

dicey *adj* risky, chancy, unpredictable, uncertain, tricky, iffy (*inf*), dodgy (*inf*).

dicky *adj* unsound, unsteady, unstable, unreliable.

dictate *verb* **1** read, read out, speak. **2** command, order, ordain, lay down, decree, prescribe, impose.
➤*noun* **1** command, order, injunction, behest, edict, word. **2** rule, precept, principle.

dictator *noun* tyrant, despot, autocrat, oppressor, Big Brother (*inf*).

dictatorship *noun* tyranny, despotism, totalitarianism, authoritarianism, autocracy, absolutism, police state.

diction *noun* **1** speech, enunciation, articulation, intonation, expression, pronunciation, delivery. **2** style, vocabulary, language, phraseology, wording, idiom.

dictionary *noun* lexicon, wordbook, glossary, vocabulary.

dictum *noun* **1** ruling, decree, pronouncement. **2** saying, maxim, utterance.

didactic *adj* **1** instructive, educational, educative, pedagogic, moralistic. **2** prescriptive, pedantic, moralistic.

die *verb* **1** expire, decease, perish, depart this life, pass away, pass on, breathe one's last, peg out (*inf*), snuff it (*inf*), kick the bucket (*inf*), meet one's maker (*inf*), meet one's end (*inf*), pop one's clogs (*inf*). **2** pass, disappear, vanish, finish, come to an end. **3** long, yearn, pine, hunger.

die away *verb* dwindle, fade, die down, wane, peter out, taper off.

die-hard *adj* reactionary, hard-line, conservative, ultraconservative, inflexible, immovable, intransigent, dyed-in-the-wool.
➤*noun* reactionary, hardliner, conservative, ultraconservative, fanatic, intransigent, stick-in-the-mud (*inf*).

diet[1] *noun* **1** food, fare, nourishment, nutrition, sustenance, provisions, menu. **2** fast, regimen, regime, abstinence.
➤*verb* slim, lose weight, watch one's weight, fast, reduce.

diet[2] *noun* parliament, congress, assembly, legislature.

differ *verb* **1** vary, diverge, contrast. **2** argue, disagree, demur, dissent, conflict, oppose, take issue, clash, quarrel, fall out.

difference *noun* **1** dissimilarity, dissimilitude, unlikeness, contrast, imbalance, diversity, variation, variety. **2** distinction, disparity, discrepancy, divergence, imbalance, gap. **3** disagreement, argument, dispute, misunderstanding, conflict, quarrel, row, set-to, contretemps, tiff. **4** balance, remainder, residue, rest.

different adj 1 dissimilar, unlike, contrasting, disparate, divergent, incompatible, inconsistent, conflicting, opposed, poles apart (inf). 2 distinct, separate, individual, discrete. 3 other, various, diverse, miscellaneous, sundry, assorted. 4 unusual, unique, original, distinctive, special, rare, remarkable, extraordinary, out of the ordinary, new, novel, unconventional, atypical, anomalous, bizarre, strange, odd.

differentiate verb distinguish, contrast, set apart, set off, separate, mark off, individualize, tell apart, discriminate, tell the difference.

difficult adj 1 hard, arduous, demanding, uphill, tough, backbreaking, gruelling, tiring, taxing, demanding, formidable, complex, complicated, abstruse, obscure, dark, baffling, perplexing, intractable, knotty, thorny, ticklish, problematical. 2 awkward, uncooperative, fractious, refractory, perverse, obstinate, stubborn, troublesome, trying, demanding, fastidious, fussy, finicky, perfectionist, particular.

difficulty noun 1 arduousness, laboriousness, awkwardness, hardness, complexity, complicatedness, intricacy, delicacy, knottiness, obscurity, abstruseness, challenge, strain, struggle, trouble. 2 problem, trouble, predicament, hole (inf), fix (inf), mess (inf), spot (inf), jam (inf), pickle (inf), hot water (inf). 3 problem, obstacle, hitch, hurdle, stumbling-block, hindrance, impediment, complication, snag.

diffident adj shy, bashful, timid, meek, modest, humble, nervous, hesitant, apprehensive, reluctant, unsure, tentative, self-conscious, self-effacing, inhibited, unassertive, unassuming.

diffuse verb spread, scatter, disperse, send out, radiate, broadcast, transmit.
➤adj 1 scattered, disconnected, dispersed, spread out. 2 wordy, verbose, long-winded, waffling, rambling, wandering, digressive, roundabout, imprecise, vague.

diffusion noun dispersion, scattering, spread, spreading, dissemination, radiation, broadcasting, transmission.

dig verb 1 excavate, gouge, grub, burrow, hollow out, tunnel, quarry, mine. 2 turn over, break up, work, till, cultivate. 3 poke, prod, jab, punch. 4 investigate, delve, probe, go into.
➤noun 1 poke, prod, jab, punch. 2 gibe, taunt, jeer, sneer, insinuation, slur.

dig up 1 discover, find, retrieve, track down, uncover, bring to light, unearth. 2 disinter, exhume.

digest verb 1 assimilate, absorb, ingest, process, convert, break down, macerate. 2 take in, absorb, grasp, assimilate, understand, ponder, think about.
➤noun abridgment, summary, outline, abstract, synopsis, précis.

digestion noun assimilation, absorption, conversion, breaking down, maceration, understanding, consideration.

dignified adj stately, grand, august, noble, distinguished, lofty, solemn, formal, ceremonious, composed, self-possessed.

dignify verb distinguish, adorn, grace, honour, elevate, raise.

dignitary noun notable, notability, worthy, personage, celebrity, luminary, leading light, public figure, VIP (inf), high-up (inf), big shot (inf), top brass (inf).

dignity noun 1 nobility, stateliness, grandeur, augustness, impressiveness, solemnity, ceremoniousness, formality. 2 standing, rank, status, station. 3 pride, self-respect, self-importance, self-esteem, amour propre. 4 gravity, poise, composure, self-possession, collectedness.

digress verb deviate, wander, stray, depart, ramble, meander, go off at a tangent, get off the subject.

dilapidated adj ramshackle, tumbledown, rickety, ruined, broken-down, run-down, neglected, decayed, decaying, crumbling.

dilate verb 1 expand, swell, bloat, distend. 2 widen, broaden, spread, expand. 3 develop, amplify, enlarge, elaborate, expatiate.

dilation noun expansion, enlargement, spread, widening, broadening, distension, development, amplification, expatiation.

dilatory adj 1 dawdling, slow, lackadaisical, loitering, tardy, behindhand, procrastinating. 2 delaying, postponing, stalling, time-wasting.

dilemma noun quandary, predicament, difficulty, problem, plight, vicious circle, fix (inf), spot (inf), no-win situation (inf), catch 22 (inf).

dilettante *noun* dabbler, amateur, trifler, potterer.

diligence *noun* assiduity, application, industry, industriousness, care, conscientiousness, attention, perseverance, thoroughness, concentration.

diligent *adj* assiduous, industrious, hardworking, painstaking, meticulous, thorough, attentive, careful, persevering, conscientious, dedicated, zealous, tireless.

dillydally *verb* loiter, lag, dawdle, dally, delay, procrastinate, hesitate, haver, dither, waste time, shilly-shally (*inf*).

dilute *verb* 1 adulterate, attenuate, water down, thin, weaken. 2 diminish, lessen, reduce, moderate, tone down, soften, weaken.

dim *adj* 1 dark, dusky, shadowy, sombre, crepuscular, gloomy, dull, grey, muted, lacklustre, feeble. 2 obscure, indistinct, vague, blurred, blurry, unclear, foggy, hazy, fuzzy, faint, weak, ill-defined, pale, shadowy. 3 weak, faint, bleary. 4 stupid, dense, slow, slow-witted, dumb (*inf*), thick (*inf*), dozy (*inf*).
➤*verb* lower, turn down, shade, obscure, darken, dull, weaken, cloud, blur, fade, pale.

dimension *noun* 1 extent, size, magnitude, proportions, measurements, volume, bulk, mass. 2 length, width, breadth, height, depth. 3 size, extent, magnitude, scope, scale, range, importance. 4 aspect, facet, element, factor, feature.

diminish *verb* 1 lessen, decrease, reduce, lower, shrink, contract, shorten, cut, curtail, narrow, constrict. 2 disparage, belittle, devalue, denigrate, demean, cheapen. 3 decline, wane, die away, fade, dwindle, taper off, ebb, slacken.

diminution *noun* decrease, reduction, lessening, lowering, contraction, constriction, shrinkage, shortening, abatement, slackening, weakening, decline, wane.

diminutive *adj* tiny, minute, small, small-scale, little, miniature, mini, wee, pygmy, midget, bantam, dwarf, slight, petite, undersized, teeny (*inf*), pint-sized (*inf*).

din *noun* noise, clamour, uproar, racket, row, commotion, tumult, shouting, yelling, hullabaloo, hubbub.

din into instil, drive home, drum into, inculcate.

dine *verb* eat, feed, feast, banquet.

dingy *adj* 1 dirty, grimy, soiled, faded, discoloured, dull, murky, drab, dreary. 2 shabby, squalid, seedy, tacky (*inf*).

dinky *adj* dainty, fine, small, cute, neat.

dinner *noun* 1 supper, lunch, tea, main meal, evening meal. 2 meal, feast, banquet, spread (*inf*), blowout (*inf*).

dint *noun* **by dint of** by means of, by virtue of, by force of.

dip *verb* 1 plunge, duck, submerge, immerse, dunk, steep, rinse. 2 set, sink, drop, disappear. 3 sink, drop, fall, decrease, decline, slump. 4 slope, descend, go down, fall, drop.
➤*noun* 1 incline, declivity, descent, slope. 2 hollow, depression, dent, concavity, basin. 3 decline, fall, drop, slump, blip. 4 plunge, ducking, dunking, immersion. 5 bathe, swim, paddle. 6 sauce, cream, dressing, mixture, concoction.

dip into 1 skim, browse, look at, leaf through, look through, glance at, flick through, thumb through. 2 spend, draw on, use.

diplomacy *noun* 1 statecraft, statesmanship, international relations. 2 tact, tactfulness, discretion, subtlety, delicacy, finesse, sensitivity, politeness, judiciousness, savoir faire.

diplomat *noun* 1 ambassador, envoy, emissary, plenipotentiary, consul, attaché, chargé d'affaires. 2 diplomatist, mediator, conciliator, arbitrator, negotiator, peacemaker.

diplomatic *adj* 1 tactful, discreet, sensitive, judicious, careful, polite, delicate, subtle. 2 consular, ambassadorial.

dire *adj* 1 dreadful, terrible, frightful, appalling, awful, atrocious, disastrous, catastrophic, wretched, woeful. 2 ominous, portentous, sinister, pessimistic, unfavourable, inauspicious, unpropitious. 3 desperate, urgent, pressing, vital, compelling, drastic, crying, grave, critical.

direct *adj* 1 straight, unswerving, undeviating, uninterrupted, unbroken, non-stop, through. 2 straightforward, honest, frank, candid, blunt, outspoken, open, forthright, sincere, plainspoken, straight,

explicit, clear, up-front (*inf*). **3** immediate, firsthand, face-to-face, personal.
➤*verb* **1** manage, control, run, organize, orchestrate, govern, lead, command, regulate, administer, superintend, oversee, supervise, handle, mastermind.
2 command, order, charge, enjoin, bid, instruct. **3** guide, lead, conduct, point, show, accompany, escort, usher. **4** aim, point, level, fix, focus, train, pilot, steer, turn. **5** address, aim, destine, mean.

direction *noun* **1** way, course, route, road, path, track, bearing, trend, tendency, aim, tack, bent. **2** management, control, command, conduct, administration, government, regulation, orchestration, running, handling, leadership, supervision, overseeing, masterminding, guidance. **3** order, command, instruction, guideline, recommendation, injunction, directive.

directive *noun* direction, command, instruction, order, regulation, ruling, dictate, decree, injunction.

directly *adv* **1** immediately, straightaway, at once, without delay, instantly, quickly, promptly, shortly, soon, as soon as possible, in a moment, presently. **2** straight, right.

director *noun* **1** manager, chairperson, chair, executive, chief executive, administrator. **2** manager, governor, head, chief, principal, president, chair, chairperson, superintendent, supervisor, overseer, controller, organizer, leader, boss (*inf*), gaffer (*inf*). **3** producer.

dirge *noun* requiem, elegy, lament, threnody.

dirt *noun* **1** filth, grime, muck, mire, mud, sludge, slime, dust, soot, gunge (*inf*), gunk (*inf*), crap (*inf*), crud (*inf*), grot (*inf*). **2** excrement, muck, poo (*inf*), crap (*inf*), shit (*sl*). **3** earth, soil, clay, mud, loam, dust. **4** indecency, obscenity, pornography, lewdness, coarseness, bawdiness, ribaldry, smut (*inf*), sleaze (*inf*). **5** gossip, scandal, rumour, talk, slander, libel, revelations.

dirty *adj* **1** filthy, grimy, grubby, soiled, muddy, mucky, messy, bedraggled, scruffy, shabby, dusty, sooty, greasy, slimy, nasty, unwashed, foul, contaminated, polluted, stained, spotted, unclean, unhygienic, grotty (*inf*), cruddy (*inf*). **2** obscene, inde-

cent, blue, coarse, filthy, smutty, salacious, prurient, lewd, bawdy, ribald, risqué, suggestive, pornographic, raunchy (*inf*), sleazy (*inf*). **3** mean, low, contemptible, despicable, cowardly, shabby, unscrupulous, deceitful, dishonest, treacherous. **4** abject, base, vile, nasty, sordid, squalid, ignominious. **5** unsporting, unfair. **6** malevolent, threatening, angry, resentful, bitter, indignant, annoyed, offended. **7** stormy, bad, nasty, foul, squally, rainy, unpleasant.
➤*verb* soil, begrime, foul, stain, smear, smirch, besmirch, smudge, splash, spatter, spot, mess up, spoil, muddy, blacken, contaminate, pollute, sully, tarnish, defile.

disability *noun* **1** handicap, defect, impairment, infirmity, affliction, disorder. **2** incapacity, incapability, infirmity, impotency, weakness, powerlessness.

disable *verb* **1** cripple, lame, incapacitate, paralyse, immobilize, handicap, impair, damage, hamstring. **2** immobilize, cripple, put out of action.

disabled *adj* **1** challenged, handicapped, incapacitated, impaired, crippled, lame, maimed, paralysed, bedridden. **2** crippled, out of action.

disabuse *verb* undeceive, enlighten, put straight, disillusion.

disadvantage *noun* **1** drawback, burden, hindrance, liability, impediment, handicap, limitation, inconvenience, trouble, nuisance, weakness, weak point, weak link, Achilles' heel, minus, downside. **2** damage, injury, loss, harm, detriment, prejudice.

disadvantaged *adj* deprived, poor, underprivileged, discriminated against, struggling.

disadvantageous *adj* detrimental, prejudicial, deleterious, injurious, damaging, harmful, adverse, unfavourable.

disaffected *adj* disloyal, estranged, alienated, dissatisfied, discontented, disgruntled, mutinous, rebellious.

disagree *verb* **1** dissent, take issue, dispute, object, differ, argue, squabble, fight, wrangle, quarrel, fall out (*inf*). **2** conflict, clash, differ, vary, be at variance. **3** upset, make unwell, nauseate, sicken.

disagreeable *adj* **1** unpleasant, distasteful, offensive, nasty, horrible, horrid,

obnoxious, objectionable, odious, repugnant, repulsive, revolting, abominable, disgusting, nauseating, yucky (*inf*).
2 unfriendly, churlish, surly, awkward, difficult, contrary, bad-tempered, ill-tempered, ill-natured, peevish, irritable, cross, rude, impolite, nasty, unpleasant, grouchy (*inf*), tetchy (*inf*).

disagreement *noun* **1** argument, dispute, squabble, wrangle, quarrel, row, altercation, conflict, clash, controversy, misunderstanding, disharmony, friction, discord, strife, division, falling-out (*inf*), tiff (*inf*).
2 discrepancy, difference, disparity, divergence, incompatibility, inconsistency, conflict, clash, incongruity.

disallow *verb* **1** forbid, prohibit, ban, proscribe, bar, veto. **2** reject, repudiate, dismiss.

disappear *verb* **1** vanish, fade, dissolve, evaporate, dematerialize. **2** go, depart, exit, decamp, abscond, scarper (*inf*), make oneself scarce (*inf*). **3** vanish, end, cease, pass, die out.

disappoint *verb* fail, let down, frustrate, foil, thwart, balk, disillusion, disenchant, depress, dispirit, discourage, dishearten, dismay, sadden, upset.

disappointed *adj* let down, frustrated, thwarted, foiled, upset, saddened, deflated, disheartened, downcast, depressed, dispirited, chagrined, disillusioned, dissatisfied.

disappointment *noun* **1** sadness, regret, dissatisfaction, discontent, disenchantment, disillusionment, chagrin, mortification, vexation, discouragement, frustration, thwarting, foiling, defeat, failure, comedown. **2** letdown, setback, blow, non-event, anticlimax, damp squib (*inf*).

disapprobation *noun* disapproval, displeasure, dislike, censure, blame, condemnation.

disapproval *noun* disapprobation, displeasure, dissatisfaction, blame, censure, criticism, condemnation, denunciation, deprecation, rejection, veto, objection, dislike, stick (*inf*).

disapprove *verb* **1** censure, blame, condemn, frown on, take a dim view of, deplore, deprecate, find unacceptable, object to, take exception to, criticize, dislike. **2** reject, disallow, veto, turn down.

disarm *verb* **1** unarm, deprive of weapons. **2** lay down one's arms, demilitarize, demobilize, disband. **3** win over, charm, persuade, set at ease, mollify, placate.

disarmament *noun* demilitarization, demobilization, arms control, arms reduction, arms limitation.

disarming *adj* charming, winning, persuasive, conciliatory.

disarrange *verb* disorder, confuse, disorganize, disturb, upset, untidy, mess up, mix up, muddle, jumble, dishevel, rumple, tousle.

disarray *noun* disorder, confusion, disunity, indiscipline, disorganization, muddle, jumble, mess, chaos, shambles, state.

disaster *noun* **1** calamity, catastrophe, cataclysm, act of God. **2** calamity, tragedy, blow, misfortune, reverse, setback. **3** fiasco, failure, debacle, flop (*inf*), washout (*inf*).

disavow *noun* deny, repudiate, gainsay, disclaim, renounce, recant, retract, abjure.

disband *verb* **1** disperse, break up, separate, part company. **2** break up, dismiss, disperse, let go, send home, demobilize.

disbelief *noun* unbelief, incredulity, doubt, scepticism, distrust, mistrust, suspicion, rejection.

disbelieve *verb* **1** reject, discount, doubt, question, challenge. **2** doubt, distrust, mistrust.

disburse *verb* spend, pay, expend, lay out, fork out (*inf*), shell out (*inf*).

disc *noun* circle, ring, plate, counter, discus.

discard *verb* reject, abandon, cast aside, throw away, throw out, get rid of, drop, dispense with, jettison, scrap, junk (*inf*), ditch (*inf*).

discern *verb* **1** perceive, descry, make out, identify, recognize, notice, detect, pick up. **2** detect, perceive, identify, distinguish, recognize.

discerning *adj* discriminating, judicious, wise, perceptive, perspicacious, clearsighted, eagle-eyed, sensitive, quick, sharp, penetrating, shrewd.

discharge verb 1 release, free, set free, let go, liberate, acquit, clear. 2 dismiss, cashier, get rid of, fire, sack (inf), boot out (inf), turf out (inf). 3 emit, exude, give off, let off, let out, eject, release, gush, ooze, leak. 4 fire, shoot, let off. 5 perform, execute, carry out, fulfil, accomplish, settle, clear, pay, honour, meet, satisfy.
➤noun 1 liberation, release, acquittal, dismissal, firing, sacking (inf), performance, execution, carrying out, fulfilment, accomplishment, observance, settling, clearance, payment, honouring, satisfaction. 2 emission, secretion, suppuration, pus, flow, leak, ooze, seepage. 3 blast, volley, salvo, fusillade, shot.

disciple noun 1 follower, adherent, partisan, devotee, supporter, believer, student, pupil, convert, proselyte. 2 apostle, follower.

disciplinarian noun authoritarian, hard taskmaster, stickler, martinet.

discipline noun 1 training, routine, drill, exercise, instruction, schooling, coaching. 2 regulation, control, order, orderliness, rule, direction, strictness. 3 self-control, restraint, self-restraint. 4 punishment, chastisement, correction, reprimand, rebuke, reproof, penalty. 5 subject, area, field, course, branch, speciality.
➤verb 1 train, drill, break in, exercise, coach, teach, educate, instruct, school, tutor, prepare. 2 control, restrain, check, curb, govern, regulate. 3 punish, chastise, chasten, correct, reprimand, penalize.

disclaim verb deny, disown, disavow, reject, repudiate, decline, refuse.

disclaimer noun denial, repudiation, disavowal, disowning, rejection.

disclose verb 1 divulge, confess, release, reveal, impart, communicate, broadcast, publish, make known, make public, leak, let slip, blab. 2 expose, lay bare, reveal, uncover, unveil, bring to light.

disclosure noun 1 revelation, exposé, leak, announcement, declaration, confession, admission, avowal. 2 announcement, declaration, release, broadcasting, publication, exposure, discovery, revelation.

discolour verb stain, soil, tarnish, bruise, fade, bleach, wash out, weather.

discomfit verb 1 embarrass, fluster, ruffle, abash, unsettle, perturb, worry, disconcert, rattle (inf), faze (inf). 2 thwart, frustrate, foil, balk, defeat, worst.

discomfort noun pain, soreness, ache, trouble, distress, unease, uneasiness, embarrassment, anxiety, disquiet, worry, restlessness.

discompose verb make uneasy, embarrass, perturb, agitate, fluster, ruffle, unsettle, disturb, upset, disconcert, vex, annoy, irritate.

disconcert verb discompose, ruffle, embarrass, fluster, unsettle, disturb, perturb, trouble, upset, confuse, bewilder, alarm, startle, surprise, nonplus, take aback, dismay, worry, agitate, shake, rattle (inf), faze (inf), throw (inf).

disconnect verb 1 disengage, uncouple, undo, separate, take apart, split up, sever, detach, dissociate, disunite, unhook, unhitch, unplug. 2 discontinue, interrupt, break, suspend, stop.

disconnected adj 1 unconnected, separate, detached, dissociated. 2 confused, garbled, disjointed, jumbled, mixed-up, incoherent, rambling, wandering, illogical, abrupt, staccato.

disconsolate adj unhappy, sad, desolate, despondent, dejected, heartbroken, crushed, inconsolable, griefstricken, wretched, miserable, depressed, despairing, hopeless.

discontent noun discontentment, dissatisfaction, displeasure, irritation, chagrin, pique, disaffection, restlessness, unrest.

discontented adj dissatisfied, disgruntled, vexed, complaining, querulous, fretful, irritated, annoyed, chagrined, peeved, piqued, envious, restless, unhappy, disaffected, fed up (inf), pissed off (sl), hacked off (inf), browned off (inf), cheesed off (inf).

discontinue verb 1 stop, terminate, end, cease, break off, halt, cancel, interrupt, suspend, abandon, drop, give up, refrain from, scrap (inf). 2 cease, stop, halt, leave off.

discontinuous adj broken, interrupted, intermittent, irregular, fitful, periodic, disjointed, disconnected.

discord noun 1 dissension, dissent, strife, war, contention, friction, conflict, hostility, argument, quarrelling, disagreement, wrangling, disunity, division.

2 dissonance, disharmony. **3** cacophony, din, racket, jarring, jangling.

discordant *adj* **1** conflicting, incompatible, incongruous, contradictory, different, differing, divergent, clashing, opposing, inconsistent, at odds. **2** dissonant, inharmonious, cacophonous, unmelodious, harsh, jangling, jarring, grating.

discount *noun* reduction, rebate, allowance, deduction, markdown, cut.
➤*verb* **1** disregard, ignore, overlook, pass over, disbelieve. **2** deduct, take off, cut, reduce, lower, mark down, rebate, knock off (*inf*).

discourage *verb* **1** dishearten, dispirit, deject, cast down, depress, cow, abash, daunt, put off, intimidate, demoralize, unnerve, psych out (*inf*). **2** deter, dissuade, advise against, put off, frown on, deprecate, oppose, hold back. **3** prevent, inhibit, hinder, obstruct, restrain, check, curb.

discourse *noun* **1** conversation, talk, discussion, converse, conference, communication. **2** speech, talk, sermon, lecture, address, dissertation, paper, essay, study, treatise, disquisition.
➤*verb* **1** converse, talk, speak, discuss, confer, debate. **2** talk, speak, hold forth, expatiate, lecture, preach, spout (*inf*).

discourteous *adj* rude, impolite, bad-mannered, ill-mannered, uncivil, ungentlemanly, unladylike, ill-bred, boorish, churlish, disrespectful, insolent, impertinent, impudent, curt, abrupt, brusque, offhand.

discourtesy *noun* rudeness, bad manners, impoliteness, incivility, ill-breeding, disrespect, impertinence, insolence, abruptness, curtness, brusqueness, slight, snub, insult, affront.

discover *verb* **1** find, come across, happen upon, stumble across, chance upon, light upon, unearth, dig up, ferret out, turn up, bring to light, uncover, reveal. **2** find out, learn, ascertain, establish, realize, understand, see, spot, perceive, notice, recognize, twig (*inf*), suss out (*inf*), rumble (*inf*). **3** invent, pioneer, devise, create, design, originate, conceive.

discovery *noun* **1** finding, detection, location, uncovering, finding out, realization, perception, recognition, ascertainment,

exploration, pioneering, invention, origination, introduction. **2** find, finding, invention, breakthrough, coup, innovation. **3** revelation, disclosure, divulgence.

discredit *verb* **1** dishonour, disgrace, belittle, defame, decry, vilify, smear, denigrate, slur, slander, disparage, detract from, invalidate, refute, explode, debunk.
2 disbelieve, discount, doubt, question, challenge, distrust, mistrust, reject, deny, dispute.
➤*noun* **1** dishonour, disgrace, disrepute, censure, blame, shame, reproach, stigma, scandal, infamy, ignominy, humiliation, damage, harm. **2** disgrace, shame, reproach, blot.

discreditable *adj* dishonourable, disgraceful, shameful, ignoble, degrading, scandalous, blameworthy, reprehensible, improper, unworthy.

discreet *adj* careful, tactful, diplomatic, cautious, reserved, guarded, wary, sensible, judicious, circumspect, prudent, thoughtful, considerate.

discrepancy *noun* **1** inconsistency, difference, variance, dissimilarity, disparity, incongruity, divergence, disagreement, conflict, inequality. **2** inconsistency, difference, disparity, gap.

discrete *adj* separate, distinct, detached, disconnected, individual.

discretion *noun* **1** tact, tactfulness, diplomacy, caution, sense, discernment, discrimination, judgment, judiciousness, prudence, circumspection, care, carefulness, reserve, guardedness. **2** choice, option, liberty, freedom, preference, will, wish, desire, liking.

discretionary *adj* optional, elective, voluntary, non-mandatory, open.

discriminate *verb* **1** distinguish, differentiate, tell apart, separate, isolate, judge, assess, evaluate. **2** be biased, be prejudiced, single out, victimize, disfavour.

discriminating *adj* **1** discerning, cultivated, cultured, refined, selective, critical. **2** perceptive, sensitive, subtle, shrewd.

discrimination *noun* **1** bias, prejudice, bigotry, intolerance, unfairness, favouritism, narrow-mindedness, segregation, racism, sexism, chauvinism, ageism, homophobia. **2** differentiation, discernment, selectivity. **3** discernment, judgment, acumen, perspicacity, perception, acuteness, insight, shrewdness, penetration, subtlety, sensitivity, refinement, taste, culture, cultivation.

discriminatory adj **1** biased, prejudiced, partial, inequitable, loaded, one-sided, weighted, partisan, unfair, unjust, preferential. **2** discriminating, discerning, perceptive, perspicacious, critical, analytical.

discursive adj rambling, wandering, meandering, episodic, digressive, circuitous, roundabout, wordy, long-winded, diffuse, loose.

discuss verb **1** debate, talk about, talk over, confer, converse, consult, argue, thrash out, consider, deliberate, air, ventilate, kick around (inf). **2** examine, go into, analyse, weigh up, review, study.

discussion noun **1** debate, argument, conference, talk, conversation, confabulation, confab (inf), consultation, exchange, forum, symposium, seminar. **2** consideration, deliberation, examination, review, analysis.

disdain noun scorn, contempt, superciliousness, haughtiness, hauteur, aloofness, arrogance, snobbishness, indifference, derision, disparagement, sneering.
➤verb **1** scorn, snub, rebuff, despise, deride, sneer at, belittle, look down on, slight, cold-shoulder (inf), pooh-pooh (inf). **2** scorn, spurn, reject, turn down, refuse.

disdainful adj scornful, contemptuous, supercilious, haughty, aloof, arrogant, snobbish, superior, indifferent, sneering, derisive, hoity-toity (inf).

disease noun sickness, illness, complaint, malady, ailment, disorder, condition, infection, epidemic, plague, blight, cancer, canker, bug (inf), virus (inf).

disembark verb land, arrive, go ashore, alight, get off, debark.

disembodied adj bodiless, incorporeal, immaterial, insubstantial, intangible, impalpable, ghostly, phantom, spectral.

disembowel verb eviscerate, gut, draw.

disenchant verb disillusion, undeceive, disabuse, disappoint.

disengage verb **1** disentangle, extricate, release, free, loose, unfasten, untie,

unhitch, unhook, undo, disconnect, uncouple, detach, separate. **2** withdraw, retire, retreat.

disentangle verb **1** untangle, undo, unravel, unknot, unsnarl, untwist, unwind, straighten, smooth, resolve, sort out, clear up. **2** untangle, extricate, disengage, loose, release, free, distance.

disfavour noun **1** disapproval, disapprobation, displeasure, dissatisfaction, dislike, distaste. **2** unpopularity, disgrace, disrepute, bad books (inf), doghouse (inf).

disfigure verb deface, mutilate, scar, deface, blemish, spoil, mar, damage, injure, ruin.

disgorge verb **1** discharge, empty, eject, emit, expel. **2** regurgitate, vomit, spew, throw up (inf). **3** surrender, yield, relinquish, hand over.

disgrace noun **1** shame, dishonour, humiliation, ignominy, infamy, discredit, scandal, degradation, disrepute, loss of face, opprobrium, odium. **2** shame, slur, blot, stain, blemish, smear, stigma, scandal, dishonour.
➤verb dishonour, discredit, shame, humiliate, demean, sully, stain, tarnish, besmirch.

disgraceful adj shameful, shameless, scandalous, infamous, blameworthy, culpable, discreditable, dishonourable, low, degrading, disreputable, contemptible, despicable, reprehensible, shocking, outrageous, unseemly, unworthy, appalling, awful, dreadful.

disgruntled adj discontented, displeased, dissatisfied, sulky, sullen, peeved, peevish, put out, resentful, annoyed, irritated, fed up (inf), brassed off (inf), cheesed off (inf), browned off (inf), pissed off (sl).

disguise noun **1** concealment, camouflage, guise. **2** costume, getup (inf), mask, front, facade, veneer, cover, screen, veil, semblance, masquerade, pretence, deception.
➤verb **1** camouflage, conceal, hide, screen, cover, mask, veil, dress up. **2** cover up, falsify, misrepresent, gloss over, varnish, whitewash (inf).

disgust verb sicken, nauseate, revolt, repel, offend, displease, appal, scandalize, outrage.
➤noun **1** distaste, nausea, repulsion, revulsion, repugnance, loathing, abhorrence,

detestation, aversion, hatred, antipathy.
2 offence, outrage, shock, disapproval,
displeasure.

dish noun **1** plate, saucer, platter, bowl,
vessel, salver, container. **2** food, fare,
recipe, course, delicacy, speciality.
➤ verb ruin, spoil, wreck, torpedo, muck
up (inf).
dish out 1 serve, dish up. **2** distribute,
dole out, deal out, hand out, mete out,
inflict.
dish up 1 serve, ladle, spoon. **2** offer,
present, dish out.

dishearten verb discourage, dispirit,
depress, cast down, sadden, deject, dash,
dampen, dismay, disappoint.

dishevelled adj unkempt, bedraggled,
messy, untidy, disarranged, disordered,
ruffled, rumpled, tousled.

dishonest adj untruthful, deceitful, lying,
mendacious, false, cheating, double-
dealing, fraudulent, rascally, knavish, sly,
duplicitous, devious, unscrupulous,
unprincipled, treacherous, underhand,
untrustworthy, crooked (inf), bent (inf),
shady (inf), iffy (inf), dodgy (inf).

dishonour noun **1** disgrace, shame,
humiliation, loss of face, disrepute,
discredit, ignominy, infamy, scandal,
reproach, degradation. **2** disgrace, shame,
ignominy. **3** insult, affront, offence, indignity, outrage, slight.
➤ verb **1** disgrace, discredit, shame, defile,
degrade, stain, sully, blacken. **2** refuse,
reject, bounce (inf). **3** humiliate, demean,
shame.

dishonourable adj discreditable, disgraceful, shameful, degrading, ignoble, despicable, contemptible, low, base, reprehensible,
blameworthy, unworthy.

disillusion verb disenchant, disabuse,
undeceive, disappoint.

disincentive noun deterrent, discouragement, impediment, damper.

disinclination noun reluctance, unwilling-
ness, recalcitrance, distaste, repugnance,
objection, opposition, resistance, aversion.

disinclined adj reluctant, unwilling, hesitant, indisposed, averse, loath, opposed,
resistant, unenthusiastic.

disinfect verb sterilize, sanitize, decontaminate, fumigate.

disinfectant noun antiseptic, sterilizer,
decontaminant, bactericide, germicide.

disingenuous adj insincere, deceitful,
dishonest, two-faced, false, sly, shifty,
duplicitous.

disinherit verb dispossess, deprive, cut off,
disown, reject, repudiate.

disintegrate verb **1** crumble, break up,
break apart, fall apart, separate, shatter.
2 break down, decompose, dissolve, decay,
rot.

disinterested adj impartial, unbiased,
unprejudiced, objective, dispassionate,
neutral, open-minded, even-handed,
detached, fair, just.

disjointed adj rambling, incoherent, desultory, bitty, disordered, confused, disorganized, unconnected, disconnected.

dislike verb hate, detest, loathe, abhor,
abominate, disapprove of, object to.
➤ noun hate, hatred, detestation, loathing,
abhorrence, aversion, antipathy, distaste,
repugnance, animosity, antagonism,
enmity, hostility, disapproval.

dislocate verb **1** put out, twist, sprain,
strain. **2** disrupt, disorganize, disarrange.

dislodge verb remove, displace, shift,
budge, oust, expel, force out.

disloyal adj unfaithful, faithless, perfidious, treacherous, traitorous, unpatriotic,
false, untrue, inconstant, disaffected.

dismal adj **1** gloomy, dreary, desolate,
melancholy, depressing, sombre, dull,
drab, bleak, grim, cheerless, comfortless,
inhospitable, uninviting, sad, miserable,
unhappy, low, despondent, morose,
joyless, lugubrious. **2** bad, poor, feeble,
wretched, inept, bungling, incompetent.

dismantle verb disassemble, take apart,
take to pieces, strip down.

dismay verb alarm, frighten, scare, disturb,
perturb, shock, unnerve, unsettle, upset,
distress, bother, worry, disconcert, startle,
surprise, take aback, daunt, intimidate, discourage, dishearten, depress, sadden, cast
down, disappoint.
➤ noun consternation, alarm, distress,
apprehension, dread, fear, fright, terror,
anxiety, trepidation, agitation, misgiving,
disappointment, chagrin.

dismember *verb* **1** dissect, cut up, anatomize, disjoint, amputate. **2** break up, divide up.

dismiss *verb* **1** send away, discharge, release, disband, disperse, demobilize. **2** lay off, let go, cashier, discharge, sack (*inf*), fire (*inf*), axe (*inf*), boot out (*inf*), give someone their marching orders (*inf*), give someone their cards (*inf*). **3** banish, discount, disregard, discard, reject, set aside, put away.

dismount *verb* descend, alight, get off, get down.

disobedient *adj* insubordinate, contrary, wayward, defiant, refractory, recalcitrant, undisciplined, naughty, mischievous, perverse, unruly, mutinous, rebellious.

disobey *verb* infringe, violate, contravene, transgress, break, disregard, defy, flout, resist, rebel.

disorder *noun* **1** confusion, chaos, disarray, clutter, muddle, jumble, mess, disorderliness, untidiness, disorganization, turmoil, shambles (*inf*). **2** disturbance, tumult, uproar, commotion, brouhaha, riot, rumpus, fracas, unrest, fight, brawl. **3** ailment, complaint, condition, indisposition, malady, illness, disease, affliction, sickness.
➤ *verb* disarrange, disorganize, disturb, upset, confuse, muddle, jumble, mess up, mix up, turn upside down.

disorderly *adj* **1** untidy, messy, jumbled, muddled, cluttered, disordered, disorganized, disarranged, confused, chaotic, shambolic, upside-down, higgledy-piggledy (*inf*), irregular, unsystematic. **2** unruly, undisciplined, unmanageable, ungovernable, lawless, riotous, rowdy, disruptive, turbulent, rebellious, mutinous.

disorganized *adj* **1** disordered, disorderly, topsy-turvy, upset, confused, muddled, jumbled, haphazard, random, chaotic, shambolic. **2** muddled, careless, unmethodical, unsystematic.

disorientate *verb* confuse, perplex, puzzle, bewilder, muddle, mix up.

disown *verb* **1** repudiate, disclaim, reject, retract, renounce, deny, disavow. **2** repudiate, reject, cast off, disinherit, cut off.

disparage *verb* belittle, depreciate, decry, run down, denigrate, ridicule, deride, mock, scorn, slight, defame, slander, libel, traduce, malign, impugn, asperse, criticize, vilify, calumniate, rubbish (*inf*), badmouth (*inf*), slag off (*inf*).

disparate *adj* distinct, different, separate, contrasting, dissimilar, unequal.

disparity *noun* difference, distinction, inequality, discrepancy, imbalance, incongruity, disproportion, gap.

dispassionate *adj* objective, impartial, unbiased, unprejudiced, disinterested, neutral, detached, composed, calm, collected, cool, unemotional, unruffled, self-controlled, self-possessed, impassive, unmoved, placid, equable, sober, level-headed.

dispatch *verb* **1** send, post, mail, emit, consign, convey, ship, forward. **2** conclude, finish, complete, discharge, perform, dispose of, settle, expedite, push through. **3** kill, execute, murder, put to death, eliminate, bump off (*inf*).
➤ *noun* **1** promptness, promptitude, speed, rapidity, swiftness, alacrity, haste, hurry. **2** communication, message, report, bulletin, communiqué, note, news, letter.

dispel *verb* disperse, scatter, banish, allay, dissipate, drive away, chase away, get rid of.

dispensable *adj* expendable, disposable, unnecessary, nonessential, inessential, replaceable, superfluous, redundant.

dispensation *noun* **1** exemption, immunity, indulgence, licence, permission, privilege, exception, release, relief, reprieve, remission. **2** distribution, issue, handing out, dealing out, apportionment, allotment, assignment, administration, discharge, execution, implementation, enforcement. **3** system, order, scheme, plan.

dispense *verb* **1** distribute, give out, apportion, share out, allot, assign, allocate, deal out, mete out, supply. **2** administer, apply, implement, execute, enforce, impose. **3** dispose of, get rid of, do away with, discard, abolish, omit, ignore, waive. **4** do without, forgo, give up, renounce.

disperse *verb* **1** break up, scatter, disband, dismiss. **2** disappear, vanish, melt away, dissipate. **3** distribute, scatter, spread, strew. **4** dispel, dissipate.

dispirit *verb* dishearten, discourage, damp, dash, depress, deject, cast down, disappoint.

displace *verb* **1** move, shift, disturb, disarrange, disorder, relocate, dislodge. **2** remove, dismiss, depose, eject, expel, oust, force out. **3** evict, exile, banish. **4** replace, supplant, supersede.

display *verb* **1** show, exhibit, set out, set forth, present. **2** demonstrate, betray, disclose, reveal, show, manifest. **3** parade, flaunt, show off, vaunt, flash (*inf*). **4** unfold, unfurl, spread out, open out. ➤*noun* **1** show, exhibition, demonstration, presentation, performance. **2** revelation, betrayal, disclosure, demonstration, exposure. **3** parade, show, ostentation, flourish, splash (*inf*).

displease *verb* offend, annoy, irritate, vex, irk, anger, exasperate, infuriate, nettle, pique, rile, peeve, bug (*inf*), piss off (*sl*).

displeasure *noun* annoyance, irritation, anger, exasperation, indignation, vexation, wrath, ire, pique, disapproval, dislike, dissatisfaction.

disport *verb* **1** amuse, entertain, divert, delight. **2** frolic, gambol, caper, frisk, romp, play, sport.

disposable *adj* **1** expendable, throwaway, non-returnable. **2** available, usable, liquid, accessible.

disposal *noun* removal, clearance, scrapping, dumping, discarding.
at one's disposal under one's control, at one's command, available, to hand.

dispose *verb* **1** arrange, group, place, position, set out, put, array, align, order, marshal, range, rank, line up, organize. **2** incline, lead, make, move, prompt, tempt, induce, predispose, influence, motivate. **3** get rid of, discard, jettison, throw away, throw out, scrap, bin (*inf*), dump (*inf*), junk (*inf*), chuck out (*inf*). **4** assign, transfer, give, bestow, make over, sell, auction.

disposed *adj* **1** prone, inclined, apt, liable, likely, given, willing, minded, predisposed, ready. **2** inclined, minded.

disposition *noun* **1** character, nature, temperament, make-up, temper, humour.

2 inclination, tendency, bias, bent, leaning, habit, predisposition, predilection, proclivity, propensity. **3** disposal, arrangement, distribution, grouping, marshalling, ordering, positioning, organization, placement, placing, alignment, pattern, system.

dispossess *verb* deprive, divest, strip, rob, expropriate, evict, expel, turn out, drive out, dislodge.

disproportion *noun* disparity, inequality, imbalance, lopsidedness, unevenness, asymmetry.

disproportionate *adj* unequal, out of proportion, excessive, inordinate, unreasonable, incommensurate.

disprove *verb* confute, refute, rebut, invalidate, contradict, discredit, debunk (*inf*).

disputable *adj* debatable, arguable, contestable, moot, controversial, questionable, doubtful.

disputation *noun* argument, debate, dispute, controversy.

disputatious *adj* argumentative, contentious, quarrelsome, irascible, cantankerous, captious.

dispute *verb* **1** argue, debate, disagree, quarrel, wrangle, squabble, clash. **2** question, challenge, contest, controvert, doubt, deny, oppose. ➤*noun* **1** argument, debate, discussion, controversy, contention, conflict, friction, strife. **2** quarrel, squabble, wrangle, altercation, clash, conflict, row, disagreement.

disqualify *verb* **1** debar, preclude, exclude, rule out, disentitle. **2** eliminate.

disquiet *noun* anxiety, nervousness, worry, concern, unease, uneasiness, fear, alarm, distress, perturbation, trepidation, trouble, agitation, disturbance, foreboding. ➤*verb* worry, concern, unsettle, frighten, perturb, agitate, distress, shake, ruffle, upset, disturb, bother, trouble.

disquisition *noun* dissertation, essay, treatise, paper, lecture, monograph.

disregard *verb* ignore, overlook, neglect, pass over, gloss over, discount, take no notice of, disobey, flout, forget, brush aside, slight, snub, cold-shoulder (*inf*). ➤*noun* inattention, neglect, carelessness, oversight, heedlessness, indifference, disrespect, disdain, contempt, scorn.

disrepair *noun* dilapidation, decay, ruin, rack and ruin, decrepitude.

disreputable *adj* **1** discreditable, shameful, disgraceful, ignominious, reprehensible, base, dishonourable, notorious, outrageous, shocking, scandalous, infamous, suspicious, questionable, dubious, dishonest, unsavoury, shifty, shady (*inf*), dodgy (*inf*), crooked (*inf*). **2** scruffy, shabby, bedraggled, dishevelled, unkempt, disorderly, untidy, threadbare, worn.

disrepute *noun* disgrace, dishonour, discredit, shame, infamy, ignominy, odium, opprobrium, notoriety, disfavour.

disrespect *noun* impoliteness, incivility, rudeness, discourtesy, insolence, impertinence, impudence, cheek (*inf*).

disrobe *verb* undress, unclothe, strip, divest.

disrupt *verb* **1** disturb, upset, disorganize, disorder, unsettle, agitate, break up, sabotage. **2** interrupt, intrude on, interfere with, hamper, suspend.

dissatisfaction *noun* discontent, discontentment, displeasure, dislike, unhappiness, restlessness, disappointment, chagrin, annoyance, irritation, disapproval.

dissatisfy *verb* discontent, displease, disgruntle, put out, annoy, anger, chagrin, vex, irritate, disappoint, disillusion.

dissect *verb* **1** anatomize, cut up, dismember, vivisect. **2** analyse, break down, examine, study, probe.

dissemble *verb* pretend, feign, sham, counterfeit, dissimulate.

disseminate *verb* disperse, diffuse, spread, scatter, distribute, circulate, broadcast, promulgate, publish, publicize.

dissension *noun* disagreement, discord, friction, strife, conflict, argument, wrangling, bickering.

dissent *verb* disagree, differ, object, protest.
➤*noun* disagreement, discord, friction, dissension, protest, opposition, resistance, nonconformity.

dissentient *adj* dissenting, disagreeing, dissident, differing, opposing, rebellious, heterodox, nonconformist.

dissertation *noun* discourse, treatise, essay, thesis, paper.

disservice *noun* disfavour, wrong, bad turn, damage, injury, harm, injustice, unkindness.

dissident *adj* dissenting, dissentient, nonconformist, heterodox, opposing, rebellious, revolutionary.
➤*noun* dissenter, protester, objector, rebel, revolutionary, agitator.

dissimilar *adj* unlike, unalike, different, divergent, distinct, disparate, unrelated, heterogeneous, contrasting, incompatible.

dissimulate *verb* feign, fake, sham, pretend, dissemble, lie, conceal, disguise, mask, camouflage, cover up (*inf*).

dissipate *verb* **1** spend, expend, consume, drain, deplete, use up, run through, waste, squander, fritter away. **2** scatter, drive away, disperse, break up, dispel, disappear, vanish, evaporate.

dissipated *adj* debauched, dissolute, licentious, promiscuous, profligate, abandoned, self-indulgent, wanton.

dissipation *noun* **1** debauchery, profligacy, licence, licentiousness, dissoluteness, corruption, immorality, self-indulgence, intemperance, excess. **2** depletion, squandering, waste, extravagance, excess, prodigality. **3** dispersion, dispersal, scattering, dissolution.

dissociate *verb* **1** separate, disassociate, detach, divorce, segregate. **2** distance, withdraw, separate.

dissociation *noun* separation, severance, detachment, divorce, split, break, setting apart, segregation.

dissolute *adj* dissipated, debauched, wanton, loose, profligate, abandoned, licentious, lewd, corrupt, immoral, rakish, promiscuous, self-indulgent.

dissolution *noun* **1** disintegration, break-up, collapse, decay, dispersal, disappearance, evaporation. **2** annulment, termination, discontinuation, end, ending, break-up, divorce, separation. **3** suspension, adjournment, disbandment,

winding-up, dispersal. **4** dissolving, liquefaction, melting, solution. **5** dissipation,
debauchery, profligacy, licentiousness.

dissolve *verb* **1** liquefy, melt, thaw, deliquesce. **2** disperse, diffuse, dissipate,
evaporate, fade away, melt, vanish, disappear. **3** annul, nullify, finish, terminate,
break up, wind up. **4** break up, disband,
dismiss, suspend, adjourn. **5** break, burst,
collapse.

dissonance *noun* **1** discord. **2** discordance,
cacophony, harshness, stridency, jarring,
grating. **3** discord, disagreement, dissension, disharmony, quarrelling, wrangling,
feuding.

dissuade *verb* deter, discourage, put off,
stop, talk out of, persuade against, advise
against, warn.

distance *noun* **1** space, interval, gap,
remove, separation, extent, range, stretch,
span, reach, length, width, breadth, depth,
height. **2** remoteness, farness, inaccessibil-
ity. **3** reserve, remoteness, coolness, aloofness, constraint, stiffness, reticence,
formality, unfriendliness,
unresponsiveness.
➤ *verb* **1** separate, set apart. **2** dissociate,
withdraw, break with.

distant *adj* **1** far, away, off. **2** far, remote,
outlying, faraway, far-off, out-of-the-way,
isolated. **3** reserved, cool, cold, aloof, stiff,
ceremonious, formal, haughty, condescending, standoffish, detached, withdrawn, unfriendly, unapproachable,
uncommunicative. **4** remote, faint, slight.

distaste *noun* dislike, disgust, repugnance,
disinclination, aversion, abhorrence, revulsion, antipathy.

distasteful *adj* unpleasant, displeasing,
disagreeable, offensive, revolting, repellent, repugnant, disgusting, objectionable,
hateful, abhorrent, detestable, off-putting,
unpalatable.

distend *verb* dilate, enlarge, expand, swell,
inflate, bloat, puff out.

distil *verb* **1** condense, purify, refine, separate, concentrate. **2** extract, draw out,
derive.

distinct *adj* **1** clear, sharp, clear-cut, well-
defined, plain, obvious, definite, unmistakable, marked, conspicuous, noticeable.
2 definite, decided. **3** separate, detached,

individual, discrete, disparate, unconnected, different, dissimilar.

distinction *noun* **1** differentiation, discrimination, separation. **2** difference,
division, dissimilarity, contrast. **3** fame,
renown, repute, reputation, eminence,
prestige, mark, note, prominence, importance, significance, consequence.
4 honours, credit, merit.

distinctive *adj* distinguishing, characteristic, typical, individual, particular, peculiar,
unique, special, idiosyncratic.

distinctly *adv* **1** clearly, plainly, evidently,
decidedly, definitely, obviously, patently,
palpably. **2** markedly, noticeably, remarkably, very. **3** clearly, plainly, intelligibly.

distinguish *verb* **1** differentiate, tell apart,
discriminate, tell the difference.
2 single out, set apart, characterize, particularize, stamp. **3** separate, categorize,
classify. **4** discern, perceive, see, pick out,
make out, identify, detect. **5** excel, do
well, be successful, win fame.

distinguished *adj* **1** eminent, illustrious,
notable, renowned, famous, well-known,
prominent, noted, celebrated, acclaimed,
respected. **2** dignified, refined, stately,
aristocratic, noble.

distort *verb* **1** deform, twist, buckle, warp,
misshape, wrench. **2** falsify, misrepresent,
pervert, colour, bias, slant, twist, alter,
change, tamper with.

distract *verb* **1** divert, deflect, sidetrack,
turn away, put off. **2** amuse, divert, entertain, occupy, engross, absorb.

distracted *adj* **1** abstracted, preoccupied,
inattentive, absent-minded, distrait, miles
away (*inf*). **2** agitated, flustered, harassed,
overwrought, frantic, frenzied, mad, crazy,
insane.

distraction *noun* **1** diversion, interruption, disturbance. **2** amusement, entertainment, diversion, pastime, occupation,
recreation.
drive somebody to distraction drive
somebody mad, drive somebody crazy.

distraught *adj* agitated, anxious, upset,
overwrought, distressed, worked up, beside
oneself, desperate, frantic, hysterical.

distress *noun* **1** grief, sorrow, sadness,
heartache, heartbreak, anguish, misery,
wretchedness, suffering, discomfort, pain,

trouble, worry, unease, anxiety, torment.
2 adversity, hardship, privation, need,
want, poverty, destitution, misfortune,
trouble. **3** danger, trouble, difficulty.
➤*verb* upset, grieve, sadden, afflict, pain,
hurt, trouble, worry, bother, perplex,
torment.

distribute *verb* **1** dispense, dole out, give
out, hand out, deal out, allocate, allot,
share, divide, apportion. **2** deliver, convey,
supply, issue. **3** scatter, spread, strew,
disperse.

distribution *noun* **1** dispensation, doling-
out, giving-out, handing-out, sharing,
division, apportionment, allotment,
allocation, delivery, supply, transport,
mailing, handling, conveyance, circulation, spread, dispersion, scattering.
2 spread, grouping, disposition, frequency,
incidence, density.

district *noun* **1** area, region, quarter, place,
locality, locale, neighbourhood. **2** ward,
borough, parish, precinct, zone, division,
community.

distrust *verb* doubt, mistrust, disbelieve,
question, suspect, be wary of.
➤*noun* doubt, doubtfulness, mistrust, disbelief, incredulity, suspicion, wariness,
misgiving, scepticism.

disturb *verb* **1** disrupt, interrupt, butt in
on, intrude on, pester, bother, trouble, distract, annoy, hassle (*inf*). **2** disarrange, disorganize, upset, disorder, muddle, confuse.
3 worry, concern, trouble, agitate, excite,
upset, distress, alarm, frighten, perturb,
unsettle, fluster, ruffle, shake. **4** agitate,
churn up, convulse. **5** inconvenience, put
out, trouble, bother.

disturbance *noun* **1** interruption, distraction, intrusion, nuisance. **2** disruption,
upheaval, upsetting, disordering, disorganization, discomposure, perturbation,
troubling, bothering. **3** commotion, riot,
brawl, fray, fracas, uproar, hubbub, hullabaloo, noise, racket, row, rumpus (*inf*).

disturbed *adj* unbalanced, disordered,
maladjusted, neurotic, psychotic, paranoid, screwed-up (*inf*).

disunite *verb* separate, part, divide, dis-
join, disconnect, sever, split, detach.

disuse *noun* neglect, abandonment, dis-
continuance, obsolescence, decay.

disused *adj* unused, neglected, abandoned,
discontinued, obsolete.

ditch *noun* trench, dyke, channel, drain,
gully, gutter, moat.
➤*verb* discard, dispose of, get rid of, scrap,
throw away, throw out, jettison, abandon,
drop, dump (*inf*).

dither *verb* waver, vacillate, hesitate,
haver, delay, procrastinate, faff about (*inf*),
shilly-shally (*inf*).
➤*noun* bother, flutter, panic, flap (*inf*),
stew (*inf*), tizzy (*inf*).

diurnal *adj* **1** daily, daytime, day-to-day.
2 quotidian, circadian.

divan *noun* sofa, settee, couch, chaise
longue, daybed, lounger.

dive *verb* **1** plunge, bellyflop.
2 submerge. **3** plummet, descend,
nosedive, swoop. **4** fall, drop, plummet,
nosedive. **5** dart, rush, dash, bolt, duck.
6 lunge, dash.
➤*noun* **1** plunge, bellyflop. **2** dip, descent,
fall, drop, nosedive. **3** nosedive, descent,
swoop. **4** bar, nightclub, club, pub, den,
joint (*inf*), dump (*inf*), hole (*inf*).

diverge *verb* **1** divide, subdivide, separate,
split, fork, branch, bifurcate, part, spread
out, radiate, open. **2** deviate, digress, wander, stray, depart. **3** differ, vary, conflict,
clash, disagree.

divergent *adj* diverging, differing, different, diverse, dissimilar, disagreeing, varying, conflicting, clashing, abnormal,
aberrant.

divers *adj* sundry, various, varying, manifold, some, several, many.

diverse *adj* **1** different, differing, separate,
distinct, discrete, contrasting, conflicting,
divergent. **2** varied, various, assorted,
mixed, miscellaneous, sundry, heterogeneous, variegated.

diversify *verb* **1** vary, variegate, assort,
mix, change, modify. **2** branch out,
expand.

diversion *noun* **1** deflection, redirection,
turning aside, deviation, divergence,
departure. **2** detour, deviation.
3 amusement, entertainment, sport,
recreation, pastime, game, hobby.

diversity *noun* **1** variety, assortment, mixture, medley, miscellany, multiplicity,

range. **2** difference, variance, variation, variegation, contrast, diverseness, dissimilarity, heterogeneity.

divert verb **1** redirect, reroute, deflect, switch, turn aside. **2** distract, sidetrack. **3** amuse, entertain, distract, interest, occupy, absorb, engross.

diverting adj amusing, entertaining, enjoyable, absorbing, interesting, pleasant, pleasurable, fun, funny, humorous, witty.

divest verb **1** take off, remove, doff, undress, strip. **2** dispossess, strip, deprive.

divide verb **1** separate, split, part, sever, shear, sunder, disunite, cut up, break up, bisect, halve, quarter, detach, disconnect. **2** diverge, branch, fork, ramify, separate, split. **3** partition. **4** share, apportion, portion out, distribute, deal out, allot, allocate, dole out, measure out. **5** come between, disunite, alienate, estrange, separate, set at odds. **6** classify, categorize, group, grade, rank, sort.

dividend noun **1** share, portion, cut (inf), divvy (inf). **2** bonus, extra, plus, benefit, perk (inf).

divination noun prophecy, prediction, prognostication, augury, divining, soothsaying.

divine adj **1** godlike, godly, supernatural, superhuman, spiritual, heavenly, celestial, transcendent. **2** holy, sacred, consecrated, hallowed, sanctified. **3** splendid, delightful, marvellous, wonderful, excellent, glorious, heavenly, gorgeous, lovely, beautiful, super (inf).
➤verb predict, foretell, foresee, forecast, prophesy, prognosticate, augur, deduce, infer, suspect, intuit, perceive.
➤noun cleric, ecclesiastic, theologian, clergyman, clergywoman, minister, priest.

divinity noun **1** god, goddess, deity. **2** godliness, godhood, holiness, sanctity. **3** theology, religion, religious education, religious studies, religious knowledge, scripture.

division noun **1** separation, parting, partition, dividing, disconnection, detachment, cutting up, splitting, distribution, sharing out, apportionment, allotment, allocation. **2** share, part, segment, slice, portion, section, piece, bit, chunk. **3** section, group, branch, department, sector. **4** divide, dividing-line, demarcation, border, frontier, boundary. **5** conflict, discord, disagreement, dissension, disunity.

divisive adj alienating, disruptive, troublemaking, estranging.

divorce noun **1** annulment, dissolution, break-up, separation. **2** separation, division, split, breach, rupture.
➤verb **1** break up, split up, part, separate. **2** separate, detach, disconnect, divide, dissociate, part.

divulge verb disclose, reveal, make known, communicate, tell, betray, let slip, confess, expose, publish, broadcast, leak (inf).

dizzy adj **1** giddy, light-headed, off-balance, vertiginous, shaky, unsteady, faint, woozy (inf). **2** confused, bewildered, bemused, muddled. **3** giddy, foolish, silly, scatterbrained, featherbrained, irresponsible, fickle, flighty.

do verb **1** perform, execute, carry out, fulfil, accomplish, achieve, bring about, implement, effect, put into practice, realize, complete, discharge. **2** deal with, sort out, tackle. **3** suffice, serve, be adequate, suit, answer, measure up, fit the bill, pass muster. **4** prepare, get ready, make, fix, arrange, organize, see to, deal with, look after, take care of, provide, supply. **5** work at, earn a living by, take, read, study. **6** go at, reach, travel at.
➤noun party, function, gathering, occasion, celebration, bash (inf), knees-up (inf), thrash (inf).

do away with get rid of, dispose of, dispense with, abolish, annul, repeal, revoke, rescind, eliminate, axe (inf), kill, murder, liquidate, do in (inf), bump off (inf).

do in 1 tire out, exhaust, weary, fag out (inf). **2** kill, murder, assassinate, do away with (inf), bump off (inf).

do out of deprive of, cheat of, swindle out of, con out of (inf).

do up 1 fasten, wrap, pack, tie, lace, button, zip up. **2** renovate, restore, modernize, decorate, redecorate, repair, recondition, refurbish.

do without forgo, go without, dispense with, manage without, abstain from, deny oneself, give up.

have done with finish with, give up, throw over, wash one's hands of.

docile adj tractable, manageable, amenable, compliant, cooperative, submissive, yielding, malleable, obedient, dutiful, biddable.

dock[1] *verb* **1** clip, crop, cut off, lop, shorten. **2** reduce, cut, decrease. **3** deduct, subtract, withhold.

dock[2] *noun* wharf, quay, jetty, harbour, port, marina, waterfront.
➤*verb* **1** moor, berth, anchor. **2** moor, berth, anchor, tie up, put in, land. **3** couple, join. **4** link up, hook up, rendezvous.

docket *noun* **1** document, certificate, chit, chitty. **2** ticket, label, tag. **3** receipt, tab, bill.
➤*verb* document, label, tag, tab, ticket.

doctor *noun* physician, medical officer, general practitioner, GP, surgeon, clinician, specialist, consultant, doc (*inf*), medic (*inf*), quack (*inf*).
➤*verb* **1** adapt, modify, change, alter, tamper with, interfere with. **2** falsify, misrepresent, distort. **3** fix, repair, mend, patch up. **4** neuter, spay, castrate, sterilize.

doctrinaire *adj* theoretical, ideological, unrealistic, impractical, dogmatic, rigid, pedantic, biased, fanatical.

doctrine *noun* dogma, creed, credo, tenet, principle, precept, teaching, canon, article, belief.

document *noun* paper, certificate, instrument, form, deed, affidavit.
➤*verb* **1** support, back up, substantiate, corroborate, authenticate, prove. **2** record, report, chronicle, detail.

documentary *adj* documented, recorded, detailed, written.

doddering *adj* doddery, weak, feeble, shaky, frail, infirm, unsteady, tottery, decrepit, distort. **3** fix, repair, mend, senile.

dodge *verb* **1** move, duck, sidestep. **2** evade, elude, avoid, escape, shirk, bypass, get round. **3** avoid, evade, parry, duck.
➤*noun* **1** duck, sidestep, swerve, body-swerve. **2** artifice, trick, ruse, scheme, stratagem, manoeuvre, ploy, wheeze (*inf*).

dodgy *adj* **1** risky, dangerous, chancy, dicey (*inf*), difficult, tricky. **2** dubious, suspect, dishonest, shady (*inf*). **3** unsafe, uncertain, unreliable.

doer *noun* performer, agent, executor, achiever, accomplisher, worker, organizer, live wire (*inf*), go-getter (*inf*).

doff *verb* **1** raise, lift, tip. **2** shed, cast off, slip off, slip out of, take off, remove.

dog *noun* **1** hound, cur, mongrel, pup, puppy, bitch, canine, mutt (*inf*), pooch (*inf*). **2** scoundrel, rascal, villain, cur, blackguard, knave, cad.
➤*verb* **1** follow, pursue, trail, tail (*inf*). **2** plague, haunt, trouble.

dogged *adj* determined, resolute, tenacious, persevering, persistent, pertinacious, single-minded, relentless, unflagging, unwavering, indefatigable, tireless, stubborn, obstinate.

dogma *noun* doctrine, principle, tenet, precept, teaching, belief, conviction, article of faith.

dogmatic *adj* **1** assertive, opinionated, doctrinaire, domineering, authoritarian, peremptory, dictatorial, insistent, pushy (*inf*). **2** authoritative, categorical, unquestionable, unchallengeable.

dogsbody *noun* menial, drudge, skivvy (*inf*), servant, factotum, gofer, maid-of-all-work.

doing *noun* **1** responsibility, work, handiwork. **2** action, act, activity, exploit, adventure, achievement, proceeding, transaction, dealing.

doldrums *pl noun* **in the doldrums**
1 inactive, stagnant, sluggish, flat.
2 depressed, dejected, downhearted, apathetic, listless, bored.

dole *noun* social security, unemployment benefit, jobseeker's allowance, income support.
dole out distribute, give out, hand out, dish out, share out, dispense, allocate, allot, assign.

doleful *adj* gloomy, melancholy, sad, miserable, unhappy, sorrowful, disconsolate, woebegone, dejected, depressing, distressing, dismal, lugubrious, funereal, mournful.

doll *noun* dolly (*inf*), puppet, figure, toy, plaything.

dolorous *adj* painful, harrowing, grievous, distressing, heartrending, doleful, mournful, sad, sorrowful, miserable.

dolour *noun* sorrow, sadness, misery, grief, distress, heartache, suffering.

dolt *noun* fool, idiot, imbecile, ignoramus, simpleton, dunce, dullard, ass, blockhead, berk (*inf*), dimwit (*inf*), clot (*inf*), dope (*inf*), nitwit (*inf*), numskull (*inf*), ninny (*inf*), chump (*inf*), twerp (*inf*), twit (*inf*).

domain *noun* **1** dominion, kingdom, realm, territory, demesne. **2** area, field, sphere, realm, department, province, concern, speciality.

dome *noun* cupola, rotunda, hemisphere.

domestic *adj* **1** home, family, household, private, personal, home-loving, stay-at-home, homely, domesticated. **2** domesticated, house-trained, tame, pet. **3** internal, home, native, home-grown.
➤*noun* daily, daily help, housekeeper, maid, servant, menial, skivvy (*inf*), char (*inf*).

domesticate *verb* tame, break in, housetrain.

domicile *noun* abode, home, dwelling, residence, house, address.
➤*verb* settle, house, establish.

dominant *adj* principal, chief, main, primary, leading, commanding, controlling, ruling, governing, presiding, paramount, predominant, preeminent, prevailing, supreme.

dominate *verb* **1** control, rule, govern, preside over, command, predominate, lead, domineer, overbear, intimidate, subdue, subjugate. **2** overlook, overshadow, tower above.

domineer *verb* oppress, overbear, dominate, browbeat, intimidate, bully, boss around (*inf*).

dominion *noun* **1** power, authority, sovereignty, suzerainty, supremacy, sway, rule, control, mastery, command. **2** domain, territory, province, realm, kingdom.

don *verb* put on, slip on, slip into, dress in, wear.
➤*noun* lecturer, tutor, academic, scholar, teacher, pedagogue.

donate *verb* give, give away, gift, bestow, bequeath, grant, confer, present, contribute.

donation *noun* gift, present, grant, bequest, contribution, offering, largess, charity.

done *adj* **1** finished, over, ended, completed, concluded, fulfilled, realized, accomplished. **2** cooked, ready. **3** done in, exhausted, tired out, worn out, drained. **4** conventional, acceptable, proper, right, correct, appropriate, fitting.
➤*interj* agreed, accepted, settled, right, OK (*inf*).

done for 1 dead, finished. **2** ruined, wrecked, destroyed, beaten, defeated, undone, finished, doomed.

done in done, tired out, exhausted, worn out, all in (*inf*), shattered (*inf*), dead beat (*inf*), fagged out (*inf*), knackered (*inf*), bushed (*inf*).

donkey *noun* **1** ass, jackass, burro, jenny, hinny. **2** ass, dunce, fool, idiot, blockhead, dolt, simpleton.

donnish *adj* academic, intellectual, bookish, scholarly, learned, pedantic, serious.

donor *noun* giver, provider, benefactor, benefactress, philanthropist, contributor, backer, supporter, fairy godmother (*inf*), angel (*inf*).

doom *noun* **1** fate, destiny, fortune, lot. **2** ruin, ruination, destruction, extinction, annihilation, downfall, disaster, death. **3** judgment, verdict, decision, sentence.
➤*verb* destine, predestine, ordain, preordain, fate, damn, condemn, sentence.

door *noun* **1** entrance, entry, exit, opening, hatch, gate, portal. **2** entrance, entrée, opening, opportunity, access, gateway.

dope *noun* **1** drug, narcotic, sedative, stimulant. **2** dolt, blockhead, fool, idiot, wally (*inf*), dipstick (*inf*), dickhead (*inf*), plonker (*inf*), prat (*inf*), schmuck (*inf*), berk (*inf*), charlie (*inf*), dimwit (*inf*), clot (*inf*), nitwit (*inf*), twerp (*inf*), twit (*inf*). **3** facts, information, news, gen (*inf*), info (*inf*), lowdown (*inf*).
➤*verb* sedate, drug, anaesthetize, doctor, stupefy, knock out.

dormant *adj* **1** sleeping, asleep, hibernating. **2** inactive, inert, fallow, quiescent, passive, suspended. **3** latent, potential, hidden, unrealized, undeveloped.

dose *noun* draught, measure, amount, quantity, dosage, shot.
➤*verb* **1** medicate, treat. **2** prescribe, dispense, administer.

dot *noun* **1** point, spot, speck, mark. **2** dab, jot, particle.

➤ *verb* **1** spot, speckle, fleck, speck, mark. **2** stud, pepper, sprinkle, stipple, scatter. **on the dot** punctually, promptly, precisely, exactly, sharp.

dotage *noun* senility, old age, second childhood.

dote *verb* idolize, adore, worship, love, cherish, hold dear.

double *adj* **1** twofold, dual, duplex. **2** dual, paired, twin. **3** twice, twofold, large. **4** deceitful, false, insincere, hypocritical, dishonest. **5** dual, double-edged, ambiguous, ambivalent, equivocal.
➤ *verb* **1** enlarge, magnify, increase, repeat. **2** understudy, substitute, stand in. **3** fold, bend over.
➤ *noun* twin, duplicate, copy, image, replica, clone, lookalike, doppelgänger, dead ringer (*inf*), spitting image (*inf*).
at the double quickly, rapidly, without delay, straightaway, immediately, at once.

double-cross *verb* cheat, trick, swindle, betray, con (*inf*), two-time (*inf*).

double-dealing *noun* cheating, swindling, betrayal, treachery, fraud, double-crossing, hypocrisy, deceit, deception, duplicity, trickery, dishonesty, two-facedness, two-timing (*inf*).

double entendre *noun* innuendo, wordplay, pun.

doubt *verb* **1** suspect, question, query, mistrust, distrust, disbelieve, discredit. **2** question, query, have reservations, be sceptical.
➤ *noun* **1** suspicion, mistrust, distrust, scepticism, misgiving, reservation, incredulity, disbelief. **2** uncertainty, confusion, hesitation, perplexity, irresolution.
no doubt doubtless, undoubtedly, definitely, certainly, surely, assuredly, of course, probably, most likely, presumably.

doubtful *adj* **1** uncertain, unsure, unconvinced, undecided, indecisive, unresolved, uneasy, wavering, distrustful, hesitant, suspicious, sceptical. **2** unlikely, improbable, open to question, questionable, unclear, equivocal, dubious, problematic, difficult. **3** unsettled, inconclusive. **4** dubious, questionable, suspect, iffy (*inf*), dodgy (*inf*), fishy (*inf*).

doubtless *adv* **1** certainly, surely, assuredly, unquestionably, undoubtedly, no doubt, without doubt. **2** probably, most likely, presumably.

dour *adj* **1** sullen, morose, churlish, gruff, grim, forbidding, unsmiling, unfriendly. **2** hard, inflexible, stern, austere, rigorous, harsh, strict, severe.

douse *verb* **1** souse, plunge, duck, dunk, submerge, flood, deluge, soak, drench. **2** extinguish, smother, snuff, blow out.

dovetail *verb* **1** fit together, splice, join. **2** fit together, go together, correspond, coincide, tally, accord.

dowdy *adj* shabby, drab, dull, frumpish, frumpy, frowsy, inelegant, unfashionable, old-fashioned.

down[1] *adv* **1** to the ground, to the floor. **2** downwards, low, below, beneath, under.
➤ *prep* along, through.
➤ *adj* **1** depressed, dejected, downcast, downhearted, disheartened, discouraged, dispirited, despondent, sad, miserable, unhappy, depressed, low, blue (*inf*). **2** out of order, out of action, not working, crashed.
➤ *verb* **1** knock down, bring down, floor, fell, topple, throw, trip up. **2** drink, swallow, drain, gulp, knock back (*inf*), swig (*inf*).

down[2] *noun* **1** feathers, fluff. **2** fuzz, floss, wool.

down-and-out *adj* destitute, impoverished, penniless, broke (*inf*).
➤ *noun* tramp, vagrant, beggar, dosser (*inf*), bum (*inf*).

downbeat *adj* **1** gloomy, pessimistic, negative, depressed. **2** relaxed, informal, casual, laid-back (*inf*).

downcast *adj* cast down, dejected, depressed, despondent, sad, unhappy, wretched, miserable, low, glum, melancholy, disheartened, downhearted, dispirited, disappointed.

downfall *noun* fall, ruin, destruction, collapse, overthrow, undoing, disgrace.

downgrade *verb* degrade, demote, lower, relegate, reduce in rank, depreciate, detract from.

downhearted *adj* discouraged, disheartened, dispirited, despondent, depressed, dejected, downcast, disappointed, sad, sorrowful, unhappy, miserable, glum.

downpour *noun* cloudburst, deluge, torrent, storm.

downright *adj* **1** absolute, positive, utter, categorical, outright, complete, total, thorough, thoroughgoing, sheer, unmitigated, out-and-out. **2** candid, frank, open, honest, blunt, matter-of-fact, straightforward, forthright, up-front (*inf*).
➤*adv* absolutely, plainly, utterly, completely, totally, thoroughly.

down-to-earth *adj* practical, realistic, commonsensical, hardheaded, matter-of-fact, no-nonsense, unsentimental.

downtrodden *adj* oppressed, exploited, ground down, tyrannized, victimized, abused, bullied, helpless, poor, miserable, wretched.

downward *adj* descending, declining, downhill.

dowry *noun* marriage portion, marriage settlement, portion.

doze *verb* **1** drowse, nap, catnap, snooze (*inf*). **2** drift off, drop off (*inf*), nod off (*inf*).
➤*noun* nap, catnap, forty winks (*inf*), snooze (*inf*), siesta.

drab *adj* dull, dingy, dreary, colourless, lacklustre, cheerless, depressing, boring.

draft *noun* **1** sketch, outline, plan, rough, abstract, diagram, blueprint. **2** bill of exchange, money order, letter of credit.
➤*verb* sketch, outline, draw up, put together, prepare, plan, formulate, write.

drag *verb* **1** draw, pull, haul, heave, lug, tug, tow. **2** crawl, creep, inch, plod, trudge, lag, linger, loiter, dawdle.
➤*noun* bore, nuisance, bother, pain (*inf*), pain in the neck (*inf*), bind (*inf*).
drag out prolong, protract, spin out.

dragoon *verb* force, compel, bully, browbeat, railroad (*inf*).

drain *verb* **1** empty, finish, drink up, down (*inf*). **2** draw off, pump out, extract, remove, withdraw, tap, bleed, milk. **3** evacuate, void. **4** exhaust, sap, tax. **5** deplete, consume, use up. **6** drip, trickle, seep, leak, ooze, flow.
➤*noun* **1** channel, culvert, conduit, pipe, gutter, ditch, dyke, sewer. **2** drag, strain, demand, burden.

drama *noun* **1** play, show, piece, work. **2** theatre, dramaturgy, stagecraft, acting. **3** crisis, dilemma, scene, sensation.

dramatic *adj* **1** theatrical, stage, Thespian. **2** exciting, electrifying, tense, sensational, sudden, abrupt, unexpected, startling, thrilling, breathtaking, vivid, expressive, effective, powerful. **3** striking, impressive, spectacular.

dramatist *noun* playwright, scriptwriter, screenwriter.

dramatize *verb* **1** adapt. **2** exaggerate, overdo, overstate, ham up (*inf*).

drape *verb* **1** cover, envelop, swathe, wrap, overlay, decorate, adorn, dress. **2** hang, suspend, dangle, arrange.

drastic *adj* extreme, far-reaching, radical, violent, powerful, severe, harsh, rigorous.

draught *noun* **1** current, flow, breeze. **2** drink, potion, dose, cup.

draw *verb* **1** sketch, pencil, doodle, scribble, delineate, outline, trace. **2** depict, portray, represent. **3** pull, drag, haul, tow, tug. **4** pull together, close. **5** come, advance, approach, move, proceed. **6** extract, pull out, take out, unsheathe, produce, withdraw. **7** inhale, breathe in. **8** attract, lure, entice, interest, captivate, fascinate. **9** induce, prompt, elicit, call forth. **10** reach, come to, infer, derive. **11** pick, choose, select, take. **12** get, receive, earn. **13** tie, finish together.
➤*noun* **1** attraction, enticement, pull, lure, appeal. **2** tie, stalemate, dead heat. **3** raffle, lottery, sweepstake.
draw off drain, siphon, tap, bleed, milk.
draw out protract, prolong, drag out, spin out, stretch, extend, lengthen.
draw up 1 draft, compose, frame, prepare, write. **2** halt, stop, pull up.

drawback *noun* disadvantage, snag, hitch, flaw, fault, defect, weakness, difficulty, trouble, problem, catch, shortcoming, inconvenience, limitation, deficiency, downside.

drawing *noun* sketch, picture, outline, diagram, plan, illustration, cartoon, representation, depiction, portrait.

drawl *verb* drone, twang, draw out.

drawn *adj* tired, drained, wan, washed out, worn, haggard, gaunt, hollow-cheeked, stressed, tense.

dread *verb* **1** fear, be terrified of. **2** quail at, shrink from, fear, be apprehensive about, worry about.
➤*noun* fear, terror, horror, fright, alarm, panic, anxiety, apprehension, trepidation, misgiving.
➤*adj* dreaded, dreadful, feared, fearful, terrifying, frightful.

dreadful *adj* **1** awful, terrible, fearful, frightful, terrifying, horrific, horrible, appalling, shocking, ghastly, hideous, horrendous, distressing, harrowing, tragic. **2** awful, appalling, nasty, disagreeable, unpleasant, atrocious, appalling. **3** great, terrific, terrible, tremendous.

dream *noun* **1** vision, illusion, hallucination, fantasy, nightmare. **2** ambition, goal, aspiration, ideal, aim, hope, wish, desire. **3** reverie, trance, daydream. **4** delight, gem, treasure, ideal, beauty, marvel.
➤*verb* **1** fantasize, hallucinate. **2** think, consider, imagine, conceive, suppose. **3** daydream, fantasize, imagine, muse.
dream up invent, create, devise, conceive, think up, imagine, cook up (*inf*).

dreamy *adj* **1** dreamlike, surreal, unreal, fantastic, imaginary, shadowy, intangible, phantasmagorical. **2** impractical, unrealistic, daydreaming, fantasizing, romantic, quixotic, idealistic. **3** faraway, absent, abstracted, preoccupied, musing. **4** gorgeous, marvellous, wonderful, fabulous, terrific, heavenly.

dreary *adj* dull, flat, drab, colourless, featureless, lifeless, monotonous, boring, tedious, uninteresting, uneventful, routine, humdrum, gloomy, sombre, cheerless, comfortless, bleak, dismal, depressing.

dregs *pl noun* **1** sediment, residue, lees, grounds, deposit, precipitate, remains. **2** scum, refuse, dross, scourings, rabble, riff-raff.

drench *verb* soak, wet, saturate, douse, souse, flood, swamp.

dress *noun* **1** frock, gown, robe. **2** clothes, clothing, attire, garb, apparel, garments, costume, vestments, getup (*inf*), gear (*inf*).
➤*verb* **1** clothe, garb, rig, attire, accoutre, robe. **2** get dressed, put one's clothes on.

3 arrange, adjust, straighten, tidy, fix (*inf*), prepare, groom, comb, do, adorn, decorate, embellish, trim, furbish. **4** treat, tend, clean, cover, bandage, bind up, strap up, attend to. **5** prepare, get ready, clean.
dress down reprimand, rebuke, scold, berate, tell off (*inf*), bawl out (*inf*), tear off a strip (*inf*).
dress up decorate, trim, embellish, beautify, prettify, titivate, tart up (*inf*).

dressing *noun* **1** sauce, relish, garnish. **2** bandage, plaster, compress, covering. **3** manure, fertilizer, compost.

dressmaker *noun* seamstress, needlewoman, tailor, couturier.

dribble *verb* **1** trickle, drip, ooze, seep, leak, run. **2** drool, slaver, slobber.
➤*noun* drip, trickle, leak.

drift *verb* **1** wander, meander, stray, roam, float, freewheel, coast. **2** accumulate, pile up, gather, bank.
➤*noun* **1** trend, tendency, movement, flow. **2** shift, sea change. **3** deviation, digression, variation. **4** meaning, intention, purpose, object, point, gist, thrust, implication, significance, import. **5** bank, mound, heap, mass, accumulation.

drill *verb* **1** teach, instruct, train, practise, rehearse, exercise, discipline. **2** instil, inculcate, din in. **3** bore, punch. **4** pierce, perforate, puncture.
➤*noun* **1** instruction, training, exercise, practice, repetition, discipline. **2** procedure, routine. **3** borer, awl, bit, gimlet.

drink *verb* **1** imbibe, swallow, down, quaff, sup, swill, sip, swig (*inf*), knock back (*inf*). **2** booze (*inf*), hit the bottle (*inf*), tipple, indulge, tope. **3** toast, pledge, drink the health of.
➤*noun* **1** beverage, brew, potion, liquid. **2** swallow, sip, nip, spot, glass, cup, mug, slug (*inf*), snifter (*inf*). **3** alcohol, liquor, spirits, booze (*inf*), hooch (*inf*).

drinker *noun* drunk, drunkard, alcoholic, alkie (*inf*), piss artist (*sl*), soak (*inf*), boozer (*inf*), lush (*inf*).

drip *verb* **1** drop, dribble, trickle, splash, leak, filter, percolate, seep, ooze. **2** drop, dribble, trickle, sprinkle.
➤*noun* **1** drop, splash, bead, tear, trickle, dribble. **2** weakling, milksop, wimp (*inf*), weed (*inf*), softy (*inf*), ninny (*inf*).

drum

drive *verb* **1** steer, direct, control, handle, operate, pilot. **2** take, transport, convey, carry, chauffeur. **3** strike, hammer, bang, ram, hit, dig, sink, thrust, plunge. **4** force, push, coerce, compel, impel, pressure, pressurize, persuade, motivate, goad, spur. **5** lead, prompt, provoke. **6** move, urge, propel, guide, shepherd, usher. **7** power, propel.
➤*noun* **1** ride, jaunt, outing, excursion, journey, tour, trip, run, spin (*inf*). **2** energy, vigour, verve, enterprise, initiative, push, ambition, motivation, determination, resolve, spirit, tenacity, get-up-and-go (*inf*), vim (*inf*). **3** instinct, impulse, urge, need, desire. **4** campaign, crusade, struggle, effort, push (*inf*). **5** driveway, avenue, road, roadway. **6** thrust, power, propulsion.
be driving at imply, allude to, refer to, mean, suggest, insinuate, have in mind, intend, get at (*inf*).

drivel *noun* nonsense, gibberish, rubbish, bunkum (*inf*), tosh (*inf*), tripe (*inf*), claptrap (*inf*), twaddle (*inf*), eyewash (*inf*), hogwash (*inf*), bosh (*inf*), crap (*sl*), balls (*sl*).
➤*verb* **1** dribble, slaver, slobber, drool. **2** babble, jabber, blather, blether, witter (*inf*), waffle (*inf*).

driver *noun* motorist, chauffeur, cabbie, trucker.

drizzle *noun* mist, spray, shower, mizzle.
➤*verb* **1** spit, spot, rain, mizzle. **2** sprinkle, shower, spray.

droll *adj* comic, comical, amusing, funny, humorous, entertaining, witty, whimsical, quaint, eccentric, odd.

drone *verb* **1** hum, buzz, whirr, purr, murmur. **2** intone, prattle, spout (*inf*), drivel (*inf*).
➤*noun* **1** hum, buzz, whirr, purring, murmur. **2** parasite, hanger-on, sponger (*inf*), scrounger (*inf*), idler, layabout, shirker, skiver (*inf*).

drool *verb* **1** dribble, slaver, slobber, salivate. **2** dote, gush, slobber, enthuse.

droop *verb* **1** sag, sink, drop, bow, bend, hang down. **2** wilt, fade, languish, weaken, flag, decline, slump, lose heart.

drop *verb* **1** fall, sink, descend, dive, plunge, tumble, lower, let fall, let go. **2** fall, collapse, faint, swoon. **3** lower, decrease, diminish, depreciate, dwindle, lessen, subside, fall, sink, plunge, slacken off, weaken. **4** abandon, desert, discard, chuck (*inf*), ditch (*inf*), reject, repudiate, renounce, give up, disown, jilt, run out on (*inf*). **5** stop, end, cease, finish, discontinue, interrupt. **6** omit, exclude, leave out. **7** deposit, set down, unload, let off, put off, deliver, leave.
➤*noun* **1** bead, pearl, globule, drip, bubble, blob, tear, oval. **2** sip, tot, nip, splash, mouthful, dash (*inf*), spot (*inf*). **3** sprinkle, trickle, taste, bit, speck, trace, modicum, pinch, dab, smidgen (*inf*), tad (*inf*). **4** decline, slump, plunge, falling-off, decrease, downturn, lowering, reduction, diminution.

drop off 1 decline, drop, fall off, decrease, lessen, diminish, slacken off. **2** fall asleep, doze off, drift off, nod off (*inf*).

drop out give up, withdraw, pull out, opt out, cry off, back out, quit (*inf*).

dross *noun* scum, debris, waste, dregs, slag, refuse, rubbish.

drought *noun* dry spell, dryness, aridity.

drove *noun* **1** herd, flock, pack. **2** swarm, crowd, mob, herd, horde, throng.

drown *verb* **1** submerge, engulf, inundate, flood. **2** deluge, swamp, drench. **3** drown out, overwhelm, swamp, obliterate.

drowsy *adj* **1** sleepy, tired, dozy, dozing, nodding, somnolent, half-asleep, yawning, lethargic, torpid, heavy, heavy-eyed, dopey (*inf*), groggy (*inf*). **2** sleepy, soporific, hypnotic, soothing, lulling, restful.

drub *verb* **1** beat, pummel, thrash, wallop, hammer. **2** beat, defeat, trounce, hammer, paste (*inf*), clobber (*inf*).

drudge *noun* toiler, plodder, hack, servant, slave, skivvy (*inf*), dogsbody (*inf*).

drudgery *noun* toil, hard work, hard labour, donkeywork (*inf*), slog (*inf*), grind (*inf*).

drug *noun* **1** medicine, medication, medicament, remedy, panacea. **2** narcotic, opiate, barbiturate, amphetamine, sedative, stimulant, downer (*inf*), upper (*inf*).
➤*verb* medicate, sedate, tranquillize, anaesthetize, dope (*inf*), knock out (*inf*).

drum *noun* tambour, tabor, tympanum, tom-tom.

➤*verb* **1** beat, tap, rap, knock, hammer. **2** thrum, throb, pulsate. **3** instil, din into, inculcate.

drum out cashier, discharge, expel, dismiss, oust.

drum up obtain, get, collect, attract, canvass, solicit.

drunk *adj* inebriated, intoxicated, under the influence, tipsy, tiddly (*inf*), merry (*inf*), squiffy (*inf*), pissed (*sl*), stoned (*inf*), wasted (*inf*), sloshed (*inf*), smashed (*inf*), paralytic (*inf*), tight (*inf*), legless (*inf*), plastered (*inf*), stewed (*inf*), sozzled (*inf*), tanked up (*inf*), well-oiled (*inf*), blotto (*inf*), pie-eyed (*inf*), soused (*inf*), tired and emotional (*inf*).
➤*noun* drunkard, drinker, alcoholic, dipsomaniac, alkie (*inf*), boozer (*inf*), soak (*inf*), tippler (*inf*), piss artist (*sl*), lush (*inf*).

drunken *adj* **1** drunk, inebriated, intoxicated, tipsy. **2** bibulous, crapulent, intemperate. **3** debauched, riotous, roistering, orgiastic, bacchanalian, bacchic, Dionysian.

dry *adj* **1** arid, parched, scorched, waterless, rainless, barren. **2** dried, shrivelled, withered, wilted, desiccated, dehydrated, hard. **3** dull, flat, boring, tedious, tiresome, wearisome, monotonous, uninteresting, unimaginative, prosaic, dreary, vapid, insipid. **4** laconic, terse, deadpan, sly, ironic, subtle, low-key. **5** impassive, unemotional, impersonal, remote.
➤*verb* **1** towel, wipe, blot, mop, parch, scorch, sear, desiccate, dehydrate, drain, shrivel, harden, wither, wilt. **2** dehydrate, desiccate, preserve, cure.

dry up **1** run out, give out, fail, stop, disappear. **2** fall silent, shut up, forget one's lines, forget one's words.

dual *adj* double, twofold, duplex, binary, twin, combined.

dub *verb* name, christen, label, designate, nickname.

dubiety *noun* doubt, doubtfulness, dubiosity, indecision, uncertainty, scepticism.

dubious *adj* **1** doubtful, uncertain, unsure, undecided, sceptical. **2** doubtful, unsure, unsettled, unclear, unresolved, open, equivocal, ambiguous, debatable, question-

able. **3** questionable, suspect, unreliable, untrustworthy, dodgy (*inf*), fishy (*inf*), iffy (*inf*).

duck *verb* **1** bob, crouch, stoop, bow, drop, hunch. **2** dip, dunk, immerse, plunge, submerge. **3** dodge, avoid, evade, shirk, wriggle out of.

duct *noun* conduit, pipe, tube, passage.

ductile *adj* **1** malleable, plastic, flexible, pliable. **2** biddable, malleable, yielding, tractable, amenable, cooperative.

dud *noun* failure, flop (*inf*), washout (*inf*).
➤*adj* broken, defective, inoperative, worthless, duff (*inf*).

due *adj* **1** owing, unpaid, outstanding. **2** rightful, merited, deserved. **3** right, fit, fitting, right and proper, appropriate, requisite, adequate, sufficient. **4** scheduled, expected.
➤*adv* exactly, directly, dead (*inf*).
➤*noun* **1** right, prerogative, deserts, just deserts. **2** fee, membership, charge, subscription, levy.

due to **1** caused by, attributable to, ascribable to. **2** owing to, because of.

duel *noun* **1** single combat, affair of honour. **2** contest, fight, clash, struggle.

duffer *noun* bungler, blunderer, dunce, ignoramus, numskull, fool, wally (*inf*), clot (*inf*).

dulcet *adj* sweet, pleasant, pleasing, melodious, harmonious, musical, euphonious, soothing, soft.

dull *adj* **1** murky, grey, overcast, cloudy. **2** gloomy, sombre, drab, colourless, faded, dim, leaden, lacklustre, matt. **3** muted, subdued, indistinct, muffled. **4** obtuse, stolid, stupid, slow, slow-witted, dense, dim, dim-witted, thick (*inf*), dozy (*inf*). **5** boring, uninteresting, unexciting, unimaginative, uneventful, dry, dreary, monotonous, flat, heavy, ponderous, humdrum, tedious, tiresome, pedestrian, prosaic. **6** apathetic, languid, listless, sluggish, lethargic, stagnant, slow, inactive, slack.
➤*verb* blunt, alleviate, mitigate, allay, lessen, reduce, diminish, soften, moderate, mute, tone down, numb, deaden, dim, fade, wash out, obscure, tarnish, darken.

duly *adv* rightly, rightfully, correctly, properly, fittingly, appropriately, deservedly, accordingly.

dumb *adj* **1** silent, mute, mum (*inf*), speechless, voiceless. **2** inarticulate, tongue-tied, uncommunicative. **3** stupid, foolish, unintelligent, dim, slow, ignorant, thick (*inf*), dozy (*inf*), dense (*inf*), brainless (*inf*), gormless (*inf*).

dumbfound *verb* astonish, astound, amaze, stun, stagger, take aback, disconcert, nonplus, knock for six (*inf*), knock sideways (*inf*), gobsmack (*inf*).

dummy *noun* **1** figure, model, mannequin. **2** model, mock-up, copy, duplicate, reproduction. **3** dolt, blockhead, fool, idiot, simpleton, wally (*inf*), berk (*inf*), dope (*inf*), charlie (*inf*), chump (*inf*), clot (*inf*).
➤*adj* **1** fake, sham, imitation. **2** simulated, mock, practice, trial.

dump *verb* **1** drop, deposit, put down, throw down, park, plonk (*inf*). **2** discharge, unload, empty, tip, pour. **3** scrap, jettison, get rid of, discard, dispose of, offload, throw away, throw out, chuck (*inf*), ditch (*inf*), drop, jilt, walk out on, abandon.
➤*noun* **1** tip, rubbish heap, junkyard, scrapyard. **2** hovel, slum, pigsty (*inf*), hole (*inf*).

dumps *pl noun* depression, despondency, sadness, blues (*inf*).

dun *adj* brownish, greyish-brown, khaki, mud-coloured, mousy.

dunce *noun* ignoramus, dullard, simpleton, idiot, fool, blockhead, thickhead, ass, dolt, halfwit, dummy (*inf*), dimwit (*inf*), nitwit (*inf*).

dung *noun* muck, excrement, faeces, droppings, manure, fertilizer.

dungeon *noun* cell, oubliette, prison, jail, vault.

dupe *verb* cheat, deceive, hoax, hoodwink, trick, fool, take in, humbug, bamboozle (*inf*), con (*inf*).
➤*noun* victim, fool, pawn, puppet, tool, gull, sucker (*inf*), mug (*inf*), sap (*inf*), stooge (*inf*).

duplicate *verb* **1** copy, clone, reproduce, photocopy. **2** repeat, equal.
➤*adj* **1** identical, twin, matching. **2** double, duplex, twofold.
➤*noun* **1** copy, replica, facsimile, carbon copy, photocopy, clone. **2** match, twin, fellow, counterpart.

duplicity *noun* deceit, deceitfulness, deception, double-dealing, treachery, trickery, fraud, chicanery, hypocrisy, dishonesty.

durable *adj* lasting, enduring, abiding, unfading, long-lasting, hard-wearing, heavy-duty, strong, stout, robust, sturdy, reinforced, resistant, tough, permanent, fixed, stable, fast, unchanging.

duration *noun* continuance, period, time, span, length, extent, course.

duress *noun* **1** constraint, coercion, compulsion, pressure, force. **2** imprisonment, detention, confinement, captivity, custody, restraint.

during *prep* **1** throughout, through. **2** in, within.

dusk *noun* twilight, nightfall, sunset, evening, gloaming, gloom, darkness, dark.

dusky *adj* **1** shadowy, shady, dim, dark, gloomy, murky, twilit, crepuscular. **2** swarthy, dark, dark-skinned, dark-complexioned, black, brown, tawny.

dust *noun* **1** powder. **2** grit, grime, dirt, soot. **2** earth, soil, ground.
➤*verb* **1** clean, wipe, brush, polish. **2** sprinkle, powder, dredge, scatter, strew, cover.

dusty *adj* **1** dust-covered, unswept, dirty, grubby. **2** powdery, chalky, granular, crumbly.

dutiful *adj* obedient, respectful, deferential, filial, conscientious, thoughtful, considerate, faithful, devoted.

duty *noun* **1** task, job, assignment, mission, office, obligation, responsibility, function, role. **2** obligation, responsibility, commitment. **3** tax, excise, customs, toll, tariff.
off duty off, off work, at leisure, free.
on duty working, at work, on call.

dwarf *noun* **1** midget, pygmy, manikin, homunculus. **2** gnome, goblin.
➤*adj* miniature, tiny, small, diminutive, bantam, baby, pygmy, undersized, stunted, mini (*inf*).
➤*verb* **1** dominate, overshadow, tower over, rise above. **2** stunt, retard, arrest.

dwell *verb* live, reside, lodge, stay, remain, settle.
dwell on/upon brood on, think about, meditate on, turn over, reflect on, harp on, linger over, elaborate, expatiate on.

dwelling *noun* abode, residence, house, home, lodgings, domicile, habitation.

dwindle *verb* diminish, decrease, lessen, shrink, abate, wane, ebb, decline, fade, taper off, tail off, waste away.

dye *noun* **1** colourant, pigment, tint, stain, wash. **2** colour, hue, shade.
➤*verb* stain, tint, colour.

dyed-in-the-wool *adj* entrenched, inveterate, long-standing, die-hard, hard-core, hardened, inflexible, unshakable, absolute, utter, confirmed, card-carrying.

dying *adj* **1** deathbed. **2** last, final.

dynamic *adj* forceful, powerful, energetic, vigorous, active, lively, vital, high-powered, go-ahead (*inf*), go-getting (*inf*).

dynasty *noun* house, line, succession.

each *pron* each one, every one, one and all.
➤*adj* every, every single, individual, separate.
➤*adv* apiece, per person, respectively, individually, separately.

eager *adj* keen, avid, enthusiastic, ardent, intent, earnest, impatient, anxious, desirous, longing, itching.

ear *noun* 1 attention, notice, heed, regard, consideration. 2 sensitivity, discrimination, perception, appreciation.

early *adj* 1 first, primary, opening, introductory. 2 premature, untimely, forward, advanced. 3 primitive, primordial, primeval, ancient.
➤*adv* in advance, beforehand, too soon, prematurely, in good time, ahead of schedule.

earmark *verb* 1 label, tag. 2 set aside, reserve, designate, allocate, ring-fence.

earn *verb* 1 make, be paid, collect, gross, net, take home. 2 yield, bring in. 3 get, gain, acquire, attain, win, merit, warrant.

earnest[1] *adj* serious, solemn, intense, determined, passionate, wholehearted, ardent, eager, dedicated, committed, zealous.
in earnest serious, sincere, genuine, earnestly, seriously, passionately, sincerely, ardently, eagerly, diligently.

earnest[2] *noun* 1 security, deposit. 2 token, pledge, promise, assurance, guarantee.

earnings *pl noun* pay, wages, salary, remuneration, emolument, income, revenue.

earth *noun* 1 world, globe, sphere, orb. 2 land, ground. 3 soil, dirt, clay.

earthly *adj* 1 terrestrial, telluric. 2 worldly, mundane, temporal, secular, material, physical, mortal, human. 3 possible, likely, conceivable, imaginable.

earthquake *noun* seism, quake (*inf*), tremor.

earthy *adj* coarse, crude, ribald, bawdy, vulgar, rude, unrefined, down-to-earth.

ease *verb* 1 alleviate, allay, soothe, palliate, relieve, comfort, lessen, reduce, moderate, lighten. 2 abate, moderate, subside, let up, calm, diminish, decrease, die down. 3 facilitate, help, assist, aid, simplify, smooth, expedite. 4 slide, slip, guide, steer, manoeuvre.
➤*noun* 1 facility, effortlessness, readiness, deftness, easiness, simplicity, convenience, user-friendliness. 2 calmness, tranquillity, comfort, relief, security. 3 composure, comfort, relaxation, naturalness. 4 rest, repose, relaxation, leisure, luxury.
at ease relaxed, comfortable, at home, secure, calm, composed.

easily *adv* 1 with ease, effortlessly, comfortably, simply, readily, smoothly. 2 by far, far and away, indisputably, undeniably, undoubtedly, definitely, certainly, clearly.

easy *adj* 1 simple, effortless, straightforward, uncomplicated, child's play (*inf*), a piece of cake (*inf*), light, undemanding, user-friendly. 2 peaceful, calm, untroubled, quiet, relaxed, comfortable, natural, unforced, casual. 3 leisurely, unhurried, moderate, gentle, even, steady. 4 painless, trouble-free, comfortable, relaxing, restful, contented, secure, leisured, luxurious. 5 compliant, obliging, yielding. 6 flexible, accommodating, easygoing.

easygoing *adj* 1 carefree, happy-go-lucky, relaxed, laid back (*inf*). 2 calm, placid, even-tempered, tolerant, understanding, flexible, casual, informal.

eat *verb* 1 consume, devour, scoff (*inf*), guzzle (*inf*), put away (*inf*), polish off (*inf*), munch, gnaw, swallow, ingest, feed on. 2 erode, corrode, wear away, destroy.
eat into consume, use, deplete, waste, drain.

eatable *adj* edible, comestible, wholesome, good, palatable, appetizing.

eavesdrop *verb* listen in, overhear, snoop (*inf*), monitor, tap (*inf*), bug (*inf*).

ebb *verb* 1 go out, flow back, recede, retreat, withdraw. 2 subside, abate, sink, fall, decline, weaken, fade, wane, decrease, diminish, peter out, die away.

ebullient *adj* exuberant, enthusiastic, excited, animated, irrepressible, effervescent, exhilarated, elated.

ebullition *noun* boiling, seething, bubbling, effervescence.

eccentric *adj* irregular, abnormal, strange, odd, weird, quirky, unconventional, idiosyncratic, offbeat (*inf*), wacky (*inf*).
➤*noun* character, case (*inf*), oddity, original, weirdo (*inf*), oddball (*inf*), crank (*inf*), nutter (*inf*).

ecclesiastic *noun* cleric, clergyman, clergywoman, divine, priest, minister.
➤ **ecclesiastical** *adj* ecclesiastic, clerical, sacerdotal, religious, holy, spiritual, priestly, ministerial.

echelon *noun* grade, rank, level, tier, step, degree.

echo *verb* 1 resound, reverberate, ring. 2 repeat, reflect. 3 copy, imitate, ape, parrot, repeat, reiterate.
➤*noun* 1 resonance, reverberation, repetition, reflection. 2 copy, imitation, parallel, likeness, reminder, repercussion.

éclat *noun* 1 splendour, brilliance, glory, renown. 2 show, display, ostentation, effect. 3 acclaim, applause.

eclectic *adj* diverse, varied, multifarious, comprehensive, all-embracing, catholic, broad, wide-ranging, general.

eclipse *verb* 1 obscure, hide, cover, mask, shadow, darken. 2 surpass, transcend, excel, outdo, overshadow, outshine.
➤*noun* 1 obscuration, occultation, adumbration. 2 decline, fall, deterioration, degeneration, wane, ebb.

economic *adj* 1 monetary, financial, pecuniary, budgetary, commercial, business, trade, mercantile. 2 profitable, viable, cost-effective, remunerative.

economical *adj* 1 thrifty, provident, careful, sparing, frugal, mean. 2 efficient, money-saving.

economize *verb* save, conserve, husband, cut corners (*inf*), budget, cut back, tighten one's belt (*inf*).

economy *noun* 1 financial system, wealth, resources. 2 thrift, thriftiness, husbandry, frugality, parsimony. 3 saving, cut.
➤*adj* cheap, inexpensive, low-cost, budget.

ecstasy *noun* rapture, bliss, elation, euphoria, seventh heaven (*inf*), cloud nine (*inf*), exhilaration, thrill.

ecstatic *adj* overjoyed, blissful, delighted, elated, euphoric, exhilarated, thrilled, over the moon (*inf*).

eddy *noun* whirlpool, vortex, swirl.
➤*verb* whirl, swirl, turn.

edge *noun* 1 border, verge, brink, side, outline, boundary, perimeter, limit. 2 rim, lip, margin, parsiphery, fringe, border. 3 sharpness, keenness, intensity, bite, sting, trenchancy.
➤*verb* 1 trim, bind, border, fringe. 2 creep, inch, steal, sidle, worm.
on edge nervous, anxious, tense, keyed up, ill at ease.

edging *noun* border, trimming.

edgy *adj* nervous, anxious, tense, sensitive, touchy, irritable.

edible *adj* eatable, comestible, esculent, wholesome, good.

edict *noun* decree, ordinance, ruling, proclamation, pronouncement, command, order, injunction.

edifice *noun* building, erection, structure, pile.

edify *verb* improve, uplift, elevate, enlighten, inform, educate, instruct.

edit *verb* 1 compile, prepare, redact, compose. 2 assemble, compile, cut. 3 correct, emend, revise, modify, check, censor, expurgate.

edition *noun* 1 impression, revision. 2 copy, issue, number, volume, version.

editor *noun* reviser, redactor, compiler.

educate *verb* 1 school, instruct, teach, train, coach, tutor. 2 edify, inform, enlighten, civilize, cultivate, develop, improve.

educated *adj* 1 scholarly, learned, erudite, intellectual, highbrow. 2 literate, well-read, knowledgeable, schooled, cultivated, refined, enlightened, informed.

education *noun* **1** schooling, instruction, teaching, training, coaching, tuition, enlightenment, cultivation. **2** learning, knowledge, scholarship, erudition, literacy, culture.

eerie *adj* weird, uncanny, strange, frightening, chilling, unnatural, ghostly, spooky (*inf*).

efface *verb* erase, rub out, obliterate, expunge, remove, blot out.
efface oneself withdraw, keep out of the limelight, be modest.

effect *noun* **1** result, consequence, issue, event, aftermath, repercussion. **2** power, force, effectiveness, efficacy, success, impact, influence, weight. **3** action, operation, implementation, enforcement, execution, performance.
➤*verb* **1** cause, bring about, create, produce, make, effectuate, achieve, accomplish. **2** carry out, perform, execute, implement.
in effect in fact, actually, in reality, effectively, essentially, virtually, to all intents and purposes.
take effect 1 act, work, function. **2** come into effect, come into force, come into operation, start.

effective *adj* **1** successful, productive, active, effectual, efficacious, efficient, capable, useful. **2** operative, current, valid, in force. **3** striking, impressive, powerful, potent, forceful, influential, convincing, persuasive. **4** actual, real, practical, essential.

effects *pl noun* goods, chattels, movables, property, belongings, possessions, baggage, paraphernalia, things (*inf*), stuff (*inf*).

effectual *adj* **1** successful, productive, effective, efficacious, powerful, potent, useful, functional. **2** legal, lawful, binding, in force, valid.

effectuate *verb* effect, actuate, bring about, initiate, produce, procure, carry out, execute.

effeminate *adj* unmanly, womanish, feminine, effete, camp, sissy (*inf*).

effervesce *verb* **1** bubble, fizz, sparkle, foam, froth, ferment, boil. **2** sparkle, be ebullient, be exuberant, enthuse.

effete *adj* weak, feeble, drained, spent, enervated, decadent, degenerate, dissipated.

efficacious *adj* effective, effectual, powerful, potent, successful, productive, efficient, competent.

efficient *adj* **1** competent, proficient, skilful, expert, adept, capable, organized, businesslike. **2** effective, effectual, efficacious, productive, economical, labour-saving, streamlined, rationalized.

effigy *noun* image, likeness, representation, idol, figure, model, dummy, guy.

effloresce *verb* flower, bloom, blossom.

effluent *noun* outflow, efflux, effluence, discharge, waste, sewage, emission, exhalation.

effluvium *noun* exhalation, emanation, emission, fumes, gas, miasma, smell, stench.

effort *noun* **1** exertion, energy, struggle, strain, application, pains, work, labour. **2** attempt, try, endeavour, go (*inf*), stab (*inf*), shot (*inf*). **3** achievement, accomplishment, exploit, creation, work.

effrontery *noun* audacity, temerity, nerve, gall, impertinence, insolence, cheek, shamelessness, presumption.

effulgence *noun* brilliance, radiance, dazzle, blaze, splendour, resplendence.

effusion *noun* **1** outpouring, emission, discharge. **2** outflow, stream, efflux, effluence. **3** outburst, outpouring, gush.

effusive *adj* gushing, unreserved, unrestrained, extravagant, demonstrative, exuberant, lyrical, expansive.

egg *verb* **egg on** urge, encourage, push, spur, incite, provoke.

egghead *noun* intellectual, highbrow, academic, scholar, boffin, brain, genius.

ego *noun* **1** self, oneself, identity, self-image. **2** self-esteem, amour propre, self-confidence, self-importance.

egoism *noun* **1** selfishness, self-interest, self-seeking, looking after number one (*inf*). **2** egotism, self-obsession, self-absorption, self-centredness, egocentricity, egomania, self-regard, self-importance.

egotism noun **1** conceit, vanity, pride, arrogance, boastfulness, self-praise, self-obsession, self-absorption. **2** narcissism, self-love, self-regard, self-importance, egoism, self-centredness, egocentricity, egomania.

egregious adj flagrant, blatant, glaring, gross, rank, arrant, appalling, outrageous, heinous, monstrous.

egress noun **1** exit, way out, outlet, vent. **3** emergence, issue, exodus, escape.

ejaculate verb **1** exclaim, cry, shout, blurt out. **2** discharge, emit, eject, expel, spurt, spout.

eject verb **1** emit, discharge, ejaculate, throw out, expel, spout, spew. **2** evict, dispossess, turn out, throw out, turf out (inf). **3** drive out, expel, banish, throw out, dismiss, discharge, oust, get rid of.

eke verb **eke out 1** be frugal with, go easy on (inf), save, stretch out. **2** extend, supplement, add to, augment.

elaborate adj **1** ornate, fancy, fussy, showy, laboured, complicated, intricate, complex. **2** thorough, painstaking, precise, minute, detailed.
➤verb **1** devise, work out, develop. **2** amplify, expand, flesh out, refine, embellish, embroider.

élan noun spirit, vitality, vigour, zest, dash, verve.

elapse verb pass, go by, slip away, roll on, lapse.

elastic adj **1** stretchy, extensible, flexible, pliant, resilient, springy, rubbery, plastic. **2** adaptable, adjustable, flexible, accommodating, yielding, fluid.

elate verb exhilarate, enrapture, delight, thrill, transport, excite.

elbow noun angle, corner, bend, crook, joint, flexure.
➤verb **1** push, shove. **2** nudge, knock. **3** jostle, push, shove, barge (inf).

elbowroom noun space, room, scope, leeway.

elder adj older, senior, firstborn, earlier.
➤noun senior, superior, patriarch, chief.

elderly adj old, ageing, aged, advanced in years, senescent, over the hill (inf).

elect verb **1** select, pick, appoint, vote for. **2** choose, decide on, opt for, plump for (inf).
➤adj **1** elite, choice, select, hand-picked. **2** designate, chosen, selected.

election noun **1** voting, ballot, poll. **2** appointment, selection, choice.

elector noun voter, constituent.

electric adj **1** electrical, powered, battery-operated. **2** electrifying, exciting, thrilling, stirring, stimulating, dynamic. **3** charged, tense.

electrify verb excite, thrill, charge, fire, stimulate, animate, galvanize, astound.

elegant adj **1** stylish, fashionable, chic, smart, neat, graceful, dignified, refined. **2** tasteful, aesthetic, classic, fine, exquisite, luxurious, sumptuous, opulent.

elegiac adj plaintive, mournful, sad, melancholy, dirgelike, threnodic.

elegy noun lament, dirge, threnody, requiem.

element noun **1** component, constituent, member, unit, module, part, factor, detail. **2** trace, grain, hint, soupçon. **3** medium, domain, sphere, field, environment.

elemental adj basic, fundamental, essential, rudimentary, natural, primitive.

elementary adj basic, fundamental, rudimentary, introductory, primary, simple.

elements pl noun **1** weather, climate, atmospheric conditions, wind, rain. **2** basics, fundamentals, essentials, rudiments, principles.

elephantine adj **1** huge, immense, enormous, massive, gigantic, colossal. **2** ponderous, heavy, lumbering, clumsy.

elevate verb **1** lift, raise, hoist, erect. **2** exalt, ennoble, dignify, advance, promote, upgrade.

elevated adj **1** high, lofty, raised, hoisted. **2** exalted, dignified, grand, great, high-flown, lofty.

elevation noun **1** height, altitude. **2** lifting, raising, hoisting, erection, ennoblement, aggrandizement, promotion, advancement, preferment, exaltation, loftiness, grandeur.

elf noun pixie, imp, sprite, fairy.

elfin *adj* small, petite, dainty, delicate, elf-ish, elvish, impish, puckish, mischievous, arch.

elicit *verb* evoke, call forth, draw out, extract, derive, cause.

eligible *adj* **1** qualified, fit, appropriate, suitable. **2** acceptable, worthy, desirable.

eliminate *verb* **1** remove, get rid of, dispose of, discard, throw out, do away with, eradicate, annihilate, stamp out. **2** defeat, beat, knock out, conquer, overwhelm. **3** kill, rub out (*inf*), exterminate, liquidate (*inf*).

elite *noun* best, flower, cream, crème de la crème, elect, meritocracy, aristocracy.

elixir *noun* cure, remedy, cure-all, panacea, universal remedy.

elliptical *adj* **1** oval, ovate, ovoid, egg-shaped. **2** ambiguous, cryptic, obscure, concise, terse, succinct.

elocution *noun* delivery, diction, speech, articulation, enunciation, eloquence, oratory, declamation.

elongate *verb* lengthen, extend, stretch, prolong, draw out, protract.

elope *verb* run away, run off, flee, leave.

eloquence *noun* **1** oratory, rhetoric. **2** fluency, articulacy, cogency, forcefulness, expressiveness, way with words, diction, elocution.

eloquent *adj* **1** fluent, articulate, persuasive, glib, silver-tongued, cogent, impressive, stirring, moving. **2** meaningful, significant, suggestive, expressive, revealing.

else *adv* **1** other, different. **2** besides, more, in addition.

elsewhere *adv* somewhere else, not here, not there, away.

elucidate *verb* explain, expound, clarify, illuminate, throw light on, simplify, illustrate, interpret.

elude *verb* evade, avoid, escape, get away from, lose, shake off, give the slip, dodge.

elusive *adj* **1** hard to find, slippery, tricky, deceptive. **2** fugitive, subtle, indefinable, difficult, puzzling.

emaciate *verb* waste, atrophy, wizen, pinch, attenuate, enfeeble.

emanate *verb* **1** proceed, originate, derive, stem, issue, spring, flow. **2** emit, send out, give off, discharge, radiate, exhale.

emanation *noun* **1** origination, derivation, emergence, emission, discharge, radiation, exhalation. **2** emission, discharge, effluent.

emancipate *verb* liberate, free, release, deliver, unfetter, unchain, manumit, enfranchise.

emasculate *verb* **1** castrate, geld, neuter, unman. **2** weaken, debilitate, enfeeble, soften, dilute, water down.

embalm *verb* mummify, preserve.

embargo *noun* ban, prohibition, interdiction, bar, barrier, stoppage, restriction, obstruction.
➤ *verb* ban, prohibit, proscribe, interdict, bar, debar, stop, restrict, block, obstruct.

embark *verb* **1** board, get on, go aboard. **2** begin, start, set about, undertake, take up, launch into, broach.

embarrass *verb* discomfit, disconcert, abash, shame, show up, humiliate, mortify, chagrin, distress, upset, fluster, confound.

embassy *noun* **1** consulate, legation. **2** mission, legation, ministry, deputation.

embed *verb* **1** fix, set, plant, root, sink, insert. **2** implant, drive, hammer, ram.

embellish *verb* **1** ornament, decorate, adorn, deck, garnish, trim, beautify, enhance, enrich, gild. **2** varnish, embroider, colour, dress up, elaborate, exaggerate.

ember *noun* cinder, ash.

embezzle *verb* steal, rob, pilfer, appropriate, misappropriate, peculate, defalcate, defraud.

embitter *verb* **1** sour, envenom, disillusion, disenchant, disaffect, anger, exasperate. **2** aggravate, sour, poison.

emblazon *verb* **1** adorn, decorate, ornament. **2** display, show off, flaunt, publicize, proclaim.

emblem *noun* **1** symbol, token, representation, figure, sign, mark. **2** badge, device, symbol, mark, insignia, logo.

embody verb 1 reify, express, represent, symbolize. 2 incorporate, embrace, encompass, include, comprise, assimilate, integrate, combine. 3 personify, incarnate, epitomize, exemplify.

embolden verb encourage, hearten, inspirit, rouse, stir, spur, fire, invigorate, strengthen, reassure.

embrace verb 1 clasp, hold, hug, enfold, cuddle, squeeze. 2 adopt, espouse, take up, take on board (*inf*). 3 seize, grasp, accept, welcome. 4 include, comprehend, encompass, embody, incorporate, take in, subsume, involve.
➤*noun* hug, cuddle, squeeze, clasp, hold, clinch (*inf*).

embroider verb 1 sew, stitch. 2 decorate, ornament. 3 embellish, elaborate, exaggerate, colour, varnish, dress up.

embroidery noun 1 needlework, cross stitch, crewelwork, tapestry. 2 embellishment, elaboration, exaggeration, varnishing.

embroil verb involve, implicate, incriminate, entangle, enmesh, mix up.

embryonic adj rudimentary, undeveloped, early, immature, primary, inchoate, germinal, seminal.

emend verb correct, rectify, improve, polish, edit, redact.

emerge verb 1 appear, materialize, come out, surface. 2 become known, come out, come to light, transpire. 3 arise, develop, proceed, issue.

emergency noun crisis, accident, disaster, catastrophe, exigency, extremity, pinch, contingency.
➤*adj* urgent, reserve, backup, fallback, alternative, spare.

emergent adj emerging, arising, beginning, budding, developing, embryonic.

emigrate verb migrate, move abroad, resettle, relocate, depart, leave.

eminence noun 1 distinction, illustriousness, renown, mark, note, prominence, esteem, repute, prestige, greatness, grandeur, superiority. 2 hill, mound, height, elevation.

eminent adj 1 noted, notable, prominent, conspicuous, outstanding, paramount.

2 distinguished, illustrious, celebrated, renowned, esteemed, venerable, high-ranking, great.

emissary noun agent, ambassador, envoy, representative, legate, deputy.

emission noun 1 ejection, expulsion, discharge, release, ejaculation, secretion, emanation, radiation. 2 discharge, exhalation, leak.

emit verb 1 discharge, give off, send forth, release, eject, expel, emanate, exhale, radiate, secrete. 2 utter, let out, give vent to.

emollient adj soothing, lenitive, palliative, demulcent, softening, relaxing.
➤*noun* liniment, embrocation, lotion, salve, balm, oil, unguent.

emolument noun remuneration, pay, salary, wages, fee, stipend, honorarium, revenue, income, reward.

emotion noun feeling, sentiment, reaction, response, passion.

emotional adj 1 sensitive, susceptible, feeling, sentimental, responsive, demonstrative. 2 passionate, ardent, excitable, temperamental, hot-blooded, melodramatic, hysterical, overwrought. 3 emotive, rousing, stirring, moving, touching.

emotive adj rousing, stirring, controversial, sensitive, delicate, awkward.

empathize verb identify, sympathize, understand, be on the same wavelength (*inf*).

emperor noun ruler, sovereign, imperator, tsar, kaiser, shah.

emphasis noun 1 force, stress, accent, accentuation, underlining, underscoring, insistence, urgency. 2 weight, importance, stress, priority, attention.

emphasize verb 1 stress, accent, accentuate, press home, insist on. 2 underline, underscore, mark, spotlight, point up. 3 highlight, heighten, intensify.

emphatic adj 1 categorical, unequivocal, marked, pronounced, stressed, accented. 2 forceful, insistent, earnest, vigorous, positive, determined. 3 positive, definite, decided, absolute, categorical, unequivocal.

empire noun 1 domain, dominion, realm, commonwealth, territory. 2 sovereignty, dominion, supremacy, power, sway, rule.

empirical *adj* experimental, experiential, observed, practical.

employ *verb* **1** engage, appoint, hire, recruit, take on, sign up, retain, commission. **2** use, utilize, exploit, exercise, exert, apply, occupy, take up.

employee *noun* worker, member of staff, hand, operative.

employer *noun* manager, boss, contractor, proprietor, company, business.

employment *noun* **1** work, service. **2** situation, appointment, post, job, occupation, profession. **3** engagement, appointment, hire, recruitment, use, utilization, exploitation, exercise.

empower *verb* authorize, license, accredit, qualify, entitle, sanction, permit, enable.

empty *adj* **1** void, unfilled, devoid, bare, blank, clear. **2** deserted, uninhabited, vacant, unoccupied, free. **3** trivial, frivolous, idle, vain, hollow, unsubstantial. **4** worthless, meaningless, insincere, futile, useless, ineffective, aimless, purposeless. ➤*verb* **1** drain, evacuate, void, vacate, clear, unload. **2** discharge, pour out, tip out.

emulate *verb* **1** imitate, copy, follow, take after. **2** rival, compete with, vie with.

enable *verb* **1** permit, allow, facilitate, assist. **2** capacitate, empower, equip, authorize, license, qualify, permit, entitle.

enact *verb* **1** decree, ordain, rule, pass, make law, legislate, ratify. **2** perform, act out, play, represent, portray, depict, stage.

enamour *verb* infatuate, charm, enchant, bewitch, captivate.

encamp *verb* camp, pitch camp, bivouac, lodge, settle.

encampment *noun* camp, campsite, bivouac, base, quarters.

encapsulate *verb* summarize, sum up, epitomize, condense, digest.

encase *verb* enclose, wrap, sheathe, pack, box, crate.

enchant *verb* **1** bewitch, spellbind, hypnotize. **2** attract, captivate, charm, delight, enrapture, fascinate, beguile, entrance.

enchanting *adj* attractive, captivating, charming, delightful, lovely, winsome, appealing, endearing, engaging.

encircle *verb* surround, gird, circumscribe, ring, enclose, confine.

enclose *verb* **1** surround, encircle, shut in, fence in, confine, contain, encase, envelop. **2** include, insert, put in.

enclosure *noun* **1** pen, fold, pound, paddock, corral, yard. **2** inclusion, insertion.

encomium *noun* eulogy, panegyric, praise, acclaim, homage, tribute.

encompass *verb* **1** surround, encircle, gird, circumscribe, enclose, confine. **2** include, contain, embrace, cover, span, comprehend, incorporate.

encounter *verb* **1** confront, face, be faced with, come up against, experience, undergo, grapple with, struggle with. **2** meet, happen upon, come across, run into (*inf*). ➤*noun* **1** meeting, contact, rendezvous. **2** confrontation, clash, conflict, brush (*inf*), run-in (*inf*), fight, battle, engagement, skirmish.

encourage *verb* **1** cheer, hearten, reassure, comfort, inspirit, embolden, rouse, stir. **2** persuade, urge, exhort, spur, goad, incite, stimulate, motivate. **3** support, advocate, back, aid, foster, promote, advance, boost.

encroach *verb* intrude, trespass, invade, infiltrate, infringe, impinge, muscle in (*inf*), arrogate, usurp.

encumber *verb* **1** hamper, hinder, impede, handicap, inconvenience, obstruct, burden, weigh down. **2** burden, oppress, saddle, tax.

encumbrance *noun* hindrance, impediment, handicap, inconvenience, obstacle, obstruction, burden, load, responsibility, obligation.

encyclopedic *adj* comprehensive, all-inclusive, all-embracing, universal, wide-ranging, exhaustive, broad, compendious.

end *noun* **1** finish, conclusion, termination, close, cessation, stoppage, completion, resolution. **2** finale, ending, conclusion, climax, denouement. **3** extremity, tip, point, terminus, limit. **4** stub, butt, remnant, scrap. **5** aim, object, purpose, intention, reason, goal, target, objective. **6** death, demise, downfall, ruin, destruction, annihilation, extermination,

extinction. **7** part, section, side, aspect, area, department.
➤**verb 1** finish, conclude, terminate, close, cease, stop, complete, resolve. **2** ruin, destroy, annihilate, exterminate, abolish, dissolve.

endanger verb imperil, jeopardize, hazard, risk, expose, threaten, compromise.

endearment noun soft word, sweet nothing, blandishment, pet name, diminutive.

endeavour verb try, attempt, strive, struggle, do one's best, aim, undertake, venture.
➤**noun** try, attempt, bid, go (inf), shot (inf), effort, aim, undertaking, venture, enterprise.

ending noun end, finish, conclusion, finale, climax, denouement.

endless adj **1** unlimited, immeasurable, infinite, unending. **2** interminable, never-ending, ceaseless, incessant, constant, continuous, uninterrupted, unbroken, limitless, boundless, eternal, everlasting.

endorse verb approve, sanction, ratify, authorize, support, back, advocate, champion, vouch for, uphold.

endorsement noun approval, sanction, ratification, authorization, support, backing, advocacy.

endow verb **1** bestow, bequeath, will, present, grant, award, fund, finance. **2** give, bless, provide, supply, equip, invest, endue.

endowment noun **1** bequest, legacy, grant, award, donation, benefaction. **2** talent, gift, flair, faculty, attribute, quality, ability, skill.

endurance noun fortitude, stamina, strength, tenacity, staying power, persistence, perseverance, patience, stoicism, tolerance.

endure verb **1** bear, stand, brook, tolerate, permit, allow, put up with, abide. **2** undergo, experience, go through, suffer, submit to, take, brave, cope with, weather, withstand. **3** last, persist, remain, stay, continue, hold, prevail, survive.

enduring adj lasting, durable, continuing, abiding, prevailing, unwavering, permanent, eternal.

enemy noun foe, adversary, opponent, antagonist, rival, competitor.

energetic adj vigorous, active, lively, full of beans (inf), dynamic, spirited, animated, brisk, tireless, busy, strenuous, forceful.

energy noun **1** vigour, activity, life, vitality, dynamism, spirit, get-up-and-go (inf), stamina, strength, power, force, zest. **2** power, fuel, electricity.

enervate verb weaken, debilitate, enfeeble, sap, tire, weary, fatigue, prostrate, disable, incapacitate.

enfeeble verb weaken, debilitate, enervate, unman, sap, tire, weary, wear out, exhaust, deplete, reduce, diminish.

enfold verb **1** envelop, wrap, swathe, shroud, enclose, surround. **2** embrace, hug, clasp, hold.

enforce verb **1** apply, administer, implement, execute, carry out, discharge, impose, bring to bear. **2** force, compel, require, insist on, prescribe, ordain, impose, exact.

enfranchise verb emancipate, liberate, free, release, manumit, disenthral.

engage verb **1** hire, employ, appoint, take on, recruit, sign up, commission, retain. **2** engross, absorb, grip, hold, attract, draw, catch, win. **3** pledge, promise, vow, undertake, contract, agree, commit oneself. **4** attack, take on, encounter, meet, fight, combat. **5** interlock, mesh, join, activate, apply.
engage in participate in, take part in, undertake, tackle, embark on, practise.

engaged adj **1** betrothed, affianced, pledged, promised, spoken for (inf). **2** busy, active, occupied, tied up, involved, engrossed. **3** unavailable, in use, busy, occupied, taken, reserved, booked.

engagement noun **1** betrothal, pledge, promise. **2** pledge, promise, vow, contract, bond, obligation, commitment, involvement. **3** appointment, meeting, rendezvous, date, assignation, commitment. **4** employment, appointment, job, post, situation. **5** fight, battle, skirmish, combat, conflict, clash, encounter, attack, offensive.

engaging adj charming, delightful, enchanting, captivating, winning, appealing, attractive, fetching, pleasing, likable.

engender verb produce, cause, occasion, bring about, lead to, create, generate, beget, give rise to, provoke, arouse.

engine noun motor, generator, machine, mechanism, appliance, device.

engineer noun **1** designer, inventor. **2** mechanic, technician, operator, controller, driver.
➤verb plan, devise, contrive, manoeuvre, manipulate, bring about, arrange, orchestrate, mastermind.

engrave verb **1** inscribe, etch, cut, incise, carve, chisel, chase. **2** stamp, imprint, impress, fix, set, lodge, ingrain.

engraving noun **1** print, impression, etching, woodcut, lithograph, plate. **2** cutting, carving, chiselling, etching, lithography, intaglio.

engross verb absorb, preoccupy, occupy, engage, involve, interest, fascinate, grip, rivet.

engulf verb **1** flood, deluge, inundate, swamp, immerse, submerge. **2** overwhelm, consume, swallow up, bury, envelop, swamp, inundate.

enhance verb improve, embellish, enrich, heighten, boost, elevate.

enigma noun mystery, riddle, conundrum, puzzle, paradox, problem.

enjoin verb **1** order, command, direct, instruct, require, charge, bid, urge. **2** ban, bar, forbid, prohibit, proscribe, disallow, interdict.

enjoy verb **1** like, love, appreciate, relish, savour, luxuriate in, delight in, revel in, be amused by, be entertained by. **2** have, possess, benefit from, be endowed with, use, avail oneself of. **3** experience, have, be blessed with.
  enjoy oneself have fun, have a good time, have the time of one's life (inf), have a ball (inf), party, revel, live it up (inf), let one's hair down (inf).

enlarge verb **1** expand, magnify, amplify, grow, increase, develop, extend, stretch, swell, distend, dilate, inflate. **2** blow up, expand, magnify. **3** expatiate, elaborate, expand, descant, expound, develop, amplify, flesh out.

enlargement noun expansion, magnification, amplification, increase, development, extension, swelling, distension, dilation.

enlighten verb instruct, edify, teach, educate, inform, make aware, apprise, illuminate, civilize, cultivate.

enlightened adj aware, knowledgeable, educated, wise, learned, erudite, civilized, broad-minded, open-minded, liberal.

enlightenment noun understanding, awareness, insight, education, edification, knowledge, wisdom, erudition, civilization, broad-mindedness.

enlist verb **1** volunteer, join up, sign up, recruit, enrol, conscript. **2** engage, hire, take on, employ, recruit, draft. **3** secure, obtain, procure.

enliven verb **1** animate, liven up, invigorate, vitalize, excite, rouse, refresh, exhilarate. **2** brighten up, jazz up (inf), liven up, hearten, cheer up, perk up (inf).

en masse adv all together, as one, as a group, en bloc.

enmesh verb entangle, catch, ensnare, trap, embroil, involve.

enmity noun hostility, animosity, antagonism, strife, hate, antipathy, bad blood, ill will, bitterness, acrimony.

ennoble verb **1** elevate, uplift, magnify, glorify, dignify. **2** raise, elevate, aggrandize, exalt, honour.

ennui noun boredom, tedium, dissatisfaction, languor, lassitude, listlessness.

enormity noun **1** atrocity, outrage, scandal, horror, abomination, evil, iniquity, crime. **2** outrageousness, wickedness, heinousness, cruelty, brutality, monstrousness.

enormous adj huge, immense, vast, massive, whopping (inf), colossal, gigantic, mammoth, prodigious, monumental.

enough adj sufficient, adequate, ample.
➤pron sufficiency, adequacy, plenty.
➤adv **1** sufficiently, adequately, amply, abundantly. **2** tolerably, passably, reasonably, moderately.

en passant adv in passing, by the way, incidentally.

enquire verb **1** ask, question, query, interrogate, quiz. **2** investigate, look into, study, examine, probe.

enquiry noun **1** question, query. **2** inquest, investigation, study, survey, probe.

enrage verb incense, infuriate, madden, exasperate, anger, vex, irk, rouse, inflame.

enrapture verb delight, enchant, captivate, charm, beguile, thrill, ravish, transport.

enrich verb 1 improve, enhance, embellish, refine, uplift, develop. 2 augment, supplement

enrol verb register, put one's name down, join up, sign up, enlist, recruit, admit, record, note, list.

enrolment noun registration, matriculation, recruitment, enlistment, admission, acceptance.

en route adv on the way, in transit.

ensconce verb settle, lodge, install, nestle, snuggle up.

ensemble noun 1 whole, totality, entirety, aggregate, set, assemblage, combination, composite. 2 outfit, costume, suit, coordinates. 3 band, group, company, troupe, cast, choir.
➤ adv together, en masse, as a group, in concert, at the same time, all at once.

enshrine verb 1 consecrate, dedicate, revere, venerate, idolize. 2 immortalize, cherish, treasure, preserve, protect, guard.

enshroud verb shroud, veil, cloak, envelop, wrap, cover, obscure, conceal.

ensign noun flag, pennant, standard, colours.

enslave verb subjugate, oppress, bind, chain, fetter, yoke.

ensnare verb snare, trap, catch, net, enmesh, entangle, embroil.

ensue verb follow, succeed, arise, result, derive, stem, happen, transpire.

ensure verb guarantee, assure, make sure, make certain, confirm, certify, secure, safeguard.

entail verb involve, necessitate, demand, require, cause, produce, result in, lead to.

entangle verb 1 tangle, ravel, knot, mat, intertwine, catch, snarl, ensnare, complicate, confuse, muddle. 2 embroil, enmesh, involve, implicate, mix up.

entente noun understanding, arrangement, agreement, deal, pact, treaty.

enter verb 1 go in, come in, arrive, cross the threshold, invade, infiltrate. 2 penetrate, pierce, go into, pass into. 3 record, note, register, log, put down, input, introduce, insert. 4 join, enrol, enlist, sign up for, take up, engage in. 5 go in for, participate in, take part in, engage in. 6 begin, start, commence, embark on, set about, undertake.

enterprise noun 1 undertaking, venture, operation, project, scheme, campaign, effort, endeavour. 2 business, company, firm, establishment, concern. 3 initiative, resourcefulness, gumption, ambition, drive, energy, boldness, daring, adventurousness, spirit.

enterprising adj resourceful, entrepreneurial, go-ahead (inf), self-starting (inf), adventurous, bold, daring, ambitious, keen, energetic, spirited, enthusiastic.

entertain verb 1 amuse, divert, interest, occupy, please, delight. 2 receive, welcome, accommodate, put up, host, have round, wine and dine, treat, regale, throw a party. 3 harbour, foster, nurture, hold, have, consider, contemplate.

entertainment noun amusement, diversion, recreation, play, fun, show, performance, spectacle.

enthral verb captivate, fascinate, spellbind, hypnotize, mesmerize, rivet, grip, thrill.

enthrone verb 1 crown, install, invest, induct, ordain. 2 exalt, glorify, ennoble, elevate, idolize.

enthuse verb 1 be enthusiastic, rave, wax lyrical, gush. 2 make enthusiastic, excite, inspire, fire.

enthusiasm noun 1 keenness, ardour, passion, excitement, devotion, commitment, zeal, fanaticism. 2 pastime, hobby, passion, mania, craze, rage.

enthusiast noun fanatic, devotee, fan, aficionado, buff (inf), fiend (inf).

entice verb tempt, lure, draw, attract, seduce, cajole, coax, persuade.

entire adj 1 complete, whole, full, integral. 2 total, absolute, utter, unreserved. 3 intact, unbroken, sound, perfect, unimpaired.

entirely adv 1 completely, wholly, totally, fully, altogether, perfectly, absolutely, utterly. 2 only, solely, exclusively.

entirety *noun* **1** completeness, wholeness, totality, fullness. **2** whole, total, aggregate.

entitle *verb* **1** qualify, make eligible, authorize, empower, enable, allow, warrant. **2** call, name, dub, designate.

entity *noun* thing, object, article, individual, unit, body, being.

entomb *verb* bury, inter.

entourage *noun* attendants, staff, retinue, suite, escort, bodyguard, followers, companions.

entrails *pl noun* intestines, bowels, guts (*inf*), viscera, offal, innards (*inf*).

entrance[1] *noun* **1** way in, access, approach, drive, threshold, doorway, portal, lobby, foyer. **2** admission, admittance, entry, entrée, access, ingress. **3** entry, appearance, arrival, introduction.

entrance[2] *verb* **1** charm, enchant, delight, captivate, bewitch, beguile. **2** hypnotize, mesmerize.

entrant *noun* newcomer, novice, beginner, trainee, initiate, convert, competitor, contestant, candidate, applicant.

entrap *verb* **1** catch, capture, trap, snare, net, bag, enmesh, embroil. **2** trick, deceive, lure, entice.

entreat *verb* **1** beg, implore, beseech, plead, petition. **2** ask, request, exhort, crave, solicit.

entreaty *noun* appeal, plea, prayer, supplication, request, exhortation.

entrench *verb* establish, fix, lodge, install, dig in (*inf*), plant, embed, root.

entrepreneur *noun* businessman, businesswoman, executive, industrialist, tycoon, magnate, financier, impresario.

entrust *verb* commit, consign, hand over, deliver, commend, confide.

entry *noun* **1** admission, admittance, entrance, access. **2** entrance, way in, ingress, door, gate, portal, passage, opening. **3** appearance, arrival, entrance, introduction. **4** item, note, record, minute, memorandum, listing. **5** submission, entrant, contestant, candidate, applicant.

entwine *verb* twine, intertwine, interweave, interlace, twist, wind, entangle.

enumerate *verb* **1** list, name, cite, detail, specify, itemize. **2** number, count, reckon, tally, add up, total.

enunciate *verb* **1** articulate, pronounce, vocalize, voice, utter, say, speak. **2** state, express, propound, put forward, declare, announce.

envelop *verb* wrap, swathe, swaddle, enfold, sheathe, encase, cover, shroud, cloak, blanket, surround, enclose.

envelope *noun* **1** wrapper, wrapping, case, casing, sheath, cover. **2** skin, capsule, covering.

envenom *verb* **1** poison, contaminate, pollute, taint. **2** embitter, sour, provoke, inflame, anger, enrage.

enviable *adj* desirable, covetable, tempting, sought-after, favoured, privileged, blessed.

envious *adj* covetous, desirous, jealous, green with envy, resentful, grudging, jaundiced, discontented.

environ *verb* encircle, surround, circumscribe, gird, ring, enclose.

environment *noun* **1** surroundings, milieu, circumstances, conditions, background, setting, context. **2** habitat, element, medium, territory, domain, situation, location.

environs *pl noun* surroundings, vicinity, neighbourhood, locality, district.

envisage *verb* **1** visualize, imagine, picture, conceive, envision. **2** contemplate, foresee, predict, anticipate.

envoy *noun* **1** agent, deputy, diplomat, emissary, minister. **2** representative, delegate, messenger, intermediary, go-between.

envy *verb* covet, desire, crave, resent, begrudge.
➤*noun* enviousness, covetousness, desire, jealousy, resentment, grudge, spite, discontent, dissatisfaction.

ephemeral *adj* transitory, transient, fleeting, passing, brief, momentary, short-lived, impermanent.

epic *adj* **1** heroic, legendary, historic, impressive, lofty, elevated. **2** vast, huge, ambitious, grand, large-scale, long.
➤*noun* saga, narrative, legend, myth, epopee.

epicure *noun* gourmet, gastronome, foodie (*inf*), bon vivant, connoisseur, epicurean.

epidemic *adj* widespread, extensive, prevalent, rampant, rife.
➤*noun* 1 outbreak, plague, scourge. 2 upsurge, increase, outbreak, rash, wave, spate.

epigram *noun* witticism, quip, bon mot, pun, saying, aphorism.

epilogue *noun* afterword, conclusion, coda, tailpiece, appendix.

episode *noun* 1 incident, event, affair, business, adventure, experience. 2 instalment, part, chapter, programme, show, broadcast.

episodic *adj* 1 intermittent, spasmodic, sporadic, occasional. 2 anecdotal, discursive, rambling, wandering, disjointed.

epistle *noun* letter, missive, communication, message.

epithet *noun* 1 nickname, sobriquet, appellation, designation, label, tag, description. 2 insult, oath, curse, expletive.

epitome *noun* 1 archetype, exemplar, prototype, model, embodiment, personification, incarnation. 2 summary, synopsis, précis, résumé, digest, abstract.

epitomize *verb* 1 typify, exemplify, illustrate, embody, personify, incarnate, symbolize, represent. 2 summarize, synopsize, précis, condense, digest.

epoch *noun* age, era, period, time, date.

equable *adj* 1 placid, composed, level-headed, cool, even-tempered, easygoing (*inf*). 2 moderate, temperate, even, uniform, constant, steady.

equal *adj* 1 identical, the same, like, uniform, even. 2 egalitarian, fair, impartial, comparable, equivalent, commensurate. 3 level, even, balanced, symmetrical. 4 adequate, good enough, suited, fit, competent, able.
➤*noun* peer, fellow, match, twin, counterpart, equivalent.
➤*verb* 1 add up to, amount to, total, correspond to, balance, equate to. 2 match, reach, achieve, come up to, equalize.

equality *noun* uniformity, evenness, equivalence, parity, par, identity, correspondence, egalitarianism.

equalize *verb* 1 level, even up, square, match, balance, standardize. 2 smooth, even out, make uniform.

equanimity *noun* composure, self-possession, self-control, level-headedness, presence of mind, calmness, tranquillity, cool (*inf*).

equate *verb* 1 compare, liken, identify, associate, pair, bracket, link. 2 equal, match, square, tally, balance, correspond.

equestrian *noun* rider, jockey, horseman, horsewoman.
➤*adj* riding, mounted, on horseback, in the saddle.

equilibrium *noun* 1 balance, stability, steadiness, stasis, equipoise, parity, symmetry, evenness, equality. 2 equanimity, poise, aplomb, sangfroid, composure, self-possession, level-headedness.

equip *verb* 1 supply, provide, furnish, fit out, kit out, stock, arm. 2 endow, prepare.

equipment *noun* apparatus, tackle, gear, kit, outfit, tools, supplies, resources.

equipoise *noun* 1 balance, stability, equilibrium. 2 counterbalance, counterpoise.

equitable *adj* just, fair, even-handed, unbiased, impartial, objective, right, proper.

equity *noun* justice, fairness, even-handedness, equitableness, impartiality, objectivity, propriety, reasonableness.

equivalent *adj* 1 commensurate, tantamount, on a par, equal, like, the same, identical. 2 comparable, corresponding, homologous, similar, interchangeable, substitutable, synonymous.
➤*noun* equal, parallel, homologue, match, twin, counterpart, opposite number.

equivocal *adj* 1 ambiguous, two-edged, vague, indefinite, evasive, roundabout. 2 suspicious, suspect, shady (*inf*), doubtful, dubious, questionable.

equivocate *verb* prevaricate, hedge, evade, tergiversate, quibble, vacillate, beat about the bush (*inf*), sit on the fence (*inf*).

era *noun* age, period, epoch, time, day, date.

eradicate *verb* annihilate, extirpate, exterminate, wipe out, root out, get rid of, abolish, eliminate, stamp out.

erase *verb* **1** rub out, wipe off, expunge, efface, obliterate, delete, cross out. **2** remove, wipe off, excise, delete. **3** expunge, obliterate, blot out, eradicate.

erect *verb* **1** build, construct, assemble. **2** put up, raise, set upright, stand up. **3** establish, set up, found, initiate, institute.
➤ *adj* **1** upright, vertical, perpendicular, raised. **2** stiff, rigid, straight, standing. **3** hard, firm, tumid, tumescent.

erection *noun* **1** building, construction, structure, edifice, pile (*inf*). **2** raising, elevation, building, construction, establishment, foundation. **3** hardness, firmness, tumidity, tumescence, hard-on (*sl*).

ergo *adv* therefore, hence, consequently, then, so, thus.

erode *verb* **1** wear away, abrade, excoriate, grind down. **2** eat into, gnaw away at, consume, devour. **3** destroy, disintegrate, fragment, weaken, undermine.

erosion *noun* wear, attrition, abrasion, excoriation, destruction, disintegration.

erotic *adj* titillating, stimulating, arousing, aphrodisiac, sexy (*inf*), sensual, voluptuous, pornographic.

err *verb* **1** be wrong, make a mistake, slip up (*inf*), blunder, miscalculate, misjudge. **2** sin, transgress, do wrong, misbehave, go astray.

errand *noun* commission, assignment, task, charge, undertaking, message.

errant *adj* **1** erring, wrong, misbehaving, delinquent. **2** straying, wayward. **3** wandering, roving, travelling, itinerant, peripatetic, nomadic.

erratic *adj* **1** changeable, variable, irregular, inconsistent, unreliable, unpredictable, capricious, eccentric. **2** rambling, wandering, meandering, wayward.

erratum *noun* error, mistake, misprint, corrigendum, correction, amendment.

erroneous *adj* wrong, incorrect, mistaken, untrue, false, inaccurate, faulty, fallacious.

error *noun* **1** mistake, inaccuracy, miscalculation, slip, gaffe, misprint, solecism, erratum, misunderstanding, fallacy. **2** wrong, wrongdoing, misbehaviour, misconduct, offence, transgression, sin, fault.

ersatz *adj* substitute, imitation, simulated, artificial, synthetic, fake.

erudite *adj* learned, scholarly, academic, well-read, lettered, cultured, intellectual, highbrow.

erupt *verb* **1** burst open, gush, spout, spew, belch. **2** explode, burst forth, break out, flare up.

eruption *noun* **1** explosion, ejection, discharge, outburst, outbreak. **2** rash, inflammation, spot, pimple.

escalate *verb* increase, grow, mushroom, snowball, intensify, accelerate, soar, spiral, rocket (*inf*).

escapade *noun* adventure, exploit, scrape (*inf*), prank, caper, stunt.

escape *verb* **1** get away, break free, flee, fly, run off, bolt, decamp, abscond, do a runner (*inf*). **2** avoid, evade, dodge, sidestep, shirk, elude. **3** leak, seep, ooze, discharge, flow, drain.
➤ *noun* getaway, breakout, flight, decampment, avoidance, evasion, leak, seepage, discharge, emission.

escapism *noun* fantasy, dreaming, wishful thinking, escape, getting away from it all (*inf*), recreation, diversion, distraction.

eschew *verb* shun, avoid, abstain from, forgo, refrain from, renounce, abjure.

escort *noun* **1** partner, companion, beau, gigolo. **2** chaperon, guide, bodyguard, retinue, entourage, convoy, protection.
➤ *verb* accompany, conduct, usher, guide, take, see, partner, chaperon, guard.

escutcheon *noun* shield, scutcheon, coat of arms.

esoteric *adj* **1** arcane, private, secret, recondite, hidden, occult. **2** abstruse, cryptic, obscure, unfathomable, mysterious, enigmatic.

especial *adj* **1** special, particular, distinctive, singular, peculiar. **2** exceptional, extraordinary, unusual, notable, marked. **3** individual, personal, own, exclusive.

especially *adv* **1** exceptionally, extraordinarily, unusually, notably, very, extremely. **2** particularly, in particular, above all, chiefly, primarily, specifically.

espionage *noun* spying, intelligence, secret service, undercover work, reconnaissance, surveillance.

espousal *noun* adoption, support, backing, defence, championship, advocacy.

espouse *verb* adopt, embrace, take up, support, maintain, defend, champion, advocate.

espy *verb* spot, catch sight of, glimpse, see, notice, perceive, discern, detect.

essay *noun* **1** composition, dissertation, treatise, paper, discourse, tract, commentary, critique. **2** attempt, try, endeavour, effort, venture, trial.
➤*verb* attempt, endeavour, try, strive, venture, undertake.

essence *noun* **1** nature, character, quintessence, quiddity, substance, heart, marrow, pith, spirit, significance. **2** concentrate, extract, distillate, spirits, tincture.
in essence essentially, basically, fundamentally, in effect.
of the essence crucial, essential, vital, indispensable.

essential *adj* **1** vital, indispensable, necessary, requisite, crucial. **2** basic, fundamental, inherent, intrinsic, elemental, principal.
➤*noun* necessity, requisite, must (*inf*), basic, fundamental, rudiment, sine qua non.

establish *verb* **1** found, institute, set up, create, inaugurate, build. **2** settle, install. **3** lodge, secure, fix, plant. **4** prove, verify, substantiate, corroborate, demonstrate, authenticate, certify.

establishment *noun* **1** foundation, institution, creation, inception, inauguration. **2** business, enterprise, company, firm, corporation, organization, institute, institution. **3** household, house, residence. **4** authorities, powers that be, system, ruling class, bureaucracy, officialdom.

estate *noun* **1** development, area, park, centre. **2** land, property, demesne, manor. **3** property, assets, effects, possessions, holdings, wealth, fortune. **4** status, position, station, condition, rank, class.

esteem *verb* **1** respect, admire, think highly of, revere, value, prize, treasure, appreciate. **2** deem, regard, consider, judge, think, hold, rate, reckon.
➤*noun* respect, admiration, estimation, regard, honour, appreciation, approval, favour.

estimable *adj* admirable, respected, esteemed, valued, worthy, deserving, commendable, creditable.

estimate *verb* **1** reckon, gauge, assess, evaluate, rate, guess. **2** judge, think, believe, conclude.
➤*noun* **1** reckoning, approximation, educated guess, assessment, evaluation, appraisal. **2** judgment, opinion, view, estimation, consideration, reckoning.

estimation *noun* **1** evaluation, assessment, reckoning. **2** estimate, judgment, opinion, view. **3** esteem, respect, admiration, regard.

estrange *verb* alienate, disaffect, separate, part, divide, disunite.

estuary *noun* inlet, mouth, firth, fjord.

et cetera *adv* and so on, and so forth, and the rest, and the like.

etch *verb* **1** corrode, eat into, cut, incise, engrave, inscribe. **2** stamp, impress, imprint.

eternal *adj* **1** everlasting, immortal, undying, indestructible, enduring, abiding, never-ending. **2** interminable, incessant, endless, continuous, constant, perpetual. **3** timeless, unchanging, immutable, infinite.

eternity *noun* **1** perpetuity, infinity, evermore. **2** immortality, indestructibility, timelessness, endlessness. **3** afterlife, hereafter, next world, heaven. **4** ages, long time, donkey's years.

ethereal *adj* **1** light, airy, delicate, dainty, fine, diaphanous, subtle, rarefied. **2** heavenly, celestial, empyreal, otherworldly, spiritual.

ethical *adj* moral, right, proper, seemly, just, fair, good, honourable.

ethics *pl noun* morals, standards, principles, scruples.

ethnic *adj* **1** racial, national, tribal, cultural. **2** native, indigenous. **3** traditional, folk.

ethos *noun* beliefs, principles, standards, ethics, code, spirit, character.

etiquette *noun* propriety, decorum, code of conduct, protocol, form, convention, usage, custom.

etymology *noun* origin, derivation, source, word history.

Eucharist *noun* Communion, Lord's Supper, Mass.

eulogize *verb* praise, extol, laud, panegyrize, exalt, glorify.

eulogy *noun* **1** panegyric, encomium, accolade, plaudit, compliment, tribute. **2** praise, extolment, laudation, exaltation, glorification, acclaim.

euphonious *adj* euphonic, melodious, tuneful, harmonious, musical, dulcet, mellifluous, sweet.

euphony *noun* melody, harmony, music, sweetness, softness, smoothness, mellowness.

euphoria *noun* ecstasy, bliss, elation, jubilation, exultation, rapture, transport, exhilaration.

evacuate *verb* **1** leave, quit, flee, vacate, clear, empty, abandon. **2** purge, eject, expel, discharge, eliminate, excrete.

evade *noun* **1** avoid, escape, elude, dodge, duck (*inf*), get out of (*inf*), sidestep, get round (*inf*). **2** fence, hedge, parry, equivocate, beat about the bush (*inf*).

evaluate *noun* appraise, assess, value, estimate, size up, judge, rate, reckon, measure, determine.

evanescent *adj* fading, disappearing, brief, short-lived, ephemeral, fleeting, fugitive, transient.

evangelical *adj* **1** biblical, scriptural, canonical, orthodox. **2** evangelistic, missionary, crusading, converting, reforming, zealous, Bible-bashing (*inf*).

evangelist *noun* preacher, gospeller, missionary, crusader, revivalist, Bible-basher (*inf*).

evangelize *verb* preach, spread the word, crusade, convert, proselytize.

evaporate *verb* **1** vaporize, dry, dehydrate. **2** disappear, vanish, fade, evanesce, dissolve, dissipate.

evasion *noun* avoidance, escape, dodging, prevarication, equivocation, sophistry, subterfuge.

evasive *adj* **1** equivocal, indirect, oblique, roundabout, devious, misleading, tricky,

slippery (*inf*), unforthcoming, cagey (*inf*). **2** avoiding, escaping, dodging, sidestepping.

eve *noun* threshold, brink, verge.

even *adj* **1** level, flat, horizontal, plane. **2** smooth, uniform. **3** flush, square, aligned. **4** uniform, consistent, regular, stable, steady, unvarying. **5** calm, placid, equable, imperturbable. **6** equal, abreast, drawn, tied, same, identical. **7** symmetrical, balanced.
➤*adv* **1** yet, still, all the more. **2** so much as, at all.
➤*verb* level, flatten, plane, smooth, square, align, balance, equalize.

even as just as, at the very moment that.

even so nevertheless, nonetheless, all the same, yet, still.

evenhanded *adj* fair, just, equitable, impartial, dispassionate.

evening *noun* close of day, dusk, twilight, sunset, nightfall, night, eventide.

event *verb* **1** happening, occurrence, incident, episode, phenomenon. **2** occasion, affair. **3** contest, competition, fixture, meeting, race, game. **4** case, contingency, eventuality, possibility.

at all events come what may, whatever happens, regardless, in any event, in any case, anyway.

eventful *adj* busy, action-packed (*inf*), full, memorable, notable, significant, historic.

eventual *adj* final, ultimate, closing, consequent, ensuing, prospective, future, impending.

eventuality *noun* contingency, event, case, possibility, probability, emergency.

eventuate *verb* result, follow, ensue, happen, occur.

ever *adv* **1** always, at all times, continually, perpetually, constantly, eternally, to the end of time. **2** at any time, in any circumstances, by any chance, at all, before, until now.

ever so/such very, extremely, really.

everlasting *adj* **1** eternal, immortal, undying, indestructible. **2** infinite, endless, enduring, abiding. **3** interminable, incessant, never-ending, constant, perpetual, unremitting.

evermore *adv* always, forever, till the end of time, eternally, perpetually.

every *adj* each, all possible.

everyday *adj* ordinary, common, usual, familiar, habitual, routine, daily, quotidian, regular, standard, plain, workaday.

everyone *pron* everybody, all, one and all, the whole world.

everything *pron* all, the lot, the whole shooting match (*inf*).

everywhere *adv* all around, the world over, near and far, high and low, left right and centre (*inf*).

evict *noun* expel, eject, turn out, throw out, remove, dislodge, dispossess.

evidence *noun* 1 proof, verification, substantiation, corroboration, documentation, testimony. 2 indication, sign, mark, demonstration, manifestation.
➤*verb* evince, indicate, show, demonstrate, denote, signify.
in evidence evident, obvious, conspicuous, visible.

evident *adj* apparent, plain, clear, obvious, visible, manifest, conspicuous, noticeable, indisputable.

evidently *adv* 1 apparently, seemingly, to all appearances, outwardly, ostensibly. 2 plainly, clearly, obviously, patently, manifestly.

evil *adj* 1 wicked, villainous, bad, sinful, vile, immoral, malevolent, malignant, nefarious, heinous. 2 devilish, demonic, diabolic. 3 harmful, injurious, pernicious, noxious, bad, destructive. 4 foul, vile, offensive, noisome. 5 unpleasant, disagreeable, nasty.
➤*noun* 1 bad, wrong, sin, vice, immorality, wickedness, villainy, malevolence. 2 harm, ill, bane, mischief, adversity, affliction, calamity, catastrophe.

evince *verb* indicate, show, reveal, demonstrate, manifest, display, exhibit.

eviscerate *verb* disembowel, exenterate, gut, draw.

evocative *adj* suggestive, expressive, reminiscent, redolent.

evoke *verb* 1 summon, call, conjure up, invoke, raise. 2 call forth, elicit, rouse, provoke, stimulate. 3 recall, reawaken, rekindle.

evolution *noun* 1 development, progression, maturation, growth, elaboration. 2 derivation, descent, natural selection, Darwinism.

evolve *verb* develop, unfold, progress, mature, grow, elaborate, result, derive.

exacerbate *verb* aggravate, worsen, intensify, inflame, irritate, provoke.

exact *adj* 1 precise, accurate, spot on (*inf*), correct, true, faithful, literal, strict, specific. 2 careful, meticulous, scrupulous, punctilious, painstaking, methodical, rigorous.
➤*verb* extort, extract, wring, wrest, force, impose, levy, demand, require, insist on.

exacting *adj* difficult, hard, arduous, demanding, challenging, taxing, rigorous, stringent, strict.

exaction *noun* extortion, extraction, imposition, levy, demand, requisition.

exactly *adv* 1 altogether, entirely, precisely, strictly, absolutely, in every respect. 2 quite, just so, absolutely, indeed, certainly, of course.

exaggerate *verb* 1 overstate, inflate, magnify, blow out of all proportion (*inf*), stretch, embroider, embellish, overestimate. 2 emphasize, stress, overemphasize, overstress.

exalt *verb* 1 elevate, raise, upgrade, promote, advance, aggrandize, ennoble, honour, uplift, exhilarate. 2 praise, laud, extol, glorify, worship, acclaim.

exaltation *noun* 1 elevation, promotion, advancement, aggrandizement, ennoblement, praise, glorification, worship, acclamation. 2 exhilaration, elation, jubilation, exultation, grandeur, loftiness.

examination *noun* 1 inspection, scrutiny, observation, study, analysis, investigation, assessment, check-up. 2 exam, test, paper, quiz. 3 questioning, interrogation, cross-examination, third degree (*inf*).

examine *verb* 1 look at, scrutinize, observe, study, peruse, analyse, inspect, vet, check, investigate, consider, assess. 2 test, quiz. 3 question, interrogate, cross-examine, pump (*inf*), grill (*inf*).

example *noun* 1 sample, specimen, illustration, exemplification, instance, case.

2 model, pattern, standard, criterion, precedent, exemplar, paradigm, ideal. **3** warning, caution, admonition, lesson. **for example** for instance, say, such as.

exasperate *verb* anger, incense, infuriate, enrage, madden, vex.

excavate *verb* **1** dig, delve, burrow, tunnel, scoop, gouge. **2** dig out, quarry, mine. **3** dig up, unearth, disinter, exhume, uncover, reveal.

exceed *verb* **1** surpass, outstrip, outdo, beat, better, outshine, eclipse, cap, top. **2** pass, go beyond, overstep.

exceedingly *adv* very, extremely, exceptionally, extraordinarily, greatly, highly, enormously, tremendously.

excel *verb* lead, predominate, be outstanding, succeed, surpass, outclass, transcend, outshine, eclipse.

excellent *adj* superior, first-rate, exceptional, outstanding, superb, prime, supreme, sterling, fine, great, splendid, wonderful.

except *prep* but, excepting, save, other than, apart from, excluding, bar.
➤*verb* omit, exclude, leave out, reject, bar, rule out.

exception *noun* **1** omission, exclusion, rejection, debarment. **2** anomaly, odd one out, freak, peculiarity, special case.
take exception to object to, disagree with, be offended by, take offence at.

exceptionable *adj* objectionable, unpleasant, disagreeable, offensive, obnoxious.

exceptional *adj* **1** abnormal, anomalous, irregular, special, unusual, atypical, out of the ordinary, singular. **2** outstanding, remarkable, extraordinary, excellent, phenomenal, superior.

excerpt *noun* extract, passage, quotation, citation, fragment, clip.
➤*verb* extract, take, quote, select.

excess *noun* **1** surfeit, overabundance, glut, surplus, remainder, residue, overflow. **2** immoderation, intemperance, overindulgence, unrestraint, extravagance, dissipation. **3** extra, additional, surplus, residual, leftover.

excessive *adj* extreme, immoderate, inordinate, undue, disproportionate, unreasonable, superfluous, exorbitant, over the top (*inf*).

exchange *verb* **1** trade, barter. **2** swap, interchange, transpose, switch, bandy. **3** substitute, replace, change.
➤*noun* **1** trade, traffic, barter, swap, substitution, replacement. **2** conversation, fight. **3** change, conversion. **4** market, fair.

excise[1] *noun* duty, tax, levy, tariff.

excise[2] *verb* **1** cut out, remove, extract. **2** delete, expurgate, bowdlerize, eliminate.

excitable *adj* volatile, mercurial, nervous, highly-strung, sensitive, passionate, fiery, temperamental, irascible, touchy.

excite *verb* **1** rouse, animate, move, inspire, thrill, exhilarate, titillate, turn on (*inf*). **2** stimulate, provoke, arouse, awaken, stir up, kindle, elicit, cause. **3** incite, foment.

excited *adj* **1** animated, in high spirits, eager, enthusiastic, fired up (*inf*), thrilled, exhilarated, wild, frenzied. **2** agitated, disturbed, restless, worked up, overwrought.

exclaim *verb* cry, shout, roar, shriek, call, declare, ejaculate, vociferate.

exclamation *noun* cry, shout, call, ejaculation, interjection, vociferation.

exclude *verb* **1** omit, leave out, except, rule out, eliminate, reject, ban, bar, blackball, ostracize. **2** expel, eject, throw out, oust, evict, remove.

exclusion *noun* omission, exception, elimination, rejection, ban, bar, expulsion, ejection.

exclusive *adj* **1** excluding, not counting, omitting, excepting, barring. **2** individual, single, sole, only. **3** undivided, total, full, absolute. **4** limited, restricted, closed, selective. **5** private, cliquish, clannish, snobbish. **6** elegant, fashionable, chic, up-market, posh (*inf*), classy (*inf*).

excommunicate *verb* exclude, bar, expel, cast out, denounce, execrate, proscribe, interdict.

excoriate *verb* **1** denounce, condemn, censure, reprove, berate, castigate, attack, revile, vilify. **2** skin, flay. **3** strip, peel, scrape, abrade.

excrement *noun* excretion, excreta, faeces, dung, droppings, guano.

excrescence *noun* 1 lump, growth, swelling, tumour, protuberance, protrusion. 2 eyesore, monstrosity, disfigurement, blot.

excrete *verb* discharge, eject, expel, eliminate, pass, defecate, urinate.

excruciating *adj* 1 agonizing, racking, harrowing, exquisite, searing, piercing. 2 severe, intense, acute, extreme. 3 awful, unbearable, insufferable, atrocious.

exculpate *verb* exonerate, vindicate, clear, absolve, pardon, acquit, discharge.

excursion *noun* trip, outing, jaunt, tour, drive, ride.

excuse *verb* 1 pardon, forgive, exonerate, exculpate, let off. 2 overlook, condone, indulge, make allowances for, absolve. 3 vindicate, justify, explain, defend. 4 free, release, discharge, dismiss. 5 exempt, spare, relieve, let off.
➤*noun* 1 explanation, reason, grounds, justification, vindication, defence, plea. 2 pretext, front, cover-up (*inf*).
excuse me pardon, sorry.

execrable *adj* abominable, detestable, loathsome, odious, vile, repulsive, appalling, atrocious.

execrate *verb* 1 abominate, abhor, detest, loathe. 2 revile, deplore, condemn, denounce.

execute *verb* 1 kill, put to death, hang, behead, electrocute, shoot. 2 perform, carry out, fulfil, complete, accomplish, discharge. 3 implement, effect, enforce, enact.

executive *noun* 1 administration, management, directorate, leadership. 2 administrator, official, manager, director.
➤*adj* 1 administrative, managerial, directorial. 2 governing, controlling, decision-making.

exegesis *adj* explanation, clarification, exposition, interpretation.

exemplar *noun* example, specimen, type, exemplification, model, pattern, ideal, epitome.

exemplary *adj* 1 model, ideal, perfect, faultless, estimable, commendable, praise-worthy, meritorious. 2 cautionary, warning, admonitory. 3 typical, characteristic, representative, illustrative.

exemplify *verb* 1 illustrate, instance, demonstrate, show. 2 represent, characterize, typify, epitomize, embody.

exempt *verb* excuse, release, free, relieve, except, exclude, spare, let off.
➤*adj* exempted, excused, free, excluded, immune, privileged.

exercise *verb* 1 drill, train, work out, keep fit, limber up, warm up. 2 use, exert, apply, bring to bear, implement, wield, practise. 3 worry, trouble, disturb, upset, annoy, vex. 4 tax, preoccupy.
➤*noun* 1 practice, drill, training. 2 exertion, activity, workout, warm-up, keep fit, walking, sports, PE. 3 task, lesson, problem, piece of work. 4 use, exertion, application, implementation, discharge, performance. 5 drill, manoeuvre, operation, assignment, mission.

exert *verb* use, employ, exercise, apply, bring to bear, wield, expend.
exert oneself strive, labour, make an effort, put oneself out, apply oneself, try hard, do one's best.

exhale *verb* 1 breathe out, expire. 2 emit, expel, emanate, give off.

exhaust *verb* 1 consume, use up, finish, empty, drain, expend, dissipate. 2 tire, weary, fatigue, wear out, prostrate, debilitate, enervate, sap, drain.

exhaustion *noun* 1 tiredness, weariness, fatigue, collapse, prostration, debility, enervation, lassitude. 2 consumption, expenditure, depletion, dissipation.

exhaustive *adj* comprehensive, all-embracing, full, thorough, detailed, extensive, wide-ranging, encyclopedic, in-depth.

exhibit *verb* 1 display, show, set out, present, demonstrate, parade, air. 2 show, display, demonstrate, indicate, manifest, reveal, disclose.
➤*noun* display, array, presentation, demonstration, model.

exhibition *noun* 1 display, show, fair, exposition, presentation, demonstration, parade. 2 indication, manifestation, revelation, expression. 3 scholarship, grant, bursary, allowance.

exhilarate verb 1 elate, delight, cheer, excite, thrill. 2 enliven, invigorate, stimulate.

exhort verb urge, implore, entreat, beseech, press, prevail upon, advise, encourage.

exhume verb disinter, dig up, unearth.

exigency noun 1 urgency, emergency, crisis, extremity, predicament, quandary. 2 need, necessity, demand, requirement, pressure, constraint.

exigent adj 1 urgent, pressing, critical, imperative, importunate, insistent. 2 demanding, taxing, exacting, difficult, rigorous, stringent.

exiguous adj scanty, meagre, paltry, tiny, slender, slight, trifling, negligible.

exile verb expel, banish, expatriate, deport, eject, cast out.
➤noun 1 expulsion, banishment, expatriation, deportation, ejection. 2 deportee, refugee, émigré, expatriate, displaced person, outcast.

exist verb 1 be, be real, be present, occur. 2 survive, be extant, endure, abide, prevail, obtain. 3 live, breathe. 4 subsist, survive, stay alive, eke out an existence.

existence noun 1 being, life, animation, reality, actuality, presence, survival, continuance. 2 life, way of life, lifestyle.

existent adj existing, in existence, being, living, real, actual, present, current, prevailing, abiding, surviving, extant.

exit noun 1 way out, egress, door, gate, outlet. 2 departure, leaving, going, withdrawal, flight.
➤verb depart, leave, go, withdraw.

exodus noun exit, departure, withdrawal, retreat, flight, migration, evacuation, hegira.

exonerate verb 1 absolve, acquit, clear, exculpate, excuse, pardon. 2 exempt, excuse, let off, spare, release, relieve.

exorbitant adj excessive, immoderate, inordinate, unreasonable, undue, extreme, extortionate, prohibitive, steep (inf).

exorcize verb 1 expel, drive out, cast out. 2 free, rid, deliver, purify.

exotic adj 1 foreign, alien, non-native, tropical, imported, introduced. 2 strange, unusual, outlandish, striking, colourful, impressive, glamorous, fascinating, mysterious.

expand verb 1 enlarge, stretch, extend, spread, augment, inflate. 2 grow, increase, multiply, swell, dilate, develop, diversify. 3 open, unfold, unroll, unfurl. 4 expatiate, elaborate, enlarge, amplify, develop.

expanse noun stretch, extent, spread, area, range, sweep.

expansion noun enlargement, extension, spread, growth, increase, multiplication, swelling, dilation, development, diversification, elaboration, expatiation.

expansive adj 1 expandable, extendable, elastic, stretchy, spreading, swelling. 2 large, vast, wide, broad, extensive, far-reaching, universal. 3 talkative, communicative, outgoing, extrovert, sociable, affable, unreserved, open.

expatiate verb enlarge, expand, dilate, elaborate, descant, discourse.

expatriate verb exile, deport, banish, expel.
➤noun exile, deportee, emigrant, expat (inf), refugee, displaced person.

expect verb 1 suppose, presume, believe, think, imagine, guess (inf). 2 anticipate, foresee, predict, envisage, contemplate, await, look forward to, hope for, bargain for, count on. 3 require, demand, insist on, call for, want.

expectant adj 1 expecting, anticipating, hopeful, eager, anxious, ready, curious, on tenterhooks. 2 pregnant, with child, expecting (inf), in the family way (inf).

expectation noun 1 anticipation, readiness, expectancy, contemplation, supposition, presumption, probability, likelihood. 2 hope, trust, reliance, assurance, confidence, belief. 3 prospect, outlook, prediction, forecast, requirement, demand.

expedient adj 1 appropriate, suitable, apt, desirable, worthwhile, valuable. 2 useful, advantageous, convenient, practical, pragmatic, advisable, politic, opportune.
➤noun means, device, shift, resource, scheme, ploy, ruse, dodge (inf).

expedite verb accelerate, precipitate, step up, hasten, facilitate, dispatch.

expedition noun **1** journey, voyage, excursion, mission, quest, campaign. **2** team, crew, company, party. **3** haste, speed, dispatch, promptness.

expeditious adj prompt, punctual, speedy, hasty, swift, brisk, efficient.

expel verb **1** eject, evict, throw out, kick out (inf), banish, deport, oust, dismiss. **2** discharge, eject, evacuate, eliminate, spew, belch.

expend verb **1** spend, disburse, pay out, fork out (inf), squander, fritter away. **2** use, consume, use up, exhaust, deplete, drain.

expendable adj dispensable, replaceable, disposable.

expenditure noun **1** spending, disbursement, expense, payment, outlay. **2** outgoings, expenses, costs.

expense noun **1** payment, expenditure, disbursement, outlay. **2** sacrifice, cost, price, loss.

expenses pl noun spending, expenditure, costs, outgoings, incidentals.

expensive adj dear, costly, pricey (inf), exorbitant, steep (inf), extravagant, valuable.

experience verb undergo, suffer, go through, encounter, face, participate in, know.
>noun **1** event, incident, episode, adventure, encounter, ordeal. **2** knowledge, understanding, familiarity, acquaintance, practice. **3** contact, exposure, involvement, participation, observation.

experienced adj knowledgeable, familiar, acquainted, expert, practised, proficient, veteran, seasoned.

experiment noun **1** trial, test, investigation, study, observation, demonstration. **2** try, venture, trial run, pilot study. **3** experimentation, research, analysis, trial and error.
>verb try, test, investigate, research, study, explore.

experimental adj **1** empirical, speculative, exploratory, test, trial, pilot. **2** tentative, provisional, preliminary.

expert noun specialist, consultant, authority, pundit, connoisseur, professional, master, dab hand (inf).
>adj proficient, adept, skilled, practised,

experienced, masterly, ace (inf), crack (inf), professional, specialist.

expertise noun skill, proficiency, mastery, command, ability, facility, professionalism, experience.

expiate verb atone for, make amends for, redeem, pay for.

expire verb **1** lapse, run out, end, terminate. **2** die, pass away, breathe one's last, give up the ghost (inf). **3** exhale, breathe out.

expiry noun end, cessation, termination, expiration.

explain verb **1** define, describe, interpret, expound, clarify, solve, illustrate, demonstrate. **2** account for, justify, warrant, excuse, defend, rationalize.

explanatory adj descriptive, illustrative, interpretative, expository, explicative, exegetic.

expletive noun oath, curse, swearword, four-letter word (inf), obscenity, profanity, epithet.

explicable adj explainable, accountable, justifiable, definable, interpretable, solvable.

explicit adj **1** plain, clear, distinct, unambiguous, definite, positive. **2** direct, forthright, blunt, frank. **3** precise, specific, full, detailed.

explode noun **1** blow up, detonate, go off, go up. **2** burst, fly apart, erupt, go bang (inf). **3** detonate, set off, let off, fire, blast, blow up. **4** erupt, flare up, blow one's top (inf), flip one's lid (inf). **5** discredit, invalidate, refute, disprove, debunk, belie, blow sky-high (inf). **6** boom, mushroom, escalate, rocket.

exploit verb **1** use, utilize, tap, draw on, capitalize on, turn to account, profit from, cash in on (inf). **2** take advantage of, misuse, abuse, use, impose on, oppress.
>noun feat, deed, act, achievement, adventure, stunt.

explore verb **1** travel, tour, range over, search, prospect, survey, reconnoitre. **2** examine, study, analyse, investigate, look into, probe, plumb, inspect, research, consider.

explosion noun **1** blast, detonation, burst, eruption, discharge, report, bang, pop.

2 outburst, outbreak, fit, paroxysm.
3 boom, mushrooming, escalation, rocketing.

explosive *noun* bomb, mine, charge, gunpowder, dynamite, gelignite.
➤ *adj* **1** volatile, unstable, flammable, inflammable. **2** tense, charged, fraught, volatile, violent, stormy. **3** touchy, sensitive, controversial.

exponent *noun* **1** advocate, supporter, backer, champion, promoter, proponent. **2** interpreter, commentator, expounder, expositor. **3** practitioner, performer, player, artist.

export *verb* ship, send abroad, sell overseas.
➤ *noun* foreign trade, international trade.

expose *verb* **1** show, exhibit, display, reveal, air, uncover, bare, strip. **2** make known, denounce, blow the whistle on (*inf*), uncover, bring to light, take the lid off (*inf*). **3** lay open, put at risk, make vulnerable, endanger, jeopardize.
expose oneself display one's genitals, flash (*inf*).

exposé *noun* exposure, revelation, disclosure.

exposed *adj* **1** uncovered, bare, naked, unsheltered, unprotected, open. **2** vulnerable, susceptible, subject, liable.

exposition *noun* **1** explanation, explication, interpretation, commentary, exegesis, dissertation, analysis, presentation. **2** display, show, exhibition, demonstration, fair, market.

expostulate *verb* object, protest, argue, remonstrate, reason.

exposure *noun* **1** exhibition, display, airing, broadcasting, publication, unveiling, presentation, exposition, publicity, advertising. **2** revelation, disclosure, betrayal, unmasking, denunciation, whistle-blowing (*inf*). **3** uncovering, laying open, vulnerability, susceptibility, introduction, contact.

expound *verb* explain, define, spell out, detail, develop, interpret, explicate.

express *verb* **1** utter, speak, voice, articulate, word, communicate, convey, state, air, show, demonstrate, indicate. **2** denote, depict, represent, symbolize.
➤ *adj* **1** fast, rapid, high-speed, direct, non-

stop, through. **2** explicit, precise, plain, clear, unambiguous, definite, positive, categorical. **3** particular, specific.

expression *noun* **1** look, face, countenance, air, aspect. **2** phrase, locution, word, term, saying, idiom. **3** utterance, verbalization, articulation, communication, statement, airing. **4** manifestation, exhibition, demonstration, show, indication, sign, symbol, token. **5** feeling, emotion, passion, spirit, modulation, intonation.

expressive *adj* **1** eloquent, meaningful, significant, pregnant, vivid, graphic. **2** emotional, passionate, powerful, evocative, suggestive. **3** showing, indicative, demonstrative, revealing.

expropriate *verb* **1** seize, take, appropriate, usurp, assume, arrogate. **2** requisition, commandeer, impound, confiscate, sequester.

expulsion *noun* ejection, eviction, exile, banishment, expatriation, deportation, dismissal, discharge, evacuation, elimination.

expunge *verb* **1** erase, rub out, efface, delete, cross out, cancel. **2** obliterate, blot out, eradicate, extirpate.

expurgate *verb* bowdlerize, censor, cut, purge, sanitize, clean up.

exquisite *adj* **1** fine, delicate, dainty, beautiful, excellent, outstanding. **2** beautiful, delightful, fine, superb, rare, valuable. **3** refined, sophisticated, sensitive, appreciative, discriminating, selective. **4** intense, sharp, keen, acute, piercing, excruciating.

extant *adj* existing, existent, present, living, surviving, remaining.

extemporaneous *adj* extemporary, extempore, spontaneous, impromptu, ad-lib, improvised, unrehearsed, off-the-cuff (*inf*).

extempore *adj and adv* extemporaneously, spontaneously, on the spur of the moment (*inf*), off the top of one's head (*inf*).

extemporize *verb* ad-lib, improvise, make up.

extend *verb* **1** enlarge, lengthen, elongate, add to. **2** prolong, protract, draw out, spin out, continue. **3** spread, stretch, reach, range, expand, increase, widen, broaden, develop, augment. **4** stretch out, hold out, put out, spread. **5** pull out, draw out, unfold, unfurl, unroll, unwind. **6** offer, proffer, tender, give, present, bestow.

extension noun **1** enlargement, lengthening, elongation, stretching, prolongation, protraction, expansion, increase. **2** addendum, supplement, appendix, codicil, annex, wing.

extensive adj large, sweeping, broad, wide, wide-ranging, all-embracing, thorough, comprehensive, lengthy, protracted.

extent noun **1** amount, size, magnitude, length, breadth, depth, area, expanse, range, scope. **2** limit, boundary.

extenuate verb mitigate, palliate, diminish, reduce, play down, minimize, excuse, justify.

exterior noun **1** outside, surface, shell, skin. **2** facade, front, appearance, aspect.
➤adj outer, external, outside, outward, superficial, surface.

exterminate verb kill, destroy, eradicate, wipe out.

external adj **1** outer, exterior, outside, outward, superficial, apparent. **2** extraneous, extrinsic, alien, foreign.

extinct adj **1** dead, defunct, wiped out, lost. **2** extinguished, quenched, put out.

extinction noun annihilation, eradication, destruction, suppression, extermination, death.

extinguish verb **1** quench, snuff, douse, blow out. **2** annihilate, extirpate, eliminate, destroy, end, terminate, suppress, quash.

extirpate verb destroy, wipe out, annihilate, eradicate, abolish, extinguish.

extol noun praise, laud, sing the praises of, rave about (inf), exalt, glorify, magnify, acclaim.

extort verb extract, wring, wrest, squeeze, force, exact.

extortionate adj **1** exorbitant, excessive, unreasonable, steep (inf), inflated, usurious. **2** hard, severe, grasping, rapacious.

extra adj additional, supplementary, more, other, spare, reserve, surplus, excess.
➤noun **1** addition, adjunct, accessory, supplement, bonus. **2** supernumerary, walk-on, spear-carrier.

➤adv especially, exceptionally, particularly, in addition, over and above, on top.

extract verb **1** remove, pull out, draw out, take out, withdraw, wrest, wring, force, obtain, elicit. **2** derive, draw, distil, separate, press. **3** select, excerpt, abstract, quote, reproduce.
➤noun **1** excerpt, abstract, quotation, passage, selection. **2** essence, concentrate, distillate, juice.

extraction noun **1** removal, pulling, withdrawal, derivation, distillation, separation. **2** parentage, descent, ancestry, lineage, stock, origin.

extradition noun surrender, delivery, handing over, repatriation, deportation, expulsion.

extraneous adj **1** extrinsic, external, exterior, alien, foreign, adventitious. **2** irrelevant, immaterial, unrelated, incidental, nonessential, superfluous.

extraordinary adj **1** strange, peculiar, odd, curious, unusual. **2** outstanding, exceptional, striking, remarkable, phenomenal, wonderful.

extravagant adj **1** lavish, wasteful, profligate, prodigal, spendthrift, improvident. **2** immoderate, unrestrained, inordinate, excessive, exaggerated, reckless, wild. **3** expensive, costly, overpriced, exorbitant, extortionate, steep (inf). **4** flamboyant, ostentatious, pretentious, flashy (inf), over the top (inf).

extreme adj **1** great, intense, severe, acute, exceptional, extraordinary. **2** radical, hard-line, fanatical, zealous, immoderate, excessive. **3** drastic, dire, draconian, rigid, severe, strict, harsh, stringent. **4** farthest, outermost, most distant, last, final, endmost. **5** utter, downright, out-and-out. **6** ultimate, maximum, greatest, supreme, utmost.
➤noun **1** extremity, end, edge, limit, top, bottom, zenith, nadir, pole. **2** height, maximum, peak, climax.

extremism noun radicalism, militancy, fanaticism, zealotry, fundamentalism.

extremity noun **1** extreme, limit, boundary, edge. **2** emergency, crisis, exigency, predicament, adversity, trouble.

extricate *verb* disentangle, disengage, detach, free, release, deliver, rescue, remove, extract, withdraw.

extrinsic *adj* **1** extraneous, foreign, alien, unrelated. **2** external, exterior, outside.

extrovert *noun* socializer, mixer, joiner.

extrude *verb* eject, force out, squeeze out, expel.

exuberant *adj* **1** vivacious, ebullient, effervescent, bubbly, bouncy (*inf*), elated, high-spirited, enthusiastic, irrepressible, unrestrained, effusive. **2** abundant, copious, profuse, rich, luxuriant. **3** extravagant, exaggerated, flamboyant, lavish.

exude *verb* **1** ooze, seep, leak, trickle, drip, discharge, secrete. **2** display, exhibit, ooze, emanate.

exult *verb* rejoice, triumph, crow, gloat, glory, revel.

eye *noun* **1** perception, awareness. **2** appreciation, taste, discernment, discrimination.
➤*verb* look at, scrutinize, scan, gaze at, stare at, ogle.
keep an/one's eye on watch, mind, look after, supervise, monitor.
see eye to eye agree, concur, get along, be on the same wavelength (*inf*).

eye-catching *adj* striking, arresting, noticeable, conspicuous, showy, attractive, beautiful, stunning.

eyesight *noun* sight, vision, eyes.

eyesore *noun* monstrosity, sight (*inf*), scar, blight, excrescence, carbuncle, blot on the landscape.

fable noun **1** allegory, parable, apologue, tale, story. **2** myth, legend, saga, epic, fantasy.

fabric noun **1** cloth, material, stuff, textile. **2** structure, frame, construction. **3** organization, structure, framework, makeup, constitution.

fabricate verb **1** construct, make, assemble, manufacture, produce, put together. **2** make up, concoct, hatch, devise, invent, coin, think up, formulate.

fabulous adj **1** extraordinary, incredible, unbelievable, fantastic, amazing, astounding. **2** wonderful, marvellous, superb, great. **3** legendary, mythical, fantastic, unreal, imaginary, fictitious.

facade noun **1** front, exterior, face, frontage, outside. **2** mask, veneer, show, appearance, guise, pretence, semblance.

face noun **1** countenance, visage, physiognomy, features. **2** expression, appearance, look, air, grimace, scowl, pout. **3** surface, front, facade, exterior, outside. **4** aspect, side.
➤verb **1** confront, brave, oppose, meet, encounter, come up against, deal with, face up to. **2** overlook, front on, be opposite. **3** cover, surface, veneer, dress, finish.
face to face opposite, facing.
face up to confront, deal with, come to terms with, get to grips with, cope with.

facet noun **1** aspect, angle, slant, element. **2** face, plane, surface, side.

facetious adj **1** frivolous, flippant. **2** joking, jocular, witty, tongue-in-cheek, playful, humorous.

facile adj **1** glib, superficial, shallow, slick. **2** easy, simple, effortless.

facilitate verb assist, aid, further, advance, accelerate, expedite, ease, smooth.

facility noun **1** amenity, convenience, resource, aid. **2** skill, proficiency, ability, knack, talent, aptitude. **3** ease, effortlessness, smoothness, fluency.

facing noun **1** lining, reinforcement. **2** covering, coating, cladding.

facsimile noun copy, reproduction, duplicate, photocopy, fax.

fact noun **1** event, occurrence, incident. **2** datum, given, truth, point, detail, particular. **3** actuality, reality, circumstance, deed, act.
in fact actually, in reality, really, as a matter of fact.

faction noun group, party, camp, gang, band, clique, set, splinter group.

factious adj disagreeing, disputatious, dissenting, conflicting, warring, seditious, dissident, divisive, schismatic.

factitious adj artificial, false, simulated, sham, mock, unreal, fake.

factor noun **1** element, part, feature, ingredient, detail, point, circumstance, determinant. **2** agent, middleman, intermediary, proxy, representative, broker.

factory noun plant, shop, works, assembly line, mill.

factotum noun odd job man, jack of all trades, man Friday.

factual adj authentic, genuine, true, real, actual, accurate, correct, certain, faithful.

faculty noun **1** power, capacity, capability, sense, attribute, feature. **2** ability, aptitude, facility, knack, talent, skill. **3** department, school, discipline, division.

fad noun **1** vogue, trend, craze, rage, mania. **2** taste, whim, fancy.

faddy adj fussy, finicky, particular, choosy (inf), picky (inf).

fade verb **1** pale, dim, dull, bleach, discolour, decolorize, wash out. **2** diminish, dwindle, wane, decline, fail, disperse, vanish, disappear, die away.

faeces *pl noun* stools, excreta, excrement, dung, droppings, crap (*sl*), shit (*sl*).

fag[1] *noun* cigarette, smoke, cig (*inf*), ciggie (*inf*).

fag[2] *noun* chore, drag (*inf*), bother, nuisance, bind (*inf*).

fagged out *adj* weary, tired out, exhausted, jaded, worn out.

fail *verb* **1** be unsuccessful, blow it (*inf*), miscarry, fall through, come to nothing, flop (*inf*). **2** omit, neglect, forget. **3** break down, stop, cut out, malfunction, pack up (*inf*), crash (*inf*). **4** decline, wane, weaken, flag. **5** dwindle, fade, die, disappear. **6** go bankrupt, crash (*inf*), collapse, go to the wall (*inf*), go under, fold (*inf*). **7** fall short, miss. **8** let down, leave, desert, forsake, abandon.

failing *noun* flaw, fault, defect, weakness, frailty, shortcoming, foible.

failure *noun* **1** miscarriage, frustration, defeat, collapse, ruin. **2** fiasco, washout (*inf*), disappointment, letdown, flop (*inf*), loser, no-hoper (*inf*), also-ran (*inf*). **3** omission, neglect, default, nonperformance. **4** breakdown, malfunctioning, crash (*inf*).

faint *adj* **1** dim, pale, weak, feeble, indistinct, soft, subdued, low. **2** dizzy, giddy, light-headed, weak, woozy (*inf*). **3** slight, small, remote, vague.
➤*verb* collapse, pass out, black out, swoon, keel over (*inf*).
➤*noun* blackout, collapse, unconsciousness, swoon, syncope.

faint-hearted *adj* timid, weak, spiritless, cowardly, fearful, chicken (*inf*).

fair[1] *adj* **1** just, equitable, impartial, evenhanded, unbiased, honest. **2** legitimate, right, proper, above board. **3** blond, flaxen, light, pale. **4** attractive, beautiful, handsome, pretty, comely, good-looking. **5** sunny, clear, bright, fine, dry. **6** reasonable, moderate, decent, adequate, satisfactory, average, all right, not bad.

fair[2] *noun* **1** fete, festival, carnival, bazaar. **2** show, exhibition, exposition.

fairly *adv* **1** quite, rather, somewhat, pretty (*inf*). **2** positively, absolutely, really, veritably. **3** justly, equitably, impartially, honestly. **4** rightly, properly, legally, lawfully.

fairy *noun* elf, sprite, pixie, brownie, imp, fay, peri.

fairy story *noun* **1** fairy tale, myth, legend, folk tale. **2** lie, fib, tall story (*inf*), yarn (*inf*).

faith *noun* **1** belief, confidence, assurance, trust, reliance, credence, conviction, faithfulness, allegiance, devotion. **2** religion, creed, doctrine, dogma, church, denomination, sect, cult.

faithful *adj* **1** loyal, true, devoted, steadfast, committed, trustworthy, reliable, unswerving. **2** accurate, exact, close, strict, true, literal, factual.
➤*noun* followers, believers, adherents.

faithless *adj* **1** unfaithful, disloyal, untrue, false, treacherous, untrustworthy, fickle, inconstant. **2** unbelieving, doubting, sceptical, agnostic.

fake *adj* counterfeit, forged, false, bogus, phoney (*inf*), reproduction, synthetic, pseudo (*inf*).
➤*verb* **1** counterfeit, forge, pirate, falsify. **2** pretend, feign, affect, put on, dissemble.
➤*noun* **1** counterfeit, forgery, imitation, reproduction, copy. **2** fraud, impostor, charlatan, quack (*inf*).

fall *verb* **1** descend, drop, sink, plunge, dive, plummet. **2** trip, tumble, topple, come a cropper (*inf*), over, fall down. **3** drop, hang, slope. **4** surrender, capitulate, be defeated, be taken. **5** fail, lose power. **6** decline, go down, abate, decrease, lessen, dwindle. **7** become, grow, turn. **8** happen, occur, take place.
➤*noun* **1** drop, plunge, dive, trip, tumble. **2** waterfall, cascade, cataract, rapids. **3** descent, slope, declivity, incline. **4** decline, decrease, reduction, slump. **5** surrender, capitulation, failure, defeat, downfall, ruin, destruction, collapse, breakdown.
fall back withdraw, retreat.
fall back on resort to, have recourse to, turn to, call on, look to, make use of.
fall behind drop back, lag, trail.
fall for 1 fall in love with, take to, desire, fancy (*inf*). **2** be fooled by, accept, swallow (*inf*).
fall in collapse, cave in, subside.
fall in with 1 meet, encounter, join, get involved with, associate with, go around with. **2** agree to, accept, go along with, support.

fall off decrease, lessen, decline.
fall on attack, assail, descend on, set upon, lay into.
fall out quarrel, argue, disagree, fight.
fall through fail, come to nothing, collapse, flop (inf).

fallacy noun misconception, misapprehension, mistake, error, delusion.

fallen adj **1** dead, killed, slaughtered, slain. **2** immoral, loose, promiscuous.

fallible adj imperfect, erring, flawed, weak, unreliable.

fallow adj **1** uncultivated, untilled, unsown, undeveloped. **2** dormant, inactive, idle, resting.

false adj **1** untrue, inaccurate, wrong, incorrect, mistaken. **2** invalid, faulty, unsound, fallacious. **3** treacherous, disloyal, traitorous, unfaithful, untrustworthy, duplicitous, dishonest, perfidious. **4** fake, imitation, counterfeit, artificial, mock, sham, bogus, fictitious. **5** unreal, illusory, deceptive, misleading.

falsehood noun **1** lie, fib, untruth, fabrication, fiction. **2** falsity, mendacity, untruthfulness, deceit.

falsify verb misrepresent, distort, doctor, alter, forge, cook (inf), fiddle (inf).

falter verb **1** hesitate, waver, vacillate. **2** stumble, totter, dodder, tremble. **3** stammer, stutter.

fame noun renown, celebrity, distinction, note, repute, glory, acclaim, stardom.

familiar adj **1** well-known, recognizable, usual, common, household, everyday, ordinary, accustomed. **2** conversant, acquainted, versed in, no stranger to. **3** intimate, close, confidential, friendly, sociable, informal. **4** forward, bold, presumptuous, overfamiliar, disrespectful.

familiarize verb acquaint, accustom, habituate, make, train, teach.

family noun **1** household, ménage, people, folk. **2** children, offspring, progeny, kids (inf). **3** relations, kin, clan, tribe, house, dynasty, ancestors, descendants. **4** group, class, subdivision, system.

famine noun starvation, hunger, want, lack, dearth, scarcity.

famished adj starving, ravenous, hungry, empty.

famous adj well-known, renowned, celebrated, famed, illustrious, eminent, distinguished, notable, great, legendary.

fan¹ verb **1** ventilate, air-condition, freshen, cool. **2** agitate, arouse, stimulate, stir up, inflame, incite.
➤ noun ventilator, aerator, blower.

fan² noun devotee, enthusiast, aficionado, buff (inf), fiend (inf), admirer, supporter, fanatic.

fanatic noun **1** zealot, extremist, radical, militant. **2** enthusiast, addict, devotee.

fanciful adj **1** capricious, flighty, impractical, visionary, romantic, imaginative, inventive. **2** fantastic, fabulous, chimerical, imaginary, unreal, mythical. **3** elaborate, ornate, extravagant, whimsical, curious.

fancy verb **1** want, feel like, desire, crave, like, have a crush on (inf). **2** think, reckon, believe, suppose, guess. **3** imagine, conceive, picture, visualize.
➤ noun **1** inclination, liking, fondness, desire, wish, hankering. **2** caprice, whim, notion, idea. **3** conception, image, picture, impression. **4** imagination, dreaming, fantasy.
➤ adj **1** ornamental, decorative. **2** ornate, ornamented, decorated, elaborate, showy. **3** capricious, whimsical, fanciful, fantastic.

fanfare noun **1** flourish, fanfaronade. **2** show, ostentation, display, razzmatazz.

fantasize verb imagine, dream.

fantastic adj **1** fanciful, imaginary, unreal, mythical, legendary. **2** tremendous, formidable, far-fetched, preposterous, incredible. **3** weird, bizarre, outlandish, wild, extravagant, unrealistic, crazy. **4** wonderful, splendid, marvellous, excellent, great, superb.

fantasy noun fancy, imagination, image, dream, hallucination, vision, romance, flight of fancy.

far adj distant, remote, faraway, far-flung, outlying, out of the way.
➤ adv **1** a long way, afar, miles. **2** greatly, considerably, much, very much, extremely.
far and away easily, decidedly, markedly.
so far up to this point, until now, to date.

farce noun 1 comedy, burlesque, slapstick, buffoonery. 2 mockery, travesty, sham. 3 absurdity, nonsense, joke.

farcical adj ludicrous, ridiculous, absurd, laughable, comic, funny, amusing, droll.

fare noun 1 charge, fee, price, cost. 2 food, diet, menu, provisions.
➤verb manage, get along, do, make out, progress.

farewell interj goodbye, au revoir, adieu, cheerio (inf), so long (inf).
➤noun departure, leave-taking, valediction, goodbye, parting.

far-fetched adj improbable, implausible, unlikely, unbelievable, unconvincing, fantastic.

farm noun 1 land, holding, ranch, plantation. 2 farmstead, grange, homestead, croft.
➤verb till, cultivate, work.

farmer noun agriculturalist, smallholder, crofter, rancher.

farrago noun hotchpotch, miscellany, potpourri, mishmash.

far-reaching adj sweeping, extensive, broad, wide-ranging.

farsighted adj forward-looking, wise, shrewd, prudent.

farther adv further, beyond, past.

farthest adj furthest, last, remotest, most distant, extreme.

fascinate verb 1 charm, captivate, enchant, delight, attract, allure, enthral, spellbind, engross, absorb. 2 hypnotize, mesmerize, transfix.

fashion noun 1 vogue, mode, look, style, trend, craze, fad, custom, convention. 2 way, method, manner, style, approach.
➤verb make, form, mould, shape, design, create, forge, construct, tailor.
after a fashion approximately, roughly, to some extent.

fashionable adj stylish, modish, in vogue, à la mode, chic, smart, trendy (inf), all the rage (inf), in (inf), cool (inf).

fast adj 1 rapid, swift, quick, speedy, brisk, fleet. 2 secure, fixed, firm, immovable, tight, fastened. 3 loose, immoral, promiscuous, wanton.

➤adv 1 rapidly, swiftly, quickly, speedily, briskly, in haste. 2 securely, firmly, tightly. 3 deeply, soundly.

fasten verb 1 secure, fix, make fast, tie, attach, connect, do up, pin, clip. 2 aim, direct, focus, bend, fix, concentrate.

fastidious adj hard to please, particular, fussy, finicky, hypercritical, squeamish.

fat adj 1 stout, overweight, plump, obese, podgy, chubby, rotund, portly, corpulent. 2 wide, thick, big, large. 3 substantial, considerable, lucrative, profitable.
➤noun 1 plumpness, obesity, corpulence, overweight, flab (inf). 2 fatty tissue, blubber, grease, oil. 3 margarine, butter, lard.

fatal adj 1 deadly, lethal, mortal, incurable, terminal, malignant. 2 ruinous, calamitous, disastrous. 3 critical, crucial, decisive, fateful. 4 inevitable, destined, fated.

fatalism noun predeterminism, resignation, stoicism, acceptance.

fatality noun death, mortality.

fate noun 1 destiny, providence, fortune, kismet, predestination, foreordination. 2 end, outcome, future. 3 lot, portion, doom. 4 death, destruction, downfall, ruin.
➤verb destine, doom, predestine, foreordain.

fateful adj crucial, decisive, pivotal, momentous, disastrous, catastrophic, ruinous, deadly.

father noun 1 sire, dad (inf), daddy (inf), papa, pater, old man (inf). 2 progenitor, ancestor, forefather, forebear, predecessor. 3 creator, maker, author, inventor, founder. 4 priest, minister, padre, clergyman.
➤verb sire, beget, procreate.

fatherly adj 1 paternal, parental. 2 kind, benevolent, caring, sympathetic, protective, supportive.

fathom verb 1 measure, sound, plumb. 2 penetrate, understand, grasp, get to the bottom of.

fatigue verb exhaust, weary, tire, drain, weaken, debilitate.
➤noun exhaustion, weariness, tiredness, lassitude, debility, enervation.

fatten verb 1 stuff, cram, build up. 2 put on weight, spread, swell, bloat.

fatty *adj* **1** fat, fleshy. **2** oily, greasy, unctuous. **3** adipose, sebaceous, oleaginous.

fatuous *adj* foolish, silly, inane, stupid, idiotic, asinine.

fault *noun* **1** flaw, blemish, defect, imperfection, failing, shortcoming. **2** error, mistake, lapse, offence, wrong, transgression, misdemeanour. **3** culpability, responsibility, blameworthiness.
➤*verb* find fault with, criticize, blame.
at fault to blame, culpable, responsible, guilty, in the wrong.
to a fault exceedingly, excessively, extremely, unduly.

faulty *adj* defective, flawed, imperfect, impaired, out of order, unsound, weak, wrong.

faux pas *noun* blunder, gaffe, indiscretion, mistake, boob (*inf*).

favour *noun* **1** approval, approbation, good books (*inf*), sanction, backing, support. **2** preference, partiality, bias, favouritism. **3** goodwill, kindness, friendliness, graciousness. **4** good turn, service, courtesy, kindness. **5** gift, present, memento, keepsake. **6** token, badge, rosette.
➤*verb* **1** approve, countenance, sanction, back, support, patronize, prefer, recommend. **2** oblige, help, assist, facilitate. **3** prefer, side with, choose, like, spoil. **4** resemble, take after, look like.
in favour of for, pro, supporting, backing, behind, on the side of.

favourable *adj* encouraging, promising, auspicious, advantageous, beneficial, helpful, approving, agreeable, sympathetic, positive.

favourite *noun* pet, darling, apple of one's eye, preference, choice.
➤*adj* dearest, best-loved, special, preferred, chosen, pet.

favouritism *noun* partiality, partisanship, nepotism, bias, inequality.

fawn[1] *noun* beige, buff, yellowish brown.

fawn[2] *verb* grovel, crawl, creep, kowtow, bow and scrape, toady, flatter, curry favour.

fealty *noun* loyalty, allegiance, fidelity, faithfulness, devotion, homage.

fear *noun* **1** terror, horror, alarm, fright, trepidation, dread, foreboding, phobia.
2 anxiety, worry, concern, solicitude, misgiving, qualm.
➤*verb* **1** dread, be frightened of, shudder at. **2** worry, be anxious, feel concern, suspect. **3** revere, venerate.

fearful *adj* **1** terrified, afraid, frightened, scared, alarmed, apprehensive, nervous. **2** terrible, formidable, horrible, fearsome, harrowing, shocking. **3** awful, frightful, dreadful, appalling, atrocious.

fearsome *adj* formidable, daunting, formidable, frightening, scary (*inf*).

feasible *adj* **1** practicable, workable, viable, possible, realistic, realizable, attainable. **2** possible, likely, reasonable.

feast *noun* **1** banquet, repast, spread (*inf*), blowout (*inf*), slap-up meal (*inf*). **2** festival, holy day, saint's day, fete.
➤*verb* dine, banquet, gorge, overindulge, regale, treat.

feat *noun* deed, act, exploit, achievement, accomplishment, stroke, coup.

feather *noun* plume, quill, penna, aigrette.

feature *noun* **1** characteristic, trait, attribute, property, quality, aspect, highlight, attraction, focal point. **2** article, story, item, piece, column, report.
➤*verb* **1** highlight, emphasize, accentuate, spotlight, star. **2** participate, appear, have a place.

features *pl noun* face, countenance, physiognomy, lineaments.

fecund *adj* fruitful, productive, fertile, rich, prolific, abundant.

federal *adj* confederated, federated, associated, allied, united.

federate *verb* confederate, ally, combine, unite.

federation *noun* **1** confederation, confederacy, union. **2** league, alliance, coalition.

fee *noun* price, charge, payment, remuneration, hire, emolument, honorarium.

feeble *adj* **1** weak, frail, infirm, delicate, sickly, puny, faint, slight. **2** ineffectual, unavailing, inadequate, poor, weak, lame.

feed *verb* **1** nourish, sustain, cater for, provision, suckle. **2** graze, pasture, eat, dine, subsist. **3** satisfy, gratify. **4** support,

encourage, strengthen. **5** supply, provide, give, introduce.
➤*noun* fodder, forage, food.

feel *verb* **1** touch, handle, finger, stroke, rub. **2** experience, undergo, suffer, enjoy. **3** sense, perceive, be aware of. **4** think, consider, believe, judge. **5** fumble, grope.
➤*noun* **1** texture, surface, finish. **2** atmosphere, quality, air, mood, aura. **3** knack, touch, talent, skill.
feel for sympathize with, commiserate with, pity, be sorry for, weep for.
feel like want, desire, fancy.

feeler *noun* **1** antenna, tentacle, palp. **2** approach, advance, overture.

feeling *noun* **1** emotion, sentiment. **2** sensibility, sensitivity. **3** sense, impression, perception. **4** hunch, suspicion, idea, notion, opinion, belief, sentiment, thought. **5** premonition, presentiment, inkling. **6** touch, sensation, consciousness, awareness. **7** sympathy, affection, passion, ardour. **8** atmosphere, quality, air, mood, aura.
➤*adj* **1** passionate, intense, ardent, fervent. **2** sentient, sensitive. **3** emotional, sympathetic, caring, compassionate.

feign *verb* **1** affect, put on, assume, dissemble, act, sham, simulate, fake. **2** pretend, make believe, play-act.

felicitations *pl noun* congratulations, compliments, best wishes, greetings.

felicitous *adj* apt, appropriate, well-chosen, suitable, pertinent, apposite, timely.

felicity *noun* **1** aptness, appropriateness, suitability, pertinence. **2** happiness, joy, bliss, ecstasy, rapture, delight.

feline *adj* catlike, sleek, graceful, slinky, stealthy.

fell *verb* **1** hew, cut down, knock down, level, flatten, raze. **2** prostrate, knock down, floor, kill.

fellow *noun* **1** man, boy, chap (*inf*), bloke (*inf*), guy (*inf*). **2** equal, peer, colleague, partner. **3** mate, match, twin, counterpart. **4** companion, comrade, friend, associate.

fellowship *noun* **1** companionship, comradeship, camaraderie, friendship, amity, intimacy, communion. **2** association, society, club, guild.

felon *noun* criminal, [illegible] wrongdoer.

felony *noun* crime, offence, misdemeanour.

female *noun* woman, girl, she, cow, doe, hen.
➤*adj* feminine, woman, lady.

feminine *adj* womanly, girlish, ladylike, gentle, graceful, effeminate, womanish.

feminism *noun* women's rights, women's lib, women's movement.

fen[1] *noun* bog, marsh, swamp, morass, quagmire.

fence *noun* railing, barrier, enclosure, palisade
➤*verb* enclose, shut in, surround, encircle, confine.
sit on the fence hedge, prevaricate, equivocate, tergiversate, shilly-shally.

fend *verb* **fend for** provide for, support, look after, take care of.
fend off ward off, avert, deflect, parry, beat off, repel.

feral *adj* **1** wild, untamed, unbroken, undomesticated. **2** savage, ferocious, vicious.

ferment *verb* **1** foam, froth, effervesce, brew, rise, leaven. **2** rouse, stir up, excite, inflame, incite, foment.
➤*noun* commotion, tumult, uproar, turmoil, agitation, unrest.

ferocious *adj* fierce, savage, vicious, violent, bloodthirsty, merciless, intense, extreme.

ferret *verb* search, rummage, scour, forage.
ferret out discover, find, track down, unearth.

ferry *noun* ferryboat, shuttle, packet.
➤*verb* transport, carry, convey, shuttle.

fertile *adj* **1** fruitful, productive, prolific, abundant. **2** fecund, productive, rich. **3** creative, original, imaginative, resourceful.

fertilize *verb* **1** impregnate, inseminate, fecundate, pollinate. **2** enrich, dress, feed, manure, mulch.

fertilizer *noun* manure, mulch, compost, top-dressing.

fervent *adj* ardent, passionate, enthusiastic, earnest, zealous, intense, impassioned, heartfelt.

fervour *noun* ardour, passion, enthusiasm, emotion, spirit, zeal.

fester *verb* 1 suppurate, ulcerate. 2 putrefy, rot, decay, decompose. 3 rankle, gall, rile, irritate.

festival *noun* 1 celebration, commemoration, anniversary. 2 feast, saint's day, holiday, fete. 3 gala, carnival, fair.

festive *adj* happy, merry, jolly, convivial, hearty, joyous.

festivity *noun* 1 merriment, conviviality, revelry, celebration, party, entertainment. 2 festival, feast, carnival.

festoon *verb* decorate, adorn, array, deck, garland, drape, hang.

fetch *verb* 1 bring, convey, deliver, get, retrieve. 2 realize, yield, make, sell for.

fetching *adj* attractive, becoming, sweet, winsome, charming.

fete *noun* 1 fair, bazaar, gala, garden party. 2 holiday, feast day, saint's day, festival.

fetid *adj* foul, rank, malodorous, stinking.

fetish *noun* 1 obsession, mania, fixation, compulsion. 2 charm, talisman, amulet.

fetter *verb* 1 shackle, manacle, chain, tie, bind. 2 restrain, restrict, confine, trammel. *noun* shackle, manacle, chain, bond.

fettle *noun* condition, shape, order, state.

feud *noun* vendetta, hostility, animosity, bad blood, strife, conflict, quarrel.

fever *noun* 1 feverishness, pyrexia, high temperature, temperature (*inf*). 2 agitation, excitement, heat, passion, fervour, frenzy.

few *adj* rare, scarce, sporadic.
➤*noun* not many, hardly any, one or two, a handful.

fiasco *noun* failure, disaster, flop (*inf*), washout (*inf*).

fiat *noun* order, decree, edict, proclamation.

fib *noun* lie, untruth, falsehood, whopper (*inf*).

fibre *noun* 1 thread, strand, filament, fibril. 2 spirit, constitution, temperament, strength, stamina, toughness.

fickle *adj* changeable, capricious, mercurial, flighty, unpredictable, vacillating, inconstant, unreliable.

fiction *noun* 1 stories, novels. 2 story, legend, fantasy, romance, invention, fabrication, lie, falsehood.

fictitious *adj* 1 false, invented, imaginary, made-up, bogus, assumed. 2 sham, feigned.

fiddle *verb* 1 falsify, cook (*inf*). 2 contrive, manoeuvre, wangle (*inf*).
➤*noun* swindle, fraud, racket, scam (*inf*).
fiddle with play with, tinker with, tamper with, meddle with.

fiddling *adj* trifling, trivial, small, insignificant, petty.

fidelity *noun* 1 faithfulness, loyalty, devotion, allegiance, constancy, steadfastness. 2 closeness, exactness, accuracy.

fidget *verb* squirm, twitch, wriggle, move about.

field *noun* 1 meadow, pasture, grassland, common. 2 ground, pitch. 3 domain, province, department, discipline, speciality, territory, area. 4 competitors, participants, candidates.
➤*verb* 1 catch, stop. 2 deal with, answer, handle, parry.

fiend *noun* 1 demon, devil, evil spirit. 2 monster, brute, beast, ogre. 3 enthusiast, devotee, fanatic, aficionado, fan, buff (*inf*), freak (*inf*).

fiendish *adj* 1 devilish, diabolical, infernal. 2 wicked, evil, malevolent, cruel, inhuman, monstrous. 3 complex, intricate, involved.

fierce *adj* 1 savage, ferocious, vicious, wild, feral, menacing, aggressive, combative. 2 wild, violent, raging, furious, unrestrained, uncontrollable. 3 intense, severe, powerful, strong, passionate, ardent.

fiery *adj* 1 burning, blazing, flaming. 2 spicy, hot, pungent. 3 ardent, vehement, passionate. 4 temperamental, violent, fierce.

fight *verb* 1 battle, combat, war, clash, grapple, wrestle, brawl. 2 quarrel, dispute, argue, wrangle. 3 strive, struggle. 4 defy, attack, take issue with. 5 oppose, resist, campaign against. 6 suppress, repress, control, check.

➤**noun 1** battle, combat, engagement, bout, brawl, punch-up (*inf*), scrap (*inf*). **2** dispute, argument, quarrel, row. **3** campaign, battle, struggle, drive, crusade. **4** spirit, determination, resolve, aggression.
fight back retaliate, resist, defend oneself.
fight off repel, resist, rebuff.

fighter *noun* warrior, soldier, boxer, pugilist.

figment *noun* invention, fabrication, creation, fancy.

figurative *adj* **1** metaphorical, allegorical. **2** emblematic, symbolic, representative.

figure *noun* **1** number, numeral, digit. **2** shape, form, body, build, physique, frame, outline, silhouette. **3** diagram, drawing, illustration, chart. **4** personage, notable, dignitary, celebrity, worthy.
➤*verb* **1** calculate, reckon, compute, work out, add up. **2** appear, feature. **3** represent, depict, portray. **4** think, believe, consider.
figure out solve, understand, grasp, fathom.

figurehead *noun* **1** bust, carving, sculpture. **2** mouthpiece, puppet.

filament *noun* strand, thread, fibre, hair, wire.

filch *verb* steal, pilfer, purloin, nick (*inf*), pinch (*inf*).

file¹ *noun* **1** folder, portfolio, cabinet. **2** dossier, documents, information.
➤*verb* **1** classify, put in order. **2** record, register.

file² *noun* line, row, queue, column.
➤*verb* march, troop, parade, pass.

file³ *verb* rasp, grind, abrade, smooth, shape.

fill *verb* **1** stuff, cram, pack. **2** stock, load, supply, replenish. **3** plug, bung, stop, close, block. **4** satiate, glut, sate. **5** satisfy, fulfil, perform, execute. **6** pervade, suffuse, cover. **7** occupy, hold, take up.
➤*noun* enough, sufficiency, plenty.
fill in 1 complete, answer. **2** replace, substitute, stand in, deputize. **3** inform, advise, apprise, acquaint.
fill out 1 become fatter, put on weight. **2** complete, answer.

fillip *noun* boost, stimulus, incentive, impetus.

film *noun* **1** picture, movie, feature, video. **2** covering, coating, skin, membrane, pellicle.
➤*verb* **1** photograph, shoot, video. **2** blur, cloud, mist.

filmy *adj* fine, sheer, gauzy, light, translucent, diaphanous.

filter *verb* **1** strain, clarify, purify, screen, sieve, sift. **2** seep, trickle, leach, percolate.
➤*noun* strainer, screen, sieve, net, mesh, gauze.

filth *noun* **1** dirt, muck, grime, sewage, refuse. **2** obscenity, pornography, smut, porn (*inf*), sleaze (*inf*).

filthy *adj* **1** dirty, mucky, grimy, foul, polluted. **2** obscene, pornographic, smutty. **3** mean, nasty, vile, lewd.

final *adj* **1** ultimate, last, terminal, concluding, closing. **2** conclusive, decisive, definitive, irrevocable.

finale *noun* **1** end, conclusion, finish. **2** climax, culmination.

finality *noun* conclusiveness, decisiveness, completeness, definitiveness, irrevocability.

finalize *verb* conclude, complete, decide, settle, wrap up (*inf*).

finally *adv* ultimately, eventually, at last, in the end.

finance *noun* banking, economics, accounting, commerce, investment, money.
➤*verb* fund, bankroll, pay for, back, subsidize, underwrite.

finances *pl noun* resources, wealth, means, funds, money, cash, capital.

financial *adj* monetary, fiscal, economic, commercial, budgetary, pecuniary.

find *verb* **1** discover, come across, happen upon, encounter. **2** locate, track down, ferret out, unearth. **3** perceive, detect, realize, learn, observe. **4** attain, reach, achieve, obtain. **5** think, consider, judge, feel.
➤*noun* discovery, strike, catch.
find fault complain, carp, cavil, criticize.
find out 1 ascertain, learn, discover, realize. **2** unmask, expose, uncover.

finding *noun* verdict, judgment, decision, conclusion, result.

fine[1] *adj* **1** excellent, choice, select, superior, first-class. **2** splendid, magnificent, grand, showy, beautiful. **3** sunny, cloudless, dry, bright, clear, fair. **4** healthy, fit, well. **5** acceptable, satisfactory, all right, OK (*inf*). **6** smart, stylish, elegant, refined, tasteful, exquisite, pure. **7** delicate, precise. **8** thin, slender, sheer, light. **9** powdery, ground, crushed. **10** slight, small, little, minute. **11** keen, acute, sharp. **12** sensitive, subtle, nice.

fine[2] *noun* penalty, mulct, forfeit, damages.
➤*verb* penalize, punish, mulct.

finery *noun* trappings, trinkets, ornaments, splendour, Sunday best, glad rags (*inf*).

finesse *noun* **1** refinement, delicacy, grace, polish, mastery, craft. **2** subtlety, diplomacy, discretion, delicacy, skill, adroitness.

finger *verb* feel, touch, handle, manipulate, toy with.

finicky *adj* finical, fussy, particular, fastidious, hard to please, choosy (*inf*).

finish *verb* **1** end, close, terminate, conclude, finalize, wind up. **2** stop, cease. **3** consume, use up, eat, drink, drain, empty, polish off (*inf*). **4** complete, fulfil, achieve, do, perfect, consummate, round off. **5** polish, varnish, face, dress, veneer, coat. **6** destroy, ruin, defeat, overwhelm, do away with.
➤*noun* **1** completion, conclusion, close, termination, end, finale. **2** polish, varnish, lacquer, veneer, coating. **3** surface, lustre, shine, texture, grain. **4** refinement, polish, culture, suavity, urbanity.

finite *adj* limited, restricted, circumscribed, demarcated, measurable.

fire *noun* **1** burning, combustion, spark, flame. **2** blaze, conflagration, inferno, holocaust. **3** gunfire, sniping, fusillade, cannonade, bombardment, shelling. **4** heater, radiator, convector. **5** ardour, heat, passion, enthusiasm, spirit, force.
➤*verb* **1** ignite, light, set fire to. **2** discharge, detonate, explode. **3** shoot, hurl, launch. **4** kindle, stimulate, inspire. **5** rouse, stir, inspire, excite. **6** dismiss, discharge, sack (*inf*).
on fire alight, ablaze, burning, in flames. **2** eager, enthusiastic, passionate, ardent, excited.

firearm *noun* gun, handgun, revolver, pistol, rifle.

firebrand *noun* agitator, troublemaker, rabble-rouser, revolutionary, demagogue, agent provocateur.

firm[1] *adj* **1** hard, compact, dense, rigid, inelastic, unyielding, solid, set. **2** secure, fixed, fast, immovable, steady, stable, sturdy. **3** strong, vigorous, tight. **4** steadfast, unwavering, unshakable, dogged. **5** definite, settled, fixed, established. **6** constant, loyal, staunch, steady, enduring, long-standing. **7** resolute, determined, decided, adamant, inflexible, strict.

firm[2] *noun* company, business, establishment, house, corporation, partnership.

firmament *noun* sky, heavens, empyrean, space, universe.

first *adj* **1** initial, opening, introductory, primary. **2** earliest, primeval, primordial, original. **3** highest, top, supreme. **4** greatest, foremost, leading, principal.
➤*adv* **1** beforehand, initially, at first. **2** firstly, to begin with, in the first place.

first-hand *adj* direct, immediate.
➤ **at first hand** directly, straight from the horse's mouth (*inf*).

first-rate *adj* excellent, superb, outstanding, second to none, supreme, fine, A1 (*inf*), top-notch (*inf*).

fish *verb* **1** angle, trawl. **2** search, hunt. **3** solicit, angle.
fish out take out, pull out, extract, produce.

fishy *adj* odd, suspicious, dubious, questionable, unlikely.

fission *noun* splitting, parting, division, rupture, cleavage.

fissure *noun* opening, rift, cleft, crevice, crack, fault, split, gap.

fit[1] *adj* **1** healthy, sturdy, strong, well. **2** capable, competent, trained, qualified, eligible, worthy. **3** suitable, fitting, appropriate, apt, right, proper.
➤*verb* **1** insert, position, install, adjust, adapt. **2** equip, rig, furnish, supply. **3** match, tally with, correspond to, agree with, meet. **4** qualify, prepare, equip, arm.
fit in slot in, find time for, find room for, pack in. **2** conform, be compatible.
fit out equip, supply, provide, accoutre.

fit² *noun* **1** convulsion, paroxysm, spasm, seizure. **2** attack, turn. **3** bout, spell, outburst.
by/in fits and starts fitfully, spasmodically, irregularly, intermittently.

fitful *adj* irregular, intermittent, spasmodic, erratic, inconstant.

fitted *adj* **1** built-in, fixed. **2** suitable, appropriate, adapted, qualified.

fitting *adj* appropriate, apt, suitable, proper, seemly.
➤*noun* component, part, accessory, attachment.

fix *verb* **1** secure, make fast, install, locate, fasten, attach, stick, pin. **2** settle, establish, decide on, arrange, appoint, set. **3** mend, repair, restore, rectify. **4** direct, focus, level. **5** dress, tidy, groom, straighten. **6** prepare, make, get ready, cook. **7** rig, tamper with, manipulate, fiddle (*inf*).
➤*noun* dilemma, predicament, quandary, spot (*inf*).
fix up 1 provide, supply, furnish.
2 arrange, settle, decide, agree on, plan, organize.

fixation *noun* obsession, compulsion, mania, fetish, preoccupation, thing (*inf*).

fixed *adj* **1** secure, stable, firm, fast.
2 stationary, immovable. **3** established, set, constant, unchanging. **4** intent, resolute, unwavering.

fixture *noun* **1** appliance, installation.
2 event, match, race, contest.

fizz *verb* sparkle, effervesce, bubble, froth, foam.

fizzle *verb* **fizzle out** fail, collapse, die away, peter out, flop (*inf*).

fizzy *adj* effervescent, sparkling, carbonated, gassy.

flabbergast *verb* amaze, astound, dumbfound, stun, daze, stagger.

flabby *adj* flaccid, limp, floppy, loose, slack, soft.

flaccid *adj* limp, drooping, floppy, soft.

flag¹ *noun* standard, ensign, pennant, jack.
➤*verb* **1** mark, tag, label. **2** wave down, signal to.

flag² *verb* **1** droop, languish, fail, tire, wilt.
2 weaken, drop, fade, decline, fall.

flagellate *verb* scourge, flog, lash, whip, beat.

flagon *noun* **1** jug, pitcher. **2** bottle, carafe, flask.

flagrant *adj* blatant, glaring, bold, barefaced, arrant, conspicuous, open, outrageous.

flail *verb* wave, thrash, thresh.

flair *noun* **1** talent, gift, knack, faculty, facility, aptitude. **2** style, panache, elegance, taste.

flake *noun* **1** scale, chip, sliver, shaving, peeling. **2** fragment, particle.
➤*verb* scale, peel, chip, desquamate, exfoliate.
flake out faint, pass out, collapse, keel over.

flamboyant *adj* **1** showy, ostentatious, flashy. **2** brilliant, colourful, gaudy.
3 ornate, elaborate, fancy.

flame *noun* **1** fire, blaze, spark, light.
2 ardour, passion, heat, intensity.
➤*verb* burn, blaze, flare, flash.

flaming *adj* **1** burning, blazing, ablaze, on fire. **2** bright, brilliant, blazing, intense.
3 furious, violent, raging, passionate.

flank *noun* **1** side, loin. **2** side, wing.
➤*verb* border, edge, fringe, skirt.

flannel *noun* nonsense, blarney, waffle (*inf*), baloney (*inf*).
➤*verb* prevaricate, equivocate, waffle (*inf*), sweet-talk (*inf*).

flap *verb* wave, wag, flutter, shake, beat, flail.
➤*noun* **1** fold, tab, overlap, fly. **2** waving, fluttering. **3** commotion, fuss, panic, fluster, tizzy (*inf*).

flare *verb* **1** blaze, flash, gleam, flame.
2 widen, broaden, splay, spread out.
➤*noun* **1** blaze, glare, gleam, flash, flame.
2 signal, light, beacon, rocket. **3** widening, spread, broadening, splay.
flare up explode, blow one's top (*inf*), lose control, fly off the handle (*inf*).

flash *verb* **1** flare, flame, shine, beam, sparkle, gleam, glint, glitter. **2** dash, tear, shoot, dart, streak, fly. **3** show off, display, flaunt, brandish.
➤*noun* **1** beam, ray, flare, blaze, gleam,

spark. **2** burst, outbreak, display, show.
➤*adj* showy, ostentatious, flamboyant,
loud, garish, tawdry.

flashy *adj* showy, ostentatious, flamboyant, loud, garish, pretentious, tasteless,
tawdry.

flat[1] *adj* **1** level, horizontal. **2** even,
smooth, plane. **3** low, shallow. **4** vapid,
uninteresting, dull, bland, boring, spiritless. **5** fixed, set, standard. **6** punctured,
burst, deflated, blown out. **7** outright,
direct, straight, downright, positive,
categorical.
➤*adv* outright, directly, absolutely,
categorically.
➤*noun* **1** lowland, plain, marsh. **2** shallow,
shoal, sandbank.
flat out at top speed, all out.

flat[2] *noun* apartment, penthouse, maison-
ette, rooms.

flatten *verb* **1** level, smooth, even out,
press, roll, crush, squash. **2** demolish,
knock down, tear down, raze. **3** knock
down, floor. **4** beat, overwhelm, crush,
subdue.

flatter *verb* **1** praise, compliment, eulogize, fawn, adulate, court, sweet-talk (*inf*).
2 suit, become, enhance, show to
advantage.

flattery *noun* **1** fawning, sycophancy, ser-
vility, adulation, blarney, sweet-talk (*inf*).
2 praise, compliments, blandishments.

flatulent *adj* **1** windy, gassy. **2** verbose,
bombastic, pompous, pretentious, inflated.

flaunt *verb* display, show off, parade, flash,
brandish, flourish.

flavour *noun* **1** taste, savour, tang, smack.
2 essence, spirit, tone, character.
➤*verb* season, spice.

flavouring *noun* seasoning, relish, extract,
essence, additive.

flaw *noun* **1** defect, fault, blemish, imperfection, weakness, failing. **2** crack, split,
fault, defect.

flay *verb* **1** skin, excoriate, peel, strip.
2 criticize, pan (*inf*), castigate, tear a strip
off (*inf*).

fleck *verb* speckle, spot, dot, streak, dapple,
mottle.
➤*noun* spot, dot, streak, speck, mark.

flee *verb* fly, run away, abscond, make off,
escape, bolt, decamp, beat it (*inf*).

fleece *noun* coat, wool, down.
➤*verb* swindle, cheat, diddle (*inf*), overcharge, rob, rip off (*inf*).

fleet[1] *noun* armada, squadron, task force,
flotilla.

fleet[2] *adj* rapid, swift, fast, quick, speedy,
nimble.

fleeting *adj* transitory, transient, ephemeral, passing, brief, short, momentary.

flesh *noun* **1** tissue, muscle, meat, fat.
2 mortality, carnality, physicality, corporeality, sensuality.
➤ **in the flesh** in person, in real life, in
bodily form.

fleshly *adj* carnal, sensual, animal, physical, bodily, corporeal, earthly, worldly.

fleshy *adj* fat, plump, corpulent, stout,
podgy, chubby.

flex *noun* wire, cable, cord, lead.
➤*verb* **1** bend, bow, crook. **2** tense,
tighten, contract.

flexible *adj* **1** pliable, pliant, bendable,
supple. **2** yielding, compliant, amenable,
tractable. **3** adaptable, adjustable, variable.

flexuous *adj* winding, serpentine, sinuous,
twisting, bending, curving.

flick *verb* rap, tap, flip, snap, click.
flick through scan, skim, browse, flip
through, thumb through.

flicker *verb* **1** flash, twinkle, sparkle, blink.
2 waver, fluctuate, quiver, tremble.
➤*noun* flash, gleam, glimmer, spark.

flight[1] *noun* **1** flying, gliding, aviation,
aeronautics. **2** journey, trip, shuttle.
3 swarm, flock. **4** squadron, unit, formation. **5** staircase, stairs, steps.

flight[2] *noun* fleeing, escape, getaway, exodus, retreat, migration.
take (to) flight flee, run away, escape,
abscond, make off, decamp.

flighty *adj* frivolous, capricious, irresponsible, scatterbrained, giddy, wild.

flimsy *adj* **1** frail, fragile, delicate, slight,
insubstantial, rickety. **2** thin, sheer, light.
3 weak, feeble, poor, inadequate, unconvincing, implausible.

flinch *verb* **1** wince, shrink, cower, quail,
blench, recoil. **2** balk, dodge, shirk, flee.

fling verb hurl, toss, throw, sling, chuck (*inf*).
➤*noun* spree, binge, debauch.

flip verb **1** toss, pitch, turn, spin. **2** flick, rap, tap.
flip through skim, flick through, scan, thumb through, browse.

flippant adj frivolous, offhand, superficial, irreverent, glib, disrespectful.

flirt verb philander, make advances, lead on, ogle, chat up (*inf*).
➤*noun* philanderer, coquette, vamp, tease.
flirt with 1 toy with, entertain, consider. **2** dally with, trifle with.

flit verb fly, dart, skim, flash.

float verb **1** sail, drift, waft, glide, bob, hang. **2** suggest, put forward, propose, present.

flock noun **1** herd, pack, flight, swarm. **2** crowd, throng, group, company, gathering, assembly.
➤*verb* congregate, gather, converge, swarm, throng, cluster.

flog verb whip, lash, beat, scourge, flagellate, cane. **2** sell, trade in.

flood verb **1** inundate, deluge, submerge, drown, swamp, engulf. **2** overflow, brim over, rise, swell. **3** pour, surge, rush, gush, flow, stream. **4** saturate, swamp, glut, overwhelm.
➤*noun* **1** inundation, deluge, overflow, spate. **2** abundance, profusion, excess, glut, torrent, plethora.

floor noun **1** ground, bottom, base. **2** storey, level.
➤*verb* **1** knock down, fell, prostrate. **2** confound, stump, disconcert, nonplus, perplex, throw (*inf*).

flop verb **1** collapse, fall, drop, slump. **2** droop, sag, hang, dangle. **3** fail, founder, crash (*inf*), bomb (*inf*).
➤*noun* failure, fiasco, debacle, washout (*inf*).

floppy adj droopy, sagging, hanging, limp, loose.

flora noun plants, vegetation, botany.

florid adj **1** ruddy, red, flushed, rosy, rubicund. **2** flowery, ornate, overelaborate, fussy, flamboyant, high-flown.

flounce[1] verb stamp, storm, fling, jerk.

flounce[2] noun frill, ruffle, valance.

flounder verb **1** wallow, struggle, thrash. **2** stumble, blunder, falter, grope, fumble.

flourish verb **1** thrive, grow, burgeon, bloom, blossom. **2** prosper, succeed, do well, boom. **3** brandish, wield, wave, swing, flaunt.
➤*noun* **1** show, display, wave, twirl, panache. **2** ornament, decoration, swirl, curlicue.

flout verb **1** defy, disregard. **2** mock, jeer, scoff at.

flow verb **1** run, pour, stream, ooze, gush, spout, cascade. **2** move, proceed, circulate. **3** originate, issue, arise, derive, spring, result.
➤*noun* stream, course, drift, movement, circulation, surge, gush, outpouring, discharge.

flower noun **1** bloom, blossom, floret, inflorescence. **2** prime, peak, height, zenith. **3** cream, pick, best, elite.
➤*verb* **1** bloom, blossom, blow, come out. **2** develop, mature, flourish, thrive.

flowery adj florid, ornate, high-flown, rhetorical, grandiloquent, bombastic.

fluctuate verb **1** swing, seesaw, oscillate, undulate. **2** vacillate, waver, vary, change, shift.

flue noun chimney, passage, channel, duct, vent, shaft.

fluent adj **1** smooth, flowing, fluid, graceful, easy, effortless. **2** articulate, eloquent.

fluff[1] noun **1** down, pile, fur. **2** lint, dust.

fluff[2] verb botch, bungle, mess up, boob (*inf*).

fluffy adj furry, fuzzy, fleecy, woolly, downy.

fluid noun liquid, solution, gas, vapour.
➤*adj* **1** liquid, gaseous, molten, flowing. **2** changeable, shifting, mobile, protean. **3** flexible, adaptable, adjustable. **4** smooth, flowing, fluent, easy, effortless, graceful.

fluke noun accident, chance, stroke of luck, lucky break.

flunky noun **1** footman, lackey, servant, valet. **2** underling, menial, minion, drudge. **3** sycophant, toady, yes-man, bootlicker (*inf*), hanger-on.

flurry noun **1** bustle, stir, commotion, ado, whirl, fuss. **2** squall, gust. **3** outbreak, burst, bout, spell.
➤verb fluster, agitate, ruffle, upset, rattle (inf), faze (inf), confuse, bewilder.

flush[1] verb **1** blush, colour, go red. **2** clean out, rinse, drench, douse, cleanse.
➤noun **1** blush, redness, rosiness, bloom, glow, radiance. **2** thrill, excitement, exhilaration, animation.

flush[2] adj **1** even, level, flat, plane. **2** wealthy, rich, affluent.

flush[3] verb chase, drive, expel, eject.

fluster verb agitate, ruffle, disconcert, perturb, bother, upset, panic, confuse.
➤noun agitation, flap (inf), panic, flurry, turmoil.

flute verb groove, furrow, corrugate, channel.

flutter verb **1** flap, bat, beat. **2** wave, flap, shake, waver, ripple, flicker. **3** palpitate, vibrate, quiver, tremble.
➤noun **1** quiver, tremble, shake, flap. **2** fluster, flurry, stir, commotion, agitation, confusion. **3** tremor, palpitation. **4** bet, gamble, wager.

flux noun **1** flow, fluidity, motion. **2** transition, change, alteration, mutation, fluctuation, instability.

fly[1] verb **1** wing, flutter. **2** glide, float. **3** flap, wave. **4** pilot, control, manoeuvre. **5** dash, dart, shoot, tear, race, speed, career, zoom. **6** escape, flee, bolt, abscond.
fly at attack, lay into, go for, fall upon.

fly[2] adj artful, shrewd, astute, canny, cunning, sharp.

flying adj **1** airborne, hovering, soaring, gliding. **2** brief, quick, hasty, fleeting.

foam noun froth, spume, bubbles, suds, lather.
➤verb froth, lather, bubble, effervesce.

fob verb **fob off 1** put off, deceive, trick, mislead. **2** get rid of, unload, foist, palm off (inf).

focus noun centre, core, pivot, hub, nucleus, focal point.
➤verb **1** aim, direct, concentrate, centre. **2** line up, converge, meet.

fodder noun feed, food, forage, silage, hay, provender.

foe noun enemy, opponent, adversary, antagonist.

fog noun **1** mist, haze, murk, smog, pea-souper (inf). **2** obscurity, vagueness, haziness, daze, stupor, confusion, bewilderment.
➤verb **1** cloud, mist, steam up. **2** confuse, bewilder, mystify, obscure, obfuscate.

foggy adj **1** misty, hazy, murky. **2** obscure, vague, blurred, indistinct, confused, unclear.

foible noun weakness, failing, fault, shortcoming, quirk, idiosyncrasy.

foil[1] verb **1** thwart, balk, outwit, hamper, impede. **2** frustrate, defeat, counter.

foil[2] noun **1** contrast, antithesis. **2** leaf, lamina, sheet, film.

foist verb pass, fob off, palm off, dump, unload, get rid of, impose.

fold[1] verb **1** bend, double, overlap, crease, pleat, tuck. **2** enfold, envelop, wrap, enclose. **3** clasp, embrace. **4** collapse, fail, go under (inf), go bust (inf), close, shut down.
➤noun **1** crease, bend. **2** pleat, tuck, overlap, layer.

fold[2] noun enclosure, pen, compound, stockade, corral.

folder noun binder, file, portfolio, wallet, envelope.

foliage noun leaves, greenery, vegetation.

folk noun **1** people, public, nation, race. **2** relations, family, kin.

folklore noun **1** mythology, legends, stories, lore. **2** custom, tradition, popular belief.

follow verb **1** succeed, come after, go after, replace. **2** pursue, chase, shadow, hunt, stalk, trail. **3** obey, observe, heed, comply with. **4** copy, imitate, ape, emulate. **5** ensue, result, spring, develop, proceed. **6** keep up with, keep abreast of. **7** support, be a fan of. **8** understand, grasp.
follow through pursue, see through, continue, complete.
follow up investigate, look into, research, check out.

follower noun **1** disciple, adherent, partisan, pupil. **2** supporter, enthusiast, devotee, fan. **3** servant, attendant, companion.

following *adj* next, subsequent, ensuing, coming.
➤ *noun* entourage, train, circle, audience, supporters, fans.

folly *noun* foolishness, stupidity, madness, lunacy, rashness, recklessness, imprudence.

foment *verb* encourage, stimulate, incite, provoke, stir up, promote.

fond *adj* 1 loving, affectionate, amorous, adoring, devoted, doting. 2 foolish, empty, vain, deluded, naive.
fond of partial to, attached to, keen on, enamoured of.

fondle *verb* caress, stroke, pet, pat.

food *noun* 1 nourishment, nutriment, aliment, fodder, fare, diet, foodstuffs, provisions, comestibles, eats (*inf*), grub (*inf*), nosh (*inf*). 2 stimulation, stimulus, nourishment, sustenance.

fool *noun* 1 blockhead, dunce, simpleton, idiot, twit (*inf*), clot (*inf*), dope (*inf*), prat (*sl*). 2 jester, clown, buffoon.
➤ *verb* 1 deceive, dupe, trick, hoodwink, delude, con (*inf*). 2 jest, joke, kid (*inf*). 3 meddle, fiddle, tamper, trifle, toy.

foolhardy *adj* reckless, rash, daredevil, madcap, bold, daring, adventurous.

foolish *adj* 1 silly, unwise, imprudent, ill-advised, senseless, inane, stupid, crazy, daft (*inf*), barmy (*inf*). 2 absurd, ridiculous, ludicrous, laughable.

foolproof *adj* fail-safe, idiot-proof, guaranteed, never-failing.

foot *noun* 1 paw, hoof, trotter, pad. 2 bottom, base, pedestal, end.
➤ *verb* pay, settle.

foothold *noun* basis, foundation, position, status.

footing *noun* 1 foothold, support, grip. 2 standing, position, basis, foundation. 3 status, rank, relationship.

footstep *noun* 1 footprint, footmark, track, trace. 2 footfall, step, tread.

for *prep* 1 towards, to. 2 during, throughout. 3 in favour of, pro, with, in support of. 4 because of, owing to, due to.
➤ *conj* since, as, because.

forage *noun* fodder, food, feed, provender, herbage.
➤ *verb* scavenge, search, hunt, rummage.

foray *noun* raid, incursion, invasion, sally, sortie, assault.

forbear *verb* refrain, abstain, hold back, restrain oneself.

forbearance *noun* 1 abstinence, self-restraint, self-control, patience, endurance. 2 tolerance, leniency, clemency.

forbid *verb* 1 prohibit, ban, proscribe, outlaw, veto, disallow. 2 impede, hinder, prevent, rule out.

forbidding *adj* 1 menacing, threatening, sinister, grim, daunting. 2 hostile, unfriendly, stern, harsh.

force *verb* 1 compel, constrain, oblige, make, drive, coerce, press, pressure. 2 prise, break open. 3 push, thrust, drive. 4 strain, wrench.
➤ *noun* 1 compulsion, constraint, coercion, duress, pressure, violence. 2 power, might, strength, vigour, drive, energy, dynamism. 3 army, squadron, troop, unit, division, corps. 4 cogency, weight, significance, thrust, impact. 5 influence, power, authority.

forced *adj* 1 compulsory, obligatory, mandatory, compelled. 2 unnatural, strained, artificial, mannered, laboured, stiff.

forceful *adj* strong, powerful, compelling, persuasive, effective, dynamic, vigorous, energetic.

forcible *adj* 1 forced, compulsory, obligatory, violent, aggressive, coercive. 2 forceful, compelling, powerful, strong.

fore *noun* front, head, top, bow.

forebear *noun* ancestor, forefather, progenitor, predecessor, forerunner.

foreboding *noun* premonition, presentiment, dread, omen, portent, prediction, prophecy.

forecast *verb* predict, foretell, prognosticate, estimate, calculate, plan, project.
➤ *noun* prediction, prognosis, projection, outlook.

foreclose *verb* exclude, rule out, preclude, prevent.

forefather *noun* ancestor, forebear, progenitor.

forefront *noun* front, fore, vanguard, spearhead.

foregoing *adj* preceding, prior, previous, former, antecedent, aforesaid.

foreground *noun* fore, front, forefront, prominence, limelight.

foreign *adj* **1** overseas, exotic. **2** international, overseas. **3** extrinsic, extraneous. **4** alien, strange, unfamiliar. **5** irrelevant, unconnected, unrelated.

foreigner *noun* **1** alien, visitor, immigrant. **2** stranger, outsider, incomer.

foreknowledge *noun* prescience, foresight, precognition, premonition, clairvoyance.

foreland *noun* cape, headland, promontory.

foreman *noun* supervisor, overseer, superintendent, chargehand.

foremost *adj* **1** first, leading, head, front. **2** chief, principal, primary, premier, preeminent, supreme, paramount, prime.

forerunner *noun* **1** precursor, predecessor, prototype. **2** harbinger, herald, omen, portent.

foresee *verb* anticipate, expect, envisage, forecast, predict, prophesy, divine.

foreshadow *verb* augur, presage, predict, prefigure, portend, bode.

foresight *noun* forethought, anticipation, precaution, prudence, caution, farsightedness.

forest *noun* wood, grove, copse.

forestall *verb* anticipate, thwart, preempt, intercept, prevent, hinder.

foretaste *noun* **1** portent, forewarning. **2** preview, sample, appetizer.

foretell *verb* predict, prophesy, augur, forecast.

forethought *noun* **1** anticipation, foresight, planning. **2** precaution, prudence, farsightedness.

forever *adv* **1** evermore, always, eternally, indefinitely. **2** continually, constantly, incessantly, all the time.

forewarn *verb* warn, alert, advise, tip off.

foreword *noun* preface, introduction, preamble.

forfeit *verb* lose, surrender, hand over, give up.
➤*noun* loss, forfeiture, confiscation, sequestration.

forge[1] *verb* **1** shape, form, mould, work, hammer out, beat. **2** make, create, fabricate, construct. **3** fake, counterfeit, falsify, imitate.
➤*noun* smithy, foundry, furnace.

forge[2] *verb* advance, progress, press on, make headway.

forgery *noun* **1** falsification, imitation. **2** fake, counterfeit.

forget *verb* **1** neglect, disregard, fail, omit. **2** overlook, disregard, ignore, pass over.

forgetful *adj* absentminded, inattentive, negligent, careless, unmindful.

forgive *verb* **1** let bygones be bygones, bury the hatchet. **2** pardon, absolve, excuse, exonerate, overlook.

forgiveness *noun* pardon, absolution, exoneration, clemency, amnesty, mercy.

forgiving *adj* merciful, lenient, clement, tolerant, forbearing, magnanimous.

forgo *verb* surrender, give up, renounce, do without, refrain from, abstain from.

fork *verb* branch, bifurcate, divide, split, diverge.
➤*noun* bifurcation, division, parting of the ways.

forked *adj* branching, diverging, divided, split, pronged, Y-shaped.

forlorn *adj* **1** miserable, wretched, sad, desolate, woebegone, pathetic, abandoned, forsaken. **2** desperate, hopeless, futile, vain.

form *noun* **1** shape, configuration, arrangement, structure, frame, outline. **2** body, figure. **3** type, kind, sort, variety, style, model. **4** mould, frame, pattern, matrix. **5** document, order, application, blank. **6** manner, method, system, convention, etiquette, protocol. **7** condition, health, fitness, shape. **8** class, grade, year.
➤*verb* **1** make, construct, produce. **2** shape, mould, model, fashion. **3** create, set up, establish. **4** take shape, materialize, appear, develop. **5** compose, make up, constitute, serve as. **6** arrange, assemble, dispose, organize. **7** train, educate, develop, school, discipline.

formal *adj* **1** conventional, customary, standard, approved, official, set. **2** punctilious, ceremonious, stiff, solemn, dignified. **3** symmetrical, methodical, orderly.

formality *noun* **1** convention, custom, usage, practice, procedure. **2** ceremony, protocol, etiquette, decorum.

format *noun* design, layout, arrangement, organization, style, order, pattern, composition.

formation *noun* **1** creation, production, construction, composition, establishment, development. **2** arrangement, grouping, organization, configuration, pattern, structure.

formative *adj* influential, dominant, significant.

former *adj* **1** earlier, preceding, foregoing, past, old, bygone. **2** previous, prior, past, one-time, erstwhile, late.

formerly *adv* previously, in the past, heretofore, hitherto, once, at one time.

formidable *adj* **1** daunting, intimidating, redoubtable, terrifying, menacing, threatening. **2** strong, powerful, indomitable, overwhelming.

formula *noun* **1** rule, principle. **2** code, expression, equation. **3** recipe, prescription. **4** procedure, method. **5** ritual, convention.

formulate *verb* **1** define, specify, detail, itemize. **2** devise, draw up, invent, think up, create, work out.

forsake *verb* **1** desert, abandon, leave in the lurch **2** give up, relinquish, forgo, renounce.

forsaken *adj* **1** desolate, deserted, abandoned, isolated. **2** abandoned, neglected, forlorn.

fort *noun* fortress, stronghold, citadel, garrison, castle.

forte *noun* strength, strong point, talent, gift, métier, speciality.

forth *adv* **1** forwards, onwards. **2** out, away, off, abroad.

forthcoming *adj* **1** future, prospective, approaching, imminent, impending.
2 available, ready, accessible, obtainable. **3** communicative, open, talkative, responsive.

forthright *adj* direct, plain-spoken, candid, blunt.

forthwith *adv* directly, immediately, at once, straight away, without delay.

fortification *noun* defence, rampart, battlement, barricade, bulwark, stronghold.

fortify *verb* **1** strengthen, reinforce, buttress, protect, guard, secure, defend. **2** encourage, cheer, hearten, invigorate, revive, sustain.

fortitude *noun* endurance, forbearance, courage, bravery, resolution, perseverance.

fortuitous *adj* accidental, unplanned, chance, unexpected, random, arbitrary.

fortunate *adj* **1** lucky, happy, blessed, prosperous. **2** auspicious, propitious, favourable, advantageous, promising, timely.

fortune *noun* **1** wealth, affluence, assets, treasure, king's ransom, packet (*inf*). **2** luck, chance, providence, fortuity, fate, destiny. **3** future, prospects, lot, doom.

fortune-teller *noun* soothsayer, seer, augur, sibyl, clairvoyant, psychic.

forum *noun* **1** meeting, arena, assembly, debate. **2** marketplace, square.

forward *adj* **1** onward, advancing, leading. **2** front, first, head, anterior, fore. **3** bold, brash, pert, impudent, presumptuous, overfamiliar, fresh (*inf*), confident, assertive, pushy (*inf*). **4** early, premature, advanced, precocious. **5** advanced, progressive. **6** future, prospective, advance.
➤*adv* **1** forwards, on, onwards, ahead. **2** out, forth, into view, to the fore.
➤*verb* **1** advance, further, promote, help, expedite. **2** send, dispatch, mail, post, ship.

foster *verb* **1** promote, further, encourage, facilitate, stimulate, cultivate, maintain. **2** raise, rear, bring up, take care of, look after. **3** cherish, nurture, harbour.

foul *adj* **1** disgusting, nauseating, putrid, fetid, stinking, offensive, rank, noisome. **2** wicked, evil, ignoble, despicable, shameful, heinous, base, low. **3** bad, nasty, unpleasant, disagreeable, vile, horrible.

4 vulgar, obscene, profane, filthy, offensive, abusive. **5** unfair, dishonourable, dishonest, unsportsmanlike. **6** dirty, filthy, impure, contaminated, polluted.
➤**verb 1** soil, dirty, pollute, contaminate. **2** block, clog, jam, choke.

found *verb* **1** establish, set up, institute, inaugurate, create. **2** build, erect, base, ground, set, place.

foundation *noun* **1** base, footing, groundwork, underpinning, substructure, bedrock. **2** establishment, institution, inauguration, endowment. **3** basis, support, base, starting point. **4** proof, support, backup, reason, justification.

founder[1] *verb* **1** sink, go down. **2** stumble, fall, trip, stagger. **3** collapse, fail, miscarry, come to nothing.

founder[2] *noun* originator, creator, benefactor, architect, designer, builder.

foundling *noun* waif, stray, orphan, outcast.

fountain *noun* **1** jet, spout, spray. **2** spring, well. **3** fountainhead, fount, source, wellspring.

fowl *noun* bird, chicken, cock, hen, goose, duck, turkey.

foxy *adj* wily, artful, cunning, sly, crafty, sharp, shrewd.

foyer *noun* entrance hall, lobby, vestibule, reception area.

fracas *noun* quarrel, row, brawl, disturbance, rumpus.

fraction *noun* part, piece, bit, portion, proportion, section.

fractious *adj* irritable, peevish, cross, fretful, unruly, refractory.

fracture *verb* **1** break, crack. **2** split, rupture.
➤*noun* **1** break, crack. **2** rift, division, split, fissure, breach, rupture.

fragile *adj* **1** brittle, frangible, breakable, frail, delicate, flimsy. **2** dainty, light, fine, delicate. **3** weak, feeble, unwell, ailing.

fragment *noun* piece, part, bit, particle, scrap, sliver.
➤*verb* **1** break, splinter, shatter, break up. **2** disintegrate, collapse, come to pieces, fall apart.

fragrance *noun* **1** scent, perfume, aroma, redolence, bouquet. **2** perfume, scent, cologne.

fragrant *adj* perfumed, scented, balmy, aromatic, sweet-smelling.

frail *adj* **1** weak, feeble, infirm, delicate. **2** fragile, flimsy, vulnerable.

frailty *noun* **1** weakness, infirmity, fragility, vulnerability. **2** failing, fault, foible, weakness.

frame *noun* **1** border, setting, mount, case. **2** structure, framework, skeleton, shell. **3** build, physique, shape, figure.
➤*verb* **1** enclose, surround, border, mount. **2** devise, invent, formulate, draft, plan. **3** make, form, construct, build, fabricate. **4** trap, incriminate, set up (*inf*), fit up (*inf*).
frame of mind mood, temper, humour, disposition.

frame-up *noun* conspiracy, trap, put-up job (*inf*), fit-up (*inf*).

framework *noun* **1** frame, structure, skeleton, shell, casing, support. **2** structure, system, scheme.

franchise *noun* **1** vote, suffrage, enfranchisement. **2** licence, authorization, dealership. **3** right, privilege, prerogative, freedom.

frank *adj* **1** honest, direct, forthright, candid, blunt, open, sincere. **2** undisguised, unconcealed, apparent, obvious, plain.

frankly *adv* candidly, bluntly, plainly, honestly, straight.

frantic *adj* **1** mad, hysterical, panic-stricken, distraught, beside oneself. **2** frenzied, wild, berserk, furious, frenetic.

fraternity *noun* **1** brotherhood, fellowship, association, society, guild, union. **2** companionship, camaraderie, fellowship.

fraternize *verb* associate, socialize, mix, mingle, consort.

fraud *noun* **1** deception, deceit, trickery, swindling, sharp practice. **2** trick, swindle, hoax, con (*inf*), scam (*inf*). **3** impostor, charlatan, quack, confidence trickster, fake, phoney (*inf*).

fraudulent *adj* deceitful, dishonest, cheating, swindling, crooked (*inf*), shady (*inf*).

fraught *adj* **1** filled, full, charged, laden. **2** anxious, tense, distraught, stressed.

fray[1] *noun* fight, battle, combat, brawl, mêlée, fracas.

fray[2] *verb* wear, unravel, shred, tatter.

freak *noun* 1 aberration, anomaly, oddity, curiosity, mutant, monster. 2 enthusiast, addict, fanatic, fiend (*inf*). 3 oddball (*inf*), weirdo (*inf*), nut (*inf*). 4 phenomenon, quirk, whim, caprice.
➤*adj* abnormal, anomalous, unnatural, exceptional, unpredictable, unexpected.

free *adj* 1 independent, liberated, enfranchised, emancipated, self-governing, autonomous. 2 unconfined, loose, unshackled, at liberty, at large. 3 exempt, immune, relieved, released. 4 idle, at leisure, unoccupied, unattached. 5 spare, available. 6 clear, unobstructed, unimpeded, open. 7 vacant, empty, available. 8 unfettered, unshackled, unrestrained, unrestricted. 9 gratis, on the house (*inf*), complimentary. 10 liberal, generous, lavish, extravagant, prodigal. 11 voluntary, unforced, willing, spontaneous. 12 rough, loose, broad, imprecise.
➤*verb* liberate, release, loose, let go, emancipate, relieve, discharge, exempt.
free and easy informal, relaxed, casual, unceremonious, familiar, uninhibited.

freebooter *noun* pirate, buccaneer, brigand, raider, marauder.

freedom *noun* 1 liberty, emancipation, independence, release, deliverance. 2 exemption, immunity, impunity. 3 right, privilege. 4 latitude, leeway, licence, authority, carte blanche.

freeze *verb* 1 solidify, congeal, harden, ice. 2 stop, stand still, hold, fix, suspend. 3 numb, anaesthetize.

freezing *adj* icy, bitter, raw, wintry, arctic, polar, glacial.

freight *noun* 1 transportation, haulage, carriage, shipping. 2 cargo, load, lading, consignment, shipment, goods.

frenetic *adj* frantic, frenzied, wild, mad, uncontrolled.

frenzy *noun* 1 agitation, excitement, fury, passion, madness, wildness. 2 fit, paroxysm, outburst.

frequency *noun* 1 repetition, recurrence. 2 incidence, prevalence.

frequent *adj* 1 recurrent, repeated, continual, constant, numerous. 2 habitual, persistent.
➤*verb* visit, attend, patronize, haunt.

fresh *adj* 1 new, recent, latest, more, other. 2 novel, original, innovative, different, unfamiliar. 3 natural, unprocessed, uncured, raw. 4 pure, clean, unpolluted, sweet. 5 cold, windy, cool, chilly, crisp. 6 brisk, bracing, refreshing, invigorating, bracing, crisp. 7 energetic, vigorous, alert, revived, refreshed, rested. 8 healthy, blooming, glowing, clear. 9 bright, clear. 10 clean, spruce. 11 inexperienced, green, callow, artless, unsophisticated. 12 overfamiliar, forward, presumptuous, bold, impudent, disrespectful.

freshen *verb* 1 air, clean, clear, purify, deodorize. 2 refresh, invigorate, revitalize, enliven, renew.
freshen up get washed, tidy oneself up.

fret *verb* 1 worry, brood, agonize, grieve, pine. 2 rub, chafe, wear, abrade. 3 erode, corrode, eat away.

fretful *adj* irritable, peevish, restless, troubled, touchy, fractious, anxious, distressed.

friable *adj* crumbly, powdery, brittle.

friction *noun* 1 rubbing, grating, scraping. 2 disagreement, discord, dispute, conflict, disharmony, animosity.

friend *noun* 1 companion, intimate, comrade, crony, chum (*inf*), buddy (*inf*), pal (*inf*), mate (*inf*). 2 benefactor, patron, backer, supporter.

friendly *adj* 1 amiable, amicable, kind, neighbourly, sociable, approachable, convivial, intimate, pally (*inf*), matey (*inf*). 2 favourable, propitious, advantageous, beneficial, helpful.

fright *noun* fear, alarm, terror, scare, shock, start, panic, dismay.

frighten *verb* alarm, scare, terrify, shock, startle, dismay, daunt, intimidate, unnerve, put the wind up (*inf*).

frightful *adj* 1 frightening, terrifying, fearsome, fearful, dreadful, awful, horrifying, shocking, appalling, monstrous. 2 awful, dreadful, terrible, unpleasant, horrible, ghastly.

frigid *adj* 1 cold, chilly, icy, glacial, bitter, freezing. 2 cool, unfriendly, frosty, unfeeling, indifferent, unenthusiastic. 3 unresponsive, passionless.

frill noun **1** flounce, ruche, ruffle, valance. **2** decoration, embellishment, extra, trimming.

fringe noun **1** border, edging, trimming. **2** edge, border, margin, periphery, outskirts.
➤verb edge, trim, border, skirt.

frisk verb **1** frolic, gambol, caper, skip, leap, dance, cavort. **2** search, inspect, check.

frisky adj frolicsome, sportive, playful, lively, coltish, full of beans (inf).

fritter verb waste, squander, dissipate, misspend.

frivolous adj **1** foolish, silly, childish, flippant. **2** idle, light, trivial, petty, unimportant.

frolic verb gambol, caper, frisk, romp, cavort, play, sport.
➤noun **1** gambol, caper, romp, game, lark. **2** fun, amusement, merriment, jollity.

front noun **1** anterior, forepart, foreground, face, head, lead, vanguard. **2** facade, frontage. **3** aspect, appearance, exterior, facade, mask, disguise, cover, pretext.
➤adj foremost, leading, head, first, anterior, frontal, forward.
➤verb face, be opposite, overlook.
in front of ahead of, before.

frontier noun **1** boundary, border, marches, bounds. **2** limits, confines, edge.

frost noun hoarfrost, rime.

frosty adj **1** icy, freezing, cold, wintry. **2** hoary, rimy. **3** unfriendly, indifferent, cool, frigid, distant, aloof.

froth noun **1** foam, spume, bubbles, lather, suds, head. **2** triviality, superficiality, humbug, flummery.
➤verb foam, lather, bubble, effervesce.

frown verb scowl, glower, glare, lower.
frown on disapprove of, dislike, discourage, take a dim view of.

frowzy adj unkempt, untidy, slovenly, slatternly, sloppy.

frugal adj thrifty, sparing, economical, careful, provident, abstemious, parsimonious.

fruit noun product, result, consequence, effect, yield, outcome, reward, benefit.

fruitful adj **1** prolific, productive, fertile, rich, plentiful, abundant. **2** profitable, worthwhile, effective, successful, useful, productive, rewarding.

fruition noun fulfilment, achievement, realization, completion, success, maturation.

fruitless adj futile, vain, useless, ineffective, unproductive, unsuccessful, abortive, idle.

fruity adj **1** rich, mellow, deep, resonant, full. **2** bawdy, suggestive, risqué, ribald.

frustrate verb **1** disappoint, discourage, dishearten, upset, annoy. **2** thwart, foil, balk, check, defeat, impede, prevent. **3** dash, confound, undo, block, prevent.

fuddle verb confuse, muddle, stupefy, inebriate, intoxicate.

fuddy-duddy noun conservative, old fogey, stick-in-the-mud (inf), stuffed shirt (inf).

fuel noun **1** combustible, wood, coal, gas, oil, petrol. **2** food, nourishment, sustenance, encouragement.

fugitive noun runaway, escapee, deserter, refugee.
➤adj **1** runaway, escaping, deserting, refugee. **2** fleeting, transitory, transient, passing, ephemeral, elusive.

fulcrum noun pivot, support.

fulfil verb **1** complete, accomplish, achieve, realize. **2** effect, carry out, perform, execute. **3** satisfy, fill, meet, answer, comply with.

full adj **1** filled, brimming, packed, chock-a-block (inf), satisfied, replete, sated, gorged, bursting (inf). **2** complete, entire, whole, integral, unabridged, comprehensive. **3** greatest, maximum, highest, top. **4** rounded, curvaceous, plump, buxom, ample. **5** wide, puffy, baggy, loose-fitting, voluminous. **6** resonant, rich, deep, loud.
➤adv directly, right, squarely, exactly, smack bang (inf).
in full fully, completely, wholly, entirely.

full-scale adj **1** full-size, life-size. **2** complete, full, thorough, comprehensive, wide-ranging.

fully adv completely, entirely, wholly, totally, utterly, absolutely, altogether.

fully-fledged *adj* **1** developed, mature. **2** experienced, trained, qualified.

fulminate *verb* **1** denounce, condemn, decry, rail, inveigh, censure, remonstrate, protest. **2** rage, fume. **3** explode, detonate, blow up, burst.

fulsome *adj* excessive, extravagant, adulatory, fawning, ingratiating, insincere, cloying, over-the-top (*inf*).

fumble *verb* **1** grope, feel, scrabble, search. **2** botch, bungle, muff.

fume *verb* **1** rage, storm, rant, rave, seethe, fret. **2** smoke, emit, exhale.

fumes *pl noun* gas, vapour, smoke, exhaust, effluvium, exhalation.

fumigate *verb* smoke, disinfect, purify, cleanse, sterilize, sanitize.

fun *noun* amusement, entertainment, diversion, recreation, sport, pleasure, good time, enjoyment, merriment, jollity.
➤*adj* enjoyable, entertaining, amusing, pleasurable.
in fun as a joke, for a laugh, in jest.
make fun of/poke fun at ridicule, laugh at, mock, jeer, taunt, satirize, lampoon, send up (*inf*).

function *noun* **1** purpose, use, role, duty, job, office. **2** ceremony, party, reception, affair, do (*inf*).
➤*verb* **1** work, operate, run, go. **2** serve, work, act, perform, operate, behave.

functional *adj* **1** useful, practical, utilitarian, serviceable, plain. **2** operational, working, running.

functionary *noun* official, bureaucrat, civil servant.

fund *noun* **1** reserve, collection, kitty, endowment, foundation. **2** stock, supply, store, reserve, hoard, pool.
➤*verb* finance, pay for, subsidize, bankroll, endow, capitalize.

fundamental *adj* **1** important, essential, principal, key, indispensable, cardinal. **2** basic, rudimentary, primary, elementary, underlying, organic, integral.
➤*noun* basic, rudiment, essential, principle, foundation.

funds *pl noun* cash, capital, means, money, resources, finance.

funeral *noun* burial, interment, inhumation, cremation, obsequies.

funereal *adj* mournful, gloomy, solemn, sombre, dark, lugubrious.

funk *noun* fear, panic, terror, fright.
➤*verb* flinch, recoil, take fright, chicken out (*inf*).

funny *adj* **1** amusing, comical, humorous, droll, witty, facetious, entertaining, hilarious. **2** odd, strange, weird, curious, peculiar, mysterious.

fur *noun* hair, coat, hide, skin, pelt.

furious *adj* **1** angry, enraged, fuming, livid, incensed, irate, infuriated, raging, up in arms (*inf*), hopping mad (*inf*). **2** wild, stormy, violent, agitated, turbulent, tempestuous.

furl *verb* roll, wrap, fold, wind.

furnish *verb* **1** equip, rig out, fit out, appoint. **2** give, supply, provide, bestow. **3** endow, supply, provide, equip.

furniture *noun* movables, appliances, fixtures, fittings, furnishings, effects.

furore *noun* outcry, uproar, commotion, stir, hullabaloo, ado.

furrow *noun* **1** trench, trough, channel. **2** groove, flute, rebate. **3** wrinkle, crease, line.
➤*verb* wrinkle, crease.

further *adj* additional, more, extra, new, other.
➤*adv* **1** furthermore, besides, moreover, in addition, also, yet. **2** farther, beyond, past.
➤*verb* advance, promote, forward, help, foster, encourage, facilitate, expedite.

furthermore *adv* moreover, yet, in addition, besides, what's more, further, also.

furthest *adj* farthest, utmost, outermost, uttermost, extreme, ultimate.

furtive *adj* secret, clandestine, hidden, covert, sly, stealthy, surreptitious, underhand.

fury *noun* **1** rage, anger, wrath, ire, passion, temper. **2** violence, force, intensity, ferocity, wildness, turbulence.

fuse *verb* **1** unite, combine, amalgamate, blend, merge, weld, solder. **2** melt, liquefy.

fusion *noun* **1** union, amalgamation, coalescence. **2** synthesis, blend, merger, amalgam.

fuss *noun* **1** agitation, commotion, bustle, bother, ado, palaver. **2** complaint, objection, protest, trouble.
➤*verb* fret, worry, flap (*inf*), get worked up (*inf*).

fussy *adj* **1** pernickety, nit-picking, exacting. **2** fastidious, hard to please, particular, finicky, faddy, choosy (*inf*). **3** ornate, busy, cluttered, overelaborate.

fusty *adj* **1** musty, mouldy, damp, frowsty, stale, stuffy. **2** old-fashioned, out-of-date, antiquated, archaic.

futile *adj* useless, vain, fruitless, unavailing, unsuccessful, unproductive, pointless.

future *adj* forthcoming, coming, prospective, impending, eventual, ultimate, subsequent, later.
➤*noun* **1** prospect, outlook. **2** offing, hereafter.

fuzzy *adj* **1** frizzy, fluffy, woolly, downy. **2** blurred, indistinct, out of focus, misty, vague, obscure.

gab *verb* chatter, gossip, prattle, natter (*inf*), yak (*inf*), talk, jaw, prate.
➤*noun* chat, talk, small talk, chitchat, gossip, prattle, tittle-tattle, waffle (*inf*).

gabble *verb* jabber, gibber, spout, chatter, babble, burble, blether, rabbit (*inf*).
➤*noun* drivel, gibberish, chatter, babble, blether, prattle, jabber, nonsense.

gad *verb* gallivant, roam, rove, range, travel, wander.

gadabout *noun* pleasure-seeker, rover, globe-trotter, traveller, wanderer.

gadget *noun* device, contraption (*inf*), gizmo (*inf*), widget (*inf*), contrivance, appliance, tool, implement.

gaffe *noun* mistake, error, blunder, clanger (*inf*), boob (*inf*), indiscretion, faux pas.

gaffer *noun* **1** boss, foreman, manager, supervisor, overseer. **2** old man, old fellow, old boy (*inf*), old geezer (*inf*), old-timer (*inf*).

gag *verb* **1** smother, muffle, muzzle, silence. **2** muzzle, stifle, silence, suppress, curb, restrain. **3** retch, heave, vomit.
➤*noun* joke, quip, one-liner, witticism, wisecrack (*inf*).

gaiety *noun* **1** joy, glee, cheerfulness, happiness, mirth, jollity, merriment, exuberance, high spirits, joie de vivre. **2** merrymaking, festivity, revelry, celebration, fun, jollification.

gain *verb* **1** earn, make, get, secure, attain, win, capture, reap. **2** catch up, approach, close in, narrow the gap, overtake, leave behind. **3** develop, pick up, increase, gather, add, build up, improve. **4** acquire, procure, obtain, get. **5** reach, arrive at, get to. **6** profit, benefit, advance, progress.
➤*noun* **1** profit, advantage, benefit, earnings, winnings, revenue, return, reward, yield, interest. **2** increase, rise, increment, augmentation. **3** acquisition, achievement, attainment.

gainful *adj* profitable, lucrative, remunerative, money-making, rewarding, productive, worthwhile, advantageous.

gainsay *verb* deny, contradict, disagree with, dispute, challenge, oppose, rebut.

gait *noun* walk, step, stride, tread, bearing, carriage.

gala *noun* celebration, festival, carnival, fete, jamboree.

galaxy *noun* **1** star system, constellation, cluster, nebula. **2** host, array, assembly, collection, bevy.

gale *noun* **1** wind, hurricane, blast, storm. **2** burst, outburst, peal, roar, eruption, scream, shriek, fit.

gall[1] *noun* **1** impudence, insolence, effrontery, impertinence, audacity, temerity, cheek (*inf*), nerve (*inf*), face (*inf*), brass neck (*inf*). **2** rancour, bitterness, malice, resentment, acrimony, bile, spleen, ill feeling.

gall[2] *noun* **1** irritation, exasperation, vexation, annoyance, nuisance, bother, pest, irritant, plague, torment. **2** sore, abrasion, chafe.
➤*verb* irritate, exasperate, vex, annoy, infuriate, irk, rile, pique, peeve (*inf*), mortify, chagrin.

gallant *adj* **1** brave, courageous, valiant, heroic, intrepid, fearless, doughty, noble. **2** polite, courteous, gracious, chivalrous, gentlemanly, courtly, magnanimous, obliging, considerate, attentive. **3** fine, dashing, elegant, splendid.
➤*noun* dandy, beau, fop, ladies' man, lady-killer, man about town, buck (*inf*).

gallantry *noun* **1** courage, bravery, valour, heroism, fearlessness, mettle, spirit, pluck. **2** courtesy, politeness, chivalry, graciousness, courtliness, nobility, honour, gentlemanliness, attentiveness, consideration.

gallery noun **1** corridor, passage, hallway, landing, cloister, loggia, veranda. **2** balcony, circle, gods (inf).

gallivant verb gad, rove, roam, range, wander, travel.

gallop verb **1** canter, lope. **2** race, rush, run, dash, speed, sprint, fly, career, tear, shoot.

gallows noun scaffold, gibbet.

galore adj aplenty, in abundance, in profusion, lots of, loads of (inf), heaps of (inf).

galvanize verb electrify, excite, stimulate, fire, rouse, stir, animate, invigorate, shock, jolt, kick-start, spur.

gambit noun ruse, ploy, stratagem, trick, device, manoeuvre, move, tactic.

gamble verb **1** game, play for money. **2** bet, wager, stake, have a flutter (inf), risk, chance. **3** speculate, venture.
➤noun **1** bet, wager, flutter (inf). **2** risk, venture, speculation, chance, pot luck, lottery, leap in the dark.

gambol verb frolic, frisk, romp, caper, dance, leap, play, sport, skip, prance.

game¹ noun **1** pastime, recreation, diversion, amusement, match, sport, play, prank, lark (inf). **2** match, contest, competition, meeting, event, fixture. **3** round, bout. **4** activity, enterprise, adventure, undertaking, business. **5** quarry, prey, wild animals, wild fowl. **6** scheme, plan, ploy, strategy, tactics, ruse, trick.

game² adj **1** brave, courageous, plucky, resolute, persevering, dogged, spirited, heroic, dauntless, feisty (inf). **2** ready, willing, inclined, eager, enthusiastic, interested.

gamut noun compass, range, scope, series, sweep, spectrum.

gang noun **1** band, pack, mob, ring. **2** circle, set, coterie, camp, lot. **3** team, squad, troop, crew, shift, detachment.

gangling adj lanky, gangly, gawky, stringy, awkward, ungainly, rangy, leggy.

gangster noun mobster, heavy (inf), hoodlum, hood (inf), racketeer, mafioso, thug, desperado.

gap noun **1** opening, break, breach, rift, cleft, crevice, chink. **2** space, hole, cavity, void, interstice, blank, omission, lacuna.

3 break, interval, pause, hiatus, lull, intermission, rest. **4** breach, divide, gulf, chasm, difference, divergence, disparity.

gape verb **1** stare, gaze, gawk (inf), gawp (inf), goggle, rubberneck (inf). **2** open, yawn, part, split.

garb noun dress, attire, clothes, garments, wear, gear (inf), apparel, outfit, costume, style, fashion, mode.
➤verb clothe, dress, kit out (inf), rig out (inf), array, attire, apparel.

garbage noun **1** rubbish, refuse, waste, trash, junk, litter, scraps. **2** nonsense, rubbish, gibberish, drivel, twaddle, balderdash, bullshit (sl), claptrap (inf), cobblers (inf), rot (inf).

garble verb confuse, jumble, scramble, distort, twist, warp, slant, spin, misrepresent, misreport.

gargantuan adj enormous, huge, immense, colossal, massive, gigantic.

garish adj gaudy, flashy, showy, brash, flamboyant, glaring, lurid, loud, bold, tawdry.

garland noun wreath, festoon, decoration, crown, laurels, bays, honours.
➤verb festoon, crown, decorate, deck, adorn.

garner verb **1** gather, collect, accumulate, amass, assemble. **2** hoard, store, lay in, reserve, stockpile.

garnish verb decorate, ornament, embellish, trim, enhance, grace.
➤noun decoration, ornament, embellishment, trimming, enhancement, relish.

garret noun attic, loft, mansard.

garrison noun **1** detachment, unit, platoon, squadron, militia, troops. **2** fort, stronghold, citadel, station, post, barracks, camp.
➤verb defend, guard, fortify, man, post, station.

garrulous adj talkative, loquacious, voluble, chatty, effusive, babbling, jabbering, gossipy, gabby (inf), mouthy (inf).

gas noun vapour, fume, exhalation, effluvium.

gash noun cut, incision, slash, slit, tear, rent, laceration, wound.
➤verb cut, slash, slit, lacerate, split, incise.

gasp *verb* 1 gulp, catch one's breath.
2 pant, puff, blow, wheeze, choke.
➤*noun* gulp, intake of breath, pant, puff,
blow, wheeze.

gastric *adj* stomach, intestinal, abdominal,
enteric.

gate *noun* 1 door, portal, wicket, postern.
2 gateway, entrance, exit, opening.

gather *verb* 1 assemble, congregate, collect, meet, cluster, flock together, rally.
2 collect, assemble, accumulate, amass,
garner, stockpile, round up, convene, marshal. 3 summon up, muster. 4 understand,
conclude, infer, surmise, believe, learn,
hear. 5 pick, pluck, glean, reap, harvest,
cull. 6 increase, build up, accumulate,
develop. 7 ruffle, shirr, pucker, wrinkle,
pleat, tuck.

gathering *noun* assembly, meeting, rally,
muster, party, convention, congress, convocation, company, congregation.

gauche *adj* awkward, gawky, clumsy, shy,
inept, graceless, unsophisticated, insensitive, tactless, maladroit.

gaudy *adj* bright, colourful, garish, flashy,
showy, flamboyant, loud, brilliant,
multicoloured.

gauge *verb* 1 assess, weigh, evaluate,
judge, rate, estimate, guess, figure, reckon.
2 measure, calculate, compute, determine,
ascertain.
➤*noun* 1 measure, standard, norm, yardstick, touchstone, rule, meter. 2 thickness,
width, depth, diameter. 3 size, magnitude,
bore, span.

gaunt *adj* 1 thin, lean, lank, spare, drawn,
emaciated, wasted, bony, angular, haggard.
2 bleak, desolate, bare, barren, harsh, forbidding, forlorn, stark.

gawk *verb* gape, gawp (*inf*), goggle, stare,
gaze, rubberneck (*inf*), ogle, look.

gawky *adj* awkward, ungainly, gangling,
lanky, gauche, graceless, uncoordinated.

gay *adj* 1 merry, jolly, cheerful, blithe,
carefree, happy, joyful, elated, lively.
2 bright, colourful, vivid, brilliant, sparkling, gaudy, showy. 3 homosexual, lesbian, queer (*inf*), bent (*inf*).
➤*noun* homosexual, lesbian, queer (*inf*),
poof (*inf*), dyke (*inf*).

gaze *verb* stare, gape, gawk, gawp (*inf*),
contemplate, watch, regard, view.
➤*noun* stare, look, gape.

gazette *noun* journal, periodical, newspaper, newssheet, organ, dispatch, notice.

gear *noun* 1 gearwheel, cog, ratchet.
2 mechanism, machinery, works.
3 equipment, apparatus, trappings, paraphernalia, tools, instruments, kit, outfit,
rig, tackle, stuff (*inf*), things (*inf*).
4 clothes, garments, wear, dress, attire,
garb, togs (*inf*).

gelatinous *adj* viscous, glutinous, jelly-
like, gooey (*inf*), gummy, sticky, rubbery,
mucilaginous.

geld *verb* castrate, neuter, emasculate.

gelid *adj* icy, freezing, frozen, frigid, glacial, cold, wintry, bitter, arctic, polar.

gem *noun* 1 gemstone, jewel, precious
stone, brilliant. 2 jewel, treasure, prize,
pearl.

genealogy *noun* pedigree, family tree,
ancestry, descent, extraction, line, lineage,
family, stock.

general *adj* 1 collective, universal, overall,
total, across-the-board, all-inclusive, indiscriminate, comprehensive, encyclopedic.
2 widespread, extensive, common, popular, prevailing, prevalent, typical, accepted.
3 universal, generic, broad, blanket,
sweeping, unspecific, imprecise, loose.
➤*noun* commander, leader, chief, head.

generality *noun* 1 generalization, general
principle, sweeping statement, vague
notion. 2 universality, all-inclusiveness.
3 prevalence, commonness, imprecision,
looseness.

generally *adv* 1 usually, normally, in general, as a rule, by and large, on the whole,
ordinarily, typically, mainly, mostly.
2 universally, collectively, as a whole.
3 in general, broadly, loosely, approximately.

generate *verb* 1 produce, create, make.
2 engender, beget, create, produce, initiate, originate. 3 cause, bring about, give
rise to, occasion, arouse, stir up.

generation *noun* 1 age group, peer group.
2 procreation, breeding, reproduction,
genesis, begetting, propagation.
3 production, creation, formation,
engenderment, initiation, origination.

generic *adj* **1** collective, general, common, sweeping, blanket, all-inclusive, universal, nonspecific. **2** unbranded, nonproprietary.

generous *adj* **1** liberal, lavish, prodigal, open-handed, unstinting, munificent, charitable, bountiful, hospitable. **2** magnanimous, noble, benevolent, philanthropic, public-spirited, unselfish, altruistic, kind, good, big (*inf*). **3** abundant, plentiful, copious, full, lavish, rich, ample.

genesis *noun* beginning, origin, birth, outset, start, source, creation, dawn, generation, foundation, initiation, inception.

genial *adj* hearty, cordial, warm, friendly, amiable, affable, jovial, cheery, agreeable, good-humoured, kindly, benevolent.

genius *noun* **1** prodigy, virtuoso, maestro, master, expert, intellectual, egghead (*inf*), brains (*inf*), boffin (*inf*). **2** brilliance, intelligence, intellect, cleverness, wisdom, gift, talent, aptitude, knack, endowment.

genre *noun* category, class, group, school, style, type, sort, kind.

genteel *adj* **1** polite, civil, courteous, gracious, courtly, polished, cultivated, mannerly. **2** respectable, well-bred, aristocratic, noble, gentlemanly, ladylike, well-born, blue-blooded, cultured, refined.

gentility *noun* **1** politeness, civility, courtesy, good manners, propriety, decorum, etiquette, graciousness, cultivation. **2** aristocracy, nobility, gentry, upper class, ruling class, rank, breeding, high birth, blue blood.

gentle *adj* **1** tender, kind, compassionate, benign, charitable, humane, sweet-tempered, meek, mild. **2** soft, delicate, light, soothing, smooth. **3** gradual, easy, slow, slight, moderate, undemanding. **4** light, moderate, pleasant, temperate, balmy, clement.

gentry *noun* aristocracy, nobility, gentility, upper class, upper crust (*inf*).

genuine *adj* **1** real, authentic, original, pure, natural, true, veritable, actual, bona fide, legitimate, pukka (*inf*), kosher (*inf*). **2** honest, sincere, earnest, heartfelt, artless, unaffected, unfeigned, frank, candid.

genus *noun* **1** subdivision, taxon. **2** order, class, set, category, genre.

germ *noun* **1** microbe, bacterium, bacillus, virus, micro-organism, bug (*inf*). **2** beginning, start, root, source, origin, spark. **3** egg, ovum, ovule, seed, embryo, nucleus, bud, spore.

germane *adj* relevant, pertinent, connected, related, apposite, apropos, appropriate, fitting, to the point, apt, applicable, material.

germinate *verb* **1** sprout, shoot, grow, vegetate, bud, take root, spring up, burgeon. **2** originate, develop, evolve, begin, start.

gestation *noun* **1** pregnancy, gravidity, incubation, maturation. **2** conception, planning, development, evolution.

gesticulate *verb* gesture, sign, signal, wave.

gesture *noun* **1** gesticulation, signal, sign, action, motion, movement, wave, flourish. **2** demonstration, action, deed, act.
➤*verb* gesticulate, motion, signal, sign, wave, beckon, point, nod.

get *verb* **1** obtain, acquire, procure, secure, gain, earn, buy, win, receive, come by, make. **2** fetch, pick up, collect, bring, go for. **3** catch, seize, capture, take, grab, collar, arrest, nab (*inf*), bag (*inf*). **4** become, grow, turn, go, wax. **5** catch, contract, go down with, be afflicted with, fall victim to, pick up, develop. **6** contact, communicate with, speak to, phone, ring, reach. **7** attain, earn, win, score, receive, take. **8** understand, grasp, see, hear, follow, fathom, twig (*inf*), work out, comprehend, catch on (*inf*). **9** persuade, induce, coax, prevail upon, influence, urge. **10** arrive, come, go, make it (*inf*). **11** manage, arrange, succeed, contrive, wangle (*inf*). **12** prepare, cook, get ready, put together, rustle up (*inf*), fix (*inf*). **13** punish, get even with, get back at, pay back, take revenge on, settle the score with.

get across communicate, put across, put over, get over, make clear, bring home, impart, convey, transmit.

get along 1 get on, hit it off (*inf*), see eye to eye, agree. **2** manage, cope, fare, do, survive, make out (*inf*), progress, advance.

get at 1 reach, attain, find, get hold of, discover, obtain. **2** criticize, knock (*inf*), pick on, nag, tease, taunt. **3** suggest, imply, insinuate, intend, mean. **4** bribe, buy off, corrupt, influence, tamper with, suborn.

get away escape, get out, break free, run away, flee, leave, depart.

get back return, come back, arrive, come home.

get back at get, pay back, retaliate against, get even with, settle the score with, take revenge on.

get by get along, cope, manage, survive, make ends meet (*inf*), scrape by (*inf*), keep one's head above water (*inf*), weather the storm (*inf*), exist, subsist.

get down 1 descend, get off, step down, alight, dismount, disembark. **2** depress, discourage, dishearten, dispirit, sadden.

get off 1 leave, depart, start, begin. **2** escape, avoid punishment, be acquitted, be excused, be let off (*inf*).

get on 1 get along, manage, cope, make out (*inf*). **2** succeed, prosper, thrive, do well, make good, progress, advance, go places (*inf*).

get out 1 escape, break out, get away, flee, leave, depart, quit (*inf*), withdraw, extricate oneself, evacuate, vacate. **2** circulate, spread, leak out, become known.

get out of avoid, dodge (*inf*), evade, escape, shirk, skive (*inf*).

get over 1 recover from, recuperate from, shake off, survive, pull through, forget, come to terms with. **2** surmount, overcome, master, get round, defeat, deal with. **3** communicate, get across, make clear, make understood, convey, put across, put over, impart, explain.

get round 1 circumvent, bypass, evade, avoid, skirt. **2** persuade, win over, prevail upon, coax, cajole, wheedle.

get together meet, meet up, see one another, assemble, congregate, rally, converge, collect, gather.

get up 1 stand, rise. **2** rise, stir, wake up. **3** increase, intensify, strengthen.

getaway *noun* escape, breakout, flight, departure.

get-together *noun* meeting, party, gathering, function, reception, knees-up (*inf*), do (*inf*), bash (*inf*), social, rally, reunion.

get-up *noun* outfit, clothing, dress, garb, garments, costume.

ghastly *adj* **1** dreadful, frightful, terrible, awful, shocking, appalling, hideous, horrible, terrifying, horrendous, grim, gruesome. **2** horrid, appalling, abominable, nasty, odious, loathsome, contemptible, awful, dreadful, terrible. **3** pale, ashen, cadaverous, deathly, livid, pallid, wan, pasty, white.

ghost *noun* **1** spectre, phantom, phantasm, apparition, ghoul, spook (*inf*), spirit, soul, wraith, shade, revenant. **2** glimmer, trace, shadow, suggestion, hint, possibility.

ghostly *adj* eerie, creepy, unearthly, otherworldly, supernatural, spooky (*inf*), haunted, spectral, phantom, phantasmal.

giant *noun* **1** colossus, ogre, titan. **2** monster, behemoth, leviathan.
➤*adj* gigantic, colossal, huge, immense, massive, mammoth, jumbo (*inf*), whopping (*inf*), gargantuan, titanic.

gibber *verb* gabble, jabber, prattle, babble, chatter, blabber, waffle (*inf*).

gibberish *noun* nonsense, rubbish, twaddle, drivel, gobbledygook (*inf*), mumbo-jumbo, claptrap, rot (*inf*), prattle, chatter, blather, humbug.

gibe *noun* taunt, jeer, dig (*inf*), sneer, quip, crack (*inf*).
➤*verb* jeer, scoff, mock, sneer, deride, taunt, tease, ridicule, make fun of.

giddy *adj* **1** dizzy, faint, light-headed, reeling, unsteady, woozy (*inf*), vertiginous. **2** flighty, fickle, capricious, silly, scatterbrained, frivolous, skittish, impulsive, excitable, irresponsible, carefree, thoughtless.

gift *noun* **1** present, offering, donation, contribution, handout, freebie (*inf*), benefaction, gratuity, boon, bequest. **2** talent, knack, genius, faculty, aptitude, flair, bent, facility, skill, ability.
➤*verb* **1** give, offer, contribute, donate, bestow, will. **2** present, endow.

gifted *adj* **1** talented, accomplished, expert, masterly, adept, able, proficient, skilful, skilled, endowed. **2** brilliant, clever, intelligent, bright, sharp, smart (*inf*).

gigantic *adj* giant, huge, enormous, immense, colossal, gargantuan, jumbo (*inf*), king-size, whopping (*inf*), great, big, large.

giggle *verb* snigger, titter, laugh, chortle, chuckle, snicker.

gild *verb* adorn, decorate, ornament, garnish, embellish, dress up, embroider, disguise, camouflage, window-dress.

gimcrack *adj* cheap, tacky (*inf*), shoddy, tatty (*inf*), kitsch, showy, flashy, tawdry.

gimmick *noun* device, contrivance, attraction, stunt, novelty, gambit, ploy, scheme, ruse, trick.

gingerly *adv* cautiously, warily, carefully, daintily, delicately, gently, hesitantly, reluctantly, tentatively, suspiciously.

gird *verb* encircle, surround, ring, encompass, hem in, enclose, confine, strap, fasten, bind.

girdle *noun* 1 corset, foundation, stays. 2 belt, sash, cummerbund, waistband.
➤*verb* gird, encircle, surround, ring, encompass, bind.

girl *noun* 1 lass, miss, schoolgirl, daughter. 2 maiden, maid, lass, miss, young lady, young woman, wench, damsel, bird (*inf*), babe (*inf*), chick (*inf*). 3 girlfriend, sweetheart, lover, date, fiancée, inamorata.

girth *noun* 1 circumference, perimeter, size, measure. 2 strap, band.

gist *noun* substance, essence, pith, marrow, core, nub, crux, idea, meaning, import, sense, drift.

give *verb* 1 hand, pass, slip, present, grant, bestow, confer, award, contribute, donate, bequeath, make over. 2 suggest, present, show, display, exhibit, demonstrate, reveal, indicate. 3 offer, proffer, supply, provide, furnish. 4 express, communicate, tell, transmit, impart, convey, announce, declare, propose, put forward. 5 concede, allow, grant, cede, relinquish, surrender, yield. 6 cause, make, provoke, occasion. 7 produce, yield, afford, provide. 8 arrange, organize, stage, host, put on, lay on, provide, supply. 9 let out, utter, emit. 10 collapse, give way, break, yield, bend, buckle, sag, sink.

give away 1 expose, divulge, reveal, disclose, let slip, leak. 2 betray, inform on, shop (*inf*), grass on (*inf*), rat on (*inf*).

give in 1 surrender, yield, capitulate, submit, give way, give up, quit (*inf*), throw in the towel (*inf*). 2 concede, admit defeat.

give off emit, exude, exhale, produce, send out, discharge, release, vent.

give out 1 distribute, hand out, dole out, dish out (*inf*), allocate, allot, apportion, issue, deal, mete out. 2 fail, run out, run dry, come to an end, be exhausted.

give up 1 stop, cease, renounce, forgo, desist, leave off, quit (*inf*), kick (*inf*), discontinue, cut out (*inf*). 2 surrender, yield, give in, capitulate, resign, throw in the towel (*inf*), despair, lose heart, abandon hope.

given *adj* 1 inclined, disposed, likely, apt, wont, liable, prone. 2 specified, specific, particular, stated, fixed, set, arranged, appointed.

glacial *adj* 1 icy, frozen, freezing, arctic, polar, raw, bitter, biting, piercing, cold, chilly, wintry. 2 cold, frigid, unfeeling, hostile, unfriendly.

glad *adj* 1 happy, pleased, delighted, contented, satisfied, relieved, cheerful, joyful, thrilled, over the moon (*inf*), ready, willing. 2 pleasing, gratifying, cheering, encouraging, welcome, pleasant.

gladden *verb* please, gratify, delight, cheer, encourage, hearten, brighten.

glamour *noun* 1 attraction, fascination, allure, appeal, excitement, sparkle, glitter, glitz (*inf*), magic, spell, prestige 2 allure, charm, fascination, beauty, elegance, loveliness, attractiveness, sex appeal.

glance *verb* 1 look, glimpse, peek, peep, view, cast an eye over, browse. 2 scan, skim, flick. 3 bounce, rebound, ricochet.
➤*noun* glimpse, peek, peep, look, butchers (*inf*), dekko (*inf*), gander (*inf*), once-over (*inf*).

glare *verb* 1 glower, scowl, frown, glower, look daggers (*inf*). 2 dazzle, blind, blaze, flame, flare, beam, shine.
➤*noun* 1 scowl, frown, glower, black look (*inf*), dirty look (*inf*). 2 dazzle, blaze, brilliance, brightness, flare, beam, flame.

glaring *adj* conspicuous, prominent, obvious, manifest, patent, overt, blatant, flagrant, open.

glass *noun* tumbler, beaker, goblet, flute, schooner, balloon.

glasses *pl noun* spectacles, specs (*inf*), eyeglasses, bifocals.

glassy *adj* 1 glasslike, shiny, smooth, polished, glossy, mirrorlike, clear, crystalline, transparent, icy, slippery. 2 blank, expressionless, vacant, empty, glazed, vacuous, lifeless, dull.

glaze *verb* 1 lacquer, varnish, gloss, enamel, polish, burnish. 2 coat, cover, ice, frost, candy.

➤*noun* **1** lacquer, varnish, gloss, lustre, shine, sheen, polish, patina. **2** coating, icing, frosting.

gleam *noun* **1** glint, flash, beam, ray, shaft, flash, flare, flicker. **2** glow, shine, lustre, gloss, sheen. **3** glimmer, flicker, ray, trace, suggestion, hint, inkling, spark.
➤*verb* glint, glitter, shine, flash, beam, shimmer, sparkle, twinkle, coruscate.

glean *verb* **1** gather, collect, harvest, garner. **2** amass, gather, collect, find out, learn, pick up.

glee *noun* delight, pleasure, joy, merriment, gaiety, gladness, happiness, high spirits, elation, exultation, jubilation, triumph.

gleeful *adj* delighted, pleased, happy, merry, joyful, high-spirited, jubilant, exultant, triumphant, elated, exhilarated.

glib *adj* **1** easy, facile, quick, ready, slick, superficial. **2** smooth, fluent, plausible, insincere, suave, voluble, sweet-talking, silver-tongued, unctuous.

glide *verb* slide, slip, sail, skate, fly, float, drift, coast, roll.

glimmer *noun* **1** gleam, glint, flash, flicker, shimmer, twinkle, sparkle, glow. **2** flicker, gleam, ray, hint, suggestion, inkling, trace, grain.
➤*verb* gleam, glint, flicker, shimmer, glitter, twinkle, sparkle, blink, wink, shine, glow.

glimpse *noun* glance, peep, peek, look, sight, squint, view.
➤*verb* spot, catch sight of, sight, view, spy, descry.

glint *verb* gleam, flash, shine, glitter, sparkle, twinkle, blink, wink, scintillate.
➤*noun* gleam, glimmer, flash, sparkle, twinkle, reflection.

glisten *verb* shine, gleam, glitter, sparkle, twinkle, shimmer.

glitter *verb* sparkle, twinkle, shimmer, spangle, gleam, glint, glisten, flash, blink, wink, scintillate, coruscate.
➤*noun* **1** sparkle, twinkle, shimmer, scintillation, coruscation, brilliance, brightness, sheen, lustre. **2** glamour, pageantry, tinsel, flashiness, gaudiness, glitz (*inf*), razzmatazz (*inf*), ostentation, showiness.

gloat *verb* revel, exult, triumph, crow, rejoice, glory, delight, relish, boast, vaunt, rub it in (*inf*).

global *adj* **1** worldwide, international, universal. **2** general, wide-ranging, comprehensive, all-inclusive, exhaustive, thorough, total, across-the-board.

globe *noun* **1** world, earth. **2** sphere, orb, ball.

globule *noun* bead, ball, drop, droplet, bubble, pearl, pellet.

gloom *noun* **1** dark, darkness, blackness, shadow, obscurity, dimness, murk, cloudiness, dusk, twilight. **2** melancholy, depression, dejection, despondency, despair, glumness, misery, woe, downheartedness, low spirits, pessimism, blues (*inf*).

gloomy *adj* **1** dull, dark, overcast, murky, dismal, dreary, sombre, dingy. **2** depressed, despondent, blue (*inf*), melancholy, glum, downcast, miserable, pessimistic, cheerless, depressing, hopeless, dispiriting.

glorify *verb* **1** praise, exalt, honour, reverence, adore, worship, extol, bless, magnify, laud. **2** ennoble, dignify, elevate, praise, acclaim, celebrate, revere, venerate. **3** romanticize, idealize, aggrandize, lionize, immortalize.

glorious *adj* **1** illustrious, renowned, celebrated, great, eminent, distinguished, glittering, noble, exalted, triumphant, victorious. **2** beautiful, splendid, magnificent, superb, perfect, fine, brilliant, resplendent, excellent, wonderful, marvellous.

glory *noun* **1** honour, renown, greatness, prestige, credit, distinction, eminence, celebrity, recognition, praise, acclaim, kudos (*inf*). **2** magnificence, splendour, resplendence, grandeur, majesty, dignity, pomp, stateliness, radiance, brilliance, beauty. **3** praise, worship, adoration, exaltation, veneration, homage, tribute, thanksgiving, blessing.
➤*verb* **1** triumph, exult, rejoice. **2** revel, delight, relish, bask, boast, crow, gloat, preen oneself.

gloss[1] *noun* **1** lustre, sheen, polish, shine, brightness, brilliance, sparkle, glaze, varnish. **2** appearance, facade, front,

veneer, show, window-dressing, semblance, surface.
➤ *verb* polish, burnish, shine, varnish,
glaze, lacquer.
gloss over disguise, mask, hide, conceal,
cover up, whitewash (*inf*), veil, explain
away, dismiss.

gloss² *noun* **1** note, annotation, explanation, elucidation, comment, definition,
translation. **2** interpretation, construction,
slant, spin.
➤ *verb* annotate, comment on, define,
translate, explain, elucidate, interpret,
construe.

glossy *adj* shiny, lustrous, brilliant, sparkling, glassy, polished, burnished, glazed,
smooth, sleek, silky.

glow *noun* **1** light, luminosity, incandes-
cence, phosphorescence, shine, lustre,
brightness, radiance, effulgence.
2 richness, vividness, brightness, brilliance, colourfulness. **3** passion, ardour,
fervour, eagerness, enthusiasm, intensity,
vehemence, excitement, thrill, contentment, happiness, satisfaction. **4** warmth,
burning, blush, flush, redness, rosiness.
➤ *verb* **1** shine, radiate, burn, smoulder,
phosphoresce. **2** redden, colour, blush,
flush, bloom.

glower *verb* glare, scowl, frown, lour, look
daggers (*inf*).
➤ *noun* glare, scowl, frown, lour, black look
(*inf*), dirty look (*inf*).

glue *noun* adhesive, gum, paste, cement,
fixative.
➤ *verb* stick, paste, affix, cement, gum,
seal, adhere, bond.

glum *adj* morose, melancholy, gloomy,
despondent, dejected, doleful, downcast,
pessimistic, sad, miserable, sullen, moody.

glut *noun* surfeit, excess, surplus, superfluity, overabundance, plethora, oversupply.
➤ *verb* **1** cram, gorge, stuff, sate, satiate,
surfeit. **2** flood, inundate, deluge, saturate,
overload, oversupply.

glutinous *adj* sticky, gummy, gluey, adhesive, mucilaginous, mucous, viscous,
viscid.

glutton *noun* gourmand, gormandizer,
gannet (*inf*), guzzler (*inf*), pig (*inf*).

gluttony *noun* greed, greediness, vora-
ciousness, insatiability, rapacity,
gourmandism.

gnarled *adj* **1** knotty, lumpy, nodular,
twisted, crooked. **2** wrinkled, rough, leathery, twisted, bent.

gnash *verb* grind, grate, scrape.

gnaw *verb* **1** bite, nibble, chew, munch,
masticate. **2** erode, corrode, wear, eat, consume, devour. **3** worry, trouble, bother,
nag, niggle, plague, torment.

go *verb* **1** move, proceed, advance, pass,
progress, travel, head. **2** set off, start,
leave, depart, quit (*inf*), make tracks (*inf*),
go away, beat it (*inf*), withdraw, retreat.
3 vanish, disappear, cease, stop. **4** work,
operate, perform, function, run. **5** develop,
progress, proceed, happen. **6** turn out,
work out, end up, pan out (*inf*). **7** become,
grow, get, turn. **8** fit, slot in, lie, stand,
belong. **9** extend, stretch, reach, run,
spread, span, lead. **10** emit, sound, send
out, release. **11** elapse, pass, fly, go by, roll
on. **12** match, blend, coordinate, belong,
complement, suit, harmonize, fit.
13 comply, conform, match, correspond,
chime, accord. **14** collapse, break down,
give way, cave in, crumble, disintegrate,
fall to pieces.
➤ *noun* **1** try, attempt, bid, effort, shot
(*inf*), crack (*inf*), turn, chance. **2** drive, get-
up-and-go (*inf*), energy, vigour, dynamism,
spirit, enterprise, force, pep (*inf*), oomph
(*inf*), life, vitality.
go about set about, begin, approach,
address, tackle, undertake, do, perform.
go ahead 1 begin, start, commence.
2 proceed, advance, progress, continue,
carry on.
go along with comply with, cooperate
with, accept, agree with, support, abide by,
assent to.
go back on renege on, default on, deny,
repudiate, retract, break.
go by pass, elapse, proceed, move on.
go down 1 descend, sink, set. **2** decrease,
reduce, drop, fall, decline, deteriorate,
degenerate. **3** lose, fail, go under, come a
cropper (*inf*). **4** sink, founder, crash.
go for 1 attack, assault, rush at, set about,
lay into. **2** like, love, admire, enjoy.
3 prefer, favour, choose, select.
go in for 1 engage in, take up, adopt,
practise, pursue, follow. **2** enter, take part
in, participate in, compete in.

go into probe, enquire into, look into, examine, investigate, research, study, analyse, scrutinize, check out.

go off 1 explode, blow up, detonate, blast, fire, go bang (*inf*). **2** rot, decompose, go bad, turn, sour, deteriorate.

go on 1 continue, persist, last, carry on, proceed. **2** take place, happen, occur. **3** ramble, chatter, witter (*inf*), rabbit (*inf*).

go out 1 be extinguished, die down, expire, fade. **2** date (*inf*), go steady (*inf*), court, see one another.

go over 1 examine, look over, peruse, scan, inspect, check. **2** repeat, reiterate, discuss, review, think about. **3** study, read, revise, rehearse.

go round circulate, spread.

go through 1 examine, look through, search, check, review, discuss. **2** undergo, endure, suffer, experience, brave, bear, weather. **3** spend, use, consume, get through, exhaust, use up.

go under collapse, fail, fold (*inf*), go bust (*inf*), go to the wall (*inf*), founder, succumb.

go with 1 accompany, escort, take, usher. **2** go out with, see, date (*inf*), court.

go without do without, abstain from, forgo, lack, want.

goad *verb* **1** spur, prick, prod, drive. **2** incite, prompt, stimulate, motivate, impel, urge, spur, drive, hound, harass, nag, pressurize.
➤*noun* **1** spur, prod. **2** incentive, spur, stimulus, motivation, impetus, incitement, provocation, pressure.

go-ahead *noun* permission, consent, authorization, clearance, leave, approval, OK (*inf*), thumbs-up (*inf*), green light (*inf*).
➤*adj* ambitious, aspiring, up-and-coming, enterprising, pioneering, progressive, forward-looking, dynamic, energetic, aggressive.

goal *noun* **1** aim, objective, target, object, purpose, end, intent, ambition, aspiration. **2** destination, end, end.

gobble *verb* bolt, gulp, guzzle, wolf (*inf*), scoff (*inf*), swallow, devour, consume, put away (*inf*), gorge, cram, stuff.

gobbledygook *noun* jargon, officialese, nonsense, drivel, twaddle, gibberish (*inf*), mumbo-jumbo, prattle, babble, verbiage.

go-between *noun* intermediary, middleman, third party, negotiator, mediator, arbitrator, liaison, contact, messenger, agent, broker, factor.

goblin *noun* imp, gnome, dwarf, elf, gremlin, sprite, bogey, demon.

god *noun* deity, divinity, spirit, genius, idol, icon.

God *noun* Lord, Almighty, Supreme Being, Holy One, Creator, Jehovah, Allah.

godforsaken *adj* **1** desolate, remote, isolated, bleak, lonely, deserted. **2** lonely, abandoned, forlorn, neglected, miserable, wretched.

godless *adj* **1** pagan, heathen, atheistic, agnostic, faithless, unbelieving, ungodly, impious. **2** unprincipled, depraved, profane, sacrilegious, sinful, bad, wicked, evil.

godly *adj* **1** divine, holy, heavenly, exalted, superhuman, transcendent. **2** pious, devout, religious, holy, saintly, God-fearing, believing, righteous, virtuous.

godsend *noun* blessing, boon, bonanza, miracle, windfall, stroke of luck.

goggle *verb* stare, gaze, gape, gawp (*inf*), gawk (*inf*), peer, rubberneck (*inf*), wonder.

goings-on *pl noun* **1** happenings, events, activities, affairs, business. **2** misbehaviour, mischief, misconduct, hanky-panky (*inf*), funny business (*inf*).

gold *noun* **1** bullion, nuggets, ingots. **2** money, wealth, treasure, riches, fortune.

golden *adj* **1** gold, gilt. **2** yellow, flaxen, blond, fair, tow-coloured. **3** prosperous, successful, flourishing, bright, brilliant, glorious, great, classic, halcyon, palmy. **4** favourable, propitious, excellent, auspicious, fortunate, timely, opportune, promising, rosy, advantageous.

good *adj* **1** virtuous, righteous, moral, upright, honest, honourable, admirable, worthy, exemplary, ethical. **2** pleasing, satisfying, gratifying, desirable, cool (*inf*), great (*inf*), super (*inf*), favourable, propitious, auspicious, convenient. **3** fine, excellent, first-rate, first-class, marvellous, fantastic, splendid, wonderful. **4** nice, pleasant, enjoyable, agreeable, amusing. **5** beneficial, advantageous, worthwhile, useful, wholesome, healthy, healthful, salutary, salubrious, nutritional. **6** proficient, competent, capable, able, skilful, skilled, adept, adroit, expert, accomplished, gifted, talented. **7** kind, considerate, friendly, benevolent, obliging,

gracious, generous, well-disposed, charitable, philanthropic. **8** well-behaved, well-mannered, polite, obedient, orderly, decorous, tractable, compliant. **9** suitable, appropriate, apt, fit. **10** correct, right, proper, seemly. **11** authentic, bona fide, legitimate, real, valid, genuine. **12** reliable, dependable, sound, secure, well-founded, true. **13** well, fine, fit, healthy, robust, sound, strong, hale and hearty. **14** adequate, sufficient, ample, satisfactory, reasonable, acceptable, passable. **15** thorough, complete, exhaustive, whole, entire, full.
➤*noun* **1** advantage, benefit, welfare, interest, behalf, sake. **2** use, service, purpose, worth, merit, avail. **3** virtue, righteousness, goodness, excellence, ethics, morality, integrity, honour.
for good always, forever, evermore, till the end of time, permanently, in perpetuity, finally, once and for all.
make good 1 make up for, compensate, put right, make amends for, pay for, reimburse. **2** succeed, go far, get on in the world, make it. **3** fulfil, realize, carry out, live up to, discharge, effect.

goodbye *interj* farewell, adieu, so long (*inf*), bye (*inf*), bye-bye (*inf*), cheerio (*inf*), ta-ta (*inf*), see you (*inf*), ciao (*inf*).
➤*noun* farewell, adieu, leave-taking, parting, swan song, valediction.

good-for-nothing *adj* useless, worthless, lazy, idle, irresponsible, no-good, feckless.
➤*noun* ne'er-do-well, idler, layabout, loafer, waster, reprobate, bum (*inf*).

good-humoured *adj* affable, amiable, friendly, cheerful, jovial, genial, easygoing, pleasant, good-tempered.

good-looking *adj* attractive, fair, pretty, lovely, beautiful, handsome, personable, presentable.

goodly *adj* sizeable, considerable, substantial, large, ample, good, significant, tidy (*inf*).

good-natured *adj* kind, kindly, benevolent, generous, helpful, gentle, good-tempered, approachable, friendly, well-disposed, tolerant, patient.

goodness *noun* **1** virtue, nobility, benevolence, generosity, humanity, excellence, superiority, merit, worth, quality. **2** nourishment, nutrition, wholesomeness, benefit.

goodwill *noun* **1** benevolence, kindness, compassion, goodness, generosity, graciousness, friendship. **2** acquiescence, willingness, zeal. **3** favour, custom, patronage.

gore *verb* pierce, stab, spear, stick, impale, transfix, wound.
➤*noun* blood, bloodshed, carnage, slaughter, butchery.

gorge *noun* ravine, canyon, fissure, defile, pass, rift, chasm, gully, abyss.
➤*verb* **1** stuff, cram, fill. **2** devour, bolt, wolf (*inf*), guzzle, gobble, gulp, overeat, gormandize, pig out (*inf*), sate, surfeit.

gorgeous *adj* **1** beautiful, lovely, glamorous, stunning (*inf*), ravishing (*inf*), magnificent, splendid, brilliant, fine, rich, luxurious, opulent. **2** good, marvellous, wonderful, terrific (*inf*), lovely, glorious, excellent, great, delightful.

gory *adj* **1** bloodthirsty, grisly, bloody, sanguinary, brutal, horrific, savage, violent, murderous. **2** bloodstained, blood-soaked, bloody, bloodied.

gospel *noun* **1** message of Christ, teachings of Christ, good news, New Testament. **2** truth, fact, certainty. **3** doctrine, creed, credo, belief, ethic, principle, tenet.

gossamer *adj* delicate, fine, light, flimsy, insubstantial, diaphanous, silky, gauzy, sheer.

gossip *noun* **1** prattle, tittle-tattle, small talk, chitchat (*inf*), scandal, mudslinging (*inf*), rumour, hearsay, report, whisper. **2** chat, talk, natter, chinwag (*inf*). **3** scandalmonger, chatterbox, prattler, tattler, blabbermouth (*inf*), busybody, nosy parker (*inf*).
➤*verb* **1** prattle, tattle, blab, whisper, dish the dirt (*inf*). **2** chat, chatter, talk, natter, gab (*inf*), gas (*inf*), yak (*inf*), chew the fat (*inf*).

gouge *verb* scratch, claw, scoop, hollow, dig, chisel, cut, incise, score, gash, groove.

gourmet *noun* gastronome, connoisseur, foodie (*inf*), bon vivant, epicure.

govern *verb* **1** rule, reign, hold office, direct, manage, administer, lead, head, preside over, command. **2** control, regulate, guide, steer, influence, sway. **3** restrain, contain, check, curb, control, hold back, dominate, master, subdue, discipline, tame.

government *noun* **1** rule, sovereignty, dominion, direction, management, administration, control, command, charge, leadership, authority, power. **2** state, parliament, executive, leadership, administration, cabinet, ministry, congress, authorities, Establishment, powers that be (*inf*).

governor *noun* **1** ruler, president, head, chief, leader, commander. **2** director, manager, chief executive, warden. **3** viceroy, commissioner. **4** employer, supervisor, boss (*inf*), old man (*inf*). **5** controller, regulator.

gown *noun* **1** robe, habit. **2** dress, frock, evening gown, ball gown.

grab *verb* **1** grasp, grip, clutch, clasp, seize, snatch, pluck, take, lay hold of, catch. **2** seize, snatch, steal, nab (*inf*), swipe (*inf*), snap up, bag (*inf*), commandeer, usurp, appropriate.
➤*noun* snatch, clutch, grip, grasp, capture.
up for grabs available, on offer, for sale, obtainable, for the asking (*inf*), to be had.

grace *noun* **1** gracefulness, elegance, fluidity, agility, suppleness, smoothness, ease, fluency, poise. **2** charm, refinement, finesse. **3** postponement, delay, deferral, reprieve. **4** favour, approval, prestige, goodwill. **5** decency, courtesy, manners, consideration, tact, kindness, goodness. **6** benevolence, beneficence, compassion, clemency, mercy, pardon. **7** blessing, benediction, thanksgiving, prayer.
➤*verb* **1** adorn, embellish, decorate, ornament, deck, trim, garnish, enhance, enrich. **2** honour, favour, distinguish, dignify.

graceful *adj* elegant, easy, smooth, flowing, supple, agile, lithe, deft, refined, charming, attractive.

graceless *adj* **1** clumsy, awkward, ungainly, unattractive, inelegant, gauche, gawky. **2** uncouth, coarse, boorish, ill-mannered, improper, indecorous, rude.

gracious *adj* **1** kindly, benevolent, beneficent, obliging, cordial, courteous, compassionate, considerate, sweet, charitable, generous, magnanimous. **2** elegant, tasteful, comfortable, refined, luxurious, sumptuous.

grade *noun* **1** degree, level, stage, position, rank, status, station, echelon, step, rung,

quality, standard. **2** rating, mark, score. **3** category, class, group, type. **4** gradient, hill, slope.
➤*verb* **1** sort, group, class, classify, categorize, label, brand. **2** arrange, order, rank, size, graduate. **3** evaluate, assess, mark, rate.
make the grade measure up, pass muster, come up to scratch (*inf*), pass, qualify, succeed.

gradient *noun* **1** slope, incline, rise, acclivity, declivity. **2** hill, ramp, slope.

gradual *adj* **1** slow, leisurely, unhurried, steady, step-by-step, progressive, piecemeal. **2** gentle, moderate, easy.

graduate *verb* **1** qualify, pass. **2** mark off, divide, calibrate, measure out, proportion. **3** progress, move up, advance.
➤*noun* bachelor, master, professional, alumnus.

graft[1] *verb* **1** join, unite, splice, engraft. **2** implant, insert, transplant. **3** attach, affix, add.
➤*noun* **1** shoot, bud, sprout, slip, scion. **2** implant, implantation, transplant.

graft[2] *noun* effort, hard work, toil, industry, labour, sweat of one's brow (*inf*), slog (*inf*).

grain *noun* **1** cereals, crops, corn. **2** seed, kernel, grist. **3** particle, granule, crumb, piece. **4** bit, iota, atom, jot, scrap, trace, modicum, whit. **5** texture, marking, weave, fibre.

grand *adj* **1** impressive, great, imposing, striking, monumental, palatial, sublime. **2** opulent, splendid, magnificent, fine, sumptuous, lavish, luxurious. **3** majestic, august, lofty, exalted, lordly, noble, dignified, stately, haughty. **4** pompous, pretentious, ostentatious, showy, grandiose. **5** excellent, wonderful, marvellous, splendid, very good, first-class, great (*inf*), super (*inf*), cool (*inf*). **6** chief, principal, head, supreme, arch, highest, senior.

grandeur *noun* **1** splendour, magnificence, sumptuousness, opulence, glory, pomp, stateliness, majesty, greatness, impressiveness. **2** greatness, eminence, nobility, dignity, illustriousness, prominence, fame, renown.

grandfather *noun* **1** grandad (*inf*), grandpa (*inf*). **2** forefather, forebear, ancestor, progenitor.

grandiloquence *noun* bombast, rhetoric, periphrasis, euphuism, magniloquence.

grandiose *adj* **1** pretentious, extravagant, ostentatious, showy, flamboyant, pompous, affected, bombastic, high-flown. **2** grand, impressive, imposing, monumental, striking, ambitious.

grandmother *noun* grandma (*inf*), granny (*inf*), gran (*inf*), nan (*inf*), nana (*inf*).

grant *verb* **1** give, award, present, allot, allocate, provide. **2** donate, bestow, transfer, transmit. **3** admit, concede, acknowledge, allow, accept, agree.
➤*noun* award, bursary, scholarship, endowment, allowance, donation, handout, subsidy.

granule *noun* grain, particle, crumb, speck, piece, bead.

graph *noun* diagram, chart, table, line, curve.

graphic *adj* **1** vivid, expressive, striking, descriptive, picturesque, detailed, realistic, clear, explicit. **2** visual, pictorial, representational.

grapple *verb* **1** wrestle, fight, clash, engage, close. **2** contend, struggle, get to grips, confront, address, tackle, attack. **3** grasp, seize, grab, lay hold of, fasten on.

grasp *verb* **1** grip, clasp, hold, clutch, grab, seize, catch, snatch. **2** understand, comprehend, take in, realize, see, follow, get (*inf*).
➤*noun* **1** grip, clasp, hold, clutches, embrace, possession. **2** power, command, control, rule, dominion. **3** reach, scope, range, limits, extent, capacity. **4** understanding, comprehension, awareness, perception, ken, knowledge, mastery.

grasping *adj* greedy, avaricious, acquisitive, rapacious, mercenary, miserly, mean.

grate *verb* **1** shred, grind, mince, pulverize. **2** rasp, rub, scrape, scratch. **3** annoy, irritate, rankle, rile, jar, set one's teeth on edge, get on one's nerves (*inf*).

grateful *adj* thankful, appreciative, obliged, beholden, indebted.

gratify *verb* **1** please, delight, gladden, cheer, satisfy. **2** satisfy, fulfil, indulge, humour, pander to, pacify, appease, give in to.

grating *adj* harsh, strident, raucous, rasping, hoarse, croaky, scraping, grinding, jarring, irritating.

gratis *adv and adj* free, free of charge, for nothing, without payment, complimentary, on the house (*inf*).

gratitude *noun* gratefulness, thankfulness, appreciation, obligation, indebtedness, thanks, acknowledgment, recognition.

gratuitous *adj* **1** unwarranted, unjustified, uncalled-for, unnecessary, undeserved, unprovoked, unsolicited, superfluous, irrelevant. **2** free, gratis, voluntary, spontaneous, complimentary.

gratuity *noun* **1** tip, gift, reward, perk (*inf*), benefaction, baksheesh. **2** pension, lump sum, bonus, golden handshake.

grave[1] *adj* **1** serious, significant, important, weighty, vital, crucial. **2** critical, dangerous, hazardous, threatening, life-and-death, urgent, pressing, acute, severe. **3** solemn, sober, dignified, staid, sedate, serious, unsmiling.

grave[2] *noun* **1** burial place, pit, barrow, tumulus. **2** tomb, sepulchre, crypt, vault, mausoleum.

graveyard *noun* cemetery, churchyard, burial ground, boneyard (*inf*), necropolis, God's acre.

gravitate *verb* descend, sink, drop, fall, precipitate, settle.
gravitate towards tend towards, drift towards, move towards, be drawn to.

gravity *noun* **1** solemnity, dignity, gravitas, sobriety, sedateness, staidness, reserve, restraint. **2** importance, significance, weight, moment, seriousness, severity, enormity, urgency, acuteness, danger, exigency.

graze[1] *verb* feed, browse, crop, pasture, ruminate.

graze[2] *verb* **1** scrape, scratch, skin, chafe, bark, abrade. **2** brush, shave, touch, skim, glance off, kiss.
➤*noun* scratch, scrape, abrasion.

greasy *adj* **1** slimy, slippery, smeary. **2** oily, waxy, oleaginous, sebaceous. **3** fatty, oily, buttery. **4** unctuous, oily, slimy, smooth, slick, smarmy (*inf*), fawning, ingratiating, gushing, sycophantic.

great *adj* **1** big, large, huge, vast, immense, massive, enormous, colossal, tremendous, gigantic, mega (*inf*), whopping (*inf*). **2** considerable, substantial, pronounced, high, strong, exceptional, extreme, excessive. **3** important, significant, weighty, momentous, critical, crucial, essential, vital, paramount, major, serious. **4** eminent, illustrious, distinguished, renowned, noted, famed, famous, celebrated, prominent. **5** grand, august, noble, aristocratic, exalted, sublime, glorious, heroic, lofty. **6** main, chief, principal, primary, leading. **7** expert, skilled, accomplished, masterly, brilliant, gifted, able, adroit, proficient, ace (*inf*). **8** keen, enthusiastic, dedicated, devoted, zealous. **9** excellent, wonderful, marvellous, fine, splendid, enjoyable, super (*inf*), smashing (*inf*), cool (*inf*), wicked (*inf*).

greed *noun* **1** greediness, gluttony, voracity, hunger, ravenousness, insatiability, omnivorousness. **2** desire, craving, covetousness, avarice, rapacity, acquisitiveness, cupidity, miserliness.

greedy *adj* **1** gluttonous, voracious, insatiable, hungry, starving, ravenous, omnivorous. **2** desirous, acquisitive, covetous, avaricious, rapacious, grasping.

green *adj* **1** grassy, leafy, verdant, fresh, lush. **2** unripe, immature. **3** undried, unseasoned, unfinished. **4** inexperienced, callow, raw, naive, ingenuous, gullible, wet behind the ears (*inf*). **5** envious, jealous, covetous, grudging, resentful. **6** wan, pale, pallid, ashen, sick, ill, sickly, unhealthy. **7** environmentally friendly, eco-friendly, non-polluting. **8** ecological, environmental, conservationist.
➤*noun* **1** grassland, common, field, village green. **2** lawn, grass, turf, sward.

greenhouse *noun* glasshouse, hothouse, conservatory.

greet *verb* hail, salute, address, acknowledge, accost, welcome, receive, meet.

greeting *noun* salutation, acknowledgment, address, welcome, salute, hello, nod, handshake.

greetings *pl noun* respects, compliments, regards, good wishes, salutations.

gregarious *adj* sociable, outgoing, friendly, companionable, extrovert, clubbable.

grey *adj* **1** ashen, leaden. **2** dull, drab, gloomy, sombre, cloudy, murky, sunless, overcast. **3** neutral, anonymous, uninteresting, nondescript, characterless, colourless. **4** doubtful, arguable, debatable, uncertain, unclear, ambiguous. **5** hoary, grizzled, white.

grief *noun* sorrow, sadness, misery, unhappiness, woe, heartache, lamentation, mourning, despair, distress, anguish, affliction.

grievance *noun* **1** complaint, objection, protest, grudge, moan, gripe (*inf*), grouse (*inf*), beef (*inf*). **2** injury, damage, wrong, injustice, offence, affront, insult.

grieve *verb* **1** sorrow, lament, mourn, cry, weep, bewail, bemoan, mope, brood, pine away, eat one's heart out. **2** sadden, dismay, distress, upset, offend, hurt, wound, pain.

grievous *adj* **1** serious, severe, grave, acute, intense, heavy, appalling, outrageous, monstrous, dire. **2** tragic, distressing, lamentable, sad, sorrowful, mournful, devastating, unbearable, overwhelming, injurious, painful, agonizing.

grim *adj* **1** stern, severe, harsh, dour, formidable, forbidding, hard, cruel, fierce, menacing. **2** dire, dreadful, terrible, horrendous, ghastly, grisly, gruesome, macabre, sinister. **3** resolute, firm, dogged, unrelenting, obstinate, persistent, tenacious, unflinching, unyielding, unwavering. **4** horrible, horrid, awful, unpleasant, nasty.

grimace *noun* frown, scowl, pout, face.
➤*verb* frown, scowl, pout, pull a face.

grime *noun* dirt, filth, muck, crud (*inf*), smut, soot, dust, mud.
➤*verb* begrime, dirty, soil, foul.

grin *verb* smile, beam, smirk, leer.

grind *verb* **1** pulverize, triturate, comminute, powder, crush, pound, mill, grate. **2** sharpen, whet, sand, file, smooth, polish. **3** rub, grate, rasp, scrape.
➤*noun* routine, toil, slog, labour, drudgery.
grind down oppress, tyrannize, persecute, crush, torture, harass.

grip *noun* **1** hold, clasp, grasp, clutch, purchase. **2** control, mastery, command, power, domination, clutches, hold, influence, possession. **3** grasp, understanding,

comprehension, perception, awareness. **4** bag, case, holdall.
➤*verb* **1** hold, clutch, clasp, grasp, cling to, grab, seize, catch. **2** fascinate, engross, absorb, enthral, thrill, spellbind, mesmerize, rivet.
come/get to grips with 1 tackle, handle, deal with, cope with. **2** confront, face, meet head on, take on, grapple with, close with.

gripe *verb* complain, moan, grumble, protest, bleat, whine (*inf*), beef (*inf*), bellyache (*inf*).
➤*noun* complaint, objection, protest, grievance, moan, grumble, beef (*inf*).

grisly *adj* grim, gruesome, gory, macabre, horrifying, shocking, terrible, sickening.

grit *noun* **1** gravel, sand, pebbles, shingle. **2** courage, nerve, mettle, spirit, determination, tenacity, resolve, fortitude, backbone (*inf*), bottle (*inf*), guts (*inf*), balls (*sl*).
➤*verb* clench, gnash, grate, grind.

gritty *adj* **1** grainy, gravelly, granular, sandy, pebbly, shingly, dusty, coarse, rough. **2** determined, resolute, brave, courageous, feisty, plucky, tough, dogged, tenacious, spirited.

grizzled *adj* grey, greying, hoary.

groan *noun* moan, sigh, cry, murmur, whine, whimper, wail, lament, complaint, grumble.
➤*verb* moan, sigh, cry, murmur, whine, whimper, wail, lament, complain, grumble.

groggy *adj* dazed, confused, befuddled, stupefied, dopey, unsteady, wobbly, shaky, woozy (*inf*), muzzy (*inf*), dizzy, faint.

groom *verb* **1** tidy, neaten, spruce up, smarten up, smooth, preen, clean, comb, arrange. **2** rub, brush, curry, clean, tend. **3** prepare, prime, train, coach, drill, school, teach, instruct.
➤*noun* **1** bridegroom, husband-to-be, newlywed. **2** stable boy, stable man, stable hand, ostler.

groove *noun* **1** furrow, channel, rut, gutter, trench, trough, track, flute, rebate, slot. **2** rut, routine, habit, grind (*inf*).

grope *verb* **1** fumble, feel, scrabble, search, hunt, fish. **2** fondle, pet, paw, touch up (*inf*).

gross *adj* **1** big, large, fat, obese, bloated, corpulent, overweight, bulky, heavy, massive, lumpish. **2** coarse, vulgar, crude, rude, indecent, offensive, loutish, yobbish (*inf*), insensitive, crass, boorish. **3** disgusting, revolting, repulsive, foul, vile, nasty, yucky (*inf*). **4** flagrant, glaring, blatant, arrant, outrageous, sheer, utter, rank, serious, grievous. **5** all-inclusive, total, complete, whole, aggregate.
➤*verb* earn, make, take, bring in, accumulate, aggregate.

grotesque *adj* **1** freakish, monstrous, unnatural, deformed, misshapen, distorted, hideous, ugly, repugnant. **2** bizarre, weird, odd, fantastic, fanciful, absurd, ludicrous, outlandish, incongruous, surreal.

ground *noun* **1** earth, terra firma, surface, floor, deck (*inf*). **2** soil, earth, dirt, clay. **3** land, terrain. **4** stadium, arena, field, pitch, park, site, plot. **5** basis, foundation, reason, motive, cause, occasion, justification, premise, rationale, argument.
➤*verb* **1** base, found, establish, set. **2** instruct, teach, train, coach, drill, tutor, prepare, introduce, initiate.

groundless *adj* baseless, unfounded, unsubstantiated, unsupported, idle, empty, false, unjustified, unreasonable, unwarranted.

groundwork *noun* preparation, research, homework, spadework, fundamentals, preliminaries, foundation, basis.

group *noun* **1** category, class, batch, set, party, body, gang, pack, gathering, cluster, club, society. **2** band, ensemble. **3** unit, squad, detachment.
➤*verb* **1** collect, assemble, gather, congregate, cluster, mass, bunch, clump. **2** sort, classify, categorize, arrange, rank, grade, band, bracket.

grouse *verb* complain, grumble, moan, beef (*inf*), bellyache (*inf*), gripe (*inf*).
➤*noun* complaint, grumble, moan, beef (*inf*), gripe (*inf*), grievance, objection, protest.

grove *noun* wood, copse, coppice, thicket, spinney, brake, arbour, plantation.

grovel *verb* **1** fawn, toady, crawl, creep, bow and scrape, suck up (*inf*), bootlick (*inf*), curry favour, flatter, abase oneself, ingratiate oneself. **2** crawl, creep, kowtow, bow down, kneel, stoop, slither, prostrate oneself.

grow *verb* **1** increase, expand, lengthen, broaden, wax, swell, spread, multiply, escalate, mushroom. **2** germinate, sprout, shoot, vegetate, develop, mature, thrive, get bigger. **3** become, turn, go, get. **4** cultivate, produce, raise, sow, plant, propagate, farm.

growl *verb* snarl, rumble, roar, snap, bark.

grown-up *adj* adult, mature, of age, fully-grown, fully-developed, fully-fledged.

growth *noun* **1** germination, cultivation, development, maturation, increase, rise, expansion, enlargement, spread, multiplication, proliferation. **2** development, evolution, improvement, advance, progress, headway. **3** vegetation, crop, produce. **4** tumour, lump, swelling, protuberance.

grub *verb* **1** dig, root, forage. **2** uproot, unearth. **3** search, rummage, delve, probe, hunt, scour, ferret out, uncover.
➤*noun* **1** maggot, larva, caterpillar, worm, pupa, chrysalis. **2** food, nosh (*inf*), eats (*inf*), refreshment, victuals.

grubby *adj* **1** dirty, soiled, grimy, mucky (*inf*), unwashed, unkempt, slovenly. **2** disreputable, seedy, squalid, sordid.

grudge *noun* grievance, resentment, envy, jealousy, pique, spite, ill will, bitterness, rancour, hard feelings, animosity, antipathy.
➤*verb* **1** begrudge, resent, envy, covet. **2** hold back, stint.

gruelling *adj* arduous, strenuous, hard, difficult, harsh, stiff, tough, exhausting, taxing, demanding, punishing, backbreaking.

gruesome *adj* grim, grisly, macabre, ghastly, hideous, repugnant, revolting, sickening, horrible, appalling, horrific.

gruff *adj* **1** surly, curt, brusque, abrupt, stern, sour, grumpy, cross, rude, uncivil. **2** throaty, guttural, harsh, raucous, husky, hoarse, croaking, rough, thick, low.

grumble *verb* **1** complain, object, protest, moan, bleat, carp, grouse (*inf*), gripe (*inf*), beef (*inf*), whinge (*inf*). **2** growl, rumble, roar, murmur.
➤*noun* **1** complaint, grievance, protest,

objection, moan, gripe (*inf*), beef (*inf*). **2** growl, rumble, roar, murmur.

grumpy *adj* cantankerous, irascible, crabby, crusty, testy, surly, crotchety (*inf*), bad-tempered, ratty (*inf*), cross, irritable, grouchy (*inf*).

guarantee *noun* **1** warranty, assurance. **2** covenant, bond. **3** assurance, promise, word, pledge. **4** security, collateral, surety, pledge, earnest.
➤*verb* **1** warrant, assure, insure, protect. **2** pledge, promise, swear, undertake. **3** assure, ensure. **4** underwrite, secure, vouch for, answer for, back, endorse, sponsor.

guarantor *noun* underwriter, sponsor, backer, angel (*inf*), surety, guarantee, referee.

guard *verb* **1** protect, defend, shield, secure, patrol, police, mind, escort. **2** watch over, supervise.
➤*noun* **1** protection, defence, security, supervision, surveillance. **2** shield, screen, barrier, buffer, cushion, safeguard. **3** sentry, sentinel, watchman, lookout, picket, warder, guardian, defender, bodyguard, minder (*inf*), escort, patrol. **4** watchfulness, vigilance, wariness, caution, heed, attention, alertness, awareness, readiness, preparedness.
guard against mind, beware.

guarded *adj* careful, cautious, circumspect, watchful, wary, discreet, reticent, non-committal, cagey (*inf*).

guardian *noun* protector, defender, keeper, custodian, caretaker, steward, trustee, curator, warder, guard.

guerrilla *noun* freedom fighter, resistance fighter, terrorist, irregular, partisan.

guess *verb* **1** estimate, guesstimate (*inf*), hypothesize, postulate, speculate, judge, gauge. **2** solve, work out, fathom, predict, conjecture, surmise, divine. **3** reckon, think, believe, suppose, fancy, dare say.
➤*noun* estimate, guesstimate (*inf*), shot in the dark (*inf*), conjecture, hypothesis, theory, belief, feeling, idea, hunch, prediction, reckoning.

guesswork *noun* speculation, estimation, conjecture, surmise, prediction, supposition.

guest *noun* **1** visitor, caller, company. **2** lodger, boarder, resident, patron.

guidance *noun* **1** leadership, instruction, direction, advice, counselling, assistance, help, recommendation, suggestion. **2** direction, control, handling, management.

guide *verb* **1** lead, direct, navigate, shepherd, conduct, usher, escort, show, accompany. **2** control, regulate, handle, manage, point, direct, steer, manoeuvre, pilot, manipulate. **3** advise, counsel, influence, teach, inform, instruct.
➤*noun* **1** leader, usher, escort, adviser, counsellor, mentor, teacher, instructor, guru. **2** courier, cicerone. **3** mark, marker, pointer, sign, beacon, landmark, signpost, lodestar. **4** guidebook, travelogue, handbook, manual, vade mecum. **5** principle, credo, model, pattern, example, ideal, inspiration, benchmark, yardstick, standard.

guideline *noun* recommendation, suggestion, instruction, direction, advice, principle, standard, criterion, measure, benchmark, yardstick, parameter.

guild *noun* **1** fellowship, fraternity, sorority, society, club, association, organization. **2** union, league, lodge, order, company, corporation.

guile *noun* deceit, deception, duplicity, artfulness, craftiness, cunning, artifice, wiles, trickery.

guilt *noun* **1** guiltiness, culpability, criminality, delinquency, sin, iniquity, misconduct, wrongdoing, blame, responsibility. **2** remorse, shame, contrition, regret, self-reproach, self-accusation, self-condemnation, compunction, guilty conscience.

guilty *adj* **1** culpable, at fault, blameworthy, reprehensible, responsible, offending, delinquent, wicked, sinful. **2** convicted, condemned, criminal, culpable. **3** conscience-stricken, guilt-ridden, ashamed, remorseful, contrite, regretful, rueful, sorry, bad. **4** sheepish, shamefaced, hangdog.

guise *noun* **1** front, facade, semblance, likeness, pretence, show, disguise, mask, cover. **2** appearance, exterior, form, shape, air, aspect.

gulf *noun* **1** bight, bay, cove, inlet, sound. **2** chasm, abyss, fissure, gorge, gully, crevice, canyon, ravine. **3** gap, chasm, abyss, breach, rift, split, difference, separation.

gullet *noun* throat, craw, crop, oesophagus.

gullible *adj* credulous, suggestible, impressionable, unsuspecting, trusting, naive, innocent, green, wet behind the ears (*inf*), born yesterday, simple, foolish.

gully *noun* **1** channel, watercourse, ravine, gorge, canyon, valley. **2** gutter, ditch, trench.

gulp *verb* swallow, swig, quaff, knock back (*inf*), guzzle, gobble, bolt, wolf (*inf*).
➤*noun* swallow, draught, mouthful, swig.

gum *noun* glue, adhesive, paste, cement, fixative.
➤*verb* glue, stick, paste, affix, cement.
gum up block, clog, obstruct, hinder, impede, stop, halt.

gumption *noun* **1** initiative, enterprise, spirit, get-up-and-go (*inf*). **2** common sense, resourcefulness, savvy (*inf*), nous (*inf*), acumen, shrewdness, wit.

gun *noun* firearm, pistol, revolver, rifle, shotgun, shooting iron (*inf*), machine gun, flintlock, musket, blunderbuss.

gunman *noun* sniper, gunfighter, hit man (*inf*), hired gun (*inf*), assassin, killer, gunslinger, gangster, hood (*inf*).

gurgle *verb* **1** bubble, babble, burble, ripple, lap, tinkle, splash, purl. **2** chuckle, burble, crow, babble, murmur.

guru *noun* **1** maharishi, swami, mahatma, pandit. **2** master, teacher, tutor, mentor, guide. **3** leader, expert, authority, pundit, sage, luminary.

gush *verb* **1** flow, rush, pour, stream, spurt, spout, cascade, jet, surge, flood. **2** enthuse, wax lyrical, chatter, babble, effervesce, bubble over, fuss.
➤*noun* flow, rush, spurt, spout, jet, outburst, outpouring, stream, surge, torrent, cascade, flood.

gushy *adj* gushing, effusive, demonstrative, emotional, sentimental, cloying, sickly, mawkish, excessive, overenthusiastic.

gust *noun* **1** blast, puff, flurry, breeze, wind, squall. **2** outburst, burst, outbreak, eruption, explosion, fit, rush, surge.
➤*verb* blow, puff, blast, bluster.

gusto *noun* relish, zest, enjoyment, pleasure, delight, appetite, enthusiasm, energy, verve.

gut *noun* **1** stomach, belly, abdomen, paunch. **2** intestine, bowel, innards (*inf*), entrails, viscera.
➤ *verb* **1** disembowel, dress, clean, draw, eviscerate. **2** strip, empty, clear, loot, sack, lay waste, destroy, ravage.

gutless *adj* cowardly, chicken (*inf*), yellow (*inf*), lily-livered, spineless, feeble, weak, timid, submissive, fainthearted, craven, abject.

guts *pl noun* courage, bravery, daring, pluck, nerve, audacity, bottle (*inf*), spunk (*inf*), fortitude, mettle, spirit, determination.

gutter *noun* **1** conduit, duct, drain, culvert, sluice, sewer. **2** channel, furrow, trough, trench, ditch.

guttersnipe *noun* urchin, street arab, waif, ragamuffin, mudlark.

guttural *adj* hoarse, husky, gruff, croaking, gravelly, harsh, throaty, thick, deep, low.

guy *noun* man, boy, lad, fellow, chap (*inf*), bloke (*inf*), person, customer, individual, character.

guzzle *verb* gobble, bolt, scoff (*inf*), wolf (*inf*), devour, polish off (*inf*), gulp, quaff, swig, knock back (*inf*).

gypsy *noun* Romany, traveller, wanderer, rover, nomad, transient, vagrant, tinker, didicoi, tzigane.

gyrate *verb* circle, revolve, rotate, turn, spiral, pirouette, spin, twirl, whirl, wheel.

habit *noun* **1** practice, custom, usage, wont, routine, quirk, mannerism, pattern, tendency, propensity. **2** addiction, dependence, weakness, compulsion. **3** clothing, clothes, costume, dress, garb, uniform, robes.

habitable *adj* inhabitable, fit to live in, livable-in.

habitat *noun* **1** environment, surroundings, territory, home, haunt. **2** home, milieu, home ground, stamping ground.

habitation *noun* **1** occupation, occupancy, inhabitation, residence, residency, tenancy. **2** home, house, dwelling, dwelling place, abode, domicile, residence, quarters.

habitual *adj* **1** customary, usual, wonted, accustomed, established, standard, routine, ordinary, familiar. **2** chronic, inveterate, hardened, confirmed, persistent. **3** recurrent, frequent, repeated, regular, fixed, set, constant, continual.

habituate *verb* accustom, familiarize, acclimatize, adapt, harden, inure, school, discipline.

habitué *noun* regular, patron, frequenter.

hack[1] *verb* cut, chop, hew, slash, lacerate, mutilate, mangle.

hack[2] *noun* **1** scribbler, journalist, newsman, newswoman, drudge, plodder, hireling, mercenary. **2** horse, nag, workhorse, jade.

hackneyed *adj* banal, commonplace, trite, clichéd, stale, worn-out, overworked, over-used, unoriginal, stock, stereotyped, corny (*inf*).

hag *noun* crone, battle-axe, old bat (*inf*), harridan, vixen, shrew, nag, scold, witch.

haggard *adj* gaunt, drawn, hollow-cheeked, weary, pale, wan, ghastly, pinched, wasted, drained.

haggle *verb* **1** bargain, barter, negotiate, beat down. **2** wrangle, squabble, quarrel, quibble.

hail[1] *verb* **1** greet, salute, accost, call out to, halloo, shout to, wave to. **2** signal, flag down, wave down. **3** acclaim, acknowledge, recognize, praise.
hail from come from, originate from, be a native of.

hail[2] *noun* shower, rain, storm, volley, barrage.
➤*verb* pelt, bombard, volley, shower, rain, pepper.

hair *noun* **1** locks, tresses, mop, shock, mane, coat, fur, wool, pelt.
let one's hair down relax, enjoy oneself, let off steam (*inf*) let it all hang out (*inf*).
not turn a hair not bat an eyelid, remain calm, keep one's cool (*inf*).

hair-raising *adj* frightening, terrifying, horrifying, shocking, bloodcurdling, spine-chilling, petrifying.

hairy *adj* **1** hirsute, shaggy, bushy, furry, bearded, whiskery. **2** dangerous, hazardous, risky, frightening, scary (*inf*).

halcyon *adj* peaceful, tranquil, serene, balmy, unruffled, mild, temperate, carefree, palmy, blissful, golden.

hale *adj* healthy, hearty, robust, strong, sound, well, fit, blooming, vigorous, in the pink.

half *noun* **1** fifty per cent. **2** equal part, equal share.
➤*adj* **1** halved, divided in two, equally divided. **2** partial, part, incomplete, slight.
➤*adv* partly, in part, partially, slightly, moderately. **2** almost, nearly.
not half 1 not a bit, not at all. **2** really, very, very much, certainly. **3** not nearly, nowhere near.

half-baked *adj* impractical, stupid, harebrained, ill-conceived, ill-judged, shortsighted, premature, silly, crackpot (*inf*).

halfhearted *adj* cool, lukewarm, unenthusiastic, apathetic, perfunctory, cursory, superficial, tame.

halfway *adj and adv* **1** equidistant, middle, mid, midway, in the middle, intermediate, mean. **2** almost, just about, part, partly, partially, in some measure, minimally.

half-wit *noun* fool, idiot, cretin, imbecile, dunce, blockhead, fathead, dimwit, simpleton, ignoramus, moron, wally (*inf*), berk (*inf*), prat (*inf*), plonker (*inf*), pillock (*inf*), chump (*inf*), clot (*inf*), dope (*inf*), twit (*inf*), twerp (*inf*).

hall *noun* **1** hallway, entrance-hall, vestibule, lobby, foyer. **2** corridor, passage. **3** concert hall, church hall, auditorium, amphitheatre, assembly room, chamber.

hallmark *noun* **1** assay mark, stamp of authenticity, authentication, seal. **2** mark, trademark, feature, stamp, sign, indication, indicator, characteristic, badge.

hallow *verb* **1** make holy, sanctify, consecrate, bless. **2** honour, revere, venerate.

hallucinate *verb* dream, imagine, see things, fantasize, freak out (*inf*), trip (*inf*).

hallucination *noun* delusion, illusion, dream, fantasy, mirage, vision, apparition, figment, trip (*inf*).

halo *noun* **1** ring of light, nimbus, radiance, glory, aureole, aureola. **2** corona, aureole, aureola.

halt[1] *verb* stop, pull up, draw up, pause, wait, cease, break off, finish, desist, discontinue, end, bring to an end, come to an end, curb, stem.
➤*noun* break, interruption, hiatus, stop, end, standstill, rest, pause, interval, intermission.

halt[2] *verb* limp, hobble, stumble.

halting *adj* hesitant, faltering, stumbling, stammering, stuttering, broken.

halve *verb* bisect, cut in half, cut in two.

hammer *verb* **1** beat, pound, batter, pummel, strike, hit, knock, drive, bang, clobber (*inf*), wallop (*inf*). **2** beat, defeat, trounce, annihilate, rout, slaughter (*inf*), clobber (*inf*). **3** pound away, persevere, keep at, beaver away, plug away.
➤*noun* sledgehammer, beetle, mallet, gavel.

hammer into force, drum, drive, din, instil, inculcate.
hammer out thrash out, work out, sort out, negotiate, agree, resolve, settle.

hamper *verb* **1** hinder, impede, slow down, hold up, obstruct, check, curb, prevent, frustrate, balk, foil, thwart. **2** hinder, impede, encumber, handicap, hamstring, inhibit, cramp, restrict.
➤*noun* basket, box, container.

hamstring *verb* **1** lame, cripple, disable, incapacitate, hock. **2** hinder, impede, hold up, stop, frustrate, prevent, foil, balk, stymie, block, cripple, paralyse.

hand *noun* **1** palm, fist, paw (*inf*), mitt (*inf*). **2** help, aid, assistance, support. **3** pointer, indicator, needle. **4** labourer, worker, workman, operative, employee, assistant, helper, crew member. **5** handwriting, writing, script, penmanship, fist (*inf*). **6** ovation, clap, round of applause. **7** clutches, grasp, grip, supervision, command, disposal, power, control. **8** possession, keeping, custody, care.
verb give, hand over, present, offer, deliver, pass.

at hand coming, approaching, imminent, nearby, close, handy, to hand, on hand, within reach.
by hand manually, with one's hands.
hand down bequeath, will, transfer, pass on, pass down, leave.
hand in glove closely, in partnership, in collaboration, in association, in league, in cahoots (*inf*).
hand in hand holding hands, with hands clasped. **2** together, side by side, in association, in cooperation, conjointly.
hand out distribute, dispense, give out, deal out, dole out, pass out, dish out (*inf*).
hand to mouth in poverty, on the breadline, precariously, from day to day.
in hand receiving attention, being attended to, being dealt with.
to hand near, close, handy, accessible, available, ready.
turn one's hand to attempt, try, have a go at (*inf*), have a stab at (*inf*).
win hands down win easily, win by a mile, walk it (*inf*).

handbill *noun* circular, leaflet, pamphlet, flyer, notice, advertisement.

handbook *noun* manual, instructions, directions, ABC, guide, companion, prospectus.

handcuff *verb* fetter, shackle, manacle, secure.

handcuffs *pl noun* cuffs (*inf*), bracelets (*inf*), darbies (*inf*), manacles.

handful *noun* **1** few, small number, sprinkling, scattering. **2** nuisance, headache, pest, pain (*inf*).

handicap *noun* disability, disadvantage, impairment, hindrance, drawback, impediment, encumbrance, millstone, constraint, restriction, limitation, penalty.
➤*verb* disable, impair, hamstring, hinder, hamper, impede, burden, encumber, disadvantage, restrict, hold back.

handicraft *noun* **1** craft, skill, craftsmanship, workmanship. **2** craftwork, handiwork.

handiwork *noun* **1** action, doing, achievement, work, creation, design, invention, product. **2** craftsmanship, craftwork, handicraft.

handle *noun* knob, grip, stock, hilt, shaft.
➤*verb* **1** feel, touch, finger, pick up, hold, grasp, grip, manipulate. **2** deal with, cope with, manage, tackle, treat. **3** control, conduct, direct, manage, supervise. **4** drive, steer, hold the road. **5** deal in, sell, trade in, market, carry, stock. **6** treat, deal with, discuss.

handout *noun* **1** charity, gift, alms, dole. **2** leaflet, pamphlet, circular, flyer, notice, press release, brochure.

handover *noun* delivery, transfer, presentation, surrender, yielding, release.

handpicked *adj* choice, chosen, select, élite.

handsome *adj* **1** good-looking, attractive, personable, gorgeous, dishy (*inf*), hunky (*inf*). **2** good-looking, attractive, elegant, majestic, stately, statuesque. **3** generous, magnanimous, gracious, noble. **4** large, considerable, sizeable.

handwriting *noun* writing, script, hand, penmanship, calligraphy, scrawl (*inf*), scribble (*inf*), fist (*inf*).

handy *adj* **1** nearby, near, close, on hand, to hand, within reach, available, accessible, convenient. **2** convenient, useful, practical, helpful, serviceable, neat.

3 dexterous, skilful, skilled, deft, nimble-fingered, practical, expert.

hang *verb* **1** dangle, swing, droop, trail, hang down, loll. **2** suspend, put up, dangle, drape. **3** stick, glue, paste. **4** hover, float, be suspended. **5** lynch, execute, put to death, string up (*inf*).
get the hang of master, understand, grasp, get the knack of, catch on to (*inf*).
hang about 1 hang around, wait, stay, linger, loiter, dawdle. **2** associate with, keep company with.
hang back hold back, hesitate, shrink, recoil, demur.
hang on 1 cling, hold, grip, grasp. **2** persevere, carry on, persist, hold out, endure. **3** wait, hold on, hang about.

hangdog *adj* abject, guilty, ashamed, shamefaced, embarrassed, cowed, abashed, sheepish, crestfallen, furtive.

hanger-on *noun* follower, henchman, minion, lackey, toady, sycophant, parasite, sponger (*inf*), groupie (*inf*).

hangover *noun* morning after (*inf*), after-effects, crapulence.

hang-up *noun* inhibition, phobia, mental block, problem, obsession, preoccupation, fixation, thing (*inf*).

hank *noun* coil, loop, twist, skein.

hanker *verb* long, yearn, yen (*inf*), pine, itch, hunger, thirst, crave, desire.

haphazard *adj* random, chance, arbitrary, indiscriminate, aimless, casual, careless, disorganized, unmethodical, unsystematic, hit-or-miss.

hapless *adj* unfortunate, unlucky, luckless, ill-fated, ill-starred, unhappy.

happen *verb* **1** occur, take place, come about, come to pass, arise, transpire, result, develop, ensue, eventuate, befall, betide. **2** chance, crop up, materialize.
happen on/upon chance on, stumble on, discover, come across, hit on.

happening *noun* event, occurrence, incident, eventuality, episode, case, circumstance, chance, accident.

happy *adj* **1** joyful, delighted, pleased, content, contented, satisfied, glad, gleeful, ecstatic, elated, euphoric, blissful, jolly, lighthearted, cheerful, gay, smiling, radiant, carefree, untroubled, unworried, in good spirits, over the moon (*inf*). **2** glad, pleased, delighted, gratified, thrilled, tickled pink (*inf*). **3** fortunate, lucky, favourable, advantageous, beneficial, auspicious, propitious, convenient, opportune, timely. **4** appropriate, apt, fitting, good, felicitous.

happy-go-lucky *adj* easygoing, free and easy, carefree, casual, nonchalant, devil-may-care, insouciant, unconcerned, reckless, irresponsible, improvident.

harangue *noun* lecture, sermon, tirade, diatribe, philippic, broadside.
➤*verb* lecture, rant, preach, spout (*inf*), berate, castigate, lambaste.

harass *verb* plague, torment, persecute, harry, pester, hassle (*inf*), nag, hector, badger, hound, bother, trouble, worry, annoy, irritate, vex, provoke, tire, stress, wear out.

harbinger *noun* precursor, forerunner, herald, messenger, warning, sign, omen, portent.

harbour *noun* port, anchorage, dock, mooring, marina, haven.
➤*verb* **1** protect, shelter, hide, conceal, shield, take in. **2** cherish, foster, nurture, nurse, cling to, retain, entertain.

hard *adj* **1** firm, rigid, stiff, solid, solidified, dense, compact, compacted, resistant, impenetrable, strong, tough, stony. **2** difficult, arduous, laborious, gruelling, uphill, strenuous, onerous, formidable, heavy, taxing, tiring, demanding, exhausting, backbreaking. **3** puzzling, baffling, difficult, insoluble, incomprehensible, complicated, complex, knotty, thorny. **4** harsh, severe, stern, strict, unrelenting. **5** tyrannical, cruel, oppressive, ruthless, merciless. **6** hardhearted, cold-hearted, callous, unfeeling, unsympathetic, unkind. **7** painful, distressing, unpleasant, tough, harsh, severe, austere, grim, bad, uncomfortable, unbearable, unendurable. **8** hardworking, industrious, diligent, persevering, tireless, assiduous, conscientious, zealous, keen, enthusiastic. **9** heavy, sharp, powerful, forceful, strong, intense, fierce, violent. **10** close, careful, searching. **11** definite, firm, factual, certain, reliable, verifiable. **12** addictive, habit-forming, narcotic.
➤*adv* **1** diligently, industriously, assiduously, conscientiously, determinedly, earnestly, vigorously, energetically, strenuously, steadily, busily. **2** violently, forcefully, strongly, powerfully, roughly, sharply, heavily, fiercely, severely, harshly, badly, painfully. **3** closely, carefully, intently, sharply, attentively. **4** tightly, firmly.

hard up poor, short, penniless, impoverished, in difficulties, broke (*inf*), skint (*inf*), strapped (*inf*).

hard-and-fast *adj* fixed, binding, definite, rigid, set, strict, stringent, unalterable, unchangeable.

hard-bitten *adj* hardened, hard-boiled, hard-nosed, tough, callous, cynical, down-to-earth, practical, realistic, unsentimental.

hard-boiled *adj* tough, cynical, hardened, hardheaded, down-to-earth, unsentimental.

hard-core *adj* **1** diehard, dyed-in-the-wool, intransigent, rigid, uncompromising, extreme. **2** explicit, blatant, obscene.

harden *verb* solidify, compact, set, stiffen, freeze, bake, congeal, clot, strengthen, toughen, fortify, reinforce, inure, habituate, accustom, acclimatize, discipline.

hardheaded *adj* shrewd, astute, sharp, sensible, rational, businesslike, down-to-earth, realistic, practical, pragmatic, unsentimental, hard-bitten, tough.

hardhearted *adj* cold, callous, hard, indifferent, insensitive, unfeeling, uncaring, unkind, unsympathetic, cold-hearted, heartless, cruel, pitiless, merciless.

hard-hitting *adj* tough, uncompromising, unsparing, no-holds-barred (*inf*), direct, blunt, vigorous, effective, forceful.

hard-line *adj* uncompromising, strict, extreme, inflexible, intransigent, militant.

hardly *adv* **1** scarcely, barely, only just. **2** not at all, by no means.

hard-pressed *adj* **1** harried, hounded, under attack. **2** hard-pushed, hard put, under pressure, beleaguered, up against it (*inf*).

hardship *noun* trouble, difficulty, trial, burden, tribulation, affliction, suffering, distress, misery, misfortune, adversity, privation, deprivation, want, need, poverty, destitution.

hardy adj strong, tough, sturdy, robust, resistant, fit, healthy, hardened, inured, stoical.

harebrained adj 1 daft, foolish, silly, empty-headed, featherbrained, flighty, foolhardy, rash, reckless, mad, half-baked, ill-conceived, ill-thought-out, crackpot (inf).

hark verb listen, hear, give ear, hearken, pay attention, mark.
hark back recall, go back, turn back, look back, think back, revert.

Harlequin noun jester, fool, clown, buffoon.

harlot noun prostitute, whore, trollop, strumpet, fallen woman, scarlet woman, tart (inf), hooker (inf), scrubber (inf).

harm verb 1 hurt, injure, wound, damage, destroy, ruin, maltreat, ill-treat, ill-use, abuse, molest. 2 impair, mar, spoil, injure, damage.
➤noun 1 hurt, pain, injury, damage, impairment, destruction, loss, abuse, disservice, detriment, misfortune. 2 evil, ill, wrong, mischief, wrongdoing, sinfulness, immorality, vice.

harmless adj safe, non-toxic, non-irritant, mild, gentle, innocuous, inoffensive, unobjectionable, innocent.

harmonious adj 1 harmonic, tuneful, melodious, euphonious, mellifluous, musical, sweet-sounding, pleasant. 2 matching, well-matched, coordinated, balanced, compatible, concordant, consistent. 3 amiable, amicable, friendly, congenial, cordial, sympathetic, cooperative, peaceful, trouble-free.

harmonize verb 1 agree, accord, correspond, match, suit, fit in, blend, go together, go well with. 2 reconcile, balance, coordinate, adapt, attune.

harmony noun 1 tunefulness, melodiousness, mellifluousness, euphony. 2 accord, concord, accordance, agreement, unison, unity, amity, friendliness, friendship, fellowship, comradeship, peace, understanding, cooperation, goodwill. 3 balance, symmetry, consonance, congruity, compatibility, correspondence, coordination.

harness noun tackle, tack, reins, straps, bridle.

➤verb 1 saddle, bridle. 2 hitch up, couple, yoke. 3 control, utilize, exploit, employ, mobilize.
in harness working, at work, employed, active, busy.

harp verb dwell, go on about, repeat, reiterate, labour, press, insist.

harridan noun hag, virago, battleaxe, witch, dragon, shrew, vixen, nag, scold, tartar, old bag (inf).

harrow verb distress, disturb, alarm, perturb, upset, torment, traumatize, terrify, chill, horrify.

harry verb 1 ravage, raid, plunder, pillage. 2 badger, pester, hassle (inf), nag, chivvy, harass, plague, torment, annoy, bother, bedevil.

harsh adj 1 rough, coarse, gravelly, hoarse, raucous, grating, rasping, strident, ear-piercing, dissonant, discordant, jarring, jangling, glaring, dazzling, acrid, bitter, unpleasant, disagreeable. 2 bold, crass, crude, vulgar, unrefined, showy, gaudy, garish, lurid. 3 severe, strict, stern, merciless, pitiless, unrelenting, ruthless, unfeeling, brutal, cruel, punitive, unforgiving, despotic, tyrannical, draconian, barbarous, savage. 4 severe, extreme, hard, bitter, freezing, arctic, austere, bleak, stark, grim, comfortless, inhospitable, spartan. 5 abrasive, strong, astringent, caustic.

harvest noun 1 harvesting, reaping, gathering-in. 2 crop, yield, produce, fruits.
➤verb 1 gather, reap, mow, pick. 2 garner, collect, amass, gather, bring in.

hash noun mess, jumble, muddle, mishmash, hotchpotch, mix-up, botch, bungle, screw-up (inf).

hassle noun 1 trouble, inconvenience, bother, nuisance, difficulty, problem. 2 harassment, persecution, trouble, bother, pestering, nagging, badgering, vexation, unpleasantness, aggro (inf).
➤verb harass, bother, bug (inf), pester, trouble, worry, annoy, badger, plague, hound, harry.

haste noun 1 speed, rapidity, swiftness, quickness, celerity, velocity, dispatch, hurry, promptitude, alacrity, briskness, urgency. 2 hastiness, hurriedness, hurry, rush, precipitateness, recklessness, rashness, impetuosity, impulsiveness, carelessness.

hasten *verb* **1** quicken, speed up, accelerate, precipitate, expedite, urge on, push forward, step up. **2** make haste, hurry, rush, dash, race, tear, run, scurry, scamper, hotfoot it (*inf*).

hasty *adj* **1** quick, fast, rapid, speedy, swift, brisk, prompt, expeditious, hurried, rushed, superficial, cursory, perfunctory, fleeting, passing, brief, short. **2** reckless, rash, impetuous, impulsive, impatient, precipitate.

hatch *verb* **1** incubate, brood, sit on. **2** contrive, devise, concoct, conceive, think up, invent, dream up (*inf*), cook up (*inf*).

hatchet *noun* axe, chopper, cleaver, tomahawk.

hate *verb* detest, despise, loathe, abhor, abominate, execrate, dislike.
➤*noun* hatred, detestation, loathing, abhorrence, abomination, execration, aversion, dislike, antipathy, hostility, animosity, rancour, enmity, revulsion, repugnance.

hateful *adj* detestable, loathsome, abhorrent, abominable, odious, execrable, contemptible, despicable, horrible, vile, evil, heinous, disgusting, repulsive, revolting.

hatred *noun* hate, detestation, loathing, abhorrence, abomination, execration, aversion, dislike, antipathy, hostility, animosity, rancour, ill will, antagonism, revulsion, repugnance.

haughty *adj* arrogant, self-important, lofty, superior, vain, conceited, proud, presumptuous, supercilious, disdainful, condescending, snobbish, snooty (*inf*), stuck-up (*inf*).

haul *verb* **1** drag, lug, pull, tow, tug. **2** carry, convey, transport, ship.
➤*noun* harvest, yield, takings, spoils, booty, loot, swag (*inf*).

haunt *verb* **1** roam, walk, visit. **2** frequent, visit, patronize. **3** obsess, possess, prey on, oppress, weigh on, torment, worry.
➤*noun* retreat, resort, meeting-place, stamping ground.

haunted *adj* **1** ghostly, eerie, spooky (*inf*). **2** troubled, obsessed, preoccupied, worried, anguished.

haunting *adj* **1** evocative, nostalgic, poignant, wistful. **2** persistent, recurrent, recurring.

have *verb* **1** own, possess, hold, keep. **2** show, display, demonstrate, exhibit, express. **3** experience, undergo, go through, suffer, endure, enjoy. **4** arrange, organize, hold, give. **5** arrange for, get, cause, induce, ask, tell, order, instruct, command, bid, make, force, compel. **6** eat, take, consume, drink. **7** receive, obtain, get, be given, be sent. **8** bear, give birth to, bring into the world.
be had be cheated, be swindled, be taken in (*inf*), get done (*inf*).
have on 1 wear, be dressed in. **2** have arranged, have planned. **3** tease, trick, kid (*inf*), wind up (*inf*), pull someone's leg (*inf*).

haven *noun* **1** harbour, port, anchorage, dock. **2** shelter, refuge, sanctuary, retreat, oasis.

haversack *noun* backpack, rucksack, knapsack.

havoc *noun* **1** damage, destruction, devastation, desolation, ruin. **2** confusion, disorder, chaos, mayhem.

hawk *verb* peddle, sell, tout.

hawker *noun* pedlar, door-to-door salesman, tout, huckster.

haywire *adj* wrong, out of control, erratic, crazy, berserk, chaotic, confused, mixed up, topsy-turvy.

hazard *noun* **1** danger, risk, peril. **2** danger, threat, menace, death trap, pitfall. **3** chance, luck, accident, fluke.
➤*verb* **1** advance, venture, put forward, offer, volunteer, conjecture, risk, gamble. **2** put at risk, endanger, imperil, jeopardize, expose.

hazardous *adj* **1** dangerous, risky, perilous, unsafe, precarious, dicey (*inf*). **2** uncertain, unpredictable, speculative, chancy (*inf*).

haze *noun* **1** mist, mistiness, fog, cloud, vapour, film. **2** blur, confusion, bewilderment, uncertainty, befuddlement, vagueness, indistinctness.

hazy adj 1 misty, foggy, cloudy, milky, smoky, filmy. 2 vague, indistinct, faint, fuzzy, blurred, dim, unclear, ill-defined, indefinite, nebulous.

head noun 1 skull, cranium, pate (inf), nut (inf), noddle (inf), mind, brain, intellect, loaf (inf). 2 leader, chief, controller, administrator, principal, headteacher, boss, director, manager, chairman, chair, superintendent, supervisor. 3 front, forefront, vanguard, lead, start, top. 4 source, fount, rise, spring. 5 froth, foam, lather, suds, bubbles.
> verb 1 lead, go first, precede. 2 lead, command, direct, control, run, manage, administer, superintend, supervise, oversee. 3 make for, steer for, aim for, go towards, set out for.
> adj leading, first, chief, principal, main, supreme, top, foremost, preeminent.
go to somebody's head 1 intoxicate, inebriate, make drunk. 2 puff up (inf), excite, dizzy, intoxicate.
head off intercept, cut off, divert, turn aside, avert, ward off, forestall, prevent.
head over heels completely, utterly, passionately, madly (inf).
keep one's head keep calm, keep cool, keep one's cool (inf).
lose one's head panic, get excited, lose control, lose it (inf), freak out (inf).

headache noun 1 migraine, neuralgia, thick head (inf). 2 bother, nuisance, problem, trouble, worry, pain (inf), pain in the neck (inf).

heading noun title, rubric, caption, headline, head, category, topic.

headland noun cape, promontory, foreland, point.

headlong adv and adj 1 headfirst, head-on. 2 hasty, rash, precipitate, reckless, heedless, thoughtless, impetuous, impulsive, foolhardy, hastily, hurriedly, precipitately, pell-mell, wildly, impetuously, impulsively, recklessly, rashly, without thinking.

head-on adv and adj directly, straight-on, full-frontal, face-to-face, eyeball-to-eyeball (inf).

headquarters noun HQ, base, centre of operations, nerve centre, head office.

headstrong adj wilful, self-willed, obstinate, stubborn, stiff-necked, pigheaded, perverse, contrary, rash, reckless, foolhardy.

headway noun progress, advance, ground, improvement, development.

heady adj 1 intoxicating, strong, potent. 2 exciting, thrilling, exhilarating, stimulating, rousing, intoxicating, overpowering.

heal verb 1 cure, remedy, treat, make well. 2 restore, repair, mend, put right, reconcile, patch up. 3 assuage, soothe, allay, alleviate, mitigate. 4 mend, get better, get well, recover, improve.

health noun 1 fitness, well-being, soundness, strength, vigour. 2 condition, welfare, state, shape, fettle.

healthy adj 1 fit, fine, well, sound, hale, sturdy, strong, vigorous, robust, blooming, flourishing, thriving, right as rain (inf). 2 healthful, health-giving, wholesome, nutritious, nourishing, beneficial, wholesome, invigorating, salubrious, salutary.

heap noun 1 pile, mound, mountain, stack. 2 abundance, plenty, great deal, lots, loads (inf), stacks (inf), tons (inf), pots (inf), oceans (inf).
> verb 1 pile, stack, amass, accumulate, gather, collect, stockpile. 2 pile up, stack up. 3 load, burden, shower, pour, supply. 4 shower, pour, lavish.

hear verb 1 listen to, catch, make out, overhear, latch on to (inf). 2 listen to, heed, attend to. 3 learn, gather, understand, find out, hear tell, get wind of (inf). 4 try, judge, consider.

hearing noun 1 aural perception, ear. 2 audience, interview, examination. 3 trial, tribunal. 3 earshot, range, sound.

hearsay noun rumour, gossip, word of mouth, talk, tittle-tattle.

heart noun 1 core, centre, kernel, nucleus, nub, essence, crux. 2 tenderness, warmth, benevolence, compassion, sympathy, pity, responsiveness, goodwill, humanity, kindness. 3 passion, emotion, feeling, love, affection. 4 courage, bravery, heroism, guts (inf), backbone, spirit, resolution, determination, enthusiasm. 5 spirit, soul.
by heart by rote, parrot-fashion, off pat, from memory.

take heart cheer up, rally, buck up (*inf*), perk up (*inf*).

heartache *noun* distress, anguish, grief, sadness, sorrow, heartbreak, remorse, pain, torment, suffering, affliction, anxiety, worry.

heartbreaking *adj* heartrending, distressing, sad, pitiful, tragic, harrowing, agonizing, bitter, harsh, painful, cruel.

heartbroken *adj* brokenhearted, heartsick, sad, miserable, grieving, suffering, devastated, desolate, crushed.

hearten *verb* cheer, cheer up, buoy up, buck up, comfort, reassure, encourage, embolden, animate, energize, rouse, invigorate, revitalize.

heartfelt *adj* sincere, profound, deep, genuine, unfeigned, hearty, earnest, ardent, fervent, wholehearted.

heartily *adv* 1 warmly, cordially, sincerely, wholeheartedly, gladly, eagerly, enthusiastically. 2 completely, absolutely, totally, thoroughly.

heartless *adj* cruel, unkind, unfeeling, uncaring, hard, hardhearted, cold, coldhearted, callous, harsh, brutal, ruthless, cold-blooded, inhuman.

heartrending *adj* heartbreaking, harrowing, distressing, pitiful, sad, tragic, moving, poignant.

heartsick *adj* sad, heartsore, heavyhearted, despondent, disappointed, devastated, desperate.

heart-warming *adj* cheering, heartening, encouraging, uplifting, gratifying, pleasing, touching, moving.

hearty *adj* 1 warm, cordial, friendly, enthusiastic, vigorous, ebullient, exuberant,. 2 heartfelt, sincere, profound, wholehearted, genuine, unfeigned. 3 strong, hale, healthy, well, robust, sound, vigorous, lusty. 4 nourishing, nutritious, filling, substantial, square, solid.

heat *noun* 1 warmth, hotness, high temperature, torridness. 2 passion, warmth, zeal, ardour, eagerness, enthusiasm, fervour, vehemence, intensity, violence, rage, fury, fieriness, excitement.
➤*verb* 1 warm, warm up, heat up, cook, boil, toast, microwave. 2 excite, inflame, stir, rouse, arouse, impassion, anger, enrage.

heated *adj* furious, angry, passionate, impassioned, stormy, fierce, intense, vehement, violent, excited, aroused, worked up.

heathen *noun* pagan, infidel, unbeliever, idolater.
➤*adj* pagan, unbelieving, infidel, idolatrous, godless, irreligious.

heave *verb* 1 haul, drag, pull, tug, hoist, lift, heft. 2 throw, cast, fling, hurl, sling, chuck (*inf*). 3 surge, swell, billow, roll. 4 breathe, utter, give, let out. 5 retch, gag, vomit, throw up (*inf*), spew (*inf*).

heaven *noun* 1 paradise, hereafter, afterlife, next world, better place, kingdom of God, Elysium, Valhalla, happy hunting-ground, nirvana. 2 paradise, nirvana, utopia, ecstasy, rapture, bliss. 3 sky, skies, firmament.

heavenly *adj* 1 celestial, cosmic, extraterrestrial. 2 celestial, holy, angelic, godlike, blessed, beatific, divine, immortal, supernatural. 3 wonderful, marvellous, delightful, lovely, beautiful, enchanting, ravishing, exquisite, perfect, sublime, glorious, divine.

heavily *adv* 1 hard, laboriously, painfully, ponderously, slowly, with difficulty, dully. 2 greatly, very, extremely, seriously, excessively, severely, decisively, thoroughly, soundly.

heavy *adj* 1 weighty, hefty, bulky, big, massive, enormous, mighty, substantial, fat, ponderous, cumbersome, burdensome, awkward, unmanageable, unwieldy. 2 laborious, arduous, tough, strenuous, difficult, hard, demanding, taxing. 3 harsh, grievous, oppressive, burdensome, demanding, exacting, onerous, taxing, crushing, unbearable. 4 hard, forceful, powerful, severe, intense, sharp, stinging, violent. 5 intense, intensive, fierce, vigorous, concentrated, severe, excessive, extreme, great, serious, considerable. 6 dull, boring, tedious, dry, uninteresting, wearisome. 7 difficult, profound, deep, complex, abstruse. 8 sluggish, torpid, listless, apathetic, slow, ponderous, laborious, lumbering. 9 large, big, fat, bulky, stout, overweight, obese, hulking. 10 stodgy, filling, solid, indigestible, starchy. 11 dense, thick, solid, impenetrable. 12 coarse, clumsy, ungraceful.

heavy-handed *adj* **1** clumsy, awkward, blundering, maladroit, inexpert, unskilful, ham-handed (*inf*), ham-fisted (*inf*), cack-handed (*inf*), insensitive, tactless, unsubtle. **2** harsh, severe, ruthless, hard, oppressive, overbearing, domineering.

heckle *verb* interrupt, disrupt, shout down, boo, barrack, catcall.

hectic *adj* feverish, frenetic, frantic, frenzied, bustling, busy, fast, furious, excited, exciting, animated, chaotic.

hector *verb* bully, browbeat, cow, intimidate, threaten, harass, badger, chivvy.

hedge *noun* **1** hedgerow, fence, barrier, windbreak. **2** safeguard, protection, insurance.
➤*verb* **1** surround, enclose, encircle, fence, protect. **2** evade, dodge, sidestep, hum and haw, stall, equivocate, prevaricate, quibble, fudge. **3** protect, safeguard, cover, insure.

heed *verb* mind, attend to, pay attention to, listen to, take notice of, bear in mind, note, observe, obey, follow.
➤*noun* attention, notice, note, regard, respect, mind, thought, care, caution.

heedless *adj* unmindful, regardless, oblivious, unconcerned, thoughtless, unthinking, careless, inattentive, negligent, rash, reckless.

heel[1] *noun* stiletto, platform, wedge.
down at heel shabby, poor, ill-dressed, tattered, ragged, dowdy, run-down, tatty (*inf*).

heel[2] *verb* lean, list, tilt, cant.

hefty *adj* heavy, weighty, bulky, big, large, huge, massive, burly, hulking, beefy, muscular, brawny, strapping, sturdy, powerful, mighty, substantial, sizeable, expensive.

height *noun* **1** altitude, elevation, highness, loftiness. **2** tallness, stature. **3** mountain, hill, high ground, cliff. **4** top, summit, crest. **5** climax, consummation, culmination, high point, peak, zenith, acme, maximum, utmost.

heighten *verb* **1** raise, elevate, uplift. **2** increase, augment, build up, amplify. **3** intensify, sharpen, enhance, enrich, improve, boost, strengthen.

heinous *adj* wicked, evil, iniquitous, infamous, atrocious, scandalous, outrageous, shocking, monstrous, abominable, odious, loathsome, hateful, hideous, deplorable, contemptible, despicable, detestable, revolting, abhorrent, unspeakable.

heir *noun* **1** heiress, child, inheritor, beneficiary, legatee. **2** successor, inheritor.

helix *noun* spiral, screw, corkscrew, whorl.

hell *noun* **1** underworld, perdition, inferno, abyss, Hades, Gehenna. **2** purgatory, torture, torment, agony, ordeal, trial, nightmare.

hell-for-leather *adv and adj* fast, quickly, at full speed, all-out, full tilt.

hellish *adj* infernal, diabolical, fiendish, satanic, demonic, devilish, brutal, barbarous, barbaric, monstrous, savage, ferocious, vicious, ruthless, inhuman, cruel, wicked, evil, heinous, abominable, atrocious, appalling, awful, dreadful, horrible.
➤*adv* very, extremely, unpleasantly, terribly, ever so (*inf*).

helm *noun* **1** rudder, wheel, tiller. **2** charge, control, command, driving seat.

help *verb* **1** assist, aid, lend a hand, abet, back, support, stand by, rally round, succour. **2** encourage, boost, promote, further, serve. **3** assist, benefit, facilitate, be of use. **4** relieve, alleviate, mitigate, soothe, ease, cure, heal, remedy. **5** avoid, resist, refrain from. **6** stop, prevent, control. **7** steal, take, appropriate, nick (*inf*), pinch (*inf*).
➤*noun* **1** assistance, aid, helping hand, succour, backing, backup, support, encouragement, advice, guidance, service, use, cooperation, collaboration. **2** relief, remedy, cure, alleviation, mitigation, improvement. **3** helper, assistant, servant, maid, employee, hand, worker.

helpful *adj* useful, serviceable, timely, beneficial, advantageous, favourable, practical, constructive, friendly, sympathetic, kind, supportive, cooperative, obliging.

helping *noun* serving, portion, plateful, bowlful, spoonful, dollop (*inf*).

helpless *adj* **1** invalid, bedridden, laid-up (*inf*), dependent, feeble, incapable, incompetent, weak, unfit, powerless. **2** unprotected, defenceless, vulnerable, exposed.

helpmate *noun* helper, partner, companion, spouse.

hem *noun* edge, border, edging, trimming.
➤*verb* **1** edge, border, bind, trim. **2** border,
skirt, fringe, edge. **3** surround, encircle,
enclose, confine, restrict, shut in, box in,
trap.

hence *adv* therefore, thus, accordingly,
consequently.

henceforth *adv* henceforward, hereafter,
subsequently, from now on, hence.

henchman *noun* attendant, servant, flun-
key, toady, minion, follower, supporter,
aide, associate, right-hand man, crony
(*inf*).

henpecked *adj* bullied, browbeaten,
nagged, dominated, meek, docile, under
someone's thumb (*inf*).

herald *noun* **1** messenger, courier, runner,
crier. **2** harbinger, forerunner, precursor,
usher-in, sign, signal, indication, omen,
portent.
➤*verb* **1** announce, proclaim, trumpet,
make known, make public. **2** precede,
usher in, pave the way for, portend, indicate, promise, presage.

herculean *adj* laborious, arduous, backbreaking, onerous, formidable, daunting,
gruelling, demanding, great, enormous,
prodigious, colossal, gigantic, tremendous,
mammoth, massive, powerful, strong,
mighty, muscular, brawny.

herd *noun* **1** drove, pack, flock. **2** horde,
host, crowd, throng, multitude, mob,
mass, swarm, rabble, riffraff, hoi polloi.
➤*verb* **1** drive, round up, shepherd, lead,
guide. **2** gather, huddle, assemble, flock,
congregate.

here *adv* **1** hereabouts. **2** hither. **3** now, at
this stage, at this point.

hereafter *adv* after this, henceforth,
henceforward, from now on, in future.
➤*noun* afterlife, life to come, next world,
heaven.

hereditary *adj* **1** inheritable, hereditable,
genetic, congenital, inborn, innate, inherited, transmissible. **2** ancestral, family,
inherited.

heresy *noun* unorthodoxy, heterodoxy,
nonconformity, dissent, misbelief, schism,
revisionism.

heretic *noun* dissenter, misbeliever, apostate, nonconformist, revisionist,
schismatic.

heritage *noun* **1** history, past, tradition,
culture. **2** inheritance, birthright, legacy,
bequest, patrimony.

hermit *noun* **1** recluse, loner, solitary.
2 monk, anchorite, anchoress.

hermitage *noun* retreat, refuge, hideaway,
sanctum, sanctuary, haven.

hero *noun* **1** champion, victor, icon, ideal,
idol, celebrity, star, superstar, pinup, heart-
throb (*inf*). **2** protagonist, central character, lead, leading actor.

heroic *adj* **1** courageous, brave, valiant,
intrepid, fearless, dauntless, bold, adventurous, daring, gallant, noble, chivalrous,
selfless. **2** legendary, mythological, fabulous, Homeric. **3** epic, grand, impressive,
titanic, monumental.

heroine *noun* **1** champion, victor, ideal,
idol, celebrity. **2** leading lady, female lead,
prima donna, protagonist.

heroism *noun* courage, bravery, valour,
fortitude, fearlessness, daring, spirit, gallantry, determination, selflessness.

hero worship *noun* admiration, idolization, idealization, adoration, adulation.

hesitant *adj* uncertain, unsure, doubtful,
dubious, indecisive, irresolute, vacillating,
wavering, tentative, reluctant, wary, diffident, halting, stammering, stuttering.

hesitate *verb* **1** pause, wait, delay, hold
back, hang back, waver, vacillate, dither,
shilly-shally, stall, temporize, doubt, be
uncertain, demur. **2** shrink, hang back, be
reluctant, scruple, think twice, balk.

heterodox *adj* unorthodox, heretical, dissenting, freethinking, revisionist, unsound.

heterogeneous *adj* dissimilar, different,
unlike, unrelated, disparate, varied,
diverse, divergent, contrasting, mixed,
assorted, motley, miscellaneous.

hew *verb* **1** chop, chop down, hack, cut
down, fell, lop, sever. **2** carve, whittle,
chisel, sculpt, shape, fashion, form, make.

heyday *noun* prime, peak, pinnacle,
bloom, flowering, culmination, golden
age, salad days.

hiatus *noun* gap, break, interruption, lapse,
lull, respite, pause, rest, interval, blank,
discontinuity, breach.

hide[1] *verb* **1** conceal, cloak, shroud, cover, screen, mask, veil, disguise, camouflage, secrete, stash away (*inf*), bury, stow away, obscure, eclipse, darken, cloud, block, obstruct. **2** suppress, hush up, bottle up (*inf*), sweep under the carpet (*inf*), keep under wraps (*inf*). **3** take cover, conceal oneself, shelter, lurk, lie low, go to ground, go into hiding, hole up (*inf*).

hide[2] *noun* skin, pelt, fur, coat, leather.

hideaway *noun* hiding place, hideout, hidey-hole (*inf*), retreat, refuge, den, lair.

hidebound *adj* narrow-minded, intolerant, bigoted, prejudiced, reactionary, set, rigid, entrenched, conventional, conservative, ultraconservative, fundamentalist.

hideous *adj* **1** ugly, grotesque, unsightly, repulsive, repellent, ghastly, gruesome, disgusting, grisly, grim. **2** horrible, horrid, dreadful, terrible, terrifying, horrific, horrifying, appalling, shocking, monstrous, heinous, odious, loathsome, vile.

hideout *noun* hiding place, hideaway, hidey-hole (*inf*), retreat, refuge, den, lair.

hiding *noun* beating, thrashing, flogging, whipping, caning, spanking, drubbing, belting (*inf*), tanning (*inf*).

hierarchy *noun* social order, class system, pecking order, ladder, ranking, scale.

higgledy-piggledy *adv and adj* untidily, confusedly, haphazardly, indiscriminately, topsy-turvy, anyhow, disorderly, haphazard, indiscriminate, confused, disorganized, jumbled, untidy.

high *adj* **1** tall, lofty, elevated, towering, soaring. **2** great, intense, good, excellent, top, top-class, fine, outstanding, superior, first-rate, first-class, expensive, dear, excessive, exorbitant, extortionate, steep (*inf*). **3** strong, powerful, vigorous, forceful. **4** shrill, piercing, high-pitched, soprano, treble, falsetto. **5** high-ranking, top, senior, leading, chief, eminent, prominent, important, powerful, distinguished, noble. **6** happy, merry, joyful, elated, excited, exhilarated, ecstatic, euphoric, hyped up (*inf*). **7** drugged, intoxicated, stoned (*inf*), bombed (*inf*), blitzed (*inf*), out of it (*inf*), spaced out (*inf*). **8** smelly, niffy (*inf*), whiffy (*inf*), gamy, bad, off, tainted, rancid, putrid.
➤*noun* **1** record level, height, peak, zenith. **2** euphoria, intoxication, ecstasy, trip (*inf*).

high and dry *adv* abandoned, stranded, marooned, helpless, destitute, bereft.

high-and-mighty *adj* arrogant, conceited, haughty, proud, self-important, superior, overbearing, overweening, snobbish, supercilious, condescending, stuck-up (*inf*).

highborn *adj* aristocratic, noble, gentle, wellborn, blue-blooded, patrician.

highbrow *adj* intellectual, academic, scholarly, bookish, sophisticated, cultured, cultivated.

high-flown *adj* high-sounding, florid, flowery, extravagant, elaborate, flamboyant, pretentious, overblown, inflated, bombastic, pompous, affected, highfalutin (*inf*), la-di-da (*inf*).

high-handed *adj* bossy (*inf*), domineering, overbearing, arrogant, imperious, cavalier, dictatorial.

highland *noun* upland, plateau, tableland, heights, mountains, hills.

highlight *noun* climax, peak, best part, high spot, high point.
➤*verb* stress, emphasize, accentuate, underline, point up, call attention to, focus on.

highly *adv* **1** extremely, very, very much, greatly, immensely, tremendously, exceptionally. **2** favourably, well, appreciatively, approvingly, enthusiastically.

highly-strung *adj* sensitive, temperamental, neurotic, nervous, nervy, jumpy, edgy, on edge, excitable, tense, twitchy (*inf*), uptight (*inf*).

high-minded *adj* noble, moral, ethical, principled, idealistic, lofty, elevated, virtuous, honourable.

high-powered *adj* powerful, forceful, vigorous, aggressive, assertive, dynamic, ambitious, enterprising, energetic, go-getting (*inf*).

high-spirited *adj* spirited, exuberant, boisterous, bouncy, buoyant, ebullient, cheerful, animated, lively, vital, vivacious, dashing, full of beans (*inf*).

high spirits *pl noun* spirit, exuberance, ebullience, boisterousness, animation, energy, exhilaration, vitality, bounce (*inf*), cheerfulness, vivacity, joie de vivre.

hijack *verb* commandeer, seize, take over.

hike *verb* **1** walk, tramp, trek, ramble, backpack. **2** lift, hitch, pull, tug, hoist, jerk, yank (*inf*). **3** increase, put up, jack up (*inf*).
➤ *noun* walk, tramp, trek, ramble.

hilarious *adj* **1** funny, amusing, comical, humorous, uproarious, rollicking, merry, sidesplitting, hysterical (*inf*), killing (*inf*).

hilarity *noun* merriment, jollity, mirth, laughter, fun, amusement, gaiety, levity, conviviality, cheerfulness, glee.

hill *noun* mound, knoll, hillock, rise, mountain, mount, fell, tor, height, eminence, prominence, incline, slope, ascent, heap, pile, stack.

hillock *noun* mound, knoll, hummock.

hilt *noun* handle, grip, shaft, haft.
to the hilt fully, completely, totally, to the full, to the end, all the way (*inf*).

hind *adj* back, rear, posterior, tail.

hinder *verb* impede, obstruct, block, hamper, handicap, encumber, thwart, foil, frustrate, balk, retard, delay, hold up, hold back, slow down, check, stop, halt, forestall, stymie, prevent, deter, interfere with.

hindmost *adj* last, final, rear, rearmost, tail, furthest.

hindrance *noun* **1** impediment, encumbrance, handicap, obstacle, obstruction, block, stumbling block, deterrent, barrier, bar, hitch, snag, difficulty. **2** delay, stoppage, restriction, limitation, thwarting, interference, interruption.

hinge *verb* turn, hang, depend, rest, pivot.

hint *noun* **1** suggestion, intimation, implication, insinuation, clue, cue, reminder, indication. **2** tip, pointer, suggestion, piece of advice. **3** trace, suspicion, suggestion, undertone, tinge, soupçon, dash, breath, whisper, whiff.
➤ *verb* suggest, intimate, imply, indicate, insinuate, tip off, signal.

hire *verb* **1** rent, charter, lease. **2** employ, take on, sign up, contract, appoint, engage, recruit. **3** let, rent out, lease out.
➤ *noun* **1** rental, renting, leasing. **2** rent, rental, charge.

hirsute *adj* hairy, shaggy, bearded.

hiss *verb* whistle, sibilate, wheeze, boo, hoot, catcall, jeer.
➤ *noun* hissing, whistle, sibilance, wheeze, boo, hoot, catcall.

historian *noun* chronicler, recorder, antiquarian, historiographer, annalist.

historic *adj* famous, celebrated, notable, memorable, remarkable, important, significant, momentous, epoch-making.

historical *adj* **1** ancient, former, past, bygone, of yore. **2** attested, documented, chronicled, recorded, authentic, true, verifiable.

history *noun* **1** chronicle, chronology, annals, record, account, story, saga, memoir, biography. **2** antiquity, the past, former times, days of old, times gone by, yesteryear. **3** background, experience, record.

histrionic *adj* theatrical, melodramatic, sensational, exaggerated, affected, hammy (*inf*).

hit *verb* **1** strike, knock, beat, batter, pound, smack, slap, tap, punch, thump, box, cuff, buffet, hammer, pummel, whack (*inf*), bash (*inf*), clobber (*inf*), clout (*inf*), sock (*inf*), wallop (*inf*). **2** bump, bang, crash into, run into, plough into, collide with. **3** reach, attain, achieve, arrive at, strike. **4** affect, damage, hurt, upset, devastate, overwhelm, knock for six (*inf*).
➤ *noun* **1** stroke, blow, knock, smack, slap, rap, tap, thump, punch, cuff, box, bash, bump, clout (*inf*), whack (*inf*), wallop (*inf*). **2** success, triumph, winner, sell-out, smash (*inf*).
hit it off get along, get on, become friends, take to.
hit on find, discover, come on, happen upon, stumble on, think of, arrive at.
hit out lash out, strike out, attack, denounce, criticize, inveigh against.

hitch *verb* **1** tie, fasten, make fast, attach, join, couple, tether, moor, harness. **2** pull, tug, jerk, hoist, hike, hoick (*inf*).
➤ *noun* impediment, obstacle, hindrance, stumbling block, problem, difficulty, snag, catch, setback, hiccup, mishap.

hitherto *adv* up to now, until now, so far, previously.

hit-or-miss *adj* random, haphazard, disorganized, indiscriminate, trial-and-error, aimless, unplanned, careless, casual.

hoard *verb* gather, collect, amass, accumulate, store, stockpile, save, keep, set aside, put away, put by, squirrel away, stash away (*inf*).
➤*noun* collection, accumulation, store, supply, reserve, fund, stash (*inf*).

hoarse *adj* husky, throaty, croaky, guttural, gruff, gravelly, harsh, rasping.

hoary *adj* **1** grey, silvery, white, grizzled. **2** old, aged, ancient, venerable. **3** hackneyed, trite, antiquated, old hat (*inf*).

hoax *noun* trick, practical joke, prank, bluff, cheat, swindle, fraud, humbug, leg-pull (*inf*), con (*inf*), spoof (*inf*).
➤*verb* trick, deceive, take in, delude, dupe, fool, bluff, cheat, swindle, con (*inf*), have on (*inf*), wind up (*inf*).

hobble *verb* **1** limp, stumble, totter, stagger. **2** fetter, shackle, tie, bind.

hobby *noun* pastime, recreation, amusement, relaxation, interest, leisure activity, pursuit, sideline.

hobgoblin *noun* goblin, imp, gnome, dwarf, bogey, bogeyman.

hobnob *verb* fraternize, socialize, associate, mingle, mix, keep company, go around.

hocus-pocus *noun* nonsense, gibberish, gobbledygook, mumbo jumbo, rigmarole, magic, conjuring, abracadabra, charm.

hog *noun* **1** pig, swine, porker, boar. **2** glutton, pig (*inf*), gannet (*inf*).
➤*verb* monopolize, corner, keep for oneself.

hogwash *noun* rubbish, nonsense, drivel, tripe, twaddle, claptrap, bunk (*inf*), bunkum (*inf*), cobblers (*inf*), bosh (*inf*), tosh (*inf*), rot (*inf*), piffle (*inf*), eyewash (*inf*), poppycock (*inf*), bollocks (*sl*).

hoi polloi *pl noun* masses, common people, riffraff, rabble, common herd, populace, proletariat, great unwashed (*inf*).

hoist *verb* raise, lift, winch, jack, heave.
➤*noun* jack, winch, crane, pulley, tackle, lift.

hold *verb* **1** grip, grasp, clutch, clasp, seize, cling to, support, sustain, bear, carry. **2** keep, retain, maintain, prop. **3** carry, take, contain, accommodate. **4** detain, arrest, imprison, lock up. **5** occupy, fill, hold down. **6** think, believe, consider, regard, view, reckon, assume, presume. **7** maintain, entertain. **8** embrace, hug, enfold, clasp. **9** last, endure, remain, stay, persist, go on, continue, keep up, carry on, stand. **10** convene, call, organize, conduct, run, give, officiate at, preside over.
➤*noun* **1** grip, grasp, clasp, purchase. **2** anchorage, footing, foothold. **3** influence, control, power, authority, grip, sway, mastery.

hold back 1 keep back, restrain, control, curb, check, inhibit, restrain, hinder, impede, delay. **2** smother, repress, suppress, keep back, stifle. **3** hesitate, shrink, refrain, desist, restrain oneself.

hold down keep, have, occupy, continue in

hold forth speak, talk, preach, lecture, declaim, spout (*inf*).

hold off 1 fend off, fight off, ward off, stave off, keep at bay, repel. **2** delay, postpone, defer, put off, put on hold.

hold on continue, endure, last out, persevere, carry on, keep going, survive.

hold one's own hold out, stand one's ground, stay put, keep one's head above water (*inf*), keep pace.

hold out 1 offer, proffer, extend, present. **2** hang on (*inf*), carry on, last out, continue, endure, resist, stand firm.

hold over defer, put off, postpone, suspend.

hold up 1 delay, retard, detain, set back, slow down, hinder, impede. **2** put forward, show, present. **3** stick up (*inf*), mug (*inf*), rob, steal from.

holdup *noun* **1** delay, wait, interruption, hitch, setback, snag, problem, stoppage, traffic jam. **2** stick-up (*inf*), robbery, heist (*inf*), mugging (*inf*).

hole *noun* **1** aperture, opening, gap, space, break, breach, gash, slit, slot, split, tear, rent, puncture, perforation. **2** hollow, dip, depression, excavation, cavity, pocket, pit, crater, pothole. **3** hovel, slum, dive (*inf*), dump (*inf*), pigsty (*inf*), tip (*inf*). **4** predicament, difficulty, tight corner, dilemma, plight, fix (*inf*), mess (*inf*), jam (*inf*), spot (*inf*), tight spot (*inf*), hot water (*inf*).
➤*verb* puncture, perforate, pierce, breach, break, slit, gash.

hole up hide, hide out, take cover, lie low, lie up, go to ground, go to earth, go into hiding, take refuge.

holiday noun 1 vacation, time off, leave, day off, break, rest, recess, furlough. 2 festival, feast day, bank holiday, public holiday.

holier-than-thou adj sanctimonious, goody-goody (inf), self-righteous, self-satisfied, smug.

holiness noun piety, devoutness, sacredness, saintliness, godliness, sanctity, goodness, righteousness, blessedness.

hollow adj 1 empty, vacant, void, unfilled. 2 sunken, deep-set, indented, depressed, caved-in, concave. 3 muffled, muted, rumbling, echoing, reverberant, flat, dull, dead, expressionless, toneless. 4 meaningless, pointless, futile, empty, vain, worthless, pyrrhic. 5 insincere, hypocritical, feigned, pretended, sham, false.
➤noun 1 depression, dip, basin, cavity, concavity, pit, groove, recess, dent, dimple, indentation, valley, dale, glen, dell. 2 cavity, void, hole.
➤verb dig out, excavate, scoop out, gouge out, furrow, groove, pit.
beat somebody hollow annihilate, defeat, crush, rout, hammer (inf), thrash (inf), slaughter (inf), trounce (inf).

holocaust noun massacre, carnage, butchery, mass murder, genocide, ethnic cleansing, slaughter, annihilation, extermination, destruction, devastation.

holy adj 1 devout, pious, saintly, godly, God-fearing, good, virtuous, righteous, sinless, pure. 2 sacred, hallowed, consecrated, sanctified, sacrosanct. 3 divine, spiritual, blessed, sublime.

homage noun honour, respect, deference, praise, reverence, esteem, admiration, tribute.

home noun 1 house, abode, dwelling, dwelling place, residence, domicile, habitat, territory, natural element, domain. 2 birthplace, hometown, homeland, native land, fatherland, mother country, origin, roots, fount, source, cradle. 3 residential home, retirement home, nursing home, old people's home, institution, hospice, hostel, asylum.
adj 1 domestic, family, familiar, household. 2 domestic, internal, inland, national.
at home comfortable, relaxed, at ease, in one's element, on home ground.
bring home to somebody make aware, convince, persuade, impress on, emphasize, stress.
home in on focus on, concentrate on, zero in on, pinpoint.

homeland noun native land, country of origin, fatherland, mother country.

homeless adj of no fixed abode, itinerant, vagrant, travelling, rootless, displaced, dispossessed, evicted, outcast, destitute, down-and-out (inf).

homely adj 1 ordinary, everyday, homey, comfortable, informal, relaxed, familiar. 2 simple, plain, modest, unpretentious, unsophisticated, homespun, folksy. 3 plain, unattractive, ugly, unprepossessing. 4 warm, welcoming, affectionate.

homespun adj plain, simple, modest, unpolished, unsophisticated, rustic, homely, folksy, crude.

homicide noun manslaughter, murder, assassination, killing, slaying.

homily noun sermon, lecture, lesson, harangue.

homogeneous adj 1 uniform, consistent, unvaried. 2 identical, alike, similar, akin, analogous.

homogenize verb coalesce, fuse, unite, blend.

homosexual noun gay, lesbian, queer (inf), poof (inf), poofter (inf), fairy (inf), queen (inf), homo (inf), faggot (inf), nancy (inf), dyke (inf).

hone verb sharpen, point, edge, whet, strop.

honest adj 1 good, upright, righteous, virtuous, honourable, upstanding, reputable, respectable, law-abiding, moral, worthy, just, decent, high-minded, principled, incorruptible, conscientious, trustworthy, reliable. 2 truthful, sincere, candid, frank, blunt, open, direct, straightforward. 3 right, moral, ethical, fair, just, lawful, legal, legitimate, above-board.

honestly adv **1** to be honest, truthfully, sincerely, frankly, candidly, straight up (inf). **2** legally, lawfully, legitimately, ethically, fairly, justly, honourably, in good faith.

honesty noun **1** virtue, uprightness, worthiness, integrity, morality, morals, ethics, principles, righteousness, incorruptibility, reputability, conscientiousness, trustworthiness, reliability, probity, goodness. **2** truthfulness, sincerity, frankness, candour, straightforwardness.

honorarium noun fee, recompense, remuneration.

honorary adj titular, voluntary, unofficial, unpaid.

honour noun **1** repute, reputation, good name, pride, dignity, prestige, standing, credit. **2** honesty, integrity, probity, goodness, rectitude, righteousness, sincerity, trustworthiness, truthfulness, uprightness, worthiness, virtue, principles. **3** fame, glory, renown, praise, acclaim, applause, adulation, admiration, respect, deference, acknowledgment, recognition. **4** award, accolade, decoration, distinction, prize, trophy, title, tribute. **5** privilege, pleasure, joy. **6** virginity, chastity.
➤verb **1** respect, esteem, appreciate, value, prize, admire, revere, venerate, praise, acclaim, applaud, celebrate, commemorate, pay homage to, pay tribute to, acknowledge, recognize. **2** keep, observe, respect, discharge, fulfil, carry out. **3** pay, cash, clear, accept.

honourable adj **1** honest, upright, moral, ethical, principled, upstanding, good, decent, righteous, virtuous, worthy, trustworthy, truthful, respectable, reputable, just, fair. **2** noble, glorious, distinguished, creditable, illustrious, respected, renowned.

hood noun cowl, scarf, capuche.

hoodlum noun hood (inf), gangster, heavy (inf), hatchet man, gunman, criminal, lawbreaker, felon, delinquent, thug, tough (inf).

hoodwink verb dupe, deceive, delude, mislead, trick, hoax, fool, con (inf), take for a ride (inf), bamboozle (inf).

hook noun **1** hasp, clasp, catch, clip, fastener, peg, holder. **2** billhook, sickle. **3** punch, blow.
➤verb **1** catch, capture, bag, snare, trap. **2** fasten, clasp, fix, secure, join, link, connect. **3** curve, bend, curl.
off the hook cleared, acquitted, exonerated, in the clear, let off.

hooked adj **1** bent, curved, crooked, aquiline. **2** addicted, dependent. **3** obsessed, devoted.

hooligan noun lout, vandal, delinquent, rowdy, tough, rough, yob (inf).

hoop noun band, ring, circle, round, loop.

hoot verb **1** tu-whit tu-whoo, screech, shriek, call. **2** toot, beep. **3** boo, catcall, jeer.
➤noun **1** tu-whit tu-whoo, screech, shriek, call, cry, toot, beep, howl, yell, cry, whoop, boo, catcall, jeer, raspberry (inf). **2** scream (inf), laugh (inf).

hop verb skip, jump, leap, frisk, prance, dance.
➤noun **1** jump, leap, spring, bound, skip. **2** flight, trip, journey. **3** dance, disco, knees-up (inf).

hope noun **1** expectation, anticipation, confidence, assurance, faith, trust, conviction, optimism. **2** ambition, dream, aspiration, desire. **3** prospect, promise, chance.
➤verb **1** desire, wish, trust, believe, assume. **2** expect, count on, reckon on, rely on. **3** await, long, yearn, dream, look forward to.

hopeful adj **1** optimistic, sanguine, expectant, positive, confident, assured, bullish (inf). **2** promising, encouraging, positive, favourable, heartening, auspicious, bright, rosy.

hopefully adv **1** with luck, if all goes well, all being well, probably. **2** expectantly, eagerly, optimistically, in anticipation.

hopeless adj **1** despairing, desperate, despondent, demoralized, disconsolate, negative, pessimistic, defeatist. **2** lost, irretrievable, irredeemable, irreversible, irreparable, insoluble, incurable, terminal, fatal, unattainable, no-win (inf), vain, futile, useless, pointless, forlorn. **3** incompetent, bad, awful, lousy (inf), pathetic (inf), no good.

horde noun crowd, multitude, throng, mob, host, army, swarm, herd.

horizon *noun* **1** skyline, field of view. **2** scope, perspective, perception, ken, knowledge.

horizontal *adj* flat, level, plane, prone, supine.

horrendous *adj* horrific, horrifying, appalling, shocking, awful, frightful, dreadful, terrible.

horrible *adj* **1** horrid, harrowing, blood-curdling, terrifying, hair-raising, horrifying, horrific, ghastly, grisly, gruesome, heinous, hideous, revolting, disgusting. **2** unpleasant, disagreeable, horrid, nasty, terrible, dreadful, awful, beastly, mean, unkind.

horrid *adj* **1** horrible, awful, dreadful, unpleasant, disagreeable, nasty, mean, unkind, hateful, beastly. **2** horrifying, ghastly, bloodcurdling, hair-raising, repulsive, revolting, gruesome, hideous, dreadful, abominable, frightening, terrifying.

horrific *adj* horrifying, grisly, gruesome, frightening, alarming, terrifying, shocking, appalling, dreadful, ghastly, bloodcurdling, harrowing.

horrify *verb* **1** shock, appal, disgust, sicken, outrage, scandalize, offend, revolt. **2** alarm, frighten, scare, terrify, petrify, scare to death (*inf*), scare stiff (*inf*).

horror *noun* **1** terror, fear, fright, alarm, dread, dismay. **2** loathing, hatred, detestation, abomination, abhorrence, repugnance, revulsion, disgust.

horse *noun* mount, steed, stallion, gelding, mare, filly, colt, foal, pony, hack, nag, gee-gee (*inf*).

horseplay *noun* clowning, foolery, fooling around, skylarking, high jinks, rough-and-tumble, shenanigans (*inf*).

horticulture *noun* gardening, cultivation.

hose *noun* pipe, tube, tubing, siphon.

hosiery *noun* stockings, tights, socks, hose.

hospitable *adj* **1** welcoming, friendly, neighbourly, sociable, warmhearted, kind, generous. **2** congenial. **3** amenable, receptive, responsive.

hospital *noun* infirmary, clinic, sanatorium.

hospitality *noun* hospitableness, welcome, neighbourliness, friendliness, sociability, warmheartedness, generosity.

host[1] *noun* **1** hostess, master of ceremonies, MC, emcee (*inf*). **2** compere, presenter, announcer, anchor. **3** proprietor, landlord, landlady, innkeeper.
➤ *verb* **1** present, introduce, compere, front (*inf*), emcee (*inf*). **2** give, hold.

host[2] *noun* throng, army, legion, horde, crowd, mob, swarm.

hostage *noun* prisoner, captive, pawn.

hostile *adj* **1** enemy, opposing, unfriendly, belligerent, warring, malevolent, malicious, spiteful, aggressive. **2** opposed, anti (*inf*), against, antagonistic, averse, ill-disposed, adverse, unfavourable.

hostility *noun* **1** war, warfare, battle, conflict, fighting. **2** opposition, antagonism, enmity, hatred, ill will, unfriendliness, animosity, antipathy, aversion, belligerence, aggression, malevolence.

hot *adj* **1** heated, warm, red hot, scalding, boiling, steaming, sizzling, scorching, fiery, burning, blazing, roasting, searing, blistering, baking, sweltering, torrid, tropical. **2** pungent, sharp, strong, fiery, spicy, peppery. **3** fiery, fierce, ferocious, irascible, touchy, violent. **4** lustful, horny (*inf*), randy, lecherous, libidinous. **5** recent, latest, brand new, fresh, up-to-date, exciting. **6** stolen, smuggled, contraband. **7** wanted. **8** popular, in (*inf*), in vogue, in demand, fashionable, sought-after.

hot air *noun* nonsense, blather, blether, bluster, bombast, froth, verbiage, empty talk, piffle (*inf*), bunk (*inf*), bunkum (*inf*), claptrap (*inf*), gas (*inf*), wind (*inf*).

hotbed *noun* breeding-ground, forcing-house, cradle, nursery, den, nest.

hot-blooded *adj* passionate, ardent, excitable, temperamental, fiery, eager, impulsive, impetuous, rash.

hotel *noun* guesthouse, boarding house, inn, hostel, motel, pension.

hotfoot *adv* quickly, swiftly, rapidly, promptly, without delay, hurriedly, in haste, posthaste.

hotheaded *adj* hot-tempered, quick-tempered, short-tempered, excitable, volatile, fiery, irascible, headstrong, impetuous, impulsive, hasty, rash.

hothouse *noun* greenhouse, glasshouse, conservatory, orangery.

hound *verb* chase, pursue, dog, harry, harass, badger, hassle (*inf*), bully, persecute, pester, chivvy, pressurize.

house *noun* **1** dwelling, residence, home, building, cottage, bungalow, villa, mansion, semi (*inf*). **2** family, line, race, tribe, clan, dynasty. **3** firm, business, company, partnership, concern, enterprise, establishment, corporation. **4** chamber, legislative body, assembly, parliament, congress. **5** audience, auditorium.
➤*verb* **1** accommodate, put up, lodge, board, quarter, billet. **2** contain, hold. **3** store, shelter, cover.
on the house free, free of charge, for nothing.

household *noun* family, family circle, ménage, establishment.

householder *noun* homeowner, head of the household, occupier, occupant, resident, tenant.

housekeeping *noun* domestic work, household management, homemaking, housewifery.

housing *noun* **1** accommodation, houses, homes, dwellings. **2** casing, case, holder, guard, cover, sheath, jacket.

hovel *noun* shack, shanty, slum, dump (*inf*), hole (*inf*).

hover *verb* **1** hang, float, drift. **2** linger, hang about, lurk. **3** dither, hesitate, waver, vacillate, fluctuate, oscillate, seesaw.

however *adv* nevertheless, nonetheless, notwithstanding, but, still, yet, even so, though, after all.

howl *verb* **1** bay. **2** bellow, bawl, yell, wail, shriek, scream, caterwaul. **3** bawl, wail, cry.
➤*noun* bay, yowl, bellow, yell, wail, cry, shriek, scream, caterwauling.

howler *noun* mistake, error, blunder, gaffe, boob (*inf*), bloomer (*inf*), clanger (*inf*).

hub *noun* **1** pivot, axis. **2** centre, focus, focal point, core.

hubbub *noun* noise, din, racket, uproar, commotion, hullabaloo, rumpus, bedlam, pandemonium.

huddle *verb* **1** cluster, bunch, gather, crowd, throng, cram, pack, squeeze.

2 nestle, cuddle, snuggle, curl up, hunch up.
➤*noun* **1** crowd, gathering, knot, throng, cluster, bunch. **2** conclave, conference, discussion, confab (*inf*).

hue *noun* **1** colour, shade, tint, dye. **2** complexion, cast, aspect.

hue and cry *noun* furore, uproar, commotion, fuss, hullabaloo, outcry, to-do (*inf*).

huff *noun* **in a huff** in a temper, piqued, sulky, angry, miffed (*inf*).

hug *verb* **1** embrace, cuddle, clasp, enfold, squeeze, hold. **2** hold, cling to, keep close to.
➤*noun* embrace, cuddle, squeeze, clinch (*inf*).

huge *adj* enormous, massive, tremendous, prodigious, stupendous, vast, immense, colossal, giant, gigantic, mammoth, monumental, ginormous (*inf*).

hulk *noun* **1** wreck, shell, skeleton, hull. **2** oaf, lout, gorilla, lummox (*inf*).

hulking *adj* massive, bulky, heavy, weighty, overgrown, clumsy, lumbering.

hull *noun* **1** body, frame, casing, covering, shell. **2** husk, rind, shell, pod.
➤*verb* peel, husk, shell, shuck.

hullabaloo *noun* noise, furore, din, fuss, racket, uproar, hubbub, commotion, disturbance, rumpus (*inf*), to-do (*inf*).

hum *verb* **1** buzz, whirr, purr, drone, murmur. **2** sing, croon. **3** throb, bustle, buzz, stir.
➤*noun* whirr, buzz, purr, drone, murmur.

human *adj* **1** anthropoid, manlike, mortal. **2** fallible, mortal, flesh and blood, susceptible, erring, weak, frail. **3** kind, considerate, humane, sensitive, sympathetic, understanding, approachable.
➤*noun* human being, person, individual, mortal.

humane *adj* kind, kindhearted, kindly, benevolent, benign, compassionate, sympathetic, gentle, good, charitable, humanitarian.

humanitarian *adj* humane, benevolent, kind, good, compassionate, public-spirited, philanthropic, charitable.
➤*noun* philanthropist, benefactor, do-gooder (*inf*).

humanity *noun* **1** human race, man, mankind, humankind, people. **2** mortality, human nature, flesh and blood. **3** humaneness, kindness, benevolence, compassion, sympathy, fellow feeling, mercy, pity, goodness.

humanize *verb* civilize, educate, enlighten, refine, polish, soften, mellow.

humble *adj* **1** modest, simple, plain, poor, lowly, ordinary, unpretentious, undistinguished. **2** modest, meek, submissive, unassertive, unassuming, unpretentious, self-effacing. **3** deferential, respectful, polite, subservient, obsequious.
➤*verb* **1** humiliate, bring down, bring low, abase, demean, deflate, crush. **2** defeat, overwhelm, smash, rout, trounce.

humbug *noun* **1** trick, trickery, deception, deceit, hoax, fraud, pretence, sham. **2** hypocrite, plaster saint, cheat, fraud, phoney, sham, impostor. **3** nonsense, rubbish, bunkum (*inf*), balderdash (*inf*), bosh (*inf*), eyewash (*inf*), poppycock (*inf*).

humdrum *adj* monotonous, boring, tedious, dull, routine, repetitious, uninteresting, uneventful, dreary, commonplace, ordinary, run-of-the-mill.

humid *adj* damp, moist, wet, steamy, muggy, clammy, sticky, sultry, close.

humiliate *verb* mortify, chagrin, embarrass, abash, humble, deflate, shame, abase, demean, disgrace, discredit, put down (*inf*).

humility *noun* humbleness, modesty, self-effacement, diffidence, meekness, unassertiveness, unpretentiousness, deference.

hummock *noun* knoll, hillock, mound.

humorist *noun* comic, comedian, wit, wag, joker, card (*inf*).

humorous *adj* funny, amusing, entertaining, comic, comical, witty, waggish, jocular, facetious, hilarious, sidesplitting, rib-tickling.

humour *noun* **1** comedy, wit, drollery, fun. **2** wit, gags, jokes, joking, wisecracks (*inf*), badinage, repartee, farce, satire, facetiousness. **3** mood, temper, frame of mind, state of mind, disposition, temperament.
➤*verb* placate, mollify, gratify, satisfy, indulge, tolerate, pander to, flatter, please, accommodate, go along with.

hump *noun* **1** protuberance, bulge, swelling, lump, bump, outgrowth, projection, hunch. **2** prominence, mound, knoll.
➤*verb* **1** arch, hunch, curve, crook. **2** carry, lug, heave.
get the hump sulk, mope, be depressed, be annoyed.

hunch *noun* guess, intuition, feeling, notion, idea, premonition, suspicion.
➤*verb* **1** hump, arch, bend. **2** crouch, stoop, huddle.

hunger *noun* **1** hungriness, famine, starvation, emptiness, appetite. **2** longing, yearning, desire, need, craving, thirst, appetite, yen (*inf*).
➤*verb* long, yearn, wish, want, need, crave, thirst, yen (*inf*).

hungry *adj* **1** ravenous, peckish (*inf*), starving, famished. **2** longing, yearning, craving, pining, aching, thirsty, eager, avid.

hunk *noun* **1** chunk, lump, wedge, slab, piece. **2** he-man (*inf*), dreamboat (*inf*), beefcake (*inf*).

hunt *verb* **1** chase, pursue, stalk, trail, track. **2** seek, search, look, rummage, forage, ferret.
➤*noun* chase, pursuit, search, quest.

hurdle *noun* **1** barrier, barricade, fence, railing, hedge. **2** obstacle, obstruction, barrier, difficulty, problem.

hurl *verb* throw, sling, fling, heave, chuck (*inf*), catapult, let fly.

hurly-burly *noun* commotion, hubbub, uproar, upheaval, turmoil, tumult, confusion.

hurricane *noun* gale, storm, cyclone, typhoon.

hurry *verb* **1** rush, hasten, make haste, race, dash, run, fly, scurry, scamper, step on it (*inf*), get a move on (*inf*). **2** accelerate, quicken, speed up, hasten, expedite, drive, urge, hustle.
➤*noun* rush, haste, hustle, flurry, urgency.

hurt *verb* **1** ache, be sore, be painful, throb, smart, burn, sting. **2** harm, injure, damage, wound, cut, scratch, bruise, burn, disable, incapacitate. **3** pain, grieve, wound, distress, upset, offend. **4** damage, harm.
➤*noun* **1** wound, injury. **2** distress,

anguish, misery, grief, sorrow, sadness, suffering, pain. **3** harm, damage, injury.
➤*adj* **1** injured, wounded, harmed, cut, bruised, grazed, scarred, sore, painful. **2** upset, wounded, distressed, sad, aggrieved, offended, piqued, miffed (*inf*).

hurtful *adj* wounding, upsetting, distressing, mean, unkind, cruel, vicious, nasty, spiteful, catty, offensive.

hurtle *verb* rush, dash, tear, race, shoot, career, plunge, crash.

husband *noun* spouse, partner, consort, bridegroom, old man (*inf*), hubby (*inf*).
➤*verb* conserve, preserve, save, economize, eke out, ration.

husbandry *noun* **1** agriculture, farming, cultivation, land management. **2** frugality, thrift, economy, good housekeeping.

hush *verb* **1** silence, quieten, shush, still, soothe, calm, pacify. **2** shush, be quiet, shut up (*inf*), pipe down (*inf*).
➤*noun* quiet, silence, stillness, calm, peace.
hush up suppress, smother, gag, cover up, keep secret, sit on (*inf*).

hush-hush *adj* top secret, confidential, classified.

husk *noun* shell, hull, pod, capsule, shuck, chaff.

husky *adj* hoarse, gruff, gravelly, thick, throaty, deep.

husky *adj* burly, brawny, muscular, hefty, beefy (*inf*).

hustle *verb* **1** push, shove, thrust, jostle. **2** bustle, hurry, make haste, get a move on (*inf*). **3** force, badger, coerce, pressure.
➤*noun* bustle, hurly-burly, fuss, activity, rush, haste, hurry.

hut *noun* shed, cabin, lean-to, shanty, shack, booth.

hybrid *noun* **1** cross, crossbreed, mongrel. **2** mixture, compound, combination.

hygiene *noun* cleanliness, sanitation.

hygienic *adj* clean, sanitary, sterile, uncontaminated, pure, healthy, salubrious.

hymn *noun* song of praise, psalm, anthem, carol, spiritual, paean.

hype *noun* publicity, promotion, advertising, ballyhoo, razzmatazz (*inf*).

hyperbole *noun* exaggeration, overstatement, amplification.

hypercritical *adj* faultfinding, niggling, hairsplitting, captious, fussy, pedantic, nitpicking (*inf*).

hypnotic *adj* mesmeric, mesmerizing, fascinating, compelling, irresistible, spellbinding.

hypnotize *verb* **1** mesmerize, put under. **2** spellbind, bewitch, entrance, fascinate, captivate.

hypochondria *noun* neurosis, valetudinarianism.

hypochondriac *adj* neurotic, valetudinarian.

hypocrisy *noun* insincerity, double-talk, two-facedness, dishonesty, duplicity, deceit, dissembling, cant, sanctimoniousness.

hypocrite *noun* fraud, impostor, phoney, deceiver, dissembler, pharisee.

hypothesis *noun* **1** theory, thesis, proposition, premise. **2** assumption, supposition, presumption, conjecture.

hypothetical *adj* theoretical, imaginary, assumed, conjectural, speculative.

hysteria *noun* hysterics, frenzy, panic, agitation.

hysterical *adj* **1** mad, demented, frenzied, beside oneself, frantic, distraught, neurotic. **2** comical, hilarious, sidesplitting, priceless (*inf*).

ice *noun* **1** frost, rime, pack, floe, glacier. **2** frozen water, ice cube, rocks (*inf*). **3** ice cream, sorbet, water ice, ice lolly.
➤*verb* **1** freeze, freeze over, solidify. **2** frost, chill, refrigerate, cool. **3** glaze, frost, decorate.
on ice delayed, postponed, shelved, on the back burner (*inf*).

icon *noun* **1** symbol, image, figure, representation. **2** idol.

iconoclast *noun* radical, nonconformist, dissident, extremist, rebel.

icy *adj* **1** chilly, frosty, freezing, bitter, arctic, glacial. **2** frosted, frozen, glassy, slippery. **3** unfriendly, cold, frosty, frigid, hostile, unwelcoming.

idea *noun* **1** plan, scheme, suggestion, proposition. **2** belief, conviction, principle. **3** thought, concept, conception, notion, brain wave. **4** thought, opinion, view, theory, hypothesis. **5** impression, inkling, clue, hint, conjecture, approximation, guess, guesstimate (*inf*).

ideal *noun* **1** epitome, model, paragon, example, pattern, perfection. **2** standard, principle, benchmark.
➤*adj* **1** perfect, exemplary, model, classic, flawless, supreme. **2** unreal, imaginary, illusory, unattainable, utopian, impracticable, theoretical, visionary, idealistic.

idealism *noun* **1** perfectionism. **2** optimism, utopianism, impracticality, wishful thinking.

ideally *adv* **1** perfectly, absolutely, in every way. **2** by preference, by choice, if possible.

identical *adj* **1** same, selfsame, one and the same. **2** indistinguishable, interchangeable, similar, alike, duplicate, twin, matching.

identification *noun* **1** recognition, detection, diagnosis, spotting, pinpointing, naming, association, sympathy. **2** credentials, ID, identity card, documents.

identify *verb* **1** recognize, know, name, point out. **2** spot, pick out, make out, detect, put one's finger on (*inf*). **3** relate to, sympathize, empathize, feel for. **4** relate, associate, connect, equate.

identity *noun* **1** character, individuality, chcteristics, personality. **2** sameness, oneness, likeness, similarity, correspondence.

ideology *noun* beliefs, ideas, tenets, principles, creed, philosophy.

idiocy *noun* stupidity, senselessness, foolishness, imbecility, lunacy, craziness, insanity, absurdity.

idiom *noun* **1** language, jargon, phraseology, parlance, usage. **2** phrase, expression, locution, colloquialism.

idiosyncrasy *noun* peculiarity, characteristic, mannerism, trait, quirk, eccentricity.

idiot *noun* fool, imbecile, moron, cretin, dolt, blockhead, dimwit (*inf*), twerp (*inf*), wally (*inf*), dope (*inf*), twit (*inf*), clot (*inf*), chump (*inf*), pillock (*inf*), plonker (*inf*), prat (*sl*), dickhead (*sl*).

idle *adj* **1** inactive, inoperative, not working, out of action. **2** unemployed, jobless, unoccupied. **3** lazy, workshy, indolent, slothful, shiftless. **4** useless, vain, futile, ineffective, pointless, empty. **5** trivial, frivolous, superficial, casual.
➤*verb* **1** laze, lounge, potter, take it easy, drift, loaf, skive, shirk, bum around (*inf*). **2** tick over, run slowly.

idol *noun* **1** hero, heroine, star, icon, favourite, pinup (*inf*), blue-eyed boy (*inf*), golden girl (*inf*). **2** graven image, effigy, god.

idolatry *noun* **1** worship, adulation, adoration, glorification, hero-worship, doting. **2** paganism, heathenism, fetishism.

idolize *verb* worship, adore, hero-worship, look up to, revere, put on a pedestal.

if *conj* **1** provided, providing, on condition that. **2** assuming, supposing. **3** though, although. **4** in case, granting, admitting.

iffy *adj* **1** uncertain, unsure, doubtful, undecided, unpredictable, up in the air (*inf*). **2** dubious, chancy (*inf*), dodgy (*inf*).

ignite *verb* **1** light, set fire to, set on fire, set alight, catch fire, burn, burst into flames. **2** arouse, inflame, fire.

ignoble *adj* **1** low, base, worthless, abject, unworthy, contemptible, dishonourable, ignominious, shameful, disgraceful. **2** low, base, mean, humble, inferior.

ignominious *adj* **1** shameful, disgraceful, dishonourable, contemptible, ignoble, unworthy, base, mean, shabby. **2** degrading, humiliating, embarrassing, shameful, mortifying.

ignominy *noun* dishonour, disgrace, infamy, shame, humiliation, mortification.

ignoramus *noun* dunce, donkey, ass, blockhead, simpleton, duffer (*inf*), dimwit (*inf*), know-nothing (*inf*), lowbrow (*inf*), dummy (*inf*).

ignorant *adj* **1** unaware, unenlightened, uninformed, in the dark, uneducated, unschooled, untutored, illiterate, unintelligent, dumb (*inf*), thick (*inf*), inexperienced, green. **2** unaware, unconscious, unknowing, unwitting, blind. **3** ill-mannered, impolite, rude, crass.

ignore *verb* disregard, pay no attention to, take no notice of, shut one's eyes to, snub, cold-shoulder, send to Coventry (*inf*), skip, pass over, omit, overlook.

ill *adj* **1** sick, unwell, not very well, ailing, poorly, out of sorts, off-colour, laid up, in a bad way, infirm, unhealthy, indisposed, under the weather (*inf*). **2** adverse, unfavourable, unfortunate, unlucky, bad, harmful, detrimental, ominous, sinister, threatening. **3** unfriendly, unkind, hostile, acrimonious, resentful, rancorous, malevolent, malicious. **4** bad, disagreeable, adverse, distressing, uncomfortable.
➤*adv* **1** badly, unfavourably, adversely, unluckily, unfortunately, unsuccessfully. **2** badly, poorly, unkindly, spitefully. **3** barely, scarcely, hardly, with difficulty.
➤*noun* **1** harm, suffering, misfortune, sorrow, trouble, disaster, calamity. **2** illness, ailment, complaint, disorder, sickness, disease.

ill at ease uncomfortable, uneasy, nervous, embarrassed, self-conscious, anxious, edgy, fidgety, apprehensive.

ill-advised *adj* **1** unwise, imprudent, foolish, foolhardy, rash, reckless, thoughtless. **2** injudicious, misguided, ill-considered, ill-judged.

ill-assorted *adj* mismatched, incompatible, unsuited.

ill-bred *adj* ill-mannered, rude, impolite, boorish, churlish, uncouth, vulgar, unladylike, ungentlemanly.

ill-disposed *adj* unfriendly, hostile, opposed, averse, against, anti (*inf*), unsympathetic.

illegal *adj* unlawful, criminal, illicit, wrongful, prohibited, banned, forbidden, unauthorized, unconstitutional, contraband, bootleg, black-market, under-the-counter (*inf*).

illegible *adj* unreadable, indecipherable, unclear, scrawled, scribbly.

illegitimate *adj* **1** natural, love, born out of wedlock, bastard. **2** illegal, unlawful, illicit, unauthorized. **3** illogical, invalid, unsound, incorrect.

ill-fated *adj* ill-starred, star-crossed, doomed, unfortunate, unlucky, luckless.

ill-favoured *adj* unattractive, ugly, unsightly, plain, unprepossessing.

ill-humoured *adj* bad-tempered, cross, irritable, grumpy, moody, morose, sullen, surly, testy, cantankerous, crabby (*inf*), crotchety (*inf*).

illiberal *adj* **1** narrow-minded, intolerant, bigoted, prejudiced, hidebound, reactionary. **2** miserly, mean, stingy, close, near, tight (*inf*), tightfisted (*inf*).

illicit *adj* illegal, unlawful, criminal, unauthorized, forbidden, banned, improper, immoral, contraband, black-market, under-the-counter (*inf*), furtive, clandestine, secretive.

illimitable *adj* limitless, unlimited, inexhaustible, boundless, unbounded, infinite.

illiterate *adj* ignorant, uneducated, untutored, unlettered.

ill-mannered *adj* bad-mannered, rude, impolite, ill-bred, discourteous, uncivil, churlish, boorish.

ill-natured *adj* bad-tempered, nasty, mean, spiteful, vindictive, sullen, surly, disagreeable, unkind, malicious, vicious, malignant.

illness *noun* ailment, complaint, sickness, disease, disorder, condition, indisposition, malady.

illogical *adj* unreasonable, irrational, unsound, invalid, faulty, fallacious, unscientific, inconsistent, absurd, senseless.

ill-starred *adj* ill-fated, star-crossed, doomed, unlucky, luckless.

ill-tempered *adj* bad-tempered, cross, irascible, grumpy, irritable, tetchy, touchy.

ill-timed *adj* inopportune, inconvenient, untimely, inept, unwelcome, awkward.

ill-treat *verb* abuse, mistreat, maltreat, ill-use, harm, damage, injure, batter, knock about, wrong, persecute, oppress.

illuminate *verb* 1 light, light up, floodlight. 2 clarify, make clear, elucidate, explain, shed light on, illustrate. 3 decorate, ornament, embellish.

illumination *noun* 1 lighting, lights, floodlighting. 2 lighting, clarification, explanation, elucidation, decoration, ornamentation, embellishment.

illusion *noun* 1 misapprehension, false impression, misconception, delusion, fallacy, error, fancy. 2 hallucination, mirage, dream, fantasy, daydream, delusion, will o' the wisp, figment of the imagination.

illusory *adj* imaginary, unreal, fanciful, chimerical, deceptive, misleading, false.

illustrate *verb* 1 exemplify, clarify, demonstrate, explain, show. 2 decorate, embellish, ornament, illuminate.

illustration *noun* 1 example, instance, case, specimen, explanation. 2 explanation, clarification, elucidation, demonstration. 3 picture, plate, figure, drawing, photograph, diagram, sketch.

illustrative *adj* descriptive, explanatory, representative, graphic, pictorial.

illustrious *adj* famous, renowned, prominent, celebrated, distinguished, noted, eminent, great, noble, glorious.

ill will *noun* hostility, enmity, animosity, hatred, spite, malice, rancour, malevolence, acrimony, bitterness, bad blood.

image *noun* 1 idea, concept, notion, thought. 2 mental picture, impression, vision. 3 likeness, representation, icon, picture, photograph, portrait, statue. 4 reflection, replica, facsimile, duplicate. 5 double, twin, spitting image (*inf*), dead ringer (*inf*). 6 figure of speech, figurative expression, simile, metaphor.

imaginable *adj* conceivable, thinkable, possible, credible, likely.

imaginary *adj* unreal, fanciful, illusory, fictitious, fictional, made-up, make-believe, invented, mythical, chimerical, unsubstantial, nonexistent.

imagination *noun* 1 creativity, vision, insight, perception. 2 inventiveness, ingenuity, resourcefulness, enterprise, originality. 3 fancy, mind's eye.

imaginative *adj* 1 inventive, ingenious, resourceful, enterprising, clever. 2 creative, original. 3 visionary, dreamy, fanciful.

imagine *verb* 1 picture, visualize, envisage, conjure up, see in one's mind's eye, dream up, make believe, fancy, pretend, create, invent. 2 think, believe, suppose, assume, presume. 3 fancy, guess, surmise.

imbecile *noun* idiot, fool, lunatic, moron, cretin.
➤ *adj* idiotic, stupid, foolish, asinine, cretinous, moronic, barmy (*inf*).

imbibe *verb* 1 drink, swallow, tipple, swig (*inf*). 2 absorb, assimilate, take in, pick up.

imbroglio *noun* 1 entanglement, complication, dilemma, quandary, muddle. 2 difficulty, misunderstanding, confusion.

imbue *verb* fill, impregnate, infuse, pervade, permeate.

imitate *verb* 1 ape, copy, mimic, impersonate, parody, caricature, send up (*inf*), take off (*inf*). 2 copy, reproduce, replicate, duplicate, simulate, counterfeit. 3 copy, emulate, follow, follow in the footsteps of.

imitation *noun* 1 mimicry, impersonation, impression, takeoff (*inf*), copy, copying, replication, duplication, emulation. 2 copy, reproduction, replica, sham, simulation, forgery, fake, counterfeit.

▸*adj* simulated, artificial, synthetic, repro-duction, mock, fake, counterfeit.

imitative *adj* copycat (*inf*), unoriginal, secondhand.

immaculate *adj* **1** clean, spotless, spick-and-span, neat, pristine, squeaky-clean (*inf*). **2** pure, sinless, faultless, irreproach-able. **3** flawless, perfect. **4** spotless, unblemished, unpolluted, undefiled, unsullied.

immaterial *adj* irrelevant, insignificant, unimportant, trivial, trifling, minor.

immature *adj* unripe, undeveloped, green, young, unfinished. **2** inexperienced, callow, young, wet behind the ears (*inf*), puerile, childish, infantile.

immeasurable *adj* immense, vast, huge, limitless, boundless, unbounded, infinite, endless, never-ending, incalculable.

immediate *adj* **1** instant, instantaneous, prompt, swift. **2** present, current, latest, urgent, pressing. **3** direct, primary, first. **4** near, next, next-door, adjacent, neigh-bouring, adjoining. **5** nearest, closest, next.

immediately *adv* instantly, at once, now, right away, this minute, straightaway, forthwith.

immemorial *adj* very old, ancient, age-old, time-honoured.

immense *adj* huge, enormous, colossal, vast, gigantic, giant, massive, mammoth, tremendous, prodigious, stupendous, mega (*inf*).

immerse *verb* **1** dip, plunge, duck, dunk, submerge, sink. **2** engross, preoccupy, absorb.

immersion *noun* dipping, plunging, sub-mersion, absorption, preoccupation, involvement.

immigrant *noun* incomer, newcomer, settler.

imminent *adj* impending, forthcoming, coming, upcoming, at hand, near, close, threatening, looming, in the offing, just around the corner (*inf*).

immobile *adj* **1** immobilized, immovable, fixed, rooted. **2** motionless, stationary, still, static.

immobilize *verb* stop, halt, freeze, para-lyse, put out of action, cripple, disable.

immoderate *adj* extreme, excessive, inor-dinate, unreasonable, undue, uncalled-for, exorbitant, intemperate, unbridled, extravagant.

immodest *adj* **1** bold, brazen, shameless, forward, pushy, saucy (*inf*). **2** indecent, indecorous, improper, unchaste, lewd, bawdy.

immoral *adj* corrupt, debauched, disso-lute, profligate, licentious, lewd, obscene, indecent, wicked, bad, unprincipled, dis-honest, unethical.

immortal *adj* **1** deathless, undying, eter-nal. **2** imperishable, indestructible, eternal, everlasting, unfading, lasting, enduring. **3** unforgettable, memorable, famous. ▸*noun* **1** god, goddess, deity, Olympian. **2** great, genius, hero.

immortalize *verb* commemorate, eternal-ize, enshrine, perpetuate.

immovable *adj* **1** jammed, set, fixed, fast, secure, firm, stable, immobile. **2** resolute, determined, steadfast, staunch, inflexible, stubborn, unyielding, unshakeable.

immune *adj* exempt, free, not liable, unaffected.

immunity *noun* **1** protection, resistance, immunization, inoculation. **2** exemption, freedom, release, privilege, indemnity.

immunize *verb* inoculate, vaccinate, inject, jab (*inf*), protect.

immure *verb* imprison, confine, enclose, shut in, wall up.

immutable *adj* constant, invariable, unal-terable, unchangeable, unchanging, fixed, immovable.

imp *noun* **1** sprite, hobgoblin, demon, devil. **2** scamp, rascal, urchin, brat, minx, pickle (*inf*).

impact *noun* **1** collision, crash, smash, bump, shock. **2** impression, effect, influ-ence, burden, brunt, repercussions. ▸*verb* **1** hit, strike, collide, crash. **2** affect, influence, have an effect on.

impair *verb* damage, injure, harm, weaken, spoil, lessen, reduce, diminish.

impale *verb* skewer, spike, spit, transfix.

impalpable adj 1 intangible. 2 imperceptible, insubstantial, shadowy, airy.

impart verb 1 tell, communicate, make known, convey, pass on, reveal. 2 give, confer, bestow.

impartial adj unbiased, unprejudiced, neutral, fair, equitable, non-partisan, disinterested.

impassable adj blocked, closed, obstructed.

impasse noun deadlock, stalemate, stand-off, blind alley.

impassioned adj passionate, fervent, ardent, intense, vehement, zealous, excited, fiery, enthusiastic, animated.

impassive adj 1 emotionless, unemotional, unfeeling. 2 unmoved, inscrutable, poker-faced (inf), imperturbable, unruffled, composed, indifferent.

impatient adj 1 restless, fretful, uneasy, jumpy, anxious, excited, eager, agog, impetuous, reckless, hasty, straining at the leash (inf). 2 irritable, testy, edgy, irascible, short-tempered, snappy.

impeach verb 1 accuse, charge, indict, arraign. 2 call into question, question, impugn, challenge.

impeccable adj excellent, perfect, faultless, flawless, irreproachable.

impecunious adj poor, penniless, poverty-stricken, hard up (inf), broke (inf).

impede verb hinder, block, obstruct, clog, encumber, hamper, hold up, delay.

impediment noun 1 obstruction, hindrance, block, obstacle, bar, barrier, encumbrance. 2 handicap, defect, problem.

impedimenta pl noun equipment, gear, belongings, things, luggage, baggage, paraphernalia.

impel verb force, urge, drive, compel, incite, motivate, move, induce, persuade.

impending adj approaching, imminent, coming, forthcoming, looming, on the way.

impenetrable adj 1 thick, dense, impervious, impermeable, solid. 2 incomprehensible, unintelligible, unfathomable, baffling, inexplicable.

impenitent adj unrepentant, unabashed, defiant, incorrigible.

imperative adj 1 vital, urgent, essential, crucial, necessary. 2 commanding, authoritative, dictatorial, domineering.

imperceptible adj 1 indiscernible, impalpable, inaudible, invisible, indistinguishable. 2 microscopic, infinitesimal, tiny, minute, minuscule. 3 slight, small, gradual, fine, subtle.

imperfect adj faulty, defective, flawed, impaired, damaged, broken, chipped, incomplete, partial.

imperfection noun 1 fault, defect, flaw, blemish, weakness, failing, shortcoming, inadequacy, deficiency. 2 inadequacy, deficiency, frailty, infirmity.

imperial adj 1 sovereign, regal, royal, supreme. 2 majestic, kingly, queenly, grand, imposing, stately, lofty, noble, magnificent.

imperil verb endanger, jeopardize, risk, put at risk.

imperious adj overbearing, domineering, dictatorial, peremptory, high-handed, arrogant, haughty, lordly.

imperishable adj everlasting, enduring, lasting, undying, immortal.

impermanent adj temporary, transient, transitory, passing, short-lived.

impersonal adj 1 objective, dispassionate, detached, neutral. 2 cold, cool, aloof, distant, clinical.

impersonate verb mimic, imitate, do an impression of, pose as, masquerade as.

impertinent adj 1 impudent, insolent, rude, impolite, disrespectful, pert, saucy (inf), cheeky (inf). 2 irrelevant, inapplicable.

imperturbable adj calm, composed, collected, self-possessed, unflappable, unruffled.

impervious adj 1 immune, invulnerable, unreceptive, insensitive, thick-skinned. 2 impermeable, impenetrable, proof against, waterproof.

impetuous adj 1 hasty, precipitate, rash, reckless, impulsive, spontaneous, unplanned, unpremeditated. 2 rash, reckless, impulsive, passionate, eager.

impetus noun **1** force, energy, momentum, power, drive. **2** incentive, motivation, spur, stimulus, impulse.

impiety noun irreverence, ungodliness, profanity, blasphemy, sacrilege.

impinge verb **1** encroach on, infringe, trespass, intrude on, invade, usurp. **2** affect, influence, touch.

impious adj irreverent, ungodly, irreligious, profane, blasphemous, sacrilegious.

impish adj mischievous, naughty, roguish, puckish, waggish.

implacable adj **1** unyielding, uncompromising, unrelenting, pitiless, merciless, harsh, unforgiving. **2** inexorable, relentless, unrelenting.

implant verb **1** instil, inculcate, introduce, imbue. **2** graft, insert, transplant. **3** plant, embed, fix, root.
➤ noun insert, insertion, graft, transplant.

implausible adj improbable, unlikely, unconvincing, doubtful, farfetched, incredible.

implement noun tool, utensil, instrument, device, gadget.
➤ verb execute, carry out, perform, do, put into effect.

implicate verb incriminate, involve, embroil, entangle, associate.

implication noun **1** suggestion, insinuation, innuendo, inference. **2** meaning, significance, connotation, consequence, repercussion. **2** incrimination, entanglement, involvement, association.

implicit adj **1** implied, suggested, tacit, understood, unspoken. **2** latent, inherent. **3** absolute, total, unconditional, unqualified, unquestioning.

implore verb beg, beseech, entreat, supplicate, plead.

imply verb **1** suggest, insinuate, intimate, hint, give to understand, connote, signify, mean. **2** import, involve, entail.

impolite adj rude, bad-mannered, uncivil, discourteous, impudent, impertinent, cheeky (inf), disrespectful, churlish, boorish.

impolitic adj unwise, ill-advised, injudicious, imprudent.

import verb **1** bring in, introduce from abroad. **2** mean, signify, denote, betoken.
➤ noun **1** foreign produce, foreign commodity. **2** significance, importance, consequence, moment. **3** significance, meaning, purport.

important adj **1** significant, momentous, far-reaching, weighty, critical, crucial, urgent, serious, essential, valuable. **2** influential, powerful, prominent, eminent, leading, principal, main, chief, major.

importunate adj **1** persistent, demanding, troublesome, annoying. **2** persistent, pressing, urgent, clamorous.

importune verb harass, badger, pester, plague, dun, press, urge, entreat, beg.

impose verb **1** inflict, force, foist. **2** lay, place, set, levy, exact, charge.
impose on/upon 1 intrude on, foist on, take advantage of. **2** inconvenience, bother, put out, exploit.

imposing adj impressive, grand, majestic, stately, striking.

imposition noun **1** charge, tax, levy. **2** enforcement, infliction, institution, levying, exaction. **3** burden, trouble, intrusion, liberty.

impossible adj **1** impracticable, unattainable, unachievable, unthinkable, inconceivable, absurd, ludicrous, unreasonable, unacceptable, out of the question. **2** unbearable, intolerable, insufferable, difficult, unmanageable.

impostor noun fraud, fake, deceiver, dissembler, charlatan, quack, phoney, con-man (inf).

imposture noun deception, fraud, pretence, cheat, swindle, con (inf).

impotent adj powerless, helpless, weak, feeble, disabled, incapacitated, crippled, paralysed, incapable, ineffective.

impound verb **1** seize, confiscate, appropriate, distrain. **2** confine, shut up, pen, cage.

impoverish verb **1** beggar, ruin, bankrupt. **2** exhaust, wear out, deplete, drain, use up.

impracticable adj impossible, unworkable, unfeasible, unachievable.

impractical *adj* **1** impossible, unworkable, unrealistic, impracticable. **2** unrealistic, idealistic, airy-fairy (*inf*), romantic, starry-eyed.

imprecation *noun* curse, malediction, execration.

imprecise *adj* inexact, inaccurate, ill-defined, vague, hazy, approximate, rough, loose, woolly.

impregnable *adj* **1** strong, secure, unassailable, invulnerable, indestructible. **2** irrefutable, incontestable, incontrovertible.

impregnate *verb* **1** permeate, saturate, imbue, soak, steep, fill. **2** fertilize, make pregnant, inseminate.

impresario *noun* manager, producer, director, promoter.

impress *verb* **1** influence, move, affect, touch, stir, strike, grab (*inf*). **2** imprint, stamp, mark, print. **3** stress, emphasize, instil, inculcate.

impression *noun* **1** effect, influence, impact. **2** mark, stamp, imprint, indentation, impress. **3** feeling, sensation, sense, notion, recollection, suspicion, inkling, hunch, funny feeling. **4** view, opinion, idea, thought. **5** impersonation, imitation, takeoff (*inf*), send-up (*inf*). **6** edition, issue, printing, print run.

impressionable *adj* susceptible, receptive, open, suggestible.

impressive *adj* imposing, striking, awe-inspiring, powerful, dramatic, majestic.

imprint *noun* mark, impression, print, indentation.
▸*verb* impress, stamp, engrave, etch.

imprison *verb* jail, gaol, incarcerate, confine, lock up, detain, put behind bars, send down (*inf*), put away (*inf*), bang up (*inf*).

improbable *adj* unlikely, doubtful, dubious, questionable, unconvincing, implausible, farfetched, incredible.

impromptu *adj* extempore, extemporaneous, improvised, unrehearsed, spontaneous, off the cuff, ad-lib, spur-of-the-moment.

improper *adj* **1** unseemly, indecorous, unbecoming, indecent, rude, vulgar, risqué, obscene. **2** illegal, dishonest, unlawful, wrong, irregular, abnormal, incorrect. **3** unsuitable, inappropriate, uncalled-for, unwarranted.

impropriety *noun* unseemliness, indecency, immodesty, improper conduct, vulgarity, bad taste.

improve *verb* **1** better, ameliorate, amend, mend, reform, rectify, put right, enhance, touch up, polish, brush up, recover, rally, pick up, recuperate. **2** advance, rise, progress, increase, augment.

improvement *noun* **1** betterment, amelioration, amendment, change, correction, rectification, restoration, development, enhancement, progress. **2** increase, rise, rally, recovery.

improvident *adj* wasteful, extravagant, prodigal, unthrifty, spendthrift, imprudent, incautious, careless, reckless.

improvise *verb* **1** ad-lib, extemporize, play by ear (*inf*), wing it (*inf*), vamp (*inf*). **2** invent, devise, concoct, throw together.

imprudent *adj* unwise, injudicious, incautious, rash, hasty, careless, thoughtless, irresponsible, indiscreet, impolitic, ill-advised.

impudence *noun* rudeness, impertinence, insolence, effrontery, audacity, cheek (*inf*), sauce (*inf*), lip (*inf*).

impudent *adj* rude, disrespectful, impertinent, insolent, audacious, cocky, forward, cheeky (*inf*), saucy (*inf*).

impugn *verb* dispute, challenge, question, call into question, cast aspersions on.

impulse *noun* **1** urge, desire, drive, wish, whim, caprice. **2** impetus, thrust, boost, surge. **3** spur, stimulus, incentive, motive.

impulsive *adj* impetuous, rash, hasty, precipitate, ill-considered, spontaneous, unplanned, unpremeditated.

impunity *noun* exemption, immunity, licence.

impure *adj* **1** contaminated, polluted, infected, tainted, defiled, soiled, unclean, dirty, filthy, foul. **2** immoral, indecent, wanton, unchaste, immodest, depraved, corrupt, dissolute, sensual, carnal. **3** adulterated, mixed, alloyed, blended.

impurity *noun* **1** contamination, pollution, infection, adulteration, immorality, immodesty, indecency. **2** contaminant, pollutant, adulterant, dirt, grime, filth, foreign body.

impute *verb* ascribe, attribute, accredit, accuse, put down.

in *prep* **1** within, inside, among. **2** during, while.
➤ *adj* fashionable, popular, trendy (*inf*), all the rage (*inf*).

inability *noun* incapacity, incapability, impotence, powerlessness.

inaccessible *adj* remote, out of the way, unreachable, out of reach, ungetatable (*inf*).

inaccurate *adj* incorrect, wrong, mistaken, inexact, imprecise, out, wide of the mark, off beam (*inf*).

inactive *adj* **1** inert, immobile, idle, inoperative, unoccupied, unemployed, out of service. **2** indolent, slothful, lazy, lethargic, sluggish, sedentary.

inadequate *adj* **1** insufficient, deficient, scanty, meagre, skimpy, sparse, short, incomplete. **2** incompetent, incapable, inept, found wanting, not up to scratch (*inf*).

inadmissible *adj* immaterial, irrelevant, invalid, unacceptable.

inadvertent *adj* chance, accidental, unintentional, involuntary, unwitting.

inadvisable *adj* unwise, ill-advised, imprudent, injudicious, impolitic, inexpedient.

inalienable *adj* absolute, sacrosanct, inviolable, unassailable, nonnegotiable, nontransferable.

inane *adj* foolish, stupid, silly, fatuous, senseless, idiotic, puerile, mindless, frivolous, empty, vacuous.

inanimate *adj* **1** lifeless, dead, inert, inorganic, mineral. **2** inert, inactive, immobile, lethargic, sluggish.

inapplicable *adj* irrelevant, inapposite, immaterial, inappropriate, unsuitable, inapt, unfit, unrelated.

inapposite *adj* inappropriate, unsuitable, out of place, inapplicable, irrelevant.

inappropriate *adj* unsuitable, inapt, unfit, ill-suited, out of place, out of keeping, incongruous, unseemly, indecorous, tasteless, unbecoming.

inapt *adj* **1** inappropriate, unsuitable, unfit. **2** inept, incompetent, incapable.

inarticulate *adj* **1** incoherent, unclear, unintelligible, incomprehensible. **2** unspoken, unutterable, silent, unexpressed. **3** speechless, dumb, tongue-tied (*inf*), faltering, hesitant, stammering, stumbling, stuttering.

inattention *noun* inattentiveness, absent-mindedness, daydreaming, woolgathering, negligence, carelessness, disregard.

inaudible *adj* imperceptible, silent, quiet, low, faint, indistinct.

inaugurate *verb* **1** commence, begin, start, initiate, introduce, launch. **2** induct, invest, install. **3** open, dedicate, commission.

inauspicious *adj* unpromising, discouraging, unpropitious, ill-starred, ominous, unfavourable, bad, unlucky, unfortunate.

inborn *adj* **1** innate, congenital, inherited, hereditary. **2** innate, inherent, natural, native, in one's blood.

inbred *adj* innate, natural, inherent, inborn.

incalculable *adj* **1** countless, innumerable, numberless, untold, vast, enormous, boundless, infinite. **2** inestimable, incomputable.

incandescent *adj* glowing, white-hot, gleaming, bright, brilliant, shining.

incantation *noun* chant, charm, mantra, invocation, spell, abracadabra.

incapable *adj* unable, powerless, impotent, helpless, weak, inadequate, unequal, incompetent, ineffective, not up to it (*inf*).

incapacitate *verb* immobilize, paralyse, cripple, disable, put out of action.

incapacity *noun* inability, incapability, unfitness, powerlessness, impotence, inadequacy, incompetence, ineffectiveness.

incarcerate *verb* imprison, jail, gaol, confine, detain, lock up, put behind bars.

incarnate *adj* **1** embodied, in human form, made flesh. **2** in the flesh, personified, typified.

incarnation *noun* **1** embodiment, archetype, personification. **2** avatar.

incautious *adj* imprudent, unwise, ill-judged, injudicious, impolitic, unwary, ill-considered, careless, thoughtless, impulsive, indiscreet.

incendiary *adj* **1** inflammatory, seditious, subversive, rabble-rousing. **2** combustible, flammable, fire-raising.

incense[1] *noun* perfume, fragrance, scent.

incense[2] *verb* enrage, infuriate, anger, exasperate, provoke, make one see red (*inf*), make one's blood boil (*inf*).

incentive *noun* encouragement, inducement, lure, stimulus, spur, motivation, carrot (*inf*), sweetener (*inf*).

inception *noun* beginning, start, inauguration, outset, birth.

incessant *adj* ceaseless, continual, continuous, unremitting, nonstop, perpetual, constant, persistent, relentless, never-ending.

inchoate *adj* incipient, initial, elementary, embryonic, undeveloped.

incidence *noun* frequency, prevalence, rate, occurrence.

incident *noun* **1** occurrence, event, happening, occasion, episode. **2** encounter, confrontation, clash. disturbance, commotion, fight, contretemps, fracas.

incidental *adj* **1** chance, accidental, unplanned, fortuitous. **2** minor, unimportant, subsidiary, secondary, concomitant, related, attendant.

incidentally *adv* **1** by the way, by the bye, in passing. **2** by chance, coincidentally, unexpectedly, accidentally, by accident.

incinerate *verb* burn, cremate, reduce to ashes.

incipient *adj* inchoate, initial, nascent, developing, embryonic.

incise *verb* **1** cut, cut into, slit, gash. **2** etch, engrave, inscribe, carve.

incision *noun* cut, gash, slit, opening.

incisive *adj* **1** sharp, keen, acute, penetrating. **2** cutting, trenchant, mordant, biting.

incite *verb* **1** rouse, stir up, inflame, excite, whip up, egg on, put up to, spur, drive. **2** stimulate, instigate, provoke, foment.

incivility *noun* impoliteness, rudeness, bad manners, discourtesy, disrespect, ill-breeding.

inclement *adj* stormy, blustery, windy, rainy, squally, foul, bad, rough, severe.

inclination *noun* **1** tendency, leaning, bent, proclivity, propensity, disposition, penchant, partiality, predilection, liking, fondness. **2** slope, slant, tilt, incline.

incline *verb* **1** predispose, sway, persuade, influence, bias, prejudice. **2** slope, slant, lean, tilt. **3** bend, bow, nod.
➤*noun* slope, slant, gradient, rise, ascent.
inclined to prone to, liable to, apt to, disposed to, likely to, given to.

include *verb* **1** contain, comprise, embrace, encompass, incorporate, cover, involve. **2** add, insert, enter, introduce, incorporate.

including *prep* as well as, with, together with, counting.

inclusion *noun* addition, insertion, incorporation.

inclusive *adj* comprehensive, all-embracing, global, overall, blanket, general, across-the-board.

incognito *adv and adj* disguised, in disguise, undercover, under an assumed name.

incoherent *adj* **1** unclear, unintelligible, confused, disjointed, disconnected, uncoordinated, disordered. **2** inconsistent, illogical, muddled, jumbled.

incombustible *adj* fireproof, flameproof, nonflammable, fire-resistant, flame-retardant.

income *noun* salary, pay, wages, earnings, remuneration, revenue, receipts, proceeds, yield, return, profits.

incoming *adj* **1** coming, arriving, entering, approaching, returning. **2** succeeding, new.

incommensurate *adj* unequal, disproportionate, insufficient, inadequate.

incommode *verb* hinder, inconvenience, put out, bother, disturb, trouble.

incommodious *adj* inconvenient, awkward, cramped.

incomparable *adj* matchless, peerless, unmatched, unequalled, unrivalled, unique, inimitable.

incompatible *adj* **1** antipathetic, at odds, unsuited, mismatched, like chalk and cheese. **2** irreconcilable, conflicting, clashing, contrary, contradictory.

incompetent *adj* inexpert, unskilful, inept, bungling, botched, clumsy, incapable, unfit, inadequate, inefficient, useless, ineffectual.

incomplete *adj* unfinished, partial, short, defective, fragmentary, abridged, shortened.

incomprehensible *adj* unintelligible, unfathomable, impenetrable, obscure, mysterious, inexplicable, over one's head, baffling, puzzling, perplexing.

inconceivable *adj* unthinkable, unimaginable, incomprehensible, impossible, incredible, unheard-of, preposterous, out of the question, absurd.

inconclusive *adj* undecided, unsettled, uncertain, open, open to question, up in the air (*inf*).

incongruous *adj* out of place, out of keeping, inappropriate, at odds, inconsistent, incompatible, discordant, absurd.

inconsequential *adj* **1** insignificant, unimportant, trifling, petty, minor, piddling (*inf*). **2** immaterial, irrelevant.

inconsiderable *adj* **1** small, slight, minor, negligible. **2** insignificant, inconsequential, unimportant, trifling.

inconsiderate *adj* thoughtless, unkind, uncaring, tactless, insensitive, ungracious, rude, selfish.

inconsistent *adj* **1** self-contradictory, paradoxical, irreconcilable, incompatible, incongruous. **2** irregular, changeable, unpredictable, variable, erratic, fickle, capricious.

inconsolable *adj* brokenhearted, heartbroken, disconsolate, forlorn, miserable, desolate, despairing, wretched.

inconspicuous *adj* unobtrusive, ordinary, unremarkable, unostentatious, modest, muted, low-key.

inconstant *adj* changeable, variable, vacillating, fluctuating, wavering, uncertain,

unsteady, unstable, volatile, fickle, capricious, wayward, unreliable.

incontestable *adj* indisputable, incontrovertible, unquestionable, indubitable, undeniable, irrefutable, unassailable.

incontinent *adj* unrestrained, unbridled, ungovernable, uncontrollable, dissolute, lustful, promiscuous.

incontrovertible *adj* indisputable, incontestable, undeniable, irrefutable, unquestionable, indubitable, certain.

inconvenience *noun* **1** trouble, bother, difficulty, hassle (*inf*). **2** nuisance, bore, bind, pain (*inf*), drag (*inf*).
➤*verb* bother, trouble, upset, annoy, worry, disturb, put out.

incorporate *verb* **1** include, absorb, subsume, take in, comprise. **2** integrate, merge, blend, mix, combine, unite, assimilate.

incorporeal *adj* disembodied, immaterial, insubstantial.

incorrect *adj* **1** wrong, erroneous, false, untrue, inaccurate, out, mistaken, wide of the mark (*inf*). **2** improper, unseemly, inappropriate, unsuitable.

incorrigible *adj* **1** hardened, inveterate, obdurate. **2** incurable, irremediable, beyond redemption, hopeless.

incorruptible *adj* **1** honest, upright, honourable, straight, straight as a die (*inf*), above suspicion. **2** imperishable, immortal, deathless.

increase *verb* grow, enlarge, expand, swell, extend, lengthen, add to, escalate, heighten, rise, spiral, climb, rocket, soar, build up, develop, spread, mushroom, snowball, intensify, multiply, boost, improve, bump up.
➤*noun* growth, rise, enlargement, expansion, extension, development, addition, gain, increment, intensification, boost, upsurge.

incredible *adj* **1** unbelievable, inconceivable, improbable, unlikely, impossible, implausible. **2** extraordinary, marvellous, wonderful, amazing, fantastic, fabulous, awesome (*inf*), great (*inf*), terrific (*inf*).

incredulous *adj* disbelieving, sceptical, distrustful, doubtful, dubious, unconvinced.

increment *noun* increase, addition, rise, step-up (*inf*).

incriminate *verb* blame, implicate, point the finger at (*inf*), inculpate, accuse.

inculcate *verb* instil, teach, drum, din, drill.

incumbent *adj* binding, obligatory, compulsory.
➤ *noun* office-holder, office-bearer.

incur *verb* bring, bring upon oneself, sustain, suffer, lay oneself open to.

incurable *adj* fatal, terminal, inoperable, untreatable, incorrigible, inveterate, hardened, dyed-in-the-wool.

incursion *noun* attack, raid, invasion, onslaught.

indebted *adj* obliged, beholden, grateful, thankful.

indecent *adj* **1** offensive, obscene, crude, vulgar, filthy, coarse, smutty, lewd, pornographic, blue (*inf*). **2** improper, unseemly, tasteless, inappropriate, unsuitable.

indecipherable *adj* illegible, unreadable, unintelligible, crabbed.

indecision *noun* indecisiveness, irresolution, hesitancy, shilly-shallying (*inf*), vacillation, wavering, dithering, uncertainty.

indecisive *adj* **1** irresolute, hesitant, wavering, vacillating, undecided, dithering, uncertain, doubtful. **2** inconclusive, undecided, unsettled, open.

indecorum *adj* impropriety, unseemliness, immodesty, ill-breeding, incivility, bad manners, rudeness.

indeed *adv* **1** really, truly, surely, without doubt, undoubtedly, undeniably, certainly. **2** in fact, in point of fact

indefatigable *adj* tireless, untiring, inexhaustible, unflagging, unfailing, indomitable, dogged, persistent, persevering.

indefensible *adj* inexcusable, unjustifiable, unwarrantable, unpardonable, unforgivable.

indefinable *adj* indescribable, inexpressible, vague, hazy.

indefinite *adj* **1** unspecified, undefined, unlimited, indeterminate. **2** unclear, vague, loose, general, inexact, imprecise, ambiguous, unsettled.

indelible *adj* permanent, unfading, lasting, ingrained, ineradicable.

indelicate *adj* **1** indecent, embarrassing, coarse, crude, suggestive, risqué. **2** tasteless, untoward, insensitive, undiplomatic, tactless.

indemnify *verb* **1** secure, guarantee, insure. **2** compensate, reimburse, recompense, repay.

indemnity *noun* **1** insurance, protection, security, guarantee, safeguard. **2** compensation, reimbursement, reparation, repayment. **3** exemption, immunity, impunity, amnesty.

indent *verb* **1** ask for, order, requisition. **2** cut, nick, notch, serrate. **3** move away from the margin, move right.

indentation *noun* notch, nick, serration, dent, hollow, dimple, depression.

indenture *noun* agreement, contract, compact, certificate, deed, bond.

independent *adj* **1** autonomous, free, sovereign, self-governing. **2** free, self-reliant, self-sufficient, self-supporting, self-confident, unaided. **3** separate, unconnected, self-contained, unattached, freestanding.

indescribable *adj* inexpressible, indefinable, unutterable.

indestructible *adj* durable, unbreakable, shatterproof, tough, resistant, permanent, lasting, enduring, everlasting.

indeterminate *adj* indefinite, unknown, ill-defined, uncertain, unspecified, unsettled, vague, unclear, ambiguous, ambivalent, equivocal.

index *noun* **1** key, guide, list, catalogue, directory. **2** guide, indication, sign, token. **3** pointer, needle, hand.
➤ *verb* sort, tabulate, alphabetize, catalogue.

indicate *verb* **1** show, mark, signify, mean, suggest, imply, represent, be symptomatic of. **2** state, declare, make known, announce. **3** designate, point out, point to.

indicative *adj* characteristic, symptomatic, suggestive.

indicator *noun* **1** gauge, meter, display. **2** marker, pointer, needle, hand.

indict *verb* charge, accuse, arraign, prosecute, summons.

indictment *noun* charge, accusation, arraignment, summons.

indifferent *adj* 1 unconcerned, uninterested, uncaring, cool, cold, aloof, distant, detached, impassive, unmoved. 2 mediocre, passable, middling, so-so (*inf*), undistinguished, no great shakes (*inf*).

indigenous *adj* native, original, home-grown.

indigent *adj* poor, needy, destitute, penniless, poverty-stricken, impoverished, impecunious, penurious, without two pennies to rub together (*inf*).

indigestion *noun* dyspepsia, heartburn, upset stomach, acidity, wind.

indignant *adj* angry, irate, incensed, wrathful, furious, livid, annoyed, disgruntled, hot under the collar (*inf*), pissed off (*sl*), peeved (*inf*).

indignation *noun* anger, ire, wrath, rage, fury, exasperation, annoyance.

indignity *noun* 1 humiliation, embarrassment, insult, affront, slight, snub, slap in the face (*inf*). 2 abuse, mistreatment, humiliation.

indirect *adj* 1 roundabout, circuitous, meandering, winding. 2 roundabout, circuitous, oblique, circumlocutory. 3 secondary, ancillary, subsidiary, subordinate, incidental. 4 underhand, backhanded, devious, deceitful, evasive.

indiscernible *adj* 1 imperceptible, indistinguishable, undetectable, hidden, invisible, subtle, slight. 2 indistinguishable, indistinct, indefinite, shadowy.

indiscreet *adj* unwise, injudicious, imprudent, ill-judged, incautious, ill-considered, foolish, unthinking, tactless, undiplomatic, unseemly, indelicate.

indiscretion *noun* folly, imprudence, carelessness, tactlessness, unseemliness, indelicacy, faux pas, breach of etiquette, impropriety, misdemeanour, lapse, mistake.

indiscriminate *adj* 1 broad, wide, wholesale, general, sweeping, unselective, random, hit-or-miss. 2 aimless, careless, undiscriminating, unsystematic, unmethodical.

indispensable *adj* essential, vital, key, crucial, fundamental, basic, necessary.

indisposed *adj* 1 unwell, ill, sick, ailing, poorly, under the weather (*inf*), out of sorts (*inf*). 2 disinclined, reluctant, loath, averse.

indisputable *adj* undeniable, beyond doubt, incontestable, certain, sure, positive.

indissoluble *adj* permanent, indestructible, indivisible, unbreakable, lasting, enduring, binding.

indistinct *adj* 1 dim, faint, hazy, misty, foggy, vague, blurred, out of focus. 2 vague, indefinite, ill-defined, obscure, uncertain, unclear, ambiguous.

indistinguishable *adj* identical, twin, same, alike, like as two peas in a pod (*inf*).

individual *adj* 1 separate, distinct, discrete, lone. 2 specific, respective, particular, peculiar, characteristic, distinctive, personal, own. 3 idiosyncratic, singular, unique, special.
➤ *noun* person, party, soul, head, unit.

individualism *noun* independence, free-thinking, nonconformity, egoism.

individuality *noun* uniqueness, originality, particularity, peculiarity, distinctiveness.

indoctrinate *verb* brainwash, drill, imbue, inculcate, instil, school.

indolent *adj* idle, lazy, slothful, shiftless, workshy, lethargic.

indomitable *adj* invincible, unconquerable, indefatigable, staunch, steadfast, resolute, determined, courageous.

indubitable *adj* unquestionable, beyond doubt, undoubted, indisputable, undeniable, evident, obvious, certain.

induce *verb* 1 persuade, influence, move, prevail upon, impel, prompt, spur. 2 cause, bring about, produce, lead to, generate, set in motion.

inducement *noun* 1 incentive, enticement, bait, motive, stimulus, spur, persuasion, carrot (*inf*). 2 bribe, sweetener (*inf*), backhander (*inf*).

induct *verb* 1 inaugurate, install, swear in, invest. 2 initiate, introduce.

induction *noun* **1** inauguration, investiture, swearing in, installation. **2** reasoning, inference, generalization.

indulge *verb* **1** pamper, cosset, spoil, gratify, humour. **2** gratify, satisfy, give way to. **3** treat oneself, splash out, go to town, splurge (*inf*).

indulgence *noun* **1** gratification, satisfaction, fulfilment, spoiling, mollycoddling, pampering, humouring, dissoluteness, excess. **2** luxury, treat, extravagance. **3** kindness, leniency, tolerance, forbearance.

indulgent *adj* lenient, permissive, tolerant, liberal, forgiving, forbearing, understanding, easygoing, soft.

industrial *adj* business, commercial, trade, manufacturing.

industrialist *noun* manufacturer, producer, captain of industry, magnate, tycoon.

industrious *adj* hardworking, diligent, assiduous, busy, active, energetic, persevering, conscientious, zealous.

industry *noun* **1** business, commerce, trade, manufacture, production. **2** diligence, assiduity, work, effort, energy, zeal, application, conscientiousness, perseverance.

inebriated *adj* drunk, intoxicated, the worse for drink, under the influence (*inf*), tight (*inf*), plastered (*inf*), well-oiled (*inf*), blotto (*inf*).

inedible *adj* unfit to eat, uneatable, unpalatable, bad, off.

ineffable *adj* indescribable, inexpressible, beyond words, indefinable.

ineffective *adj* **1** ineffectual, unavailing, useless, vain, futile, unsuccessful, abortive, fruitless. **2** ineffectual, inept, incompetent, inefficient, impotent, powerless.

ineffectual *adj* **1** ineffective, unavailing, useless, futile, fruitless, vain, abortive. **2** inept, impotent, powerless, weak, feeble, inadequate, inefficient, incompetent.

inefficient *adj* incompetent, inept, inexpert, disorganized, negligent, lax, uneconomical, wasteful, time-wasting.

inelegant *adj* unrefined, unattractive, graceless, uncouth, ungainly, gauche, clumsy, awkward, crude, vulgar.

ineligible *adj* unqualified, disqualified, ruled out, incompetent.

inept *adj* incompetent, inefficient, unskilful, inexpert, bungling, bumbling, clumsy, cack-handed (*inf*), ham-fisted (*inf*).

inequality *noun* disparity, imbalance, disproportion, difference, imparity, prejudice, discrimination, unfairness, injustice.

inequitable *adj* unfair, unjust, biased, one-sided, discriminatory.

inequity *noun* unfairness, injustice, partiality, discrimination.

inert *adj* **1** immobile, motionless, static, inanimate. **2** inactive, lifeless, unresponsive, leaden, idle, lazy, sluggish.

inertia *noun* immobility, inactivity, lifelessness, unresponsiveness, passivity, stagnation, idleness, indolence, laziness, sloth, sluggishness.

inescapable *adj* unavoidable, inevitable, inexorable, unpreventable.

inessential *adj* unnecessary, superfluous, surplus, redundant, extraneous, unimportant, dispensable.
➤*noun* nonessential, extra, luxury, extravagance.

inestimable *adj* **1** incalculable, immeasurable, infinite. **2** invaluable, priceless.

inevitable *adj* unavoidable, inescapable, ineluctable, fated, certain, destined, unalterable, inexorable.

inexact *adj* inaccurate, incorrect, wrong, imprecise, approximate.

inexcusable *adj* indefensible, unjustifiable, unpardonable, unforgivable.

inexhaustible *adj* **1** unlimited, limitless, boundless, infinite, endless, abundant. **2** tireless, unwearied, untiring, indefatigable, unflagging, unfailing.

inexorable *adj* **1** relentless, unrelenting, unavoidable, inevitable, inescapable, certain, sure. **2** adamant, obdurate, inflexible, unyielding, immovable, intransigent, implacable.

inexpensive *adj* cheap, low-priced, economical, low-cost, reasonable, modest, budget, bargain.

inexperience *noun* ignorance, unfamiliarity, greenness, rawness, naivety, innocence.

inexpert *adj* unskilled, amateur, blundering, bungling, cack-handed (*inf*).

inexplicable *adj* unexplainable, unaccountable, insoluble, unfathomable, incomprehensible, mysterious, puzzling, bewildering, baffling.

inexpressible *adj* indescribable, unutterable, ineffable.

inexpressive *adj* expressionless, blank, empty, vacant, deadpan, poker-faced, inscrutable.

inextinguishable *adj* unquenchable, ever-burning, indestructible, undying, eternal.

inextricable *adj* inseparable, indivisible, indistinguishable, tangled, complicated, knotty, involved, intricate, convoluted.

infallible *adj* **1** faultless, unerring, impeccable, perfect. **2** unfailing, sure, certain, foolproof.

infamous *adj* **1** notorious, disreputable, nefarious. **2** shameful, disgraceful, shocking, scandalous, outrageous, heinous, monstrous.

infamy *noun* notoriety, ignominy, shame, disgrace, dishonour, wickedness.

infancy *noun* **1** babyhood, early childhood. **2** beginning, start, dawn, early stages, inception.

infant *noun* baby, babe, babe in arms, bairn, toddler, tot, child.

infantile *adj* babyish, childish, puerile, juvenile.

infantry *noun* infantrymen, foot soldiers, foot.

infatuate *verb* enamour, enrapture, captivate, fascinate, bewitch, obsess, possess.

infect *verb* **1** contaminate, pollute, poison. **2** pass on, spread to. **3** taint, mar, blight, corrupt, defile, vitiate.

infection *noun* **1** disease, illness, contagion, germ, bug (*inf*), virus. **2** contamination, pollution, defilement, tainting, fouling, poisoning.

infectious *adj* **1** contagious, catching, communicable, transmittable, infective, virulent. **2** contagious, catching, irresistible.

infelicitous *adj* unfortunate, unlucky, unhappy, inapt, inappropriate, unsuitable.

infer *verb* conclude, deduce, derive, gather, understand, guess, conjecture.

inference *noun* conclusion, deduction, corollary, guess, conjecture.

inferior *adj* **1** lower, lesser, subordinate, minor, junior, secondary, subsidiary, lowly, humble. **2** unimportant, insignificant, substandard, second-rate, second-class, mediocre, poor, bad, shoddy.
➤ *noun* subordinate, junior, underling.

infernal *adj* **1** demonic, devilish, diabolical, fiendish, hellish. **2** atrocious, abominable, damned, wretched, confounded, dratted (*inf*), blasted (*inf*), blooming (*inf*).

infertile *adj* **1** sterile, barren, childless. **2** barren, unfruitful, unproductive.

infest *verb* overrun, swarm, invade, plague.

infidel *noun* **1** pagan, heathen, misbeliever. **2** unbeliever, atheist, sceptic, freethinker.

infidelity *noun* **1** unfaithfulness, adultery, playing around (*inf*), affair, cheating, disloyalty, betrayal. **2** disbelief, unbelief, scepticism.

infiltrate *verb* **1** penetrate, enter, insinuate oneself into, subvert. **2** filter, seep, percolate, permeate.

infinite *adj* **1** limitless, unlimited, boundless, unbounded, endless, never-ending, countless, numberless, innumerable. **2** vast, immense, enormous, extreme.

infinitesimal *adj* microscopic, minuscule, minute, tiny, imperceptible.

infinity *noun* **1** eternity, perpetuity. **2** limitlessness, endlessness, vastness, immensity.

infirm *adj* weak, feeble, frail, doddering, doddery, shaky.

infirmity *noun* **1** weakness, feebleness, frailty, ill health, disability. **2** ailment, disorder, illness, disease, sickness.

inflame *verb* **1** arouse, excite, fire, animate, incite, provoke, rouse, madden, enrage, stir up, whip up. **2** aggravate, exacerbate, intensify. **3** redden, flush, swell, infect.

inflammable *adj* flammable, combustible, burnable.

inflammation *noun* redness, rash, swelling, pain, soreness, tenderness, infection.

inflammatory *adj* **1** provocative, rabble-rousing, inflaming. **2** sore, painful, allergic, irritant.

inflate *verb* **1** expand, swell, blow up, dilate, distend. **2** overestimate, exaggerate, overstate, boost, hike up (*inf*).

inflated *adj* **1** puffed up, blown up, swollen, bloated, distended. **2** exaggerated, overstated, disproportionate, exorbitant. **3** pompous, bombastic, high-flown.

inflect *verb* **1** curve, bend, flex. **2** modulate, intonate, vary.

inflection *noun* **1** modulation, intonation, pitch, accent. **2** conjugation, declension.

inflexible *adj* **1** rigid, stiff, hard, firm, inelastic. **2** firm, unchangeable, unalterable, hard and fast. **3** stubborn, obstinate, intractable, obdurate, immovable, unbending, unyielding.

inflict *verb* impose, enforce, apply, mete out, wreak, exact, visit.

influence *noun* **1** power, sway, hold, control, effect, weight. **2** connections, prestige, standing, importance, clout (*inf*). ➤*verb* affect, modify, persuade, induce, control, direct, lead, sway, incline, dispose, prompt, impel.

influential *adj* powerful, potent, significant, effective, cogent, persuasive, controlling, leading, authoritative, weighty, important.

influx *noun* inflow, inrush, arrival.

inform *verb* **1** tell, apprise, advise, let know, notify, acquaint, keep posted (*inf*), put in the picture (*inf*). **2** characterize, typify, distinguish, permeate, pervade. **inform on** betray, denounce, grass on (*inf*), tell on (*inf*), blow the whistle on (*inf*), snitch (*inf*).

informal *adj* **1** casual, unceremonious, easygoing, relaxed, natural, everyday, unofficial. **2** familiar, colloquial, vernacular.

information *noun* **1** knowledge, intelligence. **2** facts, data, details, input, gen (*inf*), info (*inf*), lowdown (*inf*). **3** news, word, report.

informative *adj* instructive, illuminating, enlightening, revealing.

informed *adj* **1** well-informed, up to date, abreast, conversant, familiar, au fait, clued-up (*inf*). **2** authoritative, expert, well-researched,.

informer *noun* informant, source, traitor, spy, sneak, telltale, mole (*inf*), grass (*inf*), whistle-blower (*inf*), squealer (*inf*), nark (*inf*).

infraction *noun* violation, breach, infringement, contravention.

infrequent *adj* occasional, rare, unusual, uncommon, few and far between.

infringe *verb* violate, break, disobey, flout, breach, contravene. **infringe on** encroach on, trespass on, impinge on.

infuriate *verb* enrage, incense, madden, anger, exasperate, make one see red (*inf*), make one's blood boil (*inf*).

infuse *verb* **1** instil, inculcate, impart. **2** imbue, pervade, permeate, saturate. **3** brew, steep, soak.

infusion *noun* **1** instillation, inculcation, saturation, brewing, steeping. **2** brew.

ingenious *adj* clever, shrewd, astute, skilful, brilliant, inventive, resourceful, innovative, creative, original, cunning, subtle, crafty.

ingenuity *noun* cleverness, skill, flair, inventiveness, resourcefulness, innovativeness, creativity, imagination, shrewdness.

ingenuous *adj* **1** artless, naive, unsophisticated, simple, innocent, trusting. **2** direct, honest, frank, candid, straightforward.

inglorious *adj* disgraceful, dishonourable, ignominious, ignoble, discreditable.

ingrain *verb* instil, impress, implant, imprint, fix.

ingrained *adj* **1** rooted, deep-rooted, deep-seated, inveterate, inherent. **2** fixed, embedded, indelible.

ingratiate *verb* flatter, fawn, crawl, curry favour, get in with, get into someone's good books (*inf*), suck up to (*inf*).

ingratitude *noun* ungratefulness, thanklessness, unappreciativeness.

ingredient *noun* constituent, component, part, factor.

ingress *noun* **1** entrance, entry, way in. **2** admittance, access, entrée.

inhabit *verb* occupy, live in, reside in, populate, people.

inhale *verb* **1** breathe in, respire. **2** breathe in, sniff, take in, draw in.

inherent *adj* intrinsic, built-in, inborn, innate, natural, native, congenital, fundamental.

inherit *verb* **1** come into, be left. **2** assume, succeed to, take over.

inheritance *noun* legacy, bequest, patrimony, birthright.

inhibit *verb* **1** restrain, suppress, repress, curb, hold back, hinder, obstruct, frustrate, hamper, impede, prevent, stop. **2** deter, discourage, constrain. **3** prohibit, forbid, ban.

inhibition *noun* **1** constraint, hang-up (*inf*). **2** prohibition, ban, embargo, curb, restriction. **3** restraint, repression, reserve, shyness, reticence, embarrassment, self-consciousness.

inhospitable *adj* **1** unfriendly, cold, unwelcoming, unsociable. **2** barren, sterile, desolate, bleak, uninviting, forbidding.

inhuman *adj* **1** inhumane, unkind, cruel, heartless, unfeeling, hardhearted, callous, pitiless, merciless, ruthless, sadistic, savage, barbarous, barbaric. **2** nonhuman, alien, animal.

inhumane *adj* unkind, insensitive, unfeeling, cold-hearted, heartless, hardhearted, ruthless, brutal, cruel, harsh, savage.

inhumanity *noun* unkindness, hardheartedness, callousness, pitilessness, brutality, cruelty, harshness, savagery, barbarity, sadism.

inimical *adj* **1** harmful, injurious, detrimental, destructive. **2** hostile, antagonistic, adverse, unfavourable.

inimitable *adj* unique, peerless, perfect, unmatched, matchless, unparalleled, incomparable.

iniquity *noun* **1** sin, vice, wickedness, evil, wrongdoing, unrighteousness, injustice, unfairness. **2** wrong, crime, offence, misdeed, transgression.

initial *adj* **1** first, primary, opening, early, inaugural. **2** first, introductory, opening.
➤*verb* sign, endorse, countersign.

initiate *verb* **1** begin, start, commence, open, inaugurate, launch, trigger, prompt, get under way (*inf*). **2** teach, instruct, prime, ground, break in. **3** introduce, admit, enrol, induct, install.
➤*noun* member, recruit, entrant, newcomer, beginner, neophyte.

initiative *noun* **1** lead, first move, opening gambit, first step. **2** enterprise, drive, dynamism, get-up-and-go (*inf*), resourcefulness, inventiveness.

inject *verb* **1** immunize, inoculate, vaccinate, jab (*inf*). **2** shoot (*sl*), shoot up (*sl*), mainline (*sl*). **3** introduce, insert, infuse, instil.

injection *noun* **1** immunization, vaccination, inoculation, introduction, insertion, instilling. **2** dose, jab (*inf*), shot (*inf*), fix (*sl*).

injudicious *adj* imprudent, unwise, ill-judged, ill-advised, indiscreet, rash, incautious, misguided.

injunction *noun* instruction, order, directive, command, warning, admonition.

injure *verb* **1** hurt, wound, harm, maim, cripple, disable. **2** harm, damage, undermine. **3** damage, ruin, mar, spoil, deface, disfigure, besmirch, tarnish.

injurious *adj* **1** hurtful, damaging, harmful, detrimental, destructive, unfavourable, adverse. **2** abusive, offensive, slanderous, libellous.

injury *noun* **1** hurt, wound, sore, bruise, gash, laceration, cut. **2** damage, loss, wrong, injustice, abuse, offence.

injustice *noun* **1** unfairness, inequity, discrimination, prejudice, bias, favouritism, partiality, one-sidedness. **2** offence, wrong, injury, affront.

inkling *noun* **1** intimation, suggestion, hint, clue. **2** suspicion, idea, notion, glimmering.

inland *adj* **1** internal, interior, up-country. **2** internal, home, domestic.

inlay *verb* **1** set, inset, enchase. **2** decorate, stud, tile, line.

inlet *noun* **1** bay, bight, cove, creek, arm, fiord. **2** opening, entrance.

inmate *noun* prisoner, convict, detainee, patient, resident.

inmost *adj* innermost, deepest, central, private, personal, secret, basic, fundamental.

inn *noun* pub, public house, tavern, hotel.

innards *pl noun* **1** insides, guts, intestines, entrails, offal, viscera. **2** inner workings, mechanism, works.

innate *adj* **1** inborn, inbred, congenital, native, natural. **2** instinctive, intuitive, untaught, spontaneous. **3** inherent, intrinsic, essential, basic.

inner *adj* **1** interior, internal, inward, innermost. **2** central, restricted, exclusive, privileged. **3** spiritual, emotional, psychological, mental. **4** secret, private, unexpressed, unspoken.

innermost *adj* **1** inmost, deepest, central. **2** private, intimate, personal, confidential, secret.

innkeeper *noun* landlord, landlady, publican.

innocent *adj* **1** guiltless, blameless, in the clear, not guilty. **2** pure, chaste, sinless, virtuous, upright, unsullied, spotless, uncorrupted. **3** harmless, innocuous, inoffensive, safe. **4** naive, unsophisticated, artless, ingenuous, trusting, unworldly, green (*inf*).
➤ *noun* beginner, novice, ingenue, greenhorn, babe, child.

innocuous *adj* harmless, safe, innocent, inoffensive, unobjectionable, bland, mild.

innovate *verb* make changes, branch out, progress, restructure.

innuendo *noun* insinuation, allusion, slur, implication, suggestion.

innumerable *adj* countless, numberless, myriad, umpteen (*inf*).

inoculate *verb* vaccinate, immunize, inject.

inoffensive *adj* innocent, harmless, innocuous, mild, retiring, quiet.

inoperable *adj* incurable, untreatable, terminal.

inoperative *adj* broken, not working, defective, out of order, out of commission, unserviceable, kaput (*inf*), invalid, null and void, ineffective.

inopportune *adj* untimely, inconvenient, awkward, unsuitable, inappropriate.

inordinate *adj* excessive, immoderate, outrageous, extreme, exorbitant, disproportionate, unreasonable.

inorganic *adj* **1** inanimate, mineral. **2** chemical, artificial, man-made.

inquest *noun* inquiry, investigation, hearing, postmortem.

inquisition *noun* interrogation, cross-examination, questioning, grilling (*inf*), third degree (*inf*).

inquisitive *adj* **1** enquiring, questioning, curious, probing. **2** curious, nosy (*inf*), prying, snooping, meddlesome, interfering.

inroad *noun* **1** incursion, raid, foray. **2** irruption, invasion, intrusion, encroachment.

insalubrious *adj* unhealthy, unwholesome, insanitary, unhygienic, dirty.

insane *adj* **1** mentally ill, mad, crazy, deranged, out of one's mind, demented, unbalanced, unhinged, non compos mentis, not all there (*inf*), nuts (*inf*), barking (*inf*). **2** foolish, daft (*inf*), stupid, crazy, mad, senseless, idiotic, irresponsible, irrational, absurd, ridiculous.

insanitary *adj* unhygienic, unhealthy, unclean, dirty, insalubrious, filthy, contaminated.

insatiable *adj* unquenchable, rapacious, voracious, ravenous, greedy, gluttonous.

inscribe *verb* **1** engrave, carve, cut, etch, incise, imprint, stamp, write. **2** sign, autograph, dedicate.

inscription *noun* **1** engraving, etching. **2** legend, words, writing, lettering, epitaph. **3** dedication, autograph.

inscrutable *adj* enigmatic, deadpan, poker-faced, sphinxlike, cryptic, inexplicable, unfathomable, incomprehensible, mysterious.

insecure *adj* **1** uncertain, unsure, diffident, hesitant. **2** apprehensive, anxious, nervous, afraid. **3** unsafe, dangerous, exposed, vulnerable, unprotected, unguarded, defenceless. **4** unstable, unsteady, shaky, wobbly, rickety, loose.

insensible *adj* **1** unaware, oblivious, heedless, unconscious, ignorant, indifferent, insensitive, unaffected, unmoved. **2** numb, unfeeling. **3** unconscious, anaesthetized, out (*inf*), knocked out.

insensitive *adj* **1** uncaring, unfeeling, thick-skinned, callous, tactless, indifferent, unaffected, unmoved, unappreciative, unresponsive. **2** immune, proof, unsusceptible, unreactive.

inseparable *adj* **1** indivisible, undividable, inextricable, indissoluble. **2** devoted, intimate, close, bosom.

insert *verb* **1** introduce, enter, interpolate, inject, interject, inset, implant. **2** stick in, push in, put in.
>*noun* insertion, enclosure, supplement.

insertion *noun* **1** insert, inset, supplement. **2** entry, inclusion, addition, intercalation.

inside *noun* interior, contents, centre.
>*adj* **1** interior, inner, internal, inward. **2** secret, classified, confidential, restricted, private.
>*adv* **1** indoors, within. **2** internally, privately, secretly.

insider *noun* member, participant, one of us (*inf*).

insides *pl noun* innards (*inf*), guts, intestines, stomach, tummy (*inf*), belly (*inf*).

insidious *adj* stealthy, subtle, surreptitious, gradual, sneaky, sly, cunning, deceitful, treacherous.

insight *noun* **1** realization, understanding, explanation, revelation. **2** penetration, perspicacity, acumen, discernment, shrewdness, awareness.

insignia *noun* badge, sign, emblem, mark, symbol.

insignificant *adj* **1** unimportant, trivial, immaterial, irrelevant, minor, inconsequential, petty, of no account. **2** meagre, small, trifling, nugatory, negligible, not worth mentioning, piddling (*inf*).

insincere *adj* hypocritical, dissembling, two-faced, deceitful, dishonest, disingenuous, false, phoney (*inf*), hollow, empty.

insinuate *verb* **1** intimate, hint, suggest, imply. **2** introduce, squeeze in, slip. **3** ingratiate, curry favour, worm one's way.

insinuation *noun* **1** intimation, hint, suggestion, implication, innuendo. **2** introduction, infiltration, implanting.

insipid *adj* **1** bland, tasteless, flavourless, watery, wishy-washy (*inf*). **2** bland, colour-

less, anaemic, vapid, dull, boring, uninteresting, jejune, banal, trite, tame.

insist *verb* **1** demand, require, command. **2** stand one's ground, be firm, put one's foot down, not take no for an answer. **3** maintain, assert, stress, emphasize.

insistent *adj* **1** emphatic, determined, persistent, dogged, relentless. **2** incessant, persistent, repeated.

insobriety *noun* drunkenness, intoxication, intemperance.

insolent *adj* impudent, impertinent, rude, bold, brazen, disrespectful, presumptuous, arrogant, saucy (*inf*), cheeky (*inf*).

insoluble *adj* **1** indissoluble. **2** unfathomable, inexplicable, mystifying, baffling.

insolvent *adj* bankrupt, failed, ruined, gone to the wall (*inf*), bust (*inf*), penniless, broke (*inf*), in queer street (*inf*).

insomnia *noun* sleeplessness, wakefulness, restlessness.

insouciance *verb* nonchalance, unconcern, casualness, airiness, lightheartedness, jauntiness.

inspect *verb* examine, scrutinize, scan, study, check, vet, investigate, view, visit, tour.

inspector *noun* examiner, checker, vetter, auditor, investigator, observer, supervisor.

inspiration *noun* **1** creativity, originality, genius, inventiveness, insight. **2** stimulus, motivation, influence, muse, spur, incitement, incentive. **3** idea, bright idea, brain wave, stroke of genius, revelation.

inspire *verb* **1** stimulate, provoke, trigger, arouse, kindle, give rise to, spark off, prompt. **2** motivate, encourage, spur on, move, impel, stir, rouse, fire.

inspired *adj* brilliant, superlative, outstanding, marvellous, memorable.

inspirit *verb* encourage, inspire, stimulate, arouse.

instability *noun* unreliability, impermanence, insecurity, fluidity, unsteadiness, precariousness, shakiness, flimsiness, capriciousness, flightiness, fickleness, changeableness, volatility.

install verb **1** place, put in, put in place, fix, lodge. **2** invest, induct, instate. **3** ensconce, settle, position, establish.

installation noun **1** placing, positioning, siting, fitting, fixing. **2** plant, equipment, machinery. **3** base, post, camp, headquarters.

instalment noun **1** part payment, payment, repayment. **2** episode, chapter, section, part.

instance noun **1** example, case, illustration, occurrence. **2** situation, stage, step. ➤ verb cite, quote, adduce, mention, refer to.

instant noun moment, second, minute, twinkling, flash, jiffy (inf). ➤ adj **1** immediate, instantaneous, prompt. **2** ready-prepared, ready-made, convenience. **3** urgent, demanding, pressing, critical.

instantaneous adj instant, immediate, on-the-spot, abrupt.

instantly adv immediately, at once, now, forthwith, straightaway.

instead adv alternatively, preferably, as a substitute.

instead of prep in lieu of, rather than, in preference to, in place of.

instigate verb **1** start, initiate, foment. **2** incite, provoke, spur, prompt, impel, encourage, influence, persuade.

instil verb infuse, implant, inculcate, introduce, teach.

instinct noun intuition, feeling, hunch, sixth sense, gut feeling (inf), inner prompting, inclination, tendency, predisposition.

instinctive adj **1** intuitive, unlearned, unthinking, automatic, spontaneous, involuntary, reflex. **2** natural, inherent, native, innate.

institute verb **1** found, establish, set up, initiate, introduce, organize, start, inaugurate. **2** appoint, install, invest. ➤ noun institution, school, college, academy, association, organization, foundation.

institution noun **1** institute, school, college, university, hospital, asylum, home, reformatory, prison, establishment, organization, foundation. **2** custom, tradition, usage, convention. **3** regular feature, familiar sight.

instruct verb **1** tell, order, command, direct. **2** teach, educate, train, coach, drill. **3** inform, notify, tell, advise, brief.

instruction noun **1** order, command, direction, directive. **2** advice, guideline, recommendation, guide, manual, handbook. **3** teaching, education, tuition, training.

instructive adj informative, educational, enlightening, illuminating, helpful, useful.

instructor noun teacher, lecturer, tutor, schoolmaster, schoolmistress, coach, trainer.

instrument noun **1** implement, tool, utensil, device, gadget, gizmo (inf). **2** indicator, gauge, meter. **3** agent, agency, vehicle, medium, way, means. **4** pawn, puppet, creature, tool, dupe, stooge (inf).

instrumental adj helpful, useful, contributory, conducive, involved.

insubordinate adj disobedient, defiant, rebellious, mutinous, rude, unruly, undisciplined.

insubstantial adj **1** frail, weak, flimsy, tenuous, slight, thin. **2** unreal, illusory, imaginary, immaterial, spectral.

insufferable adj unbearable, intolerable, impossible, too much.

insufficient adj inadequate, deficient, lacking, not enough, short, scanty, scarce.

insular adj **1** narrow-minded, narrow, petty, parochial, provincial, inward-looking, blinkered. **2** isolated, detached, separate, remote.

insulate verb **1** isolate, separate, cut off, shield, cocoon, shelter. **2** isolate, separate, heatproof, soundproof, lag.

insult verb abuse, affront, offend, hurt the feelings of, hurt, injure, wound, slight, slander, slag off (sl). ➤ noun affront, offence, snub, put-down (inf), gibe, barb, dig (inf), slight, slur, slander, aspersion, humiliation, indignity.

insuperable adj insurmountable, impassable, overpowering, impossible, overwhelming, hopeless.

insupportable *adj* intolerable, unendurable, unbearable, insufferable, more than flesh and blood can stand.

insurance *noun* **1** assurance, protection, provision, cover, security. **2** safeguard, precaution, protection, provision.

insure *verb* **1** cover, underwrite, guarantee, assure. **2** protect, safeguard.

insurgent *noun* rebel, revolutionary, insurrectionist.
➤*adj* rebellious, revolutionary, insurrectionary, mutinous.

insurmountable *adj* insuperable, impassable, overpowering, impossible, overwhelming, hopeless.

insurrection *noun* rebellion, revolt, uprising, rising, coup, insurgency.

insusceptible *adj* insensitive, unresponsive, proof against, immune.

intact *adj* whole, complete, perfect, unbroken, sound, in one piece, unhurt, uninjured, unharmed, undamaged, unscathed.

intangible *adj* **1** impalpable. **2** insubstantial, vague, indefinite, shadowy.

integral *adj* **1** intrinsic, essential, indispensable, component, constituent. **2** intact, integrated, whole, complete.

integrate *verb* incorporate, combine, consolidate, amalgamate, mix, blend, merge, desegregate.

integration *noun* unification, merger, incorporation, assimilation, amalgamation, consolidation.

integrity *noun* **1** honesty, truthfulness, uprightness, rectitude, probity, honour, principle. **2** unity, wholeness, completeness, cohesion.

intellect *noun* **1** mind, intelligence, brains, brainpower, reason, understanding. **2** intellectual, thinker, mind.

intellectual *adj* **1** learned, erudite, academic, scholarly, donnish, highbrow, intelligent. **2** mental, cerebral. **3** academic, logical, rational, bookish.
➤*noun* scholar, academic, thinker, egghead (*inf*).

intelligence *noun* **1** intellect, mind, brains, brainpower, grey matter (*inf*), cleverness, understanding, perception, acumen, sense, nous (*inf*). **2** information, facts, news, word. **3** espionage, surveillance, spying.

intelligent *adj* clever, smart, bright, quick, sharp, alert, astute, perceptive, discerning, brainy (*inf*), well-informed, educated, sensible, rational.

intelligentsia *noun* academics, literati, intellectuals, brains (*inf*).

intelligible *adj* comprehensible, understandable, clear, plain, distinct, legible.

intemperate *adj* **1** uncontrolled, unrestrained, unbridled, extravagant, self-indulgent, wild. **2** excessive, immoderate, inordinate, drunken, alcoholic.

intend *verb* **1** mean, propose, have in mind, contemplate, plan, aim. **2** mean, earmark, design.

intended *adj* designated, planned, future, prospective.
➤*noun* betrothed, fiancé, fiancée, husband-to-be, wife-to-be.

intense *adj* **1** ardent, burning, consuming, fervent. **2** acute, severe, extreme, harsh, deep, profound, violent, fierce, consuming, great, strong, powerful. **3** concentrated, intensive. **4** earnest, serious, passionate, impassioned, enthusiastic, emotional.

intensify *verb* heighten, enhance, deepen, strengthen, sharpen, concentrate, step up, raise.

intensity *noun* fierceness, acuteness, harshness, concentration, depth, strength, power, force, vigour, energy, seriousness, tenseness, fraughtness, enthusiasm, eagerness, ardour, fervour, vehemence.

intensive *adj* thorough, concentrated, in-depth, all-out, intense.

intent *adj* **1** concentrated, focused, intense, eager, absorbed, engrossed, rapt, preoccupied, wrapped up. **2** set, determined, resolute, bent, hell-bent, committed.
➤*noun* intention, aim, goal, object, purpose, plan.
to all intents and purposes nearly, almost, virtually, practically, as good as.

intention *noun* aim, goal, object, objective, intent, plan, purpose.

intentional *adj* intended, premeditated, planned, deliberate, meant, calculated.

inter *verb* bury, lay to rest, entomb.

intercede *verb* mediate, intervene, interpose, plead.

intercept *verb* interrupt, stop, block, head off, cut off, catch, seize.

intercession *noun* mediation, intervention, plea, prayer, entreaty, supplication.

interchange *verb* 1 exchange, swap, trade, replace. 2 switch, substitute, transpose, exchange.
➤ *noun* 1 exchange, swap, trade, give and take. 2 junction, intersection, crossroads.

intercourse *noun* 1 communication, dealings, commerce, trade, traffic, contact. 2 sex, copulation, coitus, carnal knowledge, intimacy, lovemaking, nookie (*inf*), screwing (*sl*), shagging (*sl*), bonking (*sl*), fucking (*sl*).

interdict *verb* prohibit, embargo, ban, forbid, veto, bar.
➤ *noun* interdiction, prohibition, embargo, ban, veto, bar.

interest *noun* 1 curiosity, attention, concern, regard, notice, heed, fascination, involvement. 2 appeal, fascination, importance, consequence, concern, significance, hobby, pastime, activity, pursuit, amusement. 3 benefit, advantage, good, profit, gain. 4 share, stake, stock, investment, part, right, claim, involvement. 5 premium, dividend, percentage, profit, return, revenue.
➤ *verb* engage, absorb, captivate, rivet, grip, fascinate, intrigue, attract, excite, affect, concern, touch, involve.

interested *adj* 1 curious, intrigued, attracted, drawn, attentive, held, absorbed, fascinated. 2 concerned, involved, affected, prejudiced, biased, partial.

interesting *adj* intriguing, curious, absorbing, fascinating, thought-provoking, compelling, gripping, appealing, attractive.

interfere *verb* 1 intervene, meddle, intrude, butt in, stick one's nose in (*inf*). 2 hinder, impede, hamper, get in the way of (*inf*), inhibit, cramp. 3 molest, abuse, sexually assault.

interference *noun* intervention, meddling, prying, sticking one's nose in (*inf*), hampering, obstruction.

interim *noun* interval, meantime, meanwhile.
➤ *adj* temporary, provisional, stopgap, caretaker, acting.

interior *adj* 1 internal, inner, inside, inward. 2 inland, central, upcountry. 3 home, domestic. 4 inner, mental, personal, emotional, spiritual.
➤ *noun* inside, heart, core, centre.

interject *verb* throw in, put in, introduce.

interjection *noun* exclamation, ejaculation, cry, remark, interruption.

interlace *verb* interweave, intertwine, plait, braid.

interlock *verb* join, lock, interconnect, interlink.

interloper *noun* intruder, trespasser, gate-crasher.

interlude *noun* 1 intermission, entr'acte. 2 interval, break, pause, letup (*inf*), respite.

intermediary *noun* negotiator, arbitrator, mediator, go-between, middleman.

intermediate *adj* intervening, transitional, halfway, midway, in-between.

interment *noun* burial, funeral.

interminable *adj* endless, never-ending, everlasting, long, protracted, long-winded, monotonous, boring.

intermingle *verb* mingle, mix, blend, merge, mix up, combine, amalgamate.

intermission *noun* 1 interlude, interval, entr'acte. 2 break, pause, breathing-space, rest, respite, lull, let-up (*inf*).

intermittent *adj* spasmodic, irregular, fitful, sporadic, periodic, occasional, discontinuous.

intern *verb* confine, jail, imprison, detain, hold.

internal *adj* 1 inner, interior, inside, inward. 2 domestic, home. 3 private, personal, intimate, mental, psychological.

international *adj* global, worldwide, intercontinental, universal.

internecine *adj* 1 destructive, violent, deadly. 2 internal, civil, domestic.

interpolate *verb* insert, introduce, put in, intercalate.

interpose verb 1 insert, introduce, put in. 2 introduce, interject, interpolate, inject. 3 intervene, mediate, interfere, meddle, butt in.

interpret verb 1 explain, expound, elucidate, clarify, unravel, solve, decode, decipher. 2 render, translate. 3 construe, take to mean, take, understand, read. 4 depict, portray, perform.

interpretation noun 1 decoding, deciphering, translation, explanation, expounding, elucidation, clarification. 2 explanation, reading, translation. 3 rendition, portrayal, performance.

interpreter noun translator, linguist.

interrogate verb question, quiz, pump, cross-examine, examine, grill (inf).

interrogative adj questioning, quizzical, interrogatory, probing.

interrupt verb 1 intrude, break in, butt in, interpose, chip in (inf), interfere. 2 discontinue, suspend, break off, halt, hinder, obstruct, block, impede, interfere with.

intersect verb 1 divide, cut. 2 cross, meet.

intersection noun interchange, crossroads, junction.

intersperse verb 1 scatter, sprinkle, distribute. 2 pepper, dot, diversify.

interstice noun gap, chink, cranny, crevice, space, interval.

intertwine verb twine, entwine, twist, interweave, interlace.

interval noun 1 interlude, intermission, halftime. 2 pause, rest, hiatus, gap, lull, interim, period, space.

intervene verb 1 interpose, step in, intrude, interfere, mediate, intercede. 2 happen, occur, take place, ensue.

intervention noun involvement, intrusion, interference, mediation, stepping-in.

interview noun 1 meeting, talk, discussion, conference, audience, appraisal. 2 assessment.
➤verb examine, question, talk to, sound out, vet.

interweave verb 1 interlace, intertwine, braid, plait. 2 intermingle, blend, mix.

intestines pl noun bowels, guts, entrails, viscera, innards (inf), insides (inf).

intimacy noun close relationship, closeness, friendship, familiarity, affection, love, warmth, understanding.

intimate[1] adj 1 close, cherished, dear, bosom, familiar (inf). 2 warm, snug, cosy, comfy (inf). 3 confidential, personal, private, secret. 4 deep, profound, thorough, detailed, personal, firsthand.
➤noun friend, confidant, confidante, familiar, crony (inf), bosom friend.

intimate[2] verb 1 suggest, imply, tip someone the wink (inf), insinuate, hint. 2 make known, declare, announce.

intimidate verb 1 frighten, scare, daunt, cow, overawe. 2 deter, warn off, bully, browbeat, pressurize, threaten, get at (inf), lean on (inf).

intolerable adj unbearable, insufferable, unendurable, impossible, too much, the limit (inf), the last straw (inf), the end (inf).

intolerant adj narrow-minded, illiberal, bigoted, biased, self-opinionated, small-minded, prejudiced, chauvinistic, dogmatic.

intonation noun modulation, accentuation, cadence, inflection, lilt.

intone verb chant, recite, speak, utter.

intoxicate noun 1 inebriate, make drunk. 2 exhilarate, elate, excite.

intractable adj 1 stubborn, obstinate, unbending, obdurate, intransigent, perverse, contrary, unmanageable, awkward, difficult. 2 unmanageable, awkward, difficult, troublesome.

intransigent adj uncompromising, unbending, unyielding, intractable, stubborn, obstinate, rigid, immovable.

intrepid adj fearless, dauntless, daring, brave, courageous, audacious, bold, heroic, gallant, plucky, spirited.

intricate adj complex, convoluted, involved, complicated, labyrinthine, entangled, knotty, thorny, tortuous.

intrigue verb 1 attract, interest, fascinate, captivate, rivet. 2 conspire, plot, scheme, machinate.
➤noun 1 conspiracy, plot, scheme, machination. 2 scheming, plotting, subterfuge, double-dealing. 3 affair, liaison, amour.

intriguing adj fascinating, captivating, absorbing, riveting, interesting, tantalizing.

intrinsic adj inherent, essential, basic, built-in, innate.

introduce verb **1** present, acquaint, make known. **2** institute, begin, start, initiate, inaugurate, launch, establish, originate. **3** bring in, usher in, pioneer. **4** propose, put forward, advance, submit, offer, moot, suggest, bring up. **5** insert, inject, interpose, interpolate, interject, add.

introduction noun **1** presentation, announcement, acquaintance, familiarization, institution, start, beginning, commencement, initiation, inauguration, launch, establishment, insertion, injection, interposition, infusion, addition. **2** preface, proem, foreword, intro (inf), preamble, prologue. **3** fundamentals, basics, rudiments, guide, handbook.

introductory adj preliminary, prefatory, preparatory, opening, initial, rudimentary, basic, fundamental.

introspection noun self-analysis, introversion, reserve, reflection, meditation, brooding.

intrude verb obtrude, push in, butt in, break in, interrupt, interfere, meddle, gatecrash, trespass.

intruder noun trespasser, invader, burglar, robber, thief, interloper, gate-crasher.

intrusion noun encroachment, infringement, invasion, trespass, gate-crashing, obtrusion, meddling, interference.

intrusive adj intruding, invasive, unwelcome, interfering, meddlesome, nosy (inf).

intuition noun **1** instinct, clairvoyance, sixth sense. **2** presentiment, hunch, feeling, inkling, gut feeling (inf).

intuitive adj instinctive, spontaneous, untaught, innate, automatic, involuntary.

inundate verb flood, deluge, swamp, submerge, engulf, overwhelm.

inure verb harden, toughen, accustom, habituate, familiarize, acclimatize.

invade verb **1** enter, penetrate, attack, assault, storm, occupy, seize, overrun. **2** intrude, encroach, infringe, violate.

invalid[1] noun patient, convalescent, sufferer.

invalid[2] adj **1** unsound, fallacious, untrue, false, incorrect, wrong, illogical, unscientific, unfounded. **2** illegal, null, void, inoperative, null and void.

invalidate verb refute, rebut, disprove, undermine, weaken, annul, nullify, void, repeal, rescind, quash, cancel.

invaluable adj priceless, inestimable, precious, indispensable, useful.

invariable adj unchanging, unchangeable, unalterable, unvarying, constant, fixed, permanent.

invasion noun **1** attack, assault, raid, incursion, penetration, occupation. **2** interruption, intrusion, encroachment, infringement, violation.

invective noun abuse, obloquy, vituperation, diatribe, harangue, philippic, tirade, scolding, tongue-lashing.

inveigh verb rail, vituperate, expostulate, protest, condemn, censure, denounce, berate, lambaste.

inveigle verb beguile, coax, cajole, persuade, entice, sweet-talk (inf), lure, wheedle.

invent verb **1** originate, create, design, discover, think up, devise, improvise. **2** concoct, fabricate, make up, cook up (inf).

invention noun **1** origination, creation, discovery, design, development. **2** creation, brainchild, innovation, discovery, machine, device, contrivance. **3** fabrication, deceit, lie, fib (inf), falsehood, sham, fiction. **4** inventiveness, originality, resourcefulness, creativity, imagination.

inventive adj creative, imaginative, original, innovative.

inventory noun list, checklist, catalogue, register, roll, record.

inverse noun opposite, contrary, converse, reverse.
   ➤ adj opposite, reverse, converse, reversed, transposed, inverted.

inversion noun reversal, transposition, reverse, converse.

invert verb **1** turn upside down, overturn, upset, capsize, turn inside out. **2** reverse, transpose.

invest[1] verb **1** spend, deposit, put in, sink. **2** expend, devote, give, dedicate.

invest[2] verb **1** install, induct, instate, swear in. **2** give, grant, bestow, confer.

investigate verb explore, examine, probe, study, research, inspect, look into, check out (inf).

investiture noun installation, induction, instatement, coronation.

investment noun risk, venture, speculation, stake, contribution.

inveterate adj **1** chronic, habitual, confirmed, dyed-in-the-wool. **2** ingrained, deep-seated, incurable, established.

invidious adj **1** unpleasant, awkward, difficult, impossible. **2** unfair, discriminating, prejudicial, deleterious.

invigorate verb enliven, animate, stimulate, brace, refresh, energize, revitalize, rejuvenate, give a new lease of life to.

invincible adj unconquerable, indomitable, unassailable, impregnable, insuperable, insurmountable, indestructible.

inviolable adj inalienable, untouchable, sacrosanct, sacred.

inviolate adj intact, whole, undamaged, unsullied, undefiled, unspoiled, untouched, undisturbed.

invisible adj **1** unseen, hidden, concealed, out of sight. **2** imperceptible, indiscernible, inconspicuous.

invitation noun **1** summons, call, request, bidding, invite (inf). **2** attraction, enticement, temptation, come-on (inf).

invite verb **1** ask, bid, summon, request, ask for, call for. **2** attract, encourage, court, tempt, provoke.

inviting adj attractive, tempting, alluring, enticing, seductive, appealing, irresistible.

invocation noun prayer, supplication, entreaty, petition.

invoice noun bill, charges, statement, reckoning.

invoke verb **1** call on, appeal to, implore, pray to. **2** implement, apply, put into effect. **3** summon, conjure up, raise.

involuntary adj **1** automatic, mechanical, reflex, spontaneous, instinctive, unintentional, unconscious. **2** forced, compulsory, obligatory.

involve verb **1** entail, require, mean, necessitate, presuppose. **2** include, affect, embrace, cover, implicate, incriminate, associate, embroil, mix up. **4** absorb, engross, preoccupy, engage, occupy.

involved adj **1** complex, complicated, difficult, confused, intricate, elaborate. **2** concerned, mixed up in, taking part, implicated, in on (inf).

invulnerable adj **1** safe, secure, unassailable, impregnable. **2** proof, immune.

inward adj **1** inner, internal, interior, inside. **2** inner, innermost, private, personal, intimate, secret, mental, spiritual.

iota noun atom, jot, bit, scrap, grain, trace.

irascible adj irritable, touchy, testy, hot-tempered, quick-tempered, short-tempered, cross, prickly.

irate adj angry, furious, incensed, enraged, livid, fuming, indignant.

ire noun anger, rage, fury, wrath, indignation.

iridescent adj shimmering, pearly, nacreous, opalescent.

irk verb irritate, annoy, vex, nettle, rile, anger, rub up the wrong way (inf), peeve (inf), miff (inf).

irksome adj tiresome, annoying, irritating, trying, troublesome, bothersome.

iron adj inflexible, unyielding, rigid, determined, firm, strong, tough.
➤ verb press, flatten, smooth.
➤ noun chains, bonds, fetters, manacles, shackles.

iron out clear up, resolve, sort out, put right, smooth out.

ironic adj ironical, sarcastic, sardonic, paradoxical, incongruous, coincidental.

irony noun **1** sarcasm, satire, ridicule. **2** paradox, incongruity.

irradiate verb **1** brighten, illuminate, light up. **2** treat with radiation, X-ray.

irrational *adj* **1** illogical, unreasonable, absurd, preposterous, ridiculous, nonsensical, muddled, confused, foolish. **2** unthinking, idiotic, stupid, brainless, insane, demented.

irreconcilable *adj* incompatible, conflicting, at odds, diametrically opposed, implacable, unappeasable, deadly.

irrecoverable *adj* irretrievable, lost, irredeemable, unsalvageable.

irrefutable *adj* incontrovertible, undeniable, incontestable, indisputable, conclusive.

irregular *adj* **1** uneven, rough, bumpy, pitted, jagged, ragged, crooked, lopsided, unsymmetrical, asymmetric. **2** variable, fluctuating, spasmodic, sporadic, occasional, intermittent, haphazard, random. **3** dishonest, fraudulent, deceitful, false, cheating, against the rules, out of order, unconventional, unorthodox, unusual, eccentric, abnormal, deviant, immoral, improper. **4** guerrilla, volunteer, partisan, mercenary.

irrelevant *adj* inapplicable, inapposite, inappropriate, inapt, beside the point, unimportant.

irreligion *noun* godlessness, unbelief, impiety, irreverence, blasphemy.

irremediable *adj* irreparable, irreversible, irredeemable, incurable.

irreparable *adj* irreversible, beyond repair, irremediable, incurable.

irreplaceable *adj* unique, precious, indispensable, vital, essential.

irrepressible *adj* uncontrollable, unstoppable, uninhibited, animated, boisterous, ebullient.

irreproachable *adj* beyond reproach, unimpeachable, blameless, faultless, impeccable.

irresistible *adj* overwhelming, overpowering, compelling, powerful, uncontrollable, unavoidable, inescapable, tempting, seductive, alluring, fascinating.

irresolute *adj* undecided, unresolved, uncertain, in two minds, indecisive, hesitant, vacillating, wavering, faltering.

irrespective *adj* **irrespective of** regardless of, despite, in spite of, notwithstanding, setting aside, ignoring.

irresponsible *adj* **1** unreliable, untrustworthy, careless, flighty, scatterbrained, immature. **2** thoughtless, careless, inconsiderate, reckless, rash.

irretrievable *adj* irrecoverable, lost, unsalvageable, irreparable.

irreverence *noun* disrespect, discourtesy, rudeness, impiety, blasphemy, sacrilege, profanity.

irreversible *adj* unalterable, irrevocable, permanent, final, incurable, irreparable.

irrevocable *adj* irreversible, unalterable, unchangeable, final.

irrigate *verb* **1** water. **2** wet, moisten, soak, wash, bathe.

irritable *adj* touchy, testy, irascible, peppery, petulant, impatient, bad-tempered, short-tempered, quick-tempered, prickly, cross, stroppy (*inf*), shirty (*inf*).

irritate *verb* **1** annoy, vex, nettle, needle, rile, anger, get on one's nerves (*inf*), rub up the wrong way (*inf*), get (*inf*), bug (*inf*). **2** inflame, rub, chafe, aggravate.

irrupt *verb* invade, rush in, burst in.

island *noun* isle, islet, atoll, cay, key, ait, eyot.

isolate *verb* **1** separate, set apart, keep apart, insulate, cut off, detach, disconnect, exclude. **2** segregate, quarantine.

isolated *adj* **1** solitary, lonely, out-of-the-way, off-the-beaten-track, remote, outlying. **2** exceptional, uncommon, freak, single, solitary.

issue *noun* **1** topic, subject, question, problem, matter. **2** edition, number, impression, printing, instalment. **3** issuance, publication, supply, delivery, distribution, circulation, sending out. **4** offspring, progeny, children, descendants. **5** outflow, discharge, egress, exit.
➤ *verb* **1** deliver, supply, give out, distribute, send out, circulate. **2** publish, put out, release. **3** come out, appear, emerge, emanate, flow, pour forth, gush.
at issue under discussion, in question, to be decided.

itch *verb* **1** tingle, prickle, tickle. **2** yearn, long, ache, crave, hanker.
➤ *noun* **1** itchiness, irritation, tingling, prickling. **2** yearning, longing, craving, hankering, yen (*inf*).

itchy *adj* itching, prickly, tingling.

item *noun* **1** article, thing, piece, element. **2** story, report, feature, article. **3** couple, partners.

itemize *verb* detail, specify, list, inventory.

iterate *verb* repeat, reiterate, restate, recapitulate.

itinerant *adj* wandering, travelling, nomadic, migratory.

itinerary *noun* route, schedule, programme, timetable.

jab *verb* **1** poke, prod, dig, nudge, stab. **2** punch.
➤*noun* **1** poke, prod, dig, stab, punch. **2** injection, shot.

jabber *verb* chatter, babble, blather, witter (*inf*).

jack up *verb* **1** lift, raise, hoist. **2** increase, raise, hike up.

jacket *noun* **1** coat, blazer, anorak, cardigan. **2** cover, casing, wrapper, lagging.

jackpot *noun* first prize, bonanza, pot.

jaded *adj* weary, tired, fatigued, cloyed, sated, satiated, bored, fed up (*inf*), stale.

jagged *adj* uneven, irregular, rough, notched, toothed, serrated.

jail *noun* gaol, prison, penitentiary, nick (*inf*), clink (*inf*), cooler (*inf*), slammer (*inf*), stir (*inf*).
➤*verb* gaol, imprison, lock up, send down (*inf*), put away (*inf*), bang up (*inf*).

jailer *noun* gaoler, warder, guard, screw (*sl*).

jam¹ *verb* **1** cram, stuff, pack, squash, wedge, ram. **2** cram, stuff, pack. **3** block, obstruct, clog, congest. **4** stick, stall, stop.
➤*noun* **1** blockage, congestion, gridlock. **2** press, crush, crowd. **3** predicament, plight, trouble, fix (*inf*), spot (*inf*).

jam² *noun* preserve, conserve, jelly.

jangle *verb* **1** clang, clank, clink, jingle. **2** upset, disturb, irritate.

janitor *noun* caretaker, doorkeeper, concierge.

jar¹ *noun* pot, vessel, container, bottle.

jar² *verb* **1** jolt, jerk, rattle, shake. **2** jangle, grate. **3** clash, conflict, disagree, quarrel.

jargon *noun* vocabulary, phraseology, lingo (*inf*), idiom, argot, slang, mumbo jumbo.

jaunt *noun* excursion, outing, trip, spin (*inf*).

jaunty *adj* **1** breezy, airy, bouncy, carefree, sprightly. **2** smart, stylish, natty (*inf*).

jaw *noun* mandible, chap, chop. **2** mouth, maw, threshold.
➤*verb* chat, gossip, natter (*inf*).

jazz up *verb* brighten up, liven up, ginger up.

jealous *adj* **1** envious, covetous, grudging, resentful, green-eyed. **2** suspicious, distrustful, possessive. **3** protective, watchful, vigilant.

jeer *verb* scoff, mock, sneer, taunt, barrack, boo.
➤*noun* sneer, taunt, gibe, catcall, boo.

jejune *adj* **1** immature, callow, childish, puerile, juvenile. **2** dull, vapid, insipid, tame, boring, trite.

jeopardize *verb* endanger, imperil, threaten.

jeopardy *noun* danger, peril, risk.

jerk *verb* **1** pull, tug, yank, wrench, jolt. **2** twitch, convulse, shake.
➤*noun* **1** pull, tug, yank, jolt, bump, lurch. **2** fool, idiot, dope (*inf*), prat (*sl*).

jerky *adj* convulsive, twitchy, jumpy, uncontrolled, uncoordinated, spasmodic, irregular.

jersey *noun* jumper, sweater, pullover.

jest *noun* **1** joke, quip, witticism. **2** fun, sport, play.
➤*verb* **1** joke, quip. **2** joke, banter, chaff, tease, kid (*inf*), have on (*inf*).

jester *noun* clown, fool, buffoon, zany.

jet *noun* gush, stream, spout, spurt, squirt, spray, fountain.
➤*verb* gush, stream, pour, shoot, spurt, squirt, spray.

jettison *verb* offload, dump, throw away, discard, get rid of, scrap.

jetty noun 1 breakwater, groyne, mole. 2 pier, wharf, landing stage.

jewel noun 1 gem, precious stone, rock (inf), sparkler (inf). 2 pride, boast, pearl, treasure.

jib verb jib at balk at, recoil from, refuse.

jiffy noun instant, moment, second, tick, flash.

jilt verb abandon, desert, leave, throw over, drop, dump (inf).

jingle verb ring, tinkle, clink, chink.
➤noun 1 ringing, tinkle, clink, chink. 2 song, tune, slogan, rhyme.

jingoism noun nationalism, chauvinism, flag-waving.

jinx noun curse, spell, hoodoo, hex.
➤verb curse, bewitch, hex.

job verb 1 work, employment, position, occupation, profession. 2 task, chore, assignment, commission, project, undertaking. 3 duty, responsibility, role, business.

jockey noun rider, horseman, horsewoman.
➤verb manipulate, engineer, finagle (inf).

jocose adj merry, jovial, jolly, joking, playful.

jocular adj joking, facetious, waggish, droll, comical, funny, humorous.

jog verb 1 jolt, jerk, jostle, nudge, shake. 2 prompt, stir, stimulate. 3 trot, run.

join verb 1 attach, fasten, bind, unite, connect, link, combine, merge, amalgamate. 2 unite, connect, meet, merge. 3 enrol, enlist, sign up, become a member. 4 contribute, participate, take part, muck in (inf).

joint noun junction, connection, link, join.
➤adj 1 common, communal, shared, mutual. 2 combined, concerted, united.

joke noun 1 jest, quip, witticism, crack (inf), gag (inf). 2 prank, trick, hoax, leg-pull (inf).
➤verb 1 jest, quip. 2 tease, kid (inf), have on (inf).

joker noun comedian, comic, wag, humorist.

jollity noun fun, joviality, merriment, gaiety.

jolly adj jovial, merry, happy, joyful, cheerful, lively, convivial, festive.

jolt verb 1 jerk, bounce, lurch. 2 jar, jog, jostle, push, bump, knock. 3 shock, startle, shake, upset, disconcert.
➤noun jerk, bump, knock, surprise, upset, shock.

jostle verb push, shove, elbow, barge, jolt, bump.

jot noun iota, bit, scrap, whit.
➤verb write, scribble, note.

journal noun 1 periodical, magazine, review. 2 diary, chronicle, record, daybook.

journalism noun news, reporting, the press, Fleet Street.

journalist noun reporter, correspondent, editor, newspaperman, newspaperwoman, hack (inf).

journey noun voyage, trip, expedition, tour, drive, ride, flight.
➤verb travel, voyage, go, roam, drive, ride, fly, sail.

jovial adj jolly, genial, convivial, hearty, cheerful, good-humoured.

joy noun 1 happiness, gladness, glee, delight, ecstasy, elation, exultation, jubilation, joyfulness. 2 treat, delight, pleasure. 3 luck, success.

joyful adj happy, glad, gleeful, delighted, overjoyed, elated, euphoric, exultant, jubilant, joyous, over the moon (inf), in seventh heaven (inf).

jubilant adj exultant, triumphant, overjoyed, elated, ecstatic, euphoric, thrilled.

jubilation noun exultation, triumph, rejoicing, celebration, elation.

judge verb 1 adjudicate, referee, arbitrate. 2 try, hear, sit in judgment. 3 determine, ascertain, decide, reckon, gauge, estimate, assess, evaluate. 4 deem, consider, regard, think.
➤noun 1 justice, magistrate, beak (inf). 2 adjudicator, referee, arbiter. 3 authority, expert, connoisseur.

judgment noun 1 verdict, finding, decision, conclusion, sentence. 2 discernment, perspicacity, discrimination, taste, insight, understanding, sense, wisdom, acumen, shrewdness. 3 assessment, evaluation, diagnosis, estimation, opinion. **4** doom, retribution, punishment.

judicial *adj* judiciary, juridical, legal.

judicious *adj* wise, prudent, careful, cautious, sensible, shrewd, astute, clever.

jug *verb* pitcher, ewer, urn, flagon.

juggle *verb* manipulate, alter, rearrange, falsify, rig.

juice *noun* liquid, fluid, sap.

juicy *adj* **1** succulent, lush. **2** sensational, colourful, scandalous, racy, spicy.

jumble *verb* disorder, disarrange, mix up, muddle, confuse.
➤*noun* hotchpotch, mishmash (*inf*), disorder, muddle, mess.

jump *verb* **1** leap, spring, bound, skip, hop. **2** clear, vault, hurdle, leap. **3** start, flinch, recoil, jerk. **4** miss, omit, skip, leave out, pass over, disregard. **5** attack, pounce on, set upon.
➤*noun* **1** leap, spring, bound, vault. **2** hurdle, fence, obstacle, barrier. **3** start, jerk, jolt, lurch, flinch. **4** rise, increase, hike (*inf*).

jump at grab, snatch, pounce on.

jumper *noun* sweater, pullover, woolly (*inf*).

jumpy *adj* nervous, agitated, jittery, twitchy, on edge, tense, apprehensive.

junction *noun* **1** joint, connection, link, join. **2** intersection, crossroads, crossing.

juncture *noun* point, stage, time, moment, crux.

junior *adj* minor, lesser, lower, subordinate.

junk *noun* rubbish, refuse, scrap, waste, bric-a-brac.

jurisdiction *noun* **1** power, authority, control, dominion. **2** domain, realm, area, territory.

just *adj* **1** fair, equitable, impartial, unbiased, upright, honest, honourable, righteous, good, virtuous, moral, ethical, principled. **2** right, legal, legitimate, valid.. **3** deserved, merited, justified, rightful, due, appropriate, condign. **4** accurate, correct, factual, well-founded.
➤*adv* **1** exactly, precisely, absolutely, perfectly. **2** barely, hardly, scarcely, by the skin of one's teeth. **3** only, merely, simply, no more than. **4** recently, not long ago, a moment ago.
just about almost, nearly, virtually, practically.

justice *noun* **1** fairness, equity, impartiality, integrity, honesty, righteousness, legality, legitimacy, lawfulness, validity.

justifiable *adj* excusable, defensible, warrantable, reasonable, legitimate, valid.

justify *verb* excuse, explain, defend, support, bear out, vindicate, warrant.

jut *verb* project, protrude, stick out, overhang.

juvenile *adj* **1** young, junior. **2** immature, puerile, infantile, childish.
➤*noun* minor, child, youth, adolescent.

keel over *verb* **1** overturn, capsize, turn turtle. **2** faint, collapse, pass out.

keen *adj* **1** enthusiastic, ardent, eager, diligent, impatient, longing. **2** sharp, acute, cutting, biting, penetrating. **3** shrewd, astute, sharp, quick, perceptive. **4** intense, strong, deep.
keen on fond of, devoted to, into (*inf*).

keep *verb* **1** retain, hold on to, hang on to (*inf*). **2** continue, carry on, go on, persist. **3** store, put, place, deposit. **4** save, hoard, store, collect. **5** sell, deal in, stock, carry. **6** tend, look after, mind. **7** sustain, support, maintain, provide for. **8** guard, protect, defend, shield. **9** fulfil, honour, abide by, observe, obey. **10** hide, conceal, withhold, suppress. **11** detain, delay, hold back, prevent, hinder. **12** stay fresh, last.
➤*noun* **1** board, subsistence, maintenance, livelihood. **2** tower, stronghold, citadel, donjon.
for keeps for ever, for good, permanently.
keep back **1** restrain, check, curb, hold back.
2 suppress, hide, conceal, hush up.
keep from avoid, abstain from, refrain from.
keep on go on, continue, carry on, persist.
keep up **1** maintain, keep going, continue with. **2** keep pace, keep abreast, compete.

keeper *noun* custodian, curator, caretaker, guard, guardian.

keeping *noun* **1** custody, care, possession, safekeeping. **2** conformity, accord, agreement, harmony.

keepsake *noun* memento, souvenir, reminder, token.

keg *noun* barrel, cask, butt.

ken *noun* knowledge, comprehension, understanding, grasp.

kernel *noun* **1** core, nucleus, centre. **2** centre, heart, core, gist, essence.

key *noun* **1** solution, answer, guide, clue, explanation. **2** tonality. **3** tone, mood, vein, style.
➤*adj* crucial, vital, essential, main, basic, fundamental.

kick *verb* **1** boot, punt. **2** recoil, kick back. **3** give up, abandon, quit. **4** oppose, resist, defy, rebel.
➤*noun* **1** boot, punt. **2** strength, potency, punch (*inf*), bite (*inf*). **3** thrill, buzz (*inf*), excitement, pleasure.
kick off start, begin, get going.
kick out eject, expel, throw out, get rid of, dismiss, fire, sack (*inf*), boot out (*inf*).

kid *noun* child, baby, boy, girl, adolescent, teenager.
➤*verb* **1** trick, fool, have on (*inf*). **2** tease, rib (*inf*), pull someone's leg (*inf*).

kidnap *verb* abduct, seize, snatch, take hostage.

kill *verb* **1** slaughter, slay, murder, assassinate, execute, put to death, exterminate, liquidate, butcher, massacre, do in (*inf*), bump off (*inf*), top (*inf*). **2** deaden, smother, negate, neutralize, cancel. **3** exhaust, tire out, wear out, overtire. **4** pass, spend, occupy, while away.

killing *noun* **1** slaughter, butchery, carnage, massacre, murder, manslaughter, homicide, assassination, execution. **2** coup, success, profit, fortune.
➤*adj* **1** deadly, fatal, lethal. **2** tiring, exhausting, taxing, punishing. **3** hilarious, side-splitting, rib-tickling, uproarious.

killjoy *noun* spoilsport, misery, wet blanket (*inf*), party-pooper (*inf*).

kin *noun* kindred, relations, relatives, family.

kind¹ *adj* **1** benevolent, charitable, generous, helpful, friendly, obliging, neighbourly. **2** humane, gentle, warm-hearted, compassionate, sympathetic, understanding, good, nice, considerate, thoughtful.

kind² *noun* **1** sort, type, class, variety, species, genus, breed, ilk. **2** nature, character, make, stamp.

kindle *verb* **1** ignite, light, set alight, set fire to. **2** arouse, stimulate, excite, provoke.

kindly *adj* kind, kind-hearted, warm-hearted, sympathetic, compassionate, benevolent, good, nice.
➤*adv* benevolently, generously, graciously, humanely, compassionately, sympathetically, well, considerately.

kindness *noun* **1** benevolence, generosity, humanity, compassion, sympathy, goodness, consideration. **2** favour, service, good turn.

kindred *noun* **1** kin, relations, relatives, family. **2** kinship, consanguinity, relationship.
➤*adj* **1** related, kin. **2** akin, allied, similar, like.

king *noun* **1** monarch, ruler, sovereign, prince. **2** star, leader, leading light.

kingdom *noun* monarchy, realm, dominion, country.

kink *noun* **1** bend, twist, curl, wrinkle. **2** flaw, fault, defect, snag. **3** quirk, eccentricity, perversion, foible.
➤*verb* bend, twist, curl, crimp, wrinkle.

kinky *adj* **1** wavy, curly, crinkled, bent, twisted. **2** deviant, perverted, unnatural, abnormal. **3** unconventional, weird, bizarre, quirky.

kinship *noun* **1** consanguinity, relationship, kindred. **2** connection, affinity, similarity, likeness.

kiosk *noun* booth, stall, stand.

kismet *noun* destiny, fate, fortune.

kiss *verb* **1** embrace, peck (*inf*), neck (*inf*), snog (*inf*). **2** touch, caress, brush.
➤*noun* embrace, peck (*inf*), smacker (*inf*).

kit *noun* **1** set, parts. **2** tools, implements, instruments. **3** equipment, apparatus, gear, tackle, clothes, uniform, strip (*inf*).
verb equip, supply, fit out, clothe, rig out.

kitchen *noun* cookhouse, galley.

knack *noun* **1** flair, talent, gift, ability, skill, expertise, dexterity, trick, hang (*inf*). **2** propensity, proneness, aptness.

knave *noun* rascal, rogue, scoundrel, blackguard, villain, dastard.

knead *verb* **1** work, press, squeeze. **2** manipulate, massage, shape, mould.

kneel *verb* genuflect, kowtow.

knell *noun* toll, ring, chime.

knickers *pl noun* pants, panties, bloomers, drawers, undies (*inf*).

knick-knack *noun* ornament, trinket, bauble.

knife *noun* blade, carver, scalpel, dagger.
➤*verb* stab, cut, slash.

knight *noun* horseman, cavalier, lord, chevalier.

knit *verb* **1** join, unite, bind, link. **2** heal, mend. **3** furrow, wrinkle, crease.

knob *noun* **1** protuberance, projection, boss, bump, lump. **2** handle, switch, button.

knock *verb* **1** hit, strike, tap, rap, thump, pound, hammer. **2** bump, collide, crash, hit. **3** hit, strike, hammer, beat, dash. **4** criticize, attack, run down, slate (*inf*), slam (*inf*), pan (*inf*).
➤*noun* blow, hit, tap, rap, bang, bump, collision.
knock about beat, batter, abuse, ill-treat, damage.
knock down demolish, level, raze, fell, floor.
knock off 1 stop, finish, clock off. **2** kill, murder, do in (*inf*), bump off (*inf*). **3** steal, pinch (*inf*), nick (*inf*).
knock out 1 eliminate, defeat, beat. **2** stun, astound, impress, overwhelm, bowl over (*inf*).
knock up 1 improvise, put together. **2** reach, achieve, clock up (*inf*). **3** warm up, practise.

knoll *noun* hill, hillock, mound.

knot *noun* **1** fastening, bow, hitch. **2** bunch, clump, cluster, group. **3** protuberance, lump, swelling, nodule.
➤*verb* **1** tie, secure, fasten, join, splice. **2** entwine, entangle, ravel.

knotty *adj* **1** complicated, difficult, thorny, tricky. **2** gnarled, nodular, lumpy.

know *verb* **1** understand, comprehend, realize, see, be aware, be conscious. **2** have learned, be familiar with, be conversant with, have at one's fingertips (*inf*). **3** be acquainted with, have met, socialize with. **4** recognize, identify, distinguish, tell. **5** experience, undergo, go through.

knowing *adj* **1** meaningful, significant, expressive. **2** shrewd, astute, clever, subtle, cunning. **3** deliberate, intentional, conscious.

knowledge *noun* **1** erudition, learning, scholarship, wisdom, acquaintance, familiarity, understanding, comprehension, grasp, skill, expertise, know-how. **2** information, facts, data. **3** awareness, consciousness, realization, recognition.

knowledgeable *adj* erudite, learned, well-informed, acquainted, familiar, conversant.

kowtow *verb* **1** bow, kneel, prostrate oneself. **2** grovel, toady, bow and scrape.

kudos *noun* prestige, glory, fame, renown.

label *noun* **1** tag, ticket, tab, sticker. **2** mark, brand, logo, trademark, proprietary name. **3** epithet, name, title, description, characterization, classification.
➤*verb* **1** mark, stamp, tag, ticket. **2** call, dub, brand, describe, characterize, categorize.

laborious *adj* hard, arduous, strenuous, tiring, painstaking, thorough.

labour *noun* **1** work, toil, drudgery, grind (*inf*), effort, exertion. **2** workers, labourers, employees, staff, workforce. **3** confinement, childbirth, parturition, delivery.
➤*verb* **1** work, toil, drudge, slave. **2** overdo, overemphasize, dwell on, belabour. **3** struggle, strive.

laboured *adj* strained, forced, stiff, unnatural, contrived, overdone.

labourer *noun* workman, hand, navvy, manual worker, unskilled worker.

labyrinth *noun* maze, warren, jungle, network, tangle.

lace *noun* **1** netting, web, mesh, filigree, openwork, tatting. **2** string, cord, thong, tie.
➤*verb* **1** tie, fasten, do up, thread, string. **2** mix, flavour, fortify, spike (*inf*). **3** interlace, interweave, intertwine.

lacerate *verb* tear, rip, rend, gash, slash, cut, mangle, mutilate.

lack *noun* need, want, shortage, deficiency, dearth, absence.
➤*verb* **1** require, be without. **2** need, want, be short of.

lackadaisical *adj* lethargic, listless, apathetic, unenthusiastic, lukewarm, languid.

lackey *noun* **1** sycophant, toady, yes-man (*inf*), parasite, hanger-on, minion, pawn. **2** servant, valet, footman, flunky.

lacklustre *adj* uninteresting, boring, unimaginative, uninspired, flat, dry, bland.

laconic *adj* terse, succinct, concise, short, pithy, curt.

lad *noun* boy, youngster, youth, young man.

laden *adj* loaded, burdened, weighed down, full.

ladylike *adj* refined, polished, genteel, dignified, proper, seemly, polite.

lag *verb* dawdle, loiter, fall behind, trail, straggle, bring up the rear.

laggard *noun* dawdler, loiterer, straggler, sluggard, slowcoach (*inf*).

laid back *adj* relaxed, casual, informal, easygoing (*inf*), leisurely, calm, cool, unflappable (*inf*).

lair *noun* **1** den, hole, cave. **2** hideaway, retreat, refuge.

lambaste *verb* scold, chide, reprimand, rebuke, upbraid, berate, criticize, censure.

lame *adj* **1** crippled, disabled, handicapped, limping, hobbling, halting. **2** weak, feeble, flimsy, unconvincing, inadequate.
➤*verb* cripple, disable, handicap, hamstring.

lament *verb* **1** mourn, sorrow, grieve, cry, wail. **2** bemoan, regret, rue, deplore.
➤*noun* **1** lamentation, cry, wail, complaint. **2** dirge, requiem, elegy, threnody.

lamentable *adj* **1** regrettable, unfortunate, sad, grievous, distressing. **2** deplorable, pitiful, poor, miserable, wretched.

lamp *noun* light, lantern.

lampoon *noun* satire, parody, caricature, skit, spoof.
➤*verb* satirize, ridicule, mock, parody, send up (*inf*).

lance *noun* spear, pike, javelin.
➤*verb* pierce, puncture, cut, incise.

land *noun* **1** earth, ground, terra firma. **2** estate, property, realty, grounds. **3**

country, nation, state, region, area, territory, realm.
> *verb* **1** disembark, alight. **2** dock, berth. **3** alight, settle, touch down, come down. **4** arrive, end up. **5** get, obtain, secure, gain, win. **6** saddle, burden, encumber.

landmark *noun* **1** monument, prominent feature, signpost, beacon. **2** turning point, watershed, milestone, crisis.

landscape *noun* scene, panorama, view, vista, scenery.

lane *noun* track, path, way, road, passage, alley.

language *noun* **1** tongue, dialect, idiom, parlance, lingo (*inf*). **2** slang, cant, jargon, terminology. **3** style, wording, phraseology, expression. **4** speech, utterance, talk, communication.

languid *adj* **1** listless, lethargic, sluggish, torpid, apathetic, spiritless, unenthusiastic. **2** weak, feeble, limp, drooping, flagging, tired, weary.

languish *verb* **1** weaken, flag, droop, fail, wilt. **2** decay, rot, decline, go downhill (*inf*). **3** pine, long, yearn, sigh, mope, grieve.

languor *noun* **1** weakness, tiredness, weariness, fatigue, listlessness, lassitude, lethargy. **2** stillness, tranquillity, calm, quiet, silence.

lank *adj* limp, dull, lustreless, straight.

lanky *adj* gangling, gawky, rangy, tall, thin, lean, gaunt, angular.

lap *noun* **1** circuit, round, tour, circle. **2** stage, part, section, leg.
> *verb* wrap, envelop, enfold, swathe, swaddle.

lapse *noun* **1** slip, error, mistake, failing, oversight. **2** interval, gap, break, pause. **3** drop, fall, decline, deterioration.
> *verb* **1** end, stop, cease. **2** expire, become invalid, run out. **3** drop, fall, sink, decline, slip, slide. **4** pass, elapse, go by.

large *adj* big, great, extensive, broad, ample, considerable, substantial.
at large 1 free, loose, at liberty, on the run. **2** as a whole, in general.

largely *adv* chiefly, mainly, mostly, on the whole, by and large.

largesse *noun* **1** generosity, bounty, charity, philanthropy, beneficence. **2** gift, donation, benefaction, endowment.

lark *noun* prank, joke, trick, escapade, caper, sport, fun.
> *verb* play, sport, frolic, romp, fool about, have fun.

lascivious *adj* lecherous, lustful, lewd, randy (*inf*), horny (*inf*), prurient, salacious, licentious, depraved, dirty.

lash[1] *verb* **1** beat, whip, flog, cane, birch. **2** hit, strike, beat, pound, buffet. **3** flick, whip, switch.
noun **1** whip, scourge, cat-o'-nine-tails. **2** stroke, blow, stripe.

lash[2] *verb* tie, bind, fasten, tether, hitch.

lass *noun* girl, young woman, miss, maid, maiden, bird (*inf*), chick (*inf*).

lassitude *noun* languor, lethargy, listlessness, apathy, tiredness, weariness, fatigue, torpor.

last[1] *adj* **1** ultimate, final, closing, terminal, endmost, rearmost. **2** latest, most recent. **3** previous, preceding.
> *adv* **1** at the end, in the rear, behind. **2** lastly, finally.
> *noun* end, finish, conclusion, close.
at last/at long last finally, eventually, in the end.
on one's last legs worn out, exhausted, all in (*inf*), failing, at death's door (*inf*).

last[2] *verb* **1** continue, carry on, go on, persist. **2** survive, hold out, live, exist. **3** endure, wear, keep.

last-ditch *adj* desperate, frantic, final, eleventh-hour (*inf*).

lasting *adj* abiding, enduring, persisting, long-term, perennial, lifelong, permanent, never-ending, undying, indestructible.

lastly *adv* finally, ultimately, in conclusion, to sum up.

last word *noun* **1** ultimatum, final statement. **2** latest, newest, dernier cri, epitome, quintessence.

latch *noun* catch, lock, bolt.
> *verb* fasten, secure, lock, bolt, bar.
latch on understand, realize, twig (*inf*).

late *adj* **1** unpunctual, delayed, tardy, belated, overdue, behind. **2** recent, up-to-the-minute, current, new. **3** dead,

deceased, departed. **4** former, ex, previous, past, old.
➤*adv* behind schedule, unpunctually, tardily, belatedly.
of late lately, recently, latterly.

lately *adv* recently, latterly, of late.

latent *adj* potential, dormant, quiescent, inactive, undeveloped, hidden, secret, invisible.

later *adv* **1** after, afterwards, subsequently. **2** by and by, in a while.

lateral *adj* side, sideward, sidelong, indirect, oblique.

lather *noun* **1** suds, foam, froth, bubbles. **2** fuss, fluster, state (*inf*), flap (*inf*), tizzy (*inf*).
➤*verb* foam, froth.

latitude *noun* freedom, liberty, licence, carte blanche, leeway, scope.

latter *adj* **1** second, last-mentioned. **2** later, final, last, closing. **3** latest, recent.

latterly *adv* recently, lately, of late.

lattice *noun* **1** trellis, mesh, grid, grille, grating. **2** network, fretwork, openwork, tracery.

laud *verb* praise, extol, eulogize, panegyrize, acclaim, glorify.

laudable *adj* praiseworthy, commendable, admirable, estimable, worthy.

laugh *verb* giggle, chuckle, titter, chortle, guffaw, split one's sides (*inf*), fall about (*inf*).
➤*noun* **1** giggle, chuckle, titter, guffaw. **2** fun, sport, lark. **3** joke, jest, hoot (*inf*), scream (*inf*).
laugh at mock, ridicule, make fun of, deride, scoff at.
laugh off belittle, minimize, play down, make light of, pooh-pooh (*inf*).

laughable *adj* ludicrous, ridiculous, absurd, risible, funny, comical, farcical.

laughter *noun* laughing, giggling, chuckling, mirth, merriment, hilarity.

launch *verb* **1** propel, send off, fire, release, hurl. **2** begin, start, initiate, inaugurate, institute.

launder *verb* wash, clean, iron, press.

laundry *noun* **1** wash, washing, clothes, linen, cleaning. **2** launderette, washhouse, cleaner's.

lavatory *noun* toilet, WC, loo (*inf*), public convenience, privy, latrine.

lavish *adj* **1** abundant, plentiful, profuse, copious, ample, prolific. **2** extravagant, prodigal, thriftless, generous, liberal, unstinting.
➤*verb* shower, pour, heap, squander.

law *noun* **1** statute, rule, regulation, decree, ordinance, act. **2** code, charter, constitution. **3** principle, formula, axiom, truth. **4** jurisprudence, legislation, litigation. **5** police, cops (*inf*), bill (*inf*).

law-abiding *adj* honest, upright, upstanding, virtuous, decent, honourable, obedient, dutiful.

lawful *adj* legal, licit, legitimate, constitutional, rightful, just, valid, permissible.

lawless *adj* **1** anarchic, unruly, disorderly, wild, riotous, revolutionary. **2** unlawful, illegal, illicit, illegitimate.

lawsuit *noun* litigation, suit, action, case, proceedings.

lawyer *noun* solicitor, barrister, counsel, advocate, attorney.

lax *adj* **1** negligent, remiss, permissive, tolerant, indulgent, easygoing (*inf*). **2** loose, limp, flaccid, flabby, slack.

laxative *noun* purgative, cathartic, aperient.

lay¹ *verb* **1** put, place, set down, deposit, rest. **2** arrange, dispose, position, set out, lay out. **3** put forward, advance, bring, submit, lodge. **4** attribute, ascribe, assign, allocate. **5** bet, wager, gamble, stake. **6** have sex with, sleep with, shag (*sl*), bonk (*sl*), screw (*sl*).
lay aside set aside, put off, postpone, discard, dismiss.
lay down 1 give up, sacrifice, surrender. **2** stipulate, set down, formulate, ordain, prescribe, state.
lay in collect, amass, accumulate, store, hoard, stockpile.
lay into attack, assail, set about, lambaste.
lay off 1 discharge, dismiss, let go, make redundant. **2** stop, desist from, refrain from.
lay on provide, supply, give, organize.
lay out 1 set out, arrange, dispose, plan, design. **2** spend, pay, disburse, shell out (*inf*), fork out (*inf*). **3** knock down, fell, floor, knock out.

lay[2] *adj* **1** laic, secular, nonclerical.
2 amateur, nonprofessional, nonspecialist.

layabout *noun* good-for-nothing, wastrel, idler, loafer, skiver (*inf*).

layer *noun* stratum, seam, vein, ply, thickness, tier, covering, coating.

laze *verb* idle, loaf, lounge, loll about.

lazy *adj* **1** slothful, idle, indolent, workshy.
2 sluggish, torpid, lethargic, slow.

lead *verb* **1** guide, precede, usher, show.
2 conduct, escort, marshal, steer. **3** head, rule, preside over. **4** govern, command, direct, supervise. **5** cause, move, prompt, influence, induce, dispose. **6** outstrip, outrun, outdistance, surpass, excel. **7** pass, spend, live, experience, undergo.
8 contribute, produce, bring on, provoke.
➤*noun* **1** first place, front, vanguard. **2** supremacy, edge, advantage, initiative.
3 leadership, direction, guidance, example.
4 clue, hint, tip, guide, indication, pointer, tip-off (*inf*). **5** principal part, starring role, title role. **6** leash, tether, chain. **lead on** entice, lure, seduce, flirt with, deceive, string along (*inf*).

leaden *adj* **1** heavy, weighty, burdensome.
2 stiff, wooden, sluggish, torpid, lifeless, spiritless. **3** grey, dark, gloomy, overcast, louring.

leader *noun* **1** head, chief, ruler, boss (*inf*), commander, captain, principal, number one (*inf*). **2** guide, pioneer, trailblazer, pathfinder, innovator. **3** front-runner, pacemaker.

leading *adj* principal, chief, first, foremost, front, best, greatest, highest, ruling, governing.

leaf *noun* **1** bract, frond, needle. **2** page, sheet, folio.

leaflet *noun* booklet, brochure, pamphlet, circular, flyer.

league *noun* **1** association, federation, alliance, coalition, consortium, syndicate, guild, fellowship. **2** class, category, group, level.
verb associate, confederate, ally, unite, band together.
in league collaborating, hand in glove (*inf*), in collusion, in cahoots (*inf*).

leak *verb* **1** seep, ooze, drip, escape.

2 divulge, disclose, reveal, give away, let slip.
➤*noun* **1** crack, split, hole, puncture.
2 leakage, seepage, escape, discharge.

lean[1] *verb* **1** rest, recline. **2** bend, slant, slope, tilt, list, incline. **3** depend, rely, count. **4** tend, incline.

lean[2] *adj* **1** thin, slim, spare, skinny, bony, angular, emaciated. **2** meagre, scanty, sparse, poor, barren.

leaning *noun* tendency, inclination, propensity, disposition, partiality, predilection, proclivity, penchant.

leap *verb* **1** jump, bound, spring, hop.
2 vault, clear, jump over. **3** surge, escalate, soar, shoot up, skyrocket.
➤*noun* **1** jump, bound, spring, vault, hop.
2 rise, increase, escalation, upsurge.
by/in leaps and bounds rapidly, swiftly, quickly, speedily.

learn *verb* **1** master, grasp, study, take in, assimilate, acquire, pick up. **2** memorize, get off pat. **3** discover, find out, hear, ascertain.

learned *adj* scholarly, erudite, lettered, well-read, academic, intellectual.

learning *noun* scholarship, erudition, education, schooling, knowledge, study.

lease *verb* let, rent, hire, charter.

leash *noun* lead, tether, chain.

least *adj* smallest, slightest, lowest, fewest, minimum.

leave[1] *verb* **1** depart, set off, go, exit, vacate, evacuate, quit (*inf*). **2** abandon, desert, forsake, ditch (*inf*). **3** retire, withdraw, pull out. **4** forget, omit, exclude, miss. **5** bequeath, will, make over, transfer, convey, devise. **6** allot, commit, entrust, hand over.
leave off stop, cease, desist from, refrain from.

leave[2] *noun* **1** permission, consent, sanction, authorization. **2** holiday, vacation, time off, sabbatical.
take one's leave say goodbye, part, depart, leave.

leavings *pl noun* scraps, leftovers, remains, residue, refuse.

lechery *noun* lust, lewdness, lasciviousness, concupiscence, prurience, depravity, debauchery.

lecture *noun* **1** talk, speech, address, lesson, discourse. **2** reprimand, reproof, dressing-down (*inf*), tirade.
➤*verb* **1** teach, tutor, talk, speak, hold forth, expound. **2** reprimand, reprove, chide, berate.

ledge *noun* shelf, sill, ridge, projection, overhang.

lee *noun* shelter, protection, cover, refuge.

leech *noun* parasite, bloodsucker, hanger-on, freeloader (*inf*), sponger (*inf*), scrounger (*inf*).

leer *verb* stare, eye, ogle.

lees *pl noun* residue, sediment, deposit, precipitate.

leeway *noun* scope, room, latitude, slack, margin.

leg *noun* **1** limb, shank, pin (*inf*). **2** upright, support, prop. **3** part, portion, stage, stretch.
leg it **1** walk, go on foot. **2** run, hurry, hightail it (*inf*), hotfoot it (*inf*).

legacy *noun* **1** bequest, gift, endowment. **2** inheritance, heritage, patrimony.

legal *adj* **1** lawful, licit, legitimate, authorized, above-board, legit (*inf*). **2** judicial, juridical, forensic. **3** constitutional, statutory.

legalize *verb* decriminalize, legitimate, authorize, ratify, license.

legate *noun* envoy, ambassador, emissary, plenipotentiary.

legation *noun* embassy, ministry, mission, deputation, delegation.

legend *noun* **1** myth, tale, story, saga. **2** inscription, motto, caption, key.

legendary *adj* **1** mythical, fictional, fabled, traditional, fabulous, heroic. **2** famous, celebrated, great, immortal.

legible *adj* readable, decipherable, clear, plain, neat.

legion *noun* **1** army, regiment, troop, division, unit. **2** crowd, throng, multitude, host.
➤*adj* numerous, many, myriad, countless, innumerable.

legislation *noun* lawmaking, codification, law, statute, charter, constitution.

legislature *noun* assembly, parliament, congress, senate.

legitimate *adj* **1** legal, lawful, licit, authorized, sanctioned, permissible, legit (*inf*). **2** proper, rightful. **3** genuine, real, true. **4** recognized, approved. **5** reasonable, logical, rational, sound, valid.

leg-up *noun* help, assistance, boost, advancement.

leisure *noun* rest, recreation, freedom, liberty, free time, spare time, holiday, break.

leisurely *adj* unhurried, slow, relaxed, easy, gentle.

lend *verb* **1** loan, advance. **2** give, bestow, impart, contribute, add.

length *noun* **1** extent, reach, span, measure, distance. **2** duration, stretch, period, term. **3** piece, portion, section.
at length **1** in detail, in depth, fully, thoroughly. **2** interminably, on and on, for ages. **3** eventually, finally, at last, in the end.

lengthen *verb* stretch, extend, elongate, prolong, protract, draw out.

lengthy *adj* **1** long, extended, protracted. **2** long-winded, wordy, rambling, interminable.

lenient *adj* tolerant, indulgent, clement, merciful, mild, gentle, kind, generous.

leper *noun* outcast, pariah, untouchable, undesirable, persona non grata.

lesbian *noun* homosexual, gay, sapphist, dyke (*sl*).

lessen *verb* **1** reduce, lower, decrease, shorten. **2** diminish, decrease, abate, ease, subside, wane.

lesser *adj* smaller, lower, inferior, minor, secondary, subordinate.

lesson *noun* **1** class, period, tutorial, seminar. **2** example, deterrent, warning.

let[1] *verb* **1** permit, allow, sanction, authorize. **2** cause, make, enable. **3** lease, rent, hire.
let down betray, fail, abandon, leave in the lurch (*inf*).
let in admit, accept, receive.
let off **1** excuse, exempt, pardon, forgive, reprieve. **2** set off, fire, detonate, explode.
let on **1** reveal, divulge, tell, let slip, give away. **2** pretend, make out, feign, affect.

let out 1 release, free, liberate, let go. **2** utter, emit, give vent to.

let up abate, subside, ease, diminish, die down.

let² *noun* obstruction, impediment, restriction, constraint.

lethal *adj* **1** fatal, deadly, mortal, murderous, toxic. **2** destructive, devastating, dangerous, virulent.

lethargy *noun* **1** sluggishness, inertia, apathy, listlessness, lassitude, languor. **2** sleepiness, drowsiness, somnolence, stupor, narcosis.

letter *noun* **1** note, line, message, communication, missive, epistle. **2** character, symbol, grapheme.
to the letter exactly, precisely, strictly, literally.

letters *pl noun* learning, scholarship, erudition, culture, literature, humanities.

level *adj* **1** flat, even, smooth. **2** horizontal, plane. **3** flush, aligned. **4** equal, level pegging, neck and neck. **5** steady, stable.
➤ *verb* **1** flatten, smooth, plane. **2** raze, demolish, lay waste, pull down, bulldoze. **3** aim, point, train. **4** direct, aim, focus. **5** be frank, speak plainly, tell the truth, put one's cards on the table (*inf*).
➤ *noun* **1** horizontal, flat. **2** position, rank, grade, station, status, degree, amount, quantity. **3** height, altitude, elevation. **4** layer, plane, stratum, floor, storey.
on the level honest, above-board, genuine, sincere, candid.

lever *noun* **1** bar, crowbar, jemmy. **2** handle, switch, joystick.
➤ *verb* prise, jemmy, force, shift, lift.

leverage *noun* force, power, weight, influence, pull (*inf*), clout (*inf*).

levity *noun* flippancy, facetiousness, jocularity, fun, humour, light-heartedness, frivolity, triviality.

levy *verb* impose, exact, demand, charge, raise, collect.
➤ *noun* **1** imposition, exaction, collection. **2** charge, fee, tax, duty, toll, tariff.

lewd *adj* lecherous, lascivious, prurient, salacious, obscene, indecent, suggestive, smutty (*inf*).

liability *noun* **1** responsibility, answerability, accountability. **2** debt, due, obligation, duty. **3** handicap, hindrance, impediment, burden, disadvantage, drawback.

liable *adj* **1** responsible, answerable, accountable, blameworthy, culpable. **2** subject, susceptible, exposed, open, vulnerable. **3** likely, apt, prone, inclined, disposed.

liaise *verb* communicate, network, interface, collaborate, cooperate, interact.

liaison *noun* **1** communication, contact, collaboration, cooperation. **2** connection, link, bond, tie. **3** relationship, affair, romance, intrigue.

libel *noun* defamation, traducement, denigration, vilification, mudslinging (*inf*).
➤ *verb* defame, traduce, denigrate, vilify, smear.

liberal *adj* **1** progressive, forward-looking, enlightened, broad-minded, permissive, tolerant. **2** general, wide-ranging, broad-based. **3** generous, open-handed, munificent, unstinting, charitable, magnanimous. **4** ample, abundant, plentiful, copious, lavish. **5** broad, loose, free.

liberate *verb* free, set free, emancipate, manumit, unshackle, unfetter, release, deliver.

libertine *noun* profligate, debauchee, rake, roué, playboy, philanderer.

liberty *noun* **1** freedom, independence, autonomy, self-determination. **2** right, privilege, dispensation, exemption, immunity. **3** licence, latitude, carte blanche. **4** choice, option, free will, volition. **5** familiarity, impropriety, presumption.

libidinous *adj* lecherous, lustful, lascivious, randy (*inf*), horny (*inf*), concupiscent, prurient, salacious.

libido *noun* sex drive, sexual appetite, passion, ardour, lust.

licence *noun* **1** certificate, permit, warrant. **2** authorization, permission, charter, franchise, right. **3** liberty, freedom, latitude, carte blanche.

license *verb* permit, authorize, warrant, empower, certify, accredit, charter, franchise.

licentious *adj* dissolute, debauched, depraved, loose, wanton, promiscuous, immoral, lewd.

lick *verb* 1 wash, clean, taste, lap, moisten, wet. 2 play, flicker, dart. 3 beat, defeat, trounce, thrash (*inf*), hammer (*inf*).

lid *noun* top, cap, cover, stopper.

lie¹ *verb* 1 tell untruths, fib (*inf*). 2 fabricate, dissemble, falsify, misrepresent.
➤*noun* untruth, falsehood, fabrication, fib (*inf*), whopper (*inf*), porky (*inf*).
give the lie to disprove, contradict, negate, refute.

lie² *verb* 1 recline, be recumbent, rest, repose, lounge. 2 stretch out, sprawl. 3 remain, stay, continue, be. 4 be located, be found, reside.
lie low hide, take cover, go to ground, keep a low profile, skulk.

lieu *noun* **in lieu** instead, as an alternative, as a substitute.

life *noun* 1 being, existence, viability, animation. 2 living things, living beings, flora, fauna. 3 lifestyle, way of life, existence, circumstances, situation.

lifeless *adj* 1 dead, deceased, defunct. 2 inanimate, inorganic, inert. 3 dull, flat, lacklustre, stiff, sluggish, listless. 4 barren, sterile, uncultivated, uninhabited.

lifelike *adj* realistic, true-to-life, vivid, graphic, accurate, faithful, authentic.

lifetime *noun* life, span, days.

lift *verb* 1 raise, elevate, hoist, jack. 2 uplift, exalt, boost, improve. 3 revoke, rescind, annul, cancel, terminate, remove. 4 steal, copy, plagiarize, take.
➤*noun* 1 elevator, hoist. 2 run, drive, ride, transportation. 3 boost, stimulus, pick-me-up, shot in the arm (*inf*).

light¹ *noun* 1 illumination, luminosity, radiance, brightness, ray, beam, glow, flash. 2 lamp, lantern, candle, torch, beacon. 3 daylight, sunshine. 4 enlightenment, elucidation, explanation. 5 understanding, insight, knowledge, awareness. 6 aspect, viewpoint, angle, perspective.
➤*adj* 1 bright, sunny, well-lit, illuminated. 2 pale, pastel, faded, fair.
➤*verb* 1 ignite, kindle, set alight. 2 illuminate, brighten, light up.

in the light of considering, in view of.

light² *adj* 1 weightless, airy, buoyant. 2 thin, flimsy, lightweight, insubstantial. 3 easy, simple, effortless, undemanding. 4 amusing, entertaining. 5 frivolous, superficial, trivial, petty. 6 gentle, soft, weak, faint. 7 slight, mild, moderate. 8 agile, nimble, sprightly, graceful, deft. 9 cheerful, blithe, carefree, happy, merry.
➤*verb* land, settle, alight.
light on come across, find, discover, stumble upon, happen upon.

lighten¹ *verb* 1 illuminate, brighten, light. 2 bleach, whiten, fade.

lighten² *verb* 1 lessen, reduce, ease, relieve, disencumber, unload. 2 cheer, brighten, gladden, hearten, buoy up, uplift.

light-headed *adj* faint, dizzy, giddy, woozy (*inf*).

light-hearted *adj* 1 cheerful, bright, merry, jolly, happy, carefree. 2 playful, amusing, entertaining.

likable *adj* nice, pleasant, agreeable, friendly, charming.

like¹ *adj* similar, alike, same, akin, corresponding, equivalent.
➤*noun* equal, peer, match, counterpart, twin.

like² *verb* 1 enjoy, relish, appreciate, be partial to, care for, love, be fond of, approve of. 2 prefer, choose, wish, want, care.
➤*noun* liking, preference, partiality, predilection.

likelihood *noun* possibility, probability, prospect, chance.

likely *adj* 1 probable, odds-on (*inf*), expected, on the cards, liable, apt. 2 plausible, convincing, credible, feasible, reasonable, rational. 3 promising, hopeful, suitable, acceptable.

liken *verb* compare, equate, link, relate.

likeness *noun* 1 similarity, resemblance, correspondence, analogy. 2 image, representation, portrait, effigy, copy, reproduction. 3 semblance, guise, appearance, form.

likewise *adv* 1 similarly, the same. 2 moreover, furthermore, also, in addition, besides.

liking noun **1** love, affinity, appreciation, admiration. **2** fondness, partiality, predilection, taste, relish, fancy, soft spot (inf).

lilt noun rhythm, inflection, cadence.

limb noun **1** leg, arm, wing, member. **2** bough, branch. **3** offshoot, extension, branch, arm.
out on a limb isolated, alone, exposed, vulnerable.

limber adj lithe, lissom, supple, flexible.
➤ **limber up** warm up, loosen up, exercise, prepare.

limelight noun public eye, attention, fame, celebrity, stardom, prominence, spotlight.

limit noun **1** boundary, frontier, border, edge, end, cut-off point. **2** extreme, extremity, utmost. **3** maximum, ceiling. **4** confine, bound, parameter, restriction, restraint.
➤ verb **1** restrict, restrain, confine, bound, delimit, demarcate. **2** curb, check, control, curtail.

limitation noun **1** restriction, restraint, control, curb, check. **2** weakness, defect, flaw, shortcoming.

limited adj restricted, controlled, qualified, confined, finite, fixed.

limp[1] verb hobble, shuffle, falter, stagger.
➤ noun hobble, claudication, lameness.

limp[2] adj flaccid, soft, flexible, slack, relaxed, drooping.

limpid adj **1** clear, transparent, pellucid, crystalline. **2** plain, lucid, clear, simple.

line noun **1** row, rank, file, queue, column. **2** stroke, rule, dash, stripe, band, bar. **3** crease, wrinkle, furrow, groove. **4** string, rope, cord, thread. **5** wire, cable, flex, cord. **6** limit, boundary, frontier, border. **7** outline, contour, shape. **8** way, policy, procedure, course, direction, tack. **9** field, area, business, profession, specialty. **10** brand, type, range. **11** series, sequence, succession, ancestry, descent, lineage, family, stock.
➤ verb **1** border, edge, fringe, skirt. **2** rule, score, hatch, crease, wrinkle.
line up 1 align, range, straighten, array. **2** queue up, fall in. **3** organize, arrange, assemble, marshal, prepare, secure.
on the line at risk, in danger, in jeopardy.

lineage noun ancestry, descent, extraction, parentage, family, pedigree, genealogy.

linger verb **1** loiter, wait, tarry, hang around. **2** dally, dawdle, take one's time. **3** delay, procrastinate. **4** persist, continue, survive, remain.

lingo noun **1** language, tongue, idiom, vernacular, dialect. **2** jargon, terminology.

link verb **1** connect, join, couple, unite, tie, fasten. **2** associate, relate, connect.
➤ noun **1** connection, coupling, tie, bond, member, element. **2** association, relationship, connection, correspondence.

lip noun **1** edge, brim, rim. **2** impudence, impertinence, insolence, cheek (inf).

liquefy verb liquidize, liquesce, melt, dissolve.

liquid noun liquor, fluid, juice, solution.
➤ adj **1** fluid, flowing, running, watery, wet. **2** liquefied, molten, melted. **3** smooth, flowing, fluid. **4** pure, clear, sweet.

liquidate verb **1** pay, settle, discharge, clear. **2** sell, cash, realize. **3** dissolve, break up, close down, wind up. **4** kill, murder, assassinate, eliminate, rub out (inf).

liquidize verb blend, process, purée.

list[1] noun catalogue, inventory, index, roll, enumeration, series.
➤ verb enumerate, catalogue, index, record, log.

list[2] verb lean, slant, incline, tilt, tip, heel.

listen verb **1** hark, attend, hear, give ear. **2** heed, mind, take notice, concentrate.
listen in eavesdrop, overhear, tap, bug (inf).

listless adj lethargic, sluggish, inactive, enervated, spiritless, unenthusiastic, apathetic.

literal adj **1** strict, faithful, authentic, actual, true, unvarnished. **2** verbatim, word-for-word, exact, precise.

literally adv **1** verbatim, word for word, strictly, exactly, faithfully. **2** positively, absolutely, really, truly.

literary adj scholarly, erudite, academic, intellectual, highbrow.

literate adj **1** educated, cultured, learned, scholarly. **2** skilled, knowledgeable.

literature noun **1** literary works, books, novels, poetry, plays, writings. **2** printed matter, brochures, leaflets, bumf (inf).

lithe adj lissom, limber, supple, flexible, agile, nimble, graceful.

litter noun **1** rubbish, refuse, waste, junk, trash. **2** clutter, mess, disorder, jumble. **3** brood, young, progeny, offspring. **4** bedding, straw, hay.
➤verb strew, scatter, clutter, mess up.

little adj **1** small, short, petite, diminutive, miniature, dwarf, pygmy. **2** young, small, baby. **3** short, brief, fleeting. **4** trivial, trifling, petty, paltry, slight, minor. **5** meagre, scant, skimpy, sparse.
➤adv barely, scarcely, hardly.
➤noun **1** dash, pinch, drop, spot, trace, touch, tad (inf), smidgen (inf). **2** moment, second, minute, bit.
little by little gradually, slowly, progressively, bit by bit, by degrees.

liturgy noun service, ceremony, office, sacrament, rite, form.

live[1] verb **1** be, exist, be alive, breathe. **2** survive, remain, endure, continue, last. **3** subsist, survive, support oneself, make ends meet. **4** reside, dwell, abide, inhabit. **5** pass, spend, lead.

live[2] adj **1** alive, living, breathing, animate, real. **2** unrecorded, unedited. **3** connected, charged. **4** burning, alight, glowing, hot. **5** unexploded, explosive. **6** topical, current, active.

livelihood noun occupation, job, work, living, income, subsistence.

lively adj **1** active, energetic, dynamic, vivacious, bouncy, frisky, spry, sprightly. **2** animated, spirited, brisk, quick, vigorous. **3** alert, keen, enquiring, perceptive. **4** busy, bustling, astir, exciting, eventful. **5** vivid, graphic, colourful, striking.

liven verb enliven, animate, invigorate, vitalize, stimulate.

livery noun uniform, costume, dress, regalia, vestments.

livid adj **1** angry, furious, enraged, incensed, fuming, seething. **2** ashen, pale, pallid, white, bloodless, ghastly. **3** discoloured, bruised, black-and-blue.

living adj **1** alive, live, breathing, animate.
2 current, contemporary, active, in use, extant, surviving.
➤noun keep, maintenance, subsistence, income, livelihood, work, job.

load noun **1** cargo, freight, lading, burden, charge. **2** shipment, consignment, contents. **3** burden, onus, weight, responsibility, cross, millstone. **4** lot, heap (inf), pile (inf), stack (inf).
➤verb **1** fill, pack, lade, freight. **2** charge, prime. **3** weight, bias, rig.

loaded adj **1** laden, full, stacked, crammed, charged, primed. **2** rich, wealthy, affluent, well-off, rolling in it (inf).

loaf[1] noun **1** block, slab, cake, lump. **2** head, brains, common sense.

loaf[2] verb lounge, idle, laze, hang around, waste time.

loafer noun idler, sluggard, shirker, skiver (inf), layabout.

loan noun **1** advance, credit. **2** lending, usury.
➤verb lend, advance.

loath adj unwilling, reluctant, disinclined, averse.

loathe verb detest, abhor, abominate, hate.

loathing noun detestation, abhorrence, hatred, aversion, repugnance, disgust.

loathsome adj detestable, abhorrent, execrable, odious, hateful, disgusting, obnoxious, vile.

lob verb throw, fling, hurl, pitch.

lobby noun **1** foyer, entrance hall, vestibule, anteroom. **2** campaign, pressure group.
➤verb **1** campaign, push. **2** urge, press.

local adj **1** regional, parochial, municipal. **2** neighbourhood, community, resident, nearby. **3** limited, restricted, confined, contained.

locality noun **1** neighbourhood, vicinity, environment, district, area. **2** position, location, place.

localize verb limit, restrict, contain, confine.

locate verb **1** find, discover, unearth, track down, pinpoint. **2** situate, place, put, set, establish.

location noun position, whereabouts, place, spot, site, venue, setting.

lock¹ *noun* bolt, bar, latch, padlock.
➤*verb* **1** fasten, secure, bolt, padlock.
2 clasp, embrace, hug, hold.
lock up jail, imprison, incarcerate, put behind bars.

lock² *noun* tress, curl, ringlet, tuft, wisp, strand.

locomotion *noun* movement, motion, progress, travel.

lodge *verb* **1** live, dwell, stay, room, board. **2** accommodate, house, billet, quarter, put up. **3** submit, register, file. **4** fix, implant, embed, stick. **5** put, place, deposit.
➤*noun* **1** gatehouse, cottage. **2** hut, cabin, chalet. **3** branch, chapter, group. **4** den, lair.

lodger *noun* boarder, paying guest, tenant.

lodgings *pl noun* accommodation, quarters, rooms, digs (*inf*).

lofty *adj* **1** high, tall, towering, soaring. **2** elevated, exalted, noble, grand, august, dignified. **3** arrogant, haughty, high-and-mighty (*inf*), lordly, overbearing, supercilious, condescending, snooty (*inf*).

log *noun* **1** branch, trunk, billet, piece. **2** record, register, diary, journal.
➤*verb* **1** record, register, write down. **2** cover, travel, do, hit, achieve, attain.

loggerhead *noun* **at loggerheads** at variance, at odds, quarrelling, fighting.

logic *noun* **1** reasoning, argumentation, dialectics. **2** rationality, reason, sense, coherence.

logical *adj* **1** reasoned, rational, sound, valid, coherent, consistent. **2** reasoning, thinking, rational, sensible, wise.

logistics *pl noun* planning, organization, management, coordination, strategy.

logo *noun* logotype, emblem, symbol, sign, trademark, badge, insignia.

loiter *verb* **1** hang around, skulk, tarry, linger. **2** dawdle, dilly-dally (*inf*), lag.

loll *verb* **1** lounge, sprawl, slouch, flop, lie, recline. **2** hang, dangle, droop, flap.

lone *adj* **1** single, sole, only. **2** isolated, separate. **3** solitary, alone, solo, by oneself, on one's own.

lonely *adj* **1** friendless, lonesome, alone, forlorn, bereft. **2** solitary, withdrawn, sequestered, reclusive. **3** remote, isolated, out-of-the-way, off the beaten track (*inf*), deserted, unfrequented.

long¹ *adj* **1** lengthy, extensive, stretched, elongated. **2** protracted, prolonged, sustained, interminable.

long² *verb* yearn, crave, hunger, thirst, hanker, dream.

longing *noun* yearning, desire, urge, hankering, yen (*inf*), hope, dream.

long-standing *adj* well-established, old, time-honoured, enduring, lasting, continuing.

long-suffering *adj* patient, forbearing, stoical, uncomplaining, resigned, tolerant.

long-winded *adj* lengthy, long-drawn-out, wordy, verbose, diffuse, rambling.

look *verb* **1** watch, observe, survey, view, examine, scan. **2** gaze, stare, peer, glance, peep. **3** seem, appear.
➤*noun* **1** examination, view, gaze, stare, glance, peep, shufti (*inf*), butcher's (*inf*), gander (*inf*), dekko (*inf*). **2** expression, face, countenance, features. **3** appearance, aspect, air, demeanour, semblance, facade. **4** fashion, vogue, style, design.
look after mind, take care of, attend to, supervise, protect.
look back remember, recall, reminisce.
look down on despise, scorn.
look for seek, search for, hunt for.
look into investigate, explore, study, research, enquire about, check out (*inf*).
look out beware, watch out, take care, pay attention.
look over inspect, examine, check, scan.
look up 1 refer to, turn to, search for, find. **2** improve, get better, pick up, advance.
look up to admire, respect, revere, worship.

lookalike *noun* double, doppelgänger, twin, clone, image, spitting image (*inf*), dead ringer (*inf*).

lookout *noun* **1** watch, guard, vigil, qui vive. **2** guard, sentry, sentinel. **3** watchtower, observation post. **4** business, concern, responsibility, problem.

loom *verb* **1** appear, emerge, materialize, bulk, threaten, menace. **2** tower, rise, hover, hang over, overshadow, dominate.

loop noun circle, ring, noose, curl, coil, whorl.
➤ **verb 1** encircle, ring, surround. **2** wind, coil, spiral, curl, twist.

loose adj **1** baggy, sloppy. **2** slack, lax, relaxed, drooping, sagging, floppy. **3** free, at large, at liberty, on the loose. **4** untied, undone, detached, floating, hanging, insecure, wobbly. **5** vague, indefinite, broad, general, imprecise, inexact. **6** dissolute, debauched, degenerate, immoral, wanton, promiscuous.
➤ **verb 1** set free, release, let go, unleash. **2** unfasten, detach, disengage, disconnect.
at a loose end idle, unoccupied, bored.

loosen verb slacken, relax, ease, undo, unfasten, let out.

loot noun spoils, booty, plunder, haul, swag (inf).
➤ **verb** pillage, plunder, sack, ransack, raid, maraud.

lop verb **1** cut off, chop off, sever, detach. **2** prune, clip, trim.

lope verb run, stride, bound, lollop.

lopsided adj **1** asymmetrical, unbalanced, uneven. **2** askew, skew-whiff (inf), crooked, awry.

loquacious adj talkative, voluble, garrulous, chatty, gabby (inf).

lord noun **1** peer, noble, aristocrat, baron, earl, marquess, viscount. **2** ruler, monarch, sovereign, chief. **3** master, governor, commander, leader.
lord it over domineer, oppress, pull rank on, boss around (inf).

lordly adj **1** haughty, arrogant, overbearing, domineering, lofty, high-and-mighty (inf), condescending, supercilious. **2** noble, dignified, regal, majestic, imperial.

lore noun knowledge, wisdom, traditions, superstitions, sayings, stories.

lorry noun truck, juggernaut, pantechnicon, artic (inf), van.

lose verb **1** mislay, misplace, drop. **2** miss, pass up (inf), waste, squander. **3** be deprived of, be divested of, forfeit, sacrifice. **4** dissipate, expend, get rid of, shed. **5** elude, dodge, escape, throw off, shake off, give the slip. **6** be defeated, be beaten, fail.

loser noun **1** runner-up, also-ran. **2** failure, flop (inf), nonstarter (inf), no-hoper (inf).

loss noun **1** dispossession, forfeiture, sacrifice, dissipation. **2** privation, disadvantage, detriment, harm, death, bereavement. **3** casualty, fatality. **4** failure, defeat, waste. **5** deficit, shortfall.
at a loss puzzled, perplexed, bewildered, confused, uncertain.

lost adj **1** disoriented, astray. **2** bewildered, confused, puzzled, at a loss. **3** absorbed, preoccupied, engrossed, rapt, abstracted, absent.

lot noun **1** abundance, great deal, load (inf), heap (inf), pile (inf), stack (inf). **2** collection, assortment, set, group, batch. **3** fate, destiny, fortune, luck, doom. **4** chance, hazard, lottery. **5** share, portion, part, ration. **6** plot, piece, patch, tract.
a lot 1 much, a great deal. **2** often, frequently.

lotion noun ointment, cream, embrocation, liniment.

lottery noun **1** draw, raffle, sweepstake. **2** gamble, game of chance, risk, speculation.

loud adj **1** noisy, deafening, roaring, blaring, resounding, strident, shrill, raucous, vociferous. **2** garish, gaudy, lurid, flashy, showy.

lounge verb rest, relax, loll, sprawl, loaf, idle, laze.
➤ **noun** living room, sitting room, drawing room, parlour.

lour verb **1** darken, blacken, threaten, menace. **2** frown, scowl, glower, glare, look daggers (inf).

lousy adj **1** poor, bad, inferior, incompetent, awful (inf), terrible (inf), rotten (inf). **2** mean, base, low, dirty, despicable, rotten (inf).

lout noun boor, churl, brute, barbarian, yahoo, yob (inf).

lovable adj adorable, endearing, charming, sweet, cute, appealing.

love verb **1** adore, cherish, hold dear, be fond of, care for, dote on, desire, fancy (inf), like, adore, delight in, appreciate, be mad on (inf). **2** enjoy, like, adore, delight in, appreciate, be mad on (inf).
➤ **noun 1** affection, attachment, fondness, tenderness, care, devotion, adoration.

2 passion, infatuation, ardour, desire, lust.
3 liking, enjoyment, appreciation, taste.
4 dear, darling, sweetheart, beloved, pet.
make love have sex, go to bed, have it off (*sl*), bonk (*sl*), shag (*sl*).

lovely *adj* **1** beautiful, attractive, pretty, good-looking, enchanting, exquisite.
2 delightful, enjoyable, pleasant, nice.

lovemaking *noun* sexual intercourse, sex, coition, nooky (*inf*), rumpy-pumpy (*inf*), petting, foreplay.

lover *noun* **1** boyfriend, girlfriend, sweetheart, partner, gigolo, toy boy (*inf*), mistress, bit on the side (*inf*). **2** fan, devotee, aficionado, enthusiast, buff (*inf*).

low[1] *adj* **1** short, small, shallow, squat, stunted. **2** low-lying, depressed, sunken.
3 inadequate, deficient, paltry, scant, moderate, reduced, inferior, substandard.
4 poor, lowly, humble, common, simple, modest. **5** base, abject, mean, contemptible, ignoble, coarse, vulgar. **6** quiet, soft, subdued, muted, hushed. **7** deep, bass.
8 depressed, blue (*inf*), down in the dumps (*inf*), despondent, gloomy, miserable.

low[2] *verb* moo, bellow.

lowdown *noun* information, intelligence, data, gen (*inf*), dope (*inf*).

lower *verb* **1** drop, let down, bring down.
2 reduce, decrease, lessen, cut, moderate, turn down, abate. **3** abase, degrade, humble, demean, debase, devalue.
➤*adj* inferior, lesser, subordinate, minor, junior, under, nether, bottom.

low-key *adj* restrained, muted, subdued, subtle, understated, quiet.

lowly *adj* **1** humble, simple, unpretentious, modest, unassuming, meek. **2** lowborn, plebeian, poor, common.

loyal *adj* faithful, devoted, committed, staunch, steadfast, reliable.

loyalty *noun* allegiance, faithfulness, fidelity, fealty, devotion, duty.

lubricate *verb* **1** oil, grease. **2** moisturize, smooth.

lucid *adj* **1** clear, plain, intelligible, comprehensible, simple, obvious. **2** sane, rational, clear-headed, compos mentis.

luck *noun* **1** chance, fortune, hazard, fortuity, serendipity, providence, fate, lot.
2 success, prosperity, blessing, windfall.

luckless *adj* unlucky, unfortunate, hapless, wretched, unsuccessful, ill-fated, cursed, jinxed.

lucky *adj* fortunate, happy, blessed, charmed, favoured, jammy (*inf*), propitious, auspicious, fortuitous, providential.

lucrative *adj* remunerative, well-paid, gainful, profitable, economic.

lucre *noun* wealth, riches, money, dosh (*inf*), profit, gain, proceeds, spoils.

ludicrous *adj* absurd, ridiculous, preposterous, comical, laughable, droll, zany, crazy.

lug *verb* pull, drag, heave, haul, carry, tote, hump (*inf*).

luggage *noun* baggage, bags, cases, impedimenta.

lugubrious *adj* mournful, doleful, sombre, funereal, gloomy, melancholy.

lukewarm *adj* **1** tepid, warm, at room temperature. **2** indifferent, uninterested, apathetic, cool, unenthusiastic, half-hearted.

lull *verb* abate, moderate, diminish, wane, subside, let up.
➤*noun* pause, break, respite, letup (*inf*).

lumber[1] *verb* burden, encumber, saddle, land (*inf*).
➤*noun* jumble, rubbish, junk, clutter, odds and ends.

lumber[2] *verb* plod, trudge, stomp, clump, shamble, shuffle.

luminary *noun* star, leading light, celebrity, personage, worthy, VIP, bigwig (*inf*).

luminous *adj* glowing, incandescent, luminescent, phosphorescent, bright, shining, radiant.

lump *noun* **1** piece, chunk, ball, nugget, cake, clod. **2** bump, boss, swelling, growth, tumour, protuberance, bulge.
➤*verb* gather, mass, aggregate, merge, combine, group.

lumpish *adj* clumsy, awkward, ungainly, heavy, ponderous, lumbering, oafish.

lumpy *adj* bumpy, knobbly, nodose, granular, clotted.

lunacy *noun* **1** madness, craziness (*inf*), stupidity, folly, absurdity. **2** insanity, derangement, dementia, mania, psychosis.

lunatic *noun* maniac, psychopath, nutter (*inf*), loony (*inf*), basket case (*inf*).

lunge *noun* thrust, stab, jab, pounce.
➤*verb* thrust, stab, jab, lash out, pounce, charge.

lurch *verb* **1** pitch, roll, toss, rock. **2** sway, reel, stagger, totter.

lure *verb* tempt, entice, attract, draw, allure, seduce.
➤*noun* temptation, enticement, attraction, draw, decoy, bait, carrot (*inf*).

lurid *adj* **1** sensational, melodramatic, graphic, explicit, grisly, shocking. **2** bright, brilliant, vivid, dazzling, garish, gaudy.

lurk *verb* skulk, prowl, hide, lie in wait.

luscious *adj* **1** delicious, delectable, appetizing, mouth-watering, succulent, juicy, fragrant, aromatic. **2** beautiful, gorgeous, voluptuous, sensual.

lush *adj* **1** luxuriant, dense, rank, exuberant, flourishing, verdant. **2** luxurious, sumptuous, plush (*inf*), opulent, lavish, extravagant.

lust *noun* **1** sex drive, sexual desire, passion, ardour, lechery, lasciviousness, lewd-ness, randiness (*inf*), horniness (*inf*).
2 desire, longing, yearning, craving, hunger, thirst, greed.
➤*verb* desire, long, yearn, crave.

lustre *noun* **1** sheen, gloss, shine, glitter, glow, brilliance. **2** glory, honour, distinction, prestige.

lustrous *adj* shiny, glossy, polished, gleaming, shimmering, glowing.

lusty *adj* strong, robust, sturdy, rugged, hardy, healthy, hearty, vigorous, energetic.

luxuriant *adj* lush, dense, thick, abundant.

luxuriate *verb* bask, revel, wallow, indulge, enjoy, delight, relish.

luxurious *adj* **1** sumptuous, opulent, rich, expensive, ritzy (*inf*), plush (*inf*), grand, de luxe. **2** voluptuous, sensual, self-indulgent, hedonistic, sybaritic.

luxury *noun* **1** opulence, grandeur, affluence, comfort, ease, self-indulgence, hedonism. **2** indulgence, extravagance, treat. **3** frill, extra.

lynch *verb* hang, string up (*inf*), execute, put to death.

lyrical *adj* **1** poetic, expressive, songlike, musical. **2** enthusiastic, rhapsodic, effusive, rapturous.

lyrics *pl noun* words, libretto.

macabre *adj* gruesome, grim, grisly, morbid, eerie.

mace *noun* staff, club, cudgel.

macerate *verb* soak, steep, soften, pulp.

Machiavellian *adj* crafty, cunning, sly, devious, unscrupulous, scheming.

machinate *verb* plot, plan, scheme, intrigue.

machination *noun* scheme, ruse, stratagem, tactic, manoeuvre.

machine *noun* **1** instrument, tool, device, gadget. **2** mechanism, apparatus, appliance, contraption. **3** automaton, robot, zombie.

machinery *noun* **1** equipment, plant, machines, hardware. **2** workings, organization, set-up (*inf*), system.

machismo *noun* maleness, masculinity, manliness, virility.

macho *adj* male, masculine, manly, virile.

macrocosm *noun* universe, cosmos, creation, totality.

mad *adj* **1** insane, deranged, demented, unbalanced, unhinged, psychotic, non compos mentis, out of one's mind (*inf*), off one's head (*inf*), crazy (*inf*), nuts (*inf*), mental (*inf*). **2** absurd, ridiculous, stupid, idiotic, senseless, reckless, harebrained. **3** frenzied, frenetic, frantic, wild. **4** angry, enraged, furious, livid. **5** fanatical, infatuated, crazy (*inf*).
like mad madly, wildly, fast, intensely.

madcap *adj* foolhardy, rash, reckless, daredevil, hotheaded.

madden *verb* **1** anger, enrage, incense, infuriate, make someone's blood boil (*inf*). **2** craze, derange, unbalance, unhinge.

maelstrom *noun* **1** whirlpool, vortex. **2** confusion, tumult, turmoil, chaos.

maestro *noun* master, expert, virtuoso.

magazine *noun* journal, periodical, review, glossy (*inf*).

magic *noun* **1** sorcery, witchcraft, necromancy, voodoo. **2** conjuring, prestidigitation, sleight of hand, illusion. **3** charm, enchantment, fascination, spell.
➤*adj* **1** magical, occult, supernatural, miraculous. **2** enchanting, charming, bewitching, spellbinding. **3** wonderful, marvellous, great, terrific (*inf*), fantastic (*inf*).

magician *noun* **1** sorcerer, wizard, enchanter, enchantress. **2** conjurer, illusionist.

magisterial *adj* **1** authoritative, commanding, imperious, lofty. **2** bossy (*inf*), dictatorial, domineering, high-handed.

magnanimous *adj* generous, big-hearted, gracious, noble, high-minded, unselfish, merciful, forbearing.

magnate *noun* tycoon, baron, mogul, captain of industry, capitalist, fat cat (*inf*), big shot (*inf*).

magnetic *adj* charismatic, captivating, fascinating, irresistible, mesmeric.

magnetism *noun* charisma, charm, fascination, allure.

magnificent *adj* **1** grand, stately, majestic, regal, noble, imposing, impressive. **2** splendid, superb, glorious, sublime, wonderful, marvellous. **3** gorgeous, sumptuous, opulent, lavish.

magnify *verb* **1** enlarge, increase, amplify, expand. **2** exaggerate, overstate, inflate, blow up, overplay.

magniloquent *adj* grandiloquent, highflown, bombastic, pompous, overblown.

magnitude *noun* **1** greatness, importance, significance, seriousness. **2** extent, size, dimensions, proportions, immensity.

maid *noun* servant, housemaid, maidservant.

maiden noun girl, lass, maid, young woman, virgin, spinster.
➤adj **1** first, initial, inaugural. **2** single, unmarried, unwed, virgin, spinster.

mail noun post, correspondence, letters, parcels.
➤verb post, send, dispatch, forward.

maim verb disable, incapacitate, cripple, mutilate.

main adj chief, principal, leading, primary, supreme, pre-eminent, essential, vital.
➤noun pipe, conduit, line, cable.
in the main mainly, mostly, on the whole.

mainly adv chiefly, principally, primarily, mostly, for the most part, in the main.

mainspring noun motive, driving force, cause.

mainstay noun prop, backbone, linchpin.

maintain verb **1** keep, retain, preserve, continue, carry on. **2** look after, tend, take care of, keep up. **3** support, keep, provide for. **4** state, assert, declare, allege, contend. **5** defend, uphold, champion, back.

maintenance noun **1** conservation, preservation, continuation, upkeep, repairs, care. **2** allowance, alimony, support.

majestic adj **1** regal, kingly, queenly, dignified, noble, lofty, grand, stately. **2** magnificent, splendid, impressive, imposing.

majesty noun **1** regality, nobility, loftiness, grandeur, stateliness. **2** magnificence, splendour, glory.

major adj **1** larger, greater, main. **2** great, considerable, leading, key, crucial, important, serious, radical.

majority noun **1** bulk, preponderance, greater part, most. **2** adulthood, maturity, coming of age.

make verb **1** create, fabricate, manufacture, produce, turn out, build, construct, assemble, put together, fashion, form, prepare. **2** cause, effect, bring about, occasion, give rise to. **3** do, execute, carry out. **4** force, oblige, compel, constrain, impel, induce, prevail upon. **5** earn, clear, gain. **6** act as, serve as, function as. **7** head for, aim for, proceed towards, be bound for. **8** lead to, contribute to, enable, be conducive to.
noun brand, marque, type, sort, kind.

make believe pretend, play-act, imagine, fantasize.

make do cope, manage, get by, improvise.

make it arrive, get there, succeed, prosper, get on.

make off run away, decamp, clear off (inf), beat it (inf), scarper (inf).

make out 1 see, perceive, discern, detect, distinguish, decipher, understand, work out, figure out. **2** claim, allege, assert, suggest, imply. **3** draw up, write out, fill in, complete. **4** fare, get on, manage.

make up 1 invent, fabricate, manufacture, concoct, cook up (inf). **2** assemble, build, construct, put together. **3** constitute, compose, comprise, form. **4** make good, compensate, make amends, atone. **5** be reconciled, make peace, bury the hatchet (inf).

make-believe noun pretence, play-acting, imagination, dream, fantasy.

makeshift adj temporary, provisional, stopgap, make-do, improvised.

make-up noun **1** cosmetics, greasepaint, war paint (inf). **2** constitution, composition, form, structure, organization. **3** character, personality, nature, temperament.

making noun **1** creation, manufacture, production, construction. **2** potential, capacity, ability, essentials, materials, ingredients.
in the making potential, coming, budding.

maladjusted adj disturbed, unstable, neurotic, mixed-up (inf).

maladminister verb mismanage, misgovern, misrule.

maladroit adj clumsy, awkward, inept, incompetent, ham-fisted (inf), cack-handed (inf).

malady noun illness, sickness, complaint, disorder, disease.

malaise noun **1** unease, anxiety, depression, ennui. **2** lassitude, weakness, enervation, indisposition.

malcontent noun grumbler, complainer, rebel, troublemaker.

male *noun* man, gentleman, boy, cock, buck, bull, ram, stag, stallion.
 ➤*adj* masculine, virile, manly.

malediction *noun* curse, anathema, imprecation, execration.

malefactor *noun* **1** criminal, felon, lawbreaker, offender. **2** wrongdoer, miscreant, evildoer.

malevolent *adj* malignant, malign, ill-disposed, spiteful, malicious, vindictive, hostile.

malfunction *verb* go wrong, break down, fail.

malice *noun* malevolence, spite, vindictiveness, resentment, grudge, enmity, hostility, ill will.

malicious *adj* malevolent, malignant, spiteful, vindictive, vicious, bitchy (*inf*), catty (*inf*).

malign *verb* defame, denigrate, run down, badmouth (*inf*).
 ➤*adj* malignant, malevolent, evil, pernicious, destructive.

malignant *adj* **1** malign, malevolent, spiteful, malicious, vindictive. **2** deadly, fatal, incurable, life-threatening, cancerous.

malleable *adj* **1** plastic, pliant, flexible. **2** impressionable, amenable, tractable.

malnutrition *noun* undernourishment, poor diet, hunger.

malpractice *noun* misconduct, malfeasance, negligence, dereliction.

maltreat *verb* mistreat, ill-treat, abuse, misuse, mishandle.

mammoth *adj* enormous, huge, immense, colossal, massive, gigantic, giant, jumbo (*inf*).

man *noun* **1** male, gentleman, fellow, chap (*inf*), bloke (*inf*), guy (*inf*). **2** person, human being, individual. **3** mankind, humankind, humanity. **4** employee, worker, labourer, hand.
 ➤*verb* staff, crew, work, operate.
 to a man without exception, as one, unanimously.

manacle *verb* **1** handcuff, shackle, fetter. **2** restrain, confine, curb.
 ➤*noun* handcuff, shackle, fetter, iron.

manage *verb* **1** administer, direct, run, conduct, supervise, superintend. **2** contrive, succeed, bring off, achieve, accomplish. **3** cope, fare, get along, make do.

management *noun* **1** executive, board, employers, bosses (*inf*). **2** administration, direction, running, control, supervision, handling.

manager *noun* administrator, executive, director, supervisor, boss (*inf*).

mandate *noun* **1** command, order, direction, instruction. **2** warrant, authority, authorization.

mandatory *adj* compulsory, obligatory, binding.

mangle *verb* **1** mutilate, hack, crush, destroy. **2** bungle, ruin, murder (*inf*).

manhandle *verb* **1** treat roughly, maul, knock about (*inf*). **2** heave, haul, hump (*inf*), lug (*inf*).

manhood *noun* **1** adulthood, maturity. **2** masculinity, manliness, machismo.

mania *noun* **1** frenzy, hysteria, dementia, insanity, madness. **2** passion, obsession, fixation, compulsion, craze.

maniac *noun* **1** lunatic, nutter (*inf*), loony (*inf*). **2** enthusiast, fanatic, freak (*inf*).

maniacal *adj* **1** frenzied, frantic, wild, raving. **2** mad, crazy (*inf*), insane, deranged, demented.

manifest *verb* show, exhibit, display, demonstrate, evince.
 ➤*adj* obvious, evident, plain, clear, apparent.

manifestation *noun* display, demonstration, exhibition, evidence, sign, indication.

manifesto *noun* policy statement, platform, programme.

manifold *adj* numerous, many, multiple, various, diverse, varied.

manipulate *verb* **1** handle, wield, use. **2** manage, influence, exploit, falsify, rig.

mankind *noun* man, humankind, humanity, the human race.

manly *adj* virile, masculine, macho (*inf*), strong, courageous, chivalrous.

man-made *adj* synthetic, artificial, imitation.

manner *noun* **1** way, method, system, technique, fashion. **2** behaviour, bearing, demeanour. **3** kind, sort, type, variety. **4** politeness, courtesy, breeding. **5** etiquette, protocol, the done thing (*inf*).

mannered *adj* unnatural, artificial, stilted, affected.

mannerism *noun* idiosyncrasy, characteristic, peculiarity, quirk.

mannerly *adj* polite, courteous, civil.

mannish *adj* unfeminine, masculine, butch (*inf*).

manoeuvre *verb* **1** steer, pilot, guide, manipulate, handle. **2** plan, scheme, intrigue.
➤*noun* **1** move, movement. **2** plan, scheme, tactic, gambit, ploy. **3** training, exercise.

manse *noun* vicarage, rectory, parsonage.

mansion *noun* palace, villa, hall, stately home.

mantle *noun* **1** cloak, cape, wrap. **2** covering, layer, blanket, pall, shroud.
➤*verb* cloak, wrap, envelop, cover, blanket.

manual *noun* handbook, instructions, guide, companion.
➤*adj* **1** physical, labouring. **2** human, hand-operated.

manufacture *verb* **1** make, produce, fabricate, mass-produce. **2** invent, make up, concoct, fabricate.
➤*noun* making, production, fabrication, mass-production.

manumit *verb* liberate, free, emancipate.

manure *noun* fertilizer, compost, dressing, dung.

many *adj* numerous, manifold, countless, umpteen (*inf*), lots of (*inf*).
➤*pronoun* large numbers, plenty, hundreds, thousands, lots (*inf*), loads (*inf*).

map *noun* chart, plan, guide, atlas.
➤*verb* **1** chart, plot. **2** plan, set out, lay out.

mar *verb* spoil, damage, detract from, disfigure, ruin, wreck.

maraud *verb* **1** foray, forage. **2** raid, plunder, pillage.

march *verb* **1** parade, file, process. **2** walk, stride, strut, stalk. **3** advance, proceed, progress.
➤*noun* **1** parade, procession, demonstration. **2** step, pace, stride, gait.

margin *noun* **1** border, edge, limit, boundary. **2** rim, brink, verge. **3** allowance, extra, leeway, latitude, scope.

marginal *adj* **1** borderline, peripheral, fringe. **2** slight, small, minimal, negligible.

marijuana *noun* cannabis, hashish, grass (*inf*), pot (*inf*).

marinate *verb* marinade, soak.

marine *adj* **1** sea, oceanic, saltwater. **2** nautical, maritime, seafaring.

mariner *noun* sailor, seaman, seafarer.

marital *adj* conjugal, matrimonial, wedded, married.

maritime *adj* **1** marine, nautical, seafaring. **2** coastal, littoral, seaside.

mark *noun* **1** spot, speck, stain, smudge, blemish, bruise, dent, scar, scratch, trace. **2** sign, symbol, indication, evidence. **3** brand, stamp, badge, emblem, logo. **4** symbol, sign, character. **5** characteristic, trait, feature. **6** grade, score, percentage, assessment. **7** line, point, level, standard. **8** target, objective, goal, aim.
➤*verb* **1** spot, stain, smudge, blemish, bruise, dent, scar, scratch. **2** label, tag, identify, flag. **3** characterize, distinguish, denote, designate. **4** note, heed, mind. **5** correct, grade, assess. **6** celebrate, commemorate, observe. **7** demarcate, delimit, mark off.
mark down reduce, lower, discount.
mark up raise, increase, put up.
of mark of note, eminent, prominent.

marked *adj* obvious, evident, noticeable, conspicuous, pronounced.

market *noun* **1** mart, bazaar, fair, exchange. **2** demand, call, need. **3** trade, commerce, business.
➤*verb* sell, retail, peddle, deal.

maroon *verb* abandon, desert, strand.

marriage *noun* **1** wedlock, matrimony. **2** wedding, nuptials. **3** union, amalgamation, combination.

marry *verb* **1** wed, get hitched (*inf*), tie the knot (*inf*). **2** join, unite, merge, combine.

marsh *noun* bog, swamp, quagmire, morass.

marshal *verb* **1** arrange, dispose, deploy, organize, assemble. **2** lead, guide, usher, shepherd.

martial *adj* warlike, military, soldierly.

marvel *verb* wonder, stare, goggle, be amazed.
➤*noun* wonder, prodigy, miracle.

marvellous *adj* **1** wonderful, splendid, magnificent, superb, fantastic (*inf*), fabulous (*inf*). **2** wondrous, miraculous, incredible, astonishing.

masculine *adj* manly, virile, macho (*inf*), mannish, butch (*inf*).

mash *verb* crush, pulp, purée.
➤*noun* mush, pulp, purée.

mask *noun* disguise, camouflage, front, facade, pretence, veil.
➤*verb* disguise, camouflage, hide, veil, cloak, screen.

masquerade *noun* **1** masked ball, fancy dress party. **2** pretence, charade.
verb pose as, pass oneself off as, play.

mass *noun* **1** lump, chunk, block, piece. **2** crowd, throng, swarm. **3** weight, bulk, volume. **4** majority, body, bulk, preponderance. **5** populace, common people, proletariat, rabble, riffraff. **6** plenty, lots (*inf*), loads (*inf*), heaps (*inf*), piles (*inf*).
➤*adj* **1** large-scale, widespread, extensive. **2** universal, general, popular.
➤*verb* collect, gather, assemble, crowd, swarm, throng.

massacre *noun* slaughter, butchery, carnage, blood bath, genocide.
➤*verb* kill, slaughter, butcher, mow down.

massage *verb* rub, knead, pummel, manipulate.
➤*noun* rub, rubdown, manipulation, physiotherapy.

massive *adj* huge, enormous, colossal, immense, gigantic, bulky, heavy.

master *noun* **1** lord, ruler, governor, leader, captain. **2** owner, proprietor, keeper. **3** teacher, instructor, tutor, guru. **4** expert, past master, maestro, virtuoso, ace (*inf*).
➤*adj* **1** chief, principal, main. **2** expert, experienced, qualified, professional.

3 controlling, directing, commanding, ruling.
➤*verb* **1** conquer, vanquish, subdue, subjugate. **2** learn, grasp, get the hang of (*inf*).

masterful *adj* authoritative, commanding, dominating, domineering, bossy (*inf*).

masterly *adj* expert, consummate, accomplished, first-rate, crack (*inf*).

mastermind *noun* planner, organizer, prime mover, brains (*inf*).
➤*verb* plan, organize, direct.

masterpiece *noun* masterwork, chef d'oeuvre, magnum opus.

mastery *noun* **1** command, control, domination, supremacy. **2** upper hand, superiority. **3** knowledge, command, grasp, proficiency, expertise, virtuosity.

masticate *verb* chew, munch, crunch.

masturbation *noun* autoeroticism, onanism, self-abuse, wanking (*sl*).

mat *noun* **1** rug, carpet. **2** pad, coaster.
➤*verb* tangle, entangle, ravel.

match *noun* **1** game, contest, bout, event. **2** equal, peer, counterpart, equivalent. **3** fellow, mate, twin. **4** marriage, union.
➤*verb* **1** fit, suit, accord, agree, correspond, tally. **2** oppose, pit, set. **3** equal, measure up to, rival.

matchless *adj* peerless, unequalled, unrivalled, unmatched, incomparable.

mate *noun* **1** spouse, husband, wife, partner. **2** friend, pal (*inf*), buddy (*inf*). **3** assistant, helper, apprentice.
➤*verb* pair, couple, copulate, breed.

material *noun* **1** substance, matter, stuff. **2** fabric, cloth, textile.
➤*adj* **1** physical, corporeal, earthly, temporal. **2** relevant, applicable, pertinent. **3** important, significant, essential, key.

materialize *verb* appear, take shape, emerge, turn up, happen.

maternal *adj* motherly, protective, caring, loving.

matrimony *noun* marriage, wedlock.

matter *verb* signify, be relevant, count, make a difference.
➤*noun* **1** substance, material, stuff. **2** subject, topic, question, issue, case. **3** trouble, problem, difficulty.
as a matter of fact in fact, actually, to tell the truth.

no matter never mind, it doesn't matter.

matter-of-fact *adj* down-to-earth, straightforward, unsentimental, unemotional, factual, prosaic.

mature *adj* 1 grown-up, adult, of age, fully grown. 2 responsible, sensible, wise, level-headed. 3 ripe, seasoned, aged, ready.
➤*verb* ripen, develop, grow up, become adult.

maudlin *adj* sentimental, tearful, weepy (*inf*), mawkish.

maul *verb* 1 claw, lacerate, wound, savage. 2 paw, manhandle, mistreat, molest, knock about (*inf*).

mausoleum *noun* tomb, vault, sepulchre.

maverick *noun* individualist, nonconformist, rebel.

mawkish *adj* sentimental, maudlin, soppy (*inf*), slushy (*inf*).

maxim *noun* saying, aphorism, axiom.

maximum *noun* peak, summit, limit, ceiling, utmost.
➤*adj* maximal, highest, greatest, supreme.

maybe *adv* perhaps, possibly, perchance.

mayhem *noun* chaos, havoc, commotion, tumult, uproar.

maze *noun* labyrinth, network, web, mesh.

meadow *noun* field, paddock, pasture, lea.

meagre *adj* 1 scanty, sparse, skimpy, inadequate, paltry, niggardly, measly (*inf*). 2 thin, skinny, bony, emaciated.

meal *noun* repast, snack, feast, banquet.

mean *verb* 1 signify, denote, represent, symbolize, stand for, indicate, imply, involve, entail. 2 intend, aim, purpose, plan. 3 destine, design, intend.

mean[1] *adj* 1 miserly, niggardly, parsimonious, penny-pinching, tight-fisted, stingy (*inf*). 2 unkind, nasty, spiteful, malicious, petty, small-minded, shabby. 3 cross, irritable, bad-tempered, vicious. 4 poor, lowly, humble, wretched. 5 common, ordinary, inferior.

mean[2] *noun* average, norm, median, middle.
➤*adj* 1 medium, average, normal. 2 middle, intermediate.

meander *verb* 1 wind, zigzag, snake. 2 wander, ramble, stray.

meaning *noun* 1 sense, signification, significance, import, implication, gist, drift, definition. 2 value, worth, point, purpose. 3 expressiveness, significance, suggestiveness.

meaningful *adj* 1 significant, important, serious. 2 worthwhile, useful, material, relevant. 3 expressive, significant, suggestive, pregnant.

meaningless *adj* 1 senseless, unintelligible, incomprehensible, nonsensical. 2 pointless, futile, empty, hollow.

means *pl noun* 1 method, way, vehicle, instrument, agency, measure, expedient. 2 resources, funds, money, wherewithal.
by all means certainly, of course, definitely, absolutely.
by means of through, via, using.
by no means not at all, certainly not, no way (*inf*).

meanwhile *adv* 1 in the meantime, for the time being. 2 at the same time, simultaneously.

measure *verb* 1 quantify, weigh, survey, size up, gauge, assess, calculate, determine. 2 distribute, dispense, deal out, share out, allocate.
➤*noun* 1 rule, ruler, gauge, meter. 2 unit, standard, norm. 3 portion, share, ration, quota, allocation. 4 certain amount, degree, quantity. 5 step, action, proceeding, procedure. 6 act, bill, statute, law.
measure up pass muster, come up to standard, make the grade.

measured *adj* 1 slow, leisurely, unhurried, deliberate, steady, rhythmical. 2 well-thought-out, planned, premeditated, studied, considered.

measureless *adj* immeasurable, limitless, boundless, unbounded, infinite.

measurement *noun* 1 dimension, length, breadth, width, height, depth, area, volume, weight. 2 mensuration, quantification, assessment, calculation.

mechanical *adj* 1 automatic, automated, mechanized, power-driven. 2 involuntary, instinctive, automatic.

mechanism *noun* 1 works, workings, machinery, machine, appliance, device. 2 means, method, technique, procedure, process.

meddle verb interfere, intervene, intrude, stick one's nose in (inf).

medial adj middle, central, intermediate, median.

mediate verb arbitrate, moderate, intercede, intervene, conciliate.

medicinal adj therapeutic, healing, curative, restorative, medical.

medicine noun 1 medicament, medication, remedy, drug. 2 medical science, healing art.

mediocre adj average, middling, so-so (inf), indifferent, undistinguished, nothing special (inf), inferior, second-rate.

meditate verb reflect, ponder, muse, contemplate, brood, ruminate, plan, intend.

meditation noun reflection, contemplation, rumination, consideration, thought.

medium adj average, middling, mean, middle.
➤noun 1 average, mean, middle. 2 means, vehicle, agency, instrument, channel. 3 spiritualist, psychic, clairvoyant.

medley noun mixture, assortment, miscellany, mixed bag (inf).

meek adj mild, unassuming, humble, submissive, acquiescent, spineless, timid, weak.

meet verb 1 encounter, come across, run into, bump into (inf). 2 join, converge, cross, intersect. 3 fulfil, satisfy, measure up to, discharge, carry out. 4 face, confront, encounter, experience, undergo, endure.

meeting noun 1 encounter, confrontation, introduction, rendezvous, assignation, date. 2 gathering, assembly, session, convention, conference, reunion, get-together (inf).

melancholy noun melancholia, depression, dejection, despondency, sadness, sorrow, unhappiness.
➤adj 1 sad, sorrowful, unhappy, melancholic, depressed, dejected, despondent, glum, gloomy, downcast, miserable. 2 sad, sorrowful, unhappy, dismal, depressing.

mêlée noun fight, brawl, scuffle, free-for-all.

mellifluous adj smooth, flowing, euphonious, melodious, musical.

mellow adj 1 ripe, soft, tender, sweet, full-flavoured, rich, smooth. 2 genial, affable, good-natured, pleasant, easygoing.
➤verb age, develop, mature, ripen, soften, sweeten.

melodious adj tuneful, musical, harmonious, euphonious, sweet.

melodramatic adj histrionic, theatrical, stagy, hammy (inf), overdone.

melody noun tune, music, theme, air, song.

melt verb 1 liquefy, thaw, dissolve. 2 fade, disappear, disperse, dissolve. 3 touch, soften, disarm.

member noun 1 adherent, associate, subscriber. 2 part, component, constituent, element. 3 limb, arm, leg, organ.

membrane noun film, layer, sheet, skin.

memento noun keepsake, souvenir, reminder, token.

memoir noun 1 record, account, biography, essay. 2 reminiscences, recollections, autobiography, life.

memorable adj unforgettable, outstanding, impressive, notable, historic, significant, momentous.

memorandum noun 1 memo, note, message. 2 record, minute, reminder.

memorial noun monument, shrine, plaque.

memorize verb learn by heart, commit to memory.

memory noun 1 recall, recollection, remembrance. 2 recollection, remembrance, reminiscence.

menace verb threaten, intimidate, bully, browbeat, scare, frighten.
➤noun 1 threat, intimidation, warning. 2 threat, danger, peril, hazard, risk, nuisance, pest.

mend verb 1 repair, fix, put back together, darn, patch. 2 correct, put right, reform, improve. 3 recover, get better, recuperate.
on the mend improving, getting better, recovering, recuperating.

mendacious adj lying, untruthful, dishonest, insincere.

mendicant noun beggar, vagrant, tramp.

menial *adj* humble, lowly, degrading, demeaning, unskilled, routine.
➤*noun* servant, domestic, drudge, skivvy (*inf*).

menstruation *noun* menses, period, curse (*inf*).

mensuration *noun* measurement, measuring, surveying.

mental *adj* 1 intellectual, cerebral, abstract. 2 psychological, psychiatric. 3 insane, mad, crazy (*inf*), barking (*inf*), nuts (*inf*).

mentality *noun* 1 frame of mind, mindset, attitude. 2 intellect, intelligence, mind, brains.

mention *verb* refer to, allude to, touch on, bring up, point out, say, breathe a word of (*inf*).
➤*noun* 1 reference, allusion, remark, observation. 2 tribute, citation, acknowledgment.

mentor *noun* adviser, counsellor, guru, teacher.

mercantile *adj* commercial, trade, trading.

mercenary *adj* greedy, acquisitive, money-grubbing (*inf*), materialistic, venal.

merchandise *noun* goods, wares, commodities, produce.
➤*verb* market, promote, advertise, push (*inf*).

merchant *noun* trader, dealer, seller, distributor, wholesaler.

merciful *adj* compassionate, soft-hearted, forgiving, forbearing, lenient, humane, gracious.

merciless *adj* pitiless, unforgiving, unkind, harsh, hard, callous, heartless, ruthless, unrelenting, implacable.

mercurial *adj* volatile, fickle, changeable, unpredictable, temperamental, flighty.

mercy *noun* 1 clemency, grace, pardon, forgiveness, forbearance, leniency, pity, humanity. 2 blessing, godsend, stroke of luck.
at the mercy of defenceless against, prey to, exposed to.

mere *adj* sheer, plain, pure, utter, total.

merely *adv* only, just, solely, simply, purely.

meretricious *adj* showy, flashy, gaudy, tawdry.

merge *verb* 1 join, unite, combine, coalesce. 2 blend, mingle, mix, fuse.

merger *noun* amalgamation, combination, union.

merit *verb* deserve, be worthy of, earn, be entitled to, warrant.
➤*noun* 1 excellence, goodness, worthiness. 2 virtue, good point, strong point, advantage.

meritorious *adj* deserving, worthy, commendable, creditable, admirable.

merriment *noun* mirth, hilarity, laughter, jollity, gaiety, fun, merrymaking, conviviality.

merry *adj* 1 jolly, happy, cheerful, carefree, light-hearted, gay, convivial. 2 tipsy, tiddly (*inf*), squiffy (*inf*).
make merry party, celebrate, have fun.

mesh *noun* net, netting, network, web.
➤*verb* 1 engage, interlock. 2 dovetail, harmonize, match.

mesmerize *verb* hypnotize, fascinate, captivate, enthral, bewitch, spellbind.

mess *noun* 1 untidiness, disorder, disarray, clutter, litter, muddle, confusion, chaos, shambles (*inf*). 2 difficulty, trouble, predicament, pickle (*inf*).
➤*verb* untidy, disorder, muddle, confuse, disarrange, tangle, dirty.
mess about fool about, play about, muck about (*inf*).
mess up bungle, make a mess of, make a hash of (*inf*), screw up.
mess with fiddle, tamper, interfere, meddle.

message *noun* 1 communication, note, memorandum, memo (*inf*), dispatch, communiqué. 2 meaning, point, moral, theme.
get the message understand, follow, see, get it (*inf*), catch on (*inf*).

messenger *noun* courier, runner, envoy, go-between, herald.

messy *adj* untidy, disordered, cluttered, littered, dirty, grubby, unkempt, dishevelled, disarranged, disorganized.

metamorphosis *noun* change, alteration, mutation, transformation.

metaphor *noun* allegory, image, figure of speech, analogy.

metaphysical *adj* abstract, theoretical, intangible, supernatural, transcendental.

mete *verb* **mete out** dispense, administer, deal, allot, inflict.

meteoric *adj* rapid, swift, lightning, sudden, overnight.

method *noun* **1** way, manner, means, technique, procedure, process, system. **2** order, orderliness, organization, planning.

methodical *adj* systematic, organized, orderly, businesslike, efficient, logical, planned.

meticulous *adj* scrupulous, punctilious, particular, conscientious, painstaking, thorough.

metropolis *noun* capital, city.

mettle *noun* **1** character, temperament, spirit, courage. **2** stamina, fortitude, backbone (*inf*).

miasma *noun* vapour, smell, stench.

microscopic *adj* minute, tiny, minuscule, infinitesimal.

midday *noun* noon, twelve o'clock, lunchtime.

middle *noun* centre, midpoint, heart, core, midst.
➤*adj* **1** central, midway, halfway. **2** intermediate, medium.

middleman *noun* broker, agent, intermediary, go-between.

middling *adj* average, medium, fair, passable, so-so (*inf*), OK (*inf*).

midget *noun* dwarf, pygmy.
➤*adj* dwarf, pygmy, miniature, pocket, baby.

midst *noun* middle, centre, heart, thick.

midway *adv* halfway, in the middle.

mien *noun* bearing, demeanour, manner, air.

miff *verb* annoy, vex, irk, displease, upset, put out.

might *noun* power, force, strength.
with might and main powerfully, forcefully, with all one's strength.

mighty *adj* **1** powerful, forceful, strong, sturdy, muscular. **2** huge, enormous, immense, colossal.

migrant *noun* traveller, wanderer, itinerant.

migrate *verb* move, relocate, resettle, emigrate, immigrate.

mild *adj* **1** gentle, tender, soft-hearted, kind, compassionate, merciful, easygoing (*inf*). **2** moderate, light, slight. **3** warm, temperate, balmy, fair. **4** bland, smooth, insipid.

mildew *noun* mould, fungus, blight.

milieu *noun* environment, surroundings, setting, background.

militant *adj* aggressive, active, radical, extremist.

military *adj* soldierly, armed, martial, warlike.
➤*noun* forces, services, armed forces.

militate *verb* **militate against** oppose, counter, conflict with, be detrimental to.

milky *adj* **1** white, whitish, off-white, creamy. **2** cloudy, opaque.

mill *noun* **1** factory, plant, works. **2** grinder, crusher, roller.
➤*verb* **1** grind, pulverize, powder, crush. **2** crowd, throng, move about.

millstone *noun* burden, weight, responsibility, cross.

mime *noun* dumb show, pantomime, sign language.
➤*verb* gesture, signal, act out.

mimic *verb* **1** imitate, ape, copy. **2** parody, caricature, take off (*inf*). **3** simulate, mirror, echo.
➤*noun* imitator, copycat (*inf*), impersonator, impressionist.

mince *verb* **1** chop, hash, grind. **2** walk affectedly, pose, attitudinize.

mind *noun* **1** intellect, intelligence, brain, reason. **2** head, wits, senses, understanding, imagination, brain, psyche. **3** memory, recollection, remembrance. **4** opinion, view, viewpoint, way of thinking. **5** inclination, disposition, tendency, desire, wish, purpose, intention. **6** genius, intellectual, thinker.
➤*verb* **1** object, take offence, disapprove of, dislike. **2** care, be bothered. **3** be careful, take care, pay attention, watch out, look out. **4** heed, listen to, take notice of,

miscarry

follow. **5** be sure to, remember to, take care that. **6** look after, take care of, guard, keep an eye on (*inf*).
bear/keep in mind remember, note, consider, take into account.

mindful *adj* aware, conscious, attentive, heedful.

mindless *adj* **1** heedless, inattentive, oblivious, neglectful. **2** foolish, stupid, brainless, senseless, gratuitous. **3** mechanical, automatic, routine.

mine *noun* **1** pit, colliery, shaft, quarry. **2** source, fund, treasury, wealth, abundance.
➤ *verb* dig, bore, excavate, quarry, extract.

mingle *verb* **1** mix, merge, blend, fuse, coalesce, combine. **2** hobnob, socialize, circulate.

miniature *adj* small, little, tiny, mini, pygmy, dwarf, midget, baby, toy.

minimal *adj* minimum, least, smallest, lowest.

minimize *verb* **1** reduce, cut, keep to a minimum. **2** play down, make light of, belittle.

minimum *noun* **1** least, lowest. **2** bottom, nadir.
➤ *adj* minimal, least, smallest, lowest.

minion *noun* underling, menial, lackey, toady, yes-man (*inf*).

minister *noun* **1** cleric, clergyman, clergywoman, preacher, vicar, parson, pastor, rector, priest. **2** politician, statesman, stateswoman, secretary. **3** ambassador, diplomat, plenipotentiary.
➤ *verb* attend, wait on, take care of, look after, tend, nurse, help.

ministration *noun* help, aid, assistance, care.

ministry *noun* department, office, bureau, secretariat.

minor *adj* **1** lesser, smaller, secondary, subordinate, junior. **2** slight, trivial, trifling, petty, insignificant, unimportant.

minstrel *noun* musician, singer, troubadour, bard.

mint *verb* **1** coin, stamp, strike, make. **2** formulate, invent, make up, coin.
➤ *adj* perfect, pristine, brand-new, unused.
➤ *noun* fortune, king's ransom (*inf*), packet (*inf*).

minus *adj* less, take away, without.

minute[1] *noun* **1** moment, second, instant, flash, twinkling, tick (*inf*), jiffy (*inf*). **2** notes, record, transcript, proceedings.

minute[2] *adj* **1** tiny, minuscule, microscopic, infinitesimal, small, negligible. **2** detailed, exact, strict, meticulous, scrupulous, painstaking, thorough.

minutia *noun* detail, particular, nicety, subtlety.

miracle *noun* wonder, marvel, prodigy, phenomenon.

miraculous *adj* **1** wonderful, marvellous, fantastic (*inf*), phenomenal, extraordinary, remarkable, incredible. **2** inexplicable, unaccountable, supernatural, divine.

mire *noun* marsh, bog, swamp, quagmire, morass, slough.

mirror *noun* **1** glass, looking-glass, reflector. **2** reflection, copy, replica, double, image.
➤ *verb* reflect, echo, imitate, copy, mimic.

mirth *noun* merriment, jollity, hilarity, laughter, amusement, fun, glee, gaiety, merrymaking.

misadventure *noun* misfortune, mischance, mishap, setback, accident, calamity.

misanthrope *noun* cynic, recluse, grouch.

misapprehend *verb* misunderstand, misconceive, misconstrue, misinterpret, misread, mistake.

misappropriate *verb* embezzle, peculate, steal, thieve.

misbegotten *adj* **1** ill-conceived, ill-advised, harebrained. **2** dishonourable, contemptible, despicable.

misbehave *verb* behave badly, be naughty, get up to mischief, play up (*inf*), act up (*inf*).

miscalculate *verb* misjudge, overestimate, underestimate, make a mistake, slip up (*inf*).

miscarriage *noun* **1** abortion. **2** failure, breakdown, perversion.

miscarry *verb* **1** abort. **2** fail, go wrong, founder, come to grief.

miscellaneous *adj* mixed, varied, assorted, diverse, various, heterogeneous, motley.

miscellany *noun* mixture, assortment, collection, medley, mixed bag, hotchpotch.

mischance *noun* misfortune, bad luck, mishap, accident, disaster.

mischief *noun* **1** naughtiness, misbehaviour, devilment, pranks, tricks, monkey business (*inf*). **2** harm, hurt, injury, damage, nuisance, trouble.

mischievous *adj* **1** naughty, roguish, impish, badly behaved, troublesome. **2** arch, playful, waggish, teasing. **3** harmful, hurtful, damaging, detrimental, pernicious.

misconception *noun* misunderstanding, misapprehension, mistake, error, delusion.

misconduct *noun* **1** misbehaviour, wrongdoing. **2** malpractice, malfeasance, impropriety.

misconstrue *verb* misinterpret, misread, take the wrong way, misunderstand.

miscreant *noun* wrongdoer, malefactor, scoundrel, blackguard, reprobate.

misdeed *noun* misdemeanour, crime, offence, fault, sin, transgression.

misdemeanour *noun* misdeed, violation, infringement, peccadillo.

miser *noun* niggard, skinflint, scrooge, penny-pincher (*inf*).

miserable *adj* **1** unhappy, sad, sorrowful, wretched, woebegone, mournful, melancholy, depressed, dejected, downcast, despondent. **2** contemptible, despicable, ignominious, base, low. **3** paltry, meagre, pathetic, poor, mean. **4** sordid, squalid, shabby, wretched, sorry, pathetic, pitiful, cheerless, joyless, gloomy, dismal, dreary.

miserly *adj* **1** mean, niggardly, stingy (*inf*), parsimonious, penny-pinching (*inf*), tight-fisted, grasping, avaricious. **2** meagre, paltry, miserable, measly (*inf*).

misery *noun* **1** unhappiness, sadness, sorrow, wretchedness, depression, dejection, despondency, gloom, distress, anguish. **2** poverty, need, want, deprivation, destitution, hardship. **3** moaner, complainer, grouch, pessimist, wet blanket (*inf*), spoilsport, killjoy.

misfit *noun* eccentric, nonconformist, maverick, square peg (*inf*).

misfortune *noun* **1** bad luck, mischance, adversity, trouble. **2** mishap, accident, blow, setback, calamity, disaster.

misgiving *noun* doubt, hesitation, uncertainty, suspicion, qualm, scruple, reservation.

misguided *adj* imprudent, ill-advised, unwise, injudicious, mistaken, wrong.

mishap *noun* accident, misfortune, setback, calamity, disaster.

mishmash *noun* hotchpotch, hodgepodge, jumble, farrago.

misinterpret *verb* misconstrue, misread, distort, garble, misunderstand.

misjudge *verb* **1** miscalculate, misread, get wrong. **2** underestimate, underrate, wrong, do an injustice.

mislay *verb* lose, misplace.

mislead *verb* misguide, lead astray, throw off the scent (*inf*), misinform, deceive, delude, fool.

mismanage *verb* maladminister, mishandle, botch, bungle, mess up, screw up (*sl*).

misprint *noun* mistake, erratum, literal, typo (*inf*).

misquote *verb* misreport, misstate, misrepresent.

misrepresent *verb* falsify, distort, twist, garble.

misrule *noun* **1** misgovernment, maladministration, mismanagement. **2** anarchy, lawlessness, turmoil.

miss[1] *verb* **1** fail, go wide. **2** lose, let slip. **3** fail to attend, play truant from, skip. **4** escape, avoid, dodge. **5** want, need, long for, yearn for. **6** misunderstand, overlook, disregard. **7** skip, pass over, omit, leave out, overlook, disregard.
➤ *noun* failure, omission, loss.

miss[2] *noun* girl, young woman, young lady.

misshape *verb* deform, twist, contort, warp, distort.

missile *noun* projectile, shot, arrow, rocket.

missing *adj* lost, mislaid, misplaced, gone, unaccounted for.

mission *noun* **1** task, job, assignment, responsibility, charge, operation, campaign, quest. **2** embassy, legation. **3** delegation, deputation, task force. **4** vocation, calling.

missionary *noun* evangelist, proselytizer, preacher.
➤*adj* evangelistic, campaigning, crusading, zealous.

missive *noun* letter, epistle, message.

misspend *verb* misuse, misapply, squander, waste.

misstate *verb* misreport, misquote, misrepresent, distort.

mist *noun* **1** haze, fog, vapour. **2** condensation, film.
verb steam up, fog over, blur.

mistake *noun* **1** error, slip, fault, blunder, oversight, omission, gaffe, faux pas, slip-up (*inf*), boob (*inf*), howler (*inf*), clanger (*inf*), cock-up (*sl*). **2** misunderstanding, misapprehension, misconception.
➤*verb* **1** misinterpret, misconstrue, misread, misjudge, misunderstand. **2** confuse, mix up. **3** err, be wrong, miscalculate, slip up (*inf*).

mistaken *adj* **1** wrong, erroneous, incorrect, wide of the mark (*inf*), false, untrue, faulty. **2** wrong, in error, at fault, misguided.

mistreat *verb* maltreat, ill-treat, misuse, abuse, molest, harm, injure, damage.

mistress *noun* **1** lover, girlfriend, kept woman, bit on the side (*inf*). **2** lady-love, inamorata, paramour. **3** head, owner, proprietor, employer. **4** teacher, tutor, governess.

mistrust *verb* distrust, doubt, suspect, disbelieve.
➤*noun* distrust, doubt, scepticism, suspicion, misgiving.

misty *adj* **1** hazy, foggy, murky. **2** bleary, blurred, vague, indistinct.

misunderstand *verb* **1** misinterpret, misconstrue, misread. **2** mistake, mishear, misjudge.

misunderstanding *noun* **1** misinterpretation, misconception, mistake, mix-up, crossed wires (*inf*). **2** disagreement, difference, quarrel, dispute, tiff (*inf*), spat (*inf*).

misuse *verb* **1** misemploy, misapply, squander, waste. **2** abuse, mistreat, illtreat, exploit.
➤*noun* **1** misemployment, misapplication, waste. **2** abuse, mistreatment, exploitation.

mitigate *verb* **1** moderate, lessen, alleviate, allay, ease, relieve. **2** moderate, temper, soften. **3** extenuate, remit.

mix *verb* **1** combine, blend, merge, amalgamate, unite. **2** combine, blend, mingle, intermingle. associate, consort, hobnob, socialize.
➤*noun* mixture, combination, blend, compound.
mix up **1** confuse, mistake. **2** jumble, muddle, scramble, garble.

mixed *adj* **1** assorted, varied, diverse, motley, heterogeneous. **2** ambivalent, conflicting, equivocal. **3** multiracial, coeducational.

mixed-up *adj* confused, muddled, puzzled, perplexed, disturbed, maladjusted.

mixer *noun* **1** blender, liquidizer, processor. **2** socializer, mingler, extrovert.

mixture *noun* **1** combination, blending, amalgamation, mixing. **2** blend, mix, assortment, variety, medley, miscellany, pot-pourri, hotchpotch, mixed bag.

moan *verb* **1** complain, grumble, whine, protest, make a fuss, grouse (*inf*), whinge (*inf*), gripe (*inf*), bellyache (*inf*). **2** groan, cry, whine.
➤*noun* **1** complaint, grumble, grouse (*inf*), gripe (*inf*). **2** groan, cry. **3** wail, howl.

mob *noun* **1** crowd, throng, horde, herd, swarm. **2** populace, rabble, riffraff, hoi polloi.

mobile *adj* **1** movable, portable, travelling. **2** changeable, lively, animated. **3** flexible, adaptable.

mobilize *verb* call up, muster, marshal, assemble.

mock *verb* **1** ridicule, jeer at, scoff at, laugh at, make fun of, take the mickey out of (*inf*). **2** lampoon, parody, satirize, send up (*inf*). **3** thwart, frustrate, foil.
➤*adj* imitation, synthetic, artificial, sham, feigned, pretended.

mockery noun **1** ridicule, jeering, scoffing, scorn, derision. **2** travesty, joke, apology.

mode noun manner, way, method, means, technique, fashion.

model noun **1** example, archetype, original. **2** pattern, template, mould. **3** exemplar, paragon, ideal. **4** copy, replica, mock-up, dummy. **5** version, mark, design, variety. **6** sitter, subject. **7** mannequin, clothes-horse (inf).
➤verb **1** make, mould, shape, fashion. **2** plan, design, base. **3** wear, show, display.
➤adj exemplary, ideal, perfect.

moderate adj **1** reasonable, restrained, sober, middle-of-the-road. **2** temperate, equable, mild, calm. **3** average, medium, mediocre, passable.
➤verb **1** temper, subdue, restrain, mitigate, ease, reduce, tone down, let up, die down. **2** arbitrate, preside over, chair.

moderation noun **1** temperance, restraint, self-control, self-restraint. **2** decrease, reduction, mitigation.
in moderation within reason, within limits, moderately.

modern adj **1** contemporary, current, present, present-day. **2** recent, latest, up-to-date, state-of-the-art, advanced, new, newfangled, fashionable, trendy (inf).

modernize verb update, upgrade, renew.

modest adj **1** humble, unassuming, unpretentious, self-effacing, diffident, unassertive. **2** demure, decent, decorous, chaste. **3** moderate, small, limited, simple, humble, unpretentious.

modicum noun bit, pinch, drop, scrap, shred.

modification noun **1** change, alteration, adjustment, revision, refinement. **2** limitation, restriction, qualification.

modify verb **1** adjust, adapt, revise, tweak (inf). **2** change, alter, remodel, recast. **3** limit, restrict, qualify.

modulate verb **1** tune, vary, inflect, **2** adjust, regulate, temper, moderate.

mogul noun magnate, tycoon, captain of industry.

moist adj **1** damp, clammy, dewy, wet. **2** humid, muggy.

moisten verb wet, damp, dampen.

moisture noun liquid, damp, dampness, vapour, steam, condensation.

mole^1 noun spot, mark, freckle.

mole^2 noun breakwater, groyne, pier.

mole^3 noun infiltrator, spy, secret agent.

molest verb disturb, trouble, bother, assault, abuse, sexually assault, rape.

mollify verb **1** calm, pacify, appease. **2** moderate, temper, allay, soften.

mollycoddle verb pamper, cosset, spoil, baby, spoonfeed.

moment noun **1** minute, second, instant, flash, tick (inf). **2** instant, second, minute, point, stage. **3** importance, significance, consequence, note, concern.

momentarily adv briefly, fleetingly, for an instant.

momentary adj brief, short, short-lived, transitory, fleeting.

momentous adj important, significant, weighty, crucial, major, historic, epoch-making.

momentum noun impetus, impulse, force, thrust.

monarch noun ruler, sovereign, king, queen.

monastery noun friary, abbey, priory, cloister.

monastic adj reclusive, solitary, cloistered, ascetic, celibate, monkish.

monetary adj financial, pecuniary, fiscal.

money noun **1** currency, coin, cash, finance, funds, capital, wherewithal, dosh (sl), dough (sl), bread (sl), lolly (inf). **2** wealth, riches, means.

moneyed adj rich, wealthy, affluent, well-off.

mongrel noun cross, crossbreed.

monitor noun **1** screen, VDU. **2** observer, watchdog, scanner, security camera, CCTV.
➤verb check, observe, watch, keep under surveillance, keep track of.

monk noun friar, abbot, prior, brother.

monkey noun **1** simian, primate. **2** imp, rascal, scamp.
➤verb fiddle, tinker, tamper, interfere.

monologue *noun* soliloquy, speech.

monomania *noun* fixation, obsession, bee in one's bonnet (*inf*).

monopolize *verb* dominate, corner, hog (*inf*), engross.

monopoly *noun* control, domination, sole rights.

monotonous *adj* boring, tedious, dull, uninteresting, humdrum, repetitive, samey (*inf*).

monster *noun* **1** freak, mutant, monstrosity. **2** dragon, bogey. **3** brute, beast, fiend, ogre. **4** giant, colossus, leviathan.
➤*adj* giant, gigantic, colossal, huge, whopping (*inf*).

monstrosity *noun* **1** eyesore, blot on the landscape, horror. **2** monster, freak, mutant.

monstrous *adj* **1** dreadful, awful, appalling, shocking, outrageous, atrocious. **2** vicious, cruel, barbaric, inhuman. **3** abnormal, unnatural, freakish, grotesque. **4** huge, enormous, immense, gigantic.

monument *noun* **1** memorial, cenotaph, shrine, column, obelisk, cross, statue. **2** reminder, testament, witness.

monumental *adj* **1** great, enormous, colossal, tremendous. **2** grand, impressive, striking, outstanding, major, historic. **3** commemorative, memorial, lapidary.

mood *noun* **1** temper, humour, disposition, frame of mind. **2** bad temper, sulk, fit of pique.

moody *adj* **1** glum, gloomy, morose, broody, sullen, sulky, bad-tempered, grumpy. **2** temperamental, unpredictable, changeable, mercurial.

moor[1] *noun* moorland, heath, upland.

moor[2] *verb* tie up, berth, anchor.

moot *adj* debatable, questionable, doubtful, unresolved, undecided.
➤*verb* broach, bring up, introduce, put forward.

mop *verb* swab, clean, wipe, sponge.
➤*noun* **1** swab, sponge. **2** shock, mane.

mope *verb* brood, fret, sulk, moon.

moral *adj* ethical, good, virtuous, decent, right, just, honest, upright, principled.
➤*noun* **1** lesson, teaching, message, point. **2** morality, ethics, principles, ideals, standards.

morale *noun* confidence, spirit, mood.

morality *noun* **1** ethics, rights and wrongs. **2** morals, ethics, principles. **3** goodness, virtue, decency, honesty, integrity, rectitude.

morass *noun* **1** swamp, bog, quagmire. **2** muddle, confusion, tangle.

moratorium *noun* suspension, halt, freeze.

morbid *adj* **1** unhealthy, unwholesome, sick, ghoulish. **2** sombre, melancholy, lugubrious, gloomy. **3** pathological, diseased, infected.

mordant *adj* biting, caustic, cutting, sarcastic, acerbic.

more *adj* further, increased, additional, extra, other.
➤*adv* **1** further, longer, harder. **2** besides, in addition.
➤*noun* increase, addition, extra.

moreover *adv* furthermore, further, besides.

morgue *noun* mortuary, funeral parlour, chapel of rest.

moribund *adj* **1** dying, on one's deathbed, not long for this world. **2** declining, decaying, on its last legs (*inf*).

morning *noun* **1** daybreak, sunrise, dawn. **2** morn, forenoon.

moron *noun* idiot, imbecile, cretin, fool, blockhead.

morose *adj* **1** gloomy, glum, melancholy. **2** saturnine, dour, sullen, surly.

morsel *noun* **1** bit, piece, fragment, scrap. **2** bite, crumb, mouthful, titbit.

mortal *adj* **1** human, physical, worldly, earthly, temporal. **2** passing, transient. **3** deadly, fatal, lethal. **4** great, extreme, intense, dire. **5** sworn, bitter, irreconcilable, implacable.
➤*noun* human being, person.

mortality *noun* **1** humanity, earthliness, temporality, transience. **2** death, loss of life, carnage.

mortify *verb* **1** humiliate, humble, shame, abash, embarrass, chasten. **2** discipline, control, subdue. **3** fester, putrefy.

mortuary noun morgue, funeral parlour, chapel of rest.

most adj 1 nearly all. 2 greatest, highest, utmost, maximum.
➤adv greatly, highly, very, extremely.
➤noun majority, greater part, nearly all, bulk.

mostly adv 1 mainly, chiefly, principally. 2 usually, normally, ordinarily, generally.

mother noun 1 mum (inf), mummy (inf), ma (inf), parent, dam. 2 source, origin, cause.
➤verb look after, care for, pamper, indulge, spoil.

motherly adj maternal, kind, loving, caring, protective.

motion noun 1 movement, action, travel, progress. 2 mobility, motility, locomotion. 3 gesture, gesticulation, signal, sign. 4 proposal, proposition, suggestion, idea.
➤verb signal, gesticulate, gesture, wave, beckon.

motivate verb prompt, move, lead, impel, drive, stimulate, persuade, induce, inspire.

motivation noun 1 stimulus, inspiration, inducement, incentive, motive. 2 stimulation, incitement. 3 drive, ambition.

motive noun reason, cause, grounds, inspiration, incentive, inducement, motivation.

motley adj 1 mixed, varied, assorted, miscellaneous. 2 multicoloured, kaleidoscopic, variegated.

mottle verb speckle, dapple, streak, fleck, marble.

motto noun slogan, watchword, maxim.

mould¹ noun 1 die, form, matrix, pattern. 2 shape, form, pattern, format. 3 type, sort, nature.
➤verb 1 shape, form, model, fashion. 2 influence, affect, shape, form.

mould² noun mildew, fungus, rot.

moulder verb rot, decay, decompose, crumble.

mouldy adj 1 mildewed. 2 musty, fusty, stale.

mound noun 1 hill, hillock, knoll, hummock. 2 embankment, rampart, earthwork, barrow. 3 heap, pile, stack.

mount verb 1 climb, ascend, go up. 2 board, get on. 3 increase, grow, intensify, rise. 4 produce, stage, put on, organize, arrange. 5 frame, set, instal.
➤noun 1 mounting, stand, base, support. 2 horse, steed.

mountain noun 1 fell, alp, mount, peak. 2 heap, pile, stack, lot.

mountainous adj 1 highland, upland, hilly. 2 lofty, towering, huge, massive.

mountebank noun charlatan, quack, impostor, fake.

mourn verb lament, grieve, sorrow, weep, wail, keen.

mournful adj 1 sad, sorrowful, gloomy, funereal, elegiac, lugubrious, plaintive. 2 sad, sorrowful, depressing, distressing, unhappy, miserable.

mourning noun grief, sadness, sorrow, lamentation.

mousy adj 1 timorous, timid, shy. 2 brownish-grey, dun-coloured, dull, lacklustre.

mouth noun 1 jaws, lips, gob (inf), trap (inf). 2 orifice, opening, entrance, door. 3 estuary, delta. 4 boasting, bragging, hot air (inf). 5 impudence, insolence, impertinence, lip (inf).

mouthful noun bite, nibble, sip, taste, morsel.

mouthpiece noun spokesperson, agent, representative, organ.

movable adj mobile, portable, transportable, adjustable.

move verb 1 stir, budge, shift. 2 go, advance, proceed, pass, carry, transport, shift. 4 relocate, remove, migrate. 5 prompt, drive, impel, induce, motivate, act, take action, do something. 6 touch, affect, impress. 7 propose, put forward, suggest.
➤noun 1 movement, motion, gesture. 2 act, action, step, measure, manoeuvre. 3 relocation, removal, change of address. 4 turn, go.
get a move on hurry up, make haste, step on it (inf).
on the move 1 moving, in motion, under way. 2 advancing, progressing.

movement noun 1 motion, progress, advance, carriage, transportation, transfer,

removal. **2** move, motion, gesture, shift.
3 campaign, crusade, drive, faction, party.
4 drift, trend. **5** part, section. **6** works,
workings, mechanism.

moving *adj* **1** touching, affecting, poignant, pathetic, stirring. **2** mobile, movable,
driving, impelling, motivating.

mow *verb* cut, trim, clip.
mow down slaughter, massacre, butcher.

much *adj* abundant, plentiful, great,
considerable.
➤*adv* **1** greatly, considerably, a great deal.
2 often, frequently.
➤*noun* plenty, a great deal, a lot (*inf*), lots
(*inf*).

muck *noun* **1** manure, dung, droppings,
slurry. **2** dirt, filth, grime, gunge (*inf*).
3 mud, mire, sludge.
muck about fool around, play around,
mess about.
muck up botch, bungle, spoil.

mud *noun* soil, dirt, muck, mire.

muddle *verb* **1** confuse, mix up, jumble,
disorder. **2** confuse, mix up. **3** perplex,
bewilder, confuse, baffle.
➤*noun* **1** jumble, disorder, disarray, mess.
2 perplexity, bewilderment, confusion,
bafflement.

muddy *adj* **1** boggy, swampy, marshy,
mucky, dirty. **2** murky, dull, dingy.
3 obscure, confused, muddled.

muffle *verb* **1** envelop, wrap, swathe.
2 deaden, damp, mute, soften, dull, stifle.

mug *noun* **1** beaker, tankard, pot, cup.
2 fool, simpleton, sucker (*inf*).
➤*verb* assault, rob, beat up.

muggy *adj* humid, clammy, sticky, sultry,
close.

mulish *adj* stubborn, obstinate, obdurate,
refractory.

mull over *verb* think about, reflect on,
meditate, ponder.

multifarious *adj* manifold, varied,
assorted, miscellaneous, motley.

multiple *adj* many, numerous, manifold,
various.

multiply *verb* **1** increase, expand, extend,
spread, proliferate. **2** breed, reproduce,
propagate.

multitude *noun* crowd, throng, mob,
horde, swarm.

mum *adj* quiet, silent, tight-lipped, shtum
(*inf*).

mumble *verb* mutter, murmur.

munch *verb* chew, champ, chomp, crunch.

mundane *adj* **1** banal, ordinary, everyday,
humdrum. **2** worldly, earthly, temporal.

municipal *adj* civil, civic, town, city.

munificent *adj* generous, bountiful, charitable, philanthropic.

munitions *pl noun* ammunition, armaments, weapons, matériel.

murder *verb* **1** kill, slay, assassinate, bump
off (*inf*), eliminate (*inf*), waste (*sl*). **2** ruin,
spoil, mangle, mutilate.
➤*noun* **1** homicide, manslaughter, killing,
assassination, hit (*inf*). **2** ordeal, nightmare, hell (*inf*).

murderous *adj* **1** homicidal, cruel, ferocious, bloodthirsty. **2** deadly, lethal, fatal.
3 difficult, arduous, exhausting, killing
(*inf*). **4** dangerous, perilous.

murky *adj* **1** dark, gloomy, dull, dim.
2 cloudy, turbid, muddy, dirty. **3** shady,
dark, obscure, questionable.

murmur *verb* **1** mutter, mumble, whisper.
2 whisper, sigh, rustle, babble. **3** complain, moan, whinge (*inf*), carp, grumble.
➤*noun* **1** mutter, mumble, whisper.
2 complaint, protest, grumble.

muscle *noun* **1** tendon, ligament, sinew.
2 power, force, influence, clout (*inf*).
muscle in interfere, intrude, butt in (*inf*).

muscular *adj* **1** brawny, sinewy, beefy
(*inf*), strapping, sturdy, athletic.

muse *verb* ruminate, reflect, ponder,
meditate.

mushroom *verb* spring up, shoot up,
sprout, snowball.

music *noun* tune, melody, harmony.

musical *adj* tuneful, melodious, harmonious, lyrical.

musician noun player, instrumentalist, performer.

must noun essential, necessity, requirement, requisite.

muster verb **1** marshal, call up, mobilize, assemble. **2** assemble, congregate, meet, gather.
➤noun meeting, rally, assembly, gathering.
pass muster measure up, suffice, come up to scratch (inf).

musty adj **1** mouldy, mildewy. **2** stale, fusty, smelly.

mutable adj changeable, inconstant, fickle, vacillating, wavering.

mutant noun mutation, anomaly, freak.

mutation noun change, alteration, variation, transformation.

mute adj **1** silent, dumb, speechless. **2** wordless, unexpressed, unspoken.
➤verb soften, quieten, subdue, tone down, muffle.

muted adj soft, subdued, low-key, understated.

mutilate verb **1** maim, disable, cripple, disfigure. **2** mar, spoil, ruin, butcher, bowdlerize.

mutinous adj rebellious, insurgent, insubordinate, disobedient, unmanageable.

mutiny noun rebellion, insurrection, revolt, uprising, insubordination.
➤verb rebel, revolt, rise up, disobey.

mutter verb **1** mumble, murmur, talk under one's breath. **2** complain, carp, grumble.

mutual adj **1** reciprocal, interchangeable, interactive. **2** joint, shared, common.

muzzle verb gag, silence, censor, stifle.

myopia noun **1** short-sightedness, near-sightedness. **2** narrow-mindedness, short-sightedness, insularity.

myriad adj innumerable, countless, untold.
➤noun multitude, host, swarm, thousands (inf), millions (inf).

mysterious adj **1** inexplicable, unaccountable, enigmatic, puzzling, baffling, mystifying. **2** strange, curious, weird, uncanny.

mystery noun **1** enigma, riddle, conundrum, secret. **2** secrecy, obscurity, inexplicability, inscrutability.

mystical adj **1** occult, esoteric, abstruse, arcane. **2** supernatural, metaphysical, transcendental. **3** mysterious, enigmatic, cryptic.

mystify verb puzzle, baffle, perplex, stump (inf).

myth noun **1** legend, saga, tale. **2** fallacy, fabrication, fiction, delusion.

mythical adj **1** mythological, legendary, fabulous. **2** fictitious, make-believe, made-up, imaginary.

mythology noun myths, legends, folklore.

nab *verb* **1** arrest, catch, capture, collar (*inf*), nick (*inf*). **2** seize, grab, snatch.

nadir *noun* low point, bottom, rock bottom, zero, depths.

nag *verb* **1** find fault, complain, grumble, criticize, carp. **2** scold, henpeck, pester, plague, harass, go on at (*inf*). **3** niggle, annoy, bother, trouble, bug (*inf*).
➤*noun* shrew, termagant, virago, scold.

nail *noun* **1** pin, tack, brad, spike. **2** fingernail, toenail, claw, talon.
➤*verb* **1** fasten, tack, fix, pin. **2** catch, arrest, nab (*inf*), collar (*inf*). **3** expose, uncover, detect, reveal, unmask.

naive *adj* **1** guileless, ingenuous, artless, unsophisticated, simple, innocent, childlike. **2** credulous, gullible, trusting, unsuspicious, callow, wet behind the ears (*inf*).

naivety *noun* artlessness, ingenuousness, simplicity, innocence, unworldliness, inexperience, gullibility, credulousness.

naked *adj* **1** nude, unclothed, undressed, exposed, bare, starkers (*inf*), in the altogether (*inf*), in the buff (*inf*), in one's birthday suit (*inf*). **2** barren, bare, stripped, denuded, leafless, hairless. **3** unshaded, uncovered, exposed, unguarded. **4** plain, stark, bald, open, blatant, flagrant, undisguised. **5** defenceless, unprotected, vulnerable, unarmed, helpless, powerless.

name *noun* **1** appellation, denomination, designation, title, term, label, tag, nickname, sobriquet, handle (*inf*), moniker (*inf*). **2** reputation, character, credit, honour, fame, renown. **3** star, celebrity, luminary, VIP, dignitary, personage, big noise (*inf*), big shot (*inf*).
➤*verb* **1** call, baptize, christen, dub, style, term, label. **2** identify, mention, cite. **3** designate, nominate, appoint, select. **4** specify, pick, fix.

nameless *adj* **1** anonymous, unnamed, unidentified, unknown, unspecified. **2** inexpressible, unspeakable, indescribable.

namely *adv* that is, i.e., viz., to wit.

nap[1] *noun* doze, catnap, snooze (*inf*), sleep, kip (*inf*), forty winks (*inf*).
➤*verb* doze, catnap, snooze (*inf*), sleep, nod off.

nap[2] *noun* pile, down, fibre, shag.

narcissism *noun* self-love, self-admiration, vanity, egotism, egocentricity, self-centredness.

narcotic *noun* drug, opiate, sedative, soporific, analgesic, anaesthetic.
➤*adj* **1** soporific, hypnotic, sedative. **2** opiate, anaesthetic, analgesic.

narrate *verb* tell, relate, recite, recount, report, describe.

narrative *noun* account, story, tale, report, chronicle.

narrow *adj* **1** thin, slender, fine. **2** tight, cramped, constricted, close, confined, restricted, limited. **3** narrow-minded, intolerant, insular, parochial, inflexible, hidebound.
➤*verb* **1** taper, attenuate, constrict, tighten. **2** confine, restrict, limit.

narrowly *adv* **1** scarcely, barely, only just, by a whisker (*inf*). **2** carefully, closely, attentively.

narrow-minded *adj* prejudiced, bigoted, illiberal, intolerant, insular, parochial, provincial, conservative, hidebound.

nasty *adj* **1** unpleasant, disagreeable, offensive, repugnant, close, vile, foul, awful, grotty (*inf*). **2** spiteful, malicious, mean, vicious, unkind, cruel. **3** dangerous, serious, critical, threatening.

nation *noun* **1** people, race, society, population. **2** country, land, republic, state.

national adj **1** civil, nationwide, country-wide, domestic, internal. **2** state, public.
➤*noun* citizen, resident, inhabitant, subject.

nationalism *noun* patriotism, chauvinism, jingoism.

nationality *noun* ethnic group, race, clan, tribe.

nationwide *adj* national, countrywide, general, coast-to-coast.

native *noun* **1** inhabitant, citizen, national. **2** aborigine, autochthon, indigene. **3** resident, local.
➤*adj* **1** home, mother, original. **2** local, indigenous, aboriginal, autochthonous, ethnic. **3** inborn, innate, congenital, natural, inherent.

natter *verb* chat, gossip, chatter, talk, gab (*inf*), jaw (*inf*).
➤*noun* chat, gossip, talk, conversation, chinwag (*inf*).

natty *adj* smart, neat, trim, dapper, spruce, stylish, snazzy (*inf*).

natural *adj* **1** normal, typical, usual, logical, reasonable, expected. **2** inborn, innate, inherent, intrinsic, fundamental, instinctive, intuitive. **3** artless, guileless, sincere, unaffected, relaxed, spontaneous. **4** pure, unprocessed, unrefined, whole, organic.

naturalist *noun* botanist, biologist, zoologist, life scientist, ecologist.

naturalize *verb* adapt, assimilate.

naturally *adv* **1** of course, obviously, certainly, needless to say. **2** inherently, innately, normally, by nature. **3** unaffectedly, spontaneously, artlessly, sincerely.

nature *noun* **1** essence, character, identity, constitution. **2** kind, sort, type, class. **3** creation, natural world, environment. **4** disposition, temper, humour, temperament, character, personality.

naughty *adj* **1** bad, mischievous, disobedient, defiant, wayward, unruly. **2** rude, improper, indecent, bawdy, ribald, risqué.

nausea *noun* **1** biliousness, queasiness, sickness. **2** disgust, revulsion, repugnance.

nauseate *verb* sicken, disgust, revolt, offend.

nauseous *adj* **1** queasy, sick, ill, unwell. **2** nauseating, sickening, disgusting, revolting, repulsive.

nautical *adj* naval, marine, maritime, seafaring, sailing.

navigable *adj* passable, negotiable, clear, unobstructed.

navigate *verb* **1** direct, guide, pilot, steer, plot, plan. **2** cross, traverse, sail, voyage.

navy *noun* fleet, flotilla, armada, marine.

near *adj* close, nearby, neighbouring, adjacent, imminent, impending, approaching, coming, immediate, intimate.
➤*adv* close, nigh, nearby, at close quarters, within reach.
➤*prep* close to, within reach of, a stone's throw from (*inf*).
➤*verb* approach, draw near to, move towards, come close to.

nearly *adv* almost, practically, all but, virtually, well-nigh, just about.

neat *adj* **1** tidy, orderly, spick-and-span, trim, smart, spruce, well-groomed. **2** clever, convenient, ingenious, apt. **3** straight, pure, undiluted.

neaten *verb* tidy, smarten, straighten, spruce up, groom, order.

nebulous *adj* **1** vague, indefinite, indistinct, unformed, amorphous. **2** hazy, misty, cloudy, fuzzy.

necessarily *adv* automatically, certainly, by definition, of course, inevitably, perforce.

necessary *adj* **1** needed, required, requisite, essential, vital, indispensable, imperative, compulsory. **2** certain, unavoidable, inescapable, inevitable.

necessitate *verb* cause, require, entail, demand, call for, oblige, force, compel.

necessity *noun* **1** essential, fundamental, requisite, requirement, sine qua non. **2** need, want, demand, exigency. **3** indispensability, inevitability. **4** compulsion, obligation.

necromancy *noun* **1** magic, sorcery, witchcraft, voodoo. **2** spiritualism, divination.

need *verb* **1** lack, want, require, demand, call for, necessitate. **2** must, have to, be obliged to.
➤*noun* **1** necessity, essential, requisite,

requirement. **2** want, lack, shortage.
3 requirement, demand, obligation, exigency, urgency. **4** poverty, indigence, penury, destitution, distress, privation.

needful *adj* needed, necessary, required, requisite, essential.

needless *adj* unnecessary, gratuitous, redundant, superfluous, pointless, uncalled-for.

needy *adj* poor, indigent, poverty-stricken, destitute, deprived, disadvantaged, underprivileged.

nefarious *adj* wicked, evil, bad, iniquitous, villainous, criminal, atrocious, monstrous.

negate *verb* **1** nullify, annul, cancel, invalidate. **2** repudiate, deny, contradict, refute, disprove, oppose.

negation *noun* **1** denial, contradiction, repudiation, annulment, cancellation, invalidation. **2** nothing, nullity, void, opposite, converse, antithesis.

negative *adj* **1** denying, contradictory, opposing. **2** opposite, converse, contrary, antagonistic. **3** pessimistic, cynical, unhelpful, unenthusiastic, defeatist.
➤*noun* **1** contradiction, denial. **2** negation, opposite.

neglect *verb* **1** ignore, spurn, slight, abandon, forsake. **2** omit, miss, overlook, skip, forget. **3** disregard, ignore, spurn, shirk.
➤*noun* **1** negligence, inattention, carelessness, heedlessness. **2** disregard, oversight, omission, default, dereliction.

neglectful *adj* negligent, remiss, careless, regardless, heedless, unmindful, thoughtless, forgetful.

negligence *noun* **1** disregard, inattention, forgetfulness, carelessness, heedlessness, thoughtlessness. **2** neglect, omission, default, dereliction, laxity.

negligible *adj* insignificant, inconsequential, trifling, minor, slight, small.

negotiable *adj* **1** open to discussion, open to question, arguable. **2** passable, navigable, open, clear, unobstructed.

negotiate *verb* **1** bargain, deal, discuss, mediate, arbitrate, conciliate, compromise, haggle, transact. **2** arrange, work out, settle, complete. **3** navigate, get through, get round, clear, pass.

neighbourhood *noun* **1** locality, community, neck of the woods (*inf*). **2** vicinity, environs, district, area.
in the neighbourhood of about, approximately, almost, close to.

nemesis *noun* punishment, retribution, vengeance, destruction, downfall, ruin, destiny, fate.

neophyte *noun* **1** beginner, tyro, novice, learner, greenhorn, rookie (*inf*). **2** convert, proselyte. **3** initiate, novice.

nepotism *noun* favouritism, patronage, bias, preferential treatment.

nerve *noun* **1** courage, bravery, mettle, pluck, guts (*inf*), fortitude, will, resolution. **2** audacity, effrontery, impertinence, gall, cheek (*inf*), chutzpah (*inf*).
➤*verb* steel, brace, strengthen, fortify, embolden.

nerve-racking *adj* tense, stressful, worrying, anxious, nail-biting (*inf*).

nerves *pl noun* nervousness, tension, strain, anxiety, apprehension, butterflies in one's stomach (*inf*).

nervous *adj* **1** tense, anxious, worried, apprehensive, uneasy, agitated, on edge, jumpy, jittery (*inf*). **2** excitable, highly strung, sensitive, timorous.

nest *noun* **1** shelter, refuge, breeding ground, hole, burrow. **2** den, haunt, refuge, retreat, hideout.

nestle *verb* snuggle, cuddle, huddle, curl up, settle, shelter.

net[1] *noun* mesh, web, netting, network, openwork, lace.
➤*verb* catch, bag, trap, ensnare, enmesh, entangle.

net[2] *adj* **1** take-home, after tax, after deductions, clear. **2** final, closing, ultimate.
➤*verb* bring in, take home, clear, earn, get, make, realize.

nether *adj* lower, under, bottom, inferior.

nettle *verb* vex, annoy, irk, pique, chafe, provoke, goad, sting.

network *noun* **1** mesh, net, web. **2** grid, matrix. **3** system, organization, complex, maze, labyrinth.

neurosis *noun* nervous disorder, mental illness, obsession, phobia.

neurotic *adj* disturbed, deranged, maladjusted, irrational, paranoid, obsessive, compulsive, phobic.

neuter *verb* emasculate, castrate, geld, doctor, spay.

neutral *adj* 1 non-partisan, non-aligned. 2 impartial, unbiased, disinterested, dispassionate, objective, uninvolved. 3 bland, unremarkable, nondescript, anodyne, inoffensive, indeterminate. 4 pale, colourless, achromatic, grey, beige.

neutralize *verb* counteract, balance, offset, compensate for, cancel, negate.

never *adv* 1 at no time, not ever, not once. 2 certainly not, under no circumstances, on no account, not on your life (*inf*), no way (*inf*), not in a million years (*inf*).

nevertheless *adv* nonetheless, however, yet, but, still, even so.

new *adj* 1 latest, recent, modern, advanced, novel, state-of-the-art, avant-garde. 2 innovative, original, revolutionary, experimental, pioneering, unconventional. 3 fresh, unused, clean, blank. 4 changed, different, other, better, improved. 5 refreshed, renewed, regenerated. 6 unfamiliar, unaccustomed, unknown, different. 7 inexperienced, unacquainted, ignorant.

newcomer *noun* 1 incomer, new arrival, settler, immigrant, outsider, stranger. 2 novice, learner, beginner, recruit, trainee, probationer.

newly *adv* recently, just, lately, of late.

news *noun* report, information, bulletin, announcement, word, tidings.

newspaper *noun* paper, daily, broadsheet, tabloid, gazette, rag (*inf*).

next *adj* 1 following, succeeding, subsequent, ensuing. 2 neighbouring, adjacent, nearest, contiguous.
➤*adv* 1 then, after. 2 later, subsequently.

nibble *verb* bite, gnaw, pick at.
➤*noun* bite, morsel, mouthful, taste.

nice *adj* 1 pleasant, agreeable, enjoyable, good, lovely. 2 charming, likable, kind, sympathetic, considerate. 3 polite, refined, civil, decent. 4 subtle, fine, delicate, minute. 5 exact, precise, strict, scrupulous, fastidious, particular.

nicety *noun* 1 distinction, nuance, subtlety, refinement, detail. 2 precision, accuracy, rigour.

niche *noun* 1 recess, alcove, nook, cubbyhole. 2 position, place, slot.

nick *noun* notch, indentation, cut, chip, groove.
➤*verb* 1 notch, cut, chip. 2 steal, take, pinch (*inf*). 3 arrest, catch, collar (*inf*).

nickname *noun* tag, diminutive, epithet, sobriquet.

niggardly *adj* 1 penny-pinching, mean, miserly, stingy, parsimonious, tightfisted (*inf*). 2 meagre, scanty, paltry, frugal, sparing.

niggle *verb* 1 bother, irritate, worry, nag, bug (*inf*). 2 carp, cavil, complain, grumble, moan.

nigh *adj and adv* near, close, nearly, almost.

nightfall *noun* sunset, dusk, twilight, evening.

nightmare *noun* ordeal, trial, agony, horror, torment.

nil *noun* nothing, nought, zero, zilch (*inf*).

nimble *adj* 1 agile, sprightly, spry, lively, quick, brisk, deft. 2 alert, clever, smart, quick.

nip[1] *verb* 1 pinch, squeeze, tweak, catch, grip. 2 pop, rush, hurry, go, dash.

nip[2] *noun* dram, draught, drop, shot (*inf*).

nipple *noun* teat, mamilla, pap.

nippy *adj* chilly, cold, raw, sharp.

nirvana *noun* paradise, heaven, bliss, tranquillity, peace.

nitty-gritty *noun* essentials, basics, fundamentals, brass tacks (*inf*).

no *interj* certainly not, no way (*inf*), not on your life (*inf*).

nobble *verb* 1 bribe, influence, persuade, threaten, intimidate. 2 drug, dope, disable, incapacitate.

nobility *noun* 1 gentry, aristocracy, upper class, peerage, nobles. 2 nobleness, dignity, eminence, greatness, grandeur, honour, integrity.

noble *noun* aristocrat, patrician, nobleman, noblewoman, peer.
➤*adj* 1 aristocratic, patrician, highborn,

blue-blooded, titled. **2** magnanimous, generous, worthy, honourable, virtuous.
3 dignified, distinguished, eminent, lordly.
4 stately, grand, magnificent, impressive.

nobody *noun* nonentity, nothing, cipher.

nocturnal *adj* night, nightly.

nod *verb* bow, incline, agree, approve, assent, signal.
nod off fall asleep, drop off, doze, nap.

node *noun* protuberance, nodule, knob, knot, bulge, swelling, lump.

noise *noun* sound, din, row, racket, uproar, hubbub.

noisome *adj* offensive, disgusting, repugnant, foul, fetid, noxious.

noisy *adj* loud, clamorous, boisterous, rowdy, uproarious, deafening, earsplitting.

nomad *noun* **1** traveller, itinerant, migrant. **2** wanderer, rover, vagrant.

nominal *adj* **1** titular, formal, so-called, self-styled. **2** token, minimal, small, inconsiderable.

nominate *verb* **1** propose, put forward, suggest. **2** choose, select, elect, appoint.
3 name, designate.

nonchalant *adj* unconcerned, indifferent, blasé, insouciant, carefree, cool, easy, offhand.

nonconformist *noun* dissident, rebel, individualist, maverick.

nondescript *adj* indeterminate, unremarkable, unexceptional, characterless, dull, bland, ordinary.

none *pronoun* **1** not one, not any, zero.
2 nobody, no one, not a soul.
➤*adv* not at all, in no way.

nonentity *noun* nothing, nobody, cipher.

nonetheless *adv* nevertheless, however, yet, still, but, even so.

non-existent *adj* **1** unreal, imaginary, hypothetical, fictitious, fanciful, illusory.
2 absent, missing.

nonplus *verb* perplex, bewilder, confuse, puzzle, disconcert, take aback, flummox (*inf*), faze (*inf*).

nonsense *noun* **1** rubbish, drivel, gibberish, claptrap (*inf*), gobbledygook (*inf*), mumbo-jumbo (*inf*). **2** absurdity, stupidity,

foolishness, fatuity. **3** rot, balderdash, crap (*sl*), bullshit (*sl*), cobblers (*inf*).

non-stop *adj* continuous, incessant, constant, uninterrupted, never-ending, interminable, unremitting.

nook *noun* corner, recess, niche, alcove, cranny, cubbyhole, retreat.

noon *noun* midday, twelve o'clock, noontide.

norm *noun* **1** standard, criterion, yardstick, benchmark, type, model. **2** average, mean, rule, usual, measure, gauge.

normal *adj* usual, common, general, average, conventional, customary, regular, standard, typical, healthy, natural.

nose *noun* **1** snout (*inf*), hooter (*inf*), schnozzle (*inf*), conk (*inf*). **2** instinct, intuition, sixth sense, feel, sense.
➤*verb* **1** search, pry, snoop (*inf*). **2** scent, detect, sniff out (*inf*).

nose-dive *verb* plummet, fall, drop, dive, plunge.

nostalgia *noun* **1** yearning, longing, pining. **2** reminiscence, wistfulness, sentimentality.

nosy *adj* inquisitive, curious, prying, interfering, eavesdropping, snooping (*inf*).

notable *adj* **1** remarkable, noteworthy, special, significant, marked, outstanding, impressive, memorable, extraordinary, distinctive. **2** distinguished, celebrated, famous, illustrious, eminent, prominent.
➤*noun* personage, celebrity, VIP, dignitary, luminary, big shot (*inf*).

notably *adv* **1** particularly, especially, noticeably, significantly. **2** remarkably, unusually, memorably, impressively.

notation *noun* symbols, signs, characters, system, alphabet, code, script, shorthand.

notch *noun* **1** cut, nick, indentation, serration. **2** groove, gouge, score, slit. **2** step, level, stage, rung, degree, grade.
➤*verb* cut, nick, indent, serrate.
notch up score, achieve, attain, register, chalk up (*inf*).

note *noun* **1** memorandum, memo, record, minute, jotting. **2** message, letter, missive, epistle. **3** banknote, bill, paper money.
4 annotation, gloss, footnote, explanation, comment, observation. **5** quality, tone, inflection, hint.

➤*verb* **1** notice, perceive, observe, see. **2** heed, pay attention. **3** write down, log, register, record, enter, jot down.
of note 1 famous, renowned, distinguished, eminent, great. **2** significant, important, of consequence.
take note heed, pay attention, note, observe.

notebook *noun* notepad, jotter, exercise book.

noted *adj* famous, renowned, celebrated, acclaimed, notable, great, well-known, illustrious.

noteworthy *adj* remarkable, notable, memorable, exceptional, unusual, significant, striking.

nothing *pronoun and noun* **1** nought, zero, nil, love. **2** naught, zilch (*inf*), sod all (*sl*), sweet FA (*sl*). **3** nonentity, cipher.
for nothing 1 free, gratis, without charge, on the house (*inf*). **2** in vain, to no purpose, needlessly.

nothingness *noun* **1** nullity, nonexistence. **2** void, emptiness.

notice *noun* **1** attention, observation, note, heed, regard. **2** warning, information, notification, advice. **3** notification, instruction, dismissal, discharge. **4** poster, placard, sign, bill, advertisement. **5** announcement, declaration, news. **6** review, critique, write-up.
➤*verb* perceive, observe, see, detect, mark, note, take notice of.

noticeable *adj* perceptible, appreciable, discernible, conspicuous, distinct, clear, visible.

notify *verb* inform, tell, advise, warn, alert, acquaint, apprise.

notion *noun* **1** idea, concept, thought, opinion, belief, theory. **2** impression, conception, apprehension, understanding. **3** whim, impulse, desire, caprice, fancy, inclination.

notional *adj* **1** theoretical, hypothetical, conceptual, speculative. **2** unreal, illusory, imaginary.

notorious *adj* infamous, disreputable, ill-famed, ignominious.

notwithstanding *prep* despite, in spite of.
➤*adv* nevertheless, however, even so, nonetheless.

nought *noun* zero, nil, love, nothing.

nourish *verb* **1** feed, sustain. **2** nurture, nurse, bring up, rear. **3** maintain, entertain, harbour, cherish, foster, encourage.

nourishment *noun* food, nutrition, nutriment, sustenance, subsistence.

novel *adj* **1** new, fresh, innovative. **2** original, different, unfamiliar.
➤*noun* story, book, narrative, romance.

novelist *noun* writer, author.

novelty *noun* **1** newness, freshness, originality, unfamiliarity. **2** bagatelle, trinket, knick-knack, toy.

novice *noun* beginner, tyro, neophyte, learner, student, apprentice, trainee, amateur.

now *adv* **1** at present, at the moment, nowadays, today, currently. **2** immediately, at once, straightaway, promptly.

nowadays *adv* at the present time, now, today, in this day and age.

noxious *adj* poisonous, toxic, harmful, deleterious, deadly, noisome, foul.

nuance *noun* shade, gradation, degree, distinction, subtlety, nicety.

nucleus *noun* centre, focus, core, kernel, heart, nub, pivot.

nude *adj* naked, bare, unclothed, undressed, au naturel, in the buff (*inf*), in one's birthday suit (*inf*).

nudge *verb* **1** poke, prod, dig, jab, elbow. **2** push, shove.
➤*noun* push, shove, poke, prod, jog.

nugget *noun* piece, lump, mass, chunk.

nuisance *noun* annoyance, bother, pest, pain (*inf*), bore, trouble, inconvenience, drag (*inf*).

null *adj* void, invalid, worthless, cancelled, annulled.

nullify *verb* annul, abrogate, revoke, quash, invalidate, void.

numb *adj* dead, benumbed, insensible, frozen, paralysed, unfeeling.
➤*verb* deaden, benumb, freeze, paralyse, anaesthetize.

number *noun* **1** figure, numeral, digit, integer. **2** quantity, collection, several, many. **3** copy, issue, edition.
➤

➤*verb* **1** total, add up to, amount to.
2 enumerate, count, calculate. **3** include,
count, reckon.

numberless *adj* countless, innumerable,
infinite, incalculable, untold, myriad.

numeral *noun* number, figure, digit, integer, symbol, character.

numerous *adj* many, manifold, several,
lots of (*inf*), multiple, abundant.

nuptial *adj* conjugal, connubial, matrimonial, marital, bridal, wedding.

nurse *verb* **1** tend, look after, care for,
treat. **2** suckle, feed, nurture, rear.
3 harbour, hold, have, entertain, cherish.

nurture *verb* **1** nourish, feed, sustain,
nurse. **2** rear, bring up, raise, train.

3 cultivate, develop, encourage, help,
foster.
➤*noun* care, support, training, discipline,
education, upbringing.

nut *noun* **1** kernel, pip, stone, seed.
2 fanatic, enthusiast, devotee, fan, buff
(*inf*), freak (*inf*). **3** maniac, lunatic, psycho
(*inf*), weirdo (*inf*), crackpot (*inf*).
nuts and bolts basics, fundamentals,
essentials, nitty-gritty (*inf*).

nutrition *noun* nourishment, alimentation, subsistence.

nutritious *adj* nutritive, nourishing, good,
wholesome, healthy.

nuts *adj* mad, crazy, deranged, barmy (*inf*).

nymph *noun* sylph, dryad, naiad, oread.

oaf *noun* dolt, blockhead, idiot, bungler, lout, clod.

oasis *noun* refuge, retreat, haven, sanctuary.

oath *noun* **1** vow, pledge, promise, word, bond. **2** blasphemy, profanity. **3** curse, expletive, swearword, obscenity, four-letter word.

obdurate *adj* **1** hard, hardhearted, cold, callous, unfeeling, insensitive. **2** inflexible, adamant, firm, stubborn, obstinate, pigheaded.

obedient *adj* compliant, acquiescent, submissive, dutiful, biddable, amenable.

obeisance *noun* **1** homage, deference, reverence, honour, worship. **2** salutation, bow, curtsy, genuflection, salaam.

obelisk *noun* pillar, column, shaft.

obese *adj* fat, stout, overweight, heavy, gross, corpulent.

obey *verb* comply with, observe, follow, abide by, adhere to, respect, discharge, fulfil.

obfuscate *verb* obscure, cloud, blur, confuse, scramble, muddle.

object *noun* **1** thing, article, item, entity, body. **2** aim, purpose, objective, goal, end, point. **3** butt, victim, recipient, target. ➤*verb* **1** protest, demur, remonstrate, expostulate, oppose, complain. **2** mind, disapprove, take exception.

objection *noun* protest, complaint, expostulation, exception, disapproval, opposition, scruple, qualm.

objectionable *adj* unpleasant, disagreeable, offensive, repulsive, obnoxious, loathsome, nasty, odious.

objective *adj* impartial, unbiased, neutral, detached, disinterested, dispassionate. ➤*noun* aim, purpose, goal, end, target, intention, design, ambition.

oblation *noun* offering, sacrifice, gift, donation.

obligate *verb* constrain, compel, require, bind, oblige, impel.

obligation *noun* **1** duty, responsibility, necessity, requirement. **2** pledge, promise, contract, bond, commitment.

obligatory *adj* compulsory, mandatory, required, necessary, essential, imperative.

oblige *verb* **1** compel, force, bind, require, make, obligate. **2** accommodate, serve, help, please, indulge.

obliging *adj* accommodating, amenable, willing, cooperative, helpful, gracious.

oblique *adj* **1** slanting, diagonal, angled, sloping, inclined. **2** indirect, evasive, devious, furtive, sidelong.

obliterate *verb* **1** eradicate, annihilate, wipe out, expunge. **2** delete, cross out, efface, erase, rub out.

oblivion *noun* **1** disregard, heedlessness, obliviousness, unawareness, unconsciousness. **2** abeyance, neglect. **3** extinction, non-existence.

oblivious *adj* unaware, unconscious, insensible, blind, deaf, heedless, neglectful, careless.

obloquy *noun* **1** censure, denunciation, condemnation, invective, abuse, vilification. **2** dishonour, discredit, shame, disgrace, infamy, ignominy.

obnoxious *adj* objectionable, unpleasant, nasty, disgusting, repugnant, odious, loathsome, insufferable.

obscene *adj* **1** indecent, immoral, improper, offensive, dirty, blue, pornographic, vulgar. **2** shocking, atrocious, outrageous, scandalous, wicked, sickening.

obscenity noun 1 indecency, immorality, offensiveness, vulgarity, atrocity, wickedness. 2 swearword, expletive, four-letter word, curse.

obscure adj 1 unclear, vague, abstruse, arcane, cryptic, impenetrable, incomprehensible. 2 unknown, insignificant, undistinguished, unheard-of, minor, humble. 3 faint, dim, hazy, indistinct, dark.
➤verb 1 hide, conceal, cover, screen, veil, cloak. 2 blur, confuse, muddle, scramble, garble, obfuscate.

obsequious adj servile, fawning, sycophantic, slavish, ingratiating, grovelling, unctuous, smarmy (inf).

observance noun 1 obedience, adherence, compliance, discharge, regard, respect. 2 rite, ritual, ceremony, service, custom, practice, convention, tradition.

observant adj 1 eagle-eyed, alert, sharp, perceptive. 2 attentive, vigilant, watchful. 3 heedful, mindful, dutiful, obedient.

observation noun 1 notice, attention, perception, watching, monitoring. 2 surveillance, scrutiny, study. 3 comment, remark, statement, finding, note, reflection, opinion.

observe verb 1 watch, contemplate, look at, view, witness, see, perceive, notice, detect. 2 remark, comment, say, mention. 3 follow, honour, respect, abide by, comply with, conform to. 4 celebrate, mark, keep, commemorate. 5 study, monitor, keep under surveillance.

observer noun watcher, viewer, spectator, onlooker, witness, bystander, reporter.

obsess verb preoccupy, dominate, rule, consume, possess, grip, plague, haunt.

obsession noun preoccupation, fixation, passion, mania, compulsion, fetish, thing (inf).

obsessive adj compulsive, uncontrollable, overwhelming.

obsolete adj 1 discontinued, disused, extinct, archaic. 2 outmoded, antiquated, passé, old-fashioned, superannuated.

obstacle noun barrier, bar, hurdle, obstruction, impediment, stumbling block.

obstinate adj stubborn, mulish, pigheaded, opinionated, adamant, unshakable, obdurate, unyielding.

obstreperous adj 1 riotous, unruly, disorderly, refractory, bolshie (inf), stroppy (inf). 2 boisterous, rowdy, clamorous, noisy.

obstruct verb 1 block, clog, choke, bar, barricade. 2 hinder, impede, hamper, prevent, check, retard, thwart.

obstruction noun blockage, obstacle, barricade, hindrance, impediment, stumbling block.

obtain verb 1 get, acquire, come by, receive, secure, gain, attain, achieve. 2 prevail, exist, rule, be the case.

obtrusive adj 1 conspicuous, obvious, unmistakable, blatant, flagrant, prominent. 2 officious, importunate, forward, assertive, pushy (inf).

obtuse adj slow, dull, stupid, dim (inf), insensitive, thick-skinned.

obviate verb preclude, forestall, avert, prevent, get rid of, do away with.

obvious adj evident, manifest, patent, clear, plain, apparent, noticeable, conspicuous.

occasion noun 1 time, occurrence, instance, event. 2 function, affair, party, celebration. 3 opportunity, chance, opening. 4 reason, cause, motive, grounds, excuse, justification.
➤verb cause, bring about, prompt, elicit, provoke, lead to, result in, produce.

occasional adj intermittent, sporadic, irregular, infrequent.

occult adj 1 mystical, supernatural, magic. 2 arcane, esoteric, recondite, hidden, secret. 3 abstruse, obscure, mysterious.
➤noun magic, sorcery, witchcraft, wizardry, mysticism, supernatural.

occupancy noun occupation, tenure, tenancy, possession, residence.

occupant noun 1 owner, occupier, tenant, resident, inhabitant, inmate. 2 holder, incumbent.

occupation noun 1 job, profession, work, trade, business, métier. 2 activity, pursuit. 3 occupancy, tenure, tenancy, residence. 4 conquest, invasion, possession, capture.

occupational adj professional, vocational, work, business.

occupy verb 1 inhabit, live in, dwell in, reside in. 2 fill, take up, use. 3 conquer, seize, capture, invade, take over. **4** absorb, engross, engage, monopolize, entertain.

occur *verb* **1** happen, take place, come about, befall, transpire, arise. **2** appear, materialize, be present, exist.
occur to strike, dawn on, come to mind.

occurrence *noun* **1** happening, event, incident, episode, instance. **2** incidence, existence, presence.

ocean *noun* sea, main, deep.

odd *adj* **1** unusual, strange, peculiar, funny, curious, unconventional, weird, bizarre. **2** occasional, incidental, casual, random, various, sundry. **3** unmatched, single, spare, leftover.

oddity *noun* **1** peculiarity, oddness, strangeness. **2** curiosity, eccentric, misfit, freak, idiosyncrasy.

oddment *noun* bit, piece, scrap, remnant, offcut, leftover.

odds *pl noun* **1** probability, likelihood, chances. **2** advantage, edge, difference, disparity.
at odds in disagreement, conflicting, at loggerheads.
odds and ends bits and pieces, oddments, scraps, leftovers, odds and sods (*inf*).

odious *adj* obnoxious, objectionable, repulsive, abhorrent, disagreeable, detestable, horrid, nasty.

odium *noun* disfavour, antipathy, abhorrence, repugnance, condemnation, disgrace, obloquy, opprobrium.

odour *noun* **1** smell, scent, aroma, perfume, stench, redolence, whiff (*inf*). **2** air, aura, quality, flavour.

odyssey *noun* journey, voyage, trek, travels, peregrination.

off *adj* **1** bad, rotten, sour, mouldy, rancid. **2** cancelled, postponed.

off and on *adv* on and off, occasionally, periodically, intermittently, now and then, every so often, from time to time.

offbeat *adj* unconventional, unorthodox, unusual, bizarre, wacky (*inf*).

off-colour *adj* **1** unwell, out of sorts, poorly, ill, below par, under the weather (*inf*). **2** risqué, indecent, improper, vulgar, smutty (*inf*).

offence *noun* **1** wrongdoing, fault, sin, transgression, misdeed, misdemeanour. **2** violation, infringement, crime. **3** affront, insult, slight, injury, injustice, indignity. **4** indignation, displeasure, anger, resentment, umbrage. **5** attack, assault, charge, offensive.
take offence be offended, be hurt, feel resentment, take umbrage, take exception.

offend *verb* **1** upset, hurt, wound, wrong, affront, insult, slight. **2** outrage, disgust, repel, sicken, anger. **3** do wrong, sin, transgress, err.

offensive *adj* **1** insulting, abusive, rude, disrespectful, annoying, hurtful. **2** unpleasant, nasty, repugnant, disgusting, revolting, vile. **3** aggressive, attacking, invading, belligerent.
➤*noun* attack, assault, charge, onslaught, invasion, incursion.

offer *verb* **1** present, hold out, tender, proffer, propose, put forward, submit, bid. **2** provide, give, supply, afford, impart, yield. **3** volunteer, come forward, show willing (*inf*).
➤*noun* **1** bid, tender, proposal. **2** proposition, suggestion, advance.
on offer 1 reduced, discounted, cheap. **2** available, for sale.

offering *noun* present, gift, donation, contribution, sacrifice, oblation.

offhand *adv* impromptu, extempore, ad lib, off the cuff (*inf*).
➤*adj* **1** abrupt, curt, brusque, rude, discourteous. **2** casual, informal, unceremonious, cavalier, nonchalant.

office *noun* **1** workplace, room, study, bureau. **2** place of business, firm, company. **3** post, position, situation, appointment, commission, role, capacity, function. **4** service, work, support, help. **5** duty, task, responsibility.

officer *noun* official, functionary, administrator, bureaucrat, executive.

official *adj* **1** authorized, legitimate, approved, accredited, endorsed, licensed, proper, authentic, bona fide. **2** formal, ceremonial, ritual, solemn.
➤*noun* officer, functionary, administrator, bureaucrat, executive.

officiate *verb* preside, chair, conduct, direct, manage, take charge.

officious *adj* importunate, interfering, meddlesome, intrusive, bustling, forward, pushy (*inf*), overzealous.

offing *noun* **in the offing** imminent, impending, forthcoming, approaching, at hand, on the cards (*inf*), near, close, looming, brewing.

offload *verb* **1** unload, discharge, jettison, deposit. **2** get rid of, dump (*inf*).

off-putting *adj* disconcerting, discouraging, disheartening, unnerving, unsettling, disturbing.

offset *verb* counterbalance, make up for, compensate for, cancel out, counteract, neutralize.

offshoot *noun* **1** branch, outgrowth. **2** development, derivative, by-product, spin-off, consequence.

offspring *noun* children, young, family, progeny, issue, descendants, posterity.

often *adv* frequently, repeatedly, time after time, again and again.

ogle *verb* eye up, make eyes at, leer at, stare at.

ogre *noun* **1** giant, monster, brute, bogeyman. **2** demon, bogey, beast.

oil *noun* **1** grease, lubricant. **2** ointment, lotion, balm, unguent.
➤ *verb* lubricate, grease, anoint.

oily *adj* **1** greasy, fatty, oleaginous. **2** smooth, suave, unctuous, glib, servile, obsequious.

ointment *noun* balm, salve, lotion, liniment, embrocation, cream, unguent.

OK *adj* satisfactory, acceptable, adequate, passable, fair, all right, so-so (*inf*), not bad (*inf*).
➤ *interj* all right, fine, yes, very well, agreed.
➤ *noun* approval, authorization, endorsement, agreement, permission, consent, green light (*inf*), thumbs-up (*inf*).
➤ *verb* approve, authorize, sanction, endorse, pass.

old *adj* **1** aged, elderly, getting on, past one's prime, over the hill (*inf*), long in the tooth (*inf*). **2** ancient, antique, early, primitive, bygone. **3** long-standing, lasting, enduring, time-honoured, traditional. **4** former, previous, one-time, erstwhile, quondam. **5** worn-out, shabby, broken-down, dilapidated. **6** discarded, cast-off, outdated, antiquated, obsolete.

old-fashioned *adj* outmoded, outdated, dated, unfashionable, passé, démodé, antiquated, superannuated.

omen *noun* portent, sign, foretoken, warning, harbinger, presage.

ominous *adj* threatening, menacing, sinister, portentous, foreboding, inauspicious, premonitory.

omission *noun* **1** exclusion, exception, deletion, negligence, default. **2** oversight, gap, failure.

omit *verb* **1** exclude, except, drop, delete, leave out, miss out, skip, pass over. **2** neglect, forget, fail, overlook.

omnipotent *adj* almighty, all-powerful, supreme, sovereign, absolute.

omnipresent *adj* **1** ubiquitous, pervasive. **2** all-present, universal.

on and off *adv* off and on, occasionally, periodically, intermittently, now and then, every so often, from time to time.

once *adv* formerly, previously, at one time, long ago.
➤ *conj* when, after, as soon as.
at once 1 immediately, instantly, straightaway, directly, now. **2** together, simultaneously, at the same time.
once in a while occasionally, sometimes, now and then, infrequently.

oncoming *adj* approaching, coming, advancing, imminent.

one *adj* **1** single, individual, lone, sole, only, unique. **2** united, like-minded.

onerous *adj* burdensome, oppressive, heavy, weighty, arduous, difficult, taxing.

one-sided *adj* uneven, unbalanced, unequal, unfair, biased, prejudiced.

one-time *adj* former, earlier, previous, erstwhile, quondam.

ongoing *adj* **1** continuing, in progress, current. **2** developing, growing.

onlooker *noun* bystander, observer, spectator, eyewitness.

only *adj* sole, solitary, lone, single, unique.
➤ *adv* **1** just, merely, simply, purely. **2** scarcely, barely.

onset *noun* **1** beginning, start, inception, commencement, outbreak. **2** onslaught, onrush, attack, assault, charge.

onslaught *noun* attack, assault, charge, raid, push, drive.

onus *noun* burden, load, responsibility, liability, duty, obligation.

onwards *adv* forwards, ahead, on.

ooze *verb* **1** seep, percolate, filter, leak, drip, trickle. **2** secrete, exude, discharge.
➤*noun* sludge, slime, silt, mud, deposit, sediment.

opacity *noun* **1** cloudiness, haziness, murkiness. **2** obscurity, unintelligibility, incomprehensibility.

opalescent *adj* opaline, iridescent, pearly, nacreous.

opaque *adj* **1** cloudy, hazy, murky, muddy, turbid, dull. **2** obscure, unclear, abstruse, incomprehensible, unintelligible.

open *adj* **1** unclosed, gaping, ajar, unlocked. **2** unenclosed, unfenced, extensive, sweeping. **3** clear, unobstructed, free, unrestricted. **4** unfolded, spread out, stretched out, unfurled. **5** unfastened, unsealed. **6** uncovered, unprotected, exposed. **7** public, accessible, general, overt, manifest, unconcealed. **8** liable, prone, susceptible, vulnerable. **9** vacant, free, available, unoccupied. **10** undecided, unsettled, unresolved, debatable, moot. **11** receptive, responsive, flexible, accommodating. **12** frank, candid, honest, direct, forthright. **13** broad-minded, liberal, tolerant, unbiased, unprejudiced. **14** holey, porous, cellular, honeycombed.
➤*verb* **1** unfasten, unlock, unbolt, separate, part, split. **2** undo, unwrap, unseal, uncover. **3** spread out, expand, extend, unfold, unfurl. **4** begin, start, commence. **5** launch, inaugurate.

opening *noun* **1** gap, aperture, orifice, hole, space, slot, vent, crack. **2** beginning, start, launch, inauguration, outset. **3** opportunity, chance, occasion, break (*inf*). **4** vacancy, place, job, position.
➤*adj* beginning, first, initial, introductory, inaugural.

openly *adv* frankly, candidly, honestly, directly, forthrightly, unreservedly.

open-minded *adj* receptive, tolerant, catholic, broad-minded, reasonable, unprejudiced.

operate *verb* function, work, act, go, run, handle, control, manipulate.

operation *noun* **1** running, performance, working, action, motion, manipulation. **2** procedure, process, task, job, business, undertaking, enterprise, venture. **3** exercise, manoeuvre, mission.

operational *adj* functioning, in operation, going, running, active, in use, working, functional.

operative *adj* **1** in force, effective, active, in operation, operational. **2** significant, key, crucial, relevant.
➤*noun* **1** worker, hand, employee, labourer, mechanic, operator. **2** secret agent, spy, mole (*inf*).

operator *noun* **1** worker, operative, machinist, technician. **2** contractor, trader, handler, manager. **3** manipulator, machinator, wheeler-dealer (*inf*).

opinion *noun* **1** belief, judgment, assessment, view, point of view, standpoint. **2** idea, notion, fancy, impression, feeling, theory, conjecture.

opinionated *adj* dogmatic, doctrinaire, cocksure, arrogant, pompous, self-important, obdurate, bigoted.

opponent *noun* **1** adversary, antagonist, foe, rival, competitor. **2** dissenter, disputant, opposer.

opportune *adj* **1** timely, seasonable, convenient, auspicious. **2** appropriate, apt, suitable, fitting, good, felicitous.

opportunism *noun* exploitation, expediency, pragmatism, unscrupulousness.

opportunity *noun* **1** occasion, time, moment. **2** chance, opening, break (*inf*).

oppose *verb* **1** resist, withstand, counter, disapprove of, take issue with, obstruct, prevent, thwart. **2** fight, contest, combat, attack, confront, defy. **3** contrast, counterbalance, offset.

opposite *adj* **1** facing, corresponding, reverse, far. **2** opposed, opposing, conflicting, antagonistic, hostile. **3** contrary, different, antithetical, incompatible.
➤*noun* converse, inverse, reverse, contrary, contradiction, antithesis.

opposition *noun* 1 counteraction, conflict, competition, confrontation. 2 antagonism, hostility, defiance, resistance, disapproval, obstruction. 3 opponents, rivals, competition, other side, enemy.

oppress *verb* 1 subjugate, subdue, crush, suppress, persecute, tyrannize, enslave. 2 burden, trouble, afflict, weigh down, discourage, depress.

oppressive *adj* 1 tyrannical, despotic, harsh, severe, authoritarian, draconian. 2 sultry, stuffy, stifling, close, muggy, airless. 3 burdensome, onerous, overwhelming, overpowering.

opprobrious *adj* scornful, contemptuous, reproachful, vituperative, derogatory, unfavourable, offensive, abusive.

oppugn *verb* dispute, contest, question, oppose, attack.

opt *verb* choose, select, decide, settle.

optimism *noun* hopefulness, confidence, bullishness, cheerfulness, idealism, positive thinking.

optimum *adj* ideal, perfect, best, top, peak,.

option *noun* 1 choice, alternative. 2 selection, preference, wish, will, discretion.

optional *adj* voluntary, unforced, discretionary, elective.

opulent *adj* rich, wealthy, affluent, prosperous, sumptuous, luxurious, lavish, plush (*inf*).

opus *noun* work, production, piece, creation, oeuvre.

oracle *noun* seer, prophet, soothsayer, sage, sibyl, augur.

oracular *adj* 1 prophetic, sibylline, vatic, mantic, divinatory, predictive. 2 wise, authoritative, dogmatic, obscure, mysterious, cryptic, ambiguous.

oral *adj* verbal, spoken, vocal, unwritten.

oration *noun* speech, address, lecture, discourse, declamation, harangue.

orator *noun* public speaker, demagogue, lecturer, rhetorician.

oratory *noun* rhetoric, eloquence, delivery, declamation, grandiloquence, magniloquence.

orb *noun* ball, sphere, globe.

orbit *noun* 1 revolution, rotation, cycle, circle, circuit, track, path, course, trajectory. 2 field, compass, sphere, domain.
➤*verb* circle, revolve around.

orchestrate *verb* 1 organize, coordinate, arrange, stage-manage, mastermind. 2 arrange, score.

ordain *verb* 1 consecrate, anoint, induct, invest. 2 destine, predestine, fate, doom, foreordain. 3 order, command, decree, rule, prescribe.

ordeal *noun* trial, test, trouble, torture, torment, nightmare.

order *noun* 1 command, injunction, instruction, direction, decree, mandate, edict, directive. 2 discipline, control, law and order, peace, calm. 3 request, demand, commission, booking, reservation. 4 system, method, organization, structure, neatness, tidiness, orderliness. 5 arrangement, disposition, grouping, layout. 6 association, society, brotherhood, sisterhood, community, fellowship, sect, denomination. 7 class, caste, rank, stratum. 8 rank, grade, level, degree. 9 kind, sort, type, class, category. 10 sequence, progression, classification.
➤*verb* 1 command, instruct, direct, bid, enjoin. 2 decree, ordain, prescribe, demand, require. 3 request, commission, book, reserve, send for. 4 arrange, organize, systematize, rank, group, sort.

out of order 1 broken, inoperative, not working, on the blink (*inf*). 2 wrong, unseemly, improper, not done.

orderly *adj* 1 neat, tidy, shipshape. 2 systematic, methodical, well-organized. 3 well-behaved, disciplined, peaceful, quiet.

ordinance *noun* 1 decree, edict, order, rule, regulation, law, statute. 2 ceremony, rite, observance, usage.

ordinary *adj* 1 usual, typical, customary, habitual, regular, routine. 2 commonplace, everyday, unexceptional, run-of-the-mill (*inf*), plain, standard, common, average.
out of the ordinary unusual, uncommon, exceptional, remarkable, rare, noteworthy, extraordinary.

organ *noun* 1 part, structure. 2 agency, forum.

organic *adj* **1** natural, biological, living. **2** basic, fundamental, structural, integral, constitutional. **3** systematic, ordered, structured.

organism *noun* **1** creature, being, living thing, animal, plant. **2** system, organization, structure.

organization *noun* **1** association, institution, society, corporation, company, group. **2** management, coordination, arrangement, classification. **3** system, structure, plan, composition.

organize *verb* **1** order, systematize, arrange, dispose, classify, categorize, structure. **2** coordinate, manage, run, plan.

orgy *noun* **1** debauch, revel, carousal, bacchanalia. **2** spree, binge (*inf*).

orientate *verb* **1** familiarize, get one's bearings. **2** orient, direct, position, align, angle. **3** adjust, adapt, accommodate.

orientation *noun* **1** inclination, leaning, tendency, preference. **2** adjustment, adaptation, familiarization. **3** position, direction, arrangement, alignment, bearings.

orifice *noun* opening, aperture, hole, mouth, vent, fissure.

origin *noun* **1** source, root, spring, cause, derivation, provenance, beginning, starting-point. **2** ancestry, extraction, parentage, birth.

original *adj* **1** first, initial, earliest, primal. **2** fresh, new, novel, innovative, creative, inventive, unconventional. **3** real, genuine, authentic. **4** archetypal, prototypical, master.
➤*noun* master, prototype, archetype, model, pattern, standard.

originality *noun* **1** freshness, novelty. **2** creativity, inventiveness, imaginativeness, resourcefulness.

originate *verb* **1** proceed, begin, spring, issue, result, arise, derive, stem. **2** initiate, start, create, conceive, pioneer, found.

ornament *noun* **1** decoration, embellishment, garnish, trimming, frill, accessory. **2** trinket, knick-knack. **3** ornamentation, decoration, embellishment, adornment.
➤*verb* adorn, decorate, embellish, garnish, beautify.

ornamental *adj* decorative, attractive, showy, ornate.

ornate *adj* **1** elaborate, fancy, showy, baroque, rococo. **2** florid, flowery.

orotund *adj* **1** resonant, sonorous, rich, full, ringing, booming. **2** pompous, bombastic, grandiloquent, magniloquent.

orthodox *adj* **1** conventional, traditional, accepted, approved, official, proper, standard, regular. **2** faithful, strict, true, devout, conformist, established.

oscillate *verb* **1** swing, sway, vibrate. **2** vacillate, fluctuate, vary, waver.

ostensible *adj* outward, superficial, alleged, apparent, seeming, specious.

ostentation *noun* display, show, parade, showiness, flamboyance, affectation.

ostracize *verb* exclude, bar, banish, expel, blackball, reject, shun, cold-shoulder (*inf*), send to Coventry.

other *adj* **1** different, variant, alternative, diverse. **2** separate, distinct. **3** further, more, extra, additional, spare.

otherwise *adv* **1** or else, if not. **2** in other respects, in other ways, apart from that, except for that. **3** differently, in a different way.

oust *verb* **1** eject, expel, evict, dispossess. **2** depose, unseat, replace, supplant.

out *adv* **1** away, absent, abroad, elsewhere. **2** unconscious, knocked out. **3** exposed, revealed, disclosed, published, known, broadcast. **4** unfashionable, passé, dated, old-fashioned. **5** extinguished, dead, finished.

out-and-out *adj* absolute, thorough, complete, utter, downright, arrant.

outbreak *noun* eruption, explosion, flare-up, rash, epidemic.

outburst *noun* **1** fit, tantrum, eruption, explosion, outpouring. **2** burst, surge, rush.

outcast *noun* pariah, exile, displaced person, refugee, leper.

outclass *verb* surpass, beat, excel, outdo, outrank, outshine, eclipse.

outcome *noun* consequence, result, issue, upshot.

outcry *noun* protest, complaint, uproar, clamour, fuss, hullabaloo.

outdated *adj* old-fashioned, outmoded, out-of-date, passé, démodé, obsolete, antiquated, superannuated.

outdistance *verb* outrun, outstrip, overtake, leave behind.

outdo *verb* surpass, beat, top, outshine, outclass, outstrip, outsmart.

outdoors *adv* outside, out, in the open air, alfresco.

outer *adj* 1 external, exterior, outward, superficial. 2 remote, outlying, peripheral, fringe.

outfit *noun* 1 clothes, ensemble, costume, dress, suit. 2 kit, set, equipment, gear. 3 organization, group, team, company, firm, business.
➤*verb* fit out, equip, supply, rig out.

outgoing *adj* 1 retiring, withdrawing, former, ex-. 2 departing, leaving, ebbing. 3 extrovert, demonstrative, sociable, gregarious, friendly, affable.

outgoings *pl noun* expenditure, outlay, expenses, costs, overheads.

outing *noun* excursion, trip, jaunt.

outlandish *adj* unconventional, bizarre, curious, weird, extraordinary, odd, unfamiliar, exotic.

outlaw *noun* bandit, brigand, pirate, freebooter, fugitive, criminal.
➤*verb* ban, bar, prohibit, forbid.

outlay *noun* expenditure, cost, expense, spending, disbursement.

outlet *noun* 1 vent, escape, exit, way out, opening. 2 shop, store, market. 3 safety valve, release, vent.

outline *noun* 1 draft, sketch, plan, skeleton, framework. 2 contour, shape, form, delineation. 3 summary, synopsis, résumé, abstract.
➤*verb* 1 draft, sketch, trace, delineate. 2 summarize, recapitulate, show, indicate.

outlook *noun* 1 attitude, viewpoint, perspective, slant, angle. 2 prospect, future, prognosis, forecast. 3 view, vista, prospect, scene.

outlying *adj* distant, remote, outer, peripheral, far-flung.

out-of-date *adj* outdated, old-fashioned, outmoded, obsolete, obsolescent, antiquated.

out-of-the-way *adj* distant, remote, faraway, isolated, inaccessible, off the beaten track.

outpouring *noun* flood, deluge, torrent, flow, spurt, stream.

output *noun* 1 productivity, production, manufacture. 2 yield, harvest, fruits.

outrage *noun* 1 anger, fury, horror, indignation, shock. 2 scandal, violation, offence, affront, insult, indignity. 3 atrocity, enormity, crime, barbarism.
➤*verb* 1 anger, infuriate, incense, disgust, shock, horrify. 2 abuse, violate, desecrate.

outrageous *adj* 1 shocking, scandalous, terrible, dreadful, monstrous, disgraceful, offensive, intolerable. 2 immoderate, excessive, extravagant, extreme.

outright *adj* 1 total, complete, utter, absolute, thorough, downright. 2 direct, unconditional, unqualified.
➤*adv* 1 totally, completely, utterly, absolutely. 2 instantly, immediately, at once, instantaneously, on the spot.

outrun *verb* 1 outstrip, outpace, outdistance, leave behind. 2 beat, surpass, outdo.

outset *noun* start, beginning, opening, inception.

outshine *verb* eclipse, overshadow, surpass, excel, transcend, outclass, outdo, put in the shade.

outside *noun* 1 exterior, surface, edge, border. 2 appearance, facade.
➤*adj* 1 exterior, external, outer, outward, superficial. 2 remote, unlikely, slim.
➤*adv* outdoors, out, in the open air, alfresco.

outsider *noun* stranger, alien, foreigner, newcomer, intruder, interloper, visitor, non-member.

outskirts *pl noun* suburbs, periphery, environs, purlieus, edge.

outspoken *adj* candid, frank, blunt, open, unreserved, direct, forthright.

outspread *adj* outstretched, open, unfurled, extended, spread out.

outstanding *adj* 1 excellent, superb, exceptional, great, distinguished, impressive. 2 striking, prominent, noticeable, conspicuous. 3 owing, due, unpaid. 4 unsettled, unresolved, remaining.

outstrip verb **1** outrun, outpace, outdistance. **2** outdo, surpass, excel, beat.

outward adj **1** outer, external, exterior, outside. **2** superficial, apparent, visible, ostensible.

outweigh verb exceed, override, prevail over, surpass, outbalance.

outwit verb trick, dupe, outfox, outsmart (inf), outmanoeuvre, get the better of.

oval adj egg-shaped, ovoid, ovate, elliptical.

ovation noun applause, clapping, cheering, acclamation.

oven noun stove, cooker, kiln.

over prep **1** above, on top of, higher than. **2** exceeding, in excess of, more than, greater than. **3** across, through.
➤adv **1** above, beyond. **2** across, through. **3** extra, surplus, remaining, left, in excess. **4** finished, at an end, past.
over and above in addition to, as well as, on top of.

overact verb exaggerate, ham it up (inf).

overall adj general, global, comprehensive, all-inclusive, total, sweeping.
➤adv in general, broadly speaking, on the whole.

overawe verb intimidate, cow, daunt, disconcert, frighten, alarm.

overbalance verb lose one's balance, fall over, topple, capsize.

overbearing adj domineering, imperious, lordly, high-handed, bossy (inf), autocratic, dictatorial, oppressive.

overcast adj cloudy, grey, dull, murky, dark, leaden.

overcharge verb surcharge, cheat, short-change, fleece (inf), swindle, rip off (inf), diddle (inf).

overcome verb **1** conquer, master, surmount, rise above. **2** overpower, overwhelm, crush, quash, subdue. **3** defeat, beat, best, worst, lick (inf).

overcrowd verb pack, cram, congest, overpopulate.

overdo verb **1** go overboard (inf), do to death (inf), lay it on thick (inf). **2** exaggerate, overstate. **3** overcook, burn.

overdue adj **1** late, behind, delayed, tardy. **2** owing, in arrears.

overeat verb overindulge, stuff oneself, gorge oneself, guzzle, gormandize, pig out (inf).

overestimate verb overrate, overvalue, think too much of.

overflow verb **1** spill over, run over, brim over, flood, swamp. **2** be full of, abound, swarm, teem.
➤noun excess, surplus, overspill, overabundance.

overhang verb jut out, stick out, protrude, extend, project, beetle.

overhaul verb **1** inspect, examine, check, service, repair. **2** overtake, pass, get ahead of, outstrip.

overhead adv above, up, over, on high.

overindulge verb **1** overeat, gorge, binge (inf). **2** pamper, mollycoddle, cosset, spoil, pander to.

overjoyed adj delighted, ecstatic, elated, thrilled, over the moon (inf).

overload verb overburden, strain, weigh down, overtax, oppress, encumber.

overlook verb **1** look out on, front onto, face, dominate. **2** miss, neglect, omit, forget. **3** disregard, ignore, pardon, excuse, condone, blink at.

overly adv too, excessively, inordinately.

overpower verb **1** defeat, overcome, conquer, vanquish, beat, crush, quell, subdue. **2** overwhelm, overcome, fill, affect.

overrate verb overestimate, overvalue, think too much of.

overreach verb outwit, outsmart (inf), cheat, swindle, trick, dupe.
overreach oneself overstretch oneself, go too far, bite off more than one can chew (inf).

override verb **1** outweigh, prevail over. **2** overrule, supersede, annul, reverse.

overriding adj main, chief, major, principal, prevailing, paramount.

overrule verb disallow, reject, override, annul, reverse, rescind, countermand, revoke.

overrun *verb* **1** attack, invade, occupy. **2** infest, inundate, swarm over, spread over. **3** exceed, go beyond, overshoot.

oversee *verb* supervise, superintend, watch, observe, monitor, direct.

overshadow *verb* **1** eclipse, outshine, exceed, outweigh, dominate, tower over. **2** cloud, darken, dim, obscure, spoil, blight.

oversight *noun* **1** omission, lapse, slip, mistake, error. **2** supervision, surveillance, management, control, care, charge, custody.

overt *adj* plain, manifest, patent, open, unconcealed, undisguised, conspicuous, blatant.

overtake *verb* **1** pass, leave behind, outstrip, outdistance, overhaul. **2** befall, come upon, surprise, take unawares.

overthrow *verb* **1** oust, depose, unseat, dethrone, bring down. **2** overturn, quash, abolish, upset, topple.
➤*noun* defeat, fall, downfall, deposition.

overtone *noun* suggestion, hint, implication, nuance, connotation.

overture *noun* **1** introduction, prelude, opening, preface. **2** advance, approach, offer, proposal, invitation.

overturn *verb* **1** upset, tip over, upend, invert. **2** capsize, turn turtle, overbalance, topple, spill. **3** overrule, override, annul,

reverse, cancel. **4** overthrow, subvert, bring down, depose, destroy, abolish.

overweening *adj* **1** arrogant, haughty, supercilious, presumptuous, lordly, pompous. **2** excessive, immoderate, extravagant, exaggerated.

overweight *adj* obese, fat, plump, stout, portly, heavy.

overwhelm *verb* **1** overcome, move, touch, affect, stir, dumbfound, bowl over (*inf*). **2** engulf, submerge, inundate, flood, deluge, swamp. **3** overpower, overthrow, conquer, overcome, vanquish, defeat.

overwork *verb* overdo it, do too much, strain oneself, burn oneself out.

overwrought *adj* **1** distraught, overexcited, frantic, worked up (*inf*), wound up (*inf*). **2** fancy, ornate, flowery, overelaborate.

owe *verb* **1** be in debt, be in arrears. **2** be indebted, be beholden.

owing *adj* due, unpaid, payable, outstanding, in arrears.

own *adj* personal, private, individual, particular.
➤*verb* **1** possess, have, hold. **2** acknowledge, admit, recognize, grant, concede.
on one's own 1 alone, by oneself, solo, unaccompanied. **2** independently, unaided.
own up confess, come clean (*inf*).

pace *noun* **1** step, stride. **2** gait, walk. **3** speed, rate, tempo, momentum, progress, quickness.
➤*verb* **1** walk, stride, step, tramp, march, patrol. **2** measure, mark.

pacific *adj* conciliatory, placatory, propitiatory, peacemaking, peaceable, non-violent, gentle, friendly.

pacify *verb* **1** appease, conciliate, propitiate, placate, mollify, calm, soothe, assuage. **2** crush, subdue, repress, tame.

pack *noun* **1** packet, package, carton, container. **2** herd, flock, drove. **3** troop, band, group, company. **4** crowd, mob, bunch. **5** bundle, set, lot, collection. **6** backpack, rucksack, haversack, knapsack, kitbag.
➤*verb* **1** cram, stuff, jam, fill, wedge, ram, compact, compress. **2** load, stow, box, crate. **3** wrap, parcel, package, bundle, cover, protect. **4** crowd, cram, squeeze, press.
pack in draw, pull, attract.
pack off send, dismiss, dispatch, bundle off, send packing (*inf*).
pack up break down, fail, stop working, malfunction.

package *noun* **1** bundle, pack, parcel, packet, box, consignment. **2** deal, whole, unit, set, combination.
➤*verb* **1** pack, box, wrap, parcel. **2** group, batch, combine.

packaging *noun* wrapping, wrapper, packet, packing, covering, container.

packet *noun* **1** box, carton, case, bag, container, wrapper. **2** pack, package, parcel. **3** lot, fortune, bundle (*inf*), pile (*inf*), pretty penny (*inf*), tidy sum (*inf*).

pact *noun* agreement, compact, covenant, bond, contract, treaty, entente, convention, bargain, deal.

pad¹ *noun* **1** cushion, bolster, wad, stuffing, stiffening, protection. **2** block, jotter, notepad, notebook, tablet. **3** paw, foot, sole, print. **4** home, place, house, flat, rooms, quarters.
➤*verb* cushion, stuff, pack, wad, line, protect.
pad out fill out, expand, flesh out, amplify, lengthen, stretch out, spin out.

pad² *verb* tiptoe, creep, walk, tread, tramp, plod.

padding *noun* packing, filling, stuffing, wadding, lining, protection.

paddle¹ *noun* oar, scull.
➤*verb* row, scull, propel, steer.

paddle² *verb* wade, splash.

paddock *noun* field, meadow, yard, compound, stockade, corral.

padre *noun* chaplain, pastor, minister, priest, cleric, clergyman.

paean *noun* hymn, song of praise, psalm, anthem, eulogy, panegyric.

pagan *noun* **1** heathen, unbeliever, infidel, idolater, atheist, agnostic. **2** polytheist, pantheist.

page¹ *noun* **1** leaf, sheet, folio, side. **2** event, episode, chapter, period, time, era, epoch.

page² *noun* **1** bellboy, messenger. **2** servant, attendant, footman.
➤*verb* call, summon, send for, ask for.

pageant *noun* parade, procession, tableau, spectacle, show, display, play, representation, extravaganza.

pageantry *noun* pomp, ceremony, magnificence, splendour, spectacle, parade, show, display, showiness, ostentation, theatricality, extravagance.

pain *noun* **1** hurt, discomfort, suffering, agony, ache, throb, cramp, pang, twinge, smart, soreness, tenderness. **2** distress, anguish, suffering, trouble, affliction, torment, heartache, sorrow. **3** nuisance,

bother, pest, pain in the neck (*inf*), drag (*inf*), bore (*inf*).
>*verb* hurt, ache, throb, distress, trouble, afflict, torment, agonize, grieve, sadden, upset.

pained *adj* hurt, injured, wounded, stung, offended, aggrieved, distressed, upset, worried, reproachful.

painful *adj* 1 sore, tender, aching, throbbing, raw, agonizing, excruciating, distressing, harrowing, upsetting, traumatic, uncomfortable. 2 hard, difficult, tough, arduous, laborious, toilsome.

painkiller *noun* anaesthetic, sedative, palliative, analgesic, anodyne, lenitive.

painless *adj* 1 pain-free, comfortable. 2 effortless, easy, trouble-free, simple, straightforward, undemanding.

pains *pl noun* effort, bother, trouble, care, diligence.

painstaking *adj* careful, scrupulous, punctilious, meticulous, assiduous, thorough, conscientious, diligent, persevering, industrious.

paint *noun* colour, pigment, emulsion, gloss, distemper, oil.
>*verb* 1 colour, wash, tint, decorate, coat, cover, spray. 2 daub, smear, slap on (*inf*). 3 depict, portray, represent, draw. 4 describe, conjure up, draw, sketch, evoke, represent.
paint the town red celebrate, carouse, make merry, revel, go on the razzle (*inf*), live it up (*inf*), have a ball (*inf*).

painter *noun* artist, portraitist, dauber.

painting *noun* picture, watercolour, oil painting, portrait, landscape, still life, miniature, fresco, mural.

pair *noun* 1 brace, duo, doublet, set. 2 couple, twosome, duo, twins.
>*verb* match, couple, mate, twin, partner, yoke, marry, wed.

pal *noun* friend, chum (*inf*), mate (*inf*), comrade, companion, buddy (*inf*), crony (*inf*).

palace *noun* castle, château, stately home, mansion.

palatable *adj* 1 tasty, appetizing, mouthwatering, toothsome, delicious, yummy

(*inf*), scrumptious (*inf*), edible, eatable. 2 pleasant, agreeable, acceptable, satisfactory, attractive, nice.

palate *noun* taste, appreciation, liking, relish, enjoyment, enthusiasm.

palatial *adj* grand, stately, majestic, imposing, splendid, magnificent, sumptuous, luxurious, opulent, posh (*inf*), ritzy (*inf*).

palaver *noun* 1 rigmarole, procedure, business (*inf*), performance (*inf*), fuss, song and dance (*inf*), carry-on (*inf*). 2 chatter, babble, prattle, blather.

pale *adj* 1 wan, pallid, pasty, ashen, livid, colourless, anaemic, bloodless, white. 2 light, whitish, muted, pastel, bleached, faded, washed-out. 3 dim, faint, feeble, weak, thin, insipid.
>*verb* 1 blanch, whiten. 2 fade, dim, lessen, diminish, dwindle, melt.

pall¹ *noun* shroud, mantle, veil, cloak, shadow, cloud.

pall² *verb* cloy, bore, weary, sicken, jade.

palliate *verb* 1 alleviate, mitigate, allay, ease, relieve, dull, blunt. 2 extenuate, lighten, lessen, diminish, moderate, tone down.

palliative *noun* analgesic, anodyne, sedative, tranquillizer, painkiller.

pallid *adj* 1 pale, wan, ashen, pasty, whey-faced, cadaverous, peaky, sickly, white. 2 dull, tedious, unexciting, colourless, vapid, bland, boring, tame.

pallor *noun* paleness, pallidness, pastiness, peakiness, whiteness.

palm *noun* hand, paw (*inf*), mitt (*inf*).
palm off foist, fob off, offload, unload, get rid of.

palmistry *noun* fortune-telling, clairvoyance.

palmy *adj* prosperous, thriving, flourishing, halcyon, golden, glorious.

palpable *adj* 1 obvious, evident, manifest, clear, plain, perceptible, apparent. 2 tangible, real, concrete, solid, substantial, material.

palpitate *verb* 1 pulsate, pulse, beat, throb, pound, thump. 2 tremble, quiver, shake, vibrate, flutter.

paltry adj **1** trivial, trifling, small, slight, meagre, poor, derisory, measly (inf). **2** contemptible, despicable, mean, petty, base, low.

pamper verb indulge, humour, gratify, spoil, mollycoddle, cosset, baby.

pamphlet noun booklet, leaflet, brochure, handout, tract, treatise.

pan[1] noun **1** saucepan, pot, skillet, casserole. **2** container, vessel, receptacle.
➤verb criticize, censure, blast, lambaste, hammer (inf), slam (inf), slate (inf).
pan out work out, turn out, come out, result, culminate.

pan[2] verb scan, sweep, follow, track, swing, turn.

panacea noun cure-all, elixir, universal remedy, nostrum.

panache noun flamboyance, dash, flourish, style, flair, élan, pizzazz (inf), verve, brio.

pandemic adj widespread, universal, global, general, rife, rampant.

pandemonium noun chaos, confusion, tumult, turmoil, bedlam, riot, uproar, commotion, rumpus, hullabaloo.

pander verb **pander to** humour, gratify, satisfy, indulge, please.

panegyric noun eulogy, homage, accolade, tribute, encomium, paean.

panel noun **1** sheet, board, plank, beam, timber, slab. **2** board, council, committee, commission.

pang noun **1** pain, stab, prick, twinge, spasm, throe. **2** twinge, qualm, scruple, feeling, attack.

panic noun terror, alarm, fright, flap (inf), fear, frenzy, hysteria, agitation, nervousness, confusion, turmoil.
➤verb overreact, go to pieces (inf), lose one's head (inf), get the wind up (inf), alarm, frighten, unnerve, startle, agitate.

panoply noun array, display, trappings, show, regalia, splendour.

panorama noun **1** view, vista, prospect, landscape, scene, spectacle. **2** survey, appraisal, overview, perspective.

pant verb **1** puff, blow, gasp, wheeze, breathe, sigh, heave. **2** long, pine, yearn, desire, ache, thirst, hunger, lust, crave, hanker.

pants pl noun **1** underpants, briefs, panties, knickers, boxer shorts, Y-fronts. **2** trousers, slacks, jeans, strides (inf).

pap noun rubbish, trash, pulp, trivia.

paper noun **1** newspaper, gazette, daily, rag (inf), broadsheet, tabloid, weekly, periodical, journal, magazine. **2** document, authorization, ID, certificate, instrument, deed. **3** article, study, report, monograph, treatise, essay, dissertation, thesis.
➤verb wallpaper, line, decorate.
on paper 1 in writing, in black and white, on the record. **2** in theory, theoretically, hypothetically.
paper over hide, conceal, cover up, gloss over, disguise, camouflage.

papers pl noun documents, credentials, file, dossier.

papery adj paper-thin, light, lightweight, flimsy, fragile, delicate.

par noun **on a par with** equal to, equivalent to, the same as, as good as.
par for the course average, typical, normal, standard, usual, predictable, to be expected.

parable noun fable, allegory, tale, story, lesson.

parade noun **1** procession, train, column, file, march, cavalcade, motorcade. **2** show, display, array, exhibition, demonstration, succession, progression.
➤verb **1** march, file, process. **2** flaunt, vaunt, show off, display, exhibit, flourish, brandish. **3** swagger, strut.

paradigm noun **1** model, ideal, example, exemplar, paragon. **2** pattern, model, standard, norm, criterion, archetype, framework.

paradise noun **1** heaven, afterlife, hereafter, next world, happy hunting ground, Elysium. **2** utopia, fairyland, Shangri-la, bliss, ecstasy, rapture, seventh heaven (inf).

paradox noun contradiction, incongruity, inconsistency, absurdity, oxymoron, riddle, enigma.

paragon noun model, paradigm, ideal, epitome, quintessence, exemplar, nonpareil, apotheosis.

paragraph *noun* division, section, part, subdivision, subsection, clause, passage.

parallel *adj* 1 equidistant, aligned, side by side, collateral. 2 corresponding, similar, like, akin, matching, analogous, comparable, equivalent.
➤*noun* 1 counterpart, equivalent, equal, match, analogue. 2 analogy, correspondence, similarity, likeness, equivalence, correlation, comparison.
➤*verb* 1 echo, correspond with, correlate with, compare with, resemble. 2 match, equal, rival, emulate, surpass.

paralyse *verb* 1 deaden, numb, anaesthetize, incapacitate, disable, cripple, lame. 2 immobilize, halt, stop, transfix, freeze, shock, stun, terrify, petrify.

paralysis *noun* 1 paraplegia, quadriplegia, palsy, incapacity, immobility. 2 immobilization, standstill, stoppage, breakdown, arrest, stagnation.

paralytic *adj* 1 paralysed, crippled, disabled, incapacitated, immobile, palsied, paraplegic, quadriplegic, powerless. 2 drunk, inebriated, legless (*inf*), plastered (*inf*), pissed (*sl*), wasted (*inf*), wrecked (*inf*), blotto (*inf*).

parameter *noun* 1 constant, specification, criterion, variable. 2 limit, boundary, limitation, restriction.

paramount *adj* supreme, pre-eminent, chief, cardinal, main, principal, leading, primary, highest, predominant.

paranoia *noun* 1 mania, obsession, psychosis, delusions, persecution complex. 2 distrustfulness, suspiciousness, insecurity.

parapet *noun* 1 wall, rail, barrier. 2 rampart, barricade, fortification, defence, bulwark, embankment.

paraphernalia *noun* stuff, things, gear, equipment, apparatus, tackle, impedimenta, appurtenances, trappings.

paraphrase *verb* reword, rephrase, restate, explain, translate, interpret.
➤*noun* rewording, rephrasing, restatement, explanation, interpretation, translation.

parasite *noun* hanger-on, leech, sponger (*inf*), scrounger (*inf*), cadger (*inf*), freeloader (*inf*), bum (*inf*).

parcel *noun* 1 package, packet, box. 2 batch, bunch, pack, group, collection, assortment. 3 piece, plot, tract, patch, lot, area.
➤*verb* 1 package, wrap, pack, do up, bundle, box. 2 divide, share, apportion, allot, carve up, dole out, distribute.

parched *adj* 1 dry, arid, waterless, torrid, scorched, baked. 2 thirsty, dehydrated, dry, gasping (*inf*).

pardon *verb* 1 forgive, excuse, condone, overlook. 2 let off, acquit, clear, exonerate, reprieve, absolve, exculpate, vindicate.
➤*noun* 1 forgiveness, excuse, mercy, grace, clemency, indulgence, absolution, remission. 2 acquittal, exoneration, discharge, release, reprieve, amnesty.

pare *verb* 1 peel, skin, shave, shear. 2 clip, trim, cut, crop, whittle. 3 reduce, decrease, diminish, lessen.

parent *noun* 1 father, mother. 2 dam, sire, progenitor. 3 source, root, origin, originator, creator, author, architect.
➤*verb* bring into the world, produce, beget, procreate, nurture, rear, bring up, raise.

parentage *noun* ancestry, lineage, descent, extraction, derivation, birth, family, stock, pedigree.

pariah *noun* outcast, leper, exile, outlaw, undesirable, persona non grata.

parish *noun* 1 district, community, commune, canton. 2 parishioners, churchgoers, congregation, flock.

parity *noun* equality, equivalence, uniformity, identity, sameness, correspondence, congruence, conformity.

park *noun* 1 public garden, recreation ground, play area. 2 grounds, estate, parkland, woodland, grassland. 3 ground, stadium, arena, field, pitch.
➤*verb* 1 pull up, stop. 2 put, leave, deposit, plonk (*inf*).

parlance *noun* idiom, vernacular, jargon, language, lingo (*inf*), speech, talk, vocabulary, phraseology.

parley *verb* talk, discuss, negotiate, confer, confabulate, deliberate.
➤*noun* talk, discussion, meeting, conference, dialogue, powwow, palaver.

parliament *noun* 1 House of Commons, House of Lords. 2 legislature, assembly, council, congress, senate, diet.

parliamentary *adj* legislative, lawmaking, governmental, congressional, senatorial.

parlour *noun* **1** living room, sitting room, lounge, drawing room. **2** establishment, salon, shop, store.

parochial *adj* provincial, small-town, parish-pump, insular, small-minded, blinkered, narrow, limited.

parody *noun* **1** burlesque, lampoon, pastiche, satire, spoof (*inf*), skit, send-up (*inf*). **2** travesty, mockery, perversion, distortion.
➤*verb* burlesque, lampoon, satirize, spoof (*inf*), send up (*inf*), ape, mock, mimic, imitate.

paroxysm *noun* **1** fit, seizure, attack, spasm, convulsion. **2** outburst, eruption, flare-up, explosion.

parrot *verb* copy, repeat, echo, imitate, mimic, ape.

parry *verb* **1** deflect, ward off, fend off, repulse, rebuff. **2** avoid, evade, duck (*inf*), sidestep, circumvent.

parsimonious *adj* mean, stingy (*inf*), miserly, penny-pinching (*inf*), niggardly, close-fisted, tight (*inf*), frugal, sparing, scrimping.

parsimony *noun* meanness, miserliness, frugality, cheeseparing.

parson *noun* clergyman, cleric, priest, minister, chaplain, vicar, preacher.

part *noun* **1** piece, portion, share, section, division, proportion, percentage, fraction, fragment, bit. **2** ingredient, constituent, element, factor, aspect, facet, dimension. **3** component, module. **4** limb, organ, member, branch. **5** episode, chapter, instalment, section, volume, passage, scene. **6** role, character, lines, words. **7** contribution, involvement, participation, interest, role, function, responsibility, job. **8** region, area, territory, quarter, sector, neighbourhood, vicinity. **9** talent, ability, skill, attribute, accomplishment.
➤*verb* **1** divide, separate, split, break, cleave, sever, disunite, disconnect, detach. **2** leave, say goodbye, divorce, separate, break up, split up.
in part partly, partially, up to a point, to a certain extent, in some measure, somewhat.

part with relinquish, give up, let go of, discard, sacrifice, surrender.
take part join in, participate, partake, play a role, share, contribute, help.

partake *verb* take part, participate, share, be involved, engage, enter, contribute.

partial *adj* **1** incomplete, fragmentary, unfinished, imperfect, limited, part. **2** biased, prejudiced, partisan, discriminatory, preferential, inequitable, affected, interested.
partial to fond of, keen on, mad about (*inf*), taken with.

partiality *noun* **1** bias, prejudice, partisanship, favouritism, preference, discrimination. **2** liking, fondness, love, inclination, penchant, proclivity, soft spot, predilection, taste.

participate *verb* take part, share, partake, play a role, join in, be involved, help, enter, contribute, cooperate, have a hand.

particle *noun* grain, speck, atom, molecule, bit, piece, fragment, iota, whit, scrap, shred.

particular *adj* **1** specific, precise, distinct, peculiar, separate, individual, single. **2** notable, noteworthy, remarkable, special, exceptional, singular, unusual. **3** exact, close, detailed, blow-by-blow. **4** careful, meticulous, painstaking, thorough, minute, punctilious. **5** fussy, finicky, choosy (*inf*), pernickety (*inf*), discriminating, selective, difficult, exacting.
➤*noun* particularity, detail, specific, point, feature, fact.
in particular particularly, especially, specifically, exactly, precisely.

particularize *verb* specify, stipulate, detail, itemize, enumerate, list.

particularly *adv* **1** especially, exceptionally, unusually, markedly, decidedly, notably, remarkably. **2** specifically, expressly, explicitly, distinctly.

parting *noun* **1** farewell, goodbye, valediction, leave-taking, departure, separation, severance. **2** division, separation, cleavage, rift, split, break, rupture.

partisan *noun* **1** adherent, follower, disciple, champion, supporter, upholder, enthusiast, stalwart, devotee, votary. **2** guerrilla, irregular, freedom fighter, resistance fighter.

partition noun **1** division, dividing, sub-division, separation, segregation. **2** screen, barrier, wall, panel, divider.
➤verb **1** divide, separate, segregate, split up, break up. **2** subdivide, divide, divide up. **3** separate, screen off, wall off, fence off.

partly adv in part, not wholly, somewhat, up to a point, to a certain extent, to some degree, fractionally.

partner noun **1** ally, comrade, colleague, associate, co-worker, confederate, collaborator, accomplice, mate. **2** spouse, other half (inf), significant other (inf), consort, lover.

partnership noun **1** association, collaboration, collusion, cooperation, companionship. **2** company, firm, cooperative, combine, syndicate, society. **3** alliance, confederation, fellowship, union.

party noun **1** social, soirée, reception, at-home, celebration, function, get-together (inf), do (inf), knees-up (inf), rave-up (inf), bash (inf), shindig (inf). **2** group, band, gang, team, crew, squad, unit, contingent, detachment. **3** faction, grouping, circle, association, caucus, cabal. **4** side, camp, set. **5** person, individual. **6** participant, litigant, plaintiff, defendant.

pass[1] verb **1** go, move, proceed, travel, flow, run, make one's way, cross, traverse. **2** hand, transfer, transmit, convey, spread. **3** go past, overtake, overhaul, lap, surpass, exceed, outdo, outstrip. **4** go by, elapse, advance, roll by, slip away. **5** end, cease, die, fade, disappear, go, blow over. **6** devolve, go, be transferred. **7** spend, fill, occupy, employ, while away. **8** change, develop, evolve, progress, go, turn. **9** succeed, get through, qualify, graduate, do, come up to scratch (inf). **10** approve, accept. **11** enact, legislate, sanction, authorize, ratify, vote for, agree to. **12** throw, kick, hit. **13** pronounce, deliver, declare. **14** utter, express. **15** discharge, eliminate, void, evacuate, excrete, expel.
➤noun **1** authorization, permission, warrant, permit, ID, documents, papers, safe conduct. **2** ticket, passport, visa. **3** advance, approach, overture, proposition. **4** throw, kick, hit, move. **5** success, qualification.

pass as/for be taken for, be mistaken for, be regarded as, qualify as.

pass away pass on, die, expire, kick the bucket (inf).

pass off turn out, go off, happen, occur, take place.

pass out faint, black out, lose consciousness, collapse, keel over (inf).

pass over ignore, gloss over, disregard, overlook, omit, skip, miss.

pass up forgo, refuse, reject, decline, let slip, waive.

pass[2] noun col, defile, gap, passage.

passable adj **1** fair, all right, OK (inf), so-so (inf), acceptable, satisfactory, adequate, tolerable, admissible, average, unexceptional, mediocre. **2** clear, unobstructed, open, navigable.

passage noun **1** passing, course, flow, progression, advance, transition, development, transfer. **2** route, way, path, track, lane, alley, pass, thoroughfare, channel. **3** passageway, corridor, hall, lobby, vestibule, aisle. **4** journey, voyage, trip, crossing, trek. **5** access, admission, entry. **6** section, piece, excerpt, extract, clause, paragraph, quotation, text.

passé adj out-of-date, dated, outmoded, old-fashioned, obsolete, obsolescent, antiquated, archaic, old hat (inf).

passenger noun **1** fare, rider, traveller, commuter. **2** drone, parasite, hanger-on, idler.

passer-by noun bystander, onlooker, witness.

passing adj **1** short-lived, temporary, transitory, transient, fleeting, momentary, ephemeral. **2** brief, hasty, quick, cursory, superficial, casual, incidental.
➤noun death, demise, loss, decease, departure.

passion noun **1** emotion, feeling, ardour, fervour, zeal, heat, fire, intensity, vehemence. **2** love, adoration, ardour, infatuation. **3** desire, lust. **4** rage, fury, wrath, ire, temper, fit, tantrum, storm, outburst, explosion. **5** enthusiasm, craze, mania, obsession, fascination.

passionate adj **1** loving, affectionate, amorous, lustful, sexy (inf), hot, intense, vehement, impassioned, emotional, stormy, wild, irate, incensed. **2** enthusiastic, eager, keen, avid, ardent, fervent, fanatical, zealous.

passive *adj* **1** submissive, unresisting, acquiescent, compliant, yielding. **2** inactive, inert, apathetic, lethargic, lifeless, still. **3** uninvolved, non-participating, receptive, unassertive.

passport *noun* visa, pass, laissez-passer, identity card, ID.

password *noun* watchword, signal, open sesame, shibboleth.

past *adj* **1** over, finished, ended, done. **2** erstwhile, sometime, bygone, olden, obsolete, early, extinct, forgotten. **3** recent, late, latter, last. **4** preceding, former, previous, prior, foregoing.
➤*noun* **1** history, antiquity, long ago, olden days, former times, yesteryear, days gone by. **2** life, background, record, history, experience, memories.
➤*adv* by, on, beyond, over, across.
➤*prep* **1** above, over, beyond. **2** after, beyond. **3** outside, beyond.

paste *noun* **1** adhesive, glue, gum, cement. **2** puree, spread, pâté.
➤*verb* stick, glue, gum.

pastel *adj* pale, soft, delicate, light, subtle, muted, subdued, low-key.

pastille *noun* lozenge, sweet, drop, gum.

pastime *noun* hobby, recreation, leisure activity, sport, game, entertainment, diversion, amusement.

pastor *noun* minister, priest, rector, parson, vicar, preacher, clergyman, clergywoman.

pastoral *adj* **1** rural, rustic, country, agricultural, bucolic. **2** idyllic, Arcadian. **3** ministerial, priestly.

pasture *noun* grazing, grassland, meadow, field, paddock, grass, pasturage, herbage.

pasty *adj* pale, pallid, sallow, wan, whey-faced, anaemic, sickly, unhealthy.

pat *verb* tap, dab, hit, slap, stroke, pet, touch.
➤*noun* tap, dab, slap, touch, stroke.
➤*adj* **1** ready, prompt, immediate, automatic. **2** slick, glib, facile, simplistic.
a pat on the back compliment, commendation, praise, congratulations.

patch *noun* **1** piece, scrap, bit. **2** cover, pad, shield. **3** plot, bed, area, parcel, tract, lot. **4** phase, time, period, stretch, spell.
➤*verb* mend, repair, reinforce, cover.

patchwork *noun* medley, mixture, potpourri, mosaic, miscellany, hotchpotch, farrago, mishmash (*inf*).

patchy *adj* **1** sketchy, bitty, uneven, irregular, inconsistent, erratic. **2** random, fitful, variable.

patent *adj* obvious, plain, clear, manifest, evident, conspicuous, overt, blatant, visible, apparent.
➤*noun* copyright, licence, certificate, invention.

paternal *adj* fatherly, patriarchal, protective, solicitous, benevolent, vigilant.

path *noun* **1** footpath, pathway, bridleway, walk, track, trail. **2** trajectory, course, route, way, avenue, approach.

pathetic *adj* **1** moving, touching, poignant, plaintive, piteous, pitiful, poor, sorry, wretched, sad, distressing, harrowing. **2** feeble, contemptible, deplorable, derisory, miserable, worthless, paltry, meagre, measly, inadequate, pitiful, lamentable.

pathological *adj* compulsive, habitual, chronic, inveterate, persistent, obsessive, irrational, unreasonable, illogical.

pathos *noun* poignancy, pitifulness, piteousness, plaintiveness, sadness.

patience *noun* tolerance, forbearance, composure, equanimity, endurance, stoicism, resignation, perseverance, persistence, tenacity, fortitude.

patient *adj* tolerant, forbearing, understanding, accommodating, calm, composed, enduring, long-suffering, uncomplaining, stoical, philosophical, resigned.
➤*noun* invalid, sufferer, case, inmate, client.

patois *noun* **1** dialect, vernacular, local parlance, lingo (*inf*). **2** jargon, cant, argot, slang.

patrician *noun* aristocrat, noble, lord, lady, peer.

patrimony *noun* heritage, birthright, inheritance, legacy, bequest.

patriot *noun* nationalist, loyalist, flag-waver, jingoist, chauvinist.

patrol *verb* guard, protect, defend, police, watch, inspect, monitor, go the rounds, pound the beat.
➤*noun* **1** watch, guard, vigil, surveillance,

policing, protection, defence, round, beat. **2** guard, patrolman, patrolwoman, sentry, garrison, watchman, security guard, police officer.

patron noun **1** sponsor, promoter, backer, supporter, champion, advocate, friend, benefactor, philanthropist, angel (inf). **2** customer, client, regular (inf), frequenter, habitué, shopper, subscriber.

patronage noun **1** sponsorship, backing, funding, financing, help, aid, support, protection, benefaction. **2** trade, custom, business.

patronize verb **1** frequent, use, shop at, buy from, deal with, sponsor, promote, champion, back, finance, support, protect. **2** condescend, stoop, talk down to, look down on, despise, scorn, disdain.

patter[1] verb **1** tap, pat, pitter-patter, drum, pound, beat. **2** scuttle, scurry, skip, tiptoe. ➤noun pattering, tapping, drumming, pitter-patter, pit-a-pat, beating, pounding.

patter[2] noun **1** chatter, jabber, line, pitch, spiel (inf), harangue, monologue. **2** jargon, lingo (inf).

pattern noun **1** design, motif, figure, device, decoration, marking. **2** arrangement, order, sequence, plan, system, method, style. **3** model, stencil, template, mould, diagram, blueprint, design. **4** exemplar, ideal, paragon, paradigm, standard, archetype, prototype, original. **5** sample, swatch, specimen. ➤verb **1** decorate, ornament, print, mark. **2** model, style, mould, shape, order, form.

paucity noun dearth, lack, want, scarcity, shortage, deficiency, inadequacy, poverty.

paunch noun potbelly, beer gut (inf), spare tyre (inf), stomach, abdomen, belly.

pauper noun down-and-out, have-not, bankrupt, insolvent, indigent, beggar.

pause verb stop, halt, cease, let up (inf), break, rest, take a breather (inf), take five (inf), hesitate, interrupt, discontinue, adjourn. ➤noun stop, halt, suspension, discontinuation, break, rest, lull, let-up (inf), gap, interval, interruption, delay.

pave verb flag, cobble, tile, floor, concrete, surface. **pave the way for** prepare for, get ready for, lead up to, introduce, clear the way

for, lay the foundations for, do the spadework for, set the scene for, facilitate.

pavement noun **1** footpath, footway, walkway, sidewalk. **2** floor, bed, causeway.

paw noun **1** foot, pad. **2** hand, mitt (inf). ➤verb maul, touch, stroke, manhandle, molest, touch up (inf).

pawn[1] verb deposit, pledge, hock (inf), stake, mortgage.

pawn[2] noun instrument, tool, stooge (inf), dupe, puppet, cat's-paw (inf).

pay verb **1** remunerate, reimburse, reward, compensate, indemnify. **2** spend, remit, pay out, fork out (inf), shell out (inf), cough up (inf), stump up (inf), foot the bill (inf), pick up the tab (inf). **3** repay, pay back, pay off, defray, settle, clear, discharge, liquidate, honour. **4** give, offer, proffer, bestow. **5** suffer, answer, atone, make amends. ➤noun salary, wages, remuneration, earnings, payment, hire, fee, commission, stipend, honorarium, emoluments, reward. **pay back 1** repay, pay off, return, refund, reimburse, settle, square. **2** punish, get even with, avenge oneself, get one's own back, retaliate. **pay off 1** pay in full, discharge, settle, clear, square. **2** dismiss, discharge, lay off, let go, make redundant, sack (inf), fire (inf). **3** succeed, be effective, work, get results, pay dividends. **pay out** pay, spend, lay out, fork out (inf), shell out (inf), part with, hand over.

payment noun **1** settlement, discharge, liquidation, defrayal. **2** instalment, contribution, donation, advance, premium, remittance, fee, pay. **3** reward, recompense, remuneration, punishment, retribution.

peace noun **1** calm, tranquillity, quiet, silence, stillness, peacefulness, nonviolence. **2** concord, harmony, friendship, amity, goodwill, accord, agreement, conciliation. **3** truce, ceasefire, armistice. **4** contentment, calmness, composure, repose, rest, serenity.

peaceable adj **1** pacific, peace-loving, non-aggressive, non-belligerent, inoffensive, easygoing, friendly, irenic, dovish, conciliatory, placatory. **2** peaceful, non-violent, quiet, serene, tranquil, undisturbed, harmonious, amicable, cordial.

peaceful adj **1** calm, tranquil, serene, quiet, still, restful, relaxing, unruffled, undisturbed, untroubled. **2** non-violent, strife-free, pacific, peaceable. **3** friendly, cordial, harmonious, amicable, peace-loving, peacemaking.

peak noun **1** top, summit, crest, mountain. **2** high point, apex, pinnacle, acme, apogee, zenith, meridian, heyday. **3** climax, maximum, culmination.
➤ verb climax, culminate, come to a head.

peaky adj pale, pallid, wan, pasty, whey-faced, drawn, drained, sickly, unwell, off-colour, washed-out (inf).

peal verb **1** ring, chime, toll, tintinnabulate. **2** roar, roll, thunder, boom, crash, rumble, reverberate. **3** resound, resonate.
➤ noun **1** chime, toll, knell, ringing, tintinnabulation, carillon. **2** rumble, roll, roar, boom, crash, reverberation.

peasant noun **1** countryman, countrywoman, rustic, bumpkin, yokel, provincial, hick (inf). **2** oaf, boor, lout, churl.

peccadillo noun error, fault, indiscretion, lapse, slip, misdeed, misdemeanour, infraction.

peck verb **1** tap, rap, bite, nip, poke, jab. **2** nibble, pick at, play with.

peculiar adj **1** strange, odd, queer, curious, funny, weird, bizarre, abnormal, unusual, singular, exceptional, extraordinary. **2** unique, exclusive, characteristic, representative, typical. **3** specific, particular, distinctive, special, individual, personal.

peculiarity noun **1** characteristic, trait, attribute, feature, mark, stamp, property, quality, quirk, idiosyncrasy. **2** strangeness, oddness, abnormality, curiosity, bizarreness, weirdness, individuality, particularity, singularity.

pecuniary adj monetary, financial, fiscal, commercial.

pedagogue noun teacher, educator, educationalist, tutor, instructor, lecturer, don.

pedant noun purist, formalist, dogmatist, literalist, quibbler, pettifogger, nit-picker (inf), hair-splitter (inf), intellectual, academic, scholar, egghead (inf).

peddle verb **1** sell, hawk, vend, tout, flog (inf). **2** traffic, deal, push (inf).

pedestal noun plinth, platform, podium, base, stand, support.

pedestrian noun walker, foot-traveller, hiker.
➤ adj dull, boring, unimaginative, uninspired, prosaic, mundane, banal, run-of-the-mill, commonplace.

pedigree noun **1** race, stock, breed, blood. **2** descent, line, ancestry, parentage, family, extraction, genealogy. **3** origin, history, background, derivation, provenance.
➤ adj purebred, thoroughbred, pure-blooded, full-blooded.

pedlar noun hawker, street-trader, vendor, seller, dealer, peddler.

peek verb peep, glance, glimpse, peer, spy, sneak a look (inf).
➤ noun peep, glance, glimpse, look, dekko (inf), shufti (inf).

peel verb **1** pare, skin, excoriate, decorticate. **2** strip, remove, take off. **2** scale, flake.
➤ noun peeling, skin, rind.

peep[1] verb **1** peek, glimpse, glance, spy, peer, squint. **2** emerge, appear, show, spring up, pop up.
➤ noun look, peek, glimpse, glance.

peep[2] verb cheep, chirp, chirrup, tweet, twitter, pipe, squeak, squeal.

peephole noun spyhole, aperture, opening, slit, chink, crack.

peer[1] noun **1** noble, aristocrat, patrician, lord, duke, marquess, earl, viscount, baron. **2** equal, coequal, match, counterpart, compeer, mate, fellow.

peer[2] verb squint, gaze, stare, look, scan, scrutinize, examine, inspect, peep, peek, spy, snoop.

peerage noun aristocracy, nobility, titled classes, upper crust (inf), top drawer (inf).

peerless adj matchless, unequalled, unparalleled, unrivalled, unsurpassed, unbeatable, second to none (inf), nonpareil, superlative, supreme, incomparable, beyond compare.

peeve verb annoy, irritate, rile, exasperate, irk, bug (inf), provoke, upset, vex, pique, put out, miff (inf).

peevish *adj* irritable, fretful, fractious, crotchety, cross, ratty (*inf*), touchy, crabby, grumpy, petulant, captious, querulous.

peg *noun* **1** pin, nail, spike, skewer, dowel, bolt, marker, post, stake. **2** hook, knob.
➤*verb* **1** pin, fasten, secure, fix, attach, join. **2** fix, set, freeze, hold, control, limit.
peg away persevere, persist, plug away, beaver away (*inf*), keep going, stick at (*inf*).
take somebody down a peg or two humble, humiliate, cut somebody down to size, put somebody in their place.

pejorative *adj* derogatory, deprecatory, depreciatory, disparaging, insulting, critical, negative, bad.

pellet *noun* **1** pill, tablet, capsule. **2** ball, shot, bullet.

pell-mell *adv* in chaos, in disarray, in confusion, in disorder, anyhow, haphazardly, recklessly, hastily, headlong, helter-skelter (*inf*).

pellucid *adj* **1** transparent, translucent, clear, limpid, crystalline, glassy, bright. **2** clear, plain, straightforward, lucid, coherent, comprehensible, understandable, intelligible.

pelt[1] *verb* **1** bombard, pepper, shower, attack, assail, hit, strike, throw, hurl, cast, sling. **2** dash, race, run, rush, speed, shoot, career, hare, belt (*inf*), charge, tear. **3** pour, teem, bucket, rain cats and dogs (*inf*).

pelt[2] *noun* skin, hide, fur, fleece, coat.

pen[1] *noun* ballpoint, Biro®, felt-tip, fountain pen, quill.
➤*verb* write, jot down, scribble, draft, compose.

pen[2] *noun* enclosure, compound, pound, corral, fold, stall, sty, coop, hutch.
➤*verb* enclose, confine, shut up, coop up, fence in, cage.

penal *adj* punitive, disciplinary, corrective, retributive, retaliatory.

penalize *verb* **1** punish, discipline, correct, castigate, fine. **2** handicap, disadvantage.

penalty *noun* **1** punishment, sentence, retribution, castigation, penance, forfeit, fine. **2** disadvantage, handicap, drawback, downside (*inf*), cost, price.

penance *noun* punishment, penalty, amends, atonement, reparation, contrition, self-abasement, mortification, humiliation, sackcloth and ashes.

penchant *noun* inclination, proclivity, propensity, liking, preference, predilection, predisposition, partiality, fondness, love, taste, weakness.

pendant *noun* locket, medallion, necklace.

pendent *adj* hanging, suspended, dangling, swinging, drooping, pendulous.

pending *prep* until, till, awaiting, waiting for, during, throughout.
➤*adj* **1** unsettled, undecided, unresolved, in abeyance, up in the air (*inf*), on the back burner (*inf*). **2** imminent, impending, coming, approaching, in the offing, in the pipeline.

penetrate *verb* **1** pierce, puncture, perforate, stab, prick, impale, bore. **2** enter, get into, infiltrate, invade. **3** permeate, saturate, imbue, suffuse, pervade, seep, percolate. **4** decipher, crack (*inf*), unravel, understand, fathom, get to the bottom of (*inf*), grasp, work out, solve, discern, perceive, see. **5** register, get through, sink in, make an impression.

penetrating *adj* **1** piercing, shrill, strident, sharp, harsh, keen, biting, intrusive, pervasive, penetrative. **2** acute, incisive, perceptive, discerning, smart, shrewd, astute, searching, probing, in-depth.

penetration *noun* **1** piercing, puncturing, perforation, incision, infiltration, invasion, entry, permeation, pervasion, suffusion. **2** discernment, perception, perspicacity, insight, discrimination, acumen, astuteness, sharpness, shrewdness, understanding, comprehension.

penitent *adj* contrite, repentant, regretful, remorseful, rueful, abject, humble, sorry, ashamed, apologetic.

pen name *noun* pseudonym, alias, assumed name, nom de plume.

pennant *noun* flag, standard, banner, streamer, ensign, jack.

penniless *adj* poor, impecunious, penurious, broke (*inf*), skint (*inf*), bankrupt, ruined, destitute, down and out (*inf*), poverty-stricken, on the breadline (*inf*).

penny-pinching *adj* mean, stingy (*inf*), grasping, miserly, money-grubbing, tight-fisted, frugal, skimping, scrimping, parsimonious, niggardly, cheeseparing.

pension *noun* annuity, allowance, benefit.

pensioner *noun* retired person, old-age pensioner, OAP, senior citizen.

pensive *adj* thoughtful, reflective, contemplative, meditative, ruminative, absorbed, preoccupied, wistful, brooding.

pent-up *adj* repressed, inhibited, suppressed, held back, restrained, bridled, confined, stifled, smothered, bottled-up (*inf*).

penurious *adj* **1** poor, penniless, impecunious, impoverished, poverty-stricken, destitute, broke (*inf*). **2** frugal, mean, miserly, niggardly, cheeseparing, penny-pinching (*inf*), parsimonious.

penury *noun* poverty, destitution, impoverishment, indigence, bankruptcy, insolvency, need, want, privation, beggary, pauperism.

people *noun* **1** persons, individuals, human beings, souls, folk, human race, mankind, humanity, humankind. **2** nation, race, tribe, clan, society, population, inhabitants. **3** populace, crowd, mob, general public, masses, multitude, commonalty, rank and file, rabble, hoi polloi, plebs (*inf*). **4** citizens, electorate. **5** family, folks (*inf*), kinsfolk, kith and kin, relations, relatives.
➤*verb* **1** populate, settle, colonize. **2** inhabit, occupy.

pep *noun* energy, vigour, verve, spirit, sparkle, vitality, animation, life, exuberance, ebullience, high spirits.

pepper *verb* **1** season, flavour, spice, spice up. **2** bombard, pelt, riddle, blitz. **3** sprinkle, dot, scatter, spatter, strew, stud.

perceive *verb* **1** sense, feel, be aware of, see, glimpse, notice, discern, detect, make out, understand, realize, recognize. **2** regard, consider, see, view.

perceptible *adj* perceivable, discernible, detectable, appreciable, apparent, noticeable, distinct, evident, palpable, tangible.

perception *noun* **1** awareness, consciousness, appreciation, recognition, cognizance, understanding, apprehension, knowledge, grasp. **2** insight, intuition, feeling, sensitivity, awareness, discernment, discrimination, percipience.

perceptive *adj* sharp-eyed, observant, vigilant, alert, aware, quick-witted, sharp, acute, discerning, sensitive, percipient, perspicacious.

perch *noun* pole, bar, branch, roost, rest.
➤*verb* alight, land, settle, rest, sit, roost, balance.

perchance *adv* perhaps, maybe, possibly, peradventure.

percipient *adj* perceptive, perspicacious, astute, shrewd, sharp, discerning, intuitive, knowing, alert, sensitive, aware.

percolate *verb* **1** strain, filter, drip, seep, leach, penetrate, trickle, leak. **2** permeate, pervade, spread, filter, pass.

perdition *noun* damnation, destruction, ruin, doom, hell.

peregrination *noun* journey, voyage, odyssey, expedition, trek, travel, globetrotting, wandering, roaming, roving.

peremptory *adj* **1** imperious, high-handed, overbearing, dogmatic, authoritative, dictatorial, despotic, assertive, overweening, lordly. **2** imperative, urgent, pressing. **3** incontrovertible, irreversible, binding, absolute, final, conclusive, definitive, categorical, irrefutable, obligatory, mandatory.

perennial *adj* lasting, enduring, persistent, abiding, constant, continual, perpetual, everlasting, undying, imperishable, recurrent, chronic.

perfect *adj* **1** pure, unblemished, flawless, immaculate, spotless, faultless, impeccable, exemplary, model, exact, accurate. **2** ideal, excellent, superlative, wonderful, consummate, expert, masterly. **3** complete, entire, full, whole. **4** total, utter, absolute, sheer, thorough, downright, out and out, unmitigated.
➤*verb* **1** finish, complete, consummate, effect, fulfil, realize, achieve, accomplish. **2** polish, refine, hone, improve, ameliorate.

perfection *noun* **1** improvement, polishing, refinement, consummation, fulfilment, realization, perfectness, purity, flawlessness, impeccability, excellence. **2** ideal, model, paragon, acme, crown, pinnacle.

perfectionism noun idealism, purism, pedantry.

perfectly adv 1 completely, totally, entirely, fully, altogether, quite, thoroughly, utterly, absolutely. 2 flawlessly, faultlessly, immaculately, superlatively, wonderfully, admirably, ideally, exactly, precisely.

perfidious adj treacherous, traitorous, false, faithless, unfaithful, disloyal, untrustworthy, untrue, double-dealing, duplicitous.

perfidy noun perfidiousness, treachery, betrayal, treason, falseness, faithlessness, unfaithfulness, infidelity, disloyalty, double-dealing, duplicity.

perforate verb hole, puncture, stab, pierce, penetrate, punch, bore, drill, prick, burst, rupture.

perforce adv necessarily, of necessity, unavoidably, inevitably.

perform verb 1 do, carry out, discharge, execute, effect, achieve, complete, fulfil, conduct, transact. 2 play, act, stage, put on, present, appear.

performance noun 1 accomplishment, achievement, execution, discharge, act, deed, conduct, behaviour, practice. 2 production, presentation, show, act, entertainment, portrayal, interpretation, play, concert, recital, gig (inf). 3 operation, functioning, running, working, efficiency. 4 fuss, bother, business, carry-on (inf), rigmarole.

perfume noun 1 scent, fragrance, essence, cologne, toilet water, eau de toilette. 2 aroma, scent, fragrance, smell, bouquet, sweetness, redolence.

perfunctory adj cursory, superficial, desultory, brief, quick, fleeting, hasty, careless, casual, automatic, mechanical.

perhaps adv maybe, possibly, conceivably, feasibly, perchance.

peril noun danger, jeopardy, risk, hazard, threat, pitfall, vulnerability, exposure, insecurity, uncertainty.

perimeter noun 1 circumference, boundary, edge. 2 boundary, border, frontier, confines, limits, edge, margin, periphery, fringe.

period noun 1 time, term, spell, span, interval, stretch, stint, duration, season, session, stage, phase. 2 age, era, epoch, time, days, years, generation. 3 lesson, class, session, lecture, seminar, tutorial. 4 menstruation, menses, time of the month (inf), curse (inf). 5 full stop, stop, point, dot, end, finish.

periodic adj 1 intermittent, recurrent, regular, occasional, sporadic, spasmodic. 2 repeated, recurring, cyclic, seasonal.

periodical noun magazine, journal, paper, weekly, monthly, quarterly.

peripatetic adj 1 itinerant, wandering, roving, travelling, nomadic, migrant. 2 travelling, mobile, supply.

peripheral adj 1 outlying, outer, outermost, surrounding. 2 secondary, subsidiary, marginal, borderline, lesser, minor, unimportant, inessential, incidental, tangential.

periphery noun 1 boundary, border, outskirts, edge, perimeter, limits, outside. 2 edge, fringe, margin.

perish verb 1 die, expire, pass away, be killed. 2 go off, go bad, rot, decay, moulder, decompose. 3 disintegrate, collapse, crumble, fade, fail, vanish.

perishable adj decomposable, biodegradable, destructible, frail, fragile, short-lived.

perjure verb **perjure oneself** commit perjury, lie under oath, bear false witness, forswear oneself.

perjury noun false witness, false testimony.

perk noun perquisite, fringe benefit, extra, bonus, advantage, dividend, gratuity, tip, freebie (inf).
perk up cheer up, liven up, buck up (inf), rally, recover, revive.

perky adj jaunty, sprightly, lively, bouncy, buoyant, bubbly, upbeat (inf), bright, cheerful, chirpy (inf).

permanent adj lasting, enduring, imperishable, indestructible, everlasting, perpetual, constant, fixed, established, stable, unchanging, indelible.

permeable adj porous, absorbent, spongy, pervious, penetrable.

permeate verb 1 penetrate, soak into, seep through, percolate through, infiltrate, saturate, impregnate. **2** pervade, fill, spread through, diffuse through, imbue, suffuse.

permissible *adj* allowable, allowed, permitted, legitimate, authorized, sanctioned, acceptable, admissible.

permission *noun* authorization, sanction, clearance, leave, approval, consent, assent, agreement, go-ahead, green light (*inf*), thumbs-up (*inf*).

permissive *adj* liberal, broad-minded, easygoing (*inf*), tolerant, indulgent, lenient, lax, free, unrestricted.

permit *verb* **1** allow, let, authorize, give leave, license, enable, empower. **2** consent to, agree to, approve of, tolerate, countenance, brook, sanction, authorize. ➤*noun* licence, warrant, permission, authorization, pass, visa.

permutation *noun* alteration, transformation, change, transposition, rearrangement, configuration.

pernicious *adj* deadly, fatal, lethal, mortal, ruinous, destructive, injurious, harmful, damaging, dangerous.

pernickety *adj* fussy, particular, overparticular, finicky, exacting, difficult, punctilious, fastidious.

peroration *noun* summary, summing-up, conclusion, closing remarks, recapitulation.

perpendicular *adj* **1** upright, vertical, straight, plumb, erect, standing, on end. **2** steep, sheer, precipitous, abrupt.

perpetrate *verb* commit, do, execute, perform, carry out, pull off (*inf*), effect, bring about, wreak, inflict.

perpetual *adj* **1** eternal, everlasting, never-ending, permanent, lasting, enduring, constant, uninterrupted, continuous. **2** persistent, constant, recurrent, repeated, continual, perennial.

perpetuate *verb* continue, keep up, maintain, sustain, preserve, conserve, keep alive, immortalize, eternalize.

perpetuity *noun* eternity, all time, infinity, permanence.

perplex *verb* puzzle, baffle, mystify, nonplus, stump, flummox, bewilder, confuse, confound.

perquisite *noun* perk (*inf*), fringe benefit, extra, bonus, advantage, dividend, gratuity, tip.

persecute *verb* **1** victimize, oppress, tyrannize, torment, torture, martyr, afflict, maltreat, abuse. **2** harass, hassle (*inf*), hound, pester, plague, badger, bother, worry, vex, annoy.

persevere *verb* persist, continue, carry on, go on, keep going, struggle on, soldier on, plug away (*inf*), peg away (*inf*), stick at (*inf*), endure, hold fast.

persist *verb* **1** continue, carry on, go on, keep on, persevere, soldier on, plug away (*inf*). **2** insist, stand firm. **3** last, linger, endure, abide, remain, survive, continue, carry on.

persistent *adj* **1** persevering, tenacious, assiduous, determined, resolute, dogged, stubborn, obstinate. **2** continual, continuing, recurring, recurrent, perpetual, repeated, frequent. **3** incessant, never-ending, perennial, chronic. **4** lasting, enduring. **5** constant, unchanging, unvarying, continuous.

person *noun* individual, body, soul, mortal, human being, man, woman, child, somebody, character, type.

persona *noun* **1** character, role, part, personality. **2** front, image, face, facade, mask, public face.

personable *adj* pleasing, agreeable, likable, nice, attractive, presentable, good-looking, charming.

personage *noun* celebrity, notable, VIP (*inf*), worthy, dignitary, luminary, somebody (*inf*), public figure, big shot (*inf*), bigwig (*inf*).

personal *adj* **1** private, individual, own, confidential, secret, intimate. **2** personalized, individual, subjective, idiosyncratic, unique, peculiar, characteristic, distinctive, special, particular, exclusive. **3** insulting, rude, derogatory, critical, disparaging, offensive, upsetting, hurtful, disrespectful, pejorative.

personality *noun* **1** character, nature, make-up, disposition, temperament, temper, psyche, individuality, identity. **2** charisma, magnetism, attractiveness, charm, dynamism. **3** celebrity, star, personage, notable, dignitary, luminary, worthy, VIP (*inf*).

personally *adv* **1** in person, in the flesh, individually, privately, confidentially, exclusively, solely, alone, independently. **2** insultingly, offensively, as personal criticism.

personify *verb* embody, incarnate, exemplify, epitomize, represent, symbolize, typify.

personnel *noun* staff, employees, workforce, crew, manpower, human resources.

perspective *noun* **1** viewpoint, point of view, vantage point, standpoint, stance, outlook, angle, aspect, slant, attitude. **2** view, vista, outlook, prospect, scene, panorama. **3** proportion, balance, context, relation.

perspicacious *adj* perceptive, observant, alert, quick-witted, astute, shrewd, sharp, acute, penetrating, discerning, clever, intuitive.

perspicuous *adj* lucid, clear, limpid, transparent, plain, distinct, intelligible, comprehensible, understandable, explicit, unambiguous, obvious.

perspiration *noun* **1** sweating, secretion, exudation, diaphoresis. **2** sweat, moisture, wetness.

perspire *verb* sweat, secrete, exude, drip, swelter, glow.

persuade *verb* move, induce, coax, cajole, urge, influence, sway, win over, convince, bring round (*inf*), prevail upon, lean on (*inf*).

persuasion *noun* **1** persuading, convincing, cajolery, wheedling, urging, arm-twisting (*inf*). **2** opinion, viewpoint, belief, tenet, conviction, certitude. **3** faith, creed, sect, cult, denomination, philosophy, school of thought.

persuasive *adj* convincing, credible, cogent, effective, potent, forceful, weighty, influential, plausible, sound, compelling, winning.

pert *adj* **1** impudent, impertinent, cheeky, saucy, bold, brazen, forward, fresh. **2** jaunty, smart, spruce, natty (*inf*), stylish, chic, trim, dapper.

pertain *verb* **1** relate, apply, regard, concern, refer, have a bearing, appertain. **2** belong, go along with.

pertinacious *adj* tenacious, dogged, persistent, insistent, firm, unshakable, stubborn, obstinate, obdurate, pig-headed, inflexible, intransigent.

pertinent *adj* relevant, germane, apposite, apropos, apt, appropriate, applicable, fitting, suitable, proper, to the point, to the purpose.

perturb *verb* **1** trouble, disturb, upset, worry, alarm, bother, ruffle, fluster, unsettle, disconcert. **2** confuse, muddle, disorder, disarrange, jumble.

peruse *verb* study, scrutinize, examine, inspect, read, pore over, scan, look through.

pervade *verb* permeate, spread through, diffuse through, fill, charge, saturate, impregnate, penetrate, infiltrate, imbue, infuse, suffuse.

perverse *adj* **1** wrongheaded, stiff-necked, stubborn, obstinate, mulish, obdurate, pig-headed, pertinacious, intransigent, unreasonable, cussed (*inf*). **2** contrary, bloody-minded, contumacious, disobedient, refractory, wayward, headstrong, awkward, difficult, intractable, uncooperative, stroppy (*inf*).

perversion *noun* **1** corruption, depravity, debauchery, kinkiness (*inf*), immorality, vice, deviance, abnormality. **2** distortion, deviation, misinterpretation, misconstruction, misrepresentation, travesty, falsification, misapplication, misuse.

pervert *verb* **1** corrupt, warp, deprave, debauch, lead astray, debase, degrade, vitiate. **2** twist, distort, misrepresent, falsify, misconstrue, misinterpret, garble. **3** divert, deflect, turn aside, misdirect, misuse, misapply.
➤ *noun* deviant, perv (*inf*), degenerate, debauchee, weirdo (*inf*).

perverted *adj* corrupt, depraved, debauched, deviant, kinky (*inf*), abnormal, unnatural, unhealthy, warped, twisted, sick, immoral.

pessimism *noun* hopelessness, defeatism, fatalism, cynicism, despair, resignation, gloom, alarmism, distrust, doubt, suspicion, misanthropy.

pest *noun* nuisance, bother, irritant, annoyance, vexation, trial, trouble, inconvenience, bore, drag (*inf*), pain (*inf*), thorn in the flesh (*inf*).

pester *verb* plague, torment, bedevil, trouble, worry, bother, disturb, annoy, harass, hassle (*inf*), badger, nag.

pestilence *noun* plague, bubonic plague, Black Death, epidemic, pandemic, disease, contagion, scourge, blight, canker, cancer.

pestilential *adj* **1** destructive, ruinous, deadly, fatal, hazardous, noxious, toxic, poisonous, unhealthy, insalubrious. **2** pernicious, dangerous, detrimental, harmful, corrupting, evil. **3** annoying, irritating, infuriating, bothersome, vexatious, irksome, troublesome, tiresome.

pet[1] *noun* favourite, darling, apple of one's eye (*inf*), blue-eyed boy (*inf*), treasure, jewel.
➤*adj* **1** tame, domestic, domesticated, house-trained. **2** favourite, favoured, preferred, chosen, dearest, beloved, cherished, prized, treasured. **3** particular, special, personal.
➤*verb* **1** stroke, pat. **2** kiss, embrace, fondle, caress, cuddle, snog (*inf*), neck (*inf*).

pet[2] *noun* mood, bad temper, ill humour, sulk, tantrum, huff (*inf*), paddy (*inf*), hump (*inf*).

peter *verb* peter out dwindle, diminish, fade, fizzle out (*inf*), run out, die away, evaporate, taper off, wane, ebb, cease, come to an end.

petition *noun* **1** appeal, protest, round robin. **2** request, entreaty, plea, supplication, prayer, invocation. **3** application, suit.
➤*verb* **1** appeal to, call upon, beg, implore, crave, entreat, bid, urge, press. **2** ask, request, solicit, apply, sue.

petrify *verb* **1** harden, solidify, turn to stone, calcify, ossify, fossilize. **2** terrify, horrify, alarm, frighten, stun, daze, numb, paralyse, immobilize, transfix, astound, amaze.

petticoat *noun* slip, underskirt.

pettish *adj* peevish, petulant, sulky, touchy, testy, waspish, cross, bad-tempered, irritable, ratty (*inf*), querulous, fractious.

petty *adj* **1** trivial, trifling, paltry, contemptible, piffling (*inf*), slight, small, inconsiderable, negligible. **2** minor, lesser, secondary, subordinate, unimportant, insignificant. **3** small-minded, narrow-minded, mean, shabby, spiteful.

petulant *adj* peevish, pettish, grumpy, crabby, touchy, huffy (*inf*), irritable, fretful, captious, querulous, sulky, moody.

phantom *noun* **1** ghost, spectre, apparition, spirit, spook (*inf*), wraith, phantasm, shade, revenant. **2** illusion, chimera, figment, hallucination, vision.
➤*adj* phantasmal, spectral, ghostly, illusory, unreal, fictitious, non-existent.

pharisaic *adj* pharisaical, sanctimonious, self-righteous, holier-than-thou, goody-goody (*inf*), hypocritical, insincere.

phase *noun* **1** period, time, spell, season, chapter, part, point, juncture, stage, step. **2** aspect, facet, side, angle, state, position.
phase in introduce, incorporate, bring in, start.
phase out discontinue, axe (*inf*), close, terminate, wind down, run down, eliminate, remove, withdraw.

phenomenal *adj* sensational, extraordinary, prodigious, stupendous, mind-blowing (*inf*), mind-boggling (*inf*), remarkable, exceptional, outstanding, unprecedented, unheard-of.

phenomenon *noun* **1** occurrence, event, incident, episode, fact, circumstance, experience. **2** marvel, wonder, prodigy, miracle, sensation, spectacle, rarity, curiosity.

philander *verb* flirt, womanize (*inf*), dally, trifle, play around, sleep around (*inf*).

philanthropy *noun* humanitarianism, public-spiritedness, social conscience, altruism, selflessness, benevolence, beneficence, charity, munificence, bounty, patronage, sponsorship.

philippic *noun* diatribe, tirade, harangue, fulmination, denunciation, condemnation, attack, onslaught, invective, obloquy, vituperation.

philistine *noun* boor, barbarian, lowbrow, ignoramus, yahoo, vulgarian.

philosopher *noun* thinker, theorist, metaphysician, logician, sage, guru, scholar, pundit.

philosophical *adj* 1 wise, learned, erudite, thinking, contemplative, meditative, reflective, logical, rational, theoretical, metaphysical, abstract. 2 resigned, calm, composed, impassive, unruffled, self-possessed, serene, stoical, patient, phlegmatic, realistic, practical.

philosophy *noun* 1 logic, reasoning, metaphysics, aesthetics, knowledge, wisdom, thought, thinking. 2 ideology, doctrine, beliefs, values, ideas, tenets, convictions, principles, attitudes, opinions.

phlegmatic *adj* calm, placid, impassive, imperturbable, lethargic, indolent, stolid, bovine.

phobia *noun* fear, terror, neurosis, obsession, hang-up (*inf*), thing (*inf*), anxiety, horror, dread, aversion.

phone *noun* telephone, blower (*inf*), receiver, handset, mobile.
➤*verb* telephone, call, ring, dial, give a bell (*inf*).

phoney *adj* 1 fake, bogus, sham, counterfeit, forged, false, imitation, mock, simulated. 2 pretentious, affected, contrived, put-on, feigned, pseudo (*inf*).
➤*noun* impostor, pretender, fraud, fake, counterfeit, forgery, imitation, sham, pseud (*inf*), quack (*inf*).

phosphorescence *adj* luminosity, radiance, glow, fluorescence, luminescence.

photocopy *noun* copy, duplicate, Photostat®, Xerox®, facsimile.
➤*verb* copy, duplicate, Photostat®, Xerox®, run off.

photograph *noun* picture, shot, photo (*inf*), snapshot, snap (*inf*), print, still, slide, transparency, image.
➤*verb* take, snap (*inf*), shoot, film.

phrase *noun* expression, locution, idiom, saying, remark, utterance.
➤*verb* express, put, word, style, couch, frame, say, voice.

phraseology *noun* 1 idiom, language, parlance, speech, words, jargon, terminology, vocabulary. 2 style, phrasing, wording, expression, syntax.

physical *adj* 1 material, solid, substantial, tangible, concrete, real, visible, actual. 2 natural, earthly, material. 3 bodily, corporeal, corporal. 4 carnal, fleshly, mortal.

physician *noun* doctor, quack (*inf*), healer, medic (*inf*), general practitioner, GP, MD, specialist, consultant.

physiognomy *noun* face, mug (*inf*), countenance, visage, features, lineaments, look, appearance.

physique *noun* build, frame, figure, body, shape, form, constitution, make-up.

pick *verb* 1 choose, select, pick out, single out, decide on, settle on, go for, opt for, plump for (*inf*), prefer, favour. 2 pluck, gather, pull, remove, cut, collect, harvest. 3 open, crack, force, break into. 4 rob, steal from. 5 provoke, incite, instigate, prompt, cause, start.
➤*noun* 1 choice, selection, option, decision, favour, preference. 2 best, choicest, cream, flower, pride, prize, élite, elect.

pick at nibble at, peck at, play with, push round the plate.

pick off shoot, aim at, fire at, hit, kill, take out.

pick on bully, persecute, tease, torment, nag, hector, criticize, blame, find fault with.

pick out choose, select, cull, single out, separate out, distinguish, discriminate, discern, spot.

pick up 1 lift, raise, hoist, take up. 2 call for, collect, fetch, give a lift. 3 buy, purchase, collect, get. 4 acquire, gain, obtain, find, grasp, master, discover, learn, glean. 5 take up with, fall in with, meet, get off with (*inf*). 6 receive, detect, hear, get. 7 resume, start again, carry on, continue, go on. 8 improve, perk up (*inf*), get better, mend, rally, recover, make progress.

picket *noun* 1 striker, demonstrator, protester, objector. 2 guard, sentry, sentinel, patrol, watch, lookout. 3 post, stake, spike, peg, upright, paling, pale, stanchion.
➤*verb* blockade, demonstrate at, protest at.

pickle *noun* 1 relish, chutney. 2 mess, fix (*inf*), spot (*inf*), jam (*inf*), predicament, trouble, difficulty, quandary.
➤*verb* marinade, souse, steep, preserve, cure, salt.

pick-me-up *noun* tonic, boost, shot in the arm (*inf*), bracer, restorative, refreshment, stimulant.

pickpocket *noun* thief, dip (*inf*).

picnic *noun* piece of cake (*inf*), doddle (*inf*), pushover (*inf*), breeze (*inf*), cinch (*inf*), child's play (*inf*).

pictorial *adj* illustrated, illustrative, representational, graphic, diagrammatic, schematic, photographic.

picture *noun* **1** drawing, sketch, painting, engraving, photograph, print, illustration, portrait, representation, image. **2** account, description, depiction, portrayal, impression. **3** film, movie, motion picture.
➤*verb* **1** imagine, envisage, visualize, see, conceive of. **2** depict, portray, draw, illustrate, represent, reproduce, show, paint, photograph.
in the picture informed, acquainted, au fait, up to date.

pictures *pl noun* cinema, movies, flicks (*inf*), picture house, film theatre, multiplex.

picturesque *adj* **1** scenic, quaint, attractive, pretty, lovely, charming, idyllic. **2** colourful, vivid, graphic, strong, striking.

piddling *adj* minor, small, piffling (*inf*), trifling, trivial, unimportant, insignificant, petty, paltry, derisory, contemptible, measly (*inf*).

pie *noun* pastry, tart.
pie in the sky fantasy, romance, illusion, mirage, dream, pipe dream, reverie, castle in the air (*inf*).

piebald *adj* pied, black and white, dappled, mottled, brindled, spotted.

piece *noun* **1** part, element, component, bit, fragment, scrap, length, chunk, lump, slice, portion, share. **2** bit, part, segment, section, division, unit, item, example, specimen. **3** work, composition, opus, creation, production, painting, sculpture, article, report.
➤*verb* **1** join, unite, connect, put together, fit together, assemble. **2** fix, mend, repair, patch.
go to pieces break down, panic, lose control, lose one's head, collapse, crack up (*inf*), fall apart.
in one piece intact, unbroken, whole, complete, undamaged, sound, unharmed, unhurt.

pièce de résistance *noun* masterpiece, showpiece, magnum opus, chef d'oeuvre, prize, jewel.

piecemeal *adv* piece by piece, bit by bit, little by little, gradually, by degrees, in stages, at intervals.

pied *adj* piebald, mottled, dappled, speckled, brindled, spotted, flecked, skewbald, motley, variegated, parti-coloured.

pier *noun* **1** jetty, quay, wharf, breakwater, landing stage. **2** support, upright, pillar, post, pile, column.

pierce *verb* **1** puncture, perforate, impale, spear, skewer, stab, lance, prick, hole, punch, bore, drill. **2** penetrate, enter, burst through, pervade, shatter.

piercing *adj* **1** shrill, high-pitched, earsplitting, loud. **2** keen, penetrating, probing, searching. **3** cold, freezing, arctic, wintry, raw, keen, sharp, biting, bitter, fierce. **4** hurtful, wounding, lacerating, scathing. **5** sharp-witted, discerning, perceptive, percipient, perspicacious, shrewd, astute.

piety *noun* piousness, devoutness, godliness, saintliness, holiness, sanctity, religiousness, spirituality, faith, devotion, reverence.

pig *noun* **1** hog, swine, sow, boar, porker (*inf*). **2** animal, slob (*inf*), glutton, hog (*inf*), boor, beast.
➤*verb* **1** guzzle, wolf (*inf*). **2** gorge, stuff.

pigeonhole *noun* **1** cubbyhole, locker, cubicle, compartment, box. **2** category, classification, compartment, slot (*inf*), niche.
➤*verb* classify, categorize, label, tag, compartmentalize.

pigheaded *adj* obstinate, stubborn, obdurate, self-willed, stiff-necked, inflexible, intransigent, unyielding.

pigment *noun* colour, colouring, tint, tincture, dye, paint, stain, colourant.

pile[1] *noun* **1** heap, mound, mountain, stack, mass, hoard, accumulation, collection. **2** load, lot, heap, ton, great deal. **3** fortune, bomb (*inf*), mint (*inf*), packet (*inf*), bundle (*inf*), wad (*inf*). **4** mansion, building, edifice, structure.
➤*verb* **1** heap, stack. **2** amass, mass, stockpile, load, hoard, accumulate, build up, collect. **3** crowd, flock, pack, squeeze, flood, stream, tumble, rush.
pile it on exaggerate, overemphasize, overplay, overstate, overdo, lay it on (*inf*).
pile up mount up, increase, grow, accumulate, escalate, soar.

pile² *noun* post, pillar, column, support, pier, upright.

pile³ *noun* nap, shag, fur, hair, fuzz, fluff.

pile-up *noun* crash, smash (*inf*), collision, accident.

pilfer *verb* steal, purloin, filch, pinch (*inf*), nick (*inf*), knock off (*inf*), swipe (*inf*), lift (*inf*).

pilgrim *noun* 1 worshipper, devotee, palmer, hajji. 2 traveller, wanderer, wayfarer.

pilgrimage *noun* expedition, journey, voyage, peregrination, crusade, mission, hajj.

pill *noun* tablet, capsule, pellet, bolus.

pillage *verb* ransack, rifle, rob, plunder, loot, maraud, raid, sack, despoil, strip, rape, ravage.
➤*noun* plundering, looting, pillaging, sack, raid, depredation, spoliation.

pillar *noun* 1 column, shaft, post, pole, mast, pier, upright, stanchion, pile. 2 bastion, mainstay, rock, support, prop, leading light (*inf*).

pillory *verb* brand, denounce, show up, stigmatize, ridicule, laugh at, mock, shame.

pillow *noun* cushion, bolster, headrest.

pilot *noun* 1 aviator, airman, airwoman, aeronaut, flier. 2 navigator, steersman, helmsman, guide. 3 trial, test, experiment, model.
➤*verb* fly, drive, operate, control, handle, manoeuvre, navigate, steer, guide, direct.

pimple *noun* spot, zit (*inf*), pustule, eruption.

pin *verb* 1 staple, clip, tack, nail, fasten, join, fix, attach. 2 hold, confine, restrain, bind, tie, immobilize.
➤*noun* 1 peg, bolt, nail, tack, spike, dowel. 2 clip, staple. 3 brooch, badge.
pin down 1 pressure, pressurize, force, compel, nail down. 2 pinpoint, locate, identify, define, specify, determine.

pinch *verb* 1 nip, tweak, squeeze. 2 hurt, crush, cramp, constrict, confine, press, compress. 3 steal, take, filch, pilfer, purloin, snatch, swipe (*inf*), nick (*inf*), knock off (*inf*). 4 arrest, apprehend, detain, catch, run in (*inf*), pick up (*inf*), nick (*inf*), nab (*inf*), collar (*inf*). 5 cut back, economize, save, stint, scrimp, skimp.
➤*noun* 1 squeeze, nip, tweak. 2 bit, smidgen (*inf*), tad (*inf*), dash, jot, touch, soupçon. 3 hardship, difficulty, stress, pressure, privation, necessity.
at a pinch if necessary, if need be, in an emergency.

pine *verb* 1 long, yearn, ache, sigh, hanker, crave. 2 languish, fret, flag, wilt, weaken, decline, fade, fail, grieve, mourn.

pinion *verb* pin, hold, constrain, restrain, immobilize, bind, tie, shackle, fetter.

pink¹ *adj* rose, pale red, salmon, flesh, rosy, flushed.
in the pink 1 flourishing, thriving, prospering. 2 fit, fighting fit (*inf*), healthy, in rude health, hale and hearty, in good shape, in fine fettle, right as rain (*inf*).

pink² *verb* cut, notch, serrate.

pinnacle *noun* 1 peak, summit, height, crown, top, apex, apogee, acme, zenith. 2 mountain, peak, height, summit, top, cap, crest. 3 spire, steeple, turret, needle, pyramid, cone.

pinpoint *verb* identify, pin down, specify, define, distinguish, determine, locate, home in on, zero in on (*inf*).

pioneer *noun* 1 settler, colonist, explorer, frontiersman, frontierswoman. 2 innovator, pathfinder, trailblazer, groundbreaker, founder, architect, discoverer, inventor, developer, leader.
➤*verb* launch, introduce, invent, discover, originate, instigate, start, found, establish, spearhead.

pious *adj* 1 devout, godly, God-fearing, saintly, holy, spiritual, religious, reverent. 2 righteous, virtuous, devoted, dutiful, respectful, reverential. 3 sanctimonious, self-righteous, holier-than-thou (*inf*), unctuous, pietistic, hypocritical, insincere, goody-goody (*inf*).

pipe *noun* 1 tube, line, pipeline, main, hose, piping, tubing, duct, conduit, channel. 2 clay, brier, meerschaum, hookah. 3 whistle, flute, fife, recorder.
➤*verb* 1 channel, funnel, siphon, duct, supply. 2 carry, convey, transmit, deliver. 3 squeak, tweet, chirp, cheep, peep, whistle, warble, trill, shrill.
pipe down stop talking, be quiet, hush, shut up (*inf*), belt up (*inf*).

pipe dream *noun* dream, mirage, castle in the air (*inf*), pie in the sky (*inf*), fantasy, reverie, romance.

pipeline *noun* pipe, main, tube, line, conduit, channel, passage, duct.
in the pipeline under way, forthcoming, imminent, in preparation, in production, planned.

piquant *adj* **1** pungent, sharp, biting, tart, tangy, flavoursome, savoury, spicy, hot, peppery, seasoned. **2** lively, spirited, sparkling, scintillating, interesting, stimulating, provocative, intriguing, fascinating.

pique *verb* **1** wound, hurt, offend, affront, upset, put out, annoy, nettle (*inf*), gall, irk, anger, rile. **2** excite, arouse, awaken, kindle, stimulate, provoke, stir, whet.
➤*noun* offence, umbrage, resentment, indignation, annoyance, displeasure, anger.

piracy *noun* **1** buccaneering, freebooting, robbery. **2** plagiarism, infringement, theft.

pirate *noun* corsair, buccaneer, sea rover, freebooter, robber, plagiarist.
➤*verb* plagiarize, copy, reproduce, poach, steal, crib (*inf*), lift (*inf*).

pit *noun* **1** hole, cavity, crater, pothole, ditch, trench, shaft, well, abyss, chasm. **2** mine, quarry, diggings, workings. **3** pockmark, dimple, dent, depression, hollow.
➤*verb* indent, dent, dimple, pothole, pockmark, scar, mark.
pit against match, oppose, set against.

pitch *verb* **1** hurl, fling, throw, chuck (*inf*), cast, toss, lob, sling. **2** erect, raise, put up, set up, establish, locate, place. **3** plunge, plummet, topple, tumble, fall, drop. **4** roll, reel, lurch, list, sway, rock, flounder, wallow, heave. **5** set, fix.
➤*noun* **1** level, degree, height, depth, point, extent, intensity. **2** gradient, slope, incline, tilt, slant, inclination, steepness, angle. **3** list, lurch, roll, reeling, swaying, rocking. **4** tone, timbre, sound, frequency, level, modulation. **5** field, ground, park, arena, stadium. **6** patter, jargon, talk, line, spiel (*inf*).
pitch in join in, muck in (*inf*), chip in (*inf*), do one's bit (*inf*), participate, contribute, cooperate, help, assist, lend a hand.

pitch-black *adj* black, dark, jet-black, coal-black, ebony, inky, stygian.

pitcher *noun* jug, jar, ewer, urn, crock.

piteous *adj* pitiable, pitiful, pathetic, plaintive, sorrowful, doleful, sorry, wretched, moving, affecting, distressing, harrowing.

pitfall *noun* **1** hazard, danger, catch, snag, drawback, difficulty. **2** trap, snare.

pith *noun* **1** essence, quintessence, crux, nub, core, heart, kernel, meat, marrow. **2** meaning, substance, gist, point, import, significance.

pithy *adj* terse, succinct, concise, compact, cogent, expressive, meaningful, weighty, forceful, telling.

pitiable *adj* piteous, pitiful, pathetic, poor, sad, sorry, wretched, miserable, doleful, lamentable, deplorable.

pitiful *adj* **1** pathetic, pitiable, sorry, sad, wretched, piteous, affecting, moving, poignant, heartbreaking, harrowing. **2** contemptible, miserable, meagre, poor, pathetic, inadequate, worthless, paltry.

pitiless *adj* merciless, harsh, severe, callous, cold, unfeeling, uncaring, unsympathetic, heartless, inhuman, brutal, cruel.

pittance *noun* allowance, ration, modicum, trifle, peanuts (*inf*), chicken feed (*inf*).

pity *noun* **1** compassion, mercy, forgiveness, clemency, humanity, understanding, sympathy, fellow feeling, commiseration, condolence, regret, sorrow. **2** disappointment, shame, misfortune, bad luck, bummer (*sl*).
➤*verb* sympathize with, feel for, feel sorry for, grieve for, weep for, bleed for.

pivot *noun* **1** axis, fulcrum, axle, spindle, pin, hinge. **2** hub, centre, focus, focal point.
➤*verb* **1** revolve, rotate, spin, swivel, swing, turn. **2** depend, hang, rely, hinge.

pixie *noun* elf, fairy, sprite, brownie, leprechaun.

placard *noun* notice, poster, advertisement, sign.

placate *verb* pacify, appease, mollify, conciliate, soothe, lull, calm down, assuage, propitiate, win over.

place *noun* **1** spot, location, scene, site, position, situation, point, whereabouts, venue. **2** area, region, district, locality, town, city, village, hamlet. **3** position, station, status, standing, rank, grade. **4** job, task, duty, responsibility, role, function, business, right, prerogative. **5** house, flat, home, pad (*inf*), abode, dwelling, residence, accommodation, lodgings. **6** seat, position, space, area, post, station, niche. **7** position, location.

➤*verb* **1** put, lay, set, deposit, plant, position, fix, locate, situate, stand, rest, leave. **2** arrange, dispose, sort, order. **3** rank, grade, classify, categorize, bracket, pinpoint, identify, recognize. **4** entrust, put, lay, rest, consign, invest. **5** install, establish, accommodate, appoint, assign, allocate.

in place of instead of, in lieu of, in exchange for, as an alternative to, as a substitute for.

put somebody in their place humble, humiliate, shame, mortify, crush, deflate, cut down to size (*inf*), take down a peg or two.

take place happen, occur, come to pass, crop up, befall, transpire, go on.

take the place of replace, substitute for, supersede, stand in for, cover for, act for.

placid *adj* calm, cool, serene, tranquil, unexcitable, unflappable, even-tempered, easygoing, equable.

plagiarize *verb* pirate, borrow, crib (*inf*), lift (*inf*), poach, steal, appropriate, copy, reproduce, imitate, forge, counterfeit.

plague *noun* **1** epidemic, pandemic, pestilence, disease, sickness, infection, contagion. **2** infestation, invasion, influx, swarm.

➤*verb* **1** torment, torture, trouble, afflict, bedevil, haunt. **2** harass, harry, hassle (*inf*), badger, hound, pester, annoy, irritate, bother, disturb, worry.

plain *adj* **1** unadorned, undecorated, unembellished, unornamented, unpatterned, self-coloured. **2** pure, natural. **3** clear, distinct, obvious, apparent, evident, manifest, simple, intelligible, comprehensible, accessible, lucid, unambiguous. **4** forthright, plain-spoken, frank, candid, open, blunt, direct, sincere, guileless, artless, ingenuous. **5** ordinary, average, commonplace, typical, everyday, homely, modest, unaffected, unpretentious. **6** straightforward, uncomplicated, unsophisticated, simple. **7** basic, austere,

Spartan, restrained, muted. **8** unattractive, unprepossessing, ill-favoured, ugly.

➤*adv* completely, totally, utterly, thoroughly, downright, positively, simply, quite.

➤*noun* plateau, tableland, lowland, flat, grassland, prairie, steppe, pampas, savannah.

plain-spoken *adj* candid, frank, blunt, direct, forthright, up-front (*inf*), open, honest, truthful.

plaintive *adj* mournful, doleful, sad, melancholy, sorrowful, woebegone, piteous, pitiful, pathetic, heart-rending.

plan *noun* **1** scheme, programme, schedule, plot, device, strategy, method, system, procedure, design, formula. **2** idea, intention, aim, hope, ambition, aspiration, project, proposal. **3** map, chart. **4** diagram, chart, drawing, representation, outline. **5** blueprint, layout, drawing.

➤*verb* **1** arrange, organize, prepare, schedule, programme, mastermind, scheme, plot. **2** intend, propose, mean, aim, resolve, determine, envisage, contemplate, want, wish, seek. **3** design, outline, draft, map out, sketch, devise, work out, frame.

plane *adj* flat, level, even, flush, smooth, horizontal.

➤*noun* **1** flat, level. **2** level, stratum, condition, degree, stage. **3** aeroplane, aircraft, airliner, jet.

➤*verb* **1** glide, fly, float, drift. **2** skim, skate.

plant *noun* **1** flower, vegetable, herb, shrub, tree, weed. **2** factory, mill, foundry, works, yard. **3** machinery, equipment, apparatus.

➤*verb* **1** sow, set out, bury, root, transplant. **2** put, set, place, position, settle. **3** lodge, fix, implant, insert, establish. **4** conceal, hide, secrete.

plaque *noun* plate, tablet, slab, panel, sign, brass.

plaster *noun* **1** mortar, cement, stucco, gypsum. **2** dressing, Elastoplast®, Band-aid®.

➤*verb* daub, bedaub, smear, spread, cover, coat.

plastic *adj* **1** soft, ductile, mouldable, malleable, pliable, pliant, supple, tensile, flexible. **2** artificial, synthetic, unnatural, false, sham, bogus.

plate | 314

plate *noun* 1 dish, platter, salver, trencher. 2 sheet, layer, coating. 3 plaque, sign, tablet, brass. 4 illustration, picture, print.
➤*verb* coat, cover, gild, silver.

plateau *noun* 1 highland, tableland, upland, mesa. 2 lull, respite, break, let-up, level, stability.

platform *noun* 1 stage, dais, podium, rostrum, soapbox. 2 policy, manifesto, programme, plan, strategy, principles, objectives, party line.

platitude *noun* truism, cliché, commonplace, banality, bromide (*inf*).

platonic *adj* non-physical, spiritual, intellectual.

platter *noun* plate, dish, tray, salver, trencher, charger.

plaudits *pl noun* applause, ovation, acclamation, accolade, congratulations, compliments, praise, commendation, approval, approbation.

plausible *adj* 1 reasonable, logical, likely, probable, possible, imaginable, conceivable, credible, believable, convincing, cogent. 2 smooth-talking, glib, persuasive, specious.

play *verb* 1 have fun, amuse oneself, enjoy oneself, romp, frolic, gambol, sport. 2 compete, contend, participate, take part, join in. 3 challenge, oppose, take on, vie with. 4 perform, act, portray, represent. 5 toy, trifle, fiddle. 6 flicker, twinkle, flash, dance, flit, dart.
➤*noun* 1 fun, revelry, amusement, merrymaking, enjoyment, entertainment, diversion, recreation, leisure, game, sport, jest. 2 drama, comedy, tragedy, farce, melodrama, piece, entertainment, show, performance. 3 action, move, movement, motion, activity. 4 freedom of movement, flexibility, give (*inf*), slack, leeway, margin, sweep, swing, function, operation. 5 scope, range, room, space, latitude, freedom, liberty, licence. 6 conduct, behaviour, action, activity, interaction, interplay.
play about *fun*, clown, fool, mess, meddle. 2 womanize, philander, flirt, trifle, dally.
play down minimize, diminish, make light of, gloss over, downplay, understate, underestimate, belittle, disparage.
play up 1 emphasize, stress, accentuate, exaggerate, magnify, highlight, spotlight, underline, underscore, point up. 2 trouble,

bother, hurt. 3 misbehave, annoy, provoke, give trouble. 4 malfunction, go wrong.
play up to flatter, ingratiate oneself with, suck up to (*inf*), butter up (*inf*), curry favour with, pander to, fawn over.

playboy *noun* philanderer, womanizer, ladies' man, lady-killer, rake, man-about-town (*inf*), socialite, libertine, roué.

player *noun* 1 competitor, contestant, contender, participant, sportsman, sportswoman. 2 musician, performer, instrumentalist, accompanist, virtuoso, artist, artiste.

playful *adj* 1 sportive, frolicsome, frisky, coltish, skittish, lively, high-spirited, fun-loving, merry, jolly. 2 humorous, joking, light-hearted, teasing, tongue-in-cheek, facetious, arch, roguish, mischievous, puckish.

playground *noun* play area, park, recreation ground.

playwright *noun* dramatist, dramaturge, scriptwriter, screenwriter.

plea *noun* 1 request, entreaty, appeal, petition, prayer, supplication. 2 excuse, explanation, vindication, justification, defence. 3 allegation, suit, case, claim.

plead *verb* 1 appeal, entreat, beg, beseech, crave, implore, supplicate. 2 declare, state. 3 argue, reason. 4 present, put forward, allege, maintain, claim.

pleasant *adj* 1 delightful, agreeable, enjoyable, pleasing, nice, lovely. 2 charming, friendly, likable, affable, agreeable, good-humoured.

pleasantry *noun* remark, comment.

please *verb* 1 delight, gratify, humour, gladden, cheer, content, satisfy, amuse, entertain, charm, appeal to, suit. 2 like, wish, want, desire, choose, prefer, see fit.

pleased *adj* 1 contented, satisfied, gratified, delighted, thrilled, overjoyed, chuffed (*inf*), over the moon (*inf*), tickled pink (*inf*). 2 willing, happy, glad.

pleasure *noun* 1 gratification, contentment, satisfaction, enjoyment, delight, happiness, gladness, joy. 2 amusement, recreation, diversion, entertainment, enjoyment, fun.

plebeian *adj* **1** common, vulgar, coarse, unrefined, uncultured, uncultivated, base, low, mean, ignoble. **2** working-class, lower-class, proletarian, low-born, common.
➤*noun* commoner, proletarian, worker, peasant, pleb (*inf*), prole (*inf*), man in the street.

pledge *noun* **1** promise, vow, oath, bond, covenant, guarantee, undertaking, commitment, assurance, word. **2** surety, security, collateral, deposit, earnest, bail. **3** token, symbol, sign, mark, testimony, evidence. **4** toast, health.
➤*verb* **1** promise, vow, give one's word, swear, engage, contract, guarantee. **2** mortgage, put up, pawn. **3** toast, drink to.

plenary *adj* full, entire, thorough, general, absolute, unqualified, unconditional, unrestricted.

plentiful *adj* **1** abundant, plenteous, bountiful, copious, ample, bumper, profuse, lavish, generous, full, large, infinite. **2** prolific, fruitful, productive.

plenty *noun* **1** abundance, bounty, profusion, wealth, fund, mine, enough, sufficiency, excess, superfluity, plethora, glut. **2** great deal, lots (*inf*), piles (*inf*), heaps (*inf*), oodles (*inf*). **3** plentifulness, plenteousness, plenitude, copiousness, amplitude, fullness, fruitfulness, prosperity.

plethora *noun* superfluity, excess, surplus, surfeit, glut, overabundance.

pliable *adj* **1** pliant, flexible, bendable, bendy (*inf*), elastic, supple, lithe, limber, ductile, tensile, malleable, plastic. **2** yielding, amenable, compliant, docile, biddable, tractable, adaptable, flexible, accommodating, responsive, receptive.

plight[1] *noun* predicament, quandary, dilemma, fix (*inf*), spot (*inf*), extremity, dire straits, difficulty, trouble, state, position, circumstances.

plight[2] *verb* promise, vow, swear, pledge, engage, contract.

plod *verb* **1** trudge, tread, stump, stomp, tramp, clump, lumber. **2** drudge, toil, labour, slog, grind, persevere, plug away (*inf*), peg away (*inf*), soldier on.

plot *noun* **1** plan, scheme, conspiracy, intrigue, machination, ruse, stratagem.

2 story, storyline, narrative, theme, thread, action, scenario. **3** patch, allotment, parcel, tract, area, lot.
➤*verb* **1** plan, scheme, conspire, intrigue, collude, connive, machinate, contrive, hatch, brew, cook up (*inf*). **2** devise, conceive, think up, frame, draft. **3** chart, map, mark, record. **4** locate, compute, calculate. **5** draw, outline.

plough *verb* **1** till, work, dig, break up, cultivate, furrow, turn. **2** hurtle, career, run, crash, smash, bulldoze. **3** plod, trudge, wade, make one's way.

ploy *noun* manoeuvre, tactic, stratagem, scheme, gambit, contrivance, device, ruse, subterfuge, artifice, trick.

pluck *verb* **1** draw, extract, pull out, remove, snatch. **2** pick, gather, collect, harvest. **3** tug, tweak, jerk, pull, yank (*inf*). **4** strum, pick, thrum, twang.
➤*noun* courage, bravery, valour, mettle, spirit, nerve (*inf*), guts (*inf*), daring, intrepidity, determination, resolution.

plucky *adj* courageous, brave, mettlesome, spirited, game (*inf*), bold, intrepid, gutsy (*inf*), fearless, doughty, feisty, determined.

plug *noun* **1** bung, stopper, cork, seal, wad, ball. **2** publicity, promotion, mention, advertisement, puff.
➤*verb* **1** stop, close, block, clog, fill, pack, choke, obstruct, bung, cork, seal. **2** publicize, promote, mention, advertise, tout, puff, push (*inf*). **3** slog, grind, toil, labour, persevere, plod on, soldier on.

plumb *adj* vertical, perpendicular, true. *adv* exactly, precisely, right, dead.
➤*verb* **1** measure, sound, fathom. **2** probe, penetrate, delve into, explore, examine, investigate.

plummet *verb* plunge, dive, nosedive, crash, drop, fall, tumble.

plump[1] *adj* fat, stout, portly, rotund, round, fleshy, chubby, podgy, tubby, well-upholstered (*inf*).

plump[2] *verb* **1** put down, dump (*inf*), plonk (*inf*), deposit. **2** drop, fall, flop, slump, sink, collapse.
plump for choose, pick, select, opt for, decide on, back, support, favour.

plunder *verb* **1** loot, pillage, rob, ransack, sack, rape, despoil, ravage, raid, maraud. **2** steal, thieve, make off with.

➤*noun* **1** booty, spoils, pickings, loot, swag (*inf*). **2** pillage, rapine, sack.

plunge *verb* **1** dive, fall, plummet, swoop, jump, dash, charge, hurtle. **2** plummet, nosedive, drop, fall, sink, tumble, go down, decrease. **3** immerse, submerge, dip, duck, douse. **4** throw, cast, pitch.
➤*noun* **1** dive, swoop, jump, swim, bathe. **2** fall, drop, plummet, dive, nosedive, tumble.

plus *prep* and, with, in addition to, as well as, coupled with.
➤*noun* bonus, extra, benefit, advantage, credit, asset.

plush *adj* luxurious, luxury, de luxe, lavish, sumptuous, palatial, opulent, ritzy (*inf*), classy (*inf*), posh (*inf*).

ply¹ *noun* **1** strand, fibre, filament, thread. **2** layer, thickness, fold, sheet.

ply² *verb* **1** practise, carry on, pursue, follow, work at, engage in. **2** manipulate, handle, wield, apply, use, operate. **3** provide, supply, furnish, lavish, shower, feed, load, heap. **4** bombard, assail, beset, harass, importune. **5** travel, go, ferry, shuttle.

poach *verb* **1** trespass, encroach, intrude. **2** steal, take, appropriate, pirate, lift (*inf*), borrow (*inf*).

pocket *noun* **1** bag, pouch, sack, envelope, compartment, cavity, hollow. **2** finances, resources, funds, budget, means, money. **3** patch, island, area, zone.
➤*adj* **1** small, little, miniature, mini (*inf*), pint-size (*inf*). **2** potted, compact, concise, portable.
➤*verb* take, misappropriate, steal, purloin, filch, pilfer, nick (*inf*), pinch (*inf*).

pod *noun* shell, husk, case, hull, shuck.

podgy *adj* fat, stout, chubby, tubby, dumpy, plump, roly-poly, rotund, squat, chunky.

podium *noun* platform, stage, stand, rostrum, dais.

poem *noun* verse, rhyme, ode, sonnet, lyric, ballad, elegy, limerick.

poet *noun* versifier, rhymer, lyricist, sonneteer, balladeer, elegist, bard, rhymester, poetaster.

poetic *adj* **1** poetical, lyric, lyrical, elegiac, metrical, rhythmical, rhyming. **2** imaginative, creative, flowery, figurative, symbolic, aesthetic, artistic, graceful, flowing, elegant, expressive.

poetry *noun* **1** poems, poesy, verse, rhyme. **2** versification, rhyming.

poignant *adj* emotional, sentimental, affecting, evocative, distressing, harrowing, painful, plaintive, sad, sorrowful, mournful, tragic.

point *noun* **1** tip, top, end, extremity, apex, spike, spur, nib, prong, tine. **2** dot, mark, speck, spot. **3** full stop, dot, period. **4** spot, place, position, site, location. **4** moment, instant, juncture, stage, phase, period, time. **5** aim, end, object, objective, goal, intention, reason, motive, purpose, use. **6** crux, nub, heart, core, essence, thrust, significance, question, matter, issue, subject, topic. **7** detail, item, element, particular, characteristic, feature, aspect, facet, quality, property. **8** mark, run, hit, goal. **9** cape, headland, bluff, promontory, bill, foreland.
➤*verb* **1** show, indicate, signal, gesture, designate, specify, point out. **2** direct, aim, level, train. **3** face, head. **4** sharpen, taper, edge, whet.

beside the point irrelevant, immaterial, incidental, inconsequential, unrelated, unconnected, neither here nor there (*inf*).
on the point of on the verge of, on the brink of, about to.
point out indicate, draw attention to, show, reveal, identify, specify, mention.
point to indicate, show, suggest, evidence.
point up emphasize, stress, underline, underscore, accentuate, highlight, spotlight, bring to the fore, draw attention to.
to the point relevant, related, pertinent, connected, germane, applicable, appropriate, apt, apropos, apposite.
up to a point to a certain extent, to some degree, slightly, partly, somewhat.

point-blank *adv* **1** outright, directly, straight, bluntly, frankly, candidly, abruptly, brusquely, unequivocally, plainly, explicitly, openly. **2** at close range, close up.

pointed *adj* **1** incisive, cutting, trenchant, pertinent, accurate, sharp, keen, acute, penetrating, forceful, striking, telling. **2** marked, obvious, conspicuous, evident. **3** sharp, barbed, peaked, tapering, edged.

pointer *noun* **1** hand, indicator, needle, arrow. **2** tip, hint, suggestion, recommendation, warning, guideline, advice, indicator, clue, sign. **3** stick, rod, cane, pole.

pointless *adj* meaningless, irrelevant, ridiculous, senseless, aimless, vain, futile, useless, fruitless, unavailing, empty, worthless.

point of view *noun* **1** opinion, view, belief, judgment, attitude, feeling, sentiment. **2** viewpoint, perspective, outlook, angle, slant, stance, standpoint, position.

poise *noun* **1** composure, self-possession, aplomb, self-assurance, presence of mind, cool (*inf*), sang-froid, calmness, equanimity, serenity, dignity. **2** elegance, grace, bearing, carriage. **3** balance, equilibrium, steadiness, stability.
➤*verb* **1** balance, steady. **2** support, brace, hold, hang, suspend. **3** hover, hang, float.

poised *adj* **1** composed, serene, self-possessed, self-assured, calm, cool, dignified, unperturbed, self-confident, graceful, suave, elegant. **2** ready, prepared, set, waiting, expectant.

poison *noun* **1** venom, toxin. **2** contagion, pollution, contamination, corruption, blight, canker, bane.
➤*verb* **1** infect, contaminate, pollute, taint. **2** corrupt, deprave, subvert, undermine, warp, blight, spoil, vitiate.

poisonous *adj* **1** venomous, toxic, deadly, fatal, lethal, mortal. **2** malicious, spiteful, pernicious, malevolent, corrupting, harmful, virulent, noxious.

poke *verb* **1** jab, prod, dig, nudge, elbow, stab, stick, push, shove. **2** stick out, jut out, project, protrude, extend, overhang. **3** rummage, forage, search.
➤*noun* prod, dig, jab, nudge, shove, push.
poke one's nose into meddle in, interfere with, pry into, intrude on.

poky *adj* confined, cramped, narrow, tight, small.

polar *adj* **1** Arctic, Antarctic, frozen, icy, extreme. **2** opposite, contradictory, contrary, conflicting, diametrically opposed, antagonistic.

polarity *noun* opposition, oppositeness, contradiction, conflict, difference, antagonism, duality, dichotomy, ambivalence, paradox.

pole[1] *noun* post, upright, rod, stick, staff, mast, prop, stanchion, stake, shaft, bar, spar.

pole[2] *noun* extremity, extreme, limit.
poles apart at opposite extremes, incompatible, irreconcilable, completely different.

polemic *noun* attack, dispute, argument, refutation.

polemics *pl noun* debate, discussion, argumentation, disputation, controversy, contention.

police *noun* police force, constabulary, the law (*inf*), the fuzz (*inf*), the Bill (*inf*).
➤*verb* **1** patrol, guard, protect, defend, keep in order, keep the peace. **2** regulate, control, monitor, check, observe, supervise.

police officer *noun* policeman, policewoman, officer, constable, cop (*inf*), copper (*inf*), bobby (*inf*), rozzer (*inf*), pig (*sl*).

policy *noun* **1** strategy, method, tactic, course, line, approach. **2** plan, programme, scheme, schedule, theory, practice, system, procedure, code, protocol, rule, guideline.

polish *verb* **1** buff, burnish, shine, rub up, wax, smooth, brighten. **2** refine, cultivate. **3** finish, perfect, improve, enhance, brush up.
➤*noun* **1** shine, lustre, sheen, gloss, smoothness, brilliance, brightness, sparkle. **2** wax, varnish. **3** refinement, sophistication, cultivation, finesse, urbanity, suavity, elegance, grace, poise, style.
polish off finish, eat up, consume, devour, put away, dispose of, bolt, down, gobble, wolf (*inf*).

polite *adj* **1** courteous, well-mannered, mannerly, civil, respectful, deferential, tactful, diplomatic, gallant, gentlemanly, ladylike, well-bred. **2** genteel, refined, cultured, cultivated, polished, sophisticated, urbane, suave.

politic *adj* **1** expedient, opportune, advisable, judicious, wise, prudent, sensible, advantageous. **2** wise, sagacious, shrewd, astute, tactful, diplomatic, discreet.

political *adj* **1** civil, civic, public, state, governmental, parliamentary, constitutional, executive, ministerial. **2** party political, partisan, factional.

politics *pl noun* **1** government, affairs of state, public affairs, civic affairs, party politics. **2** statecraft, statesmanship, political science. **3** machination, manipulation, opportunism, diplomacy.

poll *noun* **1** vote, voting, ballot, show of hands, referendum, plebiscite. **2** tally, count, return. **3** survey, canvass, census, market research.
➤*verb* **1** win, receive, get, obtain. **2** record, register, return, receive. **3** canvass, survey, ballot, question, interview.

pollute *verb* **1** contaminate, taint, adulterate, poison, infect, dirty, soil, foul. **2** corrupt, warp, pervert, deprave, defile, debauch.

pollution *noun* **1** contamination, adulteration, poisoning, corruption, perversion, depravity, defilement. **2** dirt, filth, muck, waste, rubbish, refuse, fumes, impurities.

pomp *noun* **1** display, state, ceremony, pageantry, parade, spectacle, grandeur, solemnity, formality, splendour, majesty, glory. **2** ostentation, show, showiness, exhibitionism, pomposity, grandiosity, vainglory.

pompous *adj* **1** pretentious, self-important, arrogant, haughty, puffed up, lofty, presumptuous, overbearing, supercilious, grandiose, imperious, affected. **2** bombastic, high-flown, inflated, elaborate, flowery, ostentatious, showy, grandiloquent.

pond *noun* pool, puddle, lake, mere, tarn.

ponder *verb* **1** think about, reflect on, mull over, consider, contemplate, brood over, puzzle over, weigh up. **2** meditate, ruminate, cogitate, think, reflect, deliberate, brood.

ponderous *adj* **1** huge, massive, bulky, hefty, heavy, weighty, unwieldy, awkward, clumsy, lumbering. **2** dull, boring, tedious, monotonous, dreary, dry, laboured, stilted, plodding, pedestrian, long-winded, verbose.

pontificate *verb* hold forth, declaim, sound off, expound, preach, sermonize, lecture, harangue, moralize, dogmatize.

pool[1] *noun* **1** puddle, patch, splash, pond. **2** swimming pool, lido, baths.

pool[2] *noun* **1** pot, kitty, bank, purse, stakes. **2** supply, reserve, fund. **3** syndicate, consortium, cartel, ring, group, collective.
➤*verb* combine, merge, amalgamate, put together, share.

poor *adj* **1** needy, in need, penniless, impoverished, necessitous, impecunious, poverty-stricken, indigent, destitute, deprived, underprivileged, disadvantaged. **2** meagre, sparse, scant, skimpy, measly, paltry, inadequate, insufficient. **3** deficient, lacking, short. **4** inferior, third-rate, low-grade, substandard, unsatisfactory, shoddy, weak, bad, worthless, rotten (*inf*), lousy (*inf*), pathetic (*inf*). **5** unlucky, unfortunate, ill-fated, ill-starred, unhappy, hapless, wretched, miserable, sad, sorry, pitiable, pitiful.

poorly *adj* sick, ill, unwell, off colour, under the weather (*inf*), out of sorts (*inf*), indisposed, ailing.
➤*adv* badly, inadequately, insufficiently, unsatisfactorily, incompetently, shoddily, feebly.

pop *verb* **1** burst, explode, detonate, bang, snap, crack. **2** put, slip, drop, tuck, stick, shove. **3** go, nip (*inf*), drop, visit.
➤*noun* **1** burst, explosion, detonation, report, bang, snap, crack. **2** fizzy drink, fizz (*inf*), soda, soft drink.

pop off die, pass away, pass on, snuff it (*inf*), kick the bucket (*inf*).

pope *noun* pontiff, Holy Father, Bishop of Rome, Vicar of Christ.

populace *noun* public, general public, people, society, community, masses, rank and file, proletariat, rabble, plebs (*inf*), hoi polloi, commonalty.

popular *adj* **1** well-liked, favoured, approved, well-received, admired, accepted, fashionable, in vogue, cool (*inf*), trendy (*inf*), in demand, sought-after. **2** middle-of-the-road, middlebrow, low-brow, accessible, understandable, general, non-specialist, non-technical, ordinary, pop, mass-market, down-market. **3** common, familiar, public, general, civic, universal. **4** prevailing, prevalent, widespread, ubiquitous, current, accepted, usual, conventional, standard, customary.

popularize *verb* **1** familiarize, make accessible, simplify. **2** universalize, generalize, spread, propagate, disseminate, give currency to.

populate *verb* **1** inhabit, occupy, live in, dwell in. **2** colonize, settle, people.

population *noun* inhabitants, residents, occupants, denizens, citizenry, populace, people, folk, society, community.

populous *adj* crowded, overpopulated, densely populated, packed, teeming, swarming, crawling, thronged.

porch *noun* entrance hall, lobby, foyer, vestibule.

pore[1] *verb* **1** study, examine, scrutinize, peruse, scan, read. **2** ponder, meditate, reflect, think, muse, deliberate, contemplate, brood.

pore[2] *noun* opening, orifice, aperture, perforation, hole, outlet, vent, stoma.

pornography *noun* porn (*inf*), erotica, sexploitation, titillation, obscenity, smut.

porous *adj* **1** permeable, pervious, penetrable, absorbent. **2** spongy, spongelike, honeycombed, cellular, open.

port *noun* harbour, dock, haven, anchorage.

portable *adj* light, lightweight, compact, handy, convenient, manageable, movable, transportable.

portend *verb* forebode, bode, foretoken, foreshadow, forecast, predict, prognosticate, augur, presage, indicate, herald, announce.

portent *noun* **1** omen, sign, token, harbinger, augury, precursor, forerunner, prognostication, presage, premonition, presentiment, foreboding. **2** phenomenon, marvel, wonder, prodigy, miracle.

portentous *adj* **1** ominous, foreboding, sinister, alarming, threatening, inauspicious, unpropitious, momentous, fateful, crucial, pivotal. **2** pompous, ponderous, solemn, weighty, self-important, pontifical.

porter[1] *noun* doorman, doorkeeper, gatekeeper, commissionaire, concierge, janitor, caretaker.

porter[2] *noun* bearer, carrier, baggage-handler.

portion *noun* **1** share, division, part, cut (*inf*), lot, allotment, allocation, quota, ration, helping, serving. **2** fate, lot, destiny, fortune.
➤ *verb* **1** apportion, share, divide, split, partition, carve up (*inf*), parcel out, distribute, deal out, hand out, dole out (*inf*), mete out. **2** allot, allocate, assign.

portly *adj* stout, corpulent, rotund, fat, plump, tubby (*inf*), overweight, burly, stocky, well-built, large, heavy.

portrait *noun* **1** picture, likeness, image, study, painting, caricature, miniature, photograph. **2** portrayal, representation, characterization, account, description, depiction, sketch, vignette.

portray *verb* **1** draw, paint, sketch, depict, delineate. **2** describe, depict, picture, represent. **3** act, play, perform, impersonate, characterize.

pose *verb* **1** model, sit, stand, arrange, dispose, place, position, set out. **2** feign, pretend, impersonate, pass oneself off, masquerade, act. **3** posture, attitudinize, show off, play-act, put on airs. **4** ask, put, present, put forward, propose, submit, set, posit, postulate, propound, advance, suggest. **5** constitute, present, create, produce, cause, give rise to, lead to, result in.
➤ *noun* **1** posture, bearing, attitude, position, stance, air. **2** pretence, masquerade, act, role, posture, sham, facade, front, affectation, airs.

poser *noun* riddle, enigma, mystery, puzzle, problem, dilemma, conundrum, brainteaser (*inf*).

poseur *noun* poser, posturer, exhibitionist, show-off, pseud (*inf*), phoney (*inf*), sham, impostor, charlatan.

posh *adj* **1** smart, elegant, fancy, luxurious, de luxe, luxury, grand, lavish, sumptuous, plush (*inf*), ritzy (*inf*), swish (*inf*). **2** upper-class, aristocratic, la-di-da (*inf*), up-market, stylish, fashionable, exclusive, select, high-class, classy (*inf*).

position *noun* **1** place, situation, location, spot, point, site, locality, bearings, whereabouts. **2** posture, pose, stance, attitude, arrangement, disposition, layout. **3** opinion, stance, standpoint, stand, view, point of view, viewpoint, angle, outlook, attitude, feeling, belief. **4** situation, case, state of affairs, state, condition, circumstances, background, predicament. **5** job, post, situation, employment, appointment, place, office, role, function,

capacity. **6** status, standing, station, rank, ranking, class, grade, level.
➤*verb* place, arrange, dispose, lay out, deploy, station, put, set, stand, locate, situate, site.

positive *adj* **1** certain, sure, assured, confident, convinced, definite, categorical, emphatic. **2** constructive, practical, helpful, useful, productive, beneficial, substantial, real, actual. **3** optimistic, encouraging, favourable, hopeful, heartening, promising, cheerful, upbeat (*inf*). **4** utter, complete, perfect, absolute, thoroughgoing, downright, rank, out-and-out, veritable, consummate.

possess *verb* **1** own, have, hold, enjoy, acquire, obtain, get, gain, seize, take. **2** consume, obsess, control, influence, dominate. **3** enter, take over, control, bewitch. **4** be endowed with, have, be gifted with.

possessed *adj* consumed, obsessed, infatuated, cursed, bedevilled, bewitched, hagridden, demented, crazed, raving, mad.

possession *noun* **1** ownership, proprietorship, custody, control, hold, grip. **2** tenure, tenancy, occupancy, holding, title.

possessions *pl noun* wealth, assets, property, estate, goods, chattels, belongings, effects, things (*inf*).

possessive *adj* **1** selfish, greedy, grasping, covetous, acquisitive. **2** clinging, controlling, domineering, jealous, overprotective.

possibility *noun* **1** likelihood, liability, probability, odds, chance, prospect, risk, hope, potentiality, practicability, feasibility, conceivability. **2** promise, potential, expectation, prospect, advantage, capability. **3** option, alternative, recourse, choice.

possible *adj* **1** conceivable, imaginable, credible, likely, probable, potential, hypothetical. **2** feasible, practicable, attainable, achievable, realizable, doable, viable, workable, deliverable.

possibly *adv* **1** perhaps, maybe, perchance, peradventure, God willing. **2** conceivably, at all, by any chance.

post[1] *noun* pole, shaft, stake, pale, picket, prop, strut, leg, upright, pillar, column, stanchion.
➤*verb* **1** affix, attach, fasten, put up, stick up, pin up, hang, display. **2** announce,

make known, publish, broadcast, publicize, advertise, promulgate, circulate.

post[2] *noun* **1** place, station. **2** position, situation, job, office, employment, appointment, vacancy, place.
➤*verb* **1** station, place, position, locate. **2** transfer, relocate, move, send, second, assign.

post[3] *noun* **1** mail, correspondence, letters, parcels. **2** collection, delivery. **3** postal service, postal system, mail.
➤*verb* **1** mail, send, dispatch, forward. **2** enter, fill in, record, register, note, write up.
keep somebody posted inform, notify, keep up to date, fill in (*inf*), brief, advise.

poster *noun* placard, bill, notice, advertisement, sticker, sign, announcement.

posterior *noun* rear, behind, bottom, seat, haunches, hindquarters, rump, buttocks, backside, bum (*inf*).
➤*adj* **1** rear, rearward, back, hind, hinder. **2** after, later, following, succeeding, ensuing, subsequent.

posterity *noun* descendants, successors, heirs, progeny, offspring, issue, children, family.

postmortem *noun* **1** autopsy, necropsy, dissection. **2** review, analysis, examination.

postpone *verb* delay, defer, shelve, table, reschedule, put off, put back.

postscript *noun* PS, addendum, afterthought, appendix, supplement, addition, epilogue, codicil.

postulate *verb* assume, suppose, presume, presuppose, propose, take for granted, posit, theorize, hypothesize, predicate.

posture *noun* **1** position, attitude, pose, stance, bearing, carriage, deportment. **2** attitude, position, viewpoint, standpoint, disposition, frame of mind, feeling, inclination, opinion.
➤*verb* **1** pose, strut, show off, put on airs. **2** strike an attitude, attitudinize, play-act, affect.

posy *noun* bouquet, nosegay, bunch, spray.

pot *noun* **1** container, receptacle, vessel, pan, cauldron, casserole, bowl, jar, urn, tankard, jug. **2** kitty, purse. **3** fund, reserve.

potent *adj* powerful, strong, effective, efficacious, intoxicating, heady (*inf*), forceful, mighty, influential, dominant, authoritative, compelling.

potentate *noun* ruler, sovereign, monarch, mogul, overlord, chieftain, dictator.

potential *adj* possible, likely, probable, future, prospective, promising, budding, developing, embryonic, aspiring, would-be, latent.
➤*noun* **1** aptitude, talent, flair, promise, the makings (*inf*). **2** potentiality, possibility, capacity, capability, ability.

potion *noun* drink, draught, dose, brew, mixture, concoction, elixir, philtre, medicine, tonic.

potter *verb* **1** tinker, play, dabble, fiddle, fool about, mess about (*inf*). **2** dawdle, amble, loiter, dally, dilly-dally (*inf*), toddle (*inf*).

pottery *noun* ceramics, earthenware, crockery, china, terracotta, stoneware.

pouch *noun* bag, sack, purse, wallet, satchel. **2** pocket, sac.

pounce *verb* swoop, dive, descend, drop, fall, spring, bound, lunge, surprise, ambush, attack, strike.
➤*noun* swoop, spring, bound, lunge, assault, attack.

pound[1] *verb* **1** thump, bang, beat, drum, batter, pummel, pelt, hammer, strike, smash. **2** pulverize, powder, crush, grind, comminute, triturate, mash. **3** throb, pulsate, pulse, pump, beat, thump, thud. **4** walk, pace, tramp, plod, tread, trudge, stomp, clump.

pound[2] *noun* pound coin, pound sterling, quid (*inf*), nicker (*inf*), smacker (*inf*).

pound[3] *noun* compound, pen, enclosure, fold.

pour *verb* **1** flow, stream, course, cascade, run, gush, spout, jet, spill, spew, emit, discharge. **2** emerge, issue, come out, stream, flood, spill, crowd, swarm, throng. **3** serve, decant. **4** rain, teem, pelt, rain cats and dogs (*inf*), bucket down (*inf*).

pout *verb* frown, scowl, glower, grimace, sulk.

poverty *noun* **1** want, need, impoverishment, indigence, destitution, beggary, pauperism, penury, privation, deprivation,
distress, hardship. **2** dearth, scarcity, shortage, lack. **3** deficiency, inadequacy, insufficiency, paucity, depletion, barrenness, sterility.

powder *noun* dust, grains, particles, triturate.
➤*verb* **1** pulverize, pound, crush, grind, mash, granulate, comminute, triturate. **2** dust, dredge, sprinkle, scatter, strew.

power *noun* **1** ability, capability, capacity, potential, aptitude, faculty, effectiveness, force, strength, potency. **2** capacity, authority, competence, right, prerogative, warrant, licence. **3** control, command, authority, domination, clutches, grip, influence, clout (*inf*), muscle (*inf*), pull (*inf*). **4** rule, sovereignty, mastery, dominion, sway, ascendancy, supremacy. **5** powerfulness, force, strength, energy, might, vigour. **6** effectiveness, forcefulness, intensity, potency, cogency, weight, conviction.

powerful *adj* **1** influential, authoritative, commanding, controlling, dominant, leading, high-powered, supreme, prevailing. **2** strong, mighty, vigorous, energetic, robust, tough, forceful, intense. **3** potent, strong, effective, overwhelming, cogent, compelling, impressive.

powerless *adj* **1** helpless, disabled, incapacitated, weak, feeble, defenceless, vulnerable. **2** impotent, ineffectual, ineffective, incapable.

practicable *adj* possible, feasible, attainable, achievable, doable, workable, viable.

practical *adj* **1** actual, real, hands on, applied. **2** useful, expedient, realistic, sensible, practicable, workable, feasible. **3** utilitarian, functional, serviceable, workaday, handy. **4** businesslike, efficient, down-to-earth, matter-of-fact, pragmatic, sensible, realistic, hard-headed, hard-nosed (*inf*). **5** virtual, effective, essential.

practically *adv* **1** virtually, in effect, almost, nearly, well-nigh, all but, just about, essentially, fundamentally, to all intents and purposes. **2** realistically, pragmatically, sensibly, reasonably, rationally.

practice *noun* **1** exercise, drill, training, study, preparation, repetition. **2** rehearsal, run-through. **3** performance, effect, action, application, operation, use. **4** custom, habit, routine, wont, rule. **2** tradition, convention, way, method, system, procedure, usage. **5** profession, work, pursuit, occupation, vocation. **6** partnership, firm, business, surgery.

practise verb **1** do, perform, carry out, execute, implement, apply, put into practice. **2** rehearse, repeat, exercise, drill, train, prepare, polish, refine, perfect, go over, run through. **3** work at, engage in, ply, pursue, specialize in, carry on, undertake.

practised adj expert, masterly, proficient, adept, accomplished, consummate, skilled, versed, experienced, veteran, trained, qualified.

pragmatic adj practical, realistic, expedient, down-to-earth, matter-of-fact, unsentimental, hard-headed, hard-nosed (inf).

praise verb **1** commend, applaud, cheer, acclaim, hail, admire, approve, congratulate, compliment, extol, eulogize, panegyrize. **2** worship, glorify, honour, exalt, magnify, laud.
➤noun **1** commendation, accolade, eulogy, panegyric, acclamation, plaudits, congratulations, compliments, flattery, admiration, adulation, approval. **2** worship, tribute, homage, glory, honour, exaltation, devotion, adoration.

praiseworthy adj commendable, laudable, meritorious, admirable, estimable, creditable, reputable, fine, excellent, exemplary, sterling.

prance verb **1** leap, spring, jump, bound, gambol, frolic, frisk. **2** swagger, strut, stalk, show off, parade, skip, dance, cavort.

prank noun trick, practical joke, caper, lark (inf), hoax, stunt.

prattle verb chat, chatter, gossip, babble, blather, gab (inf), rabbit (inf), witter (inf), prate.

pray verb invoke, call on, commune with, offer prayers, worship, beseech, confess, thank.

prayer noun **1** collect, litany. **2** communion, devotion, invocation, intercession. **3** appeal, plea, request, entreaty, petition, supplication, hope, wish, desire.

preach verb **1** evangelize, spread the gospel, proclaim, promulgate, disseminate, teach, address. **2** sermonize, moralize,

pontificate, lecture, harangue. **3** recommend, advise, advocate, urge, exhort.

preamble noun introduction, preface, prologue, foreword, preliminaries.

precarious adj **1** unstable, shaky, unsteady, insecure, unsafe, dangerous, perilous, hazardous, hairy (inf). **2** uncertain, unsure, unpredictable, doubtful, unreliable, unsettled, risky, vulnerable, dodgy (inf), dicey (inf), iffy (inf).

precaution noun safeguard, safety measure, preventive measure, provision, protection, insurance, security.

precede verb **1** go ahead of, lead, head, usher in, herald, come before, antedate, predate. **2** begin, open, introduce, preface, prefix.

precedence noun priority, preference, seniority, superiority, supremacy, primacy, preeminence, ascendancy.

precedent noun **1** antecedent, parallel. **2** example, model, pattern, standard, criterion, yardstick.
➤adj preceding, foregoing, previous, prior, earlier, past, former.

precept noun rule, principle, canon, instruction, direction, order, command, directive, dictum, edict, tenet, ordinance.

precinct noun **1** centre, mall, zone, sector, district, area. **2** close, enclosure, court. **3** boundary, ambit, limit, bound, confines.

precincts pl noun environs, purlieus, region, area, vicinity, neighbourhood, locality.

precious adj **1** valuable, expensive, costly, dear, high-priced, priceless, invaluable, fine, exquisite. **2** dear, darling, cherished, beloved, prized, treasured, esteemed, adored, idolized, revered. **3** affected, pretentious, mannered, contrived, artificial, overrefined, effete, twee (inf).

precipice noun cliff, rockface, bluff, crag, escarpment, height, drop.

precipitate verb **1** hasten, hurry, accelerate, expedite, advance, bring on, induce, trigger, cause, occasion. **2** throw, hurl, fling, cast, heave, propel.
➤adj hurried, hasty, rash, reckless, rapid, swift, headlong, abrupt, sudden, unexpected, impetuous, impulsive.

prefer

precipitous *adj* **1** steep, sheer, perpendicular, vertical, dizzy, high. **2** abrupt, sudden, rapid, headlong, violent. **3** hurried, hasty, rash, reckless, precipitate.

précis *noun* summary, synopsis, abstract, résumé, digest, condensation, epitome, outline.
➤*verb* condense, shorten, synopsize, abridge, digest, abstract, summarize, sum up, encapsulate, epitomize.

precise *adj* **1** exact, accurate, correct, detailed, minute, explicit, unambiguous, express, definite, specific, strict, literal. **2** particular, rigorous, finicky, nice, meticulous, scrupulous, conscientious, careful. **3** exact, actual, very, specific, particular. **4** punctilious, rigid, severe, inflexible, stiff, formal.

preclude *verb* rule out, forestall, eliminate, obviate, prohibit, debar, prevent, stop, impede, inhibit.

precocious *adj* **1** advanced, mature, bright, clever, smart, quick. **2** premature, early, forward, ahead.

preconception *noun* **1** presupposition, presumption, assumption, preconceived idea. **2** bias, prejudice, prejudgment.

precondition *noun* condition, stipulation, prerequisite, requirement, essential, necessity, must (*inf*).

precursor *noun* harbinger, forerunner, herald, usher, antecedent, prelude, sign, indication.

predatory *adj* **1** predacious, rapacious, voracious, carnivorous, hunting, preying. **2** plundering, pillaging, robbing, thieving, marauding, greedy, rapacious, exploitative.

predecessor *noun* forerunner, precursor, antecedent.

predestination *noun* predetermination, foreordination, fate, destiny.

predestine *verb* destine, fate, doom, foreordain, preordain, predetermine.

predetermine *verb* prearrange, set, fix, preordain, foreordain, ordain, decree.

predicament *noun* plight, quandary, dilemma, crisis, difficulty, problem, trouble, mess, fix (*inf*), jam (*inf*), spot (*inf*), corner (*inf*).

predicate *verb* assert, aver, affirm, maintain, declare, state, contend, postulate, posit.

predict *verb* foretell, foresee, forecast, prophesy, prognosticate, augur, divine, foreshadow, presage, portend.

predictable *adj* foreseeable, expected, anticipated, probable, likely, certain, sure, on the cards (*inf*).

prediction *noun* **1** prophecy, forecast, forewarning, prognosis. **2** prognostication, augury, soothsaying, divination.

predilection *noun* inclination, predisposition, proclivity, propensity, preference, partiality, liking, fondness, soft spot, weakness, taste, penchant.

predispose *verb* dispose, incline, prompt, induce, sway, move, influence, prepare.

predominant *adj* **1** chief, main, primary, principal, preponderant. **2** ruling, leading, controlling, prevailing, preeminent, ascendant, supreme.

predominate *verb* **1** preponderate, outnumber, outweigh. **2** dominate, prevail, hold sway, rule, reign.

preeminent *adj* supreme, transcendent, paramount, matchless, unrivalled, unsurpassed, superior, distinguished, excellent, leading, predominant, foremost.

preempt *verb* **1** prevent, forestall, anticipate. **2** acquire, secure, appropriate, assume, commandeer, seize, take over, usurp.

preen *verb* **1** groom, clean, arrange, smooth, slick. **2** array, deck out, doll up, dress up, tart up (*inf*), beautify, prink, primp, titivate.
preen oneself pride oneself, congratulate oneself, pat oneself on the back (*inf*), bask, exult, gloat.

preface *noun* **1** introduction, foreword, prologue, preamble. **2** prelude, preliminary.
➤*verb* **1** introduce, open, begin, prefix. **2** precede, lead up to.

prefer *verb* **1** favour, like better, choose, pick, opt for, go for, fancy (*inf*), desire, want, wish. **2** bring, press, lodge, file. **3** advance, promote, upgrade, elevate, raise, honour, aggrandize.

preferable *adj* better, superior, more desirable, nicer, preferred, favoured, chosen, advisable, recommended.

preferably *adv* rather, sooner, from choice, for preference, first.

preference *noun* **1** favourite, choice, option, wish, desire, selection, pick. **2** liking, fancy, inclination, bias, predilection, partiality, weakness. **3** favour, priority, precedence, preferential treatment, favouritism.

preferential *adj* special, superior, better, partial, biased, advantageous, favourable, favoured, privileged.

preferment *noun* advancement, promotion, upgrading, betterment, aggrandizement, elevation, exaltation.

pregnancy *noun* gestation, gravidity.

pregnant *adj* **1** expectant, expecting (*inf*), in the club (*inf*), in the family way (*inf*), up the duff (*inf*), with child, gravid. **2** meaningful, significant, loaded, charged, eloquent, expressive, fraught, full, rich.

prehistoric *adj* **1** primeval, primitive, primordial, early. **2** antiquated, ancient, archaic, obsolete, old, old-fashioned, superannuated, antediluvian.

prejudice *noun* **1** bias, discrimination, favouritism, partiality, partisanship, injustice. **2** preconception, prejudgment. **3** bigotry, intolerance, narrow-mindedness, chauvinism, racism, sexism, ageism, xenophobia, anti-Semitism. **4** harm, damage, injury, mischief, detriment, disadvantage, loss.
➤*verb* **1** bias, colour, warp, distort, predispose, load, weight, slant, influence, dispose, jaundice, poison. **2** harm, damage, impair, ruin, hurt, injure, mar, hinder, undermine.

prejudicial *adj* harmful, damaging, injurious, pernicious, detrimental, deleterious, counter-productive, disadvantageous, unfavourable, inimical.

preliminary *adj* introductory, beginning, opening, first, primary, initial, precursory, prefatory, preparatory, exploratory.
➤*noun* preparation, groundwork, foundation, introduction, opening, beginning, preface, preamble, prelude.

prelude *noun* **1** preliminary, preparation, beginning, opener, curtain-raiser, precur-

sor, harbinger, herald, forerunner. **2** introduction, intro (*inf*), overture. **3** preface, preamble, prologue, foreword.

premature *adj* **1** early, untimely, unseasonable, incomplete, undeveloped, half-formed, embryonic. **2** hasty, precipitate, impulsive, impetuous, rash, previous (*inf*).

premeditate *verb* plan, plot, calculate, contrive, intend, predetermine, prearrange.

premier *adj* principal, leading, prime, cardinal, primary, first, foremost, preeminent, supreme, chief, highest, top.

première *noun* first performance, first showing, opening, opening night.

premise *noun* **1** proposition, hypothesis, thesis, assertion, postulate, argument, basis, ground. **2** assumption, presumption, supposition, surmise.
➤*verb* **1** postulate, posit, predicate, presuppose, assume. **2** stipulate, assert, state.

premises *pl noun* **1** property, grounds, estate, site. **2** building, establishment, office.

premium *noun* **1** instalment, payment. **2** bonus, extra, tip, perquisite, perk (*inf*), commission, percentage.
at a premium expensive, dear, in short supply, scarce, rare, hard to come by, like gold dust (*inf*).

premonition *noun* foreboding, presentiment, suspicion, feeling, hunch, intuition, sixth sense.

preoccupation *noun* **1** absorption, engrossment, pensiveness, concentration, abstraction, reverie, brown study, oblivion. **2** concern, interest, enthusiasm, hobby-horse, obsession, fixation, thing (*inf*), bee in one's bonnet (*inf*).

preoccupied *adj* engrossed, obsessed, absorbed, involved, taken up, wrapped up, immersed, engaged, intent, abstracted, pensive, lost in thought.

preoccupy *verb* occupy, absorb, engross, engage, take up, involve, obsess, distract.

preordain *verb* foreordain, destine, predestine, predetermine, fate, doom.

preparation *noun* **1** groundwork, spadework, planning, organization, development, anticipation, expectation, coaching, training, grooming. **2** preliminary, foundation, provision, plan. **3** mixture, compound, concoction, medicine, potion, tincture.

preparatory *adj* preparative, preliminary, prefatory, precursory, primary, introductory, elementary, fundamental.
preparatory to in preparation for, in advance of, in anticipation of, before, prior to.

prepare *verb* **1** get ready, make ready, arrange, make provision, take steps, gear up (*inf*), adjust, adapt, study, practise, train, coach. **2** ready, brace, steel. **3** plan, work out, map out, arrange, organize, develop, devise, think up. **4** make, concoct, put together, throw together, fix (*inf*). **5** draft, draw up, compile, put together, compose, produce.

preparedness *noun* readiness, willingness, ability, inclination, disposition.

preponderant *adj* **1** predominant, prevalent, in the majority. **2** dominant, superior, in the ascendant.

preponderate *verb* predominate, dominate, prevail, hold sway, outweigh, outnumber, prevail, reign supreme.

prepossessing *adj* attractive, fetching, good-looking, pretty, fair, charming, engaging, winning, appealing, pleasing.

preposterous *adj* ridiculous, ludicrous, absurd, laughable, farcical, crazy, unreasonable, nonsensical, outrageous, monstrous, unthinkable, impossible.

prerequisite *noun* condition, precondition, proviso, qualification, requirement, requisite, necessity, essential, must (*inf*).

prerogative *noun* privilege, right, liberty, choice, due, entitlement, advantage, exemption, immunity.

presage *verb* **1** indicate, point to, announce, herald, warn of, foreshadow, threaten, augur, bode, portend, betoken. **2** predict, forecast, prophesy, foretell, forebode, foresee, divine, feel, sense.

prescience *noun* foreknowledge, precognition, clairvoyance, second sight, foresight.

prescribe *verb* **1** direct, specify, stipulate. **2** advise, urge, recommend, suggest. **3** lay down, require, stipulate, define, dictate, rule, specify, set, fix, ordain, decree.

prescription *noun* **1** direction, instruction, order, formula, recipe, medicine, drug, preparation, mixture, remedy, treatment. **2** prescribing, stipulation, specification, ruling.

presence *noun* **1** being, existence, attendance. **2** company, proximity, vicinity, nearness, closeness, propinquity. **3** spirit, manifestation, apparition, ghost, phantom, spectre. **4** magnetism, charisma, aura, personality. **5** poise, bearing, demeanour, dignity, self-assurance, self-possession.

presence of mind aplomb, composure, poise, calm, cool (*inf*), sang-froid, self-assurance, self-possession, level-headedness, quick-wittedness.

present[1] *adj* **1** existing, existent, extant. **2** current, immediate, contemporary, present-day. **3** here, there, attending, in attendance, at hand, available.
at present at the moment, now, at this time, currently.
for the present for the moment, for the time being, for now, in the meantime, pro tem.

present[2] *verb* **1** give, donate, bestow, award, confer, grant, hand over, extend, offer, proffer, tender. **2** introduce, make known, acquaint with. **3** stage, put on, produce, perform, mount, organize. **4** compère, host, introduce, announce, emcee (*inf*). **5** show, display, exhibit, demonstrate. **6** submit, set forth, put forward, offer, advance, suggest, state, pose. **7** depict, portray, represent, describe, explain, expound.
present itself crop up, occur, arise, happen, transpire, materialize, come about.
present oneself be present, arrive, appear, attend, show up, turn up.

present[3] *noun* gift, prezzie (*inf*), donation, offering, hand-out, tip, freebie (*inf*), sweetener (*inf*), award, endowment, benefaction.

presentable *adj* **1** neat, tidy, smart, clean, respectable, decent. **2** acceptable, satisfactory, passable, good enough, OK (*inf*).

presentation *noun* **1** arrangement, organization, disposition, layout, format, structure, performance, production, representation, delivery. **2** award, conferral, bestowal, endowment, donation, offering, submission, introduction, launch. **3** talk, address, lecture, seminar, demonstration, display.

presentiment *noun* premonition, foreboding, intuition, hunch, feeling, suspicion.

presently *adv* **1** soon, shortly, in a minute, before long, in a while, by and by, later. **2** at present, now, currently, at the moment, these days.

preserve *verb* **1** conserve, keep, save, store, put away, protect, care for, look after. **2** maintain, uphold, keep up, keep alive, sustain, perpetuate, continue, retain. **3** protect, defend, shield, guard, safeguard, look after, take care of, save. **4** bottle, can, tin, pickle, cure, smoke, salt, dry, freeze.
➤*noun* **1** jam, jelly, marmalade, conserve. **2** domain, sphere, realm, field, area, speciality. **3** reserve, reservation, park, sanctuary.

preside *verb* **1** officiate, chair, conduct. **2** lead, head, control, direct, run, manage, administer, supervise.

president *noun* **1** head of state, ruler. **2** chief, head, managing director, chief executive, principal. **3** leader, director, chairman, controller.

press *verb* **1** push, depress, force down. **2** squeeze, crush, mash, compress, pinch, hug, clasp, clutch, cram, crowd. **3** iron, smooth. **4** flatten, mould. **5** urge, beg, entreat, exhort, importune, harass, constrain, force, coerce, pressure, pressurize. **6** petition, campaign, clamour, call, demand, insist on. **7** pursue, push, advance, put forward.
➤*noun* **1** journalists, reporters, correspondents, paparazzi, media, fourth estate. **2** newspapers, papers, magazines, Fleet Street, journalism. **3** review, criticism, comment, coverage. **4** crowd, throng, mob, swarm, pack, herd, crush, push.
be pressed for lack, be short of, be strapped for (*inf*).
press on 1 go on, carry on, continue, proceed, advance. **2** persevere, go ahead, push on, hasten, hurry, rush.

pressing *adj* urgent, crucial, high-priority, serious, critical, key, vital, essential, important, imperative, burning, exigent.

pressure *noun* **1** load, weight, stress, strain, force, compression, squeezing.

2 constraint, duress, compulsion, coercion, force, power, influence. **3** insistence, urgency, harassment, obligation. **4** stress, strain, tension, trouble, problems, hassle (*inf*), aggro (*inf*).

pressurize *verb* pressure, press, force, compel, coerce, bully, browbeat, bulldoze, dragoon, lean on (*inf*), put the screws on (*inf*).

prestige *noun* **1** status, reputation, esteem, regard, credit, authority, influence, weight, eminence, distinction, standing, stature. **2** fame, renown, celebrity, kudos, cachet, credit, superiority.

presumably *adv* no doubt, doubtless, probably, most likely, apparently, on the face of it.

presume *verb* **1** assume, imagine, suppose, surmise, guess, conjecture, hypothesize, postulate. **2** take for granted, take it, think, believe, judge, conclude, deduce, infer. **3** venture, dare, undertake, make so bold as, have the temerity, have the audacity. **4** take advantage, exploit.

presumption *noun* **1** assumption, supposition, surmise, deduction, inference, conjecture, belief, hypothesis, premise. **2** presumptuousness, boldness, audacity, temerity, effrontery, impertinence, cheek (*inf*), nerve (*inf*), assurance, overconfidence, bumptiousness, arrogance.

presumptive *adj* believable, credible, reasonable, conceivable, probable, likely, assumed, supposed.

presumptuous *adj* bold, audacious, impertinent, insolent, disrespectful, forward, pushy (*inf*), bumptious, overbearing, arrogant, overconfident, cocky (*inf*).

presuppose *verb* assume, presume, take for granted, suppose, postulate, posit.

pretence *noun* **1** make-believe, playacting, feigning, dissembling, dissimulation, invention, affectation. **2** show, charade, semblance, masquerade, veneer, cover, appearance, guise, facade. **3** claim, aspiration, profession, excuse, ruse, lie, bluff.

pretend *verb* **1** play-act, put on an act, bluff, dissemble, dissimulate, go through the motions, make believe, imagine, suppose. **2** sham, fake, feign, simulate, put on, affect, assume. **3** claim, profess,

purport, allege. **4** aspire, aim, lay claim.
➤*adj* make-believe, imaginary, fictitious.

pretender *noun* claimant, aspirant, candidate.

pretension *noun* **1** pretentiousness, pomposity, self-importance, airs, conceit, vanity, affectation, show, flamboyance, ostentation. **2** claim, profession, demand, assertion. **3** aspiration, ambition, pretence.

pretentious *adj* ostentatious, showy, flamboyant, affected, extravagant, exaggerated, high-flown, overambitious, grandiose, highfalutin (*inf*), pompous, self-important.

preternatural *adj* **1** extraordinary, out of the ordinary, unnatural, abnormal, unusual, exceptional, singular, strange, weird, inexplicable. **2** unearthly, supernatural, paranormal.

pretext *noun* excuse, reason, claim, allegation, pretence, guise, semblance, cover, ploy, ruse.

pretty *adj* attractive, beautiful, fair, bonny, lovely, appealing, pleasing, charming, dainty, picturesque.
➤*adv* **1** fairly, moderately, reasonably, rather, somewhat. **2** quite, very.

prevail *verb* **1** win, triumph, be victorious, succeed, conquer, overcome, gain ascendancy, carry the day (*inf*). **2** abound, predominate, preponderate, hold sway.
prevail on/upon persuade, sweet-talk (*inf*), influence, lean on (*inf*), urge, exhort, cajole, coax, convince, win over, bring round.

prevailing *adj* **1** usual, established, dominant, controlling, principal, chief, main. **2** prevalent, predominant, widespread, universal, general, common, current, popular, fashionable.

prevalent *adj* prevailing, frequent, general, common, widespread, universal, endemic, rife, rampant, ubiquitous, extensive.

prevaricate *verb* equivocate, evade, sidestep, dodge (*inf*), hedge (*inf*), quibble, cavil, waffle (*inf*), flannel (*inf*), beat about the bush (*inf*), tergiversate, shilly-shally (*inf*).

prevent *verb* **1** stop, preclude, block, obstruct, avert, avoid, ward off, stave off, anticipate, forestall, nip in the bud.

2 arrest, check, impede, inhibit, deter, restrain, hold back, thwart, frustrate.

preventive *adj* **1** preventative, precautionary, protective, prophylactic, inhibitory, deterrent. **2** preemptive, anticipatory.
➤*noun* **1** precautionary measure, prevention, protection, protective, prophylactic, remedy, safeguard, shield, deterrent.

previous *adj* **1** former, preceding, prior, foregoing, antecedent, precursory, past, erstwhile, sometime, earlier. **2** premature, precipitate, hasty, presumptuous.

prey *noun* **1** quarry, game, kill. **2** victim, target, mark.
prey on/upon **1** hunt, seize, catch, devour, eat, feed on, live off. **2** victimize, intimidate, bully, terrorize, exploit, take advantage of, con (*inf*), fleece (*inf*). **3** oppress, weigh down, burden, trouble, worry, distress, torment, plague, haunt.

price *noun* **1** cost, fee, rate, charge, value, worth, sum, figure, valuation, assessment, estimate, quotation. **2** penalty, loss, forfeit, sacrifice, cost, consequence, result.
➤*verb* rate, cost, assess, estimate, appraise, value.
at a price expensively, dearly, at a high price, at considerable cost.
at any price regardless, anyhow, at any cost, whatever it takes.

priceless *adj* **1** invaluable, inestimable, beyond price, precious, prized, treasured, dear, expensive, costly, unique, rare, irreplaceable. **2** hilarious, riotous, sidesplitting, funny, amusing, rich (*inf*).

prick *verb* **1** pierce, spike, jab, stab. **2** puncture, perforate, punch, lance, cut. **3** prickle, sting, tingle, smart, itch, stab. **4** raise, erect, stand up, point.
➤*noun* **1** jab, stab, prickle, tingle, pang, spasm, twinge. **2** puncture, perforation, pinhole.

prickle *verb* tingle, smart, prick, sting.
➤*noun* **1** thorn, spike, spine, barb, spur, point, needle. **2** prick, sting, twinge, pang, itch, tickle, tingle, pins and needles.

prickly *adj* **1** thorny, spiky, spiny, barbed, bristly, brambly, scratchy, rough. **2** prickling, tingling, itchy, pricking, smarting, stinging, creeping, crawling. **3** irritable, irascible, ratty (*inf*), crotchety (*inf*), touchy, edgy, fractious, peevish, waspish, grumpy, bad-tempered, cantankerous.

pride *noun* **1** vanity, conceit, self-love, egotism, boastfulness, bigheadedness, smug-
ness, complacency, arrogance, hauteur,
self-importance, presumption. **2** dignity,
self-respect, self-esteem, self-worth, ego,
honour. **3** pleasure, delight, joy, satisfaction, gratification. **4** treasure, jewel, gem,
prize, boast. **5** cream, pick, elite.
pride oneself congratulate oneself, flatter
oneself, preen oneself, take pride, take satisfaction, exult, revel, glory, boast, brag.

priest *noun* clergyman, clergywoman,
cleric, ecclesiastic, minister, vicar, pastor,
father, padre.

prim *adj* formal, proper, decorous, stiff,
staid, strait-laced, stuffy, starchy (*inf*), particular, precise. **2** prudish, puritanical,
priggish, fussy, fastidious, prissy, demure,
modest, po-faced.

primarily *adv* chiefly, principally, mainly,
mostly, first and foremost, basically, fundamentally, predominantly, on the whole.

primary *adj* **1** prime, principal, cardinal,
supreme, paramount, foremost, top, chief,
main, leading. **2** basic, fundamental,
elementary, rudimentary, essential.
3 introductory, preparatory, initial, early,
opening, beginning. **4** earliest, first, original, primeval, primitive, primordial,
primal.

prime *adj* **1** primary, first, paramount,
major, principal, leading, chief, main.
2 first-rate, first-class, excellent, fine, classic, ideal. **3** superior, best, top-quality,
high-grade, choice, select. **4** basic, fundamental, elemental, rudimentary, primary.
➤*noun* zenith, peak, pinnacle, height, heyday, flower, bloom.
➤*verb* **1** prepare, make ready, equip, supply, provide, furnish, fill, charge. **2** brief,
inform, fill in (*inf*), notify, tell.

primeval *adj* primordial, original, aboriginal, primitive, primal, primary, first, earliest, ancient, prehistoric.

primitive *adj* **1** rudimentary, crude, rough,
rude, simple, undeveloped, unsophisticated, unrefined, primal, primary, original.
2 uncivilized, uncultured, barbarian, savage, preliterate, preindustrial. **3** self-taught,
naive, simple, natural, unsophisticated.

primordial *adj* primeval, primitive, primal, primary, first, earliest.

prince *noun* ruler, lord, monarch, sovereign, potentate.

princely *adj* **1** noble, imperial, royal, regal,
majestic, stately, august, imposing, gracious, dignified. **2** magnificent, grand, lavish, rich, sumptuous. **3** generous, liberal,
large, ample.

principal *adj* chief, main, controlling,
dominant, leading, first, foremost,
supreme, primary, cardinal, key.
➤*noun* **1** chief, leader, head, master, boss
(*inf*), director, manager. **2** head, headmas-
ter, headmistress, headteacher. **3** capital,
fund, money, assets, resources. **4** lead, star.

principle *noun* **1** law, rule, standard, criterion, formula, precept, theory, proposition,
truth, tenet, doctrine, dogma. **2** code,
canon, rule, law, belief, credo, philosophy,
maxim, axiom. **3** morals, morality, ethics,
standards, conscience, scruples, decency,
honour, probity, integrity, virtue, honesty.
in principle theoretically, in theory, ideally, in essence, basically.

print *verb* **1** reproduce, copy, run off.
2 stamp, mark, impress, imprint. **3** publish, issue.
➤*noun* **1** impression, imprint, mark,
indentation. **2** type, lettering, letters,
typescript. **3** reproduction, copy, replica,
duplicate, photograph, picture.
in print printed, published, current, available, obtainable, in circulation.

prior *adj* preceding, antecedent, earlier,
anterior, previous, former, foregoing.
prior to before, preceding, earlier than,
until, up to.

priority *noun* **1** prime concern, main
thing, essential, requirement. **2** preference,
urgency, precedence, preeminence,
supremacy. **3** superiority, seniority, prerogative, right of way.

priory *noun* abbey, cloister, monastery,
convent, religious house.

prise *verb* **1** lever, force, jemmy, raise, lift.
2 dislodge, shift, extricate, winkle.

prison *noun* jail, cell, dungeon, penitentiary, nick (*inf*), inside (*inf*), can (*inf*), clink
(*inf*), slammer (*inf*), cooler (*inf*).

prisoner *noun* convict, captive, hostage, internee, detainee, jailbird (*inf*), con (*inf*), lag (*inf*).

pristine *adj* **1** perfect, immaculate, unblemished, unmarked, spotless, clean, fresh, pure, new, in mint condition. **2** original, earliest, first, former, primitive, unspoilt.

privacy *noun* **1** seclusion, retirement, retreat, solitude, isolation, sequestration. **2** peace, secrecy, confidentiality.

private *adj* **1** exclusive, personal, particular, own, special, individual, separate. **2** secret, confidential, personal, intimate, unofficial, off the record, classified, hush-hush (*inf*). **3** reserved, uncommunicative, secretive, retiring, withdrawn, solitary. **4** secluded, quiet, out-of-the-way, sequestered, isolated, remote. **5** independent, privatized, denationalized, self-governing.

privation *noun* deprivation, want, need, necessity, lack, hardship, disadvantage, poverty, penury, austerity, beggary, pauperism.

privilege *noun* **1** right, prerogative, due, entitlement, benefit, advantage, honour, favour. **2** immunity, exemption, dispensation, concession, freedom, liberty, indulgence.

privileged *adj* **1** favoured, advantaged, protected, sheltered, pampered, honoured, ruling, immune, exempt, special. **2** confidential, private, classified, secret, hush-hush (*inf*), unofficial, off the record.

privy *adj* private, personal, secret, confidential.
privy to informed about, acquainted with, aware of, cognizant of, in on (*inf*).
➤ *noun* lavatory, toilet, loo (*inf*), bog (*inf*), latrine, WC.

prize *noun* **1** winnings, jackpot, purse, trophy, medal, award, palm, laurels, reward, premium, haul, spoils. **2** goal, aim, desire, treasure, jewel.
➤ *adj* **1** best, top, champion, winning, prize-winning, award-winning. **2** choice, select, first-class, excellent, outstanding.
➤ *verb* value, treasure, cherish, hold dear, esteem, revere, hold in high regard.

probability *noun* **1** chance, odds, likelihood, likeliness, possibility. **2** likelihood, prospect, expectation, possibility.

probable 1 likely, expected, anticipated, odds-on (*inf*), predictable, foreseeable. **2** credible, believable, plausible, feasible, possible, reasonable.

probation *noun* test period, trial, try-out, apprenticeship.

probe *verb* **1** explore, search, sound, plumb, pierce, prod. **2** investigate, enquire into, study, scrutinize, examine, analyse, research.
➤ *noun* investigation, enquiry, examination, scrutiny, study, research, analysis.

probity *noun* integrity, rectitude, honesty, sincerity, truthfulness, trustworthiness, honour, virtue, morality, principle.

problem *noun* **1** difficulty, complication, snag, trouble, predicament, quandary, dilemma, issue. **2** question, poser, riddle, enigma, puzzle, conundrum, teaser (*inf*).

problematic *adj* **1** difficult, troublesome, awkward, complicated, puzzling, perplexing, ticklish, tricky. **2** dubious, doubtful, questionable, debatable, arguable, moot, uncertain, unsettled.

procedure *noun* **1** methodology, system, technique, plan of action, strategy, scheme, approach, way. **2** formula, routine, rigmarole, steps, actions, processes, operations. **3** process, method, means, modus operandi, policy, custom, practice, rule.

proceed *verb* **1** advance, progress, go, move on, make one's way. **2** continue, carry on, resume. **3** act, go ahead, move, start, begin. **4** prosecute, litigate, take steps, take action. **5** arise, originate, spring, stem, issue, derive, come, result, follow.

proceedings *pl noun* **1** activities, events, action, procedure, happenings, goings-on (*inf*), affairs, dealings, business. **2** minutes, record, report, account, transactions. **3** action, case, lawsuit, trial, process, litigation.

proceeds *pl noun* **1** takings, receipts, returns, yield. **2** profit, gain, income, earnings.

process *noun* **1** procedure, operation, action, system, method, routine, steps, measures. **2** development, evolution, advance, progress, progression, growth,

formation. **3** proceedings, action, case, lawsuit, trial.
➤*verb* **1** handle, deal with, dispose of, fulfil. **2** treat, prepare, refine, convert.
in the process of 1 in the middle of, at the stage of. **2** during, in the course of, in the performance of, in the execution of.

procession *noun* **1** parade, march, column, file, cavalcade, cortège, motorcade. **2** stream, string, series, sequence, run, succession.

proclaim *verb* **1** declare, announce, make known, give out, advertise, publish, broadcast. **2** pronounce, declare, hail. **3** reveal, indicate, show, prove, blazon, trumpet.

proclivity *noun* bent, leaning, inclination, tendency, propensity, predisposition, penchant, predilection, liking, fondness, partiality.

procrastinate *verb* defer, put off, postpone, adjourn, delay, stall, play for time, temporize.

procreate *verb* reproduce, beget, engender, propagate, breed, conceive, generate, produce.

procure *verb* **1** obtain, acquire, secure, gain, come by, get hold of, buy, earn, win. **2** effect, bring about, cause, fix (*inf*), contrive, manage, manipulate.

prod *verb* **1** poke, jab, dig, nudge, push. **2** urge, goad, spur, prompt, stimulate, incite, stir, impel.
➤*noun* **1** poke, jab, dig, nudge, push. **2** goad, spike, stick. **3** prompt, reminder, cue, stimulus, spur, goad, incitement.

prodigal *adj* **1** extravagant, wasteful, spendthrift, thriftless, improvident, reckless, wanton, profligate. **2** generous, liberal, lavish, bountiful, profuse, copious.

prodigious *adj* **1** huge, immense, massive, enormous, colossal, gigantic, vast, immeasurable, tremendous, monumental. **2** wonderful, marvellous, phenomenal, miraculous, extraordinary, exceptional, amazing, astounding, staggering, impressive, remarkable, spectacular.

prodigy *noun* **1** genius, wunderkind, virtuoso, whiz kid (*inf*). **2** marvel, wonder, phenomenon, miracle, sensation. **3** paragon, ideal, epitome, exemplar, paradigm.

produce *verb* **1** bring about, effect, result in, give rise to, generate, engender, occasion, cause, beget, yield. **2** make, manufacture, create, construct, fabricate, build, put together, assemble, turn out. **3** bring out, offer, advance, present, set out, supply, provide, show, reveal. **4** stage, mount, put on, present, perform, direct.
➤*noun* **1** crop, harvest, fruit, vegetables, foodstuffs. **2** product, yield, output.

product *noun* **1** commodity, merchandise, goods, wares, produce, output, article, artefact. **2** result, consequence, effect, outcome, offshoot, spin-off, by-product, legacy.

production *noun* **1** making, creation, manufacture, construction, assembly, preparation, formation, development, presentation. **2** output, yield, harvest, fruit, return, productivity, performance. **3** show, play, concert, film, presentation, performance.

productive *adj* **1** fertile, fecund, rich, fruitful, prolific, creative, busy. **2** profitable, worthwhile, valuable, beneficial, gainful, fruitful, useful. **3** effective, efficient, efficacious, constructive.

productivity *noun* **1** productiveness, fertility, fecundity, fruitfulness. **2** production, output, yield, capacity, work rate, efficiency.

profane *adj* **1** sacrilegious, irreverent, irreligious, impious, ungodly, heathen, pagan, idolatrous. **2** blasphemous, foul, obscene, vulgar, indecent. **3** secular, lay, unhallowed, unsanctified, worldly, temporal.
➤*verb* **1** desecrate, violate, defile. **2** debase, corrupt, pervert, abuse, misuse, vitiate.

profanity *noun* **1** blasphemy, obscenity, indecency. **2** swearword, four-letter word (*inf*), expletive, curse, obscenity, oath. **3** profaneness, sacrilege, idolatry, irreverence, irreligion, impiety, ungodliness.

profess *verb* **1** claim, maintain, allege, make out, pretend, fake, feign. **2** assert, proclaim, declare, announce, affirm, aver, acknowledge, admit. **3** declare, avow, confess, confirm, acknowledge.

professed *adj* **1** acknowledged, self-confessed, confirmed, declared, avowed. **2** self-styled, so-called, would-be. **3** pretended, feigned, sham, fake, false, supposed, alleged, purported.

profession *noun* **1** business, trade, occupation, job, métier, vocation, career, line, walk of life, sphere. **2** declaration, announcement, affirmation, averment, acknowledgment, admission. **3** declaration, statement, confession, avowal, testimony, claim, assertion, protestation.

professional *adj* **1** skilled, trained, qualified, licensed, chartered. **2** competent, businesslike, expert, masterly, skilful, proficient, polished, refined. **3** paid, career, vocational.
➤ *noun* **1** specialist, authority. **2** expert, master, virtuoso, pro (*inf*), ace (*inf*).

proffer *verb* offer, tender, advance, extend, give, hold out, present.

proficient *adj* skilled, expert, masterly, adept, deft, practised, experienced, capable, able, accomplished, talented, good.

profile *noun* **1** silhouette, outline, shape, form, contour, figure. **2** study, analysis, biography, characterization, curriculum vitae, thumbnail sketch, portrait, vignette.

profit *noun* **1** excess, surplus, gain, return, yield, proceeds, interest, dividend. **2** advantage, benefit, good, gain, dividend, use, value, worth.
➤ *verb* **1** gain, make money, benefit, capitalize on, cash in on, take advantage of, exploit, put to good use. **2** pay, serve, help, avail, benefit.

profitable *adj* lucrative, remunerative, cost-effective, economic, commercial, money-making, profit-making, productive, rewarding, worthwhile, useful, beneficial, advantageous.

profligate *adj* **1** dissolute, dissipated, debauched, abandoned, loose, licentious, promiscuous, wanton, immoral, degenerate, depraved, corrupt. **2** extravagant, prodigal, wasteful, spendthrift, thriftless, reckless, immoderate, improvident.
➤ *noun* rake, roué, libertine, degenerate, reprobate, wastrel, spendthrift, prodigal.

profound *adj* **1** deep, bottomless, fathomless, abysmal. **2** sagacious, wise, learned, erudite, intellectual, knowledgeable, thoughtful, philosophical. **3** abstruse, abstract, complex, difficult, impenetrable, recondite, esoteric. **4** intense, keen, great, extreme, heartfelt, deep, utter, absolute.

profuse *adj* **1** generous, liberal, unstinting, open-handed, lavish, extravagant, prodi-

gal. **2** abundant, copious, ample, full, plentiful, bountiful, luxuriant, exuberant.

progeny *noun* **1** descendants, issue, offspring, children, family. **2** offspring, young.

prognosis *noun* **1** assessment, evaluation, prognostication, expectation, outlook, prospect. **2** forecast, speculation, prediction, projection.

programme *noun* **1** listing, line-up, schedule, timetable, agenda, calendar. **2** prospectus, curriculum, syllabus. **3** show, production, episode, broadcast, transmission. **4** plan, scheme.
➤ *verb* **1** arrange, organize, plan, map out. **2** schedule, line up, book, list, bill.

progress *noun* **1** advance, movement, progression, headway, course. **2** evolution, growth, development, improvement, amelioration, furtherance, advancement, promotion, breakthrough.
➤ *verb* **1** advance, proceed, go on, move forward, make headway, travel. **2** grow, develop, advance, make strides, flourish, prosper, improve, ameliorate.

progression *noun* **1** progress, passage, advance, headway, development. **2** succession, series, string, chain, sequence.

progressive *adj* **1** advancing, continuous, forward, onward. **2** growing, increasing, escalating, intensifying, developing. **3** forward-looking, modern, avant-garde, advanced, enlightened, liberal, enterprising, go-ahead, innovative, reformist, revisionist, revolutionary.

prohibit *verb* **1** forbid, disallow, ban, outlaw, proscribe, veto, bar, interdict. **2** stop, prevent, hamper, impede. **3** preclude, exclude, rule out, obstruct.

prohibition *noun* **1** forbidding, banning, proscription, interdiction, prevention. **2** ban, bar, veto, embargo, boycott, injunction.

prohibitive *adj* **1** restrictive, preventive, repressive, proscriptive, prohibitory, forbidding. **2** exorbitant, extortionate, excessive, steep (*inf*).

project noun **1** proposal, plan, scheme, design, idea. **2** campaign, operation, enterprise, undertaking, venture, task, job, assignment.
➤verb **1** propose, intend, contemplate, devise, contrive, design, frame. **2** plan, calculate, estimate, gauge, reckon, extrapolate, predict, forecast. **3** cast, throw, hurl, fling, propel, shoot, eject, launch. **4** jut out, protrude, stick out, bulge, overhang, extend.

projectile noun missile, shell, shot, bullet, ball.

projection noun **1** protrusion, protuberance, bulge, prominence, overhang, ledge, shelf, ridge. **2** estimate, prediction, forecast, extrapolation, plan, proposal, blueprint, design. **3** diagram, representation.

proletariat noun working class, lower class, plebs (inf), proles (inf), commonalty, masses, mob, herd, rank and file, hoi polloi, common people, great unwashed (inf).

proliferate verb **1** reproduce, breed, multiply, burgeon, run riot. **2** increase, expand, spread, escalate, mushroom, snowball.

prolific adj **1** fertile, fecund, fruitful, copious, profuse, abundant, rank, teeming. **2** productive, fertile, inventive, creative.

prolix adj **1** long-winded, lengthy, prolonged, protracted, long-drawn-out, tedious, boring. **2** verbose, wordy, diffuse, rambling, discursive, digressive.

prologue noun **1** introduction, preface, foreword, preamble. **2** preliminary, prelude.

prolong verb **1** protract, draw out, spin out, drag out, continue, sustain, perpetuate, carry on, keep up. **2** extend, lengthen, stretch, elongate.

prominence noun **1** protuberance, projection, bulge, mound, hump, lump, swelling, elevation, protrusion, overhang. **2** conspicuousness, importance, precedence, eminence, illustriousness, distinction, greatness, note, prestige, fame, renown.

prominent adj **1** conspicuous, noticeable, marked, pronounced, striking, eye-catching, obvious, evident. **2** eminent, distinguished, respected, notable, famous, celebrated, renowned, illustrious, well-

known, popular, leading. **3** projecting, bulging, jutting, protruding, protuberant.

promiscuous adj loose, wanton, abandoned, profligate, dissolute, immoral, debauched, unchaste.

promise verb **1** pledge, vow, swear, give one's word, undertake, engage, contract, guarantee, vouch. **2** augur, presage, betoken, suggest, indicate, signify.
➤noun **1** pledge, vow, oath, word, assurance, guarantee, commitment, undertaking, contract, covenant, bond. **2** potential, capacity, capability, aptitude, talent, flair, sign, indication.

promising adj hopeful, likely, encouraging, optimistic, favourable, auspicious, propitious, able, gifted, budding, up-and-coming (inf).

promontory noun **1** headland, foreland, cape, point, peninsula, cliff, bluff. **2** projection, prominence, ridge, spur.

promote verb **1** further, advance, forward, support, sponsor, boost, encourage, espouse, champion, foster, nurture, cultivate. **2** upgrade, raise, elevate, prefer, aggrandize, kick upstairs (inf). **3** advertise, publicize, market, sell, push, plug (inf), hype (inf), advocate, recommend, endorse.

promotion noun **1** advancement, preferment, elevation, upgrading, aggrandizement. **2** advocacy, recommendation, endorsement, encouragement, furtherance, development, support, backing, publicity, advertising, marketing, propaganda.

prompt adj **1** immediate, instant, instantaneous, direct, quick, brisk, sharp, smart. **2** ready, eager, alert, willing, swift, quick. **3** punctual, timely, on time.
➤adv promptly, punctually, sharp, precisely, to the minute, on the dot.
➤verb **1** make, induce, impel, move, spur, incite, stimulate, motivate, inspire. **2** cause, occasion, provoke, urge, encourage. **3** cue, remind, help, hint, prod.
➤noun cue, reminder, prod, jolt, hint, spur, stimulus, encouragement.

promulgate verb **1** make known, announce, proclaim, declare, cry, trumpet, broadcast, publish. **2** proclaim, decree, enact, ordain. **3** publicize, spread, disseminate, circulate, advertise, promote.

propose

prone *adj* **1** apt, inclined, disposed, liable, likely, given, subject, susceptible. **2** prostrate, flat, horizontal, recumbent.

prong *noun* point, tip, spike, spur, tine.

pronounce *verb* **1** utter, articulate, enunciate, voice, vocalize, say, speak, sound. **2** proclaim, declare, announce, decree.

pronounced *adj* marked, distinct, noticeable, conspicuous, obvious, striking, definite, clear, strong, positive.

pronunciation *noun* speech, diction, elocution, enunciation, articulation, vocalization, delivery, accent, stress, inflection, intonation, modulation.

proof *noun* **1** evidence, documentation, testimony, demonstration. **2** confirmation, substantiation, verification, validation, authentication, corroboration. **3** sample, galley, print, impression.
➤*adj* resistant, repellent, impervious, impenetrable, tight, proofed, treated.

prop *noun* **1** support, brace, upright, buttress, stay, column, pillar, post, pole, strut. **2** supporter, pillar, mainstay, anchor, rock, backbone, support.
➤*verb* **1** support, hold up, underpin, shore up, brace, bolster, buttress, reinforce. **2** lean, rest, stand, lay, balance, steady.
prop up sustain, uphold, support, maintain, subsidize, finance.

propaganda *noun* **1** publicity, promotion, advertising, ballyhoo (*inf*), indoctrination, brainwashing. **2** information, disinformation, agitprop.

propagate *verb* **1** reproduce, breed, increase, multiply. **2** disseminate, spread, circulate, publish, broadcast, communicate, transmit, distribute. **3** promulgate, proclaim, make known, advertise, publicize, promote.

propel *verb* **1** drive, impel, push, thrust, move, launch, start, shoot, throw, send. **2** urge, drive, impel, spur, motivate.

propensity *noun* tendency, disposition, inclination, proclivity, leaning, aptness, liability.

proper *adj* **1** correct, right, accurate, strict, accepted, established, customary, conventional, orthodox. **2** appropriate, suitable, right, fitting. **3** acceptable, seemly, becoming, decorous, decent, polite, respectable, genteel, prim, formal. **4** own, special, specific, respective, individual, particular, peculiar, personal. **5** real, actual, genuine, true. **6** complete, total, utter, thorough.

property *noun* **1** possessions, effects, belongings, goods, chattels, assets, means, wealth. **2** land, realty, estate, holding, house, building, premises. **3** attribute, quality, ability, power, characteristic, feature, trait, peculiarity.

prophecy *noun* **1** prediction, forecast, prognostication, augury. **2** clairvoyance, fortune-telling, soothsaying, second sight.

prophesy *verb* predict, foresee, divine, prognosticate, forecast, augur, presage.

prophet *noun* soothsayer, seer, clairvoyant, fortune-teller, augur, oracle, sibyl, diviner, forecaster, prognosticator.

prophetic *adj* predictive, prognostic, oracular, augural, divinatory, prescient, portentous.

propinquity *noun* **1** nearness, closeness, proximity, vicinity, contiguity, adjacency. **2** affiliation, kinship, consanguinity, relationship, connection.

propitiate *verb* pacify, placate, appease, mollify, satisfy, conciliate.

propitious *adj* **1** auspicious, bright, rosy, promising, optimistic, encouraging. **2** favourable, advantageous, beneficial, timely, opportune, lucky, fortunate.

proponent *noun* advocate, supporter, upholder, promoter, champion, defender, apologist.

proportion *noun* **1** ratio, relationship, distribution. **2** balance, symmetry, harmony. **3** agreement, correspondence, uniformity, congruity. **4** share, portion, quota, ration, part. **5** fraction, percentage.
➤*verb* **1** adjust, fit. **2** arrange, balance, harmonize.

proportional *adj* proportionate, relative, balanced, symmetrical, corresponding, commensurate, equivalent.

proportions *pl noun* dimensions, measurements, size, magnitude, scale, extent, capacity, volume.

proposal *noun* proposition, presentation, suggestion, recommendation, offer, tender, bid, motion, plan, idea.

propose *verb* **1** suggest, recommend, move, put forward, submit, table, present, introduce, offer, tender, propound. **2** nominate, name, put up, recommend, suggest. **3** plan, intend, aim, mean, have in mind. **4** pop the question (*inf*), plight one's troth.

proposition *noun* **1** proposal, suggestion, theory, idea, scheme, plan, project, programme. **2** challenge, problem, undertaking, job, task, venture. **3** advance, overture, approach, pass, come-on (*inf*).
➤*verb* accost, solicit.

propound *verb* propose, present, put forward, set forth, advance, submit, contend, postulate, state, declare.

proprietor *noun* owner, possessor, holder, landowner, freeholder, leaseholder, landlord, landlady.

proprieties *pl noun* etiquette, protocol, manners, formalities.

propriety *noun* **1** correctness, fitness, appropriateness, orthodoxy. **2** seemliness, decorum, courtesy, politeness, respectability, modesty, decency.

propulsion *noun* drive, motive force, power, thrust, momentum, impetus.

prosaic *adj* dry, flat, commonplace, mundane, bland, vapid, dull, boring, pedestrian, everyday, trite, banal.

proscribe *verb* **1** condemn, denounce, censure, interdict, prohibit, forbid, ban, bar. **2** outlaw, exile, banish, expel, deport, expatriate, blackball, ostracize.

prosecute *verb* **1** sue, take to court, prefer charges, summon, charge, arraign, indict, accuse, try. **2** pursue, follow through, proceed with, discharge, see through, bring to an end. **3** conduct, carry on, engage in, pursue.

prospect *noun* **1** chance, possibility, probability, likelihood, expectation, hope, promise, anticipation. **2** thought, idea, outlook. **3** view, vista, scene, landscape, panorama.
➤*verb* explore, examine, inspect, survey, search.

prospective *adj* **1** imminent, impending, planned, forthcoming, expected, anticipated, likely, probable. **2** future, intended, destined, to-be, potential, likely, possible, eventual, would-be, aspiring.

prospectus *noun* syllabus, manifesto, programme, plan, announcement, statement, notice, list, catalogue, brochure.

prosper *verb* thrive, flourish, boom, succeed, do well, make good, advance, progress, flower, bloom.

prosperity *noun* success, boom, fortune, plenty, affluence, wealth.

prosperous *adj* thriving, flourishing, successful, booming, rich, wealthy, affluent, well-off.

prostitute *noun* whore, harlot, fallen woman, courtesan, call girl, streetwalker, tart (*inf*), hooker (*inf*).
➤*verb* devalue, cheapen, debase, degrade, demean, misuse, profane.

prostrate *verb* **1** lie down, stretch out. **2** bow, kneel, kowtow, grovel. **3** overcome, overpower, overwhelm, crush, exhaust, weary, fatigue, sap.
➤*adj* **1** flat, horizontal, lying down, stretched out, recumbent. **2** prone, face down. **3** overcome, overwhelmed, crushed, devastated, helpless, laid low, exhausted, weary, all in (*inf*), desolate, heartbroken. **4** procumbent, trailing.

protagonist *noun* **1** hero, heroine, principal, lead, title role. **2** supporter, advocate, exponent, champion, promoter, leader, prime mover.

protect *verb* **1** defend, guard, escort, safeguard, secure, shield, shelter, look after, take care of. **2** screen, cover, shield, mask, conceal. **3** keep, save, preserve, conserve.

protection *noun* **1** safety, safekeeping, conservation, preservation, security, defence, insurance, guardianship, aegis, care, custody, charge. **2** shield, barrier, screen, cover, shelter, guard, safeguard, precaution.

protective *adj* defensive, insulating, prophylactic, fatherly, motherly, watchful, possessive.

protector *noun* defender, champion, guard, guardian, bodyguard, minder, safeguard, shield.

protégé *noun* pupil, student, ward, dependant, charge.

protest *verb* **1** object, complain, appeal, oppose, disagree, demur, expostulate, kick up a fuss (*inf*). **2** demonstrate, march, rally,

strike. **3** maintain, contend, insist, profess, argue, assert, aver, attest, declare, proclaim.
➤*noun* **1** objection, complaint, appeal, disapproval, opposition, demurral, dissent, exception, disagreement, expostulation, outcry. **2** demonstration, demo (*inf*), march, riot, boycott.

protestation *noun* **1** declaration, profession, assertion, affirmation, assurance, asseveration, avowal, pledge. **2** protest, objection, complaint, outcry, opposition, dissent, disagreement.

protocol *noun* procedure, etiquette, custom, convention, formalities, proprieties, decorum, good form.

prototype *noun* **1** original, model, mock-up, pattern, standard. **2** archetype, exemplar, ideal, paradigm.

protract *verb* prolong, draw out, spin out, drag out (*inf*), extend, lengthen, elongate, stretch.

protrude *verb* project, point, stick out, stand out, jut out, extend, bulge.

protuberant *adj* bulging, swollen, bulbous, prominent, proud, protruding, protrusive.

proud *adj* **1** satisfied, contented, gratified, pleased, happy, delighted, thrilled. **2** conceited, vain, self-satisfied, smug, egotistic, self-important, bigheaded (*inf*), arrogant, haughty, supercilious. **3** self-respecting, dignified, noble, high-minded, honourable. **4** memorable, notable, red-letter (*inf*), glorious, pleasing, gratifying, satisfying, rewarding. **5** noble, majestic, stately, grand, magnificent, splendid, imposing, distinguished.

prove *verb* **1** demonstrate, show, verify, certify, attest, confirm, authenticate, corroborate, substantiate, justify, validate, bear out. **2** turn out, end up, transpire, eventuate. **3** test, try, assay, examine, analyse, check.

proverb *noun* saying, maxim, aphorism, adage, saw, precept.

proverbial *adj* **1** axiomatic, self-evident, traditional, time-honoured. **2** acknowledged, accepted, famous, well-known, legendary.

provide *verb* **1** supply, contribute, provision, purvey, stock, maintain, support, sus-
tain, keep. **2** furnish, equip, outfit, kit out. **3** give, lend, afford, impart, yield, produce. **4** prepare, take precautions, anticipate, allow, make provision, plan, cater, arrange. **5** stipulate, specify, lay down, state, require.

provided *conj* providing, given, as long as, on condition, on the understanding, with the proviso, contingent on, subject to, if.

providence *noun* **1** fate, destiny, fortune, luck, divine intervention, God. **2** prudence, wisdom, sagacity, circumspection, foresight, forethought, caution, economy, frugality, thrift.

provident *adj* **1** judicious, farsighted, prudent, wise, sagacious, circumspect, careful, cautious, shrewd, canny, well-prepared. **2** economical, frugal, thrifty.

providing *conj* provided, given, as long as, on condition, on the understanding, with the proviso, contingent on, subject to, if.

province *noun* **1** region, area, district, division, zone, colony, dependency, county, shire, department. **2** field, area, patch, domain, turf (*inf*), role, function, duty, concern, responsibility, business, pigeon (*inf*). **3** discipline, speciality, field, sphere, area, line.

provincial *adj* **1** regional, state, local, rural, country. **2** unsophisticated, unrefined, uncouth, rustic. **3** parochial, insular, limited, narrow, parish-pump, small-town, bigoted, prejudiced, narrow-minded, small-minded.
➤*noun* bumpkin, country cousin, yokel, rustic, peasant.

provision *noun* **1** preparation, precaution, measure, step, arrangement, allowance, concession. **2** providing, supply, facility, amenity, service. **3** clause, term, requirement, stipulation, specification, condition, proviso, reservation, restriction, limitation, qualification, rider.

provisional *adj* temporary, interim, pro tem (*inf*), transitional, stopgap, makeshift, conditional, contingent, provisory, tentative.

provisions *pl noun* food, foodstuffs, victuals, comestibles, groceries, rations, supplies, stores.

proviso *noun* **1** clause, term, specification, provision, restriction, limitation, rider.

2 requirement, stipulation, condition, reservation, qualification.

provocation *noun* **1** harassment, irritation, aggravation (*inf*), incitement, stimulus, motivation, instigation, encouragement. **2** taunt, insult, affront, offence, injury, challenge.

provocative *adj* offensive, insulting, irritating, aggravating (*inf*), alluring, tantalizing, suggestive, seductive, titillating, erotic, stimulating.

provoke *verb* **1** anger, enrage, infuriate, aggravate (*inf*), incense, madden, exasperate, tease, taunt, wind up (*inf*), insult, offend. **2** inspire, prompt, excite, rouse, induce, encourage, stimulate, motivate, spur, move. **3** instigate, cause, occasion, bring about, stir up, evoke, elicit, call forth, engender, produce, lead to, precipitate.

prow *noun* bow, sharp end (*inf*), fore, stem, front, head, nose.

prowess *noun* **1** skill, ability, expertise, mastery, genius, talent, dexterity, aptitude, facility, competence, proficiency, accomplishment. **2** strength, might, bravery, heroism, valour, gallantry, courage, fortitude.

prowl *verb* roam, rove, range, steal, sneak, creep, skulk, lurk, scavenge, search, hunt, snoop (*inf*).

proximity *noun* nearness, closeness, propinquity, vicinity, contiguity, adjacency, juxtaposition.

proxy *noun* substitute, agent, representative, deputy, surrogate, stand-in.

prude *noun* prig, old maid, puritan, goody-goody (*inf*).

prudence *noun* **1** wisdom, judgment, sagacity, shrewdness, common sense, farsightedness, foresight, forethought. **2** caution, cautiousness, discretion, circumspection, care, carefulness, wariness, vigilance. **3** providence, thrift, economy, saving, husbandry, frugality.

prune *verb* **1** trim, thin out, cut back, shape, clip, lop, remove. **2** cut, pare down, trim, shorten, reduce, condense.

prurient *adj* lustful, lecherous, lewd, salacious, lubricious, concupiscent, voyeuristic, erotic, obscene, pornographic, indecent.

pry *verb* meddle, interfere, question, enquire, nose, snoop (*inf*), ferret, dig, spy, peep.

psalm *noun* hymn, song, canticle, chant, anthem, paean.

pseudo *adj* false, sham, phoney (*inf*), mock, simulated, feigned, fake, bogus, quasi, spurious.

pseudonym *noun* alias, incognito, assumed name, false name, pen name, nom de plume, nom de guerre, stage name, sobriquet, nickname.

psyche *noun* **1** soul, self, ego, anima, personality, individuality. **2** mind, intellect, intelligence, understanding, awareness, consciousness, subconscious.

psychiatry *noun* psychoanalysis, psychotherapy, psychology.

psychic *adj* **1** supernatural, paranormal, extrasensory, mystic, occult, clairvoyant, telepathic, telekinetic, spiritualistic. **2** spiritual, psychological, mental, cognitive.

psychological *adj* mental, cerebral, intellectual, psychic, cognitive, subconscious, unconscious, subjective, emotional, psychosomatic, all in the mind.

psychology *noun* **1** behaviourism, science of the mind, study of personality. **2** mind, mindset, thought processes, behavioural characteristics, mental chemistry, way of thinking.

psychopath *noun* lunatic, maniac, psychotic, sociopath.

pub *noun* public house, bar, local (*inf*), boozer (*inf*), inn, tavern, hostelry (*inf*).

puberty *noun* pubescence, adolescence, teens, youth.

public *adj* **1** communal, common, open, unrestricted, accessible. **2** state, government, nationalized, civic, civil, official. **3** national, community, social. **4** general, universal, widespread, popular. **5** open, overt, plain, exposed, unconcealed. **6** known, acknowledged, recognized, published. **7** famous, well-known, celebrated, prominent, eminent, illustrious, influential.
➤*noun* **1** population, people, nation, community, society, populace, commonalty, hoi polloi, multitude, masses, citizens,

electorate. **2** followers, supporters, fans, admirers, audience, spectators.

in public publicly, openly, in the open, for all to see.

publication *noun* **1** publishing, printing, production, distribution, circulation, dissemination, announcement, promulgation, disclosure, appearance. **2** book, title, magazine, newspaper, journal, pamphlet, brochure, edition, issue.

publicity *noun* **1** promotion, advertising, marketing, hype (*inf*). **2** public attention, media interest.

publicize *verb* announce, make known, disseminate, promulgate, promote, advertise, market, push (*inf*), plug (*inf*), hype (*inf*).

publish *verb* **1** produce, issue, release, bring out, distribute, circulate. **2** print, report. **3** announce, declare, proclaim, make public. **4** communicate, disclose, reveal, divulge, leak, expose.

pucker *verb* gather, wrinkle, crease, ruffle, pleat, furrow, purse, screw up, knit.

pudding *noun* dessert, sweet, afters (*inf*), pud (*inf*).

puerile *adj* childish, babyish, infantile, juvenile, immature, silly, irresponsible, frivolous.

puff *noun* **1** gust, blast, whiff, breath, draught, waft. **2** pull, drag. **3** praise, commendation, publicity, promotion, plug (*inf*).
➤*verb* **1** blow, breathe, exhale. **2** pant, wheeze, gasp, gulp. **3** swell, dilate. **4** inflate, blow up, distend, bloat. **5** smoke, suck, draw, pull, drag (*inf*). **6** praise, flatter, advertise, promote, push (*inf*), plug (*inf*), hype (*inf*), crack up (*inf*).

puffy *adj* puffed up, swollen, bloated, enlarged, dilated, distended.

pugnacious *adj* belligerent, hostile, combative, aggressive, irascible, bad-tempered, quarrelsome, argumentative, contentious, disputatious, petulant, choleric.

pull *verb* **1** draw, heave, tug, jerk, yank (*inf*). **2** drag, haul, tow, trail. **3** pluck, pick, withdraw, uproot, extract, remove, detach. **4** take out, bring out, draw, produce. **5** strain, wrench, sprain, dislocate. **6** tear, rip, rend. **7** attract, seduce, allure, entice.
➤*noun* **1** drag, tow, haul, tug, jerk, yank

(*inf*). **2** power, force, draw, magnetism, attraction, lure, appeal, influence, weight, clout (*inf*).

pull apart 1 take to pieces, tear apart, dismantle, separate, break, dismember. **2** criticize, take apart, pull to pieces (*inf*), blast, slate (*inf*), slam (*inf*).

pull back withdraw, fall back, retreat, retire, disengage.

pull down knock down, demolish, level, raze, bulldoze, destroy.

pull in 1 pull up, stop, draw up, park. **2** attract, draw, bring in, lure. **3** arrest, apprehend, detain, take into custody, run in (*inf*), nick (*inf*). **4** earn, receive, make, clear, net, take home, pocket, rake in (*inf*).

pull off accomplish, achieve, bring off, execute, carry out.

pull out leave, quit, withdraw, retreat, back out, give up.

pull up 1 stop, halt, brake, draw up, pull in, park. **2** reprimand, rebuke, admonish, scold, take to task, tell off (*inf*), tick off (*inf*).

pulp *noun* **1** flesh, soft part. **2** paste, purée. **3** mash, mush, pap, slop.
➤*verb* crush, squash, mash, pulverize, liquidize, purée.

pulsate *verb* **1** beat, pulse, pound, drum. **2** throb, palpitate, vibrate, oscillate, quiver.

pulse *noun* **1** beat, throb, thud, thump. **2** rhythm, beating, throbbing, pulsation, vibration, oscillation.
➤*verb* beat, throb, pound, pulsate, palpitate, vibrate.

pulverize *verb* **1** powder, pound, crush, mash, grind, mill, crumble, comminute, triturate. **2** destroy, annihilate, crush, defeat, trounce, thrash (*inf*), hammer (*inf*), lick (*inf*).

pummel *verb* batter, beat, thump, pound, hammer, punch, belabour.

pump *verb* **1** drive, force, push, send, draw. **2** inflate, blow up, fill. **3** interrogate, question, quiz, cross-examine, grill (*inf*).

pun *noun* play on words, double entendre, witticism, quip.

punch[1] *verb* hit, box, thump, pummel, batter, cuff, jab, slug (*inf*), bash (*inf*), wallop (*inf*), sock (*inf*).
➤*noun* **1** blow, thump, box, cuff, jab, bash (*inf*), sock (*inf*), slug (*inf*). **2** strength, force,

power, impact, effectiveness, forcefulness, energy, vigour, bite (*inf*), oomph (*inf*).

punch[2] *verb* pierce, puncture, perforate, prick, bore, drill, stamp.

punctilious *adj* 1 strict, precise, correct, proper, formal, ceremonious. 2 meticulous, scrupulous, conscientious, careful, particular, fussy, finicky, pernickety (*inf*), nice, minute.

punctual *adj* 1 prompt, on time, in good time, on the dot (*inf*). 2 exact, precise, regular.

punctuate *verb* interrupt, break up, intersperse, sprinkle, pepper.

puncture *noun* hole, perforation, rupture, prick, opening, leak.
➤*verb* 1 burst, rupture, pierce, penetrate, prick, perforate, cut, punch. 2 deflate, prick, let down, flatten, put a dent in (*inf*).

pundit *noun* authority, expert, master, guru, teacher, sage, savant.

pungent *adj* 1 acrid, sharp, biting, strong, powerful, hot, spicy, piquant, bitter, sour. 2 cutting, sharp, incisive, caustic, stinging, biting, barbed, trenchant, acerbic, mordant. 3 pointed, telling.

punish *verb* 1 discipline, penalize, correct, chastise, castigate, beat, flog, execute, imprison, fine. 2 misuse, abuse, maltreat, mistreat, damage, harm.

punishing *adj* arduous, demanding, strenuous, taxing, hard, harsh, severe, gruelling, exhausting, backbreaking.

punishment *noun* 1 discipline, correction, chastisement, castigation, retribution. 2 penalty, sentence. 3 abuse, misuse, mistreatment, maltreatment, manhandling, damage, harm.

punitive *adj* 1 penal, disciplinary, corrective, castigatory, retaliatory, retributive. 2 punishing, crippling, crushing, hard, harsh, severe, gruelling, demanding, taxing, stiff.

puny *adj* 1 weak, feeble, frail, sickly, small, slight, stunted, undersized, diminutive, minor, insignificant, inferior. 2 meagre, paltry, measly (*inf*), piddling (*inf*).

pupil *noun* student, scholar, schoolchild, learner, beginner, novice, apprentice, trainee.

puppet *noun* 1 marionette, dummy. 2 pawn, stooge, poodle, cat's-paw, tool, instrument, figurehead.

purchase *verb* buy, pay for, procure, acquire, pick up, invest in.
➤*noun* 1 acquisition, buy, investment. 2 grasp, grip, hold, foothold, footing.

pure *adj* 1 unadulterated, unmixed, unalloyed. 2 undiluted, neat, real, authentic, genuine, natural, solid, perfect, flawless. 3 clear, fresh, clean, unpolluted, uncontaminated, untainted, sterile, aseptic, hygienic, sanitary. 4 chaste, virginal, immaculate, undefiled, unsullied. 5 moral, uncorrupted, unblemished, impeccable, spotless, virtuous, honourable, noble, righteous, innocent, blameless. 6 sheer, downright, utter, unmitigated, out-and-out, mere, perfect, thorough, absolute. 7 theoretical, conceptual, abstract, conjectural, academic.

purgative *noun* laxative, emetic, enema, purge, cathartic, aperient.

purge *verb* 1 cleanse, purify, clear. 2 rid, clear, empty, free. 3 expel, eject, oust, depose, remove, weed out, eliminate, dismiss, do away with, kill.
➤*noun* purgation, cleansing, purification, eradication, elimination, liquidation, witch hunt, removal, ejection, expulsion.

purify *verb* 1 cleanse, clean, wash, distil, filter, clarify, refine, decontaminate, disinfect, sanitize, sterilize, fumigate. 2 purge, redeem, sanctify, exculpate, clear, absolve, shrive.

purist *noun* pedant, dogmatist, literalist, formalist, stickler.

puritan *noun* moralist, disciplinarian, zealot, fanatic, prude, killjoy, goody-goody (*inf*).

purity *noun* pureness, clarity, cleanliness, spotlessness, perfection, authenticity, simplicity, chastity, virginity, virtue, honour, innocence.

purloin *verb* steal, pilfer, pinch (*inf*), nick (*inf*), lift (*inf*), knock off (*inf*), pocket (*inf*), filch (*inf*), embezzle, appropriate.

purport *verb* claim, profess, seem, pretend, allege, maintain, assert, declare, imply, suggest.
➤*noun* 1 meaning, significance, import,

implication, drift, point, gist, thrust.
2 purpose, intention, object, aim, design, scheme, goal, plan.

purpose noun **1** reason, basis, point, motivation, cause, justification, rationale, intention. **2** aim, object, objective, end, goal, target, ambition, desire, wish, plan, design. **3** resolution, resolve, determination, will, drive, perseverance, tenacity, doggedness, single-mindedness, dedication, zeal. **4** avail, effect, good, use, advantage, benefit, gain, profit, value.
➤*verb* mean, intend, plan, propose, aim, aspire, resolve, decide, determine.
on purpose purposely, deliberately, intentionally, wilfully, wittingly, knowingly, consciously, by design.

purposeful adj determined, decided, resolved, resolute, positive, deliberate, firm, set, dogged, tenacious, single-minded, strong-willed.

purposely adv on purpose, intentionally, with intent, by design, deliberately, expressly, consciously, wilfully, knowingly, wittingly.

purse noun **1** wallet, moneybag, pouch. **2** funds, finances, resources, coffers, treasury, exchequer, means, wherewithal. **3** prize, reward, award, present, gift.
➤*verb* pucker, pout, wrinkle, knit, compress, contract, tighten, close.

pursue verb **1** follow, chase, go after, run after, hunt, stalk, trail, track, shadow, tail (*inf*). **2** seek, search for, aspire to, aim for, strive for, work towards. **3** proceed with, continue with, carry on with, persist with, see through. **4** practise, engage in, conduct, prosecute, ply, work at, apply oneself to. **5** follow up, chase up, maintain, hold to.

pursuit noun **1** chase, hunt, hue and cry, search, quest. **2** occupation, business, profession, trade, craft, hobby, pastime, activity, interest, recreation.

purvey verb provide, supply, stock, cater, provision, sell, retail, deal in, trade in.

push verb **1** shove, thrust, press, squeeze, prod, nudge, elbow, ram, butt. **2** drive, propel, move, force, squash, cram, manhandle. **3** press, urge, encourage, egg on (*inf*), incite, impel, spur, goad, persuade, pressurize, force, coerce. **4** promote, market, advertise, plug (*inf*), hype (*inf*).

➤*noun* **1** shove, thrust, nudge, prod, poke, butt. **2** effort, endeavour, drive, attack, offensive, onslaught. **3** energy, vigour, dynamism, drive, determination, forcefulness, ambition, enterprise, initiative, enthusiasm, spirit, gumption (*inf*).

push around bully, terrorize, domineer, intimidate, victimize, trample on, browbeat, tyrannize.

push off go away, depart, leave, get out, shove off, buzz off (*inf*), clear off (*inf*), beat it (*inf*), get lost (*inf*).

pushover noun **1** walkover, child's play (*inf*), picnic (*inf*), doddle (*inf*), piece of cake (*inf*), cinch (*inf*), breeze (*inf*). **2** dupe, sap, soft touch (*inf*), sucker (*inf*), mug (*inf*).

pushy adj forward, bold, ambitious, enterprising, go-ahead, dynamic, forceful, assertive, aggressive, presumptuous, arrogant, bumptious.

pusillanimous adj timid, timorous, fearful, cowardly, gutless (*inf*), faint-hearted, lily-livered, chicken (*inf*), spineless, craven, weak, feeble.

pustule noun abscess, ulcer, eruption, gathering, blister, pimple, spot, zit (*inf*), boil, carbuncle.

put verb **1** place, set, lay, deposit, dump (*inf*), plonk (*inf*), situate, locate, position, stand, install, fix. **2** impose, inflict, subject, condemn, sentence, consign, doom. **3** apply, use, employ, utilize, assign, allocate, devote, dedicate, invest, spend, give, contribute. **4** value, evaluate, assess, calculate, estimate, reckon, guess. **5** advance, put forward, propose, present, offer, submit, tender, utter, state, formulate, express.

put about tell, spread, make known, circulate, publicize, broadcast, announce, disseminate, propagate, bandy about.

put across communicate, get across, put over, convey, make clear, explain, express.

put aside 1 save, reserve, put by, set aside, lay down, put away, hoard, stockpile, store, stash (*inf*). **2** ignore, disregard, set aside, discard, dispense with, abandon, drop, forget.

put away 1 save, keep, reserve, set aside, put by, store, lay in, stockpile. **2** consume, devour, eat, drink, down, bolt, gobble, wolf (*inf*), guzzle (*inf*), scoff (*inf*), polish off (*inf*). **3** imprison, jail, lock up, send down (*inf*), confine, shut away, incarcerate, certify, institutionalize.

put back replace, put away, tidy up.

put down 1 record, write down, set down, jot down, make a note of, inscribe. **2** enter, log, register, list. **3** suppress, quash, quell, crush, stamp out, extinguish, stop. **4** kill, destroy, put to sleep, put out of its misery. **5** disparage, slight, belittle, criticize, deprecate, knock (*inf*), humiliate, humble, mortify, deflate, squash, crush.

put down to attribute to, ascribe to, impute to, blame on.

put forward propose, move, table, submit, offer, tender, present, advance, suggest, recommend, nominate.

put off 1 postpone, defer, delay, put back, hold over, shelve, suspend, adjourn, reschedule. **2** deter, dissuade, discourage, dishearten, demoralize, daunt, intimidate, faze, repel, disgust, revolt, repulse. **3** distract, divert, sidetrack, deflect, disconcert, unsettle, rattle (*inf*), confuse, throw (*inf*).

put on 1 don, change into, get into, slip into, try on, wear, dress in. **2** feign, fake, simulate, sham, pretend, assume, affect. **3** present, produce, mount, stage, perform. **4** switch on, turn on, illuminate, activate.

put out 1 extinguish, douse, quench, snuff, blow out, stamp out. **2** announce, make known, disclose, publish, broadcast, circulate, release. **3** annoy, irritate, vex, irk, anger, exasperate, infuriate, upset, hurt, offend. **4** inconvenience, trouble, bother, discommode, incommode.

put up 1 erect, build, construct, raise, assemble. **2** accommodate, house, lodge, board, shelter, entertain. **3** offer, give, provide, supply, present, submit. **4** put forward, propose, nominate, recommend, suggest, choose, select.

put up with tolerate, endure, stand, suffer, bear, abide, accept, swallow, stomach, brook.

put upon impose on, take advantage of, exploit, take for granted.

putative *adj* accepted, acknowledged, recognized, alleged, hypothetical, theoretical, suppositional, conjectural, supposed, assumed.

put-down *noun* snub, rebuff, slight, insult, gibe, barb, affront, sneer.

putrefy *verb* rot, perish, decompose, decay, go bad, spoil, moulder, fester.

putrid *adj* **1** rotten, decomposed, decayed, bad, off, mouldy. **2** rancid, fetid, rank, foul, offensive.

puzzle *verb* **1** perplex, baffle, mystify, confuse, confound, nonplus, bewilder, flummox (*inf*), floor (*inf*), stump (*inf*), beat (*inf*). **2** ponder, meditate, brood, mull, muse, cudgel one's brains.
➤ *noun* **1** enigma, mystery, paradox, dilemma. **2** riddle, conundrum, poser, brainteaser, question, problem.

pygmy *noun* dwarf, midget, manikin, homunculus, shrimp (*inf*).
➤ *adj* miniature, dwarf, midget, pocket, toy, baby.

quack *noun* **1** charlatan, fake, mountebank. **2** doctor, doc (*inf*), medic (*inf*).

quaff *verb* drink, swig (*inf*), swallow, down.

quagmire *noun* **1** swamp, bog, marsh, morass. **2** muddle, tangle, imbroglio, predicament.

quail *verb* shrink, recoil, blench, flinch, cower, cringe, get cold feet (*inf*).

quaint *adj* **1** picturesque, charming, old-fashioned, olde-worlde (*inf*). **2** strange, unusual, curious, odd, peculiar, eccentric.

quake *verb* **1** tremble, shake, quiver. **2** shudder, shiver, quail.

qualification *noun* **1** certificate, diploma. **2** attainment, skill, expertise, knowledge, know-how (*inf*), experience, suitability, fitness, eligibility. **3** requirement, prerequisite. **4** restriction, limitation, modification, condition, proviso.

qualify *verb* **1** pass, graduate. **2** prepare, fit, equip, train. **3** modify, alter, restrict, limit. **4** restrain, moderate, mitigate, temper.

quality *noun* **1** characteristic, property, attribute, feature, aspect, trait. **2** character, nature, grade, condition, standard. **3** distinction, excellence, superiority, supremacy, value, worth, merit.

qualm *noun* **1** scruple, doubt, uncertainty, misgiving, hesitation, second thought. **2** spasm, nausea, queasiness.

quandary *noun* dilemma, cleft stick, uncertainty, perplexity, predicament, plight, mess.

quantity *noun* **1** amount, number, sum, total, proportion. **2** extent, measure, size, magnitude, mass.

quarantine *noun* isolation, seclusion, segregation.

quarrel *noun* argument, disagreement, dispute, squabble, tiff, spat (*inf*), row, altercation, misunderstanding, difference, clash, fight, set-to (*inf*), barney (*inf*).
➤*verb* **1** argue, disagree, squabble, row, fight, bicker, fall out (*inf*). **2** object to, take exception to, find fault with, criticize, disagree with, disapprove of.

quarrelsome *adj* argumentative, disputatious, combative, pugnacious, quick-tempered, choleric, irascible.

quarry[1] *noun* pit, mine, excavation.
➤*verb* mine, extract, obtain.

quarry[2] *noun* **1** prey, victim. **2** prize, object, aim, goal.

quarter *noun* **1** fourth, fourth part. **2** district, region, area, neighbourhood. **3** mercy, pity, clemency, pardon. **4** lodgings, accommodation, housing, residence, rooms, billet, barracks. **5** station, post.
➤*verb* accommodate, house, lodge, billet.

quash *verb* **1** suppress, subdue, crush, put down, quell. **2** annul, nullify, invalidate, cancel, repeal, revoke, reverse.

quasi- *adv* **1** supposedly, seemingly, apparently. **2** partly, virtually, almost, semi-.

quaver *verb* tremble, shake, quiver, flutter, waver.
➤*noun* tremor, trembling, shake, quiver.

quay *noun* wharf, landing stage, jetty, dock.

queasy *adj* ill, sick, bilious, nauseous, green about the gills (*inf*).

queen *noun* **1** monarch, ruler, sovereign. **2** consort. **3** star, diva, belle, idol.

queer *adj* **1** odd, curious, strange, weird, funny, unusual, peculiar, singular. **2** dubious, questionable, suspect, shady (*inf*), fishy (*inf*). **3** unwell, ill, sick, queasy, dizzy, giddy, faint.

➤*noun* homosexual, gay.
➤*verb* spoil, mar, thwart, frustrate, endanger, threaten.

quell *verb* 1 suppress, subdue, repress, put down, crush. 2 allay, assuage, alleviate, soothe, calm, pacify, silence.

quench *verb* 1 slake, satisfy. 2 extinguish, douse, put out. 3 sate, satiate, suppress, smother, stifle.

querulous *adj* peevish, petulant, whining, plaintive, complaining, dissatisfied, discontented, fretful, irritable, fractious.

query *noun* question, enquiry, doubt, uncertainty, reservation.
➤*verb* 1 question, dispute, challenge. 2 question, doubt, mistrust, suspect.

quest *noun* search, hunt, pursuit, expedition, journey, crusade.

question *noun* 1 query, enquiry, interrogation. 2 matter, issue, controversy. 3 matter, issue, subject, topic. 4 problem, difficulty. 5 doubt, uncertainty, dispute, argument, controversy.
➤*verb* 1 interrogate, examine, interview, probe, sound out, grill (*inf*), pump (*inf*). 2 query, challenge, dispute, doubt, mistrust, suspect.
out of the question impossible, unthinkable, preposterous, absurd.

questionable *adj* 1 debatable, doubtful, uncertain, moot, controversial. 2 dubious, suspicious, suspect, shady (*inf*).

questionnaire *noun* survey, opinion poll, form.

queue *noun* line, column, file, tailback.

quibble *verb* cavil, carp, split hairs, nitpick (*inf*).
➤*noun* criticism, objection, complaint, niggle, equivocation.

quick *adj* 1 fast, swift, rapid, speedy, brisk. 2 nippy, nimble, agile, prompt, sudden, instant, immediate. 3 hasty, hurried, cursory, brief, momentary. 4 sharp, keen, alert, quick-witted, bright, smart, clever.
➤*adv* fast, swiftly, rapidly, speedily, at the double, promptly, immediately.

quicken *verb* 1 accelerate, speed up, hasten, hurry. 2 stimulate, rouse, kindle, inspire, excite, enliven.

quick-tempered *adj* touchy, irascible, irritable, snappy, impatient, fiery.

quick-witted *adj* sharp, alert, quick on the uptake (*inf*), bright, intelligent, clever.

quiescent *adj* still, inactive, dormant, quiet.

quiet *adj* 1 silent, soundless, hushed, soft, muffled, muted. 2 tranquil, peaceful, undisturbed. 3 calm, serene, still. 4 reticent, reserved, shy, retiring, taciturn, mild, gentle, placid. 4 private, secret, secluded, unfrequented, sleepy. 5 subdued, sober, restrained.
➤*noun* silence, hush, peace, calm, tranquillity, serenity.

quieten *verb* quiet, silence, hush, shush, shut up (*inf*), muffle, mute, soften, stifle, still, calm, pacify, subdue.

quilt *noun* 1 bedspread, coverlet, counterpane. 2 eiderdown, duvet.

quintessence *noun* 1 essence, heart, core, soul. 2 embodiment, personification.

quip *noun* joke, witticism, sally, wisecrack (*inf*).

quirk *noun* idiosyncrasy, peculiarity, trait, mannerism, oddity, eccentricity, whim, caprice, vagary, foible.

quit *verb* 1 stop, cease, desist, leave off, give up, pack in (*inf*). 2 leave, depart, go. 3 retire, resign.

quite *adv* 1 completely, totally, entirely, wholly, altogether, utterly, absolutely. 2 fairly, moderately, rather, pretty (*inf*).

quiver *verb* tremble, shake, quake, shiver, shudder, flutter, vibrate.
➤*noun* tremor, trembling, shake, shiver, shudder, vibration, flutter.

quixotic *adj* impractical, unrealistic, idealistic, utopian, fanciful, crazy (*inf*).

quiz *noun* test, examination, questionnaire.
➤*verb* interrogate, question, examine, grill (*inf*).

quizzical *adj* puzzled, questioning, enquiring, curious.

quondam *adj* former, one-time, past.

quota *noun* share, portion, allocation, allowance, ration.

quotation *noun* **1** citation, quote (*inf*), extract, excerpt, passage, reference, allusion. **2** estimate, quote (*inf*), tender, price.

quote *verb* cite, mention, refer to, instance, adduce.
> *noun* **1** estimate, quotation, tender, price. **2** citation, quotation, extract, excerpt, passage, reference, allusion.

quotidian *adj* **1** daily, diurnal, everyday, routine, regular. **2** common, commonplace, ordinary.

R

rabble *noun* **1** mob, crowd, horde, herd. **2** masses, common people, common herd, proletariat, plebs (*inf*), hoi polloi, riffraff, great unwashed (*inf*).

rabid *adj* **1** mad, hydrophobic. **2** wild, raving, frenzied, hysterical, maniacal, fanatical, extreme, fervent, overzealous, overenthusiastic, unreasoning, irrational.

race¹ *noun* **1** contest, competition, chase, dash, sprint, relay, marathon, steeplechase. **2** contest, competition, quest, rivalry. **3** stream, channel, sluice.
➤*verb* **1** run, dash, dart, bolt, sprint, tear, fly, hare, career, speed, zoom, hurry, rush. **2** compete, contend, run.

race² *noun* **1** people, nation, tribe, ethnic group. **2** blood, bloodline, stock, descent, extraction, ancestry, parentage.

racial *adj* ethnic, ethnological, tribal, national.

racism *noun* racialism, discrimination, prejudice, apartheid, xenophobia.

rack *noun* stand, support, holder, shelf.
➤*verb* torture, torment, agonize, pain, afflict, distress.

racket *noun* **1** din, noise, uproar, clamour, hubbub, hullabaloo, commotion, pandemonium. **2** scheme, fraud, fiddle, con (*inf*), scam (*inf*). **3** business, game, line.

racy *adj* **1** lively, spirited, animated, vigorous, vivacious, exciting, fast-moving. **2** risqué, suggestive, bawdy, ribald, blue (*inf*), smutty, dirty, naughty, off-colour.

raddled *adj* haggard, wasted, worn out, unkempt, dishevelled.

radiant *adj* **1** bright, shining, brilliant, resplendent, dazzling, sparkling, glittering, gleaming, lustrous, glowing, luminous. **2** beaming, glowing, happy, joyful, delighted, elated, ecstatic, blissful, on top of the world (*inf*).

radiate *verb* **1** give off, give out, send out, emit, emanate, diffuse, shed. **2** diverge, branch out, spread out. **3** show, display, exude.

radiation *noun* **1** emanation, emission, propagation. **2** rays, waves.

radical *adj* **1** basic, fundamental, profound, deep-seated, complete, total, thorough, thoroughgoing, comprehensive, exhaustive, sweeping, far-reaching, drastic, severe, extreme. **2** fanatical, revolutionary, militant, extreme, extremist, leftist, left-wing.
➤*noun* extremist, fanatic, militant, revolutionary, reformer.

raffle *noun* lottery, draw, sweepstake, sweep.

rag¹ *noun* **1** cloth, scrap, remnant. **2** shreds, tatters.

rag² *verb* tease, badger, mock, ridicule, taunt, poke fun at, make fun of, rib (*inf*).

rage *noun* **1** anger, fury, wrath, ire, passion. **2** passion, fit, frenzy, temper, tantrum, paroxysm. **3** mania, fad, craze, fashion, vogue.
➤*verb* rant, rave, seethe, fume, storm, explode, rampage, raise hell (*inf*), go mad (*inf*), do one's nut (*inf*), fly off the handle (*inf*), boil over (*inf*), lose one's temper (*inf*), lose one's rag (*inf*), lose it (*inf*).

ragged *adj* **1** tattered, ripped, torn, frayed, worn, threadbare, tatty. **2** unkempt, untidy, scruffy, shabby, down-at-heel. **3** rough, uneven, jagged, notched, serrated. **4** erratic, irregular, uneven, uncoordinated, disorganized.

raging *adj* **1** wild, violent, stormy, turbulent, tempestuous, angry, furious, enraged. **2** excruciating, painful, agonizing, piercing.

raid *noun* **1** attack, assault, onslaught. **2** incursion, invasion, foray, sortie, strike. **3** robbery, break-in, hold-up. **4** swoop, bust (*inf*), search.

➤*verb* **1** attack, assault, invade, descend upon, swoop on, forage, maraud. **2** plunder, pillage, loot, sack, rob, break into.

rail *verb* complain, criticize, denounce, declaim, fulminate, rage, inveigh, vociferate, vituperate, revile, abuse.

railing *noun* fence, barrier, paling, palisade, rail.

raillery *noun* banter, badinage, persiflage, teasing, kidding (*inf*), ribbing (*inf*), ragging (*inf*).

rain *noun* **1** rainfall, raindrops, precipitation, drizzle, mizzle. **2** shower, downpour, cloudburst, deluge, storm, thunderstorm. **3** torrent, volley, shower, deluge, hail.
➤*verb* **1** drizzle, spit, pour, teem, pelt, bucket (*inf*), come down in torrents (*inf*), piss down (*sl*). **2** pour, shower, drop, lavish.

rainy *adj* wet, damp, showery, drizzly.

raise *verb* **1** lift, lift up, elevate, hoist, heave up. **2** erect, set up, put up. **3** build, construct, erect. **4** put up, increase, jack up (*inf*), hike (*inf*). **5** increase, augment, enhance, heighten, intensify, amplify, boost. **6** promote, prefer, upgrade, elevate. **7** arouse, awaken, stir, excite, provoke, whip up, evoke, cause, occasion, produce, create, engender, conjure up. **8** rear, breed, bring up, nurture, educate. **9** cultivate, propagate, grow. **10** bring up, broach, introduce, present, put forward. **11** collect, gather, assemble, muster, rally, levy. **12** collect, amass, get, accumulate, scrape together (*inf*). **13** lift, remove, take away, end, suspend. **14** call, reach, contact, get hold of.

rake¹ *verb* **1** level, even out, smooth, flatten. **2** search, comb, scour, hunt, rifle, rummage. **3** sweep, pepper, enfilade.

rake² *noun* debauchee, libertine, roué, prodigal, profligate, playboy, womanizer, lecher.

rake in *verb* earn, receive, make, clear, amass, bring in.

rake up *verb* bring up, drag up, revive, remind.

rakish *adj* stylish, snazzy (*inf*), natty (*inf*), sporty, sharp, dashing, jaunty, breezy, debonair, nonchalant.

rally *verb* **1** come together, muster, assemble, meet, gather, collect, congregate, group, convene, bring together, get together, mobilize, organize, round up, marshal, summon. **2** regroup, reassemble, re-form. **3** recover, revive, improve, get better, mend, pick up, bounce back (*inf*).
➤*noun* **1** gathering, meeting, assembly, convention, march, demonstration. **2** recovery, revival, improvement, resurgence.

ram *verb* **1** force, drive, thrust, cram, pack, stuff, wedge, squeeze. **2** hit, strike, run into, crash into, collide with, smash into, slam into.

ramble *verb* **1** walk, hike, stroll, trek, wander, roam. **2** digress, drift, wander, maunder, waffle, blather. **3** straggle, trail, spread.
➤*noun* walk, hike, stroll, wander, trek, tramp, jaunt, tour, excursion.

rambler *noun* hiker, walker, stroller, wanderer.

ramification *noun* **1** development, consequence, upshot, result, effect, repercussion, implication. **2** branching, forking, divergence. **3** branch, limb, offshoot, subdivision.

ramp *noun* slope, incline, rise.

rampage *verb* run riot, run wild, run amok, charge, rage, go berserk.
➤*noun* rage, fury, frenzy.
on the rampage rampaging, running amok, going berserk, in a frenzy, out of control, wild.

rampant *adj* **1** unrestrained, out of control, uncontrollable, ungovernable, out of hand, unbridled, wanton, riotous. **2** luxuriant, lavish, profuse, rank, rife, widespread, epidemic. **3** erect, upright, rearing.

rampart *noun* bulwark, fortification, embankment, bank, earthwork, breastwork, parapet, bastion, defence.

ramshackle *adj* tumbledown, dilapidated, broken-down, run-down, derelict, rickety, flimsy, jerry-built.

rancid *adj* sour, off, stale, high, bad, rotten, tainted, turned, putrid, musty.

rancour *noun* malice, spite, venom, vindictiveness, ill will, ill feeling, malevolence, animosity, enmity, hostility, hatred, resentment, acrimony, animus.

random *adj* haphazard, casual, hit-or-miss, arbitrary, accidental, chance, fortuitous, unsystematic, unplanned, indiscriminate, aimless, stray.
at random randomly, haphazardly, arbitrarily, unsystematically, aimlessly, indiscriminately.

range *noun* **1** scope, reach, extent, sweep, spread, compass, area. **2** limits, bounds, parameters, span, scale, gamut, spectrum. **3** line, row, rank, chain. **4** sequence, series, succession, variety, array, assortment, selection, class, sort, kind, type. **5** stove, cooker, oven.
➤*verb* **1** align, line up, draw up, order, position, array, arrange, rank, class, classify, file, categorize, group, grade. **3** extend, stretch, reach, run, go. **4** cover, include. **5** vary, fluctuate. **6** roam, wander, traverse, travel.

rank[1] *noun* **1** position, station, level, grade, echelon. **2** nobility, status, standing, class, caste. **3** line, row, file, column, string.
➤*verb* **1** rate, class, grade, classify, categorize, sort. **2** arrange, organize, marshal, place, position, align, order, line up, draw up, dispose, array.

rank[2] *adj* **1** exuberant, luxuriant, lush, dense, profuse, abundant, prolific, overgrown, spreading. **2** foul, offensive, stinking, smelly, evil-smelling, rancid, putrid, fetid, rotten, disgusting, noisome, revolting. **3** complete, utter, total, sheer, absolute, downright, thorough, unmitigated, out-and-out. **4** blatant, flagrant, glaring, gross. **4** vile, shocking, foul, filthy, coarse, vulgar, gross.

rank and file *noun* **1** soldiers, troops, men, other ranks. **2** ordinary members, workers, grass roots.

rankle *verb* fester, annoy, vex, irk, gall, nettle, embitter, anger, bug (*inf*).

ransack *verb* **1** search, scour, comb, rummage through, rake through, turn inside out, turn upside down. **2** rifle, sack, loot, strip, raid, plunder, pillage, rob.

ransom *noun* money, payment, pay-off, price.
➤*verb* rescue, deliver, release, free, set free, liberate.

rant *verb* declaim, hold forth, shout, yell, bawl, bluster, vociferate, spout (*inf*).
➤*noun* bombast, bluster, declamation, tirade, harangue, storm, diatribe.

rap *verb* **1** tap, knock, thump, bang, hammer. **2** hit, strike, clout, whack, tap, crack. **3** rebuke, reprimand, criticize, censure, blame, scold, knock (*inf*), slam (*inf*), slate (*inf*).
➤*noun* **1** tap, knock, bang, thump, blow, hit, whack. **2** blame, flak (*inf*), responsibility, accountability. **3** rebuke, reprimand, censure, castigation, stick (*inf*).

rapacious *adj* **1** greedy, grasping, avaricious, voracious, wolfish, insatiable. **2** preying, predatory, predacious.

rape *verb* **1** ravish, violate, assault, abuse, seduce. **2** plunder, pillage, ravage, despoil, ransack, devastate.
➤*noun* **1** ravishment, violation, assault, abuse. **2** plundering, pillage, sack, devastation, spoliation, despoilation, violation.

rapid *adj* fast, quick, swift, speedy, express, hurried, hasty, precipitate, headlong, brisk, lively, prompt.

rapport *noun* sympathy, empathy, understanding, harmony, affinity, bond, link, relationship.

rapt *adj* **1** absorbed, engrossed, preoccupied, intent, lost. **2** enthralled, entranced, captivated, fascinated, spellbound, enchanted, enraptured.

rapture *noun* **1** ecstasy, bliss, enchantment, euphoria, delight, elation, joy, happiness, exaltation, exhilaration, enthusiasm. **2** transport, rhapsody.

rare *adj* **1** uncommon, unusual, unfamiliar, unique, strange, exceptional, infrequent, scarce, sparse. **2** excellent, exquisite, fine, choice, precious, special, superior, superlative, outstanding, first-rate.

rarely *adv* seldom, infrequently, occasionally, little, hardly ever, once in a blue moon (*inf*).

rarity *noun* **1** infrequency, uncommonness, unusualness, scarcity, sparseness. **2** curiosity, curio, gem, treasure, wonder, marvel.

rascal *noun* **1** scoundrel, rogue, good-for-nothing, ne'er-do-well, reprobate, blackguard, villain, rat (*inf*), rotter (*inf*). **2** imp, devil, scallywag, scamp, mischief.

rash[1] *adj* hasty, precipitate, reckless, thoughtless, heedless, careless, devil-may-care, incautious, imprudent, unguarded, indiscreet, unwary, impetuous, headstrong, hotheaded, impulsive, foolhardy.

rash[2] *noun* **1** eruption, outbreak, hives, urticaria. **2** outbreak, epidemic, plague, spate, flood, wave.

rasp *verb* **1** scrape, scratch, rub, abrade, grind, file, sand. **2** grate, jar. **3** bark, croak, screech.
➤ *noun* **1** scrape, scraping, grating, grinding. **2** file, grater.

rate *noun* **1** speed, velocity, pace, tempo. **2** pay, payment, fee, amount, figure, charge, price, cost. **3** ratio, proportion, percentage, degree.
➤ *verb* **1** regard, deem, consider, estimate, reckon. **2** esteem, admire, value. **3** judge, assess, rank, grade, categorize, class, classify. **4** assess, value, evaluate, appraise. **5** deserve, merit, warrant, justify.
at any rate in any case, anyway, anyhow, nonetheless, nevertheless, in any event.

rather *adv* **1** somewhat, fairly, moderately, relatively, slightly, quite, pretty (*inf*), sort of (*inf*). **2** sooner, preferably, for preference, instead, by choice.

ratify *verb* authorize, sanction, approve, accept, agree to, endorse, confirm, validate, certify, sign, seal.

rating *noun* **1** assessment, appraisal, evaluation, grading, ranking, classification. **2** ranking, rank, grade, standing, status, position.

ratio *noun* proportion, rate, percentage, relation.

ration *noun* **1** quota, allowance, share, portion, allocation, allotment, measure, helping, amount. **2** foodstuffs, food, provisions, supplies, stores, victuals.
➤ *verb* **1** restrict, limit, control. **2** conserve, save, economize.

rational *adj* **1** reasoning, thinking, mental, analytical, logical, sane, lucid, coherent, normal, well-balanced, compos mentis. **2** reasonable, logical, sensible, sound, practical, realistic, right, proper, wise, judicious, prudent.

rationale *noun* logic, reasoning, theory, principle, philosophy, reason, motive, basis, grounds.

rationalize *verb* **1** explain, explain away, account for, justify, excuse, vindicate. **2** trim, cut back, streamline, reduce, downsize.

rattle *verb* **1** clatter, knock, bang, clang, clank, jangle, clink. **2** bounce, bump, jolt, jar, vibrate, shake. **3** disconcert, discompose, confuse, unnerve, unsettle, fluster, shake, disturb, perturb, upset, frighten, scare, faze (*inf*), throw (*inf*). **4** reel off, recite, run through. **5** chatter, babble, prattle, jabber, yak (*inf*), rabbit (*inf*).

raucous *adj* hoarse, husky, harsh, jarring, discordant, grating, rasping, rough, strident, shrill, piercing, screeching.

ravage *verb* ruin, wreck, destroy, devastate, lay waste, desolate, pillage, plunder, sack, ransack, despoil.
➤ *noun* damage, ruin, havoc, destruction, devastation, desolation, ruination.

rave *verb* **1** ramble, babble, jabber, gibber, rage, storm, rant. **2** praise, extol, hail, acclaim, gush, enthuse, wax lyrical, go wild.
➤ *noun* **1** rave-up (*inf*), party, disco, do (*inf*), bash (*inf*). **2** rage, craze, trend, vogue, fad.

ravenous *adj* **1** starving, famished, hungry. **2** greedy, gluttonous, rapacious, voracious, insatiable.

ravine *noun* gorge, canyon, chasm, gully, gulch.

ravish *verb* **1** rape, violate, assault, deflower. **2** charm, delight, transport, captivate, enchant, entrance, bewitch, spellbind, enthral.

ravishing *adj* lovely, beautiful, stunning, gorgeous, alluring, seductive, bewitching, enchanting, entrancing, captivating, fascinating.

raw *adj* **1** uncooked, fresh. **2** natural, unprocessed, untreated, crude, coarse, unrefined. **3** green, immature, callow, new, inexperienced, naive, unsophisticated, unseasoned, untested, untried, untrained, unpractised, undisciplined. **4** tender, sore, painful, sensitive. **5** scratched, bloody, grazed, chafed, skinned, excoriated. **6** bitter, biting, piercing, penetrating, freezing, cold, chill, chilly, nippy. **7** unrefined, unvarnished, crude, plain, naked, bare, brutal, frank, explicit.

ray noun **1** beam, shaft, streak, flash, gleam, glint. **2** glimmer, flicker, spark, hint, trace.

raze verb demolish, destroy, level, flatten, bulldoze, pull down, tear down, erase, obliterate, expunge.

reach verb **1** stretch, stretch out, hold out, extend, stick out. **2** touch, grasp, seize, get hold of. **3** clutch at, grab at. **4** get to, arrive at, come to, attain, achieve, accomplish, make, amount to, hit (inf). **5** contact, get hold of, get through to, get in touch with.
➤ noun **1** grasp, distance, stretch. **2** range, extent, span, scope, compass.

react verb **1** act, behave, conduct oneself, proceed, respond, reply, answer. **2** oppose, defy, resist, rebel.

reaction noun **1** response, reply, answer, feedback, retaliation, backlash, repercussion. **2** conservatism, the right. **3** counteraction, counterbalance, reciprocation.

reactionary adj conservative, right-wing, rightist, counter-revolutionary, traditional, die-hard, dyed-in-the-wool.
➤ noun conservative, right-winger, rightist, counter-revolutionary, traditionalist, die-hard.

read verb **1** peruse, browse through, dip into, scan, skim, study, pore over, look through, look at, leaf through, thumb through, flick through, wade through. **2** interpret, decipher, deduce, understand, comprehend. **3** recite, deliver, declaim, utter, speak. **4** indicate, show, display, register, measure. **5** interpret, construe, understand, take.
➤ noun perusal, study, look.

readable adj **1** legible, decipherable, clear, intelligible, understandable, comprehensible. **2** interesting, entertaining, enjoyable, absorbing, gripping, compulsive, unputdownable (inf).

readily adv **1** willingly, gladly, happily, cheerfully, eagerly, enthusiastically, with pleasure, unhesitatingly, without hesitation. **2** easily, with ease, effortlessly, without difficulty.

reading noun **1** interpretation, construction, understanding, impression, take (inf). **2** recital, recitation, lecture. **3** level, figure, measurement.

ready adj **1** prepared, set, all set. **2** prepared, arranged, organized, done, completed, finished, handy, convenient, accessible, available, near, to hand, on hand, within reach. **3** willing, agreeable, game (inf), eager, enthusiastic, anxious, keen, happy, glad, inclined, disposed, minded. **4** prompt, quick, sharp, smart, apt, skilful, clever, bright, perceptive, alert, resourceful. **5** about, liable, likely, apt, on the brink of, on the verge of, on the point of.

real adj **1** actual, factual, existing, material, physical, tangible, true, genuine, authentic, legitimate, legal, valid, bona fide, sincere, earnest, fervent, heartfelt, honest, unfeigned. **2** complete, absolute, total, utter, thorough.

realistic adj **1** practical, pragmatic, down-to-earth, matter-of-fact, sensible, no-nonsense, rational, hard-headed, level-headed, clear-sighted, sober, objective, unromantic, unsentimental. **2** natural, naturalistic, lifelike, true-to-life, faithful, real, authentic, genuine.

reality noun **1** real world, real life. **2** actuality, existence, substantiality, corporeality, materiality, tangibility, truth, factuality, realism, genuineness, authenticity.

realize verb **1** understand, comprehend, be aware of, be conscious of, take in, catch on, grasp, learn, perceive, recognize, appreciate, discern, discover, twig (inf), cotton on (inf). **2** fulfil, accomplish, achieve, carry out, perform, effect, complete, bring about, bring off, bring to fruition, execute, implement. **3** make, earn, clear, fetch, produce, net, bring in.

really adv **1** actually, in reality, in fact, in truth, truly. **2** indeed, truly, surely, genuinely, sincerely, certainly, assuredly, positively, absolutely, categorically, unquestionably, undoubtedly, without a doubt, indubitably, very, extremely, exceptionally, remarkably, highly, thoroughly, decidedly.

realm noun **1** kingdom, country, land, principality, state, dominion, territory. **2** field, area, sphere, domain, department.

reap verb **1** cut, crop, harvest, mow, gather in, bring in. **2** get, obtain, acquire, secure, receive, gain, win, derive, realize.

rear noun **1** back, back end, tail end, stern. **2** tail, rump, behind, bottom, buttocks, posterior, backside (inf).
➤adj back, hindmost, rearmost, last, tail-end.
➤verb **1** raise, bring up, nurture, look after, care for, educate. **2** breed, keep, farm, grow, cultivate. **3** put up, set up, erect, build, construct, raise. **4** rise, tower, loom.

reason noun **1** cause. **2** ground, basis, motive, motivation, incentive, inducement. **3** excuse, justification, vindication, defence, explanation, rationale. **4** intellect, mind, brains, intelligence, understanding, sense, rationality. **5** sanity, mind, senses, wits.
➤verb **1** think, ponder, consider, deliberate, cogitate, ratiocinate. **2** conclude, deduce, infer, work out, analyse, solve. **3** argue, debate, dispute, discuss, talk over, prevail upon, plead, persuade, dissuade.
within reason in moderation, moderately, within limits.

reasonable adj **1** equitable, fair, just. **2** sensible, practical, rational, sane, sober, wise, intelligent, sound, judicious, advisable, well-advised. **3** reasoned, logical, justifiable, arguable, admissible, viable, tenable, plausible. **4** moderate, tolerable, passable, fair, acceptable, OK (inf), modest, inexpensive, cheap, low-priced.

reassure verb comfort, encourage, hearten, cheer, put one's mind at rest, calm, assuage.

rebate noun **1** refund, repayment. **2** discount, reduction, deduction, allowance.

rebel noun revolutionary, insurrectionist, insurgent, agitator, mutineer, anarchist, guerrilla, freedom fighter, traitor.
➤verb **1** revolt, rise up, mutiny, take to the streets. **2** resist, defy, disobey. **3** recoil from, shy away from, shrink from.

rebellion noun **1** revolt, revolution, insurgency, insurrection, rising, uprising, coup, mutiny, resistance. **2** defiance, resistance, opposition, disobedience, insubordination, dissent.

rebellious adj **1** revolutionary, rebel, insurgent, mutinous. **2** unruly, defiant, insubordinate, disobedient, ungovernable, unmanageable, refractory, recalcitrant.

rebound verb **1** bounce back, ricochet, recoil, spring back, return. **2** backfire, misfire, come back to haunt, come home to roost.
➤noun bounce, ricochet, recoil, return.

rebuff verb snub, reject, decline, repel, repulse, spurn, fend off, discourage, refuse, turn away, turn down, slight, cut, cold-shoulder.
➤noun rejection, refusal, spurning, discouragement, snub, repulse, slight, cold shoulder, brush-off (inf), slap in the face (inf).

rebuke verb scold, chide, upbraid, berate, castigate, reprove, reproach, reprimand, admonish, take to task, lecture, censure, remonstrate with, tell off (inf).
➤noun scolding, reproof, reproach, reprimand, admonition, lecture, telling-off (inf), dressing-down (inf), bollocking (sl).

rebut verb refute, deny, disprove, discredit, contradict, explode.

recalcitrant adj **1** disobedient, insubordinate, refractory, unruly, defiant, rebellious, mutinous, uncooperative, perverse, obstinate, stubborn, contrary. **2** intractable, ungovernable, unmanageable, uncontrollable.

recall verb **1** remember, call to mind, recollect, reminisce about, look back on, think back to, hark back to. **2** summon, call back, order back, bring back.
➤noun memory, remembrance, recollection, reminiscence.

recant verb withdraw, retract, revoke, deny, disavow, disclaim, disown, repudiate, renege on, renounce, relinquish, abjure, forswear, take back.

recapitulate verb restate, repeat, reiterate, review, go over, summarize, sum up, recap (inf).

recede verb **1** retreat, withdraw, retire, return, go back, fall back, move back, ebb. **2** lessen, decrease, diminish, decline, dwindle, wane, fall off, taper off, peter out, fade, abate, subside, slacken.

receipt noun **1** delivery, acceptance, reception, receiving. **2** proof of purchase, sales slip, slip, counterfoil, acknowledgement. **3** takings, proceeds, profits, gains, income.

receive verb **1** accept, take, be in receipt of. **2** get, obtain, acquire, derive, come by.

3 hear, learn, find out about, gather, perceive. **4** take, react to, respond to. **5** suffer, undergo, sustain, experience, endure, go through, meet with, encounter. **6** greet, welcome, entertain. **7** hold, accommodate, take, contain, admit.

recent *adj* **1** modern, contemporary, present-day, latter-day. **2** new, novel, fresh, current, up-to-date, up-to-the-minute.

receptacle *noun* container, vessel, holder, repository.

reception *noun* **1** receipt, receiving, acceptance. **2** response, welcome, recognition, reaction, treatment. **3** party, function, social, gathering, get-together, at-home, soirée.

receptive *adj* open, open-minded, amenable, accessible, approachable, sympathetic, interested, responsive, susceptible.

recess *noun* **1** alcove, niche, nook, corner, bay. **2** hollow, indentation, cavity. **3** break, interval, intermission, rest, respite, breather (*inf*), holiday, vacation. **4** depths, interior, bowels, heart.

recession *noun* **1** depression, slump, downturn, crash, trough, hard times (*inf*). **2** retreat, withdrawal, ebbing, abatement.

recipe *noun* **1** directions, instructions, guide, ingredients. **2** formula, prescription, method, procedure, means.

recipient *noun* receiver, beneficiary, legatee, assignee.

reciprocal *adj* **1** return, requited, retaliatory. **2** mutual, common, shared, exchanged, interchangeable, alternating.

reciprocate *verb* **1** return, give back, give in return, requite, repay, match, respond in kind, do the same. **2** exchange, swap, trade, interchange.

recital *noun* **1** performance, concert, solo. **2** recitation, reading, rendering, rendition, narration, relation, account, description, telling. **3** enumeration, detailing, itemization, specification.

recite *verb* **1** read aloud, speak, declaim, deliver, perform. **2** recount, rehearse, relate, detail, enumerate, specify, itemize, list, reel off, rattle off.

reckless *adj* rash, heedless, thoughtless, careless, imprudent, incautious, injudicious, ill-advised, unwise, foolish, harebrained, irresponsible, hasty, rash, impetuous, impulsive, foolhardy, irresponsible.

reckon *verb* **1** think, believe, imagine, suppose, assume. **2** consider, regard, look upon, deem, think of, count. **3** calculate, compute, work out, add up, count, estimate. **4** rely, depend, count, bank, bargain.

reckon with anticipate, expect, foresee, bargain for, take into account, allow for.

reckoning *noun* **1** calculation, computation, working-out, addition, count, estimate. **2** account, bill, score. **3** judgement, settlement, retribution, punishment, damnation. **5** summation, assessment, evaluation, judgement, appraisal.

reclaim *verb* **1** recover, retrieve, regain, get back. **2** save, salvage, recycle. **3** save, redeem, rescue, reform, rehabilitate.

recline *verb* **1** lean, lie, lie back. **2** rest, repose, loll, lounge, stretch out.

recluse *noun* hermit, solitary, loner (*inf*).

recognition *noun* identification, recall, recollection, knowledge, appreciation, realization, acknowledgement, awareness, consciousness, acceptance, admission, approval, endorsement, reward, honour, gratitude.

recognize *verb* **1** identify, know, place, pick out, tell, remember, recall. **2** acknowledge, admit, own, grant, allow, concede, confess, accept, realize. **3** acknowledge, accept, admit, endorse, concede, grant, uphold. **4** honour, respect, reward, salute, applaud, appreciate.

recoil *verb* **1** rebound, spring back, fly back. **2** shy away, draw back, shrink, flinch, balk. **3** rebound, backfire, misfire, go wrong. **4** kick, kick back.
➤*noun* kick, kickback, backlash, reaction, repercussion, rebound.

recollect *verb* remember, recall, call to mind, think of, summon up.

recommend *verb* **1** advise, counsel, suggest, propose, advocate. **2** approve, endorse, vouch for, commend.

recompense *verb* **1** repay, reimburse, indemnify, compensate, reward. **2** redress, requite, make amends.

➤*noun* compensation, indemnification, amends, redress, reparation, remuneration, reward, repayment.

reconcile *verb* **1** reunite, bring together, conciliate, appease, pacify, make peace between. **2** settle, resolve, mend, patch up, sort out, iron out. **3** accept, resign, submit, yield.

recondite *adj* obscure, abstruse, esoteric, profound, deep, hidden, secret, arcane, mysterious, inscrutable.

reconnaissance *noun* **1** recce (*inf*), reconnoitring, spying, scouting, survey, exploration. **2** probe, investigation, examination, scrutiny.

reconnoitre *verb* recce (*inf*), survey, spy out, scout, explore, investigate, check out (*inf*).

reconsider *verb* rethink, review, re-evaluate, re-examine, reassess, revise, think better of, have second thoughts.

reconstruct *verb* **1** rebuild, reassemble, remake, remodel, restore, renovate, make over. **2** recreate, re-enact, piece together. **3** reorganize, reform, re-establish.

record *noun* **1** journal, diary, history, chronicle, archives, minutes, log, document, documentation, file, dossier, memorandum, note, account, report, entry. **2** reputation, history, background, career. **3** recording, disc, CD, compact disc, album, LP, single, release. **4** souvenir, token, memorial, remembrance, testimony, witness, evidence, trace.
➤ *verb* **1** enter, note, write down, put in writing, set down, take down, enter, register, log, minute, document, file, chronicle. **2** tape, video, videotape. **3** register, read, indicate, show, display.
off the record confidential, in confidence, private, secret, unofficial.
on record recorded, documented, noted, known.

recorder *noun* **1** tape recorder, cassette recorder, video recorder. **2** registrar, archivist, annalist, clerk, stenographer, scribe, diarist, chronicler, historian.

recording *noun* record, album, disc, compact disc, CD, tape, mini disc, DVD, video.

recount *verb* narrate, relate, tell, report, recite, repeat, detail, describe, depict, portray.

recoup *verb* regain, recover, retrieve, get back, win back, make good.

recourse *noun* resort, refuge, way out, resource, option, possibility, expedient, remedy.

recover *verb* **1** regain, recoup, get back, recapture, retrieve. **2** get better, get well, pull through, come round, improve, mend, heal, revive, recuperate. **3** save, salvage, retrieve, reclaim, recycle.

recovery *noun* **1** retrieval, reclamation, recapture, recycling, salvaging, rescue, redemption, restoration. **2** recuperation, convalescence, rally, improvement, cure. **3** improvement, upturn, upswing.

recreation *noun* relaxation, fun, play, sport, enjoyment, pleasure, entertainment, amusement, distraction, diversion, leisure, hobby, pastime.

recrimination *noun* countercharge, retaliation, retort, counteraccusation.

recruit *verb* **1** enlist, draft, call up, conscript, mobilize, levy, muster. **2** enrol, sign up. **3** engage, sign up, employ, take on, appoint.
➤*noun* conscript, draftee, volunteer, newcomer, novice, rookie (*inf*), beginner, learner, trainee.

rectify *verb* correct, put right, redress, remedy, fix, mend, repair, improve, better, make good, emend.

rectitude *noun* **1** uprightness, righteousness, virtue, goodness, decency, integrity, honesty, probity. **2** correctness, accuracy, soundness.

rector *noun* cleric, clergyman, parson, vicar, minister.

recumbent *adj* lying, reclining, leaning, resting, prostrate, supine, prone.

recuperate *verb* **1** recover, convalesce, improve, get better, get well, mend, heal. **2** recover, recoup, get back, regain, make good.

recur *verb* be repeated, happen again, return, come back, reappear, persist.

recurrent *adj* recurring, repeated, frequent, regular, periodic, intermittent, chronic, persistent, continual.

recycle *verb* **1** reuse, recover, reclaim. **2** reprocess, salvage.

red adj 1 crimson, carmine, scarlet, ruby, cherry, rose, vermilion, maroon, wine, claret, coral. 2 rosy, ruddy, florid, blushing, flushed, bloodshot, inflamed. 3 ginger, auburn, Titian, sandy, carroty. 4 Communist, commie (inf), left-wing, leftist, lefty (inf).
➤noun 1 crimson, scarlet, vermilion, maroon. 2 Communist, commie (inf), socialist, left-winger, leftist, lefty (inf).
in the red overdrawn, in debt, in debit, in arrears, owing money, insolvent, broke (inf).
see red go mad, lose one's temper, explode, boil over, blow one's top (inf), hit the roof (inf), fly off the handle (inf).

redden verb blush, flush, colour, crimson.

redeem verb 1 recover, regain, get back, retrieve, recoup, buy back, ransom. 2 save, absolve, convert, rehabilitate. 3 deliver, free, set free, release, discharge, rescue. 4 exchange, cash in, trade in. 5 discharge, fulfil, perform, make good. 6 expiate, make amends for, make up for, atone for. 7 offset, compensate for, outweigh.

redemption noun recovery, reclamation, retrieval, freeing, liberation, release, ransom, rescue, salvation, deliverance, expiation, atonement, reparation, fulfilment, discharge.

redolent adj 1 fragrant, scented, smelling, reeking. 2 reminiscent, suggestive, evocative.

redoubtable adj formidable, fearsome, mighty, powerful, terrible, fearful.

redound verb 1 conduce to, contribute to, lead to, result in. 2 recoil on, rebound on.

redress verb 1 rectify, right, put right, correct, remedy, make amends for, make up for, compensate for. 2 amend, adjust, regulate, even up.
➤noun 1 rectification, correction, remedying, putting right. 2 cure, remedy, compensation, amends, reparation, restitution, satisfaction, justice.

reduce verb 1 lessen, lower, diminish, decrease, shorten, cut, curtail, shrink, slim, moderate, alleviate, mitigate, dilute, deplete, weaken, impair. 2 bring to, drive to, force to. 3 demote, downgrade, lower, degrade. 4 discount, mark down, cut, slash, knock down. 5 subdue, conquer, capture, subjugate.

reduction noun lessening, lowering, diminution, decrease, drop, fall, decline, cut, cutback, abatement, moderation, alleviation, dilution, weakening, curtailment, discount, deduction, allowance, rebate.

redundant adj 1 superfluous, unnecessary, inessential, surplus, unneeded, unwanted. 2 unemployed, laid off, out of work, jobless, on the dole (inf), idle. 3 verbose, wordy, diffuse, padded, repetitious, tautological.

reek verb smell, stink, pong (inf), hum (inf).
➤noun smell, odour, stink, pong (inf), stench.

reel verb 1 stagger, totter, lurch, sway. 2 go round, swim, spin.

refer verb 1 mention, allude, speak of, bring up, quote, cite, touch on. 2 direct, send, pass, transfer, consign. 3 consult, turn, apply, have recourse, resort.

referee noun ref (inf), umpire, arbiter, judge.
➤verb umpire, judge, adjudicate, arbitrate.

reference noun 1 mention, allusion, remark, hint, intimation. 2 regard, respect, concern, bearing, application, applicability, connection, relation, relevance. 3 testimonial, character, recommendation. 4 source, authority. 5 citation, quotation, footnote, note, bibliography.

referendum noun poll, vote, plebiscite.

refine verb 1 purify, clarify, cleanse, filter, distil, process. 2 polish, cultivate, civilize, improve, hone, perfect.

refined adj 1 cultivated, cultured, civilized, polished, genteel, well-mannered, polite, well-bred, urbane, gentlemanly, ladylike, elegant, stylish. 2 discriminating, discerning, sensitive, sophisticated, subtle, delicate, fine. 3 pure, purified, clarified, distilled, processed.

refinement noun 1 purification, processing, polish, style, elegance, finesse, sophistication, cultivation, taste, discrimination, urbanity, good manners, good breeding, politeness, gentility. 2 subtlety, nicety, nuance, detail. 3 modification, alteration, adjustment, improvement.

reflect verb 1 mirror, image, echo, reproduce. 2 throw back, send back, return, give back, echo. 3 show, display, exhibit, demonstrate, manifest, reveal, bear out, indicate, express, betray. **4** meditate, contemplate, cogitate, ponder, muse, think, deliberate, consider. **5** discredit, detract from, put in a bad light.

reflection noun **1** image, echo, likeness, expression, indication, sign, display, demonstration, manifestation. **2** thought, idea, meditation, contemplation, musing, deliberation, consideration. **3** criticism, reproach, aspersion, slur, imputation.

reflex adj automatic, mechanical, involuntary, knee-jerk.

reform verb **1** improve, better, ameliorate, amend, correct, rectify, revise, revolutionize, remodel, reorganize. **2** mend, amend, improve, rehabilitate, reclaim.
➤ noun reformation, improvement, amelioration, betterment, amendment, correction, rectification, change, revision, reorganization, rehabilitation, reclamation.

refractory adj recalcitrant, obstinate, stubborn, intractable, contrary, difficult, uncooperative, unruly, rebellious, unmanageable, uncontrollable, disobedient, naughty.

refrain[1] verb abstain, forbear, hold back, desist, stop, give up, do without, avoid, eschew.

refrain[2] noun chorus, response, burden.

refresh verb **1** revive, reanimate, reinvigorate, revitalize, perk up (inf). **2** freshen, revive, renew, restore. **3** jog, prompt, prod, arouse, stimulate, activate.

refreshing adj **1** cooling, revitalizing, reviving, invigorating, bracing, stimulating, energizing. **2** fresh, new, novel, original, different, unexpected.

refreshment noun **1** food, drink, sustenance, snacks, provisions, eats (inf). **2** freshening, revival, reanimation, reinvigoration, revitalization, rejuvenation, renewal.

refrigerate verb cool, chill, freeze.

refuge noun **1** shelter, sanctuary, asylum, haven, retreat, hideout, hideaway, bolthole. **2** resort, recourse, expedient, stopgap.

refugee noun displaced person, stateless person, exile, émigré.

refund verb repay, pay back, return, give back, reimburse.
➤ noun repayment, reimbursement, rebate, return.

refurbish verb renovate, do up (inf), make over, redecorate, spruce up, re-equip, remodel.

refusal noun **1** denial, rejection, turning-down, withholding, non-acceptance, rebuff, no, thumbs down. **2** option, choice, opportunity.

refuse[1] verb **1** decline, turn down, reject, spurn, pass up. **2** deny, withhold.

refuse[2] noun rubbish, waste, garbage, litter, trash, junk.

refute verb **1** disprove, rebut, negate, confute. **2** deny, reject.

regain verb recover, get back, retake, win back, retrieve, recoup, recapture, reclaim.

regal adj **1** royal, kingly, queenly, princely, imperial. **2** majestic, stately, august, noble, magnificent, grand.

regale verb **1** entertain, amuse, divert. **2** feast, banquet, treat, ply.

regard verb **1** watch, look at, gaze at, stare at, observe, study, scrutinize. **2** heed, notice, note, pay attention to, listen to, mind, take notice of, take into consideration. **3** consider, think of, see, view, contemplate, esteem, hold, account, deem. **4** concern, relate to, pertain to, refer to, apply to.
➤ noun **1** notice, attention, heed, thought, consideration. **2** care, concern. **3** esteem, respect, approval, estimation, appreciation, admiration, liking, fondness, affection, love. **4** look, gaze, stare. **5** respect, aspect, point, particular.

regardful adj mindful, heedful, attentive.

regarding prep about, re, concerning, in connection with, with respect to, as regards, as to, with reference to, in relation to.

regardless adj heedless, reckless, careless, indifferent, unconcerned.
➤ adv anyway, in any case, notwithstanding, nevertheless, no matter what.

regards pl noun best wishes, good wishes, greetings, respects, compliments.

regenerate verb renew, restore, revive, revitalize, rekindle, improve, reconstruct, remodel, overhaul.

regime *noun* 1 government, administration. 2 system, rule, control, leadership, management.

region *noun* 1 area, zone, territory, district, quarter, sector, neighbourhood, locality, part, section, division. 2 province, department, district, county.
in the region of around, about, approximately, roughly, something like, more or less, or thereabouts, close to, nearly.

regional *adj* local, district, provincial.

register *noun* list, listing, roster, roll, catalogue, directory, index, record.
➤*verb* 1 record, put on record, enter, write down, put in writing, note, list. 2 check in, sign in. 3 sign up, sign on, enrol, enlist. 4 show, record, indicate, display. 5 express, show, display, exhibit, reveal, reflect, betray. 5 get through, sink in, penetrate, make an impression.

regress *verb* go backwards, retreat, retrogress, revert, relapse, backslide, degenerate, deteriorate, decline.
➤*noun* regression, return, reversion, relapse, retrogression, retreat.

regret *verb* 1 rue, repent, deplore. 2 lament, mourn, grieve over, miss.
➤*noun* sorrow, grief, remorse, self-reproach, ruefulness, repentance, penitence, contrition, disappointment.

regretfully *adv* sorrowfully, sadly, apologetically, remorsefully, ruefully, contritely.

regrettable *adj* deplorable, lamentable, ill-advised, wrong, unfortunate, unwelcome, distressing, upsetting.

regular *adj* 1 normal, usual, customary, habitual, routine, standard, ordinary, common, constant, everyday, daily, unvarying. 2 formal, official, orthodox, conventional, usual, established, approved, proper, correct, traditional, time-honoured, classic. 3 rhythmic, steady, constant, recurrent, periodic, fixed, set, consistent, even, uniform. 4 real, absolute, complete, total, utter, thorough, genuine.

regulate *verb* 1 control, rule, govern, direct, manage, administer, supervise, superintend, oversee, monitor. 2 organize, systematize, methodize, order. 3 adjust, fix, set, tune, modulate, control.

regulation *noun* 1 control, rule, direction, management, administration, organiza-

tion, monitoring, supervision, adjustment, setting, tuning, modulation. 2 rule, ruling, law, statute, act, edict, decree, order.
➤*adj* formal, official, orthodox, prescribed, statutory, mandatory, fixed, set, accepted, standard, regular.

regurgitate *verb* vomit, disgorge, bring up.

rehabilitate *verb* 1 reintegrate, reinstate, retrain, reform, reclaim. 2 restore, renovate, recondition, fix up, renew, revive, reinvigorate, repair, reconstruct.

rehearsal *noun* 1 practice, run-through, drill, exercise, trial run, dry run, dummy run. 2 listing, enumeration, itemization.

rehearse *verb* 1 practise, drill, exercise, train, prepare. 1 practise, run through, try out, go over. 3 recount, relate, repeat, reiterate, recapitulate. 4 detail, list, enumerate.

reign *verb* 1 rule, govern, hold sway. 2 hold sway, predominate, prevail, obtain.
➤*noun* 1 rule, sovereignty. 2 rule, supremacy, ascendancy, sovereignty. 3 government, administration, regime, influence, dominion.

reimburse *verb* repay, pay back, give back, return, refund, compensate.

rein *noun* 1 bridle, harness. 2 restraint, restriction, limitation, control.
➤*verb* restrain, restrict, limit, check, curb, hold back, slow down, control.

reinforce *verb* strengthen, fortify, support, brace, shore up, back up, consolidate, buttress, bolster, stiffen, supplement.

reinstate *verb* restore, replace, reinstall, re-establish, recall, rehabilitate.

reiterate *verb* repeat, iterate, restate, recapitulate, recap (*inf*), say again, dwell on, harp on.

reject *verb* 1 refuse, turn down, decline, pass up, spurn, rebuff, repudiate. 2 cast out, cast off, brush off, repudiate, spurn, rebuff, jilt, abandon, exclude, expel.
➤*noun* discard, second.

rejoice *verb* exult, triumph, glory, revel, celebrate, make merry.

rejoinder *noun* reply, answer, response, riposte, retort.

relapse verb revert, slip back, lapse, backslide, regress, retrogress, go backwards, degenerate, deteriorate, decline, sink.
>*noun* reversion, regression, deterioration, setback.

relate verb 1 narrate, tell, recount, rehearse, describe, detail, report. 2 connect, link, associate, couple. 3 refer, apply, regard, respect, concern, pertain. 4 identify, sympathize, empathize, feel for, understand.

related adj 1 connected, interconnected, associated, linked, allied, affiliated, concomitant, relevant. 2 connected, akin, kindred.

relation noun 1 relationship, connection, link, association, affiliation, correlation, affinity, similarity. 2 relative, kinsman, kinswoman, kin. 3 reference, respect, regard, concern, bearing, relevance, application, applicability. 4 narration, telling, recounting, account, report, story. 5 contact, connections, dealings, intercourse, communications. 6 terms, rapport. 7 sex, intercourse, sexual intercourse, sexual relationship, intimacy, affair.

relationship noun 1 connection, association, link, bond, affinity, similarity, closeness, correspondence. 2 affair, romance, fling (inf), liaison, friendship.

relative noun relation, kinsman, kinswoman, kin, family.
>*adj* comparative, comparable, proportionate, reasonable, moderate.
relative to 1 relevant to, relating to, applicable to, pertaining to. 2 apropos, with regard to, with respect to.

relax verb 1 loosen, slacken, ease. 2 moderate, ease, soften. 3 rest, unwind, wind down, take it easy, chill out (inf), put one's feet up (inf). 4 calm down, ease up, unbend, loosen up, lighten up.

relaxation noun 1 loosening, slackening, easing, letting-up, easing-off, moderation, softening, rest, leisure, recreation, fun. 2 recreation, amusement, diversion, entertainment, hobby, pastime.

relay noun 1 relief, shift. 2 passing-on, transmission, communication.
>*verb* 1 broadcast, transmit, send. 2 communicate, circulate, pass on, hand on.

release verb 1 free, set free, turn loose, let out, let go, liberate, unshackle, untie, unbind, unchain, unfasten, unleash. 2 clear, absolve, discharge, let off, excuse, exempt. 3 publish, make public, issue, broadcast, distribute, make available, put out, reveal, disclose.
>*noun* 1 freedom, liberation, emancipation, deliverance, untying, unbinding, acquittal, discharge, publication, publishing, issue, broadcasting, dissemination, announcement, declaration. 2 record, recording, CD, disc, album, single, book, publication, film.

relegate verb demote, send down, downgrade.

relent verb 1 unbend, yield, give way, soften, come round, show mercy. 2 let up, abate, die down, drop, fall off, ease.

relentless adj 1 unrelenting, unyielding, implacable, remorseless, uncompromising, ruthless, strict, unforgiving, hard, harsh, merciless, pitiless. 2 unrelenting, unremitting, unflagging, persistent, incessant, unabated, non-stop, taxing, punishing.

relevant adj pertinent, germane, apropos, applicable, to the point, to the purpose, apposite, appropriate, apt.

reliable adj trustworthy, dependable, faithful, conscientious, honest, unfailing, tried and tested, steadfast, staunch, solid, sure, certain, infallible.

reliance noun 1 trust, confidence, faith, belief, conviction. 2 dependence, leaning.

relic noun survival, remnant, trace, vestige.

relief noun 1 alleviation, reduction, mitigation, soothing, allaying, easing, release, remedy, cure. 2 comfort, solace, consolation, reassurance. 3 help, aid, assistance, support. 4 respite, rest, remission, breather (inf), letup (inf), break, interruption, lull, diversion, variation. 5 replacement, substitute, stand-in, locum, supply, temp (inf), understudy. 6 contrast, distinctness, vividness, intensity.

relieve verb 1 ease, alleviate, mitigate, assuage, allay, soothe, soften, reduce, diminish, abate, cure, heal. 2 break up, interrupt, lighten, brighten, vary. 3 replace, take over from, stand in for, take the place of, substitute for. 4 free, release, liberate, unburden, excuse, exempt.

religious *adj* 1 holy, sacred, divine, spiritual, theological, doctrinal, devotional, church. 2 pious, godly, God-fearing, devout, churchgoing, practising, committed, faithful. 3 strict, rigorous, exact, scrupulous, meticulous, conscientious, faithful.

relinquish *verb* 1 abandon, surrender, yield, cede, abdicate, resign, sign away, hand over. 2 let go, release, drop. 3 abandon, give up, renounce, yield, waive, forgo, abstain from, discontinue.

relish *verb* 1 enjoy, delight in, revel in, luxuriate in, savour, appreciate. 2 look forward to, anticipate.
➤*noun* 1 enjoyment, pleasure, delight, gusto, zest, satisfaction, appreciation, fondness. 2 taste, flavour, savour, tang, piquancy. 3 sauce, chutney, pickle, condiment, seasoning.

reluctant *adj* unwilling, unenthusiastic, grudging, disinclined, hesitant, loath, averse, slow.

rely *verb* 1 depend, count, bank, trust, swear by, have confidence in, be sure of. 2 depend on, lean on.

remain *verb* 1 survive, last, abide, endure, be left. 2 stay, stay behind, stay put, linger, wait.

remainder *noun* rest, remnants, vestiges, leftovers, residue, balance, surplus, excess.

remains *pl noun* 1 remnants, remainder, rest, leavings, leftovers, residue, dregs, vestiges, traces, relics. 2 corpse, body, ashes.

remark *verb* 1 comment, observe, mention, say, state, assert. 2 notice, note, see, perceive, observe, regard, heed.
➤*noun* 1 comment, observation, reference, utterance, statement, assertion. 2 attention, comment, mention, heed, regard, notice.

remarkable *adj* notable, noteworthy, memorable, outstanding, impressive, striking, extraordinary, exceptional, rare, singular, signal, important, significant, peculiar, strange, amazing, surprising, wonderful.

remedy *noun* 1 cure, antidote, treatment, medicine, medication, therapy. 2 solution, answer, corrective, countermeasure.
➤*verb* cure, heal, counteract, treat, relieve, rectify, correct, put right, sort out, fix, repair, solve.

remember *verb* 1 recall, recollect, call to mind, look back on, hark back to. 2 bear in mind, keep in mind, memorize, learn, retain, hold onto. 3 commemorate, record, mark, celebrate. 4 send one's regards, send greetings.

remembrance *noun* 1 memory, recollection, recall. 2 souvenir, memento, keepsake, token, reminder. 3 commemoration, memorial, relic.

remind *verb* 1 prompt, nudge, jog somebody's memory, refresh somebody's memory. 2 bring back, call up, evoke, put one in mind.

reminisce *verb* remember, recall, think back, hark back, call to mind, review.

reminiscence *noun* 1 memory, recall, recollection, remembrance, review. 2 memoirs, memories, anecdotes.

reminiscent *adj* evocative, suggestive, redolent.

remiss *adj* negligent, careless, inattentive, thoughtless, casual, forgetful, derelict, slack, lax, lackadaisical.

remission *noun* 1 suspension, abrogation, amnesty, reprieve. 2 forgiveness, pardon, absolution. 3 sending, dispatch, forwarding, posting, mailing. 4 easing, moderation, abatement, slackening, lessening, decrease. 5 respite, suspension, abeyance.

remit *verb* 1 send, dispatch, mail, post, forward. 2 halt, stop, cancel, repeal, rescind, revoke, set aside, suspend. 3 ease, slacken, moderate, abate, dwindle, subside, decrease, diminish. 4 pass, refer, transfer, hand on. 5 pardon, forgive, absolve.

remittance *noun* payment, fee, allowance.

remnant *noun* 1 remainder, rest, remains, residue, scrap, shred, fragment, bit, trace, vestige, leftover. 2 piece, oddment.

remonstrate *verb* argue, take issue, expostulate, object, protest, reprimand, reproach.

remorse *noun* regret, sorrow, contrition, penitence, repentance, self-reproach, guilt, shame.

remorseless *adj* 1 relentless, unrelenting, unremitting, indefatigable, persistent, implacable. 2 merciless, pitiless, unforgiving, cruel, hard, ruthless.

remote *adj* **1** distant, far, far-off, faraway, far-removed. **2** sequestered, secluded, isolated, lonely, godforsaken, inaccessible, outlying, out-of-the-way, off the beaten track. **3** slight, slender, slim, small, faint, outside. **4** detached, reserved, stand-offish, distant, aloof, withdrawn, indifferent, unconcerned, uninvolved.

removal *noun* moving, move, shifting, transfer, taking away, withdrawal, relocation, departure, deletion, elimination, obliteration, eradication, destruction, extermination, firing, sacking (*inf*), expulsion, ejection, ousting, dismissal, eviction, amputation, cutting off, excision.

remove *verb* **1** move, shift, transport, transfer, convey, take away, take off, detach, doff, shed, cut off, chop off, amputate. **2** eliminate, eradicate, get rid of, abolish, do away with, obliterate, expunge, erase, delete. **3** oust, throw out, depose, unseat, dislodge, expel, eject, evict, dismiss, discharge, fire, sack (*inf*). **4** move, relocate, transfer.

remunerate *verb* pay, reward, recompense, compensate.

renaissance *noun* renascence, rebirth, revival, renewal, reappearance, resurgence, re-emergence.

rend *verb* tear, rip, split, rupture, fracture, break, crack, burst, splinter, smash, shatter.

render *verb* **1** give, supply, provide, furnish. **2** present, submit, offer, tender. **3** surrender, deliver, yield. **4** hand over, send in, submit, tender, deliver. **5** perform, act, play, interpret. **6** represent, depict, portray, do, paint, reproduce. **7** make, cause to be, leave. **8** translate, transcribe, interpret, express, put.

rendezvous *noun* **1** meeting, appointment, date, assignation. **2** meeting-place, venue.
➤*verb* come together, gather, meet, assemble, convene, rally.

rendition *noun* **1** rendering, performance, execution, presentation, delivery, interpretation, depiction, portrayal, reading. **2** translation, interpretation.

renegade *noun* traitor, apostate, turncoat, defector, betrayer, deserter, runaway, rat (*inf*).

renege *verb* go back on, break, default, back out, pull out, backslide, cop out (*inf*).

renew *verb* **1** recommence, resume, restart, repeat, continue, prolong. **2** revive, restore, reconstitute, regenerate, rejuvenate, revitalize, renovate, overhaul, modernize. **3** replenish, restock, refresh.

renounce *verb* **1** give up, forgo, waive, abandon, forswear, abdicate, resign, relinquish, yield, surrender, cede. **2** disown, repudiate, cast off, discard, reject, spurn, abandon, deny, recant, renege, abjure.

renovate *verb* restore, renew, repair, do up (*inf*), fix up, revamp, remodel, modernize, refurbish, redecorate, refit, rehabilitate.

renown *noun* fame, celebrity, illustriousness, stardom, note, eminence, prominence, reputation, distinction, prestige, honour, glory.

renowned *adj* famous, famed, well-known, celebrated, distinguished, illustrious, eminent, prominent, notable, noted.

rent[1] *verb* **1** hire, lease, charter. **2** lease, let.
➤*noun* **1** rental, lease. **2** rental, hire, lease, tariff.

rent[2] *noun* tear, rip, slit, gash, slash, hole, crack, split.

renunciation *verb* surrender, waiving, giving up, abdication, resignation, relinquishment, repudiation, rejection, disowning, abandonment, denial, abjuration.

repair[1] *verb* **1** mend, fix, put right, service, overhaul, maintain, renovate, renew. **2** remedy, rectify, patch up, redress, make good.
➤*noun* **1** mending, fixing, restoration, renovation, overhaul, servicing, refit. **2** mend, patch. **3** condition, state, shape, nick (*inf*).

repair[2] *verb* go, move, withdraw, head for, resort, betake oneself.

reparation *noun* **1** atonement, redress, requital, restitution, recompense, compensation. **2** amends, compensation, damages.

repartee *noun* banter, badinage, raillery, wordplay.

repast *noun* meal, feast, banquet, spread (*inf*).

repay *verb* **1** refund, return, pay back, give back, reimburse. **2** recompense, requite, compensate, indemnify, reward, settle up with. **3** get back at, hit back, get even with, reciprocate, retaliate, revenge, avenge.

repeal *verb* rescind, revoke, annul, nullify, void, abolish, quash, cancel, set aside.

repeat *verb* **1** say again, restate, recapitulate, recap (*inf*), go over, reiterate, quote, reproduce, echo, parrot. **2** redo, duplicate, replay, rerun, reshow.
➤ *noun* **1** repetition, recapitulation, retelling, restatement, reiteration. **2** repetition, duplication, copy, replay, rerun, reshowing, rebroadcast.

repel *verb* **1** repulse, drive back, push back, force back, fend off, ward off, hold off, stave off, resist, keep at bay. **2** disgust, nauseate, sicken, revolt, offend.

repellent *adj* repulsive, disgusting, revolting, nauseating, sickening, repugnant, abhorrent, offensive, distasteful, obnoxious, loathsome, vile.

repent *verb* **1** regret, rue, lament, deplore. **2** be penitent, be contrite, feel remorse, reproach oneself, see the light.

repercussion *noun* result, consequence, effect, reverberation, aftermath, ripple, shock wave.

repetition *noun* **1** restatement, retelling, recapitulation, recap (*inf*), repeat, recurrence, reiteration, echoing, parroting, quoting, copying, repetitiousness, tautology, redundancy. **2** duplication, reproduction, copy, rehash.

repetitious *adj* recurrent, unchanging, unvaried, boring, tedious, monotonous, samey (*inf*).

replace *verb* **1** put back, return, restore. **2** supersede, take the place of, succeed, follow, oust, supplant, relieve, take over from, substitute for, stand in for, fill in for, cover for, deputize for, understudy.

replacement *noun* substitute, stand-in, reserve, understudy, locum, supply, proxy, surrogate, successor.

replenish *verb* refill, top up, recharge, reload, restock, stock up, fill up, make up, renew.

replete *adj* **1** full, gorged, sated, satiated, stuffed, bursting. **2** packed, jam-packed, crammed, full, well-stocked, well-provided, overflowing, brimming.

replica *noun* copy, carbon copy, duplicate, reproduction, facsimile, model, clone.

reply *verb* **1** answer, respond, counter, rejoin, retort, riposte. **2** react, retaliate, acknowledge.
➤ *noun* answer, response, acknowledgement, rejoinder, comeback (*inf*), retort, riposte, reaction, retaliation.

report *noun* **1** account, statement, study, file, dossier. **2** account, article, item, story, review, write-up, description, announcement, declaration, news, word, message, communiqué, dispatch, bulletin. **3** bang, crack, boom, shot, blast, explosion, detonation, discharge.
➤ *verb* **1** tell, relate, recount, describe, detail, divulge, disclose, relay, pass on, communicate, broadcast, publish, state, announce, declare. **2** complain about, accuse, denounce, inform on, shop (*inf*), grass on (*inf*). **3** present oneself, appear, come, arrive, turn up. **4** cover, chronicle, record, document, investigate, enquire into, look into.

reporter *noun* journalist, correspondent, columnist, newspaperman, newspaperwoman, writer, hack (*inf*), newshound (*inf*).

repose[1] *noun* **1** rest, ease, relaxation, time off, sleep, slumber, inactivity, idleness, inertia, peace, quiet, calm. **2** composure, calmness, poise, aplomb, self-possession.
➤ *verb* rest, relax, laze, sleep, slumber, lie, recline, stretch out.

repose[2] *verb* place, put, set, lodge.

repository *noun* **1** store, storehouse, storeroom, depository, depot, archive, receptacle, container. **2** storehouse, treasury, reservoir.

reprehensible *adj* blameworthy, culpable, disgraceful, shameful, unworthy, dishonourable, discreditable, unpardonable, wrong, bad, remiss.

represent *verb* **1** symbolize, stand for, denote, mean, betoken, indicate, correspond to. **2** embody, exemplify, personify, typify. **3** constitute, mean, amount to. **4** depict, picture, paint, draw, sketch, portray, describe, show, express, enact. **5** act for, appear for, speak for, substitute for. **6** portray, act, appear as. **7** pose as, pass off as, describe as, claim to be.

representation noun **1** presentation, depiction, portrayal, description, performance. **2** portrait, picture, depiction, painting, drawing, image, model, likeness. **4** statement, deposition, report, declaration, allegation. **5** protest, protestation, complaint, remonstration.

representative noun **1** agent, deputy, delegate, envoy, ambassador, spokesperson, spokesman, spokeswoman, proxy, deputy, substitute. **2** salesman, commercial traveller, agent, rep (inf). **3** example, exemplar, exemplification, specimen, illustration, embodiment.
➤adj **1** typical, usual, normal, archetypal, characteristic. **2** illustrative, indicative, symbolic, emblematic. **3** elective, elected, democratic, popular.

repress verb **1** hold back, hold in, keep back, control, restrain, suppress, bottle up, stifle, smother. **2** hold in check, check, curb, inhibit, restrain. **3** put down, quell, suppress, subdue, crush, squash, stamp out, stop, oppress, subjugate.

repression noun **1** oppression, subjugation, domination, suppression, quelling, crushing, tyranny, despotism, dictatorship, authoritarianism. **2** inhibition, control, restraint, stifling, smothering.

repressive adj oppressive, tyrannical, authoritarian, dictatorial, totalitarian, harsh, severe.

reprieve verb pardon, let off, spare, forgive, amnesty.
➤noun remission, stay of execution, deferment, pardon, let-off, amnesty.

reprimand verb admonish, scold, rebuke, reprove, lecture, castigate, blame, censure, criticize, take to task, tell off (inf), tick off (inf), bawl out (inf), carpet (inf), haul over the coals (inf), rap over the knuckles (inf).
➤noun rebuke, reproof, admonition, lecture, scolding, tongue-lashing, talking-to (inf), telling-off (inf), ticking-off (inf), dressing-down (inf), rocket (inf).

reprisal noun retaliation, retribution, revenge, vengeance, tit for tat (inf).

reproach verb blame, censure, criticize, find fault with, rebuke, reprove, reprimand, scold, chide, upbraid, berate, castigate, take to task, condemn.
➤noun **1** blame, censure, criticism, disapproval, rebuke, reproof, reprimand, scolding, condemnation, opprobrium, obloquy. **2** shame, disgrace, dishonour, discredit, slur, stain, blemish, blot, stigma.

reprobate adj corrupt, depraved, degenerate, dissolute, immoral, unprincipled, sinful, shameless, wicked, vile, bad, base.
➤noun villain, degenerate, miscreant, wretch, scoundrel, ne'er-do-well, sinner, wrongdoer, evildoer, rake, roué.

reproduce verb **1** duplicate, replicate, photocopy, copy, print, Xerox®. **2** recreate, reconstruct, replicate, copy, repeat, represent, emulate, imitate, match, ape, mimic, parallel, mirror, echo. **3** propagate, multiply, breed, procreate, spawn.

reproduction noun **1** propagation, breeding, procreation, proliferation. **2** duplicate, copy, replica, facsimile, print, photocopy, Xerox®.

reproof noun reproach, rebuke, reprimand, scolding, lecture, castigation, censure, criticism, blame.

reprove verb rebuke, scold, reproach, reprimand, admonish, lecture, chide, upbraid, berate, castigate, blame, censure, criticize, take to task, tell off (inf), slate (inf).

repudiate verb **1** reject, denounce, disavow, abjure, disclaim, forswear, retract, revoke, rescind, deny. **2** disown, abandon, cast off, cut off. **3** deny, contradict, disavow, gainsay.

repugnance noun repulsion, revulsion, horror, disgust, distaste, dislike, antipathy, loathing, abhorrence, aversion.

repugnant adj repellent, repulsive, revolting, disgusting, sickening, nauseating, offensive, abominable, hateful, distasteful, horrible, horrid, odious, loathsome, vile, abhorrent.

repulse verb **1** repel, drive back, beat off. **2** reject, refuse, rebuff, snub, spurn, turn down.

repulsive adj repellent, repugnant, revolting, disgusting, nauseating, sickening, offensive, distasteful, off-putting, obnoxious, odious, loathsome, abhorrent, abominable, hideous, ugly, foul, horrible, horrid.

reputable adj respectable, respected, of good repute, well-thought-of, esteemed, good, reliable, dependable, trustworthy, honest, above-board, legitimate.

reputation *noun* **1** good name, name, good character, standing, respectability, repute. **2** fame, renown, repute, celebrity.

repute *noun* **1** good reputation, high standing, stature, good name, esteem, distinction. **2** reputation, name, character.

reputed *adj* supposed, putative, apparent, ostensible, alleged, believed, considered, thought, reckoned, held, said, rumoured.

request *verb* **1** ask for, call for, plead for, seek, solicit, demand, desire, apply for, put in for. **2** ask, beseech, appeal to, petition.
➤*noun* entreaty, behest, application, desire, appeal, plea, petition, call, prayer, demand.

require *verb* **1** need, lack. **2** desire, want, wish, crave. **3** need, necessitate, involve, take, call for, demand, entail. **4** order, command, oblige, compel, enjoin, instruct, direct, bid.

requirement *noun* **1** need, necessity, necessary, want. **2** condition, demand, must, prerequisite, requisite, stipulation, precondition.

requisite *adj* required, needed, necessary, needful, essential, indispensable, vital, called-for.
➤*noun* **1** requirement, necessity, must, essential, precondition, prerequisite. **2** article, item.

requisition *noun* **1** application, order, request, claim, demand. **2** confiscation, seizure, appropriation, commandeering.
➤*verb* put in for, order, request, demand, commandeer, appropriate, seize, confiscate.

requite *verb* **1** repay, pay back, reciprocate, return. **2** reimburse, compensate, indemnify, make good. **3** retaliate, avenge.

rescind *verb* **1** repeal, revoke, countermand, cancel, set aside. **2** annul, nullify, void, quash, invalidate.

rescue *verb* save, deliver, redeem, ransom, free, liberate, release, extricate, recover, salvage.
➤*noun* saving, salvation, deliverance, redemption, freeing, liberation, emancipation, extrication, release, recovery, salvage.

research *noun* **1** investigation, enquiry, study, analysis, examination, exploration,

testing, experiment, experimentation. **2** investigation, enquiry, study, analysis, examination, probe, review, fact-finding, groundwork
➤*verb* investigate, enquire into, look into, probe, review, study, analyse, examine, explore.

resemblance *noun* **1** likeness, similarity, sameness, correspondence, comparability, parallelism, affinity, agreement, congruity, conformity. **2** similarity, correspondence.

resemble *verb* look like, be like, be similar to, remind one of, take after, mirror, echo, duplicate, parallel.

resent *verb* begrudge, grudge, take offence at, take exception to, take amiss, object to, dislike, envy.

reservation *noun* **1** saving, putting aside, retention, booking, arrangement, pre-arrangement, order, charter, hire. **2** qualification, limitation, condition, proviso, provision, stipulation. **3** misgiving, qualm, scruple, demur, doubt, hesitation. **4** reserve, preserve, park, sanctuary, enclave, territory.

reserve *verb* **1** withhold, keep back, save, conserve, retain, set aside, put by, store, stockpile, earmark. **2** book, order, arrange, prearrange, retain, hire, charter. **3** withhold, postpone, suspend, hold over, defer, delay.
➤*noun* **1** stock, supply, store, stockpile, fund, reservoir, pool, hoard, cache. **2** park, sanctuary, reservation, preserve, enclave, territory. **3** reservation, doubt, reluctance, qualm, scruple, qualification, condition, limitation, stipulation. **4** shyness, diffidence, reticence, detachment, remoteness, aloofness, self-restraint, restraint, self-control, constraint, formality, coolness. **5** substitute, auxiliary, spare, stand-in.
in reserve available, to hand, at one's disposal, spare, stored.

reserved *adj* reticent, shy, retiring, unsociable, uncommunicative, undemonstrative, unresponsive, unforthcoming, secretive, aloof, detached, distant, remote, standoffish, formal, cautious, cool.

reservoir *noun* **1** lake, pool, pond. **2** tank, cistern, container. **3** stock, supply, reserve, repository, store, fund.

reside verb **1** live, dwell, sojourn, stay, lodge. **2** lie, rest, dwell.

residence noun **1** house, home, abode, dwelling, quarters, lodging, accommodation, domicile, seat. **2** stay, sojourn, occupancy, occupation, tenancy.

resident noun inhabitant, citizen, denizen, occupier, occupant, householder, tenant, local, dweller, sojourner, guest, inmate, patient, client.
>*adj* **1** live-in, living-in. **2** local, neighbourhood, permanent, settled.

residue noun residuum, remainder, rest, balance, leavings, leftovers, dregs, lees.

resign verb **1** leave, quit, give notice, retire, step down, stand down. **2** give up, renounce, relinquish, vacate, surrender, yield, cede.

resignation noun **1** notice, letter of resignation. **2** retirement, standing-down, stepping-down, departure, relinquishment, surrender. **3** acquiescence, submission, acceptance, endurance, stoicism.

resigned adj reconciled, acquiescent, unresisting, submissive, passive, stoical, philosophical, defeatist.

resilient adj **1** springy, bouncy, elastic, rubbery. **2** durable, resistant, tough. **3** tough, strong, adaptable.

resist verb **1** withstand, repel, repulse, defy, stand up to, hold out against, stop, stem, curb, check. **2** fight, combat, oppose, counter, stand firm, stand up to, hold out against, face, confront. **3** refrain from, abstain from, refuse, forgo.

resistance noun **1** fight, opposition, stand, defiance, struggle, avoidance, hostility, aversion. **2** immunity.

resistant adj proof, impervious, unsusceptible, unaffected, immune, tough, strong, resilient.

resolute adj steadfast, firm, set, intent, determined, resolved, decided, staunch, stalwart, unwavering, unflinching, unswerving, unyielding, stubborn, obstinate, dogged, strong-willed, single-minded, persistent, tenacious, courageous.

resolution noun **1** firmness, determination, resolve, resoluteness, steadfastness, perseverance, persistence, commitment, staunchness, tenacity, zeal, staying power, doggedness, willpower, dedication, courage. **2** decision, resolve, intention, intent, aim, plan. **3** finding, verdict, decree, declaration, statement. **4** solving, resolving, solution, answer, working-out, cracking.

resolve verb **1** determine, decide, conclude, make up one's mind. **2** solve, explain, answer, fathom, work out, crack. **3** settle, sort out, clear up. **4** break down, break up, reduce, separate.
>*noun* **1** decision, resolution, intention, intent, aim, purpose. **2** determination, resolution, resoluteness, firmness, steadfastness, staunchness, doggedness, commitment, dedication, tenacity, zeal, courage, willpower.

resonant adj **1** resounding, reverberant, echoing. **2** loud, sonorous, strong, full, ringing, rich.

resort verb **1** fall back on, turn, have recourse, use, employ. **2** go, repair, visit, frequent.
>*noun* **1** centre, spot, place, holiday destination. **2** refuge, expedient, resource, alternative, choice, option, chance, hope.

resound verb resonate, reverberate, thunder, boom, ring, echo.

resounding adj decisive, emphatic, conclusive, thorough, remarkable, memorable, outstanding, impressive.

resource noun **1** ingenuity, enterprise, ability, inventiveness, imagination, resourcefulness. **2** expedient, resort, recourse. **3** capital, money, wherewithal, funds, assets, materials, property, supplies, stores, stocks, reserves, means.

resourceful adj ingenious, inventive, innovative, original, enterprising, creative, imaginative, quick-witted, versatile.

respect verb **1** look up to, revere, venerate, esteem, admire, think highly of, appreciate, prize, value, set store by. **2** heed, follow, observe, comply with, abide by. **3** consider, show regard for, take into account, remember.
>*noun* **1** reverence, veneration, appreciation, recognition, esteem, admiration. **2** politeness, courtesy, civility, regard, deference. **3** regard, heed, consideration, attention, notice. **4** aspect, regard, particular, point, detail.

with respect to with reference to, with relation to, as regards.

respectable *adj* **1** worthy, estimable, honourable, reputable, trustworthy, honest, upright. **2** proper, decent, decorous, good, presentable. **3** acceptable, reasonable, passable, fair, adequate, satisfactory, all right, OK (*inf*). **4** considerable, sizable, substantial, goodly.

respectful *adj* courteous, polite, well-mannered, civil, considerate, deferential, reverential.

respective *adj* individual, personal, separate, various, specific, particular, own.

respects *pl noun* greetings, compliments, regards, best wishes.

respite *noun* **1** pause, lull, rest, break, interval, intermission, hiatus, relief, breather (*inf*), breathing space, letup (*inf*). **2** adjournment, postponement, suspension, deferment, reprieve, remission, stay.

resplendent *adj* splendid, glorious, bright, brilliant, radiant, shining, dazzling.

respond *verb* **1** reply, answer, acknowledge, riposte. **2** answer, reply, counter, reciprocate, retaliate.

response *noun* reply, answer, acknowledgement, rejoinder, retort, riposte, reaction, feedback, comeback (*inf*).

responsibility *noun* **1** duty, obligation. **2** role, task, affair, business, concern, baby (*inf*). **2** accountability, answerability, liability, culpability, guilt, blame, onus, maturity, common sense, authority, power, influence.

responsible *adj* **1** in charge of, in control of, managing, controlling, accountable. **2** accountable, answerable, liable, culpable, at fault, guilty. **3** mature, adult. **4** dependable, reliable, trustworthy, honest. **5** level-headed, sober, sound, sensible, rational, reasonable. **4** important, powerful, senior, high-level (*inf*), executive.

responsive *adj* sensitive, receptive, open, alert, alive, aware, sympathetic, perceptive, on the ball (*inf*), with it (*inf*).

rest[1] *noun* **1** relaxation, idleness, leisure, repose, sleep, slumber, nap, doze, siesta, snooze (*inf*), lie-down (*inf*). **2** pause, lull, respite, break, breathing-space, breather (*inf*), time off, holiday. **3** motionlessness, inertia, standstill, repose, quiet, calm,

peace. **4** support, prop, brace, stand.
▶ *verb* **1** relax, take it easy, laze, lounge, go to bed, sleep, take a nap, catnap, doze, repose, recline, lie down, sit down, put one's feet up (*inf*). **2** cease, stop, take a break, have a breather (*inf*). **3** support, prop, stand, place, position, lean, lay. **4** lie, stand, lean. **5** hinge, hang, depend, rely.

rest[2] *noun* remainder, remains, residue, balance, leftovers, others.
▶ *verb* remain, stay, continue.

restful *adj* **1** relaxing, calming, soothing. **2** calm, tranquil, quiet, still, peaceful, sleepy, relaxing.

restitution *noun* **1** restoration, return, repayment, refund. **2** reparation, amends, damages, compensation, indemnity, recompense.

restive *adj* **1** restless, unsettled, uneasy, ill at ease, edgy, on edge, nervous, tense, agitated, fretful, fidgety, jumpy (*inf*), jittery (*inf*). **2** refractory, recalcitrant, wilful, wayward, unruly.

restless *adj* **1** uneasy, ill at ease, restive, edgy, on edge, fretful, nervous, anxious, worried, agitated, troubled, impatient, fidgety. **2** disturbed, broken, sleepless, wakeful. **3** moving, active, changing, unsettled, wandering, roving, roaming.

restoration *noun* **1** renovation, repair, reconstruction, rebuilding, refurbishment. **2** revival, revitalization, reconditioning, rehabilitation, renewal, reintroduction, re-establishment, reimposition. **3** return, restitution, replacement, repayment. **4** reinstatement, reinstitution, reinstallation.

restore *verb* **1** return, give back, hand back. **2** reintroduce, bring back, reinstate, re-establish, reimpose. **3** renovate, redecorate, refurbish, repair, do up (*inf*), mend, rebuild, reconstruct, rehabilitate, renew, revive, resuscitate, revitalize, cure, return, replace, put back.

restrain *verb* **1** hold back, curb, control, hold in check, keep within bounds, bridle, moderate, contain, rein in. **2** prevent, stop, hold back, hinder, obstruct, inhibit. **3** detain, arrest, lock up, imprison. **4** hold back, tie up, fetter, manacle, pinion.

restrained *adj* controlled, self-controlled, undemonstrative, calm, cool, muted, quiet, soft, subdued, subtle, discreet, understated, low-key.

restraint noun 1 constraint, check, curb, block, barrier, hindrance, impediment, deterrent. 2 self-restraint, self-control, self-discipline, moderation, judiciousness. 3 reserve, reticence, subtlety, tastefulness, discretion, understatedness. 4 restriction, confinement, limitation, control.

restrict verb 1 impede, hamper, hinder, handicap, cramp. 2 regulate, control, limit, moderate, restrain.

restricted adj 1 cramped, confined, small, narrow, limited, tight. 2 limited, controlled, regulated. 3 off limits, out of bounds, private.

restriction noun 1 ban, embargo, regulation, condition, provision, stipulation, qualification. 2 restraint, limitation, control, confinement, constraint, cramping, hindrance.

result noun 1 consequence, outcome, issue, effect, upshot, pay-off (inf), end, conclusion, aftermath, repercussion, product, end-product, fruit. 2 answer, solution.
➤verb 1 ensue, follow, come about, issue, proceed, stem, flow, arise, emerge, spring, develop, evolve, occur, happen. 2 end, finish, culminate, terminate.

resume verb renew, recommence, restart, reopen, reinstitute, continue, proceed, carry on.

résumé noun summary, précis, abstract, synopsis, outline, overview, breakdown.

resurrect verb 1 raise, revive. 2 revive, renew, restore, resuscitate, bring back, reintroduce, re-establish.

resurrection noun revival, reappearance, comeback, restoration, return, reintroduction, re-establishment.

resuscitate verb 1 revive, bring round, save. 2 revive, revitalize, reanimate, reinvigorate, resurrect, breathe new life into.

retain verb 1 keep, maintain, save, preserve, hold, keep hold of, hang on to (inf). 2 remember, recall, recollect, keep in mind. 3 engage, employ, hire.

retainer noun 1 servant, domestic, attendant, valet. 2 fee, payment, advance.

retaliate verb strike back, hit back, fight back, pay someone back, get back at, get one's own back.

retard verb delay, slow down, slow up, hold back, hold up, set back, detain, check, restrain, hinder, impede.

retch verb gag, heave.

reticent adj reserved, restrained, shy, diffident, taciturn, uncommunicative, unforthcoming, secretive, tight-lipped.

retinue noun suite, followers, entourage, attendants, escort, staff.

retire verb 1 give up work, stop work, resign, bow out (inf). 2 withdraw, go away, leave, depart. 3 withdraw, retreat, pull back, fall back. 4 go to bed, turn in (inf).

retirement noun 1 withdrawal, departure, resignation. 2 seclusion, solitude, retreat.

retiring adj shy, reserved, reticent, quiet, diffident, modest, unassuming, unassertive, self-effacing.

retort verb answer, reply, riposte, counter, rejoin.
➤noun answer, reply, riposte, rejoinder.

retract verb 1 recant, withdraw, take back, disclaim, disavow, repudiate, disown. 2 go back on, renege on, abrogate. 3 draw back, draw in, pull in, sheathe.

retreat verb retire, withdraw, depart, leave, pull back, fall back, back off, give ground, give way, recoil, shrink, turn tail (inf), flee, take flight.
➤noun 1 retirement, withdrawal, pulling back, falling back, flight. 2 refuge, haven, harbour, hideaway, asylum.

retrench verb 1 economize, save, cut back. 2 curtail, reduce, decrease, lessen, cut, slim down, rationalize, downsize.

retribution noun punishment, justice, just deserts, nemesis, revenge, vengeance, retaliation, reprisal, tit for tat.

retrieve verb 1 recover, regain, get back, recoup. 2 salvage, rescue, save, restore, repair, set right. 3 bring back, fetch, collect.

retrograde adj 1 backward, reverse. 2 reversed, inverse. 3 backward, retrogressive.

retrogress verb decline, deteriorate, relapse, regress, return, revert, backslide.

retrospect noun review, survey.
in retrospect retrospectively, on reflection, with hindsight, looking back.

return verb 1 go back, go home, come back, come again, recur, reappear. 2 restore, replace, put back, reinstate, re-install. 3 reciprocate, requite, repay, do the same, match. 4 give back, send back, repay, refund, remit. 5 yield, earn, bring in, make, net. 6 pass back, throw back, hit back, send back. 7 elect, vote in, choose. 8 pronounce, deliver, bring in, announce, declare. 9 go back, come back, revert.
➤*noun* 1 homecoming, reappearance, arrival. 2 restoration, replacement, restitution, reinstatement, reciprocation, repayment. 3 profit, gain, income, revenue, yield, interest. 4 statement, report, account, summary.

reveal verb 1 expose, uncover, lay bare, unveil, show, display. 2 disclose, divulge, make known, make public, tell, let out, let slip, let on, publicize, betray, leak, give away.

revel verb 1 bask, luxuriate, relish, savour, rejoice, delight, take pleasure. 2 carouse, make merry, celebrate, party, live it up (*inf*).
➤*noun* carousal, spree, merrymaking, revelry, festivity, jollification, party.

revelation noun 1 uncovering, bringing to light, disclosure, exposure, divulgence, publishing, publicizing, broadcasting, leaking, betrayal, unmasking, showing. 2 disclosure, confession, admission, information, communication, announcement, leak.

revenge noun 1 vengeance, retribution, reprisal, retaliation. 2 vengefulness, spite, vindictiveness, malice, ill will, animosity, hostility, hatred.
➤*verb* avenge, repay, retaliate, exact retribution for, settle a score, get even with.

revenue noun income, receipts, return, yield, profit, gain, proceeds.

reverberate verb echo, resonate, resound, ring.

revere verb venerate, honour, worship, idolize, admire, respect, esteem, look up to.

reverence noun veneration, worship, honour, admiration, respect, esteem, deference, awe.
➤*verb* revere, admire, respect, venerate.

reverent adj reverential, solemn, pious, respectful, humble, adoring, devoted.

reverie noun 1 dream, fantasy, daydream. 2 trance, abstraction, musing, woolgathering, daydreaming, brown study.

reversal noun U-turn, turn-round, turnabout, about-turn, about-face, volte-face, exchange, change, swapping, overturning, revocation, repeal, countermanding, rescinding, cancellation, negation.

reverse verb 1 back, back up, move backwards, retreat, backtrack. 2 invert, transpose, turn round, change, exchange, swap. 3 upend, upset, invert. 4 negate, invalidate, cancel, quash, overrule, set aside, revoke, annul, declare null and void, rescind, repeal.
➤*noun* 1 opposite, contrary, converse, inverse, antithesis. 2 back, rear. 3 other side, flip side, underside. 4 setback, blow, defeat, failure, disappointment, upset, misfortune, mishap, mischance, problem, difficulty.
➤*adj* 1 opposite, contrary, converse, inverse. 2 reversed, backwards, inverted, transposed.

revert verb return, go back, relapse, backslide.

review noun 1 survey, report, study, analysis, assessment, inspection, examination, appraisal, re-examination, reassessment, re-evaluation, reconsideration, reappraisal, rethink. 2 notice, criticism, critique, commentary. 3 periodical, journal, magazine, newspaper. 4 parade, inspection, march past.
➤*verb* 1 reconsider, re-examine, reassess, re-evaluate, reappraise, revise, rethink. 2 inspect, examine, analyse, survey, study, assess, appraise, criticize, weigh up, discuss.

revile verb criticize, censure, condemn, abuse, scorn, vilify.

revise noun 1 change, alter, reconsider, review. 2 edit, rewrite, reword, correct, amend, emend, change, alter, rework, recast, update. 3 study, go over, reread, mug up (*inf*), bone up on (*inf*).

revision noun 1 correction, editing, rewriting, updating, alteration, emendation, recasting, correction, amendment, changing, reconsideration, re-examination, review. 2 study, rereading, mugging up (*inf*).

revival *noun* **1** resuscitation, revitalization, renewal, resurgence, upsurge. **2** resurrection, restoration, reintroduction, re-establishment, reinstatement.

revive *verb* **1** resuscitate, bring round, save, recover, recover consciousness, come round, wake up, rally, restore, reinvigorate, revitalize. **2** renew, restore, regenerate, rekindle, resurrect, revitalize, re-establish.

revoke *verb* rescind, repeal, annul, nullify, declare null and void, void, abolish, cancel, quash, reverse, set aside.

revolt *noun* rebellion, rising, uprising, insurrection, mutiny, coup d'état, putsch.
➤*verb* **1** rebel, rise up, rise, mutiny. **2** disgust, repel, nauseate, sicken, turn one's stomach, offend, outrage, scandalize.

revolting *adj* repulsive, repellent, repugnant, offensive, disgusting, nauseating, sickening, foul, horrid, abominable, appalling, horrible, hateful, vile.

revolution *noun* **1** revolt, rebellion, uprising, sedition, putsch, coup, coup d'état. **2** transformation, innovation, reformation, upheaval, cataclysm, sea change, change, shift. **3** rotation, turn, circle, circuit, cycle.

revolutionary *adj* **1** rebellious, rebel, mutinous, subversive, extremist, seditious, insurgent. **2** radical, complete, far-reaching, thoroughgoing, profound, drastic, progressive, innovative, new, novel.
➤*noun* rebel, revolutionist, insurgent, subversive.

revolve *verb* **1** go round, rotate, turn, wheel, whirl, spin, circle, orbit. **2** centre on, turn on, hinge on. **3** turn over, mull over, consider, think over, meditate, ponder.

revulsion *noun* repugnance, repulsion, disgust, nausea, loathing, hatred, abhorrence, aversion.

reward *noun* **1** payment, recompense, return, compensation, pay-off, benefit, prize, award, bounty. **2** punishment, retribution, retaliation, just deserts, deserts, comeuppance (*inf*).
➤*verb* recompense, repay, requite, compensate, honour.

rewarding *adj* satisfying, pleasing, gratifying, worthwhile, fulfilling, enriching, beneficial, fruitful, valuable.

rhetoric *noun* **1** eloquence, oratory, delivery. **2** grandiloquence, magniloquence, hyperbole, bombast, pomposity,.

rhetorical *adj* **1** oratorical, verbal, stylistic. **2** flowery, florid, pretentious, pompous, magniloquent, grandiloquent, high-flown, high-sounding, bombastic, declamatory, artificial, insincere, empty.

rhyme *noun* poetry, verse, poem, jingle, song, ditty.

rhythm *noun* **1** beat, pulse, tempo, throb. **2** metre, cadence, accent. **3** flow, movement, pattern, regularity.

ribald *adj* bawdy, risqué, racy, naughty, suggestive, smutty, off-colour, dirty, filthy, rude, obscene, blue (*inf*), irreverent, salacious, scurrilous, coarse, earthy.

rich *adj* **1** wealthy, affluent, moneyed, prosperous, well-off, well-to-do, well-heeled (*inf*), flush (*inf*), loaded (*inf*), rolling (*inf*). **2** fertile, productive. **3** well-provided, well-stocked, well-supplied, packed, steeped, abounding, overflowing, replete, full, rife. **4** valuable, precious, expensive, costly, priceless, dear. **5** lavish, lush, sumptuous, luxurious, splendid, gorgeous, superb, opulent, exuberant. **6** heavy, creamy, oily, spicy, fatty, full-bodied, full-flavoured. **7** bright, vivid, brilliant, intense, strong, warm, vibrant, deep. **8** deep, sonorous, resonant, full. **9** ironic, outrageous, preposterous, ridiculous.

riches *pl noun* wealth, affluence, fortune, treasure, gold, money, assets, means, resources.

richly *adv* **1** lavishly, expensively, luxuriously, gorgeously, sumptuously, splendidly, superbly, magnificently. **2** fully, thoroughly, completely, amply.

rickety *adj* shaky, unstable, insecure, unsteady, wobbly, flimsy, decrepit, ramshackle, dilapidated, broken-down.

rid *verb* clear, free, relieve, unburden, purge.
get rid of discard, throw away, throw out, dispose of, do away with, eject, expel, weed out, dump, jettison, scrap, chuck out (*inf*), ditch (*inf*), junk (*inf*).

riddle *noun* puzzle, conundrum, enigma, mystery, poser.

ride *verb* **1** sit on, mount, bestride,

control, handle, manage. **2** travel, go, journey, move.
➤*noun* journey, trip, excursion, jaunt, outing, drive, spin (*inf*), lift.

ridge *noun* crest, bank, escarpment, saddle, range, spine.

ridicule *noun* mockery, derision, scorn, laughter, taunting, teasing, jeering.
➤*verb* mock, scorn, deride, laugh at, make fun of, poke fun at, pooh-pooh (*inf*), scoff at, sneer at, jeer at, taunt.

ridiculous *adj* absurd, ludicrous, laughable, risible, comical, farcical, funny, nonsensical, senseless, foolish, stupid, fatuous, inane, pointless, silly, preposterous.

rife *adj* **1** prevalent, prevailing, common, rampant, widespread, general, universal. **2** teeming, swarming, alive, overflowing, abounding.

riffraff *noun* rabble, mob, hoi polloi, scum (*inf*).

rifle *verb* **1** ransack, rummage, rake, search. **2** rob, steal, thieve, burgle.

rift *noun* **1** split, cleft, fault, fissure, fracture, crack, breach, break. **2** difference, disagreement, quarrel, falling-out, split, breach, division.

rig *verb* **1** equip, supply, furnish, provide. **2** kit out, fit, outfit, clothe, dress, garb, turn out. **3** erect, build, put up, improvise, fix up, put together, cobble together (*inf*), knock up (*inf*).
➤*noun* **1** gear, equipment, apparatus, machinery, tackle. **2** kit, outfit, gear.

rig *verb* manipulate, falsify, fake, fix (*inf*), cook (*inf*), fiddle, twist, engineer, arrange.

right *adj* **1** just, fair, equitable, lawful, legal, good, virtuous, moral, ethical, honourable, honest. **2** true, factual, correct, accurate, exact, valid, authentic, genuine, legitimate. **3** proper, fit, fitting, apt, appropriate, suitable, advantageous, convenient, opportune, favourable. **4** fine, well, healthy, fit, sound, normal, sane, rational, all there (*inf*). **5** real, complete, absolute, total, thorough, utter. **6** conservative, Tory, true-blue, reactionary.
➤*adv* **1** properly, correctly, well, satisfactorily. **2** precisely, exactly, squarely, slap-bang (*inf*). **3** straight, directly, in a straight line. **4** immediately, quickly, directly, straightaway, without delay. **5** all the way,

totally, completely, entirely, quite.
➤*noun* **1** claim, title, privilege, prerogative, entitlement, authority, power, licence, freedom. **2** justice, fairness, equity, legality, good, goodness, righteousness, virtue, rectitude, honesty, truth, integrity, honour, morality, ethics.
➤*verb* **1** set upright, stand up, adjust. **2** straighten out, sort out, rectify, correct, redress, repair, fix, put right, tidy up. **3** avenge, settle, redress.
by rights rightfully, rightly, in fairness, justly, legally, lawfully, legitimately.

right away *adv* immediately, right now, now, straight away, at once, forthwith, without delay, without hesitation.

righteous *adj* **1** good, virtuous, moral, upright, law-abiding, honest, honourable, worthy, God-fearing, sinless, just, fair, equitable. **2** justifiable, justified, well-founded, warranted.

rightful *adj* **1** legal, lawful. **2** legitimate, genuine, valid. **3** just, fair, equitable. **4** proper, suitable, correct, right, real, fitting.

rigid *adj* **1** stiff, hard, inflexible, unbendable, inelastic. **2** fixed, set, firm, hard and fast, unalterable. **3** fixed, set, uncompromising, intransigent, unrelenting, inflexible.

rigorous *adj* **1** strict, stern, severe, hard, harsh, tough, rigid, inflexible, uncompromising, exacting, demanding. **2** severe, hard, harsh, austere, tough, stringent, demanding. **3** meticulous, painstaking, thorough, scrupulous, punctilious, exact, precise.

rigour *noun* **1** severity, hardship, harshness, ordeal. **2** strictness, firmness, sternness, severity, harshness, inflexibility, rigidity, intransigence. **3** accuracy, precision, exactitude, meticulousness, punctiliousness.

rile *verb* annoy, irritate, vex, irk, upset, exasperate, aggravate (*inf*), anger.

rim *noun* **1** edge, lip, brim. **2** edge, margin, border.

rind *noun* skin, peel, husk.

ring[1] *noun* **1** band, circle, hoop. **2** circle, halo, round, band, girdle. **3** syndicate, combine, cartel, gang, crew, clique, coterie, league, alliance. **4** arena, enclosure, area.

➤*verb* encircle, surround, gird, girdle, circle, encompass, enclose, fence in, hem in.

ring[2] *verb* **1** peal, chime, toll, knell, tinkle, jingle, clang. **2** resound, resonate, reverberate. **3** herald, signal, usher in, announce, proclaim. **4** phone, telephone, call, give a bell (*inf*), give a buzz (*inf*), give a tinkle (*inf*).

➤*noun* **1** tolling, toll, ringing, peal, knell, chime, clang, tinkle. **2** call, buzz (*inf*), bell (*inf*), tinkle (*inf*).

rinse *verse* wash, clean, cleanse, bathe, dip, swill, flush.

riot *noun* **1** disturbance, commotion, tumult, anarchy, lawlessness, disorder. **2** display, show, splash, flourish, extravaganza.

➤*verb* **1** rampage, go on the rampage, run riot, run amok, take to the streets. **2** revel, celebrate, make merry, paint the town red (*inf*).

run riot 1 rampage, raise hell (*inf*), run amok, run wild. **2** spread, proliferate.

riotous *adj* unruly, unrestrained, disorderly, rowdy, wild, violent, lawless, anarchic, boisterous, rowdy, uproarious, tumultuous.

rip *verb* tear, rend, split, burst, cut, lacerate, gash, slash, slit.

ripe *adj* **1** mature, ripened, fully developed, fully grown, ready. **2** right, ideal, favourable, advantageous, opportune, propitious, suitable, fit. **3** prepared, arranged, set, ready.

ripen *verb* develop, mature, mellow, age.

riposte *noun* retort, rejoinder, comeback (*inf*), reply.

➤*verb* retort, rejoin, come back, reply.

ripple *verb* **1** undulate, flow, lap. **2** ruffle, pucker, wrinkle.

➤*noun* **1** wave, undulation, eddy. **2** lapping, splash, burble, gurgle, purl. **3** repercussion, shock wave (*inf*), effect, reverberation.

rise *verb* **1** arise, get up, stand up, jump up. **2** arise, ascend, mount, climb, go up, move up, soar. **3** go up, increase, grow, swell, escalate, soar, rocket. **4** get up, arise, wake up, get out of bed, surface (*inf*). **5** advance, progress, get on, prosper,

thrive. **6** adjourn, go into recess, be suspended. **7** respond, react. **8** rebel, revolt, mutiny, riot. **9** emerge, spring, issue, originate.

➤*noun* **1** ascent, rising, climb. **2** increase, growth, intensification, upsurge, upswing, upturn, improvement. **3** slope, incline, acclivity, hill. **4** elevation, hill, hillock. **5** raise, pay increase.

risible *adj* ridiculous, ludicrous, absurd, laughable, farcical, comical, funny.

risk *noun* **1** hazard, threat, peril, danger. **2** chance, possibility.

➤*verb* **1** hazard, imperil, endanger, jeopardize. **2** run the risk of, expose oneself to.

risky *adj* hazardous, perilous, dangerous, fraught, unsafe, precarious, uncertain, chancy (*inf*), dicey (*inf*).

risqué *adj* indecent, off-colour, naughty, rude, suggestive, crude, smutty, bawdy, blue (*inf*), dirty, racy, salacious, ribald, adult, near the knuckle (*inf*).

rite *noun* ritual, ceremony, ceremonial, observance, practice, custom, tradition, convention.

ritual *noun* **1** rite, ceremony, ceremonial, service, solemnity. **2** ceremony, custom, habit, routine, practice, tradition, convention.

adj **1** ceremonial, ceremonious, formal. **2** customary, conventional, traditional, routine, habitual.

rival *noun* **1** competitor, opponent, antagonist, adversary, challenger. **2** equal, match, peer.

verb compete with, equal, match, measure up to, compare with.

road *noun* **1** street, thoroughfare, highway, motorway, avenue, lane, boulevard. **2** path, way, route.

roam *verb* wander, rove, range, ramble, drift, stray.

roar *verb* **1** bellow, yell, bawl, shout, scream, cry, bay, howl, growl, rumble, thunder. **2** guffaw, howl, hoot, fall about.

➤*noun* **1** bellow, growl, cry. **2** bellow, growl, yell, shout, howl, hoot, scream. **3** thunder, boom, rumble.

rob *verb* **1** burgle, steal from, break into, hold up, mug. **2** swindle, cheat, rip off (*inf*), fleece (*inf*). **3** deprive, dispossess, strip.

robbery *noun* burglary, housebreaking, theft, stealing, larceny, hold-up, raid, break-in, mugging, stick-up (*inf*), heist (*inf*).

robe *noun* **1** gown, vestment, habit, dress. **2** bathrobe, dressing-gown.
➤*verb* clothe, dress, garb, attire.

robot *noun* automaton, android, machine.

robust *adj* **1** strong, powerful, muscular, healthy, sound, vigorous, athletic, fit, hardy, tough, rugged, brawny, well-built, strapping, sturdy. **2** strong, tough, rugged, durable, hard-wearing. **3** forceful, strong, determined. **4** direct, straightforward, practical, realistic, hard-headed, no-nonsense, down-to-earth.

rock¹ *noun* **1** stone, boulder, pebble. **2** cliff, crag, outcrop.

rock² *verb* **1** sway, swing, wobble, totter. **2** sway, reel, roll, pitch, lurch, shake, quake. **3** shock, stun, stagger, astound, amaze, shake.

rocket *verb* **1** shoot, speed, zoom. **2** sky-rocket (*inf*), soar, shoot up, go through the ceiling (*inf*).

rocky¹ *adj* stony, craggy, pebbly, rough.

rocky² *adj* shaky, unsteady, wobbly, unstable, tottering, teetering.

rod *noun* **1** stick, cane, switch, birch. **2** stick, staff, baton. **3** bar, shaft, strut, pole.

rogue *noun* **1** rascal, scoundrel, villain, crook (*inf*), fraud, swindler, cheat, knave. **2** rascal, scamp, imp, little devil.

roguish *adj* mischievous, cheeky, impish, waggish, arch, playful, coquettish.

role *noun* **1** part, character. **2** function, purpose, job, task, capacity.

roll *verb* **1** go round, revolve, rotate, turn. **2** flow, run, go, pass. **3** wrap, enfold, envelop, wind, twist, coil. **4** flatten, level, smooth, press. **5** rock, sway, pitch, toss. **6** rumble, thunder, roar, boom.
➤*noun* **1** revolution, rotation, turn. **2** rumble, thunder, roar, boom. **3** sway, rocking, tossing, pitching, swell.

roll *noun* **1** cylinder, drum, reel, spool, scroll. **2** register, roster, list, record, index, directory. **3** bun, bap.

rollicking *adj* boisterous, spirited, exuberant, lively, jolly, light-hearted, merry, care-free, swashbuckling.

romance *noun* **1** love, passion, courtship. **2** love affair, affair, relationship, liaison, attachment. **3** story, tale, love story, tear-jerker (*inf*). **4** glamour, mystery, allure.
➤*verb* court, woo, go out with.

romantic *adj* **1** tender, loving, fond, passionate, amorous. **2** glamorous, mysterious, attractive. **3** fanciful, idealistic, unrealistic, starry-eyed, optimistic, utopian, imaginary, quixotic, impractical.
➤*noun* romanticist, idealist, dreamer, visionary, utopian.

romp *verb* play, frolic, frisk, sport, rollick.

roof *noun* cover, top, ceiling, canopy.

room *noun* **1** chamber, apartment. **2** space, volume, area, leeway, margin, capacity. **3** scope, chance, opportunity.

roomy *adj* spacious, capacious, voluminous, generous, ample, extensive, large, broad.

root *noun* **1** rhizome, tuber, stem. **2** base, basis, foundation, source, origin, starting-point, seat, cause, motive, reason, rationale, ground, bottom, heart.
➤*verb* fix, plant, implant, embed, anchor, base, establish.
root and branch completely, entirely, thoroughly, totally, radically.
root around dig, delve, burrow, forage, rummage, ferret, hunt, search, poke, pry.
root out uproot, weed out, remove, get rid of, eliminate, eradicate.

rope *noun* cable, cord, line, string, painter, hawser.
➤*verb* tie, bind, fasten, hitch, secure, lash.

rope in *verb* enlist, engage, talk into, involve.

roster *noun* rota, list, listing, roll, register, table, schedule.

rostrum *noun* platform, dais, podium, stage.

rosy *adj* **1** pink, pinkish, rose, roseate. **2** pink, rubicund, ruddy, blushing, flushed, florid. **3** optimistic, hopeful, bright, cheerful, encouraging, reassuring, favourable.

rot *verb* decay, decompose, perish, putrefy, go bad, go off, spoil, moulder.
➤*noun* **1** decay, decomposition, putrefaction, mould, mildew. **2** nonsense, rubbish, garbage, twaddle, drivel, claptrap, bosh (*inf*), tosh (*inf*), codswallop (*inf*).

rotary *adj* rotating, rotational, revolving, spinning, turning.

rotate *verb* **1** go round, revolve, turn, spin, wheel. **2** alternate, take turns, switch.

rotation *noun* **1** revolution, turn, gyration, cycle, orbit. **2** alternation, sequence, succession.

rotten *adj* **1** rotting, decayed, decaying, decomposing, putrid, bad, off, mouldy, mouldering, fetid, foul, tainted, spoiled, corroded, crumbling. **2** immoral, corrupt, degenerate, unprincipled, dishonest, untrustworthy, despicable, mean, low, base, crooked (*inf*). **3** miserable, awful, unpleasant, disagreeable, beastly. **4** bad, poor, inadequate, inferior, disappointing, substandard, unsatisfactory, lousy (*inf*). **5** guilty, ashamed, conscience-stricken.

rotter *noun* cad, bounder (*inf*), swine (*inf*), rat (*inf*), stinker (*inf*).

rotund *adj* plump, corpulent, portly, roly-poly, podgy, chubby, tubby.

rough *adj* **1** uneven, irregular, bumpy, lumpy. **2** bristly, unshaven, shaggy, bushy, coarse. **3** bad, stormy, squally, inclement. **4** choppy, agitated, turbulent, tempestuous. **5** violent, savage, harsh, cruel, brutal, drastic, careless, clumsy, unkind. **6** rude, impolite, discourteous, uncivil, unmannerly, ill-mannered, ill-bred, churlish, loutish, boorish, uncouth, coarse, crude, vulgar, unrefined, uncultured, insensitive. **7** hard, tough, nasty, difficult, severe, unpleasant, disagreeable. **8** crude, raw, unfinished, unrefined, unprocessed, unpolished, undressed, uncut. **9** husky, gruff, hoarse, throaty, rasping, harsh, guttural. **10** preliminary, rudimentary, basic, sketchy, general, vague, imprecise, hazy, approximate.
➤*noun* **1** draft, outline, sketch. **2** ruffian, thug, yob (*inf*), bully, hooligan, tough (*inf*).
rough out draft, sketch, outline.
rough up beat up, knock about, bash (*inf*), manhandle.

rough-and-tumble *noun* horseplay, scuffle, scrap (*inf*), fight, brawl, dust-up (*inf*), punch-up (*inf*).

round *adj* **1** circular, annular, ring-shaped. **2** curved, convex, rounded. **3** spherical, globular, ball-shaped. **4** chubby, plump, portly, well-rounded, ample, rotund, tubby. **5** complete, entire, whole, full. **6** candid, frank, blunt, plain, direct. **7** rough, approximate, ball-park (*inf*). **8** full, rich, resonant, sonorous, mellow, plummy.
➤*noun* **1** circle, disc, ring, sphere, ball, orb, globe, cylinder. **2** cycle, series, succession, sequence. **3** circuit, beat, course, route. **4** heat, level, stage. **5** bullet, cartridge, shell.
➤*prep* **1** around, about. **2** surrounding, encircling.
➤*verb* **1** go round, circumnavigate, skirt, flank, bypass. **2** complete, finish, conclude, crown. **3** plane, smooth, sand.
round on attack, turn on, set upon, lay into (*inf*).
round up bring together, gather, collect, assemble, marshal, muster.

roundabout *adj* indirect, winding, tortuous, circuitous, meandering, long-winded.

rouse *verb* **1** wake, awaken, stir, call. **2** stir, bestir, move, start, provoke, incite, agitate, stimulate, animate, galvanize. **3** kindle, stir up, evoke, provoke, excite, stimulate.

rousing *adj* stimulating, inspiring, exciting, stirring, moving, exhilarating, inflammatory.

rout *noun* **1** defeat, conquest, beating, thrashing, trouncing, drubbing, debacle, pasting (*inf*). **2** flight, retreat, stampede.
➤*verb* defeat, vanquish, conquer, beat, crush, thrash, trounce, slaughter (*inf*), hammer (*inf*).

route *noun* way, road, path, course, direction, itinerary.

routine *noun* **1** system, method, pattern, order, convention, custom, practice, habit, wont, procedure, programme. **2** act, spiel (*inf*), patter (*inf*).
➤*adj* **1** customary, habitual, wonted, regular, standard, usual, normal, ordinary, typical, everyday. **2** boring, humdrum, familiar, banal, run-of-the-mill, predictable, hackneyed.

rove *verb* wander, roam, range, stray, drift, travel.

rover *noun* wanderer, drifter, nomad, gadabout (*inf*).

row[1] *noun* line, rank, tier, bank, file, column, queue, rank, string, series, sequence, succession.

row[2] *noun* **1** quarrel, dispute, argument, disagreement, squabble, tiff, fight, altercation, brawl, scrap (*inf*), set-to (*inf*), dust-up (*inf*). **2** noise, din, racket, disturbance, commotion, fuss, hubbub, rumpus, uproar, pandemonium.
➤ *verb* quarrel, argue, bicker, squabble, wrangle, fight, brawl, scrap (*inf*).

rowdy *adj* noisy, loud, boisterous, obstreperous, rough, unruly, disorderly.

royal *adj* **1** regal, kingly, queenly, princely, imperial, sovereign. **2** majestic, impressive, imposing, noble, stately, grand, magnificent, superb. **3** excellent, first-rate, first-class.

rub *verb* **1** knead, massage, stroke, caress, fondle, polish, burnish, buff up, shine, wipe, clean, scrub, scour. **2** apply, smear, spread, work in. **3** chafe, abrade, scrape, grate.
➤ *noun* **1** massage, kneading, friction, stroke, caress, polish, clean, wipe, scrub. **2** difficulty, trouble, problem, hitch, snag, drawback.
rub out 1 erase, efface, expunge, delete, cancel. **2** kill, murder, do in (*inf*), bump off (*inf*), eliminate (*inf*), waste (*inf*).

rubbish *noun* **1** waste, refuse, garbage, litter, trash, junk, lumber, rubble, scrap, debris. **2** nonsense, stuff and nonsense, twaddle, drivel, claptrap, rot (*inf*), codswallop (*inf*), hogwash (*inf*), tosh (*inf*), tripe (*inf*), crap (*sl*), bullshit (*sl*), shit (*sl*).

ruddy *adj* **1** red, rubicund, florid, flushed, rosy, fresh, healthy. **2** red, reddish, scarlet, crimson.

rude *adj* **1** impolite, discourteous, uncivil, ill-mannered, bad-mannered, disrespectful, insolent, impudent, impertinent, cheeky, saucy, short, brusque, offhand, insulting, abusive, offensive. **2** simple, oafish, uncouth, unrefined, uncultured, uncivilized, untutored, uneducated, illiterate, ignorant. **3** crude, rudimentary, simple, rough, rough-and-ready. **4** crude, coarse, vulgar, obscene, smutty, dirty, filthy, blue (*inf*), indecent, risqué, ribald, bawdy. **5** nasty, violent, unexpected, sudden, abrupt.

rudiment *noun* basics, fundamentals, essentials, principles, beginnings.

rudimentary *adj* **1** basic, fundamental, elementary, primary. **2** crude, simple, primitive, rough. **3** undeveloped, immature, vestigial.

rue *verb* regret, repent, lament, deplore.

rueful *adj* regretful, remorseful, apologetic, sorry, sorrowful, sad, contrite, repentant, penitent, lugubrious, woebegone, mournful.

ruffian *noun* thug, tough (*inf*), rough (*inf*), hooligan, yob (*inf*), bully, brute, bruiser, scoundrel.

ruffle *verb* **1** rumple, disarrange, disorder, mess up, muss up (*inf*), tousle, dishevel, crease, crumple. **2** agitate, disturb, upset, put out, rattle (*inf*), shake up (*inf*), unsettle, disconcert, discompose, fluster, perturb.

rugged *adj* **1** rough, uneven, irregular, broken, bumpy, stony, rocky. **2** strong, craggy, manly, weather-beaten. **3** tough, strong, sturdy, robust, husky (*inf*), beefy (*inf*), burly, brawny, muscular, well-built, solid, durable, hard-wearing. **4** tough, hard, harsh, difficult, austere, punishing, demanding, taxing, arduous, rigorous.

ruin *noun* **1** shell, wreck, skeleton, wreckage, rubble, remains. **2** ruination, disrepair, dilapidation, decay, damage, disintegration. **3** defeat, overthrow, collapse, failure, fall, downfall, undoing. **4** ruination, collapse, failure, bankruptcy, insolvency, impoverishment, destitution, penury.
➤ *verb* **1** destroy, devastate, desolate, wreck, shatter, break, smash. **2** spoil, mar, mess up, wreck. **3** bankrupt, impoverish, pauperize.

ruinous *adj* **1** ruined, in ruins, derelict, dilapidated, decaying, broken-down, in disrepair, wrecked, devastated. **2** destructive, devastating, disastrous, calamitous, catastrophic, damaging, crippling, excessive, extortionate, exorbitant.

rule *noun* **1** regulation, statute, ordinance, law, by-law, tenet, order, decree, commandment, directive, instruction, guideline, principle, precept. **2** government,

reign, sovereignty, regime, administration, control, command, authority, ascendancy, sway, mastery, supremacy, power. **4** routine, custom, practice, convention, protocol, standard.
➤*verb* **1** govern, reign, hold sway. **2** dominate, direct, guide, manage, administer, preside over, lead, command, control. **3** control, restrain, curb. **4** decree, judge, adjudge, decide, determine, resolve, pronounce, lay down, direct, order.
as a rule generally, in general, usually, ordinarily, normally, mainly.

rule out *verb* **1** exclude, eliminate, ban, disqualify. **2** dismiss, disregard, ignore. **3** prevent, preclude, forbid.

ruler *noun* **1** monarch, sovereign, king, queen, emperor, empress, potentate, head of state, president, lord, chief, leader, commander, governor. **2** measure, rule.

ruling *adj* **1** reigning, sovereign, governing, dominant, leading, supreme. **2** prevailing, prevalent, leading, chief, principal, main, predominant.
➤*noun* decree, judgment, decision, verdict, pronouncement.

rumble *verb* thunder, roar, growl.

ruminate *verb* meditate, cogitate, ponder, think, deliberate, chew over.

rummage *verb* search, hunt, root, forage, delve, poke around.

rumour *noun* gossip, hearsay, talk, word, whisper, report, story, buzz (*inf*).
➤*verb* give out, put about, pass around, say, tell, report, hint.

rumple *verb* crease, crumple, scrunch up, crinkle, ruffle, tousle, dishevel, disarrange, mess up.

rumpus *noun* commotion, uproar, disturbance, row, ruction, kerfuffle (*inf*), fuss, fracas.

run *verb* **1** sprint, race, gallop, lope, jog, trot. **2** hasten, hurry, rush, charge, dash, dart, tear, bolt, career, hare (*inf*), speed, scamper, scurry, get a move on (*inf*), step on it (*inf*). **3** go, work, function, operate. **4** flow, stream, spill, pour, gush, cascade, spurt, issue, leak, drip, bleed, trickle. **5** manage, administer, conduct, direct, govern, control, lead, head, supervise, superintend, oversee, look after, carry on, own. **6** go on, continue, last. **7** drive, take,

convey, transport. **8** smuggle, traffic, bootleg. **9** compete, enter, take part in. **10** stand, be a contender. **11** drive, keep, use, own, have. **12** publish, print, carry, feature.
➤*noun* **1** sprint, race, gallop, jog, canter. **2** trip, journey, excursion, outing, jaunt, ride, drive, spin (*inf*). **3** route, line, course. **4** series, sequence, succession, string, spell, stretch, period. **5** rush, pressure, demand. **6** sort, kind, type, class, variety. **7** coop, pen, pound, enclosure. **8** ladder, hole, snag, tear, rip.

run across run into, meet, encounter, come across, chance upon, stumble upon, bump into (*inf*).

run away 1 run off, make off, flee, bolt, clear off (*inf*), scarper (*inf*), abscond, escape, elope. **2** avoid, evade, ignore, disregard, neglect.

run down 1 run over, knock down. **2** reduce, cut, cut back, pare down, trim, curtail, decrease, dwindle, diminish, wane, drop. **3** criticize, attack, denounce, disparage, belittle, denigrate, defame, knock (*inf*), slag off (*inf*), slate (*inf*), rubbish (*inf*). **4** track down, run to earth, ferret out, find.

run into 1 bump into, crash into, collide with, ram. **2** meet, encounter, run across, bump into (*inf*).

run on go on, continue, carry on, keep going, extend, last.

run out finish, end, close, expire, fail, give out, dry up.

run out of exhaust, consume, use up.

run out on desert, abandon, forsake, jilt, chuck (*inf*), ditch (*inf*), dump (*inf*), walk out on (*inf*).

run over 1 run down, knock down. **2** run through, go over, go through, look over.

run through go through, go over, run over, look over.

runaway *noun* fugitive, escapee, absconder, truant.
➤*adj* **1** escaped, fugitive, loose, uncontrolled. **2** easy, effortless.

rundown *noun* summary, run-through, résumé, synopsis, review, sketch, outline.

run-down *adj* **1** dilapidated, neglected, ramshackle, tumbledown, broken-down, ruined. **2** weak, unhealthy, tired, worn-out, exhausted, drained, debilitated, below par, peaky (*inf*).

run in *verb* arrest, jail, take into custody, nick (*inf*), bust (*inf*), collar (*inf*).

runner *noun* **1** racer, sprinter, athlete, competitor, participant, jogger. **2** messenger, courier, dispatch rider. **3** shoot, offshoot, tendril, sprig.

running *noun* **1** racing, race, sprinting, sprint, jogging. **2** administration, management, leadership, conduct, direction, control, supervision, operation, working, functioning.
➤*adj* continuous, constant, unbroken, uninterrupted.
➤*adv* in a row, in succession, consecutively, on the trot (*inf*).

run-of-the-mill *adj* ordinary, normal, common, commonplace, average, mediocre, middling, so-so (*inf*), everyday, unexceptional.

rupture *noun* fracture, fissure, break, burst, crack, split, breach, rift, bust-up (*inf*), break-up, quarrel, falling-out (*inf*).
➤*verb* break, burst, crack, split, fracture, breach, tear, puncture.

rural *adj* country, rustic, bucolic.

ruse *noun* wile, trick, artifice, stratagem, scheme, subterfuge, blind, hoax, deceit, deception, manoeuvre, ploy, tactic, dodge (*inf*).

rush *verb* **1** hurry, hasten, race, run, dash, bolt, dart, speed, shoot, sprint, tear, fly. **2** press, push, hustle, dispatch, expedite. **2** charge, attack, storm.
➤*noun* **1** dash, scramble, stampede, flood, stream, gush, surge. **2** bustle, urgency, hurry, haste, commotion, stir, activity. **3** run, demand, clamour, call. **4** surge, flow, spurt.

rust *noun* corrosion, oxidation.
➤*verb* corrode, oxidize, tarnish.

rustic *adj* **1** rural, country, countrified, provincial, pastoral, bucolic. **2** simple, plain, homely, homespun, crude, unsophisticated.
➤*noun* peasant, countryman, countrywoman, provincial, bumpkin, yokel, clodhopper, hick (*inf*).

rustle *verb* whisper, sigh, swish, crackle.
➤*noun* rustling, whisper, swish, susurration, crackle.

rusty *adj* **1** rusted, rust-covered, corroded, tarnished, oxidized. **2** russet, copper, coppery, auburn, sandy, tawny, reddish, reddish-brown. **3** out of practice, stale, stiff, off form, below par.

rut *noun* **1** groove, furrow, channel, hollow. **2** daily grind, dead end, treadmill, routine.

ruthless *adj* pitiless, merciless, hard, harsh, cruel, brutal, heartless, unfeeling, callous, relentless, unrelenting, unforgiving, unsparing, remorseless, implacable.
in the long run eventually, ultimately, at last, in the end, at the end of the day (*inf*).

sable *adj* black, jet-black, pitch-black, coal-black, inky, ebony, dark, dusky.

sabotage *noun* **1** vandalism, destruction, damage, incapacitation, impairment. **2** thwarting, ruining, wrecking, disruption, subversion.
➤*verb* vandalize, destroy, damage, disable, incapacitate, spoil, thwart, scupper, wreck, ruin, disrupt, subvert.

saccharine *adj* **1** sweet, sugary. **2** sickly-sweet, sentimental, mawkish, schmaltzy (*inf*), mushy (*inf*), sloppy (*inf*), syrupy, honeyed, cloying, nauseating.

sack[1] *noun* **1** bag, pack, pouch. **2** dismissal, discharge, boot (*inf*), push (*inf*), notice, marching orders, cards (*inf*).
➤*verb* dismiss, discharge, lay off, fire (*inf*), kick out (*inf*).

sack[2] *verb* plunder, pillage, despoil, raid, ransack, rape, rob, loot, rifle, strip.
➤*noun* plunder, pillage, despoliation, rape, rapine, looting.

sacred *adj* **1** holy, consecrated, dedicated, hallowed, sanctified, blessed. **2** religious, church, devotional, ecclesiastical, spiritual. **3** divine, godly, holy. **4** venerable, revered, respected, sacrosanct, inviolable, untouchable, protected, defended.

sacrifice *noun* **1** offering, oblation, immolation, slaughter. **2** surrender, renunciation, loss, destruction, forfeiture, relinquishment.
➤*verb* **1** offer, offer up, slaughter, immolate. **2** surrender, renounce, give up, forgo, relinquish, yield, cede, forfeit, lose, destroy.

sacrilege *noun* **1** desecration, profanation, violation, blasphemy, heresy. **2** outrage, irreverence, disrespect, mockery.

sad *adj* **1** unhappy, upset, sorrowful, downcast, dejected, low, down (*inf*), melancholy, glum, miserable, woebegone, grief-stricken. **2** distressing, upsetting, depressing, heartbreaking, tragic, grievous, pitiful, poignant, dismal, cheerless, sombre. **3** lamentable, deplorable, grievous, unfortunate, regrettable, shameful, disgraceful, sorry, wretched, pitiful, pathetic (*inf*).

sadden *verb* upset, distress, grieve, deject, depress, dismay, dispirit, dishearten.

saddle *verb* burden, encumber, load, charge, tax, lumber (*inf*), land (*inf*).

safe *adj* **1** secure, protected, invulnerable, immune, out of harm's way (*inf*), in good hands (*inf*). **2** unharmed, unhurt, uninjured, unscathed, all right, out of danger, sound, undamaged, intact. **3** sheltered, impregnable, unassailable. **4** harmless, innocuous, non-poisonous, non-toxic, uncontaminated. **5** unadventurous, cautious, timid, circumspect, prudent, conservative. **6** sure, certain, proven, dependable, reliable, trustworthy, tried and tested, sound, reputable, responsible.
➤*noun* strongbox, chest, coffer, depository, vault.

safeguard *verb* protect, guard, defend, shield, shelter, preserve, secure, look after.
➤*noun* protection, guard, defence, shield, security, precaution, preventive, guarantee, insurance.

safekeeping *noun* protection, care, charge, trust, keeping, custody, guardianship, surveillance.

safety *noun* **1** safeness, security, immunity, shelter, sanctuary, refuge, reliability, dependability. **2** protection, safeguard.

sag *verb* **1** bend, give, subside, sink, droop, hang. **2** flag, fail, falter, wilt, weaken, decline, drop, fall, slump, decrease.

saga *noun* **1** chronicle, epic, history, legend, romance, narrative. **2** story, tale, yarn, adventure.

sagacious *adj* **1** wise, sage, perceptive, percipient, perspicacious, insightful, knowing, sapient. **2** prudent, judicious, shrewd, astute, discerning, penetrating, clever, smart, canny, wily, quick-witted, far-sighted.

sage *noun* philosopher, thinker, savant, wise man, guru, master, expert, authority, pundit, elder.
➤ *adj* wise, judicious, shrewd, intelligent, discerning, perspicacious, sagacious, sapient, learned, knowledgeable.

sail *verb* **1** set sail, put to sea, embark, weigh anchor, ship, leave port. **2** travel, journey, voyage. **3** boat, yacht. **4** drift, float, glide, plane, skim, scud, fly, coast, cruise. **5** pilot, steer, captain, skipper, navigate.
➤ *noun* cruise, trip, voyage, crossing.
sail through romp through, walk (*inf*).

sailor *noun* **1** seaman, seafarer, mariner, boatman, salt, tar (*inf*). **2** deckhand, rating, matelot (*inf*). **3** yachtsman, yachtswoman.

sake *noun* account, interest, behalf, welfare, benefit, good, purpose, reason.

salacious *adj* **1** lecherous, lascivious, licentious, lustful, randy (*inf*), horny (*inf*), libidinous, concupiscent, prurient. **2** lewd, bawdy, ribald, dirty, smutty, blue (*inf*), obscene, indecent, erotic, pornographic.

salary *noun* pay, wage, remuneration, income, earnings, emolument, honorarium, stipend.

sale *noun* **1** selling, marketing, vending, trade, traffic, disposal, transaction, deal. **2** market, clearance, auction.
on/for sale on the market, up for grabs (*inf*), available, obtainable, purchasable.

salient *adj* **1** important, main, principal, prominent, striking, conspicuous, noticeable, outstanding, signal. **2** projecting, jutting, protruding.

sallow *adj* yellow, yellowish, pale, pallid, wan, waxen, jaundiced, pasty, sickly, unhealthy.

sally *noun* **1** sortie, charge, foray, attack, offensive, raid, incursion, onslaught. **2** retort, riposte, joke, jest, quip, crack (*inf*), witticism, bon mot.
➤ *verb* set out, venture forth, rush, charge.

salt *noun* **1** sodium chloride, seasoning, flavouring, relish, savour. **2** sailor, seaman, mariner, seafarer, sea dog, tar (*inf*).
➤ *adj* salty, saline, salted, briny, brackish.
➤ *verb* preserve, cure, season, flavour.

salty *adj* **1** salt, salted, saline, briny, brackish. **2** lively, animated, spicy, piquant, witty.

salubrious *adj* wholesome, healthy, healthful, invigorating, bracing, refreshing, sanitary, hygienic, beneficial, salutary.

salutary *adj* **1** beneficial, advantageous, useful, helpful, valuable, practical, edifying, timely. **2** healthy, healthful, wholesome, salubrious, invigorating.

salutation *noun* greeting, salute, homage, address, reverence, obeisance.

salute *verb* **1** greet, hail, address, accost, welcome, acknowledge. **2** praise, celebrate, honour, mark, recognize, pay tribute to.
➤ *noun* **1** greeting, salutation, address, welcome, acknowledgement. **2** gesture, wave, nod, bow, homage, tribute, recognition, honour, celebration.

salvage *verb* **1** save, rescue, redeem, reclaim, recover, retrieve. **2** preserve, conserve, retain.

salvation *noun* saving, rescue, deliverance, redemption, reclamation, preservation, conservation, restoration.

salve *noun* lotion, cream, ointment, balm, liniment, embrocation.

salvo *noun* fusillade, broadside, volley.

same *adj* identical, indistinguishable, twin, duplicate, matching, interchangeable, equal, like, consistent, uniform.
all/just the same nonetheless, nevertheless, anyway, still, yet, however, even so, in any case, for all that, be that as it may.

sameness *noun* **1** consistency, invariability, uniformity, changelessness, monotony, tedium, predictability, repetition. **2** resemblance, similarity, likeness, identity, duplication.

sample *noun* **1** specimen, example, instance, illustration, demonstration, model, pattern, piece, swatch. **2** sampling, selection, cross-section.
➤ *verb* try, test, taste, experience.

sanctify *verb* **1** consecrate, bless, dedicate, hallow. **2** absolve, purify, cleanse.

3 sanction, authorize, ratify, approve, allow, permit, accredit, warrant, license, legitimate.

sanctimonious *adj* **1** hypocritical, pharisaic, pious, pietistic. **2** self-righteous, smug, superior, holier-than-thou, goody-goody (*inf*).

sanction *noun* **1** permission, consent, agreement, authorization, approval, accreditation, acceptance, ratification. **2** ban, embargo, restriction, prohibition. **3** penalty, deterrent, punishment.
➤*verb* **1** permit, allow, authorize, warrant, license, accredit, approve. **2** ratify, validate, confirm, legitimate.

sanctity *noun* **1** holiness, sacredness, inviolability. **2** saintliness, godliness, grace, piety, devoutness, virtue, purity, spirituality.

sanctuary *noun* **1** shrine, sanctum, church, temple. **2** refuge, asylum, haven, retreat, shelter, hiding place. **3** immunity, impunity, shelter, protection, security, safety. **4** reserve, reservation, preserve, park.

sane *adj* **1** rational, normal, compos mentis, lucid, of sound mind, all there (*inf*). **2** sound, sober, prudent, wise, sensible, intelligent, rational, level-headed.

sangfroid *noun* composure, calmness, self-possession, self-control, presence of mind, poise, aplomb, equanimity, cool (*inf*).

sanguinary *adj* **1** bloody, gory, grisly. **2** bloodthirsty, murderous, brutal, savage, cruel.

sanguine *adj* **1** hopeful, optimistic, assured, confident, cheerful, buoyant. **2** ruddy, rosy, rubicund, red, florid.

sanitary *adj* **1** hygienic, clean, germ-free, aseptic, sterile, disinfected, uncontaminated. **2** salubrious, healthy, wholesome.

sanity *noun* **1** saneness, mental health, soundness of mind, reason, sense, normality, rationality, lucidity. **2** wisdom, prudence, sagacity, judiciousness, soundness, good sense.

sap[1] *noun* **1** juice, fluid. **2** energy, vigour, pep (*inf*), vitality, spirit, lifeblood. **3** fool, dupe, idiot, simpleton, sucker, twit (*inf*).
➤*verb* drain, bleed, enervate, devitalize.

sap[2] *verb* **1** undermine, erode, wear away, reduce, impair, destroy. **2** weaken, enfeeble, debilitate, exhaust.

sapient *adj* wise, sagacious, perspicacious, discerning, judicious, knowing, intelligent, shrewd.

sarcasm *noun* irony, satire, cynicism, sardonicism, mockery, scorn, derision, acerbity, mordancy, trenchancy, bitterness, resentment.

sardonic *adj* sarcastic, ironic, cynical, scornful, mocking, sneering, derisive, contemptuous, wry, bitter, malicious, caustic.

satanic *adj* devilish, diabolic, fiendish, demonic, hellish, infernal, wicked, evil, black.

sate *verb* **1** satisfy, gratify, fill, slake, gorge, satiate. **2** satiate, surfeit, cloy, glut, overfill.

satellite *noun* **1** moon, planet. **2** spacecraft, space station, sputnik. **3** follower, disciple, minion, underling, subordinate, attendant, aide, dependant, dependency, colony, dominion, protectorate.

satire *noun* **1** irony, ridicule, sarcasm, mockery. **2** lampoon, burlesque, parody, caricature, travesty, skit, spoof (*inf*), send-up (*inf*).

satirical *adj* **1** irreverent, burlesque. **2** ironic, sarcastic, sardonic, cynical, trenchant, mordant, caustic, biting, mocking, taunting, derisive, critical.

satirize *verb* mock, ridicule, make fun of, lampoon, burlesque, caricature, parody, send up (*inf*), criticize, attack.

satisfaction *noun* **1** gratification, fulfilment, contentment, pleasure, happiness, pride, comfort, ease. **2** reparation, restitution, compensation, indemnification, requital, recompense, atonement, redress. **3** settlement, payment.

satisfactory *adj* **1** acceptable, all right, good, fine, up to scratch, up to standard. **2** adequate, passable, average, fair.

satisfy *verb* **1** gratify, indulge, content, please, sate, satiate, quench. **2** meet, fulfil, comply with, answer, resolve, solve, suffice, serve. **3** convince, persuade, assure, reassure, appease, pacify. **4** discharge, settle, pay.

satisfying *adj* gratifying, pleasurable, fulfilling, enjoyable.

saturate *verb* **1** soak, drench, wet
through, douse, steep, waterlog, flood.
2 sate, satiate, fill, glut, surfeit, overfill.
3 suffuse, imbue, pervade, permeate,
infuse, impregnate.

saturnine *adj* gloomy, morose, glum, melancholy, moody, sombre, grave, dour, sullen, uncommunicative.

sauce *noun* **1** condiment, relish, dip, dressing, ketchup. **2** impertinence, impudence,
insolence, disrespect, boldness, brashness,
temerity, gall, cheek (*inf*).

saunter *verb* stroll, walk, amble, dawdle,
meander, wander, mooch (*inf*), mosey
(*inf*).
➤*noun* stroll, walk, amble, wander, constitutional, turn, airing.

savage *adj* **1** fierce, ferocious, vicious,
cruel, brutal, inhuman, barbaric, bloodthirsty. **2** untamed, undomesticated, wild,
feral. **3** uncivilized, barbarian, primitive,
rude, boorish. **4** uncultivated, wild, rough,
rugged.
➤*noun* **1** barbarian, primitive, native, aborigine. **2** beast, brute, boor, monster,
yahoo.
➤*verb* **1** maul, mangle, bite, claw, lacerate,
attack. **2** criticize, denounce, slate (*inf*),
slam (*inf*), tear to pieces (*inf*).

savant *noun* sage, philosopher, scholar,
intellectual, man of letters, woman of letters, expert, authority.

save *verb* **1** rescue, free, deliver, redeem,
recover, reclaim, salvage. **2** protect, guard,
safeguard, shield, preserve, conserve.
3 keep, retain, reserve, hoard, store, stockpile, set aside, put by, salt away. **4** budget,
cut back, economize, tighten one's belt
(*inf*). **5** spare, prevent, obviate, forestall.

savings *pl noun* capital, investments,
assets, reserves, nest-egg.

saviour *noun* redeemer, deliverer, liberator,
rescuer, protector, defender, guardian,
champion.

savoir-faire *noun* finesse, style, poise,
aplomb, confidence, assurance, discretion,
diplomacy, suaveness, urbanity.

savour *noun* **1** flavour, taste, tang, smack.
2 smell, aroma, bouquet. **3** suggestion,
hint, trace, touch.

➤*verb* **1** relish, enjoy, appreciate, delight
in, revel in, wallow in, luxuriate in.
2 smack, suggest, indicate, hint.

savoury *adj* salty, spicy, piquant, appetizing, tasty, flavoursome.

saw *noun* saying, adage, dictum, proverb,
axiom, maxim, aphorism, cliché, platitude.

say *verb* **1** utter, speak, pronounce, articulate, enunciate, voice, vocalize. **2** state,
declare, profess, aver, announce, answer,
reply, remark, observe, mention, specify,
designate. **3** express, communicate, tell,
reveal, disclose, convey. **4** recite, read,
deliver, repeat, declaim, perform, rehearse.
5 indicate, show, read. **6** allege, claim,
report, rumour. **7** estimate, guess, reckon,
judge. **8** assume, suppose, imagine, speculate, conjecture, surmise.
➤*noun* **1** word, voice, turn, chance, vote,
opinion, view. **2** influence, weight, clout
(*inf*), power, input.
that is to say that is, in other words, to
put it another way.

saying *noun* saw, adage, dictum, proverb,
axiom, maxim, epigram, slogan, motto,
catchphrase.

scaffold *noun* **1** scaffolding, framework,
gantry. **2** platform, gallows, gibbet.

scale[1] *noun* **1** plate, lamina, lamella,
squama. **2** limescale, incrustation, deposit,
coating. **3** tartar, plaque. **4** flake, scurf.

scale[2] *noun* scales, balance, weighing
machine.

scale[3] *noun* **1** range, gradation, series,
sequence, progression, order, ranking,
hierarchy, spectrum, gamut. **2** scope,
range, spread, reach, extent, compass,
degree. **3** ratio, proportion, measure.
➤*verb* climb, ascend, mount, clamber,
scramble, shin up.
scale down/back decrease, reduce, cut
down, cut back.

scaly *adj* **1** rough, scabrous. **2** flaky, scurfy.

scamp *noun* scallywag, rascal, rogue, monkey, whippersnapper (*inf*), tyke, imp, devil.

scamper *verb* scurry, scuttle, scoot (*inf*),
run, dash, rush, dart.

scan *verb* **1** examine, scrutinize, inspect,
study. **2** search, scour, survey, sweep.
3 skim, browse, flick through, read

through, look over, glance at, glance through, run one's eye over.

scandal noun **1** crime, offence, wrong-doing, misconduct, impropriety, outrage, disgrace, shame, dishonour, ignominy. **2** gossip, rumour, talk, furore, muck-raking, defamation, slander, libel, slur, smear, aspersion.

scandalize verb horrify, appal, shock, out-rage, offend, disgust.

scant adj little, scanty, limited, minimal, negligible, bare, insufficient, inadequate.

scanty adj meagre, paltry, scant, limited, insufficient, inadequate, deficient, little, small, sparse, poor.

scapegoat noun victim, fall guy (inf), whipping-boy, patsy (inf).

scar noun **1** mark, disfigurement, lesion, blemish, cicatrix. **2** wound, injury, trauma, damage, upset.
➤verb **1** mark, disfigure, deface, blemish. **2** traumatize, shock, damage, injure, upset.

scarce adj **1** rare, infrequent, uncommon, unusual, few, sparse, scanty, few and far between (inf). **2** lacking, deficient, short, insufficient, inadequate, in short supply.

scare verb frighten, alarm, rattle (inf), put the wind up (inf), startle, shock, panic, ter-rify, daunt, intimidate, unnerve.
➤noun **1** fright, start, shock, terror. **2** alarm, panic, hysteria.

scared adj frightened, afraid, fearful, terri-fied, nervous, anxious, alarmed, startled, panicky, jittery.

scarf noun muffler, neckerchief, cravat, bandanna.

scary adj **1** frightening, fearsome, alarm-ing, disturbing, terrifying, hair-raising, spine-chilling, shocking, daunting, forbid-ding, formidable. **2** weird, eerie, creepy, spooky (inf).

scathing adj caustic, vitriolic, stinging, biting, cutting, virulent, sarcastic, wither-ing, severe, bitter, harsh, savage.

scatter verb **1** disperse, disband, separate, break up, divide, disunite, dispel, dissipate. **2** sprinkle, strew, broadcast, diffuse, shower, spread, disseminate, throw, toss.

scavenge verb forage, rummage, search, hunt.

scenario noun **1** outline, plot, script, screenplay, synopsis, summary, résumé, storyline. **2** scheme, plan, projection, run-down, sequence of events, situation, state of affairs.

scene noun **1** place, spot, locality, site, location, setting. **2** background, backdrop, set. **3** incident, episode, passage, sequence, clip. **4** view, vista, landscape, panorama, spectacle, tableau. **5** fuss, row, commotion, to-do (inf), performance, drama, outburst, tantrum, display, exhibition. **6** field, area, sphere, world, milieu. **7** speciality, interest.

scenery noun **1** landscape, panorama, view, vista, setting, surroundings. **2** set, backdrop, mise en scène, flats.

scenic adj picturesque, attractive, pleasing, striking, impressive, grand, spectacular, breathtaking, panoramic.

scent noun **1** smell, odour, aroma, bou-quet, perfume, fragrance. **2** trail, track, trace, spoor. **3** perfume, fragrance, essence, toilet water, cologne.
➤verb **1** sniff, smell, nose out. **2** detect, discern, perceive, sense, get wind of.

sceptic noun **1** doubter, disbeliever, dis-senter, cynic, pessimist, scoffer, questioner. **2** doubting Thomas, agnostic, unbeliever, atheist.

schedule noun **1** plan, programme, scheme. **2** agenda, itinerary, timetable, diary, calendar. **3** list, inventory, catalogue, record, register, table.
➤verb **1** time, timetable, organize, arrange, programme, plan, appoint, book. **2** table, list, record, register.

scheme noun **1** plan, programme, sched-ule, system, procedure, project, proposal. **2** design, diagram, layout, outline, chart, map. **3** stratagem, tactic, device, ploy, ruse, shift, racket (inf), game (inf), man-oeuvre, machination, plot, conspiracy.
➤verb **1** plot, plan, manoeuvre, machi-nate, conspire, intrigue, conspire, connive. **2** plan, project, devise, formulate, design.

scheming adj calculating, designing, crafty, cunning, sly, wily, conniving, unscrupulous, devious, Machiavellian.

schism noun disunion, separation, divi-sion, split, breach, rift, rupture, severance, disagreement, estrangement.

scholar noun **1** authority, expert, specialist. **2** intellectual, academic, don, man of letters, woman of letters, savant, egghead (*inf*).

scholarly adj learned, erudite, academic, intellectual, highbrow (*inf*), studious, bookish, literary, scientific.

scholarship noun **1** erudition, learning, knowledge, wisdom, letters, schooling, education, attainments, achievements. **2** grant, bursary, fellowship, exhibition, award, endowment.

scholastic adj academic, educational, pedagogic.

school noun **1** college, academy, institute, institution. **2** faculty, department, discipline, division, unit. **3** movement, association, circle, set, group, sect, faction, denomination, persuasion, belief, doctrine, opinion.
➤*verb* **1** teach, educate. **2** coach, train, tutor, instruct, drill, verse.

schooling noun education, tuition, teaching, instruction, training, learning.

schoolteacher noun teacher, master, mistress, instructor, tutor, educator, pedagogue.

science noun **1** physics, chemistry, biology, technology. **2** discipline, speciality, field of study.

scientific adj **1** technical, technological. **2** logical, systematic, methodical, controlled, analytical, accurate, precise.

scintillate verb **1** spark, burn. **2** sparkle, twinkle, coruscate, glitter, flash, glint.

scintillating adj **1** sparkling, shining, bright, dazzling, glittering, flashing. **2** lively, stimulating, spirited, animated, vivacious, brilliant, sparkling, effervescent.

scion noun **1** shoot, twig, branch, cutting, graft. **2** descendant, heir, successor, offspring, child, progeny.

scoff[1] verb mock, jeer, sneer, poke fun, laugh, belittle, disparage, deride, scorn, pooh-pooh (*inf*).

scoff[2] verb devour, consume, bolt, guzzle, gobble, gorge, wolf (*inf*), put away (*inf*).

scold verb upbraid, berate, reprimand, admonish, rebuke, reprove, reproach, chide, take to task, tell off (*inf*), criticize, nag.

scoop noun **1** ladle, spoon. **2** bucket, shovel. **3** exclusive, coup, sensation, inside story, revelation, exposé.
➤*verb* **1** ladle, shovel. **2** dig, excavate, hollow, gouge. **3** gather, pick, lift.

scope noun **1** opportunity, freedom, latitude, leeway, capacity, space, room. **2** range, extent, reach, compass, area, field, ambit, limits.

scorch verb **1** burn, singe, char, sear, discolour. **2** bake, parch, shrivel, wither, dry up, sear.

score noun **1** record, tally, reckoning, total, points, goals, result. **2** lot, multitude, host. **3** notch, incision, nick, cut, scratch, line, groove, gouge.
➤*verb* **1** gain, win, get, make, chalk up (*inf*), notch up (*inf*). **2** keep a tally, keep count. **3** cut, incise, engrave, scratch, gouge, groove, nick, notch.
score out strike out, cross out, cancel, delete, efface, obliterate.

scorn noun contempt, disdain, derision, mockery, ridicule, sarcasm, disparagement.
➤*verb* **1** despise, disdain, look down on, deride, mock, scoff at, sneer at, hold in contempt. **2** refuse, reject, spurn, shun.

scoundrel noun rogue, rascal, villain, reprobate, good-for-nothing, blackguard, cad, bounder (*inf*), rotter (*inf*), rat (*inf*).

scour[1] verb rub, abrade, scrub, clean, polish, burnish, cleanse, purge.

scour[2] verb search, hunt, ransack, comb, rake, sweep.

scourge noun **1** punishment, torment, plague, affliction, bane, curse, evil, trial, nuisance. **2** whip, lash, cat o' nine tails, switch, rod, birch.
➤*verb* **1** afflict, curse, plague, torment, torture, punish. **2** whip, lash, beat, flog, thrash, cane.

scout noun lookout, spy.
➤*verb* **1** reconnoitre, recce (*inf*), inspect, examine, spy out, survey, scan. **2** search, hunt, seek, ferret around. **3** explore, investigate, check out (*inf*), observe, case (*inf*).

scowl verb frown, glower, glare, grimace, lour, pout.
➤*noun* frown, glower, glare, black look, grimace, pout.

scraggy *adj* scrawny, lean, thin, skinny, bony, spare, lanky.

scramble *verb* 1 clamber, climb, scale, crawl, scrabble. 2 struggle, jostle, strive, compete, battle, vie, jockey. 3 hasten, hurry, rush, race, bustle, scurry. 4 mix, jumble, muddle, confuse, disorder.
➤*noun* 1 struggle, tussle, battle, free-for-all, climb, rush. 2 muddle, mess, jumble, confusion.

scrap[1] *noun* 1 piece, fragment, remnant, snippet, bit, iota, atom, grain. 2 morsel, crumb, sliver, leftover, scraping. 3 waste, rubbish, refuse, junk, remains, remnants.
➤*verb* discard, throw away, reject, abandon, ditch (*inf*), dump, get rid of, axe, cancel.

scrap[2] *noun* fight, scuffle, brawl, run-in (*inf*), dust-up (*inf*), row, quarrel, argument.
➤*verb* fight, row, brawl, quarrel, squabble, wrangle.

scrape *verb* 1 grate, rasp, grind, scratch. 2 scratch, graze, skin, bark, scuff. 3 clean, remove. 4 file, rub, abrade, scrub, scour, sandpaper.
➤*noun* 1 rasp, scratch, creak, squeak, grating, grinding. 2 graze, scratch, abrasion, scuff. 3 difficulty, predicament, dilemma, quandary, mess, fix (*inf*), trouble, pickle (*inf*).
scrape by manage, get by, scrimp, keep the wolf from the door.

scratch *verb* 1 cut, lacerate, gouge, claw, mark, score, scrape, scuff. 2 graze, scrape, skin, bark. 3 rub, scrape, chafe. 2 delete, cross out, strike out, cancel, erase, expunge, obliterate.
➤*noun* cut, laceration, graze, abrasion, scrape, score, scuff.
up to scratch up to par, up to standard, satisfactory, good enough, adequate, acceptable, passable.

scrawl *verb* scribble, doodle, scratch, dash off, jot down.
➤*noun* scribble, squiggle, writing, sketch.

scrawny *adj* scraggy, skinny, thin, lanky, bony, emaciated, undernourished.

scream *noun* 1 screech, shriek, cry, yell, shout, wail, squeal, howl. 2 laugh, hoot (*inf*), caution (*inf*), riot (*inf*), card (*inf*).
➤*verb* 1 screech, shriek, wail, squeal, howl. 2 cry, call, yell, shout, bawl.

screech *noun* shriek, howl, yell, squeal, squawk, scream.
➤*verb* shriek, howl, cry, yell, squeal, scream.

screen *noun* 1 partition, divider, curtain, shade, blind. 2 cover, shelter, protection, guard, shield, mask, veil, cloak, shroud. 3 mesh, netting.
➤*verb* 1 divide, partition, separate, conceal, shroud, cloak. 2 shelter, shade, cover, protect, guard, shield. 3 test, check, vet, sift, filter, process, sort, evaluate, select. 4 scan, examine, test, check.

screw *noun* bolt, pin, tack, nail.
➤*verb* 1 fasten, attach, fix, clamp. 2 tighten, adjust. 3 twist, wind, turn, spiral.
screw up 1 wrinkle, pucker, twist, knit, contort, crumple. 2 mess up, botch, bungle, mishandle, mismanage, cock up (*inf*), spoil, ruin.

scribble *verb* 1 scrawl, jot down, dash off, doodle. 2 write, pen.
➤*noun* scrawl, squiggle, writing, doodle.

scribe *noun* 1 copyist, amanuensis, secretary, clerk. 2 writer, author, pen-pusher, hack (*inf*).

scrimp *verb* stint, pinch, restrict, limit, economize, save, cut back, skimp.

script *noun* 1 text, lines, words, dialogue, libretto, screenplay. 2 hand, handwriting, writing, penmanship. 3 characters, letters, alphabet.

scripture *noun* Bible, testament, word of God, holy writ, gospel.

scrounge *verb* beg, cadge, freeload, sponge (*inf*), bum (*inf*), blag (*inf*).

scrub[1] *verb* 1 rub, brush, scour, wash, clean. 2 cancel, call off, drop, give up, scrap, abandon, delete.

scrub[2] *noun* brush, undergrowth, coppice, thicket, bush.

scruffy *adj* untidy, dishevelled, bedraggled, unkempt, disreputable, shabby, seedy, slovenly, sloppy (*inf*).

scrumptious *adj* delicious, tasty, yummy (*inf*), appetizing, mouth-watering, succulent, luscious, delectable.

scrunch verb crumple, crush, squash, crunch, screw up, twist.

scruple noun **1** qualm, reservation, moral, ethic, principle, standard. **2** misgiving, compunction, doubt, hesitation, uneasiness, reluctance.
➤verb hesitate, falter, waver, think twice, demur, shrink, balk, be loath.

scrupulous adj **1** punctilious, strict, exact, precise, meticulous, painstaking, rigorous, minute, thorough. **2** honest, honourable, upright, moral, ethical, principled.

scrutinize verb examine, study, peruse, pore over, scan, search, inspect, analyse.

scrutiny noun examination, study, perusal, search, investigation, enquiry, inspection, analysis.

scud verb run, race, fly, sail, skim.

scuffle verb fight, struggle, scrap (inf), grapple, tussle, brawl.
➤noun fight, tussle, brawl, scrap (inf), fracas, affray, disturbance, clash.

sculpture noun statue, bust, figurine, bronze, carving, bas-relief, cast.

scum noun **1** froth, foam, film, crust. **2** dregs, dross, riffraff, undesirables.

scupper verb **1** wreck, destroy, ruin, foil, defeat. **2** scuttle, sink, submerge.

scurrilous adj abusive, offensive, insulting, defamatory, slanderous, libellous, disparaging.

scurry verb scamper, scuttle, scoot, dash, dart, run, hurry, bustle.
➤noun rush, bustle, flurry, hurry, scuttling, scampering.

scuttle verb scamper, scurry, scoot, dash, dart, run, hurry, bustle.

sea noun **1** ocean, main, deep, briny (inf). **2** profusion, mass, host, multitude, expanse.
at sea lost, at a loss, disorientated, bewildered, puzzled, confused.

seal verb **1** fasten, secure, close, plug, stop. **2** confirm, secure, settle, finalize, complete. **3** validate, authenticate, ratify. **4** stamp, endorse.
➤noun **1** stamp, insignia, signet, emblem, crest, monogram. **2** pledge, guarantee, assurance, confirmation, ratification, warranty, cachet.

seal off close, cut off, cordon off, isolate, segregate, quarantine.

seam noun **1** joint, join, weld, line, suture. **2** stratum, vein, layer, lode.

seaman noun sailor, rating, mariner, tar (inf), matelot (inf).

seamy adj unpleasant, unattractive, nasty, sordid, squalid, sleazy (inf), unsavoury, disreputable, rough.

sear verb **1** burn, scorch, singe, char, cauterize, brand. **2** fry, brown.

search verb **1** seek, look, examine, study, survey, explore, probe, investigate, enquire. **2** hunt, rummage, sift, comb, scour, ransack. **3** inspect, check, examine, frisk (inf).
➤noun hunt, rummage, examination, exploration, investigation, enquiry, pursuit, quest.

searching adj penetrating, intent, thorough, enquiring, probing, analytic.

season noun **1** quarter, term, trimester. **2** time, period, spell, interval.
➤verb **1** flavour, spice, salt, pepper. **2** enliven, pep up (inf), leaven. **3** age, mature, harden, toughen, mellow. **4** prepare, inure, harden, habituate, train.
in season ready, plentiful, available, obtainable, on the market.

seasonable adj **1** suitable, appropriate, fitting, apt. **2** opportune, timely, well-timed, convenient.

seasoning noun flavouring, spice, salt, pepper, herbs, relish, condiment.

seat noun **1** chair, bench, stool, pew (inf). **2** place, centre, hub, heart, cradle, site, location. **3** residence, country house, mansion, stately home.
➤verb **1** accommodate, hold, take. **2** place, set, put, sit, install, establish, settle.

secede verb withdraw, retire, resign, leave, quit, break away, split, separate.

secluded adj **1** isolated, remote, out-of-the-way, cut off, solitary, lonely, sequestered, cloistered. **2** sheltered, private, hidden, concealed.

seclusion noun privacy, solitude, isolation, retreat, retirement, remoteness, hiding, secrecy.

second[1] *adj* **1** next, following, subsequent, succeeding. **2** further, extra, additional, supplementary. **3** alternate, other. **4** secondary, subordinate, inferior, lower, lesser, minor.
➤*noun* attendant, assistant, helper, aide, supporter, backer.
➤*verb* **1** support, back, help, assist, encourage. **2** endorse, back up, support, approve, agree with.

second[2] *noun* instant, moment, trice, flash, sec (*inf*), tick (*inf*).

second[3] *verb* transfer, move, relocate, assign.

secondary *adj* **1** subordinate, subsidiary, ancillary, auxiliary, inferior, lesser, lower, back-up, reserve. **2** resultant, derivative, derived, indirect.

second-class *adj* second-rate, mediocre, inferior, lesser.

secondhand *adj* used, worn, old, hand-me-down (*inf*).

second-in-command *noun* deputy, number two, assistant, subordinate, substitute.

second-rate *adj* inferior, second-class, substandard, mediocre, poor-quality, low-grade, shoddy.

secret *adj* **1** hidden, concealed, disguised, camouflaged, private, classified, restricted, confidential, hush-hush (*inf*). **2** unseen, covert, clandestine, undercover, surreptitious, stealthy, cloak-and-dagger (*inf*). **3** secluded, remote, out-of-the-way, unfrequented, solitary, retired, sequestered. **4** cryptic, occult, arcane, esoteric, recondite. **5** secretive, reticent, uncommunicative, discreet.
➤*noun* **1** confidence, private matter. **2** mystery, enigma, puzzle, riddle. **3** key, formula, recipe, solution, answer.

secretary *noun* personal assistant, PA, aide, clerk, typist, scribe, amanuensis.

secrete[1] *verb* discharge, emit, exude, emanate, give off.

secrete[2] *verb* hide, conceal, cache, stow, stash (*inf*).

secretion *noun* discharge, release, emission, exudation, emanation.

secretive *adj* tight-lipped, reticent, cagey (*inf*), uncommunicative, unforthcoming, reserved, quiet, secret.

sect *noun* **1** cult, denomination, order. **2** faction, schism, splinter group, party, school, camp, wing.

sectarian *adj* **1** factional, denominational, partisan, bigoted, intolerant. **2** insular, narrow, limited, exclusive, parochial.

section *noun* **1** part, segment, bit, fragment, fraction, portion. **2** subdivision, part, chapter, passage, paragraph. **3** component, piece. **4** division, department, branch, wing. **5** slice, piece.

sector *noun* **1** part, field, division, area. **2** area, district, zone, region.

secular *adj* **1** temporal, worldly, earthly. **2** state, civil, profane. **3** lay, laic.

secure *adj* **1** safe, protected, immune, invulnerable. **2** fortified, impregnable. **3** firm, stable, steady, sound, dependable, reliable. **4** fast, fixed, fastened, immovable. **5** strong, tight, closed, locked, sealed. **6** calm, relaxed, settled. **7** confident, reassured, contented, happy. **8** assured, sure, certain.
➤*verb* **1** obtain, get hold of, procure, acquire, come by (*inf*), land (*inf*). **2** fix, attach, fasten, make fast, tie, lash, bind, close, lock, seal. **3** defend, guard, safeguard, protect, fortify. **4** guarantee, assure, insure, cover. **5** underwrite, sponsor.

security *noun* **1** safety, immunity, invulnerability, confidence, peace of mind. **2** protection, safekeeping, defence, guarding. **3** collateral, guarantee, warranty, surety, pledge.

sedate *adj* calm, composed, serene, placid, staid, dignified, sober, slow, measured.
➤*verb* tranquillize, calm, pacify, relax.

sedative *noun* tranquillizer, narcotic, opiate, barbiturate, calmative, depressant, downer (*inf*).
➤*adj* calming, soothing, soporific, narcotic, tranquillizing, relaxing.

sedentary *adj* seated, sitting, inactive, immobile, idle, deskbound.

sediment *noun* **1** dregs, lees, grounds, residue. **2** deposit, silt.

sedition *noun* incitement, agitation, rabble-rousing, subversion, treason, rebellion, revolt, insurrection, mutiny.

seduce verb 1 allure, entice, charm, attract, pull (inf), deflower, ravish, dishonour. 2 tempt, lure, lead astray, mislead, inveigle, beguile, deceive.

seductive adj tempting, tantalizing, alluring, inviting, appealing, attractive, irresistible, provocative, flirtatious, sexy (inf).

sedulous adj 1 painstaking, persevering, persistent, tireless, determined, resolved. 2 assiduous, diligent, conscientious, scrupulous, industrious, busy.

see verb 1 perceive, make out, distinguish, discern, spot, spy, glimpse, notice. 2 look at, behold, observe, watch, view, witness. 3 understand, grasp, learn, discover, know, feel, appreciate, realize, recognize. 4 predict, foresee, envisage, visualize, imagine. 5 ascertain, determine, consider, deliberate, decide. 6 meet, receive, interview. 7 visit, call on. 8 consult, speak to, confer with. 9 go out with, date (inf), take out, court, keep company with. 10 escort, accompany, usher, show.
see about deal with, attend to, sort out, look after, fix.
see to attend to, cope with, deal with, take care of, look after.

seed noun 1 germ, ovule, spore, grain, pip, stone. 2 source, origin, beginning, embryo. 3 sperm, semen. 4 offspring, children, young, issue, progeny.
go/run to seed deteriorate, decay, decline, go downhill (inf).

seedy adj 1 shabby, scruffy, unkempt, untidy, dirty, grubby. 2 run-down, dilapidated, tatty, squalid, sleazy (inf), grotty (inf), crummy (inf).

seek verb 1 hunt, look for, search for. 2 ask for, request, solicit, want. 3 pursue, strive for. 4 try, attempt, endeavour, aim.

seem verb appear, look, sound, feel.

seemingly adv 1 apparently, on the face of it. 2 ostensibly, outwardly, superficially, on the surface.

seemly adv proper, decent, nice, fitting, becoming, decorous.

seep verb ooze, trickle, leak, drip, percolate, leach.

seer noun prophet, soothsayer, augur, clairvoyant, sibyl.

seesaw verb 1 swing, yo-yo (inf). 2 alternate, fluctuate, oscillate, vacillate.

seethe verb 1 boil, bubble, foam, froth, fizz, churn. 2 rage, rant, rave, fume, smoulder, simmer.

segment noun 1 piece, bit, fragment, portion, slice, wedge. 2 part, division, section.

segregate verb separate, isolate, set apart, cut off, quarantine, sequester.

segregation noun separation, isolation, sequestration, partition, apartheid.

seize verb 1 grab, snatch, clutch, clasp, grasp, grip, hold. 2 capture, catch, kidnap, hijack, take, usurp, commandeer, appropriate. 3 confiscate, impound, sequester.

seizure noun 1 confiscation, sequestration, appropriation, capture, arrest. 2 convulsion, fit, spasm, paroxysm, attack.

seldom adv rarely, infrequently, hardly ever, once in a blue moon (inf).

select verb pick, choose, single out, opt for, decide on.
➤adj 1 selected, hand-picked, preferred, chosen. 2 choice, best, finest, prime, excellent, superior, high-quality, first-rate. 3 elite, exclusive, privileged.

selection noun 1 pick, choice, option, preference. 2 collection, assortment, variety, miscellany, medley, anthology.

selective adj particular, discerning, discriminating, fussy, choosy (inf), picky (inf).

self-assurance noun assurance, confidence, self-confidence, self-reliance, assertiveness, cockiness (inf), self-possession, aplomb.

self-centred adj egotistic, egoistic, egocentric, narcissistic, selfish, self-absorbed, self-interested, self-seeking, self-serving.

self-confidence noun confidence, assurance, self-assurance, self-reliance, self-possession, aplomb, assertiveness, cockiness (inf).

self-conscious adj shy, bashful, embarrassed, ill at ease, awkward, uncomfortable.

self-control noun self-restraint, self-discipline, self-denial, willpower, composure, cool (inf).

self-denial noun self-discipline, abstinence, asceticism, moderation, temperance, self-abnegation, self-sacrifice.

self-esteem noun self-respect, self-confidence, ego, pride, dignity, amour-propre.

self-indulgence noun extravagance, intemperance, self-gratification, pleasure-seeking, dissipation, profligacy, hedonism.

selfish adj self-centred, egocentric, self-seeking, self-interested, greedy, miserly, mean, inconsiderate.

selfless adj unselfish, generous, altruistic, self-sacrificing, magnanimous, philanthropic, liberal.

self-possessed adj calm, collected, composed, poised, self-assured, self-confident.

self-respect noun self-esteem, pride, dignity, amour-propre.

self-righteous adj sanctimonious, holier-than-thou, pious, pietistic, unctuous, mealy-mouthed, smug, complacent.

self-sacrifice noun self-denial, selflessness, unselfishness, altruism, self-abnegation.

self-satisfaction noun complacency, smugness, self-congratulation, self-righteousness, pride.

self-seeking adj self-serving, self-interested, selfish, opportunistic, ambitious, mercenary, calculating, on the make (inf).

self-styled adj would-be, so-called, self-appointed, pretended.

self-willed adj wilful, stubborn, obstinate, pig-headed, bloody-minded, headstrong, stiff-necked, intransigent.

sell verb 1 put up for sale, vend, dispose of, flog (inf), exchange, barter, trade. 2 trade in, traffic in, deal in, hawk, peddle, tout, retail, stock. 3 promote, advertise, push (inf).
sell out 1 run out, have none left. 2 betray, double-cross, stab in the back (inf).

seller noun vendor, trader, merchant, dealer, retailer, supplier, stockist, salesperson, representative, pedlar.

semblance noun appearance, look, aspect, air, guise, mask, pretence, show, front, veneer.

send verb 1 direct, dispatch. 2 forward, dispatch, address, mail, post, transmit, broadcast, relay, communicate, convey. 3 hurl, throw, fling, drive, propel, fire, launch. 4 emit, discharge, cast, direct.
send for summon, call, order, request.
send up lampoon, satirize, mock, ridicule, parody, caricature.

senile adj aged, old, doting, failing, doddering, gaga (inf).

senior adj 1 superior, high-ranking, chief. 2 older, elder.

sensation noun 1 feeling, sense, impression, awareness, consciousness, perception. 2 commotion, fuss, furore, ado, excitement, stir. 3 triumph, hit (inf), smash (inf).

sensational adj 1 exciting, stirring, thrilling, shocking, scandalous, melodramatic, lurid, startling. 2 marvellous, superb, wonderful, fantastic (inf), excellent, remarkable, impressive, spectacular.

sense noun 1 meaning, import, signification, connotation, nuance. 2 sensation, perception, sensibility, faculty. 3 feeling, sensation, sentiment, awareness, consciousness, impression. 4 appreciation, awareness, understanding, comprehension. 5 sanity, wit, reason, mind. 6 common sense, gumption (inf), wisdom, prudence, judgment, intelligence. 7 point, purpose, reason, logic
➤ verb 1 perceive, notice. 2 feel, suspect, divine, appreciate, realize. 3 grasp, comprehend, understand. 4 detect, pick up, recognize.

senseless adj 1 foolish, stupid, silly, idiotic, crazy, mad. 2 meaningless, nonsensical, absurd, irrational, illogical, pointless, futile. 3 unconscious, insensible, out cold, stunned, anaesthetized.

sensibility noun 1 taste, discrimination, discernment, appreciation. 2 feeling, susceptibility, emotion, sentiment. 3 sensitivity, perceptiveness, insight, awareness, responsiveness.

sensible adj 1 wise, judicious, prudent, well-advised, sober, responsible, sane, level-headed, rational, commonsense, down-to-earth, intelligent. 2 practical, utilitarian, plain. 3 perceptive, sensitive, responsive. 4 aware, conscious, cognizant, mindful.

sensitive *adj* **1** receptive, responsive, sentient, sensitized. **2** touchy, thin-skinned, emotional, susceptible, impressionable, vulnerable. **3** sympathetic, diplomatic, considerate, perceptive, discerning, discriminatory. **4** tender, delicate, soft, allergic. **5** delicate, fine. **6** difficult, tricky, awkward, ticklish, delicate, controversial.

sensual *adj* carnal, fleshly, bodily, physical, voluptuous, sexy, erotic, pleasurable, sybaritic, luxurious.

sensuous *adj* aesthetic, gratifying, pleasing, tasteful, beautiful, rich.

sentence *noun* **1** judgment, ruling, decision, condemnation. **2** punishment, penalty.
➤ *verb* judge, condemn, punish, penalize.

sententious *adj* pompous, canting, sanctimonious, moralistic, judgmental.

sentiment *noun* **1** feeling, emotion, tenderness, sentimentality, mawkishness, emotionalism. **2** thought, idea, attitude, feeling, view, opinion. **3** romanticism, nostalgia, schmaltz (*inf*).

sentimental *adj* **1** emotional, tender, softhearted, nostalgic, touching, pathetic. **2** romantic, over-emotional, maudlin, mawkish, soppy (*inf*), sloppy (*inf*), mushy (*inf*), slushy (*inf*), schmaltzy (*inf*), corny (*inf*).

sentry *noun* guard, sentinel, picket, watch, lookout.

separate *verb* **1** divide, part, split, come apart, break off, diverge. **2** split up, break up, part, divorce. **3** come between, divide, segregate, keep apart, partition, split. **4** distinguish, sort, categorize, classify. **5** detach, isolate. **6** sunder, cleave, sever, disconnect.
➤ *adj* **1** apart, detached, discrete, separated, isolated, alone. **2** individual, own, distinct, particular. **3** independent, autonomous. **4** unconnected, unrelated. **5** distinct, different, disparate.

separation *noun* **1** division, partition, severance, cleavage, detachment, disconnection, segregation, isolation. **2** break-up, split, estrangement, divorce.

septic *adj* infected, poisoned, festering, suppurating, putrefying.

sepulchral *adj* funereal, lugubrious, mournful, sombre, grave, dismal, solemn, gloomy.

sepulchre *noun* tomb, grave, vault, mausoleum, burial place.

sequel *noun* **1** development, continuation, follow-up, aftermath. **2** result, consequence, outcome, upshot, conclusion, end.

sequence *noun* **1** series, set, cycle. **2** progression, run, string, succession, train. **3** order, arrangement, pattern, course.

serendipity *noun* chance, luck, good fortune, fortuity, coincidence.

serene *adj* **1** tranquil, calm, peaceful, quiet, still, undisturbed, placid, composed, untroubled. **2** clear, fine, bright, fair, halcyon.

series *noun* sequence, succession, run, line, chain, string, progression, course.

serious *adj* **1** grave, solemn, thoughtful, pensive, sober, dour, unsmiling, humourless, poker-faced. **2** earnest, sincere, honest, genuine. **3** committed, resolved, determined, fervent. **4** bad, severe, dangerous, worrying, urgent, grievous, acute, critical. **5** important, consequential, weighty, momentous.

seriously *adv* **1** earnestly, sincerely, solemnly, gravely, soberly. **2** acutely, severely, critically, dangerously, grievously, sorely, badly. **3** very, extremely.

sermon *noun* oration, address, discourse, homily, lecture, diatribe, harangue.

serpentine *adj* **1** snaky, sinuous, coiled, spiral. **2** winding, meandering, twisting, tortuous.

serrated *adj* notched, jagged, saw-edged, toothed, indented.

serried *adj* close, compact, dense, crowded, massed.

servant *noun* domestic, home help, valet, maid, retainer, hireling, menial, skivvy (*inf*), slave, serf.

serve *verb* **1** work for, be in the service of. **2** attend to, help, assist. **3** dish up, distribute, dole out, provide, supply. **4** wait on, look after, cater to. **5** function, perform, act. **6** suit, suffice, do (*inf*), answer, fulfil, satisfy. **7** help, aid, benefit. **8** attend, minister to, oblige, obey, support. **9** present, deliver, execute

service *noun* **1** employment, work, duty, business. **2** good turn, favour, help, aid, assistance. **3** maintenance, overhaul, check. **4** ceremony, rite, sacrament, observance, worship. **5** amenity, facility, resource, utility.
➤*verb* check, maintain, overhaul.

serviceable *adj* **1** usable, operative, functioning. **2** practical, functional, utilitarian, useful, efficient, reliable, durable, tough, strong, hard-wearing.

services *pl noun* armed forces, army, navy, air force, military.

servile *adj* **1** obsequious, slavish, submissive, subservient, grovelling, fawning, sycophantic, abject. **2** humble, lowly, menial, mean, base, low.

serving *noun* helping, portion, ration, share.

servitude *noun* bondage, chains, slavery, serfdom, captivity, enslavement, thrall, subjection, subjugation, domination, vassalage, villeinage.

session *noun* **1** meeting, sitting, gathering, assembly. **2** period, time, spell, stretch.

set *verb* **1** place, put, position, locate, lay, deposit. **2** stipulate, specify, decide on, determine, fix, appoint, name, choose, impose. **3** establish, create, institute. **4** assign, allocate, give, dispense, mete out, prescribe. **5** adjust, regulate, synchronize, calibrate. **6** lay, prepare, get ready, arrange. **7** arrange, organize, lay out. **8** mount, fix, lodge, embed, insert. **9** solidify, harden, stiffen, thicken, congeal, gel. **10** sink, go down, drop, disappear.
➤*noun* **1** collection, array, assemblage, series, batch, outfit, kit. **2** circle, group, band, gang, crowd, party, faction, clique, coterie. **3** scenery, flats, backdrop, background, mise en scène. **4** bearing, carriage, posture, attitude, hang, cast, turn.
➤*adj* **1** fixed, established, prescribed, specified, prearranged, ordained, appointed, scheduled, agreed, accepted, customary, traditional. **2** determined, resolute, intent. **3** rigid, firm, fixed, rooted, inflexible, immovable. **4** ready, prepared,

organized, fit, equipped. **5** standard, conventional, stock, stereotyped, hackneyed, routine, habitual.

set about 1 start, begin, commence, embark on, tackle, undertake, get down to (*inf*). **2** attack, assault, belabour.

set apart differentiate, distinguish, characterize, mark off, single out, separate.

set aside 1 put aside, cast aside, abandon, discard, reject, drop. **2** override, overrule, overturn, reverse, annul, quash, revoke.

set back retard, slow down, delay, hold up, thwart, hinder, obstruct.

set down write down, put in writing, note, record, register.

set forth 1 set out, set off, start, depart, leave. **2** present, advance, submit, declare, state, explain, expound, describe, detail.

set in arrive, begin, start, commence.

set off 1 set out, set forth, start, leave, depart, hit the road (*inf*). **2** detonate, explode, blow up, trigger, ignite. **3** cause, prompt, incite, encourage. **4** enhance, embellish, show off, display, contrast, throw into relief, bring out.

set on set upon, attack, assault, fall upon, go for, beat up (*inf*).

set out 1 set off, set forth, start, embark, depart, leave, hit the road (*inf*). **2** present, set forth, state, detail, describe, explain.

set up 1 raise, elevate, put up. **2** build, erect, construct, assemble. **3** establish, found, inaugurate, institute, form, start.

setback *noun* reverse, check, delay, holdup, impediment, obstruction, stumblingblock, hitch, problem, snag (*inf*), blow (*inf*).

setting *noun* **1** background, environment, surroundings, location, site, scene, context, milieu. **2** frame, mounting.

settle *verb* **1** clear up, solve, resolve, reconcile, straighten out, close, conclude, clinch (*inf*). **2** calm down, quieten down, be still, subside, abate. **3** arrange, adjust, make comfortable. **4** take up residence, set up home, put down roots, populate, people, colonize, inhabit. **5** calm, soothe, relax, pacify, sedate, tranquillize. **6** land, alight, light, lodge, rest. **7** come down, drop, fall, descend. **8** sink, subside. **9** pay, discharge, liquidate, clear, square. **10** decide, choose, select, appoint, set, fix, establish, agree on.

settlement *noun* **1** payment, discharge. **2** colonization, occupation, arrangement, adjustment, conclusion. **2** agreement, resolution, reconciliation. **3** community, encampment, hamlet, village, outpost, colony.

settler *noun* colonist, pioneer, frontiersman, frontierswoman, immigrant.

sever *verb* **1** cut, split, cleave, sunder, cut off, amputate. **2** part, divide, separate, disunite. **3** discontinue, break off, end, terminate, dissolve, suspend.

several *adj* **1** some, sundry, various, assorted, diverse. **2** separate, disparate, distinct, different, own, individual, particular, respective.

severe *adj* **1** stern, grim, cold, dour, serious, disapproving, forbidding, austere, unsmiling. **2** strict, harsh, draconian, rigid, inflexible, merciless, hard-hearted, cruel, tough, hard, stringent, rigorous. **3** plain, simple, stark, bare, blank, unadorned, restrained, modest, sober. **4** extreme, sharp, acute, harsh, violent, fierce, intense, strong. **5** hard, difficult, arduous, tough, demanding, punishing, taxing, onerous. **6** serious, grave, acute, critical, dangerous, dire.

sew *verb* **1** stitch, tack, seam, embroider. **2** darn, mend.

sex *noun* **1** gender, sexuality. **2** sexual reproduction, facts of life, the birds and the bees (*inf*), sexuality, sexual chemistry, sexual appetite, libido. **3** sexual intercourse, coitus, copulation, mating, carnal knowledge. **4** sexual relations, intimacy, lovemaking.

sexuality *noun* **1** gender, sex. **2** sexual appetite, sexual urge, sexual desire, lust, sexiness, sensuality.

sexy *adj* **1** seductive, attractive, desirable, alluring, sensual, voluptuous, shapely, nubile, flirtatious, inviting. **2** erotic, pornographic, salacious, provocative, titillating, suggestive, arousing, stimulating. **3** exciting, stylish, desirable, trendy, fashionable.

shabby *adj* **1** ragged, frayed, tatty, worn-out, threadbare, faded, scruffy, disreputable. **2** dilapidated, ramshackle, run-down, dingy, seedy. **3** mean, base, low, cheap, dirty, rotten (*inf*), ignoble, despicable, contemptible, shameful.

shackle *verb* **1** bind, tie, chain, fetter, handcuff, manacle. **2** tether, secure, fasten. **3** restrict, limit, constrain, impede, hinder, hamper, thwart.

shackles *pl noun* manacles, handcuffs, fetters, chains, bonds.

shade *noun* **1** shadow, cover, shelter. **2** darkness, shadiness, shadowiness, gloom, dimness, obscurity. **3** degree, nuance, gradation. **4** colour, tone, hue, tint, tinge.
➤*verb* **1** shadow, eclipse, darken, dim, obscure, cloud. **2** screen, shelter, shield, protect. **3** veil, cover, hide, conceal.
a shade slightly, marginally, a little, a bit, a touch, a trifle.

shadow *noun* **1** outline, silhouette, shape, image. **2** shade, shadowiness, darkness, gloom, dimness, obscurity. **3** trace, touch, dash, hint, suspicion, ghost, shade, bit, modicum. **4** vestige, remnant. **5** cloud, blight. **6** companion, intimate, follower, sidekick (*inf*).
➤*verb* **1** overshadow, eclipse, darken, shade, screen. **2** follow, trail, stalk, dog, hound. **3** watch, observe.

shadowy *adj* **1** shady, shaded, dark, murky, gloomy, tenebrous, dim, obscure. **2** imaginary, illusory, unreal, insubstantial, intangible, ethereal, ghostly, spectral. **3** faint, indistinct, ill-defined, vague, indeterminate, hazy, nebulous.

shady *adj* **1** shaded, shadowy, dark, leafy, screened, shielded, covered, sheltered. **2** dubious, questionable, unreliable, suspect, iffy (*inf*). **3** suspicious, shifty, disreputable, dishonest, unscrupulous, devious, underhand, crooked, fishy (*inf*).

shaft *noun* **1** handle, shank, staff, stem. **2** rod, pole, bar. **3** ray, beam, streak, pencil. **4** tunnel, passage, flue, duct.

shaggy *adj* **1** hairy, hirsute, long-haired, bushy, rough, coarse. **2** unkempt, untidy, dishevelled, tangled, matted.

shake *verb* **1** vibrate, oscillate, wave, swing, rock, sway, wobble, joggle, rattle, judder. **2** tremble, quiver, quake, shudder, shiver, convulse. **3** raise, brandish, wave, wield, swing, flourish. **4** shock, alarm, agitate, upset, unsettle, unnerve, rattle (*inf*), faze (*inf*). **5** weaken, impair, undermine, reduce.

➤ *noun* wave, vibration, tremor, shudder, shiver, quiver, rattle, judder, jolt, jerk, twitch.

shake off elude, lose, leave behind, out-distance, escape from, get away from, give the slip.

shake up 1 shake, upset, shock, agitate, discompose, unnerve, alarm, distress. **2** rouse, stir up. **3** reorganize, rearrange, reshuffle (*inf*).

shaky *adj* **1** shaking, trembling, tremulous, quivery, unstable, wobbly, unsteady, rick-ety. **2** unsound, unsupported, unsubstanti-ated, unreliable, suspect, questionable, precarious, flimsy. **3** tentative, uncertain, faltering, weak.

shallow *adj* superficial, empty, idle, trivial, petty, frivolous.

sham *noun* **1** counterfeit, forgery, fake, imitation, hoax. **2** pretence, imposture, simulation, falseness. **3** impostor, fraud, phoney (*inf*), charlatan, pretender, dissembler.
➤ *adj* **1** false, counterfeit, fake, phoney (*inf*), bogus, spurious, mock, artificial, syn-thetic, imitation. **2** pretended, feigned, simulated, contrived, affected.
➤ *verb* pretend, feign, simulate, affect, put on, fake, counterfeit.

shamble *verb* shuffle, falter, dodder, totter, limp, hobble.

shambles *noun* chaos, mess, muddle, con-fusion, disorder, disarray, havoc.

shame *noun* **1** mortification, humiliation, embarrassment, chagrin, guilt, remorse. **2** disgrace, dishonour, ignominy, scandal, opprobrium, discredit, disrepute, obloquy. **3** pity, bad luck, misfortune, disap-pointment.
➤ *verb* disgrace, discredit, dishonour, debase, degrade, stain, taint, sully.
put to shame 1 mortify, humiliate, hum-ble, embarrass, abash, confound. **2** put in the shade, show up, upstage, outshine, eclipse, outclass.

shamefaced *adj* ashamed, embarrassed, red-faced, humiliated, abashed, mortified, remorseful, regretful, contrite, apologetic.

shameful *adj* **1** disgraceful, scandalous, discreditable, dishonourable, despicable, contemptible, heinous, outrageous, shock-ing, wicked. **2** embarrassing, humiliating, mortifying, ignominious.

shameless *adj* **1** unabashed, unashamed, unrepentant, impenitent, brazen, bold, audacious, insolent, brash, barefaced, fla-grant, blatant. **2** immodest, improper, unbecoming, unseemly, indecorous, inde-cent, unprincipled, wanton.

shanty *noun* shack, hut, cabin, shed, hovel.

shape *noun* **1** appearance, contour, profile, outline, silhouette, design, structure. **2** guise, form, appearance, likeness, sem-blance, image. **3** figure, build. **4** form, condition, trim, state, fettle, health. **5** model, pattern, mould.
➤ *verb* mould, model, cast, forge, form, fashion.
shape up take shape, develop, make head-way, progress.

shapeless *adj* **1** amorphous, nebulous, unstructured, formless. **2** deformed, mis-shapen, irregular, ill-proportioned.

shapely *adj* well-proportioned, neat, trim, attractive, elegant, graceful, curvaceous.

shard *noun* fragment, chip, piece, bit, splinter, sliver, shaving.

share *noun* portion, part, lot, ration, quota, proportion, percentage, cut (*inf*), whack (*inf*), allocation, contribution.
➤ *verb* **1** divide, split, apportion, allocate, allot, distribute, ration. **2** participate, take part, partake, contribute.

sharp *adj* **1** pointed, edged, keen, thin, fine, cutting, jagged, serrated. **2** sudden, abrupt, smart, vigorous, forceful, violent, fierce. **3** keen, acute. **4** intelligent, smart, shrewd, astute, quick, alert, perceptive, penetrating. **5** extreme, intense, severe, acute, piercing, excruciating, stabbing, shooting. **6** biting, cutting, incisive, barbed, caustic, trenchant, acerbic, scath-ing, brusque, curt. **7** tart, acrid, sour, bit-ter, piquant, pungent. **8** harsh, shrill, piercing.
➤ *adv* **1** suddenly, abruptly, unexpectedly, without warning. **2** punctually, promptly, exactly, precisely, on the dot.

sharpen *verb* file, hone, grind, whet.

shatter *verb* **1** break, smash, splinter, shiver, split, crack, burst, disintegrate. **2** dash, blight, wreck, ruin, devastate, crush.

shave

shave *verb* 1 cut, shear, trim, clip, crop. 2 pare, whittle. 3 scrape, graze, brush, touch, skim.

shear *verb* fleece, poll, clip, trim, cut, shave.

sheath *noun* 1 scabbard, case. 2 sleeve, envelope, cover, case. 3 condom, contraceptive, rubber (*inf*).

shed[1] *noun* outhouse, lean-to, hut, shack.

shed[2] *verb* 1 cast, slough, moult, drop. 2 remove, doff, take off, strip off. 3 get rid of, dispense with, drop, discard. 4 spill, discharge, pour forth. 5 emit, radiate, diffuse, disperse, send forth, scatter, spread. 6 drop, throw off, let fall.

sheen *noun* lustre, gloss, polish, shine, brightness.

sheepish *adj* abashed, ashamed, shamefaced, embarrassed, mortified, chastened.

sheer[1] *adj* 1 steep, precipitous, perpendicular, vertical. 2 utter, downright, absolute, total, thorough, rank, unadulterated, pure. 3 thin, fine, light, transparent, see-through, diaphanous.

sheer[2] *verb* deviate, veer, swerve, slew, drift, turn.

sheet *noun* 1 panel, pane, slab, plate, veneer, film. 2 piece, page, folio, leaf. 3 expanse, stretch, sweep, layer, covering, blanket, carpet.

shelf *noun* 1 ledge, sill. 2 sandbank, bar, reef, ledge, step.

shell *noun* 1 casing, husk, pod, capsule. 2 carapace, case, covering. 3 skeleton, framework, structure, hull, chassis. 4 explosive, missile, shot. ➤*verb* 1 husk, pod. 2 bomb, bombard, strafe, blitz.

shell out pay, spend, fork out (*inf*), cough up (*inf*).

shelter *noun* 1 screen, cover, shade, shield, refuge, haven, retreat. 2 protection, cover, security, defence, refuge, sanctuary, asylum. ➤*verb* 1 cover, shade, shield, screen, protect. 2 conceal, hide, harbour, protect, defend, guard.

sheltered *adj* protected, cloistered, secluded, quiet, cosy, snug.

shelve *verb* postpone, defer, put aside, put off, put on the back-burner (*inf*).

shepherd *verb* escort, conduct, usher, guide, steer, marshal, herd.

shield *noun* 1 buckler, targe. 2 escutcheon, device. 3 emblem, badge. 4 protection, defence, safeguard, shelter, rampart, bulwark. 5 guard, cover, screen. ➤*verb* 1 protect, guard, defend, shelter. 2 screen, cover, hide.

shift *verb* 1 move, transfer, relocate, reposition, switch, transpose. 2 change, alter, move, veer. 3 remove, get rid of, dislodge, budge. ➤*noun* 1 move, movement, relocation, transposition. 2 change, alteration, variation, reversal, about-turn. 3 stint, period, spell, time. 4 device, contrivance, expedient, resource, scheme, strategy. 5 artifice, trick, wile, ruse, dodge.

shift for oneself manage, fend for oneself, get by.

shiftless *adj* lazy, idle, indolent, unambitious, lackadaisical (*inf*), worthless, good-for-nothing, irresponsible.

shifty *adj* crafty, sly, tricky, slippery (*inf*), evasive, furtive, dishonest, devious, dubious, untrustworthy.

shimmer *verb* glimmer, glisten, gleam, glitter, flicker, dance, twinkle, sparkle. ➤*noun* glow, lustre, iridescence, glimmer, glitter, flicker, twinkle, sparkle, scintillation.

shine *verb* 1 beam, glow, radiate, sparkle, twinkle. 2 gleam, glint, glisten, glitter. 3 excel, stand out. 4 polish, burnish, buff, wax. ➤*noun* 1 brightness, light, radiance, luminosity, glow, lustre, sheen, gloss, glaze, gleam, sparkle. 2 splendour, brilliance, resplendence.

shiny *adj* bright, shining, gleaming, glossy, sleek, lustrous, polished, burnished.

ship *noun* vessel, craft, liner, boat, ferry.

shipshape *adj* neat, tidy, orderly, trim, spick and span, well-organized.

shirk *verb* evade, avoid, dodge, get out of, duck (*inf*), skive off (*inf*), play truant, slack, idle, malinger.

shiver[1] *verb* tremble, shudder, shake, quiver, quake. ➤*noun* shudder, tremor, twitch, quiver, shake.

shiver² *noun* sliver, splinter, fragment, bit, chip, shard.
➤*verb* shatter, splinter, smash, break, fragment.

shock *verb* **1** horrify, appal, disgust, offend, scandalize, outrage, disturb, distress, upset, dismay, stun, shake. **2** traumatize, daze, numb, paralyse, agitate.
➤*noun* **1** horror, fright, stupefaction, astonishment, consternation, perturbation. **2** upset, blow, bombshell (*inf*), revelation, surprise, eye-opener. **3** trauma, collapse, prostration. **4** impact, blow, bump, collision, crash. **5** jolt, jar, jerk, shake.

shocking *adj* **1** horrifying, appalling, outrageous, scandalous, disgraceful, shameful, disgusting, offensive, distressing, upsetting, disturbing. **2** awful, terrible, dreadful, atrocious, abominable.

shoot *verb* **1** fire, discharge. **2** gun down, pick off, snipe at, hit, wound, kill, bag, blast, zap (*inf*). **3** dash, rush, race, speed, charge, fly, hurtle, bolt, propel, project, launch, hurl. **4** aim, direct. **5** germinate, sprout, bud, grow. **6** film, photograph, video.
➤*noun* sprout, bud, scion, branch, cutting.

shop *noun* store, supermarket, boutique, emporium, retail outlet.
➤*verb* **1** buy, purchase. **2** betray, inform on, grass on (*inf*), blow the whistle on (*inf*).

shore¹ *noun* seashore, foreshore, beach, strand, waterfront, promenade, coastline, littoral.

shore² *noun* support, prop, brace, buttress, strut, stay.
➤*verb* support, prop, brace, reinforce, buttress, underpin.

short *adj* **1** little, small, diminutive, dwarfish, pint-sized (*inf*), stubby, squat. **2** brief, fleeting, passing, momentary, cursory, short-lived. **3** scant, scarce, insufficient, inadequate, limited, tight (*inf*). **4** deficient, lacking, wanting, low. **5** concise, succinct, terse, laconic, pithy, compact. **6** contracted, abbreviated, truncated, summarized, condensed, abridged. **7** abrupt, curt, sharp, brusque, gruff. **8** snappy, short-tempered, irascible, testy.
➤*adv* abruptly, unexpectedly, suddenly, without warning, out of the blue.

in short briefly, in a word, in a nutshell (*inf*).

shortage *noun* dearth, shortfall, lack, need, scarcity, deficiency, deficit, insufficiency.

shortcoming *noun* defect, flaw, fault, failing, weakness, foible, deficiency, drawback.

shorten *verb* cut, curtail, truncate, reduce, decrease, dock, trim, abbreviate, abridge, condense, contract.

short-lived *adj* brief, momentary, fleeting, passing, temporary, transitory, ephemeral.

shortly *adv* **1** soon, presently, directly, by and by, before long, in a little while. **2** briefly, succinctly, concisely, tersely. **3** abruptly, brusquely, curtly, gruffly.

short-sighted *adj* **1** myopic, near-sighted. **2** rash, ill-considered, ill-advised, imprudent, unwise, careless, hasty.

short-tempered *adj* quick-tempered, hot-tempered, irascible, impatient, touchy (*inf*), testy (*inf*).

shot *noun* **1** report, blast, bang, crack, discharge, explosion. **2** ball, pellet, bullet, slug (*inf*), projectile, missile. **3** try, attempt, go (*inf*), crack (*inf*), stab (*inf*), bash (*inf*). **4** kick, hit, stroke, throw. **5** photograph, photo, picture, snapshot, snap. **6** vaccination, inoculation, injection, jab (*inf*).
like a shot unhesitatingly, without delay, immediately, right away, at once.

shoulder *verb* **1** assume, accept, take on, bear, carry. **2** push, shove, jostle, thrust, press.
shoulder to shoulder together, as one, jointly, united, side by side.

shout *verb* **1** yell, cry, scream, shriek. **2** call, cry, exclaim, roar, bawl, bellow.
➤*noun* cry, call, yell, scream, shriek, exclamation.

shove *verb* **1** push, move, propel, drive. **2** put, thrust, push, barge, jostle, elbow.
➤*noun* push, thrust.

shovel *noun* spade, scoop.
➤*verb* dig, excavate, scoop, dredge, shift, clear.

show *verb* **1** present, produce, reveal, uncover, expose. **2** appear, be visible, stand out. **3** display, exhibit, parade, show

off. **4** express, demonstrate, register, betray, disclose, make known, evince. **5** indicate, point out. **6** demonstrate, explain, expound, teach, instruct. **7** prove, evidence, establish. **8** usher, escort, conduct, accompany, guide, lead, direct, steer. **9** turn up, show up, appear, come, arrive.
➤*noun* **1** production, entertainment, spectacle, pageant, performance, showing. **2** programme, broadcast. **3** display, exhibition, exposition, presentation, demonstration, parade. **4** demonstration, manifestation, representation, display, indication, sign. **5** pretence, semblance, air, appearance, facade, front, affectation, ostentation, window-dressing (*inf*), play-acting (*inf*). **6** business, operation, organization, affair, enterprise, venture.
show off 1 display, exhibit, advertise, parade, brandish, flaunt. **2** swagger, boast, brag, strut.
show up 1 reveal, expose, lay bare, put to shame, outshine, upstage. **2** embarrass, humiliate, mortify, let down, shame, disgrace. **3** appear, arrive, come, turn up, materialize (*inf*).

showdown *noun* confrontation, clash, crisis, face-off, moment of truth.

shower *noun* **1** fall, cloudburst, flurry, sprinkling. **2** barrage, fusillade, volley, hail, flood, deluge, torrent.
➤*verb* **1** rain, fall, spray, sprinkle, pour. **2** inundate, deluge, load, overwhelm.

show-off *noun* exhibitionist, poseur, braggart, boaster, swaggerer.

showy *adj* **1** attractive, fancy, ornate, gaudy. **2** flamboyant, flashy, swanky (*inf*), garish, loud, ostentatious, pretentious, pompous.

shred *noun* **1** piece, snippet, strip, ribbon, rag, tatter. **2** atom, grain, bit, scrap, jot, whit, trace.
➤*verb* tear up, cut up, grate, slice.

shrew *noun* nag, scold, termagant, virago, harridan, dragon.

shrewd *adj* **1** astute, sharp, smart, clever, wise, sagacious, judicious, canny. **2** artful, crafty, cunning, sly, wily, calculating.

shriek *verb* screech, scream, squeal, yell, cry, shout.

shrill *adj* sharp, piercing, ear-splitting, penetrating, high-pitched, strident.

shrine *noun* **1** temple, holy place, church, chapel, sanctuary, tabernacle. **2** reliquary, tomb, sepulchre. **3** memorial, monument.

shrink *verb* **1** contract, shorten, narrow, shrivel, decrease, reduce. **2** recoil, draw back, flinch, wince, cower, quail. **3** shy away, balk.

shrivel *verb* wither, wilt, wrinkle, shrink, contract, dry up, dehydrate, desiccate.

shroud *noun* **1** winding-sheet, cerement. **2** mantle, blanket, cloak, pall, veil, cover.
➤*verb* wrap, swathe, envelop, cover, conceal, mask, veil, screen, cloak, blanket.

shrug off *verb* disregard, brush aside, ignore, dismiss, minimize, play down, make light of.

shudder *verb* shiver, shake, tremble, quiver, quake.

shuffle *verb* **1** shamble, falter, hobble, toddle. **2** drag, scrape, scuff. **3** mix, jumble, rearrange, reorder. **4** rearrange, reorganize, shift, switch. **5** equivocate, hedge, fence, parry, evade, quibble, prevaricate, beat about the bush.

shun *verb* avoid, evade, spurn, ignore, ostracize, cold-shoulder (*inf*), shirk, shrink from, eschew, steer clear of.

shut *verb* **1** pull to, close, slam, draw. **2** lock, latch, bolt, seal, fasten. **3** confine, enclose, immure, cage.
➤*adj* closed, drawn, locked, sealed, fastened.
shut down stop, close down, switch off, inactivate.
shut out exclude, bar, lock out, banish, exile, keep out.
shut up 1 imprison, incarcerate, jail, confine, coop up, cage. **2** hush, be quiet, pipe down, clam up, silence, gag.

shutter *noun* shade, blind, screen.

shuttle *verb* commute, go to and fro, ply, shunt.

shy *adj* **1** bashful, retiring, reserved, diffident, self-effacing, introverted, inhibited, coy, self-conscious. **2** timid, timorous, nervous, fearful. **3** hesitant, reluctant, wary, cautious, distrustful, suspicious.
➤*verb* **1** rear, buck, balk, swerve. **2** avoid, shrink, flinch, quail, recoil, back away.

sick *adj* **1** ill, unwell, ailing, poorly (*inf*), indisposed, laid up (*inf*). **2** queasy, bilious, nauseated. **3** tired, bored, fed up (*inf*), jaded, satiated. **4** annoyed, angry, disgruntled, disgusted, fed up (*inf*), pissed off (*sl*). **5** disappointed, upset, miserable, cheesed off (*inf*). **6** morbid, sadistic, tasteless, macabre, black.

sicken *verb* **1** nauseate, disgust, revolt, shock, appal. **2** catch, contract, pick up, go down with (*inf*).

sickening *adj* **1** nauseating, revolting, disgusting, offensive, foul, stomach-turning. **2** annoying, infuriating.

sickly *adj* **1** unhealthy, delicate, infirm, ailing. **2** weak, feeble, frail, puny. **3** pale, wan, peaky, unhealthy. **4** unpleasant, revolting, nauseating. **5** sentimental, soppy (*inf*), syrupy, cloying, mawkish, slushy (*inf*).

sickness *noun* **1** ill health, indisposition, infirmity. **2** disease, illness, ailment, disorder, complaint, malady, bug (*inf*). **3** nausea, queasiness, biliousness.

side *noun* **1** edge, border, boundary, margin. **2** face, surface, facet, end, profile. **3** part, half, wing, flank, area, region, sector, zone, bank, shore. **4** aspect, angle, facet, perspective. **5** attitude, position, standpoint, opinion, point of view, part. **6** party, group, faction, camp, interest, cause. **7** team, squad, line-up.
➤*adj* **1** lateral, flanking. **2** subordinate, secondary, incidental, minor, marginal.
➤*verb* ally, associate, team up, support, agree with, take the part of.

sidelong *adj and adv* sideways, indirect, oblique.

sidestep *verb* avoid, evade, dodge, bypass, circumvent, duck (*inf*).

sidetrack *verb* divert, deflect, head off, distract.

sideways *adv and adj* **1** askance, indirectly, obliquely, sidelong. **2** edgeways, crabwise, lateral.

siege *noun* blockade, besiegement, encirclement.

siesta *noun* nap, rest, relaxation, snooze (*inf*), forty winks (*inf*).

sieve *noun* colander, strainer, sifter, screen, riddle.

sift *verb* **1** sieve, strain, filter, riddle, screen. **2** sprinkle, scatter. **3** remove, sepa-

rate. **4** study, analyse, examine, scrutinize, investigate. **5** screen, sort, winnow.

sigh *verb* **1** breathe, exhale, moan. **2** lament, mourn, grieve, long, pine, yearn.

sight *noun* **1** vision, eyesight, seeing. **2** look, view, glimpse, glance, perception, observation. **3** range, view. **4** spectacle, scene, show, display, appearance. **5** feature, curiosity, wonder, beauty. **6** mess, fright (*inf*), eyesore, monstrosity.
➤*verb* see, glimpse, catch sight of, spot, perceive, notice.
set one's sights on aim at, aspire to, strive after, work towards.

sign *noun* **1** token, indication, manifestation, symptom, pointer, clue, evidence, proof, trace, vestige. **2** symbol, mark, character, cipher. **3** signal, gesture, motion, movement. **4** omen, portent, augury, harbinger, presage, warning. **5** signpost, marker, indicator, board, notice.
➤*verb* **1** initial, autograph, countersign, endorse, subscribe, validate, authenticate, certify. **2** write, inscribe. **3** recruit, hire, employ, engage, appoint, take on.
4 signal, gesture, motion, beckon, wave, nod.
sign on sign up, enlist, enrol, register.
sign over make over, hand over, surrender, transfer, assign, convey.

signal *noun* **1** cue, sign, gesture, indicator. **2** sign, beacon, flag, siren, warning, alert.
➤*adj* conspicuous, noteworthy, remarkable, notable, memorable, striking, outstanding, impressive, exceptional, extraordinary.
➤*verb* **1** gesture, motion, nod, beckon, wave, sign. **2** communicate, express, show, indicate.

significance *noun* **1** meaning, sense, point, gist, import, implication, connotation. **2** importance, consequence, matter, moment, weight, force, relevance.

significant *adj* **1** important, consequential, noteworthy, relevant, weighty, momentous, impressive, appreciable, material, key. **2** meaningful, indicative, symptomatic. **3** suggestive, eloquent, expressive, telling, pregnant.

signify verb **1** mean, denote, symbolize, represent, stand for. **2** indicate, show, signal, betoken, imply, suggest. **3** express, communicate, impart, convey, indicate, show. **4** matter, count, be significant, carry weight.

silence noun **1** quiet, hush, peace, stillness, soundlessness. **2** muteness, dumbness, wordlessness, voicelessness, taciturnity, reticence, secrecy.
➤verb **1** quieten, hush, mute, muffle, smother, deaden. **2** suppress, muzzle, gag, cut short.

silent adj **1** quiet, still, hushed, peaceful, soundless, noiseless. **2** dumb, mute, tight-lipped, tongue-tied, speechless, wordless, mum (inf). **3** taciturn, reticent, reserved, uncommunicative. **4** tacit, unspoken, understood, implicit, implied. **5** voiceless, mute.

silhouette noun outline, contour, profile, shape, form, shadow.
➤verb outline, profile, stand out, delineate.

silky adj silken, fine, velvety, soft, smooth, glossy, sleek, lustrous.

silly adj **1** stupid, daft (inf), mad, crazy (inf), idiotic, foolish, senseless, irresponsible, reckless, foolhardy, unwise, imprudent. **2** frivolous, trifling, trivial, absurd, ridiculous, preposterous.

silt noun deposit, sediment, ooze, sludge, alluvium.

similar adj like, alike, comparable, equivalent, corresponding, analogous, akin, related, allied.

similitude noun similarity, resemblance, likeness, sameness, relation, comparability, agreement, congruence, correspondence, equivalence.

simmer verb **1** boil, seethe, bubble. **2** cook, stew. **3** fume, rage, seethe, smoulder.
simmer down calm down, control oneself, cool off.

simper verb smile, smirk, giggle.

simple adj **1** easy, effortless, uncomplicated, uninvolved, straightforward, elementary, clear, plain, comprehensible, intelligible. **2** plain, basic, ordinary, pure, natural, primitive, classic, unadorned, uncluttered, bare. **3** unpretentious, unaf-

fected, unfussy, restrained, modest. **4** unsophisticated, artless, guileless, naive, ingenuous. **6** simple-minded, feeble-minded, backward, slow, retarded, unintelligent. **7** humble, lowly.

simplicity noun simpleness, easiness, effortlessness, straightforwardness, plainness, clarity, intelligibility, naturalness.

simplify verb clarify, explain, paraphrase, shorten, abridge, condense, streamline.

simplistic adj oversimplified, simple, facile, superficial, shallow, naive.

simply adv **1** plainly, straightforwardly, clearly, intelligibly. **2** unpretentiously, naturally, informally, modestly, humbly, with restraint. **3** merely, only, just, purely, solely. **4** absolutely, utterly, certainly, positively, categorically, unreservedly, altogether, really, quite, unquestionably.

simulate verb **1** pretend, feign, sham, fake, counterfeit, affect, assume. **2** reproduce, duplicate, imitate, mimic, copy.

simultaneous adj concurrent, concomitant, coincident, synchronous, contemporaneous, coexistent.

sin noun **1** trespass, transgression, lapse, fault, offence, wrongdoing. **2** crime, wrong, iniquity, immorality, evil, wickedness, sacrilege, outrage.
➤verb transgress, trespass, do wrong, err, offend, lapse, stray, fall from grace.

sincere adj honest, real, true, heartfelt, wholehearted, genuine, unaffected, earnest, serious, truthful, frank, candid.

sincerely adv earnestly, seriously, without reservation, wholeheartedly, genuinely, really, truly, honestly.

sinewy adj strong, powerful, muscular, brawny, strapping, sturdy, wiry, athletic.

sinful adj bad, wicked, evil, wrong, iniquitous, criminal, immoral, ungodly, sacrilegious.

sing verb **1** warble, croon, serenade, intone, chant, yodel. **2** trill, warble, chirp, pipe. **3** cry, call, shout, yell.

singe verb burn, scorch, char, sear.

single adj **1** sole, only, one, lone, solitary. **2** separate, distinct, individual, particular, singular, unique, exclusive. **3** unmarried, unwed, unattached, free, available.

single out choose, select, pick, decide on, separate, isolate, highlight, pinpoint, distinguish, identify.

single-minded *adj* determined, resolute, purposeful, set, dogged, persevering, unwavering, unswerving, dedicated, devoted, committed, obsessive.

singular *adj* 1 remarkable, outstanding, exceptional, notable, eminent, striking, distinctive. 2 unusual, odd, curious, peculiar, strange, weird. 3 single, unique.

sinister *adj* 1 ominous, portentous, inauspicious, unlucky, disturbing, worrying, menacing, threatening. 2 evil, wicked, bad, villainous, malign, malevolent.

sink *verb* 1 go under, capsize, submerge, immerse, dip, plunge, dive. 2 go down, scuttle, scupper, wreck, drown. 3 penetrate, drive, embed. 4 bore, drill, dig, excavate, put down, lay. 5 fall, drop, descend, slip, slump, subside, sag, collapse, plunge, plummet, ebb, recede. 6 disappear, vanish. 7 decrease, lessen, diminish, decline, deteriorate, go downhill (*inf*). 8 fail, fade, weaken, succumb. 9 overwhelm, defeat, ruin, destroy. 10 invest, put, venture, risk, plough.
sink in penetrate, register (*inf*), be understood.

sinuous *adj* 1 serpentine, winding, bending, flexuous, crooked, curving, twisting, coiling, wavy, undulating. 2 tortuous, convoluted, intricate, devious. 3 supple, lithe, slinky.

sip *verb* taste, sample, sup, drink.
➤*noun* taste, drink, drop, mouthful.

siren *noun* 1 alarm, bell, buzzer, warning. 2 temptress, seductress, femme fatale, vamp (*inf*).

sit *verb* 1 be seated, take a seat. 2 squat, crouch. 3 rest, stand, lie, place, position. 4 seat, accommodate, hold, contain. 5 meet, assemble, convene, deliberate.

site *noun* 1 place, location, position, situation, setting, scene. 2 plot, lot, ground. 3 spot, point, location, place.
➤*verb* place, locate, position, situate, set, put, install.

sitting *noun* 1 meeting, session, hearing, assembly. 2 period, spell, session.

situate *verb* place, locate, position, site.

situation *noun* 1 position, place, location, site, spot, environment, setting, context. 2 status, position, standing, condition, state, plight. 3 circumstances, case, state of affairs. 4 post, job, appointment, position.

size *noun* 1 dimensions, measurements, proportions, magnitude, area, volume, height, length, extent, scale. 2 bigness, largeness, vastness, immensity.
size up 1 rate, appraise, judge, evaluate. 2 gauge, estimate, assess, weigh up.

skeleton *noun* 1 bare bones, plan, outline, sketch. 2 structure, framework, support, shell, chassis.
➤*adj* minimum, basic, essential.

sketch *noun* 1 drawing, cartoon, plan, design, delineation, representation, draft. 2 outline, summary, précis, résumé, vignette.
➤*verb* 1 draw, pencil, draft, block out, delineate, represent. 2 outline, summarize, précis.

sketchy *adj* unfinished, incomplete, rough, preliminary, vague, bitty, superficial, cursory, scanty, deficient.

skilful *adj* skilled, adept, proficient, expert, masterly, adroit, talented, clever, able, competent, accomplished, good.

skill *noun* proficiency, expertise, mastery, facility, competence, talent, faculty, ability, accomplishment, aptitude.

skilled *adj* skilful, talented, gifted, accomplished, competent, expert, proficient, able, qualified, trained, experienced, professional.

skim *verb* 1 glide, fly, skate, plane, graze, touch, brush. 2 glance, scan, browse, flick, flip, leaf, thumb. 3 cream, separate.

skimp *verb* economize, be frugal, scrimp, stint, limit, cut corners (*inf*).

skimpy *adj* meagre, scanty, insufficient, inadequate, small, short, brief, sketchy, insubstantial.

skin *adj* 1 epidermis, cuticle, integument. 2 hide, pelt, fleece, fell. 3 peel, rind, shell, husk, pod, casing. 4 covering, casing, outside. 5 layer, film, membrane, crust.
➤*verb* 1 peel, pare, strip. 2 graze, scrape, bark.
by the skin of one's teeth by a hair's breadth, by a whisker (*inf*), narrowly, barely, only just.

skinny *adj* thin, lean, scrawny, scraggy, emaciated, skeletal.

skip *verb* 1 hop, spring, leap, bound, caper, frisk, gambol, dance. 2 omit, exclude, leave out, miss out, pass over, jump.

skirmish *noun* 1 battle, fight, engagement, combat. 2 conflict, clash, confrontation, tussle, scrap (*inf*), brush, encounter. 3 dispute, altercation, quarrel, row.
➤*verb* fight, battle, clash, tussle, brawl, scuffle, quarrel, argue, dispute, wrangle.

skirt *verb* 1 edge, border, flank, encircle. 2 avoid, evade, dodge, sidestep, bypass, circumvent.

skit *noun* burlesque, parody, caricature, satire, take-off (*inf*), send-up (*inf*), spoof (*inf*).

skittish *adj* 1 nervous, jumpy, excitable, highly strung, restive, fidgety. 2 lively, playful, frisky, sportive. 3 fickle, capricious, variable, unpredictable.

skulk *verb* 1 lurk, loiter, lie in wait. 2 prowl, slink, sidle, sneak, steal, creep.

sky *noun* heavens, firmament, ether, azure, air, upper atmosphere, outer space.

slab *noun* block, piece, chunk, brick, wedge, slice.

slack *adj* 1 loose, lax, limp, relaxed, flaccid, baggy, sagging. 2 sluggish, slow, indolent, lazy, idle. 3 negligent, neglectful, slipshod, remiss, careless, offhand, inattentive, lax. 4 inactive, quiet.
➤*verb* 1 shirk, skive (*inf*), dodge, evade. 2 neglect, idle, loaf.

slacken *verb* 1 loosen, relax, ease. 2 lessen, moderate, abate, let up, reduce, diminish, decrease, slow.

slake *verb* quench, satisfy, relieve, allay, gratify.

slam *verb* 1 bang, shut. 2 slap, bang, thump, hurl, throw. 3 smash, dash, crash. 4 criticize, denounce, attack, slate (*inf*), blast (*inf*), pan (*inf*).

slander *noun* 1 defamation, misrepresentation, calumny, disparagement, denigration, vilification. 2 aspersion, slur, smear.
➤*verb* defame, calumniate, vilify, malign, disparage, denigrate, smear, badmouth (*inf*).

slang *noun* 1 colloquialism, vulgarism. 2 jargon, cant, argot, patter.

slant *verb* 1 slope, incline, lean, tilt, list. 2 angle, bias, twist, distort, colour, skew, weight.
➤*noun* 1 slope, tilt, inclination, list, ramp, gradient, pitch, angle. 2 view, opinion. 3 bias, twist, distortion, spin.
➤*adj* oblique, aslant, slanting, sloping, angled, tilted, diagonal.

slap *verb* 1 hit, strike, smack, spank, whack, cuff, clip (*inf*). 2 slam, bang, thump. 3 daub, dollop, plaster, stick, plonk, toss.
➤*noun* 1 blow, hit, smack, whack, cuff, clip (*inf*). 2 bang, smack, thump.
➤*adv* right, smack (*inf*), straight, bang (*inf*), dead.
slap in the face insult, snub, rebuff, put-down.

slapdash *adj* slipshod, careless, negligent, offhand, untidy, disorderly, hasty, cursory, perfunctory, haphazard.

slash *verb* 1 cut, gash, hack, score, slit, lacerate, knife. 2 reduce, cut, drop, lower, axe (*inf*).
➤*noun* cut, gash, slit, laceration.

slate *verb* criticize, censure, lambaste, pan (*inf*), slam (*inf*), tear to pieces (*inf*).

slaughter *noun* 1 killing, butchery. 2 massacre, extermination, bloodshed, carnage.
➤*verb* 1 kill, butcher. 2 slay, massacre, murder, assassinate, exterminate, annihilate.

slave *noun* 1 bondservant, serf, vassal, villein. 2 drudge, skivvy (*inf*), menial, lackey.
➤*verb* toil, labour, slog, drudge, sweat.

slaver *verb* slobber, drool, dribble.

slavery *noun* 1 bondage, thrall, serfdom, servitude, enslavement, subjugation. 2 drudgery, toil, labour, slog, grind.

slavish *adj* 1 servile, obsequious, sycophantic, fawning, grovelling, abject. 2 unoriginal, imitative, unimaginative, literal.

slay *verb* 1 kill, slaughter, butcher, massacre. 2 murder, do away with, rub out (*inf*), assassinate, execute, dispatch.

sleek *adj* 1 smooth, shiny, glossy, lustrous, silky. 2 well-groomed, smooth, slick. 3 flourishing, thriving, prosperous, well-heeled (*inf*). 4 stylish, elegant, streamlined.

sleep *verb* slumber, doze, drowse, nap, snooze (*inf*), kip (*inf*), rest, hibernate.
➤*noun* **1** slumber, kip (*inf*), shut-eye (*inf*), rest, hibernation. **2** nap, doze, siesta, snooze (*inf*), forty winks (*inf*).

sleepless *adj* **1** insomniac, wakeful, alert, awake. **2** restless, disturbed.

sleepy *adj* **1** drowsy, somnolent, tired, weary. **2** sluggish, slow, lazy, torpid, languorous, lethargic, comatose. **3** quiet, peaceful, tranquil, still.

slender *adj* **1** slim, thin, willowy, svelte, trim, slight. **2** narrow, thin. **3** faint, remote, slim, slight, flimsy, fragile, meagre, paltry, insubstantial.

sleuth *noun* detective, private detective, private eye (*inf*), gumshoe (*inf*).

slice *noun* **1** piece, slab, wedge, sliver, rasher, segment. **2** share, part, portion, cut (*inf*).
➤*verb* cut, carve, chop, divide.

slick *adj* **1** skilful, deft, smooth, polished, efficient, well-organized, streamlined, professional. **2** fluent, glib, plausible, smooth-talking, urbane, suave, oily, smarmy, unctuous. **3** smooth, sleek, glossy, shiny, slippery.

slide *verb* **1** slip, glide, skate, slither, skid, plane. **2** deteriorate, decline, lapse, worsen, drop, fall.

slight *adj* **1** small, little, inconsiderable, imperceptible, modest, subtle. **2** slim, slender, diminutive, petite, elfin, dainty, delicate, frail. **3** flimsy, rickety, fragile. **4** petty, insignificant, unimportant, inconsequential, trivial, trifling. **5** superficial, negligible, minor.
➤*verb* snub, spurn, ignore, neglect, cold-shoulder (*inf*), rebuff, insult, affront, scorn, despise.
➤*noun* snub, rebuff, insult, affront.

slim *adj* **1** slender, thin, trim, lean, spare, willowy, svelte. **2** slight, remote, faint, small, scanty, meagre, flimsy, tenuous.
➤*verb* lose weight, diet.

slime *noun* **1** mud, mire, ooze, sludge. **2** mucus, goo (*inf*).

slimy *adj* **1** muddy, sludgy, greasy, oily, slippery, sticky, mucous, mucilaginous, viscous. **2** oily, unctuous, servile, obsequious, sycophantic, ingratiating, smarmy (*inf*).

sling *verb* throw, fling, hurl, toss, cast, chuck (*inf*).
➤*noun* bandage, strap, support, loop.

slink *verb* sneak, steal, creep, prowl, skulk, sidle, slip.

slip[1] *verb* **1** slide, glide, slither, skid, skate, stumble, lose one's footing. **2** fall, drop, slide. **3** sneak, steal, creep, slink. **4** put on, take off, change into. **5** decline, deteriorate, worsen, fall, drop, slide.
➤*noun* **1** slip-up, error, mistake, blunder, oversight, omission. **2** petticoat, underskirt.
give somebody the slip get away from, shake off, evade, elude, dodge, outwit.
let slip let out, disclose, reveal, divulge, leak, give away, betray.
slip up err, blunder, miscalculate, go wrong.

slip[2] *noun* **1** paper, note, chit, card, coupon, voucher. **2** cutting, shoot, sprig, twig, scion.

slippery *adj* **1** smooth, glassy, icy, greasy, slippy (*inf*). **2** slimy, oily, lubricated. **3** treacherous, perfidious, untrustworthy, shifty, foxy, tricky, sneaky, crafty, devious.

slipshod *adj* negligent, careless, lax, slapdash, sloppy, disorganized, unmethodical, untidy, slovenly.

slit *verb* cut, slash, gash, slice, split.
➤*noun* cut, incision, slash, gash, split, opening, vent, fissure, aperture.

slither *verb* **1** slide, glide. **2** slip, skid.

sliver *noun* flake, chip, splinter, fragment, shard, slice, wafer, shaving.

slobber *verb* slaver, drool, dribble, salivate.

slog *verb* **1** hit, strike, belt, thump, whack, bash (*inf*), wallop (*inf*), sock (*inf*). **2** slave, labour, toil, plough. **3** trudge, tramp, trek, hike, plod.
➤*noun* **1** struggle, effort, labour, grind. **2** hike, tramp, trek, trudge.

slogan *noun* **1** jingle, catchphrase. **2** watchword, motto. **3** rallying cry, war cry, battle-cry.

slop *verb* **1** spill, overflow. **2** splash, slosh.

slope *verb* incline, slant, lean, tilt, tip, list.
➤*noun* **1** inclination, gradient, pitch, angle, slant, tilt, acclivity, declivity. **2** hill, bank, rise. **3** incline, ramp.

slope off slip away, slink off, sneak off, steal away, make oneself scarce (*inf*).

sloppy *adj* 1 wet, watery, runny, slushy, soggy. 2 careless, slapdash, slipshod, slovenly, clumsy, amateurish, messy, untidy. 3 sentimental, emotional, mawkish, maudlin, gushing, slushy (*inf*), soppy (*inf*), corny (*inf*).

slot *noun* 1 opening, aperture, hole, slit, crack, groove. 2 place, position, niche, window (*inf*), gap, opening, vacancy.

sloth *noun* laziness, indolence, idleness, inertia, inactivity, lethargy, sluggishness, torpor.

slouch *verb* stoop, slump, hunch, shuffle, shamble.

slovenly *adj* 1 scruffy, slatternly, sluttish, dirty, messy, untidy, unkempt. 2 careless, slipshod, slapdash, sloppy, negligent.

slow *adj* 1 plodding, crawling, dawdling, lagging, lazy. 2 leisurely, unhurried, easy, measured. 3 gradual, protracted, lingering. 4 unintelligent, stupid, dense, dull, dim, obtuse, bovine. 5 slow-moving, ponderous, sleepy, inert, inactive. 6 tedious, monotonous, boring, dull, uninteresting, uneventful. 7 slack, sluggish, quiet, inactive, dead. 8 late, tardy, unpunctual, backward, dilatory, reluctant, hesitant, unwilling, disinclined.
➤*verb* retard, delay, hold up, hold back, check, curb, brake, decelerate.

sluggish *adj* 1 slow, slack, slow-moving, stagnant. 2 lazy, slothful, indolent, idle. 3 torpid, apathetic, heavy, dull, sleepy, lethargic, listless, inactive, inert.

slumber *noun* sleep, rest, repose, nap, snooze (*inf*).
➤*verb* sleep, rest, nap, doze, drowse, snooze (*inf*).

slump *verb* 1 flop, collapse, fall, drop, sink. 2 plunge, plummet, nosedive, drop. 3 decline, slide, collapse, crash, fail.
➤*noun* 1 recession, depression, decline, stagnation, downturn, trough. 2 drop, fall, plunge, nosedive, collapse, crash, failure.

slur *noun* slight, insult, aspersion, insinuation, slander, libel, smear.

slut *noun* whore, tart (*inf*), scrubber (*inf*), sloven, slattern.

sly *adj* 1 artful, cunning, crafty, wily, foxy, tricky, devious. 2 furtive, stealthy, clandestine, surreptitious, secretive. 3 roguish, impish, arch, mischievous.
on the sly secretly, in secret, furtively, surreptitiously, covertly, under cover.

smack¹ *noun* 1 flavour, taste, savour, tang, smell, aroma. 2 suggestion, trace, hint, nuance, tinge, touch, dash, whiff.
➤*verb* 1 taste, savour, smell. 2 resemble, suggest, hint, evoke.

smack² *verb* 1 slap, spank, hit, strike, cuff, box, clout (*inf*). 2 clap, bang, tap, pat.
➤*noun* 1 slap, blow, hit, cuff, punch, clip (*inf*). 2 clap, bang, thud, tap.
➤*adv* slap-bang, straight, right, directly, suddenly.

small *adj* 1 little, tiny, short, undersized, diminutive, miniature, compact, pocket-sized (*inf*). 2 insignificant, unimportant, inconsequential, minor, trifling, trivial, paltry. 3 petty, mean, small-minded, narrow-minded. 4 limited, meagre, scanty, inconsiderable, slight, inappreciable, negligible. 5 humble, base, inferior, poor. 6 modest, unpretentious, simple, lowly, minor.

small-minded *adj* 1 narrow-minded, hidebound, insular, parochial. 2 petty, mean, intolerant, ungenerous.

smart *adj* 1 neat, tidy, presentable, spruce, dapper, natty (*inf*), well-dressed, well-groomed, elegant, stylish. 2 fashionable, chic. 3 bright, intelligent, gifted, adept, sharp, acute, quick-witted, alert, ready. 4 clever, shrewd, astute, ingenious. 5 quick, fast, swift, brisk, lively, spirited, jaunty, agile. 5 vigorous, energetic, forceful.
➤*verb* sting, prick, bite, burn, tingle, twinge, pain, hurt.

smash *verb* 1 break, shatter, splinter, shiver, pulverize, crush, disintegrate. 2 drive, dash. 3 destroy, demolish, wreck, ruin. 4 crash, collide, bump, plough. 5 bang, thump, strike, knock, hit, bash.
➤*noun* 1 crash, collision, bump, shunt, prang (*inf*). 2 wreck, pile-up.

smashing *adj* marvellous, wonderful, excellent, sensational, cool (*inf*), great (*inf*), fantastic (*inf*), super (*inf*), terrific (*inf*).

smattering *noun* 1 elements, basics, rudiments. 2 modicum, dash, bit.

smear *verb* **1** besmear, daub, plaster, streak. **2** rub, spread, apply. **3** slander, libel, defame, malign, vilify, sully, tarnish, stain, blacken. **4** smudge, blur.
➤*noun* **1** smudge, streak, splodge, daub, patch, spot. **2** slander, libel, slur, stain, blot, aspersion.

smell *verb* **1** scent, detect. **2** sniff, inhale. **3** stink, reek, pong (*inf*).
➤*noun* **1** odour, scent, aroma, perfume, fragrance, whiff. **2** stink, stench, reek, pong (*inf*).

smelly *adj* malodorous, stinking, reeking, foul, putrid, fetid.

smile *noun* grin, beam, smirk, simper.

smirk *verb* simper, grimace, grin, smile, leer, sneer.

smoke *noun* fumes, exhaust, vapour.
➤*verb* **1** puff, draw, inhale, exhale, light up. **2** cure, preserve.

smooth *adj* **1** level, even, plane, horizontal, flat, uniform, shiny, polished, sleek, glassy. **2** easy, effortless, trouble-free, problem-free, simple, clear. **3** steady, even, regular, flowing, fluid. **3** suave, urbane, gracious, courteous, sophisticated. **4** fluent, facile, glib, plausible, slick, oily, smarmy (*inf*).
➤*verb* **1** level, plane, even. **2** flatten, iron, roll, press. **3** groom, slick. **4** calm, soothe, appease, pacify, allay, alleviate. **5** ease, facilitate, assist, aid.

smother *verb* **1** suffocate, stifle, asphyxiate, choke. **2** suppress, hold back, muffle, stifle, conceal. **3** cover, heap, pile, wrap, envelop, cocoon. **4** inundate, overwhelm, oppress. **6** extinguish, snuff out, put out, stamp out.

smoulder *verb* **1** burn, smoke. **2** fume, rage, smart, simmer, seethe.

smudge *verb* **1** smear, streak, daub, blur. **2** soil, blacken, besmirch, stain, blemish.
➤*noun* smear, streak, spot, mark, blot.

smug *adj* complacent, self-satisfied, conceited, proud, superior, self-righteous.

snack *noun* refreshment, light meal, bite, nibble, little something (*inf*).

snag *noun* drawback, disadvantage, difficulty, problem, catch, hitch, setback, obstacle.
➤*verb* catch, rip, tear.

snap *verb* **1** break, crack, split. **2** bite, nip. **3** growl, bark, snarl. **4** pop, click. **5** photograph, take, shoot, film.
➤*noun* **1** crack, pop, click. **2** bite, nip. **3** spell, period, stretch. **4** snapshot, photograph, photo, picture, shot, print. **5** catch, clasp, fastener.

snap up grab, grasp, snatch, seize, take, pounce on.

snappy *adj* **1** snappish, waspish, testy, touchy, irritable, peevish, grumpy, crotchety, bad-tempered. **2** brisk, lively, quick, sharp, brusque, curt, concise. **3** smart, fashionable, chic, stylish, snazzy (*inf*), natty (*inf*).

snare *noun* trap, gin, wire, noose.
➤*verb* catch, capture, trap, ensnare.

snarl¹ *verb* **1** growl, threaten. **2** bark, snap, grumble, complain.

snarl² *verb* **1** tangle, entangle, enmesh, intertwine, knot. **2** confuse, muddle, jumble, complicate, embroil.

snatch *verb* **1** pluck, grasp, clutch, pounce on. **2** grab, seize, nab (*inf*), swipe (*inf*), steal, kidnap, abduct. **3** take, seize, grab, wrest, pull.
➤*noun* **1** bit, fragment, scrap, snippet. **2** spell, period, fit, bout.

sneak *verb* **1** steal, creep, slip, sidle, slink, slide. **2** tell tales, snitch (*inf*), inform, grass (*inf*), squeal (*inf*), split (*inf*).
➤*noun* tell-tale, snitch (*inf*), informer, grass (*inf*), rat (*inf*).
➤*adj* secret, covert, furtive, surreptitious, quick.

sneer *verb* smirk, jeer, scoff, mock, scorn, deride.
➤*noun* smirk, jeer, gibe, taunt, scorn, disdain, contempt.

sniff *verb* **1** inhale, breathe in. **2** smell, scent, nose.
➤*noun* **1** smell, scent. **2** whiff, hint, suggestion, trace.

sniff at scorn, sneer at, disparage, disdain, look down on, turn one's nose up at, spurn, reject, refuse.

snigger *verb* laugh, titter, giggle, chortle, snicker.

snip *verb* cut, clip, trim, prune.
➤*noun* **1** cut, incision, nick, slit. **2** bit,

piece, scrap, remnant, snippet, cutting, clipping. **3** bargain, good buy, giveaway (*inf*), steal (*inf*).

snippet *noun* bit, piece, scrap, clipping, cutting, fragment, snatch.

snivel *verb* **1** whine, whimper, grizzle, cry, complain, moan. **2** sniff, sniffle, snuffle.

snoop *verb* spy, pry, nose, interfere, meddle.
➤*noun* **1** snooper, spy, nosy parker (*inf*), busybody, meddler. **2** look, nose.

snooty *adj* **1** condescending, patronizing, arrogant, haughty, supercilious, disdainful, high and mighty. **2** snobbish, stuck-up (*inf*), toffee-nosed (*inf*).

snooze *verb* doze, drowse, nap, sleep, drop off, nod off.
➤*noun* doze, nap, catnap, sleep, forty winks (*inf*).

snub *verb* slight, rebuff, brush off, shun, ignore, cut (*inf*), cold-shoulder (*inf*).
➤*noun* slight, rebuff, brush-off (*inf*), put-down (*inf*), insult, humiliation.

snug *adj* **1** cosy, comfortable, intimate, homely, warm, sheltered, safe, secure. **2** small, tight, close-fitting, figure-hugging.

snuggle *verb* **1** nestle, curl up. **2** cuddle, hug, nuzzle.

soak *verb* **1** wet, drench, saturate. **2** steep, immerse, marinate. **3** permeate, penetrate. **4** absorb, take in.

soar *verb* **1** fly, rise, climb, mount, ascend. **2** escalate, skyrocket, spiral. **3** tower, dominate.

sob *verb* cry, weep, blubber (*inf*), bawl, howl.

sober *adj* **1** teetotal, abstinent, temperate, on the wagon (*inf*), dry (*inf*). **2** solemn, serious, thoughtful, grave, earnest. **3** staid, dignified, sedate, sedate, steady, composed. **4** sombre, dark, drab, dull, subdued, plain.

sobriety *noun* **1** temperance, abstinence, soberness, teetotalism. **2** seriousness, gravity, solemnity, staidness, sedateness, composure, sombreness, restraint.

so-called *adj* professed, self-styled, alleged, supposed, would-be.

sociable *adj* **1** friendly, genial, affable, companionable, communicative, gregarious, outgoing, approachable. **2** convivial, congenial, social.

social *adj* **1** community, group, communal, collective, public, civic. **2** sociable, congenial, convivial.

socialize *verb* mix, mingle, fraternize, hob-nob (*inf*).

society *noun* **1** association, club, circle, guild, union, fraternity, sorority, fellowship. **2** company, companionship, fellowship, friendship, camaraderie. **3** humanity, humankind, human race. **4** community, people, population, civilization, culture. **5** high society, smart set, beau monde, gentry, aristocracy, nobility.

sodden *adj* soaked, soaking, saturated, waterlogged, drenched, sopping.

soft *adj* **1** squashy, mushy, spongy, yielding. **2** elastic, pliable, flexible, ductile, malleable, plastic. **3** pleasant, sweet, mellow. **4** smooth, silky, velvety, downy. **5** dim, diffuse, muted, subdued, light, pale, pastel, delicate. **6** quiet, low, faint, muted, mellifluous, dulcet. **7** gentle, light, mild, moderate, temperate. **8** tender, kind, soft-hearted, compassionate, sensitive, lenient, indulgent, permissive, lax. **9** easy, effortless, cushy (*inf*), comfortable, cosy. **10** spoilt, pampered, privileged.

soften *verb* cushion, pad, ease, lighten, muffle, mellow, diminish, reduce, moderate, temper.
soften up weaken, work on, win over, persuade, disarm.

soggy *adj* wet, soaked, saturated, waterlogged, sodden, sopping, damp, moist.

soil[1] *verb* **1** dirty, begrime, smudge, smear, foul, defile. **2** tarnish, besmirch, stain, blot, sully, blacken.

soil[2] *noun* earth, ground, dirt, clay.

sojourn *verb* stay, stop, tarry, rest, dwell, lodge, visit.
➤*noun* stay, visit, holiday.

solace *noun* consolation, comfort, relief, cheer.
➤*verb* console, comfort, cheer, support.

soldier *noun* **1** warrior, fighter, mercenary, trooper, serviceman, servicewoman. **2** private, regular.
soldier on persevere, continue, persist, keep going.

sole *adj* **1** only, single, one, lone, solitary, unique. **2** exclusive, individual.

sordid

solecism *noun* **1** mistake, error, slip, blunder, howler (*inf*). **2** faux pas, gaffe, impropriety, gaucherie.

solemn *adj* **1** serious, grave, sober, staid, sedate, pensive. **2** sombre, gloomy, grim, unsmiling. **3** grand, stately, dignified, formal, ceremonial, ritual. **4** sincere, committed, genuine, earnest, formal.

solemnity *noun* **1** solemnness, gravity, dignity, grandeur, stateliness, seriousness, pensiveness. **2** observance, celebration. **3** formality, ceremony, ceremonial, rite, ritual.

solemnize *verb* observe, celebrate, commemorate, honour.

solicit *verb* **1** beseech, implore, entreat, supplicate, petition. **2** ask for, request, seek, canvass, crave, beg. **2** accost, importune.

solicitous *adj* concerned, caring, attentive, anxious, worried, nervous.

solicitude *noun* care, concern, regard, worry, anxiety, trouble.

solid *adj* **1** hard, dense, compact, compressed, firm, thick, solidified, set. **2** strong, sturdy, substantial, well-built. **3** reliable, stable, sure, sound, weighty, well-founded. **4** pure, unalloyed, unmixed, unadulterated. **5** uninterrupted, unbroken, continuous. **6** whole, undivided. **7** united, unanimous.

solidarity *noun* unity, accord, agreement, consensus, unanimity, fellowship, camaraderie, team spirit.

solidify *verb* harden, set, congeal, coagulate, gel, crystallize.

solitary *adj* **1** reclusive, unsociable, introverted. **2** lonely, friendless, bereft. **3** alone, solo, companionless, cloistered. **4** sole, single, one, only. **5** secluded, isolated, separate, remote, out-of-the-way, unfrequented.

solitude *noun* loneliness, isolation, remoteness, seclusion.

solution *noun* **1** answer, result, explanation, key, remedy. **2** resolution, clarification. **3** mixture, compound, blend, emulsion, suspension.

solve *verb* answer, work out, puzzle out, crack (*inf*), resolve, unravel, clear up.

solvent *adj* sound, creditworthy, in the black.

sombre *adj* **1** dark, dim, dingy, gloomy, shadowy. **2** dull, drab, dark, funereal. **3** sober, grave, serious. **4** melancholy, depressed, doleful, mournful, lugubrious.

somebody *noun* personage, notable, dignitary, VIP, celebrity, bigwig (*inf*), big shot (*inf*).

sometimes *adv* occasionally, once in a while, now and then, from time to time, every so often.

somnolent *adj* drowsy, sleepy, dozy, slumberous, torpid.

song *noun* ballad, lay, shanty, ditty, carol, hymn.

sonorous *adj* resonant, loud, deep, rich, full, booming, ringing.

soon *adv* **1** shortly, before long, anon, presently, in a minute. **2** promptly, quickly, speedily, pronto (*inf*).

soothe *verb* **1** calm, lull, pacify, tranquillize. **2** moderate, mitigate, ease, allay, alleviate, relieve. **3** comfort, solace, reassure.

soothsayer *noun* prophet, seer, augur, sibyl.

sophisticated *adj* **1** refined, cultured, cultivated, polished. **2** worldly-wise, cosmopolitan, urbane, seasoned, experienced, blasé. **3** complex, elaborate, advanced, developed.

sophistry *noun* **1** equivocation, casuistry. **2** sophism, fallacy.

soporific *adj* sleep-inducing, sedative, narcotic, somniferous.
➤*noun* sleeping pill, sedative, tranquillizer, narcotic, opiate.

soppy *adj* sentimental, emotional, mawkish, slushy (*inf*), sloppy (*inf*), schmaltzy (*inf*).

sorcerer *noun* magician, wizard, warlock, witch, sorceress.

sorcery *noun* magic, black magic, witchcraft, wizardry, necromancy.

sordid *adj* **1** dirty, filthy, foul, grimy, squalid, seedy, seamy, sleazy. **2** corrupt, immoral, despicable, dishonourable, disreputable, ignoble, base, low, shabby, vile.

3 greedy, avaricious, grasping, self-seeking, mean, miserly, niggardly, mercenary, venal.

sore *adj* **1** tender, painful, raw, sensitive, inflamed, hurting, aching, injured. **2** dire, pressing, urgent, desperate, severe, acute, critical. **3** annoyed, irritated, aggrieved, upset, angry, offended.
➤*noun* wound, abrasion, lesion, inflammation, swelling, ulcer, abscess.

sorrow *noun* **1** sadness, grief, woe, heartache, misery, anguish, unhappiness, distress, regret, remorse. **2** trouble, misfortune, affliction.
➤*verb* mourn, grieve, weep, lament.

sorry *adj* **1** apologetic, penitent, contrite, remorseful, regretful, sheepish, ashamed, upset, distressed, moved, concerned, sympathetic. **2** wretched, miserable, heartrending, pitiful, pathetic, abject, poor, mean.

sort *noun* kind, class, category, genre, ilk, variety, type, make, brand, style.
➤*verb* **1** categorize, classify, class, group, rank, grade. **2** arrange, order, organize, systematize, catalogue, file.
out of sorts 1 unwell, sick, ill, poorly, below par (*inf*), under the weather (*inf*). **2** irritable, cross, grumpy, snappy, crotchety, grouchy.
sort out 1 separate, pick, select, segregate, sift. **2** resolve, solve, clear up, put right.

sortie *noun* **1** sally, charge, rush. **2** raid, foray, attack, offensive.

soul *noun* **1** spirit, psyche, mind, life, heart, essence. **2** person, individual, man, woman, mortal, being, creature. **3** energy, vitality, animation. **4** character, nature. **5** feeling, emotion, sensitivity, sympathy, humanity, understanding. **6** personification, epitome, embodiment, incarnation.

sound[1] *noun* **1** noise, resonance, reverberation. **2** earshot, hearing, range.
➤*verb* **1** pronounce, enunciate, ring, go off. **2** resound, echo, reverberate, resonate. **3** seem, appear.

sound[2] *adj* **1** fit, healthy, hale, hearty, strong, robust, sturdy. **2** undamaged, unimpaired, perfect, solid, whole, intact, unbroken. **3** logical, rational, valid, cogent, plausible, correct, right, true. **4** authoritative, well-founded, well-grounded, substantial, reliable, dependable, proven, secure. **5** sensible, reasonable, sane, wise, astute, shrewd, responsible, level-headed.

sound[3] *verb* **1** fathom, measure, plumb. **2** probe, test, examine.
sound out investigate, examine, survey, canvass, research, explore, look into.

sound[4] *noun* **1** estuary, inlet, firth. **2** channel, strait, passage.

sour *adj* **1** tart, acid, bitter, sharp, pungent, vinegary. **2** bad, rancid, curdled, off (*inf*). **3** acrimonious, embittered, disenchanted, disillusioned, resentful, surly, ill-tempered.
➤*verb* ferment, turn, curdle, go off.

source *noun* **1** origin, beginning, derivation. **2** cause, root. **3** informant, contact, authority, reference. **4** spring, fountainhead, wellhead.

souse *verb* **1** pickle, marinate, steep. **2** plunge, immerse, submerge, dip. **3** douse, drench, soak, saturate.

souvenir *noun* keepsake, memento, reminder, remembrance, token, relic.

sovereign *noun* ruler, monarch, king, queen, emperor, empress.
➤*adj* **1** ruling, supreme, chief, royal, imperial. **2** independent, autonomous, self-governing.

sovereignty *noun* **1** supremacy, primacy, ascendancy, power, dominion, sway. **2** independence, autonomy.

sow *verb* **1** plant, scatter, strew, spread. **2** instigate, foster, promote.

space *noun* **1** room, area, expanse, extent, capacity, volume. **2** freedom, leeway, latitude, scope, range. **3** place, seat, berth. **4** gap, blank, omission. **5** interval, period, spell, duration, span, stretch. **6** universe, cosmos, infinity.
➤*verb* arrange, dispose, array, string out, range, set apart.

spacious *adj* capacious, ample, roomy, commodious, extensive, vast, immense, large.

span *noun* **1** extent, stretch, reach, spread, compass. **2** interval, period, spell, term, duration, time.
➤*verb* bridge, cross, bestride, extend, reach, vault, arch.

spank *verb* smack, slap, thrash, wallop (*inf*), whack (*inf*).

spar *verb* argue, bicker, quarrel, squabble, wrangle, fight, scrap (*inf*).

spare *verb* **1** pardon, reprieve, let off, release, free. **2** save, rescue, protect. **3** give, grant, allow, afford, part with, relinquish.
➤*adj* **1** extra, supplementary, reserve, emergency. **2** surplus, left over, unwanted, unused. **3** free, unoccupied, available, leisure. **4** thin, slim, slender, lean, wiry.
to spare left over, surplus, available.

sparing *adj* **1** economical, thrifty, frugal, careful, prudent. **2** meagre, scant, skimpy, mean, miserly, niggardly.

spark *noun* **1** flash, sparkle, gleam, glint. **2** flicker, glimmer, scintilla, trace, scrap, hint, suggestion, germ.
➤*verb* excite, stimulate, kindle, prompt, trigger, set off, start, precipitate.

sparkle *verb* **1** glitter, twinkle, shine, gleam, glint, flash, flicker, scintillate. **2** be lively, be animated, be spirited, be witty, be brilliant.
➤*noun* **1** twinkle, spark, glint, gleam, glitter, flash, flicker. **2** liveliness, animation, vivacity, spirit, panache, pizzazz (*inf*), ebullience, effervescence.

sparse *adj* scattered, scanty, thin, few, scarce, infrequent.

spartan *adj* austere, harsh, bleak, ascetic, abstemious, frugal, plain, simple.

spasm *noun* **1** convulsion, contraction, twitch, cramp, seizure, paroxysm. **2** burst, fit, frenzy, attack, bout.

spasmodic *adj* **1** fitful, irregular, periodic, sporadic, intermittent, occasional. **2** jerky, convulsive.

spate *noun* flood, rush, deluge, torrent, outpouring.

spatter *verb* **1** splash, sprinkle, shower, spray, speckle, spot. **2** scatter, strew.

speak *verb* **1** talk, chat, converse, communicate, express, voice. **2** say, utter, articulate, enunciate, declare, state. **3** discourse, address, lecture, orate, hold forth, harangue.

speaker *noun* talker, lecturer, orator.

special *adj* **1** distinctive, characteristic, individual, unique, select, exclusive, exceptional, extraordinary, outstanding. **2** important, significant, particular, especial. **3** singular, peculiar, rare, unusual, uncommon. **4** specific, express, certain, precise.

specialist *noun* expert, authority, professional, consultant, connoisseur.

speciality *noun* **1** strength, forte, talent, gift. **2** field, area, domain, sphere.

species *noun* sort, kind, type, variety, class, category.

specific *adj* **1** particular, specified, distinct, definite, set. **2** explicit, express, detailed, exact, precise, unambiguous.

specification *noun* **1** particulars, details, requirements, description. **2** stipulation, designation, identification, definition.

specify *verb* **1** name, designate, indicate, identify, define. **2** state, spell out, stipulate. **3** itemize, list, detail, describe, set out.

specimen *noun* **1** sample, representative, model, type. **2** case, instance, example, illustration.

specious *adj* misleading, deceptive, fallacious, false, unsound, sophistic, casuistic.

speck *noun* **1** spot, dot, fleck, speckle. **2** bit, iota, atom, shred, grain, particle.

speckle *verb* spot, dot, fleck, mottle, dapple, stipple.

spectacle *noun* show, display, exhibition, parade, pageant, extravaganza, spectacular.

spectacles *pl noun* glasses, specs (*inf*).

spectacular *adj* impressive, striking, stunning, breathtaking, grand, glorious, splendid, magnificent, sensational, dramatic, dazzling.

spectator *noun* onlooker, observer, bystander, watcher, viewer, witness.

spectre *noun* ghost, apparition, phantom, spook (*inf*), spirit, wraith, revenant, shade.

speculate *verb* **1** conjecture, guess, surmise, suppose, theorize, hypothesize, wonder. **2** gamble, bet, risk, hazard, venture.

speculative *adj* conjectural, theoretical, hypothetical, suppositional, academic, unproven, tentative, abstract.

speech *noun* **1** address, talk, oration, lecture, discourse, spiel (*inf*). **2** utterance, talk, communication, conversation, dialogue. **3** language, tongue, dialect, jargon, parlance. **4** diction, elocution, articulation, enunciation, pronunciation, accent, delivery, voice.

speechless *adj* **1** mute, dumb, silent, voiceless. **2** tongue-tied, dumbfounded, astounded, thunderstruck, aghast.

speed *noun* **1** velocity, pace, rate, tempo. **2** rapidity, swiftness, quickness, alacrity, haste, dispatch.
➤*verb* hasten, hurry, rush, dash, race, career, tear (*inf*), pelt (*inf*).

speedy *adj* fast, quick, rapid, swift, express, prompt, hasty, hurried.

spell[1] *noun* **1** charm, incantation. **2** enchantment, bewitchment, magic. **3** influence, power, magnetism, allure, attraction, fascination.

spell[2] *noun* **1** period, time, stretch, span, patch, interval, session, stint, turn. **2** fit, bout.

spell[3] *verb* imply, indicate, amount to, add up to, mean, signify, signal, promise, threaten.
spell out clarify, make clear, explain, elucidate, stipulate, specify, detail, itemize.

spellbind *verb* fascinate, rivet, grip, enthral, bewitch, captivate, mesmerize, transfix.

spend *verb* **1** disburse, pay out, expend, fork out (*inf*), squander, fritter away. **2** exhaust, wear out, weary, tire, drain, knacker (*inf*). **3** pass, fill, occupy, while away.

spendthrift *noun* wastrel, prodigal, profligate, squanderer, big spender (*inf*).

spew *verb* **1** vomit, throw up (*inf*), puke (*inf*), regurgitate. **2** pour, gush, spurt, discharge, eject.

sphere *noun* **1** ball, globe, orb, round. **2** field, area, domain, province, department, discipline, speciality, territory.

spherical *adj* round, ball-shaped, globular.

spice *noun* **1** seasoning, flavouring. **2** excitement, interest, colour, kick (*inf*), pep (*inf*), piquancy, zest, relish.

spicy *adj* **1** piquant, pungent, aromatic, sharp, peppery, hot. **2** well-seasoned, savoury, flavoursome. **3** racy, bawdy, ribald, risqué, raunchy (*inf*), juicy (*inf*), scandalous, sensational.

spike *noun* point, projection, prong, spine, barb, nail.
➤*verb* **1** prick, pierce, impale, spear, skewer. **2** drug, adulterate, lace.

spill *verb* **1** upset, overturn, overflow, slop. **2** pour, tip, discharge.
➤*noun* tumble, fall, accident, header (*inf*), cropper (*inf*).
spill the beans inform, tell, divulge, disclose, let the cat out of the bag (*inf*).

spin *verb* **1** rotate, revolve, turn, twirl, whirl, wheel, pirouette, swivel, gyrate. **2** tell, recount, narrate, invent, make up.
➤*noun* **1** ride, drive, run, trip, outing. **2** turn, revolution, rotation, gyration, whirl.
spin out protract, prolong, extend, drag out, stretch out.

spine *noun* **1** backbone, vertebral column, spinal column. **2** point, spike, needle, prickle, thorn. **3** barb, quill.

spine-chilling *adj* bloodcurdling, frightening, terrifying, eerie, scary (*inf*), spooky (*inf*).

spineless *adj* weak, feeble, irresolute, ineffective, timid, timorous, pusillanimous, cowardly.

spinney *noun* coppice, thicket, grove, wood.

spiral *noun* **1** helix, coil, corkscrew. **2** twist, whorl, convolution.
➤*adj* coiled, winding, twisting, helical.
➤*verb* **1** twist, coil, wind, screw. **2** rise, increase, mount, escalate, soar, skyrocket.

spirit *noun* **1** soul, psyche, mind, will. **2** enthusiasm, zeal, fire, ardour, vigour, energy, liveliness, animation, zest, courage, backbone, resolution. **3** essence, substance, character, nature, feeling, attitude. **4** significance, meaning, gist, tenor, implication, intent. **6** ghost, apparition, spectre, phantom, wraith, revenant, visitant, shade. **7** angel, demon, fiend, fairy, sprite, imp, goblin.
spirit away carry off, remove, snatch, seize, steal away with.

spirited *adj* lively, animated, energetic, vigorous, enthusiastic, fervent, passionate, courageous, valiant, bold, determined.

spirits *pl noun* **1** alcohol, liquor, hard stuff (*inf*). **2** feelings, emotions, mood, humour, temper, morale, frame of mind.

spiritual *adj* **1** incorporeal, immaterial, intangible, ethereal, ghostly, supernatural, unworldly, otherworldly. **2** holy, sacred, religious, ecclesiastical, divine, devotional.

spit *verb* **1** expectorate, hawk. **2** discharge, eject. **3** hiss, rasp.
➤*noun* spittle, saliva, dribble, phlegm.

spite *noun* spitefulness, malice, malevolence, ill will, bitterness, animosity, vindictiveness, vengeance, resentment, grudge, spleen, rancour.
➤*verb* annoy, vex, provoke, irritate, irk, upset.
in spite of despite, notwithstanding, regardless of, in defiance of.

spitting image *noun* spit, dead ringer (*inf*), double, twin, clone, lookalike, image, picture.

splash *verb* **1** spatter, splatter, sprinkle, spray, shower, squirt, slop. **2** paddle, dabble, wallow, wade. **3** blazon, plaster, trumpet, broadcast, display, publicize, headline.
➤*noun* **1** spot, splodge, daub, smudge, smear. **2** burst, streak, patch. **3** dash, touch. **4** sensation, splurge (*inf*).
splash out spend, invest, splurge (*inf*), push the boat out (*inf*).

spleen *noun* spite, rancour, bitterness, acrimony, venom, gall, bile, pique, ill will, bad temper, anger, wrath.

splendid *adj* **1** brilliant, dazzling, glittering, radiant. **2** superb, sublime, excellent, first-class, marvellous, wonderful. **3** magnificent, grand, stately, lavish, opulent, sumptuous, rich, glorious. **4** illustrious, distinguished, great.

splendour *noun* **1** magnificence, grandeur, stateliness, majesty, pomp, glory, opulence, luxury. **2** brilliance, brightness, radiance, resplendence.

splenetic *adj* spiteful, malicious, peevish, petulant, irritable, irascible, bad-tempered, choleric, sour, rancorous.

splice *verb* **1** braid, plait, interweave, intertwine, interlace. **2** join, fasten, unite, connect, bind, graft. **3** marry, wed.

splinter *verb* shatter, shiver, split, cleave, break up, disintegrate.
➤*noun* piece, bit, fragment, sliver, shiver, shard, chip.

split *verb* **1** separate, divide, partition. **2** part, divide, branch, fork, tear, rend, cleave, cut, crack, halve, bisect. **3** rupture, burst. **4** divorce, break up, separate, part company, disband. **5** share, divide, apportion, parcel out, carve up (*inf*). **6** inform, tell, betray, shop (*inf*), grass (*inf*), squeal (*inf*).
➤*noun* **1** crack, fissure, crevice, cleft, break, gap, cut, rent, slash, tear. **2** rift, rupture, breach, divergence, schism, dissension, alienation, estrangement. **3** separation, division, partition, break-up, parting.

spoil *verb* **1** ruin, mar, harm, damage, destroy. **2** wreck, mess up (*inf*), impair, disfigure, deface, blemish. **3** overindulge, ruin. **4** indulge, pamper, mollycoddle, cosset, baby. **5** deteriorate, go bad, go off (*inf*), decay, rot, turn, sour.

spoils *pl noun* booty, loot, plunder, haul, prize, pickings (*inf*).

sponge *verb* **1** wipe, mop, wash, rub, clean. **2** erase, rub out, efface, expunge. **2** cadge, beg, scrounge (*inf*), bum (*sl*), freeload (*inf*).

spongy *adj* porous, absorbent, soft, light, yielding, squashy, springy.

sponsor *noun* patron, backer, supporter, guarantor, underwriter.
➤*verb* back, support, finance, fund, bankroll, guarantee, underwrite.

spontaneous *adj* natural, instinctive, impulsive, spur-of-the-moment (*inf*), voluntary, unforced, impromptu, unrehearsed, off-the-cuff (*inf*).

sporadic *adj* random, occasional, intermittent, fitful, spasmodic, infrequent, scattered, isolated.

sport *noun* **1** games, exercise, physical activity, athletics. **2** play, recreation, amusement, pleasure, enjoyment, entertainment, fun.
➤*verb* **1** frolic, gambol, romp, caper, play, amuse oneself. **2** wear, display, show off, exhibit.

sporting *adj* sportsmanlike, fair, decent, considerate, generous, honourable.

sportive *adj* playful, frolicsome, high-spirited, frisky, skittish, mischievous, lively.

spot *noun* **1** dot, speckle, fleck, speck, patch. **2** stain, mark, smudge, blot, splash. **3** pimple, blackhead, boil, pustule, blemish. **4** bit, morsel, trace, smidgin (*inf*). **5** place, site, point, location, position, area. **6** slot, niche, place, time.
➤*verb* **1** discern, detect, notice, catch sight of, see. **2** recognize, identify. **3** observe, watch. **4** dot, speckle, fleck, mark, stain, blemish.
in a spot in a predicament, in trouble, in difficulties, in a fix (*inf*).

spotless *adj* **1** immaculate, clean, unmarked, spick and span. **2** pure, chaste, virginal, unsullied, unblemished, stainless, perfect, irreproachable.

spotlight *noun* limelight, public eye, publicity, attention.
➤*verb* **1** highlight, illuminate, focus on. **2** emphasize, accentuate, point up, feature.

spotty *adj* **1** pimply, blotchy, acned. **2** spotted, mottled, dappled, pied, flecked, speckled. **3** patchy, bitty, uneven, irregular, erratic, inconsistent.

spouse *noun* husband, wife, consort, partner, mate, other half (*inf*).

spout *verb* **1** gush, spurt, jet, squirt, spray, stream, pour. **2** hold forth, speechify, pontificate, rant, orate. **3** declaim, recite.

sprain *verb* wrench, twist, strain, rick.

sprawl *verb* **1** recline, loll (*inf*), lounge (*inf*), slouch, slump, flop. **2** spread, straggle, stretch, trail.

spray[1] *noun* **1** mist, drizzle, spindrift. **2** shower, jet. **3** aerosol, atomizer, sprinkler.
➤*verb* **1** jet, spout, gush, sprinkle, scatter, atomize. **2** shower, spatter, splash, sprinkle.

spray[2] *noun* **1** sprig, shoot, branch. **2** posy, bouquet, corsage.

spread *verb* **1** unfold, unfurl, unroll, open, stretch, extend. **2** distribute, scatter, strew, disperse, radiate, diffuse. **3** stretch, extend, sprawl, expand, grow, mushroom. **4** coat, cover, daub, smear, plaster. **5** disseminate, circulate, communicate, promulgate.
➤*noun* **1** distribution, dissemination, dispersion, diffusion, extent, expanse, sweep. **2** stretch, reach, span, gap. **3** range, gamut, compass. **4** feast, banquet, meal, repast, blow-out (*inf*).

spree *noun* fling, bout, orgy, binge (*inf*), splurge (*inf*).

sprig *noun* spray, twig, branch, stem, shoot.

sprightly *adj* spry, agile, nimble, active, energetic, lively, spirited.

spring *verb* **1** jump, leap, bound, hop, bounce. **2** originate, derive, stem, start, arise, emanate, flow, proceed.
➤*noun* **1** jump, leap, bound, hop, bounce. **2** elasticity, resilience, springiness, bounce, give (*inf*). **3** well, fountainhead, wellhead, fount, source, origin.
spring up appear, develop, sprout, shoot up, grow.

springy *adj* bouncy, elastic, rubbery, spongy, resilient.

sprinkle *verb* **1** scatter, strew, spray, trickle, dredge. **2** spray, shower, spatter, dust, dot, pepper.

sprinkling *noun* scattering, dusting, handful, trickle, few.

sprint *verb* race, run, dash, fly, tear (*inf*), hare (*inf*).

sprite *noun* elf, fairy, pixie, brownie, leprechaun.

sprout *verb* **1** bud, burgeon, germinate, shoot. **2** spring up, shoot up, grow. **3** develop, grow, appear, emerge.

spruce *adj* smart, neat, well-dressed, well-groomed, trim, dapper, natty (*inf*).

spry *adj* brisk, nimble, agile, active, lively, sprightly, energetic.

spur *noun* **1** prick, prod, goad. **2** stimulus, motivation, incentive, inducement, encouragement, goad, prompt.
➤*verb* **1** prick, prod, goad. **2** prompt, goad, drive, impel, stimulate, motivate, incite, induce, encourage.
on the spur of the moment on impulse, impetuously, spontaneously, impromptu, suddenly, unexpectedly.

spurious *adj* **1** false, fake, phoney (*inf*), bogus, fictitious, sham. **2** specious, fallacious.

spurn *verb* reject, rebuff, repudiate, turn down, slight, scorn, despise, disdain.

spurt *verb* gush, spout, squirt, jet, shoot, burst, surge, stream.
➤*noun* **1** gush, spout, squirt, jet, stream. **2** burst, rush, surge, increase.

spy *noun* **1** snooper, private detective, scout. **2** secret agent, fifth columnist, mole (*inf*).
➤*verb* see, catch sight of, spot, glimpse, discern, detect, notice.
spy on observe, watch, keep under surveillance, shadow, tail (*inf*).

squabble *verb* quarrel, row, bicker, wrangle, argue, fight.
➤*noun* quarrel, row, altercation, argument, barney (*inf*), tiff (*inf*).

squad *noun* **1** band, gang, crew, team, group. **2** company, platoon, troop, unit, force.

squalid *adj* **1** foul, filthy, dirty, dingy, seedy, run-down, ramshackle, dilapidated, grotty (*inf*). **2** sordid, sleazy (*inf*), disreputable, nasty, obscene, disgraceful.

squall¹ *verb* cry, bawl, yell, scream, howl, wail.

squall² *noun* gust, blast, wind, gale, storm, tempest.

squalor *noun* squalidness, filth, dirt, neglect, decay, dinginess, seediness, sordidness, sleaziness (*inf*).

squander *verb* waste, dissipate, fritter away, blow (*inf*), throw away, misuse, misspend.

square *noun* **1** rectangle, quadrilateral. **2** place, plaza, piazza.
➤*adj* **1** rectangular, quadrilateral, right-angled. **2** perpendicular, normal. **3** level, even, parallel, straight, true. **4** conservative, conventional, straitlaced, old-fashioned, stuffy, fuddy-duddy (*inf*).
➤*verb* **1** straighten, level, align. **2** reconcile, accommodate, tailor, fit, adapt, adjust. **3** settle, pay, discharge, balance, tally.

squash *verb* **1** squeeze, press, crush, mash, compress, flatten, trample. **2** suppress, put down, quash. **3** silence, humiliate, put down.

squat *verb* crouch, kneel, hunker down, sit.
➤*adj* short, dumpy, stubby, chunky, stocky, broad.

squeak *verb* creak, whine, squeal, yelp, peep, cheep.
➤*noun* creak, whine, squeal, yelp, peep, cheep.

squeal *verb* **1** cry, shriek, scream, wail, howl, squeak. **2** inform, tell, split (*inf*), snitch (*inf*), grass (*inf*).
➤*noun* cry, shriek, scream, wail, howl, squeak.

squeamish *adj* **1** queasy, delicate, dainty, fastidious. **2** prudish, straitlaced.

squeeze *verb* **1** compress, squash, press, pinch, constrict, grip, hug. **2** press, extract, force. **3** pack, cram, stuff, squash, jam, wedge. **4** wring, wrest, extract, force.
➤*noun* **1** hug, embrace, cuddle. **2** squash, crush, press, jam, crowd, congestion.

squirm *verb* writhe, wriggle, fidget, twist, turn.

squirt *verb* spout, spray, spurt, gush, jet, shoot, emit, eject, ejaculate, discharge.
➤*noun* spout, spray, spurt, gush, jet.

stab *verb* **1** pierce, puncture, knife, spear, bayonet, gore, cut, wound. **2** jab, thrust.
➤*noun* **1** wound, cut, puncture, slash. **2** jab, thrust. **3** spasm, pang, ache, throb. **4** pang, twinge, prick.
stab somebody in the back betray, sell out, inform on, double-cross, deceive.

stability *noun* secureness, soundness, firmness, solidity, steadiness, regularity, constancy.

stable *adj* **1** firm, steady, fast, immovable, sound, sturdy, solid, secure. **2** sound, secure, established, well-founded, durable, enduring, lasting, sure, dependable, reliable. **3** constant, steady, regular, unchanging, invariable.

stack *noun* **1** pile, heap, mound, mountain. **2** load, lot, ton (*inf*), heap (*inf*), pile (*inf*).
➤*verb* **1** pile, heap. **2** load, fill.
stack up amass, accumulate, gather, collect.

stadium *noun* **1** ground, arena, field, pitch. **2** track, ring.

staff *noun* **1** employees, workers, personnel, workforce, team, teachers, officers. **2** stick, cane, crook, crutch, club. **2** rod, mace, baton, wand.
➤*verb* man, people, equip, provide, supply.

stage noun **1** phase, step, point, juncture, period. **2** lap, leg. **3** platform, dais, rostrum, podium. **4** background, scene, setting, arena, forum.
➤verb **1** produce, present, put on, perform, direct. **2** mount, arrange, organize, lay on. **3** orchestrate, engineer.
the stage theatre, dramatics, the boards (*inf*), show business.

stagger verb **1** totter, reel, sway, lurch, pitch, roll. **2** astound, astonish, amaze, flabbergast (*inf*), bowl over (*inf*), dumbfound, stupefy, stun.

stagnant adj **1** standing, still, motionless. **2** stale, foul. **3** quiet, dull, sluggish, slow, inert, inactive.

stagnate verb stand, vegetate, idle, languish, decline, degenerate.

staid adj sedate, sober, demure, prim, stiff, starchy.

stain verb **1** mark, spot, discolour, soil, dirty, blot. **2** dye, tint, colour. **3** smear, tarnish, taint, defile, corrupt, disgrace.
➤noun **1** mark, spot, blot, discoloration. **2** dye, tint. **3** blemish, taint, stigma, slur, smear, disgrace.

stake[1] noun pale, picket, stick, spike, post, pole.
➤verb **1** prop, support, brace, secure. **2** demarcate, mark out, define, delimit, lay claim to.

stake[2] noun **1** bet, wager, ante (*inf*), pledge. **2** interest, concern, share, involvement, investment.
➤verb bet, wager, gamble, pledge, chance, hazard, risk, venture.
at stake at risk, in jeopardy.

stakes pl noun **1** race, contest, competition. **2** prize, winnings, purse.

stale adj **1** old, hard, dry, mouldy. **2** musty, fusty, foul. **3** trite, banal, hackneyed, platitudinous, overused, unoriginal. **4** jaded, tired, worn out.

stalemate noun deadlock, impasse, stand-off, draw, tie.

stalk verb **1** hunt, track, trail, chase, pursue. **2** follow, shadow. **3** strut, stride, march, flounce.

stall[1] noun **1** stand, table, counter. **2** sideshow, booth, kiosk. **3** cubicle, pen, enclosure, compartment.
➤verb **1** stop, cut out.

stall[2] verb **1** hedge, equivocate, delay, prevaricate, play for time. **2** obstruct, hold up, delay.

stalwart adj **1** strong, sturdy, rugged, strapping, stout, resolute, courageous, indomitable. **2** staunch, trusty, faithful, loyal, steadfast, reliable, dependable.

stamina noun strength, energy, vigour, fortitude, endurance, indefatigability.

stammer verb stutter, falter, hesitate, stumble.
➤noun stutter, speech impediment.

stamp verb **1** tread, step, trample, crush, squash. **2** tramp, stomp (*inf*). **3** pound, crush, beat, mash. **4** print, imprint, impress, emboss, brand. **5** leave, fix. **6** characterize, identify, categorize. **7** mark, label, brand, tag.
➤noun **1** mark, brand, seal, print, imprint, impression. **2** characteristic, hallmark. **3** mould, cast, sort, kind, type, character.
stamp out quell, crush, eliminate, eradicate, destroy, extinguish.

stampede noun rush, charge, flight, rout.
➤verb charge, rush, dash, flee, take flight, scatter.

stance noun **1** posture, bearing, deportment, carriage. **2** position, standpoint, viewpoint, opinion, attitude, policy, line.

stand verb **1** rise, get up, straighten up. **2** place, put, set, rest, upend, erect. **3** stop, halt, pause, stay. **4** hold, persist, continue, remain, prevail. **5** bear, tolerate, endure, abide, put up with. **6** resist, withstand, cope with. **7** suffer, experience, undergo.
➤noun **1** standpoint, stance, attitude, position, policy, line. **2** frame, support, rest, rack, base, pedestal. **3** opposition, resistance, defiance.
stand by support, side with, champion, defend, stand up for, stick by.
stand for 1 represent, symbolize, betoken, denote, mean. **2** tolerate, bear, brook, countenance, permit, allow.
stand in substitute, replace, deputize, cover, understudy.
stand out be prominent, be conspicuous, stick out, catch the eye.
stand up hold up, hold water, wash (*inf*).
stand up to 1 defy, oppose, challenge, face, confront. **2** resist, withstand, endure.

standard noun **1** quality, level, grade. **2** requirement, specification. **3** model,

example, paradigm, criterion, yardstick, benchmark, norm, average. **4** principle, moral, scruple, ethic, code. **5** flag, banner, ensign, colours.
➤*adj* **1** regular, average, normal, basic. **2** common, universal, prevailing, usual, stock, staple. **3** ordinary, conventional, orthodox, set, fixed, established. **4** definitive, authoritative, classic, official, accepted, recognized.

standardize *verb* equalize, normalize, regulate, homogenize, stereotype.

stand-in *noun* deputy, substitute, understudy, proxy, delegate, surrogate.

standing *noun* **1** rank, status, position, station, reputation. **2** duration, existence, continuance.
➤*adj* **1** still, motionless, stagnant. **2** perpetual, permanent, regular, fixed, constant.

standpoint *noun* **1** vantage point, viewpoint, angle, perspective. **2** point of view, opinion, stance, position.

standstill *noun* stop, halt, pause, rest, hold-up, jam, impasse, stalemate, deadlock.

staple *adj* **1** basic, standard, essential, major, primary. **2** principal, chief, key, main.

star *noun* **1** heavenly body, celestial body, sun, moon, planet. **2** celebrity, personage, big name (*inf*), luminary, idol. **3** lead, leading man, leading woman, principal.
➤*adj* brilliant, great, outstanding, leading, principal.

starchy *adj* stiff, formal, prim, straitlaced.

stare *verb* gaze, gape, goggle, gawp (*inf*), look, watch, glare.
➤*noun* gaze, look, glare.

stark *adj* **1** absolute, sheer, arrant, downright, utter, pure. **2** plain, clear, blunt, bald, harsh, severe. **3** bare, barren, bleak, desolate.

start *verb* **1** originate, arise, begin, commence. **2** get under way, depart, set off, activate, trigger, turn on. **3** embark on, found, establish, set up, institute, pioneer, launch. **4** jump, flinch, wince, twitch, jerk, shy.
➤*noun* **1** beginning, commencement, outset, launch, opening, inception, origin,

dawn, birth. **2** lead, advantage, head start. **3** jump, twitch, jerk, spasm.

startle *verb* **1** scare, frighten, disturb, surprise, shock. **2** alarm, agitate, perturb.

starve *verb* **1** hunger, fast. **2** be famished, be ravenous.

state *noun* **1** condition, situation, position, circumstances. **2** panic, fluster, flap (*inf*), tizzy (*inf*). **3** pomp, ceremony, grandeur, majesty, dignity. **4** nation, country, republic, kingdom. **5** government, parliament, administration, politics.
➤*verb* utter, declare, assert, maintain, announce, proclaim, specify, set out.

stately *adj* grand, magnificent, splendid, glorious, dignified, solemn, imposing, impressive, majestic.

statement *noun* **1** utterance, announcement, disclosure, communication. **2** declaration, announcement, proclamation, bulletin, communiqué. **3** account, report, record, testimony.

static *adj* stationary, still, motionless, immobile, fixed, inert, unchanging, constant, steady.

station *noun* **1** depot, terminus, stop, halt. **2** place, position, location, situation. **3** post, office. **4** status, standing, level, rank, class, grade.
➤*verb* post, assign, appoint, place, locate, garrison.

stationary *adj* motionless, still, static, immobile, fixed.

statue *noun* sculpture, bronze, carving, figurine, statuette, bust, effigy, idol.

statuesque *adj* imposing, impressive, dignified, stately, majestic, noble, well-proportioned.

stature *noun* **1** height, tallness, size. **2** prestige, reputation, renown, rank, standing, consequence.

status *noun* **1** position, condition, standing. **2** station, rank, degree, level, grade, class. **3** importance, consequence, prestige, eminence, distinction.

statute *noun* **1** law, ordinance, act, decree, edict. **2** rule, regulation.

staunch *adj* loyal, faithful, devoted, true, trusty, reliable, steadfast, firm, sound, unwavering.

stave off *verb* avert, ward off, fend off, keep at bay.

stay[1] *verb* **1** wait, remain, linger, stop, pause, rest, tarry. **2** keep, remain, continue, endure, persist, last. **3** lodge, put up, board, visit. **4** live, reside, dwell. **5** defer, delay, suspend, put off, obstruct, prevent.
➤*noun* **1** visit, sojourn, holiday. **2** postponement, deferment, suspension, delay, remission, reprieve.

stay[2] *noun* prop, support, brace, buttress.

steadfast *adj* **1** steady, fixed, firm, immovable. **2** constant, loyal, faithful, staunch, dependable, stable, unwavering, unswerving.

steady *adj* **1** motionless, fixed, immovable, secure, solid, firm, balanced, stable. **2** sure, unwavering, unfaltering. **3** even, regular, uniform, unchanging, unvarying, continuous. **4** level-headed, calm, imperturbable, unflappable (*inf*). **5** constant, reliable, dependable, consistent.
➤*verb* **1** brace, balance, stabilize, secure, fix, support. **2** check, restrain, control, calm, settle, compose, subdue, still, tranquillize, soothe, relax.

steal *verb* **1** take, pocket, pilfer, purloin, filch, nick (*inf*), pinch (*inf*), knock off (*inf*), poach, thieve, rob, shoplift,. **2** creep, tiptoe, slip, sneak.

stealth *noun* stealthiness, furtiveness, surreptitiousness, secrecy.

stealthy *adj* furtive, sly, surreptitious, clandestine, unobtrusive, covert, secret.

steam *noun* **1** vapour, smoke, exhalation. **2** mist, haze, condensation. **3** energy, power.
get steamed up get angry, get agitated, lose one's cool (*inf*).
steam up mist up, fog up.
under one's own steam independently, by oneself, unaided.

steamy *adj* **1** misty, hazy. **2** humid, muggy, sticky, close, sultry, hot, sweltering. **2** erotic, sexy (*inf*), raunchy (*inf*), passionate.

steel *verb* brace, fortify, harden, nerve, prepare.

steely *adj* grey, strong, hard, unyielding.

steep[1] *adj* **1** sheer, abrupt, precipitous, vertical. **2** sudden, sharp. **3** extortionate, exorbitant, dear, expensive, overpriced, high, stiff. **4** unreasonable, extreme, excessive, inordinate.

steep[2] *verb* **1** soak, macerate, souse, drench, immerse, submerge. **2** imbue, fill, permeate, pervade.

steer *verb* **1** pilot, direct, control, drive, navigate, cox. **2** guide, conduct, lead, usher.
steer clear of shun, eschew, avoid, evade.

stem[1] *noun* stalk, trunk, shaft, stock.
➤*verb* arise, come, flow, spring, originate, derive.

stem[2] *verb* **1** stop, halt, arrest, check, curb, block. **2** contain, dam, staunch.

stench *noun* stink, smell, reek, pong (*inf*).

stentorian *adj* loud, strong, thunderous, booming, ringing, powerful, resonant, strident.

step *noun* **1** pace, stride. **2** footfall, gait, tread. **3** phase, stage. **4** move, action, proceeding, measure, advance, development. **5** stair, rung. **6** rank, degree, grade, level.
➤*verb* walk, stride, pace, tread.
in step 1 in unison, together. **2** in harmony, in agreement.
out of step at odds, at loggerheads.
step down stand down, resign, retire, abdicate, quit.
step in intervene, intercede, mediate, interfere.
step up increase, raise, augment, boost, accelerate, intensify.

sterile *adj* **1** bare, arid, barren, infertile. **2** infertile, barren, childless. **3** unproductive, unfruitful. **4** sterilized, disinfected, clean, germ-free, aseptic, uncontaminated.

sterilize *noun* **1** disinfect, cleanse, purify, fumigate. **2** neuter, castrate, spay, doctor, geld, vasectomize.

sterling *adj* genuine, true, sound, reliable, trustworthy, loyal, outstanding, exemplary.

stern *adj* **1** strict, severe, harsh, relentless, inexorable, unsparing, authoritarian. **2** tough, cruel, grim, forbidding, austere, unsmiling. **3** firm, adamant, rigorous, stringent, inflexible, uncompromising.

stew *verb* **1** simmer, boil, braise. **2** fret, fuss, worry, agonize.

➤*noun* **1** casserole, ragout. **2** bother, panic, fluster, flap (*inf*), tizzy (*inf*).

steward *noun* **1** attendant, air hostess. **2** official, functionary, organizer. **3** housekeeper, major-domo, butler, bailiff, agent, manager, caretaker.

stick[1] *noun* **1** rod, staff, wand, baton, cane, club. **2** twig, branch. **3** criticism, flak (*inf*), abuse, reproof.

stick[2] *verb* **1** stab, pierce, prick, puncture. **2** spear, skewer, transfix, impale. **2** poke, thrust, push. **3** fasten, attach, join, fix, glue, gum, paste, cement. **4** adhere, bond, fuse. **5** put, place, drop, deposit, plonk (*inf*). **6** stand, bear, abide, stomach (*inf*). **7** lodge, jam.

be stuck on be fond of, be obsessed with, be infatuated with, be keen on, be crazy about.

stick around stay, remain, linger.

stick at continue, carry on, persist, persevere.

stick by 1 stand by, support, defend. **2** uphold, adhere to, honour.

stick it out endure, persist, continue, hang in there (*inf*).

stick out protrude, project, jut out, poke out, bulge.

stick up for support, champion, defend, fight for, stand up for.

sticky *adj* **1** adhesive, gummed, tacky. **2** gluey, glutinous, viscous, gooey (*inf*). **3** muggy, close, oppressive, humid, sultry. **4** clammy, sweaty. **5** difficult, embarrassing, tricky, thorny, delicate, sensitive, awkward.

stiff *adj* **1** rigid, inflexible, unyielding, inelastic, firm, hard, taut, tense. **2** thick, solid. **3** formal, strict, precise, ceremonious, chilly, aloof, constrained. **4** awkward, clumsy, graceless. **5** brisk, keen, strong, forceful, vigorous. **6** potent, strong, alcoholic, intoxicating. **7** harsh, severe, stringent, tough, rigorous, draconian. **8** difficult, hard, arduous, strenuous, exacting, demanding.

stiffen *verb* set, harden, solidify, thicken, congeal, strengthen, brace, reinforce, fortify.

stifle *verb* **1** suffocate, asphyxiate, choke, smother, strangle. **2** suppress, muffle, subdue, keep in. **3** restrain, check, curb, repress.

stigma *noun* shame, disgrace, dishonour, stain, blemish, slur.

still *adj* **1** motionless, unmoving, immobile, inert, stationary, static. **2** calm, tranquil, serene, peaceful, undisturbed, smooth, quiet.
➤*noun* silence, quiet, hush, peace, calm, stillness.
➤*verb* hush, quieten, silence, calm, soothe, allay, settle, subdue.
➤*adv* **1** yet, even. **2** however, nevertheless, notwithstanding, even so, for all that.

stilted *adj* laboured, forced, stiff, wooden, artificial, formal.

stimulant *noun* tonic, restorative, pick-me-up (*inf*).

stimulate *verb* **1** arouse, excite, prompt, provoke, trigger, induce. **2** motivate, animate, inspire, interest, challenge, encourage, rouse, incite.

stimulus *noun* incentive, fillip, motive, spur, impetus, incitement, inducement, encouragement, shot in the arm (*inf*).

sting *verb* **1** prick, bite. **2** burn, smart, tingle, hurt. **3** injure, wound, pain, distress, upset, offend, provoke, needle, nettle. **4** goad, spur. **5** swindle, cheat, trick, fleece, rip off (*inf*), con (*inf*).
➤*noun* prick, bite, wound, pain, tingle.

stingy *adj* **1** mean, niggardly, ungenerous, miserly, tight (*inf*). **2** meagre, scanty, small, measly (*inf*).

stink *noun* **1** smell, odour, stench, fetor, reek, pong (*inf*). **2** furore, outcry, uproar, row, fuss, hoo-ha (*inf*).
➤*verb* reek, smell, pong (*inf*).

stint *verb* **1** limit, restrict, restrain. **2** skimp, begrudge, withhold. **3** scrimp, economize, save.
➤*noun* period, spell, stretch, shift, turn, bit, share, ration, quota.

stipend *noun* salary, remuneration, emolument, honorarium, allowance.

stipulate *verb* **1** specify, set down. **2** require, demand.

stir *verb* **1** mix, blend, beat. **2** rustle, twitch, tremble. **3** disturb, agitate. **4** move, budge, shift. **5** wake, awaken. **6** rouse, stimulate, provoke, spur, drive, impel, prompt, galvanize.
➤*noun* excitement, commotion, ado, fuss.

stirring *adj* rousing, stimulating, inspiring, moving, emotive, impassioned, exciting, thrilling.

stitch *verb* 1 sew, tack, seam. 2 embroider, work.

stock *noun* 1 store, supply, hoard, stockpile, repertoire, reserve, fund. 2 goods, wares, merchandise, commodities, inventory, range, selection. 3 livestock, animals, cattle. 4 trunk, stalk, stem. 5 parentage, extraction, genealogy, lineage, descent, pedigree, ancestry, family, blood. 6 breed, strain, variety, species.
➤ *adj* 1 standard, regular, average, normal, usual. 2 staple, basic, essential. 3 commonplace, hackneyed, usual, routine, conventional, traditional.
➤ *verb* 1 keep, carry, deal in, sell, handle. 2 equip, supply, fill, load.
in stock available, on the shelves, on sale.
stock up amass, accumulate, lay in, buy, hoard, stockpile.
take stock assess, appraise, weigh up, review, evaluate.

stockpile *verb* hoard, store, save, collect, accumulate, amass, lay in.

stocky *adj* thickset, chunky, sturdy, solid, squat, dumpy, short, broad.

stoical *adj* philosophical, patient, longsuffering, uncomplaining, resigned, indifferent.

stoicism *noun* patience, long-suffering, fortitude, endurance, resignation, fatalism.

stolid *adj* dull, obtuse, bovine, slow, apathetic, impassive, unemotional, phlegmatic.

stomach *noun* 1 abdomen, belly, tummy (*inf*), gut, paunch. 2 appetite, hunger, relish, taste. 3 desire, inclination, liking, proclivity.
➤ *verb* tolerate, bear, endure, abide, brook, stand.

stone *noun* 1 pebble, rock, cobble. 2 gem, jewel. 3 seed, pip.

stony *adj* 1 pebbly, rocky, shingly, gravelly. 2 hard, flinty. 3 unresponsive, unfeeling, indifferent, cold, frosty, heartless, merciless, severe, stern, expressionless, deadpan, blank.

stoop *verb* 1 bend, lower, bow, duck, crouch, squat. 2 slouch, hunch.

3 condescend, deign, yield, acquiesce.
4 descend, sink, lower oneself, resort.
➤ *noun* hunch, bow.

stop *verb* 1 finish, conclude, end, terminate, knock off (*inf*). 2 halt, pause, stall. 3 frustrate, thwart, prevent, obstruct, hinder, impede. 4 prevent, avert, avoid, intercept. 5 cease, abandon, desist, pack in (*inf*), quit (*inf*), discontinue, suspend, interrupt. 6 check, curb, restrain, suppress, arrest. 7 stem, staunch, plug, bung, seal, block.
➤ *noun* 1 halt, standstill, pause, break, end, finish. 2 halt, terminus, station.

stoppage *noun* 1 stop, interruption, cessation, discontinuation, arrest. 2 blockage, obstacle, obstruction. 3 industrial action, walk-out, sit-in, strike. 4 deduction, subtraction, withdrawal, removal.

stopper *noun* bung, plug, cork, cap, top.

store *verb* amass, accumulate, collect, hoard, stockpile, save, reserve, put by, lay in.
➤ *noun* 1 stock, supply, hoard, cache, reserve. 2 collection, accumulation, fund, mine, reservoir. 3 shop, supermarket, retail outlet, emporium.
set store by value, admire, regard, appreciate.

storm *noun* 1 tempest, squall, hurricane, blizzard. 2 outburst, outbreak, outcry, clamour, tumult, furore, riot.
➤ *verb* 1 rage, roar, thunder, rant, rave, bellow, fume. 2 rush, charge, tear, stamp, stalk, flounce. 3 charge, rush. 4 assault, attack, raid.

stormy *adj* 1 squally, windy, blustery, choppy, rough. 2 tempestuous, turbulent, wild, raging, furious.

story *noun* 1 tale, narrative, legend, myth, fable, anecdote, yarn (*inf*), account, history. 2 lie, fib (*inf*), falsehood. 3 article, report, feature, item.

stout *adj* 1 fat, corpulent, portly, rotund, plump, stocky, tubby, heavy, thickset, burly. 2 sturdy, strong, solid, tough, robust, durable. 3 brave, courageous, heroic, valiant, bold, plucky, intrepid, dauntless, staunch, stalwart.

stove *noun* cooker, oven, range.

stow *verb* 1 pack, put away, store. 2 fill, load.

straggle *verb* **1** spread, scatter, deviate, stray, meander, wander, drift. **2** lag, trail, fall behind.

straight *adj* **1** direct, undeviating, unswerving. **2** level, horizontal, vertical, upright, erect, true, aligned, symmetrical. **3** tidy, orderly, shipshape, arranged, organized. **4** honest, honourable, upright, decent, respectable, just, fair. **5** right, correct. **6** plain, clear, simple, straightforward. **7** forthright, candid, frank, blunt. **8** consecutive, successive, uninterrupted, unbroken, continuous. **9** neat, undiluted, unmixed, pure, unadulterated.
▸adv **1** directly, as the crow flies. **2** immediately, at once, right away, without delay.

straighten *verb* flatten, smooth, neaten, tidy, put in order, adjust, arrange.
straighten out clear up, sort out, settle, resolve.
straighten up stand upright, sit up straight.

straightforward *adj* **1** honest, truthful, sincere, genuine. **2** frank, candid, forthright, direct, straight. **3** simple, easy, uncomplicated, routine.

strain[1] *verb* **1** exert, force, drive. **2** wrench, sprain, twist, pull, rick, tear. **3** overtax, overexert, exhaust, fatigue, weaken. **4** tighten, stretch, extend. **5** filter, percolate, sieve, sift, separate, purify.
▸noun **1** tension, stress, pressure, force, effort, exertion. **2** wrench, sprain, injury. **3** tension, stress, pressure, duress, anxiety, worry, burden. **4** tune, melody, air.

strain[2] *noun* **1** race, stock, breed, pedigree, variety, type. **2** trait, streak, tendency, quality, characteristic.

strained *adj* **1** uneasy, awkward, uncomfortable, embarrassed, tense. **2** stiff, wooden, laboured, forced, artificial, unnatural.

strait *noun* **1** channel, sound, narrows. **2** dilemma, quandary, predicament, plight, difficulty, problem, trouble, distress.

straitened *adj* distressed, embarrassed, reduced, restricted, impoverished, destitute.

straitlaced *adj* stuffy, starchy, prim, prudish, puritanical, moralistic, proper, strict.

strand[1] *verb* **1** shipwreck, beach, ground, run aground. **2** maroon, cast away, abandon, desert.
▸noun shore, beach, coast, waterfront.

strand[2] *noun* **1** thread, fibre, filament, string, wire. **2** ingredient, element, component, theme.

strange *adj* **1** unfamiliar, unknown, exotic, foreign, alien, new, novel. **2** odd, curious, remarkable, extraordinary, fantastic, surreal, weird, bizarre, unaccountable, inexplicable.

stranger *noun* alien, foreigner, visitor, guest, newcomer, outsider, incomer.

strangle *verb* **1** throttle, choke, asphyxiate. **2** suppress, hold back, stifle, smother. **3** repress, inhibit.

strap *noun* belt, thong, strip, band, tie.
▸verb **1** tie, bind, truss, lash, fasten, secure. **2** beat, flog, belt.

stratagem *noun* ruse, artifice, trick, wile, scheme, ploy, gambit, tactic, device.

strategic *adj* tactical, calculated, planned, deliberate, key, vital, important, essential.

strategy *noun* **1** policy, tactics, planning, programme. **2** method, approach, plan, scheme.

stratum *noun* **1** layer, bed, seam, vein, lode. **2** level, grade, tier, degree, rank, station, class.

stray *verb* wander, straggle, drift, swerve, deviate, diverge, go astray, err.
▸adj **1** lost, abandoned, homeless, wandering. **2** random, freak, chance, sporadic, scattered, isolated.

streak *noun* **1** smear, smudge, stripe, line, band, fleck. **2** strain, vein, touch, element.
▸verb **1** smear, smudge, fleck. **2** rush, race, sprint, speed, dash, tear, whistle, zoom.

stream *noun* **1** brook, beck, burn, rivulet, rill, tributary. **2** run, flow, current, tide. **3** torrent, cascade, flood, deluge.
▸verb **1** flow, issue, pour, run, course. **2** flood, cascade, rush, gush, spout. **3** trail, fly.

streamer *noun* pennant, flag, ensign, standard, banner.

street *noun* thoroughfare, road, avenue, boulevard.

strength noun 1 power, might, force, vigour, energy, stamina, muscle, brawn. 2 toughness, solidity, firmness, robustness, durability, resilience, resistance. 3 intensity, vehemence, ardour, depth, sharpness, vividness. 4 potency, concentration. 6 forte, gift, talent, asset, advantage.
on the strength of on the basis of, because of, on account of, by virtue of.

strengthen verb fortify, reinforce, brace, buttress, consolidate, toughen, fortify, invigorate, boost, intensify.

strenuous adj 1 energetic, vigorous, active, forceful, ardent, zealous, wholehearted, earnest. 2 arduous, hard, difficult, laborious, gruelling, tough, demanding, taxing.

stress noun 1 force, pressure. 2 strain, tension, worry, anxiety. 3 emphasis, accent, accentuation, weight.
➤verb 1 emphasize, highlight, underline, point up, harp on, dwell on. 2 accentuate, accent, emphasize.

stretch verb 1 pull, draw out, extend, expand, tighten, tauten, strain. 2 extend, lengthen, elongate, expand, distend, enlarge. 3 spread, cover, reach, extend, range. 4 reach, strain. 5 challenge, test, tax, try, extend.
➤noun 1 extent, spread, reach. 2 expanse, area, length, distance. 3 space, spell, period, time, term.
stretch out lie down, recline, sprawl, lounge.

strew verb 1 scatter, spread, disperse, sow, sprinkle. 2 litter, cover.

stricken adj afflicted, affected, hit, struck, injured, laid low.

strict adj 1 rigorous, stringent, rigid, inflexible. 2 stern, severe, harsh, tough, firm, disciplinarian, authoritarian. 3 complete, total, utter, absolute. 4 punctilious, scrupulous, conscientious. 5 exact, precise, faithful, literal, true, close.

stricture noun 1 censure, blame, criticism, rebuke, reproof. 2 limitation, restriction, confine, bound, constraint, restraint.

stride verb pace, step, walk, march, stalk.
➤noun 1 pace, step. 2 walk, march.
make strides progress, advance.

strident adj 1 harsh, raucous, shrill, loud. 2 clamorous, vociferous.

strife noun conflict, discord, dissension, friction, animosity, hostility, combat, rivalry.

strike verb 1 hit, tap, beat, bang, knock, punch, slap, smack, thump, collide with. 2 afflict, attack, assail. 3 delete, cross out, erase, efface, remove, cancel. 4 impress, affect, touch. 5 occur to, dawn on, hit. 6 agree, settle on, clinch (inf). 7 assume, adopt, affect. 8 reach, arrive at, achieve. 9 find, discover, come upon, chance upon, happen upon. 10 walk out, down tools.
➤noun 1 tap, knock, blow, thump, collision. 2 walk-out, sit-in, industrial action. 3 attack, assault, raid, bombardment. 4 hit, stroke.
strike up begin, start, initiate, establish.

striking adj impressive, stunning, dazzling, extraordinary, outstanding, remarkable, astonishing, memorable, arresting, noticeable, conspicuous, obvious.

string noun 1 cord, twine, rope, thread, cable, line. 2 series, succession, sequence, chain, file, stream, train.
➤verb 1 thread, link. 2 hang, suspend, festoon, loop, tie, fasten.
string along deceive, fool, bluff, take for a ride (inf), lead up the garden path (inf).
string out stretch, extend, lengthen, space out, spread out.
string up hang, lynch.

stringent adj 1 strict, severe, rigorous, demanding, rigid, inflexible. 2 hard, difficult, tight, tough.

strings pl noun qualifications, conditions, provisos, requirements, restrictions, limitations, stipulations, obligations.

stringy adj 1 chewy, tough, gristly, fibrous. 2 wiry, sinewy, lanky, gangling.

strip[1] verb 1 peel, skin, flay, excoriate, denude, expose. 2 take off, remove. 3 deprive, divest, dispossess. 4 gut, clear, empty, pillage, loot. 5 take apart, dismantle, disassemble. 6 undress, disrobe.

strip[2] noun piece, band, belt, ribbon.

stripe noun 1 band, line, streak, striation. 2 bar, chevron, flash.

stripling noun youth, lad, boy, child, kid (inf), adolescent, teenager.

strive verb **1** try, endeavour, aim, aspire, struggle, labour, toil. **2** compete, vie, contend, fight, battle.

stroke[1] verb caress, pat, fondle, pet.
➤ *noun* caress, pat.

stroke[2] noun **1** blow, hit, swipe, cuff, tap, rap, slap, smack, whack (*inf*), belt (*inf*). **2** action, feat, accomplishment, achievement, coup. **3** movement, flourish, sweep. **4** apoplexy, paralysis, seizure, collapse.

stroll verb walk, amble, saunter.
➤ *noun* walk, constitutional, saunter, airing, turn.

strong adj **1** powerful, mighty, strapping, rugged, hardy, tough, solid, sturdy, durable, heavy-duty. **2** resolute, determined, strong-willed, forceful, firm, assertive, positive. **3** effective, efficacious, efficient. **4** sound, valid, weighty, forceful, cogent, convincing, compelling. **5** rich, concentrated, powerful, potent, heady, intoxicating, spicy, piquant, highly-flavoured. **6** intense, deep, bright, vivid. **7** vigorous, forceful, fierce, violent. **8** vehement, fervent, passionate, ardent, zealous, enthusiastic, devoted, committed..

stronghold noun fortress, fort, castle, citadel, bastion.

structure noun **1** building, edifice, erection, construction. **2** framework, arrangement, organization, set-up, composition, constitution.
➤ *verb* construct, assemble, put together, order, organize, arrange.

struggle verb **1** strive, labour, toil, endeavour, strain, do one's utmost. **2** compete, vie, fight, battle, contend.
➤ *noun* **1** effort, exertion, strain. **2** endeavour, attempt. **3** fight, battle, conflict, strife, contention, contest, competition, encounter. **4** trouble, labour.

strut verb prance, parade, stalk, swagger.

stub noun butt, end, stump.

stubborn adj obstinate, pig-headed, stiff-necked, obdurate, wilful, contrary, recalcitrant, intractable, inflexible, unyielding, dogged, tenacious.

stubby adj short, squat, stumpy, thick.

student noun **1** undergraduate, postgraduate, pupil, scholar. **2** learner, apprentice, trainee.

studied adj **1** prepared, calculated, premeditated, planned, considered. **2** contrived, affected, forced, artificial, deliberate, conscious.

studious adj **1** scholarly, academic, intellectual, bookish. **2** serious, thoughtful, reflective, diligent, assiduous, meticulous, thorough.

study verb **1** learn, read, research, cram, revise, swot (*inf*), mug up (*inf*). **2** read, peruse, pore over, scrutinize, examine, contemplate, consider, ponder.
➤ *noun* **1** learning, reading, research, scholarship, education, revision. **2** examination, survey, investigation, analysis, scrutiny. **3** office, den (*inf*), library.

stuff verb **1** fill, pack, load, cram. **2** pad, wad, upholster. **3** thrust, ram, push, press, squeeze, force, wedge. **4** gorge, fill, overindulge, sate.
➤ *noun* **1** matter, substance. **2** articles, equipment, kit, tackle, paraphernalia, gear (*inf*). **3** possessions, belongings, effects, things. **4** objects, things, articles, items.

stuffing noun padding, packing, wadding, filling.

stuffy adj **1** close, muggy, airless, unventilated, suffocating, oppressive, musty, stale. **2** dull, dreary, uninteresting, stodgy (*inf*). **3** straitlaced, staid, prim, starchy, fuddy-duddy (*inf*), conservative, conventional.

stumble verb **1** trip, fall, slip. **2** lurch, stagger, lumber, blunder. **3** stammer, stutter, falter, hesitate. **4** happen upon, chance upon, come across, run across, find, discover, encounter.

stump noun **1** trunk, bole. **2** remnant, remains, stub, butt, end.
➤ *verb* **1** baffle, mystify, puzzle, bewilder, perplex, outwit, defeat. **2** stamp, stomp (*inf*), trudge, plod, clump, clomp.
stump up pay up, fork out (*inf*), hand over, cough up (*inf*).

stun verb **1** daze, stupefy, knock out. **2** amaze, astonish, shock, overwhelm, flabbergast (*inf*), bowl over (*inf*), stagger, dumbfound.

stunning adj brilliant, dazzling, wonderful, splendid, sensational, spectacular, amazing, staggering, striking, impressive, beautiful, gorgeous.

stunt[1] *noun* feat, exploit, trick, turn, act, performance.

stunt[2] *verb* retard, check, restrict, slow, hinder, arrest.

stupefy *verb* 1 daze, numb, stun, confuse. 2 shock, amaze, astound, stagger, dumbfound, bowl over (*inf*).

stupendous *adj* astounding, astonishing, staggering, stunning, wonderful, marvellous, extraordinary, phenomenal, tremendous, fantastic (*inf*), superb, breathtaking.

stupid *adj* 1 unintelligent, dim, dumb (*inf*), simple, slow-witted, thick (*inf*), crass, foolish, silly, idiotic, mad, unwise. 2 stupefied, dazed, groggy, semiconscious.

stupor *noun* 1 oblivion, insensibility, coma, stupefaction, daze, trance, unconsciousness. 2 torpor, lethargy, sluggishness, apathy.

sturdy *adj* 1 strong, powerful, brawny, strapping, robust, hardy, healthy, vigorous. 2 solid, stout, tough, substantial, durable, heavy-duty. 3 determined, resolute, firm, unyielding, tenacious, staunch, steadfast, stalwart.

stutter *verb* stammer, hesitate, falter, stumble.

style *noun* 1 manner, mode, method, way, approach. 2 design, cut, shape, form, fashion, vogue. 3 stylishness, elegance, chic, flair, dash, panache, polish, taste, refinement, culture, sophistication, urbanity. 4 grandeur, comfort, luxury.
➤*verb* 1 design, fashion, cut, shape, tailor, arrange. 2 name, call, term, designate, dub, tag, label, title.

stylish *adj* smart, elegant, fashionable, chic, modish.

suave *adj* 1 smooth, glib, gracious, charming, polite. 2 urbane, sophisticated, debonair, refined, elegant.

subconscious *adj* innermost, deep, latent, underlying, repressed, unconscious, subliminal, instinctive.

subdue *verb* 1 reduce, moderate, soften, tone down, mute. 2 overcome, master, control, discipline, check, curb, restrain, suppress. 3 conquer, vanquish, subjugate, crush, defeat.

subject *noun* 1 topic, theme, substance, gist, matter, affair, issue, question.

2 patient, client, case, guinea pig (*inf*). 3 object, victim. 4 dependant, subordinate, citizen, national. 5 course, discipline, field.
➤*adj* 1 subordinate, dependent, subservient, subjugated, answerable, accountable. 2 exposed, vulnerable, open, liable. 3 susceptible, prone. 4 conditional, dependent, contingent.
➤*verb* 1 put through, submit. 2 expose, lay open. 3 subdue, subjugate, conquer, crush, master, control.

subjective *adj* 1 personal, individual, biased, prejudiced, idiosyncratic. 2 internal, mental, emotional.

subjugate *verb* conquer, vanquish, overpower, master, crush, subdue, tame, discipline, subject, enslave, oppress.

sublimate *verb* 1 refine, purify, exalt, uplift, elevate. 2 divert, redirect, transfer, channel.

sublime *adj* 1 exalted, noble, dignified, eminent, lofty, elevated. 2 glorious, superb, magnificent, grand, august, majestic. 3 great, supreme, intense, extreme.

submerge *verb* 1 submerse, immerse, plunge, dive, duck, sink. 2 inundate, flood, deluge, engulf, swamp, drown.

submission *noun* 1 surrender, capitulation, yielding, resignation, compliance, acquiescence. 2 tender, proposal, contribution, entry, suggestion, presentation.

submissive *adj* docile, tractable, biddable, yielding, unresisting, compliant, acquiescent, obedient, deferential, meek, self-effacing, passive.

submit *verb* 1 yield, surrender, capitulate, acquiesce, bow, defer, obey, comply. 2 send, present, hand in, tender, offer. 3 propose, advance, put forward, table, suggest.

subordinate *adj* 1 inferior, junior, lower, lowly, menial. 2 minor, lesser, secondary, subsidiary, ancillary.
➤*noun* inferior, junior, subaltern, underling (*inf*), assistant, sidekick (*inf*), dependant, subject.

subscribe *verb* 1 pledge, promise, contribute, give, donate, underwrite. 2 pay, shell out (*inf*), fork out (*inf*). 3 support, back, endorse, agree, approve.

subscription *noun* **1** fee, dues, payment, membership. **2** pledge, donation, contribution, offering.

subsequent *adj* succeeding, following, ensuing, future, later, next.

subservient *adj* **1** obsequious, servile, submissive, fawning, deferential, slavish, sycophantic, ingratiating. **2** subordinate, subsidiary, auxiliary.

subside *verb* **1** abate, let up, moderate, lessen, decrease, diminish, wane, die down. **2** cave in, collapse. **3** fall, drop. **4** sink, descend, settle.

subsidence *noun* sinking, settling, fall, decrease, abatement.

subsidiary *adj* **1** auxiliary, supplementary, ancillary, supporting, contributory, accessory, subservient. **2** inferior, lesser, minor, secondary, subordinate.

subsidize *verb* support, back, underwrite, sponsor, fund, finance, aid, promote.

subsidy *noun* grant, allowance, assistance, aid, sponsorship, investment, finance, funding, contribution.

subsist *verb* **1** live, exist, survive, make ends meet. **2** last, continue, endure, remain.

subsistence *noun* **1** food, sustenance, maintenance, keep. **2** living, existence, survival.

substance *noun* **1** matter, material, stuff, fabric, body. **2** validity, truth, foundation, basis. **3** solidity, reality, actuality, substantiality. **4** essence, gist, pith, burden, meaning, significance, import, point. **5** wealth, means, assets, resources, property.

substantial *adj* **1** large, considerable, sizable, ample, generous. **2** firm, strong, solid, stout, sturdy, well-built. **3** real, actual, material, tangible, corporeal, concrete. **4** basic, fundamental, essential. **5** wealthy, prosperous, affluent, well-to-do, influential, successful.

substantiate *verb* prove, establish, confirm, verify, authenticate, corroborate, back up, bear out.

substitute *verb* **1** exchange, swap (*inf*). **2** replace, deputize, stand in, understudy. ➤*noun* alternative, replacement, surrogate, proxy, understudy, reserve, stand-in, locum.

subterfuge *noun* **1** artifice, stratagem, wile, ruse, trick, device. **2** intrigue, deception, trickery, evasion.

subtle *adj* **1** faint, delicate, slight, mild, understated, low-key. **2** indistinct, indefinite, elusive, fine, deep, profound. **3** astute, shrewd, acute, penetrating, discerning, discriminating.

subtlety *noun* **1** faintness, delicacy, understatement, sensitivity, perception, discernment, shrewdness, astuteness, acumen. **2** nicety, distinction.

subtract *verb* deduct, take away, remove.

suburban *adj* bourgeois, middle-class, provincial, insular, parochial, narrow-minded.

suburbia *noun* suburbs, outskirts, edge, periphery.

subversive *adj* **1** seditious, inflammatory, incendiary, undermining. **2** revolutionary, insurrectionary, treacherous, traitorous, disruptive, riotous. ➤*noun* rebel, revolutionary, insurrectionary, troublemaker, traitor.

subvert *verb* **1** overthrow, overturn, upset, disrupt, sabotage, undermine. **2** corrupt, deprave, pervert, demoralize.

succeed *verb* **1** triumph, prevail, work, thrive, flourish. **2** realize, accomplish, achieve, bring off, pull off (*inf*). **3** prosper, make good, get on (*inf*). **4** follow, ensue, supervene, come next. **5** replace, supersede, take over from. **6** inherit, come into.

success *noun* **1** triumph, victory. **2** achievement, accomplishment, fulfilment, realization. **3** prosperity, fame. **4** celebrity, star, hit (*inf*), winner, bestseller.

successful *adj* **1** triumphant, victorious, winning. **2** prosperous, booming, thriving, flourishing, leading, top, famous, eminent. **3** profitable, rewarding, fruitful.

succession *noun* **1** chain, run, train, string, series, cycle. **2** sequence, progression, order. **3** accession, elevation, promotion.
in succession successively, consecutively, running, on the trot (*inf*).

succinct *adj* brief, short, concise, terse, pithy.

succour noun **1** help, aid, assistance, support. **2** relief, comfort, solace, reassurance.
➤verb help, aid, assist, support, relieve, comfort.

succulent adj **1** juicy, moist, luscious, mouth-watering. **2** sappy, fleshy.

succumb verb surrender, yield, give in, submit, capitulate.

suck verb **1** draw in, take in. **2** absorb, blot up, soak up.
suck up fawn, toady, curry favour.

sudden adj **1** sharp, unexpected, unforeseen, startling, dramatic. **2** abrupt, hasty, impulsive, quick, swift, prompt, immediate.

sue verb **1** prosecute, summon, take to court, prefer charges against. **2** solicit, petition, appeal, beg, implore, beseech.

suffer verb **1** undergo, experience, feel, endure, go through, meet with, sustain. **2** bear, tolerate, abide, brook, put up with (inf).

suffice verb do, serve, answer, satisfy, be sufficient.

sufficient adj enough, adequate, ample, satisfactory, decent (inf).

suffocate verb asphyxiate, smother, stifle, choke.

suffrage noun franchise, vote.

suffuse verb cover, mantle, bathe, imbue, permeate, pervade.

sugary adj sentimental, mawkish, syrupy, soppy, slushy (inf), mushy (inf), schmaltzy (inf), sickly (inf).

suggest verb **1** propose, submit, put forward, advance, advise, recommend. **2** hint, intimate, imply, insinuate. **3** evoke, bring to mind.

suggestion noun **1** proposal, proposition, idea, advice, recommendation. **2** implication, insinuation, intimation. **3** hint, trace, touch, suspicion, indication.

suggestive adj **1** evocative, reminiscent, redolent, expressive. **2** ribald, dirty, lewd, smutty, indecent, indelicate, improper, risqué, crude.

suit verb **1** befit, become, flatter, complement, match, harmonize with. **2** please, satisfy, gratify, conform with, accord with. **3** adapt, adjust, accommodate, fit.

➤noun **1** outfit, ensemble, costume, clothing. **2** lawsuit, case, action, proceeding, litigation. **3** petition, appeal, plea, prayer, request, entreaty. **4** addresses, courtship.

suitable adj appropriate, apt, fitting, right, seemly, proper, convenient, opportune.

suitor noun beau, gallant, admirer, lover.

sulk verb pout, mope, brood.
➤noun mood, huff (inf).

sulky adj moody, brooding, moping, disgruntled, miffed (inf), put out, sullen.

sullen adj sulky, morose, gloomy, scowling, cross, moody, surly, uncommunicative, unsociable.

sully verb soil, dirty, stain, blemish, taint, tarnish, defile, disgrace.

sultry adj **1** close, oppressive, muggy, humid, hot, sticky. **2** voluptuous, sexy, sensual, seductive, provocative, alluring, passionate.

sum noun **1** total, aggregate, tally, score, reckoning, result. **2** amount, quantity. **3** whole, entirety, totality.
➤verb add, total, tot up, tally, reckon.
sum up 1 summarize, recapitulate. **2** epitomize, encapsulate.

summarize verb sum up, epitomize, encapsulate, recapitulate, outline, abstract, précis.

summary noun abstract, synopsis, précis, outline, résumé, recapitulation.
➤adj **1** quick, speedy, swift, hasty, prompt, immediate. **2** concise, succinct, compendious, compact.

summit noun **1** top, crown, cap, peak, pinnacle. **2** height, peak, zenith, acme, apogee.

summon verb **1** call, send for, beckon, invite. **2** convene, muster, assemble, mobilize, rally.
summon up arouse, muster, collect, gather, call up, invoke.

sumptuous adj costly, expensive, extravagant, lavish, luxurious, rich, opulent, magnificent, splendid.

sundry adj various, diverse, assorted, miscellaneous.

sunken adj **1** submerged, buried. **2** hollow, recessed, concave.

sunny *adj* 1 bright, sunshiny, sunlit, clear, cloudless, fine, summery. 2 cheerful, blithe, happy, radiant, buoyant, optimistic.

sunrise *noun* dawn, daybreak, first light, sunup.

sunset *noun* nightfall, dusk, twilight, sundown.

super *adj* wonderful, marvellous, great, excellent, magnificent, splendid, smashing (*inf*), cool (*inf*), wicked (*inf*).

superannuated *adj* old, antiquated, passé, obsolete.

superb *adj* 1 excellent, first-rate, peerless, outstanding, superlative, fine, exquisite, choice. 2 magnificent, splendid, sumptuous, grand.

supercilious *adj* arrogant, haughty, disdainful, lofty, lordly, overbearing, snooty (*inf*), patronizing, condescending.

superficial *adj* 1 surface, exterior, external, outer. 2 apparent, seeming, ostensible, outward. 3 shallow, empty-headed. 4 casual, cursory, careless, perfunctory. 5 slight, trivial, frivolous, insignificant.

superfluity *noun* superabundance, surfeit, surplus, excess, glut.

superfluous *adj* excessive, surplus, redundant, unnecessary.

superhuman *adj* 1 prodigious, stupendous, herculean, phenomenal, miraculous. 2 supernatural, paranormal, divine.

superintend *verb* supervise, manage, administer, oversee, direct, control.

superintendent *noun* supervisor, overseer, director, manager, gaffer (*inf*).

superior *adj* 1 higher, greater, better. 2 excellent, first-rate, exclusive, quality, superlative, choice, select, prize, fine. 3 haughty, arrogant, condescending, patronizing, supercilious, disdainful, pretentious, snobbish, stuck-up (*inf*). ➤*noun* senior, chief, boss (*inf*).

superlative *adj* supreme, best, greatest, highest, transcendent, matchless, unparalleled, excellent, first-rate.

supernatural *adj* 1 paranormal, unnatural, extraordinary, miraculous, uncanny. 2 spiritual, mystical, occult, metaphysical, otherworldly, unearthly. 3 ghostly, phantom, spectral, spiritual, magic.

supernumerary *adj* extra, surplus, excess, spare, odd.

supersede *verb* replace, succeed, supplant, oust, usurp.

supervise *verb* oversee, watch over, observe, guide, superintend, administer, direct, manage.

supine *adj* recumbent, flat, horizontal.

supper *noun* dinner, evening meal, tea.

supplant *verb* replace, supersede, oust, usurp, topple, overthrow.

supple *adj* 1 pliable, pliant, flexible, elastic, plastic. 2 lithe, lissom, limber.

supplement *noun* 1 addition, additive, add-on, extra, postscript, rider. 2 addendum, appendix. ➤*verb* add to, augment, extend, top up, complement.

supplementary *adj* supplemental, additional, complementary, extra, added, ancillary, auxiliary.

suppliant *adj* supplicant, entreating, beseeching, imploring, begging, importunate.

supplicate *verb* solicit, beg, crave, beseech, implore, entreat.

supply *verb* 1 provide, furnish, equip, stock. 2 satisfy, meet, fulfil. ➤*noun* 1 stock, store, reserve, fund. 2 provision, supplying.

support *verb* 1 bear, carry, hold up, prop, brace, buttress, reinforce, strengthen. 2 maintain, keep, provide for, look after, sustain, feed. 3 endure, bear, tolerate, brook. 4 help, aid, comfort, befriend, subsidize, sponsor. 5 approve, countenance, encourage, promote, advocate. 6 uphold, maintain, endorse, champion, defend. 7 authenticate, confirm, corroborate, substantiate, back up, bear out. 8 back, second, vote for. 9 encourage, follow. ➤*noun* 1 prop, brace, stay, upright, underpinning, substructure, base, foundation. 2 help, encouragement, maintenance, keep, sustenance, subsistence, sponsorship, patronage, backing, evidence, corroboration, substantiation.

supportive *adj* encouraging, helpful, caring, comforting, reassuring, attentive, sympathetic, understanding.

suppose *verb* 1 postulate, hypothesize. 2 believe, opine. 3 think, imagine, presume, conclude, judge, surmise, conjecture. 4 assume, presuppose, require.

supposed *adj* hypothetical, assumed, so-called, professed, alleged, putative.

supposition *noun* assumption, presumption, presupposition, postulate, hypothesis, theory, conjecture, idea, notion.

suppress *verb* 1 restrain, hold back, curb, check, smother, stifle. 2 quash, quell, subdue, crush, stamp out, extinguish. 3 withhold, conceal, cover up, censor, muzzle, silence.

supremacy *noun* ascendancy, superiority, preeminence, primacy, sovereignty, mastery, dominion, sway.

supreme *adj* 1 highest, top, first, leading, chief, sovereign. 2 greatest, best, superlative, paramount, predominant, prevailing, principal, main.

sure *adj* 1 certain, positive, definite, convinced, satisfied, confident, assured. 2 reliable, dependable, trusty, guaranteed, infallible, foolproof, secure, safe. 3 bound, destined, certain, inevitable, unavoidable.

surely *adv* certainly, assuredly, definitely, undoubtedly, without fail, inevitably.

surety *noun* 1 security, guarantee, indemnity, pledge, bond, bail. 2 guarantor, sponsor.

surface *noun* 1 exterior, top. 2 outside, covering, coating, veneer. 3 appearance, front, facade.
➤*verb* 1 come up, rise. 2 emerge, crop up, arise, appear, materialize.
➤*adj* superficial, outer, external, exterior.
on the surface superficially, externally, apparently, ostensibly, seemingly.

surfeit *noun* excess, surplus, glut, superabundance, plethora.
➤*verb* sate, satiate, glut, gorge, overfeed, fill, stuff, cram.

surge *noun* 1 rush, stream, flow, outpouring. 2 upsurge, rise, escalation, increase. 3 swell, billow, wave, breaker, roller.
➤*verb* 1 rush, pour, flow, stream, swell, billow, roll, heave, undulate. 2 rise, increase, escalate.

surly *adj* sullen, cross, irritable, morose, grumpy, irascible, bad-tempered, gruff, brusque, churlish, rude.

surmise *verb* infer, guess, conjecture, suppose, imagine, suspect, assume, conclude, deduce.
➤*noun* inference, assumption, supposition, guess, conjecture.

surmount *verb* 1 overcome, conquer, vanquish, get over. 2 top, cap.

surpass *verb* exceed, transcend, beat, excel, outstrip, outdo, outshine, eclipse.

surplus *noun* excess, surfeit, superabundance, superfluity, remainder, rest, balance.

surprise *verb* 1 amaze, astound, astonish, flabbergast, bowl over (*inf*). 2 startle, shock, disconcert, confuse.
➤*noun* 1 amazement, astonishment, incredulity, wonder. 2 shock, bombshell (*inf*), thunderbolt (*inf*), bolt from the blue.

surprising *adj* amazing, astounding, astonishing, startling, unexpected, extraordinary.

surrender *verb* 1 capitulate, submit, yield, give in, concede, quit (*inf*). 2 relinquish, part with, hand over. 3 give up, renounce, waive.
➤*noun* capitulation, submission, relinquishment, renunciation.

surreptitious *adj* clandestine, stealthy, covert, furtive, sly, secret.

surrogate *noun* substitute, replacement, stand-in, proxy, deputy, agent, representative.

surround *verb* encircle, encompass, enclose, ring, gird, fence in.

surroundings *pl noun* environment, milieu, setting, background, environs, habitat, vicinity, neighbourhood.

surveillance *noun* watch, observation, scrutiny, supervision, control, superintendence.

survey *verb* 1 scrutinize, look over, study, examine. 2 view, scan, observe, look at, contemplate, consider. 3 examine, inspect, assess, appraise, value. 4 measure, plot, map, chart.
➤*noun* 1 examination, inspection, assessment, appraisal, valuation. 2 study, enquiry, poll.

survive verb 1 live, subsist, hold out, persist, last, remain. 2 outlive, outlast.

susceptibility noun liability, tendency, propensity, openness, vulnerability, sensitivity, impressionability, gullibility.

susceptible adj 1 open, vulnerable, subject, given, liable, prone. 2 receptive, responsive, sensitive, impressionable, gullible, suggestible.

suspect verb 1 doubt, mistrust, distrust, disbelieve. 2 think, believe, imagine, guess, suppose, assume, presume.
➤adj suspicious, questionable, doubtful, dubious, unreliable.

suspend verb 1 hang, dangle, swing. 2 adjourn, stop, arrest, interrupt, discontinue, cease. 3 postpone, defer, delay, put off. 4 shelve, put on ice (inf). 5 dismiss, debar, expel, exclude, remove.

suspense noun 1 uncertainty, doubt, indecision, insecurity, anxiety. 2 expectancy, anticipation, excitement.

suspension noun adjournment, interruption, postponement, moratorium, stay, respite, remission, dismissal, expulsion, debarment.

suspicion noun 1 distrust, mistrust, scepticism, wariness, caution. 2 doubt, uncertainty, misgiving, qualm, feeling, hunch (inf). 3 trace, hint, touch, soupçon.

suspicious adj 1 distrustful, mistrustful, sceptical, wary, chary, uneasy, unsure. 2 dubious, questionable, suspect, irregular, shifty, shady (inf), dodgy (inf), iffy (inf), fishy (inf).

sustain verb 1 support, hold up, carry, bear. 2 help, relieve, comfort, support. 3 maintain, keep going, continue, prolong, nurture, nourish. 4 suffer, undergo, experience, endure. 5 uphold, endorse, verify, confirm, establish, ratify.

sustenance noun 1 nourishment, nutrition, food, provisions, victuals. 2 support, maintenance, living, keep, subsistence.

swagger verb strut, prance, parade.
➤noun boasting, bragging, showing off, braggadocio, bravado.

swallow verb 1 eat, drink, gulp, down (inf). 2 absorb, assimilate, engulf, envelop. 3 accept, believe, fall for (inf), buy (inf). 4 suppress, contain, hold back, smother, stifle.

swamp noun marsh, bog, morass, fen, slough, quagmire.
➤verb 1 submerge, flood, waterlog. 2 overwhelm, inundate, deluge.

swap verb 1 exchange, barter, trade. 2 switch, transpose, substitute, replace interchange.

swarm noun mass, throng, crowd, host, horde, drove, herd, flock.
➤verb 1 throng, crowd, cluster, flock. 2 teem, abound, crawl, be overrun.

swarthy adj dark, dusky, dark-skinned, black, tanned, brown.

swathe verb 1 swaddle, bandage, bind, wrap. 2 envelop, enfold, drape, cloak, shroud.

sway verb 1 swing, rock, wave, wobble. 2 totter, reel. 3 lean, incline. 4 influence, move, persuade, convince. 5 fluctuate, vacillate, hesitate, waver. 6 govern, rule.
➤noun 1 influence, control, power, authority. 2 dominion, rule, sovereignty, ascendancy.

swear verb 1 blaspheme, curse. 2 vow, promise, pledge.
swear by believe in, have faith in, trust in, rely on.

sweat verb 1 perspire, swelter, glow. 2 drip, exude, secrete.
➤noun 1 perspiration, moisture, stickiness, diaphoresis, exudation, secretion. 2 panic, fuss, flap (inf), stew (inf), lather (inf). 3 labour, toil, drudgery.

sweaty adj sweating, perspiring, moist, clammy, sticky.

sweep verb 1 brush, clean, clear. 2 whip, whisk. 3 race, hurtle, streak, tear (inf), sail, fly.
➤noun 1 arc, curve, stroke, swing, wave. 2 expanse, stretch, span, extent. 3 compass, scope, range, reach, spread.

sweeping adj 1 comprehensive, wide-ranging, broad, extensive. 2 indiscriminate, wholesale, general, global, universal, all-inclusive, blanket (inf).

sweet adj 1 sugary, honeyed, saccharine, syrupy. 2 fragrant, aromatic, balmy, perfumed, scented. 3 fresh, clean, pure, wholesome. 4 dulcet, mellifluous, tuneful, euphonious, silvery, lovely, attractive, beautiful, pretty. 5 charming, delightful,

pleasant, agreeable, appealing, cute, adorable, winsome. **6** kind, kindly, gentle, generous. **7** dear, beloved, darling, precious.
➤*noun* **1** dessert, pudding, afters (*inf*).
2 candy, confection, bonbon.

sweeten *verb* **1** sugar, honey. **2** mellow, soothe, mollify, appease, pacify, soften.
3 soften, cushion, alleviate, ease, relieve, temper.

sweetheart *noun* love, lover, boyfriend, girlfriend, suitor, admirer, beau, beloved, darling.

swell *verb* **1** expand, dilate, distend, bloat, puff up. **2** bulge, billow, balloon. **3** increase, augment, amplify, intensify, grow, rise, mount, surge.
➤*noun* **1** expansion, dilation, rise, surge, increase. **2** wave, billow, undulation.
3 dandy, fop, beau.

swelling *noun* **1** bulge, bump, lump, protuberance. **2** tumefaction, tumescence, distension, enlargement.

sweltering *adj* hot, sultry, oppressive, torrid, suffocating, humid, sticky, steamy.

swerve *verb* turn, veer, deviate, deflect, sheer.

swift *adj* **1** fast, rapid, quick, speedy, fleet, express, brisk, nimble. **2** sudden, abrupt, hasty, prompt.

swill *verb* **1** rinse, wash, clean, flush, sluice. **2** drink, swig, quaff, knock back (*inf*), swallow, gulp, guzzle.
➤*noun* **1** swallow, swig, gulp, drink.
2 slop, waste, refuse.

swim *verb* bathe, take a dip.

swimmingly *adv* smoothly, successfully, very well, like clockwork.

swindle *verb* defraud, cheat, trick, overcharge, diddle (*inf*), do (*inf*), con (*inf*), rip off (*inf*).
➤*noun* fraud, trickery, sharp practice, fiddle, racket (*inf*), con trick (*inf*), rip-off (*inf*), scam (*inf*).

swing *verb* **1** sway, wave. **2** hang, dangle.
3 curve, bend, swerve, veer, turn, wheel.
4 spin, pivot, rotate. **5** waver, seesaw, fluctuate, oscillate. **6** achieve, get, acquire, arrange, organize, fix (*inf*).
➤*noun* **1** swaying, oscillation. **2** change, shift, fluctuation, vacillation.

swirl *verb* whirl, eddy, turn, gyrate, twist, spin.

switch *noun* **1** twig, branch, rod, stick, cane. **2** change, shift, about-turn.
➤*verb* **1** change, shift. **2** transpose, exchange, swap (*inf*), substitute, replace, interchange.

swivel *verb* turn, pivot, rotate, revolve, twirl.

swoop *verb* **1** descend, dive, plunge, rush, pounce. **2** seize, snatch.
➤*noun* descent, dive, plunge, rush, pounce, snatch.

sword *noun* blade, rapier, sabre, foil, scimitar.
cross swords fight, clash, argue, quarrel.

sycophant *noun* flatterer, fawner, groveller, toady, bootlicker (*inf*).

syllabus *noun* summary, outline, prospectus, curriculum.

symbol *noun* **1** token, emblem, sign, badge, logo, representation. **2** character, figure, letter, sign, mark.

symbolic *adj* representative, emblematic, typical, allegorical, figurative, metaphorical.

symbolize *verb* represent, stand for, signify, mean, betoken, exemplify, typify.

symmetrical *adj* balanced, proportional, harmonious, regular, even, corresponding, parallel.

symmetry *noun* **1** balance, proportion, harmony. **2** regularity, evenness, congruity, correspondence, agreement.

sympathetic *adj* **1** compassionate, kind, warm, caring, considerate, concerned, solicitous, supportive, understanding.
2 pleasant, agreeable, congenial, friendly, companionable, sociable.

sympathize *verb* **1** pity, feel for, commiserate, condole, understand, empathize.
2 agree, support, back, side, identify.

sympathy *noun* **1** compassion, concern, pity, commiseration, consolation, condolence, comfort, support, understanding, appreciation. **2** agreement, accord, harmony, rapport, affinity, empathy.

symptom *noun* sign, indication, mark, characteristic, signal, warning, expression, manifestation.

symptomatic *adj* indicative, characteristic, typical, suggestive, associated.

synchronous *adj* simultaneous, coincident, concurrent, contemporaneous.

syndicate *noun* trust, cartel, group, combine, ring, alliance, federation, association.

synonymous *adj* **1** interchangeable, substitutable. **2** equivalent, corresponding, tantamount, similar, comparable.

synopsis *noun* outline, summary, précis, résumé, abstract, digest, condensation.

synthesis *noun* combination, amalgamation, union, fusion, integration, coalescence.

synthetic *verb* artificial, man-made, imitation, simulated, mock, ersatz, fake.

system *noun* **1** network, organization, structure, set-up, arrangement. **2** method, procedure, process, technique, approach, way, means, mode, practice, routine. **3** planning, order, logic, systematization, methodology.

systematic *adj* **1** regular, ordered, structured, logical, planned, systematized. **2** methodical, efficient, orderly, organized.

tab *noun* loop, flap, tag, label.

table *noun* **1** board, counter, bar, bench, desk. **2** index, inventory, list, catalogue, register.
➤*verb* propose, submit, put forward.

tableau *noun* **1** representation, portrayal, picture. **2** arrangement, scene, diorama.

tablet *noun* **1** panel, slab, stone. **2** pill, capsule, lozenge.

taboo *noun* ban, prohibition, veto, curse.
➤*adj* prohibited, banned, forbidden, unacceptable, frowned on, unmentionable.

tabulate *verb* order, arrange, list, sort, classify, table.

tacit *adj* implied, implicit, understood, unspoken, unstated.

taciturn *adj* silent, quiet, reserved, unforthcoming, uncommunicative, tight-lipped, close-mouthed.

tack *noun* **1** nail, pin, drawing-pin. **2** direction, bearing, heading, course. **3** approach, method, plan, strategy.
➤*verb* **1** nail, pin, fasten, fix. **2** stitch, sew. **3** append, annex, add, attach.

tackle *noun* gear, equipment, apparatus, tools, implements, things, stuff.
➤*verb* **1** undertake, begin, set about, go about, attend to, deal with, take on, get to grips with, address. **2** face, confront, challenge, accost. **3** challenge, intercept, obstruct, seize, grab, bring down.

tacky¹ *adj* sticky, gluey, gummy.

tacky² *adj* tasteless, vulgar, tawdry, kitsch, naff (*inf*).

tact *noun* diplomacy, discretion, sensitivity, savoir faire, understanding, thoughtfulness, consideration.

tactful *adj* diplomatic, discreet, careful, sensitive, thoughtful, understanding, considerate.

tactic *noun* manoeuvre, move, stratagem, scheme, plan, ploy, method, approach, tack.

tactical *adj* planned, calculated, skilful, clever, politic.

tactics *pl noun* strategy, plan, scheme, method, approach, policy.

tag *noun* **1** label, sticker, ticket, tab. **2** flap, tab, loop. **3** saying, proverb, maxim, moral, dictum, quotation, platitude, cliché.
➤*verb* **1** label, mark. **2** call, label, brand, term, designate. **3** add, append, affix, tack. **4** follow, go along with, go with, accompany.

tail *noun* **1** brush, scut, dock. **2** bottom, rear, end, tail-end. **3** shadow, detective, sleuth (*inf*), private eye (*inf*).
➤*verb* **1** follow, trail, track, shadow, dog. **2** decrease, decline, fade, wane, dwindle, taper off, peter out.
turn tail run away, flee, bolt, retreat, cut and run, scarper (*inf*).

tail end *noun* end, rear, back, extremity.

tailor *noun* outfitter, couturier, costumier, clothier.
➤*verb* fit, cut, fashion, shape, adapt, adjust, modify, alter.

taint *verb* **1** contaminate, infect, pollute, putrefy, spoil, blight. **2** tarnish, stain, sully, blemish, blacken, corrupt, shame, disgrace, dishonour.
➤*noun* **1** spot, stain, blot, blemish, flaw, defect, shame, disgrace, dishonour. **2** hint, suggestion, trace, touch.

take *verb* **1** grasp, grip, clasp, clutch, lay hold of. **2** get, obtain, acquire, secure, gain, capture, win, seize, catch, arrest, kidnap. **3** hold, accommodate, contain, seat. **4** pick, select, choose, opt for, decide on. **5** subtract, deduct, take away, remove. **6** steal, make off with, pocket, purloin, pinch (*inf*), nick (*inf*), swipe (*inf*). **7** use, make use of, go by. **8** have, eat, consume,

drink. **9** stand, put up with, tolerate, stomach, bear, endure. **10** carry, convey, transport, bring, escort, accompany, lead, conduct, guide, see. **11** require, need, call for, demand, necessitate. **12** receive, cope with, deal with, handle, react to, respond to. **13** regard, look upon, consider, reckon, view. **14** claim, accept, shoulder, bear. **15** study, learn, read.
➤*noun* **1** catch, haul, bag. **2** proceeds, takings, receipts, profits, earnings, gains, income, yield.

take after resemble, look like, be like, favour.

take against dislike, object to, disapprove of.

take it assume, presume, suppose, gather, understand.

take to 1 start, begin, resort to. **2** develop a liking for, like, get on with, appreciate.

take back *verb* **1** retract, withdraw, repudiate, recant, disavow. **2** return, swap, exchange, trade.

take down *verb* **1** write down, jot down, set down, note down, make a note of, record, minute. **2** remove, take apart, take to pieces, dismantle, disassemble, demolish, tear down.

take in *verb* **1** understand, comprehend, grasp, realize, appreciate, perceive, notice, take note of. **2** include, incorporate, embrace, cover, comprise, contain. **3** accommodate, receive, lodge, board, put up, shelter. **4** fool, deceive, con (*inf*), mislead, trick, dupe, cheat, swindle, hoodwink.

takeoff *noun* **1** lift-off, departure. **2** impersonation, imitation, parody, caricature, send-up (*inf*), spoof (*inf*).

take off *verb* **1** remove, strip off, peel off, shed, discard, throw off, doff. **2** lift off, leave the ground, depart. **3** subtract, deduct, take away. **4** go, leave, run away, do a runner (*inf*), split (*inf*), scarper (*inf*). **5** impersonate, mimic, caricature, parody, satirize, send up (*inf*), spoof (*inf*). **6** catch on, work, succeed, make it (*inf*).

take on *verb* **1** employ, hire, engage, recruit. **2** undertake, accept, tackle.

take out *verb* **1** extract, remove, pull out, cut out. **2** invite out, go out with, date (*inf*), see, escort.

take over *verb* gain control of, take charge of, assume responsibility for.

take up *verb* **1** lift up, raise, pick up. **2** occupy, cover, fill, use up. **3** continue, carry on, pick up, resume. **4** start, begin, pursue, embark on.

taking *adj* charming, captivating, appealing, attractive, winning, lovable, winsome, fetching.

takings *pl noun* proceeds, receipts, earnings, profit, gain, gate money.

tale *noun* **1** story, yarn (*inf*), anecdote, narrative, account, novel, romance, saga, fable, myth, legend. **2** lie, untruth, falsehood, story, tall story, fib (*inf*), whopper (*inf*), porky (*inf*).

talent *noun* **1** gift, faculty, flair, aptitude, ability, skill, feel, knack, bent, forte, expertise. **2** genius, ability.

talk *verb* **1** speak, articulate, utter, say, lecture, discourse, prattle, babble, jabber, rabbit (*inf*), yak (*inf*). **2** communicate, converse, confer, discuss, chat, chatter, speak, gossip, natter (*inf*), jaw (*inf*), rap (*inf*). **3** confess, tell, blab (*inf*), split (*inf*), squeal (*inf*), sing (*inf*), spill the beans (*inf*). **4** persuade, influence, sway, convince, dissuade, discourage, put off, deter.
➤*noun* **1** speech, lecture, address, discourse, harangue, disquisition, sermon. **2** conversation, dialogue, discussion, conference, tête-à-tête, chat, gossip, confab (*inf*), jaw (*inf*), natter (*inf*), chinwag (*inf*). **3** rumour, scandal, gossip, hearsay, tittle-tattle.

talk back answer back, retort.

talk big boast, brag, bluster, exaggerate, crow, show off, swank, vaunt, blow one's own trumpet (*inf*).

talk down 1 patronize, look down on, condescend to. **2** drown, silence.

talking-to lecture, reprimand, reproof, telling-off (*inf*), ticking-off (*inf*).

talk round persuade, convince, win over, bring round.

talkative *adj* garrulous, loquacious, communicative, forthcoming, expansive, vocal, voluble, chatty, gossipy.

tall *adj* **1** high, lofty, towering, big, giant. **2** exaggerated, far-fetched, unlikely, unbelievable, incredible, improbable, implausible.

a tall order difficult, demanding, challenging, unreasonable.

tally *noun* **1** score, total. **2** count, record, register, reckoning.
➤*verb* **1** agree, correspond, accord, coincide, concur, conform. **2** total, count, reckon, tot up.

tame *adj* **1** domesticated, broken, trained. **2** gentle, docile, tractable, submissive, meek, obedient, amenable, biddable. **3** dull, flat, uninteresting, unexciting, uninspired, unadventurous, insipid, lifeless, weak, feeble.
➤*verb* **1** domesticate, house-train, break in. **2** discipline, master, curb, bridle, control, bring to heel, subdue, subjugate, pacify.

tamper *verb* meddle, interfere, tinker, mess about, fiddle (*inf*), fool around (*inf*), monkey (*inf*).

tan *adj* light brown, brown, yellow-brown, tawny.
➤*verb* suntan, brown, bronze, sunburn.

tang *noun* **1** flavour, taste, savour, relish, piquancy, pungency, sharpness, bite. **2** hint, trace, suggestion, touch, tinge.

tangible *adj* **1** palpable, touchable, visible, perceptible. **2** material, substantial, physical, real, actual, solid.

tangle *verb* entangle, ravel, snarl, mat, knot, tousle, intertwine, interlace.
➤*noun* knot, twist, coil, mesh, mat. **2** mess, jumble, muddle, snarl-up, complication, mix-up.

tank *noun* **1** container, receptacle, reservoir, cistern, vat. **2** aquarium. **3** armoured car, armoured vehicle.

tantalize *verb* torment, tease, bait, titillate, tempt, entice.

tantamount *adj* equivalent, equal, commensurate.

tantrum *noun* outburst, temper, rage, fury, pet, paddy (*inf*).

tap *verb* rap, pat, touch, knock, hit, strike.
➤*noun* rap, pat, touch, knock, blow.

tap *noun* **1** stopcock, spout, valve. **2** bug, listening device, wire (*inf*).
➤*verb* **1** siphon, draw off, drain, bleed, exploit, extract, make use of, draw on, milk. **2** bug, wire (*inf*).
on tap on hand, handy, ready, available.

tape *noun* **1** sticky tape, Sellotape®, parcel tape, masking tape, insulating tape. **2** ribbon, strip, string, band. **3** audiotape, videotape, video, videocassette, cassette.
➤*verb* **1** fasten, tie, bind, stick, Sellotape®. **2** record, video, video-record, tape-record.

taper *verb* **1** narrow, thin. **2** diminish, decrease, dwindle, fade, subside, die away, tail off, peter out.

tardy *adj* **1** late, belated, overdue, delayed, behindhand. **2** slow, leisurely, sluggish, dilatory.

target *noun* **1** mark, bull's eye. **2** objective, object, ambition, aim, goal. **3** prey, quarry, game. **4** victim, butt.

tariff *noun* **1** tax, duty, levy. **2** price list, schedule, rate.

tarnish *verb* **1** discolour, rust, dull, corrode. **2** stain, sully, soil, taint, blemish, blacken.
➤*noun* discoloration, rust, patina, oxidation.

tarry *verb* **1** linger, remain, stay, rest, wait. **2** loiter, dally, dawdle, delay.

tart *noun* **1** pie, pastry, flan. **2** prostitute, hooker (*inf*), whore, harlot, streetwalker, call girl. **3** slut, scrubber (*inf*), slag (*inf*).
tart up 1 doll up (*inf*), dress up, make up. **2** do up (*inf*), jazz up (*inf*) renovate, redecorate.

tart *adj* **1** sour, acid, sharp, vinegary. **2** biting, cutting, caustic, scathing, mordant, sharp, barbed, sarcastic, sardonic.

task *noun* job, duty, charge, assignment, mission, undertaking, errand, chore.
take to task rebuke, reprimand, tell off (*inf*), tick off (*inf*), reprove, reproach, criticize.

taste *noun* **1** flavour, savour, relish, tang. **2** bit, morsel, piece, mouthful, bite, sip, drop, dash, soupçon. **3** liking, fondness, love, predilection, inclination, partiality, preference, penchant, fancy. **4** discernment, discrimination, judgement, culture, refinement, elegance, delicacy, propriety, decorum, discretion, tact.
➤*verb* **1** smack, savour. **2** try, sample, test, sip, nibble. **3** tell, make out, discern, distinguish. **4** experience, undergo, know, feel.

tasteful *adj* refined, cultured, cultivated, elegant, stylish, artistic, restrained, decorous, proper, seemly, appropriate, fitting.

tasteless *adj* **1** insipid, vapid, flavourless, unappetizing, bland, flat, weak, thin, watery. **2** vulgar, tawdry, cheap, kitsch, garish, flashy, inelegant, tacky (*inf*), naff (*inf*), unseemly, improper, impolite, rude, indecorous, indelicate, coarse, crass, tactless.

tasty *adj* savoury, flavourful, mouth-watering, appetizing, delicious, delectable, luscious, scrumptious (*inf*), yummy (*inf*).

tattered *adj* ragged, frayed, threadbare, tatty, shabby, torn, ripped.

tattle *verb* **1** gossip, tittle-tattle, chatter, prattle, natter (*inf*). **2** blab, tell tales.

taunt *verb* **1** tease, torment, provoke, goad, bait, mock, make fun of, jeer at, gibe at.
➤ *noun* gibe, jeer, sneer, insult, dig (*inf*).

taut *adj* **1** tight, stretched, rigid, tensed. **2** tense, strained, drawn, stressed.

tautology *noun* repetition, repetitiousness, duplication, redundancy, pleonasm.

tawdry *adj* flashy, showy, meretricious, loud, gaudy, garish, cheap, tacky (*inf*), kitsch.

tax *noun* **1** levy, duty, excise, customs, toll, charge. **2** burden, weight, drain, strain, imposition.
➤ *verb* **1** charge duty on, impose a toll on. **2** burden, strain, stretch, try, overburden, wear out, exhaust, sap, drain.

taxing *adj* demanding, exacting, burdensome, difficult, tough, trying, onerous, punishing, heavy, tiring, exhausting, draining.

teach *verb* educate, school, instruct, tutor, lecture, coach, train, drill, inform, enlighten, indoctrinate, inculcate, explain, tell, show, demonstrate.

teacher *noun* master, mistress, tutor, lecturer, professor, don, educator, pedagogue, mentor, guru, instructor, coach, trainer.

team *noun* **1** group, squad, gang, shift, crew. **2** side, squad, line-up.
➤ *verb* **1** join, unite, combine, come together, band together, work together. **2** cooperate, ally with, collaborate.

tear *verb* **1** rip, rend, split, divide, pull apart, break apart, pull to pieces, shred, lacerate, gash, slash, cut, wound. **2** snatch, seize, grab, pull, rip, wrench, wrest. **3** race, speed, sprint, rush, career, shoot, dash, dart, bolt, belt (*inf*), whizz (*inf*).
➤ *noun* rip, rent, split, slit, hole, gash, slash, cut, laceration, wound.

tear *noun* drop, droplet, bead.
in tears weeping, crying, sobbing, blubbing (*inf*), tearful, upset.

tearful *adj* **1** weeping, crying, sobbing, in tears, weepy (*inf*), upset, distressed. **2** poignant, emotional, upsetting, pathetic, sad, distressing.

tease *verb* **1** torment, plague, harass, provoke, goad, needle, taunt, bait, rag (*inf*), rib (*inf*). **2** tantalize.

technical *adj* **1** technological, mechanical, practical, scientific, professional. **2** specialist, specialized, scientific.

technique *noun* **1** manner, style, fashion, method, approach, system, procedure, knack, touch. **2** skill, art, artistry, craft, craftsmanship, ability, know-how, proficiency, mastery, expertise.

tedious *adj* **1** boring, monotonous, dull, tiresome, wearisome, long-drawn-out, overlong, prosaic, banal, uninteresting, unexciting, uninspired, dreary, deadly (*inf*). **2** boring, dull, tiresome, long-winded.

tedium *noun* tediousness, boredom, ennui, tiresomeness, wearisomeness, dullness, dreariness, monotony, sameness.

teem *verb* swarm, bristle, crawl, be alive, be full of, overflow, be bursting.

teenage *adj* teenaged, adolescent, young, immature.

teenager *noun* teen (*inf*), adolescent, young person.

teeter *verb* **1** sway, rock, totter, tremble, wobble, shake. **2** waver, hesitate, dither, vacillate.

teetotaller *noun* abstainer, non-drinker.

telepathy *noun* clairvoyance, mind-reading, sixth sense, extrasensory perception.

telephone *noun* phone, blower (*inf*), cell phone, mobile.

➤*verb* phone, call, ring, give a bell (*inf*), give a tinkle (*inf*).

telescope *verb* **1** concertina, crush, squash, compress. **2** condense, shrink, reduce, compress, abridge, shorten.

television *noun* TV, telly (*inf*), set, box (*inf*), gogglebox (*inf*).

tell *verb* **1** relate, narrate, report, recount, recite, describe. **2** notify, let know, inform, acquaint, apprise, impart, communicate, make known, announce, disclose, reveal, divulge, say, declare, state. **3** command, order, instruct, direct. **4** distinguish, discern, ascertain, perceive, see, make out, discover. **5** distinguish, tell apart, identify, differentiate, discriminate. **6** take its toll, exhaust, drain, affect.
tell off reprimand, tick off (*inf*), scold, chide, censure, give a talking-to (*inf*).
tell on betray, denounce, inform on, shop (*inf*), grass up (*inf*), blow the whistle on (*inf*).

telling *adj* significant, striking, forceful, effective, cogent, substantial, powerful, weighty, decisive.

temerity *noun* rashness, recklessness, audacity, impudence, impertinence, effrontery, presumption, nerve (*inf*), cheek (*inf*).

temper *noun* **1** nature, disposition, temperament, character, frame of mind, mind-set, attitude. **2** rage, fury, anger, passion, bad mood, tantrum, paddy (*inf*). **3** ill humour, irritability, irascibility, peevishness, petulance, surliness.
➤*verb* **1** moderate, mitigate, abate, lessen, allay, assuage, soften, tone down, qualify. **2** toughen, harden, strengthen.

temperament *noun* character, personality, nature, disposition, make-up, temper, frame of mind, mindset, attitude, mettle.

temperamental *adj* **1** excitable, emotional, fiery, passionate, volatile, mercurial, highly-strung, sensitive, moody, irritable, explosive, touchy. **2** erratic, unpredictable, unreliable, inconsistent.

temperance *noun* teetotalism, abstinence, abstemiousness, sobriety.

temperate *adj* **1** mild, moderate, clement, cool, pleasant. **2** moderate, controlled, self-controlled, restrained, self-denying, abstinent, abstemious, sober, teetotal.

tempest *noun* storm, squall, hurricane, tornado, typhoon, gale.

tempestuous *adj* **1** stormy, squally, windy, blustery. **2** stormy, turbulent, tumultuous, violent, wild, rough, intense, fierce, passionate, impassioned.

temple *noun* shrine, sanctuary, church, mosque, pagoda.

tempo *noun* **1** rhythm, beat, time. **2** pace, rate, velocity, speed.

temporal *adj* **1** secular, lay. **2** earthly, worldly, mortal, passing, transient, transitory.

temporary *adj* impermanent, passing, transient, transitory, fleeting, brief, short, short-lived, provisional, makeshift, stop-gap, short-term.

temporize *verb* delay, procrastinate, hedge, hum and haw, equivocate, play for time, stall.

tempt *verb* **1** allure, attract, entice, draw, tantalize, invite. **2** persuade, coax, cajole, entice, incite, urge, provoke, influence.

temptation *noun* attraction, appeal, lure, draw, pull, inducement, enticement, come-on (*inf*), bait.

tempting *adj* attractive, alluring, inviting, enticing, appealing, seductive, tantalizing, mouth-watering, appetizing.

tenable *adj* sound, rational, reasonable, viable, plausible, arguable, defensible.

tenacious *adj* **1** tight, firm, secure, strong, iron, powerful, unshakeable. **2** stubborn, obstinate, dogged, persistent, determined, strong-willed, single-minded, set, firm, unyielding. **3** sticky, clinging, adhesive.

tenancy *noun* occupation, occupancy, lease, tenure, incumbency.

tenant *noun* lodger, renter, lessee, lease-holder, occupant, occupier, resident.

tend[1] *verb* **1** incline, lean, be inclined, be disposed. **2** go, move, head, gravitate.

tend[2] *verb* **1** care for, take care of, look after, watch over, keep an eye on, mind, protect, guard. **2** attend to, see to, minister to, wait on, nurse, treat.

tendency *noun* **1** leaning, inclination, disposition, predisposition, propensity, proclivity. **2** trend, movement, drift, gravitation.

tender[1] *adj* **1** soft, delicate, fragile, breakable. **2** gentle, kind, kindly, humane, merciful, compassionate, sympathetic, caring, considerate, soft-hearted. **3** warm, affectionate, loving, fond, romantic. **4** young, youthful, early, susceptible, vulnerable. **5** sore, painful, raw, sensitive, red, inflamed, smarting, bruised. **6** succulent, soft, juicy.

tender[2] *verb* proffer, offer, present, extend, give, propose, put forward, submit.
➤*noun* offer, bid, estimate, quotation, proposal, proposition.

tenet *noun* dogma, doctrine, principle, precept, rule, belief, conviction, teaching.

tenor *noun* **1** meaning, purport, sense, essence, substance, gist, drift. **2** course, direction, trend.

tense *adj* **1** tight, taut, rigid, stretched. **2** nervous, keyed up, on tenterhooks, jumpy, edgy, on edge, anxious, worried, apprehensive, jittery, uneasy, wound up (*inf*), uptight (*inf*), strung up (*inf*). **3** stressful, nerve-racking, nail-biting, fraught, worrying, strained, exciting.
➤*verb* brace, tighten, strain, stiffen.

tension *noun* **1** tightness, tautness, rigidity, strain, stress. **2** apprehension, stress, strain, nervousness, apprehensiveness, jumpiness, nerves (*inf*), anxiety, distress, worry, uneasiness, edginess. **3** suspense, excitement. **4** strain, antagonism, hostility, ill feeling, friction, conflict, opposition.

tentative *adj* **1** experimental, exploratory, trial, test, pilot, unproven, unconfirmed, provisional. **2** hesitant, cautious, uncertain, undecided, diffident, timid.

tenuous *adj* **1** flimsy, shaky, insubstantial, slight, weak, doubtful, questionable, hazy, nebulous, vague. **2** slender, slim, thin, fine.

tenure *noun* holding, possession, occupancy, tenancy, incumbency, term.

tepid *adj* **1** lukewarm, warm, cool. **2** cool, lukewarm, half-hearted, unenthusiastic.

term *noun* **1** name, designation, word, phrase, expression, epithet. **2** phrases, words, expressions, language, terminology, phraseology. **3** conditions, clauses, provisions, stipulations, specifications, particulars, details, prices, charges, rates. **4** time, period, spell, span, duration, season, session. **5** end, conclusion, limit, finish, period, culmination, close.
➤*verb* call, name, designate, denominate, style, label, tag, entitle.
come to terms accept, learn to live, reconcile oneself, resign oneself.
in terms of as regards, with regard to, regarding, in respect of, in relation to.

terminal *adj* **1** incurable, fatal, lethal, deadly. **2** boundary, bounding, limiting, concluding, last, final.
➤*noun* **1** workstation, console, monitor, keyboard. **2** depot, terminus.

terminate *verb* **1** end, conclude, complete, finish, close, stop, discontinue, wind up. **2** end, conclude, expire, lapse, run out.

terminology *noun* phraseology, vocabulary, language, terms, jargon.

terminus *noun* terminal, depot, end of the line.

terrestrial *adj* earthly, worldly, mundane, temporal.

terrible *adj* **1** extreme, great, severe, terrific, intense. **2** awful, appalling, dreadful, frightful, fearful, frightening, terrifying, horrifying, horrific, shocking, horrible, hideous, gruesome, harrowing. **3** awful, dreadful, frightful (*inf*), abominable, bad, foul, obnoxious, vile, nasty, unpleasant, repulsive, revolting, horrid, horrible. **4** awful, dreadful, bad, poor, dire, rotten (*inf*), useless (*inf*), crap (*sl*). **5** awful, dreadful, bad, rotten (*inf*).

terribly *adv* very, extremely, exceedingly, desperately, seriously, terrifically (*inf*), awfully (*inf*), dreadfully (*inf*), frightfully (*inf*).

terrific *adj* **1** great, huge, gigantic, intense, enormous, tremendous. **2** great, excellent, superb, outstanding, marvellous, sensational, tremendous, wonderful, amazing, brilliant, fantastic (*inf*), fabulous (*inf*), wicked (*inf*).

terrify *verb* frighten, scare, scare stiff, shock, appal, panic, dismay, petrify, put the wind up (*inf*).

territory *noun* **1** country, province, state, land. **2** area, region, tract, zone, district. **3** area, field, province, department, preserve. **4** area, patch, beat.

terror noun 1 fear, fright, horror, dread, awe, panic, alarm, consternation. 2 rascal, rogue, horror, monster, hooligan, tearaway. 3 monster, horror, devil, bogeyman.

terrorize verb frighten, terrify, petrify, scare, intimidate, oppress, threaten, menace, bully, browbeat, victimize.

terse adj 1 concise, succinct, pithy, incisive, brief, short, laconic. 2 curt, abrupt, brusque, short, blunt, snappy.

test verb 1 put to the test, try, try out, trial, sample, check, examine, analyse, assess, appraise, evaluate. 2 try, tax, strain, stretch, drain, exhaust, sap.
➤noun 1 trial, try, try-out, check, checkup, assessment, evaluation, appraisal, inspection, analysis. 2 examination, exam, quiz, exercise. 3 criterion, yardstick, standard, measure, touchstone.

testament noun testimony, evidence, proof, witness, tribute, demonstration.

testify verb 1 give evidence, bear witness, swear, depose, certify, assert, affirm, attest. 2 bear out, prove, corroborate, confirm, show, demonstrate.

testimonial noun 1 recommendation, reference, character. 2 tribute, gift, presentation.

testimony noun 1 evidence, statement, deposition, affidavit, declaration, submission. 2 demonstration, proof, evidence, confirmation.

testy adj irritable, quick-tempered, touchy, tetchy, crotchety (inf), peevish, snappy, grumpy, grouchy, cantankerous, crabby, cross, crusty, ratty (inf), stroppy (inf).

tether noun rope, chain, cord, leash, restraint.
➤verb tie, tie up, bind, fasten, secure, chain, restrain.

text noun 1 contents, matter, words, wording. 2 passage, verse, chapter. 3 set book, textbook.

texture noun 1 surface, feel, grain, weave, consistency. 2 character, structure, composition.

thank verb give thanks, acknowledge, recognize, credit.

thankful adj 1 grateful, appreciative, obliged, indebted, beholden. 2 pleased, glad, relieved.

thankless adj 1 ungrateful, unappreciative. 2 unappreciated, unrewarding, unprofitable. 3 vain, useless.

thanks pl noun 1 gratitude, gratefulness, appreciation, acknowledgment, recognition. 2 thank you, many thanks, much obliged, ta (inf).
thanks to because of, as a result of, on account of, owing to, due to.

thaw verb 1 melt, liquefy, defrost, unfreeze. 2 relax, loosen up.

theatre noun 1 playhouse, auditorium, hall. 2 show business, the stage, drama, the boards (inf).

theatrical adj 1 dramatic, stage, thespian. 2 affected, artificial, mannered, stilted. 3 exaggerated, stagy, melodramatic, histrionic, hammy (inf).

theft noun stealing, thieving, pilfering, robbery, burglary, larceny, embezzlement, misappropriation, shoplifting.

theme noun 1 subject, topic, argument, gist, essence, idea, thread, keynote. 2 motif, leitmotif, melody, tune.

then adv 1 at that time, at that point, at that moment, on that occasion, in those days. 2 next, after that, afterwards, subsequently, later. 3 in addition, additionally, also, as well, too, besides, moreover. 4 that being so, in that case, under those circumstances. 5 therefore, thus, accordingly, consequently.

theoretical adj 1 abstract, conceptual. 2 speculative, suppositional, notional. 3 hypothetical, conjectural, presumed, academic.

theorize verb hypothesize, conjecture, speculate, propound, suppose.

theory noun 1 hypothesis, postulation. 2 conjecture, speculation, assumption, supposition, notion, surmise, guess.

therapeutic adj curative, healing, medicinal, restorative, health-giving, beneficial, salutary.

therapy noun treatment, remedy, cure, healing.

thereabouts adv 1 near there, around there, roundabout. 2 approximately, roughly.

thereafter adv after that, afterwards, subsequently.

therefore *adv* consequently, as a result, hence, then, so, thus, ergo.

thesaurus *noun* dictionary, lexicon, vocabulary.

thesis *noun* **1** dissertation, treatise, disquisition, paper. **2** theory, hypothesis, idea, supposition. **3** proposition, argument, subject, theme, topic.

thick *adj* **1** wide, broad, deep, large, bulky, solid, substantial. **2** dense, crowded, packed, bristling, teeming, swarming, bursting, stiff, impenetrable, impassable. **3** viscous, glutinous, gelatinous, clotted. **4** dense, heavy, impenetrable, opaque. **5** abundant, plentiful, numerous. **6** stupid, unintelligent, slow, dull, obtuse, dumb (*inf*), dense (*inf*), dim (*inf*). **7** throaty, hoarse, indistinct, muffled, unclear, inarticulate. **8** pronounced, marked, broad, strong, obvious. **9** friendly, close, intimate, matey (*inf*), pally (*inf*).

thicken *verb* **1** set, solidify, congeal, gel, jell, stiffen, cake, clot. **2** deepen, intensify.

thicket *noun* coppice, copse, brake.

thickness *noun* **1** width, depth, breadth, density, diameter. **2** layer, stratum, sheet, lamina, ply.

thickset *adj* heavily built, well-built, heavy, burly, sturdy, stocky.

thick-skinned *adj* **1** insensitive, unfeeling, callous, hard-boiled. **2** impervious, invulnerable, inured.

thief *noun* robber, burglar, pilferer, housebreaker, shoplifter, pickpocket, mugger, swindler, embezzler, crook (*inf*).

thieve *verb* steal, rob, make off with, pilfer, filch, shoplift, misappropriate, nick (*inf*), pinch (*inf*), swipe (*inf*).

thin *adj* **1** narrow, fine, attenuated. **2** slim, slender, lean, slight, svelte, spare, skinny, scraggy, scrawny, lanky, emaciated, undernourished, anorexic, bony, skeletal, spindly. **3** sparse, scattered, scarce, scanty. **4** delicate, fine, gossamer, light, sheer, diaphanous, gauzy, filmy. **5** watery, diluted, dilute, weak, wishy-washy (*inf*), runny. **6** weak, quiet, small, feeble, faint. **7** poor, inadequate, weak, feeble, lame, flimsy, unconvincing. **8** few, sparse, scanty, deficient, meagre.

➤*verb* water, water down, dilute, weaken, reduce, decrease, diminish, prune, trim, weed out.

thing *noun* **1** object, article, item, entity. **2** deed, act, action, feat, exploit. **3** idea, notion, thought, theory. **4** event, occurrence, happening, episode, incident, phenomenon. **5** something, thingummy (*inf*), thingamabob (*inf*), thingamajig (*inf*), whatsit (*inf*). **6** creature, wretch, soul. **7** fashion, trend, style. **8** belongings, possessions, goods, effects, luggage, baggage, paraphernalia, stuff (*inf*), bits and bobs (*inf*), clothes, clothing, gear (*inf*), clobber (*inf*), togs (*inf*). **9** circumstance, matter, affair, situation. **10** equipment, apparatus, implements, tools, gear, tackle.

think *verb* **1** believe, suppose, expect, anticipate, foresee, imagine, surmise, fancy, guess, presume. **2** consider, judge, deem, regard, reckon. **3** ponder, meditate, reason, reflect, muse, brood, cerebrate, cogitate, ruminate, weigh up, mull over, review, contemplate, consider. **4** ponder, meditate, contemplate, consider, imagine, picture, visualize, envisage. **5** contemplate, reflect upon, consider, weigh up, meditate, ponder, chew over, mull over. **6** devise, contrive, invent, create, dream up, imagine, concoct, come up with. **7** consider, believe, reckon.
think better of reconsider, think twice about, rethink, have second thoughts about, decide against, change one's mind about.
think nothing of consider routine, take in one's stride, dismiss.

thinking *noun* thought, opinion, view, assessment, appraisal, evaluation.
➤*adj* rational, reasoning, sensible, intelligent, intellectual, cultured, sophisticated, thoughtful.

thin-skinned *adj* touchy, temperamental, vulnerable, sensitive, oversensitive, hypersensitive.

third-rate *adj* inferior, poor, poor-quality, low-quality, low-grade, mediocre, bad, awful.

thirst *noun* **1** thirstiness, dryness, dehydration. **2** craving, desire, lust, hunger, yearning, longing, yen (*inf*).
➤*verb* crave, desire, hunger, yearn, long, hanker.

thirsty adj **1** dry, dehydrated, parched (inf), gasping (inf). **2** eager, avid, longing, hungry, covetous.

thorn noun prickle, spine, barb.

thorny adj **1** prickly, spiny, barbed, spiky. **2** problematic, difficult, hard, tricky, complicated, knotty, tough, controversial, awkward, delicate, ticklish.

thorough adj **1** exhaustive, extensive, intensive, in-depth, detailed, comprehensive, full, complete, sweeping, meticulous, painstaking, methodical, scrupulous, careful, conscientious. **2** complete, total, downright, out-and-out, unmitigated, unqualified, absolute, pure, sheer, utter.

thoroughbred adj pedigree, pure-bred, pure-blooded, full-blooded.

thoroughfare noun road, street, highway, way, path, access, passage.

though conj although, albeit, while, despite the fact that, even if, admitting, granting.
➤adv nevertheless, nonetheless, even so, still, yet, however, all the same.

thought noun **1** idea, concept, conception, fancy, notion, opinion, view, sentiment, belief, plan, aim, intention, purpose. **2** thinking, reasoning, brainwork, cerebration, reflection, cogitation, meditation, contemplation, consideration, deliberation, rumination. **3** hope, expectation, anticipation, prospect. **4** attention, heed, consideration, thoughtfulness, care, regard, concern.

thoughtful adj **1** considerate, caring, kind, concerned, attentive, solicitous, helpful. **2** pensive, absorbed, abstracted, rapt, lost in thought, reflective, ruminative, contemplative, meditative, introspective. **3** serious, deep, profound, considered.

thoughtless adj **1** inconsiderate, unkind, insensitive, careless, uncaring, tactless, undiplomatic, indiscreet, selfish, remiss. **2** unthinking, mindless, careless, negligent, rash, reckless, foolish, imprudent, unwise, injudicious, ill-advised.

thrash verb **1** beat, whip, horsewhip, flog, lash, cane, birch, belt (inf), tan (inf), wallop (inf). **2** defeat, beat, crush, trounce, clobber (inf), hammer (inf), slaughter (inf). **3** thresh, flail, jerk, writhe, squirm.

thrash out verb discuss, debate, negotiate, hammer out, settle, resolve.

thread noun **1** yarn, cotton, fibre, filament, strand. **2** theme, motif, plot, story line, train of thought.
➤verb pass, ease, move, weave, wind.

threadbare adj worn, worn-out, ragged, holey, frayed, tatty (inf), tattered, scruffy, shabby, moth-eaten, old, thin.

threat noun **1** warning, menace, caution, ultimatum. **2** warning, omen, foreboding, portent. **3** danger, peril, hazard, risk, menace.

threaten verb **1** intimidate, menace, bully, browbeat, pressurize, terrorize, warn, caution, lean on (inf). **2** impend, loom, foreshadow, portend, forebode, augur. **3** menace, endanger, jeopardize, imperil, put at risk.

threesome noun trio, triumvirate, triad, trinity, trilogy, troika.

threshold noun **1** door, doorstep, doorway, entrance. **2** start, beginning, outset, opening, brink, verge, dawn.

thrift noun economy, frugality, thriftiness, husbandry, conservation, saving, carefulness, sparingness, prudence, parsimony.

thrifty adj economical, frugal, provident, prudent, careful, sparing, parsimonious.

thrill noun **1** excitement, stimulation, titillation, sensation, tingle, kick (inf), buzz (inf). **2** tremor, frisson, quiver, flutter, shudder, vibration, throb.
➤verb excite, exhilarate, stimulate, electrify, move, stir, arouse, titillate, agitate.

thrive verb **1** prosper, succeed, do well, make good, get on, flourish. **2** grow, flourish, bloom, blossom.

throat noun gullet, oesophagus, windpipe, craw.

throb verb beat, pulsate, pulse, palpitate, pound, thump, drum.
➤noun beat, beating, pulse, pulsation, palpitation, vibration.

throe noun **1** pang, pain, agony, anguish, suffering, torture, distress. **2** upheaval, turmoil, disruption, chaos, confusion.

throng *noun* crowd, multitude, mob, horde, host, mass, gathering, congregation, swarm.
➤*verb* crowd, flock, swarm, pack, cram, jam, fill.

throttle *verb* strangle, choke, suffocate, smother, stifle, asphyxiate.

through *prep* **1** across, from one end to the other. **2** because of, on account of, owing to, as a result of, due to, thanks to. **3** by, by virtue of, via, by means of. **4** during, throughout.
➤*adj* finished, done, completed, ended, fed up, tired of.
through and through completely, utterly, thoroughly, totally, altogether.

throughout *prep* **1** all over, in every part of, everywhere in. **2** through, all through, during the whole of.
➤*adv* **1** right through, all through, all over, everywhere, in every part. **2** all the time, until the end, from start to finish.

throw *verb* **1** cast, fling, toss, hurl, sling, pitch, lob, heave (*inf*), chuck (*inf*) , shy, launch. **2** catapult, propel, send, fling, hurl. **3** cast, shed, project, send. **4** floor, fell, bring down. **5** unseat, unsaddle, unhorse. **6** disconcert, disturb, put out, confuse, baffle, perplex, surprise, astonish, dumbfound, floor (*inf*). **7** put, move, operate. **8** organize, put on, give, lay on, host. **9** put, commit, exert.
➤*noun* cast, fling, toss, pitch, shy, heave (*inf*).

throw away *verb* **1** throw out, discard, dispense with, get rid of, scrap, dump, ditch (*inf*). **2** waste, squander, fritter away, blow (*inf*).

throw out *verb* **1** expel, eject, evict, kick out (*inf*), turf out (*inf*). **2** throw away, discard, dispose of, get rid of, scrap, dump, ditch (*inf*). **3** dismiss, reject, turn down.

thrust *verb* **1** push, shove, drive, ram, propel, poke, jab, lunge. **2** impose, force, press, inflict, foist. **3** push, shove, force, shoulder, elbow.
➤*noun* **1** push, shove, poke, prod. **2** drive, force, pressure, impetus, momentum. **3** lunge, stab, jab, poke, prod. **4** attack, assault, offensive, raid, incursion, drive, advance, push. **5** gist, drift, substance, point, essence, tenor.

thud *verb* thump, bang, wallop (*inf*), knock, smack, crash, clonk, clunk.

thug *noun* ruffian, hooligan, tough, rough, roughneck, heavy (*inf*), gangster, hoodlum, bandit, robber, murderer, mugger.

thumb *verb* leaf through, skim, browse, flick through, flip through, peruse, scan, glance at.

thump *verb* **1** hit, strike, knock, bang, crash. **2** slap, punch, smack, pummel, thrash, wallop (*inf*), whack (*inf*), clout (*inf*). **3** beat, pound, thud, throb.
➤*noun* blow, punch, slap, smack, knock, bang, thud, wallop (*inf*), whack (*inf*), clout (*inf*).

thunder *verb* **1** resound, reverberate, rumble, roll, boom, crash. **2** roar, bellow, bark, shout.
➤*noun* reverberation, rumble, roll, boom, roar, crash, bang, blast, crack, clap, peal.

thunderous *adj* booming, resounding, reverberating, deafening, loud, noisy, ear-splitting.

thunderstruck *adj* stunned, startled, shocked, staggered, amazed, astonished, astounded, dazed, dumbfounded, disconcerted, flabbergasted (*inf*), bowled over (*inf*), knocked for six (*inf*), gobsmacked (*inf*).

thus *adv* **1** so, in this way, like this, as follows. **2** therefore, consequently, accordingly, so, hence, ergo.

thwart *verb* frustrate, balk, foil, block, stop, cross, hinder, hamper, impede, prevent, stymie.

tic *noun* twitch, spasm, jerk.

tick *noun* **1** tick-tock, ticking, click, tap, beat. **2** moment, instant, minute, sec (*inf*), second, flash, trice, jiffy (*inf*). **3** stroke, mark, line.
➤*verb* **1** tick-tock, click, tap, beat. **2** mark, check, indicate.
tick off tell off (*inf*), scold, reprimand, reproach, reprove, rebuke, lecture, censure, take to task.

ticket *noun* **1** pass, token, certificate, coupon, voucher. **2** slip, label, tag, sticker.

tickle *verb* **1** stroke, pet, touch. **2** delight, amuse, gratify, please, thrill, excite.

ticklish *adj* sensitive, delicate, awkward, tricky, difficult, problematic, thorny.

tide *noun* **1** ebb, flow, stream. **2** current, drift, trend, tendency.
tide over help out, keep going, see through.

tidings *pl noun* news, word, information, report.

tidy *adj* **1** neat, orderly, well-ordered, well-kept, uncluttered, spruce, shipshape. **2** neat, orderly, well-organized, organized, efficient, methodical, businesslike. **3** considerable, sizeable, good, largish, substantial, respectable, healthy.
➤*verb* neaten, straighten, straighten up, smarten, spruce up, arrange, put in order, clear up, clean up.

tie *verb* **1** bind, truss, knot, fasten, join, connect, unite, link, attach, fix, secure, tether, lash. **2** restrict, confine, limit, constrain, cramp, shackle, hinder, hamper.
➤*noun* **1** bond, link, tape, fastening, fastener, connection, union, friendship, relationship. **2** draw, dead heat, stalemate.
tie up 1 tether, secure, truss, bind, moor, rope, attach, fasten, connect. **2** occupy, engage, keep busy. **3** conclude, complete, finish, finalize, wrap up.

tier *noun* **1** row, rank, line, bank. **2** layer, level, rank, echelon.

tiff *noun* quarrel, row, squabble, words, argument, falling-out (*inf*), spat (*inf*).

tight *adj* **1** fixed, fast, secure. **2** taut, stretched, tense, rigid. **3** tight-fitting, close-fitting, figure-hugging, skin-tight, snug. **4** compact, compressed, cramped, restricted, constricted, limited. **5** mean, miserly, stingy, niggardly, tightfisted (*inf*), parsimonious, penny-pinching. **6** short, limited, sparse, inadequate, insufficient, in short supply. **7** strict, rigorous, exacting, inflexible, rigid, stringent, tough. **8** close, even, well-matched, hard-fought. **9** drunk, intoxicated, tipsy (*inf*), tiddly (*inf*), blotto (*inf*), sloshed (*inf*), plastered (*inf*), smashed (*inf*), legless (*inf*), sozzled (*inf*), pissed (*sl*).

tighten *verb* stiffen, tense, tauten, secure, screw down, narrow, constrict, cramp.

till[1] *prep* until, up to, to, before.

till[2] *verb* farm, cultivate, work, plough.

tilt *verb* slope, slant, incline, lean, tip.
➤*noun* **1** slope, slant, incline, angle. **2** joust, tournament, tourney, lists.

at full tilt at full speed, at top speed, full pelt, all out, flat out.

timber *noun* wood, plank, board, beam.

timbre *noun* tone, tonality, tone colour, tone quality.

time *noun* **1** duration, period, span, space, spell, while. **2** period, era, epoch, age. **3** occasion, instance. **4** point, juncture, moment, instant, hour. **5** tempo, beat, rhythm.
➤*verb* **1** count, measure, clock. **2** set, fix, arrange, schedule, timetable, programme.
behind the times old-fashioned, out of date, dated, outmoded, passé, antiquated, fuddy-duddy (*inf*), old hat (*inf*).
for the time being for now, at the moment, for the present, at present, temporarily, in the meantime, meanwhile.
in time in good time, punctually, early enough, on schedule.
on time punctually, promptly, on the dot, spot on (*inf*), early enough.

timeless *adj* **1** ageless, immortal, undying, deathless, enduring, lasting, imperishable. **2** eternal, everlasting, endless.

timely *adj* opportune, seasonable, well-timed, punctual, at the right time, convenient.

timetable *noun* schedule, programme, calendar, agenda, curriculum.
➤*verb* schedule, programme, set, arrange.

timid *adj* timorous, shy, bashful, coy, nervous, diffident, retiring, shrinking, unself-confident, fearful, frightened, scared, afraid, fainthearted, apprehensive, irresolute.

timorous *adj* timid, fearful, scared, frightened, afraid, apprehensive, cowardly, trembling, nervous, shrinking, irresolute, shy, diffident.

tinge *noun* **1** tint, tincture, shade, hue, tone, stain, wash, dye, colour. **2** touch, trace, hint, suggestion, soupçon.
➤*verb* **1** tint, colour, shade, suffuse, dye, stain. **2** imbue, flavour.

tingle *verb* prickle, smart, itch, tickle, tremble, quiver, thrill.
➤*noun* tingling, prickling, tickle, quiver, thrill, trembling, goosepimples, pins and needles (*inf*).

tinker *verb* fiddle, play, toy, dabble, meddle, tamper, fool about, mess about.

tinkle *verb* jingle, jangle, ring, chime, clink.
➤*noun* **1** ring, jingle, jangle, chime, clink. **2** call, phone (*inf*), ring (*inf*), buzz (*inf*), bell (*inf*).

tint *noun* **1** colour, hue, shade, tone, tinge. **2** dye, stain, rinse, wash, colourant.
➤*verb* colour, stain, dye, tinge, streak.

tiny *adj* minute, minuscule, infinitesimal, microscopic, miniature, diminutive, small, little, wee, teeny (*inf*), teeny-weeny (*inf*), itsy-bitsy (*inf*), insignificant, trifling, negligible.

tip[1] *noun* point, head, top, end, extremity.
➤*verb* cap, crown, top, surmount.

tip[2] *verb* **1** tilt, incline, lean, list. **2** upset, upend, overturn, capsize. **3** empty, pour, spill, dump, unload.
➤*noun* rubbish dump, dump, rubbish heap.

tip[3] *noun* gratuity, baksheesh, bonus, reward.
➤*verb* reward, remunerate.

tip[4] *noun* hint, suggestion, recommendation, clue, pointer, forecast, advice, information.
➤*verb* recommend, predict, back.

tip off *verb* warn, forewarn, advise, tell, inform.

tip-off *noun* warning, hint, lead, clue, pointer, information, notification.

tipple *verb* drink, imbibe, booze (*inf*), indulge (*inf*).
➤*noun* drink, alcohol, liquor, poison (*inf*).

tipsy *adj* drunk, intoxicated, tight (*inf*), squiffy (*inf*), tiddly (*inf*), happy (*inf*), merry (*inf*), mellow (*inf*).

tirade *noun* diatribe, harangue, rant, lecture, denunciation, fulmination, philippic.

tire *verb* **1** weary, wear out, fatigue, exhaust, drain, flag, droop, weaken. **2** get bored with, get fed up with (*inf*), weary.

tired *adj* **1** weary, wearied, fatigued, exhausted, drained, worn out, jaded, fagged out (*inf*), done in (*inf*), dead beat (*inf*), dog-tired (*inf*), knackered (*inf*), shattered (*inf*), all in (*inf*), whacked (*inf*), bushed (*inf*), pooped (*inf*). **2** weary, bored,

sick, fed up (*inf*), irritated, exasperated, annoyed. **3** corny (*inf*), clichéd, stale, hackneyed, trite, banal.

tireless *adj* untiring, unwearied, unflagging, indefatigable, diligent, dogged, determined, resolute.

tiresome *adj* wearisome, wearing, boring, tedious, monotonous, annoying, irritating, irksome, exasperating, trying.

tissue *noun* **1** gauze, gossamer. **2** mesh, net, network, web. **3** paper handkerchief, paper hankie, disposable handkerchief, Kleenex.

titanic *adj* huge, gigantic, giant, colossal, enormous, massive, mighty, monumental, herculean, stupendous.

titbit *noun* morsel, treat, snack, delicacy, dainty, goody (*inf*).

titillate *verb* tickle, excite, thrill, arouse, turn on (*inf*), tease, tantalize, fascinate, intrigue, please.

titivate *verb* groom, smarten, spruce up, doll up (*inf*), tart up (*inf*), do up (*inf*), touch up, refurbish.

title *noun* **1** name, form of address, appellation, sobriquet, rank, position, status. **2** name, heading. **3** claim, right, entitlement, ownership, possession, proprietorship. **4** championship, trophy, prize.
➤*verb* name, call, style, designate, label.

titter *noun* snigger, snicker, chuckle, chortle, giggle.

titular *adj* nominal, token, in name only.

toast *verb* drink to, drink the health of, pledge.
➤*noun* **1** health, pledge. **2** hero, heroine, darling, favourite.

today *noun* **1** this day, this very day. **2** now, nowadays, these days.

toddle *verb* **1** totter, stagger, waddle, wobble, teeter, walk. **2** stroll, saunter, go, amble.

together *adv* **1** collectively, jointly, side by side, shoulder to shoulder, in concert, in conjunction, as a team. **2** as one, at the same time, simultaneously, in unison. **3** in a row, on the trot (*inf*), consecutively, in succession, one after the other, without a break.
➤*adj* composed, calm, cool, level-headed,

down-to-earth, sensible, stable, well-adjusted, well-organized, organized, efficient.

toil *verb* **1** work, labour, slog, grind, graft, drudge, slave, persevere. **2** labour, struggle.
➤*noun* hard work, donkeywork (*inf*), labour, slog, grind, graft, drudgery, slaving, effort.

toilet *noun* **1** lavatory, latrine, urinal, water closet, WC, privy, loo (*inf*). **2** lavatory, latrine, urinal, bathroom, washroom, powder room, cloakroom, public convenience, ladies, gents, loo (*inf*).

toilsome *adj* laborious, arduous, hard, strenuous, exhausting, backbreaking.

token *noun* **1** symbol, sign, emblem, badge, mark, indication, proof. **2** reminder, remembrance, keepsake, souvenir, memento. **3** voucher, coupon.
➤*adj* nominal, minimal, perfunctory, cosmetic.

tolerable *adj* **1** bearable, endurable, supportable. **2** passable, adequate, reasonable, fair, all right, OK (*inf*), not bad (*inf*).

tolerance *noun* **1** toleration, understanding, indulgence, permissiveness, forbearance, open-mindedness, broad-mindedness. **2** toleration, resistance, resilience.

tolerant *adj* broad-minded, open-minded, liberal, unprejudiced, unbiased, patient, forbearing, charitable, sympathetic, understanding, indulgent, permissive, easy-going.

tolerate *verb* endure, bear, take, stand, accept, put up with, stomach, permit, allow, countenance, condone.

toll[1] *verb* ring, knell, chime.

toll[2] *noun* **1** levy, tax, duty, charge. **2** loss, cost, damage.

tomb *noun* **1** vault, sepulchre, mausoleum. **2** grave.

tombstone *noun* gravestone, headstone, monument.

tome *noun* volume, book, work.

tomfoolery *noun* antics, pranks, tricks, monkey tricks (*inf*), mischief, horseplay, childishness, foolishness, silliness, nonsense.

tone *noun* **1** sound, noise, note. **2** intonation, inflection, accent, timbre, expression. **3** cast, tinge, tint, shade, hue. **4** tenor, quality, character, feel, spirit, mood, style, manner. **5** quality, style.
➤*verb* harmonize, blend, go, coordinate, match.

tone down moderate, play down, temper, restrain, soften, soft-pedal (*inf*).

tongue *noun* language, lingo (*inf*), dialect, idiom, speech.

tonic *noun* **1** stimulant, cordial, restorative, pick-me-up (*inf*). **2** boost, shot in the arm (*inf*), fillip.

too *adv* **1** also, as well, in addition, besides, likewise. **2** excessively, inordinately, unreasonably, unduly, over, overly.

tool *noun* **1** implement, instrument, gadget, gizmo (*inf*), device, contraption, contrivance, aid. **2** agent, pawn, creature, dupe, lackey, stooge, cat's-paw.
➤*verb* work, machine, shape, decorate, chase.

toothsome *adj* **1** tasty, appetizing, delicious, mouth-watering, luscious, tempting, scrumptious (*inf*), yummy (*inf*). **2** attractive, tasty (*inf*).

top *noun* **1** summit, peak, pinnacle, tip, crest, apex. **2** height, peak, pinnacle, high point, acme, zenith. **3** cap, lid, cover, stopper. **4** sweater, jumper, jersey, sweatshirt, shirt, blouse.
➤*adj* **1** highest, uppermost, upper. **2** best, finest, supreme, choicest, maximum, greatest, utmost. **3** principal, chief, main, leading, foremost, pre-eminent.
➤*verb* **1** cap, crown, tip, cover. **2** garnish, decorate, finish. **3** exceed, transcend, surpass, excel, outdo, outstrip, beat, better, best. **4** head, lead.

over the top excessive, immoderate, disproportionate, a bit much (*inf*), exaggerated, histrionic, hammy (*inf*), uncalled-for, unreasonable, OTT (*inf*).

topic *noun* subject, subject matter, theme, issue, question.

topical *adj* current, recent, up-to-date, up-to-the-minute, newsworthy.

topmost *adj* top, uppermost, upper, highest, loftiest.

topple *verb* **1** totter, overturn, overbalance, tip over, fall over, keel over, collapse.

2 upset, tip over, knock over, overthrow, overturn, bring down.

topsy-turvy *adj* **1** upside down, inverted, inside out. **2** in disorder, in chaos, confused, in a mess, muddled, untidy, disorganized, in disarray.

torment *noun* **1** agony, pain, anguish, distress, torture, hell. **2** plague, scourge, curse, bane, vexation, affliction, torture, trouble, pest, thorn in the flesh.
➤*verb* **1** torture, agonize, rack, pain, distress. **2** pester, bother, harass, harry, afflict, plague, badger, bedevil, persecute, tease.

torn *adj* ripped, split, slit, ragged, tattered.

tornado *noun* cyclone, hurricane, typhoon, whirlwind, twister (*inf*).

torpid *adj* **1** sluggish, slow, slow-moving, lethargic, languid, dull, heavy, listless, apathetic, passive, lazy, stagnant, inactive, inert, lifeless. **2** dormant, sleepy.

torpor *noun* sluggishness, lethargy, indolence, laziness, drowsiness, somnolence, sleepiness, languor, listlessness, apathy, passivity, dullness, heaviness, inactivity, stagnation, inertia.

torrent *noun* **1** flood, deluge, stream, spate, rush. **2** shower, deluge, outburst, outpouring, flood, gush, barrage, volley, storm.

torrid *adj* **1** hot, scorching, boiling, blistering, roasting, sizzling, blazing, burning. **2** parched, scorched, arid, dry, waterless. **3** passionate, ardent, sizzling (*inf*), steamy (*inf*).

tortuous *adj* **1** twisting, winding, sinuous, serpentine, zigzag, meandering, labyrinthine. **2** involved, convoluted, complicated, indirect, circuitous, roundabout.

torture *verb* persecute, torment, abuse, ill-treat, pain, distress, agonize, anguish, rack, crucify, afflict, plague.
➤*noun* **1** persecution, abuse, ill-treatment, mistreatment, punishment, pain, torment, the rack. **2** torment, agony, anguish, suffering, pain.

toss *verb* **1** throw, pitch, fling, chuck (*inf*), sling, lob, shy, flip, flick. **2** roll, rock, pitch, sway, heave, thrash, squirm, wriggle. **3** jerk, shake, throw back.
➤*noun* throw, chuck (*inf*), fling, flip.

tot *noun* **1** infant, toddler, child, baby, mite. **2** nip, dram, slug, shot (*inf*).
➤*verb* add up, count, total, reckon, calculate.

total *noun* sum, totality, entirety, whole, aggregate.
➤*adj* **1** complete, entire, full, whole, combined, aggregate. **2** complete, absolute, utter, sheer, out-and-out, downright, unqualified, unmitigated.
➤*verb* **1** reach, make, add up to, amount to, come to. **2** add up, count up, tot up.

totalitarian *adj* autocratic, authoritarian, dictatorial, undemocratic, one-party.

totality *noun* total, sum, whole, entirety, aggregate.

totter *verb* **1** stagger, stumble, reel, sway, rock, lurch. **2** tremble, quiver, shake, teeter, sway.

touch *verb* **1** feel, finger, handle, hold, fondle, caress, stroke, brush. **2** pick up, move, fiddle with, interfere with. **3** pat, tap, knock, nudge, prod, poke. **4** meet, contact, abut, adjoin. **5** affect, move, get to (*inf*), stir, soften, melt. **6** match, equal, rival, come close to, compare with, hold a candle to. **7** handle, deal with, associate oneself, use, accept, eat, drink, partake of. **8** deal with, cover, refer to, mention, allude to, broach. **9** relate to, concern, regard.
➤*noun* **1** caress, stroke, brush, pat, tap. **2** feel, feeling, tactility. **3** feel, surface, texture. **4** trace, hint, suggestion, suspicion, whiff, dash, drop, bit. **5** contact, communication, correspondence. **6** technique, method, approach, style, manner, skill, knack, flair, talent, expertise, ability, facility, dexterity, sensitivity. **7** detail, feature, point.

touch off 1 set off, trigger, detonate, ignite, set alight. **3** provoke, trigger off, spark off, set off, instigate, begin.

touch up 1 brush up, polish up, enhance, improve, retouch, fix up, repair, renovate, refurbish. **2** grope, molest, fondle.

touching *adj* moving, affecting, emotive, emotional, upsetting, sad, tender, poignant, pathetic, heart-warming.
➤*prep* regarding, respecting, apropos, with reference to, concerning.

touchstone *noun* standard, criterion, yardstick, benchmark, test, proof.

touchy *adj* testy, tetchy, irritable, irascible, quick-tempered, prickly, grumpy, bad-tempered, grouchy, sensitive, oversensitive, thin-skinned.

tough *adj* **1** strong, durable, resilient, resistant, sturdy, firm. **2** chewy, rubbery, stringy, leathery, gristly. **3** hardy, sturdy, rugged, resilient, robust, strong, vigorous, brawny, muscular, fit. **4** firm, stern, severe, harsh, determined, resolute. **5** obstinate, stubborn, tenacious, unyielding, uncompromising. **6** hardened, unsentimental, hard-boiled (*inf*), cynical. **7** rough, vicious, violent, wild, unruly, disorderly. **8** difficult, hard, arduous, heavy, laborious, strenuous, uphill, rough, exacting, taxing, stressful, troublesome, thorny, knotty, ticklish, baffling, puzzling, perplexing. **9** hard, unpleasant, distressing, regrettable, unfortunate, unlucky.
➤*noun* ruffian, thug, bruiser (*inf*), roughneck (*inf*), lout, yob (*inf*), hooligan, bully.

toughen *verb* reinforce, strengthen, fortify, harden, stiffen, beef up (*inf*).

tour *noun* **1** trip, expedition, outing, drive, ride, journey, excursion, circuit. **2** guided tour, conducted tour, visit, inspection.
➤*verb* go round, travel round, journey through, explore, visit, sightsee, inspect.

tourist *noun* holidaymaker, sightseer, traveller, visitor, tripper, globetrotter (*inf*).

tournament *noun* **1** competition, contest, championship, meeting, meet. **2** joust, tourney.

tousle *verb* ruffle, rumple, tangle, dishevel, untidy, mess up, disarrange.

tout *verb* sell, offer for sale, peddle, hawk.

tow *verb* pull, draw, drag, haul, tug.
➤*noun* pull, tug, haul.
in tow in attendance, accompanying, by one's side.

towards *prep* **1** to, for, in the direction of. **2** nearly, almost, about, around, just before, getting on for, approaching. **3** respecting, with respect to, regarding, with regard to, in relation to, concerning, for.

tower *noun* **1** steeple, turret, spire, minaret, belfry. **2** citadel, fortress, castle, stronghold, keep.
➤*verb* rise, ascend, soar, rear, mount, dominate, overshadow, overlook, loom.

towering *adj* **1** high, tall, soaring, lofty, imposing, elevated. **2** passionate, intense, fierce, violent, frenzied, mighty.

town *noun* township, burgh, borough, municipality, settlement, city, metropolis, conurbation.

toxic *adj* poisonous, venomous, noxious, harmful, unhealthy, deadly, lethal.

toy *noun* **1** plaything, game. **2** trifle, trinket, bauble, knick-knack.
➤*verb* **1** play, trifle, dally, flirt. **2** tinker, fiddle, play around, mess about.

trace *noun* **1** mark, sign, indication, vestige, remnant, relic, evidence, clue, record. **2** hint, suggestion, suspicion, touch, tinge, dash, bit, drop, spot. **3** track, trail, spoor, footprint, footstep.
➤*verb* **1** follow, pursue, trail, track. **2** hunt down, track down, run down, find, discover, detect, uncover, unearth. **3** sketch, draw, draft, rough out, outline, delineate, map.

track *noun* **1** trail, trace, mark, print, scent, spoor, footprints, footsteps, wake. **2** path, trail, route. **3** course, path, orbit, trajectory. **4** road, path, bridleway. **5** rails, line, permanent way.
➤*verb* **1** trace, trail, tail, follow, pursue. **2** keep up with, follow, check, watch, monitor, record.
track down find, discover, trace, ferret out, sniff out, bring to light, hunt down, hunt out, run down, unearth, uncover, run to earth, capture.

tract¹ *noun* area, region, stretch, expanse, zone, territory.

tract² *noun* treatise, essay, monograph, pamphlet, booklet, leaflet.

tractable *adj* amenable, complaisant, compliant, biddable, persuadable, yielding, submissive, tame, obedient, manageable, controllable.

trade *noun* **1** business, commerce, dealing, buying, selling, marketing, traffic, barter, exchange. **2** occupation, profession, calling, job, work, employment, line.
➤*verb* **1** deal, transact, buy and sell, traffic. **2** barter, exchange, swap.

trademark *noun* **1** trade name, brand name, brand, logo, symbol, label. **2** hallmark, speciality, characteristic, feature, peculiarity.

trader *noun* merchant, dealer, buyer, seller, supplier, broker, tradesman, tradeswoman, wholesaler, retailer.

tradition *noun* **1** custom, practice, routine, habit, convention, usage, ceremony, ritual, belief. **2** folklore, lore, unwritten law.

traditional *adj* folk, handed-down, accustomed, customary, habitual, usual, age-old, time-honoured, historic, ancestral, conventional, established.

traduce *verb* defame, slander, libel, misrepresent, malign, smear.

traffic *noun* **1** vehicles, cars. **2** transport, transportation, shipping, freight. **3** trafficking, dealing, trade, commerce, business, buying and selling, smuggling. ➤*verb* deal, trade, peddle, buy, sell, do business, smuggle.

tragedy *noun* disaster, catastrophe, calamity, blow, shock, misfortune.

tragic *adj* **1** disastrous, catastrophic, calamitous, dreadful, terrible, awful, shocking, appalling, unfortunate, unlucky. **2** sad, sorrowful, melancholy, unhappy, miserable, mournful, pathetic, pitiful, distressing, heart-breaking. **3** lamentable, deplorable, regrettable, terrible.

trail *noun* **1** track, trace, scent, spoor, footprint, footstep. **2** path, footpath, pathway, way, track, route. **3** queue, procession, line, column, train. ➤*verb* **1** drag, draw, pull, haul, tow. **2** drag, sweep, dangle, hang, droop. **3** lag, linger, loiter, fall behind. **4** drag, trudge, plod. **4** track, trace, follow, pursue, tail. **5** fade away, peter out, tail off, die away, diminish, decrease, dwindle.

train *noun* **1** line, file, column, convoy, procession, stream. **2** chain, series, succession, sequence, progression. **3** retinue, suite, entourage, staff, household, court, followers, attendants. ➤*verb* **1** teach, instruct, school, educate, tutor, coach, prepare, discipline. **2** study, prepare, read, learn, exercise, practise, work out. **3** direct, aim, point, level.

trainer *noun* coach, instructor, teacher, tutor, handler.

trait *noun* characteristic, attribute, feature, property, quality, idiosyncrasy, peculiarity.

traitor *noun* betrayer, deceiver, double-crosser, two-timer (*inf*), Judas, quisling, informer, renegade, apostate, turncoat, defector, collaborator, fifth columnist.

trajectory *noun* path, orbit, track, course, flight.

trammel *noun* restraint, constraint, hindrance, impediment, fetter, bond, shackle. ➤*verb* restrict, restrain, constrain, inhibit, curb, check, hinder, hamper, handicap, fetter, shackle, enmesh.

tramp *verb* **1** trudge, plod, stump, tread, march, trample. **2** trek, hike, walk, slog, footslog, ramble. ➤*noun* **1** vagrant, itinerant, bum (*inf*), dosser (*inf*), drifter, down-and-out, hobo. **2** walk, ramble, hike, trek, march. **3** tread, stamp.

trample *verb* **1** crush, squash, stamp, tread. **2** disregard, encroach, infringe, violate, defy.

trance *noun* daze, stupor, dream, reverie, rapture, ecstasy.

tranquil *adj* peaceful, calm, still, quiet, hushed, restful, undisturbed, serene, placid, relaxed, unruffled, unmoved, unperturbed, untroubled.

tranquillize *verb* calm, calm down, soothe, pacify, quiet, settle, relax, sedate.

tranquillizer *noun* sedative, sleeping pill, calmative, barbiturate, downer (*sl*).

transact *verb* conduct, carry out, carry on, do, perform, execute, conclude, dispatch, negotiate, handle, manage, take care of, settle, see to.

transaction *noun* **1** deal, bargain, business, negotiation, agreement, proceeding, matter, affair. **2** performance, execution, discharge, conduct, handling, settlement, negotiation.

transcend *verb* **1** surpass, exceed, go beyond. **2** surpass, excel, outstrip, outdo.

transcendent *adj* surpassing, unsurpassed, matchless, peerless, unrivalled, incomparable, supreme, sublime, superlative, great, magnificent, consummate.

transcendental *adj* mystic, metaphysical, otherworldly, supernatural.

transcribe *verb* **1** copy out, reproduce, write out. **2** translate, render, transliterate.

transcript *noun* copy, record, duplicate.

transfer *verb* **1** take, move, remove, transport, convey, carry, shift, switch. **2** relocate, transplant. **3** hand over, hand on, pass on, make over, convey, assign, delegate.
➤*noun* move, shift, relocation, removal, change, handover, assignment.

transfigure *verb* transform, change, alter, exalt, glorify, idealize, apotheosize.

transfix *verb* **1** rivet, stun, fascinate, mesmerize, spellbind, hold, paralyse, petrify. **2** pierce, impale, stab, spear, stick, spike, skewer, run through.

transform *verb* change, convert, transmogrify, transmute, metamorphose, transfigure, alter, modify, restructure, reorganize, renew, revolutionize.

transformation *noun* change, alteration, conversion, transmutation, metamorphosis, reorganization, remodelling, renewal.

transgress *verb* break, disobey, violate, infringe, contravene, overstep, go beyond, sin, err, do wrong.

transgression *noun* offence, crime, sin, wrong, wrongdoing, fault, misdeed, misdemeanour, contravention, infringement, violation.

transient *adj* impermanent, transitory, temporary, brief, short, passing, short-lived.

transit *noun* passage, crossing, movement, travel.

transition *noun* **1** change, change-over, conversion, development, evolution, passage, progress, progression, passing. **2** change, change-over, shift, switch, jump, leap.

transitory *adj* **1** transient, temporary, impermanent. **2** brief, short, passing, fleeting, momentary, short-lived.

translate *verb* **1** render, interpret, transcribe. **2** put, render, reword, paraphrase, simplify, explain, elucidate. **3** transform, transmute, change, transfer, relocate, transport, remove.

translation *noun* rendering, rendition, interpretation, rewording, paraphrase.

translucent *adj* sheer, pellucid, diaphanous.

transmission *noun* **1** transmittance, conveyance, carriage, transport, shipment, sending, transfer, transference, spreading, dissemination, diffusion, passing on, communication, broadcasting. **2** broadcast, programme, signal.

transmit *verb* **1** transfer, transport, take, convey, send, forward, dispatch. **2** communicate, transfer, pass on, spread. **3** broadcast, relay, send out.

transmute *verb* change, transform, convert, alter, metamorphose, transfigure.

transparency *noun* **1** clarity, clearness, limpidity, sheerness, gauziness, obviousness, plainness, openness, candidness, frankness, directness, ingenuousness, artlessness. **2** slide, photograph, picture.

transparent *adj* **1** clear, translucent, limpid, crystal-clear, crystalline, glassy. **2** diaphanous, sheer, see-through, gauzy, filmy. **3** obvious, patent, evident, apparent, unmistakable, noticeable. **4** clear, plain, distinct, obvious. **5** open, candid, frank, direct, artless, honest, ingenuous, straightforward.

transpire *verb* **1** happen, occur, arise, take place, come about, ensue. **2** become known, become apparent, come to light, come out.

transplant *verb* move, remove, transfer, relocate, resettle, uproot.

transport *verb* **1** convey, carry, bear, bring, fetch, ship, take, transfer, shift, move, remove. **2** banish, deport, exile, expatriate. **3** entrance, enrapture, enchant, bewitch, enthral, captivate, spellbind, charm, carry away.
➤*noun* **1** transportation, conveyance, carriage, shipment, haulage. **2** conveyance, vehicle, car, carriage, lorry. **3** ecstasy, rapture, elation, joy, delight.

transpose *verb* **1** interchange, exchange, switch, swap, substitute, rearrange, reorder, reverse, invert. **2** change, move, shift, transfer.

transverse *adj* crossways, crosswise, cross, diagonal.

trap *noun* **1** snare, gin, net, noose. **2** snare, pitfall, cage. **3** trick, ruse, wile, stratagem, deception, ploy, decoy.
➤*verb* **1** catch, net, snare, ensnare, enmesh. **2** trick, take in, dupe, deceive, inveigle. **3** corner, confine, cut off, imprison.

trappings *pl noun* appurtenances, accoutrements, gear, accessories, adornments, trimmings, finery.

trash *noun* **1** rubbish, refuse, garbage, waste, litter. **2** nonsense, junk, balderdash, drivel, bunkum, rubbish, garbage, bullshit (*inf*), bunk (*inf*), tripe (*inf*). **3** scum, vermin, rabble, riffraff.

trauma *noun* **1** shock, blow, jolt, upset, upheaval, ordeal. **2** shock, suffering, anguish, agony, torture, distress, pain, stress. **3** injury, wound, lesion.

travel *verb* **1** journey, take a trip, voyage, tour, go. **2** cross, traverse, journey, roam, rove, wander, explore. **3** go, move, proceed, progress, carry.
➤*noun* travelling, journeying, touring, globetrotting (*inf*).

traveller *noun* **1** voyager, wayfarer, passenger, tourist, sightseer, holidaymaker, tripper (*inf*), explorer, wanderer, globetrotter (*inf*). **2** nomad, gypsy, itinerant, drifter, vagrant, tramp.

traverse *verb* cross, pass over, travel, journey over, range, roam, wander, negotiate, bridge, span.

travesty *noun* **1** parody, caricature, lampoon, satire, send-up (*inf*), spoof (*inf*), take-off (*inf*), burlesque, mockery, misrepresentation. **2** parody, caricature, perversion, apology.

treacherous *adj* **1** traitorous, perfidious, disloyal, double-crossing, double-dealing, two-timing (*inf*), back-stabbing, faithless, unfaithful, false, deceitful, duplicitous, dishonest. **2** dangerous, hazardous, perilous, risky, dicey (*inf*). **3** unsafe, unreliable, unstable, precarious, deceptive. **4** slippery, icy.

tread *verb* **1** walk, step, pace, go, stride, march, tramp. **2** stamp, step on, trample, crush, squash, flatten.
➤*noun* **1** step, footstep, footprint, footmark, footfall. **2** pace, walk, stride, tramp, gait.

treason *noun* **1** treachery, betrayal, disloyalty, faithlessness, perfidy. **2** sedition, subversion, mutiny, rebellion.

treasure *noun* **1** riches, wealth, fortune, hoard, cache, money, gold, silver, bullion, jewels, gems, valuables. **2** darling, jewel, gem, pearl, paragon, pride and joy.
➤*verb* **1** prize, value, hold dear, esteem, cherish, dote on. **2** hoard, store, lay by, stash away (*inf*), save, collect.

treat *noun* party, entertainment, celebration, excursion, outing, surprise, indulgence, feast, present, gift, goody (*inf*).
➤*verb* **1** handle, deal with, cope with, act towards, behave towards. **2** regard, view, look upon, consider. **3** care for, look after, attend to, tend, nurse, doctor, medicate, cure, heal. **4** entertain, indulge, regale, feast, wine and dine, pay for, buy, stand. **5** cover, paint, prime, prepare, process. **6** discuss, deal with, go into, touch upon, analyse, study, consider, review. **7** negotiate, discuss terms, talk, bargain.

treatise *noun* discourse, disquisition, dissertation, essay, study, paper, monograph.

treatment *noun* **1** handling, use, usage, dealings, management, conduct, behaviour. **2** care, nursing, doctoring, medication, first aid, therapy, healing, remedy.

treaty *noun* agreement, pact, bargain, deal, contract, concordat, entente, alliance.

trek *verb* travel, journey, tramp, trudge, slog, march, walk, hike, traipse.
➤*noun* journey, expedition, trip, odyssey, safari, march, walk, hike, slog.

tremble *verb* **1** shake, quiver, quaver, quake, shiver, shudder, twitch. **2** shudder, judder, shake, vibrate, wobble.
➤*noun* tremor, shake, quiver, shiver, shudder.

tremendous *adj* **1** huge, great, vast, immense, massive, enormous, colossal, gigantic, prodigious, stupendous, mammoth, whopping (*inf*). **2** wonderful, marvellous, sensational, spectacular, extraordinary, amazing, great, incredible, fantastic (*inf*), fabulous (*inf*), terrific (*inf*), wicked (*inf*).

tremor *noun* **1** shudder, shiver, quiver, trembling, shaking, spasm, twitch. **2** earthquake, quake (*inf*), shock. **3** thrill, frisson.

tremulous *adj* 1 trembling, trembly, shaky, shaking, wavering, quavering, quaking, quivering, shivering. 2 timid, shy, diffident, fearful, apprehensive, timorous, scared, afraid, anxious, nervous, agitated, jumpy, jittery.

trench *noun* furrow, ditch, drain, cut, channel, excavation.

trenchant *adj* 1 keen, sharp, pointed, penetrating, incisive, cutting, caustic, biting, scathing. 2 clear, effective, incisive, vigorous, powerful, forceful, forthright.

trend *noun* 1 tendency, course, drift, inclination, leaning, direction, flow. 2 fashion, fad, vogue, style, craze.
➤*verb* tend, incline, drift, gravitate.

trepidation *noun* fear, fearfulness, terror, fright, alarm, dismay, dread, apprehension, apprehensiveness, anxiety, nervousness, cold feet (*inf*), qualms, misgivings, uneasiness, disquiet.

trespass *verb* 1 intrude, invade, encroach, infringe. 2 intrude, exploit, abuse, take advantage of, impose upon. 3 sin, do wrong, transgress.
➤*noun* 1 unlawful entry, intrusion, encroachment, poaching. 2 sin, offence, wrong.

trial *noun* 1 test, testing, dry run, dummy run, check, try-out, practice, rehearsal, audition, experiment, examination, analysis, probation. 2 case, lawsuit, hearing, inquiry, tribunal, appeal. 3 ordeal, suffering, distress, misery, grief, pain, hardship, trouble, adversity, tribulation, affliction, blow, worry, anxiety, burden, cross to bear.
➤*verb* test, experiment with, pilot.

tribe *noun* ethnic group, people, nation, race, clan.

tribulation *noun* 1 trial, care, hardship, ordeal, trouble, sorrow, burden. 2 pain, distress, suffering, affliction, adversity, anxiety, grief, misery, sadness, sorrow, wretchedness, unhappiness, misfortune.

tribunal *noun* court, bar, bench, board, committee, forum.

tribute *noun* 1 accolade, acclaim, applause, recognition, acknowledgment, compliment, bouquet, honour, praise, commendation, eulogy, panegyric.

2 testimony, evidence, proof. 3 payment, offering, contribution, impost, duty, tax, levy.

trice *noun* **in a trice** in a moment, in a second, quick as a flash, in a jiffy (*inf*).

trick *noun* 1 wile, stratagem, ploy, ruse, deception, feint, dodge, manoeuvre, subterfuge, trap, hoax, fraud, imposture, swindle, con (*inf*), scam (*inf*). 2 sleight of hand, legerdemain, juggling. 3 illusion, apparition, mirage. 4 trait, characteristic, idiosyncrasy, eccentricity, quirk, peculiarity, foible, mannerism.
➤*verb* dupe, cheat, defraud, trap, deceive, delude, mislead, fool, outwit, hoodwink, bluff, hoax, bamboozle, diddle, take in (*inf*), take for a ride (*inf*), lead up the garden path (*inf*), have on (*inf*), con (*inf*), pull a fast one (*inf*).

trickle *verb* drip, drop, dribble, run, leak, ooze, seep, filter, percolate.

trickster *noun* cheat, swindler, fraud, fraudster, con man (*inf*), deceiver, hoaxer, impostor, phoney, charlatan.

tricky *adj* 1 difficult, problematic, sticky, complicated, knotty, thorny, awkward, delicate, sensitive, ticklish. 2 risky, precarious, uncertain. 3 crafty, cunning, artful, scheming, sly, wily, foxy, slippery, devious, deceitful, dishonest.

trifle *noun* 1 triviality, inessential, bagatelle, nothing. 2 bit, drop, spot, dash, touch.
➤*verb* toy, play, dally, flirt, mess around.

trifling *adj* trivial, insignificant, small, tiny, paltry, piddling (*inf*), unimportant, inconsequential, petty, empty, frivolous, idle.

trigger *verb* set off, spark off, give rise to, generate, produce, bring about, cause, start, initiate, provoke.

trim *adj* neat, spruce, spick-and-span, tidy, orderly, shipshape, smart, well-turned-out, elegant.
➤*verb* 1 clip, prune, neaten, tidy up, shape. 2 shorten, clip, prune, snip, cut, lop, pare, shave. 3 curtail, cut back, scale down, reduce, decrease. 4 decorate, adorn, ornament, embellish, garnish, festoon.
➤*noun* trimming, decoration, ornamentation, embellishment, garnish, frill, fringe, edging, piping, border.

trimmings *pl noun* **1** frills, extras, accompaniments, accessories, adornments, trim. **2** clippings, cuttings, shavings, parings.

trinket *noun* bauble, gewgaw, knick-knack, ornament.

trio *noun* threesome, triumvirate, triad.

trip *noun* **1** journey, excursion, tour, jaunt, outing, ride, drive, expedition, voyage, spin (*inf*). **2** stumble, fall, tumble, slip, spill.
➤*verb* **1** stumble, fall, tumble, slip. **2** slip, slip up, err, go wrong, catch out, wrong-foot, throw (*inf*). **3** hop, skip, dance, gambol, caper, frisk.

triple *adj* threefold, treble, triplicate.
➤*noun* threesome, trio, triad.

tripper *noun* tourist, holidaymaker, traveller, sightseer, excursionist.

trite *adj* hackneyed, corny (*inf*), stale, tired, worn-out, threadbare, unoriginal, unimaginative, uninspired, stock, clichéd, overused, commonplace, ordinary, pedestrian, banal.

triumph *noun* **1** victory, win, conquest, walkover, hit (*inf*), sensation, masterstroke, coup, feat, achievement, success. **2** jubilation, exultation, elation, rejoicing, joy, pride.
➤*verb* **1** win, prevail, succeed, carry the day. **2** rejoice, exult, glory, celebrate, revel, gloat, brag, boast, crow.

triumphant *adj* **1** winning, conquering, victorious, successful. **2** exultant, jubilant, elated, celebratory, joyful, proud, gloating, boastful, cock-a-hoop (*inf*).

trivia *pl noun* trivialities, trifles, minutiae, details.

trivial *adj* trifling, unimportant, insignificant, inconsequential, negligible, small, minor, immaterial, petty, worthless.

troop *noun* **1** soldiers, army, armed forces, military, servicemen, servicewomen, men. **2** group, band, company, contingent, unit, crew (*inf*), team, squad, gang.
➤*verb* flock, throng, crowd, surge, stream, march, parade.

trophy *noun* **1** cup, prize, award, medal. **2** spoils, booty, souvenir, keepsake.

tropical *adj* hot, sultry, sweltering, stifling, boiling, humid, sticky, steamy.

trot *verb* canter, lope, run, jog, scurry, bustle.

trouble *noun* **1** difficulty, problems, danger, worry, concern, anxiety, disquiet, unease, distress, hardship, adversity, misfortune, bother, inconvenience, irritation, annoyance, hassle (*inf*). **2** worry, concern, trial, tribulation, affliction, burden, nuisance, pest, ailment, illness, disorder, disease, complaint. **3** difficulty, problem, headache (*inf*), snag, drawback, shortcoming. **4** unrest, disturbance, disorder, upheaval, strife, conflict, fighting. **5** effort, exertion, pains, work, care, attention, thought.
➤*verb* **1** worry, bother, agitate, alarm, concern, upset, distress, disturb, perturb, confuse, perplex, pester, annoy, irk, irritate, harass, hassle (*inf*), burden, weigh down, oppress, grieve. **2** bother, inconvenience, put out, disturb, impose upon.

troublemaker *noun* mischief-maker, agitator, rabble-rouser, agent provocateur, stirrer, ringleader.

troublesome *adj* annoying, irritating, irksome, upsetting, bothersome, tiresome, inconvenient, worrying, distressing, disturbing, nagging.

trough *noun* **1** trench, furrow, groove, gully, depression. **2** conduit, drain, culvert, gutter.

trounce *verb* defeat, thrash, beat, rout, crush, drub, slaughter (*inf*), wallop (*inf*), hammer (*inf*), clobber (*inf*), wipe the floor with (*inf*).

troupe *noun* company, band, group, cast.

trousers *pl noun* pants, slacks, jeans, denims, flannels, shorts, bottoms, breeches.

truant *noun* absentee, shirker, skiver (*inf*), deserter, runaway.
➤*adj* absent, missing, runaway, AWOL.
➤*verb* play truant, shirk, skive (*inf*), bunk off (*inf*), go AWOL (*inf*), play hooky (*inf*).

truce *noun* armistice, ceasefire, peace, break, interval, lull, letup (*inf*), moratorium.

truck[1] *noun* lorry, articulated lorry, heavy goods vehicle, HGV, van.

truck[2] *noun* dealings, business, commerce, trade, relations, contact, communication, connection.

truculent *adj* aggressive, hostile, obstreperous, quarrelsome, argumentative, pugnacious, belligerent, combative, defiant, sullen, surly, disrespectful, rude.

trudge *verb* plod, tramp, lumber, slog, toil, labour, traipse (*inf*).

true *adj* **1** truthful, genuine, reliable, veracious, honest, factual. **2** accurate, correct, right, valid, exact, precise. **3** real, veritable. **4** authentic, genuine, real, sincere, legitimate, bona fide, rightful, proper. **5** faithful, loyal, devoted, sincere, staunch, constant, steadfast, trusty, trustworthy, reliable, dependable.
    ➤*adv* **1** truly, sincerely, truthfully, honestly. **2** accurately, exactly, unerringly, on target.

truism *noun* platitude, commonplace, cliché.

truly *adv* **1** really, in reality, indeed, truthfully, in fact, actually, definitely, positively, undoubtedly, indubitably, unquestionably. **2** very, really, extremely, exceptionally. **3** honestly, truthfully, frankly, genuinely, sincerely, faithfully, devotedly, loyally, reliably. **4** accurately, faithfully, exactly, precisely, correctly.

trumpery *adj* **1** rubbishy, trashy, worthless, useless. **2** tawdry, shoddy, flashy, cheap.

trumpet *noun* bugle, horn, clarion.
    ➤*verb* proclaim, announce, broadcast, advertise, bellow, call out.

trump up *verb* invent, make up, fabricate, concoct, cook up (*inf*).

truncate *verb* shorten, curtail, cut, lop, clip, prune, trim, dock.

truncheon *noun* club, cudgel, baton, stick.

trunk *noun* **1** stem, stalk, stock, bole. **2** body, torso, frame. **3** chest, coffer, box, crate, portmanteau. **4** snout, nose, proboscis.

truss *verb* tie up, bind, secure, fetter, tether.
    ➤*noun* **1** support, prop, brace, strut, joist. **2** support, pad, binding.

trust *noun* **1** faith, belief, confidence, conviction, certainty, credence, assurance, reliance, credit. **2** charge, custody, care, protection, safekeeping. **3** duty, responsibility, obligation, commitment.
    ➤*verb* **1** believe, have faith in, have confidence in, swear by. **2** rely on, depend on, count on. **3** presume, assume, suppose, imagine, hope, expect, believe. **4** commit, entrust, consign, turn over.

trustworthy *adj* trusty, dependable, reliable, loyal, faithful, staunch, steadfast, honest, truthful, honourable.

trusty *adj* trustworthy, dependable, reliable, honest, faithful, loyal.

truth *noun* **1** reality, actuality, fact, factuality, veracity, truthfulness, accuracy, correctness, validity, fidelity, legitimacy, authenticity, genuineness, honesty. **2** verity, truism, proverb, saying, axiom, principle, law.

truthful *adj* **1** honest, veracious, sincere, straightforward, straight, open, trustworthy, reliable. **2** accurate, correct, valid, reliable, honest, faithful, realistic, factual, true.

try *verb* **1** attempt, endeavour, essay, undertake, venture, seek, aim, strive, have a go, have a bash (*inf*), have a shot (*inf*), have a stab (*inf*), make an effort. **2** test, experience, taste, sample, check out, try out, inspect, assess, appraise. **3** tire, wear out, strain, stress, tax. **4** hear, examine, judge, adjudicate.
    ➤*noun* **1** attempt, endeavour, effort, go, bash (*inf*), shot (*inf*), crack (*inf*), stab (*inf*). **2** trial, test, evaluation, appraisal.

try out try, test, put to the test, experiment with, check out, appraise.

trying *adj* **1** hard, difficult, tough, taxing, stressful, tiring, fatiguing, exhausting. **2** annoying, exasperating, infuriating, irksome, irritating, troublesome.

tube *noun* pipe, hose, line, spout, conduit, duct.

tuck *verb* **1** stuff, cram, push, thrust, insert. **2** fold, pleat, gather, crease. **3** put to bed, make comfortable, cover up.
    ➤*noun* **1** fold, crease, pleat, gather. **2** food, snacks, grub (*inf*), eats (*inf*), nosh (*inf*).
    tuck away stash away (*inf*), stow away, store, hoard, hide, secrete.
    tuck in eat, feast, devour, gobble up (*inf*), scoff (*inf*), wolf down (*inf*), get stuck into (*inf*).

tuft *noun* bunch, clump, cluster, knot, wisp.

tug *verb* pull, jerk, wrench, yank (*inf*), heave, pluck.
➤*noun* pull, jerk, yank (*inf*), heave.

tuition *noun* instruction, teaching, schooling, education, training, coaching.

tumble *verb* **1** fall, topple, slip, trip, stumble, sprawl. **2** plummet, drop, fall, plunge, dive, nosedive. **3** toss, roll. **4** understand, grasp, realize, latch on to, suss (*inf*), twig (*inf*), cotton on to (*inf*).
➤*noun* **1** fall, spill, trip, stumble, dive, nosedive (*inf*), plunge, drop, fall. **2** mess, chaos, disorder, jumble, confusion.

tumbledown *adj* ramshackle, dilapidated, ruined, broken-down, crumbling, decrepit, ruined, ruinous, in ruins, rickety.

tumid *adj* **1** swollen, puffy, puffed up, distended, bloated, enlarged, tumescent, bulging. **2** pompous, affected, stilted, bombastic, pretentious, turgid, rhetorical, inflated, overblown, exaggerated.

tumour *noun* swelling, lump, growth, malignancy, cancer, sarcoma.

tumult *noun* **1** uproar, commotion, racket, pandemonium, bedlam, din, noise, clamour, hubbub, hullabaloo, row, fracas, brouhaha, disturbance, rumpus. **2** confusion, turmoil, turbulence, ferment, upheaval.

tumultuous *adj* **1** noisy, loud, clamorous, uproarious, boisterous, unrestrained, vociferous, rowdy, unruly, disorderly, obstreperous. **2** passionate, raging, wild, turbulent, stormy, tempestuous, violent, fierce, frenzied, uncontrollable, unrestrained.

tune *noun* melody, air, strain, theme, motif.
➤*verb* adjust, adapt, set, regulate.
change one's tune change one's mind, change one's opinion, backtrack.

tuneful *adj* melodious, lyrical, harmonious, musical, sweet, dulcet, pleasant, catchy (*inf*).

tunnel *noun* **1** passage, underpass, subway. **2** burrow, hole.
➤*verb* dig, excavate, burrow, mine, bore.

turbid *adj* **1** muddy, cloudy, murky, dim, opaque. **2** hazy, muddled, confused, unsettled, turbulent.

turbulence *noun* tempestuousness, storminess, turmoil, agitation, confusion, commotion, chaos, instability, upheaval, disruption, disorder.

turbulent *adj* agitated, disturbed, restless, confused, disordered, tumultuous, wild, unruly, disorderly, undisciplined, boisterous, noisy, uproarious, rebellious, riotous, obstreperous, furious, violent.

turf *noun* grass, lawn, sward, green.

turf out *verb* **1** throw out, chuck out (*inf*), dump, discard, scrap, dispose of, get rid of. **2** throw out, chuck out (*inf*), kick out (*inf*), eject, expel, evict, dismiss, discharge.

turgid *adj* **1** swollen, distended, bloated, inflated, enlarged, tumescent, bulging. **2** pompous, bombastic, extravagant, pretentious, affected, stilted, inflated, overblown, high-flown, fulsome, flowery.

turmoil *noun* tumult, turbulence, uproar, commotion, stir, unrest, agitation, ferment, disturbance, chaos, disorder, disarray, upheaval, confusion.

turn *verb* **1** rotate, revolve, spin, twist, twirl, wheel, whirl, pivot, swivel, gyrate, circle, go round, flip over, reverse, invert. **2** go, go round, veer, swerve, swing, wheel, diverge, bend, curve. **3** become, go, grow, get, change, alter, modify, convert, transform, mutate. **4** curdle, sour, go off, go bad, spoil, taint. **5** fashion, form, model, carve, shape.
➤*noun* **1** rotation, revolution, circle, cycle, round, gyration, spin, twirl, swerve. **2** bend, curve. **3** corner, junction. **4** change, alteration, variation, shift, adjustment, difference. **5** move, go, try, attempt, shot (*inf*), chance, opportunity, shift, stint, spell, time, period. **6** stroll, saunter, walk, drive, ride, spin (*inf*), outing, excursion, airing, jaunt. **7** surprise, shock, start, scare, fright. **8** routine, act, performance.
turn against take a dislike to, fall out with, rebel against.
turn away 1 turn aside, avert, deflect. **2** send away, reject, repel, rebuff, cold-shoulder (*inf*).
turn down 1 lower, reduce, diminish, decrease, soften. **2** reject, refuse, decline, spurn, veto.
turn in 1 hand in, hand over, give in, deliver, surrender. **2** go to bed, go to sleep, hit the hay (*inf*), hit the sack (*inf*).

turn off 1 switch off, turn out, shut off, shut down, unplug, disconnect, extinguish. **2** leave, exit, branch off. **3** put off, alienate, repel, displease, disgust, offend, sicken, nauseate.

turn on 1 switch on, put on, start, plug in, connect, activate, operate. **2** arouse, excite, stimulate, thrill, titillate, attract, please.

turn out 1 make, manufacture, fabricate, produce, bring out, churn out (*inf*). **2** switch off, turn off, put out, extinguish. **3** empty, clear out, clean out. **4** result, ensue, transpire, pan out, happen, occur, come about, end up, emerge.

turn over 1 overturn, capsize, keel over, turn turtle, upset, overturn, upend, invert, reverse. **2** hand over, surrender, deliver, transfer. **3** consider, ponder, deliberate, mull over, think about, think over, reflect on.

turn up 1 turn out, arrive, appear, put in an appearance, show up (*inf*), attend, come, crop up, arise, transpire. **2** raise, increase, amplify, intensify. **3** discover, find, dig up, unearth, uncover, disclose, reveal, hit upon, bring to light. **4** pop up (*inf*), come to light, reappear.

turning point *noun* crossroads, crux, crisis, decisive moment, watershed, moment of truth.

turnout *noun* attendance, gate, audience, crowd, gathering, number.

turnover *noun* **1** output, volume, business, productivity, production, sales. **2** yield, income, profits, revenue. **3** change, replacement, movement.

turpitude *noun* baseness, vileness, wickedness, evil, depravity, degeneracy, immorality, criminality, villainy.

tussle *noun* **1** fight, battle, skirmish, scuffle, wrestle, set-to (*inf*), scrap (*inf*), punch-up (*inf*), dust-up (*inf*). **2** fight, battle, struggle.

tutelage *noun* **1** guardianship, charge, care, custody, protection, supervision. **2** instruction, tuition, schooling.

tutor *noun* teacher, instructor, coach, preceptor, supervisor, guide, mentor. ➤*verb* teach, instruct, coach, train, educate.

TV *noun* television, telly (*inf*), small screen, receiver, set, box (*inf*).

twaddle *noun* nonsense, rubbish, drivel, balderdash, gibberish, guff, claptrap, hogwash (*inf*), bunk (*inf*), piffle (*inf*), poppycock (*inf*), balls (*sl*).

tweak *verb* pinch, nip, squeeze, twitch, pull, tug, jerk.

twiddle *verb* **1** fiddle, finger, wiggle, play, toy. **2** twirl, twist, turn, adjust.

twig *noun* stick, stem, branch, shoot, sprig.

twilight *noun* **1** dusk, gloaming, sunset, early evening. **2** dusk, gloaming, semi-darkness, half-light. **3** decline, waning.

twin *noun* fellow, mate, match, counterpart, equivalent, double, duplicate, look-alike, likeness, spitting image (*inf*), dead spit (*inf*), dead ringer (*inf*), clone. ➤*adj* similar, like, parallel, double, dual, duplicate, paired, matching, identical. ➤*verb* join, pair, link, couple, match.

twine *noun* string, cord, yarn. ➤*verb* **1** twist, wind, turn, wrap, curl, wreathe, coil, spiral, encircle. **2** interlace, weave, entwine, twist, braid, plait.

twinge *noun* pang, spasm, throb, ache, cramp, stitch, pain, prick, tingle.

twinkle *verb* sparkle, shimmer, glimmer, shine, glint, flicker, blink, wink. ➤*noun* twinkling, sparkle, shimmer, shine, glimmer, glint, flash, flicker, blink, wink.

twinkling *noun* instant, moment, mo (*inf*), second, sec (*inf*), flash, trice, jiffy (*inf*).

twirl *verb* spin, wheel, whirl, gyrate, pirouette, swivel, twist, turn, revolve, rotate. ➤*noun* **1** turn, spin, whirl, pirouette, gyration, rotation. **2** twist, curl, coil, spiral, whorl.

twist *verb* **1** coil, curl, twine, wind, wrap. **2** wrench, bend, warp, contort, distort, deform, wring, wrest, screw, skew. **3** sprain, strain, turn, wrench, rick. **4** distort, warp, pervert, garble, falsify, misrepresent, misinterpret, misquote. **5** twine, intertwine, weave, plait, braid. **6** wind, meander, snake, worm, zigzag. **7** writhe, wriggle, squirm. **8** turn, rotate, revolve, swivel, spin. ➤*noun* **1** wrench, screw, turn, pull, jerk, yank, warp, distortion, kink. **2** turn, bend, curve, meander, zigzag. **3** coil, curl, loop, spiral. **4** surprise, turnabout, development, turn.

twit *noun* idiot, fool, simpleton, ass, block-head, chump (*inf*), dope (*inf*), clot (*inf*), twerp (*inf*).

twitch *verb* 1 jerk, jump, start, quiver, shiver, flutter, tremble, blink, jump. 2 snatch, pluck, pull, tug, tweak, jerk, yank (*inf*).
➤*noun* jerk, jump, start, spasm, convulsion, shiver, tremor, quiver, shake, flutter, jump, tic, jerk, tug, pull, yank (*inf*).

twitter *verb* 1 chirp, chirrup, cheep, tweet, warble, sing, whistle. 2 chatter, prattle, babble, witter, gossip.
➤*noun* 1 tweeting, trilling, warbling, chirrup, chirp, song. 2 chatter, babble, prattle.

two-faced *adj* deceitful, deceiving, hypocritical, insincere, false, lying, untrustworthy, treacherous, duplicitous, double-dealing.

tycoon *noun* magnate, industrialist, capitalist, entrepreneur, mogul, fat cat (*inf*).

type *noun* 1 class, order, genre, species, genus, breed, variety, kind, sort, group, category, description. 2 specimen, sample, example, exemplar, model, personification, embodiment, archetype, epitome. 3 print, face, font, fount, characters, letters.

typhoon *noun* tropical storm, cyclone, tornado, hurricane.

typical *adj* 1 representative, classic, archetypal, characteristic, standard, orthodox, stock, normal, ordinary, average, usual, routine, customary, run-of-the-mill. 2 representative, illustrative, characteristic.

typify *verb* represent, exemplify, epitomize, embody, encapsulate, personify, sum up, characterize.

tyrannical *adj* tyrannous, autocratic, despotic, dictatorial, arbitrary, absolute, domineering, overpowering, overbearing, bullying, high-handed, authoritarian, totalitarian, oppressive, repressive, harsh.

tyrannize *verb* oppress, repress, intimidate, terrorize, bully, subjugate, dictate, domineer, browbeat, coerce.

tyranny *noun* 1 dictatorship, despotism, autocracy, absolutism, authoritarianism, totalitarianism. 2 dictatorship, despotism, autocracy. 3 authoritarianism, imperiousness, high-handedness, bullying, coercion, ruthlessness, harshness, severity, brutality, cruelty, injustice.

tyrant *noun* 1 dictator, despot, autocrat, absolutist. 2 authoritarian, oppressor, bully, martinet, slave-driver, taskmaster.

ubiquitous *adj* omnipresent, universal, global, ever-present, common, frequent.

ugly *adj* **1** unattractive, plain, unsightly, ill-favoured, hideous, grotesque, unpleasant, disagreeable, offensive, revolting. **2** menacing, threatening, ominous, sinister, dangerous, nasty. **3** surly, belligerent, aggressive, quarrelsome, ill-natured, spiteful, angry, bad-tempered.

ulcer *noun* sore, abscess, boil, pustule, gathering.

ulterior *adj* hidden, concealed, underlying, undisclosed, unexpressed, secret.

ultimate *adj* **1** final, last, terminal, extreme, eventual. **2** basic, fundamental, elementary, primary. **3** maximum, utmost, supreme, paramount, greatest, best.
➤ *noun* utmost, extreme, height, peak, culmination, epitome, nonpareil, last word (*inf*).

ultra *adj* extreme, radical, excessive, fanatical.

umbrage *noun* offence, pique, resentment, indignation, huff, high dudgeon.

umpire *noun* **1** referee, ref (*inf*). **2** judge, adjudicator, arbitrator, mediator.
➤ *verb* referee, judge, adjudicate, arbitrate, mediate.

umpteen *adj and noun* numerous, thousands, millions, countless, innumerable.

unabashed *adj* unashamed, unembarrassed, undaunted, brazen, bold, confident.

unable *adj* incapable, powerless, impotent, ineffectual, incompetent, unqualified.

unabridged *adj* complete, full, uncut, unexpurgated.

unacceptable *adj* **1** unsatisfactory, inadequate. **2** intolerable, insupportable, objectionable, offensive, undesirable, inadmissible, improper.

unaccompanied *adj* alone, on one's own, by oneself, solo, unattended, unescorted.

unaccountable *adj* inexplicable, incomprehensible, puzzling, baffling, mysterious, odd, strange, extraordinary.

unaccustomed *adj* **1** unused, unacquainted, inexperienced, unpractised. **2** unusual, uncommon, strange, unfamiliar, uncharacteristic, unprecedented.

unadulterated *adj* pure, unmixed, undiluted, genuine.

unaffected *adj* **1** natural, unpretentious, simple, artless, sincere, honest, genuine, unfeigned. **2** unchanged, unaltered, untouched, impervious, proof.

unaided *adj* unassisted, single-handed, solo, by oneself.

unanimous *adj* agreeing, like-minded, concordant, united, solid, of one mind.

unanswerable *adj* **1** irrefutable, incontestable, undeniable, incontrovertible, indisputable. **2** insoluble, unsolvable.

unappetizing *adj* unappealing, unattractive, off-putting, unpleasant, unsavoury, unpalatable, tasteless, insipid.

unapproachable *adj* **1** aloof, standoffish, distant, uncommunicative, unresponsive, cold, unfriendly. **2** remote, inaccessible, out-of-the-way, off the beaten track (*inf*).

unarmed *adj* weaponless, defenceless, unprotected, vulnerable, exposed.

unasked *adj* **1** uninvited, unbidden, voluntary. **2** unsolicited, unrequested, unwanted.

unassailable *adj* **1** impregnable, invulnerable, inviolable, strong, secure. **2** undeniable, irrefutable, indisputable, incontestable, incontrovertible, certain.

unassuming *adj* modest, self-effacing, humble, meek, retiring, unassertive, unobtrusive, unpretentious.

unattached *adj* **1** loose, detached, separate, free. **2** single, unmarried, available, footloose and fancy-free. **3** uncommitted, independent, autonomous.

unattended *adj* **1** unsupervised, alone, abandoned, forsaken, neglected, untended. **2** ignored, disregarded, forgotten.

unattractive *adj* unappealing, uninviting, off-putting, plain, ugly, unsightly, undesirable, unwelcome, disagreeable.

unauthorized *adj* unofficial, illicit, unlicensed, prohibited.

unavailing *adj* vain, futile, useless, ineffectual, fruitless, unproductive, abortive, unsuccessful.

unavoidable *adj* inevitable, inescapable, ineluctable, necessary, compulsory, destined, certain.

unaware *adj* ignorant, unknowing, unacquainted, unfamiliar, unenlightened, uninformed, unconscious, oblivious.

unawares *adv* **1** unexpectedly, by surprise, off guard, unprepared, suddenly, abruptly. **2** accidentally, unintentionally, by mistake, inadvertently, unwittingly, unknowingly.

unbalanced *adj* **1** asymmetrical, lopsided, unstable, uneven, disproportionate. **2** unsound, irrational, unhinged, deranged, disturbed, insane. **3** biased, prejudiced, one-sided, partial.

unbearable *adj* intolerable, insufferable, insupportable, unendurable, too much (*inf*).

unbeatable *adj* invincible, unconquerable, indomitable, unsurpassable, matchless.

unbecoming *adj* **1** unseemly, indecorous, improper, indelicate, inappropriate. **2** unattractive, unflattering.

unbelief *noun* agnosticism, atheism, disbelief, incredulity, doubt, scepticism.

unbelievable *adj* **1** incredible, implausible, unconvincing, unlikely, improbable, impossible. **2** extraordinary, remarkable, amazing, astonishing.

unbending *adj* inflexible, rigid, unyielding, firm, intractable, intransigent, strict.

unbiased *adj* unprejudiced, impartial, dispassionate, objective, neutral, nonpartisan, fair, even-handed.

unbidden *adj* **1** spontaneous, voluntary, willing, unforced. **2** uninvited, unasked, unsolicited, unrequested.

unbind *verb* **1** untie, unfasten, undo. **2** free, release, let go.

unblemished *adj* perfect, flawless, faultless, immaculate, spotless, stainless, irreproachable.

unblushing *adj* shameless, immodest, unashamed, unabashed, unembarrassed.

unborn *adj* **1** embryonic, in utero. **2** future, to come.

unbosom *verb* **unbosom oneself** unburden oneself, confess, tell all (*inf*), make a clean breast of it (*inf*).

unbounded *adj* boundless, unlimited, immeasurable, infinite, unrestricted, unconfined, unrestrained, unbridled.

unbreakable *adj* indestructible, infrangible, shatterproof, toughened.

unbridled *adj* unrestrained, uncontrolled, unchecked, uninhibited, wild, rampant.

unbroken *adj* **1** intact, sound, undamaged, whole, complete. **2** uninterrupted, continuous, endless, non-stop. **3** unbeaten, unsurpassed, unequalled. **4** untamed, wild.

unburden *verb* **1** unload, disencumber. **2** unbosom, disclose, divulge, confess, confide.

uncalled-for *adj* **1** unnecessary, needless, unsolicited, uninvited, unwanted. **2** gratuitous, unprovoked, unjustified, unwarranted, undeserved, unfair.

uncanny *adj* **1** strange, mysterious, weird, eerie, creepy (*inf*), spooky (*inf*). **2** extraordinary, remarkable, striking, exceptional, amazing.

uncaring *adj* unconcerned, unmoved, unfeeling, unsympathetic.

unceasing *adj* ceaseless, incessant, constant, continuous, endless, never-ending.

unceremonious *adj* **1** informal, casual, relaxed, laid back (*inf*). **2** sudden, hasty, undignified, abrupt, rude, discourteous.

uncertain *adj* **1** undecided, unsettled, pending, unpredictable, up in the air (*inf*),

unknown, unconfirmed, speculative.
2 doubtful, dubious, unsure, hesitant,
irresolute, ambivalent, in two minds (*inf*).
3 unreliable, erratic, risky, iffy (*inf*).
4 changeable, variable, inconstant.

unchangeable *adj* unalterable, invariable,
immutable, fixed, permanent, unchanging.

unchanging *adj* constant, unvarying,
stable, steady, changeless, unchangeable.

uncharitable *adj* unkind, insensitive,
mean, harsh, severe, unsympathetic.

uncharted *adj* unmapped, unexplored,
unknown, unfamiliar.

uncivil *adj* rude, discourteous, impolite,
ill-mannered, ungracious, surly, boorish,
churlish.

uncivilized *adj* **1** unenlightened, primitive, barbarian, barbarous, savage. **2**
uncouth, vulgar, rude, uncivil, unrefined,
unsophisticated.

unclean *adj* **1** dirty, filthy, soiled, foul,
defiled, contaminated, tainted. **2** immoral,
impure, unchaste, corrupt, sinful, bad.

unclear *adj* vague, indistinct, hazy,
obscure, indefinite, uncertain.

uncomfortable *adj* **1** uneasy, ill at ease,
awkward, embarrassed, distressed, anxious,
nervous. **2** unpleasant, hard, rough,
cramped, ill-fitting, painful.

uncommon *adj* **1** unusual, unfamiliar,
strange, rare, infrequent, scarce. **2**
extraordinary, remarkable, exceptional,
noteworthy, outstanding.

uncommunicative *adj* reserved, reticent,
quiet, taciturn, tight-lipped, secretive,
close, unforthcoming.

uncompromising *adj* inflexible, unyielding, unbending, rigid, firm, obdurate,
intransigent, resolute.

unconcern *noun* **1** indifference, apathy,
dispassion, detachment. **2** nonchalance,
insouciance.

unconditional *adj* total, full, absolute,
categorical, unqualified, unreserved,
unrestricted.

unconnected *adj* **1** separate, independent, unrelated. **2** detached, disconnected,
disjointed.

unconquerable *adj* **1** invincible, indomitable, unbeatable. **2** insuperable, insurmountable, overwhelming.

unconscionable *adj* **1** unscrupulous,
unprincipled, amoral, unethical, dishonourable. **2** unreasonable, excessive,
immoderate, inordinate, extreme.

unconscious *adj* **1** insensible, senseless,
knocked out, comatose, asleep, stunned.
2 unaware, oblivious, unmindful, heedless,
unknowing. **3** automatic, involuntary,
reflex, instinctive. **4** unintentional, accidental, inadvertent, unwitting.

uncontrollable *adj* ungovernable,
unmanageable, wild, unruly, refractory,
mad, violent.

unconventional *adj* unorthodox, unusual, atypical, irregular, eccentric, offbeat
(*inf*), alternative, experimental.

unconvincing *adj* weak, flimsy, lame,
improbable, unlikely, implausible.

uncoordinated *adj* clumsy, awkward,
gauche, ungainly, lumbering.

uncouth *adj* coarse, vulgar, rude, rough,
loutish, oafish, ill-bred, unrefined,
unsophisticated.

uncover *verb* **1** strip, unwrap, open. **2**
bare, expose, show, reveal, unearth,
discover.

unctuous *adj* **1** insincere, gushing, effusive, smooth, glib, servile, ingratiating.
2 oily, greasy, fatty.

undaunted *adj* undismayed, undeterred,
unflinching, unshrinking, unwavering,
resolute, indomitable, dauntless.

undeceive *verb* correct, put right, set
straight, enlighten, disabuse, disillusion.

undecided *adj* **1** uncertain, unsure, doubtful, irresolute, wavering, in two minds
(*inf*). **2** unsettled, unresolved, up in the air
(*inf*), moot, undetermined.

undemonstrative *adj* reserved, unemotional, unaffectionate, formal, distant,
unresponsive.

undeniable *adj* unquestionable, indisputable, irrefutable, definite, positive, evident.

under *prep* **1** underneath, beneath, below,
lower than. **2** subject to, liable to, bound
by, controlled by. **3** subordinate to, junior

to, reporting to. **4** less than, below, lower than.
➤ *adv* down, downwards, underneath, beneath, below.

underclothes *pl noun* underwear, undergarments, underclothing, undies (*inf*), smalls (*inf*).

undercover *adj* secret, hush-hush (*inf*), covert, clandestine.

undercurrent *noun* **1** undertow, underflow. **2** undertone, hint, murmur, feeling, sense, trend.

underdog *noun* loser, victim, scapegoat.

underestimate *verb* miscalculate, misjudge, underrate, undervalue.

undergo *verb* **1** experience, go through, submit to. **2** suffer, sustain, be subjected to, endure, put up with.

underground *adj* **1** subterranean, buried, sunken. **2** secret, clandestine, undercover, covert. **3** subversive, revolutionary, unofficial, unorthodox, experimental, avant-garde.
➤ *noun* **1** metro, subway, tube (*inf*). **2** resistance, opposition.

undergrowth *noun* brush, scrub, ground cover, underwood.

underhand *adj* **1** underhanded, sly, crafty, devious, sneaky, unscrupulous. **2** clandestine, surreptitious, furtive, stealthy.

underline *verb* underscore, stress, emphasize, point up, highlight.

underling *noun* minion, lackey, subordinate, inferior, nonentity.

undermine *verb* **1** sap, weaken, subvert, destroy. **2** dig, excavate, tunnel, burrow. **3** erode, wear away.

underneath *prep and adv* under, beneath, below.
➤ *noun* bottom, underside.

undernourished *adj* malnourished, underfed, half-starved.

underprivileged *adj* deprived, disadvantaged, poor, needy.

underrate *verb* underestimate, undervalue, misprize, belittle.

undersized *adj* stunted, underdeveloped, puny, dwarf, miniature, small.

understand *verb* **1** comprehend, fathom, figure out, grasp, follow, see, get (*inf*). **2** appreciate, realize, recognize, acknowledge, sympathize. **3** believe, gather, conclude, suppose, assume, infer.

understanding *noun* **1** comprehension, grasp, awareness, perception, appreciation, realization. **2** intelligence, intellect, mind, reason, wisdom, insight. **3** interpretation, judgment, opinion, impression. **4** agreement, arrangement.
➤ *adj* sympathetic, compassionate, kind, considerate, patient, tolerant.

understate *verb* minimize, play down.

undertake *verb* **1** take on, shoulder, assume, embark on, tackle. **2** agree, promise, pledge, guarantee, engage, contract.

undertaker *noun* funeral director, mortician.

undertaking *noun* **1** venture, project, enterprise, task, mission, endeavour. **2** agreement, promise, pledge, assurance, guarantee.

undertone *noun* **1** murmur, whisper. **2** undercurrent, connotation, nuance, hint, suggestion, insinuation.

undervalue *verb* underestimate, underrate, misprize, hold cheap.

underwater *adj* subaqueous, submarine, undersea, submerged.

underwear *noun* underclothes, undergarments, lingerie, undies (*inf*), smalls (*inf*).

underwrite *verb* **1** endorse, sign, countersign, insure, guarantee. **2** back, sponsor, fund, finance, subsidize. **3** sanction, authorize, agree to, subscribe to.

undesirable *adj* unwelcome, unwanted, unenviable, unattractive, unpleasant, objectionable, unacceptable, unsuitable.

undignified *adj* unseemly, unbecoming, inelegant, ungainly.

undisciplined *adj* wild, unruly, disorderly, wayward, uncontrolled.

undisguised *adj* open, overt, evident, manifest, unconcealed, frank, sincere.

undisputed *adj* unchallenged, uncontested, unquestioned, recognized, acknowledged, accepted.

undistinguished adj ordinary, run-of-the-mill, indifferent, unexceptional, unremarkable, nothing special (inf).

undivided adj 1 full, complete, total, whole. 2 solid, unbroken, united.

undo verb 1 untie, open, unfasten, unbutton, unzip. 2 reverse, cancel, invalidate, counteract, neutralize. 3 ruin, wreck, destroy, shatter, crush.

undoing noun ruin, destruction, downfall, collapse, defeat.

undoubted adj certain, evident, undisputed, unquestioned, indubitable, undeniable.

undress verb disrobe, divest, strip. ➤noun nakedness, nudity.

undue adj excessive, immoderate, inordinate, extreme, unnecessary, unreasonable.

undulate verb roll, ripple, heave, swell, billow.

unduly adv excessively, inordinately, overmuch, overly.

undying adj eternal, everlasting, imperishable, indestructible, abiding, enduring.

unearth verb 1 excavate, dig up, exhume, disinter. 2 find, discover.

unearthly adj 1 weird, eerie, uncanny, spooky (inf). 2 unreasonable, ungodly (inf), outrageous, preposterous.

uneasy adj 1 uncomfortable, ill at ease, awkward, constrained. 2 tense, nervous, anxious, worried, apprehensive. 3 precarious, insecure, unstable.

uneconomic adj unprofitable, unremunerative, uncommercial, loss-making.

uneducated adj ignorant, illiterate, unschooled, untaught, unenlightened, benighted.

unemployed adj jobless, out of work, unwaged, on the dole (inf).

unending adj endless, interminable, incessant, unremitting, constant, perpetual.

unenthusiastic adj apathetic, half-hearted, lukewarm, unimpressed, indifferent.

unenviable adj undesirable, unpleasant, difficult, dangerous, thankless.

unequal adj 1 uneven, different, unlike, dissimilar. 2 unfair, inequitable, discriminatory, biased. 3 unbalanced, asymmetrical, disproportionate, unmatched. 4 incapable, inadequate, not up to (inf), unfit, unsuitable.

unequalled adj peerless, matchless, unparalleled, unrivalled, unsurpassed.

unequivocal adj unambiguous, explicit, clear, plain, positive, categorical, unqualified, direct.

unerring adj sure, accurate, perfect, faultless, unfailing, infallible.

unethical adj immoral, unprofessional, unscrupulous, dishonourable, underhand, wrong.

uneven adj 1 rough, lumpy, bumpy, hilly, undulating. 2 unequal, unbalanced, disproportionate, ill-matched. 3 irregular, inconsistent, variable, fluctuating, erratic.

uneventful adj ordinary, routine, unexciting, uninteresting, unexceptional, unremarkable.

unexpected adj unanticipated, unforeseen, unlooked-for, sudden, surprising, chance.

unfailing adj sure, reliable, dependable, constant, steadfast, infallible, unerring.

unfair adj 1 unjust, inequitable, unequal, biased, discriminatory, partial. 2 wrongful, undue, dishonest, unethical, unscrupulous, unsporting.

unfaithful adj 1 faithless, disloyal, false, untrue, perfidious, traitorous. 2 adulterous, inconstant, cheating (inf), two-timing (inf). 3 inaccurate, inexact, incorrect, wrong, faulty, imperfect.

unfaltering adj unswerving, unwavering, steady, constant, resolute, firm, determined.

unfamiliar adj 1 unusual, unknown, strange, alien, foreign, new. 2 unacquainted, unversed, unskilled, inexperienced, unaccustomed, unused.

unfasten adj 1 undo, open, unbutton, unzip, unlace. 2 untie, uncouple, disconnect, detach, separate.

unfathomable adj 1 deep, bottomless, unplumbed, immeasurable. 2 incomprehensible, inexplicable, baffling, impenetrable.

unfavourable *adj* **1** bad, negative, discouraging. **2** adverse, hostile, inimical, disadvantageous, unpromising, inauspicious.

unfeeling *adj* cold, callous, hard-hearted, unsympathetic, insensitive, uncaring.

unfettered *adj* free, unconfined, unrestrained, unchecked, unbridled, uninhibited.

unfinished *adj* incomplete, deficient, sketchy, rough.

unfit *adj* **1** unsuitable, inappropriate, unqualified, ineligible. **2** incompetent, incapable, inadequate, unequal, no good. **3** weak, feeble, unhealthy, out of condition.

unflagging *adj* indefatigable, tireless, unfailing, unfaltering, persistent.

unflappable *adj* cool, calm, collected, level-headed, equable, imperturbable.

unflattering *adj* uncomplimentary, critical, unfavourable, disparaging, unbecoming.

unflinching *adj* unshrinking, unfaltering, unwavering, firm, resolute, undaunted.

unfold *verb* **1** open, unfurl, unroll, spread out, flatten, straighten, stretch out, extend. **2** reveal, disclose, tell, elaborate, develop.

unforeseen *adj* unexpected, unanticipated, unpredicted, surprising.

unforgettable *adj* memorable, striking, remarkable, historic, special, distinctive.

unforgivable *adj* inexcusable, unpardonable, indefensible, reprehensible, deplorable.

unfortunate *adj* **1** unlucky, ill-fated, ill-starred, unsuccessful, disastrous. **2** luckless, hapless, poor, wretched, unhappy, tragic, regrettable, lamentable. **3** inappropriate, unsuitable, tactless, injudicious.

unfounded *adj* baseless, groundless, unproven, unsubstantiated, speculative.

unfriendly *adj* **1** hostile, antagonistic, unneighbourly, unsociable, standoffish, unapproachable. **2** inhospitable, unwelcoming, uncongenial, unpleasant.

unfurl *verb* open, unroll, unfold, spread out.

ungainly *adj* **1** clumsy, gauche, inelegant, gangling, uncoordinated, lumbering. **2** awkward, unwieldy.

ungenerous *adj* mean, niggardly, stingy (*inf*), parsimonious, tight-fisted.

ungodly *adj* **1** impious, irreverent, irreligious, profane, sacrilegious, unholy. **2** wicked, sinful, immoral, evil. **3** unreasonable, unearthly (*inf*), outrageous, preposterous.

ungovernable *adj* refractory, recalcitrant, uncontrollable, unmanageable, wild, unruly.

ungracious *adj* discourteous, impolite, rude, unmannerly.

ungrateful *adj* unthankful, unappreciative.

unguarded *adj* **1** unprotected, undefended, exposed, open. **2** careless, thoughtless, indiscreet, imprudent.

unhappy *adj* **1** miserable, sad, dejected, despondent, glum, sorrowful, melancholy. **2** unfortunate, unlucky, hapless, ill-fated. **3** inappropriate, unsuitable, ill-advised, injudicious.

unharmed *adj* safe, sound, unhurt, unscathed, undamaged, unimpaired.

unhealthy *adj* **1** unwell, ailing, ill, sickly, delicate, weak, infirm. **2** unwholesome, insalubrious, unhygienic, insanitary. **3** morbid, unnatural.

unheard-of *adj* unknown, undiscovered, obscure, unprecedented, new, extraordinary, unthinkable.

unheeded *adj* ignored, disregarded, overlooked, neglected, unnoticed.

unholy *adj* **1** impious, ungodly, sacrilegious, wicked, sinful, immoral. **2** outrageous, appalling, dreadful, awful.

unhurried *adj* slow, leisurely, easy, sedate, relaxed.

unhurt *adj* uninjured, unscathed, unharmed, undamaged.

unhygienic *adj* insanitary, insalubrious, unwholesome, unhealthy, dirty.

unidentified *adj* anonymous, unnamed, unclassified, unknown, unfamiliar, unrecognized.

unification *noun* union, merger, amalgamation, confederation.

uniform *noun* outfit, costume, dress, livery.
➤*adj* regular, even, unvarying, steady, consistent, homogeneous, same.

unify *verb* unite, combine, merge, amalgamate, consolidate.

unimaginative *adj* uninspired, unoriginal, derivative, banal, boring, uninteresting, bland.

unimpeachable *adj* blameless, irreproachable, impeccable, faultless, spotless, unassailable.

unimportant *adj* insignificant, inconsequential, trivial, trifling, petty, minor, immaterial, irrelevant.

uninhabited *adj* deserted, empty, vacant, unoccupied, unpopulated, unsettled.

uninhibited *adj* free, unconstrained, unselfconscious, relaxed, spontaneous, unreserved, open, frank.

unintelligible *adj* incomprehensible, impenetrable, incoherent, confused, garbled, illegible.

unintentional *adj* accidental, inadvertent, unpremeditated, involuntary, unwitting, chance.

uninterested *adj* indifferent, unconcerned, unresponsive, incurious, bored, unenthusiastic.

uninteresting *adj* boring, tedious, monotonous, dull, unexciting, uneventful.

uninterrupted *adj* unbroken, continuous, never-ending, non-stop, incessant, constant.

union *noun* 1 joining, connection, fusion, combination, amalgamation, merger.
2 league, alliance, coalition, confederacy, association, society, guild. 3 marriage, matrimony, wedlock, wedding.

unique *adj* 1 single, sole, only, lone, exclusive, one-off. 2 matchless, peerless, unequalled, unparalleled, incomparable, inimitable, exceptional, singular.

unit *noun* 1 part, component, element, constituent, piece, section, module.
2 measure, quantity.

unite *verb* 1 join, combine, fuse, connect, marry, wed, amalgamate, merge. 2 ally, associate, league, band, join forces, cooperate.

unity *noun* 1 wholeness, integrity, oneness. 2 concord, harmony, agreement, accord, consensus, unanimity, concert, solidarity.

universal *adj* general, comprehensive, all-embracing, all-inclusive, global.

universe *noun* 1 cosmos, macrocosm, creation. 2 world, humanity.

unjust *adj* unfair, inequitable, biased, discriminatory, wrongful, unreasonable, unwarranted, undeserved.

unkempt *adj* 1 dishevelled, tousled, rumpled, uncombed. 2 messy, untidy, slovenly, scruffy.

unkind *adj* cruel, nasty, uncharitable, mean, spiteful, callous, unsympathetic, inconsiderate.

unknown *adj* 1 undisclosed, secret, unnamed, unidentified. 2 unheard-of, obscure, unfamiliar, strange.

unlawful *adj* illegal, illicit, illegitimate, prohibited, banned, unauthorized, unlicensed.

unleash *verb* loose, free, release.

unlike *adj* different, dissimilar, disparate, distinct.
➤*prep* different from, dissimilar to, as opposed to, in contrast to.

unlikely *adj* 1 improbable, doubtful. 2 implausible, unconvincing, incredible, unbelievable.

unlimited *adj* 1 infinite, limitless, boundless, immeasurable, incalculable, never-ending. 2 absolute, total, unconditional, unqualified, unrestricted, uncontrolled.

unload *verb* 1 discharge, remove. 2 empty, unpack, disburden, disencumber.

unlock *verb* 1 open, unlatch, unbolt, unfasten. 2 free, release.

unloved *adj* unpopular, disliked, hated, uncared-for, neglected, unwanted, rejected, loveless.

unlucky *adj* 1 ill-fated, unsuccessful. 2 unfavourable, adverse, inauspicious, ominous, cursed, jinxed. 3 unfortunate, luckless, hapless, poor, wretched.

unman *verb* demoralize, dishearten, weaken, enfeeble, unnerve, daunt.

unmanageable *adj* uncontrollable, ungovernable, unruly, disorderly, difficult, awkward.

unmanly *adj* **1** cowardly, soft, weak, wet (*inf*). **2** effeminate, womanish, sissy (*inf*),

unmannerly *adj* rude, discourteous, uncivil, bad-mannered, boorish, churlish.

unmask *verb* expose, uncover, show, reveal, disclose.

unmatched *adj* matchless, peerless, unequalled, unparalleled, unrivalled, unsurpassed.

unmentionable *adj* unspeakable, unutterable, disgraceful, scandalous, shocking, embarrassing.

unmerciful *adj* merciless, pitiless, unsparing, cruel, brutal, inhuman.

unmistakable *adj* clear, distinct, plain, obvious, conspicuous, striking, positive, definite.

unmitigated *adj* **1** absolute, unqualified, veritable, consummate, utter, downright, out-and-out. **2** undiminished, intense, severe, harsh, unrelenting.

unmoved *adj* unaffected, untouched, indifferent, unfeeling, dry-eyed, impervious.

unnatural *adj* **1** abnormal, irregular, unusual, anomalous. **2** aberrant, deviant. **3** artificial, forced, laboured, stiff, affected, mannered, studied, contrived.

unnecessary *adj* needless, inessential, expendable, dispensable, superfluous, redundant, uncalled-for, gratuitous.

unnerve *verb* daunt, dismay, intimidate, unman, discourage, demoralize, disconcert, shake, upset, unsettle.

unobtrusive *adj* inconspicuous, unpretentious, unassuming, restrained, subdued, low-key, low-profile.

unoccupied *adj* **1** empty, vacant, uninhabited, untenanted. **2** idle, at leisure.

unofficial *adj* unauthorized, unlicensed, informal, unconfirmed, off-the-record, private.

unorthodox *adj* unconventional, unusual, irregular, aberrant, nonconformist, heterodox, alternative.

unpaid *adj* **1** due, outstanding, unsettled, owing, payable. **2** voluntary, honorary, unwaged.

unpalatable *adj* **1** unsavoury, unappetizing, inedible, uneatable. **2** unpleasant, disagreeable, nasty, distasteful, offensive, repugnant.

unparalleled *adj* peerless, unequalled, unmatched, unrivalled, incomparable, unprecedented, unexampled, unique.

unpardonable *adj* unforgivable, inexcusable, indefensible, reprehensible, deplorable.

unperturbed *adj* calm, composed, unruffled, unflustered, untroubled, unworried.

unpleasant *adj* disagreeable, nasty, bad, horrible, offensive, objectionable, undesirable, unattractive, unkind.

unpleasantness *noun* **1** disagreeableness, offensiveness, undesirability. **2** nastiness, ill feeling, trouble.

unpopular *adj* **1** disliked, hated, objectionable, unwelcome, undesirable, out of favour, unsought-after, unwanted. **2** friendless, unloved, cold-shouldered.

unprecedented *adj* new, unheard-of, unexampled, unparalleled, unequalled, exceptional, remarkable, unique, atypical, abnormal, freakish.

unpredictable *adj* changeable, variable, erratic, volatile, unstable, inconstant.

unprejudiced *adj* unbiased, impartial, neutral, objective, open-minded, fair, equitable, even-handed.

unpremeditated *adj* unplanned, spontaneous, impulsive, spur-of-the-moment (*inf*), impromptu, extempore.

unprepared *adj* unready, ill-equipped, unplanned, unrehearsed.

unprepossessing *adj* unattractive, plain, ugly.

unpretentious *adj* modest, simple, plain, homely, unaffected, unassuming, unostentatious.

unprincipled *adj* unscrupulous, dishonest, unethical, unprofessional, amoral, dishonourable, corrupt.

unprofessional *adj* unethical, unscrupulous, improper, amateur, unqualified, incompetent, amateurish, sloppy (*inf*).

unprofitable *adj* **1** unremunerative, unrewarding, unproductive. **2** fruitless, useless, futile, vain, unavailing.

unpromising *adj* unfavourable, adverse, unpropitious, inauspicious, gloomy, ominous, discouraging.

unprotected *adj* unguarded, unattended, defenceless, vulnerable, exposed, naked, unsheltered, uncovered.

unqualified *adj* **1** unlicensed, untrained, amateur, lay, incompetent, ineligible, unfit. **2** unconditional, unreserved, wholehearted, categorical, unequivocal, positive, absolute.

unquestionable *adj* indisputable, incontestable, incontrovertible, undoubted, irrefutable, undeniable, conclusive, certain, definite.

unravel *verb* **1** untangle, disentangle, unsnarl, undo, untwist, separate out. **2** solve, work out, fathom, decipher, resolve, clear up.

unreal *adj* **1** imaginary, fanciful, illusory, insubstantial, nonexistent, hypothetical, fictitious, false, artificial.

unrealistic *adj* impractical, unworkable, idealistic, quixotic, unreasonable, irrational, foolish, absurd, improbable, impossible.

unreasonable *adj* **1** excessive, immoderate, inordinate, undue, unwarranted. **2** irrational, illogical, senseless, crazy, absurd, ridiculous.

unrelenting *adj* **1** implacable, inexorable, ruthless, merciless, hard, unsparing. **2** continuous, relentless, unremitting, unabating, incessant.

unreliable *adj* undependable, untrustworthy, irresponsible, fickle, uncertain, suspect, unsound.

unremitting *adj* incessant, perpetual, constant, continual, relentless.

unreserved *adj* **1** unqualified, unconditional, unrestricted, wholehearted, unequivocal, absolute, total, full. **2** uninhibited, demonstrative, outgoing, open, frank, outspoken. **3** unbooked, free, vacant, available.

unrest *noun* rebellion, strife, discord, protest, discontent, agitation, turmoil, disorder.

unrestrained *adj* unchecked, unbridled, uncontrolled, unrestricted, unimpeded, free, uninhibited.

unripe *adj* **1** green, immature. **2** unready, unprepared.

unrivalled *adj* unmatched, peerless, unequalled, unparalleled, inimitable, incomparable, unsurpassed, supreme.

unroll *verb* open, unfold, unfurl, unwind, uncoil.

unruffled *adj* **1** collected, composed, poised, unperturbed, placid, serene. **2** flat, smooth, even, calm.

unruly *adj* ungovernable, unmanageable, uncontrollable, wild, refractory, insubordinate, riotous, disorderly.

unsafe *adj* **1** dangerous, hazardous, perilous, treacherous, risky, precarious, insecure, vulnerable. **2** unsound, unreliable.

unsaid *adj* unspoken, unmentioned, tacit, implicit.

unsatisfactory *adj* unacceptable, inadequate, deficient, faulty, poor, inferior, disappointing.

unsavoury *adj* **1** unpleasant, disagreeable, objectionable, offensive, nasty, distasteful, sordid, disreputable. **2** revolting, disgusting, nauseating, unpalatable, unappetizing.

unscathed *adj* unhurt, uninjured, unharmed, undamaged, safe, sound, whole, intact.

unscrupulous *adj* unprincipled, unethical, amoral, shameless, corrupt, dishonourable.

unseasonable *adj* untimely, ill-timed, inopportune.

unseat *verb* **1** unsaddle, unhorse, throw. **2** depose, dethrone, oust, dismiss, overthrow, topple.

unseemly *adj* unbecoming, undignified, improper, indecorous, inappropriate.

unseen *adj* unnoticed, unobserved, undetected, hidden, invisible.

unselfish *adj* altruistic, selfless, charitable, philanthropic, public-spirited, magnanimous, generous.

unsettle *verb* **1** destabilize, unbalance, derange, disturb. **2** upset, perturb, trouble, bother, agitate.

unsettled *adj* **1** changeable, variable, inconstant, unpredictable, unstable. **2** uneasy, tense, anxious, agitated, restless, insecure. **3** uninhabited, unoccupied, deserted, unpopulated, uncolonized. **4** unresolved, undecided, moot, pending, up in the air (*inf*). **5** unpaid, payable, owing, due, outstanding.

unshakable *adj* firm, resolute, steadfast, constant, unwavering, unswerving.

unsightly *adj* ugly, hideous, unattractive, unpleasant.

unskilful *adj* inexpert, amateurish, unprofessional, inept, incompetent, bungling.

unskilled *adj* untrained, unqualified, inexperienced, amateur.

unsociable *adj* **1** unfriendly, retiring, introverted, reclusive, standoffish. **2** uncongenial, inhospitable.

unsolicited *adj* **1** unsought, unasked, uninvited, unwanted. **2** voluntary, spontaneous, gratuitous, free.

unsophisticated **1** naive, unworldly, inexperienced, artless, ingenuous, uncultured, uncultivated. **2** simple, uncomplicated, straightforward, basic, primitive.

unsound *adj* **1** weak, frail, delicate, infirm, unhealthy, unfit, imperfect, defective. **2** unstable, shaky, rickety, wobbly, unsteady, insecure, flimsy, insubstantial. **3** faulty, flawed, illogical, unreliable, false, specious, fallacious, invalid.

unsparing *adj* **1** generous, liberal, openhanded, munificent, unstinting, ungrudging. **2** merciless, pitiless, ruthless, harsh, severe, unforgiving.

unspeakable *adj* **1** unutterable, ineffable, inexpressible, indescribable. **2** unmentionable, terrible, abominable, execrable, atrocious, deplorable, appalling.

unspoilt *adj* perfect, unharmed, unimpaired, preserved, unchanged, untouched.

unspoken *adj* tacit, understood, implicit, unexpressed, unsaid, mute, wordless.

unstable *adj* **1** insecure, unsound, unsteady, shaky, rickety, wobbly. **2** changeable, variable, inconstant, fluctuating, unsteady, irregular. **3** unbalanced, irrational, moody, mercurial, volatile, unpredictable.

unsteady *adj* **1** shaky, wobbly, tottering, unstable, unsafe, precarious. **2** irregular, erratic, inconstant, fluctuating, variable.

unstinting *adj* generous, liberal, unsparing, ungrudging, lavish, abundant.

unstudied *adj* natural, unaffected, unpretentious, unrehearsed, spontaneous.

unsubstantial *adj* light, frail, flimsy, tenuous.

unsubstantiated *adj* uncorroborated, unconfirmed, unverified, unproven.

unsuccessful *adj* futile, unavailing, ineffective, fruitless, unproductive, failed, abortive, ill-starred, losing, defeated, disappointed, unlucky.

unsuitable *adj* inappropriate, inapt, unfit, impractical, incompatible, out of keeping, unacceptable, improper.

unsung *adj* uncelebrated, unacknowledged, unrecognized, unhonoured, ignored, overlooked, anonymous, unknown.

unsure *adj* **1** uncertain, undecided, in two minds (*inf*), doubtful, sceptical, unconvinced. **2** hesitant, insecure, lacking confidence.

unsuspecting *adj* unaware, oblivious, trusting, credulous, gullible, unwary, off guard.

unswerving *adj* straight, direct, devoted, committed, constant, steadfast, unfaltering, unwavering.

untangle *verb* **1** disentangle, unsnarl, unravel, free, extricate. **2** straighten out, sort out, clear up.

untarnished *adj* **1** clean, bright, shining, polished. **2** unsullied, spotless, immaculate, stainless, unblemished, untainted.

untenable *adj* indefensible, unsound, weak, flawed, ill-founded, baseless, unacceptable, inadmissible.

unthinkable *adj* unimaginable, inconceivable, unheard-of, incredible, absurd, preposterous, impossible, out of the question.

unthinking *adj* **1** thoughtless, inconsiderate, insensitive, crass, tactless. **2** rash, careless, negligent, unmindful, heedless, inadvertent, automatic, mechanical.

untidy *adj* slovenly, scruffy, messy, careless, disorderly, littered, cluttered.

untie *verb* **1** undo, unfasten, unlace, unhitch. **2** release, loose, free, let go.

untimely *adj* **1** premature, early. **2** unseasonable, ill-timed, inopportune, inconvenient, awkward.

untold adj 1 incalculable, immeasurable, countless, innumerable, infinite. 2 extreme, indescribable, unimaginable, incredible. 3 secret, private, confidential, undisclosed, unpublished, unreported, unmentioned, unspoken.

untouched adj 1 unchanged, unaltered, unspoilt, pristine, undamaged, unused, brand-new. 2 unmoved, unaffected, indifferent, unconcerned. 3 unconsumed, uneaten.

untoward adj 1 adverse, unfavourable, contrary, hostile, unfortunate, inopportune, awkward, inconvenient. 2 unseemly, unbecoming, indecorous, improper, inappropriate. 3 unexpected, unusual, out of place, abnormal.

untried adj untested, unproven, experimental, new, novel.

untroubled adj 1 unworried, unconcerned, unruffled, unperturbed. 2 calm, peaceful, tranquil, serene.

untrue adj 1 false, untruthful, fabricated, made-up (*inf*), wrong, incorrect, inaccurate. 2 unfaithful, disloyal, treacherous, perfidious, untrustworthy.

untrustworthy adj unreliable, undependable, dishonest, deceitful, false, untrue, disloyal, unfaithful, inconstant.

untruth noun 1 falsehood, lie, fib (*inf*), whopper (*inf*), porky (*inf*). 2 lying, mendacity, untruthfulness, deceit, fabrication.

untruthful adj lying, mendacious, deceitful, false, untrue.

unused adj 1 new, pristine, untouched, intact. 2 leftover, surplus. 3 unaccustomed, unfamiliar, unacquainted, inexperienced, unpractised.

unusual adj 1 uncommon, infrequent, rare, strange, unfamiliar, unconventional, irregular, abnormal, atypical. 2 exceptional, extraordinary, remarkable.

unvarnished adj plain, simple, naked, undisguised, unembellished, unadorned, honest, frank.

unveil verb 1 reveal, expose, uncover, lay bare. 2 disclose, divulge, make known.

unwanted adj unsolicited, uninvited, unwelcome, undesirable, unnecessary, surplus, superfluous, redundant, rejected.

unwarranted adj unjustified, uncalled-for, gratuitous, unprovoked, undeserved, unreasonable, undue.

unwary adj incautious, unguarded, off guard, careless, heedless, unthinking, rash, imprudent.

unwavering adj unfaltering, unswerving, firm, unshakable, constant, steadfast.

unwelcome adj unwanted, uninvited, unpopular, undesirable, unpleasant.

unwell adj ill, sick, indisposed, poorly (*inf*), off colour, out of sorts (*inf*), unhealthy, unfit.

unwieldy adj bulky, large, heavy, cumbersome, ungainly, awkward, unmanageable.

unwilling adj reluctant, averse, loath, indisposed, disinclined.

unwind verb 1 unroll, uncoil, undo, unravel. 2 relax, wind down, take it easy (*inf*), chill out (*sl*).

unwise adj imprudent, incautious, inadvisable, injudicious, rash, foolish.

unwitting adj 1 unknowing, ignorant, unaware, unconscious, oblivious, unsuspecting. 2 accidental, inadvertent, unintentional, involuntary.

unwonted adj 1 uncharacteristic, uncustomary, atypical, abnormal. 2 unusual, uncommon, rare, unfamiliar, unaccustomed, novel..

unworldly adj 1 spiritual, metaphysical, unearthly, supernatural. 2 unsophisticated, inexperienced, naive, artless, ingenuous.

unworthy adj 1 unseemly, unbecoming, unbefitting, inappropriate. 2 dishonourable, ignoble, reprehensible, despicable, base. 3 undeserving, ineligible, unqualified. 4 inferior, second-rate, poor.

unwritten adj 1 oral, verbal, word-of-mouth, unrecorded. 2 understood, accepted, conventional, traditional.

unyielding adj 1 stiff, rigid, firm, hard, inflexible, unbending. 2 resolute, adamant, intransigent, uncompromising, stubborn, obdurate, intractable.

up-and-coming adj promising, ambitious, enterprising, go-getting (*inf*).

upbeat adj optimistic, hopeful, positive, bullish (*inf*), cheerful, buoyant, promising, encouraging.

upbraid verb scold, reprove, reproach, rebuke, castigate, berate.

upbringing adj raising, rearing, parenting, care, training, education.

update verb modernize, upgrade, renew, refresh, revise, amend.

upgrade verb 1 improve, enhance, update, modernize. 2 promote, advance, elevate, raise.

upheaval noun disruption, disturbance, upset, shake-up (inf), revolution, cataclysm.

uphill adj 1 hard, difficult, strenuous, arduous, laborious, gruelling, punishing, taxing, tough. 2 rising, ascending, upward, climbing.

uphold verb 1 sustain, maintain, keep up. 2 support, back, champion, defend.

upkeep noun 1 maintenance, conservation, preservation. 2 expenses, costs, overheads.

uplift verb 1 lift, raise, elevate, hoist. 2 exalt, edify, enrich, improve, cheer, hearten, inspire.

upper adj higher, superior, greater, senior, top.

upright adj 1 vertical, perpendicular, erect, on end. 2 righteous, good, worthy, decent, respectable, honourable, upstanding, honest, law-abiding.

uprising noun rebellion, revolt, insurrection, riot.

uproar noun 1 tumult, disturbance, pandemonium, commotion, brouhaha, rumpus. 2 outcry, furore.

uproarious adj 1 tumultuous, disorderly, riotous, noisy, clamorous, rowdy, boisterous. 2 hilarious, hysterical, side-splitting.

uproot verb 1 pull up, deracinate. 2 displace, remove. 3 destroy, eliminate, eradicate, extirpate.

upset verb 1 overturn, knock over, spill, capsize. 2 distress, sadden, hurt, dismay, alarm, worry, trouble, bother, annoy, disturb, fluster. 3 disrupt, spoil, mess up.
➤adj distressed, sad, hurt, sorry, dismayed, worried, troubled, bothered, annoyed, put out.

➤noun 1 distress, grief, dismay, alarm, worry, trouble, bother. 2 ailment, illness, disorder, complaint.

upside down adv and adj 1 inverted, wrong way up, overturned. 2 in disorder, topsy-turvy, in a mess.

up-to-date adj 1 current, up-to-the-minute. 2 modern, contemporary, fashionable, trendy (inf), latest, state-of-the-art (inf).

upturn noun upswing, improvement, recovery, rise, increase, upsurge.

urban adj civic, municipal, metropolitan, town, city, built-up.

urbane adj 1 suave, gracious, charming, polite, well-mannered. 2 elegant, refined, debonair, sophisticated, worldly, cultured.

urge verb 1 encourage, induce, persuade, beg, implore, exhort. 2 advise, recommend, advocate, demand, call for. 3 prompt, stimulate, motivate. 4 push, drive, impel, force, goad, spur.
➤noun desire, itch (inf), yen (inf), impulse, drive, compulsion.

urgent adj 1 pressing, immediate, high-priority, serious, imperative, crucial, critical, vital. 2 insistent, importunate, persistent, demanding.

urinate verb pass water, micturate, wee (inf), pee (inf), piss (sl).

usable adj exploitable, available, functional, operational, serviceable.

usage noun 1 custom, practice, tradition, convention, form, procedure, routine. 2 use, employment, application, treatment, handling.

use verb 1 operate, manipulate, wield, ply. 2 utilize, employ, apply, exercise, practise, make use of, avail oneself of. 3 consume, expend, drain, deplete. 4 abuse, misuse. 5 exploit, take advantage of, impose on. 6 treat, deal with, handle.
➤noun 1 utilization, employment, exploitation, exercise, practice, operation. 2 treatment, handling, usage. 3 purpose, reason, point. 4 utility, usefulness, good, worth, application, function, service.

used adj 1 secondhand, cast-off, hand-me-down (inf). 2 accustomed, familiar, habituated, inured, hardened.

useful *adj* helpful, serviceable, valuable, worthwhile, practical, functional, utilitarian, handy.

useless *adj* futile, vain, unavailing, ineffective, fruitless, unsuccessful, worthless, unusable.

usher *noun* guide, escort, attendant. ➤*verb* **1** guide, escort, lead, direct, conduct, show. **2** herald, announce, introduce.

usual *adj* **1** normal, typical, standard, conventional, customary, common, ordinary. **2** accustomed, habitual, wonted, routine, regular, set.

usurp *verb* seize, take over, commandeer, appropriate, arrogate, assume.

utensil *noun* implement, tool, device, appliance, gadget.

utilitarian *adj* practical, functional, useful, serviceable, plain.

utility *noun* usefulness, serviceability, practicality, convenience, use, help, service, avail.

utilize *verb* use, employ, make use of, put to use, exploit.

utmost *adj* **1** maximum, greatest, highest, supreme, paramount. **2** extreme, uttermost, farthest, furthest, ultimate. ➤*noun* maximum, most, uttermost, best, top.

utopian *adj* ideal, perfect, dream, elysian, idealistic, quixotic.

utter[1] *verb* say, speak, express, voice, vocalize, pronounce, articulate.

utter[2] *adj* complete, total, absolute, downright, out-and-out, unmitigated.

utterance *noun* **1** remark, comment, statement, declaration. **2** expression, voice, articulation.

vacancy *noun* **1** job, post, position, opening. **2** room, place. **3** void, gap, space. **4** emptiness, blankness.

vacant *adj* **1** empty, unoccupied, free, available. **2** vacuous, inane, stupid. **3** blank, expressionless, deadpan.

vacate *verb* **1** evacuate, abandon, desert. **2** quit, leave.

vacation *noun* **1** holiday, trip, leave, time off. **2** recess, break.

vaccinate *verb* inoculate, immunize.

vacillate *verb* **1** waver, falter, hesitate, dither. **2** fluctuate, oscillate, sway, rock.

vacuous *adj* vacant, stupid, inane, mindless.

vacuum *noun* void, emptiness, vacuity, space.

vagabond *noun* vagrant, tramp, beggar, nomad, itinerant, wanderer.

vagary *noun* whim, fancy, caprice, notion.

vagrant *noun* tramp, down-and-out, beggar, vagabond, nomad, itinerant, drifter, wanderer, traveller.
➤*adj* nomadic, itinerant, peripatetic, wandering, roving, rootless, homeless.

vague *adj* **1** indistinct, indeterminate, ill-defined, obscure, nebulous. **2** hazy, fuzzy, blurred, dim, faint. **3** ambiguous, rough, loose, general. **4** imprecise, woolly, unclear, indefinite. **5** uncertain, confused.

vain *adj* **1** conceited, boastful, proud, arrogant, egotistical, narcissistic, boastful, big-headed (*inf*). **2** futile, idle, unavailing, ineffectual, fruitless, unsuccessful.
in vain vainly, to no avail, ineffectually, unsuccessfully.

valediction *noun* farewell, goodbye, adieu, parting, leave-taking.

valiant *adj* valorous, brave, courageous, heroic, intrepid.

valid *adj* **1** well-grounded, justifiable, reasonable, convincing, credible, relevant. **2** logical, sound. **3** official, legal, legitimate, genuine, authentic, bona fide, binding, effective.

validate *verb* **1** ratify, certify, sanction, authorize, legalize, license. **2** substantiate, confirm, corroborate, authenticate, verify.

valley *noun* dale, dell, vale, glen.

valour *noun* bravery, courage, heroism, fortitude, pluck, spirit.

valuable *adj* **1** precious, costly, expensive, priceless. **2** helpful, advantageous, beneficial, profitable, useful, worthwhile.

value *noun* **1** use, utility, worth, merit, importance, advantage, good. **2** cost, price, worth, valuation, assessment.
➤*verb* **1** prize, esteem, appreciate, hold dear, treasure. **2** evaluate, assess, estimate, price. **3** appraise, rate.

values *pl noun* morals, principles, ethics, standards.

vanguard *noun* **1** front line, advance guard, spearhead. **2** fore, forefront, van.

vanish *verb* **1** disappear, fade, evanesce, dissipate, disperse, go away. **2** die out, end.

vanity *noun* **1** conceit, egotism, self-love, narcissism, pride, boastfulness, bigheadedness (*inf*). **2** futility, worthlessness, emptiness, idleness, pointlessness, fruitlessness.

vanquish *verb* **1** defeat, conquer, subjugate, rout, beat, crush. **2** repress, subdue, conquer, overcome, quell, master.

vapid *adj* insipid, flat, lifeless, wishy-washy, bland, banal, uninteresting.

vapour *noun* steam, smoke, fog, mist, fumes, exhalation.

variable *adj* **1** changeable, mutable, fluctuating, unsteady, unstable, shifting. **2** capricious, mercurial, fickle, inconstant.

variance *noun* **1** variation, divergence, difference. **2** disagreement, dispute, conflict, opposition. **3** discrepancy, disparity.

variant *noun* **1** variation, alternative. **2** development, modification.

variation *noun* **1** alteration, modification, change, novelty, difference, discrepancy, deviation, divergence. **2** diversity, variety. **3** variant, mutation.

varied *adj* **1** diverse, multifarious, wide-ranging, different. **2** various, assorted, mixed, miscellaneous, heterogeneous.

variegated *adj* mottled, dappled, pied, marbled, streaked.

variety *noun* **1** diversity, multiplicity, difference, dissimilarity, disparity, variation. **2** miscellany, assortment, mixture, medley, collection, range. **3** kind, type, sort. **4** breed, strain.

various *adj* **1** varying, varied, diverse, assorted, miscellaneous, motley. **2** different, unlike, dissimilar, disparate. **3** sundry, many, several, manifold.

varnish *noun* glaze, gloss, lacquer, polish, enamel, shellac.
➤*verb* glaze, lacquer, polish, enamel.

vary *verb* **1** change, alter. **2** deviate, diverge, swerve, depart, differ, disagree. **3** modify, change, alter, permute. **4** alternate, diversify

vast *adj* immense, extensive, boundless, immeasurable, huge, enormous, great, colossal.

vault[1] *noun* **1** arch, span, roof. **2** cellar, basement, chamber, cavern. **3** strong room, depository. **4** tomb, crypt, mausoleum.

vault[2] *verb* leap, jump, hurdle, clear.

vaunt *verb* boast, brag, trumpet, parade, flaunt, show off (*inf*).

veer *verb* change, swing, shift, turn, swerve, deviate, diverge.

vegetate *verb* languish, idle, do nothing, loaf, lounge, stagnate.

vehement *adj* **1** ardent, fervent, impassioned, keen, intense, violent, fierce, strong. **2** passionate, spirited, forceful, emphatic, furious, heated.

vehicle *noun* **1** conveyance, means of transport, car. **2** means, agency, medium, channel.

veil *noun* **1** screen, cloak, mantle, shroud, mask. **2** disguise, pretext, blind.
➤*verb* cover, screen, cloak, obscure, conceal, mask, disguise.

vein *noun* **1** seam, stratum, lode. **2** streak, stripe, line. **3** strain, streak, dash, trait. **4** frame of mind, mood, humour, character, tone.

velocity *noun* speed, rate, swiftness, rapidity.

venal *adj* corruptible, bribable, bent (*inf*), mercenary, grasping.

vendetta *noun* feud, rivalry, quarrel, enmity, bad blood.

vendor *noun* seller, merchant, trader, dealer, supplier, stockist.

veneer *noun* **1** layer, covering, surface, facing, finish. **2** front, facade, show, appearance.

venerable *adj* venerated, revered, respected, honoured, esteemed.

venerate *verb* revere, honour, esteem, worship.

vengeance *noun* revenge, retribution, retaliation, reprisal.
with a vengeance furiously, vehemently, violently, forcefully.

vengeful *adj* revengeful, vindictive, unforgiving, avenging, retaliatory, retributive.

venial *adj* excusable, pardonable, forgivable, minor.

venom *noun* **1** poison, toxin. **2** rancour, spite, ill will, acrimony, malevolence, hostility, gall, spleen.

venomous *adj* **1** poisonous, toxic, envenomed. **2** spiteful, vindictive, vicious, hostile, malevolent, rancorous.

vent *noun* hole, aperture, opening, outlet.
➤*verb* **1** release, emit, discharge. **2** air, express, voice.

ventilate *verb* **1** air, air-condition, cool, freshen. **2** aerate, oxygenate. **3** discuss, debate, review, examine, air.

venture *verb* **1** risk, hazard, endanger, jeopardize, chance. **2** dare, presume. **3** advance, volunteer.

➤*noun* undertaking, enterprise, mission, project, operation, speculation.

venturesome *adj* daring, bold, adventurous, enterprising, brave, fearless, spirited.

veracious *adj* **1** truthful, honest, frank, sincere, honourable, reliable. **2** true, factual, accurate, exact.

verbal *adj* **1** spoken, oral, vocal, unwritten. **2** verbatim, literal, word-of-mouth.

verbatim *adv and adj* word-for-word, to the letter, literally, exactly.

verbiage *noun* verbosity, prolixity, wordiness, waffle.

verbose *adj* **1** wordy, long-winded, circumlocutory, periphrastic. **2** prolix, loquacious, garrulous, talkative.

verdant *adj* green, grassy, leafy, lush.

verdict *noun* **1** decision, conclusion, finding. **2** judgment, opinion.

verge *noun* **1** edge, border, margin, limit, boundary. **2** brink, threshold, point.
verge on/upon approach, border on, tend towards, be close to.

verify *verb* **1** ascertain, establish, authenticate, validate. **2** confirm, corroborate, endorse, bear out, prove. **3** substantiate, attest, affirm.

veritable *adj* real, actual, positive, absolute.

verity *noun* truth, reality, actuality, fact.

vernacular *adj* native, indigenous, local, colloquial, popular, common, vulgar.
➤*noun* **1** native language, mother tongue, dialect, patois. **2** parlance, idiom, jargon, slang.

versatile *adj* **1** adaptable, all-round, flexible, resourceful. **2** all-purpose, multipurpose, handy, functional.

verse *noun* **1** rhyme, metre, poetry, doggerel. **2** stanza, canto.

versed *adj* skilled, proficient, accomplished, practised, knowledgeable.

version *noun* **1** rendering, interpretation, account, reading. **2** adaptation, translation. **3** type, model, style, design, form.

vertex *noun* apex, summit, point, tip, top, height.

vertical *adj* upright, perpendicular, erect, on end.

vertigo *noun* giddiness, dizziness, lightheadedness, wooziness (*inf*).

verve *noun* **1** vigour, energy, force, vitality, relish, gusto. **2** enthusiasm, spirit, passion, sparkle, animation.

very *adv* extremely, exceedingly, terribly (*inf*), awfully (*inf*), highly, deeply, greatly, really, truly.
➤*adj* **1** actual, selfsame, identical, genuine. **2** perfect, ideal, exact, right. **3** sheer, pure, simple, mere.

vessel *noun* **1** boat, ship, craft. **2** container, receptacle, bowl.

vestibule *noun* lobby, foyer, anteroom, hall, porch.

vestige *noun* **1** trace, mark, sign, indication. **2** hint, touch, scrap, dash, iota, glimmer.

vet *verb* check, inspect, scrutinize, investigate, examine.

veteran *noun* old hand, old-timer, past master, expert.

veto *noun* prohibition, proscription, ban, embargo, rejection.
➤*verb* reject, turn down, prohibit, proscribe, disallow, ban.

vex *verb* annoy, irritate, provoke, exasperate, infuriate, irk, anger.

vexation *noun* annoyance, bother, nuisance, pain (*inf*), problem, trouble, affliction.

vexatious *adj* annoying, irritating, exasperating, infuriating, irksome, troublesome, worrying, distressing.

viable *adj* practicable, feasible, workable, possible, achievable.

vibrant *adj* energetic, dynamic, vigorous, lively, spirited, animated, vivacious, sparkling.

vibrate *verb* **1** shake, tremble, quiver, flutter, palpitate, pulsate, throb. **2** oscillate, swing. **3** resonate, resound, reverberate, ring.

vibration *noun* shake, tremor, judder (*inf*), throb, pulsation, resonance, reverberation.

vicar *noun* minister, parson, pastor, rector, priest.

vicarious *adj* **1** indirect, secondhand, sympathetic. **2** surrogate, delegated, acting.

vice *noun* **1** immorality, corruption, depravity, degeneracy. **2** sin, wrongdoing, iniquity, evil. **3** weakness, foible, fault, flaw, failing, shortcoming.

vice versa *adv* conversely, reciprocally, the other way round, contrariwise.

vicinity *noun* neighbourhood, locality, surroundings, precincts, environs.

vicious *adj* **1** savage, ferocious, fierce, dangerous. **2** violent, brutal, cruel, sadistic, barbarous. **3** wicked, evil, sinful, immoral, corrupt, depraved, degenerate.

vicissitude *noun* variation, change, shift, alteration, fluctuation.

victim *noun* **1** sufferer, casualty, target, butt, prey, quarry. **2** dupe, sucker (*inf*). **3** sacrifice, martyr.

victimize *verb* **1** persecute, discriminate against, pick on. **2** prey on, fool, dupe, swindle, defraud.

victor *noun* winner, champion, conqueror, hero.

victorious *adj* **1** winning, conquering, champion, first, top. **2** triumphant, successful.

victory *noun* win, conquest, triumph, success.

vie *verb* strive, struggle, compete, contend, fight.

view *noun* **1** sight, vision. **2** scene, vista, prospect, outlook, panorama. **3** aspect, perspective. **4** survey, review. **5** examination, inspection, scrutiny, study, observation, contemplation. **6** opinion, belief, judgment, thinking, idea, feeling, attitude. **7** aim, intention, purpose, object.
▷*verb* **1** watch, observe, look at, survey, scan. **2** consider, regard, deem, judge. **3** examine, inspect, scrutinize. **4** contemplate, think about, consider.
in view of considering, bearing in mind, in the light of, taking into account.

viewpoint *noun* standpoint, point of view, perspective, angle, position.

vigilant *adj* watchful, observant, attentive, awake, alert, unsleeping, wary, cautious.

vigorous *adj* **1** strong, robust, lusty, hardy, sturdy, tough, fit. **2** energetic, strenuous, brisk, spirited, powerful, forceful.

vigour *noun* **1** energy, vitality, dynamism, strength, stamina, toughness, resilience. **2** power, force, forcefulness, gusto, vehemence, intensity.

vile *adj* **1** base, low, wicked, evil, immoral, villainous, heinous, despicable, loathsome, abhorrent. **2** foul, disgusting, repulsive, revolting, offensive. **3** nasty, unpleasant, disagreeable, horrible, obnoxious, objectionable.

vilify *verb* defame, denigrate, malign, slander, libel, slur, smear, badmouth (*inf*).

villain *noun* **1** scoundrel, rogue, rascal. **2** criminal, miscreant, malefactor, wrongdoer. **3** evildoer, baddy (*inf*).

vindicate *verb* **1** clear, acquit, exculpate, exonerate, absolve. **2** justify, defend, support, corroborate, confirm. **3** uphold, maintain, assert.

vindictive *adj* vengeful, revengeful, spiteful, malicious, rancorous, unforgiving.

vintage *noun* **1** crop, harvest, yield. **2** era, epoch, period.
▷*adj* **1** choice, fine, select, superior, high-quality. **2** classic, enduring, ageless.

violate *verb* **1** break, flout, contravene, infringe, breach. **2** rape, assault, molest, abuse. **3** profane, desecrate, defile, dishonour.

violence *noun* **1** aggression, brutality, savagery, roughness, fighting, bloodshed. **2** power, strength, intensity, force, wildness, turbulence. **3** vehemence, passion, fury, ferocity, fervour.

violent *adj* **1** strong, powerful, forceful, intense, wild, turbulent, destructive, devastating. **2** savage, ferocious, brutal, murderous, vicious, aggressive. **3** agonizing, painful. **4** vehement, ardent, fervent, passionate, fiery, furious.

virago *noun* shrew, termagant, harridan, battle-axe (*inf*).

virgin *adj* **1** virginal, chaste, pure, immaculate, intact, celibate. **2** virtuous, modest, maidenly. **3** undefiled, unsullied, untainted, spotless, stainless, pristine. **4** new, fresh, untouched, unspoilt, unexploited.

virginal *adj* **1** pure, chaste, celibate, virtuous. **2** new, fresh, untouched.

virile adj 1 strong, muscular, rugged, strapping. 2 manly, masculine, macho (inf). 3 powerful, forceful, vigorous, lusty.

virtual adj practical, essential, effective.

virtually adv practically, as good as, effectively, almost, nearly.

virtue noun 1 goodness, morality, rectitude, probity, integrity, honour. 2 advantage, benefit, strength, asset, quality, merit. 3 chastity, purity, virginity.
by virtue of because of, owing to, on account of, thanks to, as a result of.

virtuoso noun expert, maestro, genius.

virtuous adj 1 good, righteous, moral, honourable, incorruptible, upright, decent, respectable, exemplary, blameless. 2 pure, chaste, virginal, modest.

virulent adj 1 severe, acute, pernicious. 2 poisonous, venomous, toxic, deadly, lethal. 3 bitter, acrimonious, hostile, malicious, malignant, vitriolic.

viscous adj sticky, adhesive, mucilaginous, glutinous, thick, syrupy, gooey (inf).

visible adj 1 observable, perceptible, detectable, discernible. 2 exposed, open, unconcealed. 3 apparent, evident, noticeable, manifest, plain, conspicuous.

vision noun 1 sight, eyesight, perception, seeing. 2 foresight, farsightedness, discernment, insight, intuition. 3 apparition, phantom, dream, fantasy, hallucination, illusion, mirage. 5 imagination, creativity.

visionary adj 1 farsighted, discerning, perceptive, intuitive, imaginative, creative. 2 dreamy, romantic, idealistic, quixotic. 3 unreal, imaginary, illusory, fanciful, impracticable, unrealistic
➤noun seer, prophet, mystic, dreamer, romantic, idealist, fantasist.

visit verb 1 call on, look up, see, drop in on (inf). 2 inspect, examine. 3 assail, attack, afflict.
➤noun 1 call, stay, trip. 2 inspection, examination, visitation.

visitation noun 1 visit, inspection, examination. 2 affliction, scourge, blight, plague, disaster, ordeal.

visitor noun caller, guest, tourist, traveller, pilgrim.

vista noun view, scene, prospect, outlook.

visualize verb picture, conjure up, envisage, imagine, conceive.

vital adj 1 critical, crucial, key, essential, , necessary, imperative. 2 lively, spirited, vivacious, dynamic, energetic, animated.

vitality noun 1 liveliness, vivacity, vigour, energy, dynamism, spirit. 2 life, animation.

vitiate verb impair, harm, mar, blight, debase, corrupt, pervert, defile.

vituperate verb censure, condemn, denounce, slate (inf), revile, rail against, reprove, berate.

vivacious adj lively, animated, spirited, bubbly (inf), sparkling, ebullient.

vivid adj 1 bright, strong, rich, intense, brilliant, dazzling, glaring, lurid. 2 graphic, striking, clear, distinct, memorable. 3 powerful, dramatic, realistic, true to life.

vocal adj 1 oral, spoken, voiced. 2 noisy, vociferous, forthright, outspoken, articulate, eloquent.

vocation noun career, profession, occupation, calling, trade, work, business, job.

vociferate verb shout, yell, bellow, bawl, cry, clamour.

vociferous adj noisy, vocal, loud, strident, clamorous, insistent, vehement.

vogue noun 1 fashion, mode, style, trend, rage, craze, fad (inf). 2 favour, popularity, prevalence, currency.

voice noun 1 sound, tone, accent. 2 vocalization, verbalization, expression, utterance, speech, articulation. 3 wish, view, opinion, desire, vote, say.
➤verb express, state, say, declare.

void adj 1 empty, vacant, unoccupied, blank. 2 devoid, lacking, without. 3 invalid, null, ineffective, inoperative. 4 useless, vain, nugatory.
➤noun 1 emptiness, vacuity, vacuum. 2 space, blank, gap, opening, hole, hollow.
➤verb 1 cancel, invalidate, nullify, annul, revoke. 2 empty, evacuate, clear.

volatile adj 1 changeable, variable, inconstant, unstable. 2 fickle, capricious, flighty, mercurial, giddy, frivolous.

volition noun **1** decision, choice, preference, wish. **2** free will, discretion, determination, resolution.

volley noun **1** barrage, bombardment, fusillade, cannonade, salvo. **2** burst, shower, hail, storm.

voluble adj talkative, loquacious, garrulous, chatty (inf), articulate, fluent.

volume noun **1** capacity, size, dimensions. **2** quantity, amount. **3** mass, bulk. **4** tome, book, publication. **5** loudness, amplification.

voluminous adj spacious, roomy, capacious, big, large, vast, ample.

voluntary adj **1** free, gratuitous, unasked, unforced, unpaid, optional, willing, spontaneous. **2** intentional, conscious, deliberate.

volunteer verb offer, tender, give, put forward.

voluptuous adj **1** sensual, fleshly, hedonistic, self-indulgent, sybaritic, voluptuary. **2** erotic, sexy (inf), buxom, well-endowed, shapely, curvaceous (inf).

vomit verb be sick, disgorge, regurgitate, bring up, throw up (inf), spew (inf), puke (inf).

voracious adj **1** greedy, ravenous, gluttonous, omnivorous. **2** insatiable, avid.

vortex noun whirlpool, maelstrom, eddy, whirlwind.

votary noun devotee, adherent, disciple, worshipper, fanatic, aficionado.

vote noun **1** ballot, poll, election, referendum. **2** suffrage, franchise, voice, say.

vouch verb **1** guarantee, assure, answer for. **2** support, uphold, back, endorse. **3** attest, affirm, certify, confirm.

voucher noun **1** receipt, chit, slip, note. **2** coupon, token, ticket.

vouchsafe verb **1** grant, give, confer, accord. **2** deign, condescend.

vow noun promise, pledge, oath.
➤ verb promise, pledge, swear.

voyage noun journey, expedition, cruise, passage.
➤ verb journey, travel.

vulgar adj **1** coarse, rough, rude, boorish, uncouth, unrefined, uncultivated, common. **2** indecent, obscene, dirty, crude. **3** ordinary, general, popular, common. **4** loud, garish, tasteless, kitsch, flashy, ostentatious, pretentious.

vulnerable adj **1** assailable, defenceless, unguarded, unprotected, exposed. **2** weak, helpless, tender, sensitive, susceptible.

wad *noun* **1** lump, mass, ball, pad, plug. **2** roll, bundle.

wadding *noun* packing, padding, stuffing, filling.

waddle *verb* shuffle, toddle, sway, rock.

wade *verb* **1** ford, paddle, splash, wallow. **2** plough, labour, toil.
wade in pitch in, buckle down, set to, get stuck in (*inf*).

waffle *noun* padding, verbiage, prattle, blather, rubbish.
➤ *verb* ramble, prattle, witter (*inf*), rabbit (*inf*).

waft *verb* drift, float, glide, blow.

wag¹ *verb* wave, swing, sway, shake, twitch, wiggle, waggle.

wag² *noun* humorist, comic, comedian, wit, joker, clown.

wage *noun* **1** pay, salary, earnings, remuneration, hire, fee. **2** recompense, reward.
➤ *verb* engage in, carry on, pursue, conduct.

wager *noun* **1** stake, pledge. **2** bet, gamble, flutter (*inf*), speculation, venture.
➤ *verb* bet, gamble, punt (*inf*), risk, hazard, venture.

waggish *adj* witty, droll, humorous, comical, facetious, jocular.

waggle *verb* wag, wiggle, wobble, shake, wave, sway.

wail *verb* **1** cry, moan, howl, whine. **2** lament, keen, ululate, mourn.
➤ *noun* cry, moan, howl, whine, lamentation, ululation.

wait *verb* **1** stay, remain, await, expect, stand by, sit tight (*inf*). **2** pause, hesitate, delay, tarry. **3** hold back, mark time, hang fire (*inf*).
➤ *noun* delay, hold-up, hesitation, halt, pause, rest.
wait on serve, attend to, minister to, look after.

waiter *noun* attendant, server, steward.

waive *verb* renounce, relinquish, resign, give up, surrender, cede, forgo, set aside.

wake¹ *verb* **1** waken, awaken, rouse, come to, stir, rise. **2** realize, become aware of, become conscious of.
➤ *noun* vigil, watch.

wake² *noun* **1** wash, track. **2** path, trail, track.

wakeful *adj* **1** alert, watchful, vigilant, awake, unsleeping, insomniac. **2** sleepless, restless.

walk *verb* **1** step, stride, pace, march, stroll, hike, plod. **2** escort, accompany, conduct, shepherd.
➤ *noun* **1** stroll, promenade, ramble, hike, constitutional, airing. **2** gait, step, stride, pace. **3** walkway, footpath, pathway, pavement, esplanade, promenade, track, trail. **4** route, round, beat.
walk of life 1 occupation, line of work, trade, profession, career, job. **2** area, province, field, sphere.
walk off with steal, pilfer, nick (*inf*), pinch (*inf*).
walk out 1 storm out, flounce out. **2** strike, stop work, down tools, take industrial action.

walker *noun* pedestrian, rambler, hiker, wayfarer.

walkout *noun* industrial action, strike, stoppage.

wall *noun* **1** partition, divider, screen. **2** fence, paling. **3** barrier, obstacle, barricade, rampart, bulwark, parapet.

wallow *verb* **1** loll, roll, lie, splash, flounder. **2** bask, luxuriate, indulge, revel, delight, glory. **3** pitch, lurch.

wan *adj* **1** pale, pallid, ashen, pasty, waxen, sickly, peaky, washed-out. **2** weak, feeble, weary, worn. **3** faint, dim.

wand *noun* **1** stick, rod, baton. **2** staff, mace, sceptre.

wander *verb* **1** roam, rove, drift, range, ramble, stroll, cruise. **2** meander, wind. **3** depart, deviate, swerve, diverge, veer, stray, err, digress. **4** rave, ramble, babble, gibber.
➤*noun* saunter, stroll, ramble, peregrination.

wane *verb* **1** diminish, shrink, vanish. **2** fade, dim. **3** decline, fail, decrease, ebb, dwindle, weaken, drop, sink.
on the wane diminishing, vanishing, fading, declining, failing, decreasing, dwindling, sinking.

wangle *verb* fix, fiddle (*inf*), arrange, contrive, engineer, manoeuvre, manipulate.

want *verb* **1** desire, wish for, fancy, feel like, long for, hanker after, covet, crave. **2** lack, need, miss. **3** require, need, demand, call for.
➤*noun* **1** need, requirement, demand, wish, desire, craving, fancy, yen (*inf*). **2** lack, absence, dearth, default, deficiency, shortage, scarcity. **3** poverty, privation, indigence, penury, destitution, neediness.

wanting *adj* **1** missing, absent, lacking. **2** short, lacking, deficient. **3** inadequate, substandard, defective, faulty, inferior, poor, unsatisfactory, unacceptable.

wanton *adj* **1** promiscuous, immoral, immodest, shameless, loose, abandoned, debauched, dissolute, lustful, libidinous, lewd, lascivious. **2** needless, unnecessary, groundless, unjustified, gratuitous, uncalled-for, unprovoked, wilful, arbitrary, malicious. **3** abundant, profuse, lavish, extravagant, luxuriant.

war *noun* **1** warfare, hostilities, combat, conflict, strife, bloodshed. **2** campaign, struggle, fight, battle, crusade.
➤*verb* wage war, fight, battle, take up arms.

warble *verb* trill, sing, chirrup, twitter, pipe.

ward *noun* **1** district, precinct, division, zone, quarter, area. **2** charge, protégé, dependant, minor.

ward off avert, deflect, parry, fend off, stave off, keep at bay, repel, repulse.

warden *noun* **1** curator, guardian, keeper, custodian, protector. **2** superintendent, supervisor, overseer, official, attendant.

warder *noun* prison officer, guard, jailer, screw (*inf*).

wardrobe *noun* **1** cupboard, closet. **2** clothes, garments, gear (*inf*), togs (*inf*).

warehouse *noun* depot, depository, store, storehouse, storeroom, stockroom.

wares *pl noun* goods, products, commodities, merchandise, stock.

warfare *noun* **1** war, hostilities, fighting, combat, strife, battle. **2** struggle, conflict.

warlike *adj* **1** belligerent, bellicose, pugnacious, combative, bloodthirsty, militaristic, warmongering. **2** martial, military. **3** hostile, aggressive.

warlock *noun* sorcerer, wizard, magician, necromancer.

warm *adj* **1** tepid, lukewarm, heated, balmy, close, temperate. **2** energetic, vigorous. **3** enthusiastic, ardent, fervent, passionate, earnest, sincere, heartfelt, hearty, cordial. **4** friendly, affable, genial, loving, caring, affectionate, tender, kind, sympathetic. **5** lively, animated, heated
➤*verb* heat, reheat.
warm up exercise, prepare, loosen up, limber up.

warmth *noun* heat, warmness, ardour, fervour, sincerity, enthusiasm, passion, heartiness, friendliness, affection, tenderness, kindness.

warn *verb* **1** caution, alert, forewarn, tip off (*inf*). **2** advise, counsel, admonish, exhort, urge. **3** notify, inform, advise, alert, apprise, give notice.

warning *noun* **1** omen, portent, premonition, sign, alert, alarm, threat, admonition, caution, counsel, advice, tip-off (*inf*). **2** notice, notification, forewarning.

warp *verb* **1** twist, bend, turn, contort, misshape, deform. **2** falsify, distort, bias, pervert, corrupt.

warrant *noun* **1** authority, permit, licence, commission. **2** authorization, permission, sanction, consent.
➤*verb* **1** guarantee, swear, certify, testify, vouch for, endorse, support, uphold,

underwrite. **2** authorize, sanction, permit, allow, entitle, empower, commission, license. **3** justify, excuse, vindicate, require, call for, necessitate. **4** declare, affirm.

warrior *noun* fighter, soldier, combatant.

wary *adj* cautious, careful, chary, circumspect, guarded, watchful, vigilant, alert, suspicious, distrustful.

wash *verb* **1** bath, freshen up, shampoo, clean, launder, scrub, wipe, mop, bathe, cleanse. **2** flush, rinse, swill. **3** splash, beat, break, dash. **4** sweep, carry off. **5** pour, flow. **6** stand up, hold water, bear scrutiny, pass muster.
➤*noun* **1** bath, shower, clean, scrub, wipe. **2** washing, laundry. **3** coat, layer, film, rinse. **4** stain, paint.

washed-out *adj* **1** pale, colourless, flat, lacklustre, faded, bleached. **2** lifeless, listless, exhausted, tired out, worn out, all in (*inf*).

waspish *adj* irritable, irascible, cross, snappish, grumpy, peevish, petulant, prickly (*inf*).

waste *verb* **1** squander, fritter away, misspend, misuse, dissipate, use up, go through. **2** throw away, blow (*inf*). **3** wither, wilt, shrivel, atrophy, weaken, decline, wane, fade. **4** devastate, lay waste to, desolate, ravage, destroy, sack, despoil, raze.
➤*noun* **1** dissipation, misuse, squandering, loss, extravagance, wastefulness. **2** rubbish, refuse, trash, garbage, leftovers, leavings, scraps, slops, litter, debris. **3** wasteland, desert, wilderness.
➤ *adj* **1** unwanted, extra, superfluous, leftover, unused. **2** desolate, wild, uninhabited, unpopulated, deserted, empty. **2** uncultivated, unproductive, wild, barren.

wasteful *adj* extravagant, prodigal, profligate, lavish, thriftless, improvident, uneconomical.

watch *verb* **1** stare at, peer at, gaze at, scrutinize, examine. **2** look at, observe, view, spectate, look on, behold, contemplate, survey, scan. **3** monitor, keep tabs on (*inf*). **4** guard, protect, mind, look after, supervise, oversee, superintend, keep an eye on (*inf*). **5** be careful, take care. **6** watch out, look out, pay attention.
➤*noun* **1** wristwatch, pocket watch, timepiece, chronometer. **2** observation, surveillance. **3** vigilance, alertness, watchfulness, attention, lookout. **4** vigil, guard.
watch out **1** be vigilant, look out, keep your eyes peeled (*inf*). **2** look out, mind out, pay attention, be careful, take care.

watchdog *noun* guardian, custodian, monitor, inspector.

watchful *adj* vigilant, alert, attentive, observant, on one's guard, cautious, wary.

watchman *noun* security guard, caretaker, custodian, janitor.

watchword *noun* **1** slogan, motto, catchphrase, battle-cry, mission statement. **2** password, countersign, signal.

water *noun* sea, lake, river, pool, reservoir.
➤ *verb* **1** damp, moisten, wet, sprinkle, spray, hose, soak. **2** irrigate, flood.
water down dilute, weaken, thin, adulterate, tone down, soften, qualify.

waterfall *noun* cascade, cataract, chute.

watertight *adj* **1** waterproof, impermeable, sealed. **2** unassailable, indisputable, incontrovertible, firm, sound.

watery *adj* **1** wet, damp, moist, saturated, waterlogged, marshy, swampy. **2** liquid, fluid, aqueous, hydrous. **3** thin, runny, weak, dilute, insipid, tasteless. **4** vapid, wishy-washy (*inf*).

wave *verb* **1** gesture, gesticulate, signal. **2** shake, wag. **3** beckon, indicate, motion. **4** flourish, brandish. **5** flap, flutter, wag, swing, oscillate. **6** sway, rock, waft, stir. **7** ripple, undulate, curve, curl.
➤*noun* **1** breaker, roller, ripple, billow, swell. **2** surge, rush, flood. **3** rash, outbreak, groundswell.

waver *verb* **1** vacillate, shilly-shally (*inf*), seesaw, hem and haw (*inf*). **2** wobble, sway, rock, stagger, totter, reel. **3** flicker, quiver, shake, tremble, fluctuate, oscillate. **4** hesitate, dither, falter.

wavy *adj* undulating, rippling, ridged, curly, curvy, winding, sinuous, squiggly, zigzag.

wax *verb* grow, increase, develop, enlarge, expand, swell, spread, mount, rise.

way *noun* **1** method, manner, mode, means. **2** procedure, process, system, technique. **3** custom, practice, habit, style,

trait, peculiarity, idiosyncrasy, characteristic. **4** respect, sense, particular, aspect, point, feature. **5** course, approach, scheme, plan, strategy. **6** road, street, highway, thoroughfare, passage, path, track. **7** route, course, direction. **8** distance, journey, stretch, length.
by the way incidentally, in passing, by the by.
give way collapse, cave in, subside, break, yield, submit, capitulate.
under way in progress, in motion, begun, started, afoot.

wayfarer *noun* traveller, wanderer, walker, hiker, rambler, rover, nomad, itinerant.

waylay *verb* **1** ambush, hold up, set upon, attack. **2** buttonhole, accost, intercept, stop.

wayward *adj* **1** wilful, self-willed, perverse, contrary, uncooperative, recalcitrant, headstrong, stubborn, rebellious, unruly, intractable, ungovernable. **2** capricious, fickle, unpredictable, unstable, erratic, volatile, inconstant, changeable.

weak *adj* **1** feeble, frail, puny, weedy (*inf*), enervated, weary, sickly, unhealthy, debilitated, infirm. **2** fragile, delicate, flimsy, shaky. **3** vulnerable, unprotected, defenceless, exposed. **4** deficient, lacking, wanting. **5** poor, inadequate, imperfect, substandard, faulty, defective. **6** lame, unconvincing, inconclusive. **7** watery, dilute, insipid, tasteless, wishy-washy (*inf*). **8** faint, dim, pale, dull, soft, slight, low, muted, subdued, muffled. **9** powerless, impotent, ineffectual, useless.

weaken *verb* enervate, debilitate, enfeeble, sap, dilute, diminish, lessen, lower, moderate, soften.

weakling *noun* coward, mouse, milksop, wimp (*inf*), weed (*inf*), drip (*inf*), sissy (*inf*).

weakness *noun* **1** feebleness, frailty, debility, infirmity, fragility, vulnerability, ineffectuality, impotence. **2** fault, flaw, defect, imperfection, shortcoming, failing, foible, Achilles' heel. **3** liking, fondness, soft spot, partiality, predilection, proclivity, penchant.

wealth *noun* **1** money, cash, capital, riches, treasure, fortune, assets, property, estate. **2** affluence, opulence, prosperity, richness, means, substance. **3** abundance, plenty, profusion, bounty.

wealthy *adj* rich, prosperous, affluent, well-off, moneyed, loaded (*inf*).

wear *verb* **1** put on, dress in, don, have on, sport. **2** have, show, display, exhibit, present, assume. **3** erode, consume, eat away, abrade, rub, grind, fray, tatter. **4** last, endure. **5** tire, weary, fatigue, exhaust.
➤ *noun* **1** use, employment, service. **2** clothes, clothing, attire, dress, garb, apparel, gear (*inf*). **3** wear and tear, deterioration, damage.
wear down overcome, grind down, weary.
wear off fade, subside, weaken, decrease, diminish, disappear.
wear on pass, go by, elapse, roll on.
wear out exhaust, weary, tire, fatigue, drain, sap, weaken, prostrate, enervate.

wearing *adj* fatiguing, tiring, wearying, exhausting, stressful, taxing, trying, wearisome.

wearisome *adj* tiresome, troublesome, bothersome, irksome, fatiguing, wearing, boring, tedious.

weary *adj* **1** tired, fatigued, worn out, exhausted, spent, all in (*inf*), dead beat (*inf*), knackered (*inf*), bushed (*inf*), whacked (*inf*). **2** wearing, tiring, fatiguing, exhausting, wearisome, tiresome, laborious, dull. **3** fed up, sick and tired (*inf*), cheesed off (*inf*), jaded, bored, listless.
➤ *verb* tire, fatigue, exhaust, wear out, sap, drain, tax, bore.

weather *noun* climate, conditions, temperature, forecast, outlook.
➤ *verb* **1** erode, wear, bleach. **2** endure, withstand, resist, bear up, survive, come through, rise above, ride out.
under the weather unwell, ill, indisposed, poorly (*inf*), off colour, below par, out of sorts.

weave[1] *verb* **1** interlace, lace, intertwine, twine, interweave, braid, plait, knit. **2** make, create, produce, compose, construct, fabricate.

weave[2] *verb* swerve, wind, zigzag.

web *noun* **1** mesh, net, lattice, network, complex. **2** membrane, tissue. **3** knot, tangle, trap, snare.

wed *verb* **1** marry, tie the knot (*inf*), get hitched (*inf*). **2** join, unite, fuse, link.

wedding *noun* marriage, nuptials.

wedge *noun* lump, chunk, block, piece.
➤ *verb* **1** prop, lodge, jam. **2** cram, ram, pack, squeeze, stuff, force.

wedlock *noun* marriage, matrimony.

weed *verb* **weed out** remove, eliminate, eradicate, purge, get rid of, root out.

weekly *adj* hebdomadal, once a week.

weep *verb* cry, sob, snivel, blub (*inf*), mourn, lament, grieve, keen.

weepy *adj* tearful, lachrymose, upset.

weigh *verb* **1** balance, compare, evaluate, consider, mull over, ponder, deliberate. **2** tell, count, carry weight, have influence. **3** load, weight. **4** encumber, burden, oppress, trouble.

weight *noun* **1** heaviness, load, mass, pressure. **2** load, burden, encumbrance. **3** trouble, burden, strain, pressure, millstone, responsibility, onus. **4** influence, importance, consequence, moment, power, force, effect, impact, authority, clout (*inf*).
➤ *verb* load, weigh down, burden, oppress.

weighty *adj* **1** heavy, hefty, bulky, ponderous, massive, cumbersome. **2** burdensome, onerous, oppressive, taxing, troublesome, stressful. **3** important, consequential, momentous, serious, crucial, vital, influential, cogent, persuasive.

weird *adj* **1** uncanny, eerie, supernatural, unearthly, ghostly, spooky (*inf*), creepy (*inf*). **2** strange, bizarre, odd, peculiar, eccentric, outlandish.

welcome *adj* agreeable, delightful, pleasing, gratifying, desirable, popular, acceptable, refreshing.
➤ *noun* greeting, salutation, reception, hospitality.
➤ *verb* greet, salute, hail, receive, meet.

welfare *noun* **1** well-being, prosperity, health, happiness, comfort, security, safety. **2** benefit, income support, social security.

well[1] *noun* spring, wellspring, fountainhead, fount, reservoir, pool, source, mine.
➤ *verb* flow, gush, stream, trickle, ooze, seep, pour, issue.

well[2] *adv* **1** satisfactorily, adequately, fine, nicely, properly, correctly, rightly, suitably, fittingly, smoothly, pleasantly, successfully. **2** competently, skilfully, proficiently, ably, admirably, splendidly. **3** highly, admiringly, favourably, glowingly, warmly, kindly, generously. **4** comfortably, in luxury. **5** thoroughly, fully, completely. **6** considerably, far, much, greatly. **7** probably, possibly, conceivably, undoubtedly, certainly.
➤ *adj* **1** healthy, fit, sound, robust, strong, cured, recovered. **2** satisfactory, all right, good, fine. **3** advisable, desirable, sensible, prudent, wise.
as well also, too, in addition, furthermore, moreover, besides, to boot, into the bargain (*inf*).

well-advised *adj* sensible, wise, prudent, shrewd, sagacious, judicious, circumspect, farsighted.

well-being *noun* welfare, health, happiness, good, comfort, prosperity, security.

well-known *adj* famous, celebrated, renowned, illustrious, eminent, notable, familiar, common.

well-nigh *adv* virtually, practically, almost, nearly, all but, just about.

well-off *adj* **1** wealthy, rich, affluent, prosperous, moneyed, well-to-do, well-heeled (*inf*). **2** fortunate, lucky, comfortable, successful, flourishing, thriving.

well-read *adj* educated, knowledgeable, erudite, well-informed, lettered, cultured.

well-spoken *adj* articulate, clear, coherent, fluent, eloquent.

well-to-do *adj* wealthy, rich, well-off, well-heeled (*inf*), affluent, moneyed, prosperous.

welter *noun* jumble, muddle, tangle, confusion, mishmash (*inf*).

wet *adj* **1** damp, moist, soaked, drenched, saturated, sopping, sodden, soggy, waterlogged. **2** rainy, showery, pouring, teeming, drizzling. **3** weak, feeble, weedy (*inf*), spineless, timorous, soft, namby-pamby (*inf*), effete, ineffectual.
➤ *noun* **1** wetness, moisture, damp, condensation, humidity. **2** rain, drizzle. **3** weakling, wimp (*inf*), weed (*inf*), drip (*inf*).
➤ *verb* dampen, moisten, soak, drench, saturate, spray, splash, water, irrigate.

wharf *noun* dock, quay, pier, jetty, landing stage.

wheedle verb 1 flatter, soft-soap (inf), court, butter up (inf), beguile, charm. 2 cajole, coax, persuade, entreat, entice, influence.

wheel noun 1 disc, round, circle, ring, hoop. 2 turn, twirl, whirl, spin, roll. 3 rotation, revolution, pivot, gyration.
➤verb 1 rotate, revolve, turn, roll. 2 pivot, swivel, spin, gyrate, twirl, whirl. 3 circle, loop.

wheeze verb 1 gasp, pant. 2 rasp, hiss, whistle.
➤noun 1 gasp, pant, rasp, hiss, whistle. 2 idea, notion, scheme, plan, ruse, trick.

whereabouts pl noun location, place, position, site, locality, vicinity.

wherewithal noun means, resources, supplies, funds, cash, money, finance, capital.

whet verb 1 sharpen, hone, edge, strop, file, grind. 2 stimulate, arouse, stir, awaken, kindle, quicken, excite.

whiff noun 1 smell, scent, aroma, odour. 2 trace, hint, suggestion, touch. 3 breath, puff, gust.
➤verb 1 waft, blow, puff. 2 breathe, inhale, sniff, smell.

while noun time, period, spell, stretch, interval.
while away pass, spend, occupy.

whim noun fancy, notion, idea, impulse, urge, humour, caprice, vagary.

whimper verb cry, snivel, sniffle, grizzle (inf), whine, moan, wail.

whimsical adj 1 fanciful, curious, eccentric, quizzical, weird, bizarre, quaint, funny, droll, playful. 2 quirky, capricious, impulsive, unpredictable, quirky, freakish.

whine verb cry, wail, groan, moan, whimper, whinge (inf), complain, carp, grumble, grouse (inf), bellyache (inf).
➤noun 1 cry, wail, moan. 2 complaint, grumble, moan, grouse (inf), gripe (inf).

whip verb 1 lash, beat, flog, scourge, flagellate, thrash, discipline, chastise. 2 pull, jerk, yank (inf), whisk, snatch. 3 whisk, beat. 4 defeat, thrash, trounce.
➤noun lash, scourge, cat-o'-nine-tails, crop.
whip up stir up, rouse, provoke, excite, inflame, agitate, foment.

whirl verb 1 circle, swirl. 2 spin, twirl, pirouette, gyrate, pivot, rotate, revolve, turn, wheel. 3 reel, spin, go round.
➤noun 1 spin, rotation, revolution, turn, twirl, circle, wheel, swirl, gyration, pirouette. 2 try, attempt, go (inf), shot (inf). 3 daze, muddle, confusion, dither. 4 hurly-burly, bustle, tumult, commotion.

whirlpool noun vortex, maelstrom.

whirlwind noun tornado, cyclone, vortex.
➤ adj headlong, impulsive, impetuous, hasty, speedy, rapid, swift, quick, lightning.

whisk verb 1 beat, whip. 2 flick, twitch, wave, brandish. 3 whip, snatch, pull, jerk, yank (inf), brush, sweep. 4 dart, dash, shoot, fly, race, rush, speed, zoom.
➤noun flick, brush, sweep.

whisper verb 1 mumble, murmur, mutter, breathe, hiss. 2 rustle, murmur, sigh, swish, hiss.
➤noun 1 undertone, murmur, mumble, hiss. 2 rustle, murmur, sigh, swish, hiss. 3 rumour, report, insinuation, intimation. 4 breath, whiff, trace, hint, suggestion.

whit noun iota, jot, crumb, bit, scrap, shred, grain, atom, scintilla, modicum.

white adj 1 snowy, chalky, silvery, hoary. 2 pale, light, pallid, wan, waxen, colourless. 3 pure, spotless, immaculate, stainless, blameless, innocent.

white-collar adj professional, clerical, executive.

whiten verb bleach, blanch, blench, fade, pale, etiolate.

whitewash noun cover-up, concealment, deception.
➤verb cover up, conceal, hide, suppress, gloss over, downplay.

whittle verb 1 cut, carve, hew, shave, pare, trim. 2 reduce, cut back, eat away, consume, use up, wear away, diminish.

whole adj 1 entire, complete, total, full, integral, undivided, unabridged. 2 perfect, flawless, intact, sound, unbroken, undamaged, unhurt, unscathed.
➤noun 1 aggregate, total, all, entirety, totality. 2 ensemble, entity.
on the whole 1 all in all, all things considered, by and large. **2** as a rule, mostly, typically, generally.

wholehearted *adj* heartfelt, passionate, sincere, genuine, earnest, enthusiastic, committed, dedicated, hearty, emphatic, unreserved, unqualified.

wholesale *adj* indiscriminate, mass, comprehensive, large-scale, wide-ranging, far-reaching, sweeping, broad, all-inclusive.
➤*adv* indiscriminately, comprehensively, extensively, en bloc, without exception, on a large scale.

wholesome *adj* healthy, nourishing, nutritious, sanitary, good, beneficial, salutary, moral, uplifting, edifying.

wholly *adv* 1 entirely, completely, totally, fully, altogether, thoroughly, utterly, absolutely. 2 exclusively, purely, solely.

whoop *noun* shout, yell, cry, roar, hoot, cheer.
➤*verb* shout, yell, cry, roar, hoot, cheer.

whore *noun* prostitute, streetwalker, call girl, tart (*inf*), hooker (*inf*), slut, slag (*inf*).

wicked *adj* 1 evil, bad, wrong, sinful, villainous, unprincipled, unethical, immoral, corrupt. 2 unpleasant, nasty, cruel, vicious, abominable, reprehensible, heinous, atrocious, monstrous. 3 naughty, mischievous, impish, roguish, rascally, arch. 4 excellent, cool (*inf*), brilliant, great (*inf*).

wide *adj* 1 vast, immense, ample, spacious, roomy, capacious. 2 broad, large, thick, full. 3 comprehensive, catholic, encyclopedic, all-embracing, inclusive, compendious, general. 4 extensive, wide-ranging, far-reaching, sweeping. 5 off-course, off-target, off the mark.
➤*adv* 1 fully, completely, all the way. 2 astray, off target, off course, off the mark.

wide-awake *adj* 1 awake, conscious, roused, open-eyed. 2 alert, sharp, aware, vigilant, wary, observant, watchful, attentive, quick-witted, on the ball (*inf*).

widen *verb* broaden, extend, expand, spread, stretch, enlarge, open, augment, increase.

widespread *adj* 1 outspread, outstretched, extended. 2 rife, prevalent, common, extensive, general, universal, wholesale, epidemic.

width *noun* 1 breadth, thickness, span, diameter. 2 extensiveness, vastness, immensity, comprehensiveness, breadth, reach, scope, range, compass, extent.

wield *verb* 1 handle, manipulate, brandish, flourish, control, hold, use, ply. 2 exercise, exert, have, hold, possess, command.

wife *noun* spouse, other half (*inf*), better half (*inf*), missis (*inf*), bride, mate, consort, squaw.

wild *adj* 1 untamed, undomesticated, unbroken, feral, savage, ferocious, fierce. 2 uncultivated, waste, desert, barren, uninhabited. 3 desolate, rugged, inhospitable. 4 riotous, boisterous, rowdy, rough, lawless, unruly, undisciplined, unbridled, uncontrolled, unrestrained. 5 enthusiastic, eager, keen, passionate, crazy (*inf*), mad (*inf*). 6 angry, infuriated, incensed, seething, mad (*inf*). 7 violent, furious, raging, stormy, tempestuous, turbulent. 8 madcap, foolhardy, ill-considered, rash, outrageous, preposterous, extravagant, fantastic. 9 barbarous, barbaric, savage, brutish, primitive, uncivilized.

wilderness *noun* 1 wilds, wasteland, desert, jungle. 2 confusion, muddle, labyrinth, maze, jumble, tangle.

wile *noun* trick, ruse, ploy, dodge (*inf*), stratagem, artifice, device.

wilful *adj* 1 headstrong, obstinate, stubborn, pig-headed, refractory, recalcitrant, perverse, contrary, wayward, self-willed, dogged, persistent. 2 intentional, deliberate, premeditated, calculated, conscious, voluntary.

will *noun* 1 volition, option, choice, discretion. 2 wish, desire, fancy, inclination, preference, pleasure, decision, intention. 3 willpower, self-control, determination, resolution, single-mindedness. 4 testament, bequest.
➤*verb* 1 ordain, decree, order, command, direct, bid, desire, wish. 2 decide, determine, see fit, choose, prefer, please, want. 3 leave, transfer, bequeath, pass on, hand down.

willing *adj* 1 prepared, disposed, inclined, ready, consenting, agreeable, game (*inf*), content, happy, glad, nothing loath. 2 prompt, ready, eager, keen, obliging, amenable, cooperative, compliant.

willpower *noun* will, resolution, resolve, determination, purposefulness, doggedness, persistence, drive, commitment, single-mindedness, self-discipline, self-control.

wilt *verb* **1** wither, shrivel, droop, flop. **2** fade, flag, tire, weaken, fail.

wily *adj* artful, crafty, cunning, sly, subtle, scheming, tricky, foxy.

win *verb* **1** triumph, succeed, conquer, prevail, carry the day, come first. **2** get, gain, secure, receive, collect, pick up, attain, achieve, take, bag (*inf*).
➤*noun* victory, triumph, success, conquest.
win over/round charm, persuade, convince, convert, bring round.

wince *verb* flinch, start, jump, shrink, recoil, draw back, quail, cower, cringe, grimace.

wind[1] *noun* **1** breeze, zephyr, gale, hurricane, blast, gust, draught, puff. **2** gas, flatulence.
in the wind in the offing, on the way, approaching, impending, looming, expected, likely, probable, on the cards (*inf*).

wind[2] *verb* **1** twist, coil, curl, spiral, snake, turn, bend, curve, zigzag, meander. **2** roll, furl, coil, twine, encircle, wreathe, loop.
➤*noun* **1** coil, turn, loop, convolution, whorl. **2** bend, curve, twist, meander, zigzag.
wind down 1 unwind, relax, ease up, chill out (*inf*). **2** slow down, slacken off. **3** lessen, reduce, stop, bring to an end.
wind up 1 agitate, fluster, discompose, stress, strain, work up. **2** tease, chaff, kid (*inf*), trick, hoax, annoy, irritate. **3** end, close, conclude, finish, terminate, wrap up (*inf*). **4** close down, liquidate, dissolve. **5** arrive, end up, fetch up, find oneself.

windfall *noun* jackpot, bonanza, stroke of luck, godsend.

window *noun* pane, opening, skylight, casement.

windy *adj* **1** breezy, blowy, blustery, gusty, stormy, tempestuous, wild. **2** windswept, draughty. **3** long-winded, verbose, wordy, garrulous, prolix, loquacious, bombastic, pompous, turgid.

wing *noun* **1** arm, branch, group, set, circle, section, faction, side. **2** extension, annexe, unit.
➤*verb* **1** fly, glide, soar, flit. **2** wound, hit, clip, nick.

wink *verb* twinkle, sparkle, flash, flicker, gleam, glitter, glint, blink.
➤*noun* **1** twinkle, sparkle, flash, flicker, gleam, glitter, glint, blink. **2** instant, moment, minute, second, tick (*inf*), jiffy (*inf*).
wink at ignore, disregard, overlook, neglect, let pass, condone, connive at, turn a blind eye to (*inf*).

winkle *verb* **winkle out 1** extricate, extract, prise, remove, displace. **2** extract, draw, worm out, obtain.

winner *noun* victor, champion, conqueror.

winning *adj* **1** victorious, conquering, unbeaten, undefeated, triumphant, successful. **2** charming, enchanting, engaging, endearing, disarming, winsome, attractive, pleasing, delightful.

winnings *pl noun* proceeds, gains, spoils, booty, jackpot, prize.

winnow *verb* separate, sort, sift, select.

winsome *adj* winning, engaging, charming, pleasing, delightful, agreeable, sweet, lovely, endearing, enchanting.

wintry *adj* **1** cold, freezing, arctic, glacial, icy, snowy, frosty, hibernal, raw, harsh. **2** chilly, cool, unfriendly, hostile, bleak, cheerless.

wipe *verb* **1** rub, clean, sponge, mop, swab, dust, brush, dry. **2** remove, efface, erase, rub off, clean off.
➤*noun* rub, clean, sponge, dust, brush.
wipe out 1 destroy, demolish, eradicate, exterminate, eliminate, annihilate, massacre. **2** obliterate, erase, blot out, expunge.

wiry *adj* **1** lean, spare, sinewy, muscular, tough, vigorous. **2** coarse, rough, bristly, wavy, flexible.

wisdom *noun* **1** sagacity, sapience, discernment, insight, sense, intelligence, reason, judgment, shrewdness, circumspection, prudence, foresight. **2** knowledge, learning, erudition, enlightenment, understanding, philosophy

wise *adj* **1** sagacious, sapient, discerning, intelligent, clever, smart, rational, logical. **2** sensible, judicious, well-advised, circumspect, prudent, shrewd, astute, politic. **3** erudite, knowledgeable, learned, educated, well-informed, enlightened, experienced.

wish *verb* 1 desire, crave, long, yearn, sigh, want, prefer, fancy. 2 bid, ask, request, demand, require, order, command, direct, instruct.
➤*noun* 1 desire, longing, yearning, want, hope, aspiration, urge, yen (*inf*), craving, fancy, whim, preference. 2 demand, instruction, requirement, bidding, request, command, order, will.

wishy-washy *adj* 1 pale, wan, pallid, sickly. 2 feeble, weak, puny, namby-pamby (*inf*), irresolute, ineffectual, effete, spineless. 3 insipid, tasteless, flavourless, bland, flat, watery.

wistful *adj* 1 pensive, thoughtful, reflective, contemplative, melancholy, sad, disconsolate, mournful. 2 longing, yearning.

wit *noun* 1 humour, drollery, facetiousness, wittiness, repartee, levity, badinage, banter. 2 humorist, comic, comedian, wag, card (*inf*). 3 intelligence, intellect, cleverness, ingenuity, reason, sense, brains (*inf*), gumption (*inf*), understanding, wisdom, acumen, shrewdness.

witch *noun* sorceress, enchantress, necromancer, soothsayer.

witchcraft *noun* witchery, sorcery, magic, enchantment, divination, necromancy.

withdraw *verb* 1 remove, pull out, extract, draw back, take away, recall. 2 back out, retire, pull out, drop out. 3 leave, depart, go, retreat, fall back. 4 take back, retract, recant, unsay, revoke, rescind, cancel.

withdrawal *noun* removal, extraction, recall, retirement, departure, exodus, retreat, retraction, recantation.

withdrawn *adj* 1 shy, reserved, retiring, shrinking, introverted, self-contained, detached, distant, unsociable, uncommunicative. 2 remote, secluded, private, isolated, out-of-the-way.

wither *verb* 1 shrivel, shrink, droop, wilt, dry up, waste, atrophy. 2 fade, wane, ebb, falter, languish, die.

withhold *verb* 1 keep back, retain, reserve, deduct, refuse, decline. 2 restrain, check, curb, control, repress, hold back.

without *prep* lacking, wanting, short of, deprived of, excluding, free from.

withstand *verb* 1 endure, tolerate, bear, take, resist, weather, survive. 2 oppose, resist, fight, combat, defy, confront, face, brave.

witness *noun* 1 eyewitness, looker-on, onlooker, spectator, observer, viewer, watcher, bystander. 2 testifier, deponent. 3 testimony, attestation, deposition, statement. 4 evidence, confirmation, proof, corroboration.
➤*verb* 1 see, observe, view, watch, look on, behold, notice, attend. 2 testify, bear witness, give evidence, depose, attest, confirm, corroborate. 3 endorse, countersign.

witticism *noun* quip, riposte, bon mot, pun, joke, jest, pleasantry, wisecrack (*inf*), gag (*inf*).

witty *adj* humorous, comic, droll, facetious, funny, amusing, waggish, jocular, clever, brilliant, lively, sparkling.

wizard *noun* 1 sorcerer, warlock, necromancer, magician, magus. 2 expert, adept, dab hand (*inf*), master, virtuoso, genius, ace (*inf*), hotshot (*inf*).

wizen *verb* shrivel, shrink, dry up, wither, wrinkle, line.

wobble *verb* 1 rock, totter, teeter, sway, oscillate, shake. 2 tremble, quiver, quaver, vibrate. 3 waver, vacillate, hesitate, dither, shilly-shally (*inf*).
➤*noun* rocking, swaying, oscillation, shake, tremble, tremor, quiver, quaver, vibration.

woe *noun* 1 grief, misery, sorrow, sadness, heartache, melancholy, anguish, distress, suffering. 2 adversity, misfortune, trouble, trial, affliction, curse, ordeal, burden, disaster.

woebegone *adj* miserable, wretched, woeful, sad, sorrowful, grief-stricken, disconsolate, mournful, downcast, dejected, crestfallen, doleful.

woeful *adj* 1 sad, unhappy, sorrowful, miserable, woebegone, doleful, depressed, dejected, disconsolate, despondent, mournful, plaintive. 2 distressing, heartbreaking, grievous, lamentable, sad, tragic, terrible, pitiful, sorry, wretched, dismal, gloomy.

wolf *verb* devour, bolt, gobble, gulp, gorge, scoff (*inf*), put away (*inf*).

woman noun **1** female, lady, girl, bird (inf), chick (inf). **2** maid, domestic, housekeeper, home help.

womanhood noun women, womenfolk, womankind, sisterhood, sorority.

womanize verb philander, seduce, flirt, dally, sleep around.

womanly adj feminine, gentle, tender, kind, motherly, ladylike.

wonder noun **1** awe, wonderment, admiration, amazement, astonishment, bewilderment, curiosity, fascination. **2** marvel, phenomenon, miracle, prodigy, curiosity, rarity, sight, spectacle.
➤verb **1** meditate, ponder, reflect, muse, speculate, conjecture, doubt, question, query, puzzle, ask oneself. **2** marvel, gape, stare, boggle (inf).

wonderful adj marvellous, splendid, magnificent, sensational, excellent, terrific, admirable, remarkable, fantastic (inf), great (inf), smashing (inf), super (inf).

wont noun habit, routine, practice, custom, use, way.
➤adj accustomed, used, in the habit, given, inclined.

wonted adj habitual, customary, familiar, usual, normal, routine, regular, accustomed.

woo verb **1** court, pursue, chase after, make love to. **2** cultivate, curry favour with, seek, attract, pursue, run after, importune, coax, press, urge.

wood noun **1** woodland, thicket, coppice, spinney, grove, plantation, trees. **2** timber, planks, lumber.

wooded adj woody, forested, timbered, tree-covered, sylvan.

wooden adj stiff, rigid, leaden, stolid, awkward.

wool noun fleece, hair, down, coat.

woolly adj **1** woollen, fluffy, fleecy, furry, frizzy, shaggy, hairy. **2** unclear, ill-defined, indistinct, blurred, hazy, fuzzy, foggy, cloudy. **3** muddled, confused, vague, hazy.

word noun **1** term, name, expression. **2** remark, comment, observation, utterance, statement, declaration, chat, conversation, talk, discussion, consultation. **3** news, communication, report, notice, message, dispatch, information, intelligence, low-down (inf). **4** promise, pledge, assurance, guarantee, oath, vow. **5** command, order, instruction, signal, go-ahead, green light (inf), thumbs-up (inf).
➤verb phrase, put, express, couch, utter, say, state.
in a word briefly, in short, to sum up, in a nutshell (inf).

word-for-word adj verbatim, literal, close, faithful, exact, strict.

words pl noun lyrics, libretto, book, text, script.

wordy adj verbose, prolix, garrulous, loquacious, voluble, long-winded, rambling, protracted, discursive, diffuse.

work noun **1** toil, labour, industry, effort, exertion, drudgery, graft (inf), grind (inf), slog (inf). **2** task, job, chore, undertaking, duty, charge, function, assignment, commission, mission. **3** occupation, employment, job, business, profession, vocation, career, calling, line, field, livelihood, trade. **4** product, creation, opus, composition, piece, oeuvre, production, achievement. **5** workmanship, skill, craft, art.
➤verb **1** toil, labour, drudge, slave, slog (inf), exert oneself, be busy, be employed, have a job, earn a living, ply one's trade, do business. **2** operate, function, go, run, perform, act. **3** succeed, be effective, go well. **4** handle, manipulate, wield, ply, use, control, drive, operate. **5** accomplish, achieve, perform, pull off (inf), effect, bring about, create, produce, engineer, manoeuvre, fix (inf), wangle (inf). **6** till, cultivate, farm, mine, quarry. **7** process, knead, hammer, forge, shape, form, mould, model.

work out 1 solve, resolve, figure out, puzzle out, calculate, determine. **2** plan, arrange, organize, devise, invent, contrive, formulate, develop, elaborate. **3** succeed, go well, prosper, be effective, go as planned. **4** exercise, train, drill, keep fit.

work up 1 agitate, rouse, excite, inflame, stir, move. **2** build up, whet, create, generate, stimulate, arouse.

workable adj practicable, viable, feasible, doable, possible, realistic.

workaday adj ordinary, everyday, commonplace, familiar, mundane, routine, humdrum, run-of-the-mill (inf), dull, prosaic.

worker *noun* employee, workman, labourer, artisan, hand, operative, wage-earner, breadwinner.

working *adj* 1 in work, employed, waged, active. 2 running, functioning, operating, going.
➤*noun* 1 digging, excavation, mine, pit, quarry, shaft. 2 functioning, operation, running, routine, process, method, action, system.

workmanship *noun* 1 skill, technique, craftsmanship, artistry, expertise. 2 handiwork, execution, finish.

workout *noun* training, practice, drill, warm-up, exercise, aerobics, isometrics, callisthenics.

works *pl noun* 1 factory, mill, plant, shop. 2 machinery, mechanism, movement, action, workings, parts.

workshop *noun* 1 workroom, works, factory, plant, garage, studio. 2 seminar, symposium, study group, discussion group, training session, class.

world *noun* 1 earth, globe, humankind, humanity, everybody, everything. 2 planet, star, moon, satellite, heavenly body. 3 sphere, realm, domain, province, field, area, department, class, set. 4 people, nation, race, kingdom, epoch, era, age, period, time. 5 large amount, great deal (*inf*).

worldly *adj* temporal, earthly, terrestrial, physical, material, secular, profane, human.

worldly-wise *adj* worldly, cosmopolitan, urbane, sophisticated, knowing, experienced.

worldwide *adj* universal, international, global, widespread, pandemic, extensive, far-reaching.

worn-out *adj* 1 worn, threadbare, tattered, ragged, frayed, shabby, shiny. 2 exhausted, weary, fatigued, dog-tired, knackered (*inf*), bushed (*inf*), all in (*inf*).

worry *verb* 1 fret, be anxious, agonize, brood. 2 concern, distress, discompose, agitate, unsettle, upset, bug (*inf*). 3 disturb, bother, trouble, harass, hassle (*inf*), pester, nag, badger, importune. 4 chase, harass, attack, go for, bite, savage, shake, tease, torment.
➤*noun* 1 anxiety, unease, disquiet, agita-tion, upset, concern, trouble, distress, tension, stress, nervousness, apprehension. 2 bother, nuisance, pest, trouble, care, problem, difficulty, responsibility.

worsen *verb* deteriorate, decline, sink, slip, slide, aggravate, exacerbate.

worship *verb* 1 venerate, reverence, honour, praise, exalt, glorify, extol. 2 adore, love, cherish, treasure, dote on, esteem, revere, idolize, lionize.
➤*noun* 1 veneration, reverence, homage, devotion, praise, prayer, honour, glory, exaltation, extolment. 2 esteem, adulation, idolization, love, adoration, devotion.

worst *verb* defeat, beat, conquer, vanquish, master, overcome, overpower, best, trounce, thrash, whip (*inf*).

worth *noun* 1 cost, price, value, use, service, good, avail, gain, profit. 2 worthiness, merit, quality, virtue, excellence, eminence.

worthless *adj* 1 valueless, cheap, poor, trashy, rubbishy. 2 useless, futile, vain, pointless, nugatory, meaningless, insignificant. 3 contemptible, despicable, good-for-nothing, base, low, abject.

worthwhile *adj* valuable, useful, good, beneficial, advantageous, helpful, profitable, gainful, constructive, productive, justifiable.

worthy *adj* 1 deserving, meriting, good enough. 2 noble, admirable, good, deserving, worthwhile, commendable, creditable. 3 respectable, reputable, honourable, meritorious, moral, upright, virtuous, irreproachable.
➤*noun* dignitary, notable, personage, luminary, celebrity, VIP (*inf*), bigwig (*inf*).

wound *noun* 1 injury, cut, scratch, gash, laceration, lesion, scar. 2 hurt, blow, trauma, shock, insult, slight, affront, grief, pain.
➤*verb* injure, hurt, harm, cut, gash, stab, grieve, distress, upset, offend, pain.

wraith *noun* ghost, spirit, spectre, phantom, apparition, shade.

wrangle *noun* argument, dispute, quarrel, row, debate, controversy.
➤*verb* argue, dispute, quarrel, bicker, squabble, row, fight.

wrap verb **1** envelop, enfold, encase, sheathe, cocoon, cover, pack, parcel, package, bundle, bind, tie. **2** swathe, wind, fold. **3** surround, cover, shroud, cloak.
➤*noun* shawl, cloak, stole, cape, mantle.
wrap up 1 conclude, complete, finish, end, terminate, wind up, round off. **2** be quiet, shut up (inf), pipe down (inf), put a sock in it (inf).

wrapper noun wrapping, packaging, covering, paper, cover, sleeve, jacket, case.

wrath noun anger, ire, rage, fury, indignation, exasperation, displeasure.

wrathful adj angry, irate, incensed, enraged, furious, fuming, indignant, cross, displeased, exasperated.

wreak verb **1** inflict, execute, carry out, vent, unleash. **2** cause, bring about, create, produce.

wreath noun **1** garland, festoon, chaplet, circlet, coronet, crown. **2** ring, loop, circle, coil, spiral.

wreathe verb **1** encircle, surround, entwine, festoon, garland, crown. **2** twist, wind, coil, curl, spiral.

wreck verb **1** shipwreck, capsize, sink, run aground. **2** ruin, destroy, demolish, smash, damage, break, write off. **3** devastate, shatter, ruin, spoil, disrupt, undo, upset, play havoc with.
➤*noun* **1** ruin, destruction, devastation, demolition. **2** wreckage, debris, remains, ruins, rubble.

wreckage noun debris, detritus, pieces, shards, remnants, relics, remains, ruins, rubble.

wrench verb **1** strain, sprain, rick, twist. **2** jerk, pull, tug, yank (inf), force, twist. **3** rip, tear, wrest, snatch.
➤*noun* **1** jerk, pull, tug, yank (inf), twist. **2** strain, sprain, rick, twist. **3** blow, pang, trauma, distress, anguish, sorrow.

wrest verb **1** seize, take, pull, twist, wrench, snatch. **2** wring, extract, force.

wrestle verb fight, grapple, tussle, battle, struggle, combat.

wretch noun scoundrel, villain, rogue, rascal, reprobate, rat (inf), swine (inf), rotter (inf).

wretched adj **1** miserable, unhappy, sorry, tragic, woebegone, forlorn, cheerless,

harsh, grim. **2** bad, poor, inferior, awful, terrible, appalling, dreadful, deplorable, shocking. **3** contemptible, despicable, shameful, mean, base, vile, low, abject, squalid.

wriggle verb **1** squirm, writhe, twist, wiggle, jerk. **2** worm, snake, slink, crawl, sidle.
➤*noun* squirm, writhe, wiggle, twist, jerk.

wring verb **1** squeeze, twist, screw, mangle. **2** wrest, extract, force, extort, exact. **3** distress, harrow, rack, torment, torture, pain, hurt, wound, pierce, tear.

wrinkle verb crease, fold, crumple, crinkle, rumple, pucker, line, furrow.
➤*noun* crease, fold, crumple, crinkle, rumple, pucker, line, ridge, furrow.

writ noun court order, summons, subpoena, decree.

write verb **1** inscribe, pen, pencil, scribble, scrawl, note, record, jot down, take down, put down, transcribe. **2** draft, draw up, compose, pen, dash off (inf).
write off 1 wreck, destroy, smash, crash, demolish. **2** wipe out, cross out, delete, cancel, annul. **3** dismiss, disregard, ignore.

writer noun author, scribe, novelist, essayist, dramatist, journalist.

writhe verb wriggle, squirm, twist, turn, jerk, flail, thrash, struggle, contort.

writing noun **1** handwriting, hand, penmanship, calligraphy, script, text, print, scribble, scrawl. **2** book, publication, opus, work, composition, document, letter.

wrong adj **1** incorrect, inaccurate, inexact, false, untrue. **2** in error, erroneous, mistaken. **3** bad, sinful, iniquitous, reprehensible, unethical, immoral, wicked, evil. **4** wrongful, unlawful, illegal, dishonest, unfair, improper, inappropriate, unconventional. **5** unsatisfactory, undesirable, unacceptable, faulty, defective, amiss, awry, out of order.
➤*adv* **1** wrongly, incorrectly, inaccurately, falsely, erroneously, mistakenly. **2** improperly, inappropriately. **3** amiss, awry, out of order.
➤*noun* **1** sin, misdeed, transgression, offence, crime, infringement, injustice, grievance, outrage, atrocity, error, mistake. **2** wickedness, evil, sinfulness, iniquity, wrongdoing, immorality, unfairness.
➤*verb* **1** hurt, harm, injure, offend, abuse,

mistreat, oppress, exploit, cheat. **2** misrepresent, discredit, malign, defame, slander, libel.

in the wrong 1 at fault, in error, mistaken, incorrect. **2** guilty, culpable, blameworthy, to blame.

wrongdoer *noun* offender, lawbreaker, criminal, felon, villain, culprit, delinquent, miscreant, malefactor, sinner.

wrongful *adj* unjust, unfair, unwarranted, illegal, unlawful, criminal, illegitimate, illicit, immoral, improper, wrong.

wry *adj* **1** droll, witty, humorous, dry, ironic, sardonic, sarcastic. **2** awry, askew, crooked, lopsided, twisted, distorted, contorted, warped.

Xerox® *noun* photocopy, duplicate, Photostat®.

Xmas *noun* Christmas, Noël, Yule.

X-ray *noun* radiograph, röntgenogram.

yank *verb* pull, jerk, tug.

yap *verb* **1** yelp, bark. **2** chatter, jabber, gab (*inf*), yammer (*inf*).

yard *noun* quadrangle, court, enclosure, compound.

yardstick *noun* **1** measure, gauge, scale, rule. **2** standard, criterion, touchstone, benchmark.

yarn *noun* **1** tale, story, anecdote. **2** thread, fibre, strand.

yearly *adj* annual, once a year.

yearn *verb* long, pine, hanker, desire, wish, hunger, thirst, ache.

yell *verb* shout, scream, cry, shriek, bellow, bawl, holler (*inf*).
➤*noun* shout, scream, cry, shriek, bellow.

yelp *verb* yap, bark, cry, squeal.

yen *noun* yearning, hankering, longing, craving, fancy, desire, lust, hunger, thirst.

yes *interj* aye, sure, right, yeah (*inf*), yep (*inf*), certainly, of course, by all means.

yet *adv* **1** but, nevertheless, nonetheless, notwithstanding, however, for all that. **2** so far, far, hitherto, heretofore, until now, up to now. **3** still, even. **4** in addition, also, to boot, furthermore, besides, moreover.

yield *verb* **1** produce, bear, bring forth, give, provide. **2** return, bring in, earn, net, gross, generate, fetch, pay. **3** give up, abandon, part with, relinquish, hand over, abdicate, renounce, resign. **4** surrender, submit, capitulate, give in, admit defeat, throw in the towel (*inf*). **5** give way, bow, cave in (*inf*), knuckle under, acquiesce, agree.
➤*noun* crop, produce, harvest, output, return, revenue, proceeds, haul.

yoke *noun* **1** collar, harness, coupling. **2** link, tie, bond. **3** burden, oppression.
➤*verb* couple, link, unite, join, tie, connect, hitch, bracket.

yokel *noun* rustic, peasant, bumpkin, clodhopper (*inf*), provincial, hick.

young *adj* **1** youthful, juvenile, junior, immature, undeveloped, growing, small, baby, infant. **2** new, recent, fledgling, early, fresh.
➤*noun* offspring, progeny, issue, family, children, babies.

youngster *noun* child, kid (*inf*), nipper (*inf*), boy, girl, teenager.

youth *noun* **1** childhood, boyhood, girlhood, early life, adolescence, teens, immaturity. **2** boy, lad, adolescent, teenager, juvenile.

youthful *adj* **1** boyish, girlish, fresh, sprightly. **2** young, immature.

zany *adj* comical, funny, droll, clownish, crazy, loony (*inf*), wacky (*inf*).

zap *verb* kill, murder, liquidate, destroy, wipe out.

zeal *noun* fervour, ardour, passion, enthusiasm, eagerness, vigour, commitment, fanaticism.

zealot *noun* fanatic, enthusiast, fiend (*inf*), radical, militant, extremist.

zealous *adj* fervent, ardent, passionate, enthusiastic, eager, vigorous, committed, fanatical.

zenith *noun* height, peak, pinnacle, top, climax, apogee, acme.

zero *noun* 1 nought, nothing, nil, love. 2 bottom, nadir.
zero in 1 home in, converge. 2 focus, aim, direct, concentrate.

zest *noun* 1 spice, tang, savour, piquancy, kick (*inf*), oomph (*inf*). 2 gusto, relish, appetite, enjoyment, enthusiasm, zeal.

zigzag *adj* crooked, tortuous, twisting, winding.

zing *noun* gusto, zest, energy, vim, spirit, vitality, vigour, go (*inf*).

zip *noun* zest, energy, vigour, liveliness, vitality, pep.
➤ *verb* 1 fly, dash, race, tear, shoot, speed. 2 zoom, whizz, zing (*inf*).

zone *noun* 1 area, region, district, territory. 2 belt, section, sector.

zoom *verb* 1 shoot, fly, streak, speed, race, rush. 2 whizz, zip (*inf*), zing (*inf*).

PENGUIN POCKET REFERENCE

THE PENGUIN POCKET ENGLISH DICTIONARY

This pocket edition of the bestselling *Penguin English Dictionary* is the perfect reference book for everyday use. Compiled by Britain's foremost lexicographers, up to date and easy to use, it is the ideal portable companion for quick reference.

- Includes a wealth of words, phrases and clear definitions, with more information than other comparable dictionaries
- Covers standard and formal English, as well as specialist terms, slang and jargon
- Provides invaluable guidance on correct usage, commonly confused words and grammar and spelling

PENGUIN POCKET REFERENCE

THE PENGUIN POCKET SPANISH DICTIONARY
JOSEPHINE RIQUELME-BENEYTO

The Penguin Pocket Spanish Dictionary is an invaluable and handy wordfinder for students and travellers alike. Covering both English–Spanish and Spanish–English, it offers clear definitions in an easy-to-use format, ensuring that you find the word you need quickly and efficiently.

- Includes over 36,000 entries

- Gives entry-by-entry guidance on pronunciation

- Lists irregular verbs in both languages

PENGUIN POCKET REFERENCE

THE PENGUIN POCKET FRENCH DICTIONARY
ROSALIND FERGUSSON

The Penguin Pocket French Dictionary is an invaluable and handy
wordfinder for students and travellers alike. Covering both
English–French and French–English, it offers clear definitions in an
easy-to-use format, ensuring that you find the word you need quickly
and efficiently.

- Includes over 35,000 entries

- Gives entry-by-entry guidance on pronunciation

- Lists irregular verbs in both languages

Penguin Pocket Reference

THE PENGUIN POCKET DICTIONARY OF QUOTATIONS
EDITED BY DAVID CRYSTAL

The Penguin Pocket Dictionary of Quotations is essential reading for anyone searching for the perfect quotation – whether you need a snappy one-liner for a speech or a remark of brilliant insight for your written work. With this pithy and provocative selection of wit and wisdom, you will never be lost for words again.

- Includes quotations from a vast range of people, from film stars to politicians
- Arranged alphabetically by name of person quoted, with the original source for each quotation given
- Provides a full index of key words to help you find each quotation quickly and easily

www.penguin.com

PENGUIN POCKET REFERENCE

THE PENGUIN POCKET BOOK OF FACTS
EDITED BY DAVID CRYSTAL

The Penguin Pocket Book of Facts is a goldmine of information, figures and statistics on every conceivable subject – from the world's highest mountains and longest rivers to the gods of mythology, and from time zones to Nobel Prize winners. The ultimate one-stop factfinder, this is the essential book for browsers, crossword and trivia addicts, and for anyone who needs to check facts at home or at work.

– Up-to-date information about everything from astronomy to zoology

– Easy to use

– Illustrated throughout with maps and diagrams

www.penguin.com

PENGUIN POCKET REFERENCE

THE PENGUIN POCKET SCHOOL DICTIONARY

The Penguin Pocket School Dictionary is the perfect reference book for everyday use, whether at school or for homework. Up to date and portable, its easy-to-use format makes it the ideal way to find the words you need as quickly as possible.

- Provides clear definitions of thousands of words and phrases

- Covers not only standard everyday English, but also technical terms, slang, jargon and words that have only recently been created

- For all students aged 11+